Contents on p. 3

# 1998 ED

## Joel Whitburn's

# BUBBLING UNDER

## SINGLES & ALBUMS

Compiled from *Billboard's Bubbling Under The Hot 100* charts, 1959-1997; *Bubbling Under The Top Pop Albums* charts, 1970-1985; and *Best Selling Pop EP's* charts, 1957-1960.

Record Research

**Record Research Inc.**
**P.O. Box 200**
**Menomonee Falls, Wisconsin 53052-0200**
**U.S.A.**

Phone:     (414) 251-5408
Fax:       (414) 251-9452
E-Mail:    record@execpc.com
Web site:  http://www.recordresearch.com

# CONTENTS

*Other Books (pp. 414-415)

This third edition of the *Bubbling Under* book comes as a pleasant surprise. When I published the second edition in July of 1992, it had been seven years since *Billboard* had discontinued the chart. With the entire history of the chart covered, I thought that I had made my last dive into the *Bubbling Under* charts. Then, in December of 1992, with the book still warm off the presses, the *Bubbling Under the Hot 100* chart returned to *Billboard*!

What a thrill to once again have a forecast of the *Hot 100*! The *Bubbling Under* chart is the inside track as to which singles are gaining steam to cross over to pop music's premier singles chart, the *Hot 100*. Some make it and some do not. The latter are the fascinating focus of this book.

It was with great pleasure that I returned my focus to:

- one-hit wonders Nikita The K, Eden Kane, The Cherry Slush, Johnny October, Bing Day and The Viceroys;
- regional rock 'n' rollers Teddy and the Pandas, The Remains, The Robbs and The Coastliners;
- R&B vocal groups The Deltairs, The Diablos and The Sheppards;
- classic radio hits "The Roach," "Car Trouble" and "King Of The Surf Guitar";
- celebrity recordings by Mia Farrow, Jimmy Stewart and Leonard Nimoy;
- the dozen or more *Bubbling Under* hits by superstars Johnny Cash, Ray Charles, and Frank Sinatra;
- classic movie themes "Gidget Goes Hawaiian," "New York, New York," and "From Russia With Love";
- and valuable rarities like "Long Tall Sally" by The Kinks on Cameo or The Marvelettes singing as The Darnells on the Gordy label.

The whole new crop of *Bubbling Under*-only singles of the 1990s revealed several things about the changing nature of the singles industry. Between 1992 and 1997, several artists had quickly racked up four or more *Bubbling Under* hits. These singles were big on either the Country, Rock and R&B charts but did not garner sufficient pop radio airplay to make the leap to the *Hot 100*.

The return of the *Bubbling Under* chart gave me a chance to bring the presentation of the chart research up to par with my *Top Pop Singles* book. The many additional features lend further dimension to the *Bubbling Under* hits. The most exciting new feature is the addition of the B-sides.

This third edition of the *Bubbling Under* book offered the perfect place to introduce my research of *Billboard's Bubbling Under Albums* chart and include all of the album cuts! Now, for the first time, you can see how the debut albums by the Doobie Brothers, Barry Manilow, Red Hot Chili Peppers and Styx fared in *Billboard*, as well as the seminal albums by punk artists Dead Kennedys and Richard Hell & The Voidoids. Early New Age and World Music albums appeared on this chart before *Billboard* created their corresponding charts. An eclectic mix of artists like Mom's Apple Pie, Yellowman, the Knitters, Don Imus and Yma Sumac also found a home on the *Bubbling Under Albums* chart.

Readers of the *Bubbling Under* book are generally serious record aficionados. Likewise, EP collecting falls within the sphere of ardent collectors. So, my research of *Billboard's Best Selling Pop EP's* chart provided a fitting bridge between the singles and the albums sections. The picturesque EP covers so perfectly bring back memories of the music of the late 1950s.

Researching this book has been one of my all-time favorite projects. I am pleased to present you with the results. Many, many thanks for your interest in these charts and this work. May you have great fun reading it.

## JOEL WHITBURN

A special thanks to Bob Moke (for providing some interesting trivia notes), Malcolm Hjerstedt (for photographing all of the charted EP's from my collection) and the hard-working staff of Record Research.

# BUBBLING UNDER THE HOT 100

## THE HISTORY OF *BILLBOARD'S* *BUBBLING UNDER THE HOT 100* CHART

The first *Bubbling Under The Hot 100* chart appeared in *Billboard's* June 1, 1959 issue. On this date, *Billboard* reorganized the layout of the *Hot 100* chart and the Singles Reviews, and combined the two into a double-page spread under the heading "*The Billboard Hot 100 & Tomorrow's Tops.*" The Billboard Hot *100* occupied the first page of the spread. The second page of the spread, under the heading "*& Tomorrow's Tops,*" featured four sections: *Reviews Of This Week's Singles* which highlighted the *Spotlight Winners Of The Week; Best Buys* which listed the *Hot 100* singles with national sales breakouts; *Hot 100: A To Z* which listed *Hot 100* titles alphabetically; and *Bubbling Under The Hot 100* – a chart listing positions past #100. *Billboard* introduced the weekly *Bubbling Under* singles chart with the following explanatory note: "These records, while they have not yet developed enough strength throughout the country for inclusion on any national chart anywhere, already have stimulated considerable regional action. Rank position indicates relative potential to earn an early listing on the *Hot 100.*"

The following is a synopsis of the *Bubbling Under The Hot 100* chart:

| Chart Title | Dates Researched | # of Positions |
|---|---|---|
| Bubbling Under The Hot 100 | 6/1/59 - 12/31/60 | 15 |
| Bubbling Under The Hot 100 | 1/9/61 - 9/29/62 | average 20 |
| Bubbling Under The Hot 100 | 10/6/62 - 7/18/70 | average 30-35 |
| Bubbling Under The Hot 100 | 7/25/70 - 7/6/74 | average 20 |
| Bubbling Under The Hot 100 | 7/13/74 - 8/24/85 | 10 |
| *No Charts Published* | 8/31/85 - 11/28/92 | |
| Bubbling Under Hot 100 Singles | 12/5/92 - present | 25 |

The smallest of all *Bubbling Under The Hot 100* charts was five positions (October 16, 1971), the largest equaled 36 (April 6, 1963 and May 25, 1968).

From June 1959 through August 1985, Billboard compiled the *Bubbling Under* chart from playlists reported by radio stations and surveys of retail sales outlets. Billboard did not publish a *Bubbling Under* chart from August 31, 1985 through November 28, 1992. They resumed publication of the *Bubbling Under* chart on December 5, 1992, employing their new data capture technology in its compilation.

Still in effect today, this technology combines actual point-of-sale retail information provided by SoundScan, Inc. with input from radio stations continuously monitored by Broadcast Data Systems (BDS), and additional playlists from small-market stations. BDS is a subsidiary of *Billboard* that electronically monitors actual radio airplay. They have installed monitors throughout the country which track the airplay of songs 24 hours a day, seven days a week. These monitors can identify each song played by an encoded audio "fingerprint."

*Billboard* has not published an issue for the last week of the year since 1976. For the years 1976 through 1991, *Billboard* considered the charts listed in the last published issue of each year to be "frozen" and all chart positions remained the same for the unpublished week. This frozen chart data is included in our tabulations. Since 1992, *Billboard* has <u>compiled</u> the *Bubbling Under* chart for the last week of each year, even though an issue is <u>not published</u>. These unpublished charts are available either through *Billboard's* computerized information network (BIN), or their members-only Internet site, or by mail. Our tabulations include this unpublished chart data.

For reasons unexplained, *Billboard* did not publish a *Bubbling Under The Hot 100* chart in the following issues:

January 12, 1974
April 13, 1974
July 27, 1974
July 15, 1978

The unpublished weeks were treated as frozen weeks. However, if a *Bubbling Under* record jumped to the *Hot 100* on one of the four dates listed above, one week was not added to the record's total *Bubbling Under* weeks charted.

# WHAT'S NEW WITH THIS EDITION

We are pleased to introduce the following new features in this third edition of *Bubbling Under:*

## B-SIDES

The flip sides of the charted vinyl singles — as well as additional tracks on charted cassette singles and CD singles — are now shown, doubling the number of titles listed in any previous edition. We have commercial copies of all but nine records (see page 413) within our *Bubbling Under* record collection; rather than repeat the A-side as our promotional copies do, we do not show the B-sides for these few records.

## HOT 100 SINGLES SALES and HOT 100 AIRPLAY HITS

*For Bubbling Under* singles that hit *Billboard's Hot 100 Singles Sales* chart and/or *Hot 100 Airplay* chart, the peak positions attained on the those charts are listed directly across from the A-side title.

## CAPSULE BIOGRAPHIES ON ALL ARTISTS

Short concise biographies have been carefully researched for accuracy, with at least one line of biographical information listed for nearly every artist.

## ARTISTS CROSS REFERENCED IN BOLD TYPE

Names of artists and groups mentioned in the biographies and title notes of other artists with *Bubbling Under* singles are highlighted in bold type if they have their own discography elsewhere in the *Bubbling Under* singles section.

## SPOT EACH ARTIST'S BIGGEST HITS INSTANTLY

For an artist that charted five or more singles, their highest-charting single is underlined.

All #101 singles are shaded with a light gray background for immediate identification.

## NEW CROSSOVER CROSS-REFERENCE

A two- or three-letter abbreviation across from the artist's name alerts you to other Record Research singles books (*Top Pop Singles, Pop Memories, Pop Hits, Top Country Singles, Top R&B* Singles, *Top Adult Contemporary,* and *Rock Tracks* ) in which that artist has charted hits.

## PROMOTIONAL PICTURE SLEEVES

A special promotional picture sleeve symbol is included in this edition. Record companies issued promotional/demonstration picture sleeves for distribution to radio stations and the press, and usually marked these for promotional use. However, some companies did not stamp them as for promotional use; for these unmarked promotional sleeves, there is conjecture as to whether they may have also been issued for commercial use.

In the 1960s, many of Columbia's promotional picture sleeves were simply letters from their promotional manager, plugging the songs' hit potential, printed on the front of the sleeves. Columbia later marked their promotional sleeves as "demonstration - not for sale" on the same sleeves that they also issued commercially.

This is a guide to the *Bubbling Under The Hot 100* artist section. The artist section is organized alphabetically by artist name and lists all *Bubbling Under* singles that did not chart on the *Hot 100*. The singles are listed in chronological order and sequentially numbered (if an artist had more than one such title.

## EXPLANATION OF COLUMNAR HEADINGS

**DEBUT:** Date single first charted (*Billboard's* actual <u>issue</u> date from the chart on which it first appeared. It is not the "week ending" date which *Billboard* published on their various charts. The issue and week ending dates were different until January 13, 1962, when *Billboard* began using a one date system for both the issue and the chart inside.)

**PEAK:** Highest charted *Bubbling Under* position (highlighted in bold type)

**WKS:** Total weeks charted

**A-side:** Song title of chart hit

**B-side:** Flip side of vinyl single or additional track(s) on a cassette or CD single

**$:** Current value of near-mint commercial copy

**Pic:** ■ Indicates a custom picture sleeve was originally issued with the record
□ Indicates a promotional picture sleeve was distributed to radio stations and the press
▮ Indicates a custom picture box was originally issued with the cassette single

**LABEL & NUMBER:** Original label and number of single when charted

## EXPLANATION OF SYMBOLS

✪ indicates that the artist never hit *Billboard's Hot 100* chart (appears to the right of the artist name)

¹ Superior number to the right of a #101 peak position is the <u>total weeks</u> the single held that position

+ Indicates single peaked in the <u>year after</u> it first charted

/ Divides a <u>two-sided hit</u>. Complete chart data (debut date, peak position, etc.) is shown for both sides if each side achieved its own peak position. If a title was shown only as the B-side, then only the weeks it was shown as a "tag along" are listed.

## LETTER(S) IN BRACKETS AFTER TITLES

C - Comedy
F - Foreign language
I - Instrumental
N - Novelty

R - Re-entry, reissue, remix or re-release of a previously charted single by that artist*
S - Spoken
X - Christmas

*Includes singles that re-entered following an absence of six months from the charts, and singles re-issued with a new label number.

# CHART ABBREVIATIONS

The abbreviations listed to the right of the artist name indicate other Record Research books and yearbooks in which the artist charted hits. The abbreviations are:

| | | | |
|---|---|---|---|
| **HOT**: | Top Pop Singles 1955-1997 | **C&W**: | Top Country Singles 1944-1997 |
| **MEM**: | Pop Memories 1890-1954* | **AC**: | Top Adult Contemporary 1961-1997 |
| **POP**: | Pop Hits 1940-1954 | **ROK**: | Mainstream (Album) Rock Tracks 1981-1997 & |
| **R&B**: | Top R&B Singles 1942-1997 | | Modern Rock Tracks 1988-1997 |

*Shown only when more titles by an artist can be found other than shown in our *Pop Hits 1940-1954* book.

# ARTIST'S BIGGEST HITS

All #101 singles are shaded with a light gray background for immediate identification.

For an artist that charted five or more singles, their highest-charting single is underlined

# ARTIST NOTES

Below nearly every artist name are brief biographical notes about the artist. Names of artists mentioned in the artist notes of other *Bubbling Under* singles artists are highlighted in bold type if they have their own discography elsewhere in this artist section. A name is only shown bold the first time it appears in an artist's biography. To conserve space in some artist biographies, the abbreviation "b:" for "born on" and the abbreviation "d:" for "died on" are used. If an artist charted 20 or more hits in our *Pop Hits 1940-1954* and/or *Top Pop Singles 1955-1996* (+1997) books, the total is shown at the end of their biographies (ex.: *Top Pop Singles*: 23).

# TITLE NOTES

Directly under some song titles are notes indicating backing vocalists, titles which were Pop hits for other artists or major R&B and Country hits, the title of the movie in which the song was featured, the name of a famous songwriter or producer, etc. Duets and other important name variations are shown in bold capital letters. Names of artists mentioned in the title notes of other *Bubbling Under* artists are highlighted in bold type if they have their own discography elsewhere in this artist section. All movie, TV and album titles, and other major works, are shown in italics.

As always, we gladly welcome any corrections/updates to our artist biographies or title notes (please include verification).

# PEAK POSITIONS ATTAINED ON OTHER CHARTS

The peak position a title reached on the *R&B, Country, Adult Contemporary, Rock Tracks, Hot 100 Singles Sales* and *Hot 100 Airplay* charts are listed to the right of the A-side title. The following letter designations precede the peak position attained on these charts:

| | |
|---|---|
| **AC:** | Adult Contemporary |
| **C&W:** | Country Singles |
| **R&B:** | R&B Singles |
| **ROK:** | Album (Mainstream) Rock Tracks and Modern Rock Tracks |
| **Air:** | Hot 100 Airplay |
| **Sls:** | Hot 100 Singles Sales |

# "B-SIDES" OF CASSETTE SINGLES

B-sides for cassette singles often contain one or more mixes of the A-side along with another title which may also include one or more mixes. Mixes are shown in parentheses in lower case italicized letters in the B-side column — ex.: *(instrumental), (live), (re-mix), (album version).* A diagonal symbol (/) is used to separate A-side mixes from the other titles on the cassette [ex.: *(album version)* / *Look Alive* (Big C)]. Often an A-side and B-side are on the same side of the cassette single. Usually cassette singles repeat the same program on both sides of the cassette. If a B-side title is recorded as a duet, or is recorded by a completely different artist, the artist name is shown in parentheses after the title in non-italicized type.

# 12" VINYL SINGLES (T)

*Bubbling Under* hits released commercially as 12" vinyl singles only are listed with a "(T)" after the label number. In some instances, 7" pressings of these titles were manufactured exclusively for disk jockey or juke box use and were not commercially available. Since a 12" single usually contains four to seven mixes of the same tune, it is priced higher than a 7" single.

# CD SINGLES

*Bubbling Under* hits released commercially as CD singles only are listed with a "(CD)" after the label number of the CD single. These are priced a few dollars higher than regular cassette singles.

# CASSETTE MAXI-SINGLES (*)

*Bubbling Under* hits released commercially as cassette maxi-singles only are indicated by an asterisk after the label number. Cassette maxi-singles usually consist of four to six tracks and are packaged in a hard plastic case with a custom picture insert. These are priced a couple of dollars higher than regular cassette singles.

# RECORD PRICE GUIDE

This is the second edition of the *Bubbling Under* book to feature a price guide. The prices of singles have increased substantially since the last edition was published in 1993. The current prices of many '50s and '60s singles, valued at $8 in our last edition, are now as high as $25.

Highly collectable records such as the doo-wop, novelty, R&B groups and rockabilly singles reflect a much higher price than most records. Also, variations of the original commercial release, such as promotional copies, mistakes or differentiations on the label, colored vinyl, etc. can vastly increase, or in rare cases, decrease the price of a record. When evaluating the more common singles, the age of the record is a major determining factor. Generally, older records are more scarce and more difficult to find in good condition and thus command a higher value.

Our prices are estimates of the dealer-asking prices for *near-mint* commercial copies. Please keep in mind that this book is not intended to be an all-purpose record price guide but a novice's tool to record pricing. Remember that the condition of a record and its demand are strong determinations of its price.

# ARTIST SECTION

Lists, alphabetically by artist name, every single that hit *Billboard's Bubbling Under The Hot 100* chart, but did not go on to hit the *Hot 100* chart. This section covers the *Bubbling Under The Hot 100* chart from its inception on June 1, 1959 through December 27, 1997.

# A

**A.A.B.B.** ✪
Group is actually **James Brown**'s group, the **JB's**. Initials stand for Average American Black Band — a response to **Average White Band** and their #1 hit "Pick Up The Pieces."

| 4/12/75 | 108 | 3 | Pick Up The Pieces One By One ........................................................ *C.O.L.D.* [I] | $10 | I | Dentify 8003 |

rhythm track taken from the JB's song "Hot Pants Road" (B-side of their 1972 *Hot 100* hit "Pass The Peas"); with overdubs by **James Brown** (drums) and Maceo (**Maceo And The Macks**) Parker (sax)

**AALIYAH — see JUNIOR M.A.F.I.A.**

**ABBA**                    HOT/AC
Pop group from Stockholm, Sweden: Anni-Frid "**Frida**" Lyngstad and Agnetha Fältskog (vocals), Bjorn Ulvaeus (guitar) and Benny Andersson (keyboards). *Top Pop Singles*: 20.

| 2/12/83 | 107 | 4 | One Of Us ................................................... AC:33 *Should I Laugh Or Cry* | $5 | ■ | Atlantic 89881 |

recorded in Sweden in 1981

**ABDUL, Paula**             HOT/AC/R&B
Born on 6/19/62 in Los Angeles. Singer/dancer/choreographer. Formerly married to actor Emilio Estevez.

| 1/27/96 | 112 | 3 | Ain't Never Gonna Give You Up ...................................(2 mixes) / *Love Don't Come Easy* | $3 | ▮ | Captive/Virgin 38528 |

**ABRAHAM'S CHILDREN** ✪
Pop group from Canada: Ron Bartley (vocals), Shawn O'Shea (guitar), Bob McPherson (keyboards), Jim Bertucci (bass) and Brian Cotterill (drums).

| 2/17/73 | 119 | 4 | Gypsy .................................................................... *Fly Me To The Sky* | $7 | | Buddah 340 |

**ABSOLUTE** ✪           R&B

| 10/18/97 | 106 | 11 | Never Wanna Let You Go.................................... R&B:51 *Sexy* | $3 | ▮ | Def Jam 574925 |

from the movie *Def Jam's How To Be A Player* starring Bill Bellamy

**ACCENTS** ✪
R&B vocal group from Chicago: James Short, James Brown, Robert Hill and Oliver Jackson.

| 8/15/64 | 128 | 1 | New Girl ............................................................ *Do You Need A Good Man* | $25 | | m-pac! 7216 |

**ACCENTS, The** ✪

| 8/8/64 | 133 | 1 | Better Watch Out Boy.......................... *Tell Me (What's On Your Mind)* | $20 | | Challenge 59254 |
|  |  |  | THE ACCENTS featuring Sandi | | | |

**AC/DC**               ROK/HOT
Hard-rock group from Sydney, Australia: brothers Angus and Malcolm Young (guitars), Ron Belford "Bon" Scott (vocals), Mark Evans (bass) and Phil Rudd (drums). Bon Scott died on 2/19/80 and was replaced by Brian Johnson.

| 2/2/80 | 106 | 1 | Touch Too Much ................................................ *Walk All Over You* | $5 | | Atlantic 3644 |

**ACE OF BASE**          HOT/AC/ROK
Pop group from Gothenburg, Sweden: vocalists/sisters Jenny and Linn Berggren with keyboardists Jonas "Joker" Berggren (their brother) and Ulf "Buddha" Ekberg.

| 8/17/96 | 106 | 7 | Never Gonna Say I'm Sorry ............................................ *(radio edit)* | $3 | ▮ | Arista 13221 |

**ACID FACTOR featuring Margie M.** ✪
Dance duo: Margret McEwen (vocals) and Samantha Alvarado (spoken words).

| 2/1/97 | 106 | 6 | Fantasy ...........................................................*(remix)* | $3 | ▮ | StreetBeat 003 |

**ACKLIN, Barbara**          R&B/HOT
Born on 2/28/43 in Chicago. R&B singer/songwriter. Married Eugene Record of The Chi-Lites.

| 10/17/70 | 121 | 1 | I Did It.................................................. R&B:28 *I'm Living With A Memory* | $12 | | Brunswick 55440 |

**ACT I** ✪           R&B
R&B group assembled by producer Raeford Gerald.

| 3/31/73 | 101[1] | 3 | Friends Or Lovers        R&B:22 *I Never Had A Love Like Yours* | $8 | | Spring 132 |

**ADAMS, Johnny**          R&B/HOT
Born Lathan John Adams on 1/5/32 in New Orleans. Soul singer nicknamed "The Tan Canary."

| 1/3/70 | 121 | 2 | Proud Woman ....................................................... *Real Live Living Hurtin' Man* | $15 | | SSS International 787 |

**ADAMS, Ray** ✪
Pop vocalist.

| 5/5/62 | 119 | 2 | (Hear My Song) Violetta ........................................ *You Belong To My Heart* | $10 | | Laurie 3118 |
|  |  |  | #9 hit for Glenn Miller in 1940 | | | |

**ADC BAND** ✪          R&B
Seven-man, two-woman funk/disco band led by vocalists Kaiya Matthew and Michael Judkins.

| 12/9/78+ | 101[3] | 11 | Long Stroke           R&B:6 *That's Life* | $5 | | Cotillion 44243 |

**ADDRISI BROTHERS**          HOT/AC
Pop singing/songwriting duo: Dick (b: 7/4/41) and Don (b: 12/14/38; d: 11/13/84) Addrisi, from Winthrop, Massachusetts.

| 5/20/72 | 110 | 3 | I Can Feel You .................................................... *One Last Time* | $7 | | Columbia 45610 |

**AESOPS FABLES** ✪
Eight-man pop group led by Sonny Botarri.

| 9/14/68 | 123 | 1 | I'm Gonna Make You Love Me.......................... *They Go Out And Get It* | $8 | | Cadet Concept 7005 |
|  |  |  | #2 hit for Diana Ross And The Supremes & The Temptations in 1969 | | | |

**AFTER 7**          R&B/HOT/AC
R&B vocal trio from Indianapolis: Keith Mitchell with brothers Kevon and Melvin Edmonds. Kevon and Melvin are brothers of **Babyface**.

| 4/3/93 | 103 | 10 | 1 Can He Love U Like This................................ Sls:67 /R&B:22 *One Night / My Only Woman* | $3 | ▮ | Virgin 12643 |
| 11/25/95 | 109 | 8 | 2 Damn Thing Called Love.........................R&B:33 *(2 mixes) / I Like It Like That* | $3 | ▮ | Virgin 38521 |
|  |  |  | written by **Babyface**; produced by Jon B. and **Babyface** | | | |

| DEBUT | PEAK | WKS | A-side / B-side | $ | Pic | Label & Number |
|---|---|---|---|---|---|---|
| | | | **A-HA**           HOT/AC | | | |
| | | | Pop trio from Oslo, Norway: Morten Harket (vocals), Pal Waaktaar (guitar) and Magne "Mags" Furuholmen (keyboards). | | | |
| 7/10/93 | 111 | 4 | Dark Is The Night................................................*Between Your Mama And Yourself* | $3 | ■ | Warner 18494 |
| | | | **AIKEN, Ben** ⊙ | | | |
| | | | R&B vocalist. | | | |
| 10/23/65 | 121 | 6 | Stay Together Young Lovers ....................................*Hurry On Home* | $12 | | Roulette 4649 |
| | | | #66 hit for **Brenda & The Tabulations** in 1967 | | | |
| | | | **AKENS, Jewel**       HOT/R&B | | | |
| | | | Born on 9/12/40 in Houston. Male R&B singer/producer. | | | |
| 8/14/65 | 120 | 3 | It's The Only Way To Fly.........................................*You Sure Know How To Hurt A Fella* | $12 | | Era 3147 |
| | | | **AKINS, Rhett**       C&W | | | |
| | | | Born on 10/13/69 in Valdosta, Georgia. Country singer/songwriter/guitarist. | | | |
| 11/22/97 | 121 | 7 | More Than Everything ....................C&W:41 *Better Than It Used To Be* | $3 | ■ | Decca 72022 |
| | | | **ALABAMA**       C&W/AC/HOT | | | |
| | | | Country quartet from Fort Payne, Alabama: Randy Owen (vocals, guitar), Jeff Cook (keyboards, fiddle), Teddy Gentry (bass, vocals) and Mark Herndon (drums, vocals). Randy, Jeff and Teddy are cousins. | | | |
| 5/2/81 | 103 | 2 | 1 Old Flame........................................C&W:❶ *I'm Stoned* | $5 | | RCA 12169 |
| 3/20/82 | 101[1] | 2 | 2 Mountain Music ................................C&W:❶ *Never Be One* | $5 | ■ | RCA 13019 |
| 11/27/93 | 123 | 1 | 3 Reckless........................................C&W:❶ *Clear Water Blues* | $3 | ■ | RCA 62636 |
| 12/9/95 | 118 | 4 | 4 In Pictures....................................C&W:4 *Between The Two Of Them* | $3 | ■ | RCA 64419 |
| 1/6/96 | 122 | 1 | 5 Angels Among Us ...........................C&W:28 *Santa Claus (I Still Believe In You)* [X] | $3 | ■ | RCA 62643 |
| | | | recorded in 1993 | | | |
| | | | **ALAIMO, Steve**       HOT/AC | | | |
| | | | Born on 12/6/39 in Rochester, New York. Singer/actor. Acted in the movies *Stanley* and *Wild Rebels*. | | | |
| 8/17/63 | 125 | 1 | 1 Don't Let The Sun Catch You Crying .......................*I Told You So* | $15 | | Checker 1047 |
| 9/12/64 | 103 | 5 | 2 I Don't Know ...................................*That's What Love Will Do* | $12 | | ABC-Paramount 10580 |
| 9/16/67 | 126 | 2 | 3 New Orleans ...................................*Ooh Poo Pah Doo* | $8 | | Atco 6512 |
| | | | #6 hit for **U.S. Bonds** in 1960 | | | |
| 3/23/68 | 118 | 2 | 4 Denver .............................................*I Do* | $8 | | Atco 6561 |
| 9/6/69 | 101[2] | 3 | 5 One Woman *And Then I Tripped Over Your Goodbye* | $8 | | Atco 6710 |
| | | | **ALARM, The**       ROK/HOT | | | |
| | | | Rock quartet from Rhyl, Wales: Mike Peters (vocals), Dave Sharp (guitar), Eddie MacDonald (bass) and Nigel Twist (drums). | | | |
| 4/14/84 | 106 | 3 | 1 Sixty Eight Guns ..............................ROK:39 *Pavilion Steps* | $5 | ■ | I.R.S. 9924 |
| 7/21/84 | 104 | 2 | 2 The Deceiver ...................................*Second Generation* | $5 | ■ | I.R.S. 9929 |
| | | | **ALBERT, Eddie**       HOT | | | |
| | | | Born on 4/22/08 in Rock Island, Illinois. Played "Oliver Wendall Douglas" on TV's *Green Acres*. Acted in numerous movies. | | | |
| 1/9/65 | 119 | 3 | Fall Away...........................................*Just Waitin'* | $8 | | Hickory 1278 |
| | | | Albert sings and narrates about his "golden wedding day" | | | |
| | | | **ALBERTINE, Charles** ⊙ | | | |
| | | | Born in Passaic, New Jersey. Died on 5/18/86 (age 57). Composer/arranger. | | | |
| 8/15/64 | 112 | 5 | The Long Ships, Part 1..........................*Part 2* [I] | $12 | | Colpix 726 |
| | | | from the movie *The Long Ships* starring Richard Widmark and Sidney Poitier | | | |
| | | | **ALEONG, Aki** ⊙ | | | |
| | | | Born in Los Angeles. Male singer/actor. Acted in numerous movies including *Operation Bikini* (1963) and *The Cable Guy* (1996). | | | |
| 11/13/61 | 101[1] | 4 | Trade Winds, Trade Winds *Without Your Love* | $15 | | Reprise 20,021 |
| | | | **ALEXANDER, Arthur**       HOT/R&B | | | |
| | | | Born on 5/10/40 in Florence, Alabama. Died on 6/9/93 of a heart attack. Influential soul singer/songwriter. | | | |
| 1/12/63 | 102 | 3 | 1 Go Home Girl ...................................*You're The Reason* | $15 | | Dot 16425 |
| 8/10/63 | 118 | 4 | 2 Pretty Girls Everywhere.........................*Baby Baby* | $15 | | Dot 16509 |
| | | | #36 hit for **Eugene Church** in 1959 | | | |
| | | | **ALISHA**       HOT/R&B | | | |
| | | | Teen dance singer from Brooklyn, New York. | | | |
| 4/7/84 | 103 | 6 | All Night Passion...............................R&B:84 *Dub All Night* | $4 | | Vanguard 35244 |
| | | | **ALKAHOLIKS, Tha**       R&B/HOT | | | |
| | | | Rap trio from Los Angeles: James "J-Ro" Robinson, Rico "Tash" Smith and Eric "E-Swift" Brooks. Also see **Xzibit**. | | | |
| 10/16/93 | 108 | 6 | 1 Make Room ...................................R&B:85 *Last Call* | $3 | ■ | Loud/RCA 62579 |
| 9/13/97 | 122 | 1 | 2 Likwidation ...................................R&B:89 *(3 versions)* | $6 | ■ | Loud/RCA 64945 (T) |
| | | | **ALLEN, Chad** ⊙ | | | |
| 11/13/61 | 112 | 2 | Little Lonely ...................................*Domino* | $20 | | Smash 1720 |
| | | | **ALLEN, Lee**       HOT | | | |
| | | | Born on 7/2/26 in Pittsburg, Kansas. Died on 10/18/94 of cancer. Sax player on hits by **Fats Domino**, **Little Richard** and others. | | | |
| 10/19/59 | 102 | 3 | Cat Walk ...........................................*Creole Alley* [I] | $20 | | Ember 1057 |
| | | | **ALLEN, Peter**       AC/HOT | | | |
| | | | Born Peter Allen Woolnough on 2/10/44 in Tenterfield, Australia. Died of AIDS on 6/18/92. Cabaret-style performer. Married to **Liza Minnelli** from 1967-73. | | | |
| 8/28/76 | 108 | 4 | The More I See You .............................AC:38 *This Time Around* | $5 | | A&M 1813 |
| | | | **Herb Alpert** (trumpet solo); #16 hit for **Chris Montez** in 1966 | | | |
| | | | **ALLEN, Ricky** ⊙ | | | |
| | | | Born on 1/6/35 in Nashville. R&B singer. | | | |
| 9/21/63 | 126 | 2 | Cut You A-Loose ................................R&B:20 *Faith* | $15 | | AGE 29118 |

| DEBUT | PEAK | WKS | A-side (Chart Hit)..........................................................................................B-side | $ | Pic | Label & Number |
|-------|------|-----|---|---|---|---|

**ALLEN, Steve**     HOT/AC
Born on 12/26/21 in New York City. Comedian/actor/songwriter/author. Appeared in numerous TV shows and movies.

| 9/12/64 | 111 | 1 | How's Your Sister .............................................. *Theme From The Magic Fountain* [N] | $10 | | Dot 16645 |

Donn Trenner (orch.); features Allen's famous phrase "schmock schmock"

**ALLEN, Vee** ☺     R&B
Sister of R&B singer Al Perkins.

| 3/3/73 | 107 | 4 | Can I ..............................................**R&B:26** *Cheating Is A No No* | $8 | | Lion 140 |

**ALL-4-ONE**     R&B/HOT/AC
Male R&B vocal quartet from Southern California: Jamie Jones, Delious Kennedy, Alfred Nevarez and Tony Borowiak.

| 9/24/94 | 105 | 4 | 1 Breathless ...........................................**R&B:66** *Without You* | $3 | ■ | Blitzz/Atlantic 87202 |
| 11/4/95 | 116 | 3 | 2 I'm Your Man ...............................**R&B:71** *Christmas With My Baby* | $3 | ■ | Blitzz/Atlantic 87097 |
| 4/20/96 | 109 | 7 | 3 These Arms ................................................*Everything U R 2 Me* | $3 | ■ | Blitzz/Atlantic 87077 |

**ALLISONS, The** ☺
British pop duo of brothers Bob and John Allison.

| 4/3/61 | 102 | 4 | Are You Sure ...................................................*There's One Thing More* | $15 | ■ | London 1977 |

Harry Robinson (orch.); 1960 contest winner of BBC's "A Song for Europe"

**ALLMAN BROTHERS BAND, The**     ROK/HOT
Southern-rock band from Macon, Georgia. Numerous personnel changes. The 1979 lineup: **Greg Allman** (keyboards, vocals), Dickey Betts (guitar, vocals), Dan Toler (guitar), Rook Goldflies (bass) and the drum duo of Butch Trucks and Jai Johnny Johanson. Group inducted into the Rock and Roll Hall of Fame in 1995. Also see **Sea Level**.

| 4/20/74 | 106 | 2 | 1 Don't Mess Up A Good Thing.............................*Please Call Home* | $6 | | Capricorn 0042 |

    **GREGG ALLMAN**
#33 hit for Fontella Bass & Bobby McClure in 1965

| 7/7/79 | 105 | 4 | 2 Can't Take It With You ...............................................*Sail Away* | $5 | | Capricorn 0326 |

**ALMA** ☺

| 3/27/93 | 107 | 2 | Make It With You/Take A Chance ..................... *(sing along version)* | $4 | ■ | Original Sound 5600 |

"Make It With You" was a #1 hit for Bread in 1970; "Take A Chance" was a track on **Brenton Wood**'s 1967 album *Oogum Boogum*

**ALMIGHTY RSO, The**     R&B
Rap group from Dorchester, Massachusetts: Tony Rhome, Mack Devious, Raydog The Jackal and DJ Deff Jeff.

| 11/16/96 | 104 | 14 | You Could Be My Boo ...............**R&B:49** *(instrumental) / Sanity (2 versions)* | $3 | | Rap-A-Lot 38571 |

    **THE ALMIGHTY RSO featuring Faith Evans**

**ALPERT, Herb, & The Tijuana Brass**     AC/HOT/R&B
Born on 3/31/35 in Los Angeles. Producer/composer/trumpeter/bandleader. Formed A&M Records with Jerry Moss in 1962. Used studio musicians until early 1965, then formed own band. *Top Pop Singles*: 40.

| 3/23/63 | 102 | 1 | 1 Struttin' With Maria ...............*Marching Thru Madrid (Hot #96)* [I] | $8 | | A&M 706 |

    **HERB ALPERT'S TIJUANA BRASS**

| 5/29/65 | 116 | 4 | 2 Mae .........................................**AC:26** *El Garbanzo* [I] | $7 | | A&M 767 |

    from the movie *The Yellow Rolls-Royce* starring Rex Harrison

| 4/27/68 | 119 | 3 | 3 Slick ............................................**AC:36** *Cabaret (Hot #72)* [I] | $6 | ■ | A&M 925 |
| 8/16/69 | 118 | 3 | 4 Ob-La-Di, Ob-La-Da ..............................*Marjorine* [I] | $5 | | A&M 1102 |

    #49 hit for **The Beatles** in 1976

| 11/22/69 | 109 | 3 | 5 You Are My Life .............................**AC:34** *Good Morning, Mr. Sunshine* | $5 | ■ | A&M 1143 |
| 1/31/70 | 108 | 3 | 6 The Maltese Melody ........................**AC:14** *Country Lake* [I] | $5 | | A&M 1159 |

    recorded by Bert Kaempfert on his 1969 album *Warm And Wonderful*

| 6/12/71 | 114 | 2 | 7 Summertime ...............................**AC:28** *Hurt So Bad* | $5 | | A&M 1261 |

    from George Gershwin's 1935 folk opera *Porgy And Bess*

| 3/29/80 | 104 | 5 | 8 Street Life .................................**AC:41** *1980* [I] | $3 | ■ | A&M 2221 |

    **HERB ALPERT**
#36 hit for **The Crusaders** in 1979

**A.L.T.**     HOT
A.L.T. (Another Latin Timebomb) was born Al Trivette in Los Angeles. French-Mexican rapper. Formerly with Latin Alliance.

| 2/12/94 | 121 | 1 | All Nite Long ..................................................... *(2 versions)* | $3 | ■ | PAR 4123 |

    samples "All Night Long" by Mary Jane Girls

**ALZO** ☺
Pop singer Alzo Fronte.

| 2/12/72 | 116 | 3 | That's Alright (I Don't Mind It) ...................................*You're Gone* | $8 | | Ampex 11052 |

**AMAZING RHYTHM ACES**     C&W/HOT
Country-rock group from Memphis: Russell Smith (vocals, guitar), Barry "Byrd" Burton (guitar, dobro), Billy Earhart III (keyboards), Jeff Davis (bass) and Butch McDade (drums).

| 4/7/79 | 104 | 4 | Lipstick Traces (On A Cigarette) ...............**C&W:88** *Whispering In The Night* | $5 | | ABC 12454 |

    #48 hit for The O'Jays in 1965

**AMBASSADORS, The** ☺     R&B
Ex-gospel vocal group from Philadelphia featuring twin lead voices of Herley Johnson and Bobby Todd, with Orlando Oliphant.

| 2/15/69 | 123 | 4 | I Really Love You .........................**R&B:43** *I Can't Believe You Love Me* | $12 | | Arctic 147 |

    #78 hit for **Dee Dee Sharp** in 1965

**AMBOY DUKES, The**     HOT
Rock group formed in Chicago in 1965 by Detroit-born **Ted Nugent**. Moved to Detroit in 1967. Numerous personnel changes with Nugent the only constant.

| 3/2/68 | 106 | 4 | 1 Baby Please Don't Go ................................*Psalms Of Aftermath* | $15 | | Mainstream 676 |
| 10/12/68 | 114 | 3 | 2 You Talk Sunshine, I Breathe Fire ....................*Scottish Tea* | $15 | | Mainstream 693 |

**AMBROSE, Sammy** ☺
Sammy Ambrose is actually Tony Middleton — lead singer of the R&B group **Willows**.

| 1/9/65 | 117 | 1 | This Diamond Ring .....................................*Bad Night* | $20 | | Musicor 1061 |

    #1 hit for **Gary Lewis & The Playboys** in 1965

**AMBROSIA**            HOT/AC/ROK
Pop group from Los Angeles: David Pack (vocals, guitar), Joe Puerta (vocals, bass), Burleigh Drummond (drums) and Christopher North (keyboards; left in 1977).

| DEBUT | PEAK | WKS | A-side | B-side | $ | Pic | Label & Number |
|---|---|---|---|---|---|---|---|
| 12/11/76 | 102 | 6 | 1 Can't Let A Woman ............................................................. *The Brunt* | | $5 | | 20th Century 2310 |
| | | | produced by **Alan Parsons** | | | | |
| 7/7/79 | 107 | 4 | 2 If Heaven Could Find Me ................................................ *Apothecary* | | $4 | | Warner 8817 |
| 11/15/80 | 105 | 2 | 3 No Big Deal ................................................... *Cryin' In The Rain* | | $4 | | Warner 49590 |
| 1/31/81 | 102 | 7 | 4 Outside .............................. *I Can't Tell You Why* (Eagles-Hot #8/'80) | | $5 | | Full Moon 49654 |
| | | | from the movie *Inside Moves* starring John Savage | | | | |

**AMERICA**            AC/HOT
Soft-rock trio formed in London: Americans Dan Peek and Gerry Beckley, with Englishman Dewey Bunnell. Won the 1972 Best New Artist Grammy Award. Reduced to a duo in 1976 after Peek's departure.

| DEBUT | PEAK | WKS | A-side | B-side | $ | Pic | Label & Number |
|---|---|---|---|---|---|---|---|
| 8/25/79 | 107 | 3 | 1 Only Game In Town ......................................... *High In The City* | | $4 | | Capitol 4752 |
| 10/20/84 | 106 | 2 | 2 Special Girl ................................ **AC:15** *Unconditional Love* | | $3 | | Capitol 5398 |

**AMERICAN BREED, The**            HOT
Interracial rock quartet from Cicero, Illinois: Gary Loizzo (vocals, guitar), Al Ciner (guitar), Chuck Colbern (bass) and Lee Graziano (drums). Later members Kevin Murphy (keyboards) and Andre Fischer (drums) went on to form **Rufus**.

| DEBUT | PEAK | WKS | A-side | B-side | $ | Pic | Label & Number |
|---|---|---|---|---|---|---|---|
| 8/12/67 | 107 | 4 | 1 Don't Forget About Me ........................................ *Short Skirts* | | $12 | | Acta 808 |
| 5/3/69 | 107 | 2 | 2 Hunky Funky ............................................... *Enter Her Majesty* | | $12 | | Acta 833 |

**AMES, Ed**            AC/HOT
Born Ed Urick on 7/9/27 in Malden, Massachusetts. One of **The Ames Brothers**.

| DEBUT | PEAK | WKS | A-side | B-side | $ | Pic | Label & Number |
|---|---|---|---|---|---|---|---|
| 8/10/68 | 122 | 4 | 1 All My Love's Laughter ................. **AC:12** *I'll Stay Lonely* | | $6 | | RCA Victor 9589 |
| 2/22/69 | 130 | 4 | 2 Changing, Changing ...................... **AC:11** *Six Words* | | $6 | | RCA Victor 9726 |

**AMES, Nancy**            HOT/AC
Born in 1937 in Washington, D.C. Spanish/English singer. Cast as the "TW3 Girl" on TV's satirical revue *That Was The Week That Was*.

| DEBUT | PEAK | WKS | A-side | B-side | $ | Pic | Label & Number |
|---|---|---|---|---|---|---|---|
| 10/2/65 | 119 | 4 | 1 The Funny Thing About It................................. *Shake A Hand* | | $7 | ■ | Epic 9845 |
| 1/15/66 | 123 | 4 | 2 Friends And Lovers Forever ........... *I've Got A Lot Of Love (Left In Me)* | | $8 | | Epic 9874 |
| | | | same melody as "Hang On Sloopy" by The McCoys (#1 hit in 1965) | | | | |

**AMES BROTHERS, The**            MEM/POP/HOT
Pop vocal group from Malden, Massachusetts: **Ed Ames** and his brothers Gene, Joe and Vic (d: 1/23/78, age 51). *Pop Hits & Top Pop Singles: 43.*

| DEBUT | PEAK | WKS | A-side | B-side | $ | Pic | Label & Number |
|---|---|---|---|---|---|---|---|
| 10/26/63 | 129 | 1 | Washington Square ......................... *Knees Up! Mother Brown* | | $8 | | Epic 9630 |
| | | | Joe Sherman (orch.); #2 hit for **The Village Stompers** in 1963 | | | | |

**AMOS, Tori**            ROK/HOT
Born Myra Ellen Amos on 8/22/63 in Newton, North Carolina; raised in Maryland. Singer/songwriter/pianist.

| DEBUT | PEAK | WKS | A-side | B-side | $ | Pic | Label & Number |
|---|---|---|---|---|---|---|---|
| 5/28/94+ | 107 | 12 | 1 Cornflake Girl      **ROK:12** *Honey* | | $3 | ▌ | Atlantic 87004 |
| 6/8/96 | 119 | 1 | 2 Talula .............................. *(remix) / Samurai / Frog On My Toe / London Girls* | | $6 | | Atlantic 85504 **(CD)** |
| | | | from the movie *Twister* starring Helen Hunt and Bill Paxton | | | | |
| 7/20/96 | 108 | 3 | 3 Professional Widow ........................................ *(6 mixes)* | | $6 | | Atlantic 85499 **(CD)** |
| 10/12/96 | 120 | 1 | 4 In The Springtime Of His Voodoo .................. *(4 mixes)* | | $6 | | Atlantic 85475 **(CD)** |
| 3/1/97 | 122 | 2 | 5 Professional Widow ............................... *(6 mixes)* [R] | | $6 | | Atlantic 85499 **(CD)** |

**ANDERSON, Al** ✪
Born on 7/26/47 in Windsor, Connecticut. Blues-rock guitarist. Member of **The Wildweeds** and **NRBQ**.

| DEBUT | PEAK | WKS | A-side | B-side | $ | Pic | Label & Number |
|---|---|---|---|---|---|---|---|
| 3/24/73 | 101[2] | 2 | We'll Make Love      *I Just Want To Have You Back Again* | | $7 | | Vanguard 35168 |

**ANDERSON, Bill**            C&W/HOT
Born James William Anderson III on 11/1/37 in Columbia, South Carolina. Country singer/songwriter.

| DEBUT | PEAK | WKS | A-side | B-side | $ | Pic | Label & Number |
|---|---|---|---|---|---|---|---|
| 2/22/64 | 118 | 2 | 1 Five Little Fingers ................. **C&W:5** *Easy Come-Easy Go* (C&W #14) | | $8 | | Decca 31577 |
| 4/17/71 | 111 | 3 | 2 Always Remember ............. **C&W:6** *You Can Change My World* | | $6 | | Decca 32793 |

**ANDERSON, James** ✪
Born in Port Arthur, Texas. Bayou rock singer.

| DEBUT | PEAK | WKS | A-side | B-side | $ | Pic | Label & Number |
|---|---|---|---|---|---|---|---|
| 11/14/70 | 106 | 4 | Mama Mama ........................................ *Muskatel, Muskatel* | | $8 | | Cotillion 44097 |

**ANDERSON, John**            C&W/HOT
Born on 12/13/54 in Orlando; raised in Apopka, Florida. Country singer/guitarist.

| DEBUT | PEAK | WKS | A-side | B-side | $ | Pic | Label & Number |
|---|---|---|---|---|---|---|---|
| 8/23/97 | 115 | 3 | Somebody Slap Me ............. **C&W:22** *We've Got A Good Thing Goin'* | | $3 | ▌ | Mercury 574640 |

**ANDERSON, Jon**            ROK/HOT/AC
Born on 10/25/44 in Lancashire, England. Lead singer of **Yes**. Also recorded in the duo Jon & Vangelis.

| DEBUT | PEAK | WKS | A-side | B-side | $ | Pic | Label & Number |
|---|---|---|---|---|---|---|---|
| 1/17/81 | 109 | 2 | Some Are Born ............................................................ *Days* | | $4 | | Atlantic 3774 |

**ANDERSON, Kip** ✪
Born in Anderson, South Carolina. Male R&B singer/songwriter/pianist.

| DEBUT | PEAK | WKS | A-side | B-side | $ | Pic | Label & Number |
|---|---|---|---|---|---|---|---|
| 9/19/64 | 130 | 1 | That's When The Crying Begins ................ *I Done You Wrong* | | $15 | | ABC-Paramount 10578 |

**ANDERSON, Lynn**            C&W/HOT/AC
Born on 9/26/47 in Grand Forks, North Dakota; raised in Sacramento. Country singer. Daughter of country singer Liz Anderson.

| DEBUT | PEAK | WKS | A-side | B-side | $ | Pic | Label & Number |
|---|---|---|---|---|---|---|---|
| 12/5/70 | 112 | 1 | 1 I'm Alright ........................ **C&W:20** *Pick Of The Week* | | $7 | | Chart 5098 |
| | | | written by **Bill Anderson** | | | | |
| 7/1/72 | 107 | 1 | 2 Listen To A Country Song ............... **C&W:4** *That's What Loving You Has Meant To Me* | | $5 | | Columbia 45615 |
| 11/18/72 | 101[1] | 2 | 3 Fool Me     **C&W:4** *What's Made Milwaukee Famous* | | $5 | | Columbia 45692 |
| | | | #78 hit for **Joe South** in 1971 | | | | |
| 3/3/73 | 104 | 4 | 4 Keep Me In Mind ........................... **C&W:❶**[1] *Rodeo Cowboy* | | $4 | | Columbia 45768 |

**ANDERSON, Vicki**            HOT
R&B singer. Recorded the *Hot 100* hit "Think" with **James Brown** in 1967.

| DEBUT | PEAK | WKS | A-side | B-side | $ | Pic | Label & Number |
|---|---|---|---|---|---|---|---|
| 9/23/67 | 131 | 2 | Tears Of Joy.................... *If You Don't Give Me What I Want (I Gotta Get It Some Other Place)* | | $12 | | King 6109 |
| | | | #9 R&B hit for **The "5" Royales** in 1957 | | | | |

**ANDREWS, Ruby**            R&B/HOT
Born Ruby Stackhouse on 3/12/47 in Hollandale, Mississippi. R&B singer.

| DEBUT | PEAK | WKS | A-side | B-side | $ | Pic | Label & Number |
|---|---|---|---|---|---|---|---|
| 5/30/70 | 118 | 2 | Everybody Saw You ............................... **R&B:34** *Can You Get Away* (R&B #41) | | $10 | | Zodiac 1017 |

**ANGEL CITY** ✪           ROK
Hard-rock quintet formed in Australia in 1976: Doc Neeson (vocals), brothers Rick and John Brewster (guitars), Jim Hilbun (bass) and Brent Eccles (drums).

| 6/14/80 | 109 | 4 | Marseilles ............................................................................ *Waiting For The World* | $4 | | Epic 50881 |

**ANGELS, The**           HOT/R&B
Female pop trio from Orange, New Jersey: sisters Phyllis "Jiggs" and Barbara Allbut, and Linda Jansen (lead singer). Jansen was replaced by Peggy Santiglia in 1962. Also recorded as **The Starlets**.

| 6/20/60 | 106 | 2 | 1 P.S. I Love You .................................................................. *Where Is My Love Tonight?* | $40 | | Astro 202 |

THE STARLETS
#12 hit for Rudy Vallee in 1934; #4 hit for The Hilltoppers in 1953

| 5/26/62 | 103 | 7 | 2 Everybody Loves A Lover ................................................................ *Blow Joe* | $20 | | Caprice 116 |

Hutch Davie (orch.); #6 hit for **Doris Day** in 1958

| 9/21/63 | 119 | 1 | 3 Cotton Fields ........................................................................... *Irresistible* | $15 | | Ascot 2139 |

#13 hit for The Highwaymen in 1962; traditional American ballad, copyrighted in 1850

| 7/31/65 | 106 | 5 | 4 Out In The Sun (Hey-O) ................................................................ *Someday Soon* | $30 | | Bang 504 |

THE BEACH-NUTS (The Strangeloves & The Angels)
loosely based on Harry Belafonte's "Banana Boat (Day-O)"

**ANIMALS, The**           HOT/ROK
Rock group from Newcastle, England: Eric Burdon (vocals), Hilton Valentine (guitar), Alan Price (keyboards), Bryan "Chas" Chandler (bass; d: 7/17/96, age 57) and John Steel (drums). Group inducted into the Rock and Roll Hall of Fame in 1994.

| 9/12/64 | 102 | 2 | Baby Let Me Take You Home ................... *Gonna Send You Back To Walker* (Hot #57) | $15 | | MGM 13242 |

**ANKA, Paul**           HOT/AC/R&B
Born on 7/30/41 in Ottawa, Canada. Prolific singer/songwriter. *Top Pop Singles*: 53.

| 12/12/60 | 104 | 2 | 1 Rudolph, The Red-Nosed Reindeer .............................. *It's Christmas Everywhere* [X] | $20 | ■ | ABC-Paramount 10169 |

#1 Pop and Country hit for Gene Autry in 1949

| 1/9/61 | 108 | 3 | 2 Don't Say You're Sorry ................................... *The Story Of My Love* (Hot #16) | $15 | ■ | ABC-Paramount 10168 |
| 12/4/61 | 104 | 3 | 3 The Bells At My Wedding/ | | | |
| 12/4/61 | 110 | 1 | 4   Loveland | $15 | | ABC-Paramount 10279 |
| 1/27/62 | 103 | 4 | 5 The Fools Hall Of Fame          *Far From The Lights Of Town* | $15 | | ABC-Paramount 10282 |
| 4/7/62 | 106 | 1 | 6 I'd Never Find Another You ................................................................ *Uh Huh* | $15 | | ABC-Paramount 10311 |

Sid Feller (orch., all of above)

| 5/2/64 | 113 | 2 | 7 My Baby's Comin' Home ................................................................ *No, No* | $10 | ■ | RCA Victor 8349 |

Arthur Butler (orch.)

**ANNETTE**           HOT
Born Annette Funicello on 10/22/42 in Utica, New York. Became a Mouseketeer in 1955. Acted in several teen movies in the early '60s. Diagnosed with multiple sclerosis in 1987.

| 8/21/61 | 107 | 2 | 1 Blue Muu Muu ............................................... *Hawaiian Love-Talk (Ah-Awah-Eeay)* | $25 | ■ | Buena Vista 384 |

ANNETTE with the Afterbeats plus Four

| 11/13/61 | 106 | 2 | 2 Dreamin' About You ................................................................ *Strummin' Song* | $25 | ■ | Buena Vista 388 |

ANNETTE and the Vonnair Sisters

| 10/19/63 | 123 | 1 | 3 Promise Me Anything ................................................................ *Treat Him Nicely* | $25 | ■ | Buena Vista 427 |

from the movie *Beach Party* starring Annette and **Frankie Avalon**

**ANN-MARGRET**           HOT/AC
Born Ann-Margret Olsson on 4/28/41 in Stockholm, Sweden. Actress/dancer/singer. Acted in numerous movies.

| 1/25/69 | 113 | 3 | Sleep In The Grass ........................................................................... *Chico* | $12 | | LHI 2 |

ANN-MARGRET LEE HAZLEWOOD

**ANTELL, Peter**           HOT
Born Peter Blaise Antonio in Queens, New York. Later a composer for TV movies.

| 11/6/65 | 135 | 1 | The Times They Are A-Changing ................................. *Yesterday And Tomorrow* | $25 | | Bounty 45103 |

written and first recorded by **Bob Dylan** in 1964

**ANTHONY, Ray**           MEM/POP/HOT/AC
Born Raymond Antonini on 1/20/22 in Bentleyville, Pennsylvania. Big band leader/trumpeter. *Pop Hits & Top Pop Singles*: 28.

| 9/28/68 | 124 | 2 | I Get The Blues When It Rains ............................................ *Spanish Harlem* [I] | $6 | | Ranwood 818 |

instrumental except for 25 seconds of vocals by a chorus; #8 hit for Guy Lombardo in 1929

**ANY TROUBLE** ✪
Pub-rock group from Manchester, England: Clive Gregson (vocals), Chris Parks (guitar), Phil Barnes (bass) and Mel Harley (drums).

| 3/14/81 | 108 | 1 | Second Choice ........................................................................... *Turning Up The Heat* | $5 | | Stiff 3 |

**APPELL, Dave, and his Orchestra**           HOT
Born on 3/24/22 in Philadelphia. Orchestra leader.

| 1/13/62 | 104 | 6 | Happy Jose ........................................................................... *Noivous* [I-N] | $15 | | Cameo 207 |

#57 hit for Jack Ross in 1962

**APPLEJACKS, The** ✪
British pop/rock group: Al Jackson (vocals), Gerry Freeman, Don Gould, Phil Cash, Martin Baggott and Megan Davies.

| 6/6/64 | 135 | 1 | Tell Me When ........................................................................... *Baby Jane* | $15 | | London 9658 |

**APRIL WINE**           HOT/ROK
Rock group from Halifax, Nova Scotia, Canada: Myles Goodwyn (vocals, keyboards), Gary Moffet (guitar), Jimmy Clench (bass) and Jerry Mercer (drums). Clench left in 1975, replaced by Steve Lang. Guitarist Brian Greenway joined in 1977.

| 7/1/72 | 106 | 2 | 1 Bad Side Of The Moon ................................................................ *Believe In Me* | $6 | | Big Tree 142 |

written by **Elton John** and Bernie Taupin in 1970

| 1/12/80 | 104 | 3 | 2 Say Hello ........................................................................... *Before The Dawn* | $4 | ■ | Capitol 4802 |

**AQUATONES**           HOT/R&B
White vocal group from Long Island, New York: Lynn Nixon, Larry Vannata, David Goddard and Eugene McCarthy.

| 8/28/61 | 119 | 1 | Crazy For You ........................................... *Wanted (A Solid Gold Caddilac)* | $30 | | Fargo 1016 |

**ARBORS, The**           HOT/AC
Pop vocal group formed at the University of Michigan-Ann Arbor by two pairs of brothers: Edward and Fred Farran, and Scott and Tom Herrick.

| 2/4/67 | 113 | 1 | Just Let It Happen ........................................................................... *Dreamer Girl* | $7 | | Date 1546 |

**ARCHIES, The**            HOT/AC
Studio group created by Don Kirshner; based on the Saturday morning cartoon television series. Lead vocalist is **Ron Dante**.

| 1/9/71 | 122 | 2 | Together We Two ................................................ *Everything's Alright* | $8 | | Kirshner 5009 |

**ARDELLS, The** ○       
Pop group from West Palm Beach, Florida: Bill Ande (vocals), Tom Condra (guitar), Johnny Burgess (bass) and Dave Allen Hieronymus (drums).

| 9/28/63 | 109 | 3 | Eefananny ...................................................... *Lonely Valley* [N] | $15 | ■ | Epic 9621 |

written by **Jerry Reed**; similar to "Little Eeefin Annie" by Joe Perkins (#76 in 1963)

**ARENA, Tina**       HOT/AC
Female singer from Melbourne, Australia.

| 7/20/96 | 103 | 7 | Show Me Heaven ................................................ *Love Is The Answer* | $3 | ▌ | Epic 78357 |

produced by Peter Asher of **Peter & Gordon**

**ARGENT**       HOT
British rock quartet: Rod Argent (vocals, keyboards; **The Zombies**), Russ Ballard (guitar), Jim Rodford (bass; Argent's cousin) and Robert Henrit (drums). Rodford and Henrit later joined **The Kinks**.

| 4/17/71 | 102 | 3 | 1 Sweet Mary ..................................................... *Rejoice* | $8 | | Epic 10718 |
| 11/4/72 | 106 | 3 | 2 Tragedy ........................................................ *He's A Dynamo* | $8 | | Epic 10919 |
| 4/28/73 | 114 | 3 | 3 God Gave Rock And Roll To You ......................... *Christmas For The Free* | $8 | | Epic 10972 |

**ARGYLES, The**

| 9/21/59 | 101[1] | 5 | Vacation Days Are Over       *It Takes Time* | $30 | | Brent 7004 |

**ARMATRADING, Joan**       ROK/HOT
Born on 12/9/50 in St. Kitts, West Indies. Black singer/songwriter/guitarist.

| 1/7/78 | 110 | 1 | Show Some Emotion ........................................... *No Way Out* | $5 | ■ | A&M 1994 |

**ARMSTEAD, Jo** ○       R&B
Born Josephine Armstead on 10/8/44 in Yazoo City, Mississippi. R&B singer/songwriter. With **The Ikettes** in 1961.

| 5/25/68 | 129 | 2 | A Stone Good Lover .................. R&B:28 *The Urge Keeps Coming (Dance, Dance, Dance)* | $12 | | Giant 704 |

**ARMSTRONG, Louis**       MEM/POP/HOT/AC/R&B
Born Daniel Louis Armstrong on 8/4/01 in New Orleans. Died on 7/6/71. Highly influential trumpet player. Nicknamed "Satchmo." Won Grammy's Lifetime Achievement Award in 1972. Inducted into the Rock and Roll Hall of Fame in 1990 as a forefather of rock music.

| 5/9/64 | 122 | 2 | 1 Nomad ......................................................... *Summer Song* | $8 | | Columbia 43032 |

**LOUIS ARMSTRONG AND DAVE BRUBECK**

| 7/6/68 | 116 | 5 | 2 What A Wonderful World ............................... AC:12 *Cabaret* | $8 | | ABC 10982 |

Tommy Goodman (orch.); #32 *Hot 100* hit in 1988 due to inclusion in the movie *Good Morning, Vietnam*

**ARNELL, Ginny**       HOT
Born on 11/2/42 in New Haven, Connecticut. Female pop singer.

| 4/18/64 | 130 | 1 | I Wish I Knew What Dress To Wear ................. *He's My Little Devil* | $10 | | MGM 13226 |

**ARNOLD, Eddy**       C&W/HOT/AC/MEM/POP
Born Richard Edward Arnold on 5/15/18 near Madisonville, Tennessee. Ranked as the #1 artist in *Joel Whitburn's Top Country Singles* book. Elected to the Country Music Hall of Fame in 1966. *Pop Hits & Top Pop Singles: 32.*

| 10/23/61 | 107 | 2 | 1 One Grain Of Sand ........................... C&W:17 *The Worst Night Of My Life* | $10 | | RCA Victor 7926 |
| 3/3/62 | 102 | 4 | 2 Tears Broke Out On Me .................. C&W:7 *I'll Do As Much For You Someday* | $10 | | RCA Victor 7984 |

similar melody to "Till We Two Are One" by Georgie Shaw (#7 in 1954) and "Don't Cry Joni" by **Conway Twitty** (#63 in 1976)

| 6/23/62 | 103 | 3 | 3 A Little Heartache/       C&W:3 | | | |
| 10/6/62 | 112 | 4 | 4   After Loving You ........................................... C&W:7 | $10 | | RCA Victor 8048 |
| 8/7/65 | 135 | 1 | 5 I'm Letting You Go ................... C&W:15 / AC:33 *The Days Gone By* | $8 | | RCA Victor 8632 |

written by **Billy Grammer**

| 3/29/69 | 129 | 2 | 6 Please Don't Go ...................... C&W:10 / AC:33 *Heaven Below* | $6 | | RCA Victor 0120 |

melody is from Offenbach's "Barcarolle" from the opera *Tales Of Hoffmann*

| 6/21/69 | 125 | 4 | 7 But For Love ......................... C&W:19 / AC:31 *My Lady Of Love* | $6 | | RCA Victor 0175 |

#69 hit for Jerry Naylor in 1970; all of above produced by **Chet Atkins**

**ARRINGTON, Steve**       R&B/HOT
R&B vocalist/drummer from Dayton, Ohio. Former member of **Slave**.

| 4/27/85 | 104 | 6 | Feel So Real .................................................. R&B:17 *Willie Mae* | $4 | | Atlantic 89576 |

**ARTIFACTS** ○       R&B
Rap duo from Newark, New Jersey: El The Sensai and Tame One.

| 3/22/97 | 121 | 1 | The Ultimate ............... R&B:74 (remix) / *More Facts / Back To The Future Medley 1994-97* | $3 | ▌ | Big Beat 98027 |

**ARTISTICS, The**       R&B/HOT
R&B vocal group from Chicago: Marvin Smith, Curt Thomas, Larry Johnson, Jessie Bolian (d: 8/24/94, age 53) and Aaron Floyd.

| 9/19/64 | 118 | 4 | 1 Get My Hands On Some Lovin' .......................... *I'll Leave It Up To You* | $12 | | Okeh 7193 |

written by **Marvin Gaye**

| 12/18/65 | 115 | 3 | 2 This Heart Of Mine ................................ R&B:25 *I'll Come Running* | $12 | | Okeh 7232 |
| 5/20/67 | 111 | 2 | 3 Love Song ...................................................... *I'll Always Love You* | $10 | | Brunswick 55326 |

**ART OF NOISE**       R&B/HOT/ROK
British techno-pop trio: Anne Dudley (keyboards), Jonathan "J.J." Jeczalik (keyboards, programmer) and Gary Langan (engineer).

| 4/7/84 | 101[2] | 5 | 1 Beat Box ......................................... R&B:10 *Moment In Love* [I] | $4 | | Island 99782 |
| 8/18/84 | 102 | 2 | 2 Close (To The Edit) ........................... R&B:23 *do Donna do* [I] | $4 | ■ | Island 99754 |

**ARVON, Bobby**       AC/HOT
Born Robert Arvonio on 9/13/41 in Scranton, Pennsylvania. Singer/songwriter/pianist.

| 7/1/78 | 104 | 3 | From Now On .................................................. AC:42 *Drift Away* | $5 | | First Artists 41003 |

**A's, The** ○
Pop-rock quintet from Philadelphia: Richard Bush (vocals), Rick DiFonzo (guitar), Rocco Notte (keyboards), Terry Bortman (bass) and Mike Snyder (drums).

| 8/8/81 | 106 | 1 | A Woman's Got The Power .................................. ROK:18 *Heart Of America* | $5 | | Arista 0609 |

| DEBUT | PEAK | WKS | A-side (Chart Hit) | B-side | $ | Pic | Label & Number |
|---|---|---|---|---|---|---|---|

**ASHFORD & SIMPSON**  R&B/HOT/AC
Husband-and-wife R&B vocal/songwriting duo: Nickolas Ashford (b: 5/4/43, Fairfield, South Carolina) and Valerie Simpson (b: 8/26/48, New York City). Joined staff at Motown and wrote and produced for many of the label's top stars. They married in 1974. Valerie's brother, Ray Simpson, was the lead singer of **Village People**.

| 4/25/64 | 117 | 3 | 1 I'll Find You .................................................... Lonely Town | $20 | | Glover 3000 |

VALERIE & NICK

| 2/2/85 | 102 | 3 | 2 Outta The World ..................................... R&B:4 (dub version) | $3 | ■ | Capitol 5435 |
| 6/8/85 | 102 | 1 | 3 Babies ................................................... R&B:29 Street Corner | $3 | ■ | Capitol 5468 |

**ASHLEY, Leon ○**  C&W
Born Leon Walton on 5/18/36 in Newton County, Georgia. Country singer/songwriter/guitarist. Married **Margie Singleton** in 1965.

| 8/26/67 | 120 | 3 | 1 Laura What's He Got That I Ain't Got .......................... C&W:○[1] With The Help Of The Wine | $10 | | Ashley 2003 |

#66 hit for Frankie Laine in 1967

**ASHWORTH, Ernest ○**  C&W
Born on 12/15/28 in Huntsville, Alabama. Country singer/songwriter/guitarist.

| 9/14/63 | 101[2] | 6 | Talk Back Trembling Lips ........................ C&W:○[1] That's How Much I Care | $10 | | Hickory 1214 |

written by John D. Loudermilk; #7 hit for Johnny Tillotson in 1964

**ASSOCIATION, The**  HOT/AC
Pop group formed in Los Angeles in 1965: Terry Kirkman (plays 23 wind, reed and percussion instruments), Gary "Jules" Alexander (guitar), Brian Cole (bass; d: 8/2/72), Jim Yester (guitar), Ted Bluechel, Jr. (drums) and Russ Giguere (percussion). Larry Ramos, Jr. joined in early 1968. Richard Thompson (keyboards) replaced Giguere in 1970.

| 1/28/67 | 113 | 1 | 1 Looking Glass ................................................ No Fair At All (Hot #51) | $10 | | Valiant 758 |
| 4/26/69 | 117 | 2 | 2 Under Branches ........................................................ Hear In Here | $6 | | Warner 7277 |
| 7/19/69 | 120 | 3 | 3 Yes, I Will ................................................... I Am Up For Europe | $6 | | Warner 7305 |
| 2/28/70 | 106 | 2 | 4 Just About The Same .................................. Look At Me, Look At You | $6 | | Warner 7372 |
| 5/13/72 | 104 | 5 | 5 Darling Be Home Soon ................................ Indian Wells Woman | $6 | | Columbia 45602 |

#15 hit for The Lovin' Spoonful in 1967

**ASSORTED PHLAVORS ○**  R&B
Female R&B vocal group: Kisha, TiTi, Tiffany and Julia.

| 3/15/97 | 119 | 7 | Make Up Your Mind ......................................... R&B:58 (remix) | $3 | ■ | Hall Of Fame 78410 |

ASSORTED PHLAVORS featuring **Big Daddy Kane**
samples "You Can Turn Me Away" by Sylvia Striplin

**ASTRONAUTS, The**  HOT
Surf-rock quintet from Boulder, Colorado: guitarists Bob Demmon, Dennis Lindsey, Rich Fifield and Storm Patterson, with drummer Jim Gallagher.

| 2/15/64 | 124 | 2 | Competition Coupe ........................................................ Surf Party | $25 | | RCA Victor 8298 |

**ASYLUM CHOIR — see RUSSELL, Leon**

**ATKINS, Chet**  C&W/HOT
Born on 6/20/24 in Luttrell, Tennessee. Revered guitarist. Began recording for RCA in 1947. Entered the Country Music Hall of Fame in 1973. Won Grammy's Lifetime Achievement Award in 1993. Recipient of *Billboard's* "The Century Award" in 1997.

| 10/17/60 | 103 | 4 | 1 Theme From "The Dark At The Top Of The Stairs" ............ Hocus Pocus [I] | $12 | | RCA Victor 7796 |

with the Bob Thompson Strings; from the movie starring Robert Preston; #70 hit for Ernie Freeman in 1960

| 12/25/61 | 106 | 2 | 2 Jingle-Bell Rock ................................................. Jingle Bells [X-I] | $12 | | RCA Victor 7971 |

instrumental, except for 30 seconds of vocals by a chorus; #6 hit for Bobby Helms in 1957

| 4/2/66 | 132 | 2 | 3 From Nashville With Love ................................... Rhythm Guitar [I] | $7 | | RCA Victor 8781 |

**ATLANTA DISCO BAND, The**  R&B/HOT
Disco studio group from Atlanta assembled by producer Dave Crawford. Includes members of MFSB.

| 4/10/76 | 104 | 1 | Do What You Feel ..................................... R&B:56 I Am Trying | $5 | | Ariola America 7616 |

**ATLANTA RHYTHM SECTION**  HOT/AC/C&W/ROK/R&B
Southern-rock group from Doraville, Georgia: Ronnie Hammond (vocals), Barry Bailey and J.R. Cobb (guitars), Paul Goddard (bass), Dean Daughtry (keyboards) and Roy Yeager (drums).

| 12/15/79 | 103 | 6 | 1 Back Up Against The Wall ................................... Large Time | $5 | | Polydor 2039 |
| 10/11/80 | 101[2] | 2 | 2 I Ain't Much | Putting My Faith In Love | $5 | | Polydor 2125 |
| 12/20/80 | 101[4] | 5 | 3 Silver Eagle | C&W:75 Strictly R & R | $5 | | Polydor 2142 |

**ATLANTIC STARR**  R&B/HOT/AC
R&B band formed in 1976 in White Plains, New York, by brothers Wayne, David and Jonathan Lewis. Wayne and David on vocals with Sharon Bryant. In 1984, reduced to a quintet; Barbara Weathers replaced Bryant.

| 4/11/81 | 101[5] | 7 | 1 When Love Calls | R&B:5 Mystery Girl | $3 | | A&M 2312 |
| 7/20/85 | 110 | 1 | 2 Cool, Calm, Collected ................................... R&B:33 Island Dream | $3 | ■ | A&M 2742 |

**AUGER, Brian — see DRISCOLL, Julie**

**AUSSIE BAND ○**
Australian pop/rock duo of Dennis Dunstan and Wayne Morrison.

| 11/8/80 | 109 | 2 | Somebody Wants You .................................... Cry Your Life Away | $5 | | Real World 7309 |

**AUSTIN, Donald ○**
R&B guitar instrumentalist.

| 2/3/73 | 121 | 3 | Crazy Legs ........................................................ Nanzee [I] | $7 | | Eastbound 603 |

**AUSTIN, Patti — see JAMES, Bob / WALDEN, Narada Michael**

**AVALON, Frankie**  HOT/R&B/AC
Born Francis Avallone on 9/18/39 in Philadelphia. Singer/actor. Co-starred in many movies with **Annette**. *Top Pop Singles*: 25.

| 2/13/61 | 102 | 2 | 1 Call Me Anytime ................................... All Of Everyting (Hot #70) | $20 | ■ | Chancellor 1071 |

Bob Mersey (orch.)

| 7/3/61 | 101[2] | 3 | 2 Voyage To The Bottom Of The Sea | The Summer Of 61 | $20 | ■ | Chancellor 1081 |

from the movie starring Walter Pidgeon and Avalon

| 10/16/61 | 112 | 2 | 3 Married ......................................... True, True Love (Hot #90) | $20 | ■ | Chancellor 1087 |

Russ Faith (orch., above 2)

| | | | **AVALON, Frankie — Cont'd** | | | |
|---|---|---|---|---|---|---|
| 1/27/62 | 117 | 2 | 4 After You've Gone ...................................................*If You Don't Think I'm Leaving* | $20 | ■ | Chancellor 1101 |
| | | | there were 10 hit versions of this tune from 1918-37 | | | |
| 7/21/62 | 111 | 1 | 5 Don't Let Me Stand In Your Way .................................*A Miracle* (Hot #75) | $20 | ■ | Chancellor 1115 |
| | | | **Don Costa** (orch., above 2) | | | |
| 12/8/62 | 129 | 1 | 6 Welcome Home ....................................................*Dance The Bossa Nova* | $20 | ■ | Chancellor 1125 |
| | | | Jimmie Haskell (orch.) | | | |
| | | | **AVANT GARDE**           HOT | | | |
| | | | Duo of Chuck Woolery and Elkin "Bubba" Fowler. Woolery was the original host of TV's *Wheel of Fortune* and *Love Connection*. | | | |
| 12/14/68 | 130 | 2 | Fly With Me ........................................................*Revelation's Revolutions* | $7 | | Columbia 44701 |
| | | | **AVERAGE WHITE BAND**     R&B/HOT/AC | | | |
| | | | White soul-funk group of Scotland natives formed in London: Alan Gorrie (vocals, bass), Onnie McIntyre (guitar, vocals), Hamish Stuart (guitar, vocals), Malcolm Duncan (sax), Roger Ball (keyboards) and Steve Ferrone (drums). Also see **David Sanborn**. | | | |
| 1/15/77 | 101[1] | 1 | 1 A Love Of Your Own       R&B:35 *Soul Searching* | $5 | | Atlantic 3363 |
| | | | AWB | | | |
| 10/18/80 | 106 | 1 | 2 For You, For Love ........................................R&B:60 *Whatcha' Gonna Do For Me* | $4 | | Arista 0553 |
| | | | **AWESOME 3** ○ | | | |
| | | | British dance trio: singer Julie McDermott, with keyboardists Peter Orme and Dave Johnson. | | | |
| 11/13/93 | 105 | 8 | Don't Go! ..........................................................*Headstrong* | $3 | ▮ | American 18287 |
| | | | **AXE**        HOT/ROK/AC | | | |
| | | | Rock band from Gainesville, Florida: Bobby Barth (vocals, guitar), Edgar Riley, Jr. (keyboards), Michael Osborne (guitar; d: 7/21/84, age 34), Wayne Haner (bass) and Ted Mueller (drums). Group made the Adult Contemporary charts in 1976 as Babyface. | | | |
| 9/18/82 | 109 | 3 | 1 Rock 'N' Roll Party In The Streets .........................ROK:23 *Jennifer* | $4 | | Atco 99975 |
| 8/27/83 | 109 | 1 | 2 Heat In The Street ............................................*Midnight Drives Me Mad* | $4 | | Atco 99850 |
| | | | **AXTON, Hoyt**       C&W/HOT/AC | | | |
| | | | Born on 3/25/38 in Camanche, Oklahoma. Country singer/songwriter/guitarist. Son of songwriter Mae Axton ("Heartbreak Hotel"; d: 4/16/97, age 82). Acted in the movies *The Black Stallion* and *Gremlins*. | | | |
| 3/1/75 | 105 | 4 | 1 Speed Trap/ | [N] | | |
| 2/8/75 | 106 | 6 | 2 Nashville .........................................................C&W:61 | $6 | | A&M 1657 |
| | | | **AZ**       R&B/HOT | | | |
| | | | Born Anthony Cruz in Brooklyn. Male rapper. Also recorded as AZ The Visualiza. | | | |
| 1/13/96 | 121 | 2 | 1 Gimme Yours .....................................................R&B:51 *(remix)* | $3 | ▮ | EMI 58512 |
| | | | samples "Here We Go" by Minnie Riperton | | | |
| 8/30/97 | 117 | 3 | 2 Hey AZ .............................................................R&B:50 *(5 versions)* | $5 | ■ | EMI 58655 (T) |
| | | | **AZ Featuring SWV** | | | |
| | | | samples "Hey D.J." by The World's Famous Supreme Team | | | |

# B

| | | | **BABIES, The** ○ | | | |
|---|---|---|---|---|---|---|
| | | | Female pop quartet based in Los Angeles. | | | |
| 7/8/67 | 122 | 1 | You Make Me Feel Like Someone ..........................*The Hand Of Fate* | $15 | ■ | Dunhill 4085 |
| | | | **BABYFACE**       R&B/HOT/AC | | | |
| | | | Born Kenneth Edmonds on 4/10/59 in Indianapolis. Top R&B vocalist, songwriter and producer of the '90s. Brother of Kevon and Melvin Edmonds of After 7. | | | |
| 9/3/94 | 106 | 8 | 1 Where Is My Love? ........................Sls:68 /R&B:19 *Starlight, Moonlight, Candlelight* | $3 | ▮ | Reprise 18140 |
| | | | **EL DeBARGE featuring Babyface** | | | |
| 11/12/94 | 109 | 6 | 2 Dream Away ....................................................R&B:80 *(acoustic mix)* | $3 | ▮ | Fox 10020 |
| | | | **BABYFACE & LISA STANSFIELD** | | | |
| | | | from the movie *The Pagemaster* starring Macaulay Culkin | | | |
| | | | **BACHARACH, Burt**       AC/HOT | | | |
| | | | Born on 5/12/28 in Kansas City. Conductor/arranger/composer. With lyricist Hal David wrote most of **Dionne Warwick**'s hits. | | | |
| 2/6/71 | 116 | 4 | All Kinds Of People ...........................................AC:18 *She's Gone Away* | $5 | ■ | A&M 1241 |
| | | | vocals by a mixed chorus | | | |
| | | | **BACK PORCH MAJORITY, The** ○ | | | |
| | | | Folk group formed by **Randy Sparks** (of **The New Christy Minstrels**): Kin Vassy (d: 6/23/94, age 50), Lois Fletcher, Karen Brian, Mike Clough, Mike Crowley, Dan Dalton and Ellen Whalen. | | | |
| 3/19/66 | 104 | 6 | Second-Hand Man ............................................*That's The Way It's Gonna Be* | $8 | ☐ | Epic 9879 |
| | | | **BACKUS, Gus** ○ | | | |
| | | | Born Donald Backus on 12/12/37 in Southampton, Long Island, New York. Member of **The Dell-Vikings**. | | | |
| 7/3/61 | 102 | 2 | 1 Wooden Heart (Muss i denn zum Stadtele hinaus) ...............*Said The Old Indian Chief* | $15 | | Fono-Graf 1234 |
| | | | #1 hit for **Joe Dowell** in 1961; originally sung by **Elvis Presley** in the 1960 movie *G.I. Blues* | | | |
| 9/18/61 | 118 | 1 | 2 Auf Wiederseh'n ...............................................*Tempo Brasilliano* | $15 | | Fono-Graf 1235 |
| | | | #1 hit for **Vera Lynn** in 1952; above 2 sung in both German and English | | | |
| | | | **BAD BOYS BLUE**       HOT | | | |
| | | | Dance trio formed in Cologne, Germany: John McInerney (from Liverpool, lead vocals), Andrew Thomas (from Los Angeles) and Ova Standing (from Zaire). | | | |
| 6/19/93 | 104 | 5 | I Totally Miss You ............................................*(album version)* | $3 | ▮ | Zoo 14091 |
| | | | **BADFINGER**       HOT/AC/ROK | | | |
| | | | Rock quartet from Swansea, Wales: Pete Ham (vocals, guitar; d: 4/23/75, age 27), Tom Evans (vocals, bass; d: 11/23/83, age 36), Joey Molland (guitar) and Mike Gibbins (drums). | | | |
| 2/9/74 | 102 | 4 | Apple Of My Eye ...............................................*Blind Owl* | $20 | | Apple 1864 |

**BADGE ○**
Pop group led by singer/drummer Bill Paleselli.

| | | | | | | |
|---|---|---|---|---|---|---|
| 3/20/71 | 119 | 2 | Gettin' In Over My Head ...................................................................... *It's Straight Ahead* | $10 | | Exhibit 4600 |

**BAD YARD CLUB**
Duo of dance producers David Morales and Handell Tucker.

| 8/3/96 | 102 | 8 | 1 In De Ghetto .............................................................. *(2 mixes)* | $6 | | Mercury 578029 (T) |
|---|---|---|---|---|---|---|
| 10/18/97 | 115 | 2 | 2 In De Ghetto .............................................................. *(2 mixes)* [R] | $6 | | Mercury 578029 (T) |

Crystal Waters (lead vocal, above 2)

**BAHAMADIA ○**   R&B
Female rapper from Philadelphia.

| 3/2/96 | 105 | 9 | 1 Uknowhowwedu ........................... R&B:53 *True Honey Buns (Dat Freak Sh*t)* | $3 | ▮ | Chrysalis/EMI 58517 |
|---|---|---|---|---|---|---|
| 6/29/96 | 109 | 8 | 2 I Confess........................ R&B:45 *Uknowhowwedu (remix) / 3 Tha Hard Way (2 versions)* | $3 | ▮ | Chrysalis/EMI 58437 |

samples "Let's Get It On" by Marvin Gaye

**BAILEY, Pearl ○**   POP/MEM/R&B/AC
Born on 3/29/18 in Newport News, Virginia. Died on 8/17/90. Band vocalist from 1933-45. Acted in several movies and Broadway shows.

| 9/19/64 | 132 | 1 | I'd Rather Be Rich.......................................................... *I Was A Little Too Lonely* [N] | $8 | | Decca 31667 |
|---|---|---|---|---|---|---|

Don Redman (orch.); from the movie starring Sandra Dee

**BAJA MARIMBA BAND**   AC/HOT
Nine-man "Tijuana" band led by marimbaist Julius Wechter (b: 5/10/35 in Chicago). Wechter was a member of Herb Alpert's Tijuana Brass and The Exotic Sounds of Martin Denny.

| 3/21/64 | 121 | 3 | 1 Moonglow/Picnic Theme.......................................... *Acapulco 1922* [I] | $8 | | Almo International 203 |
|---|---|---|---|---|---|---|

#1 hit for Morris Stoloff in 1956; from the 1956 movie *Picnic* starring William Holden

| 10/22/66 | 126 | 2 | 2 The Portuguese Washerwomen ............................... AC:15 *Telephone Song* [I] | $6 | | A&M 816 |
|---|---|---|---|---|---|---|

#19 hit for Joe "Fingers" Carr in 1956

| 2/18/67 | 113 | 2 | 3 The Cry Of The Wild Goose ........................... AC:21 *Spanish Moss* [I] | $6 | ▮ | A&M 833 |
|---|---|---|---|---|---|---|

#1 hit for Frankie Laine in 1950

**JULIUS WECHTER & THE BAJA MARIMBA BAND:**

| 6/22/68 | 109 | 3 | 4 Yes Sir, That's My Baby ....................... AC:17 *Brasilia* [I] | $6 | ▮ | A&M 937 |
|---|---|---|---|---|---|---|

#1 hit for Gene Austin in 1925; #34 hit for Ricky Nelson in 1960

| 1/25/69 | 125 | 2 | 5 Flyin' High ............................................ AC:15 *Les Bicyclettes De Belsize* [I] | $6 | | A&M 1005 |
|---|---|---|---|---|---|---|
| 7/26/69 | 121 | 2 | 6 I Don't Want To Walk Without You........................ AC:21 *I'll Marimba You* [I] | $6 | | A&M 1078 |

Julius Wechter (vocal); #1 hit for Harry James with Helen Forrest in 1942

**BAKER, Anita**   R&B/AC/HOT
Born on 12/20/57 in Toledo, Ohio; raised in Detroit. Smooth R&B vocalist.

| 7/1/95 | 111 | 5 | When You Love Someone ............................ AC:39 /R&B:71 *My Funny Valentine* (Baker) | $3 | ▮ | Elektra 64415 |
|---|---|---|---|---|---|---|

**ANITA BAKER & JAMES INGRAM**
from the movie *Forget Paris* starring Billy Crystal

**BAKER, Chet, And The Mariachi Brass ○**   AC
Born Chesney Baker on 12/23/29 in Yale, Oklahoma. Died on 5/13/88. Flugelhorn player/trumpeter/bandleader. Movie biography *Let's Get Lost* was released in 1989.

| 2/5/66 | 115 | 4 | Flowers On The Wall ...................................... AC:33 *Tequila* [I] | $7 | | World-Pacific 77815 |
|---|---|---|---|---|---|---|

Jack Nitzsche (conductor); #4 hit for The Statler Brothers in 1966

**BAKER, George, Selection**   HOT/AC/C&W
Pop group from Holland: Johannes "George Baker" Bouwens, Jan Hop, Jacobus Greuter, George The and Jan Visser.

| 9/5/70 | 103 | 2 | I Wanna Love You ........................................................... *Impressions* | $6 | | Colossus 124 |
|---|---|---|---|---|---|---|

**BAKER, LaVern**   R&B/HOT
Born Delores Williams on 11/11/29 in Chicago. Died of heart failure due to diabetes on 3/10/97. One of the most popular R&B singers of the early rock era. Inducted into the Rock and Roll Hall of Fame in 1991. *Top Pop Singles*: 20.

| 1/16/61 | 103 | 4 | 1 I'll Never Be Free ............................................... *You're The Boss* (Hot #81) | $20 | | Atlantic 2090 |
|---|---|---|---|---|---|---|

**LaVERN BAKER & JIMMY RICKS**
#3 hit for Kay Starr & Tennessee Ernie Ford in 1950

| 7/18/64 | 128 | 2 | 2 You'd Better Find Yourself Another Fool.......................................... *Go Away* | $15 | | Atlantic 2234 |
|---|---|---|---|---|---|---|
| 1/1/66 | 128 | 1 | 3 Please Don't Hurt Me (I've Never Been In Love Before) ............... *Think Twice* (Hot #93) | $15 | | Brunswick 55287 |

**JACKIE WILSON And LaVERN BAKER**

| 8/27/66 | 135 | 1 | 4 Batman To The Rescue ................................................ *Call Me Darling* | $20 | | Brunswick 55297 |
|---|---|---|---|---|---|---|

vocal version of the *Batman* TV series theme; loosely based on Baker's 1957 hit "Jim Dandy"

**BAKER, Teddy ○**
Pop singer/songwriter from Atlanta.

| 10/10/81 | 101[1] | 4 | It's Over | *The Body* | $4 | | Casablanca 2340 |
|---|---|---|---|---|---|---|

**BALIN, Marty**   HOT/AC/ROK
Born Martyn Buchwald on 1/30/43 in Cincinnati. Co-founder of Jefferson Airplane.

| 5/7/83 | 102 | 6 | Do It For Love ........................................................ AC:17 *Heart Of Stone* | $4 | ▮ | EMI America 8160 |
|---|---|---|---|---|---|---|

**BALL, David**   C&W/HOT
Born on 7/9/53 in Rock Hill, South Carolina. Country singer/songwriter/guitarist.

| 12/10/94+ | 107 | 5 | When The Thought Of You Catches Up With Me .............C&W:7 *Don't Think Twice* | $3 | ▮ | Warner 18081 |
|---|---|---|---|---|---|---|

**BALL, Kenny, and his Jazzmen**   HOT/AC
Born on 5/22/30 in Ilford, England. Formed his Jazzmen, a Dixieland jazz band: Diz Disley (banjo), Johnny Bennett (trombone), Dave Jones (clarinet), Colin Bates (piano), Vic Pitts (bass) and Ron Bowden (drums).

| 11/30/63 | 119 | 3 | Heartaches ...........................................................................*High Hopes* [I] | $7 | | Kapp 554 |
|---|---|---|---|---|---|---|

#1 hit for Ted Weems in 1947; #7 hit for The Marcels in 1961

**BALLADEERS, The ○**
Pop trio: Fred Darian (lead vocals), Al DeLory and Johnny Cole.

| 4/25/60 | 104 | 3 | Roll Call Company "J" ...................................*Hurtin' (For The Love Of You)* | $15 | | Del-Fi 4138 |
|---|---|---|---|---|---|---|

## BALLARD, Hank, And The Midnighters    R&B/HOT
R&B vocal group from Detroit, formed in 1952 as The Royals: **Henry Booth**, Charles Sutton, Lawson Smith and Sonny Woods. In late 1953, Henry "Hank" Ballard (b: 11/18/36, Detroit) replaced Smith and became lead singer. Name changed to Midnighters in 1954. Ballard inducted into the Rock and Roll Hall of Fame in 1990.

| | | | | | | |
|---|---|---|---|---|---|---|
| 9/7/59 | 106 | 3 | 1 Cute Little Ways ..................................................................*House With No Windows* | $25 | | King 5245 |
| 5/15/61 | 113 | 2 | 2 Every Beat Of My Heart ...............................................................*Starting From Tonight* | $25 | | DeLuxe 6190 |

**HENRY BOOTH And The MIDNIGHTERS**
#6 hit for the **Pips** in 1961

## BALLARD, Russ    ROK/HOT
Born on 10/31/47 in Waltham Cross, England. Pop-rock singer/songwriter/producer. Guitarist of **Argent**, 1969-74.

| | | | | | | |
|---|---|---|---|---|---|---|
| 5/12/84 | 110 | 2 | 1 Voices ...........................................................ROK:15 *Living Without You* | $3 | ■ | EMI America 8204 |
| 8/4/84 | 106 | 1 | 2 Two Silhouettes ...............................................................*Playing With Fire* | $3 | ■ | EMI America 8217 |
| 7/13/85 | 105 | 3 | 3 The Fire Still Burns ...........................................ROK:15 *Hold On* | $3 | ■ | EMI America 8275 |

## BANANARAMA    HOT/AC/ROK
Female pop-rock vocal trio from London: Sarah Dallin, Keren Woodward and Siobhan Fahey.

| | | | | | | |
|---|---|---|---|---|---|---|
| 11/13/82 | 108 | 7 | 1 He Was Really Sayin' Somethin'.................................*Give Us Back Our Cheap Fares* | $5 | | London 201 |

#64 hit for the **Velvelettes** in 1965

| | | | | | | |
|---|---|---|---|---|---|---|
| 5/7/83 | 101[2] | 4 | 2 Na Na Hey Hey Kiss Him Goodbye    ROK:28 *Tell Tale Signs* | $4 | ■ | London 810115 |

#1 hit for Steam in 1969

## BAND, The    HOT
Rock group formed in Woodstock, New York: Robbie Robertson (guitar, vocals), Levon Helm (drums, vocals), Rick Danko (bass), Richard Manuel and Garth Hudson (keyboards). All from Canada (except Helm from Arkansas) and all were with **Ronnie Hawkins**'s Hawks. Manuel committed suicide on 3/4/86 (age 42). Group inducted into the Rock and Roll Hall of Fame in 1994.

| | | | | | | |
|---|---|---|---|---|---|---|
| 1/2/71 | 121 | 1 | 1 The Shape I'm In ...........................................*Time To Kill (Hot #77)* | $8 | | Capitol 2870 |
| 12/23/72 | 113 | 3 | 2 (I Don't Want To) Hang Up My Rock And Roll Shoes ....................*Caledonia Mission* | $7 | | Capitol 3500 |

#24 hit for Chuck Willis in 1958

## BANDWAGON, The ⊙    R&B
R&B vocal group from Rochester, New York. Led by Johnny Johnson.

| | | | | | | |
|---|---|---|---|---|---|---|
| 8/3/68 | 115 | 1 | Breakin' Down The Walls Of Heartache .................................*Dancin' Master* | $10 | | Epic 10352 |

## BANKS, Darrell    HOT/R&B
Born Darrell Eubanks in 1938 in Buffalo. Killed by a gunshot wound in Detroit in March 1970. R&B singer.

| | | | | | | |
|---|---|---|---|---|---|---|
| 4/1/67 | 124 | 2 | Here Come The Tears .........................................*I've Got That Feelin'* | $20 | | Atco 6471 |

## BANTON, Buju ⊙    R&B
Born Mark Myrie in Jamaica. The name Buju Banton is taken from the Jamaican word for breadfruit.

| | | | | | | |
|---|---|---|---|---|---|---|
| 7/15/95 | 117 | 3 | Champion .....................................................R&B:67 *(original version)* | $3 | ▮ | Loose Cannon 856980 |

samples "You Know How We Do It" by **Ice Cube**

## BANTON, Mega ⊙    R&B
Male dancehall/reggae singer from Jamaica.

| | | | | | | |
|---|---|---|---|---|---|---|
| 4/9/94 | 118 | 3 | Sound Boy Killing ...............................................R&B:92 *(2 versions)* | $5 | ▮ | V.P. 5280 * |

samples "Playing Your Game, Baby" by **Barry White**

## BARBARIANS, The    HOT
Garage-rock band from Provincetown, Massachusetts: Victor "Moulty" Moulton (vocals, drums), Jeff Morris and Bruce Benson (guitars), and Jerry Causi (bass).

| | | | | | | |
|---|---|---|---|---|---|---|
| 11/20/65 | 102 | 6 | What The New Breed Say .................................................*Susie-Q* | $20 | | Laurie 3321 |

## BARBIERI, Gato ⊙    R&B
Born Leandro Barbieri on 11/28/34 in Rosario, Argentina. Jazz tenor saxophonist.

| | | | | | | |
|---|---|---|---|---|---|---|
| 10/9/76 | 110 | 1 | 1 I Want You (Part I) ......................................................*(Part II)* [I] | $5 | | A&M 1857 |
| 2/26/77 | 104 | 8 | 2 Fiesta ......................................................R&B:63 *Behind The Rain* [I] | $5 | | A&M 1885 |

above 2 produced by **Herb Alpert**

## BARCLAY JAMES HARVEST ⊙
Art-rock group from Oldham, England: John Lees (vocals, guitar), Wooly Wolstenholme (keyboards), Les Holroyd (bass) and Mel Pritchard (drums).

| | | | | | | |
|---|---|---|---|---|---|---|
| 3/20/76 | 107 | 1 | Titles ...............................................................*Song For You* | $7 | | Polydor 15118 |

tune's lyrics comprised of titles from various **Beatles'** songs

## BARE, Bobby    C&W/HOT/AC
Born on 4/7/35 in Ironton, Ohio. Country singer/songwriter/guitarist.

| | | | | | | |
|---|---|---|---|---|---|---|
| 5/29/61 | 106 | 1 | 1 Book Of Love    *Lorena* | $25 | | Fraternity 878 |
| 11/17/62 | 118 | 1 | 2 I Don't Believe I'll Fall In Love Today ....................*To Whom It May Concern* | $12 | ■ | RCA Victor 8083 |

#5 Country hit for Warren Smith in 1960

| | | | | | | |
|---|---|---|---|---|---|---|
| 8/8/64 | 134 | 1 | 3 He Was A Friend Of Mine ...............................................*When I'm Gone* | $12 | | RCA Victor 8395 |
| 3/13/65 | 114 | 4 | 4 A Dear John Letter ...................................C&W:11 *Too Used To Being With You* | $12 | | RCA Victor 8496 |

**SKEETER DAVIS & BOBBY BARE**
#1 Country hit for Jean Shepard & Ferlin Husky in 1953; #44 hit for **Pat Boone** in 1960

| | | | | | | |
|---|---|---|---|---|---|---|
| 5/29/65 | 122 | 2 | 5 It's Alright.........................................C&W:7 *She Picked A Perfect Day* | $10 | | RCA Victor 8571 |
| 3/19/66 | 131 | 1 | 6 In The Same Old Way ...............................C&W:34 *The Long Black Veil* | $10 | | RCA Victor 8758 |
| 7/2/66 | 124 | 3 | 7 The Streets Of Baltimore ..........................C&W:5 *She Took My Sunshine Away* | $10 | | RCA Victor 8851 |
| 1/23/71 | 122 | 1 | 8 Come Sundown ........................C&W:7 *Woman, You Have Been A Friend To Me* | $6 | | Mercury 73148 |

written by Kris Kristofferson

## BAREFOOT JERRY ⊙    C&W
Group of Nashville session musicians led by Wayne Moss.

| | | | | | | |
|---|---|---|---|---|---|---|
| 5/31/75 | 109 | 2 | You Can't Get Off With Your Shoes On ........................*Cades Cave* | $6 | | Monument 8645 |

**BAR-KAYS**      R&B/HOT
Soul-funk group from Memphis: Larry Dodson (vocals), Lloyd Smith (guitar), Winston Stewart (keyboards), Frank Thompson, Harvey Henderson and Charles Allen (horns), James Alexander (bass) and Michael Beard (drums). Added Mark Bynum (keyboards) and Sherman Guy (percussion) in 1979.

| 2/11/78 | 102 | 5 | 1 Let's Have Some Fun ....................................................................... R&B:11 *Cozy* | $5 | | Mercury 73971 |
| 4/14/79 | 102 | 7 | 2 Shine ............................................................ R&B:14 *Are You Being Real* (R&B #61) | $5 | | Mercury 74048 |
| 12/12/81 | 101³ | 7 | 3 Hit And Run      R&B:5 *Say It Through Love* | $5 | | Mercury 76123 |

**BARRABAS** ☉
Dance/disco group: Jo Tejada (vocals), Ricky Morales (guitar), Juan Vidal (keyboards), Ernesto Duarte Duarte (percussion), Miguel Morales (bass) and Daniel Louis (drums).

| 7/12/75 | 104 | 3 | Hi-Jack .................................................................................. *Susie Wong* | $5 | | Atco 7027 |

**BARRACUDA, The** ☉
Male pop/rock group.

| 12/7/68 | 113 | 3 | The Dance At St. Francis ......................................................... *Lady Fingers* | $20 | ■ | RCA Victor 9660 |

**BARRIO BOYZZ** ☉      R&B
Hispanic vocal quintet from New York City: Hans Giraldo, Angel Ramirez, Robert Vargas, David Davilla and Louie Marrero.

| 1/20/96 | 106 | 8 | 1 How We Roll .................................................................. R&B:48 *(album snippets)* | $3 | ■ | SBK/EMI 58498 |
| | | | samples "Sucker M.C.'s" by **Run-D.M.C.** and "Oh Honey" by **Delegation** | | | |
| 6/8/96 | 121 | 4 | 2 I Wish ................................................. R&B:86 *(Spanish/English version) / Love You From The Inside* | $3 | ■ | SBK/EMI 58556 |

**BARRY, John**      HOT/AC
Born on 11/3/33 in York, England. Prolific movie soundtrack composer/conductor.

| 10/11/69 | 116 | 3 | Midnight Cowboy........................................................................ *Fun City* [I] | $6 | | Columbia 44891 |
| | | | Toots Thielemans (harmonica); from the movie starring Dustin Hoffman and Jon Voight; #10 hit for **Ferrante & Teicher** in 1970 | | | |

**BARRY, Len**      HOT
Born Leonard Borisoff on 12/6/42 in Philadelphia. Lead singer of **The Dovells** from 1957-63.

| 4/29/67 | 124 | 2 | The Moving Finger Writes ................................................................ *Our Love* | $10 | | RCA Victor 9150 |

**BARRY AND THE TAMERLANES**      HOT
Pop vocal trio from Los Angeles: songwriters Barry DeVorzon, Terry Smith and Bodie Chandler.

| 2/1/64 | 127 | 3 | Roberta ................................................................................. *Butterfly* | $15 | | Valiant 6040 |

**BARTLEY, Chris**      HOT/R&B
Born on 4/17/49 in New York City. Male R&B singer.

| 11/4/67 | 125 | 2 | Baby It's Wonderful ............................................................. *I'll Be Loving You* | $15 | | Vando 3000 |
| | | | written and produced by **Van McCoy** | | | |

**BASSEY, Shirley**      AC/HOT/R&B
Born on 1/8/37 in Cardiff, Wales. Soul singer.

| 10/16/61 | 120 | 1 | Reach For The Stars............................................................ *You'll Never Know* | $10 | | United Artists 363 |
| | | | with the Rita Williams Singers; Geoff Love (orch.) | | | |

**BATAAN** ☉      R&B
Born Bataan Nitollano in 1942 in New York City of Afro-Filipino ancestry. R&B singer. Also recorded as Joe Bataan.

| 3/29/75 | 102 | 1 | The Bottle (La Botella) .................................... R&B:59 *When You're Down (Funky Mambo)* [I] | $5 | | Salsoul 8701 |

**BAY BROTHERS, The** ☉
Pop duo from San Francisco: Lou Hokenson and Ernie Sorrentino.

| 10/11/80 | 108 | 3 | Baby Don't Give Up .......................................................... *Magic In Her Love* | $4 | | Millennium 11794 |

**BAYSIDE BOYS** ☉
Producers Carlos de Yarza and Mike Triay. Mixed the hugely popular version of "Macarena" by Los Del Rio.

| 8/24/96 | 115 | 7 | Caliente ....................................................................................... *(remix)* | $3 | ■ | Lava 98043 |
| | | | Carla Ramirez (female vocal); title is Spanish for "Hot" | | | |

**B-CODE** ☉
Italian dance producers Paolo Verianzi and Giannino Zen.

| 4/27/96 | 106 | 2 | Feel Good ...................................................................................... *(remix)* | $4 | ■ | Out Of Control 13506 |

**BEACH BOYS, The**      HOT/AC/R&B
Surf-rock group from Hawthorne, California: brothers Brian Wilson (keyboards, bass), **Carl Wilson** (guitar) and Dennis Wilson (drums); their cousin Mike Love (lead vocals, saxophone) and Al Jardine (guitar). Brian quit touring with group in December 1964, replaced briefly by **Glen Campbell** until Bruce Johnston (of **Bruce & Terry**) joined permanently in April 1965. Brian continued to write for and produce group, returned to stage in 1983. Dennis Wilson drowned on 12/28/83 (age 39). Carl Wilson died of cancer on 2/6/98 (age 51). Group was inducted into the Rock and Roll Hall of Fame in 1988. *Top Pop Singles:* 59.

| 2/29/64 | 120 | 2 | 1 Why Do Fools Fall In Love ................................................. *Fun, Fun, Fun* (Hot #5) | $15 | ■ | Capitol 5118 |
| | | | #6 hit for Frankie Lymon & The Teenagers in 1956 | | | |
| 9/12/64 | 101¹ | 3 | 2 She Knows Me Too Well      *When I Grow Up (To Be A Man)* (Hot #9) | $15 | ■ | Capitol 5245 |
| 5/16/70 | 103 | 2 | 3 Cottonfields .......................................................... *The Nearest Faraway Place* | $25 | | Capitol 2765 |
| | | | #13 hit for The Highwaymen in 1962; traditional American ballad, copyrighted in 1850 | | | |
| 7/15/72 | 110 | 3 | 4 Marcella ............................................................... *Hold On Dear Brother* | $25 | | Brother/Reprise 1101 |
| 7/26/75 | 101¹ | 3 | 5 Barbara Ann      *Little Honda* [R] | $6 | | Capitol 4110 |
| | | | Dean Torrence (of **Jan & Dean**, lead vocal); originally charted in 1966 at #2 on Capitol 5561 | | | |
| 8/16/75 | 103 | 3 | 6 Wouldn't It Be Nice ................................................... *Caroline, No* [R] | $10 | | Brother/Reprise 1336 |
| | | | originally charted in 1966 at #8 on Capitol 5706 | | | |

## BEACHNUTS, The — see ANGELS, The / STRANGELOVES, The

**BEASTIE BOYS**      R&B/HOT/ROK
White rap-punk trio from New York City: Adam Horovitz ("King Ad-Rock"), Adam Yauch ("MCA") and Michael Diamond ("Mike D").

| 7/16/94 | 101² | 6 | 1 Get It Together/      Sls:69 | | | |
| | | | samples "Headless Heroes" by Eugene McDaniels | | | |
| 8/13/94 | 115 | 5 | 2 Sabotage ..................................................................... ROK:18 | $3 | ■ | Grand Royal/Cap. 58219 |

| DEBUT | PEAK | WKS | A-side (Chart Hit)..........................................................................................B-side | $ | Pic | Label & Number |
|---|---|---|---|---|---|---|
| | | | **BEATLES, The**           HOT/AC/ROK | | | |
| | | | Rock group from Liverpool, England: **John Lennon**, **Paul McCartney**, **George Harrison** (guitars, vocals), and **Ringo Starr** (drums, vocals). Widely considered the most popular and influential rock group of all-time. Won the 1964 Best New Artist Grammy Award. McCartney publicly announced group's dissolution on 4/10/70. Won the Grammy's Trustees Award in 1972. Lennon was shot to death on 12/8/80. Group inducted into the Rock and Roll Hall of Fame in 1988. *Top Pop Singles:* 72. | | | |
| 8/3/63 | 116 | 3 | 1 From Me To You ......................................... *Thank You Girl (Hot #35/'64)* | $900 | | Vee-Jay 522 |
| | | | released in U.S. on 5/27/63; made the *Hot 100* (#41) on 3/7/64 on Vee-Jay 581; #77 hit for **Del Shannon** in 1963 | | | |
| 8/7/65 | 101¹ | 7 | 2 I'm Down          *Help! (Hot #1)* | $30 | ■ | Capitol 5476 |
| 10/23/65 | 102 | 1 | 3 Boys ............................................................. *Kansas City* | $125 | | Capitol 6066 |
| | | | recorded in 1963; one of a series of 6 singles released on Capitol's green label "The Star Line"; tune first released as the B-side of **The Shirelles'** 1961 #1 hit "Will You Love Me Tomorrow" | | | |
| | | | **BEAUMONT, Jimmy**        HOT | | | |
| | | | Born on 10/21/40 in Pittsburgh. Lead singer of **The Skyliners**. | | | |
| 12/18/65 | 123 | 1 | I Feel Like I'm Falling In Love .................................... *Tell Me* | $20 | | Bang 510 |
| | | | **BEAUTIFUL BEND** ⊙ | | | |
| | | | Disco studio group assembled by producer Boris Midney. | | | |
| 3/31/79 | 110 | 1 | Boogie Motion ................................. *Make That Feeling Come Again!* | $7 | | Marlin 3327 |
| | | | **BEAVIS & BUTT-HEAD — see CHER** | | | |
| | | | **BECK, Jeff**        ROK/HOT | | | |
| | | | Born on 6/24/44 in Surrey, England. Veteran rock guitarist. With **The Yardbirds** from 1964-66. | | | |
| 5/20/67 | 123 | 2 | Hi-Ho Silver Lining .......................................... *Beck's Bolero* [I] | $15 | | Epic 10157 |
| | | | **BECKETT** ⊙ | | | |
| | | | Born Alston Beckett Cyrus on 8/1/49 in Layou, West Indies. Disco singer/songwriter. | | | |
| 8/20/77 | 108 | 2 | Disco Calypso ................................................... *St. Thomas Mas* | $6 | | Casablanca 890 |
| | | | **BECKHAM, Bob**        HOT/C&W | | | |
| | | | Born on 7/8/27 in Stratford, Oklahoma. Pop-country singer. | | | |
| 6/20/60 | 105 | 2 | Mais Oui ..................................... *Only The Broken Hearted* | $10 | | Decca 31090 |
| | | | pronounced "may we"; French for "Why Yes" | | | |
| | | | **BEDFORD, Scott, Four** ⊙ | | | |
| | | | Pop quartet from Allentown, Pennsylvania. Led by Scott Bedford. | | | |
| 5/8/65 | 129 | 1 | Last Exit To Brooklyn ..................... *Now I'm At The Top! (How Do I Stay Here?)* | $10 | | Joy 296 |
| | | | **BEE, Molly** ⊙        C&W | | | |
| | | | Born Molly Beachboard on 8/18/39 in Oklahoma City. Country singer. | | | |
| 3/30/63 | 130 | 2 | She's New To You ...................... *All My Love All My Life* | $8 | | Liberty 55543 |
| | | | **The Johnny Mann Singers** (backing vocals); **Ernie Freeman** (orch.) | | | |
| | | | **BEE GEES**        HOT/AC/C&W | | | |
| | | | Trio of brothers from Manchester, England: Barry Gibb (b: 9/1/47) and twins Maurice and **Robin Gibb** (b: 12/22/49). To Australia in 1958, performed as the Gibbs, later as BG's, finally the Bee Gees. Returned to England in February 1967. Composed soundtracks for *Saturday Night Fever* and *Staying Alive*. Acted in the movie *Sgt. Pepper's Lonely Hearts Club Band*. Trio inducted into the Rock and Roll Hall of Fame in 1997. *Top Pop Singles:* 43. | | | |
| 7/1/67 | 128 | 1 | 1 I Can't See Nobody ......................*New York Mining Disaster 1941 (Hot #14)* | $10 | | Atco 6487 |
| 4/27/68 | 116 | 3 | 2 The Singer Sang His Song ..................... *Jumbo (Hot #57)* | $10 | | Atco 6570 |
| 6/30/73 | 115 | 5 | 3 Wouldn't I Be Someone ............................ AC:42 *Elisa* | $6 | | RSO 404 |
| 11/16/74 | 103 | 5 | 4 Charade        AC:31 *Heavy Breathing* | $6 | | RSO 501 |
| 3/12/94 | 109 | 9 | 5 For Whom The Bell Tolls ....................... AC:29 *New York Mining Disaster 1941 /* | $3 | ■ | Polydor 855332 |
| | | | *I've Gotta Get A Message To You / Massachusetts (Lights Went Out)* | | | |
| | | | **BELAND, John** ⊙ | | | |
| | | | Nashville-based guitarist/vocalist. Member of the Burrito Brothers country group in the early '80s. | | | |
| 11/8/69 | 110 | 1 | Baby You Come Rollin' 'Cross My Mind ......................... *Home Town* | $7 | | Ranwood 853 |
| | | | #59 hit for The Peppermint Trolley Company in 1968 | | | |
| | | | **BELEW, Carl** ⊙        C&W | | | |
| | | | Born on 4/21/31 in Salina, Oklahoma. Died of cancer on 10/31/90. Country singer/songwriter. | | | |
| 10/20/62 | 120 | 1 | Hello Out There ...................... C&W:8 *Together We Stand* | $10 | | RCA Victor 8058 |
| | | | **BELFAST GIPSIES, The** ⊙ | | | |
| | | | Rock group from Belfast, Ireland, led by brothers Jackie (keyboards) and Patrick (drums) McAuley. Both were former members of **Them**. | | | |
| 9/17/66 | 124 | 2 | Gloria's Dream (Round and Around) ...................... *Secret Police* | $25 | | Loma 2051 |
| | | | based on Van Morrison's classic rock hit "Gloria" | | | |
| | | | **BELL, Archie, & The Drells**        R&B/HOT | | | |
| | | | Born on 9/1/44 in Henderson, Texas. Leader of R&B vocal group, The Drells: Huey "Billy" Butler, Joe Cross and James Wise. | | | |
| 4/19/69 | 128 | 1 | 1 Just A Little Closer ...................... *I Love My Baby (Hot #94)* | $8 | | Atlantic 2612 |
| 1/31/70 | 112 | 2 | 2 Here I Go Again ...................... *A World Without Music (Hot #90)* | $8 | | Atlantic 2693 |
| | | | **BELL, William**        R&B/HOT | | | |
| | | | Born William Yarborough on 7/16/39 in Memphis. R&B singer. | | | |
| 10/20/62 | 131 | 1 | 1 Any Other Way ...................... *Please Help Me, I'm Falling* | $15 | | Stax 128 |
| 4/6/68 | 115 | 1 | 2 Every Man Oughta Have A Woman ...................... *A Tribute To A King (Hot #86)* | $10 | | Stax 248 |
| 12/28/68 | 104 | 4 | 3 My Baby Specializes ...................... R&B:45 *Left Over Love* | $10 | | Stax 0017 |
| | | | **WILLIAM BELL & JUDY CLAY** | | | |
| 7/12/69 | 106 | 4 | 4 I Need You Woman ...................... *I Can't Stop* | $10 | | Stax 0044 |
| | | | **WILLIAM BELL, CARLA THOMAS** | | | |
| 8/9/69 | 129 | 1 | 5 Happy ...................... *My Kind Of Girl* | $10 | | Stax 0038 |
| 7/7/73 | 101² | 6 | 6 Lovin' On Borrowed Time        R&B:22 *The Man In The Street* | $8 | | Stax 0157 |
| | | | **BELL & JAMES**        R&B/HOT | | | |
| | | | R&B duo of Leroy Bell and Casey James. Began as a songwriting team for Bell's uncle, producer Thom Bell. | | | |
| 6/2/79 | 103 | 4 | You Never Know What You've Got............. R&B:54 *Just Can't Get Enough (Of Your Love)* | $6 | | A&M 2137 |

**BELL BIV DeVOE**　　　　　　　　　　　　　　　　　　　　R&B/HOT
R&B trio of **New Edition** members: Ricky Bell, Michael Bivins and Ronnie DeVoe.

| | | | | | | |
|---|---|---|---|---|---|---|
| 6/19/93 | 104 | 5 | Above The Rim ................................................R&B:81 *(instrumental)* | $3 | ▮ | MCA 54620 |

samples "Blind Alley" by The Emotions

**BELLY**　　　　　　　　　　　　　　　　　　　　　　　ROK/HOT
Pop-rock group from Newport, Rhode Island: Tanya Donelly (vocals, guitar), Gail Greenwood (bass), and brothers Thomas (guitar) and Chris (drums) Gorman. Donelly was a member of **Throwing Muses** and **The Breeders**.

| | | | | | | |
|---|---|---|---|---|---|---|
| 11/20/93 | 113 | 5 | 1 Gepetto ..............................................................ROK:8 *Slow Dog* | $3 | ▮ | Sire/Reprise 18358 |
| 3/25/95 | 103 | 5 | 2 Now They'll Sleep ............................................ROK:17 *Silverfish* | $3 | ▮ | Sire/Reprise 17938 |

**BELMONTS, The**　　　　　　　　　　　　　　　　　　　　　HOT
Pop vocal trio: Angelo D'Aleo, Fred Milano and Carlo Mastrangelo. Sang with **Dion** from 1957-60.

| | | | | | | |
|---|---|---|---|---|---|---|
| 1/23/61 | 108 | 3 | 1 We Belong Together ....................................*Such A Long Way* | $30 | | Laurie 3080 |

#32 hit for **Robert & Johnny** in 1958

| | | | | | | |
|---|---|---|---|---|---|---|
| 3/2/63 | 123 | 2 | 2 Baby Doll ......................................................*Write Me A Letter* | $30 | | Laurie 3151 |

**CARLO**
The Del Satins (backing vocals)

**BELOVED, The** ☉　　　　　　　　　　　　　　　　　　　　ROK
British pop-rock duo of husband-and-wife Jon (vocals, keyboards) and Helena (guitars) Marsh.

| | | | | | | |
|---|---|---|---|---|---|---|
| 5/8/93 | 114 | 2 | Sweet Harmony ................................................ROK:23 *Dream On* | $3 | ▮ | Atlantic 87361 |

**BEN and BEA** ☉
| | | | | | | |
|---|---|---|---|---|---|---|
| 3/31/62 | 119 | 2 | Gee Baby ..................................*Let The Good Times Roll* | $15 | | Philips 40000 |

#52 hit in 1961 for Mickey & Sylvia as "Baby You're So Fine" (also see **Joe & Ann**)

**BENÉT, Eric** ☉　　　　　　　　　　　　　　　　　　　　R&B
R&B singer/songwriter from Milwaukee.

| | | | | | | |
|---|---|---|---|---|---|---|
| 5/17/97 | 107 | 10 | 1 Femininity ....................................R&B:24 *While You Were Here* | $3 | ▮ | Warner 17571 |
| 10/18/97 | 122 | 1 | 2 True To Myself ..................................................R&B:43 *(remix)* | $3 | ▮ | Warner 17328 |

from the movie *Batman & Robin* starring George Clooney and Chris O'Donnell

**BENNETT, Joe, And The Sparkletones**　　　　　　　　HOT/R&B
Rock and roll band from Spartanburg, South Carolina: Joe Bennett (vocals, guitar), Howard Childress (guitar), Wayne Arthur (bass) and Irving Denton (drums).

| | | | | | | |
|---|---|---|---|---|---|---|
| 9/14/59 | 105 | 2 | Boys Do Cry ........................................................*What The Heck* | $25 | | Paris 537 |

**BENNETT, Pete, & The Embers** ☉
Bennett was one of the leading record promotion men during the 1960s.

| | | | | | | |
|---|---|---|---|---|---|---|
| 11/13/61 | 105 | 5 | Fever ..............................................................................*Soft* [I] | $20 | | Sunset 1002 |

arrangement similar to "Last Night" by the **Mar-Keys** (#3 in 1961); #1 R&B hit for **Little Willie John** in 1956

**BENNETT, Tony**　　　　　　　　　　　　　　　　HOT/AC/MEM/POP
Born Anthony Dominick Benedetto on 8/3/26 in Queens, New York. Top jazz vocalist. *Pop Hits & Top Pop Singles*: 43.

| | | | | | | |
|---|---|---|---|---|---|---|
| 12/14/63 | 127 | 1 | 1 The Moment Of Truth ....................*The Little Boy* (Hot #52) | $10 | | Columbia 42931 |
| 2/26/66 | 104 | 6 | 2 Song From "The Oscar" AC:10 *Baby, Dream Your Dream* (AC #27) | $8 | ▮ | Columbia 43508 |

from the movie starring Eleanor Parker and Bennett

| | | | | | | |
|---|---|---|---|---|---|---|
| 9/17/66 | 119 | 2 | 3 A Time For Love ..............................AC:3 *Touch The Earth* | $8 | | Columbia 43768 |

from the movie *An American Dream* starring Stuart Whitman

| | | | | | | |
|---|---|---|---|---|---|---|
| 3/16/68 | 119 | 2 | 4 A Fool Of Fools ..............AC:12 *The Glory Of Love* (w/Dominic Germano) | $8 | | Columbia 44443 |
| 4/27/68 | 130 | 2 | 5 Yesterday I Heard The Rain ..........AC:10 *Sweet Georgie Fame* | $8 | | Columbia 44510 |
| 2/13/71 | 114 | 5 | 6 (Where Do I Begin) Love Story ......................*I'll Begin Again* | $6 | | Columbia 45316 |

from the movie *Love Story* starring Ali MacGraw and Ryan O'Neal; #9 hit for **Andy Williams** in 1971

| | | | | | | |
|---|---|---|---|---|---|---|
| 12/9/72 | 111 | 3 | 7 Living Together, Growing Together ......*The Good Things In Life* (Bennett) | $6 | | MGM/Verve 10690 |

**TONY BENNETT With The Mike Curb Congregation**
from the movie *Lost Horizon* starring Peter Finch; #32 hit for **The 5th Dimension** in 1973

**BENSON, George**　　　　　　　　　　　　　　　　　R&B/AC/HOT
Born on 3/22/43 in Pittsburgh. R&B-jazz guitarist/vocalist.

| | | | | | | |
|---|---|---|---|---|---|---|
| 9/6/69 | 113 | 2 | 1 My Woman's Good To Me ..............................*Jackie All* | $6 | | A&M/CTI 1076 |
| 6/21/75 | 105 | 2 | 2 Supership ....................................R&B:98 *My Latin Brother* | $6 | | CTI 25 |

**GEORGE "BAD" BENSON**

| | | | | | | |
|---|---|---|---|---|---|---|
| 6/4/77 | 106 | 1 | 3 Everything Must Change ......R&B:34 *The Wind And I (aka Hot Stuff)* | $5 | | Warner 8360 |
| 12/27/80 | 109 | 1 | 4 Turn Out The Lamplight ......R&B:33 *Midnight Love Affair* | $4 | | Warner 49637 |
| 4/6/85 | 102 | 6 | 5 I Just Wanna Hang Around You AC:7 /R&B:24 *Beyond The Sea (La Mer)* | $3 | | Warner 29042 |

**BENTLEY, Jay, And The Jet Set** ☉
| | | | | | | |
|---|---|---|---|---|---|---|
| 1/30/65 | 128 | 3 | Watusi '64 ..........................................................*I'll Get You* | $15 | | G.N.P. Crescendo 332 |

**BENTON, Barbi** ☉　　　　　　　　　　　　　　　　　　　C&W
Born Barbara Klein on 1/28/50 in Sacramento, California. Country singer/actress/model.

| | | | | | | |
|---|---|---|---|---|---|---|
| 10/2/76 | 108 | 2 | Staying Power ........................................*San Diego Serenade* | $6 | ▮ | Playboy 6078 |

written by **Neil Sedaka**

**BENTON, Brook**　　　　　　　　　　　　　　　　　　HOT/R&B/AC
Born Benjamin Franklin Peay on 9/19/31 in Camden, South Carolina. Died of spinal meningitis on 4/9/88. R&B singer/songwriter. *Top Pop Singles*: 50.

| | | | | | | |
|---|---|---|---|---|---|---|
| 5/5/62 | 106 | 3 | 1 Thanks To The Fool ..............................*Hit Record* (Hot #45) | $12 | ▮ | Mercury 71962 |

issued with 2 different picture sleeves: a blue background and an orange background

| | | | | | | |
|---|---|---|---|---|---|---|
| 8/18/62 | 120 | 1 | 2 With The Touch Of Your Hand ................*Lie To Me* (Hot #13) | $12 | ▮ | Mercury 72024 |
| 11/9/63 | 108 | 4 | 3 Stop Foolin'/ | | | Mercury 72207 |
| 11/16/63 | 111 | 4 | 4 Baby, You've Got It Made .......................................... | $12 | | |

**BROOK BENTON & DAMITA JO** (above 2)

| | | | | | | |
|---|---|---|---|---|---|---|
| 12/5/64 | 119 | 1 | 5 Please, Please Make It Easy ....................*Do It Right* (Hot #67) | $10 | ▮ | Mercury 72365 |
| 3/20/65 | 129 | 1 | 6 The Special Years ..............*Where There's A Will (There's A Way)* | $10 | | Mercury 72398 |
| 3/5/66 | 122 | 3 | 7 Only A Girl Like You ..........*While There's Life (There's Still Hope)* | $10 | | RCA Victor 8768 |

**BENTON, Brook — Cont'd**

| | | | | | | |
|---|---|---|---|---|---|---|
| 5/28/66 | 126 | 2 | 8 **Too Much Good Lovin' (No Good For Me)** ............................. *A Sailor Boy's Love Song* | $10 | | RCA Victor 8830 |
| 10/7/72 | 104 | 4 | 9 **If You Got The Time** *You Take Me Home Honey* | $8 | | MGM 14440 |

**BERNARD, Rod**      HOT/R&B
Born on 8/12/40 in Opelousas, Louisiana. Rock and roll singer/guitarist.

| 3/24/62 | 102 | 4 | **Colinda** ...................................................................... *Who's Gonna Rock My Baby* | $20 | | Hall-Way 1902 |
|---|---|---|---|---|---|---|
| | | | "cajun"-styled rock and roll tune written by Bernard | | | |

**BERNARDI, Herschel** ☉      AC
Born on 10/20/23 in New York City. Died on 5/9/86. Portrayed "Tevye" in Broadway's *Fiddler On The Roof.*

| 2/27/71 | 107 | 2 | **Pencil Marks On The Wall** ................................ AC:35 *In My Own Lifetime* | $6 | | Columbia 45285 |
|---|---|---|---|---|---|---|
| | | | Ernie Freeman (orch.) | | | |

**BERNSTEIN, Elmer**      HOT
Born on 4/4/22 in New York City. Composer/conductor for numerous movie soundtracks.

| 4/21/62 | 102 | 1 | **Walk On The Wild Side** ................................ *Walk On The Wild Side Jazz* [I] | $10 | | Choreo 101 |
|---|---|---|---|---|---|---|
| | | | from the movie starring Laurence Harvey and Jane Fonda | | | |

**BERRY, Chuck**      HOT/R&B
Born on 10/18/26 in St. Louis. Rock and roll singer/songwriter/guitarist. Won Grammy's Lifetime Achievement Award in 1984. Inducted into the Rock and Roll Hall of Fame in 1986. *Top Pop Singles:* 27.

| 9/28/59 | 108 | 4 | 1 **Broken Arrow** ............................................................ *Childhood Sweetheart* | $30 | | Chess 1737 |
|---|---|---|---|---|---|---|
| | | | based on the traditional song "Old MacDonald" | | | |
| 11/7/60 | 109 | 4 | 2 **Jaguar And Thunderbird** ............................................ *Our Little Rendezvous* | $25 | | Chess 1767 |

**BERRY, John** ☉      C&W
Born on 9/14/59 in Aiken, South Carolina; raised in Atlanta. Country singer/songwriter.

| 8/6/94 | 120 | 6 | 1 **What's In It For Me** ................................ C&W:5 *Your Love Amazes Me* (C&W #1) | $3 | ▌ | Liberty 58212 |
|---|---|---|---|---|---|---|
| 9/7/96 | 103 | 20 | 2 **Change My Mind**.................. Sls:75 /C&W:10 *Standing On The Edge Of Goodbye* (C&W #2/'95) | $3 | ▌ | Capitol 58577 |
| 2/15/97 | 117 | 3 | 3 **She's Taken A Shine** ................................ C&W:2 *Time To Be A Man* | $3 | ▌ | Capitol 58624 |

**BIG BROTHER AND THE HOLDING COMPANY**      HOT
Rock group formed in San Francisco: **Janis Joplin** (vocals), James Gurley and Sam Andrew (guitars), Peter Albin (bass) and David Getz (drums). Joplin died of a heroin overdose on 10/4/70 (age 27).

| 9/9/67 | 110 | 5 | 1 **Blindman** ............................................................................ *All Is Lonliness* | $15 | | Mainstream 657 |
|---|---|---|---|---|---|---|
| 9/9/67 | 118 | 4 | 2 **Bye, Bye Baby** ............................................................................ *Intruder* | $15 | | Mainstream 666 |

**BIG BUB**      R&B/HOT
Born Frederick Lee Drakeford in New Jersey. Male singer/rapper.

| 5/22/93 | 103 | 8 | **Tellin' Me Stories** ............................................ R&B:27 *Talk Dirty* | $3 | ▌ | EastWest 98451 |
|---|---|---|---|---|---|---|

**BIG HEAD TODD AND THE MONSTERS** ☉      ROK
Rock trio from Boulder, Colorado: Todd Park Mohr (guitar, keyboards), Rob Squires (bass) and Brian Nevin (drums).

| 1/15/94 | 104 | 6 | **Bittersweet**................................................ ROK:14 *Sister Sweetly* | $3 | ▌ | Giant 18369 |
|---|---|---|---|---|---|---|

**BILK, Mr. Acker**      HOT/AC
Born Bernard Stanley Bilk on 1/28/29 in Somerset, England. Clarinetist/composer.

| 2/22/60 | 104 | 3 | 1 **Summer Set** ................................................ *Acker's Away* [I] | $8 | | Atco 6160 |
|---|---|---|---|---|---|---|
| | | | #30 hit for Monty Kelly in 1960 | | | |
| 6/23/62 | 105 | 3 | 2 **Dardanella (Part 1)** ............................................ *(Part 2)* [I] | $8 | | Reprise 20,090 |
| | | | #1 hit for Ben Selvin's Novelty Orchestra in 1920 | | | |
| 2/8/64 | 125 | 1 | 3 **The Harem** ............................................ *Train Song* [I] | $8 | | Atco 6282 |
| | | | **MR. ACKER BILK and his Paramount Jazz Band** (#1 & 3) | | | |

**BILLY AND THE ESSENTIALS** ☉
Pop vocal quartet from Philadelphia: Billy Carlucci, Richie Grasso, Jimmy Sofia and Pete Torres.

| 1/19/63 | 117 | 2 | **Maybe You'll Be There** ............................................ *Over The Weekend* | $30 | | Jamie 1239 |
|---|---|---|---|---|---|---|
| | | | #3 hit for Gordon Jenkins Orchestra in 1948 | | | |

**BIONIC BOOGIE** ☉      R&B
Disco studio group assembled by producer **Gregg Diamond**.

| 7/22/78 | 105 | 2 | **Dance Little Dreamer** ............................................ *Feel Like Dancing* | $5 | | Polydor 14471 |
|---|---|---|---|---|---|---|

**BIRDWATCHERS, The** ☉
Garage-rock band from Florida: Sammy Hall, Jerry Schils, Bobby Puccetti, Eddie Martinez, Jim Tolliver, Dave Chiodo, Joey Murcia and Craig Caraglior.

| 9/3/66 | 125 | 1 | **I'm Gonna Love You Anyway**................................ *A Little Bit Of Lovin'* | $25 | | Mala 536 |
|---|---|---|---|---|---|---|
| | | | co-produced by **Steve Alaimo** | | | |

**BISHOP, Stephen**      AC/HOT
Born on 11/14/51 in San Diego. Pop singer/songwriter.

| 7/26/80 | 105 | 3 | 1 **Your Precious Love** ................................ *Redfish Blues* (Craig Hundley) | $4 | | Warner 49513 |
|---|---|---|---|---|---|---|
| | | | **STEPHEN BISHOP & YVONNE ELLIMAN** | | | |
| | | | from the movie *Roadie* starring Meat Loaf; #5 hit for **Marvin Gaye** & **Tammi Terrell** in 1967 | | | |
| 4/11/81 | 108 | 3 | 2 **Send A Little Love My Way (Like Always)** ................................ AC:31 *City Girl* | $4 | | Warner 49658 |
| | | | originally made the Adult Contemporary charts on 12/13/80 on Warner 49595 | | | |
| 9/25/82 | 108 | 1 | 3 **If Love Takes You Away** ................................ AC:22 *Search For Lina* (Basil Poledouris) | $4 | | Warner 29924 |
| | | | from the movie *Summer Lovers* starring Peter Gallagher and Daryl Hannah | | | |

**BJÖRK**      ROK/HOT
Björk pronounced: Bee-YERK. Born Björk Gudmundsdottir on 11/12/65 in Reykjavik, Iceland. Female lead singer of The Sugarcubes.

| 10/9/93 | 109 | 3 | 1 **Human Behaviour** ................................ ROK:2 *Atlantic* | $3 | ▌ | Elektra 64606 |
|---|---|---|---|---|---|---|
| 10/14/95 | 109 | 4 | 2 **It's Oh So Quiet** ................................ *You've Been Flirting Again* | $3 | ▌ | Elektra 64353 |

## BLACK('S), Bill, Combo     HOT/C&W/R&B
Born on 9/17/26 in Memphis. Died of a brain tumor on 10/21/65. Bass guitarist. Session work in Memphis; backed **Elvis Presley** on most of his early records. Formed own band in 1959. Labeled as "The Untouchable Sound."

| DEBUT | PEAK | WKS | A-side | B-side | $ | Pic | Label & Number |
|---|---|---|---|---|---|---|---|
| 12/15/62 | 114 | 2 | 1 Joey's Song | Hot Taco [l] | $12 | | Hi 2059 |
| | | | #46 hit for **Bill Haley & His Comets** in 1959 | | | | |
| 6/6/64 | 118 | 1 | 2 Raunchy ........ | Tequila (Hot #91) [l] | $12 | | Hi 2077 |
| | | | #2 hit for **Bill Justis** in 1957 | | | | |
| 2/6/65 | 124 | 4 | 3 Come On Home ........ | He'll Have To Go | $12 | | Hi 2085 |
| 8/14/65 | 135 | 1 | 4 Spootin' ........ | Crazy Feel [l] | $12 | | Hi 2094 |
| 6/11/66 | 124 | 2 | 5 Hey, Good Lookin' ........ | Mountain Of Love [l] | $12 | | Hi 2106 |
| | | | #1 Country hit for **Hank Williams** in 1951 | | | | |

## BLACK, Cilla     HOT/AC
Born Priscilla White on 5/27/43 in Liverpool, England. Female singer.

| | | | | | | | |
|---|---|---|---|---|---|---|---|
| 3/13/65 | 133 | 1 | Is It Love? ........ | One Little Voice | $12 | | Capitol 5373 |
| | | | from the movie *Ferry Cross The Mersey* starring **Gerry & The Pacemakers** and Black | | | | |

## BLACK, Clint     C&W/HOT
Born on 2/4/62 in Long Branch, New Jersey; raised in Houston. Country singer/guitarist. Married actress Lisa Hartman on 10/20/91.

| | | | | | | | |
|---|---|---|---|---|---|---|---|
| 12/25/93+ | 102 | 9 | State Of Mind ........ Sls:70 /C&W:2 | Tuckered Out (C&W #74) | $3 | ▌ | RCA 62700 |

## BLACK, Janie ⊘
Born in Mount Baldy, California. Sixteen years old in 1961. Sister of country-pop singer **Jeanne Black** (recorded together as Jeanne & Janie).

| | | | | | | | |
|---|---|---|---|---|---|---|---|
| 11/6/61 | 116 | 1 | Lonely Sixteen | A Heartache Grows | $12 | | Capitol 4633 |
| | | | Jimmie Haskell (orch.) | | | | |

## BLACK, Marion ⊘     R&B
Male R&B singer/songwriter.

| | | | | | | | |
|---|---|---|---|---|---|---|---|
| 3/20/71 | 124 | 2 | Go On Fool | R&B:39 Who Knows | $5 | | Avco Embassy 4559 |

## BLACKBYRDS, The     R&B/HOT/AC
R&B group formed in 1973 by **Donald Byrd** while teaching jazz at Howard University in Washington, D.C. Core members: Joe Hall (vocals, bass), Kevin Toney (vocals, keyboards) and Keith Killgo (vocals, drums).

| | | | | | | | |
|---|---|---|---|---|---|---|---|
| 8/17/74 | 101[1] | 3 | 1 Summer Love | Do It, Fluid (Hot #69) [l] | $5 | | Fantasy 729 |
| | | | listed strictly as the B-side during its 3 weeks on the "Bubbling Under" charts | | | | |
| 6/14/75 | 104 | 1 | 2 Think Twice ........ | We're Together | $6 | | Blue Note 650 |
| | | | DONALD BYRD | | | | |
| | | | Kay Haith (female vocal) | | | | |
| 1/7/78 | 102 | 11 | 3 Soft And Easy ........ R&B:20 | Something Special [l] | $5 | | Fantasy 809 |
| 4/22/78 | 102 | 5 | 4 Supernatural Feeling ........ R&B:19 | Lookin' Ahead | $5 | ☐ | Fantasy 819 |

## BLACKFOOT     HOT/ROK
Southern-rock band from Jacksonville, Florida: Rick Medlocke (vocals), Charlie Hargrett (guitar), Greg Walker (bass) and Jakson Spires (drums). Medlocke and Walker later joined **Lynyrd Skynyrd**.

| | | | | | | | |
|---|---|---|---|---|---|---|---|
| 9/26/81 | 108 | 1 | 1 Searchin' ........ | Payin' For It | $5 | | Atco 7338 |
| 7/30/83 | 103 | 4 | 2 Teenage Idol ........ | Run For Cover | $5 | ▌ | Atco 99851 |

## BLACKGIRL     R&B/HOT
Female R&B vocal trio from Atlanta: Tye-V Turman, Pam Copeland and Rochelle Stuart.

| | | | | | | | |
|---|---|---|---|---|---|---|---|
| 11/19/94 | 118 | 3 | 1 Where Did We Go Wrong ........ R&B:39 (remix) | | $3 | ▌ | Kaper/RCA 62964 |
| 3/18/95 | 113 | 7 | 2 Let's Do It Again ........ R&B:25 (2 mixes) | | $3 | ▌ | Kaper/RCA 64310 |
| | | | #1 hit for **The Staple Singers** in 1975 | | | | |

## BLACKHAWK ⊘     C&W
Country trio of music veterans Henry Paul (member of Southern-rock bands the **Outlaws** and the **Henry Paul Band**) with the songwriting team of Dave Robbins and Van Stephenson.

| | | | | | | | |
|---|---|---|---|---|---|---|---|
| 2/26/94 | 111 | 9 | 1 Goodbye Says It All ........ Sls:73 /C&W:11 | Let 'Em Whirl | $3 | ▌ | Arista 12568 |
| 9/16/95 | 104 | 12 | 2 I'm Not Strong Enough To Say No ........ Sls:66 /C&W:2 | A Kiss Is Worth A Thousand Words | $3 | ▌ | Arista 12857 |
| 8/23/97 | 123 | 1 | 3 Hole In My Heart ........ C&W:31 | She Dances With Her Shadow | $3 | ▌ | Arista 13092 |

## BLACK IVORY ⊘     R&B
R&B vocal trio from New York City: Leroy Burgess III, Stuart Bascombe and Russell Patterson.

| | | | | | | | |
|---|---|---|---|---|---|---|---|
| 4/8/72 | 111 | 4 | You And I ........ R&B:32 | Our Future? | $6 | | Today 1508 |

## BLACK MOON     R&B/HOT
Rap trio from Brooklyn: Buckshot Shorty, 5 Ft. Excellerator and DJ Evil Dee.

| | | | | | | | |
|---|---|---|---|---|---|---|---|
| 12/4/93 | 120 | 2 | 1 How Many Emcee's (must get dissed) ........ R&B:97 (remix) / Act Like U Want It (2 versions) | | $5 | ▌ | Wreck 20064 * |
| 10/15/94 | 124 | 1 | 2 Buck Em Down ........ R&B:81 (instrumental) / Murder MC's (2 versions) | | $5 | ▌ | Wreck 20100 * |
| | | | samples "Wind Parade" by **Donald Byrd** | | | | |

## BLACK PANTA — see BLAK PANTA

## BLACK SHEEP     R&B/HOT
Rap duo from New York City: Andre "Dres" Titus and William "Mista Lawnge" McLean.

| | | | | | | | |
|---|---|---|---|---|---|---|---|
| 10/22/94 | 103 | 11 | Without A Doubt ........ Sls:73 /R&B:67 (2 versions) / (album snippets) | | $3 | ▌ | Mercury 856170 |

## BLACKSTREET     R&B/HOT
R&B hip-hop quartet: Teddy Riley, Chauncey Hannibal, Levi Little and David Hollister. Riley, a prolific producer, was a member of Guy.

| | | | | | | | |
|---|---|---|---|---|---|---|---|
| 4/3/93 | 113 | 12 | Baby Be Mine ........ R&B:17 (instrumental) | | $3 | ▌ | MCA 54561 |
| | | | BLACKSTREET Featuring Teddy Riley | | | | |
| | | | from the movie *CB4* starring Chris Rock | | | | |

## BLACKWELLS, The ⊘
Pop duo: Dewayne and Ronald Blackwell.

| | | | | | | | |
|---|---|---|---|---|---|---|---|
| 4/10/61 | 107 | 1 | Love Or Money ........ | Big Daddy And The Cat | $15 | | Jamie 1179 |

## BLAHZAY BLAHZAY     R&B/HOT
Rap duo from Brooklyn: Outloud and DJ P.F. Cuttin.

| | | | | | | | |
|---|---|---|---|---|---|---|---|
| 6/8/96 | 115 | 1 | Pain I Feel ........ R&B:78 (radio version) | | $3 | ▌ | Fader/Mercury 127056 |

**BLAKELY, Cornell** ☉
R&B vocalist.

| 9/4/61 | 116 | 1 | You Ain't Gonna Find ............................................... *Who Knows* | $25 | | Rich 71853 |

written by Berry Gordy, Jr.; originally released on Rich 1007 in 1961 ($75)

**BLAK PANTA** ☉          R&B

| 3/18/95 | 109 | 5 | Do What U Want ..................... *R&B:78 (original mix)* | $3 | ■ | Tommy Boy 7674 |

from the movie *New Jersey Drive* starring Sharron Corley

**BLAND, Billy**          HOT/R&B
Born on 4/5/32 in Wilmington, North Carolina. R&B singer.

| 7/4/60 | 102 | 3 | Pardon Me.............................. *You Were Born To Be Loved (Hot #94)* | $20 | | Old Town 1082 |

**BLAND, Bobby**          R&B/HOT
Born on 1/27/30 in Rosemark, Tennessee. R&B/blues singer. Nicknamed "Blue." Inducted into the Rock and Roll Hall of Fame in 1992.
*Top Pop Singles:* 37.

| 12/21/63 | 106 | 4 | 1 I Can't Stop Singing ............................... *The Feeling Is Gone (Hot #91)* | $15 | | Duke 370 |
| 6/13/64 | 111 | 1 | 2 After It's Too Late ............................... *Share Your Love With Me (Hot #42)* | $15 | | Duke 377 |
| 5/15/65 | 125 | 1 | 3 Dust Got In Daddy's Eyes ............ *R&B:23 Ain't No Telling (Hot #93)* | $15 | | Duke 390 |
| 12/3/66 | 102 | 5 | 4 Back In The Same Old Bag Again............ *R&B:13 I Ain't Myself Anymore* | $12 | | Duke 412 |
| 6/28/75 | 104 | 1 | 5 Yolanda .................... *R&B:21 When You Come To The End Of Your Road* | $5 | | ABC 12105 |
| 4/10/76 | 103 | 1 | 6 Today I Started Loving You Again.................*R&B:34 Too Far Gone* | $5 | | ABC 12156 |

written in 1968 by Merle Haggard

| 7/24/76 | 101[1] | 2 | 7 Let The Good Times Roll         *R&B:20 Strange Things* | $5 | | ABC Impulse 31006 |

    **BOBBY BLAND & B.B. KING**
    "live" recording; #2 R&B hit for Louis Jordan in 1947

**BLENDTONES, The** ☉
R&B vocal group.

| 5/25/63 | 118 | 4 | Lovers .................................. *Dear Diary* | $50 | | Success 101 |

**BLESSING, Adam — see DAMNATION OF**

**BLIGE, Mary J. — see GRAND PUBA**

**BLINKY**          HOT
Female R&B singer Sandra "Blinky" Williams. Recorded duets with Edwin Starr in 1969.

| 2/15/69 | 128 | 1 | I Wouldn't Change The Man He Is ......................... *I'll Always Love You* | $7 | | Motown 1134 |

written and produced by Ashford & Simpson

**BLIZZARD** ☉
Pop vocal group.

| 4/24/71 | 106 | 1 | Baby Blue........................*Mama, The Sparrow and The Tree* | $6 | | Metromedia 215 |

**BLOODSTONE**          R&B/HOT/AC
R&B group from Kansas City: Charles Love (vocals), Willis Draffen Jr. (guitar), Charles McCormick (bass) and Harry Williams (drums).

| 11/9/74 | 108 | 2 | 1 I Need Time ................................. *I Believe You Now* | $6 | | London 1059 |
| 6/5/76 | 101[1] | 1 | 2 Do You Wanna Do A Thing      *R&B:19 Save Me* | $6 | | London 1064 |

**BLOOD, SWEAT & TEARS**          HOT/AC/R&B
Rock-jazz fusion group from New York City. Numerous personnel changes. Jerry Fisher was lead singer in 1972. David Clayton-Thomas was lead singer from 1969-71; returned in 1974.

| 12/30/72 | 103 | 4 | 1 I Can't Move No Mountains ....................... *Velvet* | $6 | | Columbia 45755 |
| 11/27/76 | 106 | 1 | 2 You're The One ....................... *AC:6 Heavy Blue* | $5 | | Columbia 10400 |

**BLOOM, Bobby**          HOT/AC
Pop singer/songwriter. Much session work in the '60s. Died from an accidental shooting on 2/28/74 (age 28).

| 2/17/73 | 123 | 3 | Sha La Boom Boom ....................... *Stay On Top* | $8 | | MGM 14437 |

**BLOSSOMS, The**          HOT/R&B
Backing female R&B vocal group for Elvis Presley, Paul Anka, Duane Eddy, Bobby Darin, Mamas & Papas, Beach Boys, Dionne Warwick and many others. Darlene Love was the featured vocalist.

| 4/2/66 | 101[1] | 3 | 1 Good, Good Lovin'/ | | | |
| 3/5/66 | 128 | 2 | 2    That's When The Tears Start ....................... | $15 | | Reprise 0436 |
| 12/16/67 | 115 | 1 | 3 Good, Good Lovin'.........................*R&B:45 Deep Into My Heart* [R] | $15 | | Reprise 0639 |

    same version as #1 above

**BLOW, Kurtis — see NADANUF**

**BLUE BELLES — see LaBELLE, Patti**

**BLUE MAGIC**          R&B/HOT/AC
R&B vocal group from Philadelphia: Theodore Mills (lead), Vernon Sawyer, Wendell Sawyer, Keith Beaton and Richard Pratt.

| 4/17/76 | 104 | 2 | Grateful.........................*R&B:15 I Like You* | $6 | | Atco/WMOT 7046 |

**BLUE NOTES, The — see MELVIN, Harold**

**BLUE RIDGE RANGERS — see FOGERTY, John**

**BLUES BROTHERS**          HOT
Joliet "Jake" (John Belushi; b: 1/24/49, d: 3/5/82) and Elwood Blues (Dan Aykroyd; b: 7/1/52); originally created for TV's *Saturday Night Live*.

| 3/7/81 | 108 | 1 | Going Back To Miami.........................*From The Bottom* | $5 | | Atlantic 3802 |

    "live" recording; written by Wayne Cochran

**BLUES MAGOOS**          HOT
Rock quintet from the Bronx, New York: Emil "Peppy" Castro Thielhelm (vocals, guitar), Mike Esposito (guitar), Ralph Scala (keyboards), Ronnie Gilbert (bass) and Geoff Daking (drums).

| 8/26/67 | 133 | 2 | 1 I Wanna Be There ....................... *Summer Is The Man* | $12 | | Mercury 72707 |
| 1/24/70 | 113 | 4 | 2 Never Goin' Back To Georgia ....................... *Feelin' Time (I Can Feel It)* | $8 | | ABC 11250 |

| DEBUT | PEAK | WKS | A-side | $ | Pic | Label & Number |
|---|---|---|---|---|---|---|

**BLUE STEEL** ☉
Rock band from Texas: Leonard Arnold (vocals, guitar), Richard Bowden and Howard Burke (guitars), Marc Durham (bass), and Mickey McGee and Michael Huey (drums). Bowden later formed country-novelty duo with Sandy Pinkard.

| 10/20/79 | 110 | 1 | No More Lonely Nights ............................................................ *Twist One Up* | $5 | | Infinity 50,029 |

**BLUR**     **ROK/HOT**
Techno-rock group from London: Damon Albarn (vocals), Graham Coxon (guitar), Alex James (bass) and Dave Rowntree (drums).

| 10/11/97 | 114 | 2 | M.O.R. .................................... *Pop Scene / Song 2 / Bustin' & Dronin'* | $6 | | Food/Virgin 38611 (CD) |

**BOATZ** ☉
Soft-rock group: Thom Flora (vocals, keyboards), Pete Carr (guitar), Gary Baker (bass) and Rick Powell (drums).

| 7/7/79 | 107 | 1 | It Was Only The Radio .............................................. *Blame It On The Future* | $5 | | Capricorn 0319 |

**BOB AND EARL**     **HOT/R&B**
R&B duo of Bob Relf and Earl Nelson. **Bobby Day** sang with Earl Nelson (as Bob & Earl) in 1960. Also see **Bobby Day** and **Jackie Lee**.

| 3/28/64 | 111 | 3 | Puppet On A String.......................................................... *My Woman* | $15 | | Marc 105 |

**BOBBETTES, The**     **HOT/R&B**
Female R&B vocal group from New York City: sisters Emma and Janice Pought, Laura Webb, Helen Gathers and Reather Dixon.

| 7/10/61 | 120 | 1 | Mr. Johnny Q .......................................................... *Teach Me Tonight* | $25 | | End 1093 |

**BOBO, Willie** ☉
Born William Correa on 2/28/34 in New York City. Died on 9/15/83. Latin-jazz percussionist.

| 12/10/66 | 107 | 2 | Sunshine Superman ................................................ *Sockit To Me* [I] | $8 | | Verve 10448 |

*#1 hit for Donovan in 1966*

**BOFILL, Angela** ☉     **R&B/AC**
Born in New York City in 1954. R&B/jazz vocalist.

| 5/12/79 | 104 | 2 | This Time I'll Be Sweeter............ R&B:23 / AC:39 *Baby, I Need Your Love* | $4 | | Arista/GRP 2500 |

**BOHANNON, Hamilton**     **R&B/HOT**
Born on 3/7/42 in Newnan, Georgia. Drummer for **Stevie Wonder** from 1965-67.

| 9/16/78 | 101[3] | 8 | Let's Start The Dance      R&B:9 *I Wonder Why* | $4 | | Mercury 74015 |

Carolyn Crawford (vocal)

**BON, Joann, and the Coquettes** ☉
Country/pop female group produced by country singer Roy Drusky.

| 9/9/67 | 105 | 5 | I'll Release You ........................................ *You're Getting Restless* | $10 | | MTA 129 |

answer song to **Engelbert Humperdinck**'s 1967 hit "Release Me"

**BONDS, Gary (U.S.)**     **HOT/R&B/ROK**
Born Gary Anderson on 6/6/39 in Jacksonville, Florida. Also see **Church Street Five**.

| 3/6/61 | 116 | 1 | 1 Not Me ............................................ *Give Me One More Chance* | $20 | | Legrand 1005 |

**U.S. BONDS**
similar arrangement as Bonds's 1960 hit "New Orleans"; #12 hit for **The Orlons** in 1963

| 10/27/62 | 101[1] | 4 | 2 I Dig This Station ................................................ *Mixed Up Faculty* | $15 | | Legrand 1022 |
| 5/7/66 | 121 | 3 | 3 Take Me Back To New Orleans.......................... *I'm That Kind Of Guy* | $15 | | Legrand 1040 |

**BONEY M**
Vocal group created in Germany by producer/composer Frank Farian. Consisted of Marcia Barrett, Maizie Williams, Liz Mitchell and Bobby Farrell. All were from the West Indies. Farian created Milli Vanilli in 1988.     **HOT/AC/R&B**

| 3/3/79 | 103 | 6 | Dancing In The Streets.............................. R&B:75 *Mary's Boy Child/Oh My Lord* (Hot #85) | $5 | | Sire 1036 |

reissued in 1979 with "Never Change Lovers In The Middle Of The Night" as the B-side on Sire 1038 (with a picture sleeve)

**BONOFF, Karla**     **AC/HOT**
Born on 12/27/51 in Los Angeles. Pop singer/songwriter/pianist.

| 12/15/79+ | 101[1] | 7 | 1 When You Walk In The Room      *Never Stop Her Heart* | $4 | | Columbia 11130 |

*#35 hit for The Searchers in 1964*

| 7/14/84 | 109 | 1 | 2 Somebody's Eyes ............................ AC:16 *Just Walk Away* | $4 | ■ | Columbia 04472 |

from the movie *Footloose* starring Kevin Bacon and Lori Singer

**BOOGIE BOYS, The** ☉     **R&B**
Rap trio from New York City: William "Boogie Knight" Stroman, Joe "Romeo J.D." Malloy and Rudy "Lil' Rahiem" Sheriff.

| 8/17/85 | 102 | 2 | A Fly Girl .................................................... R&B:6 *(dub version)* | $3 | | Capitol 5498 |

**BOOGIEMONSTERS** ☉     **R&B**
Male rap quartet formed at Virginia State University: Vex and Mondo (both from New York), and Yodared and Myntric (both born in Jamaica).

| 8/27/94 | 124 | 2 | Recognized Thresholds Of Negative Stress ................................ R&B:65 *(remix)* | $3 | ▮ | Pendulum 58184 |

samples "The Bridge" by M.C. Shan

**BOOKER T. & THE MG'S**     **HOT/R&B/AC**
Interracial R&B band formed by sessionmen from Stax Records in Memphis. Consisted of Booker T. Jones (keyboards; b: 11/12/44), Steve Cropper (guitar), Donald "Duck" Dunn (bass) and Al Jackson, Jr. (drums; murdered on 10/1/75, age 39). Cropper and Dunn later joined the **Blues Brothers**. Group inducted into the Rock and Roll Hall of Fame in 1992.

| 2/29/64 | 109 | 2 | Tic-Tac-Toe................................................ *Mo' Onions* (Hot #97) [I] | $12 | | Stax 142 |

Stax 142 also released with "Mo' Onions" and "Fannie Mae" as the A & B sides ($15)

**BOONE, Pat**     **HOT/AC/C&W/R&B**
Born Charles Eugene Boone on 6/1/34 in Jacksonville, Florida. Hosted own TV show, *The Pat Boone-Chevy Showroom*, 1957-60. Acted in numerous movies. *Top Pop Singles*: 60.

| 11/6/61 | 114 | 1 | 1 (If I'm Dreaming) Just Let Me Dream............................ *Johnny Will* (Hot #35) | $10 | | Dot 16284 |
| 5/12/62 | 113 | 2 | 2 Willing And Eager      *Quando, Quando, Quando* (Hot #95) | $10 | | Dot 16349 |

from the movie *State Fair* starring Boone

| 3/9/63 | 117 | 2 | 3 Days Of Wine And Roses ........................................ *Meditation* (Hot #91) | $10 | | Dot 16439 |

from the movie starring Jack Lemmon and Lee Remick

| 4/25/64 | 129 | 1 | 4 Rosemarie .................................... *I Understand (Just How You Feel)* [F] | $8 | | Dot 16598 |
| 6/11/66 | 127 | 1 | 5 Five Miles From Home (Soon I'll See Mary)...................... *Don't Put Your Feet In The Lemonade (We're Runnin' Short Of Water)* | $8 | | Dot 16871 |

**BOOTH, Henry — see BALLARD, Hank**

**BOOTSY'S RUBBER BAND — see PARLIAMENT**

**BORELLY, Jean-Claude, And His Orchestra ○**
French trumpet player.

| | | | | | | |
|---|---|---|---|---|---|---|
| 1/24/76 | 106 | 4 | Dolannes Melodie...................................... AC:15 *(Pipes of Pan version)* [I] | $5 | | London 228 |

**BORN JAMERICANS**    R&B/HOT
Dancehall reggae duo: Horace "Edley Shine" Payne and Norman "Natch" Howell. Both were born in U.S. to Jamaican parents.

| 4/5/97 | 112 | 7 | Yardcore...........................................................R&B:45 *(remix)* | $3 | ■ | Delicious Vinyl 4003 |

**BOSS**    R&B/HOT
Female rap duo from Los Angeles: Lichelle "Boss" Laws and Irene "Dee" Moore.

| 8/21/93 | 118 | 2 | Recipe Of A Hoe..........................................R&B:73 *(instrumental)* | $3 | ■ | DJ West/Chaos 77081 |

samples "Ain't I Been Good To You" by The Isley Brothers

**BOSTON POPS ORCHESTRA — see SHERMAN, Allan**

**BOWIE, David**    ROK/HOT/R&B
Born David Robert Jones on 1/8/47 in London. Influential singer/songwriter/actor. Acted in several movies. Formed the group Tin Machine in 1988. Inducted into the Rock and Roll Hall of Fame in 1996. *Top Pop Singles:* 27.

| 8/16/69 | 124 | 2 | 1 Space Oddity.....................................*Wild Eyed Boy From Freecloud* | $60 | | Mercury 72949 |
| | | | hit the *Hot 100* (#15) on 1/27/73 on RCA Victor 0876 | | | |
| 8/25/73 | 109 | 2 | 2 Let's Spend The Night Together........................*Lady Grinning Soul* | $7 | | RCA Victor 0028 |
| | | | #55 hit for The Rolling Stones in 1967 | | | |
| 7/28/79 | 106 | 2 | 3 D.J. ...............................................*Fantastic Voyage* | $6 | | RCA 11661 |
| 10/25/80 | 101[1] | 1 | 4 Ashes To Ashes..........................*It's No Game (Part 1)* | $6 | ■ | RCA 12078 |

**BOW WOW WOW**    HOT/ROK
New-wave group assembled in London featuring Annabella Lwin (vocals; born Myant Myant Aye in Burma).

| 10/2/82 | 103 | 3 | Baby, Oh No.......................................................*Cowboy* | $4 | ■ | RCA 13291 |

**BOYCE, Tommy, & Bobby Hart**    HOT
Songwriting/singing/production duo. Boyce was born on 9/29/39 in Charlottesville, Virginia; died a self-inflicted gunshot wound on 11/23/94. Hart was born on 2/18/39 in Phoenix.

| 1/27/62 | 118 | 2 | 1 Along Came Linda..................................*You Look So Lonely* | $20 | | RCA Victor 7975 |
| 9/10/66 | 132 | 1 | 2 Sunday, The Day Before Monday .........*Green Grass (Is Turning Brown)* | $10 | | A&M 809 |
| | | | **TOMMY BOYCE** (above 2) | | | |
| 9/30/67 | 110 | 3 | 3 Sometimes She's A Little Girl | *Love Every Day* | $8 | ■ | A&M 874 |
| 11/16/68 | 123 | 1 | 4 We're All Going To The Same Place........................*Six + Six* | $8 | ■ | A&M 993 |
| 3/15/69 | 111 | 3 | 5 L.U.V. (Let Us Vote) ...................................*I Wanna Be Free* | $8 | ■ | A&M 1031 |
| 12/20/80 | 110 | 1 | 6 Lovers For The Night..........................*You Get Smoke In Your Eyes* | $5 | | Ariola America 809 |
| | | | **BOBBY HART** | | | |

**BOYS BRIGADE ○**
Pop/rock group form Toronto: Malcolm Burn (vocals, keyboards), Tony Lester (guitar), Wayne Lorenz (bass) and Billie Brock (drums).

| 2/11/84 | 104 | 1 | Melody.............................................................*Africa* | $4 | ■ | Capitol 5311 |
| | | | produced by Geddy Lee of **Rush** | | | |

**BOYS IN THE BAND, The**    R&B/HOT
Studio group led by Herman Lewis Griffin. Griffin was married to **Mary Wells**; died on 11/11/89 (age 52).

| 9/19/70 | 103 | 5 | Money Music.........................R&B:34 *Five Fat Fast Funky Fingers* | $6 | | Spring 106 |

**BRACELETS, The ○**
Female R&B vocal group.

| 9/15/62 | 113 | 1 | Waddle, Waddle.........................................*I'll Play Along* | $25 | | Congress 104 |
| | | | Hutch Davie (orch.) | | | |

**BRADY, Bob, & The Con Chords ○**
R&B vocal group with a style similar to **Smokey Robinson & The Miracles**.

| 6/17/67 | 104 | 4 | More, More, More Of Your Love........................*It's A Better World* | $12 | | Chariot 101 |
| | | | originally recorded by **The Miracles** on their 1966 album *Away We A Go-Go* | | | |

**BRAM TCHAIKOVSKY**    HOT
Rock trio from Lincolnshire, England: Peter Bramall (vocals, guitar), Micky Broadbent (bass) and Keith Boyce (drums).

| 6/27/81 | 109 | 1 | Shall We Dance? ..........................................*Miracle Cure* | $5 | | Arista 0601 |

**BRANDT, Paul ○**    C&W
Born on 7/21/72 in Calgary, Alberta, Canada. Country singer/songwriter.

| 8/10/96 | 102 | 22 | I Do.....................................Sls:63 /C&W:2 *(instrumental)* | $3 | ■ | Reprise 17616 |

**BRANDYWINE SINGERS, The ○**
Folk group led by brothers Rick and Ron Shaw.

| 11/2/63 | 129 | 1 | Summer's Come And Gone.............................*The Brandy Stream* | $10 | | Joy 281 |

**BRANNON, Kippi ○**    C&W
Born Kippi Brinkley in 1966 in Goodlettsville, Tennessee. Female country singer.

| 4/12/97 | 120 | 9 | 1 Daddy's Little Girl/ | C&W:42 | | | |
| 6/28/97 | 120 | 2 | 2 I'd Be With You ........................................C&W:53 | $3 | ■ | Curb/Universal 56092 |

**BRANNON, Linda ○**
Pop singer.

| 1/4/64 | 115 | 5 | Don't Cross Over (To My Side Of The Street) ...............*Don't Separate Us* | $8 | | Epic 9640 |

**BRASS CONSTRUCTION**    R&B/HOT
Multi-ethnic disco group from Brooklyn: Randy Muller (keyboards), Joe Wong (guitar), Wayne Parris, Morris Price, Jesse Ward and Mickey Grudge (horn section), Sandy Billups (congas), Wade Williamston (bass) and Larry Payton (drums).

| 2/11/78 | 104 | 7 | L-O-V-E-U ..............................................R&B:18 *Get It Together* [I] | $5 | | United Artists 1120 |

**BRASS RING, The** — AC/HOT
Studio group assembled by producer/arranger/saxophonist Phil Bodner.

| | | | | | | |
|---|---|---|---|---|---|---|
| 7/23/66 | 126 | 2 | Lara's Theme (from Dr. Zhivago).................................... AC:36 *Secret Love* [I] | $7 | | Dunhill 4036 |

from the movie starring Omar Sharif; lyrical version known as "Somewhere My Love"; #65 hit for **Roger Williams** in 1966

**BRAUN, Bob** — HOT/AC
Born Robert Earl Brown on 4/20/29 in Ludlow, Kentucky.

| | | | | | | |
|---|---|---|---|---|---|---|
| 11/3/62 | 119 | 2 | Our Anniversary Of Love ....................................... *Is It Right Or Wrong?* [S] | $8 | | Decca 31430 |

Sid Bass (orch.)

**BRAXTONS, The** — R&B/HOT
R&B vocal trio of sisters from Severn, Maryland: Tamar, Trina and Towanda Braxton. Sisters of singer Toni Braxton.

| | | | | | | |
|---|---|---|---|---|---|---|
| 2/1/97 | 119 | 2 | Only Love ................................................... R&B:52 *So Many Ways* | $3 | ▮ | Atlantic 87017 |

**BREAK MACHINE** ○ — R&B
Dance/disco trio: Lindsay Blake, Lindell Blake and Cortez Jordan.

| | | | | | | |
|---|---|---|---|---|---|---|
| 4/28/84 | 105 | 7 | Street Dance ........................................................ R&B:78 *(instrumental)* | $4 | | Sire 29319 |

**BREEDERS, The** — ROK/HOT
Rock band formed in Dayton, Ohio: twin sisters/guitarists/vocalists Kim and Kelley Deal, bassist Josephine Wiggs (native of Bedfordshire, England) and drummer Jim MacPherson.

| | | | | | | |
|---|---|---|---|---|---|---|
| 4/16/94 | 104 | 5 | 1 Divine Hammer............................ROK:28 *I Can't Help It (If I'm Still In Love With You) / Hoverin'* | $3 | ▮ | 4AD/Elektra 64565 |
| 8/6/94 | 109 | 2 | 2 Saints ........................................................ROK:12 *Grunggae* | $3 | ▮ | 4AD/Elektra 64529 |

**BREMERS, Beverly** — HOT/AC
Singer/actress from Chicago.

| | | | | | | |
|---|---|---|---|---|---|---|
| 12/30/72 | 110 | 5 | Heaven Help Us All ............................................ *All That's Left Is The Music* | $5 | | Scepter 12370 |

theme from the movie *Crazies* starring Lane Carroll; written by **Melissa Manchester** and Carol Bayer Sager

**BRENDA & THE TABULATIONS** — R&B/HOT
R&B group from Philadelphia: Brenda Payton (d: 6/14/92), Pat Mercer and Deborah Martin.

| | | | | | | |
|---|---|---|---|---|---|---|
| 1/23/71 | 120 | 1 | 1 A Child No One Wanted ........................ R&B:42 *Scuse Uz Y'All* | $8 | | Top & Bottom 406 |
| 1/8/72 | 107 | 1 | 2 Why Didn't I Think Of That.................... R&B:34 *A Love You Can Depend On* | $8 | | Top & Bottom 411 |

**BRENSTEN, Jackie** ○ — R&B
Born on 8/15/30 in Clarksdale, Mississippi. Died on 12/15/79. R&B vocalist/saxophonist with **Ike Turner's** Kings Of Rhythm.

| | | | | | | |
|---|---|---|---|---|---|---|
| 3/13/61 | 118 | 1 | Trouble Up The Road ........................................... *You Ain't The One* | $20 | | Sue 736 |

Ike Turner (songwriter, guitarist and orchestra)

**BREWER, Teresa** — HOT/MEM/POP
Born Theresa Breuer on 5/7/31 in Toledo, Ohio. *Pop Hits & Top Pop Singles*: 35.

| | | | | | | |
|---|---|---|---|---|---|---|
| 7/13/59 | 115 | 1 | 1 Bye Bye Baby Goodbye ...................................... *Chain Of Friendship* | $10 | | Coral 62126 |

Dick Jacobs (orch.)

| | | | | | | |
|---|---|---|---|---|---|---|
| 3/16/63 | 122 | 3 | 2 She'll Never Never Love You (Like I Do) ..................... *The Thrill Is Gone* | $8 | | Philips 40095 |

same melody as **Allan Sherman's** 1963 hit "Hello Mudduh, Hello Fadduh!"

| | | | | | | |
|---|---|---|---|---|---|---|
| 11/9/63 | 130 | 1 | 3 He Understands Me ....................................... *Just Before We Say Goodbye* | $8 | | Philips 40135 |

#31 hit for **Johnny Tillotson** in 1964 ("She Understands Me")

| | | | | | | |
|---|---|---|---|---|---|---|
| 7/14/73 | 109 | 3 | 4 Music, Music, Music ................................................. *School Days* | $6 | | Amsterdam 85027 |

rock and roll version of Brewer's original #1 Dixieland version in 1950 on London 30023

**BRIARWOOD SINGERS, The** ○
Folk group: Dorinda Duncan, Stan Beach, Bob Hoffman, Harry Scholes and Barry Bobst.

| | | | | | | |
|---|---|---|---|---|---|---|
| 12/28/63 | 126 | 1 | He Was A Friend Of Mine .................................. *Bound For The Freedom Land* | $10 | | United Artists 686 |

a tribute to President Kennedy who was assassinated on 11/22/63

**BRICK** — R&B/HOT
Disco-jazz group from Atlanta: Jimmy Brown (vocals, sax), Reggie Hargis (guitar), Don Nevins (keyboards), Ray Ransom (bass) and Eddie Irons (drums).

| | | | | | | |
|---|---|---|---|---|---|---|
| 6/21/80 | 106 | 4 | All The Way ....................................................... R&B:38 *Spread Love* | $4 | | Bang 4810 |

written by **Paul Davis**

**BRIDES OF FUNKENSTEIN, The — see PARLIAMENT**

**BRISTOL, Johnny** — R&B/HOT/AC
Born on 2/3/39 in Morganton, North Carolina. R&B vocalist/composer/producer. Teamed with Harvey Fuqua as Motown producers until 1973.

| | | | | | | |
|---|---|---|---|---|---|---|
| 4/12/75 | 104 | 1 | 1 Leave My World ...................................... R&B:23 *All Goodbyes Aren't Gone* | $5 | | MGM 14792 |
| 3/12/77 | 106 | 1 | 2 You Turned Me On To Love ................. R&B:36 *I Sho Like Groovin' With Ya (R&B #47)* | $5 | | Atlantic 3391 |

**BRITISH WALKERS, The** ○
Rock and roll band.

| | | | | | | |
|---|---|---|---|---|---|---|
| 4/8/67 | 106 | 7 | Shake ...................................................... *That Was Yesterday* | $15 | | Cameo 466 |

#7 hit for **Sam Cooke** in 1965

**BRITT, Tina** ○ — R&B
Full name: Tina Brittingham. R&B singer from Florida.

| | | | | | | |
|---|---|---|---|---|---|---|
| 5/22/65 | 103 | 7 | The Real Thing ......................... R&B:20 *Teardrops Fell (Every Step Of The Way)* | $15 | | Eastern 604 |

**BROMBERG, David** ○
Born on 9/19/45 in Philadelphia. Folk/rock session guitarist. Backed Jerry Jeff Walker, **Bob Dylan**, Doug Kershaw and others.

| | | | | | | |
|---|---|---|---|---|---|---|
| 2/24/73 | 117 | 3 | Sharon ................................................... *Hardworkin' John* | $6 | | Columbia 45767 |

**BROOKES, Jacqui** ○
Electro-pop vocalist.

| | | | | | | |
|---|---|---|---|---|---|---|
| 2/11/84 | 105 | 1 | Lost Without Your Love .............................................. *Departures* | $4 | | MCA 52334 |

**BROOKLYN BRIDGE** — HOT/AC
Soft rock group from Long Island, New York, made up of a vocal quartet and seven-piece band. Johnny Maestro (of **The Crests**), lead singer.

| | | | | | | |
|---|---|---|---|---|---|---|
| 2/21/70 | 109 | 5 | Free As The Wind ..................................... AC:36 *He's Not A Happy Man* | $8 | | Buddah 162 |

**BROOKS, Donnie** — HOT
Born John Abahosh in Dallas; raised in Ventura, California as John Faircloth. Recorded as Johnny Faire, Dick Bush and Johnny Jordan.

| | | | | | | |
|---|---|---|---|---|---|---|
| 12/5/60 | 115 | 1 | Round Robin ...................................................... *Doll House (Hot #31)* | $15 | ▮ | Era 3028 |

| DEBUT | PEAK | WKS | A-side / B-side | $ | Pic | Label & Number |
|---|---|---|---|---|---|---|
| | | | **BROOKS & DUNN**     C&W/HOT | | | |
| | | | Country duo of Kix Brooks (b: 5/12/55 in Shreveport, Louisiana) and Ronnie Dunn (b: 6/1/53 in Texas). | | | |
| 2/22/97 | 124 | 2 | A Man This Lonely .................................... C&W:❶¹   One Heartache At A Time | $3 | ▐ | Arista 13066 |
| | | | **BROTHERS FOUR, The**     AC/HOT | | | |
| | | | Folk-pop quartet: Dick Foley, Bob Flick, John Paine and Mike Kirkland. Formed while fraternity brothers at the University of Washington. | | | |
| 10/26/63 | 114 | 5 | 1 Four Strong Winds .................................... The John B. Sails | $8 | | Columbia 42888 |
| | | | #60 hit for Bobby Bare in 1964 | | | |
| 2/27/65 | 131 | 1 | 2 Somewhere .................................... Turn Around | $8 | | Columbia 43211 |
| | | | from the Leonard Bernstein musical West Side Story | | | |
| | | | **BROTHERS JOHNSON, The**     R&B/HOT/AC | | | |
| | | | Los Angeles R&B-funk duo of brothers George (b: 5/17/53) and Louis Johnson (b: 4/13/55). With Billy Preston's band to 1975. | | | |
| 1/15/77 | 103 | 4 | 1 Free And Single .................................... R&B:26   Thunder Thumbs And Lightnin' Licks | $5 | | A&M 1881 |
| 1/14/78 | 107 | 1 | 2 Runnin' For Your Lovin' .................................... R&B:20   "Q" | $5 | ■ | A&M 1982 |
| 10/21/78 | 104 | 2 | 3 Ride-O-Rocket .................................... R&B:45   Dancin' And Prancin' | $5 | | A&M 2086 |
| | | | written by Ashford & Simpson | | | |
| 1/13/79 | 102 | 2 | 4 Ain't We Funkin' Now .................................... R&B:45   Dancin' And Prancin' | $5 | | A&M 2098 |
| | | | all of above produced by Quincy Jones | | | |
| 7/21/84 | 102 | 7 | 5 You Keep Me Coming Back    R&B:12   Deceiver | $4 | | A&M 2654 |
| | | | **BROWN, Arthur**     HOT | | | |
| | | | Born Arthur Wilton on 6/24/44 in Whitby, England. His band consisted of Sean Nicholas (guitar), Vince Crane (organ) and Carl Palmer (drums; Emerson, Lake & Palmer, Asia). | | | |
| 11/30/68 | 107 | 4 | 1 Nightmare/ | | | |
| 12/21/68 | 111 | 1 | 2 I Put A Spell On You .................................... | $12 | | Track 2582 |
| | | | THE CRAZY WORLD OF ARTHUR BROWN (above 2) | | | |
| | | | written and recorded by Screamin' Jay Hawkins in 1956; Pete Townshend (associate producer, above 2) | | | |
| | | | **BROWN, Buster**     HOT/R&B | | | |
| | | | Born Wayman Glasco on 8/15/11 in Cordele, Georgia. Died on 1/31/76. R&B singer/harmonica player. | | | |
| 5/2/60 | 105 | 4 | John Henry (The Steel Driving Man) .................................... The Madison Shuffle | $25 | | Fire 1020 |
| | | | new version of traditional folk tune written in 1873 | | | |
| | | | **BROWN, Charles**     R&B/HOT | | | |
| | | | Born on 9/13/22 in Texas City, Texas. R&B singer/pianist. Joined Johnny Moore's Three Blazers in 1944. | | | |
| 12/22/62 | 108 | 1 | Please Come Home For Christmas .................................... Christmas (Comes But Once A Year) (Amos Milburn) [X-R] | $12 | | King 5405 |
| | | | #21 R&B hit in 1960; #76 Hot 100 hit in 1961; #1 hit on Billboard's special Christmas charts in 1972 | | | |
| | | | **BROWN, Horace**     R&B/HOT | | | |
| | | | R&B singer from Charlotte, North Carolina. | | | |
| 10/8/94 | 103 | 12 | 1 Taste Your Love .................................... R&B:38   (album version) | $3 | ▐ | Uptown/MCA 54672 |
| | | | samples "Word To The Conscious" by The Cookie Crew | | | |
| 11/30/96 | 125 | 1 | 2 How Can We Stop .................................... R&B:77   Just Let Me Know (Brown) | $3 | ▐ | Motown 0586 |
| | | | HORACE BROWN featuring Faith Evans | | | |
| | | | **BROWN, James**     R&B/HOT | | | |
| | | | Born on 5/3/33 in Barnwell, South Carolina; raised in Augusta, Georgia. Formed own vocal group, the Famous Flames. His backing group, The JB's, featured various personnel, including Nat Kendrick, William "Bootsy" Collins, Maceo Parker and Fred Wesley. Inducted into the Rock and Roll Hall of Fame in 1986. Won Grammy's Lifetime Achievement Award in 1992. Ranked as the #1 artist in Joel Whitburn's Top R&B Singles book. Top Pop Singles: 99. Also see A.A.B.B. | | | |
| 11/21/60 | 105 | 3 | 1 Please, Please, Please .................................... Why Do You Do Me | $75 | | Federal 12258 |
| | | | #5 R&B hit in 1956; see the B-side of #3 below for a "live" version | | | |
| 2/13/61 | 109 | 6 | 2 Hold It .................................... The Scratch [I] | $20 | | King 5438 |
| | | | JAMES BROWN Presents His BAND | | | |
| 4/25/64 | 125 | 1 | 3 In The Wee Wee Hours (Of The Nite) .................................... Please, Please, Please (Hot #95) | $20 | | King 5853 |
| 4/25/64 | 107 | 3 | 4 Again/ | $20 | | King 5876 |
| | | | there were 6 Top 10 versions of this tune in 1949 | | | |
| 6/6/64 | 134 | 1 | 5 How Long Darling .................................... | $20 | | King 5876 |
| | | | "live" recording | | | |
| 6/27/64 | 132 | 1 | 6 So Long .................................... Dancin' Little Thing | $20 | | King 5899 |
| 10/10/64 | 107 | 2 | 7 Maybe The Last Time .................................... Out Of Sight (Hot #24) | $15 | ■ | Smash 1919 |
| | | | JAMES BROWN And His Orchestra | | | |
| 4/24/65 | 114 | 4 | 8 Devil's Hideaway .................................... Who's Afraid Of Virginia Woolf? [I] | $15 | | Smash 1975 |
| | | | JAMES BROWN At The Organ And His Orchestra | | | |
| 5/7/66 | 102 | 1 | 9 New Breed (Part I) (The Boo-Ga-Loo) .................................... (Part II) [I] | $15 | | Smash 2028 |
| 3/16/68 | 102 | 5 | 10 You've Got To Change Your Mind    R&B:47   I'll Lose My Mind (Byrd) | $12 | | King 6151 |
| | | | BOBBY BYRD & JAMES BROWN | | | |
| 6/15/68 | 104 | 2 | 11 Shhhhhhhh (For A Little While) .................................... Here I Go [I] | $12 | | King 6164 |
| | | | JAMES BROWN and The Famous Flames (#1, 3-6 & 11) | | | |
| 4/5/69 | 117 | 3 | 12 Soul Pride (Part 1) .................................... R&B:33   (Part 2) [I] | $12 | | King 6222 |
| 12/12/70 | 105 | 2 | 13 Hey America .................................... (instrumental) [X] | $10 | | King 6339 |
| | | | also released as the B-side of the Christmas chart hit "Santa Claus Is Definitely Here To Stay" on King 6340 in 1970 | | | |
| | | | **BROWN, Mara Lynn** ⚪ | | | |
| 2/10/73 | 118 | 4 | Salty Tears .................................... All The Kings Horses | $7 | | Laurie 3604 |
| | | | written and produced by Teddy Randazzo | | | |
| | | | **BROWN, Maxine**     R&B/HOT | | | |
| | | | Born in Kingstree, South Carolina. R&B singer. | | | |
| 10/30/61 | 102 | 4 | 1 After All We've Been Through .................................... My Life | $15 | | ABC-Paramount 10255 |
| 1/27/62 | 104 | 3 | 2 I Got A Funny Kind Of Feeling .................................... What I Don't Know (Won't Hurt Me) | $15 | | ABC-Paramount 10290 |
| 2/12/66 | 112 | 1 | 3 I'm Satisfied .................................... Please Don't Hurt Me | $15 | | Wand 1109 |
| | | | CHUCK JACKSON & MAXINE BROWN | | | |
| 12/10/66 | 129 | 1 | 4 I Don't Need Anything .................................... The Secret Of Livin' | $15 | | Wand 1145 |

## BROWN, Miquel ○
Disco singer/dancer/actress from Seattle. Mother of singer Sinitta.

| DEBUT | PEAK | WKS | A-side / B-side | $ | Pic | Label & Number |
|---|---|---|---|---|---|---|
| 10/8/83 | 107 | 4 | So Many Men, So Little Time .................................................... (instrumental) | $5 | ■ | TSR 102 |

## BROWN, Peter　R&B/HOT
Born on 7/11/53 in Blue Island, Illinois. Disco vocalist/keyboardist/producer.

| 2/12/83 | 104 | 4 | 1 Baby Gets High ................................................... R&B:49  The Love Game | $4 | | RCA 13413 |
| 4/28/84 | 102 | 4 | 2 They Only Come Out At Night ............................. R&B:50  (instrumental) | $3 | ■ | Columbia 04381 |
| 5/18/85 | 108 | 3 | 3 Zie Zie Won't Dance ...............................................................Hot Flash | $3 | | Columbia 04832 |

## BROWN, Shirley　R&B/HOT
Born on 1/6/47 in West Memphis, Arkansas; raised in East St. Louis. R&B vocalist.

| 4/23/77 | 102 | 1 | Blessed Is The Woman (With A Man Like Mine)........R&B:14  Lowdown, Dirty, Good Lover | $5 | | Arista 0231 |

## BROWNE, Jackson　HOT/ROK/AC
Born on 10/9/48 on a U.S. Army base in Heidelberg, Germany. Pop-rock singer/guitarist/pianist/composer. His songs were recorded by **Linda Ronstadt, Joe Cocker, The Byrds, Johnny Rivers, Bonnie Raitt** and many others. Worked with the **Eagles.**

| 12/2/78 | 109 | 1 | 1 You Love The Thunder...................................................................The Road | $5 | ■ | Asylum 45543 |
| 1/24/81 | 103 | 2 | 2 Hold On, Hold Out ........................................................................ Hold Out | $6 | ■ | Asylum 11477 (T) |
| 12/4/93 | 118 | 1 | 3 I'm Alive ...........................ROK:18 / AC:28  My Problem Is You / Sky Blue And Black | $20 | | Elektra 8853 (CD) |
| | | | released only as a CD promo single (packaged with Browne's *Retrospective* CD of his previous hits) | | | |

## BROWNS featuring Jim Edward Brown　C&W/HOT/AC
Country vocal trio from Sparkman, Arkansas: Jim Edward Brown and his sisters Maxine and Bonnie.

| 7/4/60 | 105 | 3 | 1 Lonely Little Robin ....................................... Margo (The Ninth of May) | $10 | ■ | RCA Victor 7755 |
| | | | #14 hit for the Pinetoppers in 1951 | | | |
| 8/22/60 | 112 | 2 | 2 Whiffenpoof Song................................. Brighten The Corner Where You Are | $10 | ■ | RCA Victor 7780 |
| | | | theme song of the Yale Glee Club since 1909 | | | |
| 4/7/62 | 104 | 2 | 3 Buttons And Bows　Remember Me | $8 | | RCA Victor 7997 |
| | | | #1 hit for Dinah Shore in 1948 | | | |
| 9/1/62 | 118 | 1 | 4 The Old Master Painter.................................It's Just A Little Heartache | $8 | | RCA Victor 8066 |
| | | | there were 6 Top 20 versions of this tune in 1950 | | | |
| 10/3/64 | 135 | 1 | 5 Everybody's Darlin', Plus Mine ................................C&W:40  The Outskirts Of Town | $8 | | RCA Victor 8423 |
| 7/10/65 | 120 | 3 | 6 You Can't Grow Peaches On A Cherry Tree ......... AC:35  A Little Too Much To Dream | $8 | | RCA Victor 8603 |
| | | | #34 hit in 1966 for Just Us as "I Can't Grow Peaches On A Cherry Tree" | | | |

## BROWNSTONE　R&B/HOT/AC
Female R&B vocal trio from Los Angeles: Kina Cosper, Nichole Gilbert and Charmayne Maxwell.

| 9/13/97 | 102 | 8 | Kiss And Tell ....................................................... R&B:41  (remix) | $3 | ■ | MJJ Music 78413 |

## BROWN SUGAR　HOT
Real name: Clydie King. Female singer also known as Little Clydie. Formerly in **The Raeletts.**

| 7/14/73 | 107 | 5 | Loneliness (Will Bring Us Together Again) .........................Don't Hold Back | $5 | | Chelsea 0125 |

## BRUBECK, Dave — see ARMSTRONG, Louis

## BRUCE, Ed ○　C&W
Born William Edwin Bruce, Jr. on 12/29/40 in Keiser, Arkansas. Recorded for Sun in 1957.

| 11/9/63 | 109 | 5 | See The Big Man Cry ...................................... You Need A New Love | $20 | | Wand 140 |
| | | | Bill Justis (orch.); #7 Country hit for Charlie Louvin in 1965 | | | |

## BRUCE AND TERRY　HOT
Bruce Johnston (later of **The Beach Boys**) and Terry Melcher (produced **The Byrds, Paul Revere & The Raiders**). Duo also recorded as **The Rogues.**

| 1/23/65 | 101[1] | 5 | 1 Everyday　Roger's Reef | $25 | | Columbia 43190 |
| | | | THE ROGUES | | | |
| | | | rock and roll version of Buddy Holly's 1957 classic tune (B-side of "Peggy Sue") | | | |
| 3/27/65 | 107 | 4 | 2 Carmen ..................................................... I Love You Model "T" | $25 | | Columbia 43238 |
| 9/24/77 | 109 | 1 | 3 Pipeline ...................................................... Disney Girls [I] | $10 | | Columbia 10568 |
| | | | BRUCE JOHNSTON | | | |
| | | | #4 hit for the Chantay's in 1963 (also "Bubbled Under" in 1966) | | | |

## BRUNO, Bruce ○
Pop singer.

| 9/11/61 | 103 | 2 | Hey Little One ............................................... Same Time, Same Place | $25 | | Roulette 4386 |
| | | | Marty Manning (orch.); #48 hit for Dorsey Burnette in 1960 | | | |

## BRYANT, Anita　HOT/AC
Born on 3/25/40 in Barnsdale, Oklahoma. She was second runner-up to Miss America in 1958.

| 7/3/61 | 108 | 2 | 1 Lonesome For You, Mama .........................A Place Called Happiness | $8 | | Carlton 553 |
| | | | Vic Schoen (orch.) | | | |
| 3/3/62 | 106 | 3 | 2 Step By Step, Little By Little ............................Cold Cold Winter | $7 | ■ | Columbia 42257 |
| 9/12/64 | 130 | 1 | 3 Welcome, Welcome Home .................. Laughing On The Outside (Crying On The Inside) | $6 | | Columbia 43106 |
| | | | Frankie Avalon's version "Bubbled Under" in 1962 | | | |

## BRYANT, Ray　R&B/HOT/AC
Born Raphael Bryant on 12/24/31 in Philadelphia. R&B-jazz pianist/bandleader. Uncle of *Tonight Show* guitarist Kevin Eubanks.

| 11/14/64 | 108 | 4 | Shake A Lady ...................................................... Blues March [I] | $10 | | Sue 108 |

## BRYCE, Sherry — see TILLIS, Mel

## BRYSON, Peabo　R&B/AC/HOT
Born Robert Peabo Bryson on 4/13/51 in Greenville, South Carolina. R&B singer/producer. First solo recording for Bang in 1970.

| 6/10/78 | 102 | 4 | 1 Reaching For The Sky ............................R&B:6  You Haven't Learned About Love | $4 | | Capitol 4522 |
| 1/27/79 | 109 | 1 | 2 I'm So Into You ............................................... R&B:2  Smile | $4 | | Capitol 4656 |
| 12/22/79 | 102 | 5 | 3 Gimme Some Time .................................R&B:8  Love Will Find You | $4 | | Capitol 4804 |
| | | | NATALIE COLE & PEABO BRYSON | | | |

| DEBUT | PEAK | WKS | A-side (Chart Hit) ..................................................................................................B-side | $ | Pic | Label & Number |
|---|---|---|---|---|---|---|

**B-TRIBE** ○
Group is actually dance producer Claus Zundel from Heidelberg, Germany. B-Tribe: Barcelona Tribe Of Soulsters.

| 8/27/94 | 113 | 2 | You Won't See Me Cry ........................................ *Nadie Entiende* | $3 | ▮ | Atlantic 87204 |
|---|---|---|---|---|---|---|

melody is from the 1982 Jon & Vangelis *Hot 100* hit "I'll Find My Way Home"

**BUBBLE PUPPY, The**　　　　　　　　　　HOT
Psychedelic rock quartet from Houston: Rod Price (vocals), Todd Potter (guitar), Roy Cox (bass) and David Fore (drums).

| 5/31/69 | 128 | 3 | If I Had A Reason ..............................................................*Beginning* | $25 | | International Artists 133 |

**BUCHANAN and GREENFIELD** ○
Novelty duo of Bill Buchanan and Howard Greenfield. Buchanan was the former partner of **Dickie Goodman**. Greenfield later formed a songwriting team with **Neil Sedaka**.

| 10/3/64 | 120 | 1 | The Invasion ......................................... *What A Lovely Party* [N] | $30 | | Novel 711 |

**BUCHANAN BROTHERS, The — see CASHMAN, PISTILLI & WEST**

**BUCKINGHAM, Lindsey**　　　　　　　　ROK/HOT/AC
Born on 10/3/47 in Palo Alto, California. Rock guitarist/vocalist/songwriter. Joined **Fleetwood Mac** in 1975.

| 3/20/82 | 110 | 1 | 1 It Was I ....................................... *Love From Here, Love From There* | $4 | | Asylum 47408 |
|---|---|---|---|---|---|---|

#11 hit for **Skip & Flip** in 1959

| 11/24/84 | 106 | 2 | 2 Slow Dancing ...................................................*D.W. Suite* | $4 | | Elektra 69675 |

**BUCKINGHAMS, The**　　　　　　　　　　HOT
Chicago rock quintet: Dennis Tufano (lead singer), Carl Giammarese (guitar), Nick Fortune (bass), Jon Paulos (drums; d: 3/26/80, age 32) and Dennis Miccoli (keyboards).

| 5/21/66 | 112 | 2 | 1 I'll Go Crazy ......................................... *Don't Want To Cry* | $20 | | U.S.A. 844 |
|---|---|---|---|---|---|---|

#73 hit for **James Brown** in 1966

| 11/16/68 | 117 | 3 | 2 Where Did You Come From ..................... *Song Of The Breeze* | $8 | ▮ | Columbia 44672 |

from the movie *The Guru* starring Michael York

| 9/13/69 | 126 | 2 | 3 It's A Beautiful Day (For Lovin') .......... *Difference Of Opinion* | $8 | | Columbia 44923 |

**BUCKNER & GARCIA**　　　　　　　　　　HOT
Atlanta-based duo: Jerry Buckner (keyboards) and Gary Garcia (vocals).

| 5/29/82 | 103 | 4 | Do The Donkey Kong ........................................... *(instrumental)* [N] | $4 | ▮ | Columbia 02867 |

inspired by the video game *Donkey Kong*

**BUENA VISTAS, The**　　　　　　　　　　HOT
Three-man, one-woman band that also recorded as Kathy Lynn & Play Boys. Kathy Lynn is Kathy Lynn Keppen.

| 9/7/68 | 126 | 1 | Soul Clappin .............................................................*Rappin* [I] | $10 | | Marquee 445 |

**BUFFALO SPRINGFIELD, The**　　　　　　HOT
Superstar group formed in Los Angeles in 1966: **Stephen Stills**, **Neil Young**, **Richie Furay**, Dewey Martin, Bruce Palmer and **Jim Messina**. Disbanded in 1968. Stills and Young formed Crosby, Stills, Nash & Young. Furay and Messina formed **Poco**. Group inducted into the Rock and Roll Hall of Fame in 1997.

| 8/20/66 | 110 | 4 | 1 Nowadays Clancy Can't Even Sing ......................... *Go And Say Goodbye* | $20 | | Atco 6428 |
|---|---|---|---|---|---|---|

written by **Neil Young**

| 5/18/68 | 105 | 2 | 2 Un-Mundo ................................................ *Merry-Go-Round* | $10 | | Atco 6572 |
| 9/7/68 | 107 | 1 | 3 Special Care .................................................. *Kind Woman* | $10 | | Atco 6602 |

above 2 written by **Stephen Stills**

**BUFFETT, Jimmy**　　　　　　　　　AC/C&W/HOT/ROK
Born on 12/25/46 in Pascagoula, Mississippi; raised in Mobile, Alabama. Settled in Key West in 1971.

| 3/16/74 | 105 | 4 | 1 Saxophones ........................................... *Ringling, Ringling* | $6 | | Dunhill/ABC 4378 |
|---|---|---|---|---|---|---|
| 10/5/74 | 101[1] | 7 | 2 Pencil Thin Mustache 　　　　AC:44 *Brand New Country Star* | $5 | | Dunhill/ABC 15011 |
| 4/5/75 | 101[1] | 8 | 3 A Pirate Looks At Forty 　　　　*Presents To Send You* | $5 | | ABC/Dunhill 15029 |
| 8/2/75 | 102 | 4 | 4 Door Number Three .............................. C&W:88 *Dallas* | $5 | | ABC 12113 |

inspired by Monty Hall's *Let's Make A Deal* TV game show

**BUGALOOS, The** ○
Three-man, one-woman pop group featured on the Saturday morning NBC-TV series *The Bugaloos*, 1970-72.

| 12/19/70 | 128 | 1 | For A Friend ........................................ *The Senses Of Our World* | $8 | | Capitol 2946 |

**BULLDOG**　　　　　　　　　　　　　　HOT
Rock quintet: Billy Hocher (vocals, bass), Eric Thorngren and Gene Cornish (guitars), John Turi (keyboards) and Dino Danelli (drums). Cornish and Danelli were members of **The Rascals**.

| 3/10/73 | 112 | 3 | Are You Really Happy Together ........................... *I'm A Mad Man* | $6 | | MCA 40014 |

**BULLET**　　　　　　　　　　　　　　　HOT
London-based duo of former Atomic Rooster members: John Cann (vocals) and Paul Hammond (drums).

| 6/17/72 | 107 | 2 | Little Bit O' Soul ...................................... *Up Your Sleeve* | $6 | | Big Tree 140 |

#2 hit for **The Music Explosion** in 1967

**BURCH, Vernon** ○　　　　　　　　　　R&B
R&B guitarist/vocalist from Washington, D.C. Worked with **The Delfonics** from age 13 to 15. Worked with **The Stairsteps**, then with the **Bar-Kays** for four years. Appeared as Marvin Gaye in the 1980 movie *Hollywood Nights*.

| 2/1/75 | 101[1] | 6 | Changes (Messin' With My Mind) 　　　R&B:15 *(long version)* | $5 | | United Artists 587 |

from the movie *Report To The Commissioner* starring Michael Moriarty

**BURDON, Eric, And War**　　　　　　　　HOT
Burdon was born on 5/11/41 in Newcastle-On-Tyne, England. After leaving **The Animals**, Burdon teamed up with the funk band **War** for two albums.

| 4/10/71 | 108 | 2 | Home Cookin' ............................... *They Can't Take Away Our Music* (Hot #50) | $8 | | MGM 14196 |

**BURGENS, Jan, & His New Orleans Syncopators** ○

| 2/17/62 | 111 | 1 | Midnight In Moscow ......................................... *Shine* [I] | $10 | | London 10503 |

#2 hit for **Kenny Ball** and his Jazzmen in 1962

**BURKE, Solomon**　　　　　　　　　R&B/HOT/AC
Born in 1936 in Philadelphia. Soul singer. First recorded for Apollo in 1954. *Top Pop Singles*: 26.

| 3/16/63 | 121 | 1 | 1 Words ...................................................... *Home In Your Heart* | $12 | | Atlantic 2180 |
| 8/27/66 | 109 | 3 | 2 Keep Looking ............................... R&B:38 *I Don't Want You No More* | $10 | | Atlantic 2349 |

| DEBUT | PEAK | WKS | A-side (Chart Hit) | $ | Pic | Label & Number |
|---|---|---|---|---|---|---|
| | | | **BURKE, Solomon — Cont'd** | | | |
| 12/2/67 | 104 | 7 | 3 Detroit City      R&B:47 _It's Been A Change_ | $10 | | Atlantic 2459 |
| | | | #16 hit for **Bobby Bare** in 1963 | | | |
| 3/23/68 | 112 | 1 | 4 Party People ............................................._Need Your Love So Bad_ | $10 | | Atlantic 2483 |
| 2/22/69 | 116 | 4 | 5 Up Tight Good Woman ..........................R&B:47 _I Can't Stop_ | $8 | | Bell 759 |
| | | | #93 hit in 1968 for **Laura Lee** as "Up Tight, Good Man" | | | |
| 7/12/69 | 129 | 2 | 6 That Lucky Old Sun ......................_How Big A Fool (Can A Fool Be)_ | $8 | | Bell 806 |
| | | | #1 hit for **Frankie Laine** in 1949 | | | |
| | | | **BURNETTE, Dorsey**     C&W/HOT | | | |
| | | | Born on 12/28/32 in Memphis. Died of a heart attack on 8/19/79 in Canoga Park, California. Older brother of **Johnny Burnette**. | | | |
| 6/6/60 | 102 | 3 | 1 Big Rock Candy Mountain ..................._Hey Little One_ (Hot #48) | $20 | | Era 3019 |
| | | | traditional folk song recorded by **Burl Ives** on Decca 23439 in 1945 | | | |
| 9/5/60 | 103 | 5 | 2 The Ghost Of Billy Malloo .................................._Red Roses_ | $20 | | Era 3025 |
| 11/6/61 | 117 | 1 | 3 Feminine Touch ..............................................._Sad Boy_ | $20 | | Dot 16265 |
| | | | answer song to **Gene McDaniels'** 1961 hit "A Hundred Pounds Of Clay" | | | |
| | | | **BURNETTE, Johnny**     HOT | | | |
| | | | Born on 3/25/34 in Memphis. Died on 8/1/64 in a boating accident on Clear Lake in California. Johnny, brother **Dorsey Burnette**, and Paul Burlison formed the Johnny Burnette Rock 'N Roll Trio, 1953-57. Father of **Rocky Burnette**. | | | |
| 7/31/61 | 109 | 2 | 1 I've Got A Lot Of Things To Do ............................._Girls_ | $15 | | Liberty 55345 |
| 3/3/62 | 113 | 1 | 2 Clown Shoes .........................................._The Way I Am_ | $15 | | Liberty 55416 |
| 8/25/62 | 117 | 1 | 3 I Wanna Thank Your Folks ........................._The Giant_ | $20 | | Chancellor 1116 |
| | | | **BURNETTE, Rocky**     HOT/AC | | | |
| | | | Born on 6/12/53 in Memphis. Son of **Johnny Burnette**, nephew of **Dorsey Burnette**. | | | |
| 11/1/80 | 109 | 1 | Fallin' In Love (Bein' Friends) ................._Roll Like A Wheel_ | $5 | | EMI America 8060 |
| | | | **BURRAGE, Harold** ⊙     R&B | | | |
| | | | Born on 3/30/31 in Chicago. Died of a heart attack on 11/25/66. First recorded for Decca in 1950. | | | |
| 9/25/65 | 128 | 1 | Got To Find A Way ..........R&B:31 _How To Fix Your Mouth (To Say What You Say)_ | $15 | | m-pac! 7225 |
| | | | **BURRELL, Kenny — see SMITH, Jimmy** | | | |
| | | | **BURTON, Jenny**     R&B/HOT | | | |
| | | | Born on 11/18/57 in New York City. Former lead singer of C-Bank, the R&B studio band of John Robie. | | | |
| 3/9/85 | 101[2] | 6 | Bad Habits     R&B:19 _Let's Get Back To Love_ | $4 | | Atlantic 89583 |
| | | | **BUSH BABEES — see DA BUSH BABEES** | | | |
| | | | **BUSH, Kate**     ROK/HOT | | | |
| | | | Born on 7/30/58 in Bexleyheath, Kent, England. Discovered by David Gilmour of **Pink Floyd**. | | | |
| 11/4/78 | 108 | 1 | Wuthering Heights ............................................._Kite_ | $8 | ■ | EMI America 8003 |
| | | | **BUSHWACKAS** ⊙ | | | |
| | | | Rap trio from New York City: Fish B. One, Gravedigga and B.D. Buggz. | | | |
| 8/19/95 | 120 | 1 | Caught Up In The Game ............................_Lay It On Me_ | $4 | ▌ | Pallas 357183 |
| | | | **BUSHWICK BILL**     R&B/HOT | | | |
| | | | Born Richard Stephen Shaw on 12/8/66 in Jamaica. Member of rap group **The Geto Boys**. Lost his right eye in a shooting on 5/10/91. | | | |
| 7/22/95 | 113 | 3 | Who's The Biggest ..................R&B:88 _(2 versions) / Only God Knows_ | $3 | ▌ | Rap-A-Lot 38479 |
| | | | CJ Mac (backing vocal) | | | |
| | | | **BUTLER, Billy**     R&B/HOT | | | |
| | | | Born on 6/7/45 in Chicago. **Jerry Butler**'s youngest brother. Formed group the Chanters and later the R&B group Infinity in 1969. | | | |
| 11/2/63 | 134 | 1 | 1 Found True Love ..................................._Lady Love_ | $20 | | Okeh 7178 |
| | | | **BILLY BUTLER & THE FOUR ENCHANTERS** | | | |
| 5/16/64 | 101[2] | 5 | 2 Gotta Get Away     _I'm Just A Man_ | $20 | | Okeh 7192 |
| | | | **BILLY BUTLER & THE ENCHANTERS** | | | |
| 9/26/64 | 130 | 1 | 3 Can't Live Without Her ......................._My Heart Is Hurtin'_ | $20 | | Okeh 7201 |
| 12/5/64 | 102 | 4 | 4 Nevertheless ................................._My Sweet Woman_ | $20 | | Okeh 7207 |
| | | | **BILLY BUTLER & THE CHANTERS** (above 2) | | | |
| 9/4/65 | 103 | 6 | 5 (I've Got A Feeling) You're Gonna Be Sorry ...._(You Make Me Think) You Ain't Ready_ | $15 | | Okeh 7227 |
| | | | all of above (except #3) written by **Curtis Mayfield** | | | |
| | | | **BUTLER, Jerry**     R&B/HOT/AC | | | |
| | | | Born on 12/8/39 in Sunflower, Mississippi. Older brother of **Billy Butler**. In 1957, Butler and **Curtis Mayfield** joined the Roosters; changed name to **The Impressions**. Left for solo career in autumn of 1958. Top Pop Singles: 39. | | | |
| 10/2/61 | 105 | 4 | 1 Aware Of Love ................................._Moon River_ (Hot #11) | $15 | | Vee-Jay 405 |
| 9/12/64 | 108 | 1 | 2 Ain't That Loving You Baby ............._Let It Be Me_ (Hot #5) | $15 | | Vee-Jay 613 |
| | | | **BETTY EVERETT & JERRY BUTLER** | | | |
| | | | #3 R&B hit for **Jimmy Reed** in 1956 | | | |
| 7/10/65 | 122 | 4 | 3 I Can't Stand To See You Cry ...._Nobody Needs Your Love (More Than I Do)_ | $15 | | Vee-Jay 696 |
| 7/23/66 | 103 | 4 | 4 Love (Oh, How Sweet It Is)     R&B:34 _Loneliness_ | $12 | | Mercury 72592 |
| 11/1/69 | 109 | 2 | 5 A Brand New Me ............._What's The Use Of Breaking Up_ (Hot #20) | $8 | | Mercury 72960 |
| | | | #24 hit for **Dusty Springfield** in 1969 | | | |
| 11/7/70 | 109 | 2 | 6 Special Memory ..........................R&B:36 _How Does It Feel_ | $8 | | Mercury 73131 |
| 7/3/71 | 126 | 1 | 7 Ten And Two (Take This Woman Off The Corner) ..........R&B:44 _Everybody Is Waiting_ | $8 | | Mercury 73195 |
| | | | **GENE & JERRY** (Gene Chandler) | | | |
| | | | **BUTTERFLYS, The**     HOT | | | |
| | | | Girl group is actually singer/songwriter **Ellie Greenwich** of **The Raindrops**. | | | |
| 1/23/65 | 117 | 3 | I Wonder ............................................_Gee Baby Gee_ | $25 | | Red Bird 10-016 |
| | | | **BUZZ and BUCKY — see RONNY AND THE DAYTONAS** | | | |

**BY LINERS, The** ✪
Pop mixed vocal chorus.

| 1/20/62 | 117 | 2 | Archie's Melody .................................................................... *Mary Lou Brown* | $8 | | Felsted 8631 |

**BYRD, Bobby**  R&B/HOT
Born on 8/15/34 in Toccoa, Georgia. Founder/leader of **James Brown**'s vocal group, The Famous Flames.

| 2/27/65 | 120 | 2 | 1 We Are In Love ....................................... R&B:14 *No One Like My Baby* | $15 | | Smash 1964 |
| 3/16/68 | 102 | 5 | 2 You've Got To Change Your Mind ................ R&B:47 *I'll Lose My Mind* (Byrd) | $12 | | King 6151 |
| | | | **BOBBY BYRD & JAMES BROWN** | | | |
| 6/26/71 | 117 | 2 | 3 I Know You Got Soul ... R&B:30 *It's I Who Love You (Not Him Anymore)* | $10 | | King 6378 |
| | | | written, produced and arranged by **James Brown** | | | |

**BYRD, Donald — see BLACKBYRDS, The**

**BYRD, Tracy**  C&W/HOT
Born on 12/17/66 in Beaumont, Texas; raised in Vidor, Texas. Male country singer.

| 7/2/94 | 115 | 6 | 1 Lifestyles Of The Not So Rich And | | | |
| | | |     Famous ................................ C&W:4 *You Never Know Just How Good You've Got It* | $3 | ∎ | MCA 54778 |
| 11/4/95 | 119 | 9 | 2 Love Lessons ............................ C&W:9 *Don't Need That Heartache* | $3 | ∎ | MCA 55102 |

**BYRDS, The**  HOT/ROK
Folk-rock group formed in Los Angeles in 1964. Consisted of James **Roger** McGuinn (12-string guitar), **David Crosby** (guitar), Gene Clark (percussion; d: 5/24/91), Chris Hillman (bass) and Mike Clarke (drums; d: 12/19/93). All except Clarke had folk music background. Professional debut in March 1965. Crosby left in late 1967 to form Crosby, Stills & Nash. **McGuinn, Clark & Hillman** later recorded as a trio. In 1986, Hillman later formed popular country group The Desert Rose Band. Group inducted into the Rock and Roll Hall of Fame in 1991.

| 7/24/65 | 103 | 3 | 1 I'll Feel A Whole Lot Better *All I Really Want To Do* (Hot #40) | $12 | | Columbia 43332 |
| 6/7/69 | 132 | 2 | 2 Lay Lady Lay ............................................................ *Old Blue* | $10 | | Columbia 44868 |
| | | | #7 hit for **Bob Dylan** in 1969 | | | |
| 12/19/70 | 121 | 1 | 3 Chestnut Mare ..................................................... *Just A Season* | $10 | | Columbia 45259 |
| 10/9/71 | 110 | 1 | 4 Glory, Glory ........................................................ *Citizen Kane* | $10 | | Columbia 45440 |
| 5/5/73 | 109 | 2 | 5 Full Circle ...................................................... *Long Live The King* | $10 | | Asylum 11016 |

**BYRNE, Robert** ✪
Born in Detroit. Pop session guitarist.

| 6/9/79 | 101[3] | 5 | Baby Fat *Tell Me It's Over One More Time* | $5 | | Mercury 74070 |

# C

**CADILLACS, The**  R&B/HOT
R&B vocal group formed in 1953 in Harlem, New York, as The Carnations. The first R&B vocal group to extensively use choreography in their stage routines. Consisted of Earl "Speedoo" Carroll (lead), LaVerne Drake, Earl Wade, Charles Brooks and Robert Phillips. By 1958, Drake and Brooks replaced by James Bailey and Bobby Spencer. Carroll joined The Coasters in 1961. Spencer was later the lead voice for **Crazy Elephant**.

| 8/3/59 | 105 | 3 | Romeo ..................................................... *Always, My Darling* | $40 | | Josie 866 |

**CAESAR & CLEO — see CHER**

**CAFÉ CRÉME** ✪
Disco studio group based in France.

| 7/29/78 | 105 | 4 | Discomania (Part I) ........................................... *(Part II)* | $6 | | RSO 899 |
| | | | Hey Jude/Day Tripper/Get Back/Back In The USSR/I Want To Hold Your Hand/Yellow Submarine/Ob-La-Di Ob-La-Da/Lucy In The Sky With Diamonds/Michelle/All My Loving/With A Little Help From My Friends/Penny Lane/Eleanor Rigby/Twistin' In The Sixties | | | |

**CAIN, Tané**  HOT
Born and raised in Hawaii. Former wife of Jonathan Cain (The Babys, Journey, Bad English). Daughter of late actor Doug McClure. First name pronounced: tawnee.

| 1/29/83 | 108 | 2 | My Time To Fly ................................................. *Suspicious Eyes* | $4 | ∎ | RCA 13392 |

**CAIOLA, Al**  HOT/R&B
Born on 9/7/20 in Jersey City, New Jersey. Guitarist/composer/bandleader. First recorded for Savoy in 1955. Prolific studio work.

| 4/18/64 | 120 | 3 | From Russia With Love ...................................... *Mexican Summer* [I] | $8 | | United Artists 711 |
| | | | **Don Costa** (orch.); from the James Bond movie starring Sean Connery | | | |

**CALDWELL, Bobby**  R&B/HOT/AC
Born on 8/15/51 in New York City; raised in Florida. Multi-instrumentalist/songwriter. Percussionist with **Johnny Winter**.

| 5/26/79 | 103 | 2 | 1 Can't Say Goodbye ......................... R&B:36 *Down For The Third Time* | $5 | | Clouds 15 |
| 3/27/82 | 105 | 8 | 2 Jamaica ........................................ R&B:54 *Catwalk* | $4 | | Polydor 2202 |
| 6/1/96 | 125 | 1 | 3 I Give In ........................................ R&B:53 *Promise* | $4 | ∎ | Sin-Drome 1206 |

**CALELLO, Charlie** ✪  AC
Born in Newark, New Jersey. Singer/arranger/producer. Arranger and brief member of **The 4 Seasons** in the mid-1960s.

| 3/13/76 | 104 | 6 | Dance, Dance, Dance ....................................... *(long version)* | $5 | | Ariola America 7614 |
| | | | based on the Israeli harvest song "Hava Nagila" | | | |

**CALIFORNIA EARTHQUAKE, The** ✪
Pop-rock trio: Roy Smith (vocals), Brian Griffin (organ) and Jim Gordon (drums). Style similar to **Blood, Sweat & Tears**.

| 12/20/69 | 133 | 1 | What A Beautiful Feeling ................................. *The First Day* | $7 | | World Pacific 77931 |

**CALL, Alex** ✪
Pop/rock singer/guitarist. Former member of Clover.

| 5/7/83 | 101[1] | 7 | Just Another Saturday Night *Hung Over You* | $4 | | Arista 1049 |
| | | | also released on Arista 9009 in 1983 | | | |

| | | | | | | |
|---|---|---|---|---|---|---|

### CAMEL ✪
Rock group from Surrey, England: Pete Bardens (keyboards; Them), Andy Latimer (guitar), Doug Ferguson (bass) and Andy Ward (drums).

| 7/24/76 | 109 | 2 | Another Night ..................................................................*Lunar Sea* | $6 | | Janus 262 |

### CAMEO        R&B/HOT
New York City R&B-funk band founded in 1974 as The New York City Players by Larry Blackmon (drums), with Gregory "Straps" Johnson (keyboards). Vocals by Wayne Cooper and Tomi "Tee" Jenkins.

| 3/5/77 | 103 | 2 | 1 Rigor Mortis .............................................. R&B:33 *Stay By My Side* | $5 | | Chocolate City 005 |
| 9/17/77 | 104 | 11 | 2 Funk Funk ................................................. R&B:20 *Good Times* | $5 | | Chocolate City 011 |
| 7/4/81 | 102 | 6 | 3 Freaky Dancin' ........................................... R&B:3 *Better Days* | $4 | | Chocolate City 3225 |
| 4/24/82 | 101[1] | 5 | 4 Just Be Yourself ........................................... R&B:12 *Use It Or Lose It* | $4 | | Chocolate City 3231 |

### CAMPBELL, Archie ✪        C&W
Born on 11/7/14 in Bulls Gap, Tennessee. Died on 8/29/87 in Knoxville. Chief writer and a star of the TV series *Hee Haw*.

| 5/29/65 | 132 | 1 | Rindercella ........................................ *Hockey Here Tonight* [C] | $8 | | RCA Victor 8546 |
| | | |     variation of the Jack Ross "Cinderella" #16 hit from 1962 | | | |

### CAMPBELL, Glen        C&W/AC/HOT
Born on 4/22/36 in Delight, Arkansas. Vocalist/guitarist/composer. To Los Angeles; recorded with The Champs in 1960. Became prolific studio musician; with The Hondells in 1964, The Beach Boys in 1965 and Sagittarius in 1967. Own TV show *The Glen Campbell Goodtime Hour*, 1968-72. *Top Pop Singles:* 38.

| 12/29/62 | 114 | 2 | 1 Kentucky Means Paradise ....................... C&W:20 *Truck Driving Man* | $15 | | Capitol 4867 |
| | | |     THE GREEN RIVER BOYS Featuring Glen Campbell | | | |
| 3/23/63 | 103 | 5 | 2 Prima Donna                                 *Oh My Darlin'* | $12 | | Capitol 4925 |
| 4/17/65 | 118 | 1 | 3 Tomorrow Never Comes ....................................... *Woman's World* | $10 | | Capitol 5360 |
| | | |     #3 Country hit for Ernest Tubb in 1945 | | | |
| 12/4/65 | 114 | 3 | 4 Private John Q .................................................... *Less Of Me* | $10 | | Capitol 5545 |
| | | |     written by Roger Miller; arrangement similar to Rusty & Doug's "Louisiana Man" | | | |
| 1/8/72 | 104 | 3 | 5 Oklahoma Sunday Morning ......... C&W:15 / AC:36 *Everybody's Got To Go There Sometime* | $6 | | Capitol 3254 |
| 4/1/72 | 114 | 3 | 6 Manhattan Kansas ................................... C&W:6 *Wayfarin' Stranger* | $6 | | Capitol 3305 |
| 10/20/73 | 111 | 6 | 7 Wherefore And Why ............ C&W:20 / AC:45 *Give Me Back That Old Familiar Feeling* | $5 | | Capitol 3735 |
| | | |     written by Gordon Lightfoot | | | |

### CAMP LO        R&B/HOT
Hip-hop duo from New York City: Salahadeen "Geechie Suede" Wallace and Saladine "Sonny Cheeba" Wilds.

| 2/10/96 | 104 | 4 | Coolie High ........................................... R&B:62 *World Heist* | $3 | ▌ | Profile 5445 |

### C + C MUSIC FACTORY        R&B/HOT
Dance outfit led by producers/songwriters Robert Clivilles (percussion; New York native) & David Cole (keyboards; Tennessee native). Cole died of spinal meningitis on 1/24/95 (age 32).

| 12/3/94 | 104 | 5 | 1 Take A Toke ........................................... R&B:48 *(remix)* | $3 | ▌ | Columbia 77741 |
| | | |     C+C MUSIC FACTORY "featuring" Trilogy | | | |
| 9/16/95 | 102 | 10 | 2 Robi-Rob's Boriqua Anthem ........................... Air:70 *I Found Love* [F] | $3 | ▌ | Columbia 78048 |
| 10/5/96 | 113 | 5 | 3 Shake That Body ............................ *Robi-Rob's Boriqua Anthem '96 Remix* | $3 | ▌ | Columbia 78399 |
| | | |     ROBI ROB'S CLUBWORLD | | | |
| | | |     Ya Kid K of Technotronic (lead vocal) | | | |

### CANNED HEAT        HOT
Blues-rock band formed in Los Angeles in 1966. Consisted of Bob "The Bear" Hite (vocals, harmonica; d: 4/6/81), Al "Blind Owl" Wilson (guitar, harmonica, vocals; d: 9/3/70), Henry Vestine (guitar; d: 10/20/97), Larry Taylor (bass) and Frank Cook (drums). Cook replaced by Fito de la Parra in 1968. Vestine replaced by Harvey Mandel in 1969.

| 7/29/67 | 115 | 4 | 1 Rollin' and Tumblin' ............................... *Bullfrog Blues* | $12 | ◼ | Liberty 55979 |
| | | |     written by Muddy Waters | | | |
| 8/16/69 | 119 | 4 | 2 Poor Moon ............................................. *Sic 'Em Pigs* | $10 | | Liberty 56127 |
| 3/6/71 | 105 | 1 | 3 Wooly Bully .................................... *My Time Ain't Long* | $8 | | Liberty 56217 |
| | | |     #2 hit for Sam The Sham and The Pharoahs in 1965 | | | |

### CANNIBAL and THE HEADHUNTERS        HOT
Mexican-American vocal group based in Los Angeles: Frankie "Cannibal" Garcia (d: 1/21/96, age 49), brothers Robert and Joe Jaramillo, and Richard Lopez.

| 6/26/65 | 133 | 2 | 1 Nau Ninny Nau ...................................... *Here Comes Love* | $15 | | Rampart 644 |
| 9/3/66 | 106 | 2 | 2 Land Of A Thousand Dances ............................. *Love Bird* [R] | $15 | | Date 1525 |
| | | |     new version of their #30 hit in 1965 on Rampart 642 | | | |

### CANNON, Ace        HOT/C&W/R&B
Born on 5/4/34 in Grenada, Mississippi. Saxophonist since age 10. Worked with Bill Black's Combo.

| 11/10/62 | 107 | 2 | 1 Volare ................................................ *Looking Back* [I] | $10 | | Hi 2057 |
| | | |     #1 hit for Domenico Modugno in 1958 | | | |
| 4/20/63 | 130 | 1 | 2 Since I Met You Baby ................................... *Love Letters* [I] | $10 | | Hi 2063 |
| | | |     #12 hit for Ivory Joe Hunter in 1956 | | | |
| 11/16/63 | 103 | 6 | 3 Swanee River ..................................... *Moanin' The Blues* [I] | $10 | ◼ | Hi 2070 |
| | | |     written in 1851 by Stephen Foster (also known as "The Old Folks At Home") | | | |
| 10/24/64 | 120 | 3 | 4 Empty Arms ......................................... *Sunday Blues* [I] | $10 | | Hi 2081 |
| | | |     #2 R&B hit for Ivory Joe Hunter in 1957 | | | |
| 4/24/65 | 135 | 1 | 5 Sea Cruise ........................................... *Gold Coins* [I] | $10 | | Hi 2089 |
| | | |     #14 hit for Frankie Ford in 1959 | | | |
| 2/26/66 | 102 | 4 | 6 Funny (How Time Slips Away) ......................... *Saxy Lullaby* [I] | $8 | | Hi 2101 |
| | | |     #22 hit for Jimmy Elledge in 1962 | | | |
| 4/20/68 | 110 | 4 | 7 By The Time I Get To Phoenix ........................... *Sleep Walk* [I] | $8 | | Hi 2144 |
| | | |     #26 hit for Glen Campbell in 1967 | | | |

### CANNON, Freddy        HOT/R&B
Born Frederick Picariello on 12/4/39 in Lynn, Massachusetts. Rock and roll singer, late '50s-early '60s. *Top Pop Singles:* 23.

| 4/24/61 | 114 | 1 | 1 Opportunity ........................ *Buzz Buzz A-Diddle-It* (Hot #51) | $15 | | Swan 4071 |
| 2/9/63 | 121 | 3 | 2 Four Letter Man ................................. *Come On And Love Me* | $15 | | Swan 4132 |
| 5/1/65 | 132 | 1 | 3 In The Night ................................. *Little Miss A Go Go Go* | $12 | ◼ | Warner 5615 |
| | | |     picture sleeve erroneously lists label number as 5616 | | | |

| DEBUT | PEAK | WKS | A-side (Chart Hit) ... B-side | $ | Pic | Label & Number |
|---|---|---|---|---|---|---|
| | | | **CANNON, Freddy — Cont'd** | | | |
| 11/6/65 | 127 | 1 | 4 **Let Me Show You Where It's At** ..................... *The Old Rag Man* | $12 | | Warner 5666 |
| | | | tune is similar to his 1965 hit "Action"; above 2 written by Tommy Boyce & Bobby Hart | | | |
| 7/16/66 | 111 | 2 | 5 **The Laughing Song** ... *Natalie* | $12 | | Warner 5832 |
| 6/22/68 | 121 | 2 | 6 **Rock Around The Clock** ..................... *Sock It To The Judge* | $8 | | We Make Rock'N 1601 |
| | | | **FREDDIE CANNON** | | | |
| | | | full label name: We Make Rock'N Roll Records; #1 hit for **Bill Haley & His Comets** in 1955 | | | |
| | | | **CAPALDI, Jim**  HOT/ROK/AC | | | |
| | | | Born on 8/24/44 in Evesham, England. Drummer with **Traffic**. | | | |
| 6/21/75 | 110 | 3 | 1 **It's All Up To You** ..................... *I've Got So Much Lovin'* | $5 | | Island 025 |
| 9/15/84 | 106 | 3 | 2 **I'll Keep Holding On** ... ROK:58 *Tales Of Power* | $4 | | Atlantic 89625 |
| | | | **CAPITOLS, The** | | | |
| | | | R&B vocal trio from Detroit: Sam George (murdered on 3/17/82, age 39), "Donald Norman" Storball and "Richard Mitchell" McDougall. | | | |
| 4/29/67 | 125 | 2 | **Patty Cake** ..................... *Take A Chance On Me Baby* | $10 | | Karen 1534 |
| | | | **CAPITOL SHOWBAND, The** ○ | | | |
| | | | Pop/rock group from Ireland. | | | |
| 6/12/65 | 126 | 2 | **Born To Be With You** ..................... *Far, Far Away* | $10 | | Argo 5502 |
| | | | #5 hit for **The Chordettes** in 1956 | | | |
| | | | **CAPLETON**  R&B/HOT | | | |
| | | | Born Clifton Bailey on 4/13/67 in Islington, St. Mary, Jamaica. Male dancehall/reggae DJ. | | | |
| 4/6/96 | 125 | 1 | **Heathen Rage** ..................... R&B:79 *See From Afar* | $3 | ■ | African Star 576016 |
| | | | Elisha La'verne (backing vocal); samples "Who Can I Run To" by Xscape | | | |
| | | | **CAPONE-N-NOREAGA** ○  R&B | | | |
| | | | Rap duo: Kiam "Capone" Holley and Victor "Noreaga" Santiago. Met while incarcerated at the Green Haven Correctional Facility in New York. | | | |
| 3/1/97 | 103 | 11 | 1 **T.O.N.Y. (Top Of New York)** ..................... R&B:56 *(instrumental)* | $3 | ■ | Penalty 7193 |
| 11/8/97 | 111 | 4 | 2 **Closer** ..................... R&B:63 *(instrumental)* | $3 | ■ | Penalty 7214 |
| | | | **CAPPS, Al** ○  AC | | | |
| | | | Prolific arranger/conductor. | | | |
| 5/26/73 | 119 | 2 | **Shangri-La** ..................... AC:33 *Magician* | $6 | | Bell 45,347 |
| | | | vocals are by a mixed chorus; #11 hit for **The Four Coins** in 1957 | | | |
| | | | **CAPREEZ, The** ○ | | | |
| 9/24/66 | 115 | 4 | 1 **Rosanna** ..................... *Over You* | $15 | | Sound 126 |
| | | | written by **Charlie Rich** | | | |
| 9/9/67 | 125 | 2 | 2 **Soulsation** ..................... *Time* | $20 | | Sound 171 |
| | | | **CAPTAIN & TENNILLE**  AC/HOT/R&B | | | |
| | | | Daryl "The Captain" Dragon (b: 8/27/42, Los Angeles) and his wife, Toni Tennille (b: 5/8/43, Montgomery, Alabama). Duo had own TV show on ABC, 1976-77. | | | |
| 12/20/80 | 106 | 3 | **This Is Not The First Time** ..................... *Gentle Stranger* | $4 | | Casablanca 2320 |
| | | | **CAPT. GROOVY And His Bubblegum Army** ○ | | | |
| | | | A Jerry Kasenetz and Jeff Katz studio production. **Bobby Bloom** was a member. | | | |
| 6/14/69 | 128 | 2 | **Capt. Groovy And His Bubblegum Army** ..................... *Bubblegum March or (Blowing Bubbles Through Rose Colored Glasses)* | $10 | | Super K 4 |
| | | | **CAPTAIN HOLLYWOOD PROJECT**  HOT | | | |
| | | | Captain Hollywood is Tony Harrison. Born in Newark, New Jersey; raised in Detroit. | | | |
| 9/11/93 | 118 | 1 | **Only With You** ..................... *Nothing's Gonna Stop Me* | $3 | ■ | Imago 25042 |
| | | | **CAPTAIN SKY** ○  R&B | | | |
| | | | Born Daryl L. Cameron on 7/10/57 in Chicago. R&B-funk singer/songwriter/producer. | | | |
| 8/18/79 | 105 | 1 | **Dr. Rock** ..................... R&B:35 *Saturday Night Move-Ease* | $5 | | AVI 273 |
| | | | **CARAVAN** ○ | | | |
| | | | Rock quintet from Canterbury, England: Pye Hastings (vocals, guitar), Dave Sinclair (piano), Geoff Richardson (viola), John G. Perry (bass) and Richard Coughlan (drums). | | | |
| 9/27/75 | 110 | 1 | **Stuck In A Hole** ..................... | $6 | | BTM 800 |
| | | | **CARILLO** ○ | | | |
| | | | Pop group: Frank Carillo (vocals), Rick Silechio (guitar), Kevin Keane (bass) and Dave Donen (drums). | | | |
| 8/19/78 | 101[1] | 1 | **I Wanna Live Again** ..................... *Let's Get It Up* | $4 | ■ | Atlantic 3492 |
| | | | **CARLO — see BELMONTS, The** | | | |
| | | | **CARLTON, Carl**  R&B/HOT/AC | | | |
| | | | Born in 1952 in Detroit. R&B singer. First recorded for Lando Records in 1964. | | | |
| 10/12/68 | 105 | 3 | 1 **46 Drums - 1 Guitar** ..................... R&B:19 *Why Don't They Leave Us Alone* | $8 | | Back Beat 598 |
| | | | **LITTLE CARL CARLTON 14 Year Old Sensation** | | | |
| 10/23/82 | 103 | 5 | 2 **Baby I Need Your Loving** ..................... R&B:17 *Everyone Can Be A Star* | $4 | | RCA 13313 |
| | | | #11 hit for the **Four Tops** in 1964 | | | |
| | | | **CAROLL, Yvonne, and The Roulettes** ○ | | | |
| | | | Female R&B vocal group. | | | |
| 8/31/63 | 115 | 2 | **Gee What A Guy** ..................... *Stuck On You* | $20 | | Domain 1018 |
| | | | **CAROUSELS, The** ○ | | | |
| | | | R&B vocal group. | | | |
| 3/31/62 | 117 | 1 | **If You Want To** ..................... *Pretty Little Thing* | $40 | | Gone 5118 |
| | | | **CARPENTERS**  AC/HOT/C&W | | | |
| | | | Brother-sister duo originally from New Haven, Connecticut: Richard (b: 10/15/46) and Karen Carpenter (b: 3/2/50; d: 2/4/83 of heart failure due to anorexia nervosa). Won the 1970 Best New Artist Grammy Award. *Top Pop Singles*: 29. | | | |
| 11/19/83 | 101[1] | 8 | **Make Believe It's Your First Time** ..................... AC:7 *Look To Your Dreams* | $4 | ■ | A&M 2585 |
| | | | #78 hit for **Bobby Vinton** in 1980 | | | |

| DEBUT | PEAK | WKS | A-side (Chart Hit) ... B-side | $ | Pic | Label & Number |
|---|---|---|---|---|---|---|
| | | | **CARR, Billy** ✪ | | | |
| 11/27/65 | 116 | 5 | What's Come Over This World? .......................................*(Wait Till You See) My Gidget* | $12 | | Colpix 791 |
| | | | tune is similar to **Barry McGuire**'s 1965 hit "Eve Of Destruction" | | | |
| | | | **CARR, Cathy**                         HOT | | | |
| | | | Born Angela Helen Catherine Cordovano on 6/28/36 in the Bronx, New York. Died in November 1988. | | | |
| 2/15/60 | 106 | 2 | 1 Little Sister .......................................................*Dark River* | $12 | | Roulette 4219 |
| | | | Joe Reisman (orch.); also recorded by **Connie Stevens** in 1960 (B-side of "Sixteen Reasons") | | | |
| 12/29/62 | 103 | 2 | 2 Sailor Boy ...........................................*The Next Time The Band Plays A Waltz* | $12 | | Laurie 3147 |
| | | | Glen Stuart (orch.) | | | |
| | | | **CARR, James**                  R&B/HOT | | | |
| | | | Born on 6/13/42 in Memphis. With Soul Stirrers gospel group, early 1960s. | | | |
| 6/10/67 | 106 | 5 | 1 Let It Happen .....................................R&B:30 *A Losing Game* | $15 | | Goldwax 323 |
| 8/3/68 | 112 | 2 | 2 Life Turned Her That Way ...........*A Message To Young Lovers* | $15 | | Goldwax 335 |
| | | | #1 Country hit for **Ricky Van Shelton** in 1988 | | | |
| | | | **CARR, Timothy** ✪ | | | |
| | | | R&B vocalist/songwriter. | | | |
| 4/20/68 | 112 | 2 | A Stop Along The Way ...............................*Let's Start All Over Again* | $10 | | Hot Biscuit 1454 |
| | | | full label name: The Hot Biscuit Disc Company | | | |
| | | | **CARR, Vikki**                  AC/HOT | | | |
| | | | Born Florencia Martinez Cardona on 7/19/41 in El Paso, Texas. Regular on TV's *Ray Anthony Show*, 1962. | | | |
| 9/22/62 | 115 | 3 | 1 He's A Rebel .............................................*Be My Love* | $10 | | Liberty 55493 |
| | | | Ernie Freeman (orch.); written by **Gene Pitney**; #1 hit for The Crystals in 1962 | | | |
| 6/15/68 | 114 | 2 | 2 Don't Break My Pretty Balloon ...............AC:7 *Nothing To Lose* | $7 | ■ | Liberty 56039 |
| 7/22/72 | 108 | 4 | 3 Big Hurt.....................................................AC:31 *Cabaret* | $6 | | Columbia 45622 |
| | | | Al Capps (orch.); #3 hit for Miss Toni Fisher in 1959 | | | |
| | | | **CARREY, Jim** ✪ | | | |
| | | | Born on 1/17/62 in Jacksons Point, Canada. Actor/comedian. One of the top box office attractions of the '90s. | | | |
| 8/27/94 | 117 | 3 | Cuban Pete .......................................*(movie mix)* [N] | $4 | ■ | Chaos/Columbia 77591 |
| | | | from the movie *The Mask* starring Carrey; samples "A Deeper Love" by **C + C Music Factory** | | | |
| | | | **CARROLL, David, And His Orchestra**     HOT/AC/MEM | | | |
| | | | Born Nook Schrier on 10/15/13 in Chicago. Arranger/conductor since 1951 for many top Mercury artists. | | | |
| 1/4/60 | 112 | 2 | 1 Waltzing Matilda ......................................*Sometimes I'm Happy* | $8 | | Mercury 71535 |
| | | | famous Australian Army march tune featured in the movie *On The Beach* starring Gregory Peck and Ava Gardner; | | | |
| | | | #41 hit for **Jimmie Rodgers** in 1960 | | | |
| 12/22/62 | 102 | 2 | 2 Big Girls Don't Cry Limbo .....................*Linstead Market Limbo* [I] | $7 | | Mercury 72070 |
| | | | limbo version of **The 4 Seasons**' 1962 #1 hit "Big Girls Don't Cry" | | | |
| | | | **CARROLL, Dina**                R&B/HOT | | | |
| | | | Born in Britain to an African-American father and a Scottish/English mother. R&B singer. | | | |
| 6/19/93 | 103 | 6 | Special Kind Of Love .............................*(album version)* | $3 | ■ | A&M 0298 |
| | | | **CARROLL, Jim, Band** ✪            ROK | | | |
| | | | Born in New York City in 1950. Rock singer/poet/novelist. Band included Brian Linsley and Terrell Winn (guitars), Steve Linsley (bass) and Wayne Woods (drums). The 1995 movie *The Basketball Diaries* was based on Carroll's life. | | | |
| 11/29/80 | 103 | 8 | People Who Died .....................................ROK:50 *I Want The Angel* | $4 | | Atco 7314 |
| | | | **CARSON, Jeff**                C&W/HOT | | | |
| | | | Born Jeff Herndon on 12/16/64 in Tulsa, Oklahoma; raised in Gravette, Arkansas. Country singer/songwriter/guitarist. | | | |
| 12/30/95+ | 113 | 3 | 1 The Car ................................................C&W:3 *Holdin' Onto Somethin'* | $3 | ■ | MCG/Curb 76970 |
| 8/16/97 | 101[1] | 3 | 2 Here's The Deal/                         C&W:64 | | | |
| 7/5/97 | 103 | 9 | 3   Butterfly Kisses ...................................C&W:66 | $3 | ■ | Curb 73023 |
| | | | #10 *Hot 100 Airplay* hit for Bob Carlisle in 1997 | | | |
| | | | **CARTER, Carlene**            C&W/AC/HOT | | | |
| | | | Born Rebecca Carlene Smith on 9/26/55 in Madison, Tennessee. Daughter of June Carter and **Carl Smith**. Married to **Nick Lowe**, 1979-90. Later married Howie Epstein of **Tom Petty & The Heartbreakers**. | | | |
| 12/1/79 | 108 | 2 | Do It In A Heartbeat ........................AC:36 /C&W:42 *Swap-Meat Rag* | $4 | | Warner 49083 |
| | | | **CARTER, Clarence**            R&B/HOT | | | |
| | | | Born on 1/14/36 in Montgomery, Alabama. R&B vocalist/guitarist. Blind since age one. | | | |
| 12/11/71 | 101[2] | 3 | 1 Scratch My Back (And Mumble In My Ear) .........R&B:41 *I'm The One* | $8 | | Atlantic 2842 |
| 3/17/73 | 112 | 5 | 2 Put On Your Shoes And Walk .........R&B:40 *I Found Somebody New* | $6 | | Fame 179 |
| 11/24/73 | 101[2] | 12 | 3 I'm The Midnight Special ...............R&B:15 *I Got Another Woman* | $6 | | Fame 330 |
| | | | **CARTER, Mel**               AC/HOT/R&B | | | |
| | | | Born on 4/22/39 in Cincinnati. Soul singer/actor. Named Top Gospel Tenor in 1957. Acted on TV's *Quincy, Sanford And Son, Marcus Welby, MD* and *Magnum P.I.* | | | |
| 1/23/65 | 104 | 5 | 1 The Richest Man Alive.................................*I'll Never Be Free* | $10 | | Imperial 66078 |
| 3/4/67 | 111 | 2 | 2 As Time Goes By ..................................*Look To The Rainbow* | $8 | | Imperial 66228 |
| | | | #1 hit for Rudy Vallee in 1943; featured song in the 1942 classic movie *Casablanca* | | | |
| 10/21/67 | 132 | 2 | 3 Be My Love.............................................AC:23 *I Look Into Your Eyes* | $8 | | Liberty 56000 |
| | | | #1 hit for Mario Lanza in 1951 | | | |
| 5/18/74 | 104 | 5 | 4 I Only Have Eyes For You .............AC:39 *Treasure Of Love* | $6 | | Romar/MGM 716 |
| | | | #11 hit for **The Flamingos** in 1959 | | | |
| | | | **CARTER, Valerie**            HOT/AC | | | |
| | | | Session singer. Sang backup for **Eddie Money, Randy Newman** and **James Taylor**. | | | |
| 4/2/77 | 103 | 5 | Ooh Child ...................................................*Heartache* | $5 | | Columbia 10505 |
| | | | #8 hit for **The Five Stairsteps** in 1970 | | | |
| | | | **CARTER BROTHERS, The** ✪ | | | |
| | | | R&B trio from Garland, Alabama: Roman (guitar), Jerry (piano) and Albert (guitar) Carter. | | | |
| 7/17/65 | 133 | 2 | Southern Country Boy ...............................R&B:21 *Do The Flo Show* | $15 | | Jewel 745 |

| DEBUT | PEAK | WKS | A-side (Chart Hit) .......B-side | $ | Pic | Label & Number |
|---|---|---|---|---|---|---|
| | | | **CASCADES, The**   HOT/AC&R&B | | | |
| | | | Pop group from San Diego: John Gummoe (vocals), Eddie Snyder, David Stevens, David Wilson and David Zabo. | | | |
| 8/17/63 | 116 | 1 | 1 **A Little Like Lovin'** ........................................................*Cinderella* | $15 | ■ | RCA Victor 8206 |
| 4/30/66 | 131 | 2 | 2 **Cheryl's Goin' Home** ........................................*Truly Julie's Blues* | $15 | | Arwin 132 |
| | | | written by **Bob Lind** | | | |
| | | | **CASE**   R&B/HOT | | | |
| | | | Male R&B singer/songwriter. Native of New York City; based in Mt. Vernon, New York. | | | |
| 10/12/96 | 104 | 11 | **More To Love** ........................................R&B:36 *(instrumental)* | $3 | ▌ | Spoiled Rotten 575652 |
| | | | samples "Feel The Groove" by Ultramagnetic M.C.'s and "The Payback" by James Brown | | | |
| | | | **CASEY, Al**   HOT/R&B | | | |
| | | | Born on 10/26/36 in Long Beach, California. Guitarist/pianist/bandleader/producer. Much session work with **Lee Hazlewood** productions, including **Duane Eddy**. | | | |
| 10/12/63 | 116 | 2 | **Guitars, Guitars, Guitars** ...............................*Surfin' Blues Part 1* | $20 | | Stacy 964 |
| | | | **AL CASEY With the K-C-Ettes** | | | |
| | | | **CASH, Alvin, & The Crawlers**   R&B/HOT | | | |
| | | | Born on 2/15/39 in St. Louis. Formed R&B song/dance troupe The Crawlers in 1960, with brothers Robert, Arthur and George (ages 8 to 10). | | | |
| 7/24/65 | 134 | 1 | **Un-Wind The Twine** .........................*The Penguin (Tuxedo Bird)* | $12 | | Mar-V-Lus 6006 |
| | | | sequel to Cash's early 1965 hit "Twine Time" | | | |
| | | | **CASH, Johnny**   C&W/HOT/AC | | | |
| | | | Born J.R. Cash on 2/26/32 in Kingsland, Arkansas. Formed trio with Luther Perkins (guitar) and Marshall Grant (bass) in 1955. First recorded for Sun in 1955. Own TV show for ABC from 1969-71. Elected to the Country Music Hall of Fame in 1980. Won Grammy's Living Legends Award in 1990. Inducted into the Rock and Roll Hall of Fame in 1992. Diagnosed with Parkinson's disease in July 1997. *Top Pop Singles:* 48. | | | |
| 5/23/60 | 110 | 1 | 1 **Smiling Bill McCall** ..................C&W:13 *Seasons Of My Heart (C&W #10)* [N] | $15 | | Columbia 41618 |
| 7/4/60 | 107 | 3 | 2 **The Story Of A Broken Heart** ....................*Down The Street To 301 (Hot #85)* | $20 | | Sun 343 |
| | | | **JOHNNY CASH And The Tennessee Two** | | | |
| 5/29/61 | 108 | 2 | 3 **The Rebel - Johnny Yuma** .................C&W:24 *Forty Shades Of Green* | $15 | ■ | Columbia 41995 |
| | | | theme from the TV series *The Rebel* starring Nick Adams | | | |
| 2/8/64 | 119 | 1 | 4 **Dark As A Dungeon** ..................C&W:49 *Understand Your Man (Hot #35)* | $10 | ☐ | Columbia 42964 |
| 7/3/65 | 124 | 4 | 5 **The Streets Of Laredo** .................*Mister Garfield (C&W #15)* | $10 | | Columbia 43313 |
| | | | traditional Irish melody; William Holden starred in the 1949 movie of the same title | | | |
| 8/28/65 | 119 | 5 | 6 **The Sons Of Katie Elder** ..................C&W:10 *A Certain Kinda Hurtin'* | $10 | | Columbia 43342 |
| | | | from the movie starring John Wayne | | | |
| 9/3/66 | 107 | 2 | 7 **Boa Constrictor** ..................C&W:39 *Bottom Of A Mountain* [N] | $10 | | Columbia 43763 |
| 6/19/71 | 124 | 3 | 8 **Singing In Viet Nam Talking Blues** ..........C&W:18 *You've Got A New Light Shining* [S] | $8 | | Columbia 45393 |
| 10/23/71 | 104 | 3 | 9 **Papa Was A Good Man** ..................C&W:16 *I Promise You* | $8 | | Columbia 45460 |
| 1/29/72 | 103 | 2 | 10 **A Thing Called Love** ..................C&W:2 / AC:37 *Daddy* | $8 | | Columbia 45534 |
| | | | **JOHNNY CASH And The Evangel Temple Choir** (above 2) | | | |
| 9/9/72 | 101[1] | 7 | 11 **Oney**   C&W:2 *Country Trash* | $7 | | Columbia 45660 |
| | | | **CASH, Rosanne**   C&W/AC/HOT | | | |
| | | | Born on 5/24/56 in Memphis. Daughter of **Johnny Cash** and Vivian Liberto. Married to **Rodney Crowell** from 1979-92. | | | |
| 2/20/82 | 104 | 4 | **Blue Moon With Heartache** ..................C&W:❶[1] / AC:37 *Only Human* | $4 | | Columbia 02659 |
| | | | **CASHELLES, The** ✪ | | | |
| | | | Pop female vocal group. | | | |
| 1/25/64 | 129 | 1 | **Outside City Limits** ........................................*Pretend* | $15 | | Decca 31575 |
| | | | **CASHMAN, PISTILLI & WEST**   AC/HOT | | | |
| | | | New York City trio of Dennis "Terry Cashman" Minogue, Eugene Pistilli and Thomas "Tommy West" Picardo, Jr. | | | |
| 10/21/67 | 122 | 2 | 1 **Richard & Me** ........................................*Can't Get To Stoppin'* | $8 | | ABC 10981 |
| | | | **GENE & TOMMY** | | | |
| 12/27/69 | 106 | 1 | 2 **The Last Time** ........................................*The Feelin' That I Get* | $7 | | Event 3307 |
| | | | **THE BUCHANAN BROTHERS** | | | |
| | | | #9 hit for **The Rolling Stones** in 1965. | | | |
| 4/11/70 | 105 | 2 | 3 **Goodbye Jo** ........................................*She Never Looked Better* | $6 | | Capitol 2747 |
| | | | **CASINOS, The**   HOT | | | |
| | | | Pop vocal group from Cincinnati: Gene Hughes (lead), Pete Bolton, Bob Armstrong, Tom Mathews, Ray White, Mickey Denton, Glen Hughes, Joe Patterson and Bill Hawkins. | | | |
| 6/17/67 | 121 | 1 | **How Long Has It Been** ........................................*Forever And A Night* | $12 | | Fraternity 987 |
| | | | **CASLONS, The**   HOT | | | |
| | | | White vocal group from Brooklyn. | | | |
| 1/27/62 | 120 | 1 | **For All We Know** ........................................*Settle Me Down* | $25 | | Amy 836 |
| | | | #3 hit for Hal Kemp & His Orchestra in 1934. | | | |
| | | | **CASSIDY, David**   HOT/AC | | | |
| | | | Born on 4/12/50 in New York City. Played "Keith Partridge", the lead singer of TV's *The Partridge Family*. | | | |
| 12/4/76 | 105 | 3 | **Gettin' It In The Street** ..................*I'll Have To Go Away (Saying Goodbye)* | $5 | | RCA 10788 |
| | | | **CASTAWAYS, The**   HOT | | | |
| | | | Rock and roll group of teenagers from St. Paul, Minnesota: Richard Robey (vocals, bass), Robert Folschow and Roy Hensley (guitars), James Donna (keyboards) and Dennis Craswell (drums). Craswell later joined **Crow**. | | | |
| 11/13/65 | 101[2] | 6 | **Goodbye Babe** ........................................*A Man's Gotta Be A Man* | $15 | | Soma 1442 |
| | | | **CASTELLS, The**   HOT/AC | | | |
| | | | Pop vocal quartet from Santa Rosa, California: Bob Ussery, Tom Hicks, Joe Kelly and Chuck Girard (later with **The Hondells**). | | | |
| 2/27/61 | 101[1] | 3 | **Little Sad Eyes** ........................................*Romeo* | $20 | | Era 3038 |
| | | | **CASTOR, Jimmy, Bunch**   R&B/HOT | | | |
| | | | Born on 6/22/43 in New York City. R&B singer/saxophonist/composer/arranger. Formed group in 1972, with Gerry Thomas (keyboards), Doug Gibson (bass), Harry Jensen (guitar), Lenny Fridie, Jr. (congas) and Bobby Manigault (drums). | | | |
| 8/5/72 | 105 | 3 | 1 **Luther The Anthropoid (Ape Man)** ........................................*Party Life* [N] | $6 | | RCA Victor 0763 |
| 3/12/77 | 101[1] | 5 | 2 **Space Age**   R&B:28 *Dracula Pt. II* | $5 | | Atlantic 3375 |
| 6/11/77 | 108 | 2 | 3 **I Love A Mellow Groove** ........................................*I Don't Want To Lose You* | $5 | | Atlantic 3396 |

**CASTRO, Bernadette ✪**
Pop singer. Her family founded the Castro Furniture stores in New York City.

| 9/26/64 | 123 | 4 | His Lips Get In The Way ................................................. *Sports Car Sally* | $25 | | Colpix 747 |

**CASUALS, The ✪**
Pop/rock and roll band.

| 12/5/64 | 117 | 2 | Mustang 2 + 2 (Big Mule) ........................................ *Play Me A Sad Song* | $25 | | Sound Stage 7 2534 |

**CAT MOTHER and the ALL NIGHT NEWSBOYS**   HOT
New York rock quintet produced by **Jimi Hendrix**: Larry Packer (guitar), Bob Smith (piano), Charley Chin (banjo), Roy Michaels (bass) and Michael Equine (drums).

| 9/27/69 | 115 | 2 | Can You Dance To It? ......................................................... *Marie* | $7 | | Polydor 14007 |

**CAVALIERE, Felix**   AC/HOT
Born on 11/29/43 in Pelham, New York. Lead singer of **The Rascals** after a stint with **Joey Dee**'s band.

| 6/7/80 | 105 | 4 | Good To Have Love Back ........................... AC:41 *Dancin' The Night Away* | $4 | | Epic 50880 |

**CHAD & JEREMY**   HOT/AC
British folk-pop duo formed in the early 1960s: Chad Stuart (b: 12/10/43) and Jeremy Clyde (b: 3/22/44).

| 10/23/65 | 128 | 1 | 1 Should I ............................................. *I Have Dreamed* (Hot #91) | $8 | | Columbia 43414 |
| 2/5/66 | 131 | 1 | 2 Teenage Failure ................................................ *Early Mornin' Rain* | $8 | ■ | Columbia 43490 |
| 4/16/66 | 110 | 3 | 3 The Cruel War .............................................. *I Can't Talk To You* (Chad) | $8 | ■ | Columbia 43467 |
| | | | **CHAD AND JILL STUART** | | | |
| | | | #52 hit for **Peter, Paul & Mary** in 1966 | | | |

**CHAIRMEN OF THE BOARD**   R&B/HOT
R&B vocal group formed in Detroit in 1969: General Norman Johnson, Danny Woods, Harrison Kennedy and Eddie Curtis. Johnson was leader of **The Showmen**, 1961-67.

| 5/15/71 | 111 | 3 | 1 Hanging On (To) A Memory ..................... R&B:28 *Tricked & Trapped (By A Tricky Trapper)* | $6 | | Invictus 9089 |
| 10/9/71 | 103 | 1 | 2 Try On My Love For Size.................................. R&B:48 *Working On A Building Of Love* | $6 | | Invictus 9099 |
| 12/11/71 | 104 | 1 | 3 Men Are Getting Scarce ..................................... R&B:33 *Bravo, Hooray* | $6 | | Invictus 9103 |

**CHAKIRIS, George ✪**
Born on 9/16/34 in Norwood, Ohio. Portrayed "Bernardo" (leader of the Sharks gang) in the movie *West Side Story*.

| 10/13/62 | 110 | 1 | Maria ............................................................. *Once Upon A Time* | $7 | ■ | Capitol 4844 |
| | | | Milton Raskin (orch.); from the movie *West Side Story* starring Chakiris; #78 hit for **Johnny Mathis** in 1960 | | | |

**CHAMBERS BROTHERS, The**   HOT/R&B
R&B band featuring four Mississippi-born brothers: George (bass), Willie (guitar), Lester (harmonica) and Joe (guitar) Chambers. Drummer Brian Keenan added in 1965.

| 11/18/67 | 126 | 1 | 1 Uptown ................................................. *Love Me Like The Rain* | $12 | | Columbia 44296 |
| 3/15/69 | 113 | 3 | 2 Are You Ready ........................................ *You Got The Power - To Turn Me On* | $10 | | Columbia 44779 |
| 5/30/70 | 103 | 4 | 3 Let's Do It (Do It Together) ............................................. *To Love Somebody* | $10 | | Columbia 45146 |
| 12/19/70 | 106 | 7 | 4 Funky .......................................... R&B:40 *Love, Peace & Happiness* | $10 | | Columbia 45277 |
| 3/16/74 | 106 | 7 | 5 Let's Go, Let's Go, Let's Go......................... R&B:76 *Do You Believe In Magic* | $7 | | Avco 4632 |
| | | | #6 hit for **Hank Ballard & The Midnighters** in 1960 | | | |

**CHAMPAIGN**   R&B/HOT/AC
Interracial sextet from Champaign, Illinois: Pauli Carman and Rena Jones (lead vocals), Leon Reeder (guitar), Michael Day and Dana Walden (keyboards), and Rocky Maffit (drums).

| 11/10/84 | 104 | 2 | Off And On Love .................................... R&B:10 *Laissez Le Bontemps Roulez* | $4 | | Columbia 04600 |

**CHAMPS, The**   HOT/R&B
Rock and roll instrumental band from Los Angeles featuring Chuck Rio (sax) and Dave Burgess (guitar). **Glen Campbell** and **Seals & Crofts** spent some time with the band.

| 2/2/63 | 111 | 2 | Mr. Cool ...................................................................3/4 Mash [I] | $20 | | Challenge 9180 |
| | | | melody taken from a "Mr. Clean" TV jingle | | | |

**CHANDLER, Barbara ✪**
Pop teenage vocalist.

| 7/27/63 | 114 | 7 | It Hurts To Be Sixteen ................................... *Running, Running, Johnny* | $15 | | Kapp 542 |
| | | | #45 hit for Andrea Carroll in 1963 | | | |

**CHANDLER, Gene**   R&B/HOT
Born Eugene Dixon on 7/6/37 in Chicago. R&B singer/producer. Joined The Dukays vocal group in 1957. Own label, Mr. Chand, 1969-73. *Top Pop Singles*: 25.

| 10/20/62 | 114 | 4 | 1 Tear For Tear .............................................. *Miracle After Miracle* | $20 | | Vee-Jay 461 |
| | | | **GENE "DUKE OF EARL" CHANDLER** | | | |
| 5/25/63 | 119 | 3 | 2 Check Yourself................................................... *Forgive Me* | $20 | | Vee-Jay 511 |
| 2/29/64 | 107 | 4 | 3 Think Nothing About It ...................................... *Wish You Were Here* | $15 | | Constellation 112 |
| 9/18/65 | 102 | 6 | 4 Here Come The Tears ................................... *Soul Hootenanny, Pt. 2* | $15 | | Constellation 164 |
| 6/26/71 | 116 | 3 | 5 You're A Lady.......................................... R&B:14 *Stone Cold Feeling* | $8 | | Mercury 73206 |
| 7/3/71 | 126 | 1 | 6 Ten And Two (Take This Woman Off The Corner) ................ R&B:44 *Everybody Is Waiting* | $8 | | Mercury 73195 |
| | | | **GENE & JERRY** (Jerry Butler) | | | |
| 6/14/80 | 101[1] | 6 | 7 Does She Have A Friend? .................................. R&B:28 *Let Me Make Love To You* | $5 | | Chi-Sound 2451 |

**CHANDLER, Kenny**   HOT
Born Kenneth Bolognese on 11/21/40 in Harrisburg, Pennsylvania. Pop singer. Also recorded as Kenny Beau.

| 9/4/61 | 112 | 2 | Drums ...................................................... *The Magic Ring* | $15 | | United Artists 342 |

**CHANGING FACES**   R&B/HOT
Female R&B vocal duo from New York City: Charisse Rose and Cassandra Lucas.

| 10/5/96 | 123 | 1 | I Got Somebody Else.................................... R&B:49 *(remix)* | $3 | ▌ | Big Beat 98046 |
| | | | from the movie *High School High* starring Jon Lovitz; samples "Person To Person" by the **Average White Band** | | | |

**CHANNEL, Bruce**   HOT/R&B
Born on 11/28/40 in Jacksonville, Texas. In 1959, first recorded for Teenager, then for King.

| 10/13/62 | 117 | 2 | Somewhere In This Town ................................... *Stand Tough* | $12 | ■ | Smash 1780 |
| | | | The Stephen Scott Singers (backing vocals) | | | |

| DEBUT | PEAK | WKS | A-side (Chart Hit) ... B-side | $ | Pic | Label & Number |
|---|---|---|---|---|---|---|
| | | | **CHANTAY'S**        HOT/R&B | | | |
| | | | Teenage surf-rock quintet from Santa Ana, California: Bob Spickard (lead guitar), Brian Carman (rhythm guitar), Rob Marshall (piano), Warren Waters (bass) and Bob Welsh (drums). | | | |
| 10/1/66 | 106 | 6 | Pipeline ............................................................... *Move It* [I-R] | $8 | | Dot 145 |
| | | | made the *Hot 100* (#4) on 3/2/63 on Dot 16440 ($15) | | | |
| | | | **CHANTELS, The**        HOT/R&B | | | |
| | | | Female R&B vocal group from the Bronx, New York: Arlene Smith, Sonia Goring, Rene Minus, Jackie Landry and Lois Harris. Landry died of cancer on 12/23/97 (age 56). | | | |
| 3/17/62 | 118 | 3 | 1 Here It Comes Again ....................................................... *Summertime* | $20 | | Carlton 569 |
| | | | Sammy Lowe (orch.) | | | |
| 12/6/69 | 116 | 2 | 2 Maybe ......................................................... *He's Gone* [R] | $10 | | Roulette 7064 |
| | | | made the *Hot 100* (#15) on 1/20/58 on End 1005 ($40) | | | |
| | | | **CHANTS, The** ○ | | | |
| | | | White vocal trio from New York City. | | | |
| 5/22/61 | 101¹ | 2 | Respectable      *Kiss Me Goodbye* | $20 | | MGM 13008 |
| | | | originally released on True Eko 3567 in 1961 ($50); written by The Isley Brothers; #15 hit for The Outsiders in 1966 | | | |
| | | | **CHAPIN, Harry**        HOT/AC | | | |
| | | | Born on 12/7/42 in New York City. Died in an auto accident on 7/16/81. Folk-rock balladeer. | | | |
| 2/3/73 | 118 | 2 | 1 Better Place To Be ............................................... *Winter Song* | $6 | | Elektra 45828 |
| | | | a "live" version made the *Hot 100* (#86) on 6/26/76 on Elektra 45327 ($5) | | | |
| 8/29/81 | 105 | 4 | 2 Story Of A Life ............................................... *Salt And Pepper* | $4 | | Boardwalk 119 |
| | | | **CHAPMAN, Beth Nielsen** | | | |
| | | | Born on 9/14/58 in Harlingen, Texas. Singer/songwriter. | | | |
| 11/29/97+ | 102 | 14 | Sand And Water ............................................... *Beyond The Blue* | $3 | ▌ | Reprise 17269 |
| | | | **CHAPMAN, Tracy**        HOT/AC/ROK/R&B | | | |
| | | | Born on 3/20/64 in Cleveland. Boston-based, folk-R&B singer/songwriter. Won the 1988 Best New Artist Grammy Award. | | | |
| 10/12/96 | 106 | 4 | 1 New Beginning ............................................... *Talkin' Bout A Revolution* | $3 | ▌ | Elektra 64257 |
| 12/7/96 | 119 | 2 | 2 Smoke And Ashes ............................................... *Tell It Like It Is* | $3 | ▌ | Elektra 64297 |
| | | | **CHARADE** ○ | | | |
| | | | Pop/rock vocal-instrumental group. | | | |
| 9/12/70 | 116 | 2 | And You Do ............................................... *Somebody's Watching You* | $7 | | Epic 10644 |
| | | | **CHARLENE**        HOT/AC/C&W | | | |
| | | | Born Charlene D'Angelo on 6/1/50 in Hollywood. Pop singer. | | | |
| 7/24/82 | 109 | 1 | It Ain't Easy Comin' Down ............................................... *If I Could See Myself* [R] | $4 | | Motown 1621 |
| | | | made the *Hot 100* (#97) on 3/5/77 on Prodigal 0632 ($5) | | | |
| | | | **CHARLES, Harry** ○ | | | |
| | | | Pop singer based in Nashville. | | | |
| 8/24/63 | 107 | 3 | My Laura ............................................... *Challenge Of Love* | $10 | | Rowax 802 |
| | | | **CHARLES, Ray**        R&B/HOT/AC/C&W | | | |
| | | | Born Ray Charles Robinson on 9/23/30 in Albany, Georgia. Partially blind at age five, completely blind at seven (glaucoma). Formed own band in 1954. Inducted into the Rock and Roll Hall of Fame in 1986. Won Grammy's Lifetime Achievement Award in 1987. *Top Pop Singles: 76.* | | | |
| 2/2/63 | 113 | 3 | 1 Feelin' Sad ............................................... *Carrying That Load* | $15 | | Atlantic 2174 |
| | | | originally released on Atlantic 1008 in 1953 ($40) | | | |
| 4/13/63 | 105 | 5 | 2 No Letter Today ............................... *Take These Chains From My Heart* (Hot #8) | $10 | | ABC-Paramount 10435 |
| | | | #2 Country hit for Ted Daffan's Texans in 1944 | | | |
| 9/7/63 | 102 | 3 | 3 Making Believe ............................................... *Busted* (Hot #4) | $10 | | ABC-Paramount 10481 |
| | | | #2 Country hit for Kitty Wells in 1955 | | | |
| 2/6/65 | 112 | 1 | 4 Teardrops From My Eyes ............................................... *Cry* (Hot #58) | $10 | | ABC-Paramount 10615 |
| | | | #1 R&B hit for Ruth Brown in 1950 | | | |
| 5/15/65 | 112 | 2 | 5 Without A Song (Part 1) ............................................... *(Part 2)* | $10 | | ABC-Paramount 10663 |
| | | | #6 hit for Paul Whiteman with Bing Crosby in 1930 | | | |
| 9/25/65 | 115 | 5 | 6 The Cincinnati Kid ............................... AC:19 *That's All I Am To You* | $10 | | ABC-Paramount 10720 |
| | | | from the movie starring Steve McQueen and Ann-Margret | | | |
| 3/11/67 | 112 | 2 | 7 Something Inside Me ............................................... *I Want To Talk About You* (Hot #98) | $7 | | ABC/TRC 10901 |
| 5/13/67 | 105 | 2 | 8 Somebody Ought To Write A Book About It ............... *Here We Go Again* (Hot #15) | $7 | | ABC/TRC 10938 |
| 1/11/69 | 112 | 2 | 9 When I Stop Dreaming ............... AC:25 *If It Wasn't For Bad Luck* (w/Jimmy Lewis - Hot #77) | $7 | | ABC/TRC 11170 |
| 3/8/69 | 105 | 4 | 10 I Didn't Know What Time It Was ............................................... *I'll Be Your Servant* | $7 | | ABC/TRC 11193 |
| | | | #6 hit for Benny Goodman in 1939; #92 hit for The Crampton Sisters in 1964 | | | |
| 9/13/69 | 101¹ | 4 | 11 We Can Make It      R&B:31 *I Can't Stop Loving You Baby* | $7 | | ABC/TRC 11239 |
| 12/20/69 | 111 | 4 | 12 Claudie Mae ............................................... *Someone To Watch Over Me* | $7 | | ABC/TRC 11251 |
| 12/23/72 | 115 | 1 | 13 Hey Mister ............................... R&B:47 *There'll Be No Peace Without All Men As One* | $6 | | ABC/TRC 11337 |
| 5/1/93 | 104 | 6 | 14 A Song For You ............................... AC:9 /R&B:57 *I Can't Get Enough* | $3 | ▌ | Warner 18611 |
| | | | written by Leon Russell; recorded by the Carpenters for their 1972 album *A Song For You* | | | |
| | | | **CHARLES, Ray, Singers**        AC/HOT | | | |
| | | | Born Charles Raymond Offenberg on 9/13/18 in Chicago. Arranger/conductor for many TV shows. | | | |
| 9/18/65 | 124 | 4 | 1 My Love, Forgive Me (Amore, Scusami) ............................... AC:17 *My Guitar And My Song* (Ti Regalo La Luna) | $6 | | Command 4073 |
| 2/19/66 | 134 | 1 | 2 One Of Those Songs ............................................... AC:13 *To You* | $6 | | Command 4079 |
| | | | also see Jimmy Durante's "Bubbling Under" version | | | |
| 6/3/67 | 135 | 1 | 3 Little By Little And Bit By Bit ............................................... AC:6 *Bless Your Heart* | $5 | | Command 4096 |
| | | | **CHARLES, Sonny**        HOT/R&B | | | |
| | | | R&B vocalist from Fort Wayne, Indiana. Leader of The Checkmates, Ltd. | | | |
| 10/3/70 | 116 | 1 | Half As Much ............................................... *Will You Be Easy* | $7 | | A&M 1214 |
| | | | #1 hit for Rosemary Clooney in 1952 | | | |

| DEBUT | PEAK | WKS | A-side (Chart Hit) ........................................................................................B-side | $ | Pic | Label & Number |
|---|---|---|---|---|---|---|

**CHARLES, Tina ☉**
British disco singer. Sang lead on the *Hot 100* hit "I'm On Fire" by 5000 Volts.

| 11/22/75 | 104 | 4 | You Set My Heart On Fire.............................................................................. *Fire* [I] | $5 | | Columbia 10202 |

**CHARLES & EDDIE**  HOT/AC/R&B
Soul vocal duo of Charles Pettigrew (from Philadelphia) and Eddie Chacon (from Oakland, California).

| 1/16/93 | 115 | 2 | N.Y.C. (Can You Believe This City?) ...................... *(2 versions) / Where Do We Go From Here?* | $3 | ■ | Capitol 44893 |

song includes the guitar riff from **Buffalo Springfield**'s "For What It's Worth"

**CHARMAINES, The ☉**
Female pop vocal trio.

| 9/18/61 | 117 | 1 | What Kind Of Girl (Do You Think I Am) ............................................... *All You Gotta Do* | $15 | | Fraternity 880 |

produced by **Bobby Bare**

**CHARO With The Salsoul Orchestra ☉**
Born Maria Rosario Pilar Martinez on 1/15/51 in Murcia, Spain. Singer/actress. Known as the "Cuchi-Cuchi" girl. Once married to the late bandleader Xavier Cugat.

| 1/28/78 | 104 | 3 | Dance A Little Bit Closer.............................................................................. *Cuchi-Cuchi* | $5 | | Salsoul 2048 |

**CHARTBUSTERS, The**  HOT
Rock quartet from Washington, D.C.

| 7/3/65 | 134 | 1 | New Orleans ................................................................................ *Lonely Surfer Boy* | $20 | | Crusader 118 |

"live" recording; #6 hit for **U.S. Bonds** in 1960

**CHARTS, The**  HOT
R&B vocal quintet from New York City: Joe Grier (lead), Leroy Binns and Steven Brown (tenors; d: 1/20/89), Glenmore Jackson (baritone) and Ross Buford (bass).

| 3/26/66 | 132 | 2 | Desiree ....................................................... *Fell In Love With You Baby* [R] | $25 | | Wand 1112 |

new "hot" version of the group's #88 hit "Deserie" in 1957 on Everlast 5001 ($100)

**CHASE**  HOT
Jazz-rock band organized by trumpeter Bill Chase (b: 1935 in Chicago. Chase along with three bandmates were killed in a plane crash on 8/9/74 near Jackson, Minnesota.

| 5/20/72 | 105 | 3 | I Can Feel It............................................................................... *Cronus (Saturn)* | $5 | | Epic 10853 |

**CHEAP TRICK**  HOT/ROK/AC
Rock quartet formed in 1972 in Rockford, Illinois: Robin Zander (vocals), Rick Nielsen (guitar), Tom Petersson (bass) and Bun E. Carlos (drums).

| 5/10/97 | 119 | 3 | Say Goodbye........................................................... ROK:39 *Yeah Yeah* | $4 | ■ | Red Ant 5002 |

**CHECKER, Chubby**  HOT/R&B/ROK
Born Ernest Evans on 10/3/41 in Andrews, South Carolina; raised in Philadelphia. Cover version of **Hank Ballard**'s "The Twist" started worldwide dance craze. *Top Pop Singles*: 35.

| 5/5/62 | 109 | 3 | 1 Teach Me To Twist....................................................... *Swingin' Together* [N] | $15 | ■ | Cameo 214 |

**BOBBY RYDELL  CHUBBY CHECKER**

| 6/20/64 | 116 | 2 | 2 Rosie ................................................................. *Lazy Elsie Molly* (Hot #40) | $15 | ■ | Parkway 920 |
| 5/29/82 | 104 | 2 | 3 Harder Than Diamond ............................................... ROK:33 *Your Love* | $4 | | MCA 52043 |

**CHEEKS ☉**
Buffalo-based rock quartet.

| 7/12/80 | 110 | 1 | Boney Moronie ........................................................... *Bad Reputation* | $4 | | Capitol 4883 |

from the movie *Up The Academy* starring Ralph Macchio; #14 hit for Larry Williams in 1957

**CHEMAY, Joe, Band**  HOT
Pop/rock singer/bassist Chemay was born in Baltimore. Band included Billy Walker (guitar), John Hobbs (piano), Mike Meros (organ), Louis Conte (percussion) and Paul Leim (drums).

| 6/13/81 | 105 | 3 | Love Is A Crazy Feeling ............................................................... | $5 | | Unicorn 95003 |

**CHEMICAL BROTHERS, The**  HOT/ROK
British techno-dance DJ duo: Tom Rowlands and Ed Simons.

| 4/12/97 | 105 | 27 | 1 Block Rockin' Beats ........................ ROK:40 *(remix) / Prescription Beats / Morning Lemon* [I] | $6 | | Astralwerks 6195 (CD) |

samples "Gucci Again" by Schooly D

| 9/27/97 | 122 | 1 | 2 Elektrobank ............................................................... *(2 remixes) / Not Another Drugstore / Don't Stop The Rock / These Beats Are Made For Breakin'* [I] | $6 | | Astralwerks 6204 (CD) |

**CHER**  HOT/AC/C&W/R&B
Born Cherilyn Sarkisian on 5/20/46 in El Centro, California. Adopted by stepfather at age 15 and last name changed to La Piere. Recorded with Sonny Bono as **Caesar & Cleo** in 1963, then as **Sonny & Cher** from 1965-73. Own TV series with Bono from 1971-77. Acclaimed movie actress (won Best Actress Oscar in 1987 for *Moonstruck*). *Top Pop Singles*: 30.

| 12/4/65 | 131 | 1 | 1 Love Is Strange ........................................................... *Let The Good Times Roll* | $20 | ■ | Reprise 0419 |

**Salvatore Bono & Cher LaPiere AKA CAESAR & CLEO**
#11 hit for Mickey & Sylvia in 1957; originally released in 1964 on Reprise 0308 ($25) and as the B-side of "Baby Don't Go" on Reprise 0392 (as Sonny & Cher-$15)

| 12/17/66 | 124 | 2 | 2 Mama (When My Dollies Have Babies)................................. *Dream Baby* | $8 | | Imperial 66223 |

written and produced by Sonny Bono

| 9/13/69 | 125 | 1 | 3 For What It's Worth............................... *(Just Enough To Keep Me)* Hangin' On | $6 | | Atco 6704 |

#7 hit for The Buffalo Springfield in 1967

| 5/12/73 | 111 | 1 | 4 Am I Blue ..................................................... *How Long Has This Been Going On* | $5 | | MCA 40039 |
| 12/4/93 | 108 | 1 | 5 I Got You Babe .................................................................. *Intro / Outro* [N] | $15 | | Geffen 4600 (CD) |

**CHER WITH BEAVIS AND BUTT-HEAD**
available only on a special promotional CD single; #1 hit for **Sonny & Cher** in 1965

**CHEROKEE — see ROBBS, The**

**CHERRY, Ava ☉**  R&B
R&B singer from Chicago. Toured with **David Bowie** from 1974-78.

| 3/15/80 | 107 | 1 | Love Is Good News........................................... R&B:39 *Gimme Your Lovin'* | $4 | | RSO/Curtom 1017 |

written and produced by **Curtis Mayfield**

45

| DEBUT | PEAK | WKS | A-side (Chart Hit)..........................................................................................................B-side | $ | Pic | Label & Number |
|-------|------|-----|--------------------------------------------------------------------------------------|---|-----|----------------|

**CHERRY, Don**         HOT/POP/MEM/AC/C&W
Born on 1/11/24 in Wichita Falls, Texas. Vocalist with Jan Garber band in the late '40s.

| 4/30/66 | 112 | 3 | 1 I Love You Drops........................................................................ *Don't Change* | $6 | | Monument 930 |
| | | | #30 hit for **Vic Dana** in 1966 | | | |
| 1/7/67 | 113 | 1 | 2 There Goes My Everything.................................................. *I Don't Wanna Go Home* | $6 | | Monument 989 |
| | | | #20 hit for **Engelbert Humperdinck** in 1967 | | | |

**CHERRY PEOPLE, The**         HOT
Pop-rock group: Dougy and Chris Grimes, Punky Meadows (of Angel), Rocky Isaac and Jan Zukowski.

| 3/15/69 | 134 | 2 | Feelings.................................................................................. *Mr. Hyde* | $8 | ■ | Heritage 810 |
| | | | #93 hit for **Barry Mann** in 1970 | | | |

**CHERRY SLUSH, The** ⊙
Rock group from Chicago featuring Dick Wagner.

| 2/24/68 | 119 | 3 | I Cannot Stop You.................................................................. *Don't Walk Away* | $20 | | U.S.A. 895 |
| | | | originally released on Coconut Grove 2032 in 1967 ($30) | | | |

**CHESNEY, Kenny** ⊙         C&W
Born on 3/26/68 in Knoxville; raised in Luttrell, Tennessee. Country singer.

| 10/26/96 | 112 | 6 | 1 Me And You......................................................... C&W:2 *I Finally Found Somebody* | $3 | ▌ | BNA 64589 |
| 8/2/97 | 110 | 7 | 2 She's Got It All............................................. C&W:❶³ *Lonely, Needin' Lovin'* | $3 | ▌ | BNA 64894 |

**CHESNUTT, Mark** ⊙         C&W
Born on 9/6/63 in Beaumont, Texas. Country singer. Son of regional Texas star Bob Chesnutt.

| 12/5/92 | 121 | 4 | 1 Bubba Shot The Jukebox................................................ C&W:4 *Blame It On Texas* | $3 | ▌ | MCA 54471 |
| 8/7/93 | 119 | 3 | 2 It Sure Is Monday ...................... C&W:❶¹ *I'm Not Getting Any Better At Goodbyes* | $3 | ▌ | MCA 54630 |

**CHEYNE** ⊙         R&B
Teenage female R&B singer.

| 6/15/85 | 106 | 1 | Call Me Mr. 'Telephone' (Answering Service) ........................... R&B:62 *(dub version)* | $3 | ■ | MCA 52576 |

**CHIC**         R&B/HOT/AC
R&B-disco group formed in New York City by prolific producers Bernard Edwards (bass; d: 4/18/96, age 43) and Nile Rodgers (guitar). Featured drummer Tony Thompson and vocalists Luci Martin and Norma Jean Wright.

| 1/12/80 | 101¹ | 3 | 1 My Feet Keep Dancing      R&B:42 *Will You Cry (When You Hear This Song)* | $4 | | Atlantic 3638 |
| 1/30/82 | 105 | 3 | 2 Stage Fright ................................................................... R&B:34 *So Fine* | $4 | | Atlantic 3887 |

**CHIFFONS, The**         HOT/R&B
Black female vocal group from the Bronx, New York: Judy Craig, Barbara Lee Jones (d: 5/15/92, age 48), Patricia Bennett and Sylvia Peterson.

| 3/21/64 | 105 | 4 | 1 Easy To Love (So Hard To Get) ............................................. *Tonight I Met An Angel* | $15 | | Laurie 3224 |
| 12/3/66 | 117 | 1 | 2 My Boyfriend's Back .................................................... *I Got Plenty O' Nuttin'* | $15 | | Laurie 3364 |
| | | | #1 hit for **The Angels** in 1963 | | | |

**CHILDREN, The** ⊙
Pop group led by singer Cassell Webb.

| 11/7/70 | 105 | 5 | From The Very Start ............................................................. *Such A Fine Night* | $12 | | Ode 66005 |

**CHI-LITES, The**         R&B/HOT/AC
R&B vocal group from Chicago: Eugene Record (lead), Robert "Squirrel" Lester (tenor), Marshall Thompson (baritone) and Creadel "Red" Jones (bass). Top Pop Singles: 23.

| 9/20/69 | 122 | 2 | 1 The Twelfth Of Never ..................... R&B:47 *Let Me Be The Man My Daddy Was* (Hot #94) | $8 | | Brunswick 55414 |
| | | | #9 hit for **Johnny Mathis** in 1957 | | | |
| 3/14/70 | 119 | 2 | 2 24 Hours Of Sadness .................... R&B:30 *You're No Longer Part Of My Heart* | $8 | | Brunswick 55426 |

**CHILLIWACK**         HOT/ROK
Rock band formed in Vancouver in 1969: Bill Henderson (vocals, guitar), Ab Bryant (bass) and Brian MacLeod (drums).

| 1/24/76 | 109 | 3 | 1 Last Day Of December.......................................................... *Magnolia* | $5 | | Sire 723 |
| 12/10/77 | 110 | 2 | 2 Baby Blue........................................................................ *Something Better* | $5 | | Mushroom 7028 |
| 3/12/83 | 110 | 2 | 3 Secret Information ............................................................. *You're Gonna Last* | $4 | | Millennium 13117 |

**CHILLY** ⊙
Two-man, two-woman disco group.

| 5/19/79 | 108 | 1 | For Your Love ..................................................................... *C'mon Baby* | $5 | | Polydor 14552 |
| | | | #6 hit for **The Yardbirds** in 1965 | | | |

**CHIPMUNKS, The**         HOT/AC/R&B/C&W
Cartoon characters Alvin, Simon and Theodore created by Ross Bagdasarian ("David Seville"). Bagdasarian died on 1/16/72 (age 52). His son, Ross Jr., resurrected the act in 1980.

| 11/7/64 | 134 | 1 | 1 All My Loving ............................... *Do You Want To Know A Secret* [N] | $15 | ■ | Liberty 55734 |
| | | | #45 hit for **The Beatles** in 1964 | | | |
| 8/9/80 | 101¹ | 10 | 2 You May Be Right      *Crazy Little Thing Called Love* [N] | $4 | | Excelsior 1001 |
| | | | #7 hit for **Billy Joel** in 1980 | | | |

**CHOCOLATE MILK**         R&B/HOT
R&B group from New Orleans: Frank Richard (vocals), Mario Tio (guitar), Robert Dabon (keyboards), Amadee Castanell (sax), Joe Foxx (trumpet) and Dwight Richards (drums).

| 6/10/78 | 103 | 1 | Girl Callin' .................................................................. R&B:14 *Thinking Of You* | $5 | | RCA 11222 |

**CHOCOLATE SYRUP** ⊙         R&B
Group consisted of **Jimmy Holiday**, L.J. Reynolds, Lenny Wolfe, Carl Smith and Norris Harris.

| 12/18/71 | 104 | 2 | Let One Hurt Do.................................................... R&B:31 *Stay With Me* | $8 | | Law-ton 1553 |
| | | | **L.J. REYNOLDS & CHOCOLATE SYRUP** | | | |

**CHOICE FOUR, The**         R&B/HOT
R&B vocal group from Washington, D.C.: Bobby Hamilton (lead), Ted Maduro, Pete Marshall and Charles Blagmore.

| 5/1/76 | 107 | 1 | 1 Hey, What's That Dance You're Doing ...................................... R&B:57 *Beside Me* | $5 | | RCA Victor 10602 |
| 6/12/76 | 107 | 1 | 2 A Time For Celebration ............................................................. *(long version)* | $5 | | RCA Victor 10686 |
| | | | **FAITH, HOPE & CHARITY WITH THE CHOICE FOUR** | | | |
| | | | a tribute to America's bicentennial anniversary | | | |

## CHORDETTES, The
HOT/AC

Pop female vocal group formed in 1946 in Sheboygan, Wisconsin: Janet Ertel (bass; d: 11/22/88), Carol Buschman (baritone), Dorothy Schwartz (lead) and Jinny Lockard (tenor).

| | | | | | | |
|---|---|---|---|---|---|---|
| 8/8/60 | 102 | 1 | A Broken Vow ............................................................ *All My Sorrows* | $12 | | Cadence 1382 |

Archie Bleyer (orch.)

## CHRIS and KATHY — see MONTEZ, Chris

## CHRISTIE, Lou
HOT/AC/R&B

Born Lugee Sacco on 2/19/43 in Glen Willard, Pennsylvania. Famous for his falsetto vocals.

| | | | | | | |
|---|---|---|---|---|---|---|
| 10/19/63 | 119 | 3 | 1 Shy Boy ................................................................. *It Can Happen* | $15 | | Roulette 4527 |
| 8/22/64 | 123 | 3 | 2 Guitars And Bongos................................................. *Merry-Go-Round* | $15 | | Colpix 735 |
| 9/17/66 | 118 | 2 | 3 If My Car Could Only Talk ........................................ *Song Of Lita* | $10 | ■ | MGM 13576 |
| 12/3/66 | 102 | 4 | 4 Since I Don't Have You .............. *Wild Life's Season* | $10 | | MGM 13623 |

#12 hit for The Skyliners in 1959

| | | | | | | |
|---|---|---|---|---|---|---|
| 11/28/70 | 106 | 2 | 5 Indian Lady ....................................... AC:39 *Glory River* | $8 | | Buddah 192 |

## CHRISTIE, Tony ⊙
Born on 4/25/44 in Yorkshire, England. Pop singer.

| | | | | | | |
|---|---|---|---|---|---|---|
| 3/25/72 | 121 | 1 | (Is This The Way To) Amarillo ...................... *Love Is A Friend Of Mine* | $6 | | Kapp 2161 |

#44 hit for Neil Sedaka in 1977

## CHRISTIÓN
R&B/HOT

R&B vocal duo from Oakland, California: Kenny Ski and Allen Anthony.

| | | | | | | |
|---|---|---|---|---|---|---|
| 10/4/97 | 111 | 4 | Bring Back Your Love ...................................... R&B:67 *Pimp This Love* | $3 | ■ | Roc-A-Fella 571592 |

## CHRISTY, Lauren
AC

Born on 11/19/67 in London. Female singer. As a teen, studied at the Bush Davies Ballet School.

| | | | | | | |
|---|---|---|---|---|---|---|
| 9/24/94 | 107 | 6 | The Color Of The Night ................... AC:24 *(original version)* | $3 | ■ | Mercury 858616 |

title song from the movie starring Bruce Willis

## CHURCH, Eugene
R&B/HOT

Born on 1/23/38 in St. Louis; raised in Los Angeles. Died on 4/16/93 from AIDS. Recorded with Jesse Belvin as The Cliques.

| | | | | | | |
|---|---|---|---|---|---|---|
| 11/14/60 | 106 | 4 | Good News ................................................................ *Polly* | $15 | | Rendezvous 132 |

## CHURCH STREET FIVE, The ⊙
R&B band from New Orleans led by Gene "Daddy G" Barge.

| | | | | | | |
|---|---|---|---|---|---|---|
| 2/20/61 | 111 | 2 | A Night With Daddy "G" Part 2 ............................(Part 1) [I] | $20 | | Legrand 1004 |

Gary U.S. Bonds added words to this instrumental for his #1 hit "Quarter To Three" in 1961

## CINDERELLAS, The ⊙
Female R&B vocal group led by Margaret Ross (formerly with The Cookies).

| | | | | | | |
|---|---|---|---|---|---|---|
| 5/23/64 | 134 | 1 | Baby, Baby (I Still Love You)...................... *Please Don't Wake Me* | $40 | | Dimension 1026 |

## C.J. & CO.
R&B

Disco group from Detroit: Cornelius Brown Jr., Curtis Durden, Joni Tolbert, Connie Durden and Charles Clark. Assembled by Dennis Coffey.

| | | | | | | |
|---|---|---|---|---|---|---|
| 7/22/78 | 106 | 1 | Big City Sidewalk .................................. *Call Me If You Need Me* | $5 | | Westbound 55412 |

## CLANTON, Jimmy
HOT/R&B

Born on 9/2/40 in Baton Rouge, Louisiana. Rock and roll teen idol, late '50s-early '60s. Starred in the movie Go, Johnny, Go!.

| | | | | | | |
|---|---|---|---|---|---|---|
| 12/21/63 | 115 | 6 | Red Don't Go With Blue ............................ *All The Words In The World* | $10 | | Philips 40161 |

## CLAPTON, Eric
ROK/HOT/AC/R&B/C&W

Born Eric Patrick Clapp on 3/30/45 in Ripley, England. Prolific rock-blues guitarist/vocalist. With The Yardbirds, 1963-65, and John Mayall's Bluesbreakers, 1965-66. Formed Cream in 1966, Blind Faith in 1968 and Derek & The Dominos in 1970. Top Pop Singles: 27.

| | | | | | | |
|---|---|---|---|---|---|---|
| 4/11/70 | 128 | 1 | 1 Teasin' ...................................................... *Soulin'* (Curtis) [I] | $8 | | Atco 6738 |

**KING CURTIS With Delaney Bramlett, Eric Clapton & Friends**

| | | | | | | |
|---|---|---|---|---|---|---|
| 3/3/73 | 120 | 1 | 2 Why Does Love Got To Be So Sad ........................ *Presence Of The Lord* | $6 | | RSO 400 |

**DEREK & THE DOMINOS**

| | | | | | | |
|---|---|---|---|---|---|---|
| 10/22/94 | 114 | 6 | 3 Motherless Child ...................................... ROK:23 *Driftin'* | $3 | ■ | Duck/Reprise 18044 |

## CLARK, Chris ⊙
R&B

Born in 1946 in Los Angeles. Female R&B vocalist. Worked as a receptionist at Motown. TV writer since 1969.

| | | | | | | |
|---|---|---|---|---|---|---|
| 10/1/66 | 105 | 4 | 1 Love's Gone Bad ..................................... R&B:41 *Put Yourself In My Place* | $15 | | V.I.P. 25038 |

some pressings show title as "Love's Gone Mad" ($60)

| | | | | | | |
|---|---|---|---|---|---|---|
| 4/8/67 | 114 | 3 | 2 I Want To Go Back There Again ............................ *I Love You* | $15 | | V.I.P. 25041 |

## CLARK, Dave, Five
HOT

Rock group formed in 1960 in Tottenham, England: Dave Clark (drums), Mike Smith (vocals, keyboards), Lenny Davidson (guitar), Denny Payton (sax) and Rick Huxley (bass). First recorded for Ember/Pye in 1962. Top Pop Singles: 24.

| | | | | | | |
|---|---|---|---|---|---|---|
| 4/17/65 | 128 | 1 | 1 I'm Thinking................................ *Reelin' And Rockin'* (Hot #23) | $15 | | Epic 9786 |
| 6/4/66 | 101[2] | 4 | 2 Look Before You Leap | *Please Tell Me Why* (Hot #28) | $15 | ■ | Epic 10031 |
| 5/18/68 | 115 | 4 | 3 Please Stay.................................................. *Forget* | $15 | | Epic 10325 |

#14 hit for The Drifters in 1961

## CLARK, Dee
HOT/R&B

Born Delecta Clark on 11/7/38 in Blytheville, Arkansas. Died on 12/7/90. Male R&B singer. First solo recording for Falcon in 1957.

| | | | | | | |
|---|---|---|---|---|---|---|
| 11/30/59 | 109 | 1 | 1 Blues Get Off My Shoulder ........................ *How About That* (Hot #33) | $20 | | Abner 1032 |
| 1/9/61 | 105 | 4 | 2 Because I Love You ................................ *Your Friends* (Hot #34) | $15 | | Vee-Jay 372 |
| 10/30/61 | 104 | 7 | 3 Don't Walk Away From Me ...................... *You're Telling Our Secrets* | $15 | | Vee-Jay 409 |
| 3/16/63 | 125 | 1 | 4 Shook Up Over You .................................... *I'm A Soldier Boy* | $15 | | Vee-Jay 487 |
| 8/22/64 | 119 | 5 | 5 Heartbreak .......................................... *Warm Summer Breezes* | $15 | | Constellation 132 |
| 4/10/65 | 132 | 1 | 6 T.C.B. .............................................. *It's Impossible* | $15 | | Constellation 147 |

T.C.B.: Take Care of Business

## CLARK, Michael ⊙

| | | | | | | |
|---|---|---|---|---|---|---|
| 3/23/63 | 130 | 1 | Work Out............................................... *None Of These Girls* | $15 | | Imperial 5893 |

| DEBUT | PEAK | WKS | A-side (Chart Hit) | $ | Pic | Label & Number |
|---|---|---|---|---|---|---|
| | | | **CLARK, Robin** ⊙ | | | |
| | | | Twelve-year-old female singer from Nashville. | | | |
| 3/13/61 | 120 | 1 | **Daddy, Daddy (Gotta Get A Phone In My Room)** .................*Love Has Come My Way* [N] | $12 | | Capitol 4503 |
| | | | **CLARK, Roy**         C&W/AC/HOT | | | |
| | | | Born on 4/15/33 in Meherrin, Virginia. Superb guitar, banjo and fiddle player. With the TV series *Hee Haw* from the first show in 1969. | | | |
| 1/25/64 | 128 | 2 | 1 **Through The Eyes Of A Fool**.....................C&W:31 *Sweet Violets* | $8 | | Capitol 5099 |
| | | | written by **Bobby Bare** | | | |
| 9/13/69 | 103 | 6 | 2 **September Song** .........................AC:12 /C&W:40 *For The Life Of Me* | $6 | | Dot 17299 |
| | | | #12 hit for Walter Huston in 1939; #51 hit for **Jimmy Durante** in 1963 | | | |
| 11/29/69 | 123 | 2 | 3 **Right Or Left At Oak Street** ....................C&W:21 *I Need To Be Needed* | $6 | | Dot 17324 |
| 6/13/70 | 122 | 1 | 4 **I Never Picked Cotton** ...............................C&W:5 *Lonesome Too Long* | $6 | | Dot 17349 |
| | | | **CLARK, Terri** ⊙         C&W | | | |
| | | | Born on 8/5/68 in Montreal; raised in Medicine Hat, Alberta, Canada. Female country singer. | | | |
| 1/13/96 | 122 | 2 | 1 **When Boy Meets Girl** ..................................*Flowers After The Fact* | $3 | ■ | Mercury 852388 |
| 5/11/96 | 113 | 4 | 2 **If I Were You** .....................................C&W:8 *Something You Should've Said* | $3 | ■ | Mercury 852708 |
| 11/9/96+ | 109 | 13 | 3 **Poor, Poor Pitiful Me** ...............C&W:5 *Something You Should've Said* | $3 | ■ | Mercury 578644 |
| | | | #31 hit for **Linda Ronstadt** in 1978 | | | |
| 3/8/97 | 113 | 7 | 4 **Emotional Girl**...........................C&W:10 *Something In The Water* | $3 | ■ | Mercury 574016 |
| | | | **CLASSICS, The**         HOT/R&B/AC | | | |
| | | | White doo-wop quartet from Brooklyn: Emil Stucchio (lead), Johnny Gambale, Tony Victor and Jamie Troy. First known as the Perennials. First recorded for Dart in 1959. | | | |
| 11/28/60 | 109 | 2 | 1 **Cinderella** ....................................................*So In Love* | $75 | | Dart 1015 |
| | | | first pressings show label address as Fairlawn, New Jersey | | | |
| 6/5/61 | 109 | 6 | 2 **Life Is But A Dream Sweetheart**...........R&B:27 *That's The Way* | $40 | | Mercury 71829 |
| | | | originally released on Dart 1024 ($200) in 1961 | | | |
| 9/21/63 | 120 | 3 | 3 **P.S. I Love You** .................*Wrap Your Troubles In Dreams (And Dream Your Troubles Away)* | $30 | | MusicNote 118 |
| | | | #12 hit for Rudy Vallee in 1934; #4 hit for The Hilltoppers in 1953 | | | |
| | | | **CLASSICS IV**         HOT/AC | | | |
| | | | Soft-rock quintet formed in Jacksonville, Florida: Dennis Yost (vocals), J.R. Cobb (lead guitar), Wally Eaton (rhythm guitar), Joe Wilson (bass) and Kim Venable (drums). | | | |
| 9/17/66 | 106 | 6 | 1 **Pollyanna** .................................................*Cry Baby* | $20 | | Capitol 5710 |
| | | | **THE CLASSICS** | | | |
| | | | written by **Joe South**; similar vocal style as a **4 Seasons'** recording | | | |
| 7/18/70 | 128 | 1 | 2 **God Knows I Loved Her** .........................*We Miss You* | $6 | | Liberty 56182 |
| | | | **DENNIS YOST & THE CLASSICS IV** | | | |
| | | | **CLAY, Cassius** ⊙ | | | |
| | | | Born on 1/18/42 in Louisville, Kentucky. Former world heavyweight boxing champ. Changed name to Muhammad Ali in 1966. | | | |
| 3/21/64 | 102 | 4 | 1 **Stand By Me/** | | | |
| | | | #4 hit for **Ben E. King** in 1961 | | | |
| 3/21/64 | 113 | 2 | 2 **I Am The Greatest**.......................................[N] | $25 | ■ | Columbia 43007 |
| | | | The Champ "raps" to a live audience and a musical background | | | |
| | | | **CLAY, Judy**         R&B/HOT | | | |
| | | | Real name: Judy Guion. Native of Fayetteville, North Carolina. R&B singer; sang background for many top R&B artists. | | | |
| 6/8/68 | 107 | 2 | 1 **When Do We Go** .......................................*Even Since* | $10 | | Atlantic 2515 |
| | | | **BILLY VERA & JUDY CLAY** | | | |
| 12/28/68 | 104 | 4 | 2 **My Baby Specializes** ....................R&B:45 *Left Over Love* | $10 | | Stax 0017 |
| | | | **WILLIAM BELL & JUDY CLAY** | | | |
| 4/18/70 | 122 | 2 | 3 **Greatest Love** ..........................R&B:45 *Saving All For You* | $10 | | Atlantic 2697 |
| | | | **CLAY, Otis**         R&B/HOT | | | |
| | | | Born on 2/11/42 in Waxhaw, Mississippi. To Chicago in 1957. Soul singer. | | | |
| 4/16/66 | 105 | 4 | 1 **I'm Satisfied** ..........................................*I Testify* | $10 | | One-derful! 4841 |
| 9/2/67 | 131 | 1 | 2 **That's How It Is (When You're In Love)** ...........R&B:34 *Show Place* | $10 | | One-derful! 4848 |
| 1/6/73 | 102 | 8 | 3 **Trying To Live My Life Without You** ...............R&B:24 *Let Me Be The One* | $8 | | Hi 2226 |
| | | | #5 hit for **Bob Seger** in 1981 | | | |
| | | | **CLAYTON, Merry**         R&B/HOT/AC | | | |
| | | | Real name: Mary Clayton. R&B backing vocalist from Los Angeles. In **The Raeletts**, **Ray Charles**'s backing group. Also see **Sisters Love**. | | | |
| 10/10/70 | 103 | 4 | **Country Road** .........................................*Forget It, I Got It* | $6 | | Ode 66007 |
| | | | #37 hit for **James Taylor** in 1971 | | | |
| | | | **CLAYTON THOMAS, David** ⊙         AC | | | |
| | | | Born David Thomsett on 9/13/41 in England. Lead singer of **Blood, Sweat & Tears**. | | | |
| 4/1/72 | 112 | 2 | **Sing A Song**...................................*We're All Meat From The Same Bone* | $6 | | Columbia 45569 |
| | | | **CLEFS OF LAVENDER HILL**         HOT | | | |
| | | | Rock group from Miami: brothers Fred and Bill Moss with Joseph Ximenes and his sister Lorraine. | | | |
| 10/8/66 | 114 | 2 | **One More Time** .......................................*So I'll Try* | $20 | | Date 1530 |
| | | | **CLEVELAND, James** ⊙ | | | |
| | | | Born on 12/23/32 in Chicago. Died on 2/9/91 of heart failure. Recorded with more than a dozen different choirs and gospel groups. | | | |
| 8/6/66 | 129 | 1 | **Without A Song (Part 1)**.....................................*(Part 2)* | $15 | | Savoy 4269 |
| | | | **JAMES CLEVELAND and the CLEVELAND SINGERS** | | | |
| | | | #6 hit for Paul Whiteman's Orchestra in 1930; #77 hit for **Roy Hamilton** in 1955 | | | |
| | | | **CLICK, The**         R&B/HOT | | | |
| | | | Collaboration of rappers: E-40, B-Legit, Suga T and D-Shot. | | | |
| 3/30/96 | 101[1] | 9 | **Scandalous**     Sls:72 /R&B:49 *Wolf Tickets / (album snippets)* | $3 | ■ | Sick Wid' It/Jive 42366 |
| | | | samples "Computer Love" by **Zapp** | | | |

### CLIFF, Jimmy      R&B/HOT/AC
Born James Chambers on 4/1/48 in St. James, Jamaica. Reggae singer/composer. Starred in the movies *The Harder They Come* and *Club Paradise*.

| DEBUT | PEAK | WKS | A-side | B-side | $ | Pic | Label & Number |
|---|---|---|---|---|---|---|---|
| 2/12/94 | 117 | 4 | 1 **(Your Love Keeps Liftin' Me) Higher And Higher** .........................(same version) | | $3 | ∎ | Interscope 98320 |

JIMMY CLIFF with SOULDA POP
from the movie *The Air Up There* starring Kevin Bacon; #6 hit for **Jackie Wilson** in 1967

| 5/6/95 | 105 | 6 | 2 **Hakuna Matata** ........................................ AC:26 (album version) | | $3 | ∎ | Walt Disney 60341 |

JIMMY CLIFF featuring LEBO M
co-written by **Elton John**; from the Disney animated movie *The Lion King*

### CLIFFORD, Buzz      HOT/R&B/C&W
Born Reese Francis Clifford III on 10/8/42 in Berwyn, Illinois. Pop teen idol, early '60s.

| 4/10/61 | 102 | 4 | **Three Little Fishes** ..................................................... *Simply Because* | $25 | ∎ | Columbia 41979 |

Jack Pleis (orch.); #1 hit for Kay Kyser's Orchestra in 1939

### CLIMAX BLUES BAND      HOT/AC
Blues-rock band formed in Stafford, England: Colin Cooper (sax, vocals), Peter Haycock (guitar, vocals), Derek Holt (bass) and John Cuffley (drums).

| 11/15/75 | 110 | 1 | **Using The Power**.................................................... *Running Out Of Time* | $6 | | Sire 721 |

### CLINE, Patsy      C&W/HOT/AC
Born Virginia Patterson Hensley on 9/8/32 in Gore, Virginia. Killed in a plane crash on 3/5/63. Elected to the Country Music Hall of Fame in 1973. Won Grammy's Lifetime Achievement Award in 1995.

| 7/21/62 | 107 | 3 | 1 **You're Stronger Than Me** ........................................ *So Wrong* (Hot #85) | $10 | | Decca 31406 |
| 10/27/62 | 103 | 2 | 2 **Why Can't He Be You** ........................................ *Heartaches* (Hot #73) | $10 | | Decca 31429 |
| 3/30/63 | 108 | 3 | 3 **Walking After Midnight** ................................ *That Wonderful Someone* [R] | $10 | ∎ | Everest 2020 |

same version as Cline's #12 *Top 100* hit in 1957 on Decca 30221 ($20); picture sleeve has a center-cut hole and states "Patsy Cline's On Everest"

| 3/14/64 | 123 | 3 | 4 **Someday You'll Want Me To Want You** ........................ *Your Kinda Love* | $10 | | Decca 31588 |

#5 hit for The Mills Brothers in 1949; #95 hit for Jodie Sands in 1958

### CLINTON, Buddy ☺

| 12/31/60 | 115 | 1 | **Take Me To Your Ladder (I'll See Your Leader Later)**................... *Joanie's Forever* [N] | $15 | | Madison 144 |

## CLINTON, George — see PARLIAMENT

### CLIQUE, The      HOT
Pop-rock quintet from Beaumont, Texas: Randy Shaw, David Dunham, Sid Templeton, Tommy Pena, John Kanesaw and Jerry "Function" Cope.

| 10/7/67 | 113 | 3 | **Splash 1** ..................................................................... *Stay By Me* | $20 | | Scepter 12202 |

### CLOONEY, Rosemary      MEM/POP/HOT/AC
Born on 5/23/28 in Maysville, Kentucky. Acted in several movies including *White Christmas*. Her nephew, George Clooney, is a popular TV and movie actor. *Pop Hits & Top Pop Singles*: 25.

| 11/6/61 | 108 | 5 | **Give Myself A Party** ........................ *If I Can Stay Away Long Enough* | $10 | | RCA Victor 7948 |

#46 hit for **Don Gibson** in 1958

### CLOVERS, The      R&B/HOT
R&B vocal group from Washington, D.C.: John "Buddy" Bailey (lead), Matthew McQuater, Harold Lucas (d: 1/6/94, age 61), Harold Winley, Bill Harris (d: 12/10/88, age 63) and Billy Mitchell.

| 5/22/61 | 110 | 1 | 1 **The Honeydripper** ............................................... *Have Gun* | $25 | | United Artists 307 |

#1 R&B hit (for 18 weeks) for Joe Liggins in 1945

| 8/17/63 | 134 | 1 | 2 **Stop Pretending** ............................... *One More Time (Come On)* | $25 | | Porwin 1002 |

THE CLOVERS featuring Buddy Bailey

### CLYDE AND THE BLUE JAYS ☺
R&B vocal group.

| 11/14/64 | 134 | 1 | **The Big Jerk - Pt. I** ........................................................ *Pt. II* | $15 | | Loma 2003 |

released at the same time as **The Larks'** hit version of "The Jerk"

### COACHMEN, The ☺
Five-man garage rock band from Lincoln, Nebraska: Jeff Travis, Craig Perkins, Kelly Kotera, Frank Elia and Bruce Watson. Hit the *Hot 100* in 1968 as Professor Morrison's Lollipop.

| 2/19/66 | 114 | 5 | **Mr. Moon** ................................................................... *Nothing At All* | $20 | | Bear 1974 |

### COASTLINERS, The ☺
Houston-based, surf-rock group. Leader Rex Kramer later joined **The New Christy Minstrels**.

| 10/15/66 | 121 | 2 | 1 **She's My Girl** ........................................................ *I'll Be Gone* | $25 | | Back Beat 566 |
| 4/8/67 | 115 | 1 | 2 **California On My Mind** ............................................ *I See Me* | $20 | | D.E.A.R. 1300 |

### COBB, Joyce      HOT/R&B
Born in Okmulgee, Oklahoma. Later based in Memphis. R&B singer/songwriter.

| 8/16/80 | 107 | 6 | **How Glad I Am** ........................ R&B:90 *That's What Love Will Do* | $4 | | Cream 8040 |

#11 hit for **Nancy Wilson** in 1964

### COBERT, Robert, Orchestra ☺
Prolific TV/movie score composer. Graduate of Julliard.

| 8/16/69 | 125 | 2 | **Shadows Of The Night (Quentin's Theme)** ............*I'll Be With You, Always* [S] | $6 | | Philips 40633 |

from the cult daytime TV serial *Dark Shadows*; recitation by David Selby (Quentin); #13 hit for **The Charles Randolph Grean Sounde** in 1969

### COCHRAN, Eddie      HOT/R&B
Born Edward Ray Cochran on 10/3/38 in Oklahoma City; raised in Minnesota. Killed in a car accident in England on 4/17/60; accident also injured Gene Vincent. Influential rock and roll singer/guitarist. Inducted into the Rock and Roll Hall of Fame in 1987.

| 6/6/60 | 108 | 1 | **Three Steps To Heaven** ........................................ *Cut Across Shorty* | $30 | | Liberty 55242 |

### COCHRAN, Wayne ☺
Born in Thompson, Georgia. Flamboyant rock and roll singer, with the C.C. Riders.

| 12/25/65 | 127 | 3 | **Harlem Shuffle** ................................................ *Somebody Please* | $15 | ∎ | Mercury 72507 |

#44 hit for **Bob & Earl** in 1964; #5 hit for **The Rolling Stones** in 1986

**COCHRANE, Tom**    ROK/HOT/AC
Born on 5/13/53 in Lynn Lake, Manitoba, Canada. Toronto-based rock singer/songwriter. Formed **Red Rider** in 1976.

| 11/18/95 | 101[1] | 3 | I Wish You Well                                        *(same version)* | $3 | ■ | Capitol 58505 |

**COCKBURN, Bruce**    ROK/HOT/AC
Cockburn (pronounced: CO-burn) was born on 5/27/45 in Canada. Pop-rock singer/songwriter.

| 10/25/80 | 104 | 4 | Rumours Of Glory .................................................. *You Get Bigger As You Go* | $4 | | Millennium 11795 |

**COCKER, Joe**    HOT/ROK/AC
Born John Robert Cocker on 5/20/44 in Sheffield, England. Notable spastic stage antics were based on **Ray Charles**'s movements at the piano. *Top Pop Singles*: 22.

| 6/18/83 | 104 | 5 | Threw It Away ........................................................... *Easy Rider* | $3 | | Island 99875 |

**COCONUTS, The — see KID CREOLE**

**CODAY, Bill** ☺    R&B
R&B singer from Chicago, produced by **Willie Mitchell**.

| 2/13/71 | 120 | 3 | 1 Get Your Lie Straight ............................... R&B:23 *You're Gonna Want Me* | $12 | | Crajon 48204 |
| 3/13/71 | 105 | 5 | 2 Get Your Lie Straight ............................... R&B:14 *You're Gonna Want Me* | $10 | | Galaxy 777 |
|  |  |  | above 2 are the same version | | | |

**C.O.D.'s, The**    HOT/R&B
R&B group from Chicago: Larry Brownlee (d: 1978; **The Lost Generation**), Robert Lewis and Carl Washington.

| 4/2/66 | 128 | 1 | I'm A Good Guy ........................................................ *Pretty Baby* | $12 | | Kellmac 1005 |

**COHN, Marc**    HOT/AC/ROK/C&W
Born on 7/5/59 in Cleveland. Won the 1991 Best New Artist Grammy Award.

| 6/5/93 | 121 | 1 | Walk Through The World ..................................... AC:27 *From the Station* | $3 | ■ | Atlantic 87350 |

**COLD BLOOD**    HOT
Rock group from San Francisco. Core members: Lydia Pense (vocals), Raul Matute (piano), Rod Ellicott (bass) and Danny Hull (sax).

| 3/28/70 | 125 | 3 | 1 I'm A Good Woman ............................. *I Wish I Knew How It Would Feel To Be Free* | $6 | | San Francisco 61 |
| 10/3/70 | 107 | 5 | 2 Too Many People ........................................................ *I Can't Stay* | $6 | | San Francisco 62 |

**COLDER, Ben**    C&W/HOT
Born Shelby F. Wooley on 4/10/21 near Erick, Oklahoma. Singer/songwriter/actor. Ben Colder is his comical pseudonym. Played "Pete Nolan" in the TV series *Rawhide*. Acted in the movies *High Noon*, *Rocky Mountain*, *Giant* and *Hoosiers*.

| 3/16/63 | 131 | 1 | Hello Wall No. 2 ..................................... C&W:30 *Shudders And Screams* [N] | $8 | | MGM 13122 |
|  |  |  | parody of **Faron Young**'s "Hello Walls" | | | |

**COLE, Cozy**    HOT/R&B
Born William Randolph Cole on 10/17/09 in East Orange, New Jersey. Died of cancer on 1/29/81. Lead drummer for many swing bands.

| 1/26/63 | 121 | 1 | Big Noise From Winnetka Part I ................................... *Part II* [I] | $12 | | Coral 62339 |
|  |  |  | Henry Jerome (orch.); played by Bob Crosby's band in the 1940 movie *Let's Make Music* starring Crosby | | | |

**COLE, Don & Alleyne** ☺
Don Cole was a trombone player with Erskine Hawkins and Lucky Millinder.

| 8/15/64 | 117 | 4 | Something's Got A Hold Of Me .......................... *Gotta Find My Baby* | $15 | | Tollie 9015 |
|  |  |  | recorded "live" at the Whiskey A Go-Go; #37 hit for **Etta James** in 1962 | | | |

**COLE, Jude**    AC/HOT/ROK
Native of East Moline, Illinois. Male guitarist/vocalist of **Moon Martin**'s band. Touring guitarist with **Billy Thorpe**, **Del Shannon** and **Dwight Twilley**.

| 7/17/93 | 123 | 1 | Worlds Apart ........................................ AC:37 *First Your Money (Then Your Clothes)* | $3 | ■ | Reprise 18509 |
|  |  |  | Tommy **Shaw** and Jack **Blades** (both w/Damn Yankees; backing vocals) | | | |

**COLE, Natalie**    R&B/AC/HOT
Born on 2/6/50 in Los Angeles. Daughter of **Nat "King" Cole**. Won the 1975 Best New Artist Grammy Award. Hosted own syndicated variety TV show *Big Break* in 1990.

| 3/24/79 | 108 | 2 | 1 Stand By .................................................. R&B:9 *Who Will Carry On* | $4 | | Capitol 4690 |
| 6/23/79 | 109 | 2 | 2 Sorry ...................................................... R&B:34 *You're So Good* | $4 | | Capitol 4722 |
| 12/22/79 | 102 | 5 | 3 Gimme Some Time ................................... R&B:8 *Love Will Find You* | $4 | | Capitol 4804 |
|  |  |  | **NATALIE COLE & PEABO BRYSON** | | | |

**COLE, Nat King**    HOT/MEM/R&B/POP/AC/C&W
Born Nathaniel Adams Coles on 3/17/17 in Montgomery, Alabama; raised in Chicago. Died of lung cancer on 2/15/65. Formed The King Cole Trio in 1939. The first major African-American performer to star in a network (NBC) TV variety series (1956-57). Won Grammy's Lifetime Achievement Award in 1990. *Pop Hits* & *Top Pop Singles*: 104.

| 4/18/60 | 101[1] | 4 | 1 That's You                       *Is It Better To Have Loved And Lost* | $12 | | Capitol 4369 |
|  |  |  | Nelson Riddle (orch.) | | | |
| 3/6/61 | 108 | 4 | 2 Illusion ...................................................... *When It's Summer* | $12 | | Capitol 4519 |
| 10/9/61 | 115 | 1 | 3 Cappuccina ..................................... *Let True Love Begin* (Hot #73) | $12 | | Capitol 4623 |
|  |  |  | Richard Wess (orch.) | | | |
| 1/20/62 | 106 | 4 | 4 Step Right Up (And Say You Love Me) ........................ *Magic Moment* | $12 | | Capitol 4672 |
| 3/31/62 | 110 | 3 | 5 The Right Thing To Say ...................................... *Look No Further* | $10 | | Capitol 4714 |
| 7/18/64 | 102 | 3 | 6 More And More Of Your Amor ................................... *Marnie* | $10 | | Capitol 5219 |
|  |  |  | Ralph Carmichael (orch.: #2 & 4-6) | | | |
| 12/11/65 | 123 | 5 | 7 Looking Back .................................................. AC:27 *One Sun* [R] | $10 | | Capitol 5549 |
|  |  |  | Dave Cavanaugh (orch.); new version of his #5 1958 hit on Capitol 3939 | | | |

**COLLEY, Keith**    HOT
Pop singer from Connell, Washington. Later a record executive with the Challenge label.

| 12/28/63 | 122 | 1 | Queridita Mia (Little Darlin') ................................. *Ramblin' Bee* [F] | $12 | | Unical 3011 |
|  |  |  | Spanish version of The Diamonds'/The Gladiolas' "Little Darlin'"; includes a spoken interlude in English | | | |

**COLLINS, Judy**    AC/HOT/C&W
Born on 5/1/39 in Seattle. Contemporary folk singer/songwriter. Signed to Elektra in 1961.

| 6/9/73 | 122 | 1 | Secret Gardens ........................................................ *The Hostage* | $6 | | Elektra 45849 |

| DEBUT | PEAK | WKS | A-side (Chart Hit)..........................................................................B-side | $ | Pic | Label & Number |
|---|---|---|---|---|---|---|

**COLLINS, Phil** — HOT/AC/ROK/R&B
Born on 1/30/51 in London. Pop/rock vocalist/multi-instrumentalist/composer. Joined Genesis as its drummer in 1970, became lead singer in 1975. *Top Pop Singles: 25.*

| 10/20/84 | 102 | 6 | 1 **In The Air Tonight**................................................*I Missed Again* [R] | $5 | | Atlantic 13231 |

originally made the *Hot 100* (#19) on 5/30/81 on Atlantic 3824; re-popularized through play on TV's *Miami Vice*; label is Atlantic's Oldies Series

| 4/30/94 | 125 | 1 | 2 **We Wait And We Wonder**.............................*Can't Turn Back The Years* | $3 | ■ | Atlantic 87238 |

**COLLINS, Rodger** ۞ — R&B
R&B singer from Oakland.

| 1/28/67 | 101² | 13 | **She's Looking Good** — R&B:44 *I'm Serving Time* | $12 | | Galaxy 750 |

#15 hit for **Wilson Pickett** in 1968

**COLLINS, Tommy** ۞ — C&W
Born Leonard Raymond Sipes on 9/28/30 in Bethany, Oklahoma. Joined **Buck Owens'** show in 1964. **Merle Haggard**'s song "Leonard" was about Collins.

| 2/5/66 | 105 | 7 | **If You Can't Bite, Don't Growl** ........................C&W:7 *Man Machine* | $10 | | Columbia 43489 |

**COLLINS, William "Bootsy"** — see PARLIAMENT

**COLOR ME BADD** — HOT/R&B/AC
New York City-based dance/vocal quartet: Bryan Abrams, Sam Watters, Mark Calderon and Kevin Thornton.

| 5/7/94 | 115 | 2 | 1 **Let's Start With Forever** ..........................................*(instrumental)* | $3 | ■ | Giant 18200 |
| 9/28/96 | 121 | 2 | 2 **Sexual Capacity** ..........................................*Ain't Nobody Goin' Home* | $3 | ■ | Giant 17624 |

from the movie *Striptease* starring Demi Moore

**COLOURS** ۞
British pop/rock quintet: Jack Dalton (guitar), Gary Montgomery (piano), Rob Edwards (guitar), Carl Radle (bass) and Chuck Blackwell (drums). Radle was a member of **Delaney & Bonnie** and **Derek & The Dominos**.

| 8/31/68 | 106 | 7 | **Love Heals** .................................................*Bad Day At Black Rock, Baby* | $7 | | Dot 17132 |

**COLTRANE, Chi** — HOT
Born on 11/16/48 in Racine, Wisconsin. Female vocalist/pianist. Chi pronounced: shy.

| 1/13/73 | 107 | 2 | **Go Like Elijah** ...........................................*It's Really Come To This* | $5 | | Columbia 45749 |

**COMING OF AGE** ۞ — R&B
Male vocal quintet from Los Angeles: Terrance Quaites, Israel Spencer, Ivan Shaw, Tee Kese and Marthony Tabb.

| 10/9/93 | 101² | 12 | **Coming Home To Love** — Sls:74 /R&B:27 *(album version)* | $3 | ■ | Zoo 14099 |

**COMMITTEE, The** ۞
Pop group based in San Francisco — Scott Beach, leader.

| 10/28/67 | 110 | 1 | **California My Way** ..........................................*You For Weren't It If* | $7 | | White Whale 257 |

#75 hit for **The Main Ingredient** in 1974

**COMMON SENSE** ۞ — R&B
Chicago rapper Rashied "Peteweestroe" Lynn.

| 4/29/95 | 102 | 6 | 1 **Resurrection**...............................R&B:88 *(2 remixes) / Chapter 13* | $3 | ■ | Relativity 1250 |
| 6/29/96 | 101¹ | 5 | 2 **The Bizness** — R&B:53 *(2 versions) / Stakes Is High (De La Soul)* | $6 | ■ | Tommy Boy 730 (T) |

DE LA SOUL featuring Common Sense

| 9/6/97 | 101¹ | 8 | 3 **Reminding Me (Of Sef)** — R&B:57 *(3 versions) / 1'2 Many (2 versions)* | $3 | ■ | Relativity 1627 |

COMMON Featuring Chantay Savage
samples "Mellow, Mellow Right On" by Lowrell

**COMMUTER** ۞
Pop vocal group.

| 8/25/84 | 101¹ | 1 | **Young Hearts** — *No Shelter (Broken Edge)* | $4 | | Casablanca 880141 |

from the movie *The Karate Kid* starring Ralph Macchio and Noriyuki "Pat" Morita

**COMO, Nicky** ۞
Pop singer.

| 6/20/60 | 110 | 1 | **Look For A Star** ...................................*(instrumental-Glen Stuart Orch.)* | $15 | | Laurie 3061 |

Glen Stuart (orch.); from the British movie *Circus Of Horrors*; there were 4 Top 30 versions of this tune in 1960

**COMO, Perry** — MEM/POP/HOT/AC/C&W
Born Pierino Como on 5/18/12 in Canonsburg, Pennsylvania. With Ted Weems band, 1936-42. Winner of five Emmys. *Pop Hits & Top Pop Singles: 132.*

| 6/11/66 | 128 | 1 | 1 **Coo Coo Roo Coo Coo Paloma**............................AC:12 *Stay With Me* | $6 | | RCA Victor 8823 |

Ray Charles Singers (backing vocals)

| 1/7/67 | 124 | 1 | 2 **Here Comes My Baby** ...........................AC:12 *My Own Peculiar Way* | $6 | | RCA Victor 447-0818 |

Anita Kerr Quartet (backing vocals); #10 Country hit for **Dottie West** in 1964

| 6/15/68 | 134 | 1 | 3 **Happy Man**.........................................AC:12 *Another Go Around* | $6 | | RCA Victor 9533 |
| 10/13/73 | 106 | 7 | 4 **Love Don't Care (Where It Grows)** ..............AC:16 *Walk Right Back* | $5 | | RCA Victor 0096 |

**COMPARSA UNIVERSITARIA DE LA LAGUNA** ۞
Mexican instrumental outfit.

| 5/8/65 | 107 | 4 | **Magic Trumpet (Trompeta Magica)**.............AC:12 *Mas Alla De Mombasa* [I] | $7 | | RCA Victor F4-6 |

written by Bert Kaempfert

**COMRADS, The** ۞ — R&B
Rap duo from Los Angeles: K-Mac and Gangsta.

| 6/14/97 | 102 | 9 | **Homeboyz**.............................................R&B:61 *Big Ballers* | $3 | ■ | Street Life 78109 |

**CONDITION RED** ۞ — R&B
Four-man rap outfit from Orlando.

| 9/18/93 | 122 | 1 | **Don't Get Caught Slipping** ...........................*(3 versions)* | $6 | ■ | O-Town 5002 * |

**CONFEDERATE RAILROAD** ۞ — C&W
Country-rock band from Marietta, Georgia: Danny Shirley (vocals), Michael Lamb (guitar), Gates Nichols (steel guitar), Chris McDaniel (keyboards), Wayne Secrest (bass) and Mark DuFresne (drums).

| 8/14/93 | 113 | 12 | **Trashy Women** .............C&W:10 *When You Leave That Way You Can Never Go Back* (C&W #14) | $3 | ■ | Atlantic 87357 |

**CON FUNK SHUN**　　　　　　　　　　　　　　　　　　　　　　　R&B/HOT
R&B/funk band formed as Project Soul in Vallejo, California, in 1968 by high school classmates Michael Cooper (lead vocals, guitar) and Louis McCall (drums). Moved to Memphis in 1972.

| 4/1/78 | 103 | 3 | 1 Confunkshunizeya ...................................................... R&B:31 *Who Has The Time* | $5 | | Mercury 73985 |
| 5/3/80 | 101[2] | 3 | 2 Got To Be Enough .............................................. R&B:8 *Early Morning Sunshine* | $4 | | Mercury 76051 |
| 4/7/84 | 103 | 3 | 3 Don't Let Your Love Grow Cold .................................. R&B:33 *Lovin' Fever* | $3 | | Mercury 818369 |
| 5/4/85 | 102 | 1 | 4 Electric Lady ...................................................... R&B:4 *Pretty Lady* | $3 | | Mercury 880636 |

**CONLEY, Arthur**　　　　　　　　　　　　　　　　　　　　　　　R&B/HOT
Born on 4/1/46 in Atlanta. R&B singer. Discovered by **Otis Redding** in 1965.

| 4/12/69 | 115 | 2 | 1 Run On .............................................................. *Speak Her Name* | $8 | | Atco 6661 |
| 4/18/70 | 107 | 3 | 2 God Bless .................................R&B:33 *(Your Love Has Brought Me) A Mighty Long Way* | $8 | | Atco 6747 |

**CONNIFF, Ray**　　　　　　　　　　　　　　　　　　　　　　　AC/HOT
Born on 11/6/16 in Attleboro, Massachusetts. Arranger/conductor for many of Columbia Records' top vocalists during the '50s and '60s.

| 2/29/64 | 119 | 3 | 1 Blue Moon .......................................................... *Honeycomb* | $7 | | Columbia 42967 |
| | | | **RAY CONNIFF and his Orchestra and Chorus** | | | |
| | | | #1 hit for Glen Gray's Orchestra in 1935; #1 hit for **The Marcels** in 1961 | | | |
| 12/5/64 | 126 | 4 | 2 If I Knew Then ...................................................... *Melodie D'Amour* | $6 | | Columbia 43168 |
| | | | **THE RAY CONNIFF SINGERS** | | | |
| 2/11/67 | 118 | 2 | 3 Cabaret..........................................................AC:13 *Games That Lovers Play* | $6 | | Columbia 43975 |
| | | | from the Broadway musical starring Jill Haworth | | | |

**CONNORS, Norman**　　　　　　　　　　　　　　　　　　　　　　　R&B/HOT
Born on 3/1/48 in Philadelphia. Jazz drummer with John Coltrane, Pharoah Sanders and others. Own group on Buddah in 1972.

| 7/31/76 | 101[2] | 3 | 1 We Both Need Each Other .................................... R&B:23 *So Much Love* | $5 | | Buddah 534 |
| | | | vocals by **Michael Henderson** and **Phyllis Hyman** | | | |
| 1/15/77 | 102 | 8 | 2 Betcha By Golly Wow ...................................... R&B:29 *Kwasi (Connors)* | $5 | | Buddah 554 |
| | | | **NORMAN CONNORS (Featuring PHYLLIS HYMAN)** | | | |
| | | | #3 hit for The Stylistics in 1972 | | | |

**CONRAD, Bob** ○
Born Conrad Robert Falk on 3/1/35 in Chicago. Star of many TV series including *The Wild Wild West, Hawaiian Eye* and *Baa Baa Black Sheep.*

| 12/25/61 | 113 | 1 | Bye Bye Baby ...................................................... *Love You* | $10 | ■ | Warner 5242 |

**CONSCIOUS DAUGHTERS, The**　　　　　　　　　　　　　　　　　　　　　　　R&B/HOT
Female rap duo based in Oakland, California: Carla "CMG" Green and Karryl "the Special One" Smith.

| 3/23/96 | 124 | 1 | Gamers ..............................................................R&B:65 *She's So Tight* | $3 | ▌ | Priority 53216 |
| | | | Harm (male vocal) | | | |

**CONTRASTS, The** ○

| 4/13/68 | 120 | 2 | What A Day .......................................................... *Lonely Child* | $6 | | Monument 1058 |
| | | | **THE CONTRASTS Featuring Bob Morrison** | | | |

**CONTROLLERS, The** ○　　　　　　　　　　　　　　　　　　　　　　　R&B
R&B group from Fairfield, Alabama, formed in 1965 as the Epics. Became the Soul Controllers in 1970.

| 1/21/78 | 102 | 2 | Somebody's Gotta Win, Somebody's Gotta Lose ............ R&B:8 *Feeling A Feeling* | $5 | | Juana 3414 |

**CONWAY, Russ** ○
Born Trevor Stanford on 9/2/27 in Bristol, England. Honky-tonk pianist.

| 8/3/59 | 106 | 3 | Roulette ............................................................ *Trampolina* [I] | $15 | | Cub 9034 |
| | | | Geoff Love (orch.) | | | |

**COOKE, Sam**　　　　　　　　　　　　　　　　　　　　　　　HOT/R&B/AC
Born on 1/22/31 in Clarksdale, Mississippi; raised in Chicago. Died from a gunshot wound on 12/11/64 in Los Angeles. Lead singer of the Soul Stirrers from 1950-56. Inducted into the Rock and Roll Hall of Fame in 1986. Revered as the definitive soul singer. *Top Pop Singles:* 43.

| 8/24/59 | 106 | 3 | 1 Summertime (Part 2) ............................................*(Part 1)* [R] | $25 | | Keen 2-2101 |
| | | | first charted on 11/4/57 (#81; B-side of "You Send Me") in Keen 3-4013; #12 hit for Billie Holiday in 1936; from Gershwin's folk opera *Porgy And Bess* | | | |
| 1/11/60 | 103 | 5 | 2 No One (Can Ever Take Your Place) ..................... *'T Aint Nobody's Bizness (If I Do)* | $25 | | Keen 8-2111 |
| 4/27/63 | 105 | 4 | 3 Love Will Find A Way.............................*Another Saturday Night (Hot #10)* | $15 | ■ | RCA Victor 8164 |
| 4/10/65 | 115 | 1 | 4 (Somebody) Ease My Troublin' Mind .................*It's Got The Whole World Shakin' (Hot #41)* | $15 | | RCA Victor 8539 |

**COOLIDGE, Rita**　　　　　　　　　　　　　　　　　　　　　　　AC/HOT/C&W
Born on 5/1/44 in Nashville. Moved to Los Angeles in the late '60s. With Kris Kristofferson from 1971; married to him from 1973-80.

| 4/28/73 | 106 | 3 | 1 Whiskey, Whiskey ................................................ *Donut Man* | $5 | | A&M 1414 |
| 9/19/81 | 103 | 6 | 2 The Closer You Get.............................................. *Take It Home* | $4 | | A&M 2361 |
| | | | #38 hit for **Alabama** in 1983 | | | |

**COOLIO**　　　　　　　　　　　　　　　　　　　　　　　R&B/HOT
Born Artis Ivey Jr. in 1963 in Los Angeles. Male rapper. Former member of WC And The MAAD Circle.

| 12/18/93+ | 109 | 13 | 1 County Line .........................................R&B:97 *(2 versions) / Sticky Fingers (2 versions)* | $5 | ▌ | Tommy Boy 577 * |
| | | | samples "Hit And Run" by the **Bar-Kays** | | | |
| 10/22/94 | 107 | 5 | 2 I Remember ...................................R&B:83 *(6 versions) / Mama I'm In Love Wit A Gangsta* | $5 | ▌ | Tommy Boy 635 * |
| | | | samples "Tomorrow's Dream" by Al Green | | | |
| 2/11/95 | 119 | 2 | 3 Mama, I'm In Love .................................................. *(same version)* | $3 | ▌ | Tommy Boy 7651 |
| | | | LeShaun (female rapper); samples "Mystic Voyage" by Roy Ayers and "Coolin Me Out" by **The Isley Brothers** | | | |

**COOPER, Christine** ○
R&B vocalist.

| 2/12/66 | 101[1] | 4 | S.O.S. (Heart In Distress) .......................................... *Say What You Feel* | $25 | | Parkway 971 |

**COOPER, Garnell, & The Kinfolks** ○
R&B instrumental combo.

| 8/3/63 | 132 | 1 | Green Monkey ...................................................... *Long Distance* [I] | $15 | | Jubilee 5445 |

| DEBUT | PEAK | WKS | A-side (Chart Hit) .......................................................................B-side | $ | Pic | Label & Number |
|---|---|---|---|---|---|---|
| | | | **COPELAND, Alan** ○      AC | | | |
| | | | Born on 10/6/26 in Los Angeles. Composer/arranger for several TV shows and commercials. | | | |
| 9/21/68 | 120 | 3 | 1 Mission: Impossible Theme/Norwegian Wood ................. AC:29 *Nothing To Lose* | $6 | | ABC 11088 |
| | | | medley of the TV series theme and **The Beatles**' tune | | | |
| 1/25/69 | 123 | 1 | 2 Classical Gas/Scarborough Fair ........................... AC:20 *Morgan Sebastian* | $6 | | A&M 988 |
| | | | **THE ALAN COPELAND SINGERS** | | | |
| | | | medley of the **Mason Williams** and **Simon & Garfunkel** tunes | | | |
| | | | **COPELAND, Johnny** ○ | | | |
| | | | Born on 3/27/37 in Haynesville, Louisiana. Died on 7/3/97. Moved to Houston in 1950. Blues guitarist known as "The Texas Twister." | | | |
| 9/14/63 | 105 | 6 | Down On Bending Knees .............................. *Just One More Time* | $15 | | Golden Eagle 101 |
| | | | **COPPER N' BRASS** ○ | | | |
| 3/14/70 | 103 | 1 | Does Anybody Know What Time It Is .............. *Believe It Or Not* | $7 | | Amazon 7 |
| | | | #7 hit for Chicago in 1971 | | | |
| | | | **CORBETTA, Jerry — see SUGARLOAF** | | | |
| | | | **CORNELIUS BROTHERS & SISTER ROSE**   R&B/HOT/AC | | | |
| | | | Family R&B group from Dania, Florida: Edward, Carter, Rose and Billie Jo. Carter, later known as Gideon Israel, leader of a muslim religious sect, died on 11/7/91 (age 43). | | | |
| 10/6/73 | 104 | 11 | I Just Can't Stop Loving You................ R&B:79 *These Lonely Nights* | $5 | | United Artists 313 |
| | | | **CORNERSTONE** ○ | | | |
| | | | Six-man pop band based in Phoenix. | | | |
| 3/21/70 | 104 | 4 | Holly Go Softly ............................... *Love, Nothing More* | $6 | | Liberty 56148 |
| | | | **CORRS, The**   HOT/AC | | | |
| | | | Sibling group from Ireland: Andrea (lead vocals), Jim (guitar), Sharon (violin) and Caroline (drums) Corr. | | | |
| 3/9/96 | 112 | 5 | The Right Time.......................................(acoustic version) | $3 | ▪ | 143/Lava 98085 |
| | | | **CORTEZ, Dave "Baby"**   HOT/R&B | | | |
| | | | Born David Cortez Clowney on 8/13/38 in Detroit. Rock and roll/R&B organist/pianist. First recorded (as David Clooney) for Ember in 1956. | | | |
| 10/26/59 | 103 | 2 | 1 Piano Shuffle ......................... *Its A Sin To Tell A Lie* [I] | $20 | | Clock 1014 |
| 1/2/65 | 132 | 2 | 2 Popping Popcorn............ *The Question (Do You Love Me)* [I] | $15 | | Okeh 7208 |
| 10/2/65 | 135 | 1 | 3 Tweetie Pie ...................... *Things Ain't What They Used To Be* [I] | $10 | | Roulette 4628 |
| | | | **CORY, Andy** ○ | | | |
| 5/1/61 | 121 | 1 | Hey You, What Are You, Some Kind Of Nut?............. *Lindy Hop* [N] | $20 | | Silver Bid 1023 |
| | | | **COSBY, Bill**   HOT/R&B/AC | | | |
| | | | Born on 7/12/38 in Philadelphia. Top comedian who has appeared in nightclubs, movies and on TV. Winner of five Emmys and nine Grammys. | | | |
| 1/24/70 | 124 | 2 | Hikky Burr - Part One................................ *Part Two* [N] | $8 | | Uni 55184 |
| | | | **BILL COSBY With The Bunions Bradford Band** | | | |
| | | | original theme from TV's *The Bill Cosby Show* | | | |
| | | | **COSTA, Don, And His Orchestra**   HOT/AC | | | |
| | | | Born on 6/10/25 in Boston. Died on 1/19/83. Arranger/conductor for many top artists. | | | |
| 1/9/61 | 116 | 2 | 1 The Misfits .................................... *Chi Chi* [I] | $10 | ■ | United Artists 286 |
| | | | from the movie starring Clark Gable and Marilyn Monroe | | | |
| 3/24/62 | 112 | 1 | 2 Sugar Blues ............................ *Flamenco Guitar* [I] | $7 | | Columbia 42307 |
| | | | Ernie Royal (trumpet solo); #2 hit for Clyde McCoy in 1931 | | | |
| | | | **COSTELLO, Elvis**   ROK/HOT | | | |
| | | | Born Declan MacManus on 8/25/54 in Liverpool, England. Rock singer/songwriter. | | | |
| 3/25/78 | 108 | 1 | 1 Watching The Detectives .......... *Blame It On Cain/Mystery Dance* | $15 | | Columbia 10696 |
| 4/14/79 | 101[1] | 3 | 2 Accidents Will Happen ........................ *Sunday's Best* | $6 | | Columbia 10919 |
| 3/26/94 | 115 | 4 | 3 13 Steps Lead Down ......... ROK:6 *A Drunken Man's Praise Of Sobriety* | $3 | ▪ | Warner 18214 |
| | | | **COUGAR, John — see MELLENCAMP** | | | |
| | | | **COUNT FIVE**   HOT | | | |
| | | | Psychedelic-garage-rock quintet of teenagers from San Jose, California: Kenn Ellner (vocals), John Michalski (lead guitar), Sean Byrne (rhythm guitar), Ron Chaney (bass) and Craig Atkinson (drums). | | | |
| 12/10/66 | 125 | 1 | Peace Of Mind ................................ *The Morning After* | $15 | | Double Shot 106 |
| | | | **COUNTRY JOE AND THE FISH**   HOT | | | |
| | | | San Francisco's leading political rock band of the '60s. Country Joe is singer/guitarist Joseph McDonald (b: 1/1/42). Formed the Fish in 1965 with Barry Melton and David Cohen (guitars), Bruce Barthol (bass), and Chicken Hirsch (drums). | | | |
| 2/3/68 | 114 | 3 | 1 Who Am I .................................. *Thursday* | $10 | ■ | Vanguard 35061 |
| 7/12/69 | 106 | 1 | 2 Here I Go Again ...................... *Baby, You're Driving Me Crazy* | $10 | | Vanguard 35090 |
| | | | **COUNTRY STORE** ○ | | | |
| | | | Pop vocal group. | | | |
| 1/10/70 | 103 | 3 | To Love You ....................................*Heartache* | $7 | | TA 189 |
| | | | **COUP, The** ○ | | | |
| | | | Rap trio from Oakland, California: Boots, E Roc and DJ Pam The Funkstress. | | | |
| 5/27/95 | 112 | 2 | Fat Cats-Bigga Fish (Get Down, Get Down) ............... (2 versions) | $3 | ▪ | Wild Pitch/EMI 58408 |
| | | | **COURTNEY, Peter** ○ | | | |
| 3/4/67 | 121 | 3 | The Loser....................... *Pictures Are My Only Souvenirs* | $8 | | Viva 609 |
| | | | **COUSINS, The** ○ | | | |
| | | | Instrumental quartet from Brussels, Belgium. | | | |
| 7/17/61 | 110 | 3 | St. Louis Blues............................... *No One Knows* [I] | $15 | | Parkway 823 |
| | | | there have been 15 charted versions of this W.C. Handy classic tune | | | |

**COVAY, Don**     R&B/HOT

Born in March 1938 in Orangeburg, South Carolina. R&B singer/songwriter. Member of the Rainbows in 1955. Recorded as "Pretty Boy" with **Little Richard**'s band for Atlantic in 1957. Formed The Goodtimers in 1960.

| DEBUT | PEAK | WKS | A-side | B-side | $ | Pic | Label & Number |
|---|---|---|---|---|---|---|---|
| 3/12/66 | 101[1] | 3 | 1 Watching The Late Late Show | Sookie Sookie | $12 | | Atlantic 2323 |
| 10/22/66 | 127 | 1 | 2 Somebody's Got To Love You | Temptation Was Too Strong | $12 | | Atlantic 2357 |
| | | | **DON COVAY & The Goodtimers** (above 2) | | | | |
| 2/11/67 | 133 | 1 | 3 Shingaling '67 | R&B:50 I Was There | $10 | | Atlantic 2375 |

**COVERDALE•PAGE** ☼     ROK

British hard-rock veterans David Coverdale (vocalist of **Deep Purple** and **Whitesnake**) and Jimmy Page (guitarist of **The Yardbirds**, Led Zeppelin and The Firm).

| DEBUT | PEAK | WKS | A-side | B-side | $ | Pic | Label & Number |
|---|---|---|---|---|---|---|---|
| 7/31/93 | 115 | 3 | Take Me For A Little While | ROK:15 Easy Does It | $3 | ■ | Geffen 19254 |

**COVER GIRLS, The**     HOT/R&B

New York City-based female dance trio.

| DEBUT | PEAK | WKS | A-side | B-side | $ | Pic | Label & Number |
|---|---|---|---|---|---|---|---|
| 1/30/93 | 125 | 1 | If You Want My Love (Here It Is) | (3 versions) / Wishing On A Star (2 versions) | $5 | ■ | Epic 74835 * |

**COVINGTON, Trisha** ☼     R&B

Female singer from Cleveland.

| DEBUT | PEAK | WKS | A-side | B-side | $ | Pic | Label & Number |
|---|---|---|---|---|---|---|---|
| 1/28/95 | 103 | 11 | Why You Wanna Play Me Out? | R&B:26 (remix) | $3 | ■ | Columbia 77269 |

**COWSILLS, The**     HOT/AC

Family pop group from Newport, Rhode Island: five brothers (Bill, Bob, Paul, Barry and John), with their younger sister (Susan) and mother (Barbara; d: 1/31/85, age 56).

| DEBUT | PEAK | WKS | A-side | B-side | $ | Pic | Label & Number |
|---|---|---|---|---|---|---|---|
| 7/16/66 | 118 | 4 | 1 Most Of All | Siamese Cat | $10 | ■ | Philips 40382 |
| 11/9/68 | 132 | 1 | 2 The Path Of Love | Captain Sad & His Ship Of Fools (The Cowsills) | $7 | | MGM 14003 |
| | | | **JOHN COWSILL** | | | | |
| 12/7/68 | 118 | 2 | 3 The Candy Kid (From The Mission On The Bowery) | The Impossible Years | $7 | | MGM 14011 |
| 4/3/71 | 108 | 2 | 4 On My Side | There Is A Child | $7 | | London 149 |

**CRABBY APPLETON**     HOT

Rock group from California: Michael Fennelly (vocals, guitar), Casey Foutz (keyboards), Flaco Falcon (percussion), Hank Harvey (bass) and Phil Jones (drums).

| DEBUT | PEAK | WKS | A-side | B-side | $ | Pic | Label & Number |
|---|---|---|---|---|---|---|---|
| 11/7/70 | 114 | 2 | Lucy | Some Madness | $7 | | Elektra 45702 |
| | | | also released as "My Little Lucy" on Elektra 45702 | | | | |

**CRACKER**     ROK/HOT

Rock trio formed in 1992 in Redlands, California: David Lowery (vocals), John Hickman (guitar) and Dave Faragher (bass).

| DEBUT | PEAK | WKS | A-side | B-side | $ | Pic | Label & Number |
|---|---|---|---|---|---|---|---|
| 7/30/94 | 102 | 9 | Get Off This | ROK:6 Movie Star | $3 | ■ | Virgin 38443 |

**CRACK THE SKY** ☼     ROK

Rock sextet from Steubenville, Ohio led by singer **John Palumbo**.

| DEBUT | PEAK | WKS | A-side | B-side | $ | Pic | Label & Number |
|---|---|---|---|---|---|---|---|
| 12/11/76 | 108 | 5 | (We Don't Want Your Money) We Want Mine | Invaders From Mars | $5 | | Lifesong 45016 |

**CRADDOCK, Billy "Crash"**     C&W/HOT/AC

Born on 6/13/39 in Greensboro, North Carolina. Country-rock singer.

| DEBUT | PEAK | WKS | A-side | B-side | $ | Pic | Label & Number |
|---|---|---|---|---|---|---|---|
| 4/3/71 | 113 | 4 | Knock Three Times | C&W:3 The Best I Ever Had | $6 | | Cartwheel 193 |
| | | | #1 hit for Dawn in 1971 | | | | |

**CRAFTYS, The** ☼     

R&B vocal group.

| DEBUT | PEAK | WKS | A-side | B-side | $ | Pic | Label & Number |
|---|---|---|---|---|---|---|---|
| 8/21/61 | 104 | 2 | L-O-V-E | Heartbreaking World | $20 | | 7 Arts 708 |

**CRAMER, Floyd**     HOT/AC/C&W/MEM

Born on 10/27/33 in Samti, Louisiana. Died of cancer on 12/31/97. Nashville's top session pianist. Worked with **Elvis Presley**, **Johnny Cash**, **Perry Como**, **Chet Atkins** and many others.

| DEBUT | PEAK | WKS | A-side | B-side | $ | Pic | Label & Number |
|---|---|---|---|---|---|---|---|
| 9/29/62 | 110 | 2 | 1 Swing Low/ | [I] | | | |
| | | | version of the 19th-century spiritual "Swing Low, Sweet Chariot" | | | | |
| 10/20/62 | 127 | 1 | 2 Losers Weepers | [I] | $7 | ■ | RCA Victor 8084 |
| 5/4/63 | 129 | 4 | 3 (These Are) The Young Years ... Kaapsedraai ("cop-se-dry") (The South African Cape Reel) | [I] | $7 | ■ | RCA Victor 8171 |
| 8/17/63 | 121 | 4 | 4 How High The Moon | Satan's Doll | [I] | $7 | ■ | RCA Victor 8217 |
| | | | #1 hit for Les Paul & Mary Ford in 1951 | | | | |
| 12/21/63 | 124 | 2 | 5 Heartless Heart | The Huckle Buck | [I] | $7 | | RCA Victor 8265 |
| | | | adapted from Chopin's Etude in E Major (Jo Stafford's 1950 hit "No Other Love") | | | | |
| 5/3/80 | 104 | 5 | 6 Dallas | C&W:32 / AC:34 Lover's Minuet | [I] | $4 | ■ | RCA 11916 |
| | | | theme from the TV series starring Larry Hagman and Patrick Duffy | | | | |

**CRAWFORD, Johnny**     HOT/AC

Born on 3/26/46 in Los Angeles. Played Chuck Connors's son ("Mark McCain") in the TV series The Rifleman, 1958-63.

| DEBUT | PEAK | WKS | A-side | B-side | $ | Pic | Label & Number |
|---|---|---|---|---|---|---|---|
| 4/20/63 | 126 | 1 | 1 Cry On My Shoulder | When I Fall In Love | $15 | | Del-Fi 4203 |
| 3/7/64 | 108 | 2 | 2 Sandy | Ol' Shorty | $15 | | Del-Fi 4229 |
| | | | #15 hit for Larry Hall in 1960 | | | | |

**CRAWFORD, Randy**     R&B/HOT

Born Veronica Crawford on 2/18/52 in Macon, Georgia; raised in Cincinnati. Recorded and toured Europe with **The Crusaders**. Most Outstanding Performance award at Tokyo Music Festival in 1980.

| DEBUT | PEAK | WKS | A-side | B-side | $ | Pic | Label & Number |
|---|---|---|---|---|---|---|---|
| 6/5/82 | 110 | 2 | 1 One Hello | R&B:50 That's How Heartaches Are Made | $4 | | Warner 29998 |
| | | | from the movie I Ought To Be In Pictures starring Walter Matthau and Dinah Manoff | | | | |
| 10/30/82 | 102 | 4 | 2 Your Precious Love | R&B:16 Monmouth College Fight Song (Yellowjackets) | $4 | | Warner 29893 |
| | | | **AL JARREAU AND RANDY CRAWFORD** | | | | |
| | | | #5 hit for **Marvin Gaye** & Tammi Terrell in 1967 | | | | |
| 1/29/83 | 108 | 3 | 3 Imagine | R&B:69 Monmouth College Fight Song (Yellowjackets) | $4 | | Warner 29801 |
| | | | "live" recording; accompanied by the Yellowjackets; #3 hit for **John Lennon** in 1971 | | | | |

**CRAZY ELEPHANT**     HOT

Bubblegum studio concoction. Robert Spencer (**The Cadillacs**) on lead vocals.

| DEBUT | PEAK | WKS | A-side | B-side | $ | Pic | Label & Number |
|---|---|---|---|---|---|---|---|
| 6/28/69 | 104 | 3 | 1 Sunshine, Red Wine | Pam | $8 | | Bell 804 |
| 9/13/69 | 116 | 3 | 2 Gimme Some More | My Baby (Honey Pie) | $8 | | Bell 817 |

## CRAZY JOE AND THE VARIABLE SPEED BAND ☺
Rock quintet led by "Crazy Joe" Renda.

| 2/21/81 | 105 | 3 | Eugene ...................................... *Madam Palm* [N] $5 | | | Casablanca 2298 |

co-written and co-produced by Ace Frehley of Kiss

## CRAZY PAVING ☺
Pop vocal group.

| 3/13/71 | 103 | 3 | Anytime Sunshine ..............................................*Sweet Brandy* $6 | | | Kapp 2117 |

## CREAM
**HOT**
British rock supergroup: Eric Clapton (guitar), Ginger Baker (drums) and Jack Bruce (bass). Inducted into the Rock and Roll Hall of Fame in 1993.

| 12/16/67 | 116 | 1 | I Feel Free ........................................................ *N. S. U.* $12 | | | Atco 6462 |

#88 hit for Belinda Carlisle in 1988

## CREATIVE SOURCE
**R&B/HOT**
R&B vocal group from Los Angeles: Don Wyatt, Celeste Rhodes, Steve Flanagan, Barbara Berryman and Barbara Lewis.

| 10/13/73 | 114 | 6 | 1 You Can't Hide Love.......................... R&B:48 *Lovesville* $6 | | ■ | Sussex 501 |
| 1/19/74 | 108 | 4 | 2 You're Too Good To Be True....................... R&B:88 *Oh Love* $6 | | | Sussex 508 |

## CREEP, The ☺
CREEP: Committee to Rip-off Each and Every Politician.

| 9/1/73 | 116 | 2 | Haldeman, Ehrlichman, Mitchell And Dean...........................*(stereo version)* [N] $20 | | | Mr. G 826 |

inspired by the Watergate scandal

## CRÈME CARAMAL ☺
Pop vocal group.

| 10/25/69 | 128 | 1 | My Idea ................................................ *Excursion* $7 | | | Janus 100 |

group name shown as CRÈME CARAMEL on the B-side

## CRENSHAW, Marshall
**ROK/HOT**
Born on 11/11/53 in Detroit. Rock singer/guitarist. Played John Lennon in the road show of *Beatlemania* in 1976. Appeared in the movie *Peggy Sue Got Married* and portrayed Buddy Holly in the 1987 movie *La Bamba*.

| 10/23/82 | 110 | 1 | 1 There She Goes Again ...................................... *Usual Thing* $4 | | | Warner 29894 |
| 6/18/83 | 103 | 1 | 2 Whenever You're On My Mind ................... ROK:23 *Jungle Rock* $4 | | ■ | Warner 29630 |

## CRESTONES, The ☺
Rock and roll band.

| 5/23/64 | 135 | 1 | She's A Bad Motorcycle .................................. *The Grass Hopper Dance* $30 | | | Markie 117 |

similar to The Storey Sisters' 1958 hit "Bad Motorcycle"

## CRESTS, The
Formed as an R&B vocal group in 1955 at a Manhattan junior high school, consisting of Brooklyn-born white singer Johnny Maestro, Harold Torres, Talmadge Gough, J.T. Carter and Patricia Van Dross. Van Dross (older sister of Luther Vandross) left group in 1958. Maestro left for solo work in 1960, replaced by James Ancrum.

| 12/31/60 | 102 | 3 | 1 I Remember (In The Still Of The Night) .......................... *Good Golly Miss Molly* $30 | | | Coed 543 |

**THE CRESTS with Johnny Mastro**
#24 hit for The Five Satins in 1956

| 2/2/63 | 123 | 2 | 2 Guilty ...............................................*Number One With Me* $30 | | | Selma 311 |

Herb Bernstein (orch.); #4 hit for both Ruth Etting (1931) and Margaret Whiting (1947)

## CREWE, Bob
**HOT/AC**
Born on 11/12/37 in Newark, New Jersey. Wrote many hits beginning with "Silhouettes" in 1957. One of the top producers of the 1960s.

| 7/27/59 | 111 | 4 | 1 Sweetie Pie ...............................................*Daily* $25 | | | U.T. 4000 |

rock and roll song similar to Jerry Lee Lewis's 1958 hit "Great Balls Of Fire"

| 3/18/67 | 126 | 3 | 2 After The Ball .................................. *One More Tear* $7 | | | DynoVoice 231 |

one of America's most popular songs during the 1890s

| 5/6/67 | 129 | 3 | 3 Miniskirts In Moscow or...........................AC:29 *Theme For A Lazy Girl* [I] $7 | | ■ | DynoVoice 233 |

**THE BOB CREWE GENERATION**

## CRICKETS, The
**HOT**
The post-Buddy Holly backing group: Jerry Allison, Sonny Curtis, Jerry Naylor and Glen D. Hardin.

| 12/18/61 | 105 | 3 | 1 He's Old Enough To Know Better ................................. *I'm Feeling Better* $25 | | | Liberty 55392 |
| 3/23/63 | 134 | 1 | 2 My Little Girl ...................................... *Teardrops Fall Like Rain* $25 | | | Liberty 55540 |

## CRITTERS, The
**HOT**
Pop group from New Jersey: Don Ciccone (vocals, guitar), Jimmy Ryan (guitar), Chris Darway (organ), Kenny Gorka (bass) and Jack Decker (drums).

| 2/18/67 | 111 | 6 | 1 Marryin' Kind Of Love ........................... *New York Bound* $10 | | | Kapp 805 |
| 10/21/67 | 113 | 3 | 2 Little Girl .................................. *Dancing In The Streets* $10 | | | Kapp 858 |

## CROCE, Jim
**HOT/AC/C&W**
Born on 1/10/43 in Philadelphia. Killed in a plane crash on 9/20/73 in Natchitoches, Louisiana. Vocalist/guitarist/composer.

| 4/24/76 | 110 | 1 | Mississippi Lady .................................*Maybe Tomorrow* $5 | | | Lifesong 45005 |

## CROOK, General ☺
**R&B**

| 12/8/73 | 108 | 7 | The Best Years Of My Life ........................ R&B:71 *Testification* $5 | | | Wand 11260 |

## CROSBY, Bing
**MEM/POP/HOT/R&B/AC/C&W**
One of the most popular entertainers of the 20th century. Born Harry Lillis Crosby on 5/3/03 in Tacoma, Washington. Died of a heart attack on 10/14/77 on a golf course near Madrid, Spain. Won Grammy's Lifetime Achievement Award in 1962. Ranked as the #1 artist in two of Joel Whitburn's books: *Pop Memories 1890-1954* and *Pop Hits & Top Pop Singles:* 155.

| 12/12/60 | 102 | 2 | I'll Be Home For Christmas (If Only In My Dreams) ............ *Faith Of Our Fathers* [X-R] $6 | | | Decca 23779 |

John Scott Trotter (orch.); first charted in 1943 (#3) on Decca 18570; new version above recorded in 1947

## CROSBY, Chris
**HOT/AC**
Bing Crosby's nephew. Son of the late bandleader Bob Crosby.

| 5/2/64 | 124 | 1 | Tomorrow ...............................................*All I Do Is Dream Of You* $10 | | ■ | MGM 13234 |

Bill McElhinney (orch.)

| DEBUT | PEAK | WKS | A-side (Chart Hit) | $ | Pic | Label & Number |
|---|---|---|---|---|---|---|
| | | | **CROSBY, David**     HOT/ROK/AC | | | |
| | | | Born on 8/14/41 in Los Angeles. Vocalist/guitarist with **The Byrds** from 1964-68 and later Crosby, Stills & Nash. | | | |
| 10/9/76 | 109 | 1 | Spotlight .................................................................... *Foolish Man* | $5 | | ABC 12217 |
| | | | **DAVID CROSBY/GRAHAM NASH** | | | |
| | | | **CROSSROADS** ✪ | | | |
| | | | Rock band. | | | |
| 9/5/70 | 115 | 1 | Here I Stand .................................................. *Coming Home To You Baby* | $7 | | Atco 6765 |
| | | | **CROTHERS, Scat Man** ✪ | | | |
| | | | Born Sherman Crothers on 5/23/10 in Terre Haute, Indiana. Died on 11/22/86. Movie and TV actor. | | | |
| 5/21/66 | 134 | 1 | What's A Nice Kid Like You Doing In A Place Like This? .................................. *Golly Zonk! (It's Scat Man)* | $12 | | HBR 476 |
| | | | from the TV special *The New Alice in Wonderland* | | | |
| | | | **CROW**     HOT | | | |
| | | | Rock-blues quintet from Minneapolis: Dave Waggoner (vocals), Dick Wiegand (guitar), Kink Middlemist (organ), Larry Wiegand (bass) and Denny Craswell (drums). | | | |
| 8/9/69 | 123 | 3 | 1 Time To Make A Turn .................................................. *Busy Day* | $8 | | Amaret 106 |
| 3/21/70 | 103 | 3 | 2 Slow Down .................................................. *Cottage Cheese (Hot #56)* | $8 | | Amaret 119 |
| | | | #25 hit for **The Beatles** in 1964 | | | |
| | | | **CROWDED HOUSE**     ROK/HOT/AC | | | |
| | | | New Zealand/Australian pop trio formed in 1986 by former **Split Enz** members Neil Finn and Paul Hester. | | | |
| 1/29/94 | 120 | 3 | 1 Locked Out ..................... ROK:8 *World Where You Live / It's Only Natural / Weather With You* | $6 | | Capitol 58088 (CD) |
| 7/9/94 | 113 | 2 | 2 Distant Sun ..................... ROK:26 *Pineapple Head / Locked Out (live)* | $3 | ▌ | Capitol 58136 |
| | | | **CROWELL, Rodney**     C&W/AC/HOT | | | |
| | | | Born on 8/7/50 in Houston. Country singer/songwriter/guitarist. Married to **Rosanne Cash** from 1979-92. | | | |
| 10/10/81 | 105 | 4 | Stars On The Water ..................... C&W:30 *Don't Need No Other Now* | $4 | | Warner 49810 |
| | | | **CROWN HEIGHTS AFFAIR**     R&B/HOT | | | |
| | | | R&B-disco group from New York City: Phil Thomas (vocals), William Anderson (guitar), Howard Young (keyboards), Bert Reid, James Baynard and Raymond Reid (horn section), Muki Wilson (bass) and Raymond Rock (drums). | | | |
| 4/26/80 | 102 | 2 | You Gave Me Love ..................... R&B:74 *Tell Me You Love Me* | $4 | | De-Lite 803 |
| | | | **CRUISERS, The** ✪ | | | |
| | | | R&B vocal group: Randy Hamilton, Gene Williams, Paul Long and McKinley Anthony. | | | |
| 3/14/60 | 102 | 4 | If I Knew .................................................. *Miss Fine* | $50 | | V-Tone 207 |
| | | | **CRUSADERS, The**     R&B/HOT/AC | | | |
| | | | Instrumental jazz-oriented group formed in Houston: Joe Sample (keyboards), Wilton Felder (reeds), Nesbert "Stix" Hooper (drums) and Wayne Henderson (trombone). | | | |
| 11/11/72 | 114 | 2 | 1 So Far Away ..................... AC:39 *That's How I Feel* [I] | $6 | | Blue Thumb 217 |
| | | | #14 hit for **Carole King** in 1971 | | | |
| 2/15/75 | 102 | 2 | 2 Stomp And Buck Dance ..................... R&B:41 *A Ballad For Joe (Louis)* [I] | $5 | | ABC/Blue Thumb 261 |
| | | | **CRYAN' SHAMES, The**     HOT | | | |
| | | | Rock band from Chicago: Tom Doody (vocals), Jim Fairs (lead guitar), Jerry Stone (rhythm guitar), Jim Pilster (tambourine), Dave Purple (bass) and Dennis Conroy (drums). | | | |
| 3/25/67 | 127 | 3 | 1 Mr. Unreliable .................................................. *Georgia* | $10 | | Columbia 44037 |
| 10/5/68 | 115 | 2 | 2 Greenburg, Glickstein, Charles, David Smith & Jones ..................... *The Warm* | $10 | | Columbia 44638 |
| | | | **CRYSTAL GRASS** ✪     R&B | | | |
| | | | Disco studio group assembled by producer Lee Hallyday. | | | |
| 4/26/75 | 102 | 8 | Crystal World ..................... R&B:73 *California Summer* | $5 | | Polydor 15101 |
| | | | **CUBA, Joe, Sextet**     R&B/HOT | | | |
| | | | Raunchy Latin-rock combo: Cuba (congas), Jimmy Sabater (drums, vocals), Tommy Berrios (vibes), Nick Jiménez (piano), Jose "Cheo" Feliciano (vocals) and Jules Cordero (bass). | | | |
| 8/6/66 | 115 | 3 | El Pito (I'll Never Go Back To Georgia) ..................... R&B:44 *Arecibo* | $7 | | Tico 470 |
| | | | **CULTURE BEAT**     HOT | | | |
| | | | Dance/rap duo: London vocalist Tania Evans and New Jersey rapper Jay Supreme. | | | |
| 3/5/94 | 107 | 5 | 1 Got To Get It .................................................. *Mr. Vain (radio edit)* | $3 | ▌ | 550 Music/Epic 77372 |
| 6/29/96 | 122 | 2 | 2 Inside Out .................................................. *(no rap mix)* | $3 | ▌ | 550 Music/Epic 78316 |
| 7/12/97 | 111 | 8 | 3 Take Me Away .................................................. *(remix)* | $3 | ▌ | Interhit 10165 |
| | | | **CUNNINGHAM, J.C.** ✪     C&W | | | |
| | | | Born John Collins Cunningham on 11/13/50 in Brownsville, Texas. Appeared in the movie *Day Of The Wolves*. | | | |
| 7/5/80 | 104 | 1 | The Pyramid Song ..................... C&W:85 *I'm A Lover Not A Fighter* [N] | $4 | | Scotti Brothers 601 |
| | | | **CURB, Mike, Congregation**     AC/HOT/C&W | | | |
| | | | Born on 12/24/44 in Savannah, Georgia. Pop music mogul and politician. President of MGM Records, 1969-73. Formed own company, Sidewalk Records, in 1964; became Curb Records in 1974. | | | |
| 1/16/71 | 108 | 8 | 1 Rainin' In My Heart     C&W:3 *A-eee (Williams)* | $6 | | MGM 14194 |
| | | | **HANK WILLIAMS, JR. With THE MIKE CURB CONGREGATION** | | | |
| | | | #34 hit for **Slim Harpo** in 1961 | | | |
| 8/14/71 | 115 | 1 | 2 Sweet Gingerbread Man ..................... AC:16 *Fly Me A Place For The Summer* | $5 | | MGM 14265 |
| | | | first made the Adult Contemporary charts on 7/4/70 (#16) on MGM 14140; from the movie *The Magic Garden of Stanley Sweetheart* starring Don Johnson | | | |
| 6/24/72 | 108 | 3 | 3 See You In September ..................... AC:15 *The Very Same Time Next Year* | $5 | | MGM 14391 |
| 12/9/72 | 111 | 3 | 4 Living Together, Growing Together ..................... *The Good Things In Life (Bennett)* | $6 | | MGM/Verve 10690 |
| | | | **TONY BENNETT With The Mike Curb Congregation** | | | |
| | | | from the movie *Lost Horizon* starring Peter Finch; #32 hit for **The 5th Dimension** in 1973 | | | |
| 9/1/73 | 108 | 6 | 5 It's A Small Small World ..................... AC:9 *Shinin' On Me* | $5 | | MGM 14494 |
| | | | theme music for an attraction at Walt Disney World | | | |

## CURE, The · HOT/ROK
British techno-rock group formed in 1977 by Robert Smith (vocals, guitar) and Laurence "Lol" Tolhurst (drums).

| DEBUT | PEAK | WKS | A-side / B-side | $ | Pic | Label & Number |
|---|---|---|---|---|---|---|
| 4/9/83 | 109 | 1 | 1 Let's Go To Bed ..................................... *(edit) / Just One Kiss* | $7 | ■ | Sire/Fiction 29689 (T) |

a 7" promotional single was issued on Sire 2022; reissued commercially in 1986 on Elektra 69537 with a picture sleeve

| 2/11/84 | 107 | 1 | 2 The Love Cats .................................... *Speak My Language* | $4 | | Sire/Fiction 29376 |

## CURTAIN CALLS, The ☉
Pop trio: Stan Jay, Merryl Joy and Garry Lynn.

| 5/25/68 | 116 | 3 | Sock It To Me Sunshine ........................ *Say What You See* | $6 | | Dot 17093 |

arranged by David Gates of Bread

## CURTIS, Sonny ☉ · C&W
Born on 5/9/37 in Meadow, Texas. Lead guitarist on **Buddy Holly**'s first recordings in 1956. Re-joined the post-Holly **Crickets** in 1960.

| 10/8/66 | 134 | 1 | 1 My Way Of Life ........................ C&W:49 *Last Call* | $15 | | Viva 602 |
| 3/2/68 | 120 | 3 | 2 Atlanta Georgia Stray .................. C&W:36 *Day Drinker* | $15 | | Viva 626 |

## CUTLASS, Frankie · R&B
Popular dance DJ/producer originally from Puerto Rico.

| 3/5/94 | 121 | 2 | 1 Puerto Rico ............................... *(4 versions)* | $5 | ■ | Hoody 50047 * |

Ray Boogie & The Evil Twins (rap)

| 5/25/96 | 113 | 3 | 2 You And You And You .......... R&B:84 *(3 versions)* | $3 | ■ | Relativity 1532 |

**Redman** and Sadat X (rap)

| 2/8/97 | 122 | 4 | 3 The Cypher: Part 3 ........ R&B:70 *(2 versions) / Puerto Rico/Black People* | $3 | ■ | Relativity 1576 |

Biz Markie, **Roxanne Shanté**, **Big Daddy Kane** and Craig G. (guest rappers); samples "Reach For It" by George Duke and "The Symphony" by Marly Marl

## CYMANDE · R&B/HOT
Afro-rock band from the West Indies: Ray King (vocals), Pat Patterson (guitar), Peter Serreo and Derek Gibbs (saxophones), Mike Rose (flute), Joe Dee and Pablo Gonsales (percussion), and Sam Kelly (drums).

| 6/30/73 | 102 | 2 | Bra ............................... R&B:51 *Ras Tafarian Folk Song* | $5 | | Janus 215 |

## CYMBAL, Johnny · HOT/AC
Born on 2/3/45 in Ochiltree, Scotland. Died on 3/16/93 of a heart attack. Pop singer/songwriter/producer.

| 3/27/61 | 108 | 3 | The Water Was Red ........................ *Bunny* | $20 | | MGM 12978 |

another in a series of early '60s "death" songs

## CYMONE, André ☉ · R&B
Born André Simon Anderson in Minneapolis. Former bass player of **Prince**'s band, The Revolution.

| 2/5/83 | 107 | 3 | Kelly's Eyes .............................. R&B:72 *Baby Don't Go* | $4 | | Columbia 03301 |

## CYNTHIA
Real name: Cynthia Torres. Born on 5/6/68. Native of New York.

| 2/4/95 | 107 | 9 | How I Love Him ............................ *(radio edit)* | $3 | ■ | Tommy Boy 7656 |

K7 (guest vocal)

## CYPRESS HILL · HOT/R&B
Rap trio based in Los Angeles: Senen "Sen Dog" Reyes (Cuban-born; older brother of Mellow Man Ace), Louis "B-Real" Freese and Lawrence "Mixmaster Muggs" Muggerud.

| 3/9/96 | 103 | 11 | Illusions ................................. R&B:87 *Killafornia* | $3 | ■ | Ruffhouse 78222 |

samples "Las Vegas Tango" by Gary Burton

## CYRKLE, The · HOT
Pop group: Don Dannemann (vocals, guitar), Mike Losekamp (keyboards), Tom Dawes (bass) and Marty Fried (drums).

| 12/9/67 | 112 | 1 | Turn Of The Century .................. *Don't Cry, No Fears, No Tears Comin' Your Way* | $10 | | Columbia 44366 |

written and recorded for the **Bee Gees**' *1st* album in 1967

## CYRUS, Billy Ray · C&W/HOT/AC
Born on 8/25/61 in Flatwoods, Kentucky. Country singer.

| 11/27/93+ | 104 | 6 | 1 Somebody New ................ Sls:71 /C&W:9 *Only Time Will Tell* | $3 | ■ | Mercury 862754 |
| 4/2/94 | 119 | 4 | 2 Words By Heart ................ C&W:12 *Throwin' Stones* | $3 | ■ | Mercury 858132 |
| 12/24/94+ | 108 | 4 | 3 Storm In The Heartland ........ C&W:33 *I Ain't Even Left* | $3 | ■ | Mercury 856260 |

# D

## D.A. ☉
| 6/16/79 | 102 | 3 | Ready 'N' Steady .......................................... | $40 | | Rascal 102 |

## DA BUSH BABEES ☉ · R&B
Rap trio from Flatbush, New York: Kahliyl ("Mr. Man"), Lee Major ("Babe-Face Kaos") and Jamal ("Light" or "Y-Tee").

| 10/29/94+ | 116 | 7 | 1 We Run Things (It's Like Dat) ................ R&B:99 *Original* | $3 | ■ | Reprise 18069 |
| 2/18/95 | 102 | 9 | 2 Remember We ......................... *(original version)* | $3 | ■ | Reprise 18092 |
| 10/19/96 | 117 | 2 | 3 The Love Song ........................ R&B:66 *God Complex* | $3 | ■ | Warner 17586 |

BUSH BABEES Featuring Mos Def
samples "It's Just Begun" by **Jimmy Castor**, "Onsaya Joy" by **Groove Holmes** and "Summer Madness" by **Kool & The Gang**

## dada ☉ · ROK
Pop trio from Los Angeles: Joie Calio (vocals, bass), Michael Gurley (guitar) and Phil Leavitt (drums).

| 1/2/93 | 102 | 11 | Dizz Knee Land ...................... ROK:5 *Posters* | $3 | ■ | I.R.S. 13882 |

## DAFT PUNK · HOT
Dance duo from Paris: Thomas Bangalter and Guy-Manuel de Homem Christo.

| 5/3/97 | 108 | 10 | Da Funk .............................. *(remix) / Musique* [I] | $6 | | Virgin 38587 (CD) |

### DAISIES, The ☺
Female R&B vocal group.

| 9/26/64 | 133 | 1 | I Wanna Swim With Him ........................................................ *You Just Said You Love Me* | $15 | | Roulette 4571 |
| | | | Sammy Lowe (orch.) | | | |

### DAISY, Pat ☺
C&W/AC
Born Patricia Key Deasy on 10/10/44 in Gallatin, Tennessee. Moved to Huntsville, Alabama in 1966.

| 3/11/72 | 112 | 2 | Everybody's Reaching Out For Someone ..................... C&W:20 / AC:38 *I'll Be There* | $6 | | RCA Victor 0637 |
| | | | written by **Dickey Lee**; The Jordanaires (backing vocals) | | | |

### DALE, Alan
MEM/POP/HOT
Born Aldo Sigiamundi on 7/9/25 in Brooklyn. Baritone singer formerly with Carmen Cavallaro. Hosted his own TV show in 1951.

| 5/29/61 | 101[1] | 5 | Monday To Sunday .................................................... *That's A Teenage Girl* | $20 | | Sinclair 1003 |
| | | | Vince Catalano (orch.) | | | |

### DALE, Dick, and The Del-Tones
HOT
Born Richard Monsour on 5/4/37 in Boston. Later based in Southern California. Influential surf-rock guitarist.

| 6/8/63 | 124 | 2 | King Of The Surf Guitar ........................................................ *Hava Nagila* | $20 | ■ | Capitol 4963 |

### DALE & GRACE
HOT/AC/R&B
Pop vocal duo: Dale Houston (of Ferriday, Louisiana) and Grace Broussard (of Prairieville, Louisiana).

| 8/1/64 | 114 | 4 | Darling It's Wonderful.................................................... *What's Happening To Me* | $12 | | Montel 930 |
| | | | #48 hit for The Lovers in 1957 | | | |

### DALTON, Lacy J. ☺
C&W
Born Jill Byrem on 10/13/46 in Bloomsburg, Pennsylvania. Recorded for Harbor in 1978 as Jill Croston.

| 6/5/82 | 106 | 1 | Slow Down ........................................................ C&W:13 *One Of The Unsatisfied* | $4 | | Columbia 02847 |

### DALTREY, Roger
ROK/HOT/AC
Born on 3/1/44 in London. Formed band the Detours, which later became **The Who**; Daltrey was The Who's lead singer.

| 1/24/81 | 104 | 2 | Waiting For A Friend.................................................... *Bitter And Twisted* | $4 | | Polydor 2153 |
| | | | from the movie *McVicar* starring Daltrey | | | |

### DAMITA JO
HOT/AC/R&B/MEM
Born Damita Jo DuBlanc on 8/5/30 in Austin, Texas. Featured singer with Steve Gibson & The Red Caps.

| 10/2/61 | 105 | 5 | 1 Dance With A Dolly (With A Hole In Her Stocking) *You're Nobody 'Till Somebody Loves You* | $12 | ■ | Mercury 71871 |
| | | | #3 hit for Russ Morgan in 1944 | | | |
| 11/9/63 | 108 | 4 | 2 Stop Foolin'/ | | | |
| 11/16/63 | 111 | 4 | 3 Baby, You've Got It Made ........................................................ | $12 | | Mercury 72207 |
| | | | **BROOK BENTON & DAMITA JO** (above 2) | | | |
| 3/27/65 | 124 | 3 | 4 Tomorrow Night ........................................................ *Silver Dollar* | $7 | ■ | Epic 9766 |
| 5/8/65 | 119 | 1 | 5 Gotta Travel On ....................................................*Something You Got* | $7 | | Epic 9797 |
| | | | #4 hit for Billy Grammer in 1959 | | | |

### DAMNATION OF ADAM BLESSING ☺
Rock group: Adam Blessing (vocals), Bob Kalamasz (lead guitar), Jim Quinn (rhythm guitar), Ray Benick (bass) and Bill Schwark (drums).

| 11/21/70 | 102 | 7 | Back To The River.................................................... *Driver* | $6 | | United Artists 50726 |

### DAMON, Lenny, & The Bah Humbug Band ☺
Rock and roll band with a "sound" similar to Dr. Hook.

| 3/21/70 | 107 | 2 | Tippicaw Calley ........................................................ *Sookie Mama* | $15 | | Jubilee 5688 |

### DAMONE, Vic
MEM/AC/HOT
Born Vito Farinola on 6/12/28 in Brooklyn. Hosted own TV series (1956-57). *Pop Hits & Top Pop Singles*: 39.

| 10/6/62 | 131 | 1 | 1 What Kind Of Fool Am I?........................................................*Charmaine* | $8 | | Capitol 4827 |
| | | | Billy May (orch.); from Broadway's *Stop The World-I Want To Get Off*, #17 hit for **Sammy Davis, Jr.** in 1962 | | | |
| 7/10/65 | 127 | 4 | 2 Why Don't You Believe Me ...................... AC:25 *The Thrill Of Lovin' You* | $7 | | Warner 5644 |
| | | | Ernie Freeman (orch.); #1 hit for **Joni James** in 1952 | | | |

### DANA, Vic
HOT/AC
Born on 8/26/42 in Buffalo, New York. Moved to California as a teen.

| 10/22/66 | 114 | 3 | Distant Drums............................................ AC:33 *Love Me With All Your Heart* | $8 | | Dolton 324 |
| | | | Ernie Freeman (orch.); #45 hit for **Jim Reeves** in 1966 | | | |

### DANA DANE ☺
R&B
Rapper and art alumnus of New York's High School of Music and Art. Rap partner is DJ Clark Kent.

| 1/28/95 | 115 | 4 | 1 Record Jock.................................................... Sls:74/R&B:61 *(remix)* | $3 | ▌ | Maverick/Sire 18055 |
| 4/15/95 | 118 | 5 | 2 Rollin' Wit Dane.................................................... R&B:77 *(remix)* | $3 | ▌ | Maverick/Sire 17907 |

### D&D ALL-STARS, The ☺
R&B
Producers Douglas Gramma and David Lotwin. All-Stars: DJ Premier, **Mad Lion**, **Doug E. Fresh**, **KRS-One**, Fat Joe, **Smif-N-Wessun**, Jeru the Damaja.

| 8/12/95 | 108 | 9 | 1,2 Pass It........................................ R&B:66 *(album version) / Look Alive* (Big C) | $3 | ▌ | Arista Street 12846 |

### DANIELS, Charlie, Band
C&W/HOT/ROK/AC
Born on 10/28/36 in Wilmington, North Carolina. Formed country-rock band in Nashville in 1971: Daniels (vocals, guitar, fiddle), Tom Crain (guitar), Joe "Taz" DiGregorio (keyboards), Charles Hayward (bass) and James W. Marshall and Fred Edwards (drums).

| 11/29/75 | 101[2] | 3 | 1 Birmingham Blues .................................................... *Damn Good Cowboy* | $6 | | Kama Sutra 606 |
| 7/18/81 | 110 | 2 | 2 Sweet Home Alabama..............ROK:52 /C&W:94 *Falling In Love For The Night* (w/Crystal Gayle) | $4 | | Epic 02185 |
| | | | #8 hit for **Lynyrd Skynyrd** in 1974 | | | |
| 7/17/82 | 109 | 1 | 3 Ragin' Cajun .................................................... C&W:76 *The Universal Hand* | $4 | | Epic 02995 |

### DANKWORTH, Johnny, & his Orch.
HOT
Born on 9/20/27 in London. Alto saxophonist/jazz bandleader/composer. Married singer Cleo Laine in 1958.

| 4/10/61 | 101[2] | 4 | African Waltz .................................................... *Moanin'* [I] | $8 | | Roulette 4353 |
| | | | #41 hit for Cannonball Adderley in 1961 | | | |

**DANNY BOY** ☺ — R&B
Male rapper from Los Angeles.

| DEBUT | PEAK | WKS | A-side | $ | Pic | Label & Number |
| --- | --- | --- | --- | --- | --- | --- |
| 8/10/96 | 106 | 6 | 1 Slip N' Slide .............. R&B:67 *(remix)* | $3 | ■ | Death Row 99974 |
| 5/17/97 | 101[1] | 10 | 2 It's Over Now   Sls:70 /R&B:46 *(instrumental)* | $3 | ■ | Death Row 97017 |

from the movie *Gridlock'd* starring Tupac Shakur (2 Pac)

**DANTE, Ron** ☺
Born Carmine Granito on 8/22/45 in Staten Island, New York. Ghost voice of **The Archies**, **The Pearly Gate** and **The Cuff Links**.

| 8/8/70 | 102 | 2 | Let Me Bring You Up .............. *How Do You Know* | $7 | ■ | Kirshner 1010 |
| --- | --- | --- | --- | --- | --- | --- |

**DANTÉ and the EVERGREENS** — HOT
Born Donald Drowty on 9/8/41, lead singer of pop quartet from Los Angeles. Included Bill Young, Tony Moon and Frank D. Rosenthal.

| 12/31/60 | 107 | 1 | 1 What Are You Doing New Year's Eve/   [X] | | | |
| --- | --- | --- | --- | --- | --- | --- |

#9 R&B hit for The Orioles in 1949

| 1/9/61 | 104 | 2 | 2   Yeah Baby .............. | $25 | | Madison 143 |
| --- | --- | --- | --- | --- | --- | --- |

**DAPPS, The** ☺ — R&B
White R&B instrumental group from Cincinnati.

| 7/27/68 | 103 | 3 | There Was A Time .............. *The Rabbit Got The Gun* [I] | $12 | | King 6169 |
| --- | --- | --- | --- | --- | --- | --- |

THE DAPPS FEATURING ALFRED ELLIS
#35 hit for James Brown in 1968

**D'ARBY, Terence Trent** — HOT/R&B/AC/ROK
Born on 3/15/62 in New York City. England-based R&B-pop singer. Last name originally spelled Darby.

| 2/12/94 | 111 | 5 | Let Her Down Easy .............. *Come To Me* | $3 | ■ | Columbia 77231 |
| --- | --- | --- | --- | --- | --- | --- |

**DARIN, Bobby** — HOT/AC/R&B/C&W
Born Walden Robert Cassotto on 5/14/36 in the Bronx, New York. Died of heart failure on 12/20/73 in Los Angeles. Won the 1959 Best New Artist Grammy Award. Nominated for an Oscar for his performance in the movie *Captain Newman, MD* (1963). Formed own record company, Direction. Inducted into the Rock and Roll Hall of Fame in 1990. *Top Pop Singles:* 41.

| 7/17/61 | 113 | 1 | 1 Theme From "Come September" .............. *Walk Back To Me* [I] | $15 | ■ | Atco 6200 |
| --- | --- | --- | --- | --- | --- | --- |

BOBBY DARIN & HIS ORCHESTRA
from the movie starring Darin and Sandra Dee; #73 hit for Billy Vaughn in 1961

| 10/13/62 | 105 | 4 | 2 A True, True Love   *If A Man Answers* (Hot #32) | $12 | ■ | Capitol 4837 |
| --- | --- | --- | --- | --- | --- | --- |

love theme from the movie *If A Man Answers* starring Darin and Sandra Dee

| 4/24/65 | 133 | 1 | 3 Venice Blue (Que C'est Triste Venise) .............. *A World Without You* | $10 | | Capitol 5399 |
| --- | --- | --- | --- | --- | --- | --- |
| 10/9/65 | 117 | 3 | 4 We Didn't Ask To Be Brought Here .............. *Funny What Love Can Do* | $8 | | Atlantic 2305 |
| 9/9/67 | 105 | 2 | 5 She Knows .............. *Talk To The Animals* | $8 | | Atlantic 2433 |

Atlantic 2433 originally issued as "Talk To The Animals" b/w "After Today"

| 5/10/69 | 123 | 5 | 6 Me & Mr. Hohner .............. *Song For A Dollar* | $10 | | Direction 351 |
| --- | --- | --- | --- | --- | --- | --- |
| 9/6/69 | 111 | 1 | 7 Jive .............. *Distractions (Pt. I)* | $10 | | Direction 352 |

BOB DARIN

**DARLIN, Florraine** — HOT/AC
Born Florraine Panza on 1/20/44 in Pittsburgh.

| 7/4/64 | 121 | 5 | Johnny Loves Me .............. *I'll Take You Back Again* | $12 | | RIC 105-64 |
| --- | --- | --- | --- | --- | --- | --- |

written and produced by Larry Finnegan

**DARNELLS, The — see MARVELETTES, The**

**DARRELL, Johnny** ☺ — C&W
Born on 7/23/40 in Hopewell, Alabama. Died on 10/7/97. Country singer.

| 5/25/68 | 126 | 2 | With Pen In Hand .............. C&W:3 *Poetry Of Love* | $6 | | United Artists 50292 |
| --- | --- | --- | --- | --- | --- | --- |

written by Bobby Goldsboro; #43 hit for Billy Vera in 1968

**DARREN, James** — HOT/AC/C&W
Born James William Ercolani on 10/3/36 in Philadelphia. Singer/actor. Played "Moondoggie," Gidget's boyfriend, in the *Gidget* movies. In the TV series *The Time Tunnel* and *T.J. Hooker*.

| 4/22/67 | 123 | 3 | 1 Since I Don't Have You .............. *I Miss You So* | $7 | | Warner 7013 |
| --- | --- | --- | --- | --- | --- | --- |

#12 hit for The Skyliners in 1959

| 10/30/71 | 107 | 1 | 2 Mammy Blue .............. *As Long As You Love Me* | $6 | | Kirshner 5015 |
| --- | --- | --- | --- | --- | --- | --- |

#57 hit for the Pop-Tops in 1971

**DARVELL, Barry** ☺
Teenage pop/rockabilly singer.

| 12/28/59 | 110 | 3 | How Will It End? .............. *Geronimo Stomp* | $60 | | Colt 45 107 |
| --- | --- | --- | --- | --- | --- | --- |

**DAS EFX** — R&B/HOT
Rap duo of Andre "Dray" Weston (b: 9/9/70) and Willie "Skoob" Hines (b: 11/27/70) formed at Virginia State.

| 12/19/92+ | 106 | 7 | Straight Out The Sewer .............. R&B:66 *East Coast* | $3 | ■ | EastWest 98465 |
| --- | --- | --- | --- | --- | --- | --- |

**DAVE DEE, DOZY, BEAKY, MICK AND TICH** — HOT
British pop/rock quintet: Dave "Dee" Harman, Trevor "Dozy" Davies, John "Beaky" Dymond, Michael "Mick" Wilson and Ian "Tich" Amey.

| 12/31/66 | 110 | 4 | 1 Bend It .............. *She's So Good* | $12 | | Fontana 1559 |
| --- | --- | --- | --- | --- | --- | --- |
| 4/13/68 | 123 | 2 | 2 The Legend Of Xanadu .............. *Please* | $10 | | Imperial 66287 |

**DAVID & JONATHAN** — HOT/AC
Songwriting/producing/vocal duo from Bristol, England: Roger Greenaway (David) and Roger Cook (Jonathan).

| 4/23/66 | 109 | 5 | 1 Speak Her Name .............. *I Know* | $10 | ■ | Capitol 5625 |
| --- | --- | --- | --- | --- | --- | --- |

#89 hit for Walter Jackson in 1967

| 6/24/67 | 123 | 2 | 2 She's Leaving Home .............. *One Born Every Minute* | $12 | | Capitol 5934 |
| --- | --- | --- | --- | --- | --- | --- |

written by John Lennon and Paul McCartney (from The Beatles' *Sgt. Pepper's* album)

**DAVIS, Danny, And The Nashville Brass** ☺ — C&W
Born George Nowlan on 4/29/25 in Dorchester, Massachusetts. Country trumpet player/bandleader.

| 2/15/69 | 129 | 2 | 1 I Saw The Light .............. *Maiden's Prayer* [I] | $6 | | RCA Victor 9705 |
| --- | --- | --- | --- | --- | --- | --- |

THE NASHVILLE BRASS featuring DANNY DAVIS
written and recorded by Hank Williams in 1947

| 1/24/70 | 131 | 1 | 2 Wabash Cannon Ball .............. C&W:63 *Sweet Dreams* [I] | $6 | | RCA Victor 9785 |
| --- | --- | --- | --- | --- | --- | --- |

Roy Acuff's famous theme song since 1936

| DEBUT | PEAK | WKS | A-side (Chart Hit).............................................................................................B-side | $ | Pic | Label & Number |
|---|---|---|---|---|---|---|

**DAVIS, James ☉**
Blues singer/guitarist born in Pritchard, Alabama. Nicknamed "Thunderbird." Died of a heart attack on 1/24/91 (age 53).

| 11/23/63 | 113 | 2 | **Blue Monday** ...................................................................................... *Sing* | $15 | | Duke 368 |

**DAVIS, Jan ☉**  AC
Rock and roll guitarist.

| 5/9/64 | 129 | 1 | **Fugitive**................................................................................*Boss Machine* [I] | $15 | | A&M 733 |

The Ventures' version also "Bubbled Under" in 1964

**DAVIS, John, and The Monster Orchestra**  R&B/HOT
Born on 8/31/52 in Philadelphia. Disco producer/arranger. Wrote score for the Broadway musical *Gotta Go Disco*.

| 4/10/76 | 109 | 2 | **Night And Day** ...................................R&B:100  *Night And Day - Part I* [I] | $5 | | SAM 5002 |

#1 hit for Leo Reisman with Fred Astaire in 1932

**DAVIS, Mac**  C&W/AC/HOT
Born on 1/21/42 in Lubbock, Texas. Vocalist/guitarist/composer. Wrote "In The Ghetto," "Don't Cry Daddy," hits for **Elvis Presley**. Host of own musical variety TV series, 1974-76.

| 7/18/70 | 110 | 3 | 1 **I'll Paint You A Song** ................................ AC:14 /C&W:68  *Closest I Ever Came* | $6 | | Columbia 45192 |

from the movie *Norwood* starring **Glen Campbell** and Kim Darby

| 10/24/70 | 117 | 2 | 2 **I Believe In Music** ........................................................ AC:25  *Poor Man's Gold* | $6 | | Columbia 45245 |

a new version was released by Davis in 1971 on Columbia 45456

| 9/1/73 | 105 | 7 | 3 **Kiss It And Make It Better** ................................................. C&W:29  *Sunshine* | $5 | | Columbia 45911 |
| 3/7/81 | 102 | 6 | 4 **Hooked On Music**                                C&W:2  *Me And Fat Boy* | $4 | | Casablanca 2327 |
| 11/21/81 | 106 | 1 | 5 **You're My Bestest Friend** ................................ C&W:5  *You Are So Lovely* | $4 | | Casablanca 2341 |

**DAVIS, Paul**  HOT/AC/C&W
Born on 4/21/48 in Meridian, Mississippi. Singer/songwriter/producer. Pursued country music in the '80s.

| 12/19/70 | 118 | 2 | **Can't You** ..............................................................*Gonna Keep On Lovin' You* | $7 | | Bang 581 |

**DAVIS, Sammy Jr.**  HOT/AC/MEM/POP/C&W
Born on 12/8/25 in New York City. Died of throat cancer on 5/16/90. Vocalist/dancer/actor. First recorded for Capitol in 1950. Lost his left eye and had his nose smashed in an auto accident near San Bernardino, California on 11/19/54. One of the first black entertainers to gain widespread acclaim from white audiences.

| 5/30/64 | 112 | 3 | 1 **Choose/** | | | |
| 6/27/64 | 135 | 1 | 2 **Bee-Bom** ...................................................................................... | $8 | | Reprise 0278 |
| 10/24/64 | 106 | 9 | 3 **Don't Shut Me Out** ........................................... *The Disorderly Orderly* | $8 | | Reprise 0322 |
| 2/20/65 | 135 | 1 | 4 **If I Ruled The World** ............................................... *Flash, Bang, Wallop!* | $7 | | Reprise 0345 |

from the musical *Pickwick*; #34 hit for **Tony Bennett** in 1965

| 5/22/65 | 117 | 5 | 5 **No One Can Live Forever** ................................... AC:33  *Unforgettable* | $7 | | Reprise 0370 |
| 8/10/68 | 106 | 4 | 6 **Break My Mind** ...............................................*Children, Children* | $6 | | Reprise 0757 |

written by John D. Loudermilk; #6 Country hit for **George Hamilton IV** in 1967

| 4/5/69 | 124 | 3 | 7 **Rhythm Of Life** ...............................*The Pompeii Club (Rich Man's Frug)* [I] | $6 | ■ | Decca 732470 |

**SAMMY DAVIS JR. And Ensemble**
from the movie *Sweet Charity* starring Davis

| 5/31/69 | 119 | 4 | 8 **I Have But One Life To Live** ........................................*The Goin's Great* | $6 | | Reprise 0827 |
| 5/5/73 | 116 | 3 | 9 **(I'd Be) A Legend In My Time** ............................ AC:29  *I'm Not Anyone* | $5 | | MGM 14513 |

written by Don Gibson; #1 Country hit for **Ronnie Milsap** in 1975

| 5/8/76 | 101¹ | 5 | 10 **Baretta's Theme**                                AC:42  *I Heard A Song* | $5 | | 20th Century 2282 |

"Keep Your Eye On The Sparrow"; from the TV series *Baretta* starring Robert Blake; #20 hit for **Rhythm Heritage** in 1976

**DAVIS, Skeeter**  C&W/HOT/AC/R&B
Born Mary Frances Penick on 12/30/31 in Dry Ridge, Kentucky. Country singer.

| 8/1/64 | 106 | 5 | 1 **Let Me Get Close To You**.................................... C&W:45  *The Face Of A Clown* | $12 | | RCA Victor 8397 |

written by **Carole King** and Gerry Goffin

| 11/7/64 | 123 | 1 | 2 **What Am I Gonna Do With You**...................... C&W:38  *Don't Let Me Stand In Your Way* | $12 | | RCA Victor 8450 |
| 3/13/65 | 114 | 4 | 3 **A Dear John Letter** ................................C&W:11  *Too Used To Being With You* | $12 | | RCA Victor 8496 |

**SKEETER DAVIS & BOBBY BARE**
#1 Country hit for Jean Shepard & Ferlin Husky in 1953; #44 hit for **Pat Boone** in 1960

| 4/17/65 | 126 | 2 | 4 **I Can't Help It (If I'm Still In Love With You)**............... *You Taught Me Everything That I Know* | $12 | | RCA Victor 8543 |

#2 Country hit for **Hank Williams** in 1951

| 8/28/65 | 120 | 4 | 5 **Sun Glasses**.................................................... C&W:30  *He Loved Me Too Little* | $10 | | RCA Victor 8642 |

written by John D. Loudermilk

| 8/26/67 | 121 | 2 | 6 **What Does It Take (To Keep A Man Like You Satisfied)** ...................... C&W:5  *What I Go Thru (To Keep Holding On to You)* | $10 | | RCA Victor 9242 |
| 9/22/73 | 101¹ | 4 | 7 **I Can't Believe That It's All Over**                     C&W:12  *Try Jesus* | $7 | | RCA Victor 0968 |

**DAVIS, Spencer, Group**  HOT/R&B
Born on 7/14/41. Featured **Steve Winwood** (lead vocals, lead guitar, keyboards), his brother Muff Winwood (bass) and Pete York (drums). Winwood left in 1967 to form the group **Traffic**.

| 5/11/68 | 113 | 3 | **Looking Back** ...................................................................*After Tea* | $10 | | United Artists 50286 |

**DAVIS, Tyrone**  R&B/HOT
Born on 5/4/38 in Greenville, Mississippi. R&B singer. To Chicago in 1959. First recorded for Four Brothers in 1965 as Tyrone The Wonder Boy.

| 8/9/69 | 125 | 2 | 1 **All The Waiting Is Not In Vain** ....................*Need Your Lovin' Everyday* | $8 | | Dakar 609 |
| 8/26/72 | 119 | 2 | 2 **Come And Get This Ring** .....................................*After All This Time* | $7 | | Dakar 4510 |
| 10/21/72 | 107 | 2 | 3 **If You Had A Change In Mind** ..................... R&B:28  *Was It Just A Feeling* | $7 | | Dakar 4513 |
| 7/30/77 | 102 | 2 | 4 **This I Swear** ................................................... R&B:6  *Givin' Myself To You* | $5 | | Columbia 10528 |
| 3/25/78 | 102 | 4 | 5 **Get On Up (Disco)**                              R&B:12  *It's You, It's You* | $5 | | Columbia 10684 |

**DAY, Bing ☉**
Pop/rock and roll singer.

| 6/1/59 | 104 | 3 | **Mama's Place** ...............................................................*I Can't Help It* [S] | $25 | | Mercury 71446 |

recitation by Day done in "beatnik" style

**DAY, Bobby**　　　　　　　　　　　　　　　　　　　　　　HOT/R&B
Born Robert Byrd on 7/1/30 in Ft. Worth, Texas. Died on 7/15/90 of cancer. R&B singer.

| 11/14/60 | 103 | 4 | Gee Whiz.............................................................................. *Over And Over* | $20 | | Rendezvous 136 |

**BOBBY DAY (with Earl Nelson and Orchestra)**
#28 hit for The Innocents in 1961

**DAY, Doris**　　　　　　　　　　　　　　　　　　　　　　MEM/POP/HOT/AC
Born Doris Kappelhoff on 4/3/22 in Cincinnati. Became a major star with the Les Brown band (she had 12 charted hits with Brown). Became the #1 box office star of the late '50s and early '60s. Star of own popular TV series from 1968-73. *Pop Hits & Top Pop Singles*: 46.

| 5/2/60 | 102 | 3 | 1 Please Don't Eat The Daisies........................................ *Here We Go Again* | $8 | ■ | Columbia 41630 |

Bill Marx (orch., with children's chorus); from the movie starring Day

| 7/11/60 | 111 | 1 | 2 A Perfect Understanding........................................................ *The Blue Train* | $8 | | Columbia 41703 |

Frank DeVol (orch.)

| 12/12/64 | 135 | 1 | 3 Send Me No Flowers ........................................................ *Rainbow's End* | $7 | | Columbia 43153 |

Mort Garson (orch.); from the movie starring Day; B-side produced by Day's son, Terry Melcher (**Bruce & Terry**)

**DAYNE, Taylor**　　　　　　　　　　　　　　　　　　　　　HOT/AC/R&B
Born Leslie Wundermann on 3/7/63 in Baldwin, New York. Female Adult Contemporary singer.

| 4/16/94 | 103 | 5 | I'll Wait ............................................................................. *(hot mix)* | $3 | ■ | Arista 12658 |

**DA YOUNGSTA'S**　　　　　　　　　　　　　　　　　　　　R&B/HOT
Rap trio: Tarik Dawson, Taji Goodman and Qur'an Goodman.

| 5/1/93 | 110 | 5 | Crewz Pop ............................... R&B:59 *(2 versions) / Who's The Mic Wrecka (3 versions)* | $5 | ■ | EastWest 96068 * |

**DAYTRIPPERS, The** ☉
Rock and roll band.

| 2/26/66 | 129 | 1 | That's Part Of The Game ................................................ *You Cheated* | $20 | | Karate 525 |

**DAZZ BAND**　　　　　　　　　　　　　　　　　　　　　　R&B/HOT
R&B/funk band from Cleveland featuring Bobby Harris (vocals, sax).

| 1/6/79 | 104 | 1 | 1 I Might As Well Forget About Loving You........................... R&B:46 *Dazzberry Jam* | $5 | | 20th Century 2390 |

**KINSMAN DAZZ**

| 4/4/81 | 109 | 1 | 2 Invitation To Love ................................................. R&B:51 *Magnetized* | $4 | | Motown 1507 |
| 3/23/85 | 110 | 1 | 3 Heartbeat ....................................................... R&B:12 *Rock With Me* | $4 | | Motown 1775 |

**DC TALK**　　　　　　　　　　　　　　　　　　　　　　　HOT/AC
Christian hip-hop trio from Washington, D.C.: Toby McKeehan, Michael Tait and Kevin Smith.

| 10/7/95 | 109 | 10 | Jesus Freak ...................................... *(remix) / I Wish We'd All Been Ready* | $3 | ■ | Forefront 25135 |

**DEACONS, The** ☉
Syl Johnson's backup band from Chicago, featuring Johnson's brother Jimmy on guitar.

| 12/14/68 | 121 | 1 | Sock It To Me Part I.......................................... R&B:24 *Part II* [I] | $15 | | Shama 100 |

instrumental version of **Syl Johnson**'s #12 R&B hit "Come On Sock It To Me"

**DEAL, Bill, & The Rhondels**　　　　　　　　　　　　　　　HOT
Brassy-rock band from Virginia Beach, Virginia featuring Bill Deal (vocals, organ).

| 8/19/72 | 108 | 5 | It's Too Late ...................................................... *So What If It Rains* | $8 | | Buddah 318 |

#1 hit for **Carole King** in 1971

**DEAN, Jimmy**　　　　　　　　　　　　　　　　　　　　　C&W/HOT/AC
Born on 8/10/28 in Plainview, Texas. Country singer. Own CBS-TV series, 1957-58; ABC-TV series, 1963-66.

| 6/8/59 | 106 | 3 | 1 Sing Along........................................................... *Weekend Blue* | $10 | ■ | Columbia 41395 |

vocal backing by **Mitch Miller**'s 'sing-along gang'; Jimmy Carroll (orch.)

| 4/6/63 | 128 | 3 | 2 This Ole House.................................................. *Mile Long Train* | $7 | ■ | Columbia 42738 |

#1 hit for **Rosemary Clooney** in 1954

**DEAN, Terri** ☉
Female pop vocalist.

| 6/1/59 | 107 | 3 | I'm Confessin' (That I Love You) .................................. *I Blew Out The Flame* | $20 | | Laurel 1003 |

Howie Biggs (orch.); #58 hit for **Frank Ifield** in 1963; #2 hit for Guy Lombardo in 1930

**DEAN AND JEAN**　　　　　　　　　　　　　　　　　　　　HOT
Vocal duo of Welton "Dean" Young and Brenda Lee "Jean" Jones from Dayton, Ohio.

| 6/13/64 | 123 | 2 | Thread Your Needle........................................ *I Wanna Be Loved* (Hot #91) | $10 | | Rust 5081 |

**DEARDORFF & JOSEPH** ☉
Pop vocal duo: Danny Deardorff and Marcus Joseph.

| 3/19/77 | 109 | 4 | Never Have To Say Goodbye Again........................ AC:22 *The Little Kings Of Earth* | $5 | | Arista 0230 |

#9 hit for **England Dan & John Ford Coley** in 1978

**DeBARGE, El**　　　　　　　　　　　　　　　　　　　　　R&B/HOT/AC
Born Eldra DeBarge on 6/4/61 in Grand Rapids, Michigan. Lead singer of family group DeBarge.

| 5/21/94 | 112 | 7 | 1 Can't Get Enough ..................................... R&B:21 *You To Turn Me On* | $3 | ■ | Reprise 18155 |
| 9/3/94 | 106 | 8 | 2 Where Is My Love? ............... Sls:68 /R&B:19 *Starlight, Moonlight, Candlelight* | $3 | ■ | Reprise 18140 |

**EL DeBARGE featuring Babyface**
above 2 written and produced by **Babyface**

**DeBURGH, Chris**　　　　　　　　　　　　　　　　　　　　AC/HOT/ROK
Born Christopher John Davidson on 10/15/48 of Irish parentage in Buenos Aires, Argentina. Pop-rock singer.

| 9/13/80 | 106 | 3 | The Traveller ...................................................... *Wall Of Silence* | $4 | | A&M 2259 |

**DECEMBER'S CHILDREN** ☉
Pop/rock group featuring lead singer Janet Belpulsi. Belpulsi was murdered in 1991.

| 5/18/68 | 123 | 5 | Backwards And Forwards ....................................... *Kissin' Time* | $10 | ■ | World Pacific 77887 |

**DEE, Dave — see DAVE DEE**

**DEE, Joey, & The Starliters**　　　　　　　　　　　　　　　HOT/R&B
Born Joseph DiNicola on 6/11/40 in Passaic, New Jersey. Joey & the Starliters became the house band at the Peppermint Lounge, New York City in September 1960.

| 6/16/62 | 105 | 3 | Everytime (I Think About You) Part One ................................ *Part Two* | $15 | | Roulette 4431 |

from the movie *Two Tickets to Paris* starring Dee

| DEBUT | PEAK | WKS | A-side (Chart Hit) .................................................................................B-side | $ | Pic | Label & Number |
|-------|------|-----|------|---|-----|------|

**DEE, Kiki**                     HOT/AC
Born Pauline Matthews on 3/6/47 in Yorkshire, England. Pop/rock vocalist.

| 7/13/74 | 108 | 1 | Super Cool ....................................................................... *Loving And Free* | $6 | | MCA/Rocket 40256 |

written and produced by **Elton John**

**DEE, Ricky, & the Embers** ✪
Instrumental rock and roll quintet from Philadelphia featuring Bobby Arnel.

| 6/2/62 | 103 | 4 | Work Out (Part 1) .................................................. *(Part 2)* [I] | $15 | | Newtown 5001 |

same melody as **Sam Cooke's** 1962 hit "Twistin' The Night Away"

**DEE, Tommy** ✪
Tommy Dee is a character featured in the movie *The Idolmaker* as portrayed by actor Paul Land.

| 1/10/81 | 107 | 6 | Here Is My Love .............................................. *I Know Where You're Goin'* (**Nino Tempo**) | $4 | ■ | A&M 2282 |

vocal performance by **Jesse Frederick**; from the movie *The Idolmaker* starring Ray Sharkey

**DEELE, The**             R&B/HOT/AC
R&B funk sextet from Cincinnati, led by Darnell "Dee" Bristol. Included the songwriting/production team of L.A. Reid and **Babyface**.

| 6/8/85 | 101[1] | 5 | Material Thangz            R&B:14 *Working (9 to 5)* | $4 | | Solar 69644 |

**DEEP BLUE SOMETHING**      HOT/AC/ROK
Pop-rock quartet from Dallas: brothers Todd (vocals, bass) and Toby (guitar) Pipes, Kirk Tatom (guitar) and John Kirtland (drums).

| 4/27/96 | 102 | 7 | Halo ........................................................ *(remix) / Dear Prudence* | $3 | ■ | Interscope 97000 |

**DEEP PURPLE**            ROK/HOT
British pioneer heavy-metal band formed in 1968: Ritchie Blackmore (guitar), Rod Evans (vocals), Jon Lord (keyboards), Ian Paice (drums) and Nicky Simper (bass). Evans and Simper left in 1969, replaced by Ian Gillan (vocals) and **Roger Glover** (bass). Gillan and Glover left in late 1973, replaced by **David Coverdale** (vocals) and Glenn Hughes (bass). Blackmore left in early 1975 to form **Rainbow** (which Glover later joined); replaced by American Tommy Bolin (ex-**James Gang** guitarist; d: 12/4/76). Band split in July 1976. Coverdale formed **Whitesnake**.

| 3/22/69 | 128 | 3 | 1 Emmaretta ...................................................... *The Bird Has Flown* | $10 | | Tetragrammaton 1519 |
| 8/2/69 | 108 | 3 | 2 Hallelujah (I Am The Preacher) ........................... *April (Part I)* | $10 | | Tetragrammaton 1537 |
| 6/1/74 | 105 | 4 | 3 Burn ............................................................. *Coronarias Redig* | $6 | | Warner 7809 |

**DEEP SIX, The** ✪
Five-man, one-woman folk/rock group from Southern California: Dave Gray, Don Lottermoser, Tony Scott, Don Dunn, Mac Elsensohn and Miss Dean Cannon.

| 11/27/65 | 122 | 3 | Rising Sun ............................................................... *Strollin' Blues* | $10 | | Liberty 55838 |

**DEER, John** ✪                 C&W

| 4/24/71 | 114 | 2 | The Battle Hymn Of Lt. Calley .................................... *Sittin' In Atlanta Station* | $6 | | Royal American 34 |

#37 hit for C Company Featuring Terry Nelson in 1971

**DEES, Rick**            ROK/HOT/R&B
Born Rigdon Osmond Dees III in Memphis in 1950. One of America's top radio DJs.

| 8/5/78 | 110 | 1 | 1 Bigfoot ........................................................... *Big Toe* [N] | $5 | ■ | Stax 3207 |
| 12/1/84 | 104 | 2 | 2 Get Nekked ....................................... *Eat My Shorts* (Hot #75) [N] | $4 | ■ | Atlantic 89601 |

**DEF LEPPARD**           ROK/HOT/AC
Hard-rock quintet formed in 1977 in Sheffield, England: Joe Elliott (vocals), Steve Clark (d: 1/8/91) and Pete Willis (guitars), Rick Savage (bass) and Rick Allen (drums).

| 7/5/80 | 106 | 2 | Rock Brigade ............................... *When The Walls Came Tumbling Down* | $4 | | Mercury 76064 |

**DeFRANCO FAMILY featuring TONY DeFRANCO**    HOT/AC
Pop family group from Ontario: Tony (age 13 in 1973), Merlina (16), Nino (17), Marisa (18) and Benny (19).

| 9/28/74 | 104 | 6 | Write Me A Letter ......................................................... *Baby Blue* | $5 | ■ | 20th Century 2128 |

**DEKKER, Desmond**          HOT
Born Desmond Dacris on 7/16/41 in Kingston, Jamaica. Leader of reggae group.

| 11/21/70 | 103 | 3 | You Can Get It If You Really Want ...................................... *Perserverance* | $7 | | Uni 55261 |

written by **Jimmy Cliff**

**DEL AMITRI**           HOT/ROK/AC
Pop-rock quartet formed in 1983 in Glasgow, Scotland: Justin Currie (vocals, bass)), David Cummings and Iain Harvie (guitars) and Brian McDermott (drums).

| 3/9/96 | 117 | 2 | Tell Her This .......................................................... *Food For Songs* | $3 | ■ | A&M 1322 |

**DELANEY & BONNIE & FRIENDS**    HOT/AC
Delaney Bramlett (b: 7/1/39, Pontotoc County, Mississippi) and wife Bonnie Lynn Bramlett (b: 11/8/44, Acton, Illinois). Married in 1967.

| 4/11/70 | 128 | 1 | 1 Teasin' .......................................................... *Soulin'* (Curtis) [I] | $8 | | Atco 6738 |

**KING CURTIS With Delaney Bramlett, Eric Clapton & Friends**

| 10/24/70 | 119 | 2 | 2 They Call It Rock & Roll Music .................. *Miss Ann* (w/Little Richard) | $8 | | Atco 6788 |

**DE LA SOUL**          R&B/HOT
Psychedelic-rap trio from Long Island, New York: Posdnuos, Trugoy the Dove and P.A. Pasemaster Mase.

| 6/29/96 | 101[1] | 5 | 1 The Bizness/              R&B:53 | | | |

**DE LA SOUL featuring Common Sense**

| | | 1 | 2 Stakes Is High ................................................. R&B:70 | $6 | ■ | Tommy Boy 730 (T) |

samples "Mind Power" by **James Brown** and "Swahililand" by Ahmad Jamal

| 10/12/96 | 113 | 4 | 3 Itzsoweezee (Hot) .............................. R&B:60 *Stakes Is High* (remix) | $3 | ■ | Tommy Boy 7752 |

**DELCOS, The** ✪
R&B vocal group from South Bend, Indiana — Peter Woodard, lead singer.

| 4/20/63 | 111 | 2 | Arabia ............................................... *Those Three Little Words* | $60 | | Showcase 2501 |

first pressings on green label; first released on Ebony 01 in 1962 ($150)

**DELFONICS, The**         R&B/HOT
R&B vocal group from Philadelphia: William and Wilbert Hart, Ritchie Daniels and Randy Cain. Daniels left for the service in 1968; group was replaced by Major Harris in 1971.

| 1/27/73 | 101[2] | 4 | 1 Think It Over         R&B:47 *I'm A Man* | $8 | | Philly Groove 174 |
| 2/16/74 | 101[2] | 13 | 2 I Told You So     R&B:26 *Seventeen And In Love* | $8 | | Philly Groove 182 |

| DEBUT | PEAK | WKS | A-side (Chart Hit)..........................................................B-side | $ | Pic | Label & Number |
|-------|------|-----|---------------------------------|---|-----|----------------|
| | | | **DELICATES, The** ⊘ | | | |
| 8/24/59 | 105 | 1 | 1 Ronnie Is My Lover.................................*Black And White Thunderbird* | $25 | | Unart 2017 |
| 1/30/65 | 120 | 3 | 2 I Want To Get Married.........................................*I've Been Hurt* | $20 | | Challenge 59267 |
| | | | **DELICATO, Paul** ⊘      AC/C&W | | | |
| | | | Pop singer from St. Louis. | | | |
| 3/20/76 | 108 | 2 | Cara Mia...........AC:5 *Ice Cream Sodas And Lollipops And A Red Hot Spinning Top* | $4 | | Artists of America 111 |
| | | | #4 hit for Jay & The Americans in 1965 | | | |
| | | | **DELIGHTS ORCHESTRA, The** ⊘ | | | |
| 10/26/68 | 128 | 2 | Paul's Midnight Ride.................*Baby Be Mine* (Sweet Delights) [I] | $8 | | Atco 6601 |
| | | | instrumental arrangement similar to Cliff Noble's 1968 hit "The Horse" | | | |
| | | | **DELLS, The**      R&B/HOT | | | |
| | | | R&B vocal group formed in Harvey, Illinois: Johnny Funches (d: 1/23/98, age 62), Marvin Junior, Verne Allison, Mickey McGill and Chuck Barksdale. Funches replaced by Johnny Carter (ex-**Flamingos**) in 1960. *Top Pop Singles*: 24. | | | |
| 6/12/65 | 122 | 2 | 1 Stay In My Corner......................R&B:23 *It's Not Unusual* | $15 | | Vee-Jay 674 |
| | | | a new version made the *Hot 100* (#10) on 6/29/68 on Cadet 5612 ($8) | | | |
| 11/1/69 | 108 | 2 | 2 When I'm In Your Arms.............On The Dock Of The Bay (Hot #42) | $8 | | Cadet 5658 |
| 12/20/75 | 104 | 3 | 3 We Got To Get Our Thing Together......R&B:17 *Reminiscing* | $5 | | Mercury 73723 |
| 2/7/76 | 106 | 1 | 4 The Power Of Love.......R&B:58 *Gotta Get Home To My Baby* | $5 | | Mercury 73759 |
| 7/24/76 | 102 | 4 | 5 Slow Motion.........R&B:49 *Ain't No Black And White In Music* | $5 | | Mercury 73807 |
| 9/9/78 | 108 | 3 | 6 Super Woman............R&B:24 *My Life Is So Wonderful (When You're Around)* | $5 | | ABC 12386 |
| 3/17/84 | 107 | 3 | 7 You Just Can't Walk Away.........R&B:23 *Don't Want Nobody* | $4 | | Private I 04343 |
| | | | **DEL VIKINGS, The**      HOT/R&B/AC | | | |
| | | | Interracial doo-wop group formed in Pittsburgh in 1955: Norman Wright, Corinthian "Krips" Johnson (d: 8/22/90), Donald "Gus" Backus, David Lerchey and Clarence Quick. Backus and Lerchey are white; others black. | | | |
| 5/22/61 | 101[1] | 3 | 1 Bring Back Your Heart.........*I'll Never Stop Crying* | $30 | | ABC-Paramount 10208 |
| 1/27/73 | 112 | 3 | 2 Come Go With Me.........AC:32 *When You're Asleep* [R] | $8 | | Scepter 12367 |
| | | | new version of the original 1957 *Hot 100* hit (#4) on Dot 15538 | | | |
| | | | **DELTAIRS, The** ⊘ | | | |
| | | | Female R&B vocal quintet. | | | |
| 4/17/61 | 114 | 4 | Lullaby Of The Bells.........*It's Only You, Dear* | $50 | | Ivy 101 |
| | | | Al Browne (orch.); above release on green label; originally released in 1957 on a yellow label ($300) | | | |
| | | | **DEMUS, Chaka, & Pliers**      R&B/HOT | | | |
| | | | Jamaican male dancehall reggae duo of DJ Chaka Demus and vocalist Everton "Pliers" Banner. | | | |
| 8/14/93 | 112 | 3 | I Wanna Be Your Man.........R&B:87 *Friday Evening* | $3 | ∎ | Mango 530132 |
| | | | **DENINE**      HOT | | | |
| | | | Born Denine Latanzo in Philadelphia. Female dance singer. | | | |
| 1/29/94 | 116 | 3 | I Remember You.........*(3 mixes)* | $5 | ∎ | Viper 1001 * |
| | | | **DENNIS, Gloria** ⊘ | | | |
| | | | Pop songstress. | | | |
| 9/15/62 | 115 | 3 | Richie.........*Ask* | $12 | | Rust 5049 |
| | | | **DENNY, Martin**      HOT/AC/R&B | | | |
| | | | Born on 4/10/21 in New York City. Composer/arranger/pianist. Originated "The Exotic Sounds of Martin Denny" in Hawaii. | | | |
| 12/1/62 | 124 | 3 | 1 Cast Your Fate To The Wind.........*The Payoff* [I] | $8 | | Liberty 55514 |
| | | | #22 hit for Vince Guaraldi Trio in 1963; #10 hit for **Sounds Orchestral** in 1965 | | | |
| 12/12/64 | 132 | 2 | 2 Hawaii Tattoo.........*White Silver Sands* [I] | $8 | | Liberty 55754 |
| | | | #33 hit for The Waikikis in 1965 | | | |
| | | | **DENVER, John**      AC/HOT/C&W | | | |
| | | | Born Henry John Deutschendorf on 12/31/43 in Roswell, New Mexico. Died on 10/12/97 at the controls of a light plane which crashed off the California coast. Won an Emmy in 1975 for the TV special *An Evening with John Denver*. *Top Pop Singles*: 33. | | | |
| 9/30/72 | 103 | 6 | 1 Hard Life, Hard Times | $6 | | RCA Victor 0801 |
| | | | (Prisoners).........*Late Winter, Early Spring (When Everybody Goes to Mexico)* | | | |
| 3/3/79 | 106 | 2 | 2 Downhill Stuff.........C&W:64 *Life Is So Good* | $4 | | RCA 11479 |
| 4/21/79 | 107 | 2 | 3 What's On Your Mind.........AC:10 /C&W:47 *Sweet Melinda* (C&W flip) | $4 | | RCA 11535 |
| | | | **DEREK & THE DOMINOS — see CLAPTON, Eric** | | | |
| | | | **DeSARIO, Teri — see KC And The SUNSHINE BAND** | | | |
| | | | **DeSHANNON, Jackie**      HOT/R&B | | | |
| | | | Born Sharon Myers on 8/21/44 in Hazel, Kentucky. First recorded (as Sherry Lee Myers) for Glenn in 1959. Attained prominence as a prolific songwriter. Married composer/movie scorer **Randy Edelman**. | | | |
| 4/28/62 | 108 | 1 | 1 The Prince.........*I'll Drown In My Own Tears* | $20 | | Liberty 55425 |
| | | | also released with "That's What Boys Are Made Of" on the B-side ($20) | | | |
| 9/14/63 | 110 | 3 | 2 Little Yellow Roses.........*Oh Sweet Chariot* | $20 | | Liberty 55602 |
| | | | also released with "500 Miles" on the B-side ($20) | | | |
| 4/4/64 | 112 | 4 | 3 Oh Boy.........*I'm Looking For Someone To Love* | $15 | | Liberty 55678 |
| | | | #10 hit for **The Crickets** in 1958 | | | |
| 10/29/66 | 108 | 4 | 4 Windows And Doors.........*So Long Johnny* | $10 | | Imperial 66196 |
| 2/18/67 | 121 | 4 | 5 Come On Down (From The Top Of That Hill).........*Find Me Love* | $10 | | Imperial 66224 |
| 9/30/67 | 110 | 4 | 6 It's All In The Game.........*Changin' My Mind* | $10 | | Imperial 66251 |
| | | | #1 hit for Tommy Edwards in 1958 | | | |
| 3/9/68 | 119 | 5 | 7 Me About You.........*I Keep Wanting You* | $10 | | Imperial 66281 |
| | | | #83 hit for The Mojo Men in 1967 | | | |
| 10/21/72 | 110 | 2 | 8 Paradise.........AC:33 *I Wanna Roo You* | $8 | | Atlantic 2895 |
| | | | **DETROIT — see RYDER, Mitch** | | | |

**DETROIT EMERALDS**  R&B/HOT
R&B vocal group formed in Little Rock, Arkansas by the Tilmon brothers: Abrim (d: 1982, heart attack), Ivory, Cleophus and Raymond. In 1970, group reduced to trio of Abrim, Ivory and friend James Mitchell.

| | | | | | | |
| --- | --- | --- | --- | --- | --- | --- |
| 11/11/72 | 110 | 2 | 1 Feel The Need In Me.......................................R&B:22 *There's A Love For Me Somewhere* | $8 | | Westbound 209 |
| | | | a new version "Feel The Need" made the *Hot 100* (#90) in 1977 on Westbound 55401 | | | |
| 7/14/73 | 101[1] | 7 | 2 You're Gettin' A Little Too Smart      R&B:10 *Heaven Couldn't Be Like This* | $8 | | Westbound 213 |

**DeVITO, Karla** ☉
New York-based singer/actress. Toured with Meat Loaf in 1978. Starred in the Broadway musical *The Pirates Of Penzance*. Married to actor Robby Benson.

| | | | | | | |
| --- | --- | --- | --- | --- | --- | --- |
| 11/7/81 | 109 | 2 | Midnight Confession.............................................................*Just Like You* | $4 | | Epic 02597 |
| | | | #5 hit for **The Grass Roots** in 1968 | | | |

**DEVO**  HOT/ROK
Robotic rock group formed in 1976 in Akron, Ohio: brothers Mark (synthesizers) and Bob (vocals, guitar) Mothersbaugh, brothers Jerry (bass) and Bob (guitar) Casale, and Alan Myers (drums).

| | | | | | | |
| --- | --- | --- | --- | --- | --- | --- |
| 12/20/80 | 103 | 4 | 1 Freedom Of Choice ............................................................*Snowball* | $5 | ■ | Warner 49621 |
| 11/14/81 | 102 | 5 | 2 Beautiful World .............................................................*Enough Said* | $4 | ■ | Warner 49834 |
| 4/24/82 | 107 | 2 | 3 Through Being Cool.........................................................*Going Under* | $4 | | Warner 50048 |
| 11/6/82 | 106 | 7 | 4 Peek-A-Boo!.....................................................................*Find Out* | $4 | ■ | Warner 29931 |
| 1/15/83 | 104 | 4 | 5 That's Good .............................................................*What I Must Do* | $4 | | Warner 29811 |

**DEY, Tracey**  HOT/AC
Native of Yonkers, New York. Also recorded as the "voice" of The Rag Dolls.

| | | | | | | |
| --- | --- | --- | --- | --- | --- | --- |
| 7/11/64 | 107 | 4 | Hangin' On To My Baby ...............................................*Ska-Doo-Dee-Yah* | $15 | | Amy 908 |

**DIABLOS, The** ☉  R&B
R&B vocal group from Detroit featuring brothers Nolan (b: 1/22/34; d: 2/21/77; lead) and Jimmy "Big Jim" Strong (also deceased). Nolan and Jimmy were cousins of Barrett Strong.

| | | | | | | |
| --- | --- | --- | --- | --- | --- | --- |
| 6/27/60 | 114 | 1 | 1 The Wind ...................................................................*Baby, Be Mine* | $50 | | Fortune 511 |
| | | | **THE DIABLOS Featuring Nolan Strong** | | | |
| | | | originally released in 1954 on a thick plastic, purple label ($100) (above reissue on thinner plastic) | | | |
| 11/3/62 | 112 | 3 | 2 Mind Over Matter (I'm Gonna Make You Mine) ........................*Beside You* | $40 | | Fortune 546 |
| | | | **NOLAN STRONG** | | | |
| | | | original pressings in 1962 are on a pink label | | | |

**DIAMOND, Gregg** ☉  R&B
Writer/producer for **Gloria Gaynor**, **George McCrae** and the Andrea True Connection. Also see **Bionic Boogie**.

| | | | | | | |
| --- | --- | --- | --- | --- | --- | --- |
| 1/27/79 | 102 | 8 | Star Cruiser...........................................R&B:57 *This Side Of Midnight* | $5 | | Marlin 3329 |

**DIAMOND AND THE PSYCHOTIC NEUROTICS** ☉ R&B
Diamond is a rap producer.

| | | | | | | |
| --- | --- | --- | --- | --- | --- | --- |
| 3/13/93 | 105 | 6 | Sally Got A One Track Mind ....................R&B:84 *(2 album snippets)* | $3 | ▌ | Chemistry 864850 |
| | | | samples "Sparkling In The Sand" by **Tower Of Power** | | | |

**DIAMOND HEAD** ☉
Adult Contemporary vocal group.

| | | | | | | |
| --- | --- | --- | --- | --- | --- | --- |
| 5/5/73 | 106 | 5 | If That's The Way You Want It................*What Do I Do On Sunday Morning?* | $5 | | Dunhill/ABC 4342 |

**DIAMOND REO**  HOT
Pop/rock band from Pittsburgh: Bob McKeag (vocals, guitar), Frank Czuri (keyboards), Norm Nardini (bass) and Robbie Johns (drums).

| | | | | | | |
| --- | --- | --- | --- | --- | --- | --- |
| 8/16/75 | 108 | 1 | Work Hard Labor .............................................*Sittin' On Top Of The Blues* | $5 | | Big Tree 16043 |

**DIAMOND RIO** ☉  C&W
Country band: Marty Roe (vocals), Jimmy Olander (guitar), Gene Johnson (mandolin), Dan Truman (piano), Dana Williams (bass) and Brian Prout (drums).

| | | | | | | |
| --- | --- | --- | --- | --- | --- | --- |
| 1/7/95 | 107 | 7 | 1 Night Is Fallin' In My Heart .........Sls:72 /C&W:9 *Down By The Riverside* | $3 | ▌ | Arista 12764 |
| 3/11/95 | 102 | 12 | 2 Bubba Hyde ..................................Sls:71 /C&W:16 *(dance mix)* | $3 | ▌ | Arista 12787 |

**DIBANGO, Manu**  R&B/HOT/AC
Born on 2/10/34 in Cameroon, Africa. Jazz-R&B saxophonist/pianist.

| | | | | | | |
| --- | --- | --- | --- | --- | --- | --- |
| 10/20/73 | 109 | 4 | Dangwa ..............................................R&B:77 *Obaso* [I] | $5 | | Atlantic 2983 |

**DICK & DEEDEE**  HOT/AC
Dick St. John Gosting and Deedee Sperling. Pop duo formed while students in high school at Santa Monica.

| | | | | | | |
| --- | --- | --- | --- | --- | --- | --- |
| 6/22/63 | 103 | 6 | Love Is A Once In A Lifetime Thing................*Chug-A-Chug-A Choo Choo* | $10 | | Warner 5364 |

**DICKENS, "Little" Jimmy**  C&W/AC
Born on 12/19/20 in Bolt, West Virginia. Country singer who stands only 4'11" tall.

| | | | | | | |
| --- | --- | --- | --- | --- | --- | --- |
| 2/12/66 | 103 | 5 | When The Ship Hit The Sand .........C&W:27 *Truck Load Of Starvin' Kangaroos* | $8 | | Columbia 43514 |

**DICKSON, Barbara** ☉
Born on 9/27/47 in Dunfermline, Scotland. Pop singer/songwriter.

| | | | | | | |
| --- | --- | --- | --- | --- | --- | --- |
| 7/23/77 | 110 | 1 | Who Was It Stole Your Heart Away ..............................*Stolen Love* | $5 | | RSO 875 |

**DIDDLEY, Bo**  R&B/HOT
Born Otha Ellas Bates McDaniel on 12/30/28 in McComb, Mississippi. Unique and influential R&B-rock and roll guitarist/vocalist. His first record was a two-sided #1 hit on the R&B charts: "Bo Diddley"/"I'm A Man." Inducted into the Rock and Roll Hall of Fame in 1987.

| | | | | | | |
| --- | --- | --- | --- | --- | --- | --- |
| 11/30/59 | 106 | 3 | 1 Say Man, Back Again .......................................R&B:23 *She's Alright* [N] | $25 | | Checker 936 |
| | | | sequel to Diddley's #20 hit "Say Man" in 1959 | | | |
| 6/13/60 | 111 | 1 | 2 Crawdad ......................................................*Walkin' and Talkin'* | $20 | | Checker 951 |

**DIESEL**  HOT/ROK
Rock quartet from Holland: Rob Vunderink (vocals, guitar), Mark Boon (guitars), Frank Papendrecht (bass) and Pim Koopman (drums).

| | | | | | | |
| --- | --- | --- | --- | --- | --- | --- |
| 1/16/82 | 105 | 3 | Goin' Back To China ............................................*The Harness* | $4 | | Regency 7343 |

**DIFFIE, Joe**  C&W/HOT
Born on 12/28/58 in Tulsa; raised in Duncan, Oklahoma. Country singer/guitarist.

| | | | | | | |
| --- | --- | --- | --- | --- | --- | --- |
| 10/9/93 | 122 | 1 | Prop Me Up Beside The Jukebox (If I Die).........C&W:3 *I Can Walk The Line (If It Ain't Too Straight)* | $3 | ▌ | Epic 77071 |

**DIGABLE PLANETS**       R&B/HOT
Rap trio from Washington, D.C.: Ishmael "Butterfly" Butler, Mary Ann "Ladybug" Vierra and Craig "Doodle Bug" Irving.

| 4/24/93 | 106 | 9 | Where I'm From.................................Sls:68 /R&B:60 (remix) | $3 | ▌ Pendulum 64648 |

samples "Ain't Nothin' Wrong" by K.C. And The Sunshine Band

**DILLARDS, The**       HOT
Country-rock quintet from the Ozarks in Missouri, formed by brothers Doug and Rodney Dillard.

| 7/1/72 | 111 | 3 | One A.M. .................................It's About Time (Hot #92) | $7 | Anthem 101 |

**DINK** ☉       ROK
Rock quintet: Rob Lightbody (vocals), Sean Carlin and Jer Herring (guitars), Jeff Finn (bass) and Jan Eddy Van Der Kuil (drums).

| 2/4/95 | 118 | 2 | Green Mind ...............ROK:35 (2 mixes) / Reason / Angels | $6 | Capitol 58273 (CD) |

samples "Friendly As Fascism" by Consolidated

**DINO**       HOT/R&B
Born Dino Esposito on 7/20/63 in Encino, California; raised in Hawaii and Connecticut. Former DJ/music director at KCEP in Las Vegas.

| 11/13/93 | 114 | 3 | Endlessly ...............................................(remix) | $3 | ▌ EastWest 98360 |

**DINO, DESI & BILLY**       HOT
Dino (**Dean Martin**'s son, Dean Martin, Jr.), Desi (Lucille Ball and Desi Arnaz's son, Desiderio Arnaz IV) & Billy (a schoolmate from Beverly Hills, William Hinsche). Dino was killed on 3/21/87 (age 35) when his Air National Guard jet crashed.

| 2/25/67 | 128 | 3 | 1 If You're Thinkin' What I'm Thinkin'.................Pretty Flamingo | $10 | Reprise 0544 |
| 9/16/67 | 108 | 5 | 2 Kitty Doyle ...........................Without Hurtin' Some | $10 | Reprise 0619 |

**DION**       HOT/R&B/AC
Born Dion DiMucci on 7/18/39 in the Bronx, New York. Formed vocal group, Dion & The Belmonts, in the Bronx in 1958. Dion went solo in 1960 as did **The Belmonts**. Inducted into the Rock and Roll Hall of Fame in 1989. *Top Pop Singles*: 33.

| 7/3/61 | 103 | 2 | 1 Somebody Nobody Wants ...............Could Somebody Take My Place Tonight | $20 | Laurie 3101 |
| 8/24/63 | 101[1] | 6 | 2 Lonely World                 Tag Along | $20 | Laurie 3187 |
| 3/7/64 | 113 | 3 | 3 I'm Your Hoochie Cooche Man................The Road I'm On (Gloria) | $15 | ■ Columbia 42977 |

       **DION DiMUCI**
       #3 R&B hit for Muddy Waters in 1954

| 4/11/64 | 108 | 3 | 4 Shout...................................Little Girl | $25 | Laurie 3240 |

       #6 hit for Joey Dee & The Starliters in 1962

| 12/11/71 | 103 | 4 | 5 Sanctuary ...............................Brand New Morning | $10 | ■ Warner 7537 |
| 6/5/76 | 108 | 1 | 6 Born To Be With You...............Running Close Behind You | $10 | Big Tree/Spector 16063 |

       with the Phil Spector Wall of Sound Orchestra; **Nino Tempo** (sax solo); #5 hit for **The Chordettes** in 1956

**DIPLOMATS, The**       HOT
R&B vocal group from Washington, D.C.: Ervan L. Waters, William Collier, Samuel Culley and Tom Price.

| 10/26/68 | 117 | 2 | I Can Give You Love ...............................I'm So Glad I Found You | $20 | Dynamo 122 |

**DIRE STRAITS**       ROK/HOT/AC
Rock group formed in London in 1977 by songwriter/producer Mark Knopfler (lead vocals, lead guitar).

| 4/16/83 | 105 | 3 | Twisting By The Pool ...............ROK:12 Badges, Posters, Stickers, T-Shirts | $4 | Warner 29706 |

## DIRT BAND, The — see NITTY GRITTY DIRT BAND

## DISCO and the CITY BOYZ Featuring CLAY D ☉
R&B/dance studio group from Florida featuring Clay Dixon.

| 5/18/96 | 125 | 1 | Da Train .....................................(club mix) | $3 | ▌ Krunch 5511 |

       #3 hit earlier in 1996 by **Quad City DJ's** as "C'mon N' Ride It (The Train)"

## DISCO TEX — see SEX-O-LETTES, The

**DIS 'N' DAT**       R&B/HOT
Hip-hop duo of sisters Tishea (Dis) and Tenesia (Dat) Bennett.

| 9/18/93 | 121 | 1 | 1 Whoot, Here It Is! (The Answer) ...............(instrumental) | $3 | ▌ Epic 77152 |

       **DIS 'N' DAT (featuring 95 South)**
       answer song to "Whoot, There It Is" by **95 South** earlier in 1993

| 12/3/94+ | 102 | 12 | 2 Party.................Sls:71 /R&B:59 (5 mixes) | $5 | ▌ Epic Street 77400 * |

       **69 Boyz** (backing vocals); samples "Do You Wanna Go Party" by KC And The Sunshine Band

**DISTANT COUSINS, The** ☉
Pop/rock duo: Larry Brown and Raymond Bloodworth.

| 8/27/66 | 102 | 8 | She Ain't Lovin' You ...............Here Today, Gone Tomorrow | $15 | Date 1514 |

**DIXIEBELLES, The**       HOT/R&B
Female R&B trio from Memphis: Shirley Thomas, Mary Hunt and Mildred Pratcher. Backed by pianist **Jerry Smith** (of Combread And Jerry).

| 5/16/64 | 119 | 2 | New York Town ...............................The Beale Street Dog | $8 | Sound Stage 7 2521 |

       featuring the instrumental piano refrain "Chopsticks"

**DIXIE CUPS, The**       HOT/R&B
Female R&B trio from New Orleans: Barbara Ann Hawkins, her sister Rosa Lee Hawkins and their cousin Joan Marie Johnson.

| 7/3/65 | 102 | 5 | Gee The Moon Is Shining Bright.................I'm Gonna Get You Yet | $15 | Red Bird 10-032 |

       original version "Why Don't They Let Us Fall in Love" released in 1963 by **The Ronettes** on Spector #2

**DIXIE DREGS** ☉       ROK
Instrumental rock quintet: Steve Morse (guitar), T Lavitz (piano), Allen Sloan (violin), Andy West (bass) and Rod Morgenstein (drums).

| 6/24/78 | 102 | 3 | 1 Take It Off The Top ...............................Little Kids [I] | $4 | Capricorn 0291 |
| 4/17/82 | 110 | 1 | 2 Crank It Up...............................ROK:18 Bloodsucking Leeches | $3 | Arista 0674 |

       **THE DREGS**

## DIXIE FLYERS, The — see LULU / PHILLIPS, Esther / SAM & DAVE

## DJ D-MAN & BILLY BOY ☉
Rap/dance duo.

| 4/20/96 | 101[1] | 7 | Dooky Boody ...............................(power mix) | $3 | ▌ Out Of Control 13503 |

**DJ KOOL ○**                                                                                          R&B
Born John Bowman in Washington, D.C. Male DJ/rapper.

| 9/6/97 | 106 | 5 | I Got Dat Feelin'.......................................................................R&B:80 (remix) | $3 | ■ | American 17329 |

samples "Uptown Anthem" by Naughty By Nature

**DJ TRAJIC ○**
Rap/dance duo featuring vocals by MC Peace.

| 5/25/96 | 108 | 2 | Pants R Saggin'.........................................................................Show Me Your Face | $3 | ■ | Out Of Control 13512 |

**D.O.C., The ○**                                                                                      R&B
Dallas rapper Tray Curry.

| 11/18/95 | 111 | 6 | Return Of Da Livin' Dead.................R&B:67 From Ruthless 2 Death Row (Do We All Part) | $3 | ■ | Giant 17796 |

samples "Misdemeanor" by Foster Sylvers

**DOCTOR DRÉ & ED LOVER**                                                            R&B/HOT
Rap duo from New York City. Hosted own show on MTV. Starred in the movie Who's The Man? Also see Beastie Boys.

| 4/8/95 | 118 | 5 | For The Love Of You........................................R&B:91 It's Goin' Down | $3 | ■ | Relativity 1256 |

samples "For The Love Of You" by The Isley Brothers, "Papa Was Too" by Joe Tex and "Yes You May" by Lord Finesse

**DR. JOHN THE NIGHT TRIPPER**                                                  HOT/R&B
Born Malcolm "Mac" Rebennack on 11/20/42 in New Orleans. Pioneer "swamp rock"-styled pianist/vocalist.

| 6/20/70 | 108 | 3 | Wash, Mama, Wash.............................................................................Loup Garoo | $8 | | Atco 6755 |

**DODD, Ken ○**
Born on 11/8/32 in Liverpool, England. Pop vocalist. Noted for zany stage antics.

| 12/18/65 | 107 | 5 | Tears (For Souvenirs)............................................................... You And I | $8 | | Liberty 55835 |

Geoff Love (orch.); #59 hit for Bobby Vinton in 1966

**DOKKEN**                                                                                            ROK/HOT
Heavy-metal band formed in Los Angeles in 1982: Don Dokken (vocals), George Lynch (guitar), Juan Croucier (bass) and Mick Brown (drums). Jeff Pilson replaced Croucier in late 1983.

| 2/16/85 | 105 | 2 | Just Got Lucky...............................................ROK:27 Don't Close Your Eyes | $3 | | Elektra 69664 |

**DOMINO**                                                                                            R&B/HOT
Born Shawn Ivy in St. Louis; raised in Long Beach, California. Male rapper/vocalist.

| 5/27/95 | 103 | 7 | 1 Tales From The Hood ..........Sls:56 /R&B:51 I'm Talkin' To Myself (NME & Grench The Mean 1) | $3 | ■ | MCA Soundtracks 55038 |

Chill (rap); title song from the movie starring Corbin Bernsen

| 6/22/96 | 112 | 7 | 2 So Fly.................................................................................R&B:64 (instrumental) | $3 | ■ | OutBurst 576508 |

**DOMINO, Fats**                                                          HOT/R&B/MEM/C&W
Born Antoine Domino on 2/26/28 in New Orleans. Classic New Orleans R&B piano-playing vocalist. Signed to Imperial record label in 1949. Fats had a dozen Top 10 R&B hits (1950-55) prior to his first pop hit. Inducted into the Rock and Roll Hall of Fame in 1986. Won Grammy's Hall of Fame and Lifetime Achievement Awards in 1987. Top Pop Singles: 66.

| 10/13/62 | 103 | 1 | 1 Stop The Clock .....................................Did You Ever See A Dream Walking (Hot #79) | $15 | | Imperial 5875 |
| 3/2/63 | 124 | 1 | 2 Hum Diddy Doo.......................................................................Those Eyes | $15 | | Imperial 5909 |
| 4/27/63 | 102 | 5 | 3 You Always Hurt The One You Love          Trouble Blues | $15 | | Imperial 5937 |

recorded on 8/6/60; #1 hit for the Mills Brothers in 1944; #12 hit for Clarence Henry in 1961

| 6/1/63 | 123 | 1 | 4 Can't Go On Without You .................................There Goes (My Heart Again) (Hot #59) | $12 | | ABC-Paramount 10444 |
| 8/10/63 | 114 | 3 | 5 When I'm Walking (Let Me Walk)/ | | | |
| 8/10/63 | 128 | 2 | 6   I've Got A Right To Cry ........................................................ | $12 | | ABC-Paramount 10475 |

#2 R&B hit for both Joe Liggins and Erskine Hawkins in 1946

| 11/30/63 | 114 | 5 | 7 I Can't Give You Anything But Love.............................Goin' Home | $12 | | Imperial 66005 |

recorded on 6/6/61; #1 hit for Cliff Edwards in 1928

| 12/21/63 | 108 | 2 | 8 Just A Lonely Man ...........................................Who Cares (Hot #63) | $12 | | ABC-Paramount 10512 |
| 3/14/64 | 112 | 2 | 9 Your Cheatin' Heart ......................................When I Was Young | $12 | | Imperial 66016 |

recorded on 6/20/61; #1 Country hit for Hank Williams in 1953

| 3/21/64 | 122 | 1 | 10 I Don't Want To Set The World On Fire....................Lazy Lady (Hot #86) | $12 | | ABC-Paramount 10531 |

#1 hit for Horace Heidt & His Orchestra in 1941

| 7/25/64 | 127 | 2 | 11 Mary, Oh Mary ..........................................................Packin' Up | $12 | | ABC-Paramount 10567 |

**DONNER, Ral**                                                                                    HOT/AC
Born on 2/10/43 in Chicago. Died of cancer on 4/6/84. Narrator for the movie This Is Elvis.

| 6/23/62 | 117 | 2 | 1 Loveless Life...................................................................Bells Of Love | $25 | | Gone 5129 |
| 3/30/63 | 124 | 2 | 2 I Got Burned ..................................................A Tear In My Eye | $35 | ■ | Reprise 20,141 |

**DONOVAN**                                                                                          HOT/AC
Born Donovan Phillip Leitch on 5/10/46 in Maryhill, Scotland. Singer/songwriter/guitarist. To London at age 10.

| 8/5/67 | 135 | 1 | Summer Day Reflection Song ...............................Sunny Goodge Street | $12 | | Hickory 1470 |

**DOOBIE BROTHERS, The**                                          HOT/AC/ROK/R&B
Rock group formed in 1970 in San Jose, California: Patrick Simmons (vocals, guitar), Tom Johnston (lead vocals, guitar, keyboards), Tiran Porter (bass) and John Hartman (drums). Top Pop Singles: 27.

| 7/17/71 | 122 | 2 | Nobody ...............................................................Slippery St. Paul | $8 | | Warner 7495 |

made the Hot 100 (#58) on 11/2/74 on Warner 8041

**DOONICAN, Val ○**
Born on 2/3/28 in Ireland. Hosted his own TV show in England.

| 3/2/68 | 128 | 1 | If The Whole World Stopped Lovin' ......................I'd Rather Think Of You | $8 | | Decca 32252 |

Ken Woodman (orch.)

**DOORS, The**                                                                              HOT/AC/ROK
Rock group formed in Los Angeles in 1965: Jim Morrison (b: 12/8/43, Melbourne, Florida; d: 7/3/71, Paris; lead singer), Ray Manzarek (keyboards), Robby Krieger (guitar) and John Densmore (drums). Group inducted into the Rock and Roll Hall of Fame in 1993.

| 4/8/67 | 126 | 1 | Break On Through (To The Other Side) ...............................End Of The Night | $15 | ■ | Elektra 45611 |

| DEBUT | PEAK | WKS | A-side (Chart Hit)..................................................................B-side | $ | Pic | Label & Number |
|---|---|---|---|---|---|---|
| | | | **DORSEY, Lee**      R&B/HOT | | | |
| | | | Born Irving Lee Dorsey on 12/24/24 in New Orleans. Died on 12/1/86 of emphysema. | | | |
| 10/9/65 | 121 | 3 | 1 Work, Work, Work............................................_Can You Hear Me_ | $10 | | Amy 939 |
| 2/4/67 | 105 | 4 | 2 Rain Rain Go Away..............................................._Gotta Find A Job_ | $8 | | Amy 974 |
| 12/23/67 | 110 | 1 | 3 Love Lots Of Lovin'..........................................._Take Care Of Our Love_ | $12 | | Sansu 474 |
| | | | **LEE DORSEY & BETTY HARRIS** | | | |
| | | | **DOTTIE and RAY** ✪      R&B | | | |
| | | | R&B vocal duo. | | | |
| 1/30/65 | 126 | 4 | I Love You Baby....................................R&B:35 _La La Lover_ | $15 | | Le Sage 701 |
| | | | **DOUBLE EXPOSURE**      R&B/HOT | | | |
| | | | Disco quartet from Philadelphia, featuring lead singer James Williams. | | | |
| 2/26/77 | 104 | 4 | 1 My Love Is Free...........................R&B:44 _Just Can't Say Hello_ | $4 | | Salsoul 2012 |
| 12/9/78 | 107 | 1 | 2 Newsy Neighbors......................................_Handy Man_ | $4 | | Salsoul 2069 |
| | | | #97 hit for **First Choice** in 1974 | | | |
| | | | **DOUBLE YOU** ✪      | | | |
| | | | Electro-pop artist from Germany. | | | |
| 5/20/95 | 121 | 2 | Run To Me.............................................._(3 mixes)_ | $6 | | ZYX 7314 (**CD**) |
| | | | **DOUCETTE**      HOT | | | |
| | | | Rock group from Montreal: Jerry Doucette (vocals, guitar), Mark Olson (keyboards), Donnie Cummings (bass) and Duris Maxwell (drums). | | | |
| 8/11/79 | 108 | 4 | Nobody..............................................._All Over Me_ | $4 | | Mushroom 7042 |
| | | | **DOUG E. FRESH**      R&B | | | |
| | | | Born Douglas Davis on 9/17/66 in New York City. Rapper. | | | |
| 1/8/94 | 105 | 7 | 1 I-ight (Alright)/      R&B:76 _(2 mixes)_ | | | |
| 4/9/94 | 101³ | 9 | 2 Freaks      R&B:79 _Bounce_ | $5 | ▪ | Gee Street 440583 * |
| | | | Vicious (12-year-old rapper) | | | |
| 3/4/95 | 101¹ | 11 | 3 Sittin' In My Car      Sls:54 /R&B:56 _(remix)_ | $3 | ▪ | Def Jam 853992 |
| | | | **SLICK RICK** Featuring Doug E. Fresh On The Beatbox | | | |
| | | | samples "For The Love Of You" by **The Isley Brothers** | | | |
| 9/16/95 | 108 | 7 | 4 Where's Da Party At?.........................R&B:81 _It's On! / (2 album snippets)_ | $3 | ▪ | Gee Street 447609 |
| | | | **DOUGLAS, Carol**      HOT/R&B/AC | | | |
| | | | Born Carol Strickland on 4/7/48 in Brooklyn. Disco singer. Member of **The Chantels** vocal group in the early '70s. | | | |
| 2/5/77 | 102 | 4 | 1 Midnight Love Affair.............................._(long version)_ | $4 | | Midland Int'l. 10753 |
| 2/19/77 | 110 | 1 | 2 Dancing Queen..................................._In The Morning_ | $6 | | Midland Int'l. 10870 (T) |
| | | | #1 hit for **Abba** in 1977 | | | |
| 9/17/77 | 108 | 1 | 3 We Do It............................................_Lie To Me_ | $4 | ▪ | Midsong Int'l. 10979 |
| 2/25/78 | 106 | 4 | 4 Night Fever................................._Let You Come Into My Life_ | $4 | | Midsong Int'l. 40860 |
| | | | from the movie _Saturday Night Fever_ starring **John Travolta**; #1 hit for the **Bee Gees** in 1978 | | | |
| | | | **DOUGLAS, Mike**      MEM/AC/HOT | | | |
| | | | Born Michael Dowd, Jr. on 8/11/25 in Chicago. Longtime syndicated TV talkshow host (1961-80). Singer with Kay Kyser's band, 1945-50. | | | |
| 10/29/66 | 129 | 3 | Cabaret.......................................AC:25 _A House Of Love_ | $7 | | Epic 10078 |
| | | | Frank Hunter (orch.); from the musical _Cabaret_ | | | |
| | | | **DOVE, Ronnie**      HOT/AC/C&W | | | |
| | | | Born on 9/9/40 in Herndon, Virginia; raised in Baltimore. Adult Contemporary vocalist. _Top Pop Singles_: 20. | | | |
| 3/1/69 | 131 | 3 | What's Wrong With My World.............................._That Empty Feeling_ | $7 | | Diamond 256 |
| | | | **DOVELLS, The**      HOT/R&B | | | |
| | | | Pop/rock group formed in Philadelphia featuring **Len Barry** (lead singer; left in 1963). | | | |
| 8/24/74 | 105 | 3 | Dancing In The Street............................._Back On The Road Again_ | $6 | | Event 216 |
| | | | #2 hit for **Martha & The Vandellas** in 1964 | | | |
| | | | **DOWELL, Joe**      HOT/AC | | | |
| | | | Born on 1/23/40 in Bloomington, Indiana. Signed to Mercury's Smash label by Shelby Singleton, Jr. | | | |
| 12/25/61 | 110 | 1 | A Kiss For Christmas (O Tannenbaum)........_(I Wonder) Who's Spending Xmas With You_ [X] | $12 | ▪ | Smash 1728 |
| | | | **DOWNING, Al**      C&W/HOT/R&B | | | |
| | | | Born on 1/9/40 in Lenapah, Oklahoma. R&B vocalist/pianist. Session work with **Wanda Jackson**. First recorded for White Rock in 1958. Turned to country music in 1978. | | | |
| 5/26/62 | 117 | 1 | 1 The Story Of My Life................................._I'd Love To Be Loved_ | $12 | | Chess 1817 |
| | | | **"BIG" AL DOWNING** | | | |
| | | | #15 hit for **Marty Robbins** in 1958 | | | |
| 3/30/63 | 129 | 2 | 2 If You Want It (I've Got It)..............._You Never Miss Your Water (Till The Well Runs Dry)_ (Hot #73) | $15 | | Lenox 5565 |
| | | | **"LITTLE ESTHER" PHILLIPS & "BIG AL" DOWNING** | | | |
| 5/8/76 | 107 | 1 | 3 I Love To Love................................._I'm Just Nobody_ | $6 | | Polydor 14311 |
| | | | includes a bit of "I Won't Dance" (#1 hit for Eddy Duchin in 1935) | | | |
| | | | **DOZIER, Gene, And The Brotherhood** ✪      R&B | | | |
| | | | R&B instrumental quartet: Gene Dozier (piano), Al McKay (guitar), James Wesley Smith (bass) and James Gadson (drums). | | | |
| 10/7/67 | 121 | 7 | A Hunk Of Funk...........................R&B:46 _One For Bess_ [I] | $8 | | Minit 32026 |
| | | | **DOZIER, Lamont**      R&B/HOT | | | |
| | | | Born on 6/16/41 in Detroit. R&B singer/songwriter/producer. With the brothers Brian and Eddie Holland in highly successful songwriting/production team for Motown. Inducted into the Rock and Roll Hall of Fame in 1990. | | | |
| 5/3/75 | 101¹ | 5 | All Cried Out      R&B:41 _Rose_ | $5 | | ABC 12076 |
| | | | **DRAKE, Pete, And His Talking Steel Guitar**      HOT/AC | | | |
| | | | Born Roddis Franklin Drake on 10/8/32 in Atlanta. Died on 7/29/88. Was Nashville's top steel guitar sessionman. | | | |
| 7/11/64 | 122 | 3 | I'm Sorry.............................._I'm Just A Guitar (Everybody Picks On Me)_ | $8 | | Smash 1910 |
| | | | Bill Justis (orch.); #1 hit for **Brenda Lee** in 1960 | | | |

**DRAMATICS, The**    R&B/HOT
R&B vocal group from Detroit featuring Ron Banks, lead singer.

| | | | | | | |
|---|---|---|---|---|---|---|
| 5/14/77 | 101[1] | 4 | 1 I Can't Get Over You   R&B:9 *Sundown Is Coming (Hold Back The Night)* | $5 | | ABC 12258 |
| 5/6/78 | 106 | 5 | 2 Ocean Of Thoughts And Dreams ............................... R&B:17 *Come Inside* | $5 | | ABC 12331 |

**DRAPER, Rusty**    HOT/C&W/MEM/POP/AC
Born Farrell H. Draper in Kirksville, Missouri. Began career at the age of 12, singing and playing guitar over the radio in Tulsa, Oklahoma.

| | | | | | | |
|---|---|---|---|---|---|---|
| 6/13/60 | 105 | 2 | Mule Skinner Blues ............................... *Please Help Me, I'm Falling* (Hot #54) | $12 | | Mercury 71634 |
| | | | #5 hit for **The Fendermen** in 1960; written in 1931 by country great, Jimmie Rodgers | | | |

**D:REAM** ☺
Dance outfit from Derry, Northern Ireland. Led by producer Peter Cunnah. Ream is Cockney slang for "the real thing"; D: is computer syntax.

| | | | | | | |
|---|---|---|---|---|---|---|
| 2/17/96 | 125 | 1 | Shoot Me With Your Love ............................... *(remix)* | $3 | ▮ | Sire 64369 |

**DREAMBOY** ☺    R&B
R&B vocal group formed in 1979 at Oak Park High School, Michigan: Jeff Stanton (vocals), Jeff Bass (guitar), Jimi Hunt (keyboards), Paul Stewart, Jr. (bass) and George "Dewey" Twymon (drums).

| | | | | | | |
|---|---|---|---|---|---|---|
| 11/17/84 | 106 | 2 | I Promise (I Do Love You) ............................... R&B:45 *In The Nite* | $3 | | Qwest 29190 |

**DREAMERS, The** ☺
White vocal group: Frank Cammarata, Frank Nicholas, Bruce Goldie and John Trancynger.

| | | | | | | |
|---|---|---|---|---|---|---|
| 1/30/61 | 104 | 2 | Teenage Vows Of Love ............................... *Natalie* | $30 | | Goldisc 3015 |

**DREAMLOVERS, The**    HOT
R&B vocal quintet formed while in high school in Philadelphia: Tommy Ricks (lead), Cleveland Hammock, Morris Gardner, and brothers Cliff and Ray Dunn. Backup vocal group for most of **Chubby Checker**'s hits.

| | | | | | | |
|---|---|---|---|---|---|---|
| 10/30/61 | 102 | 2 | 1 Let Them Love (And Be Loved) ............................... *Welcome Home* | $25 | | Heritage 104 |
| 6/23/62 | 115 | 1 | 2 I Miss You ............................... *If I Should Lose You* (Hot #62) | $25 | | End 1114 |
| | | | originally released on Down 2004 in 1961 ($500) | | | |
| 5/8/65 | 121 | 2 | 3 You Gave Me Somebody To Love ............................... *Doin' Things Together With You* | $20 | | Warner 5619 |

**DREGS — see DIXIE DREGS**

**DREW, Patti**    R&B/HOT
Born on 12/29/44 in Charleston, South Carolina. Lead singer of vocal group The Drew-Vels.

| | | | | | | |
|---|---|---|---|---|---|---|
| 7/12/69 | 119 | 2 | The Love That A Woman Should Give To A Man   R&B:38 *Save The Last Dance For Me* | $8 | | Capitol 2473 |

**DRIFTERS, The**    R&B/HOT/AC/MEM
R&B vocal group formed to showcase lead singer **Clyde McPhatter** on Atlantic in 1953. Many personnel changes throughout career and several groups have used the name in later years. Group inducted into the Rock and Roll Hall of Fame in 1988. *Top Pop Singles*: 36.

| | | | | | | |
|---|---|---|---|---|---|---|
| 7/13/63 | 101[1] | 3 | 1 If You Don't Come Back   *Rat Race* (Hot #71) | $15 | | Atlantic 2191 |
| 11/7/64 | 115 | 1 | 2 He's Just A Playboy ............................... *I've Got Sand In My Shoes* (Hot #33) | $12 | | Atlantic 2253 |
| 6/25/66 | 127 | 1 | 3 You Can't Love Them All ............................... *Up In The Streets Of Harlem* | $12 | | Atlantic 2336 |
| 1/6/68 | 111 | 3 | 4 Still Burning In My Heart ............................... *I Need You Now* | $10 | | Atlantic 2471 |

**DRISCOLL, Julie** ☺
Born on 6/8/47 in England. Ex-model. Sang lead with The Trinity from 1967-69.

| | | | | | | |
|---|---|---|---|---|---|---|
| 7/13/68 | 106 | 4 | This Wheel's On Fire ............................... *A Kind Of Love-In* | $10 | ▮ | Atco 6593 |
| | | |     **JULIE DRISCOLL, BRIAN AUGER & THE TRINITY** | | | |
| | | |     written by **Bob Dylan** | | | |

**DRIVER** ☺
Rock trio from Canada: Peter Glinderman (vocals, guitar), Dennis Coats (bass) and Steve Rexford (drums).

| | | | | | | |
|---|---|---|---|---|---|---|
| 9/10/77 | 109 | 2 | (I've Been Lookin' For) A New Way To Say I Love You ............ *Bring It To Me* | $5 | | A&M 1966 |

**DROGE, Pete** ☺    ROK
Rock singer/songwriter/guitarist from Portland, Oregon.

| | | | | | | |
|---|---|---|---|---|---|---|
| 3/11/95 | 119 | 1 | If You Don't Love Me (I'll Kill Myself) ............................... ROK:28 *(live version)* | $3 | ▮ | RCA 64297 |
| | | | from the movie *Dumb And Dumber* starring Jim Carrey | | | |

**DUCANES, The** ☺
Vocal sextet led by Jeff Breny and Ron Nagel.

| | | | | | | |
|---|---|---|---|---|---|---|
| 7/17/61 | 109 | 3 | I'm So Happy (Tra La La) ............................... *Little Did I Know* | $30 | | Goldisc 3024 |

**DUDLEY, Dave**    C&W/HOT/AC
Born David Pedruska on 5/3/28 in Spencer, Wisconsin. Country singer/guitarist.

| | | | | | | |
|---|---|---|---|---|---|---|
| 12/14/63 | 125 | 3 | 1 Last Day In The Mines   C&W:7 *Last Year's Heartaches* | $8 | | Mercury 72212 |
| 8/7/65 | 125 | 1 | 2 Truck Drivin' Son-Of-A-Gun ............................... C&W:3 *I Got Lost* | $7 | | Mercury 72442 |
| 4/2/66 | 127 | 2 | 3 Viet Nam Blues ............................... C&W:12 *Then I'll Come Home Again* [S] | $7 | | Mercury 72550 |
| | | | written by Kris Kristofferson | | | |

**DUKE, Billy** ☺
Pop vocalist.

| | | | | | | |
|---|---|---|---|---|---|---|
| 2/3/62 | 120 | 1 | Walking Cane ............................... *Amen* | $12 | | 20th Fox 296 |
| | | | based on the black American spiritual "Hand Me Down My Walking Cane" | | | |

**DUKE, Doris**    R&B/HOT
Born Doris Curry in Sandersville, Georgia. Recorded as Doris Willingham for Hy-Monty in 1967.

| | | | | | | |
|---|---|---|---|---|---|---|
| 5/30/70 | 109 | 4 | Feet Start Walking ............................... R&B:36 *How Was I To Know You Cared* | $8 | | Canyon 35 |

**DUKE JUPITER**    HOT/ROK
Rock quartet from Rochester, New York: Marshall James Styler (vocals, keyboards), Greg Walker (guitar), George Barajas (bass; d: 8/17/82, age 33) and David Corcoran (drums). Rickey Ellis (bass) joined in 1983.

| | | | | | | |
|---|---|---|---|---|---|---|
| 8/4/84 | 101[1] | 3 | Rescue Me   *Me And Michelle* | $4 | | Morocco 1748 |

**DUNCAN, Johnny** ☺    C&W
Born on 10/5/38 in Dublin, Texas. Country singer. Cousin of **Dan Seals** and Jim Seals (**Seals & Crofts**).

| | | | | | | |
|---|---|---|---|---|---|---|
| 8/13/77 | 105 | 1 | A Song In The Night ............................... C&W:5 *Use My Love* | $5 | | Columbia 10554 |

| DEBUT | PEAK | WKS | A-side (Chart Hit)...............................................................................................B-side | $ | Pic | Label & Number |
|---|---|---|---|---|---|---|

**DUNCAN, Tommy** ☺
R&B vocalist.

| 6/13/64 | 133 | 3 | Dance, Dance, Dance ................................................. *Let's Try It Over Again* $25 | | | Falew! 104 |

**DUPREES, The**      **HOT/AC**
Italian-American vocal quintet from Jersey City: Joseph ("Joey Vann") Canzano (lead singer; d: 2/28/84, age 40), Mike Arnone, Tom Bialablow, John Salvato and Joe Santollo.

| 4/4/64 | 114 | 4 | 1 Where Are You ..................................................... *Please Let Her Know* $15 | | | Coed 591 |

THE DUPREES featuring Joey Vann
#5 hit for Mildred Bailey in 1937

| 11/16/68 | 113 | 3 | 2 Goodnight My Love .................................................. *Ring Of Love* $10 | ■ | | Heritage 805 |

**DURAN DURAN**      **HOT/ROK/AC**
Synth-pop-dance band formed in 1978 in Birmingham, England: Simon LeBon (vocals), Andy Taylor (guitar), Nick Rhodes (keyboards), John Taylor (bass) and Roger Taylor (drums). Many personnel changes. *Top Pop Singles*: 21.

| 6/24/95 | 101[3] | 6 | Perfect Day      *White Lines (edit)* $3 | | ▌ | Capitol 58392 |

written and recorded by *Lou Reed* in 1972

**DURANTE, Jimmy**      **MEM/POP/AC/HOT**
Born on 2/10/1893 in New York City. Died on 1/29/80. One of America's all-time favorite comedians.

| 2/19/66 | 135 | 1 | One Of Those Songs ..................... **AC:26** *(I Wonder) What Became Of Life* $7 | | | Warner 5686 |

with the Girls From The Folies Bergere; **Ernie Freeman** (orch.)

**DUSK**      **HOT**
Studio group created by Dawn's producers, Hank Medress and Dave Appell. Lead vocals by Peggy Santiglia of **The Angels**.

| 11/27/71 | 106 | 3 | Treat Me Like A Good Piece Of Candy ......................... *Suburbia U.S.A.* $5 | | | Bell 45,148 |

**DUTONES, The** ☺
R&B vocal duo: Richard Parker and Jerry Brown.

| 2/16/63 | 101[2] | 7 | The Bird      *Done Got Over It* $10 | | | Columbia 42657 |

song's arrangement similar to **The Isley Brothers'** "Twist And Shout"

**DYKE AND THE BLAZERS**      **R&B/HOT**
Funk group from Buffalo: Arlester "Dyke" Christian (vocals; d: 3/30/71, age 28, shot to death), Alvester "Pig" Jacobs (guitar), Bernard Williams and Clarence Towns (saxophones), Alvin Battle (bass) and Willie Earl (drums).

| 6/17/67 | 130 | 2 | 1 So Sharp ....................................... **R&B:41** *Don't Bug Me* $8 | | | Original Sound 69 |
| 9/28/68 | 102 | 3 | 2 Funky Bull Pt. I ........................................... *Pt. II* $8 | | | Original Sound 83 |
| 1/10/70 | 121 | 2 | 3 You Are My Sunshine................................ **R&B:30** *City Dump* $8 | | | Original Sound 90 |

#19 hit for Bing Crosby in 1941

| 4/11/70 | 118 | 4 | 4 Uhh........................ **R&B:20** *Let A Woman Be A Woman - Let A Man Be A Man* (Hot #36) $8 | | | Original Sound 89 |
| 7/25/70 | 119 | 1 | 5 Runaway People ............................... **R&B:32** *I'm So All Alone* $8 | | | Original Sound 96 |

**DYLAN, Bob**      **HOT/ROK/AC**
Born Robert Allen Zimmerman on 5/24/41 in Duluth; raised in Hibbing, Minnesota. Highly influential singer/songwriter/guitarist/harmonica player. Innovator of folk-rock style. Signed to Columbia Records in October 1961. Member of the supergroup Traveling Wilburys. His son Jakob is lead singer of The Wallflowers. Inducted into the Rock and Roll Hall of Fame in 1988. Won Grammy's Lifetime Achievement Award in 1991. *Top Pop Singles*: 23. Also see **Sir Douglas Quintet**.

| 3/26/66 | 119 | 1 | 1 One Of Us Must Know (Sooner Or Later) .............. *Queen Jane Approximately* $15 | | | Columbia 43541 |
| 5/18/74 | 107 | 1 | 2 Something There Is About You ............................... *Tough Mama* $8 | | | Asylum 11035 |
| 1/15/77 | 110 | 1 | 3 Rita May/ | | | |
| | | 1 | 4    Stuck Inside Of Mobile With The Memphis Blues Again........................... $8 | | | Columbia 10454 |

"live" version of his 1966 recording on his *Blonde On Blonde* album

| 7/20/85 | 103 | 2 | 5 Tight Connection To My Heart (Has Anybody Seen | | | |
| | | |    My Love)      **ROK:19** *We Better Talk This Over* $4 | | ■ | Columbia 04933 |

**DYNAMIC SUPERIORS**      **R&B/HOT**
R&B vocal group from Washington, D.C.: Tony Washington (lead), George Spann, George Peterbark, Michael McCalphin and Maurice Washington.

| 4/5/75 | 102 | 7 | Leave It Alone ....................................... **R&B:13** *One-Nighter* $6 | | | Motown 1342 |

written and produced by **Ashford & Simpson**

**DYNASTY**      **R&B/HOT**
R&B group from Los Angeles featuring vocalists Kevin Spencer, Nidra Beard (Sylvers) and Linda Carriere (DeBlanc).

| 11/29/80 | 103 | 2 | Do Me Right........................... **R&B:34** *Adventures In The Land Of Music* $4 | | | Solar 12127 |

# E

**EARLS, The**      **HOT/R&B**
White doo-wop vocal group from the Bronx, New York: Larry Chance, Bob Del Din, Eddie Harder, Jack Wray and Larry Palumbo.

| 6/5/61 | 107 | 6 | 1 Life Is But A Dream................................................. *It's You* $150 | | | Rome 101 |

second pressings have "Without You" on the B-side ($50)

| 3/9/63 | 119 | 3 | 2 Never .......................................................... *I Keep A Tellin' You* $25 | | | Old Town 1133 |
| 7/6/63 | 123 | 1 | 3 Eyes .............................................................. *Look My Way* $25 | | | Old Town 1141 |

**EARTH, WIND & FIRE**      **R&B/HOT/AC**
Los Angeles-based R&B group formed by Chicago-bred producer/songwriter/vocalist/percussionist/kalimba player Maurice White. Co-lead singer Philip Bailey joined in 1971. Group generally contained eight to 10 members, with frequent personnel shuffling. *Top Pop Singles*: 33.

| 2/17/73 | 104 | 2 | 1 Mom ............................................................ *Power* $6 | | | Columbia 45747 |
| 1/28/84 | 103 | 4 | 2 Touch ........................... **R&B:23 / AC:36** *Sweet Sassy Lady* $4 | | ■ | Columbia 04329 |

### E-A-SKI ✪
Male rapper from Oakland.

| 11/22/97 | 103 | 14 | Showdown ................................ *Earthquake / Maddoggin / Welcome To California* | $3 | ▪ | Relativity 1643 |

**E-A-SKI Featuring Montell Jordan**

### EAST 17 ✪
Dance-pop group from London: Anthony Mortimer, John Hendy, Brian Harvey and Terry Coldwell. Group's name is part of their postal code.

| 9/11/93 | 123 | 1 | Deep.................................................... *I Disagree / (3 album snippets)* | $3 | ▪ | London 857254 |

### EAZY-E                                    R&B/HOT
Born Eric Wright on 9/7/63 in Compton, California. Died of AIDS on 3/26/95. Rapper/producer. Formerly with N.W.A.

| 6/4/94 | 103 | 8 | Luv 4 Dem Gangsta'z ........................... Sls:63 *(remix)* | $3 | ▪ | MCA 54870 |

from the movie *Beverly Hills Cop III* starring **Eddie Murphy**

### ECHOES, The                                    HOT
White vocal trio from Brooklyn: Tommy Duffy, Harry Boyle and Tom Morrissey.

| 8/21/61 | 112 | 1 | 1 Gee Oh Gee .................................................. *Angel Of My Heart* | $30 | | Seg-way 1002 |
| 10/27/62 | 112 | 4 | 2 Bluebirds Over The Mountain ........................... *A Chicken Ain't Nothing But A Bird* | $15 | | Smash 1766 |

The Stephen Scott Singers (backing vocals); #75 hit for Ersel Hickey in 1958

### ECHOES, The ✪
Pop duo: Bonnie Guitar (vocal) and Don Robertson (vocal and whistling).

| 5/23/60 | 101[1] | 4 | Born To Be With You *My Guiding Light* | $20 | | Dolton 18 |

#5 hit for **The Chordettes** in 1956

### ECSTASY, PASSION & PAIN                                    R&B/HOT
R&B group from New York City: Barbara Roy (vocals, guitar), Billy Gardner (organ), Alan Tizer (percussion), Joseph Williams (bass) and Althea "Cookie" Smith (drums).

| 3/30/74 | 102 | 7 | I Wouldn't Give You Up ........................... R&B:17 *Don't Burn Your Bridges Behind You* | $6 | | Roulette 7151 |

### EDDIE-"D" ✪                                    R&B
Eddie Drummond — rapper.

| 4/13/85 | 103 | 1 | Backstabbin' ........................... R&B:75 *(dub version)* | $4 | | Philly World 99662 |

### EDDY, Duane                                    HOT/R&B/C&W/AC
Born on 4/26/38 in Corning, New York. To Phoenix in 1955; began long association with producer/songwriter **Lee Hazlewood**. Originated the "twangy" guitar sound. Rock and roll's all-time #1 instrumentalist. Inducted into the Rock and Roll Hall of Fame in 1994. *Top Pop Singles*: 28.

| 4/3/61 | 101[1] | 2 | 1 Gidget Goes Hawaiian *Theme From Dixie (Hot #39)* [I] | $15 | ▪ | Jamie 1183 |

from the movie starring James Darren and Deborah Walley

| 1/6/62 | 101[1] | 3 | 2 The Avenger *Londonderry Air* [I] | $15 | | Jamie 1206 |

D.J. copies show B-side as "London Derriere" ($40)

| 2/10/62 | 114 | 2 | 3 The Battle ........................... *Trambone* [I] | $15 | | Jamie 1209 |

**DUANE EDDY And The Rebels** (above 2)
rock and roll instrumental version of "Battle Hymn Of The Republic"

| 1/3/70 | 110 | 4 | 4 Freight Train ........................... AC:24 *Put A Little Love In Your Heart* [I] | $10 | | Congress 6010 |

Jimmy Bowen (orch.); #6 hit for **Rusty Draper** in 1957

### EDELMAN, Randy                                    AC/HOT
Singer/songwriter/pianist. Scored movies *Ghostbusters II*, *Twins* and *Kindergarten Cop*.

| 5/24/75 | 109 | 1 | 1 Isn't It A Shame ........................... *Everybody Wants To Call You Sweetheart* | $5 | | 20th Century 2196 |
| 4/10/76 | 108 | 1 | 2 Concrete And Clay ........................... AC:11 *A Weekend In New England* | $5 | | 20th Century 2274 |

#28 hit for **Unit Four plus Two** in 1965; B-side: #10 hit for Barry Manilow in 1977

### EDMUNDS, Dave                                    ROK/HOT
Born on 4/15/44 in Cardiff, Wales. Singer/songwriter/guitarist/producer. Formed rockabilly band Rockpile in 1976.

| 9/4/71 | 104 | 2 | 1 Blue Monday ........................... *I'll Get Along* | $7 | | MAM 3611 |

#5 hit for **Fats Domino** in 1957

| 9/24/83 | 106 | 4 | 2 Information ........................... *What Have I Got To Do To Win?* | $4 | | Columbia 04080 |

produced by Jeff Lynne (ELO)

### EDWARD BEAR                                    HOT/AC
Pop trio from Toronto: Larry Evoy (vocals, drums), Roger Ellis (guitar) and Paul Weldon (keyboards).

| 9/1/73 | 115 | 1 | Walking On Back ........................... *I Love Her (You Love Me)* | $6 | ▪ | Capitol 3683 |

### EDWARDS, John ✪                                    R&B
Born in 1946 in St. Louis. With **James & Bobby Purify** in Columbus, Georgia. Replaced Philippe Wynne in the **Spinners** in 1977.

| 11/16/74 | 109 | 1 | Careful Man ........................... R&B:8 *Claim Jumpin'* [S] | $7 | | Aware 043 |

### EDWARDS, Jonathan                                    C&W/HOT/AC
Born on 7/28/46 in Aitkin, Minnesota; raised in Virginia. Formed bluegrass band Sugar Creek in 1965.

| 3/18/72 | 101[1] | 4 | 1 Train Of Glory/ | | | |
| | | 2 | 2 Everybody Knows Her | $6 | | Atco 6881 |
| 2/17/73 | 112 | 2 | 3 Stop And Start It All Again ........................... *That's What Our Life Is* | $6 | | Atco 6911 |

### EDWARDS, Vincent                                    HOT/AC
Born Vincento Eduardo Zoine III on 7/9/28 in New York City. Died on 3/11/96 of pancreatic cancer. Star of the TV series *Ben Casey*.

| 6/5/65 | 108 | | No, Not Much ........................... AC:39 *See That Girl* | $10 | ▪ | Colpix 771 |

Ernie Freeman (orch.); #2 hit for The Four Lads in 1956

### EGYPTIAN COMBO ✪

| 10/17/64 | 103 | 6 | Gale Winds ........................... *Rockin' Little Egypt* [I] | $15 | | Norman 549 |

### EIGHTBALL & MJG ✪                                    R&B
Rap duo from Memphis: Rodney "Eightball" Ellis and Marlon Jamal Goodwin.

| 2/24/96 | 110 | 8 | Space Age ........................... R&B:58 *(instrumental) / Break 'Em Off (2 versions)* | $3 | ▪ | Suave House 1545 |

**EIGHTBALL & MJG Featuring Nina Creque**

### ELBERT, Donnie
Born on 5/25/36 in New Orleans. Died on 1/26/89. Singer/multi-instrumentalist. First recorded for DeLuxe in 1957.

| 6/6/64 | 130 | 3 | Run Little Girl ........................... *Who's It Gonna Be* | $15 | | Gateway 731 |

## EL CHICANO
**HOT/AC/R&B**

Mexican-American band formed in Los Angeles as the VIP's in 1965. Core members: Mickey Lesperon (guitar), Andre Baeza (congas), Bobby Espinosa (organ), Freddie Sanchez (bass) and Johnny De Luna (drums).

| | | | | | |
|---|---|---|---|---|---|
| 7/4/70 | 115 | 3 | 1 Eleanor Rigby..................................................................... *Coming Home Baby* [I] | $6 | Kapp 2099 |
| | | | #11 hit for The Beatles in 1966 | | |
| 10/30/76 | 108 | 3 | 2 Dancin' Mama.................................................................................. *Ron Con-Con* [I] | $5 | Shady Brook 032 |

## EL CLOD ⊙

| | | | | | |
|---|---|---|---|---|---|
| 9/8/62 | 111 | 2 | Tijuana Border (Wolverton Mountain) .................................*Pedro's Piano Roll Twist* [N] | $15 | Challenge 9159 |
| | | | parody of Claude King's 1962 hit "Wolverton Mountain" | | |

## ELECTRIC LIGHT ORCHESTRA
**HOT/AC/ROK**

Orchestral rock band formed in Birmingham, England in 1971 featuring Jeff Lynne. *Top Pop Singles:* 27.

**ELO:**

| | | | | | |
|---|---|---|---|---|---|
| 1/30/82 | 101³ | 5 | 1 Rain Is Falling .......................................................................... *Another Heart Breaks* | $4 | Jet 02693 |
| 11/19/83 | 105 | 2 | 2 Stranger ......................................................................... AC:33 *Train Of Gold* | $4 | Jet 04208 |

## ELECTRIC PRUNES, The
**HOT**

Psychedelic rock quintet from Seattle: James Lowe (vocals), Ken Williams and Weasel Spagnola (guitars), Mark Tulin (bass) and Preston Ritter (drums).

| | | | | | |
|---|---|---|---|---|---|
| 7/1/67 | 128 | 3 | Dr. Do-Good ................................................................................... *Hideaway* | $20 | Reprise 0594 |

## ELEKTRAS, The ⊙

Female R&B vocal group.

| | | | | | |
|---|---|---|---|---|---|
| 6/22/63 | 126 | 2 | All I Want To Do Is Run ............................................................ *It Ain't As Easy As That* | $20 | United Artists 594 |

## ELEPHANTS MEMORY, The
**HOT**

Rock-jazz group formed in New York City's East Village: Michal Shapiro (vocals), Stan Bronstein (vocals), Richard Ayers (guitar), Richard Sussman (piano), Myron Yules (trombone), John Ward (bass) and Rick Frank (drums). Backing band for **John Lennon** and Yoko Ono.

| | | | | | |
|---|---|---|---|---|---|
| 6/7/69 | 120 | 3 | Crossroads Of The Stepping Stones ....................................... *Jungle Gym At The Zoo* | $8 | Buddah 98 |

## ELIGIBLES, The ⊙

White vocal group: Stan Farber, Ron Hicklin, Bob Zwirn and Ron Rolla. Also see **Bobby Vee.**

| | | | | | |
|---|---|---|---|---|---|
| 6/1/59 | 107 | 1 | Car Trouble ..................................................................................... *I Wrote A Song* [N] | $15 | Capitol 4203 |

## ELLIMAN, Yvonne
**AC/HOT/R&B**

Born on 12/29/51 in Honolulu. Portrayed Mary Magdalene on the concept album and in the rock opera and movie *Jesus Christ Superstar.*

| | | | | | |
|---|---|---|---|---|---|
| 1/10/76 | 109 | 1 | 1 Walk Right In ............................................................................ *Small Town Talk* | $5 | RSO 517 |
| | | | #1 hit for The Rooftop Singers in 1963 | | |
| 7/26/80 | 105 | 3 | 2 Your Precious Love .......................................... *Redfish Blues* (Craig Hundley) | $4 | Warner 49513 |
| | | | **STEPHEN BISHOP & YVONNE ELLIMAN** | | |
| | | | from the movie *Roadie* starring Meat Loaf; #5 hit for **Marvin Gaye** & Tammi Terrell in 1967 | | |

## ELLIOT, Mama Cass — see MAMAS & THE PAPAS

## ELLIS, Shirley
**R&B/HOT**

Born in 1941 in the Bronx, New York. R&B singer/songwriter. Was in the group The Metronomes.

| | | | | | |
|---|---|---|---|---|---|
| 5/9/64 | 130 | 1 | 1 Shy One ................................................................................... *Takin' Care Of Business* | $12 | Congress 210 |
| | | | "live" recording | | |
| 2/5/66 | 135 | 1 | 2 Ever See A Diver Kiss His Wife While The Bubbles | | |
| | | | Bounce About Above The Water?........................................... *Stardust* [N] | $12 | Congress 260 |

## ELLIS, Terry
**R&B/HOT**

Born on 9/5/66 in Houston. Female R&B singer. Member of En Vogue.

| | | | | | |
|---|---|---|---|---|---|
| 3/30/96 | 113 | 4 | What Did I Do To You? ................................... R&B:41 *Back Down Memory Lane* | $3 | ▮ EastWest 64323 |

## ELLISON, Lorraine
**R&B/HOT**

R&B singer/songwriter from Philadelphia. Formed gospel group, the Ellison Singers; recorded for Sharp/Savoy in 1962.

| | | | | | |
|---|---|---|---|---|---|
| 1/22/66 | 103 | 7 | 1 I Dig You Baby ................................................ R&B:22 *Don't Let It Go To Your Head* | $10 | Mercury 72472 |
| 12/31/66 | 131 | 1 | 2 A Good Love ........................................................................... *I'm Over You* | $8 | Warner 5879 |

## ELMO & PATSY
**HOT/C&W**

Husband-and-wife team of Elmo Shropshire and Patsy Trigg, originally known as The Homestead Act. Divorced in 1985.

| | | | | | |
|---|---|---|---|---|---|
| 12/26/92+ | 112 | 3 | Grandma Got Run Over By A Reindeer ................ *Percy, The Puny Poinsettia* [X-N-R] | $3 | ▮ Epic 05479 |
| | | | first released on Oink 2984 in 1979 ($8); then on Soundwaves 4658 in 1982 ($4); new version released on Epic 04703 in 1984 | | |

## ELO — see ELECTRIC LIGHT ORCHESTRA

## EL PRESIDENTE ⊙

Latin dance outfit featuring Felipe EsquiJarosa "El Presidente."

| | | | | | |
|---|---|---|---|---|---|
| 6/8/96 | 101¹ | 11 | Café Con Leché ............................................................. *(Latin instrumental)* [F] | $3 | ▮ Out Of Control 13509 |

## EMBERS, The ⊙

R&B vocal group.

| | | | | | |
|---|---|---|---|---|---|
| 6/12/61 | 103 | 3 | 1 Solitaire ........................................................................ *I'm Feeling All Right Again* | $30 | ☐ Empress 101 |
| 8/25/62 | 117 | 3 | 2 Abigail................................................................................... *I Was Too Careful* | $30 | Empress 107 |

## EMOTIONS, The
**HOT**

White male vocal quintet from Brooklyn featuring lead singer Joe Favale.

| | | | | | |
|---|---|---|---|---|---|
| 10/12/63 | 110 | 5 | A Story Untold .......................................................... *One Life, One Love, One You* | $25 | 20th Century Fox 430 |
| | | | #2 R&B hit for the Nutmegs in 1955 | | |

## EMOTIONS, The
**R&B/HOT**

Female R&B trio from Chicago: sisters Wanda (lead), Sheila and Jeanette Hutchinson.

| | | | | | |
|---|---|---|---|---|---|
| 9/13/69 | 101¹ | 4 | 1 The Best Part Of A Love Affair ......................................... R&B:27 *I Like It* | $8 | Volt 4021 |
| 3/25/72 | 113 | 5 | 2 My Honey And Me ............................................................ R&B:18 *Blind Alley* | $7 | Volt 4077 |
| | | | #55 hit for Luther Ingram in 1970 | | |
| 1/20/73 | 112 | 2 | 3 From Toys To Boys ......................................... R&B:37 *I Call This Loving You* | $7 | Volt 4088 |
| 8/12/78 | 102 | 14 | 4 Smile .......................................................................... R&B:6 *Changes* | $5 | Columbia 10791 |

| DEBUT | PEAK | WKS | A-side (Chart Hit) ... B-side | $ | Pic | Label & Number |
|---|---|---|---|---|---|---|
| | | | **ENCHANTMENT** <div style="float:right">R&B/HOT</div> | | | |
| | | | R&B vocal quintet from Detroit: Ed "Mickey" Clanton, Bobby Green, Davis Banks, Emanuel Johnson and Joe Thomas. | | | |
| 3/31/79 | 109 | 2 | Anyway You Want It .................................................... **R&B:38** *Oasis Of Love* | $5 | | Roadshow 11481 |
| | | | **ENDGAMES** ◊ | | | |
| | | | Electro-pop quartet from Glasgow, Scotland. Named after a Samuel Beckett play. | | | |
| 3/24/84 | 105 | 1 | Love Cares ......................................................... *Both Of Us* | $4 | | MCA 52338 |
| | | | **ENERGY** ◊ | | | |
| 6/15/96 | 103 | 16 | Take Me Higher............................................................ *(club mix)* | $3 | ■ | Out Of Control 13526 |
| | | | Irma Pro Compton (vocal) | | | |
| | | | **ENGLAND, Ty** ◊ <div style="float:right">C&W</div> | | | |
| | | | Born on 12/5/63. College roommate of Garth Brooks. Former member of Brooks's touring band. | | | |
| 9/16/95 | 121 | 1 | Should've Asked Her Faster ........................... **C&W:3** *A Swing Like That* | $3 | ■ | RCA 64280 |
| | | | **ENGLAND DAN & JOHN FORD COLEY** <div style="float:right">AC/HOT</div> | | | |
| | | | Pop duo from Austin, Texas: Dan Seals (b: 2/8/48) and Coley (b: 10/13/48). Dan, later a top country artist, is the brother of Jim Seals of **Seals & Crofts**. Also see **Dan Seals**. | | | |
| 9/4/71 | 103 | 4 | New Jersey ......................................................... *Tell Her Hello* | $5 | | A&M 1278 |
| | | | **ENGLISH, Michael** ◊ <div style="float:right">AC</div> | | | |
| | | | Former Contemporary Christian artist from Nashville. Left Christian music after a highly publicized extra-martial affair in April 1994. | | | |
| 1/21/95 | 120 | 4 | 1 Healing .......................................................... *(same version)* | $3 | ■ | Curb 76928 |
| | | | WYNONNA & MICHAEL ENGLISH | | | |
| | | | from the movie *Silent Fall* starring Richard Dreyfuss | | | |
| 6/22/96 | 105 | 16 | 2 Your Love Amazes Me ........................................ **AC:10** *Freedom* | $3 | ■ | Curb 76991 |
| | | | #1 Country hit for **John Berry** in 1994. | | | |
| | | | **ENGLISH BEAT** ◊ | | | |
| | | | English "ska" (reggae/R&B) sextet led by Dave Wakeling and Ranking Roger (Roger Charley). Disbanded in 1983. Wakeling and Roger formed **General Public**. | | | |
| 4/9/83 | 104 | 4 | 1 I Confess .......................................... *March Of The Swivelheads* | $4 | | I.R.S. 9913 |
| 5/21/83 | 106 | 2 | 2 Save It For Later ............................................ *Jeanette* | $4 | | I.R.S. 9909 |
| | | | **ENGLISH CONGREGATION, The** <div style="float:right">HOT</div> | | | |
| | | | British pop group. Brian Keith, lead vocals. | | | |
| 7/22/72 | 109 | 4 | Jesahel .................................................. *If I Could Have My Way* | $6 | | Signpost 70004 |
| | | | **ENRIQUEZ, Jocelyn** <div style="float:right">HOT</div> | | | |
| | | | Born on 12/28/74 in San Francisco. Female dance singer. | | | |
| 7/30/94 | 101[1] | 9 | Make This Last Forever ...................... **Air:75** *Lovely* | $3 | ■ | Classified 0203 |
| | | | **ENTWISTLE, John** ◊ <div style="float:right">ROK</div> | | | |
| | | | Born on 10/9/44 in London. Bass guitarist of **The Who**. Musical director for the movies *Quadrophenia* and *The Kids Are Alright*. | | | |
| 11/7/81 | 101[1] | 3 | Too Late The Hero ...................... *Dancin Master* | $4 | | Atco 7337 |
| | | | **ENYA** <div style="float:right">HOT/AC/ROK</div> | | | |
| | | | Born Eithne Ni Bhraonain (Gaelic spelling of Brennan) on 5/17/61 in County Donegal, Ireland. From 1980-82, she was a member of her siblings' folk-rock group, Clannad. | | | |
| 12/31/94+ | 117 | 2 | Oíche Chiún (Silent Night)............................ *Oriel Window / 'S fagaim mo bhaile* [X-F] | $6 | | Reprise 40660 **(CD)** |
| | | | **EPMD** <div style="float:right">R&B/HOT</div> | | | |
| | | | Long Island rap duo: **Erick Sermon** and Parrish Smith. EPMD: Erick and Parrish Making Dollars. By 1993, duo broke up and Sermon recorded solo and Smith recorded as PMD. | | | |
| 12/20/97 | 118 | 2 | Richter Scale............................................... *(2 versions) / Intrigued (3 versions)* | $5 | | Def Jam 568057 **(T)** |
| | | | samples "Person To Person" by Average White Band and "Jungle Boogie" by Kool & The Gang | | | |
| | | | **ERASURE** <div style="float:right">ROK/HOT</div> | | | |
| | | | British techno-soul duo formed in 1985: composer/producer/multi-instrumentalist Vince Clarke and lyricist/vocalist Andy Bell. Clarke was a member of Depeche Mode and half of the duo Yaz. | | | |
| 10/1/94 | 124 | 1 | Run To The Sun............................................. *(remix) / Tenderest Moments* | $3 | ■ | Mute/Elektra 64527 |
| | | | **ESQUIRES, The** <div style="float:right">R&B/HOT</div> | | | |
| | | | R&B vocal quintet from Milwaukee: brothers Gilbert and Alvis Moorer, Millard Edwards, Sam Pace and Shawn Taylor. | | | |
| 3/9/68 | 126 | 4 | 1 You Say .................................................. **R&B:41** *State Fair* | $10 | | Bunky 7753 |
| 3/13/71 | 120 | 3 | 2 Girls In The City ...................................... **R&B:18** *Ain't Gonna Give It Up* | $10 | | Lamarr 1001 |
| | | | **ESSEX, David** <div style="float:right">HOT</div> | | | |
| | | | Born David Cook on 7/23/47 in London. Portrayed Christ in the London production of *Godspell*. Star of British movies since 1970. | | | |
| 9/7/74 | 101[1] | 2 | 1 America .................................................. *Dance Little Girl* | $5 | ■ | Columbia 10005 |
| 12/7/74 | 105 | 4 | 2 Gonna Make You A Star ................................. *Window* | $5 | ■ | Columbia 10039 |
| | | | **ESTEFAN, Gloria** <div style="float:right">HOT/AC/R&B</div> | | | |
| | | | Born Gloria Fajardo on 12/1/57 in Havana, Cuba. Emigrated to Miami in 1960. Formed Miami Sound Machine with husband Emilio Estefan. *Top Pop Singles*: 25. | | | |
| 6/12/93 | 103 | 5 | Go Away .................................................. *(album version)* | $3 | ■ | Epic 74920 |
| | | | **ETERNITY'S CHILDREN** <div style="float:right">HOT</div> | | | |
| | | | New Orleans pop group, formerly **Charlie Rich**'s backing band, The Phantoms. Led by Bruce Blackman who later formed Starbuck. | | | |
| 9/14/68 | 117 | 1 | Sunshine Among Us ............................. *Ruppert White* | $10 | ■ | Tower 439 |
| | | | **EVANS, Adriana** ◊ <div style="float:right">R&B</div> | | | |
| | | | Female R&B singer from San Francisco. Daughter of jazz singer Mary Stallings. | | | |
| 9/27/97 | 124 | 1 | Love Is All Around .............................. **R&B:65** *(remix) / (4 album snipppets)* | $3 | ■ | PMP/Loud/RCA 64887 |
| | | | **EVANS, Barbara** ◊ | | | |
| | | | Pop songstress. | | | |
| 6/1/59 | 111 | 2 | 1 Souvenirs ............................................. *Pray For Me Mother* [N] | $15 | | RCA Victor 7519 |
| 5/29/61 | 109 | 2 | 2 Charlie Wasn't There ................................. *Nothing You Can Do* [N] | $12 | | Pioneer 71828 |

**EVANS, Elliott** ○
Pop pianist in the style of **Roger Williams**.

| 2/24/62 | 110 | 2 | Concerto For The X-15 "A Tribute To The X-15" ............................. *X-15 (Theme)* [I] | $12 | | Reprise 20,039 |

X-15: U.S. Air Force and Navy research aircraft.

**EVANS, Faith**      R&B/HOT
Female R&B singer. Married to rapper The Notorious B.I.G. until his death on 3/9/97.

| 9/7/96 | 109 | 7 | 1 Come Over................................................................ R&B:56 *(instrumental)* | $3 | ▮ | Bad Boy 79065 |
| 11/16/96 | 104 | 14 | 2 You Could Be My Boo ....................... R&B:49 *(instrumental) / Sanity (2 versions)* | $3 | ▮ | Rap-A-Lot 38571 |
| | | | **THE ALMIGHTY RSO featuring Faith Evans** | | | |
| 11/30/96 | 125 | 1 | 3 How Can We Stop ........................................... R&B:77 *Just Let Me Know* (Brown) | $3 | ▮ | Motown 0586 |
| | | | **HORACE BROWN featuring Faith Evans** | | | |
| 12/28/96+ | 108 | 6 | 4 Stressed Out ....................... R&B:56 *(4 versions)* (w/Raphael Saadiq and **Björk**) | $6 | | Jive 42420 (CD) |
| | | | **A TRIBE CALLED QUEST featuring Faith Evans** | | | |

**EVERETT, Betty**      R&B/HOT
Born on in Greenwood, Mississippi. R&B vocalist/pianist. To Chicago in the late 1950s. First recorded for Cobra in 1958.

| 7/4/64 | 126 | 3 | 1 Happy I Long To Be.............................................. *Your Loving Arms* | $20 | | C.J. Records 619 |
| | | | with the Earl Hooker Allstars | | | |
| 8/29/64 | 109 | 6 | 2 It Hurts To Be In Love............................................ *Until You Were Gone* | $15 | | Vee-Jay 610 |
| | | | #61 hit for **Annie Laurie** in 1957 | | | |
| 9/12/64 | 108 | 1 | 3 Ain't That Loving You Baby    *Let It Be Me* (Hot #5) | $15 | | Vee-Jay 613 |
| | | | **BETTY EVERETT & JERRY BUTLER** | | | |
| | | | #3 R&B hit for **Jimmy Reed** in 1956 | | | |
| 6/5/65 | 117 | 1 | 4 Gonna Be Ready ................................................. *The Real Thing* | $15 | | Vee-Jay 683 |
| 9/13/69 | 116 | 1 | 5 Maybe.............................................................. *1900 Yesterday* | $8 | | Uni 55141 |
| 5/1/71 | 113 | 3 | 6 Ain't Nothing Gonna Change Me ........................... R&B:32 *What Is It?* | $8 | | Fantasy 658 |

**EVERLY BROTHERS, The**      HOT/C&W/R&B/AC
Donald (real name: Isaac Donald) was born on 2/1/37 in Brownie, Kentucky; Philip on 1/19/39 in Chicago. Vocal duo/guitarists/songwriters. Invited to Nashville by **Chet Atkins** and first recorded there for Columbia in 1955. Signed to Archie Bleyer's Cadence Records in 1957. Duo split up in July 1973 and reunited in September 1983. Inducted into the Rock and Roll Hall of Fame in 1986. *Top Pop Singles*: 38.

| 11/14/60 | 109 | 2 | 1 Brand New Heartache..................................... *Like Strangers* (Hot #22) | $20 | | Cadence 1388 |
| 11/3/62 | 117 | 3 | 2 No One Can Make My Sunshine Smile .................. *Don't Ask Me To Be Friends* (Hot #48) | $15 | ◼ | Warner 5297 |
| 3/30/63 | 107 | 2 | 3 Nancy's Minuet/ | | | |
| 3/30/63 | 116 | 1 | 4 (So It Was...So It Is) So It Always Will Be............................. | $15 | | Warner 5346 |
| 6/1/63 | 101[1] | 4 | 5 It's Been Nice (Goodnight)    *I'm Afraid* | $15 | | Warner 5362 |
| 10/26/63 | 117 | 2 | 6 Love Her ......................................................... *The Girl Sang The Blues* | $15 | | Warner 5389 |
| 5/2/64 | 133 | 1 | 7 Ain't That Lovin' You, Baby .......................................... *Hello Amy* | $15 | | Warner 5422 |
| | | | #3 R&B hit for **Jimmy Reed** in 1956 | | | |
| 2/6/65 | 110 | 3 | 8 You're My Girl ...................................... *Don't Let The Whole World Know* | $12 | | Warner 5600 |
| 3/20/65 | 111 | 5 | 9 That'll Be The Day.................................... *Give Me A Sweetheart* | $12 | | Warner 5611 |
| | | | #1 hit for **The Crickets** in 1957 | | | |
| 5/15/65 | 104 | 3 | 10 The Price Of Love.................................. *It Only Costs A Dime* | $12 | | Warner 5628 |
| 8/21/65 | 128 | 3 | 11 Love Is Strange ..................................... *Man With Money* | $12 | ◼ | Warner 5649 |
| | | | #11 hit for **Mickey & Sylvia** in 1957 | | | |
| 11/4/67 | 114 | 2 | 12 Love Of The Common People ............................ *A Voice Within* | $12 | | Warner 7088 |
| | | | #54 hit for **The Winstons** in 1969 | | | |
| 5/18/68 | 112 | 2 | 13 It's My Time ..................................................... *Empty Boxes* | $12 | | Warner 7192 |
| | | | #51 Country hit for **John D. Loudermilk** in 1967 | | | |
| 7/20/74 | 110 | 1 | 14 Warmin' Up The Band ........................................... *Evelyn Swing* | $10 | | Ode 66046 |
| | | | **DON EVERLY** | | | |

**EXILE**      C&W/HOT/AC
Pop group formed in Lexington, Kentucky, in 1963 as The Exiles: Jimmy Stokley (vocals), J.P. Pennington (vocals, guitar), Buzz Cornelison (keyboards), Sonny Lemaire (bass) and Steve Goetzman (drums). Switched to country music in 1983.

| 1/24/70 | 104 | 3 | 1 Church St. Soul Revival ........................................... *John Weatherman* | $7 | | Columbia 44972 |
| | | | **THE EXILES** | | | |
| | | | #62 hit for **Tommy James** in 1971 | | | |
| 7/26/80 | 105 | 2 | 2 You're Good For Me ...................... AC:44 *Let's Do It All Over Again* | $4 | | Warner/Curb 49245 |
| 10/18/80 | 102 | 5 | 3 Take Me Down ........................... *It Takes Love To Make Love* | $4 | | Warner/Curb 49548 |
| | | | #1 Country hit for **Alabama** in 1982 | | | |
| 10/3/81 | 102 | 3 | 4 Heart & Soul ........................................ *Your Love Is Everything* | $4 | | Warner/Curb 49794 |
| | | | #8 hit for **Huey Lewis & The News** in 1983 | | | |

**EXITS, The** ○      R&B
R&B vocal group.

| 8/26/67 | 116 | 3 | Under The Street Lamp ...................... R&B:34 *You Got To Have Money* | $15 | | Gemini 1004 |

**EXPOSÉ**      HOT/AC/R&B
Female dance trio based in Miami: Ann Curless, Jeanette Jurado and Kelly Moneymaker.

| 2/10/96 | 117 | 4 | I'll Say Goodbye For The Two Of Us........................ *I Specialize In Love* | $3 | ▮ | Arista 12912 |

# F

**FABARES, Shelley**      HOT/AC
Born Michele Fabares on 1/19/44 in Santa Monica, California. Starred with **Elvis Presley** in three of his movies. Starred in TV's *The Donna Reed Show* and *Coach*.

| 1/19/63 | 109 | 2 | Telephone (Won't You Ring) ................................................. *Big Star* | $20 | | Colpix 667 |

### FABRIC, Bent, and His Piano    HOT/AC
Born Bent Fabricius-Bjerre on 12/7/24 in Copenhagen. Jazz pianist. Head of Metronome Records in Denmark.

| | | | | | | |
|---|---|---|---|---|---|---|
| 1/5/63 | 117 | 2 | 1 That Certain Party ....................................................... *Chicken Feed* (Hot #63) [I] | $8 | | Atco 6245 |
| | | | #8 hit for Ted Lewis in 1926; #9 hit for Benny Strong in 1948 | | | |
| 8/3/63 | 102 | 5 | 2 The Happy Puppy ....................................................... *Sermonette* [I] | $8 | | Atco 6271 |

### FABULOUS CONTINENTALS ✪
Rock and roll instrumental group from Moses Lake, Washington. Later became the Bards.

| | | | | | | |
|---|---|---|---|---|---|---|
| 10/12/63 | 128 | 1 | Undertow .................................................................... *Return To Me* [I] | $25 | | CB 5003 |

### FABULOUS FIVE — see HELTAH SKELTAH

### FAGEN, Donald    ROK/AC/HOT/R&B
Born on 1/10/48 in Passaic, New Jersey. Backup keyboardist/vocalist with Jay & The Americans. Member of Steely Dan.

| | | | | | | |
|---|---|---|---|---|---|---|
| 8/7/93 | 121 | 1 | Tomorrow's Girls ..................................... ROK:20 / AC:32  *Confide In Me* | $3 | ▮ | Reprise 18502 |

### FAITH, Percy, And His Orchestra    MEM/POP/AC/HOT
Born on 4/7/08 in Toronto. Died of cancer on 2/9/76. Orchestra leader. Moved to the U.S. in 1940. Joined Columbia Records in 1950 as conductor/arranger for company's leading singers.

| | | | | | | |
|---|---|---|---|---|---|---|
| 8/8/60 | 111 | 1 | 1 Sons And Lovers ....................................................... *Hawaiian Lullaby* [I] | $8 | | Columbia 41731 |
| | | | from the movie starring Trevor Howard and Dean Stockwell | | | |
| 10/10/60 | 101[1] | 5 | 2 Theme From "The Dark At The Top Of The Stairs" .............. *Our Language Of Love* [I] | $8 | | Columbia 41796 |
| | | | from the movie starring Robert Preston and Dorothy McGuire; #70 hit for **Ernie Freeman** in 1960 | | | |
| 9/21/63 | 111 | 2 | 3 The Sound Of Surf ....................................................... *Our Love* [I] | $7 | | Columbia 42844 |
| 7/26/69 | 111 | 1 | 4 Theme From "A Summer Place" ........................... AC:26  *Hello Tomorrow* [R] | $6 | | Columbia 44932 |
| | | | vocal version of his #1 hit in 1960 on Columbia 41490 | | | |

### FAITHFULL, Marianne    HOT/AC
Born on 12/29/46 in Hampstead, London. Discovered by **The Rolling Stones**' manager, Andrew Loog Oldham.

| | | | | | | |
|---|---|---|---|---|---|---|
| 3/11/67 | 125 | 2 | Is This What I Get For Loving You? ............................ *Tomorrow's Calling* | $10 | | London 20020 |
| | | | #75 hit for **The Ronettes** in 1965 | | | |

### FAITH, HOPE & CHARITY — see CHOICE FOUR

### FALCONS, The    R&B/HOT
R&B vocal group from Detroit featuring Eddie Floyd (replaced in 1961 by Wilson Pickett), "Sir Mack" Rice and Joe Stubbs (d: 1/19/98, age 57).

| | | | | | | |
|---|---|---|---|---|---|---|
| 10/5/59 | 107 | 3 | 1 You're Mine ....................................................... *Country Shack* | $30 | | Unart 2022 |
| | | | Joe Stubbs (lead singer) | | | |
| 11/5/66 | 107 | 5 | 2 Standing On Guard ........................... R&B:29  *I Can't Help It* | $20 | | Big Wheel 1967 |
| | | | Sonny Monroe (lead singer) | | | |

### FALLEN ANGELS ✪
Rock group from Detroit.

| | | | | | | |
|---|---|---|---|---|---|---|
| 5/3/75 | 106 | 2 | Just Like Romeo And Juliet ........................... *Ride It To The End Of The Line* | $6 | | Arista 0113 |
| | | | #6 hit for **The Reflections** in 1964 | | | |

### FANDANGO ✪
Rock group: Joe Lynn Turner (**Rainbow**, **Deep Purple**), Larry Dawson, Bob Danyls, Rick Blakemore, Santos, Chuck Burgi and Denny LaRue.

| | | | | | | |
|---|---|---|---|---|---|---|
| 2/4/78 | 110 | 1 | Headliner ....................................................... *Goin' Down For The Last Time* | $5 | | RCA 11194 |

### FANNY — see STREISAND, Barbra

### FANTASTIC FOUR, The    R&B/HOT
R&B vocal group formed in Detroit in 1955 featuring "Sweet" James Epps.

| | | | | | | |
|---|---|---|---|---|---|---|
| 4/12/69 | 111 | 3 | I Feel Like I'm Falling In Love Again ........................... *Pin Point It Down* | $15 | | Soul 35058 |

### FANTASTIC JOHNNY C, The    HOT/R&B
Born Johnny Corley on 4/28/43 in Greenwood, South Carolina. Produced and managed by **Jesse James**.

| | | | | | | |
|---|---|---|---|---|---|---|
| 3/22/69 | 130 | 2 | Is There Anything Better Than Making Love? .................... *New Love* | $10 | | Phil-L.A. of Soul 327 |

### FANTASTICS, The    HOT
R&B quartet from Brooklyn: Don Haywoode, Jerome Ramos, John Cheatdom and Richie Pitts.

| | | | | | | |
|---|---|---|---|---|---|---|
| 5/29/71 | 102 | 2 | Something Old, Something New .................... *High And Dry* | $15 | | Bell 977 |

### FANTASY ✪    R&B
R&B vocal group from New York City: Ken Robeson, Tami Hunt, Rufus Jackson and Carolyn Edwards.

| | | | | | | |
|---|---|---|---|---|---|---|
| 4/11/81 | 104 | 2 | You're Too Late ........................... R&B:28  *(instrumental)* | $5 | | Pavillion 6407 |

### FARLOWE, Chris ✪
Born John Henry Deighton on 10/13/40 in Essex, England. Rock singer/songwriter/guitarist. Joined Atomic Rooster in 1972.

| | | | | | | |
|---|---|---|---|---|---|---|
| 11/12/66 | 122 | 1 | Out Of Time ....................................................... *Baby Make It Soon* | $15 | | MGM 13567 |
| | | | produced by Mick Jagger; #81 hit for **The Rolling Stones** in 1975 | | | |

### FARMER, Jules ✪
Male Adult Contemporary vocalist.

| | | | | | | |
|---|---|---|---|---|---|---|
| 8/3/59 | 112 | 3 | Love Me Now ....................................... *Part Of Me (Is Still with You)* | $15 | | Imperial 5607 |
| | | | Henri Rene (orch. & chorus) | | | |

### FARRIS, Dionne    HOT/AC/R&B
Female singer from Bordentown, New Jersey. Worked with TLC, **El DeBarge** and Arrested Development.

| | | | | | | |
|---|---|---|---|---|---|---|
| 8/12/95 | 121 | 3 | Don't Ever Touch Me (Again) ........................... *11th Hour* | $3 | ▮ | Columbia 77905 |

### FARROW, Mia ✪    AC
Born on 2/9/45 in Los Angeles. Film actress. Had a child with actor/director Woody Allen (never married; highly publicized breakup in 1992).

| | | | | | | |
|---|---|---|---|---|---|---|
| 8/3/68 | 111 | 3 | Lullaby From "Rosemary's Baby" Part 1 .................... AC:33  *Part 2* [I] | $8 | ▮ | Dot 17126 |
| | | | from the movie *Rosemary's Baby* starring Farrow (her only vocals are "La La's") | | | |

### FASINATIONS, The    R&B/HOT
Group shown as The Fascinations on their pop and R&B hits. Female R&B vocal group: Shirley Walker, Joanne Levell, Bernadine Boswell and Fern Bledsoe.

| | | | | | | |
|---|---|---|---|---|---|---|
| 1/12/63 | 108 | 1 | Mama Didn't Lie .................................................. *Someone Like You* | $20 | | ABC-Paramount 10387 |
| | | | written and produced by **Curtis Mayfield**; #14 hit for Jan Bradley in 1963 | | | |

**FASTEST GROUP ALIVE, The ☺**
Los Angeles novelty group led by guitarist Davie Allan (The Arrows).

| 11/26/66 | 133 | 1 | The Bears .................................................................................................*Beside* [N] | $15 | | Valiant 754 |

**FAT ALBERT ORCHESTRA AND CHORUS, The ☺**
Studio group assembled by **Bill Cosby** (owner of the Tetragrammaton label).

| 4/27/68 | 120 | 3 | Fat Albert (Hey, Hey, Hey)............................................................*Cosbyianna* [I] | $8 | | Tetragrammaton 1500 |

**FATBACK ☺**                                                    **R&B**
Six-to-nine member R&B/funk band with fluctuating lineup.

| 3/27/76 | 101[1] | 7 | 1 Spanish Hustle            **R&B:12**  *Put Your Love (In My Tender Care)* [I] | $5 | | Event 229 |
| | | | THE FATBACK BAND |
| 9/9/78 | 101[1] | 7 | 2 I Like Girls            **R&B:9**  *Get Out On The Dance Floor* | $5 | | Spring 181 |

**FAT BOYS**                                                    **R&B/HOT**
Rap trio from Brooklyn: Mark "Prince Markie Dee" Morales, Darren "The Human Beat Box" Robinson (d: 12/10/95, age 28) and Damon "Kool Rock-ski" Wimbley.

| 12/22/84 | 105 | 4 | 1 Jail House Rap ..................................................................... **R&B:17**  *Stick 'Em* | $4 | | Sutra 137 |
| 3/16/85 | 101[1] | 2 | 2 Can You Feel It            **R&B:38**  *Stick 'Em* | $4 | | Sutra 139 |
| | | | above 2 written and produced by Kurtis Blow |

**FATHER MC**                                                    **R&B/HOT**
Born Timothy Brown in New York City. Dancehall reggae singer. Dropped the MC from his name in mid-1993.

| 12/5/92 | 111 | 4 | 1 One Nite Stand ................................................... **R&B:22**  *(instrumental)* | $3 | ■ | Uptown/MCA 54445 |
| | | | samples "School Boy Crush" by **Average White Band** and "Funky Sensation" by **Gwen McCrae** |
| 11/13/93 | 102 | 10 | 2 69 ...................................................................... **R&B:51**  *(instrumental)* | $3 | ■ | Uptown/MCA 54741 |
| | | | FATHER |
| | | | samples "Jungle Boogie" by **Kool & The Gang** |

**FELDER, Don**                                                    **ROK/HOT**
Born on 9/21/47 in Gainesville, Florida. Guitarist with the Eagles.

| 12/10/83 | 104 | 5 | Bad Girls ............................................................... **ROK:34**  *Night Owl* | $4 | | Asylum 69784 |

**FELDER, Wilton ☺**                                                    **R&B**
Born in Houston in 1940. R&B reed player.

| 2/16/85 | 102 | 6 | (No Matter How High I Get) I'll Still Be Lookin' Up To You................... **R&B:2**  *La Luz* | $4 | ■ | MCA 52467 |
| | | | WILTON FELDER Featuring Bobby Womack and Introducing Alltrinna Grayson |

**FELICIANO, Jose**                                                    **HOT/AC/R&B/C&W**
Born on 9/8/45 in Lares, Puerto Rico; raised in New York City. Blind since birth. Virtuoso acoustic guitarist. Won the 1968 Best New Artist Grammy Award.

| 8/2/69 | 103 | 3 | 1 She's A Woman ........................................................ *Rain* (Hot #76) | $6 | | RCA Victor 9757 |
| | | | #4 hit for **The Beatles** in 1964 |
| 5/29/71 | 122 | 2 | 2 I Only Want To Say (Gethsemane) ............................ *Watch It With My Heart* | $6 | | RCA Victor 0476 |
| | | | from the Rock Opera *Jesus Christ, Superstar* |

**FELIX Featuring JOMANDA ☺**
Felix is a techno-dance producer.

| 1/23/93 | 110 | 9 | Don't You Want Me ............................................................. *(original mix)* | $3 | ■ | Pyrotech 10107 |

**FELLER, Dick**                                                    **C&W/AC/HOT**
Born on 1/2/43 in Bronaugh, Missouri. Moved to Nashville in 1966; much session work.

| 12/29/73+ | 101[1] | 6 | 1 Biff, The Friendly Purple Bear            **C&W:22 / AC:36**  *Goodbye California* [S] | $5 | | United Artists 316 |
| 11/23/74 | 105 | 6 | 2 The Credit Card Song .................................. **C&W:10 / AC:40**  *Just Short Of The Line* [N] | $5 | | United Artists 535 |

**FEM 2 FEM ☺**
Female vocal quintet from Los Angeles: Julie Park, L.D., Christina Minna, Lynn Pompey and Altizah.

| 1/1/94 | 102 | 6 | Obsession ............................................................................. *(instrumental)* | $3 | ■ | Avenue Foch 15513 |

**FENDER, Freddy**                                                    **C&W/HOT/AC**
Born Baldemar Huerta on 6/4/37 in San Benito, Texas. Mexican-American singer/guitarist.

| 5/9/60 | 107 | 3 | 1 Holy One .........................................................................*Mean Woman* | $20 | | Imperial 5659 |
| | | | FREDDIE FENDER |
| 8/5/78 | 103 | 1 | 2 Talk To Me .................................................. **C&W:13**  *Please Mr. Sandman* | $5 | | ABC 12370 |
| | | | #20 hit for **Little Willie John** in 1958 |

**FENDERMEN, The**                                                    **HOT/C&W**
Rock and roll duo: Phil Humphrey and Jim Sundquist. Both were born on 11/26/37 in Wisconsin.

| 9/26/60 | 110 | 2 | Don't You Just Know It ...................................................*Beach Party* | $20 | | Soma 1142 |
| | | | #9 hit for **Huey (Piano) Smith** in 1958 |

**FERGUSON, Maynard**                                                    **HOT/AC/R&B**
Born on 5/4/28 in Verdun, Quebec, Canada. Jazz trumpeter. Moved to the U.S. in 1949.

| 9/3/77 | 107 | 1 | Main Title (From The 20th Century-Fox Film "Star Wars")...................*Oasis* [I] | $5 | | Columbia 10595 |
| | | | #1 hit for **Meco** and #10 hit for **John Williams** in 1977 |

**FERRANTE & TEICHER**                                                    **AC/HOT/R&B**
Piano duo: Arthur Ferrante (b: 9/7/21, New York City) and Louis Teicher (b: 8/24/24, Wilkes-Barre, Pennsylvania).

| 12/8/62 | 116 | 2 | 1 Theme From Taras Bulba (The Wishing Star)......... *Theme From The Eleventh Hour* [I] | $8 | ■ | United Artists 537 |
| | | | from the movie starring Tony Curtis and Yul Brynner; #100 hit for **Jerry Butler** in 1962 |
| 12/14/63 | 127 | 2 | 2 Crystal Fingers ........................................................*Greensleeves* [I] | $7 | | United Artists 660 |
| | | | adapted from Tchaikovsky's "Pathetique Symphony" (*Hot 100* hits known as "Where" and "In Time") |
| 7/18/64 | 124 | 4 | 3 The Seventh Dawn .................................................*You're Too Much* [I] | $7 | ■ | United Artists 735 |
| | | | from the movie starring William Holden |
| 2/27/65 | 101[2] | 8 | 4 The Greatest Story Ever Told            *To Spring* [I] | $7 | ■ | United Artists 816 |
| | | | from the movie starring Charleton Heston |

**FERRARA, Peter — see PICKETT, Bobby**

**FERRY, Bryan**              ROK/HOT/AC
Born on 9/26/45 in County Durham, England. Lead singer of **Roxy Music**.

| 6/15/85 | 109 | 1 | Slave To Love ............................................... ROK:19 *Valentine* | $4 | ■ | Warner/EG 28990 |

**FESTIVALS, The** ✪          R&B
Male R&B vocal group from Philadelphia.

| 10/29/66 | 130 | 1 | 1 Music .................................................. *I'll Always Love You* | $10 | | Smash 2056 |
| 9/19/70 | 114 | 1 | 2 You're Gonna Make It ............................. R&B:28 *So In Love* | $8 | | Colossus 122 |
| 4/24/71 | 116 | 3 | 3 Baby Show It .................................... R&B:29 *Take Your Time* | $8 | | Colossus 136 |

**FEW GOOD MEN, A**        R&B/HOT
R&B vocal quartet: Aaron Hilliard, David Morris, Tony Amey and Demail Burks.

| 10/28/95 | 118 | 3 | Tonite.......................................... R&B:44 *(instrumental)* | $3 | ▮ | LaFace 24103 |

samples "Treat Her Like A Prostitute" and "Lick The Balls" by **Slick Rick**

**FIESTAS, The**        HOT/R&B
R&B vocal group from Newark, New Jersey: Tommy Bullock, Eddie Morris, Sam Ingalls and Preston Lane.

| 11/24/62 | 123 | 1 | I Feel Good All Over ..................................... *Look At That Girl* | $25 | | Old Town 1127 |

**5TH DIMENSION, The**        HOT/AC/R&B
R&B/Adult Contemporary vocal group formed in Los Angeles in 1966: Marilyn McCoo, Billy Davis, Jr., Florence LaRue, Lamont McLemore and Ron Townson. *Top Pop Singles*: 30.

| 3/1/75 | 105 | 2 | No Love In The Room ..................... AC:11 *I Don't Know How To Look For Love* | $5 | | Arista 0101 |

**FIFTH ESTATE, The**        HOT
Pop group from Stamford, Connecticut: Wayne Wadhams (vocals, keyboards), Rick Engler and Bill Shute (guitars), Doug Ferrara (bass) and Ken Evans (drums).

| 3/16/68 | 122 | 1 | Do Drop Inn....................................................... *That's Love* | $8 | | Jubilee 5617 |

**FINDERS KEEPERS** ✪
Pop vocal group.

| 10/22/66 | 123 | 1 | (We Wear) Lavender Blue ................................. *Raggedy Ann* | $12 | | Challenge 59338 |

**FINNEGAN, Larry**        HOT
Born John Lawrence Finneran on 8/10/38 in New York City. Died of a brain tumor on 7/22/73.

| 12/19/64 | 130 | 2 | The Other Ringo (A Tribute To Ringo Starr) ................ *When My Love Passes By* [S] | $15 | | RIC 146 |

a **Beatles**' tribute based on **Lorne Greene**'s #1 hit "Ringo"

**FIREFALL**        HOT/AC
Soft-rock group from Boulder, Colorado: Rick Roberts (vocals), Larry Burnett and Jack Bartley (guitars), Mark Andes (bass) and Mike Clarke (drums; d. 12/19/93, age 49). David Muse (keyboards) joined in 1977.

| 11/5/83 | 103 | 5 | Runaway Love ...................................... *What Kind Of Love* | $4 | | Atlantic 89755 |

**FIREHOUSE**        HOT/ROK/AC
Hard-rock quartet from North Carolina: C.J. Snare (vocals), Bill Leverty (guitar), Perry Richardson (bass) and Michael Foster (drums).

| 7/29/95 | 108 | 5 | Here For You ...................... *(acoustic version) / I Live My Life For You* | $3 | ▮ | Epic 77949 |

**FIRST CHOICE**        R&B
Female R&B vocal trio from Philadelphia: Rochelle Fleming, Annette Guest and Joyce Jones. By 1977, Jones left and Ursula Herring joined.

| 12/7/74 | 103 | 3 | 1 Guilty ............................................. R&B:19 *Wake Up To Me* | $6 | | Philly Groove 202 |
| 5/12/79 | 104 | 4 | 2 Double Cross ................................. R&B:60 *Gamble On Love* | $5 | | Gold Mind 4019 |

**FIRST EDITION, The — see ROGERS, Kenny**

**FISHER, Eddie**        MEM/POP/HOT/AC
Born Edwin Jack Fisher on 8/10/28 in Philadelphia. Married to Debbie Reynolds from 1955-59. Other marriages to Elizabeth Taylor and **Connie Stevens**. Own *Coke Time* 15-minute TV series, 1953-57. Fisher was the #1 idol of bobbysoxers during the early 1950's. *Pop Hits & Top Pop Singles*: 57.

| 5/19/62 | 112 | 1 | 1 Arrivederci, Roma ........................................ *A Camminare* | $10 | | ABC-Paramount 10326 |

Eddy Samuels (orch.); #51 hit for **Georgia Gibbs** in 1955

| 6/19/65 | 119 | 5 | 2 Sunrise, Sunset.................... AC:22 *Walking In The Footsteps Of A Fool* | $8 | | Dot 16732 |

Pete King (orch.); from the musical *Fiddler On The Roof*; #84 hit for **Roger Williams** in 1967

| 6/3/67 | 131 | 2 | 3 Now I Know .................. AC:23 *I Haven't Got Anything Better To Do* | $8 | | RCA Victor 9204 |

Claus Ogerman (orch.); #73 hit for **Jack Jones** in 1967

**FITZGERALD, Ella**        MEM/POP/R&B/HOT/AC/C&W
Born on 4/25/18 in Newport News, Virginia. Died on 6/15/96. The most-honored jazz singer of all time. Won Grammy's Lifetime Achievement Award in 1967. *Pop Hits & Top Pop Singles*: 23.

| 8/14/61 | 103 | 4 | 1 Mr. Paganini (You'll Have To Swing It) ........... AC:20 *You're Driving Me Crazy* | $10 | ■ | Verve 10237 |

"live" recording; originally recorded by Ella with Chick Webb's orchestra in 1936 on Decca 1032

| 11/17/62 | 102 | 5 | 2 Desafinado (Slightly Out Of Tune)/ | | | |

#15 hit for **Stan Getz**/Charlie Byrd in 1962

| 12/15/62 | 129 | 1 | 3 Stardust Bossa Nova......................................... | $10 | | Verve 10274 |

Bossa Nova version of Hoagy Carmichael's all-time classic "Star Dust"; Marty Paich (orch., above 2)

| 6/27/64 | 125 | 1 | 4 Hello, Dolly! ......................................... *Can't Buy Me Love* | $10 | | Verve 10324 |

Johnnie Spence (orch.); from the Broadway musical starring Carol Channing; #1 hit for **Louis Armstrong** in 1964

| 1/2/65 | 127 | 1 | 5 Ringo Beat ............................................ *I'm Fallin' In Love* | $10 | | Verve 10340 |

Barney Kessel (orch.); a tribute to Ringo Starr and the music of **The Beatles**

| 10/4/69 | 126 | 2 | 6 Get Ready ......................................... *Open Your Window* | $7 | | Reprise 0850 |

#29 hit for **The Temptations** in 1966

**FIVE AMERICANS, The**        HOT
Rock and roll band from Dallas: Michael Rabon (vocals), Norman Ezell (guitar), John Durrill (keyboards), James Grant (bass) and James Wright (drums).

| 11/11/67 | 132 | 1 | 1 Stop Light ........................................ *Tell Ann I Love Her* | $12 | ■ | Abnak 125 |
| 3/1/69 | 133 | 1 | 2 Virginia Girl ............................................... *Call On Me* | $12 | | Abnak 134 |

**MICHAEL RABON and THE FIVE AMERICANS**

| DEBUT | PEAK | WKS | A-side (Chart Hit) / B-side | $ | Pic | Label & Number |
|---|---|---|---|---|---|---|
| | | | **FIVE BY FIVE**      HOT | | | |
| | | | Rock quintet: Ron Plants (vocals), Larry Andrew, Bill Merritt, Tim Milam and Doug Green. | | | |
| 3/8/69 | 133 | 2 | Apple Cider............................................................... *Fruitstand Man* | $15 | | Paula 319 |
| | | | **"5" ROYALES, The**      R&B/HOT | | | |
| | | | R&B vocal group from Winston-Salem, North Carolina: cousins Lowman Pauling (d. 1974), Clarence Pauling (d: 5/6/95) and Windsor King, with brothers Eugene and John Tanner. | | | |
| 6/8/59 | 103 | 4 | 1 I Know It's Hard But It's Fair............................... *Miracle Of Love* | $30 | | King 5191 |
| 6/27/60 | 107 | 5 | 2 I'm With You .................................. *Don't Give No More Than You Can Take* | $30 | | King 5329 |
| 11/21/60 | 114 | 2 | 3 Please, Please, Please.................................. *I Got To Know* | $25 | | Home of the Blues 112 |
| | | | #5 R&B hit for **James Brown** in 1956 | | | |
| | | | **FIVE SATINS, The**      HOT/R&B/AC | | | |
| | | | R&B vocal group from New Haven, Connecticut: Fred Parris (lead), Al Denby, Jim Freeman, Eddie Martin and Jessie Murphy (piano). | | | |
| 6/1/59 | 112 | 1 | 1 When Your Love Comes Along ......................... *Skippity Doo* | $40 | | Another First 104 |
| | | | first pressings on orange label; second pressings on green label | | | |
| 6/27/60 | 107 | 1 | 2 Your Memory....................................... *I Didn't Know* | $35 | | Cub 9071 |
| 7/21/62 | 102 | 3 | 3 The Masquerade Is Over ............................. *Raining In My Heart* | $30 | | Chancellor 1110 |
| | | | **FIVE STAIRSTEPS, The**      R&B/HOT | | | |
| | | | R&B group from Chicago: brothers Clarence, Jr., James, Kenneth, Dennis and five-year-old Cubie Burke. | | | |
| 2/15/69 | 101[1] | 7 | 1 Baby Make Me Feel So Good    R&B:12 *Little Young Lover* | $8 | | Curtom 1936 |
| | | | **FIVE STAIRSTEPS & CUBIE** | | | |
| 2/12/72 | 115 | 1 | 2 I Love You - Stop ..................... R&B:40 *I Feel A Song (In My Heart Again)* | $6 | | Buddah 277 |
| | | | **THE STAIRSTEPS** | | | |
| 3/13/76 | 102 | 8 | 3 From Us To You ................................. R&B:10 *Time* | $5 | ■ | Dark Horse 10005 |
| 7/4/76 | 106 | 5 | 4 Tell Me Why ........................................ *Salaam* | $5 | | Dark Horse 10009 |
| | | | **STAIRSTEPS** (above 2) | | | |
| | | | **FIVE WHISPERS, The** ☉ | | | |
| 10/13/62 | 115 | 3 | Midnight Sun ............................. *Moon In The Afternoon* [I] | $15 | | Dolton 61 |
| | | | first recorded by Lionel Hampton in 1948 on Decca 24429 | | | |
| | | | **FIXX, The**      ROK/HOT | | | |
| | | | Techno-pop group formed in London in 1979: Cy Curnin (vocals), Jamie West-Oram (guitar), Rupert Greenall (keyboards), Charlie Barrett (bass) and Adam Woods (drums). | | | |
| 3/12/83 | 101[1] | 5 | Red Skies    ROK:13 *Is It By Instinct* | $4 | | MCA 52167 |
| | | | **FLACK, Roberta**      R&B/AC/HOT | | | |
| | | | Born on 2/10/39 in Asheville, North Carolina. Played piano from an early age. Classmate of **Donny Hathaway**. | | | |
| 5/22/71 | 117 | 2 | 1 Do What You Gotta Do ........................ *Let It Be Me* | $6 | | Atlantic 2785 |
| 9/27/80 | 104 | 1 | 2 Don't Make Me Wait Too Long .......... R&B:67 *Only Heaven Can Wait (For Love)* | $5 | | Atlantic 3753 |
| | | | written by **Stevie Wonder** | | | |
| 6/13/81 | 108 | 5 | 3 You Stopped Loving Me.............. R&B:32 *Qual E Malindrinho (Why Are You So Bad)* | $4 | | MCA 51126 |
| | | | written by **Luther Vandross**; from the movie *Bustin' Loose* starring Richard Pryor | | | |
| | | | **FLAMING EMBER, The**      HOT/R&B | | | |
| | | | R&B-rock group from Detroit: Joe Sladich (guitar), Bill Ellis (piano), Jim Bugnel (bass) and Jerry Plunk (drums). | | | |
| 2/13/71 | 101[1] | 2 | 1 Stop The World And Let Me Off    R&B:43 *Robot In A Robot's World* | $7 | | Hot Wax 7010 |
| 5/22/71 | 117 | 2 | 2 Sunshine ....................................... *1200 Miles* | $7 | | Hot Wax 7103 |
| | | | **FLAMINGOS, The**      HOT/R&B | | | |
| | | | R&B vocal group from Chicago: cousins Zeke and Jake Carey (d: 12/10/97), **Tommy Hunt**, Nate Nelson (d: 6/1/84), Johnny Carter and Paul Wilson. | | | |
| 8/21/61 | 108 | 1 | 1 Golden Teardrops ............................. *Carried Away* | $25 | | Vee-Jay 384 |
| | | | new guitar overdub on version originally issued in 1953 on Chance 1145 ($1000) | | | |
| 10/9/61 | 117 | 1 | 2 Lovers Never Say Goodbye .................. *That Love Is You* [R] | $25 | | End 1035 |
| | | | originally made the *Hot 100* (#52) on 1/19/59 on End 1035 | | | |
| 5/4/63 | 107 | 4 | 3 I Know Better............................. *Flame Of Love* | $20 | | End 1121 |
| | | | **FLARES, The**      HOT/R&B | | | |
| | | | Los Angeles-based R&B vocal group: Aaron Collins (lead), Willie Davis, Tommy Miller and George Hollis. | | | |
| 11/9/63 | 133 | 1 | The Monkey Walk ........................... *Do It If You Wanna* | $15 | | Press 2810 |
| | | | **FLASH CADILLAC AND THE CONTINENTAL KIDS**      HOT | | | |
| | | | Fifties-styled rock act from Colorado: Sam "Flash Cadillac" McFadden (vocals, guitar), Lin "Spike" Phillips (guitar), Chris "Angelo" Moe (keyboards), Dwight "Spider" Bement (sax), Warren "Butch" Knight (bass) and Jeff "Wally" Stuart (drums; replaced in 1975 by Paul "Wheaty" Wheatbread). Group appeared as the prom band in the movie *American Graffiti*. | | | |
| 7/19/75 | 102 | 4 | Hot Summer Girls ........................... *Time Will Tell* | $6 | | Private Stock 45,026 |
| | | | **FLATT & SCRUGGS**      C&W/HOT/AC | | | |
| | | | Influential bluegrass duo: Lester Flatt (guitar; d: 5/11/79) and Earl Scruggs (banjo). Regulars on TV's *Beverly Hillbillies*. | | | |
| 4/27/63 | 113 | 3 | 1 Pearl Pearl Pearl .......................... C&W:8 *Hard Travelin'* [N] | $10 | ■ | Columbia 42755 |
| | | | **LESTER FLATT, EARL SCRUGGS and The Foggy Mountain Boys** | | | |
| | | | Cousin Pearl (Bea Benaderet) was a featured character on the TV series *The Beverly Hillbillies* | | | |
| 9/21/68 | 125 | 1 | 2 Like A Rolling Stone................... C&W:58 *I'd Like To Say A Word For Texas* | $8 | | Columbia 44623 |
| | | | #2 hit for **Bob Dylan** in 1965 | | | |
| | | | **FLEETWOOD MAC**      HOT/AC/ROK | | | |
| | | | Formed as a British blues band in 1967 by ex-**John Mayall**'s Bluesbreakers Peter Green (guitar), Mick Fleetwood (drums) and John McVie (bass), along with guitarist Jeremy Spencer. Many lineup changes followed as group headed toward rock superstardom. Christine McVie (keyboards) joined in August 1970. **Bob Welch** (guitar) joined in April 1971. Americans **Lindsey Buckingham** (guitar) and Stevie Nicks (vocals) joined in January 1975. *Top Pop Singles*: 24. | | | |
| 3/22/69 | 104 | 4 | 1 Albatross .................................... *Jigsaw Puzzle Blues* [I] | $15 | | Epic 10436 |
| | | | guitar instrumental by Peter Green | | | |
| 12/12/92 | 108 | 9 | 2 Paper Doll ....................... ROK:26 / AC:32 *The Chain* | $3 | ▌ | Warner 18661 |

| DEBUT | PEAK | WKS | A-side (Chart Hit)..................................................................................................B-side | $ | Pic | Label & Number |
|---|---|---|---|---|---|---|

**FLEETWOODS, The**      HOT/AC/R&B
Pop vocal trio from Olympia, Washington: Gary Troxel, Gretchen Christopher and Barbara Ellis.

| | | | | | | |
|---|---|---|---|---|---|---|
| 2/15/60 | 113 | 1 | 1 Magic Star ..................................................... *Outside My Window* (Hot #28) | $15 | | Dolton 15 |
| | | | written by Bonnie Guitar | | | |
| 4/13/63 | 114 | 5 | 2 You Should Have Been There ......................................... *Sure Is Lonesome Downtown* | $12 | | Dolton 74 |
| | | | written by Jackie DeShannon | | | |
| 5/16/64 | 134 | 1 | 3 Ruby Red, Baby Blue ....................................................... *Lonesome Town* | $12 | | Dolton 93 |
| 8/29/64 | 113 | 2 | 4 Mr. Sandman................................................................ *This Is My Prayer* | $12 | | Dolton 98 |
| | | | #1 hit for **The Chordettes** in 1954 | | | |

**FLEMONS, Wade**      R&B/HOT
Born on 9/25/40 in Coffeyville, Kansas. Died of cancer on 10/13/93. Electric pianist of Maurice White's pre-**Earth, Wind & Fire** group.

| | | | | | | |
|---|---|---|---|---|---|---|
| 7/13/59 | 101[1] | 4 | Slow Motion             *Walking By The River* | $25 | | Vee-Jay 321 |

**FLETCHER, Sam** ☺
Los Angeles-based R&B singer.

| | | | | | | |
|---|---|---|---|---|---|---|
| 6/22/59 | 103 | 3 | Time Has A Way ........................................................... *No Such Luck* | $25 | | Cub 9032 |
| | | | Leroy Holmes (orch.) | | | |

**FLINT, Shelby**      HOT/AC
Born on 9/17/39 in North Hollywood, California. Pop singer/songwriter.

| | | | | | | |
|---|---|---|---|---|---|---|
| 7/27/63 | 103 | 3 | Little Dancing Doll ........................................... *It Really Wouldn't Matter* | $10 | | Valiant 6031 |

**FLIRTATIONS, The**      HOT
Group consisted of Shirley and Earnestine Pearce from South Carolina, and Viola Billups from Alabama.

| | | | | | | |
|---|---|---|---|---|---|---|
| 7/26/69 | 111 | 4 | South Carolina................................................................ *Need Your Loving* | $7 | | Deram 85048 |

**FLOATERS, The**      R&B/HOT
R&B vocal group from Detroit: Charles Clarke, Larry Cunningham and brothers Paul & Ralph Mitchell.

| | | | | | | |
|---|---|---|---|---|---|---|
| 7/8/78 | 103 | 5 | I Just Want To Be With You ..................................... R&B:36 *What Ever Your Sign* | $5 | | ABC 12364 |

**FLOWERS, Phil** ☺
R&B singer based in Washington, D.C.

| | | | | | | |
|---|---|---|---|---|---|---|
| 10/11/69 | 104 | 4 | 1 Like A Rolling Stone ..................................... *Keep On Sockin' It Children* | $8 | | A&M 1122 |
| | | |      PHIL FLOWERS & THE FLOWER SHOP | | | |
| | | | #2 hit for **Bob Dylan** in 1965 | | | |
| 12/12/70 | 106 | 3 | 2 The Man, The Wife, & The Little Baby Daughter ..................... *Nothing Lasts Forever* | $7 | | Bell 928 |

**FLOYD, Eddie**      R&B/HOT
Born on 6/25/35 in Montgomery, Alabama; raised in Detroit. Original member of **The Falcons**, 1955-63.

| | | | | | | |
|---|---|---|---|---|---|---|
| 3/9/68 | 132 | 1 | 1 Big Bird ..................................................... *Holding On With Both Hands* | $8 | | Stax 246 |
| | | | written and produced by **Booker T.** Jones | | | |
| 2/8/69 | 102 | 5 | 2 I've Got To Have Your Love      R&B:50 *Girl I Love You* | $7 | | Stax 0025 |
| 7/12/69 | 107 | 4 | 3 Never, Never Let You Go ................................................. *Ain't That Good* | $7 | | Stax 0041 |
| | | |      EDDIE FLOYD, MAVIS STAPLES | | | |
| 7/18/70 | 116 | 2 | 4 My Girl ................................................................ R&B:43 *Laurie* | $7 | | Stax 0072 |
| | | | #1 hit for **The Temptations** in 1965 | | | |
| 10/17/70 | 118 | 2 | 5 The Best Years Of My Life ......................................... R&B:29 *My Little Girl* | $7 | | Stax 0077 |
| 2/26/72 | 122 | 1 | 6 Yum Yum Yum (I Want Some)................................ R&B:49 *Tears Of Joy* | $6 | | Stax 0109 |

**FLOYD, King**      R&B/HOT
Born on 2/13/45 in New Orleans. R&B singer/songwriter. First recorded for Original Sound in 1965.

| | | | | | | |
|---|---|---|---|---|---|---|
| 8/14/71 | 101[1] | 1 | Got To Have Your Lovin'      R&B:35 *Let Us Be* | $6 | | Chimneyville 439 |

**FOGERTY, John**      HOT/ROK/AC/C&W
Born on 5/28/45 in Berkeley, California. Singer/songwriter/multi-instrumentalist. With his brother Tom in the Blue Velvets in 1959. Group became the Golliwogs and recorded for Fantasy in 1964. Renamed Creedence Clearwater Revival in 1967. Went solo in 1972 and recorded as **The Blue Ridge Rangers**.

| | | | | | | |
|---|---|---|---|---|---|---|
| 10/13/73 | 107 | 1 | Back In The Hills ..................................................... *You Don't Owe Me* | $6 | | Fantasy 710 |
| | | |      THE BLUE RIDGE RANGERS | | | |

**FOGERTY, Tom** ☺
Born on 11/9/41 in Berkeley, California. Died on 9/6/90 of respiratory failure from tuberculosis. Guitarist with Creedence Clearwater Revival. Brother of **John** Fogerty.

| | | | | | | |
|---|---|---|---|---|---|---|
| 9/4/71 | 103 | 3 | Goodbye Media Man (Part I)..............................................*(Part II)* | $6 | ■ | Fantasy 661 |

**FOGHAT**      HOT/ROK
British rock quartet featuring Lonesome Dave Peverett (vocals, guitar; formerly with **Savoy Brown**).

| | | | | | | |
|---|---|---|---|---|---|---|
| 8/15/81 | 102 | 6 | Live Now-Pay Later ..................................................... ROK:15 *Love Zone* | $5 | | Bearsville 49792 |

**FOLDY, Peter** ☺
Pop singer/songwriter. Born in Australia; later moved to Canada.

| | | | | | | |
|---|---|---|---|---|---|---|
| 9/1/73 | 113 | 3 | Bondi Junction ..................................................... *Alice Mary Jane McPherson* | $6 | | Playboy 50030 |

**FOLEY, Ellen — see HUNTER, Ian**

**FONTANA, Wayne**      HOT
Born Glyn Geoffrey Ellis on 10/28/45. Leader of the English rock group The Mindbenders.

| | | | | | | |
|---|---|---|---|---|---|---|
| 7/9/66 | 117 | 2 | Come On Home ..................................................... *My Eyes Break Out In Tears* | $8 | | MGM 13516 |

**FOOL'S GARDEN** ☺
Rock group: Peter Freudenthaler (vocals), Volker Hinkel (guitar), Roland Rohl (keyboards), Thomas Mangold (bass) and Ralf Wochele (drums).

| | | | | | | |
|---|---|---|---|---|---|---|
| 7/26/97 | 113 | 4 | Lemon Tree ..................................................... *Take Me* | $3 | ▌ | Universal 56128 |

**FORCE M.D.'S**      R&B/HOT/AC
R&B/rap group from Staten Island, New York: brothers Stevie and Antoine "T.C.D." Lundy, Jesse Lee Daniels, Trisco Pearson and Charles "Mercury" Nelson (d: 3/10/95, age 30).

| | | | | | | |
|---|---|---|---|---|---|---|
| 12/15/84 | 102 | 6 | 1 Tears....................................................R&B:5 *Forgive Me Girl* | $4 | | Tommy Boy 848 |
| 6/15/85 | 105 | 3 | 2 Itchin' For A Scratch ......................................... R&B:13 *(instrumental)* | $3 | | Atlantic 89557 |
| | | | from the movie *Rappin'* starring Mario Van Peebles | | | |

**FORD, Jim** ⊙
Los Angeles-based singer/songwriter.

| 9/13/69 | 106 | 4 | Harlan County ............................................................................... *Changin' Colors* | $12 | | Sundown 115 |

**FORD, Penny** ⊙　　　　　　　　　　　　　　　　　　　　R&B
Born on 6/11/64 in Cincinnati. Multi-instrumentalist.

| 6/19/93 | 117 | 1 | Daydreaming ........................................................ *R&B:40 (remix)* | $3 | ▌ | Columbia 74891 |

#5 hit for **Aretha Franklin** in 1972

**FOREIGNER**　　　　　　　　　　　　　　　　　　HOT/ROK/AC/R&B
British-American rock group formed in New York City in 1976 featuring Mick Jones (guitar) and Lou Gramm (vocals). *Top Pop Singles*: 22.

| 12/5/92 | 103 | 6 | With Heaven On Our Side ................................................. *Head Games* | $3 | ▌ | Atlantic 87402 |

**FOR REAL**　　　　　　　　　　　　　　　　　　　R&B/HOT
Female R&B vocal group from Los Angeles: Josina Elder, Wendi Williams, LaTanyia Baldwin and Necia Bray.

| 4/30/94 | 101[1] | 9 | You Don't Wanna Miss　　　　　　*R&B:28 (remix) / I Like* | $3 | ▌ | A&M 0537 |

**FORTUNE TELLERS, The** ⊙

| 9/25/61 | 114 | 1 | Song Of The Nairobi Trio ........................................... *Camel Train* [I] | $15 | | Music Makers 105 |

The Nairobi Trio was a regular feature on TV's *Ernie Kovacs Show*

**FOTOMAKER**　　　　　　　　　　　　　　　　　　HOT
Pop-rock quintet from New York: Wally Bryson and Lex Marchesi (guitars), Frankie Vinci (keyboards), Gene Cornish (bass) and Dino Danelli (drums).

| 7/22/78 | 110 | 1 | The Other Side (So When I See You Again) ............................... *Pain* | $4 | | Atlantic 3485 |

**FOUNDATIONS, The**　　　　　　　　　　　　　　HOT/R&B
British interracial R&B-pop group: Clem Curtis (vocals), Allan Warner (guitar), Eric Allendale, Pat Burke and Michael Elliott (horns), Anthony Gomez (keyboards), Peter MacBeth (bass) and Tim Harris (drums). Colin Young replaced Curtis in 1968.

| 2/26/72 | 113 | 1 | Stoney Ground ............................................................ *I'll Give You Love* | $6 | | Uni 55315 |

**FOUNTAIN, Pete**　　　　　　　　　　　　　　　AC/HOT
Born on 7/3/30 in New Orleans. Top jazz clarinetist. With **Al Hirt**, 1956-57; **Lawrence Welk**, 1957-59.

| 7/11/64 | 115 | 2 | 1 Licorice Stick ................................................................ *Estrellita* [I] | $7 | | Coral 62413 |
| 6/26/65 | 129 | 2 | 2 Mae ........................................... *AC:27　Gotta Travel On* [I] | $7 | | Coral 62454 |

from the movie *The Yellow Rolls-Royce* starring Rex Harrison

**FOUR COACHMEN, The** ⊙
White male vocal group similar in style to The Four Lads.

| 12/21/59 | 113 | 2 | Wintertime ............................................ *That Thing Called A Girl* | $20 | | Adonis 102 |

Paul Swain (orch.)

**FOUR COINS, The**　　　　　　　　　　　　　　　HOT/MEM
Pop vocal group from Canonsburg, Pennsylvania: brothers Michael and George Mahramas, George Mantalis, and Jim Gregorakis.

| 6/1/59 | 106 | 1 | My First Love .................................... *One Love, One Heart* (Hot #82) | $12 | | Epic 9314 |

Joe Sherman (orch.)

**FOUR COQUETTES, The** ⊙
White female pop group; recorded later as The Four Cal-Quettes.

| 5/1/61 | 107 | 2 | Sparkle And Shine ................................................. *In This World* | $25 | | Capitol 4534 |

written and produced by Bruce Belland of **The Four Preps**

**FOUR-EVERS, The** ⊙
White vocal quartet from Philadelphia: Paul Verdi, Alex Barbadoro, Dominick "Steakie" Andracchio and Jackie Jacobs (d: 1993).

| 4/20/63 | 125 | 1 | Everybody South Street ....................................... *One More Time* | $15 | | Jamie 1247 |

follow-up song to **The Orlons'** 1963 hit "South Street"

**FOUR-EVERS, The**　　　　　　　　　　　　　　　HOT
White vocal quartet from Brooklyn: Joe Di Benedetto (lead), John Capriani, Steve Tudanger and Nick Zagami.

| 9/12/64 | 119 | 2 | (Say I Love You) Doo Bee Dum ............................................ *Everlasting* | $15 | | Smash 1921 |

**FOUR GENTS** ⊙
R&B vocal/instrumental group.

| 12/31/66 | 133 | 1 | Soul Sister ............................................................. *I've Been Trying* [I] | $20 | | HBR 509 |

**4 HERO** ⊙
Techno dance duo from London: Dego and Mark Mac.

| 2/3/96 | 101[1] | 7 | Mr. Kirk　　　　　　　　　　　　　　*(remix)* [F] | $3 | ▌ | Sm:)e 9030 |

Victor Alvarellos (latin chant)

**FOUR JACKS AND A JILL**　　　　　　　　　　　AC/HOT
Pop group from South Africa: Glenys "Jill" Lynne (vocals), Bruce Bark (guitar), Till Hannamann (keyboards), Clive Harding (bass) and Anthony Hughes (drums).

| 11/9/68 | 130 | 1 | Hey Mister .................................... *AC:34　Sad Little Pidgeon* | $7 | | RCA Victor 9655 |

**FOURMOST, The** ⊙
British group: Brian O'Hara (vocals, guitar), Mike Millward (guitar), Billy Hatton (bass) and Dave Lovelady (drums).

| 9/24/66 | 120 | 3 | Here, There And Everywhere ................................. *You've Changed* | $20 | | Capitol 5738 |

originally recorded by **The Beatles** on their 1966 album *Revolver*

**4 NON BLONDES**　　　　　　　　　　　　　　　ROK/HOT
Rock band formed in San Francisco in 1989: Linda Perry (vocals), Roger Rocha (guitar), Christa Hillhouse (bass) and Dawn Richardson (drums).

| 10/16/93 | 117 | 4 | Spaceman .................................... *ROK:39　Pleasantly Blue* | $3 | ▌ | Interscope 98374 |

**FOUR PENNIES, The** ⊙
Pop quartet from Lancashire, England — Lionel Morton, lead singer.

| 6/27/64 | 116 | 2 | Juliet .................................... *Tell Me Girl (What Are You Gonna Do)* | $15 | | Philips 40202 |

| DEBUT | PEAK | WKS | A-side / B-side | $ | Pic | Label & Number |
|---|---|---|---|---|---|---|
| | | | **4 P.M. (for positive music)**     R&B/HOT/AC | | | |
| | | | R&B vocal quartet from Baltimore: brothers Rene and Roberto Pena, with Larry McFarland and Marty Ware. | | | |
| 4/15/95 | 107 | 6 | 1 Lay Down Your Love ...................................................................... (remix) | $3 | ■ | Next Plateau 857970 |
| 5/24/97 | 124 | 3 | 2 I Gave You Everything ...............................................R&B:67 (remix) | $3 | ■ | Next Plateau 1422 |
| | | | 4PM | | | |
| | | | **FOUR PREPS, The**     HOT/AC/R&B | | | |
| | | | Pop vocal group formed while at Hollywood High School: Bruce Belland, Glen Larson, Ed Cobb and Marvin Ingraham. | | | |
| 7/20/59 | 111 | 1 | 1 Big Surprise.....................................................Try My Arms | $12 | | Capitol 4218 |
| | | | Joe Maphis (orch.); arrangement similar to their 1958 hit "Big Man" | | | |
| 6/29/63 | 116 | 1 | 2 Charmaine ...........................................Hi Ho Anybody Home | $10 | | Capitol 4974 |
| | | | Lincoln Mayorga (orch.); #1 hit for Guy Lombardo in 1927 | | | |
| | | | **4 RUNNER** ✪     C&W | | | |
| | | | Country vocal quartet: Craig Morris, Billy Crittenden, Lee Hilliard and Jim Chapman. | | | |
| 5/20/95 | 118 | 7 | Cain's Blood ...................................C&W:26 Ten Pound Hammer | $3 | ■ | Polydor 851622 |
| | | | **4 SEASONS, The**     HOT/AC/R&B | | | |
| | | | Vocal group formed in Newark, New Jersey featuring lead singer **Frankie Valli**. Many personnel changes; however, main hit group consisted of Valli, Bob Gaudio, Nick Massi and Tommy DeVito. Group inducted into the Rock and Roll Hall of Fame in 1990. *Top Pop Singles*: 48. | | | |
| 3/23/63 | 108 | 4 | 1 Peanuts ....................... Never On Sunday / I Can't Give You Anything But Love / La Dee Dah | $50 | ■ | Vee-Jay EP 1-901 |
| | | | "Bubbled Under" for 1 week; re-charted on 1/18/64 (3 weeks); #22 hit for Little Joe & The Thrillers in 1957 | | | |
| 4/6/63 | 123 | 2 | 2 Since I Don't Have You ............................Alone / Why Do Fools Fall In Love? / Silhouettes | $50 | ■ | Vee-Jay EP 1-902 |
| | | | #12 hit for **The Skyliners** in 1959; above 2 are from Extended Play records entitled *The 4 Seasons Sing* | | | |
| 6/13/64 | 102 | 3 | 3 Long Lonely Nights ..........................................Alone (Hot #28) | $15 | ■ | Vee-Jay 597 |
| | | | #45 hit for Lee Andrews & The Hearts in 1957 | | | |
| 10/10/64 | 106 | 3 | 4 Apple Of My Eye ...........................Happy Happy Birthday Baby | $20 | | Vee-Jay 618 |
| | | | original version made the *Hot 100* in 1956 (#62) as "You're The Apple Of My Eye" by The Four Lovers | | | |
| 4/3/65 | 105 | 2 | 5 Since I Don't Have You ...............................Tonight-Tonight [R] | $20 | | Vee-Jay 664 |
| | | | same version as on the E.P. release above | | | |
| 6/22/68 | 103 | 5 | 6 Saturday's Father................................................Good-Bye Girl | $10 | ■ | Philips 40542 |
| | | | **FOUR TOPS**     R&B/HOT/AC | | | |
| | | | Detroit R&B vocal group formed in 1953: Levi Stubbs (lead singer), Renaldo "Obie" Benson, Lawrence Payton (d: 6/20/97, age 59) and Abdul "Duke" Fakir. Group had no personnel changes since its formation. Group inducted into the Rock and Roll Hall of Fame in 1990. *Top Pop Singles*: 45. | | | |
| 5/20/72 | 102 | 3 | 1 I Can't Quit Your Love .............................Happy (Is A Bumpy Road) | $8 | | Motown 1198 |
| 1/17/76 | 107 | 1 | 2 Mama You're All Right With Me ......R&B:72 I'm Glad You Walked Into My Life (R&B #76) | $5 | | ABC 12155 |
| | | | **4U** ✪     R&B | | | |
| | | | R&B family vocal quartet: Tony, Robert, Sylvia and Eugene Owens. | | | |
| 8/31/96 | 120 | 4 | Home .......................................R&B:57 (album version) | $3 | ■ | Rip-It 2711 |
| | | | **FOXWORTHY, Jeff**     C&W/HOT | | | |
| | | | Born on 9/6/58 in Atlanta; raised in Hapeville, Georgia. Comedian/actor. Starred in own TV sitcom, 1995-97. | | | |
| 8/12/95 | 101[2] | 9 | Party All Night     Sls:60 /C&W:53 Southern Accent [N] | $3 | ■ | Warner 17806 |
| | | | JEFF FOXWORTHY With Little Texas and Scott Rouse | | | |
| | | | **FOXX, Inez & Charlie**     R&B/HOT | | | |
| | | | R&B vocal duo: Inez (b: 9/9/42 in Greensboro, North Carolina) and her brother Charlie (b: 10/23/39). | | | |
| 10/12/63 | 113 | 4 | 1 He's The One You Love ...........................Broken Hearted Fool | $12 | | Symbol 922 |
| | | | INEZ FOXX | | | |
| 8/29/64 | 124 | 5 | 2 La De Da I Love You...............................Yankee Doodle Dandy | $12 | | Symbol 201 |
| | | | arrangement is similar to **The Supremes**' "Where Did Our Love Go" | | | |
| 6/3/67 | 127 | 2 | 3 I Stand Accused ....................................R&B:41 Guilty | $10 | | Dynamo 104 |
| | | | #61 hit for **Jerry Butler** in 1964 | | | |
| | | | **FRANCIS, Connie**     HOT/AC/C&W | | | |
| | | | Born Concetta Rosa Maria Franconero on 12/12/38 in Newark, New Jersey. Pop music's #1 female vocalist from the late 1950s to the mid-1960s. *Top Pop Singles*: 56. | | | |
| 7/28/62 | 116 | 3 | 1 The Biggest Sin Of All ........................................Vacation (Hot #9) | $15 | ■ | MGM 13087 |
| 12/22/62 | 113 | 1 | 2 Baby's First Christmas ............... When The Boy In Your Arms (Is The Boy In Your Heart) (Hot #10) [X-R] | $15 | ■ | MGM 13051 |
| | | | originally made the *Hot 100* (#26) on 12/11/61 | | | |
| 3/9/63 | 127 | 1 | 3 Waiting For Billy.............................Follow The Boys (Hot #17) | $12 | ■ | MGM 13127 |
| | | | from the movie *Follow The Boys* starring Francis | | | |
| 8/10/63 | 114 | 2 | 4 Mala Femmena ........................Drownin' My Sorrows (Hot #36) [F] | $12 | ■ | MGM 13160 |
| 10/31/64 | 128 | 1 | 5 We Have Something More (Than A Summer Love) ......Don't Ever Leave Me (Hot #42) | $12 | ■ | MGM 13287 |
| 5/28/66 | 134 | 1 | 6 It's A Different World ...................................Empty Chapel | $10 | ■ | MGM 13505 |
| 7/9/66 | 105 | 3 | 7 A Letter From A Soldier (Dear Mama) ..............Somewhere, My Love (Lara's Theme From "Doctor Zhivago") | $10 | | MGM 13545 |
| | | | song is similar to her 1960 hit "Mama" | | | |
| 2/4/67 | 121 | 3 | 8 Another Page.........................Souvenir D'Italie | $10 | | MGM 13665 |
| 8/12/67 | 118 | 2 | 9 My Heart Cries For You ........... AC:12 Someone Took The Sweetness Out Of Sweetheart | $10 | ■ | MGM 13773 |
| | | | #2 hit for **Guy Mitchell** in 1951 | | | |
| 4/27/68 | 132 | 1 | 10 Why Say Goodbye (A Comme Amour) ........ AC:27 Addio Mi 'Amore (Goodbye My Love) | $10 | | MGM 13923 |
| 6/30/73 | 104 | 6 | 11 Should I Tie A Yellow Ribbon Round The Ole Oak Tree? **"The Answer"** Paint The Rain | $6 | | GSF 6901 |
| | | | answer song to **Tony Orlando** & Dawn's #1 hit from 1973 | | | |
| | | | **FRANKIE** ✪     R&B | | | |
| | | | Real name: George Franklin Jackson III. Native of Washington, D.C. Male R&B singer. | | | |
| 8/16/97 | 108 | 9 | If I Had You .........................R&B:46 (remix) / One Last Time | $3 | ■ | Chucklife/Epic 78624 |
| | | | samples "The Look Of Love" by **Isaac Hayes** | | | |

| DEBUT | PEAK | WKS | A-side / B-side | $ | Pic | Label & Number |
|---|---|---|---|---|---|---|

### FRANKLIN, Aretha     R&B/HOT/AC

Born on 3/25/42 in Memphis; raised in Buffalo and Detroit. Revered as the all-time Queen of Soul Music. Winner of 15 Grammy Awards, plus Grammy's Living Legends Award (1990) and Lifetime Achievement Award (1994). In 1987, became the first woman to be inducted into the Rock and Roll Hall of Fame. *Top Pop Singles*: 74.

| | | | | | | |
|---|---|---|---|---|---|---|
| 9/22/62 | **111** | 1 | 1 **Just For A Thrill** .............................................................. *Try A Little Tenderness* (Hot #100) | $12 | ■ | Columbia 42520 |
| | | | written by **Louis Armstrong** | | | |
| 7/6/63 | **113** | 2 | 2 **Say It Isn't So/** | | | |
| | | | #1 hit for George Olsen & His Orchestra in 1932 | | | |
| 6/22/63 | **125** | 3 | 3   **Here's Where I Came In** (Here's Where I Walk Out) ......................................... | $12 | | Columbia 42796 |
| 5/9/64 | **121** | 4 | 4 **Soulville** ................................................................................. *Evil Gal Blues* | $12 | | Columbia 43009 |
| | | | made the *Hot 100* (#83) on 2/24/68 on Columbia 44441 | | | |
| 5/15/65 | **119** | 3 | 5 **One Step Ahead** ...................................... **R&B:18** *I Can't Wait Until I See My Baby's Face* | $10 | | Columbia 43241 |
| 7/17/65 | **114** | 6 | 6 **(No, No) I'm Losing You** .......................................... **AC:34** *Sweet Bitter Love* | $10 | | Columbia 43333 |
| 12/18/65 | **109** | 3 | 7 **You Made Me Love You** .................................... **AC:32** *There Is No Greater Love* | $10 | | Columbia 43442 |
| | | | #1 hit for Al Jolson in 1913; #5 hit for Harry James Orchestra in 1941 | | | |
| 11/19/66 | **113** | 4 | 8 **Cry Like A Baby** ........................................................ **R&B:27** *Swanee* | $10 | | Columbia 43827 |
| 10/11/69 | **101**[1] | 5 | 9 Today I Sing The Blues           *People* | $10 | | Columbia 44951 |
| | | | originally made the R&B charts (#10) on 10/24/60 on Columbia 41793 | | | |
| 5/13/78 | **103** | 13 | 10 **Almighty Fire** (Woman Of The Future)............................ **R&B:12** *I'm Your Speed* | $5 | | Atlantic 3468 |
| | | | written and produced by **Curtis Mayfield** | | | |
| 10/22/94 | **114** | 3 | 11 **Honey** ................................................................ **R&B:30** *I Dreamed A Dream* | $3 | ▌ | Arista 12743 |
| 7/20/96 | **116** | 6 | 12 **It Hurts Like Hell** ........................**R&B:51** *And I Gave My Love To You* (Sonja Marie) | $3 | ▌ | Arista 13222 |
| | | | from the movie *Waiting To Exhale* starring Whitney Houston; above 2 written and produced by **Babyface** | | | |

### FRANKLIN, Carolyn ✪     R&B

Born in 1945 in Memphis. Died of cancer on 4/25/88 (age 43). Youngest sister of **Aretha Franklin**.

| | | | | | | |
|---|---|---|---|---|---|---|
| 8/16/69 | **119** | 5 | 1 **It's True I'm Gonna Miss You** ........................................ **R&B:23** *Reality* | $6 | | RCA Victor 0188 |
| 9/12/70 | **108** | 2 | 2 **All I Want To Be Is Your Woman** ..................... **R&B:46** *You Really Didn't Mean It* | $6 | | RCA Victor 0373 |

### FRANKLIN, Erma     R&B/HOT

Born in 1943 in Memphis. Younger sister of **Aretha Franklin**. Also see **Lloyd Price**.

| | | | | | | |
|---|---|---|---|---|---|---|
| 5/18/68 | **107** | 3 | **Open Up Your Soul** ............................................... *I'm Just Not Ready For Love* | $10 | | Shout 230 |

### FRASER, Andy     HOT/ROK

Born on 8/7/52 in London. Rock bassist. Formerly with **John Mayall**'s Bluesbreakers and **Free**.

| | | | | | | |
|---|---|---|---|---|---|---|
| 7/28/84 | **101**[1] | 2 | Fine, Fine Line      **ROK:43** *These Arms Of Mine* | $4 | | Island 99756 |

### FRATERNITY OF MAN ✪

Country/rock group: Lawrence "Stash" Wagner (lead singer/guitar), Elliott Ingber (guitar), Warren Klein (sitar), Martin Kibbee (bass) and Richard Hayward (drums).

| | | | | | | |
|---|---|---|---|---|---|---|
| 9/21/68 | **133** | 2 | **Don't Bogart Me** ......................................................... *Wispy Paisley Skies* [N] | $7 | | ABC 11106 |

### FRAZIER, Dallas     C&W/HOT

Born on 10/27/39 in Spiro, Oklahoma. Country singer/songwriter/multi-instrumentalist. Wrote "Alley-Oop."

| | | | | | | |
|---|---|---|---|---|---|---|
| 7/2/66 | **108** | 5 | 1 **Just A Little Bit Of You**............................................... *Walkin' Wonder* | $8 | | Capitol 5670 |
| 3/15/69 | **120** | 2 | 2 **The Conspiracy Of Homer Jones** ........................... **C&W:63** *Sundown Of My Mind* [N] | $8 | | Capitol 2402 |
| | | | parody of "Ode To Billie Joe" and "Harper Valley P.T.A." | | | |

### FRED, John, & His Playboy Band     HOT

Born John Fred Gourrier on 5/8/41 in Baton Rouge, Louisiana. Formed The Playboys in 1956 as a white band playing R&B music.

| | | | | | | |
|---|---|---|---|---|---|---|
| 7/29/67 | **125** | 5 | 1 **Agnes English** ............................................................... *Sad Story* | $8 | | Paula 273 |
| 5/25/68 | **130** | 2 | 2 **We Played Games** ..................................................... *Lonely Are The Lonely* | $8 | | Paula 303 |

### FREDDIE AND THE DREAMERS     HOT

Lead singer Freddie Garrity was born on 11/14/40 in Manchester, England. Formed The Dreamers in 1961 with Derek Quinn (lead guitar), Roy Crewsdon (guitar), Peter Birrell (bass) and Bernie Dwyer (drums).

| | | | | | | |
|---|---|---|---|---|---|---|
| 10/2/65 | **123** | 1 | **Send A Letter To Me** ..................................... *There's Not One Thing* (Just Four Men) | $12 | | Tower 163 |

### FREDERICK ✪     R&B

R&B singer/songwriter Frederick Davis from Ohio.

| | | | | | | |
|---|---|---|---|---|---|---|
| 5/18/85 | **108** | 1 | **Gentle** (Calling Your Name) ...................................... **R&B:48** *Move On* | $6 | | Heat 2022 |

### FREE     HOT

British rock band formed in 1968: **Paul Rodgers** (vocals), Paul Kossoff (guitar; d: 3/19/76), Simon Kirke (drums) and **Andy Fraser** (bass). Rodgers and Kirke formed Bad Company in 1974.

| | | | | | | |
|---|---|---|---|---|---|---|
| 6/3/72 | **119** | 1 | 1 **Little Bit Of Love** ......................................................... *Sail On* | $6 | | A&M 1352 |
| 3/10/73 | **112** | 2 | 2 **Wishing Well** ......................................................... *Let Me Show You* | $6 | | Island 1212 |

### FREE DESIGN, The ✪     AC

Vocal trio from Delevan, New York. Consisted of siblings Christopher, Bruce and Sandy Dedrick. Their father, Art Dedrick, played trumpet for Vaughn Monroe.

| | | | | | | |
|---|---|---|---|---|---|---|
| 12/23/67 | **114** | 2 | **Kites Are Fun** ......................................................... **AC:33** *The Proper Ornaments* | $7 | | Project 3 1324 |

### FREEEZ ✪     R&B

Dance outfit assembled by producer Arthur Baker.

| | | | | | | |
|---|---|---|---|---|---|---|
| 9/24/83 | **104** | 4 | 1 **I.O.U.** .................................................................. **R&B:13** *I. Dub. U.* | $5 | | StreetWise 1110 |
| | | | #1 Dance hit in 1983 on StreetWise 2210 (12") | | | |
| 1/28/84 | **104** | 1 | 2 **Pop Goes My Love** ............................................ **R&B:47** (English edit) | $5 | | StreetWise 1115 |
| | | | #5 Dance hit in 1983 on StreetWise 2215 (12") | | | |

### FREEMAN, Bobby     HOT/R&B

Born on 6/13/40 in San Francisco. R&B singer. Formed vocal group the Romancers, at age 14, and later formed R&B group the Vocaleers.

| | | | | | | |
|---|---|---|---|---|---|---|
| 4/17/65 | **131** | 3 | 1 **I'll Never Fall In Love Again** ............................................... *Friend's* | $12 | | Autumn 9 |
| | | | written by Sly Stewart (**Sly & The Family Stone**) | | | |
| 7/19/69 | **122** | 2 | 2 **Everybody's Got A Hang Up** ......................................... *Oughta Be A Law* | $8 | | Double Shot 139 |

**FREEMAN, Ernie**                                                                                      HOT/R&B/C&W
Born on 8/16/22 in Cleveland. Died of a heart attack on 5/16/81. Pianist/arranger/producer. Prominent sessionman. Musical director at Reprise Records for 10 years.

| 3/28/60 | 106 | 3 | Rockin' Red Wing.................................................................... Dark Eyes | $12 | | Imperial 5656 |

adaptation of the 1907 Indian fable tune "Red Wing"; #64 hit for Sammy Masters in 1960

**FREEWHEELERS, The ☉**
Folk quartet: Mike Matacunas, Gary Cogly, Wally Salaman and Jack McCarthy.

| 4/4/64 | 119 | 1 | Walk, Walk ............................................................ The Best Of It | $8 | | Epic 9664 |

**FRENTE!**                                                                                             ROK/HOT
Pop-rock quartet from Melbourne, Australia: Angie Hart (vocals), Simon Austin (guitar), Tim O'Connor (bass) and Mark Picton (drums).

| 8/13/94 | 106 | 3 | Labour Of Love............................ ROK:9 Thinking Darling / No Time | $3 | ▌ | Mammoth 98262 |

**FRESH AIRE ☉**
Pop group.

| 7/8/78 | 108 | 2 | Flying Over America ...................................... Living In The Space Age | $5 | | Atlantic 3482 |

**FRESH START ☉**
Rock group.

| 8/10/74 | 104 | 2 | Free...................................................... Meet Me At The Water | $5 | | Dunhill/ABC 15002 |

**FREY, Glenn**                                                                                         HOT/AC/ROK
Born on 11/6/48 in Detroit. Singer/songwriter/guitarist. Founding member of the Eagles.

| 4/3/93 | 112 | 4 | Love In The 21st Century ................................................. Delicious | $3 | ▌ | MCA 54564 |

**FRIDA**                                                                                               HOT/ROK
Born Anni-Frid Lyngstad on 11/15/45 in Narvik, Sweden. Member of Abba.

| 5/7/83 | 102 | 2 | Here We'll Stay ...................................................... Strangers | $5 | | Atlantic 89834 |

produced by Phil Collins

**FROST, The ☉**
Detroit rock quartet: Dick Wagner (lead singer, guitar), Don Hartman (guitar), Gordy Garris (bass) and Bob Riggs (drums).

| 2/21/70 | 105 | 1 | Rock And Roll Music ........................................... Donny's Blues | $10 | | Vanguard 35101 |

"live" recording

**FROST**                                                                                               HOT/R&B
Born Arturo Molina on 5/31/64 in East Los Angeles. Male rapper. Formerly known as Kid Frost.

| 5/31/97 | 108 | 6 | What's Your Name (time of the season) ........ R&B:90 (instrumental) / Get Down / (instrumental) | $3 | ▌ | Ruthless 1607 |

samples "Time Of The Season" by The Zombies

**FROST, Max, and The Troopers**                                                                        HOT
Studio group produced by Mike Curb. Paul Wybier is the lead singer.

| 12/14/68 | 123 | 2 | Fifty Two Per Cent............................... The Max Frost Theme | $15 | ■ | Tower 452 |

picture sleeve notes: "52% of the population is under 25 years old!"

**FUGEES**                                                                                              R&B/HOT/AC
Two-man, one-woman rap outfit: rappers/producers/cousins Wyclef "Clef" Jean and Prakazrel "Pras" Michel (both are of Haitian descent), and rapper/singer Lauryn Hill (from East Orange, New Jersey).

| 12/31/94+ | 108 | 8 | Vocab........................................................ R&B:91 (acoustic remix) | $3 | ▌ | Ruffhouse 77634 |

FUGEES (Tranzlator Crew)

**FULLER, Bobby, Four**                                                                                 HOT
Born on 10/22/43 in Baytown, Texas. Died on 7/18/66. Rock and roll band, formed in El Paso, consisted of Bobby (vocals, guitar) and his brother Randy (bass), with Jim Reese (guitar) and DeWayne Quirico (drums).

| 8/7/65 | 133 | 2 | 1 Let Her Dance ............................................ Another Sad And Lonely Night | $25 | | Liberty 55812 |
| 7/16/66 | 117 | 2 | 2 The Magic Touch.......................................................... My True Love | $15 | | Mustang 3018 |

**FULSOM, Lowell**                                                                                      R&B/HOT
Born on 3/31/21 in Tulsa, Oklahoma. Blues vocalist/guitarist. Also known as Tulsa Red. First recorded for Big Town in 1946.

| 10/7/67 | 118 | 2 | I'm A Drifter................................................. R&B:38 Hobo Meetin' | $10 | | Kent 474 |

**FULTON, Sonny ☉**
R&B vocalist with a style similar to Jackie Wilson.

| 5/15/61 | 106 | 4 | Locked Up ...................................................... Try, Try, Try | $25 | | Big Daddy 67511 |

**FUNKADELIC — see PARLIAMENT**

**FUNKDOOBIEST**                                                                                        HOT
Los Angeles-based rap trio: Ralph "DJ Ralph M" Medrano, Jason "Sondoobie" Vasquez and Tyrone "Tomahawk Funk" Pachenco.

| 11/29/97+ | 110 | 4 | Papi Chulo........................ (English version) / (Spanish version) / (remix) | $3 | ▌ | Buzz Tone/RCA 65317 |

FUNKDOOBIEST featuring Daz Dillinger and Cobra Red
samples "Hell" by The Squirrel Nut Zippers; title is Spanish expression for "You're The Man"

**FUNKMASTER FLEX ☉**                                                                                   R&B
Rapper/DJ from New York City. DJ for WQHT in New York.

| 1/21/95 | 101[2] | 9 | Nuttin But Flavor                                    R&B:85 (instrumental) | $3 | ▌ | Wreck 20116 |

FUNKMASTER FLEX AND THE GHETTO CELEBS Featuring Biz Markie, Charlie Brown & Old Dirty Bastard

**FURAY, Richie**                                                                                       HOT/AC
Born on 5/9/44 in Yello Springs, Ohio. Member of Buffalo Springfield, Poco, and The Souther, Hillman, Furay Band.

| 6/17/78 | 101[3] | 5 | This Magic Moment                                      Bittersweet Love | $5 | | Elektra 45487 |

#16 hit for The Drifters in 1960; #6 hit for Jay & The Americans in 1969

**FURLONG, Michael ☉**
Rock singer/songwriter.

| 9/29/84 | 103 | 2 | Use It Or Lose It....................................................... Right-A-Way | $4 | | Atlantic 89627 |

**FUZZY BUNNIES ☉**
New York-based rock quartet.

| 8/31/68 | 115 | 3 | The Sun Ain't Gonna Shine Anymore ........................................ Lemons And Limes | $8 | | Decca 32364 |

#13 hit for The Walker Bros. in 1966

# G

**GABRIEL, Peter**  HOT/R&B
Born on 2/13/50 in London. Lead singer of Genesis from 1966-75.

| 11/29/80 | 107 | 3 | I Don't Remember .................................................................. *Shosholoza* | $5 | | Mercury 76086 |

**GABRIELLE**  HOT/R&B
Born Louise Gabrielle Bobb on 4/16/70 in London. Female dance singer.

| 9/14/96 | 112 | 6 | Give Me A Little More Time ........................................*Dreams* | $3 | ▌ | London 850694 |

**GAINS, Earl** ○  R&B
Born Earl Gaines on 8/19/35 in Decatur, Alabama. Moved to Nashville in 1951.

| 8/27/66 | 133 | 1 | The Best Of Luck To You ................................*R&B:28  It's Worth Anything* | $10 | | HBR 481 |

**GALLAGHER AND LYLE**  AC/HOT
Scottish duo: Benny Gallagher and Graham Lyle. Both formerly with McGuiness Flint.

| 3/5/77 | 106 | 3 | Every Little Teardrop ..................................*AC:46  Street Boys* | $4 | | A&M 1904 |

**GALLAHADS, The** ○
R&B vocal group from Seattle.

| 8/15/60 | 111 | 1 | Lonely Guy ................................................*Jo Jo The Big Wheel* | $40 | | Del-Fi 4137 |
| | | | first released on Donna 1322 in 1960 ($60); above record is on a green label | | | |

**GALLERY featuring Jim Gold**  HOT/AC
Pop group from Detroit: Jim Gold (vocals), Brent Anderson (lead guitar), Cal Freeman (steel guitar), Bill Nova (percussion), Dennis Korvarik (bass) and Danny Brucato (drums).

| 7/14/73 | 118 | 3 | Maybe Baby ........................................*AC:40  Lady Luck* | $5 | | Sussex 259 |
| | | | #17 hit for **The Crickets** in 1958 | | | |

**GALORE, Mamie** ○
R&B songstress.

| 4/23/66 | 132 | 2 | 1 It Ain't Necessary ................................*Don't Think I Could Stand It* | $12 | | St. Lawrence 1012 |
| | | | written by Jerry Butler | | | |
| 12/14/68 | 114 | 1 | 2 By The Time I Get To Phoenix/I Say A Little Prayer ..................*All I Want For Christmas Is Your Love* | $8 | | Imperial 66334 |
| | | | **DEE IRWIN & MAMIE GALORE** | | | |
| | | | #81 hit for **Glen Campbell/Anne Murray** in 1971 | | | |

**GANG STARR**  R&B/HOT
Rap duo from Brooklyn: Christopher "DJ Premier" Martin and Keith "**Guru**" Elam.

| 7/9/94 | 123 | 2 | Code Of The Streets ................................*R&B:83  Speak Ya Clout* | $3 | ▌ | Chrysalis 58148 |
| | | | samples "Little Green Apples" by O.C. Smith | | | |

**GAP BAND, The**  R&B/HOT
R&B/funk trio from Tulsa, Oklahoma: brothers Charlie, Ronnie and Robert Wilson.

| 6/2/79 | 101[3] | 9 | 1 Shake ................................*R&B:4  Got To Get Away* | $4 | | Mercury 74053 |
| 2/2/80 | 103 | 2 | 2 Steppin' (Out) ................................*R&B:10  You Are My High* | $4 | | Mercury 76021 |
| 3/29/80 | 102 | 2 | 3 I Don't Believe You Want To Get Up And Dance (Oops, Up Side Your Head) ................................*R&B:4  Who Do You Call* | $4 | | Mercury 76037 |
| 9/10/83 | 101[1] | 4 | 4 Party Train ................................*R&B:3  (dance mix)* | $4 | | Total Experience 8209 |
| 1/12/85 | 103 | 5 | 5 Beep A Freak ................................*R&B:2  (dub version)* | $3 | ■ | Total Experience 2405 |

**GARBAGE**  ROK/HOT
Modern rock group formed in Madison, Wisconsin: Shirley Manson (vocals, guitar; native of Edinburgh, Scotland), Doug "Duke" Erikson (guitar, bass, keyboards), Steve Marker (guitar) and Butch Vig (drums).

| 12/7/96+ | 106 | 10 | Milk ................................*(3 versions)* | $3 | ▌ | Almo Sounds 89007 |

**GARCIA, Tony** ○
Dance music producer/arranger. Vocals by Noel "N.V." Figueroa.

| 3/26/94 | 120 | 2 | Girl You Hear Me Crying ................................*(4 mixes)* | $5 | | High Power 118 (T) |
| | | | **TONY "DR. EDIT" GARCIA featuring N.V.** | | | |

**GARDNER, Don**  R&B/HOT
R&B singer/organist from Philadelphia. Formed own group, the Sonotones, in 1952 and recorded for Gotham and Bruce. Had several hits as a duo with Dee Dee Ford.

| 12/24/66 | 126 | 4 | 1 My Baby Likes To Boogaloo ................................*I Wanta Know Where Did Our Love Go* | $12 | | Tru-Glo-Town 501 |
| 7/7/73 | 119 | 2 | 2 Forever ................................*R&B:30  Baby Let Me Get Close To You* | $10 | | Master Five 9103 |
| | | | **BABY WASHINGTON & DON GARDNER** | | | |

**GARDNER, J.** ○
R&B guitarist with a style reminiscent of **Duane Eddy** on his one chart hit.

| 8/14/65 | 102 | 4 | 99 Plus 1 ................................*Mustard Greens* [I] | $12 | | Blue Rock 4026 |

**GARFUNKEL**  AC/HOT
Born Art Garfunkel on 11/5/41 in Forest Hills, New York. Half of **Simon & Garfunkel** duo.

| 4/20/74 | 102 | 6 | Traveling Boy ................................*AC:30  Old Men* | $5 | | Columbia 46030 |

**GARLAND, Phil** ○
Singer/songwriter/violinist based in Boston. Leader of the group Garland.

| 3/19/83 | 109 | 1 | You Are The One ................................*Valentine's Day Massacre* | $4 | | Atlantic 99999 |
| | | | also released on Radio Records 99999 in 1983 | | | |

**GARNER, Reggie** ○
Fourteen-year-old R&B vocalist.

| 4/24/71 | 117 | 3 | Teddy Bear ................................*Traces* | $10 | | Capitol 3042 |

| DEBUT | PEAK | WKS | A-side (Chart Hit) ......................................................................................B-side | $ | Pic | Label & Number |
|---|---|---|---|---|---|---|
| | | | **GARNETT, Gale**                          HOT/AC/C&W | | | |
| | | | Born on 7/17/42 in Auckland, New Zealand. Came to the U.S. in 1951. | | | |
| 4/24/65 | 108 | 4 | I'll Cry Alone ............................................... *Where Do You Go To Go Away* | $8 | | RCA Victor 8549 |
| | | | Claus Ogerman (orch.) | | | |
| | | | **GARTRELL, Delia ☉**                          R&B | | | |
| | | | R&B songstress. | | | |
| 1/22/72 | 101[1] | 3 | See What You Done, Done (Hymn #9)     R&B:24 *Fight Fire, With Fire* | $10 | | Right-On 109 |
| | | | **GARVIN, Rex ☉** | | | |
| | | | Recorded in the R&B duo Marie & Rex in 1959. Was co-owner of J&S Records. | | | |
| 6/25/66 | 110 | 7 | Sock It To 'Em J.B. - Part I................................................. *Part II* | $20 | | Like 301 |
| | | | **REX GARVIN (And The Mighty Cravers)** | | | |
| | | | a tribute to James Bond with a James Brown-styled arrangement | | | |
| | | | **GARY, John**                          AC/HOT | | | |
| | | | Born on 11/29/32 in Watertown, New York. Died of cancer on 1/4/98. Singer on Don McNeill's radio program, *Breakfast Club*. | | | |
| 10/16/65 | 132 | 2 | Don't Throw The Roses Away.......................AC:27 *Give Me This Moment* | $6 | | RCA Victor 8677 |
| | | | Marty Paich (orch.) | | | |
| | | | **GARY & THE HORNETS**                          HOT | | | |
| | | | Brothers from Franklin, Ohio: Gary (age 11 in 1966), Gregg (13) and Steve (6) Calvert. | | | |
| 2/11/67 | 127 | 3 | Kind Of Hush .................................... *That's All For Now Sugar Baby* | $12 | ■ | Smash 2078 |
| | | | #4 hit for **Herman's Hermits** in 1967 | | | |
| | | | **GATES, Walter, and his Orchestra ☉** | | | |
| 6/20/64 | 133 | 1 | My Man .................................... *Rose Of Washington Square* [I] | $10 | | Swan 4180 |
| | | | tune's arrangement is similar to "The Stripper" by David Rose | | | |
| | | | **GATLIN, Larry**                          C&W/AC/HOT | | | |
| | | | Born on 5/2/48 in Seminole, Texas. Country singer/songwriter/guitarist. Leader of The Gatlin Brothers. | | | |
| 5/31/80 | 108 | 1 | Taking Somebody With Me When I Fall .............. C&W:12 / AC:36 *Piece By Piece* | $4 | | Columbia 11219 |
| | | | **LARRY GATLIN AND THE GATLIN BROTHERS BAND** | | | |
| | | | **GAYE, Marvin**                          R&B/HOT/AC | | | |
| | | | Born on 4/2/39 in Washington, D.C. Fatally shot by his father on 4/1/84 in Los Angeles. Inducted into the Rock and Roll Hall of Fame in 1987. Won Grammy's Lifetime Achievement Award in 1996. *Top Pop Singles*: 56. | | | |
| 2/17/79 | 106 | 5 | 1 A Funky Space Reincarnation (Part I)....................R&B:23 *(Part II)* | $4 | | Tamla 54298 |
| 3/21/81 | 101[1] | 6 | 2 Praise                          R&B:18 *Funk Me* | $3 | | Tamla 54322 |
| 5/11/85 | 101[2] | 6 | 3 Sanctified Lady                          R&B:2 *(Instrumental)* | $3 | | Columbia 04861 |
| | | | **GAYE, Nona**                          R&B/HOT | | | |
| | | | Daughter of **Marvin Gaye**. Raised in Washington D.C. | | | |
| 4/17/93 | 118 | 3 | The Things That We All Do For Love ............... R&B:51 *Only Two Can Tell* | $3 | ▌ | Third Stone 98448 |
| | | | **GAYNOR, Gloria**                          R&B/HOT/AC | | | |
| | | | Born on 9/7/49 in Newark, New Jersey. Disco singer. With the Soul Satisfiers in 1971. | | | |
| 6/1/74 | 103 | 4 | 1 Honey Bee ........................................ R&B:55 *Come Tonight* | $5 | | MGM 14706 |
| 10/28/78 | 107 | 4 | 2 Substitute........................................R&B:78 *I Will Survive* (Hot #1) | $4 | | Polydor 14508 |
| | | | #67 hit for Clout in 1978 | | | |
| 6/23/79 | 105 | 2 | 3 Anybody Wanna Party? ............................R&B:16 *Please, Be There* | $4 | | Polydor 14558 |
| 12/17/83 | 102 | 5 | 4 I Am What I Am ................................R&B:82 *More Than Enough* | $4 | | Silver Blue 04294 |
| | | | from Broadway's *La Cage aux Folles*; originally released on Silver Blue 720 (and Silver Blue 220-12") | | | |
| | | | **GEILS, J., Band**                          HOT/ROK/R&B/AC | | | |
| | | | Rock-blues band formed in Boston in 1967 featuring Jerome Geils (guitar) and Peter Wolf (vocals). | | | |
| 2/16/74 | 104 | 6 | 1 Did You No Wrong ............................ *That's Why I'm Thinking Of You* | $5 | | Atlantic 3007 |
| 2/22/75 | 106 | 1 | 2 Givin' It All Up ................................................*Gettin' Out* | $5 | | Atlantic 3251 |
| | | | **GEMINI ☉** | | | |
| | | | Pop vocal group. | | | |
| 1/17/70 | 119 | 2 | Take Her Back ................................................*Ann* | $7 | | Forward 129 |
| | | | **GENE & DEBBE**                          HOT | | | |
| | | | Duo of **Gene Thomas** and Debbe Nevills. | | | |
| 11/16/68 | 127 | 1 | 1 Make A Noise Like Love ............................ *Rings Of Gold* | $7 | | TRX 5014 |
| 2/15/69 | 114 | 5 | 2 Memories Are Made Of This ...................... *The Sun Won't Shine Again* | $7 | | TRX 5017 |
| | | | #1 hit for **Dean Martin** in 1956 | | | |
| | | | **GENE & JERRY — see CHANDLER, Gene / BUTLER, Jerry** | | | |
| | | | **GENE & TOMMY — see CASHMAN, PISTILLI & WEST** | | | |
| | | | **GENE AND WENDELL ☉**                          R&B | | | |
| | | | R&B duo: Eugene Washington and Wendell Jones, with female backing group The Sweethearts. | | | |
| 10/30/61 | 117 | 1 | The Roach ................................ R&B:14 *From Me To You* | $25 | ■ | Ray Star 777 |
| | | | **GENE AND WENDELL with The Sweethearts** | | | |
| | | | **GENERAL PUBLIC**                          HOT/ROK | | | |
| | | | British pop band formed in 1984 featuring Dave Wakeling (vocals, guitar) amd Ranking Roger (vocals, keyboards), both of **English Beat**. | | | |
| 3/16/85 | 105 | 3 | Never You Done That................................ *All The Rage* | $3 | ■ | I.R.S. 9935 |
| | | | **GENIUS**                          R&B/HOT | | | |
| | | | Born Gary Grice on 8/22/66 in Brooklyn. Male rapper. Member of **Wu-Tang Clan**. | | | |
| 10/8/94 | 122 | 1 | I Gotcha' Back ................................ *(instrumental)* | $3 | ▌ | Loud/RCA 62967 |
| | | | from the movie *Fresh* starring Samuel L. Jackson | | | |
| | | | **GENTILI, Phil ☉** | | | |
| | | | Boston-based singer/songwriter. | | | |
| 8/22/81 | 110 | 1 | Mama Lied................................ *It's Your Love I Need* | $4 | ■ | Portrait 02400 |

### GENTRY, Bobbie
HOT/AC/C&W/R&B

Born Roberta Streeter on 7/27/44 in Chickasaw County, Mississippi. Guitarist/pianist/bassist/banjo player. Won the 1967 Best New Artist Grammy Award.

| 5/31/69 | 113 | 3 | Touch 'Em With Love .......................................................... *Casket Vignette* | $6 | | Capitol 2501 |

### GENTRYS, The
HOT

Rock and roll band from Memphis featuring Larry Raspberry, Jimmy Hart and Bruce Bowles (vocals).

| 1/8/66 | 101[2] | 4 | 1 **Brown Paper Sack** *Spread It On Thick (Hot #50)* | $10 | ■ | MGM 13432 |
| 9/3/66 | 112 | 5 | 2 A Woman Of The World ....................................... *There Are Two Sides To Every Story* | $10 | | MGM 13561 |
| 3/18/67 | 130 | 2 | 3 You Make Me Feel So Good ..................................................... *There's A Love* | $10 | | MGM 13690 |
| 5/11/68 | 132 | 2 | 4 I Can't Go Back To Denver ..................................... *You Better Come Home* | $10 | | Bell 720 |
| | | | produced by Dale Hawkins | | | |
| 8/1/70 | 116 | 1 | 5 He'll Never Love You ................................................... *I Hate To See You Go* | $6 | | Sun 1118 |
| 11/21/70 | 119 | 2 | 6 Goddess Of Love ..................................................................... *Friends* | $6 | | Sun 1120 |

### GEORGE, Barbara
HOT/R&B

Born on 8/16/42 in New Orleans. R&B singer/songwriter.

| 7/21/62 | 114 | 1 | If You Think ............................. *If When You've Done The Best You Can* | $12 | | Sue 763 |

## GEORGE & GENE — see JONES, George / PITNEY, Gene

## GEORGE, JOHNNY AND THE PILOTS ☼

| 9/11/61 | 108 | 3 | Flying Blue Angels ........................... *A Fiddle And A Bow (George, Johnny And The Girlfriends)* | $15 | | Coed 555 |

### GERARD ☼

Pop group from Colorado led by singer/songwriter Gerard McMahon.

| 6/12/76 | 109 | 1 | Hello, Operator.................................................... *Who's Your Daddy O?* | $5 | | Caribou 9013 |

### GERONIMO, Mic ☼
R&B

Male rapper from Queens, New York.

| 9/10/94 | 118 | 1 | It's Real ........................................................ *R&B:89  Sh*t's Real* | $3 | ■ | Blunt/TVT 4912 |

### GERRARD, Donny
R&B/AC/HOT

Lead singer of the Canadian group Skylark.

| 7/12/75 | 104 | 1 | (Baby) Don't Let It Mess Your Mind.............. *AC:42 /R&B:65  A Woman, A Lover, A Friend* | $6 | | Rocket 40405 |
| | | | originally recorded by **Neil Sedaka** in 1972 on his *Solitaire* album | | | |

### GERRY AND THE PACEMAKERS
HOT

Pop group formed in 1959 in Liverpool, England: Gerry Marsden (vocals, guitar), Leslie Maguire (piano), Les Chadwick (bass) and Freddie Marsden (drums).

| 8/21/65 | 117 | 5 | 1 You're The Reason ............................... *Give All Your Love To Me (Hot #68)* | $12 | | Laurie 3313 |
| | | | #11 hit for Bobby Edwards in 1961 | | | |
| 12/11/65 | 103 | 4 | 2 Walk Hand In Hand ..................................................... *Dreams* | $12 | | Laurie 3323 |
| | | | #10 hit for Tony Martin in 1956 | | | |
| 12/12/70 | 112 | 1 | 3 Don't Let The Sun Catch You Crying................. *Away From You* [R] | $12 | | Laurie 3251 |
| | | | originally made the *Hot 100* (#4) on 5/23/64 | | | |

### GETO BOYS, The
R&B/HOT

Rap group from Houston featuring Brad "**Scarface**" Jordan and Richard "**Bushwick Bill**" Shaw.

| 3/6/93 | 111 | 5 | Crooked Officer............................... *Sls:75 /R&B:70  (2 versions)* | $3 | ■ | Rap-A-Lot 53818 |

### GETZ, Stan
HOT/AC

Born Stan Gayetsky on 2/2/27 in Philadelphia. Died of liver cancer on 6/6/91. Jazz tenor saxophonist. With Stan Kenton (1944-45), Jimmy Dorsey (1945-46), Benny Goodman (1946) and Woody Herman (1947-49).

| 5/23/64 | 110 | 3 | Blowin' In The Wind ............................. *The Girl From Ipanema (Getz/Gilberto - Hot #5)* [I] | $10 | | Verve 10323 |
| | | | written by **Bob Dylan**; #2 hit for **Peter, Paul & Mary** in 1963 | | | |

### GIANT SUNFLOWER ☼

Pop vocal group featuring a **Mamas & Papas** "sound."

| 6/3/67 | 106 | 1 | 1 February Sunshine ..................................................... *Big Apple* | $8 | | Ode 102 |
| 10/14/67 | 116 | 1 | 2 What's So Good About Good-Bye ................................. *Mark Twain* | $8 | | Ode 104 |
| | | | #35 hit for **The Miracles** in 1962 | | | |

### GIBB, Robin
HOT/AC

Born on 12/22/49 in Manchester, England. Twin brother of the **Bee Gees'** Maurice Gibb.

| 10/22/83 | 104 | 3 | Juliet ............................................................... *Hearts On Fire* | $4 | ■ | Polydor 810895 |

### GIBBS, Georgia
MEM/HOT/POP/AC

Born Fredda Gibbons on 8/17/20 in Worcester, Massachusetts. *Pop Hits & Top Pop Singles*: 25.

| 5/29/65 | 132 | 2 | Let Me Cry On Your Shoulder ............................. *Venice Blue (Que C'est Triste Venise)* | $8 | | Bell 615 |
| | | | Joe Sherman (orch.) | | | |

### GIBSON, Don
C&W/HOT/AC

Born on 4/3/28 in Shelby, North Carolina. Country singer/songwriter/guitarist.

| 3/6/61 | 108 | 1 | 1 The World Is Waiting For The Sunrise.......................... *What About Me (Hot #100)* | $10 | | RCA Victor 7841 |
| | | | #2 hit for **Les Paul & Mary Ford** in 1951 | | | |
| 5/26/62 | 105 | 1 | 2 I Can Mend Your Broken Heart....................... *C&W:5  I Let Her Get Lonely* | $10 | | RCA Victor 8017 |

### GIBSON, Johnny, Trio
HOT

| 6/13/64 | 116 | 2 | Beachcomber ............................................................... *Swanky* [I] | $15 | | Laurie 3256 |
| | | | originally released on Twirl 2012 in 1964 ($20); #100 hit for **Bobby Darin** in 1960 | | | |

### GIL & JOHNNY ☼

Pop vocal duo: Gil Garfield and Johnny Cole.

| 8/20/66 | 112 | 3 | Come On Sunshine ..................................................... *Mama's Little Baby* | $8 | | World Pacific 77833 |

### GILES, Eddy ☼

Full name: Elbert W. Giles. R&B vocalist/songwriter.

| 6/17/67 | 127 | 1 | Losin' Boy ..................................................................... *I Got The Blues* | $15 | | Murco 1031 |

| DEBUT | PEAK | WKS | A-side (Chart Hit)..........................................................................B-side | $ | Pic | Label & Number |
|---|---|---|---|---|---|---|

**GILL, Johnny**            R&B/HOT/AC

Born on 5/22/66 in Washington, D.C. Sang in family gospel group, Wings Of Faith, from age five. Joined New Edition in 1988. His brother Randy and cousin Jermaine Mickey are members of II D Extreme.

| 5/26/84 | 102 | 4 | 1 Baby It's You .................................... R&B:37 *50/50 Love* | $4 | | Cotillion 99750 |

STACY LATTISAW & JOHNNY GILL
#8 hit for **The Shirelles** in 1962

| 2/26/94 | 111 | 5 | 2 Quiet Time To Play ............................ R&B:25 *(LP version)* | $3 | ▮ | Motown 2236 |

Karyn White (backing vocal); recorded "live" at the Regal Theatre in Chicago

| 4/26/97 | 104 | 9 | 3 Love In An Elevator............................... R&B:59 *So Gentle* | $3 | ▮ | Motown 0626 |

**GILL, Vince**          C&W/HOT/AC

Born on 4/12/57 in Norman, Oklahoma. Country singer/guitarist. Member of Pure Prairie League, 1979-83.

| 12/31/94+ | 109 | 2 | When Love Finds You................................ C&W:3 *If I Had My Way* | $3 | ▮ | MCA 54937 |

**GILLEY, Mickey**          C&W/HOT/AC

Born on 3/9/36 in Natchez, Louisiana. Country singer/pianist. First cousin to **Jerry Lee Lewis**.

| 8/28/76 | 101[1] | 2 | 1 Bring It On Home To Me    C&W:❶ / AC:37 *How's My Ex Treating You* | $5 | | Playboy 6075 |

#13 hit for **Sam Cooke** in 1962

| 11/15/80 | 101[1] | 4 | 2 That's All That Matters    C&W:❶ *The Blues Don't Care Who's Got 'Em* | $4 | | Epic 50940 |

#34 Country hit for **Ray Price** in 1964

| 1/8/83 | 106 | 1 | 3 Talk To Me.......................... C&W:❶ *Honky Tonkin' (I Guess I Done Me Some)* | $4 | | Epic 03326 |

#20 hit for **Little Willie John** in 1958

**GILMER, Jimmy**          HOT/R&B

Born in 1940 in Raton, New Mexico. Lead singer of The Fireballs.

| 5/23/64 | 133 | 1 | 1 Look At Me ...................................... *I'll Send For You* | $10 | | Dot 16609 |

written by **Buddy Holly**

| 8/29/64 | 133 | 1 | 2 What Kinda Love?.................................... *Wishing* | $10 | | Dot 16642 |

**GIORGIO**          HOT

Full name: Giorgio Moroder. Born on 4/26/40 in Ortisel, Italy. Electronic composer/conductor/producer for numerous soundtracks.

| 10/29/77 | 109 | 3 | From Here To Eternity ............................ *Utopia Me-Giorgio* | $5 | | Casablanca 897 |

**GIOVANNI** ✪

Full name: Giovanni Gonzalez.

| 7/29/95 | 117 | 3 | Girl In My Eyes ..................................... *(Spanglish version)* | $3 | ▮ | Sire 64420 |

**GLASER, Tompall**          C&W/HOT

Born Thomas Paul Glaser on 9/3/33 in Spalding, Nebraska. Lead singer and oldest of The Glaser Brothers. Formed own Outlaw Band; toured with **Waylon Jennings** and **Willie Nelson**.

| 11/1/75 | 103 | 1 | Put Another Log On The Fire (Male Chauvinist National Anthem)................................ C&W:21 *Mendocino* [N] | $6 | | MGM 14800 |

TOMPALL

**GLASS BOTTLE, The**          HOT

Pop group featuring lead singer Gary Criss.

| 5/30/70 | 109 | 1 | Love For Living ..................................... *The First Time* | $7 | | Avco Embassy 4527 |

produced by Dickie Goodman

**GLASS HOUSE, The**          R&B/HOT

R&B vocal group from Detroit: Larry Mitchell, Pearl Jones, Scherrie Payne, **Ty Hunter** and Eric Dunham. Hunter (d: 2/24/81) was in The Originals. Payne was in **The Supremes** and is the sister of Freda Payne.

| 11/7/70 | 121 | 3 | 1 Stealing Moments From Another Woman's Life ............ R&B:42 *If It Ain't Love, It Don't Matter (R&B flip)* | $7 | | Invictus 9082 |

| 10/30/71 | 101[1] | 4 | 2 Look What We've Done To Love    R&B:31 *Heaven Is There to Guide Us* | $7 | | Invictus 9097 |

**GLASS MOON**          HOT

Pop-rock group: Dave Adams, Nestor Nunez, Chris Jones and Jaime Glaser.

| 7/19/80 | 108 | 1 | 1 (I Like) The Way You Play..................... *Killer at 25* | $5 | | Radio Records 420 |

| 6/30/84 | 103 | 2 | 2 Cold Kid ..................................... *He's Waiting For A Train* | $4 | | MCA 52402 |

GLASSMOON

**GLEAMS, The** ✪

White male vocal group led by Steve Verroca.

| 9/4/61 | 117 | 2 | You Broke My Heart .................... *I Don't Know Why You Sent For Me* | $30 | | Kip 236 |

**GLORIES, The**          R&B/HOT

Female R&B vocal trio from New York City: Francis Yvonne Gearing, Betty Stokes and Mildred Vaney.

| 9/16/67 | 124 | 2 | (I Love You Babe But) Give Me My Freedom .................... *Security* | $15 | | Date 1571 |

**GLOVER, Roger** ✪          ROK

Born on 11/30/45 in Brecon, Wales. Bass player of **Deep Purple** and **Rainbow**.

| 6/23/84 | 102 | 3 | The Mask....................................... ROK:20 *Don't Look Down* | $5 | | 21 Records 114 |

**GOD'S CHILDREN** ✪

| 3/13/71 | 112 | 1 | Hey, Does Somebody Care ...................... *Lonely Lullaby* | $7 | | Uni 55266 |

from the TV series *Matt Lincoln* starring **Vince Edwards**

**GODWIN, Peter** ✪

British disco singer. Former member of Metro with the late Duncan Browne.

| 4/2/83 | 105 | 3 | Images Of Heaven ..................................... *Emotional Disguise* | $6 | | Polydor 810065 |

**GO-GO'S**          HOT/ROK

Female rock group formed in 1978 in Los Angeles: Belinda Carlisle (vocals), Jane Wiedlin and Charlotte Caffey (guitars), Kathy Valentine (bass) and Gina Schock (drums).

| 11/19/94 | 108 | 6 | The Whole World Lost Its Head ............ ROK:21 *Skidmarks On My Heart / Forget That Day* | $3 | ▮ | I.R.S. 58290 |

**GOLDBERG, Barry, Reunion** ✪

Blues/rock band led by singer/guitarist Goldberg (b: 1941 in Chicago). Joined supergroup KGB as a keyboardist.

| 9/28/68 | 103 | 3 | Hole In My Pocket ..................................... *Sittin' In Circles* | $8 | | Buddah 59 |

## GOLDEN EARRING
`HOT/ROK`

Rock band formed in 1967 in Amsterdam, Holland: Barry Hay (vocals), George Kooymans (guitar), Rinus Gerritsen (bass) and Cesar Zuiderwijk (drums).

| DEBUT | PEAK | WKS | A-side / B-side | $ | Pic | Label & Number |
|---|---|---|---|---|---|---|
| 4/3/76 | 109 | 1 | Sleep Walkin' ..................................... *Babylon* | $6 | | MCA 40513 |

## GOLDEN GATE, The ☉

| | | | | | | |
|---|---|---|---|---|---|---|
| 3/14/70 | 105 | 2 | Diane ..................................... *Make Your Own Sweet Music* | $7 | | Audio Fidelity 161 |

## GOLDSBORO, Bobby
`AC/HOT/C&W`

Born on 1/18/41 in Marianna, Florida. Singer/songwriter/guitarist. Toured with **Roy Orbison**, 1962-64. Own syndicated TV show from 1972-75, The Bobby Goldsboro Show. *Top Pop Singles*: 27.

| | | | | | | |
|---|---|---|---|---|---|---|
| 11/7/64 | 105 | 5 | 1 I Don't Know You Anymore ..................................... *Little Drops Of Water* | $8 | | United Artists 781 |
| 7/23/66 | 114 | 3 | 2 Take Your Love ..................................... *Longer Than Forever* | $8 | | United Artists 50044 |
| 4/8/67 | 102 | 3 | 3 Goodbye To All You Women ..................................... *Abilene* | $8 | | United Artists 50138 |
| 11/25/67 | 111 | 1 | 4 Jo Jo's Place/ | | | |
| 12/23/67 | 118 | 4 | 5 Pledge Of Love | $8 | | United Artists 50224 |
| 8/1/70 | 108 | 2 | 6 It's Gonna Change .............. AC:38 *Down On The Bayou* | $7 | | United Artists 50696 |
| 11/13/71 | 107 | 2 | 7 Danny Is A Mirror To Me .............. AC:34 *A Poem For My Little Lady (AC #27)* | $6 | | United Artists 50846 |
| 4/15/72 | 108 | 5 | 8 California Wine .............. AC:36 *To Be With You* | $6 | | United Artists 50891 |
| 3/3/73 | 116 | 6 | 9 Brand New Kind Of Love .............. AC:37 *Country Feelin's* | $6 | | United Artists 51107 |
| 6/26/76 | 101[1] | 4 | 10 A Butterfly For Bucky .............. AC:7 /C&W:22 *Another Night Alone* | $6 | | United Artists 793 |
| 3/19/77 | 104 | 2 | 11 Me And The Elephants .............. AC:6 /C&W:82 *I Love Music* | $5 | | Epic 50342 |

## GOOD & PLENTY ☉

Pop vocal duo: Douglas Good and Ginny Plenty.

| | | | | | | |
|---|---|---|---|---|---|---|
| 12/23/67 | 111 | 4 | Living In A World Of Make Believe .............. *I Played My Part Well* | $10 | | Senate 2105 |

## GOODFELLAZ
`R&B/HOT`

R&B vocal trio from New York City: Angel Vasquez, DeLouie Avant and Ray Vencier.

| | | | | | | |
|---|---|---|---|---|---|---|
| 6/7/97 | 104 | 7 | If You Walk Away ..................................... R&B:59 *(remix)* | $3 | ▌ | Avatar 3638 |

## GOODMAN, Dickie
`HOT`

Born Richard Dorian Goodman on 4/19/34 in Brooklyn, New York. Died on 11/6/89 of a self-inflicted gunshot. Goodman and partner Bill Buchanan originated the novelty "break-in" recordings featuring bits of the original versions of Top 40 hits interwoven throughout the recording. Also see **Buchanan and Greenfield**, **Scott Key** and **Byron McNaughton**.

| | | | | | | |
|---|---|---|---|---|---|---|
| 10/23/61 | 116 | 1 | 1 Berlin Top Ten ..................................... *Little Tiger* [N] | $25 | | Rori 602 |
| 11/2/63 | 116 | 1 | 2 Senate Hearing ..................................... *Lock Up* [N] | $20 | | 20th Century Fox 443 |
| 9/15/73 | 119 | 3 | 3 The Purple People Eater ..................................... *Ruthie's Socks* [N] | $10 | | Rainy Wednesday 204 |

#1 hit for **Sheb Wooley** in 1958

## GOODMAN, Steve ☉

Born on 7/25/48 in Chicago. Died of leukemia on 9/20/84. Singer/songwriter/guitarist.

| | | | | | | |
|---|---|---|---|---|---|---|
| 2/5/72 | 113 | 2 | City Of New Orleans ..................................... | $7 | | Buddah 270 |

produced by **Paul Anka** and **Kris Kristofferson**; #18 hit for **Arlo Guthrie** in 1972

## GOODMAN, Tim ☉

Singer/songwriter from Boulder, Colorado. Produced by **The Doobie Brothers'** John McFee.

| | | | | | | |
|---|---|---|---|---|---|---|
| 9/19/81 | 107 | 2 | New Romeo ..................................... *Live Or Die* | $4 | | Columbia 02495 |

## GORDON, Jimmy ☉

Rock and roll instrumental guitarist.

| | | | | | | |
|---|---|---|---|---|---|---|
| 11/19/66 | 121 | 3 | Buzzzzzzz ..................................... *Somethin' Else* [I] | $12 | | Challenge 59194 |

co-written by Dave Burgess of **The Champs**

## GORE, Lesley
`HOT/AC/R&B`

Born on 5/2/46 in New York City; raised in Tenafly, New Jersey. Discovered by **Quincy Jones**.

| | | | | | | |
|---|---|---|---|---|---|---|
| 5/28/66 | 108 | 6 | 1 Off And Running ..................................... *I Don't Care* | $12 | | Mercury 72580 |
| 9/17/66 | 115 | 4 | 2 Treat Me Like A Lady ..................................... *Maybe Now* | $12 | | Mercury 72611 |
| 3/16/68 | 124 | 1 | 3 Small Talk ..................................... *Say What You See* | $12 | | Mercury 72787 |
| 6/8/68 | 119 | 3 | 4 He Gives Me Love (La La La) ..................................... *Brand New Me* | $12 | | Mercury 72819 |

## GORME, Eydie
`AC/HOT/MEM/C&W`

Born on 8/16/31 in New York City. Vocalist with the big bands of Tommy Tucker and Tex Beneke in the late 1940s. Featured on **Steve Allen's** Tonight Show from 1953. Married **Steve Lawrence** on 12/29/57.

| | | | | | | |
|---|---|---|---|---|---|---|
| 2/29/64 | 133 | 1 | 1 The Friendliest Thing ..................................... *Something To Live For* | $7 | | Columbia 42953 |

from the Broadway musical *What Makes Sammy Run?* starring **Steve Lawrence**

| | | | | | | |
|---|---|---|---|---|---|---|
| 4/10/65 | 122 | 3 | 2 Do I Hear A Waltz? ..................................... *After You've Gone* | $7 | ☐ | Columbia 43225 |

from the Broadway musical starring Elizabeth Allen

| | | | | | | |
|---|---|---|---|---|---|---|
| 6/5/65 | 124 | 3 | 3 Just Dance On By .............. AC:39 *Where Are You Now* | $7 | | Columbia 43302 |
| 6/18/66 | 120 | 3 | 4 If He Walked Into My Life .............. AC:5 *Tell Him I Said Hello* | $7 | | Columbia 43660 |

from the Broadway musical *Mame* starring Angela Lansbury

| | | | | | | |
|---|---|---|---|---|---|---|
| 1/28/67 | 117 | 1 | 5 Softly, As I Leave You .............. AC:30 *What's Good About Goodbye?* | $7 | | Columbia 43971 |

#27 hit for **Frank Sinatra** in 1964

| | | | | | | |
|---|---|---|---|---|---|---|
| 2/10/68 | 115 | 1 | 6 Life Is But A Moment (Canta Ragazzina) .............. AC:35 *What Makes Me Love Him?* | $7 | | Columbia 44299 |
| 4/26/69 | 119 | 4 | 7 Real True Lovin' .............. AC:20 *Chapter One* | $6 | | RCA Victor 0123 |

STEVE & EYDIE

Marty Manning (orch.)

## GOUDREAU, Barry ☉

Born on 11/29/51 in Boston. Lead guitarist of Boston, Orion The Hunter and RTZ.

| | | | | | | |
|---|---|---|---|---|---|---|
| 10/25/80 | 103 | 1 | Dreams ..................................... *Sailin' Away* | $4 | | Portrait 70042 |

## GOULET, Robert     AC/HOT
Born on 11/26/33 in Lawrence, Massachusetts. Broadway/movie/TV actor. Launched career as Sir Lancelot in the hit Broadway musical *Camelot*. Won the 1962 Best New Artist Grammy Award.

| DEBUT | PEAK | WKS | A-side | $ | Pic | Label & Number |
|-------|------|-----|--------|---|-----|----------------|
| 4/13/63 | 132 | 1 | 1 Two Of Us .................................................. *(These Are) The Closing Credits* | $7 | ■ | Columbia 42740 |
| | | | issued with 2 different picture sleeve photos of Goulet | | | |
| 10/3/64 | 131 | 1 | 2 I'd Rather Be Rich ......................................... *My Love, Forgive Me* (Hot #16) | $7 | □ | Columbia 43131 |
| | | | from the movie starring Sandra Dee and Goulet | | | |
| 2/27/65 | 110 | 7 | 3 Begin To Love (Cominciamo ad Amarci) .... *I Never Got To Paris* | $7 | | Columbia 43224 |
| 10/2/65 | 118 | 3 | 4 Come Back To Me, My Love/    AC:5 | | | |
| 10/16/65 | 119 | 2 | 5 On A Clear Day You Can See Forever ................... AC:13 | $7 | | Columbia 43394 |
| | | | from the Broadway musical starring Barbara Harris; #98 hit for **Johnny Mathis** in 1965 | | | |

## GQ     R&B/HOT
R&B group from New York City: Emmanuel Rahiem LeBlanc (vocals, guitar), Herb Lane (keyboards), Keith Crier (bass) and Paul Service (drums).

| DEBUT | PEAK | WKS | A-side | $ | Pic | Label & Number |
|-------|------|-----|--------|---|-----|----------------|
| 6/14/80 | 101² | 6 | Sitting In The Park    R&B:9   *It's Like That* | $4 | | Arista 0510 |
| | | | #24 hit for **Billy Stewart** in 1965 | | | |

## GRADUATES     HOT
White vocal group from New York: John Cappello, Bruce Hammond, Fred Mancuso and Jack Scorsone.

| DEBUT | PEAK | WKS | A-side | $ | Pic | Label & Number |
|-------|------|-----|--------|---|-----|----------------|
| 6/1/59 | 110 | 1 | What Good Is Graduation................................................*Lonely* | $30 | ■ | Corsican 0058 |
| | | | Corsican label formerly known as Shan-Todd | | | |

## GRADY, Don ☉
Born on 6/8/44 in San Diego. Played "Robbie Douglas" on TV's *My Three Sons*. Leader of **The Yellow Balloon**.

| DEBUT | PEAK | WKS | A-side | $ | Pic | Label & Number |
|-------|------|-----|--------|---|-----|----------------|
| 12/31/66 | 132 | 2 | The Children Of St. Monica ...................... *A Good Man To Have Around The House* | $12 | ■ | Canterbury 501 |
| | | | **DON GRADY with The Windupwatchband** | | | |

## GRAF ☉
Ohio-based pop quartet — Frank Pellino, lead singer.

| DEBUT | PEAK | WKS | A-side | $ | Pic | Label & Number |
|-------|------|-----|--------|---|-----|----------------|
| 3/14/81 | 110 | 1 | Come To My Arms............................................ *Bad Luck Mornin'* | $4 | | Precision 9805 |

## GRAHAM, Jaki ☉     R&B
Female vocalist of Jamaican descent from Birmingham, England. Did backup work with UB40. Formed half of the Kiss The Sky duo in 1992.

| DEBUT | PEAK | WKS | A-side | $ | Pic | Label & Number |
|-------|------|-----|--------|---|-----|----------------|
| 10/1/94 | 101¹ | 14 | Ain't Nobody .................................................... *(remix)* | $3 | ▮ | Avex/Critique 15529 |

## GRAHAM, Larry     R&B/HOT/AC
Born on 8/14/46 in Beaumont, Texas. Bass player with **Sly & The Family Stone** from 1966-72. Formed Graham Central Station in 1973.

| DEBUT | PEAK | WKS | A-side | $ | Pic | Label & Number |
|-------|------|-----|--------|---|-----|----------------|
| 5/29/82 | 102 | 7 | 1 Don't Stop When You're Hot.............................R&B:16 *I Love Loving You* | $4 | ■ | Warner 50068 |
| 7/31/82 | 110 | 1 | 2 Sooner Or Later ........................................R&B:27 *I Feel Good* | $4 | ■ | Warner 29956 |

## GRAHAM, Tammy ☉     C&W
Born on 2/7/68 in Little Rock, Arkansas. Country singer/pianist.

| DEBUT | PEAK | WKS | A-side | $ | Pic | Label & Number |
|-------|------|-----|--------|---|-----|----------------|
| 5/10/97 | 108 | 6 | A Dozen Red Roses ...................................C&W:37 *Tell Me Again* | $3 | ▮ | Career 13075 |

## GRANAHAN, Gerry     HOT
Born on 6/17/39 in Pittston, Pennsylvania. Formed Dicky Doo & The Don'ts and The Fireflies. Formed Caprice Records in 1958 and produced many top hits.

| DEBUT | PEAK | WKS | A-side | $ | Pic | Label & Number |
|-------|------|-----|--------|---|-----|----------------|
| 5/8/61 | 109 | 2 | Unchained Melody ........................................ *Dancing Man* | $20 | | Caprice 106 |
| | | | there were 3 Top 10 hit versions in 1955; #4 hit for **The Righteous Brothers** in 1965 | | | |

## GRAND FUNK RAILROAD     HOT/R&B
Hard-rock band formed in 1968 in Flint, Michigan: Mark Farner (guitar), Mel Schacher (bass) and Don Brewer (drums).

| DEBUT | PEAK | WKS | A-side | $ | Pic | Label & Number |
|-------|------|-----|--------|---|-----|----------------|
| 12/12/81 | 108 | 1 | Stuck In The Middle ......................................................................... | $4 | | Full Moon 49866 |

## GRANDMASTER & MELLE MEL     R&B/HOT
Rap duo. Grandmaster Flash was born Joseph Saddler on 1/1/58 in Barbados. Melle Mel was born Melvin Glover.

| DEBUT | PEAK | WKS | A-side | $ | Pic | Label & Number |
|-------|------|-----|--------|---|-----|----------------|
| 11/19/83 | 101² | 10 | White Lines (Don't Don't Do It) ..................R&B:47 *(3 versions)* | $10 | | Sugar Hill 465 (T) |

## GRAND PUBA     R&B/HOT
Born Maxwell Dixon on 3/4/66 in New York City. Former member of the rap group Brand Nubian.

| DEBUT | PEAK | WKS | A-side | $ | Pic | Label & Number |
|-------|------|-----|--------|---|-----|----------------|
| 1/9/93 | 110 | 7 | 1 Check It Out ............................................R&B:85 *That's How We Move It* | $3 | ▮ | Elektra 64671 |
| | | | **GRAND PUBA Featuring Mary J. Blige** | | | |
| 8/19/95 | 109 | 3 | 2 A Little Of This.......................................R&B:90 *I Like It (I Wanna Be Where You Are)* | $3 | ▮ | Elektra 64389 |
| | | | Kid (backing vocal); samples *"Just A Love Child"* by Bobbi Humphrey | | | |
| 2/17/96 | 108 | 13 | 3 Why You Treat Me So Bad........... R&B:52 *(club mix) / The Train Is Coming / Demand The Ride* | $3 | ▮ | Virgin 38529 |
| | | | **SHAGGY Featuring Grand Puba** | | | |
| | | | samples "Mr. Brown" by *Bob Marley* | | | |

## GRANGER, Gerri ☉
Female pop songstress.

| DEBUT | PEAK | WKS | A-side | $ | Pic | Label & Number |
|-------|------|-----|--------|---|-----|----------------|
| 12/20/75 | 108 | 2 | Can't Take My Eyes Off You......................... *Hot Ta Trot* | $6 | | 20th Century 2241 |
| | | | #2 hit for **Frankie Valli** in 1967 | | | |

## GRAPEFRUIT     HOT
British pop/rock quartet: John Perry (vocals), brothers Pete (guitar) and Geoff (drums) Swettenham, and George Alexander (bass).

| DEBUT | PEAK | WKS | A-side | $ | Pic | Label & Number |
|-------|------|-----|--------|---|-----|----------------|
| 5/4/68 | 113 | 3 | Elevator ........................................................ *Yes* | $12 | | Equinox 70005 |

## GRASS ROOTS, The     HOT/AC
Pop-rock group: Rob Grill (lead singer, bass), Warren Entner and Creed Bratton (guitars), and Rick Coonce (drums). *Top Pop Singles*: 21.

| DEBUT | PEAK | WKS | A-side | $ | Pic | Label & Number |
|-------|------|-----|--------|---|-----|----------------|
| 10/30/65 | 121 | 2 | 1 Mr. Jones (A Ballad Of A Thin Man) .................. *You're A Lonely Girl* | $20 | | Dunhill 4013 |
| | | | written and recorded by **Bob Dylan** on his 1965 album *Highway 61 Revisited* | | | |
| 2/24/68 | 123 | 3 | 2 A Melody For You.......................................*Hey Friend* | $10 | | Dunhill 4122 |
| | | | originally recorded by song's writer **P.F. Sloan** in 1966 on Dunhill 4054 | | | |
| 10/7/72 | 107 | 2 | 3 Anyway The Wind Blows .................................*Monday Love* | $8 | | Dunhill/ABC 4325 |

## GRAVEDIGGAZ     R&B/HOT
Male rap quartet: Robert Diggs (**Wu-Tang Clan**), Poetic, Paul Huston and Arnold Hamilton.

| DEBUT | PEAK | WKS | A-side | $ | Pic | Label & Number |
|-------|------|-----|--------|---|-----|----------------|
| 10/15/94 | 116 | 1 | Nowhere To Run, Nowhere To Hide ........................ *Freak The Sorceress* | $3 | ▮ | Gee Street 854104 |
| | | | samples *"Jagger The Dagger"* by **Eugene McDaniels** | | | |

| DEBUT | PEAK | WKS | A-side (Chart Hit)..................................................................................B-side | $ | Pic | Label & Number |
|---|---|---|---|---|---|---|
| | | | **GRAVES, Carl**      R&B/HOT/AC | | | |
| | | | R&B singer from Calgary, Alberta, Canada. With the group **Skylark** in 1973. | | | |
| 4/5/75 | 103 | 1 | The Next Best Thing ................................................... *Brown Skin Love* | $6 | | A&M 1673 |
| | | | **GRAY, Dobie**      HOT/R&B/C&W/AC | | | |
| | | | Born Lawrence Darrow Brown on 7/26/40 in Brookshire/Simonton, Texas. Singer/composer/actor. | | | |
| 5/3/69 | 119 | 5 | 1 Rose Garden ................................................... *Where's The Girl Gone* | $10 | | White Whale 300 |
| | | | #3 hit for **Lynn Anderson** in 1971 | | | |
| 12/1/73 | 103 | 8 | 2 Good Old Song ................................................... *Reachin For The Feelin* | $6 | | MCA 40153 |
| 9/21/74 | 107 | 1 | 3 Watch Out For Lucy ................................................... *Turning On You* | $6 | | MCA 40268 |
| | | | written by **Lonnie Mack** | | | |
| | | | **GREAN, Charles Randolph**      AC/HOT | | | |
| | | | Born on 10/1/13 in New York City. Former A&R director at RCA and Dot Records. Married singer **Betty Johnson**. | | | |
| 3/14/70 | 108 | 3 | Peter And The Wolf ..................................... AC:12 *Georgy* [I] | $6 | | Ranwood 864 |
| | | | **THE CHARLES RANDOLPH GREAN SOUNDE** | | | |
| | | | adaptation of Prokofiev's famous symphonic poem | | | |
| | | | **GREAVES, R.B.**      HOT/R&B/AC | | | |
| | | | Born Ronald Bertram Aloysius Greaves on 11/28/44 at the USAF Base in Georgetown, British Guyana. Nephew of **Sam Cooke**. | | | |
| 10/28/72 | 115 | 2 | Margie, Who's Watching The Baby ................................................... *Area Code 213* | $8 | | Sunflower 128 |
| | | | a new version by Greaves made the R&B charts (#66) on 4/2/77 on Bareback 523 ($7) | | | |
| | | | **GRECO, Buddy**      AC/MEM/POP/HOT | | | |
| | | | Born Armando Greco on 8/14/26 in Philadelphia. Former pianist/vocalist with Benny Goodman. | | | |
| 7/10/61 | 109 | 1 | 1 Around The World ................................................... *Hey, There* | $12 | | Epic 9451 |
| | | | Al Cohn (orch.); #25 hit for **Bing Crosby** in 1957 (from the movie starring David Niven) | | | |
| 8/14/65 | 132 | 1 | 2 I Can't Begin To Tell You ................................... *When The Subject Was Roses* | $10 | | Epic 9817 |
| | | | Marty Manning (orch.); #1 hit for **Bing Crosby** with Carmen Cavallaro in 1945 | | | |
| | | | **GREEN, Al**      R&B/HOT/AC | | | |
| | | | Born on 4/13/46 in Forrest City, Arkansas. R&B singer/songwriter. Inducted into the Rock and Roll Hall of Fame in 1995. *Top Pop Singles*: 20. | | | |
| 4/20/68 | 127 | 3 | 1 Don't Hurt Me No More ................................................... *Get Yourself Together* | $20 | | Hot Line 15,001 |
| | | | **AL GREENE** | | | |
| 4/10/71 | 115 | 2 | 2 Driving Wheel ..................................... R&B:46 *True Love* | $8 | | Hi 2188 |
| | | | #85 hit for **Junior Parker** in 1961 | | | |
| 2/26/77 | 101[2] | 5 | 3 I Tried To Tell Myself ..................................... R&B:26 *Something* | $5 | | Hi 2322 |
| 7/30/77 | 104 | 6 | 4 Love And Happiness ..................................... R&B:92 *Glory, Glory* | $5 | | Hi 2324 |
| | | | #58 hit for **Earnest Jackson** in 1973 | | | |
| 4/29/78 | 103 | 8 | 5 I Feel Good ..................................... R&B:36 *Feels Like Summer* | $5 | | Hi 78511 |
| | | | **GREEN, Garland**      R&B/HOT | | | |
| | | | Born Garfield Green on 6/24/42 in Leland, Mississippi. R&B singer/pianist. | | | |
| 12/27/69 | 113 | 4 | 1 Don't Think That I'm A Violent Guy ........ R&B:42 *All She Did (Was Wave Goodbye At Me)* | $10 | | Uni 55188 |
| 4/17/71 | 109 | 3 | 2 Plain And Simple Girl ..................................... R&B:17 *Hey Cloud* | $8 | | Cotillion 44098 |
| | | | arranged and produced by **Donny Hathaway** and **Syl Johnson** | | | |
| | | | **GREENE, Jack**      C&W/HOT | | | |
| | | | Born on 1/7/30 in Maryville, Tennessee. Drummer for Ernest Tubb's band, 1962-66. | | | |
| 5/27/67 | 103 | 3 | All The Time ..................................... C&W:❶5 *Wanting You But Never Having You* (C&W #63) | $8 | | Decca 32123 |
| | | | **GREENE, Jeanie** ☉ | | | |
| | | | Pop female vocalist. Did session work for **Boz Scaggs** and **Willie Nelson**. | | | |
| 10/30/71 | 114 | 1 | Only The Children Know ................................................... *Magdalene's Medley* | $7 | | Elektra 45742 |
| | | | **GREENE, Lorne**      AC/HOT/C&W | | | |
| | | | Born on 2/12/14 in Ottawa, Canada. Died on 9/11/87 of cardiac arrest. Starred in TV's *Bonanza* and *Battlestar Galactica*. | | | |
| 2/19/66 | 112 | 5 | Five Card Stud ..................................... AC:36 *Shadow Of The Cactus* | $8 | | RCA Victor 8757 |
| | | | Joe Reisman (orch.) | | | |
| | | | **GREENLEE, Lee** ☉ | | | |
| 8/31/59 | 102 | 3 | Starlight ................................................... *Cherry, I'm In Love With You* | $20 | | Brent 7003 |
| | | | **GREEN RIVER BOYS, The — see CAMPBELL, Glen** | | | |
| | | | **GREENWICH, Ellie**      HOT | | | |
| | | | Born on 10/23/40 in Long Island, New York. With former husband Jeff Barry, wrote and produced many of the top hits of the '60s. | | | |
| 5/26/73 | 122 | 2 | Maybe I Know ..................................... *Today I Met The Boy I'm Gonna Marry* | $10 | | Verve 10719 |
| | | | #14 hit for **Lesley Gore** in 1964 | | | |
| | | | **GREGG, Bobby**      HOT/R&B | | | |
| | | | Real name: Robert Grego. Jazz drummer from Philadelphia. Performed with Steve Gibson & The Red Caps, 1955-60. | | | |
| 7/6/63 | 112 | 5 | 1 Scarlet O'Hara ..................................... *Take Me Out To The Ball Game* [I] | $12 | | Epic 9601 |
| | | | rock and roll version of the #89 hit for **Lawrence Welk** in 1963 | | | |
| 2/6/65 | 133 | 1 | 2 The Hullabaloo ..................................... *Charly Ba-Ba* | $12 | | Veep 1207 |
| | | | **BOBBY GREGG AND HIS FRIENDS** | | | |
| | | | **GREGG, Ricky Lynn** ☉      C&W | | | |
| | | | Born on 8/22/62 in Longview, Texas. Country-rock singer/songwriter/guitarist. Part Native American. | | | |
| 7/10/93 | 109 | 5 | If I Had A Cheatin' Heart ..................... C&W:36 *(club mix) / Can You Feel It (2 versions)* | $3 | ∎ | Liberty 44948 |
| | | | also available as a vinyl single on Liberty 17323 | | | |
| | | | **GREGORASH, Joey** ☉ | | | |
| | | | Born in 1951 in Winnipeg. Hosted weekly TV show in Canada, *Young As You Are*. | | | |
| 10/30/71 | 113 | 1 | Down By The River ................................................... *Don't Let Your Pride Get You Girl* | $8 | | Lionel 3219 |
| | | | written and recorded by **Neil Young** on his 1969 album *Everybody Knows This Is Nowhere* | | | |
| | | | **GREY & HANKS**      R&B/HOT | | | |
| | | | Chicago-based R&B vocal/songwriting duo of Zane Grey and Len Ron Hanks. | | | |
| 11/25/78 | 104 | 4 | You Fooled Me ..................................... R&B:19 *(Part II)* | $5 | | RCA 11346 |

| | | | | | | |
|---|---|---|---|---|---|---|
| | | | **GRIER, Roosevelt** ⚪ | | | |
| | | | Born on 7/14/32 in Cuthbert, Georgia. Former all-pro football player in the NFL. | | | |
| 8/10/68 | 126 | 1 | People Make The World................................................*Hard To Forget* | $12 | | Amy 11,029 |
| | | | written by **Bobby Womack**; tribute to Robert F. Kennedy who was assassinated on 6/5/68 | | | |
| | | | **GRIFFIN** ⚪ | | | |
| | | | Los Angeles-area group consisting of former members of Aorta and H.P. Lovecraft. | | | |
| 11/4/72 | 114 | 2 | Mississippi Lady.....................................*Whatever Happens, Happens* | $8 | | Romar 707 |
| | | | **GRIFFIN, Jimmy** ⚪ | | | |
| 3/28/64 | 118 | 4 | All My Loving.........................................*My Baby Made Me Cry* | $15 | | Reprise 0268 |
| | | | originally recorded by **The Beatles** for their 1964 album *Meet The Beatles!* | | | |
| | | | **GRIFFIN, Merv**        POP/MEM/HOT | | | |
| | | | Born on 7/6/25 in San Mateo, California. Popular TV talkshow host/TV producer. Owner of TV game shows *Jeopardy!* and *Wheel Of Fortune*, and an Atlantic City casino. Featured singer with Freddy Martin, 1948-52, ("I've Got A Lovely Bunch of Coconuts"). | | | |
| 2/27/61 | 101[1] | 4 | Banned In Boston                  *The World We Love In* [N] | $10 | | Carlton 540 |
| | | | Sid Bass (orch. and chorus) | | | |
| | | | **GRIN**        HOT | | | |
| | | | Rock trio: Nils Lofgren (vocals, guitar), Bob Gordon (bass) and Bob Berberich (drums). | | | |
| 10/10/70 | 108 | 4 | We All Sung Together..............................*See What A Love Can Do* | $10 | | Thunder 4000 |
| | | | **GRIPSTA** ⚪        R&B | | | |
| | | | Female rapper from Los Angeles. Discovered by **Ice-T**. | | | |
| 1/6/96 | 109 | 1 | Pop Goz The 9.....................................**R&B:92** | $25 | | Tuff Break/A&M 8374 **(CD)** |
| | | | falsely charted due to a data-collection snafu caused by an errant bar code; originally reviewed by *Billboard* on 3/4/95, but the label (Tuff Break) was closed a short time later so no commercial single or album was ever released (number above is a promo CD only) | | | |
| | | | **GROOP, The** ⚪ | | | |
| | | | Australian pop vocal group. | | | |
| 11/29/69 | 112 | 1 | The Jet Song (When The Weekend's Over)...........**AC:35** *Nobody At All* | $10 | | Bell 822 |
| | | | **GROOVEGRASS BOYZ, The** ⚪        C&W | | | |
| | | | Country studio group assembled by producers Scott Rouse and Ronnie McCoury. Vocalists include Mac Wiseman and Doc Watson. | | | |
| 1/11/97 | 107 | 11 | Macarena (Country version)..................**C&W:70** (2 versions) | $3 | ▌ | Imprint 18007 |
| | | | #1 hit (for 14 weeks) for Los Del Rio in 1996 | | | |
| | | | **GROSS, Henry**        HOT/AC | | | |
| | | | Born on 4/1/51 in Brooklyn. Pop/rock singer. Original lead guitarist of **Sha-Na-Na**. | | | |
| 7/20/74 | 109 | 1 | 1 Come On Say It..................................*The Ever Lovin' Days* | $6 | | A&M 1534 |
| 4/23/77 | 110 | 1 | 2 Painting My Love Song..............................*String Of Hearts* | $5 | | Lifesong 45023 |
| 7/2/77 | 110 | 1 | 3 What A Sound.......................................*I Can't Believe* | $5 | | Lifesong 45024 |
| | | | **GROUP HOME**        R&B/HOT | | | |
| | | | Rap duo from New York City: Melachi The Nutcracker and Lil' Dap. | | | |
| 1/20/96 | 108 | 4 | Livin' Proof........................................*Supa Dupa Star* | $3 | ▌ | Payday 127050 |
| | | | **GUESS WHO, The**        HOT/AC | | | |
| | | | Rock group formed in 1963 in Winnipeg, Canada: Allan "Chad Allan" Kobel (vocals, guitar), Randy Bachman (guitar), Bob Ashley (piano), Jim Kale (bass) and Garry Peterson (drums). Ashley replaced by new lead singer Burton Cummings in 1966. Allan left shortly thereafter. Bachman left in 1970 to form Bachman-Turner Overdrive. *Top Pop Singles*: 21. | | | |
| 9/4/65 | 125 | 3 | 1 Hey Ho What You Do To Me.....................*Goodnight Goodnight* | $20 | | Scepter 12108 |
| | | | written by **Ashford & Simpson** | | | |
| 8/30/75 | 105 | 1 | 2 Rosanne.................................................*Dreams* | $6 | | RCA Victor 10360 |
| 11/8/75 | 102 | 4 | 3 When The Band Was Singin' "Shakin' All Over"................*Women* | $6 | | RCA Victor 10410 |
| | | | "Shakin' All Over" was the group's first *Hot 100* hit in 1965 | | | |
| | | | **GUISE, The** ⚪ | | | |
| 11/5/66 | 123 | 2 | Long Haired Music...................................*When You're Sorry* | $15 | | Musicland U.S.A. 20,011 |
| | | | THE GUISE (And Their Mod Sound) | | | |
| | | | **GURU** ⚪        R&B | | | |
| | | | Born Keith Elam on 7/18/66 in Boston. Rapper from the duo **Gang Starr**. | | | |
| 8/21/93 | 105 | 7 | Trust Me.................................**R&B:50** *Loungin'* (w/**Donald Byrd**) | $3 | ▌ | Chrysalis 24849 |
| | | | N'Dea Davenport (lead vocal) | | | |
| | | | **GUTHRIE, Arlo**        HOT/AC | | | |
| | | | Born on 7/10/47 in Coney Island, New York. Son of legendary folk singer Woody Guthrie. | | | |
| 10/24/70 | 102 | 3 | 1 Valley To Pray..................*Gabriel's Mother's Hiway Ballad #16 Blues* | $6 | ■ | Reprise 0951 |
| 6/9/73 | 105 | 8 | 2 Gypsy Davy....................................**AC:23** *Week On The Rag* | $6 | | Reprise 1158 |
| | | | written by Arlo's father, Woody Guthrie | | | |
| | | | **GUTHRIE, Gwen**        R&B/HOT | | | |
| | | | R&B singer/songwriter from Newark, New Jersey. Background vocalist for many top artists. | | | |
| 2/9/85 | 110 | 1 | 1 Love In Moderation.........................**R&B:17** *Seventh Heaven* | $4 | | Island 99685 |
| | | | produced by Deodato | | | |
| 7/6/85 | 102 | 5 | 2 Padlock.......................................**R&B:25** *Getting Hot* | $4 | | Garage 72001 |
| | | | featuring Sly Dunbar, Robbie Shakespeare, Wally Badarou and Darryl Thompson | | | |
| | | | **GYPSIES, The** ⚪        R&B | | | |
| | | | Female R&B group from New York City: sisters Betty, Shirley and Earnestine Pearce from South Carolina and Lestine Johnson. | | | |
| 5/8/65 | 111 | 4 | Jerk It....................................**R&B:33** *Diamonds Rubies Gold And Fame* | $20 | | Old Town 1180 |
| | | | written and arranged by **J.J. Jackson** | | | |
| | | | **GYPSY BAND — see WALSH, James** | | | |

## HAGGARD, Merle, And The Strangers — C&W/HOT/AC
Born on 4/6/37 in Bakersfield, California. Country singer/songwriter/guitarist.

| | | | | | | |
|---|---|---|---|---|---|---|
| 4/25/70 | 124 | 2 | 1 Street Singer ........................................ C&W:9 Mexican Rose [I] | $7 | | Capitol 2778 |
| 6/13/70 | 107 | 3 | 2 Jesus, Take A Hold ........................ C&W:3 No Reason To Quit | $7 | | Capitol 2838 |
| 10/17/70 | 106 | 5 | 3 I Can't Be Myself/ ......................................... C&W:3 | | | |
| | | 4 | 4 Sidewalks Of Chicago .................................. C&W:flip | $7 | ■ | Capitol 2891 |
| 7/31/71 | 119 | 2 | 5 Someday We'll Look Back ........ C&W:2 It's Great To Be Alive | $7 | | Capitol 3112 |

## HAIRCUT ONE HUNDRED — ROK/HOT
Pop-rock sextet formed in London in 1980: **Nick Heyward** (vocals), Graham Jones (guitar), Phil Smith (sax), Mark Fox (percussion), Les Nemes (bass) and Blair Cunningham (drums).

| | | | | | | |
|---|---|---|---|---|---|---|
| 8/28/82 | 101[1] | 8 | Favourite Shirts (Boy Meets Girl) — ROK:50 Ski Club Of Great Britain | $4 | | Arista 0708 |

## HALEY, Bill, And His Comets — HOT/MEM/POP
Born William John Clifton Haley, Jr. on 7/6/25 in Highland Park, Michigan. Died on 2/9/81 of a heart attack. Began career as a singer with a New England country band, the Down Homers. Formed the Four Aces of Western Swing in 1948. In 1949 formed the Saddlemen. The Comets band had many personnel changes. Inducted into the Rock and Roll Hall of Fame in 1987. *Pop Hits & Top Pop Singles*: 28.

| | | | | | | |
|---|---|---|---|---|---|---|
| 2/29/60 | 101[1] | 4 | 1 Tamiami ........................................... Candy Kisses [I] | $20 | | Warner 5145 |
| 6/15/68 | 118 | 2 | 2 (We're Gonna) Rock Around The Clock ...... Thirteen Women [R] | $7 | | Decca 29124 |
| | | | originally a #1 hit for 8 weeks in 1955; reissue above is on a multi-colored label; re-charted again in 1974 on MCA 60025 | | | |

## HALL, Aaron — R&B/HOT
Born on 8/10/64 in Brooklyn. R&B singer. Member of the New York City trio, Guy.

| | | | | | | |
|---|---|---|---|---|---|---|
| 1/29/94 | 113 | 6 | 1 Let's Make Love ........................ R&B:36 (instrumental) | $3 | ▌ | Silas/MCA 54783 |
| 10/22/94 | 104 | 4 | 2 When You Need Me ...................... R&B:30 (suite) | $3 | ▌ | Silas/MCA 54902 |
| 8/26/95 | 114 | 4 | 3 Curiosity .................................. R&B:36 (instrumental) | $3 | ▌ | MCA 55105 |
| | | | from the movie *Dangerous Minds* starring Michelle Pfeiffer | | | |

## HALL, Daryl, & John Oates — HOT/AC/R&B/ROK
Daryl Hall (b: 10/11/48 in Philadelphia) and John Oates (b: 4/7/49 in New York City) are the #1 charting duo of the rock era. *Top Pop Singles*: 34.

| | | | | | | |
|---|---|---|---|---|---|---|
| 3/22/80 | 110 | 3 | Who Said The World Was Fair .......... All You Want Is Heaven | $4 | | RCA 11920 |

## HALL, John, Band — HOT/ROK
Born on 10/25/47 in Baltimore. Singer/guitarist. Founder/leader of **Orleans**. Band includes Bob Leinbach (keyboards), John Troy (bass) and Eric Parker (drums).

| | | | | | | |
|---|---|---|---|---|---|---|
| 4/17/82 | 109 | 1 | You Sure Fooled Me ........................ Lovelight | $4 | | EMI America 8112 |

## HALL, Lani — AC/HOT
Lead vocalist with **Sergio Mendes & Brasil '66**. Married to **Herb Alpert**.

| | | | | | | |
|---|---|---|---|---|---|---|
| 10/22/83 | 103 | 4 | Never Say Never Again ........ AC:22 Une Chanson D'Amour (Michel Legrand) | $4 | ■ | A&M 2596 |
| | | | produced by **Herb Alpert**; title song from the James Bond movie starring Sean Connery | | | |

## HALL, Rebecca ♦ — C&W
Born in Rustburg, Virginia. Winner of *You Can Be A Star* talent competition.

| | | | | | | |
|---|---|---|---|---|---|---|
| 8/6/83 | 109 | 1 | Who Says Girls Can't Rock & Roll ........ Red Hot | $4 | | 21 Records 111 |

## HALL, Tom T. — C&W/HOT/AC
Born on 5/25/36 in Olive Hill, Kentucky. Country music storyteller. Hosted *Pop Goes The Country* TV series.

| | | | | | | |
|---|---|---|---|---|---|---|
| 6/23/73 | 101[2] | 10 | Watergate Blues — C&W:16 Spokane Motel Blues (C&W flip) [N] | $6 | | Mercury 73394 |

## HALLORAN, Jack, Singers — see VAN DYKE, Dick

## HAMILTON, George ♦ — 
Born on 8/12/39 in Memphis. Leading television/film actor.

| | | | | | | |
|---|---|---|---|---|---|---|
| 11/30/63 | 134 | 1 | Don't Envy Me ........................ Little Betty Falling Star | $10 | ■ | MGM 13178 |

## HAMILTON, George IV — C&W/HOT/AC
Born on 7/19/37 in Winston-Salem, North Carolina. Country-folk-pop singer/songwriter/guitarist.

| | | | | | | |
|---|---|---|---|---|---|---|
| 11/9/63 | 116 | 4 | There's More Pretty Girls Than One ...... C&W:21 If You Don't Somebody Else Will | $10 | | RCA Victor 8250 |

## HAMILTON, Roy — HOT/R&B/MEM
Born on 4/16/29 in Leesburg, Georgia. Died of a stroke on 7/20/69. R&B ballad singer.

| | | | | | | |
|---|---|---|---|---|---|---|
| 11/30/59 | 105 | 3 | 1 Ebb Tide ........................ R&B:5 Beware [R] | $20 | | Epic 9068 |
| | | | O.B. Masingill (orch.); #2 hit for Frank Chacksfield in 1953 | | | |
| 7/21/62 | 110 | 2 | 2 I'll Come Running Back To You ...... Climb Every Mountain | $15 | ■ | Epic 9520 |
| | | | Sammy Lowe (orch.); #18 hit for Sam Cooke in 1958 | | | |
| 5/11/63 | 129 | 1 | 3 Let Go ........................ You Still Love Him | $12 | | MGM 13138 |
| | | | Teacho Wiltshire (orch.) | | | |

## HAMILTON, JOE FRANK & REYNOLDS — HOT/AC/R&B
Pop vocal trio of Dan Hamilton (d: 12/23/94, age 48), Joe Frank Carollo and Tommy Reynolds.

| | | | | | | |
|---|---|---|---|---|---|---|
| 3/18/72 | 113 | 4 | One Good Woman ........................ Don't Refuse My Love | $6 | | Dunhill/ABC 4305 |

## HANCOCK, Herbie — R&B/HOT
Born on 4/12/40 in Chicago. Jazz electronic keyboardist. Pianist with the Miles Davis band, 1963-68.

| | | | | | | |
|---|---|---|---|---|---|---|
| 3/23/63 | 121 | 1 | 1 Watermelon Man ........................ Three Bags Full [I] | $10 | | Blue Note 1862 |
| | | | with Freddie Hubbard (trumpet) and Dexter Gordon (sax); #10 hit for **Mongo Santamaria** in 1963 | | | |
| 10/2/76 | 104 | 3 | 2 Doin' It........................ R&B:83 People Music [I] | $5 | | Columbia 10408 |
| 6/2/84 | 105 | 7 | 3 Mega-Mix (Includes: Rockit, Autodrive, Future Shock, TFS, Rough & Chameleon '84) ........ R&B:36 TFS [I] | $4 | | Columbia 04473 |
| | | | special mix of 6 tunes from his *Future Shock* album | | | |

**HANSIE** ○
Five-member Dutch rock group led by female singer Hansie.

| 1/12/80 | 109 | 2 | Automobile ................................................................................ *Lovely Love* | $5 | | Millennium 11783 |

**HAPPENINGS, The**     HOT
Pop vocal group from Paterson, New Jersey: Bob Miranda, Tom Giuliano, Ralph DiVito and Dave Libert.

| 5/11/68 | 118 | 4 | 1 Randy ........................................................................*The Love Song Of Mommy And Dad* | $10 | ■ | B.T. Puppy 540 |
| 10/26/68 | 114 | 3 | 2 Crazy Rhythm ..........................................................*The Love Song Of Mommy And Dad* | $10 | | B.T. Puppy 545 |

#10 hit for Roger Wolfe Kahn in 1928; above 2 produced by **The Tokens**

| 1/17/70 | 115 | 3 | 3 Answer Me, My Love ....................................................... *I Need A Woman* | $8 | | Jubilee 5686 |

#6 hit for **Nat King Cole** in 1954

**HARDY BOYS, The** ○
Pop vocal group used in the animated cartoon TV series *The Hardy Boys*.

| 10/4/69 | 101¹ | 7 | Love And Let Love      *Sink Or Swim* | $8 | | RCA Victor 0228 |

**HARMONICA FATS** ○
Born Harvey Blackston on 9/8/27 in McDade, Louisiana. Blues singer/harmonica player.

| 3/23/63 | 103 | 2 | Tore Up................................................................*I Get So Tired* | $25 | | Darcey 5000 |

written by **Hank Ballard**

**HARNER, Billy** ○
R&B singer from Pinehill, New Jersey.

| 8/19/67 | 118 | 4 | 1 Sally Sayin' Somethin' ...........................................*Don't Want My Lovin'* | $12 | | Kama Sutra 226 |
| 1/25/69 | 121 | 5 | 2 She's Almost You..................................................*Fool Me* | $15 | | Open 1253 |

written by **Joe South**

**HARPERS BIZARRE**     AC/HOT
Pop vocal quintet from Santa Cruz, California: Ted Templeman, Eddie James, Dick Yount, John Petersen and Dick Scoppettone.

| 6/15/68 | 123 | 2 | Both Sides Now ..........................................**AC:38** *Small Talk* | $6 | | Warner-Seven Arts 7200 |

#8 hit for **Judy Collins** in 1968

**HARPO, Slim**     R&B/HOT
Born James Moore on 1/11/24 in Lobdell, Louisiana. Died of a heart attack on 1/31/70. Blues singer/harmonica player.

| 7/23/66 | 116 | 1 | 1 Shake Your Hips ............................................. *Midnight Blues* | $15 | | Excello 2278 |
| 12/31/66 | 116 | 2 | 2 I'm Your Bread Maker, Baby ...............*Loving You (The Way I Do)* | $15 | | Excello 2282 |
| 8/12/67 | 127 | 2 | 3 Tip On In Part 1 ..............................................**R&B:37** *Part 2* [I] | $15 | | Excello 2285 |

**HARRIS, Anita** ○
British Adult Contemporary singer.

| 11/4/67 | 120 | 1 | Just Loving You ...................................**AC:20** *Butterfly With Coloured Wings* | $8 | | Columbia 44236 |

**HARRIS, Betty — see DORSEY, Lee**

**HARRIS, Bobby** ○     R&B
R&B singer.

| 2/6/65 | 107 | 1 | 1 We Can't Believe You're Gone........................**R&B:38** *More Of The Jerk* | $15 | | Atlantic 2270 |

a tribute to **Sam Cooke** who died on 12/11/64

| 9/3/66 | 101¹ | 4 | 2 Sticky, Sticky      *Mr. Success* | $20 | | Shout 203 |

**HARRIS, Brenda Jo** ○     R&B
R&B songstress.

| 10/5/68 | 131 | 1 | Standing On The Outside .....................**R&B:50** *Your Love Is Like A Hurricane* | $12 | | Roulette 7021 |

written and produced by Ronnie Savoy

**HARRIS, Eddie**     R&B/HOT
Born on 10/20/36 in Chicago. Died of cancer on 11/5/96. Jazz tenor saxophonist.

| 11/13/61 | 114 | 2 | 1 My Buddy/      [I] | | | |

#1 hit for Henry Burr in 1922

| 11/13/61 | 119 | 1 | 2   God Bless The Child ......................................... [I] | $15 | | Vee-Jay 407 |

written and recorded by blues great Billie Holiday in 1941

| 11/9/74 | 107 | 1 | 3 Is It In ..............................................**R&B:67** *Funkaroma* [I] | $6 | | Atlantic 3216 |

**HARRIS, Emmylou**     C&W/AC/HOT
Born on 4/2/47 in Birmingham, Alabama. Country singer/guitarist.

| 3/4/78 | 102 | 2 | 1 To Daddy ...........................................**C&W:3** *Tulsa Queen* | $5 | | Warner 8498 |

written by **Dolly Parton**

| 6/13/81 | 106 | 3 | 2 I Don't Have To Crawl ...................**C&W:44** *Colors Of Your Heart* | $4 | | Warner 49739 |

written by **Rodney Crowell**

**HARRIS, Richard**     AC/HOT
Born on 10/1/30 in Limerick, Ireland. Began prolific acting career in 1958.

| 10/28/72 | 107 | 5 | 1 There Are Too Many Saviours On My Cross ..............*All The Broken Children* [S] | $6 | ■ | Dunhill/ABC 4322 |

a poem by Harris pleading for peace in the Irish ("Bloody Sunday") civil war

| 2/17/73 | 106 | 2 | 2 I Don't Have To Tell You ...............................*How I Spent My Summer* | $5 | | Dunhill/ABC 4336 |

**HARRIS, Rolf**     HOT/AC
Born on 3/30/30 in Perth, Australia. Moved to England in the mid-1950s.

| 5/30/64 | 116 | 1 | 1 The Court Of King Caractacus.........................*Two Buffalos* [N] | $15 | | Epic 9682 |
| 3/21/70 | 119 | 5 | 2 Two Little Boys.............................................**AC:19** *I Love My Love* | $10 | | MGM 14103 |

written in 1903

**HARRIS, Sam**     HOT
Born in Oklahoma. Singer/actor.

| 1/26/85 | 108 | 1 | Hearts On Fire ...............................................*I Will Not Wait For You* | $3 | | Motown 1771 |

**HARRISON, George**     HOT/ROK/AC
Born in Wavertree, Liverpool, England, on 2/24/43. Lead guitarist of **The Beatles**. In 1992, became the first recipient of *Billboard's* "The Century Award."

| 8/15/81 | 102 | 5 | Teardrops .....................................................**ROK:51** *Save The World* | $8 | | Dark Horse 49785 |

| DEBUT | PEAK | WKS | A-side (Chart Hit)..........B-side | $ | Pic | Label & Number |
|---|---|---|---|---|---|---|

**HARRISON, Wilbert**                                   HOT/R&B
Born on 1/5/29 in Charlotte, North Carolina. Died on 10/26/94 of a stroke. R&B singer.

| | | | | | | |
|---|---|---|---|---|---|---|
| 2/22/60 | 102 | 6 | 1 **Good Bye Kansas City** ...................................................................... *1960* | $20 | | Fury 1028 |
| | | | new words to Harrison's 1959 #1 hit "Kansas City" | | | |
| 6/12/61 | 114 | 3 | 2 **Off To Work Again** .............................................. *After Graduation* | $15 | | Neptune 123 |
| 11/16/63 | 118 | 3 | 3 **Near To You** ........................................................... *Say It Again* | $15 | | Sea-Horn 502 |

**HARRY, Debbie**                                   HOT/ROK/R&B
Born on 7/1/45 in New York City. Lead singer of Blondie. In the movies *Roadie*, *Union City* and *Videodrome*.

| | | | | | | |
|---|---|---|---|---|---|---|
| 1/21/84 | 105 | 1 | **Rush, Rush** ......................... *Dance, Dance, Dance* (Beth Andersen) | $4 | ■ | Chrysalis 42745 |
| | | | from the movie *Scarface* starring Al Pacino | | | |

**HART, Bobby — see BOYCE, Tommy**

**HART, Susan** ✪                                   AC
Pop singer/actress. Appeared in the 1964 movie *Pajama Party*.

| | | | | | | |
|---|---|---|---|---|---|---|
| 5/9/81 | 109 | 3 | **Is This A Disco Or A Honky Tonk?** ............ AC:47 *Why Don't You Love Me?* | $6 | | Dore 967 |

**HART, Trella** ✪
Female pop singer.

| | | | | | | |
|---|---|---|---|---|---|---|
| 9/5/70 | 120 | 1 | **Two Little Rooms** ...................................... *The Way It Used To Be* | $7 | | Capitol 2881 |

**HARTMAN, Dan**                                   HOT/AC/R&B
Born on 12/8/50 in Harrisburg, Pennsylvania. Died on 3/22/94 of a brain tumor. Singer/songwriter/multi-instrumentalist/producer. Member of the Edgar Winter Group, 1972-76.

| | | | | | | |
|---|---|---|---|---|---|---|
| 3/8/80 | 104 | 3 | 1 **Relight My Fire** .............................................................. *Vertigo* | $4 | | Blue Sky 2784 |
| 9/26/81 | 110 | 3 | 2 **All I Need** ............................................ AC:41 *Forever In A Moment* | $4 | | Blue Sky 02472 |

**HARVEY**                                   R&B/HOT
R&B singer Harvey Fuqua of Harvey and The Moonglows.

| | | | | | | |
|---|---|---|---|---|---|---|
| 3/23/63 | 131 | 1 | **Any Way You Wanta** .......................................... *She Loves Me So* | $40 | | Tri-Phi 1017 |
| | | | **HARVEY (Formerly of the Moonglows)** | | | |

**HASSLES, The** ✪
Rock group from Long Island, New York: **Billy Joel**, Howie Blauvelt (d: 10/25/93, age 44), Jonathan Small, Richard McKenner and John Dizek. Joel went on to a very successful solo career.

| | | | | | | |
|---|---|---|---|---|---|---|
| 11/25/67 | 112 | 1 | **You've Got Me Hummin'** ........................................ *I'm Thinkin'* | $15 | ■ | United Artists 50215 |
| | | | #77 hit for **Sam & Dave** in 1967 | | | |

**HATFIELD, Juliana**                                   ROK/HOT
Born on 7/2/67 in Wiscasset, Maine. Female rock singer/guitarist. Also recorded with **The Lemonheads**.

| | | | | | | |
|---|---|---|---|---|---|---|
| 10/2/93 | 112 | 5 | **My Sister** ............................................ ROK:❶¹ *Put It Away* | $3 | ▮ | Atlantic/Mammoth 98392 |
| | | | the **JULIANA HATFIELD three** | | | |

**HATHAWAY, Donny**                                   R&B/HOT/AC
Born on 10/1/45 in Chicago. Committed suicide on 1/13/79. R&B singer/songwriter/keyboardist/producer/arranger.

| | | | | | | |
|---|---|---|---|---|---|---|
| 4/8/72 | 109 | 3 | 1 **Little Ghetto Boy** .............................. R&B:25 *We're Still Friends* | $7 | | Atco 6880 |
| 9/2/72 | 102 | 4 | 2 **Come Back Charleston Blue** ................................. *Bossa Nova* | $7 | | Atco 6899 |
| | | | **DONNY HATHAWAY WITH MARGIE JOSEPH** | | | |
| | | | from the movie starring Godfrey Cambridge | | | |

**HAVENS, Richie**                                   HOT/AC
Born on 1/21/41 in Brooklyn. Black folk singer/guitarist. Opening act of the 1969 Woodstock concert.

| | | | | | | |
|---|---|---|---|---|---|---|
| 6/20/70 | 115 | 4 | 1 **Handsome Johnny** ..................................................... *Sandy* | $8 | | MGM 14141 |
| 2/24/73 | 111 | 4 | 2 **Eyesight To The Blind** .......... *Underture* (London Symphony Orchestra & English Chamber Choir) | $8 | ■ | Ode 66032 |
| | | | with the London Symphony Orchestra and English Chamber Choir; from the 1972 rock opera album *Tommy*; #5 R&B hit for The Larks in 1951 | | | |
| 12/4/76 | 102 | 2 | 3 **I'm Not In Love** ............................................. *Dreaming As One* | $5 | | A&M 1882 |
| | | | #2 hit for **10CC** in 1975 | | | |

**HAWKINS', Edwin, Singers**                                   HOT/R&B/AC
Hawkins (b: August 1943) formed gospel group with Betty Watson in Oakland in 1967 as the Northern California State Youth Choir.

| | | | | | | |
|---|---|---|---|---|---|---|
| 8/9/69 | 101¹ | 2 | 1 **Ain't It Like Him** ........................... *Lord Don't Move That Mountain* | $8 | | Pavilion 20,002 |
| 11/15/69 | 109 | 2 | 2 **Blowin' In The Wind** ........................................ *Pray For Peace* | $7 | | Buddah 145 |
| | | | written by **Bob Dylan**; #2 hit for **Peter, Paul & Mary** in 1963 | | | |

**HAWKINS, Hawkshaw**                                   C&W/HOT/POP/MEM
Born Harold Hawkins on 12/22/21 in Huntington, West Virginia. Killed in a plane crash with **Patsy Cline** and Cowboy Copas on 3/5/63. Country singer.

| | | | | | | |
|---|---|---|---|---|---|---|
| 4/6/63 | 108 | 9 | **Lonesome 7-7203** ....................... C&W:❶⁴ *Everything Has Changed* | $15 | | King 5712 |

**HAWKINS, Ronnie**                                   HOT/R&B
Born on 1/10/35 in Huntsville, Arkansas. Formed The Hawks in 1952. To Canada in 1958. Assembled group later known as **The Band**.

| | | | | | | |
|---|---|---|---|---|---|---|
| 5/4/63 | 117 | 3 | 1 **Bo Diddley** ................................................... *Who Do You Love* | $20 | | Roulette 4483 |
| | | | #1 R&B hit for **Bo Diddley** in 1955 | | | |
| 4/18/70 | 118 | 1 | 2 **Bitter Green** ................................................... *Forty Days* | $8 | | Cotillion 44067 |
| | | | written by **Gordon Lightfoot** | | | |

**HAWKINS, Sam** ✪                                   R&B
R&B singer.

| | | | | | | |
|---|---|---|---|---|---|---|
| 6/19/65 | 133 | 1 | 1 **Hold On Baby** ................................. R&B:10 *Bad As They Come* | $15 | | Blue Cat 112 |
| 11/13/65 | 117 | 2 | 2 **I Know It's All Right** ..................... *It Hurts So Bad (Drip Drop)* | $15 | | Blue Cat 121 |

**HAYDEN, Ronnie** ✪
Female pop vocalist.

| | | | | | | |
|---|---|---|---|---|---|---|
| 7/17/61 | 108 | 4 | **S.O.S. (I Love You)** ............................................. *Too Late* | $25 | | Camay 2001 |
| | | | Vinny Catalano (orch.) | | | |

### HAYES, Isaac          R&B/HOT/AC
Born on 8/20/42 in Covington, Tennessee. R&B singer/songwriter/keyboardist/producer/actor.

| DEBUT | PEAK | WKS | A-side | $ | Pic | Label & Number |
|-------|------|-----|---|---|---|---|
| 4/21/73 | 104 | 2 | 1 Rolling Down A Mountainside ................ *(If Loving You Is Wrong) I Don't Want To Be Right*<br>from the *Wattstax* concert/movie | $6 | | Enterprise 9065 |
| 8/28/76 | 102 | 4 | 2 Juicy Fruit (Disco Freak) Pt. 1 ...................................................................... *Pt. 2* | $5 | | HBS/ABC 12206 |
| 1/21/78 | 107 | 3 | 3 Out Of The Ghetto ..........................................................R&B:42 *It's Heaven To Me* | $4 | | Polydor 14446 |
| 8/23/80 | 107 | 2 | 4 It's All In The Game ....................................................R&B:86 *Wherever You Are*<br>#1 hit for Tommy Edwards in 1958 | $4 | | Polydor 2102 |

### HAYES, Wade          C&W/HOT
Born on 4/20/69 on Bethel Acres, Oklahoma. Country singer/songwriter.

| DEBUT | PEAK | WKS | A-side | $ | Pic | Label & Number |
|-------|------|-----|---|---|---|---|
| 5/6/95 | 113 | 10 | 1 I'm Still Dancin' With You ........................................C&W:4 *It's Gonna Take A Miracle* | $3 | ■ | Columbia/DKC 77842 |
| 1/27/96 | 116 | 5 | 2 What I Meant To Say ...................................................C&W:5 *Kentucky Bluebird* | $3 | ■ | Columbia/DKC 78087 |

### HAYWOOD, Leon          R&B/HOT
Born on 2/11/42 in Houston. R&B singer/keyboardist. With Big Jay McNeely and **Sam Cooke** in the early '60s.

| DEBUT | PEAK | WKS | A-side | $ | Pic | Label & Number |
|-------|------|-----|---|---|---|---|
| 8/24/74 | 108 | 1 | 1 Sugar Lump ..............................................................R&B:35 *That Sweet Woman Of Mine* | $5 | | 20th Century 2103 |
| 1/31/76 | 102 | 3 | 2 Just Your Fool ..............................................................R&B:26 *Consider The Source* | $5 | | 20th Century 2264 |
| 6/19/76 | 101[1] | 5 | 3 Strokin' (Pt. II) ..................................................................R&B:13 *(Pt. I)* | $5 | | 20th Century 2285 |
| 10/16/76 | 107 | 1 | 4 The Streets Will Love You To Death - Part I ...............R&B:63 *Part II* | $5 | | Columbia 10413 |

### HAZARD, Robert          HOT
Born in Philadelphia. Rock singer/songwriter. Wrote **Cyndi Lauper's** "Girls Just Want To Have Fun."

| DEBUT | PEAK | WKS | A-side | $ | Pic | Label & Number |
|-------|------|-----|---|---|---|---|
| 6/18/83 | 106 | 2 | Change Reaction ..............................................................*Waiting For The Dream Man* | $4 | | RCA 13536 |

### HAZLEWOOD, Lee          HOT/AC
Singer/songwriter/producer. Produced majority of **Duane Eddy's** hits.

| DEBUT | PEAK | WKS | A-side | $ | Pic | Label & Number |
|-------|------|-----|---|---|---|---|
| 10/28/67 | 107 | 3 | 1 Sand..............................................................................*Lady Bird* (Hot #20)<br>**NANCY SINATRA & LEE HAZLEWOOD** | $10 | | Reprise 0629 |
| 1/25/69 | 113 | 3 | 2 Sleep In The Grass ..........................................................*Chico*<br>**ANN-MARGRET LEE HAZLEWOOD** | $12 | | LHI 2 |
| 12/13/69 | 116 | 3 | 3 Trouble Maker..............................................*Greyhound Bus Depot*<br>religious song written by Dave Somerville (The Diamonds) and Bruce Belland (**The Four Preps**) | $12 | | LHI 20 |
| 2/19/72 | 120 | 2 | 4 Down From Dover ...........................................................*Paris Summer*<br>**NANCY SINATRA AND LEE HAZLEWOOD**<br>written by Dolly Parton | $10 | | RCA Victor 0614 |

### HEAD, Roy          C&W/HOT/R&B
Born on 9/1/41 in Three Rivers, Texas. Rock-country singer/guitarist.

| DEBUT | PEAK | WKS | A-side | $ | Pic | Label & Number |
|-------|------|-----|---|---|---|---|
| 5/21/66 | 110 | 2 | Wigglin' And Gigglin'.......................................................*Driving Wheel* | $10 | | Back Beat 563 |

### HEAD EAST          HOT
Rock quintet from St. Louis: John Schlitt (vocals), Michael Somerville (guitar), Roger Boyd (keyboards), Dan Birney (bass) and Steve Huston (drums).

| DEBUT | PEAK | WKS | A-side | $ | Pic | Label & Number |
|-------|------|-----|---|---|---|---|
| 1/26/80 | 103 | 2 | Got To Be Real ...............................................................*Morning* | $5 | | A&M 2208 |

### HEART          HOT/ROK/AC
Rock band formed in Seattle featuring sisters Ann (lead singer) and Nancy Wilson. *Top Pop Singles*: 30.

| DEBUT | PEAK | WKS | A-side | $ | Pic | Label & Number |
|-------|------|-----|---|---|---|---|
| 6/14/80 | 109 | 1 | 1 Bebe Le Strange................................................................*Silver Wheels* | $4 | | Epic 50892 |
| 4/30/94 | 105 | 7 | 2 The Woman In Me ...........................................AC:24 *Risin' Suspicion*<br>#33 hit for **Donna Summer** in 1983 | $3 | ■ | Capitol 58154 |

### HEATHER B. ✪          R&B
Born Heather Gardener on 11/13/70 in Jersey City, New Jersey. Female rapper.

| DEBUT | PEAK | WKS | A-side | $ | Pic | Label & Number |
|-------|------|-----|---|---|---|---|
| 6/3/95 | 112 | 10 | All Glocks Down.......................................................R&B:63 *(remix)*<br>samples "People Make The World Go Round" by The Stylistics and "How Many MCs" by Buckshot of **Black Moon** | $3 | ■ | Pendulum 58367 |

### HEATWAVE          R&B/HOT/AC
Multi-national, interracial group formed in Germany featuring brothers Johnnie and Keith Wilder (vocals).

| DEBUT | PEAK | WKS | A-side | $ | Pic | Label & Number |
|-------|------|-----|---|---|---|---|
| 11/22/80 | 110 | 1 | Gangsters Of The Groove ...........................................R&B:21 *Find Someone Like You* | $4 | | Epic 50945 |

### HEAVEN BOUND — see SCOTTI, Tony

### HEAVEN 17          HOT/ROK
British electro-pop trio: Glenn Gregory (vocals) and former Human League co-founders/synthesists Martyn Ware and Ian Craig Marsh.

| DEBUT | PEAK | WKS | A-side | $ | Pic | Label & Number |
|-------|------|-----|---|---|---|---|
| 7/9/83 | 102 | 2 | We Live So Fast................................................................*The Best Kept Secret* | $4 | ■ | Arista/Virgin 9027 |

### HEAVY D & THE BOYZ          R&B/HOT
Rap group from Mt. Vernon, New York: leader Heavy D (Dwight Meyers), G. Whiz (Glen Parrish), Trouble T-Roy (Troy Dixon; d: 7/15/90, age 22) and DJ Eddie F (Edward Ferrell).

| DEBUT | PEAK | WKS | A-side | $ | Pic | Label & Number |
|-------|------|-----|---|---|---|---|
| 1/2/93 | 106 | 12 | 1 Who's The Man?.........................................Sls:56 /R&B:52 *(instrumental)* | $3 | ■ | Uptown/MCA 54543 |
| 5/8/93 | 107 | 8 | 2 Truthful.......................................................R&B:57 *Blue Funk* | $3 | ■ | Uptown/MCA 54593 |

### HECKSCHER, Ernie, And His Orchestra ✪

| DEBUT | PEAK | WKS | A-side | $ | Pic | Label & Number |
|-------|------|-----|---|---|---|---|
| 9/12/64 | 125 | 1 | The Girl From Ipanema ...........................................*I'll Love You Till I Die* [I]<br>#5 hit for **Stan Getz**/Astrud Gilberto in 1964 | $8 | | Columbia 43103 |

### HEDGEHOPPERS ANONYMOUS          HOT
British rock group produced by record mogul **Jonathan King**.

| DEBUT | PEAK | WKS | A-side | $ | Pic | Label & Number |
|-------|------|-----|---|---|---|---|
| 3/19/66 | 110 | 5 | Don't Push Me ...........................................*Please Don't Hurt Your Heart For Me* | $12 | | Parrot 9817 |

### HEGEL, Rob ✪
Singer/songwriter/producer. Worked the RCA promotions department in Cincinnati during the 1970s.

| DEBUT | PEAK | WKS | A-side | $ | Pic | Label & Number |
|-------|------|-----|---|---|---|---|
| 8/16/80 | 109 | 3 | Tommy, Judy & Me ................................................................*I Want You* | $4 | | RCA 12009 |

### HEINTJE ✪
Name pronounced: Hine-hee. Born Hendrik Simons on 8/12/55 in Heerlen, Holland. Male singer.

| DEBUT | PEAK | WKS | A-side | $ | Pic | Label & Number |
|-------|------|-----|---|---|---|---|
| 1/2/71 | 112 | 4 | Mama ...........................................................................*A Mother's Tears*<br>#8 hit for **Connie Francis** in 1960 | $6 | | MGM 14183 |

## HELIX ⊙                                                                ROK
Heavy-metal quintet formed in Waterloo, Canada in 1974: Brian Vollmer (vocals), Brent Doerner and Paul Hackman (guitars; d: 7/6/92), Mike Uzelac (bass; replaced by Daryl Gray in 1984) and Greg "Fritz" Hinz (drums).

| 9/1/84 | 101[1] | 5 | Rock You .................................................. ROK:32 *You Keep Me Rockin'* | $4 | ■ | Capitol 5391 |

## HELLO PEOPLE                                                          HOT
White-faced, mime-rock quartet: Greg Geddes, Robert Sedita, N.D. Smart and Laurence Tasse.

| 8/24/68 | 123 | 3 | (As, I Went Down To) Jerusalem ......................... *It's A Monday Kind Of Tuesday* | $7 | | Philips 40531 |

## HELMS, Bobby                                                    C&W/HOT/AC/R&B
Born on 8/15/35 in Bloomington, Indiana. Died on 6/19/97. Country singer/guitarist.

| 7/20/63 | 127 | 1 | Fraulein .................................................. *My Special Angel* [R] | $10 | ☐ | Columbia 42801 |
| | | | new version of his #35 hit in 1957 on Decca 30194 | | | |

## HELTAH SKELTAH                                                        R&B/HOT
Rap duo from Brooklyn: Tawl Sean (a.k.a. Ruck or Sparsky) and Da Rockness Monsta (a.k.a. Rock or Dutch).

| 1/13/96 | 103 | 3 | 1 Blah ......................................... R&B:62 *LeFlaur LeFlah Eshkoshka* (Hot #75) | $3 | ▮ | Priority 53223 |
| | | | THE FABULOUS FIVE FEATURING: HELTAH SKELTAH AND ORIGINOO GUNN CLAPPAZ | | | |
| 6/29/96 | 105 | 7 | 2 Operation Lockdown/ | R&B:64 | | |
| 6/8/96 | 108 | 3 | 3 Da Wiggy ......................................................... R&B:flip | $3 | ▮ | Priority 53232 |
| 11/9/96 | 120 | 3 | 4 Therapy ......................................... R&B:77 *Place To Be* | $3 | ▮ | Priority 53250 |

## HENDERSON, Carl ⊙
R&B vocalist.

| 3/5/66 | 126 | 2 | Sharing You .......................................... *Please Stop Laughing At Me* | $15 | | Omen 13 |

## HENDERSON, Joe                                                       HOT/R&B/AC
Born in 1937 in Como, Mississippi; raised in Gary, Indiana. Died on 10/24/64. R&B singer.

| 2/17/62 | 106 | 1 | 1 Baby Don't Leave Me ........................................ R&B:7 *Right Now* | $12 | | Todd 1066 |
| 5/30/64 | 128 | 2 | 2 You Take One Step (I'll Take Two) ................... *If We Could Start All Over Again* | $12 | | Todd 1096 |

## HENDERSON, Michael                                                     R&B/HOT
Born in 1951 in Yazoo City, Mississippi. R&B singer/bass player. Also see **Norman Connors**.

| 12/25/76+ | 101[6] | 10 | 1 Be My Girl .................................................. R&B:23 *Time* | $5 | | Buddah 552 |
| 8/6/77 | 103 | 3 | 2 I Can't Help It ........................................... R&B:27 *Make Me Feel Better* | $5 | | Budoah 578 |

## HENDERSON, Skitch ⊙                                                     AC
Born Lyle Henderson on 1/27/18 in Halstad, Minnesota. Conducted orchestra for *The Steve Allen Show* and Johnny Carson's *Tonight Show*.

| 1/27/68 | 110 | 4 | Green Green Grass Of Home .......................... AC:30 *Strangers* [I] | $7 | | Columbia 44333 |
| | | | SKITCH HENDERSON HIS PIANO AND HIS ORCHESTRA | | | |
| | | | #11 hit for **Tom Jones** in 1967 | | | |

## HENDRIX, Jimi                                                          HOT
Born on 11/27/42 in Seattle. Died of a drug overdose in London on 9/18/70. Legendary psychedelic-blues guitarist. The Jimi Hendrix Experience was inducted into the Rock and Roll Hall of Fame in 1992. Won Grammy's Lifetime Achievement Award in 1992.

| 10/18/69 | 130 | 2 | Stone Free .................................................. *If 6 Was 9* | $20 | | Reprise 0853 |
| | | | THE JIMI HENDRIX EXPERIENCE | | | |

## HENRY, Clarence                                                       HOT/R&B
Born on 3/19/37 in Algiers, Louisiana. R&B vocalist/pianist/trombonist.

| 11/20/61 | 109 | 2 | 1 Standing In The Need Of Love ..................... *On Bended Knees* (Hot #64) | $15 | | Argo 5401 |
| 5/26/62 | 112 | 1 | 2 Dream Myself A Sweetheart ............................... *Lost Without You* | $15 | | Argo 5414 |
| 12/5/64 | 135 | 1 | 3 Have You Ever Been Lonely ............................. *Little Green Frog* | $12 | | Parrot 45004 |
| | | | CLARENCE "FROGMAN" HENRY | | | |
| | | | #8 hit for Ted Lewis & His Band in 1933; #84 hit for **Teresa Brewer** in 1960 | | | |

## HERMAN'S HERMITS                                                       HOT
Pop group from Manchester, England: Peter "Herman" Noone (vocals), Derek Leckenby (d: 6/4/94, age 48) and Keith Hopwood (guitars), Karl Green (bass), and Barry Whitwam (drums).

| 8/10/68 | 101[3] | 4 | 1 Sunshine Girl .......................................... *Nobody Needs To Know* | $8 | | MGM 13973 |
| 10/12/68 | 131 | 1 | 2 The Most Beautiful Thing In My Life ........... *Ooh She's Done It Again* | $8 | | MGM 13994 |
| 3/1/69 | 130 | 2 | 3 Something's Happening ............ *Little Miss Sorrow Child Of Tomorrow* | $8 | | MGM 14035 |
| 9/14/74 | 101[1] | 2 | 4 Meet Me On The Corner Down At Joe's Cafe.... AC:22 *(Blame It) On The Pony Express* | $6 | | Casablanca 0106 |
| | | | PETER NOONE | | | |

## HERNANDO and THE ORCHESTRA ⊙
| 6/29/59 | 103 | 5 | A Very Precious Love .......................... *Across The Railroad Track* [I] | $15 | | Corsican 0059 |
| | | | #23 hit for **The Ames Brothers** in 1958 (from the movie *Marjorie Morningstar* starring Natalie Wood) | | | |

## HESITATIONS, The                                                      R&B/HOT
R&B group from Cleveland featuring lead singer George "King" Scott who was accidentally killed in February 1968.

| 7/6/68 | 112 | 4 | Who Will Answer ................................ R&B:34 *If You Ever Need A Hand* | $15 | | Kapp 926 |
| | | | #19 hit for **Ed Ames** in 1968 | | | |

## HEYWARD, Nick ⊙                                                        ROK/AC
Born on 5/20/61 in England. Lead guitarist/vocalist of **Haircut One Hundred** from 1981-83.

| 1/15/94 | 107 | 7 | Kite .................................................. ROK:4 *These Words* | $3 | ▮ | Epic 77319 |

## HICKS, Erik ⊙
R&B vocalist.

| 6/19/93 | 115 | 3 | Let's Get Into Something Sexy ..................... Air:74 *(original version)* | $3 | ▮ | Riot/RCA 62573 |

## HIDDEN STRENGTH ⊙                                                       R&B
Jazz-funk group led by singer Roy Herring Jr. and electric pianist Grover Underwood.

| 3/13/76 | 105 | 1 | Hustle On Up (Do The Bump) ............................. R&B:35 *Part 2* | $5 | | United Artists 733 |

## HIGGINS, Monk ✪
**R&B**
Born Milton Bland in 1936 in Menifee, Arkansas. Died on 7/3/86 in Los Angeles. R&B/jazz saxophonist.

| DEBUT | PEAK | WKS | A-side | B-side | $ | Pic | Label & Number |
|---|---|---|---|---|---|---|---|
| 8/6/66 | 117 | 4 | 1 Who-Dun-It?.....................................R&B:30 *These Days Are Filled With You* [I] | | $6 | | St. Lawrence 1013 |
| 6/10/72 | 105 | 1 | 2 Gotta Be Funky.....................................R&B:22 *Big Water Bed* | | $5 | | United Artists 50897 |

**MONK HIGGINS & THE SPECIALTIES**

## HIGH INERGY
**R&B/HOT**
Female R&B vocal group from Pasadena, California: sisters Vernessa and Barbara Mitchell, Linda Howard and Michelle Rumph.

| DEBUT | PEAK | WKS | A-side | B-side | $ | Pic | Label & Number |
|---|---|---|---|---|---|---|---|
| 6/16/79 | 101[1] | 9 | 1 Shoulda Gone Dancin'.....................................R&B:50 *Peaceland* | | $5 | | Gordy 7166 |
| 8/6/83 | 105 | 3 | 2 Back In My Arms Again.....................................*So Right* | | $4 | | Gordy 1688 |

#1 hit for **The Supremes** in 1965

## HIGHTOWER, Willie ✪
**R&B**
Born in Gadsen, Alabama. Blues singer.

| DEBUT | PEAK | WKS | A-side | B-side | $ | Pic | Label & Number |
|---|---|---|---|---|---|---|---|
| 4/12/69 | 130 | 2 | 1 It's A Miracle.....................................R&B:33 *Nobody But You* | | $10 | | Capitol 2226 |
| 5/30/70 | 107 | 3 | 2 Walk A Mile In My Shoes.....................................R&B:26 *You Used Me Baby* | | $8 | | Fame 1465 |

#12 hit for **Joe South** in 1970

## HI-LITES, The ✪
White vocal/instrumental rock and roll band.

| DEBUT | PEAK | WKS | A-side | B-side | $ | Pic | Label & Number |
|---|---|---|---|---|---|---|---|
| 5/1/65 | 128 | 1 | Hey Baby.....................................*Groovey* [I] | | $40 | | Wassel 701 |

#1 hit for **Bruce Channel** in 1962

## HILL, Faith
**C&W/HOT**
Born on 9/21/67 in Jackson, Mississippi. Country singer. Married **Tim McGraw** on 10/6/96.

| DEBUT | PEAK | WKS | A-side | B-side | $ | Pic | Label & Number |
|---|---|---|---|---|---|---|---|
| 4/2/94 | 115 | 6 | 1 Piece Of My Heart.....................................C&W:❶[1] *I Would Be Stronger Than That* | | $3 | ▪ | Warner 18261 |
| 10/28/95 | 122 | 2 | 2 Let's Go To Vegas.....................................C&W:5 *You Will Be Mine* | | $3 | ▪ | Warner 17817 |

#12 hit for **Big Brother And The Holding Company (Janis Joplin)** in 1968

## HILL, Vince ✪
British Adult Contemporary singer.

| DEBUT | PEAK | WKS | A-side | B-side | $ | Pic | Label & Number |
|---|---|---|---|---|---|---|---|
| 4/22/67 | 119 | 2 | Edelweiss.....................................*A Woman Needs Love* | | $8 | | Tower 323 |

with the Eddie Lester Singers; from the musical *The Sound Of Music*

## HILL, Wendy ✪
Pop songstress.

| DEBUT | PEAK | WKS | A-side | B-side | $ | Pic | Label & Number |
|---|---|---|---|---|---|---|---|
| 10/23/61 | 111 | 1 | 1 Without Your Love.....................................*Since You Went Away* | | $15 | | Era 3055 |
| 3/20/65 | 134 | 1 | 2 (Gary, Please Don't Sell) My Diamond Ring.....................................*Donna, Leave My Guy Alone* | | $10 | | Liberty 55771 |

answer song to **Gary Lewis & The Playboys'** 1965 hit "This Diamond Ring"

## HILL, Z.Z.
**R&B/HOT**
Born Arzel Hill on 9/30/35 in Naples, Texas. Died of a heart attack on 4/27/84. Blues singer/guitarist. Formed own Hill Records in 1970.

| DEBUT | PEAK | WKS | A-side | B-side | $ | Pic | Label & Number |
|---|---|---|---|---|---|---|---|
| 8/14/65 | 134 | 1 | 1 Hey Little Girl.....................................*Oh Darlin'* | | $12 | | Kent 427 |
| 10/5/68 | 129 | 2 | 2 You Got What I Need.....................................*Have Mercy Someone* | | $10 | | Kent 494 |
| 10/23/71 | 108 | 1 | 3 Chokin' Kind.....................................R&B:30 *A Man Needs A Woman* | | $7 | | Mankind 12017 |

#13 hit for **Joe Simon** in 1969

| DEBUT | PEAK | WKS | A-side | B-side | $ | Pic | Label & Number |
|---|---|---|---|---|---|---|---|
| 6/9/73 | 114 | 1 | 4 Ain't Nothing You Can Do.....................................R&B:37 *Love In The Street* | | $6 | | United Artists 225 |

#20 hit for **Bobby Bland** in 1964

| DEBUT | PEAK | WKS | A-side | B-side | $ | Pic | Label & Number |
|---|---|---|---|---|---|---|---|
| 10/26/74 | 104 | 4 | 5 I Keep On Lovin' You.....................................R&B:39 *Who Ever's Thrilling You Is Killing Me* | | $6 | | United Artists 536 |
| 8/9/75 | 109 | 1 | 6 I Created A Monster.....................................R&B:40 *Steppin' In The Shoes Of A Fool* | | $6 | | United Artists 631 |
| 9/17/77 | 102 | 6 | 7 Love Is So Good When You're Stealing It.....................................R&B:15 *Need You By My Side* | | $5 | | Columbia 10552 |

## HINES, Simone ✪
**R&B**
Female R&B singer from Trenton, New Jersey. Former backing singer for Michael Bolton.

| DEBUT | PEAK | WKS | A-side | B-side | $ | Pic | Label & Number |
|---|---|---|---|---|---|---|---|
| 9/20/97 | 110 | 8 | Yeah! Yeah! Yeah!.....................................R&B:38 *(2 mixes)* | | $3 | ▪ | Epic 78627 |

## HINTON, Joe
**R&B/HOT**
Born on 11/15/29 in Evansville, Indiana. Died on 8/13/68. R&B singer.

| DEBUT | PEAK | WKS | A-side | B-side | $ | Pic | Label & Number |
|---|---|---|---|---|---|---|---|
| 10/31/64 | 111 | 4 | 1 A Thousand Cups Of Happiness.....................................*If You Love Me* | | $15 | | Back Beat 532 |
| 2/6/65 | 132 | 1 | 2 I Want A Little Girl.....................................R&B:34 *True Love* | | $12 | | Back Beat 545 |

## HIRT, Al
**AC/HOT**
Born Alois Maxwell Hirt on 11/7/22 in New Orleans. Trumpet virtuoso. Toured with Jimmy and Tommy Dorsey.

| DEBUT | PEAK | WKS | A-side | B-side | $ | Pic | Label & Number |
|---|---|---|---|---|---|---|---|
| 6/27/64 | 103 | 1 | 1 Walkin'.....................................*Cotton Candy* (Hot #15) [I] | | $7 | | RCA Victor 8346 |

written by **Jerry Reed**

| DEBUT | PEAK | WKS | A-side | B-side | $ | Pic | Label & Number |
|---|---|---|---|---|---|---|---|
| 2/12/66 | 129 | 1 | 2 The Arena.....................................AC:28 *Yesterday* [I] | | $6 | | RCA Victor 8736 |
| 9/10/66 | 126 | 2 | 3 Green Hornet Theme.....................................*Strawberry Jam* [I] | | $6 | | RCA Victor 8925 |

Billy May (orch.); theme from the TV series *The Green Hornet* starring Van Williams

| DEBUT | PEAK | WKS | A-side | B-side | $ | Pic | Label & Number |
|---|---|---|---|---|---|---|---|
| 1/7/67 | 119 | 5 | 4 Music To Watch Girls By.....................................AC:31 *His Girl* [I] | | $6 | | RCA Victor 9060 |

**AL (He's the King) HIRT, Trumpet** (above 3)
Sid Ramin (orch.); #15 hit for **The Bob Crewe Generation** in 1967

| DEBUT | PEAK | WKS | A-side | B-side | $ | Pic | Label & Number |
|---|---|---|---|---|---|---|---|
| 6/3/67 | 129 | 1 | 5 Puppet On A String.....................................AC:18 *Big Honey* [I] | | $6 | | RCA Victor 9198 |

Al Caiola (orch.)

| DEBUT | PEAK | WKS | A-side | B-side | $ | Pic | Label & Number |
|---|---|---|---|---|---|---|---|
| 4/27/68 | 129 | 2 | 6 We Can Fly/Up-Up And Away.....................................AC:23 *The Glory Of Love* [I] | | $6 | | RCA Victor 9500 |
| 2/8/69 | 116 | 3 | 7 If.....................................AC:16 *Penny Arcade* | | $6 | | RCA Victor 9717 |

#1 hit for **Perry Como** in 1951

## HIT PARADE, The ✪
Pop vocal group headed by Sonny Casella.

| DEBUT | PEAK | WKS | A-side | B-side | $ | Pic | Label & Number |
|---|---|---|---|---|---|---|---|
| 5/10/69 | 131 | 2 | Ah, Ha, Ha, Do Your Thing.....................................*Kisses Never Die* | | $7 | | RCA Victor 9737 |

## HODGES, Eddie
**HOT**
Born on 3/5/47 in Hattiesburg, Mississippi. Played Frank Sinatra's son in the movie *A Hole In The Head*.

| DEBUT | PEAK | WKS | A-side | B-side | $ | Pic | Label & Number |
|---|---|---|---|---|---|---|---|
| 9/7/63 | 118 | 3 | 1 Halfway.....................................*Rainin' In My Heart* | | $12 | | Columbia 42811 |

produced by Terry Melcher of **Bruce & Terry**

| DEBUT | PEAK | WKS | A-side | B-side | $ | Pic | Label & Number |
|---|---|---|---|---|---|---|---|
| 11/6/65 | 134 | 1 | 2 Love Minus Zero.....................................*The Water Is Over My Head* | | $12 | | Aurora 156 |

written and recorded by **Bob Dylan** on his 1965 album *Bringing It All Back Home*; #84 hit for Turley Richards in 1970

**HOLDEN, Ron**  R&B/HOT
Born on 8/7/39 in Seattle. Died on 1/22/97. R&B vocalist. In group The Playboys in 1957.

| 8/8/60 | 106 | 3 | Gee, But I'm Lonesome...............................................*Susie Jane* | $30 | | Donna 1324 |

**HOLIDAY, Jimmy**  R&B/HOT
Born on 7/24/34 in Durant, Mississippi; raised in Waterloo, Iowa. Died of heart failure on 2/15/87. R&B singer/songwriter.

| 6/22/63 | 124 | 1 | 1 Poor Boy...........................................*Don't Laugh* | $12 | | Everest 2027 |
| 11/27/65 | 115 | 5 | 2 The New Breed.................................*Love Me One More Time* | $12 | | Diplomacy 20 |
| 4/1/67 | 116 | 5 | 3 Everybody Needs Help......................R&B:36 *Give Me Your Love* | $10 | | Minit 32016 |
| 7/29/67 | 132 | 1 | 4 I Wanna Help Hurry My Brothers Home..................*We Forgot About Love* | $10 | | Minit 32023 |

**HOLLAND, Amy**  HOT/AC
Daughter of country singer Esmereldy and opera singer Harry Boersma. Married to **Michael McDonald**.

| 6/4/83 | 110 | 1 | Anytime You Want Me......................*I'll Never Give Up* | $4 | ■ | Capitol 5228 |

produced by **Michael McDonald**

**HOLLIDAY, Jennifer**  R&B/HOT
Born on 10/19/60 in Riverside, Texas. Won 1982 Tony award for best actress in Broadway's *Dreamgirls*.

| 12/24/83 | 103 | 5 | Just Let Me Wait.............................R&B:24 *Change Is Gonna Come* | $4 | | Geffen 29432 |

**HOLLIES, The**  HOT/AC
Pop-rock group formed in Manchester, England: Allan Clarke (vocals), **Graham Nash** and Tony Hicks (guitars), Eric Haydock (bass), and Bobby Elliott (drums). *Top Pop Singles*: 23.

| 8/8/64 | 107 | 1 | 1 Here I Go Again.............................*Lucille* | $20 | | Imperial 66044 |
| 8/7/65 | 103 | 4 | 2 I'm Alive     *You Know He Did* | $15 | | Imperial 66119 |
| 11/9/68 | 129 | 1 | 3 Listen To Me................................*Everything Is Sunshine* | $8 | | Epic 10400 |
| 9/4/71 | 110 | 1 | 4 Hey Willy.....................................*Row The Boat Together* | $10 | | Epic 10754 |
| 10/4/75 | 104 | 1 | 5 I'm Down.....................................*Look Out Johnny* | $6 | | Epic 50144 |

**HOLLOWAY, Brenda**  R&B/HOT
Born on 6/21/46 in Atascadero, California. R&B singer/songwriter. Later a backup singer for **Joe Cocker**.

| 9/25/65 | 116 | 3 | 1 You Can Cry On My Shoulder......................*How Many Times Did You Mean It* | $20 | | Tamla 54121 |
| 2/26/66 | 125 | 1 | 2 Together 'Til The End Of Time.........................*Sad Song* | $20 | | Tamla 54125 |

**HOLLY, Buddy**  HOT/R&B
Born Charles Hardin Holley on 9/7/36 in Lubbock, Texas. One of rock and roll's most original and innovative performers. In February 1957, Holly assembled his backing group, **The Crickets**: Jerry Allison (drums), Niki Sullivan (rhythm guitar) and Joe B. Mauldin (bass). Holly (age 22), Ritchie Valens and the Big Bopper were killed in a plane crash near Mason City, Iowa, on 2/3/59. Holly was inducted into the Rock and Roll Hall of Fame in 1986. Also see **The Crickets**.

| 4/27/63 | 116 | 4 | 1 Bo Diddley........................................*True Love Ways* | $50 | | Coral 62352 |

#1 R&B hit for **Bo Diddley** in 1955

| 10/5/63 | 113 | 2 | 2 Brown-Eyed Handsome Man.........................*Wishing* | $40 | | Coral 62369 |

#5 R&B hit for **Chuck Berry** in 1956; above 2 originally recorded in 1956

| 4/26/69 | 105 | 3 | 3 Love Is Strange..................................*You're The One* | $25 | ■ | Coral 62558 |

recorded January 1959; #1 R&B hit for Mickey & Sylvia in 1957; all of above: overdubbed accompaniment by The Fireballs added in 1962

**HOLLYRIDGE STRINGS, The**  HOT
Arranged and conducted by Stu Phillips, later of the Golden Gate Strings.

| 7/18/64 | 134 | 1 | Love Me Do..........................*All My Loving* (Hot #93) [I] | $8 | | Capitol 5207 |

#1 hit for **The Beatles** in 1964

**HOLLYWOOD PERSUADERS, The ☉**

| 9/4/65 | 109 | 4 | Drums A-Go-Go........................*Agua Caliente (Hot Water)* [I] | $20 | | Original Sound 50 |

**HOLMAN, Eddie**  R&B/HOT/AC
Born on 6/3/46 in Norfolk, Virginia. R&B singer/songwriter. Recorded for Leopard in the early 1960s.

| 4/23/66 | 104 | 6 | 1 Don't Stop Now...............................*Eddie's My Name* | $20 | | Parkway 981 |

a new version made the *Hot 100* (#48) on 4/4/70 on ABC 11261

| 10/29/66 | 101[1] | 6 | 2 Am I A Loser (From The Start)......................R&B:17 *You Know That I Will* | $20 | | Parkway 106 |
| 6/20/70 | 115 | 3 | 3 I'll Be There...................................*Cause You're Mine Little Girl* | $10 | | ABC 11265 |

**HOLMES, Clint**  AC/HOT
Born on 5/9/46 in Bournemouth, England; raised in Farnham, New York.

| 9/15/73 | 106 | 4 | Shiddle-ee-dee..........................AC:34 *Like The Fellow Once Said* | $5 | | Epic 11033 |

**HOLMES, "Groove"**  HOT/AC/R&B
Born on 5/2/31 in Camden, New Jersey. Died on 6/29/91 of prostate cancer. Jazz organist. Discovered by **Les McCann**.

| 12/17/66 | 131 | 1 | The More I See You...........................*On The Street Where You Live* [I] | $8 | | Prestige 428 |

#16 hit for **Chris Montez** in 1966

**HOLMES, Rupert**  AC/HOT
Born on 2/24/47 in Cheshire, England. Moved to New York at age six. Member of the studio group Street People.

| 2/14/81 | 103 | 5 | 1 Blackjack.......................................*Crowd Pleaser* | $4 | | MCA 51045 |
| 11/7/81 | 103 | 5 | 2 Loved By The One You Love.................AC:35 *One Born Every Minute* | $4 | | Elektra 47225 |

**HOLY MODAL ROUNDERS, The ☉**
Country-rock group from New York City led by Steve Weber (vocals/guitar) and Peter Stampfel (fiddle).

| 2/2/74 | 103 | 4 | Boobs A Lot....................................*Black Bottom* [N] | $10 | | Metromedia 0201 |

**HOMBRES, The**  HOT
Rock group from Memphis: B.B. Cunningham, Gary Wayne McEwen, Johnny Will Hunter and Jerry Lee Masters.

| 1/13/68 | 113 | 2 | It's A Gas......................................*Am I High* | $12 | | Verve Forecast 5076 |

**HOMER AND JETHRO**  C&W/MEM/POP/HOT
Henry "Homer" Haynes (b: 7/29/17, Knoxville, Tennessee; d: 8/7/71; guitar) and Kenneth "Jethro" Burns (b: 3/10/23, Knoxville, Tennessee; d: 2/4/89; mandolin). Country music's foremost comedy duo from the 1940s until Homer's death.

| 10/3/60 | 101[1] | 2 | Please Help Me, I'm Falling     *Itsy Bitsy Teenie Weenie Yellow Polkadot Bikini* [N] | $15 | | RCA Victor 7790 |

parody of **Hank Locklin**'s #8 hit in 1960; produced by **Chet Atkins**

**HONDELLS, The**           HOT
Rock and roll studio group produced by Gary Usher and **Mike Curb**.

| 10/16/65 | 131 | 2 | 1 Sea Cruise.............................................. *You Meet The Nicest People On A Honda* | $20 | ■ | Mercury 72479 |
| | | | #14 hit for Frankie Ford in 1959 | | | |
| 8/13/66 | 118 | 4 | 2 Kissin' My Life Away........................................ *A Country Love* | $15 | | Mercury 72605 |
| | | | written by **Neil Sedaka** | | | |

**HONEY CONE, The**       R&B/HOT
Female R&B vocal trio from Los Angeles: Carolyn Willis, Edna Wright and Shellie Clark.

| 4/11/70 | 108 | 3 | 1 Take Me With You ........................................ R&B:28 *Take My Love* | $7 | | Hot Wax 7001 |
| 9/19/70 | 117 | 1 | 2 When Will It End ............................................ *Take Me With You* | $7 | | Hot Wax 7005 |
| 10/7/72 | 101¹ | 1 | 3 Innocent Til Proven Guilty      R&B:37 *Don't Send Me An Invitation* | $6 | | Hot Wax 7208 |

**HOPKIN, Mary**       HOT/AC
Born on 5/3/50 in Pontardawe, Wales. Discovered by the model Twiggy. Recorded with the group Hobby Horse in 1972.

| 1/1/72 | 113 | 1 | Water, Paper & Clay ........................................ *Streets Of London* | $8 | | Apple 1843 |

**HORATIO** ☺

| 7/26/69 | 119 | 1 | Age (Where I Started Again) ........................ *Summer Sunsets* | $8 | | Event 3304 |
| | | | written by **Jim Croce**; produced by **Cashman, Pistilli & West** | | | |

**HORNE, Jimmy "Bo"**       R&B/HOT
Born on 9/28/49 in West Palm Beach, Florida. R&B/disco singer.

| 10/6/79 | 101⁴ | 9 | You Get Me Hot      R&B:18 *They Long To Be Close To You* | $5 | | Sunshine Sound 1014 |
| | | | written and produced by Harry Casey of **KC & The Sunshine Band** | | | |

**HORNE, Lena**       MEM/HOT/R&B
Born on 6/30/17 in Brooklyn. Broadway and movie musical star. Won Grammy's Lifetime Achievement Award in 1989.

| 5/30/70 | 119 | 2 | Watch What Happens ........................................ *Rocky Raccoon* | $7 | | Skye 4523 |
| | | | Gabor Szabo (guitar); featured in the 1964 French movie *The Umbrellas Of Cherbourg* | | | |

**HORNSBY, Bruce**       AC/ROK/HOT/C&W
Born on 11/23/54 in Williamsburg, Virginia. Singer/pianist/songwriter/leader of jazz-influenced pop quintet, The Range. Won 1986 Best New Artist Grammy Award.

| 1/29/94 | 121 | 1 | Rainbow's Cadillac ........................................ AC:27 *Imagine (live)* | $3 | ▌ | RCA 62724 |
| | | | Bonnie Raitt (backing vocal) | | | |

**HORTON, Johnny**       C&W/HOT
Born on 4/30/25 in Los Angeles; raised in Tyler, Texas. Killed in an auto accident on 11/5/60. Country singer.

| 9/4/61 | 110 | 4 | Ole Slew-Foot ........................................ *Miss Marcy* | $12 | ■ | Columbia 42063 |

**HOT BUTTER**       AC/HOT
Hot Butter is Moog synthesizer player Stan Free.

| 1/20/73 | 105 | 3 | 1 Tequila........................................ *Hot Butter* [I] | $6 | | Musicor 1468 |
| | | | #1 hit for **The Champs** in 1958 | | | |
| 4/21/73 | 106 | 4 | 2 Percolator........................................ AC:19 *Tristana* [I] | $6 | | Musicor 1473 |
| | | | #10 hit for Billy Joe & The Checkmates in 1962 | | | |

**HOUNDS** ☺
Rock group from Chicago: John Hunter (vocals, keyboards), Don Griffin and Glen Rupp (guitars), Joe Cuttone (bass) and Michael Neff (drums).

| 12/8/79 | 110 | 1 | Under My Thumb........................................ *The Moth And The Fire* | $6 | | Columbia 11159 |
| | | | recorded by **The Rolling Stones** for their 1966 album *Aftermath* | | | |

**HOUSTON, Cissy**       R&B/HOT
Born Emily Houston in 1933 in Newark, New Jersey. Began career singing with a family gospel group, the Drinkard Singers, which included her nieces **Dionne** and **Dee Dee Warwick**. Lead singer of **The Sweet Inspirations**, 1967-70. Mother of Whitney Houston.

| 6/20/70 | 125 | 1 | 1 I'll Be There ........................................ R&B:45 *He - I Believe* | $7 | | Common. United 3010 |
| | | | written by **Bobby Darin**; #14 hit for Gerry & The Pacemakers in 1965 | | | |
| 10/14/78 | 106 | 4 | 2 Think It Over ........................................ R&B:32 *An Umbrella Song* | $5 | | Private Stock 45,204 |

**HOUSTON, David**       C&W/HOT/AC
Born on 12/9/38 in Bossier City, Louisiana. Died on 11/30/93. Country singer/songwriter/guitarist.

| 11/23/63 | 132 | 1 | 1 Mountain Of Love ........................................ C&W:2 *Angeline* | $10 | | Epic 9625 |
| 9/4/65 | 117 | 5 | 2 Livin' In A House Full Of Love ........................ C&W:3 *Cowpoke* | $8 | | Epic 9831 |
| 12/10/66 | 133 | 1 | 3 Where Could I Go? (But To Her)/      C&W:14 | | | |
| 12/31/66 | 135 | 1 | 4   A Loser's Cathedral ........................................ C&W:3 | $8 | ■ | Epic 10102 |

**HUDSON, Al, & The Partners** ☺       R&B
Detroit-based R&B band led by vocalist Hudson. In 1980 began recording as One Way.

| 8/25/79 | 101⁶ | 9 | You Can Do It      R&B:52 *I Don't Want You To Leave Me* | $5 | | MCA 12459 |
| | | | also released on ABC 12459 | | | |

**HUDSON, Jerry** ☺
Pop/rock vocalist/guitarist. Former member of Cognition and The Road.

| 2/10/73 | 117 | 2 | Gillian Frank ........................................ *I'll Feel A Whole Lot Better* | $7 | | Big Tree 159 |

**HUDSON BROTHERS**       HOT
Brothers Bill, Brett and Mark Hudson from Portland. Own TV variety show during the summer of 1974.

| 3/18/72 | 110 | 4 | 1 Leavin' It's Over........................................ *Someday* | $6 | | Playboy 50001 |
| | | | HUDSON | | | |
| 1/25/75 | 108 | 5 | 2 Coochie Coochie Coo ........................................ *Me And My Guitar* | $5 | | Casablanca 816 |

**HUGHES, Carol** ☺

| 2/1/60 | 114 | 1 | Let Me Go Lover ........................................ *When Did I Fall In Love* | $10 | | RCA Victor 7665 |
| | | | Hugo Peretti (orch.); #1 hit for Joan Weber in 1955 | | | |

**HUGHES, Jimmy**       R&B/HOT
Born in Florence, Alabama. Died of cancer on 4/1/97 (age 62). R&B singer. Cousin of **Percy Sledge**.

| 7/8/67 | 121 | 1 | Don't Lose Your Good Thing ........................ *You Can't Believe Everything You Hear* | $12 | | Fame 1014 |

**HUGHES, Rhetta ✪**  R&B
R&B singer/actress. Sister of keyboardist Tenison Stephens; with Stephens as a duo in Dallas. Starred on Broadway's *Dreamgirls*.

| 1/18/69 | 102 | 6 | Light My Fire ........................................................ R&B:36 *Sooky* | $8 | | Tetragrammaton 1513 |

#1 hit for **The Doors** in 1967

**HULLABALLOOS, The**  HOT
Bleached blond rock and roll quartet from England: Ricky Knight, Harry Dunn, Andy Woonton and Geoff Mortimer.

| 5/1/65 | 121 | 2 | Learning The Game ........................................................*Don't Stop* | $20 | ■ | Roulette 4612 |

written by Buddy Holly

**HUMBLE PIE**  HOT/ROK
Hard-rock band formed in Essex, England featuring Steve Marriott (vocals, guitar; **Small Faces**; d: 4/20/91, age 44). Peter Frampton was a member, 1968-71.

| 4/7/73 | 113 | 5 | 1 Black Coffee ........................................................*Say No More* | $7 | ■ | A&M 1406 |

written by Ike & Tina Turner

| 8/2/75 | 105 | 2 | 2 Rock And Roll Music ........................................................*Road Hog* | $6 | | A&M 1711 |

#8 hit for **Chuck Berry** in 1957

**HUMMERS, The ✪**  C&W

| 8/25/73 | 104 | 2 | Old Betsy Goes Boing, Boing, Boing .... C&W:38 *One Good Thing About Being Down* [N] | $6 | | Capitol 3646 |

adapted from a Mazda jingle

**HUMPERDINCK, Engelbert**  AC/HOT/C&W
Born Arnold George Dorsey on 5/2/36 in Madras, India. To Leicester, England, in 1947. *Top Pop Singles*: 23.

| 12/6/75 | 102 | 9 | This Is What You Mean To Me ........................................ AC:14 *World Without Music* | $6 | | Parrot 40085 |

**HUMPHREY, Bobbi ✪**  R&B
Born Barbara Ann Humphrey on 4/25/50 in Dallas. Jazz flutist. First recorded for Blue Note in 1971.

| 5/4/74 | 106 | 3 | Chicago, Damn........................................................ R&B:49 *Just A Love Child* | $6 | | Blue Note 395 |

**HUMPHREY, Paul**  R&B/HOT
Born on 10/12/35 in Detroit. Jazz session drummer.

| 8/14/71 | 109 | 2 | Funky L.A. ........................................................ R&B:45 *Baby Rice* | $7 | | Lizard 1009 |

PAUL HUMPHREY & His Cool Aid Chemists

**HUNT, Tommy**  HOT/R&B
Born on 6/18/33 in Pittsburgh. R&B singer. Former member of The Five Echoes and **The Flamingos**.

| 8/15/64 | 119 | 2 | 1 I Just Don't Know What To Do With Myself ................................ *And I Never Knew* | $12 | | Scepter 1236 |

#26 hit for **Dionne Warwick** in 1966

| 2/18/67 | 124 | 4 | 2 The Biggest Man ........................................ R&B:29 *Never Love A Robin* | $12 | | Dynamo 101 |

**HUNTER, Ian**  ROK/HOT
Born on 6/3/46 in Shrewsbury, England. Rock singer/guitarist. Leader of Mott The Hoople, 1969-74.

| 6/2/79 | 108 | 1 | 1 When The Daylight Comes ........................................................*Life After Death* | $5 | | Chrysalis 2324 |
| 7/5/80 | 108 | 2 | 2 We Gotta' Get Out Of Here ........................................................*Sons And Daughters* | $5 | | Chrysalis 2405 |

Ellen Foley (female vocal)

**HUNTER, Ty ✪**  R&B
Born in 1943. Died on 2/24/81. R&B singer. Member of **The Originals** and **The Glass House**.

| 1/16/61 | 110 | 2 | Free ........................................................*Everytime* | $30 | | Anna 1123 |

TY HUNTER & The Voice Masters
answer song to **Sam Cooke**'s 1960 hit "Chain Gang"

**HURRICANE G ✪**  R&B
Female rapper from Puerto Rico. G stands for Gloria.

| 10/11/97 | 119 | 2 | Somebody Else ........................................................ R&B:54 *(LP version)* | $3 | ■ | H.O.L.A. 341026 |

samples "You Gonna Make Me Love Somebody Else" by The Jones Girls

**HUTTON, Danny**  HOT
Born on 9/10/42 in Buncrana, Ireland; raised in U.S. Leader and one of the vocalists of **Three Dog Night**.

| 1/8/66 | 102 | 7 | 1 Big Bright Eyes ........................................................*Monster Shindig Pt. 2* | $15 | | HBR 453 |
| 5/28/66 | 120 | 2 | 2 Funny How Love Can Be ........................................................*Dreamin' Isn't Good For You* | $10 | ■ | MGM 13502 |

Gene Page (orch.); #74 hit for First Class in 1975

**HYLAND, Brian**  HOT/R&B
Born on 11/12/43 in Queens, New York. Pop singer. Own group, the Delphis, at age 12. In production company with **Del Shannon** in 1970. *Top Pop Singles*: 22.

| 12/31/60+ | 101[1] | 2 | 1 I Gotta Go ('Cause I Love You)/ | | | |

written by John D. Loudermilk

| 12/31/60 | 105 | 1 | 2 Lop-Sided Over-Loaded (And It Wiggled When We Rode It) ........................ [N] | $15 | ■ | Kapp 363 |
| 11/9/63 | 123 | 2 | 3 Let Us Make Our Own Mistakes ........................................................*Nothing Matters But You* | $10 | | ABC-Paramount 10494 |
| 3/21/64 | 129 | 2 | 4 Here's To Our Love........................................................*Two Kinds Of Girls* | $8 | ■ | Philips 40179 |
| 6/26/71 | 120 | 2 | 5 So Long, Marianne ........................................................*No Place To Run* | $6 | | Uni 55287 |

written and recorded by Leonard Cohen on his 1968 album *Songs Of Leonard Cohen*; produced by **Del Shannon**

**HYMAN, Dick**  HOT/R&B/MEM
Born on 3/8/27 in New York City. Pianist/composer/conductor/arranger.

| 3/9/68 | 106 | 6 | 1 In The Heat Of The Night........................................................*Respect* [I] | $8 | | Command 4114 |

DICK HYMAN And "The Group"
from the movie starring Sidney Poitier

| 9/6/69 | 109 | 4 | 2 Green Onions/ | | | [I] | | | |

#3 hit for **Booker T. & The MG's** in 1962

| 8/16/69 | 126 | 2 | 3 Aquarius ........................................................[I] | $8 | | Command/ABC 4129 |

from the rock musical *Hair*; #1 hit for **The 5th Dimension** in 1969

**HYMAN, Phyllis ✪**  R&B
Born on 7/6/41 in Philadelphia. Committed suicide on 6/30/95. R&B singer/actress.

| 1/15/77 | 102 | 8 | 1 Betcha By Golly Wow ........................................................ R&B:29 *Kwasi (Connors)* | $5 | | Buddah 554 |

NORMAN CONNORS (Featuring PHYLLIS HYMAN)
#3 hit for The Stylistics in 1972

| DEBUT | PEAK | WKS | A-side (Chart Hit)..................................................................................B-side | $ | Pic | Label & Number |
|---|---|---|---|---|---|---|

**HYMAN, Phyllis — Cont'd**

| 5/21/77 | 103 | 3 | 2 Loving You - Losing You .............................. R&B:32 *Children Of The World* | $5 | | Buddah 567 |
| 2/2/80 | 101¹ | 6 | 3 You Know How To Love Me          R&B:12 *Give A Little More* | $4 | | Arista 0463 |

**HYPNOTICS ○**
R&B vocal group.

| 4/21/73 | 115 | 5 | Beware Of The Stranger ............................................. *Memories* | $7 | | Reprise 1140 |

**IAN, Janis**                                                                    AC/HOT
Born Janis Eddy Fink on 4/7/51 in New York City. Folk-styled singer/songwriter/pianist/guitarist.

| 12/9/67 | 109 | 2 | 1 Insanity Comes Quietly To The Structured Mind .......... *Sunflakes Fall, Snowrays Call* | $10 | | Verve Forecast 5072 |
| 7/13/74 | 104 | 2 | 2 The Man You Are In Me................................. AC:33 *Jesse* | $5 | | Columbia 46034 |

**IAN AND SYLVIA ○**
Canadian folk-country duo: Ian Tyson (b: 9/25/33) and wife Sylvia Fricker (b: 9/19/40). Wrote "You Were On My Mind."

| 7/8/67 | 101¹ | 9 | Lovin' Sound          *Pilgrimmage To Paradise* | $8 | | MGM 13686 |

**IAN & THE ZODIACS ○**
Rock and roll band formed in Liverpool, England — Ian Edwards, lead singer.

| 7/31/65 | 131 | 1 | So Much In Love With You ............................. *This Empty Place* | $10 | ■ | Philips 40291 |

**ICE CUBE**                                                                    R&B/HOT
Born O'Shea Jackson on 6/15/69 in Los Angeles. Rapper/actor. Formerly with the Los Angeles rap group N.W.A.

| 2/15/97 | 107 | 11 | The World Is Mine ........................... R&B:55 *(2 versions)* | $6 | ■ | Jive 42398 (T) |

Mack 10 and K-Dee (backing vocals); from the movie *Dangerous Ground* starring Ice Cube

**ICE-T**                                                                    R&B/HOT
Born Tracy Morrow on 2/16/58 in Newark, New Jersey. Male rapper/actor.

| 6/1/96 | 114 | 3 | I Must Stand................................R&B:83 *Where The Shit Goes Down* | $3 | ▮ | Rhyme Syndicate 53210 |

Angela Rollins (backing vocal)

**IDEALS, The ○**                                                               R&B
R&B group from Chicago: Robert Tharp, Reggie Jackson, Leonard Mitchell, Sam Stewart and Eddie Williams.

| 10/12/63 | 127 | 1 | The Gorilla ........................................ *Don Juan* | $20 | | Cortland 110 |

**IDES OF MARCH, The**                                                          HOT
Rock and roll band from Chicago: Jim Peterik (vocals, guitar), Ray Herr (guitar), Larry Millas (keyboards), John Larson and Chuck Soumar (horns), Bob Bergland (bass), and Mike Borch (drums).

| 10/3/70 | 122 | 1 | 1 Melody ..................................... *The Sky Is Falling* | $7 | | Warner 7426 |
| 7/31/71 | 113 | 3 | 2 Tie-Dye Princess ................................ *Friends Of Feeling* | $7 | | Warner 7507 |

**IDOL, Billy**                                                                 ROK/HOT
Born William Broad on 11/30/55 in Stanmore, Middlesex, England. Leader of the London punk band Generation X from 1977-81.

| 9/26/81 | 107 | 3 | 1 Mony Mony ................................... *Baby Talk* | $6 | | Chrysalis 2543 |

Idol's "live" version made the *Hot 100* (#1) in 1987 on Chrysalis 43161

| 11/27/82 | 108 | 2 | 2 White Wedding ........................ROK:4 *Dead On Arrival* | $5 | | Chrysalis 2648 |

same version made the *Hot 100* (#36) on 5/21/83 on Chrysalis 42697

| 9/10/83 | 102 | 10 | 3 Dancing With Myself ...................... *Love Calling (Rub A Dub Dub Mix)* | $4 | ■ | Chrysalis 42723 |

with Generation X

| 7/3/93 | 105 | 5 | 4 Shock To The System ...................ROK:7 *Aftershock* | $3 | ▮ | Chrysalis 24825 |

**IFIELD, Frank**                                                              HOT/C&W/AC
Born on 11/30/37 in Coventry, England. Began career as a teenager in Australia with his own radio and TV shows.

| 3/30/63 | 104 | 2 | 1 The Wayward Wind ................................. *I'm Smiling Now* | $10 | | Vee-Jay 499 |

#1 hit for Gogi Grant in 1956

| 3/21/64 | 128 | 1 | 2 Don't Blame Me .............................. *Say It Isn't So* | $8 | | Capitol 5134 |

#6 hit for Ethel Waters in 1933; #20 hit for **The Everly Brothers** in 1961; Norrie Paramor (orch., above 2)

| 7/1/67 | 132 | 2 | 3 Out Of Nowhere .................................... *Kaw-Liga* | $8 | | Hickory 1454 |

Reg Guest (orch.); #1 hit for **Bing Crosby** in 1931

**IGLESIAS, Julio**                                                            AC/HOT/C&W/R&B
Born on 9/23/43 in Madrid. Spanish singer, immensely popular worldwide.

| 4/30/83 | 105 | 2 | 1 Amor ....................... AC:30 *Nostalgie (French)* | $3 | ■ | Columbia 03805 |

sung in Spanish and English; #2 hit for **Bing Crosby** in 1944; #18 hit for **Ben E. King** in 1961

| 10/20/84 | 102 | 2 | 2 Moonlight Lady.............................. AC:17 *If (E Poi)* | $3 | ■ | Columbia 04645 |

**IKETTES, The**                                                              HOT/R&B
Female R&B trio formed for the Ike & Tina Turner Revue: Vanetta Fields, Robbie Montgomery and Jessie Smith.

| 5/11/63 | 126 | 1 | 1 No Bail In This Jail (Prisoner In Love) ...................... *Those Words* | $15 | | Teena 1702 |

laughing sounds by **Tina Turner**

| 2/13/65 | 107 | 2 | 2 Camel Walk ................................ *Nobody Loves Me* | $10 | | Modern 1003 |

THE IKETTS

| 5/29/65 | 125 | 2 | 3 (He's Gonna Be) Fine, Fine, Fine ....................... *How Come* | $10 | | Modern 1008 |
| 1/22/66 | 122 | 3 | 4 (Never More) Lonely For You ...................... *Sally Go Round The Roses* | $10 | | Modern 1015 |

**ILL Featuring AL SKRATCH**                                                   R&B/HOT
Male rap duo from New York City: ILL (I Lyrical Lord) and Al Skratch.

| 5/28/94 | 103 | 13 | Where My Homiez? (Come Around My Way) .................. Sls:59 /R&B:34 *(instrumental)* | $3 | ▮ | Mercury 858462 |

| DEBUG | PEAK | WKS | A-side (Chart Hit)..............................................................................B-side | $ | Pic | Label & Number |
|---|---|---|---|---|---|---|

**ILLUSION, The**                         HOT
Rock quintet from Long Island, New York: John Vinci (vocals), Richie Cerniglia (guitar), Mike Maniscalco (keyboards), Chuck Adler (bass) and Mike Ricciardella (drums).

| 10/11/69 | **110** | 4 | How Does It Feel .................................................................... *Once In A Lifetime* | $7 | | Steed 721 |

**IMAGINATION** ⊙                  R&B
London R&B trio formed in 1981: Leee John (vocals), Ashley Ingram (keyboards) and Errol Kennedy (drums).

| 7/3/82 | **102** | 5 | Just An Illusion ...................................................... **R&B:27** *(instrumental)* | $4 | | MCA 52067 |

**IMMATURE**                      R&B/HOT
Teenage male R&B vocal trio from Los Angeles: Marques Houston, Jerome Jones and Kelton Kessee.

| 2/25/95 | **103** | 14 | 1 Is It Me? ................................................................... **R&B:32** *(smooth edit)* | $3 | ▌ | MCA 54990 |
| | | |     **MONTECO featuring Immature** | | | |
| 9/28/96+ | **102** | 13 | 2 Lover's Groove ...................................... **Sls:64 /R&B:42** *(remix)* (w/Shyheim) | $3 | ▌ | MCA 55234 |

**IMMORTALS, The** ⊙
Studio group assembled by songwriter/producer Oliver Adams.

| 9/16/95 | **118** | 4 | Mortal Kombat........................................................................ *(4 mixes)* | $6 | | Vernon Yard 38419 **(CD)** |
| | | |     title song from the movie starring Christopher Lambert | | | |

**IMPACT**                     R&B/HOT
R&B group from Baltimore: Damon Otis Harris (vocals), John Simms, Charles Timmons and Donald Tilghman. Harris was a member of **The Temptations**, 1971-75.

| 8/14/76 | **102** | 1 | 1 Give A Broken Heart A Break ................................. **R&B:36** *Love Attack* | $6 | | Atco/WMOT 7056 |
| 11/6/76 | **107** | 1 | 2 One Last Memory .................................................. *Winning Combination* | $6 | | Atco/WMOT 7064 |

**IMPRESSIONS, The**                R&B/HOT
R&B group formed in Chicago in 1957: **Jerry Butler**, **Curtis Mayfield**, Sam Gooden and brothers Arthur and Richard Brooks. Butler left in 1958, replaced by Fred Cash. The Brooks brothers left in 1962. Mayfield left in 1970, replaced by Leroy Hutson. Group inducted into the Rock and Roll Hall of Fame in 1991. *Top Pop Singles*: 39.

| 10/13/62 | **113** | 6 | 1 Minstrel And Queen ...............................................*You've Come Home* | $15 | | ABC-Paramount 10357 |
| 2/20/65 | **133** | 1 | 2 I've Been Trying ...............................**R&B:35** *People Get Ready* (Hot #14) | $12 | | ABC-Paramount 10622 |
| 2/22/69 | **104** | 3 | 3 My Deceiving Heart ..............................**R&B:23** *You Want Somebody Else* | $6 | | Curtom 1937 |
| 12/20/69 | **110** | 4 | 4 Amen (1970)/                         **R&B:44** [R] | | | |
| | | |     new version of their 1964 *Hot 100* hit (#7) on ABC-Paramount 10602 | | | |
| 1/24/70 | **128** | 2 | 5 Wherever She Leadeth Me .................................................... **R&B:31** | $6 | | Curtom 1948 |
| 2/7/76 | **103** | 5 | 6 Loving Power                 **R&B:11** *First Impressions* | $5 | | Curtom 0110 |

**INCREDIBLE BONGO BAND, The**      R&B/HOT/AC
Studio band assembled in Canada by producer Michael Viner.

| 10/20/73 | **107** | 7 | Let There Be Drums................................**R&B:90** *Dueling Bongos* [I] | $6 | | MGM 14635 |
| | | |     #7 hit for Sandy Nelson in 1961 | | | |

**INCREDIBLES, The** ⊙                R&B
R&B group formed in Los Angeles in 1963: Cal Waymon, Carl Gilbert, Jean Smith and Alda Denise Edwards.

| 12/10/66 | **108** | 2 | 1 I'll Make It Easy (If You'll Come On Home) ....................**R&B:39** *Crying Heart* | $20 | | Audio Arts! 60,001 |
| 7/29/67 | **122** | 3 | 2 Heart And Soul ...................................... **R&B:45** *I Found Another Love* | $20 | | Audio Arts! 60,007 |
| | | |     #1 hit for Larry Clinton with Bea Wain in 1938; #18 hit for The Cleftones in 1961 | | | |

**IN CROWD — see JON & ROBIN**

**INDEEP** ⊙                   R&B
Dance group led by writer/producer Michael Cleveland with female singers Reggie Megliore and Rose Marie Ramsey.

| 2/26/83 | **101**[2] | 6 | Last Night A D.J. Saved My Life      **R&B:10** *D.J. Delight* | $4 | | Sound Of New York 602 |
| | | |     also released as a 12" single on Sound Of New York 5102 | | | |

**INDEPENDENTS, The**               R&B/HOT
R&B vocal group: Chuck Jackson, Maurice Jackson, Helen Curry and Eric Thomas.

| 10/28/72 | **113** | 2 | 1 I Just Want To Be There................................**R&B:38** *Can't Understand It* | $7 | | Wand 11249 |
| 1/19/74 | **103** | 11 | 2 The First Time We Met.......................................... **R&B:20** *Show Me How* | $7 | | Wand 11267 |

**INFORMATION SOCIETY**         HOT/ROK/R&B
Techno-dance group formed in Minneapolis in 1985 featuring Paul Robb (songwriter) and Kurt Valaquen (vocals).

| 12/5/92 | **118** | 2 | Peace & Love Inc. ............................. *(4 versions) / To The City* | $5 | ▌ | Tommy Boy 544 * |

**INGRAM, James**                 R&B/AC/HOT
Born on 2/16/56 in Akron, Ohio. R&B vocalist/multi-instrumentalist/composer. Former member of the band Revelation Funk.

| 10/22/83 | **101**[1] | 3 | 1 Party Animal       **R&B:21** *Come A Da Machine (To Take A My Place)* [I] | $4 | | Qwest 29493 |
| 7/1/95 | **111** | 5 | 2 When You Love Someone ............................ **AC:39 /R&B:71** *My Funny Valentine* (Baker) | $3 | ▌ | Elektra 64415 |
| | | |     **ANITA BAKER & JAMES INGRAM** | | | |
| | | |     from the movie *Forget Paris* starring Billy Crystal | | | |

**INGRAM, Luther**                 R&B/HOT
Born on 11/30/44 in Jackson, Tennessee. R&B singer/songwriter. Sang in gospel group with his brothers.

| 11/7/70 | **110** | 3 | 1 To The Other Man ...............................**R&B:22** *I'll Just Call You Honey* | $10 | | KoKo 2106 |
| | | |     answer song to **Doris Duke**'s 1970 hit "To The Other Woman" | | | |
| 2/26/72 | **108** | 6 | 2 Missing You ...................................**R&B:26** *You Were Made For Me* (Hot #93) | $8 | | KoKo 2110 |

**INI featuring Pete Rock** ⊙         R&B
Duo of rappers Rob-O and **Pete Rock**.

| 6/15/96 | **115** | 2 | Fakin Jax ...................................................... **R&B:71** *(remix)* | $3 | ▌ | Elektra 64293 |
| | | |     samples "Give Up The Goods" by **Mobb Deep** | | | |

**INMATES, The**                   HOT
British rock group: Bill Hurley (vocals), Peter Gunn (lead guitar), Tony Oliver (rhythm guitar) and Ben Donnelly (bass).

| 2/16/80 | **107** | 2 | The Walk ...................................................... *Back In History* | $5 | | Polydor 2058 |
| | | |     #7 hit for **Jimmy McCracklin** in 1958 | | | |

**INNERVISION** ☺     R&B
R&B vocal group.

| 5/31/75 | 106 | 3 | Honey Baby (Be Mine)................................R&B:58 *We're Innervision* | $6 | | Private Stock 45,015 |

**INNOCENCE MISSION, The** ☺     ROK
Modern rock quartet from Lancaster, Pennsylvania: Don Peris (guitar) and his wife Karen (vocals) with Mike Bitts (bass) and Steve Brown (drums).

| 8/26/95 | 117 | 3 | Bright As Yellow................................ROK:33 *Let's Talk About Something Else / That Was Another Country/ Geranium Lake* | $6 | | A&M 0967 (CD) |

**INSTANT FUNK**     R&B/HOT
Funk group from Philadelphia featuring James Carmichael (vocals). Former backup band for **Bunny Sigler**.

| 2/2/80 | 103 | 4 | Bodyshine..................................R&B:41 *Scream And Shout* | $5 | | Salsoul 2112 |

**IN TRANSIT** ☺     ROK
Rock group led by singer Don Dunn and guitarist Clark Garman.

| 8/2/80 | 107 | 3 | Turn On Your Light .................................. *Too High For Heaven* | $5 | | RCA 12045 |

**INTRIGUE** ☺     R&B
R&B male vocal trio: Audley Wiggan and brothers Jason and Anthony Harper.

| 4/20/96 | 122 | 1 | Dance With Me................................R&B:91 *(remix)* | $3 | ∎ | Universal 56000 |

#15 hit for **The Drifters** in 1959

**INTRO**     R&B/HOT
R&B vocal trio from New York: Kenny Greene, Clinton Wike and Jeff Sanders.

| 3/20/93 | 111 | 8 | 1 Love Thang!!! ................................R&B:28 *(jazz version)* | $3 | ∎ | Atlantic 87416 |
| 7/31/93 | 112 | 6 | 2 Let Me Be The One................................R&B:23 *Anything For You (Don't Run Away)* | $3 | ∎ | Atlantic 87347 |

samples "Gotta Have It" by Ed O. G & Da Bulldogs and "Singing A Song For My Mother" by **Bohannon**

| 3/12/94 | 105 | 8 | 3 Ribbon In The Sky ................................Sls:72 /R&B:11 *(album version)* | $3 | ∎ | Atlantic 87269 |

#54 hit for **Stevie Wonder** in 1982

| 3/2/96 | 117 | 3 | 4 Feels Like The First Time ................................R&B:52 *Funny How Time Flies (2 versions)* | $3 | ∎ | Atlantic 87080 |

**INTRUDERS, The**     R&B/HOT
R&B vocal group from Philadelphia: Sam "Little Sonny" Brown, Eugene Daughtry (d: 12/25/94, age 55), Phil Terry and Robert Edwards.

| 2/8/69 | 104 | 3 | 1 Give Her A Transplant ................................R&B:23 *Girls Girls Girls* | $10 | | Gamble 223 |
| 6/14/69 | 101[1] | 4 | 2 Lollipop (I Like You)     R&B:22 *Don't Give It Away (Don't Be A Fool)* | $10 | | Gamble 231 |
| 3/28/70 | 119 | 2 | 3 Tender (Was The Love We Knew) ................................R&B:25 *By The Time I Get To Phoenix* | $10 | | Gamble 4001 |
| 7/3/71 | 105 | 5 | 4 Pray For Me ................................R&B:25 *Best Days Of My Life* | $10 | | Gamble 4014 |

**INVITATIONS, The** ☺     R&B
R&B group from New York City: Herman Colefield, Gary Gant, Billy Morris and Bobby Rivers.

| 7/10/65 | 111 | 5 | 1 Hallelujah ................................ *Written On The Wall* | $25 | | DynoVoice 206 |
| 6/16/73 | 110 | 4 | 2 They Say The Girl's Crazy ................................R&B:17 *For Your Precious Love* | $10 | | Silver Blue 801 |

**INXS**     ROK/HOT/AC/R&B
Rock sextet formed in Sydney, Australia: Michael Hutchence (lead singer; d: 11/22/97, age 37), Kirk Pengilly (guitar, sax), Garry Beers (bass) and brothers Tim (guitar), Andy (keyboards, guitar) and Jon (drums) Farriss.

| 12/5/92 | 101[1] | 7 | Taste It ................................ROK:5 *11th Revolution* | $4 | ∎ | Atlantic 87409 |

**IRISH ROVERS, The**     AC/HOT/C&W
Irish-born folk quintet formed in 1964 in Alberta, Canada: brothers Will (vocals, drums) and George (guitar) Millar, their cousin Joe Millar (bass), Jimmy Ferguson (vocals) and Wilcil McDowell (keyboards).

| 2/15/69 | 113 | 8 | Lily The Pink ................................AC:15 *Mrs. Crandall's Boardinghouse* [N] | $7 | | Decca 32444 |

**IRON BUTTERFLY**     HOT
Heavy-metal band from San Diego featuring Doug Ingle (vocals, keyboards).

| 10/11/69 | 118 | 2 | 1 I Can't Help But Deceive You Little Girl ................................ *To Be Alone* | $8 | | Atco 6712 |
| 12/27/75 | 108 | 3 | 2 Beyond The Milky Way ................................ *Get It Out* | $6 | | MCA 40493 |

**IRWIN, Big Dee — see GALORE, Mamie**

**ISAAK, Chris**     ROK/AC/HOT
Born on 6/26/56 in Stockton, California. Rockabilly singer/songwriter/guitarist/actor.

| 4/24/93 | 105 | 11 | 1 Can't Do A Thing (To Stop Me) ................................ROK:7 / AC:11 *Lonely With A Broken Heart* | $3 | ∎ | Reprise 18604 |
| 12/16/95+ | 102 | 9 | 2 Go Walking Down There ................................ROK:32 *Things Go Wrong* | $3 | ∎ | Reprise 17781 |

**ISLAND INSPIRATIONAL ALL-STARS** ☺     R&B
Gathering of top gospel artists: Kirk Franklin, Donald Lawrence, Karen Clark-Sheard and Hezekiah Walker.

| 1/27/96 | 108 | 2 | Don't Give Up ................................R&B:28 *The First Noel* | $3 | ∎ | Island 854478 |

from the movie *Don't Be A Menace* starring Shawn and Marlon Wayans

**ISLEY BROTHERS, The**     R&B/HOT/ROK/AC
R&B trio of brothers from Cincinnati: O'Kelly (d: 3/31/86), Ronald and Rudolph Isley. Trio added their younger brothers Ernie and Marvin Isley and brother-in-law Chris Jasper in September 1969. Ronald became the featured member beginning in 1989. Group inducted into the Rock and Roll Hall of Fame in 1992. *Top Pop Singles: 41.*

| 1/26/63 | 106 | 4 | 1 Nobody But Me ................................ *I'm Laughing To Keep From Crying* | $20 | | Wand 131 |

#8 hit for The Human Beinz in 1968

| 3/27/65 | 131 | 1 | 2 Simon Says ................................ *Wild As A Tiger* | $20 | | Atlantic 2277 |
| 9/17/66 | 110 | 1 | 3 Love Is A Wonderful Thing ................................ *Open Up Her Eyes* | $20 | | Veep 1230 |

#4 hit for Michael Bolton in 1991 (based on a court ruling)

| 8/5/67 | 125 | 3 | 4 That's The Way Love Is ................................ *One Too Many Heartaches* | $15 | | Tamla 54154 |

#7 hit for Marvin Gaye in 1969

| 4/13/68 | 121 | 5 | 5 Take Me In Your Arms (Rock Me A Little While) ...... R&B:22 *Why When Love Is Gone* | $15 | | Tamla 54164 |

#11 hit for The Doobie Brothers in 1975

| 12/6/69 | 105 | 3 | 6 Bless Your Heart ................................R&B:29 *Give The Women What They Want* | $6 | | T-Neck 912 |
| 4/25/70 | 113 | 4 | 7 If He Can, You Can ................................R&B:21 *Holdin' On* | $6 | | T-Neck 919 |
| 4/3/71 | 111 | 4 | 8 Warpath ................................R&B:17 *I Got To Find Me One* | $6 | | T-Neck 929 |
| 6/18/83 | 101[1] | 3 | 9 Between The Sheets ................................R&B:3 *(instrumental)* | $5 | | T-Neck 03797 |

## IT'S A BEAUTIFUL DAY ☺

San Francisco-based, folk-rock group led by electric violinist/vocalist David LaFlamme and female vocalist Pattie Santos.

| DEBUG | PEAK | WKS | | | | |
|---|---|---|---|---|---|---|
| 10/4/69 | 118 | 4 | White Bird ........................................................... *Wasted Union Blues* | $10 | | Columbia 44928 |

LaFlamme's version made the *Hot 100* (#89) in 1976 on Amherst 717; reissued on Columbia 45788 in 1973

## IVES, Burl          HOT/C&W/AC/MEM/POP

Born on 6/14/09 in Huntington Township, Illinois. Died on 4/14/95. Actor/author/singer. Narrated the kids' TV classic *Rudolph The Red-Nosed Reindeer*.

| 4/13/63 | 131 | 1 | 1 Baby Come Home To Me ....................................... *Roses And Orchids* | $8 | | Decca 31479 |
|---|---|---|---|---|---|---|
| 7/6/63 | 111 | 5 | 2 I'm The Boss     *The Moon Is High* | $8 | | Decca 31504 |
| 10/12/63 | 124 | 1 | 3 It Comes And Goes............................ *I Found My Best Friend In The Dog Pound* | $8 | | Decca 31543 |
| | | | written by **Bill Anderson** | | | |
| 1/23/65 | 122 | 2 | 4 My Gal Sal ............................................ *(I Hear You) Call My Name* | $8 | | Decca 31729 |
| | | | #1 hit for **Byron G. Harlan** in 1907 | | | |
| 4/10/65 | 120 | 3 | 5 Chim Chim Cheree ................................ *Lavender Blue (Dilly Dilly)* | $8 | ■ | Disneyland 130 |
| | | | from Walt Disney's movie *Mary Poppins* starring Julie Andrews; #81 hit for **The New Christy Minstrels** in 1965 | | | |
| 7/6/68 | 133 | 2 | 6 I'll Be Your Baby Tonight .................................. AC:35 *Maria (If I Could)* | $6 | | Columbia 44508 |
| | | | written and recorded by **Bob Dylan** for his 1968 album *John Wesley Harding* | | | |

# J

## JACK B. NIMBLE And The Quicks ☺

| 3/17/62 | 115 | 1 | Nut Rocker.................................................. *Never On Sunday* [I] | $30 | | Del-Rio 2302 |
|---|---|---|---|---|---|---|

also released on Dot 16319 in 1962 ($15); adapted from Tchaikovsky's *The Nutcracker*, #23 hit for **B. Bumble & The Stingers** in 1962

## JACKS, Susan/Terry       HOT/AC

Canadians Terry Jacks and wife Susan (Pesklevits) recorded solo and as **The Poppy Family**.

| 2/26/72 | 105 | 4 | 1 Good Friends? ...................................... AC:34 *Tryin'* | $6 | | London 172 |
|---|---|---|---|---|---|---|
| | | | **THE POPPY FAMILY** Vocal: Susan Jacks | | | |
| 1/27/73 | 116 | 3 | 2 I'm Gonna Love You Too ............... *Something Good Was Over Before It Ever Got To Start* | $6 | | London 188 |
| | | | first released by **Buddy Holly** on Coral 61947 in 1958; #56 hit for **The Hullaballoos** in 1965 | | | |
| 5/5/73 | 116 | 2 | 3 You Don't Know What Love Is.................. *Another Year, Another Day* | $6 | | London 182 |
| | | | **SUSAN JACKS** and The Poppy Family | | | |
| 6/7/75 | 106 | 5 | 4 Christina ............................................ *The Feelings That We've Lost* | $5 | | Private Stock 45,023 |
| | | | **TERRY JACKS** (#2 & 4) | | | |

## JACKSON, Alan       C&W/HOT

Born on 10/17/58 in Newnan, Georgia. Country singer/guitarist.

| 8/6/94 | 104 | 9 | 1 Summertime Blues ............................ Sls:60 /C&W:❶³ *Hole In The Wall* | $3 | ▮ | Arista 12697 |
|---|---|---|---|---|---|---|
| | | | #8 hit for **Eddie Cochran** in 1958 | | | |
| 10/15/94 | 101³ | 10 | 2 Livin' On Love     Sls:54 /C&W:❶³ *Let's Get Back To Me And You* | $3 | ▮ | Arista 12745 |

## JACKSON, Chuck       R&B/HOT

Born on 7/22/37 in Latta, South Carolina. R&B singer. With **The Dell-Vikings**, 1957-59. *Top Pop Singles*: 23.

| 8/11/62 | 119 | 2 | 1 Who's Gonna Pick Up The Pieces ............................ *I Keep Forgettin'* (Hot #55) | $15 | | Wand 126 |
|---|---|---|---|---|---|---|
| 6/1/63 | 110 | 6 | 2 I Will Never Turn My Back On You ............ R&B:29 *Tears Of Joy* (Hot #85) | $15 | | Wand 138 |
| | | | written and produced by **Ed Townsend** | | | |
| 12/4/65 | 105 | 7 | 3 Good Things Come To Those Who Wait     *Yah* | $15 | | Wand 1105 |
| 2/12/66 | 112 | 1 | 4 I'm Satisfied.......................................... *Please Don't Hurt Me* | $15 | | Wand 1109 |
| | | | **CHUCK JACKSON & MAXINE BROWN** | | | |
| 4/12/69 | 107 | 3 | 5 Are You Lonely For Me Baby.................... R&B:27 *Your Wonderful Love* | $12 | | Motown 1144 |
| 7/14/73 | 117 | 2 | 6 I Only Get This Feeling ........................ R&B:35 *Slowly But Surely* | $6 | | ABC 11368 |

## JACKSON, Deon       HOT/R&B

Born on 1/26/46 in Ann Arbor, Michigan. Male R&B singer/clarinetist/drummer.

| 10/1/66 | 111 | 3 | I Can't Do Without You.................... *That's What You Do To Me* | $12 | | Carla 2530 |
|---|---|---|---|---|---|---|

## JACKSON, Janet       HOT/R&B/AC

Born on 5/16/66 in Gary, Indiana. Sister of The Jacksons (youngest of nine children). Regular on TV's *Good Times*, *Diff'rent Strokes* and *Fame*. *Top Pop Singles*: 31.

| 9/8/84 | 101² | 8 | Don't Stand Another Chance .................... R&B:9 *Rock 'N' Roll* | $5 | ■ | A&M 2660 |
|---|---|---|---|---|---|---|
| | | | written and produced by **Marlon Jackson** | | | |

## JACKSON, Jerry ☺

| 7/25/64 | 134 | 1 | 1 Shrimp Boats (Jamaican Ska) ................ *Always (Jamaican Ska)* | $12 | | Columbia 43056 |
|---|---|---|---|---|---|---|
| | | | #2 hit for **Jo Stafford** in 1951 | | | |
| 12/5/64 | 114 | 4 | 2 Tell Her Johnny Said Goodbye ................ *Are You Glad When We're Apart* | $12 | | Columbia 43158 |

## JACKSON, J.J.       R&B/HOT

Born Jerome Louis Jackson on 4/8/41 in Brooklyn, New York. R&B singer/songwriter. Became permanent resident of England in 1969.

| 7/15/67 | 123 | 5 | Four Walls (Three Windows and Two Doors) ............ R&B:17 *Here We Go Again* | $10 | | Calla 133 |
|---|---|---|---|---|---|---|

## JACKSON, Joe       ROK/HOT/AC

Born on 8/11/55 in Burton-on-Trent, England. Singer/songwriter/pianist, featuring an ever-changing music style.

| 11/17/79 | 101² | 5 | It's Different For Girls     *Come On* | $5 | ■ | A&M 2186 |
|---|---|---|---|---|---|---|

## JACKSON, La Toya       R&B/HOT

Born on 5/29/56 in Gary, Indiana. Controversial sister of The Jacksons. The fifth of nine children.

| 11/15/80 | 103 | 3 | If You Feel The Funk.......................... R&B:40 *Lovely Is She* | $4 | | Polydor 2137 |
|---|---|---|---|---|---|---|

## JACKSON, Luscious — see LUSCIOUS JACKSON

## JACKSON, Mahalia     HOT/MEM

Born on 10/26/11 in New Orleans. Died on 1/27/72. One of the world's greatest gospel singers. Won Grammy's Lifetime Achievement Award in 1972. Inducted into the Rock and Roll Hall of Fame in 1997 as an early influence.

| | | | | | | |
|---|---|---|---|---|---|---|
| 12/21/63 | 116 | 1 | **In The Summer Of His Years**.......................................... *Song For My Brother* | $8 | | Columbia 42946 |

from the BBC-TV tribute to slain President John F. Kennedy; #46 hit for **Connie Francis** in 1964

## JACKSON, Michael — see MURPHY, Eddie / 3T

## JACKSON, Millie     R&B/HOT

Born on 7/15/44 in Thompson, Georgia. R&B singer/songwriter.

| | | | | | | |
|---|---|---|---|---|---|---|
| 11/13/71 | 102 | 4 | 1 **A Child Of God (It's Hard To Believe)**........................ R&B:22 *You're The Joy Of My Life* | $4 | | Spring 119 |
| 4/21/73 | 110 | 2 | 2 **Breakaway** .......................................... R&B:16 *Strange Things* | $4 | | Spring 134 |
| 3/18/78 | 102 | 2 | 3 **All The Way Lover** .......................................... R&B:12 *Cheatin' Is* | $4 | | Spring 179 |

## JACKSON, Walter     R&B/HOT

Born on 3/19/38 in Pensacola, Florida. Died on 6/20/83. R&B singer. Contracted polio at an early age, performed on crutches.

| | | | | | | |
|---|---|---|---|---|---|---|
| 10/2/65 | 120 | 4 | 1 **I'll Keep On Trying** .......................................... *Where Have All The Flowers Gone* | $10 | | Okeh 7229 |
| 1/29/66 | 103 | 6 | 2 **Funny (Not Much)** .......................................... *One Heart Lonely* | $10 | | Okeh 7236 |
| 9/3/66 | 130 | 3 | 3 **After You There Can Be Nothing** .......................... R&B:40 *My Funny Valentine* | $10 | | Okeh 7256 |
| 6/24/67 | 110 | 5 | 4 **Deep In The Heart Of Harlem** .......................... R&B:43 *My One Chance To Make It* | $10 | ■ | Okeh 7285 |

#90 hit for **Clyde McPhatter** in 1964

| | | | | | | |
|---|---|---|---|---|---|---|
| 10/21/67 | 124 | 4 | 5 **My Ship Is Comin' In** .......................................... *A Cold, Cold Winter* | $10 | | Okeh 7295 |
| 12/20/69 | 111 | 2 | 6 **Anyway That You Want Me** .......................... R&B:37 *Life Has It's Ups And Downs* | $8 | | Cotillion 44053 |

#53 hit for **Evie Sands** in 1969

## JACKSON, Wanda     C&W/HOT/AC

Born on 10/20/37 in Maud, Oklahoma. Country-rockabilly singer/songwriter/guitarist.

| | | | | | | |
|---|---|---|---|---|---|---|
| 7/14/62 | 117 | 2 | 1 **I Misunderstood** .......................................... *Between The Window And The Phone* | $15 | | Capitol 4785 |
| 9/22/62 | 117 | 2 | 2 **The Greatest Actor** .......................................... *You Bug Me Bad* | $15 | | Capitol 4833 |

## JACOBS, Debbie     HOT/R&B

Disco singer from Baltimore.

| | | | | | | |
|---|---|---|---|---|---|---|
| 9/29/79 | 106 | 4 | **Don't You Want My Love** .......................................... R&B:66 *Think I'm Fallin' In Love* | $4 | | MCA 41102 |

## JACOBS, Dick, And His Orchestra     HOT

Born on 3/29/18 in New York City. Died in 1988 (age 70). A&R director for Coral and Brunswick Records.

| | | | | | | |
|---|---|---|---|---|---|---|
| 7/10/61 | 104 | 4 | **Theme From "Come September"** .......................................... *The Villa* [I] | $8 | | Coral 62275 |

from the movie *Come September* starring **Bobby Darin** and Sandra Dee; #73 hit for **Billy Vaughn** in 1961

## JADE — see P.O.V.

## JAGGED EDGE, The ○

Rock quartet formed by Londoner Myke Gray (guitar). Includes Swedish vocalist Matt Alfonzetti, British bassist Andy Robbins and Italian drummer Fabio Del Rio.

| | | | | | | |
|---|---|---|---|---|---|---|
| 8/27/66 | 129 | 1 | **Deep Inside** .......................................... *Baby You Don't Know* | $10 | | RCA Victor 8880 |

## JAMAL ○     R&B

Male rapper Jamal Phillips. One-half of the Illegal duo.

| | | | | | | |
|---|---|---|---|---|---|---|
| 10/28/95 | 105 | 12 | **Fades Em All** .......................................... R&B:59 *(instrumental)* | $3 | ▌ | Rowdy 35042 |

samples "Ready To Die" by The Notorious B.I.G.

## JAMES     HOT

British modern rock group formed in 1983 featuring Tim Booth (vocals).

| | | | | | | |
|---|---|---|---|---|---|---|
| 6/18/94 | 105 | 7 | **Say Something** .......................................... ROK:19 *(new version) / (2 album snippets)* | $3 | ▌ | Fontana 858796 |

## JAMES, Bob     HOT

Born on 12/25/39 in Marshall, Missouri. Jazz-fusion keyboardist.

| | | | | | | |
|---|---|---|---|---|---|---|
| 7/12/75 | 105 | 2 | **I Feel A Song (In My Heart)** .......................................... *The Golden Apple* | $5 | | CTI 26 |

Patti Austin (vocal); #21 hit for **Gladys Knight & The Pips** in 1974

## JAMES, Elmore ○     R&B

Born Elmore Brooks on 1/27/18 in Richland, Mississippi. Died on 5/24/63. Blues singer/guitarist. Inducted into the Rock and Roll Hall of Fame in 1992 as an early influence.

| | | | | | | |
|---|---|---|---|---|---|---|
| 5/22/65 | 106 | 4 | **It Hurts Me Too** .......................................... R&B:25 *Bleeding Heart* | $20 | | Enjoy 2015 |

## JAMES, Etta     R&B/HOT/AC

Born Jamesetta Hawkins on 1/25/38 in Los Angeles. R&B pioneer. Nicknamed "Miss Peaches." Inducted into the Rock and Roll Hall of Fame in 1993. *Top Pop Singles:* 28.

| | | | | | | |
|---|---|---|---|---|---|---|
| 1/5/63 | 109 | 2 | 1 **How Do You Talk To An Angel** .................... *Would It Make Any Difference To You* (Hot #64) | $12 | | Argo 5430 |

#14 hit for **Eddie Fisher** in 1953

| | | | | | | |
|---|---|---|---|---|---|---|
| 11/23/63 | 118 | 1 | 2 **I Worry Bout You** .......................... *Two Sides (To Every Story)* (Hot #63) | $12 | | Argo 5452 |
| 9/28/68 | 113 | 3 | 3 **You Got It** .......................................... *Fire* | $10 | | Cadet 5620 |

written by Don Covay

| | | | | | | |
|---|---|---|---|---|---|---|
| 6/3/72 | 108 | 2 | 4 **I Found A Love** .......................... R&B:31 *Nothing From Nothing Leaves Nothing* | $7 | | Chess 2125 |

#32 hit for **Wilson Pickett** in 1967

| | | | | | | |
|---|---|---|---|---|---|---|
| 10/13/73 | 101² | 8 | 5 **All The Way Down** .......................... R&B:29 *Lay Back Daddy* | $7 | | Chess 2144 |

## JAMES, Jesse     R&B/HOT

Born James McCulland in 1943 in Eldorado, Arkansas. R&B singer/record producer.

| | | | | | | |
|---|---|---|---|---|---|---|
| 8/29/70 | 117 | 2 | **Don't Nobody Want To Get Married (Part II)** .................... R&B:18 *(Part I)* | $8 | | ZEA 50000 |

## JAMES, Jimmy, & The Vagabonds     HOT/R&B

R&B group from London: Jimmy James and Count Prince Miller (vocals), Wallace Wilson (guitar), Phil Chen (bass) and Rupert Balgobin (drums).

| | | | | | | |
|---|---|---|---|---|---|---|
| 2/15/69 | 127 | 2 | **Red Red Wine** .......................................... *No Good To Cry* | $10 | | Atco 6608 |

written by Neil Diamond; #1 hit for UB40 in 1988

| DEBUT | PEAK | WKS | A-side (Chart Hit)............................................................................B-side | $ | Pic | Label & Number |
|---|---|---|---|---|---|---|

## JAMES, Joni
**MEM/POP/HOT**

Born Joan Carmello Babbo on 9/22/30 in Chicago. Married her orchestral arranger/conductor (1958-61) Tony Acquaviva (d: 9/27/86). *Pop Hits & Top Pop Singles*: 23.

| DEBUT | PEAK | WKS | | | | |
|---|---|---|---|---|---|---|
| 9/28/59 | 102 | 4 | 1 Are You Sorry? .........................................*What I Don't Know Won't Hurt Me* | $15 | | MGM 12828 |
| | | | #9 hit for Ben Bernie's Orchestra in 1925 on Vocalion 15036 | | | |
| 11/30/59 | 108 | 1 | 2 I Laughed At Love.............................*Little Things Mean A Lot* (Hot #35) | $12 | | MGM 12849 |
| | | | #14 hit for Sunny Gale in 1952 on RCA Victor 4789 | | | |
| 3/28/60 | 101[2] | 3 | 3 You Belong To Me ........................*I Need You Now* (Hot #98) | $12 | | MGM 12885 |
| | | | **100 Strings and JONI** | | | |
| | | | original version by Joni released in 1952 on MGM 11295; #1 hit for Jo Stafford in 1952 | | | |

## JAMES, Rick
**R&B/HOT/AC**

Born James Johnson on 2/1/52 in Buffalo. Funk-rock singer/songwriter/guitarist/producer.

| DEBUT | PEAK | WKS | | | | |
|---|---|---|---|---|---|---|
| 1/30/82 | 102 | 1 | 1 Ghetto Life ..................................**R&B:38** *Below The Funk (Pass The J)* | $4 | | Gordy 7215 |
| 11/12/83 | 101[1] | 3 | 2 U Bring The Freak Out ......................**R&B:16** *Money Talks* | $4 | | Gordy 1703 |
| 7/27/85 | 106 | 2 | 3 Glow ..............................................**R&B:5** *(instrumental)* | $4 | ■ | Gordy 1796 |

## JAMES, Sonny
**C&W/HOT/AC**

Born James Loden on 5/1/29 in Hackleburg, Alabama. Country singer/songwriter/guitarist.

| DEBUT | PEAK | WKS | | | | |
|---|---|---|---|---|---|---|
| 6/29/59 | 107 | 1 | 1 Pure Love ........................................*This Love Of Mine* | $15 | | Capitol 4229 |
| | | | The Eligibles (backing vocals); written by Johnny Burnette | | | |
| 4/4/64 | 134 | 1 | 2 Baltimore ..................................**C&W:6** *Least Of All You* | $10 | ■ | Capitol 5129 |
| 4/3/65 | 116 | 3 | 3 I'll Keep Holding On (Just To Your Love) ..........**C&W:2** *I'm Getting Gray From Being Blue* | $10 | ■ | Capitol 5375 |
| 8/28/65 | *113* | 4 | 4 Behind The Tear ........................**C&W:❶**[3] *Runnin'* | $10 | ■ | Capitol 5454 |
| | | | written by Ned Miller | | | |
| 1/27/68 | 118 | 2 | 5 A World Of Our Own.......................**C&W:❶**[3] *An Old Sweetheart Of Mine* | $10 | ■ | Capitol 2067 |
| | | | #19 hit for The Seekers in 1965 | | | |
| 4/25/70 | 125 | 2 | 6 My Love ....................................**C&W:❶**[3] *Blue For You* | $7 | ■ | Capitol 2782 |
| | | | #1 hit for Petula Clark in 1966 | | | |
| 10/24/70 | 108 | 6 | 7 Endlessly ...................................**C&W:❶**[3] *Happy Memories* | $7 | ■ | Capitol 2914 |
| | | | #12 hit for Brook Benton in 1959 | | | |
| 9/9/72 | 103 | 3 | 8 When The Snow Is On The Roses **C&W:❶**[1] *Love Is A Rainbow* | $6 | ■ | Columbia 45644 |
| | | | #98 hit for Ed Ames in 1967 | | | |

## JAMES, Tommy
**HOT/AC/C&W/R&B**

Born Thomas Jackson on 4/29/47 in Dayton, Ohio. Formed pop group The Shondells at age 12. *Top Pop Singles*: 32.

| DEBUT | PEAK | WKS | | | | |
|---|---|---|---|---|---|---|
| 5/31/80 | 101[1] | 3 | You Got Me .....................................*It's All Right (For Now)* | $5 | | Millennium 11788 |

## JAMES GANG, The
**HOT**

Hard-rock band from Cleveland: Joe Walsh (vocals, guitar, keyboards), Dale Peters (bass) and Jim Fox (drums).

| DEBUT | PEAK | WKS | | | | |
|---|---|---|---|---|---|---|
| 12/13/69 | 126 | 2 | 1 Funk No. 48 ........................................*Collage* | $8 | | BluesWay 61030 |
| | | | The James Gang's "Funk #49" hit the *Hot 100* (#59) on 8/29/70 on ABC 11272 | | | |
| 5/27/72 | 108 | 5 | 2 Looking For My Lady ................................*Hairy Hypochondriac* | $6 | | ABC 11325 |
| 11/4/72 | 111 | 3 | 3 Had Enough................................................*Kick Back Man* | $6 | | ABC 11336 |
| 5/25/74 | 101[1] | 5 | 4 Standing In The Rain .........................*From Another Time* | $6 | | Atco 6966 |

## JANA ✪

Born on 5/10/74 in Charlotte, North Carolina. Female singer.

| DEBUT | PEAK | WKS | | | | |
|---|---|---|---|---|---|---|
| 4/19/97 | 117 | 3 | What Am I To You ...............................*Kind Of Love* | $3 | ▌ | Curb 73011 |

## JAN & DEAN
**HOT/R&B**

Influential surf-rock male vocal duo from Los Angeles. Jan Berry (b: 4/3/41) and Dean Torrence (b: 3/10/40). Jan was critically injured in an auto accident on 4/19/66. *Top Pop Singles*: 26.

| DEBUT | PEAK | WKS | | | | |
|---|---|---|---|---|---|---|
| 10/9/61 | 104 | 3 | 1 Wanted, One Girl..............................*Something A Little Bit Different* | $30 | | Challenge 9120 |
| 1/1/66 | 109 | 4 | 2 A Beginning From An End ...........................*Folk City* | $15 | ■ | Liberty 55849 |
| 3/18/67 | 111 | 3 | 3 Yellow Balloon ......................................*Taste Of Rain* | $30 | | Columbia 44036 |
| | | | solo performance by Dean; #25 hit for The Yellow Balloon in 1967 | | | |
| 7/24/76 | 107 | 2 | 4 Sidewalk Surfin' ...............................*Gonna Hustle You* [R] | $15 | | United Artists 670 |
| | | | originally made the *Hot 100* (#25) on 10/31/64 on Liberty 55727 | | | |

## JANKEL, Chas ✪
**R&B**

Born on 4/16/52. Former keyboardist/guitarist with Ian Dury & The Blockheads.

| DEBUT | PEAK | WKS | | | | |
|---|---|---|---|---|---|---|
| 2/20/82 | 102 | 5 | Glad To Know You...............................**R&B:57** *3,000,000 Synths* | $4 | | A&M 2396 |

## JARREAU, Al
**R&B/AC/HOT**

Born on 3/12/40 in Milwaukee. R&B/jazz-styled vocalist.

| DEBUT | PEAK | WKS | | | | |
|---|---|---|---|---|---|---|
| 7/5/80 | 102 | 5 | 1 Never Givin' Up ................................**R&B:26** *Distracted* | $4 | | Warner 49234 |
| 10/30/82 | 102 | 4 | 2 Your Precious Love ....**R&B:16** *Monmouth College Fight Song* (Yellowjackets) | $4 | | Warner 29893 |
| | | | **AL JARREAU AND RANDY CRAWFORD** | | | |
| | | | #5 hit for Marvin Gaye & Tammi Terrell in 1967 | | | |

## JAY & THE AMERICANS
**HOT/AC**

Pop group formed in late 1959 by New York University students featuring John "Jay" Traynor who was replaced by lead singer Jay Black (real name: David Blatt; b: 11/2/38) in 1962.

| DEBUT | PEAK | WKS | | | | |
|---|---|---|---|---|---|---|
| 11/27/61 | 120 | 1 | 1 Tonight.........................................*The Other Girls* | $15 | | United Artists 353 |
| | | | from the musical *West Side Story*; #8 hit for Ferrante & Teicher in 1961 | | | |
| 7/14/62 | 109 | 5 | 2 This Is It .........................................*It's My Turn To Cry* | $12 | | United Artists 479 |
| | | | Jay Traynor (lead singer, above 2) | | | |
| 5/22/65 | 129 | 1 | 3 When It's All Over ..............................*Cara, Mia* (Hot #4) | $10 | | United Artists 881 |
| 8/19/67 | 131 | 2 | 4 (We'll Meet In The) Yellow Forest................*Got Hung Up Along The Way* | $10 | | United Artists 50196 |
| 3/16/68 | 114 | 1 | 5 No Other Love ..................................*No, I Don't Know Her* | $10 | | United Artists 50282 |
| | | | from the Rodgers & Hammerstein musical *Me And Juliet*; #1 hit for Perry Como in 1953; Jay Black (lead singer, above 3) | | | |

## JAY & THE TECHNIQUES   HOT/R&B
Interracial R&B-rock group from Allentown, Pennsylvania: Jay Proctor (lead singer; b: 10/28/40), Karl Landis, Ronnie Goosly, John Walsh, George Lloyd, Chuck Crowl and Dante Dancho.

| 8/10/68 | 116 | 1 | 1 Singles Game ........................................................ *Baby How Easy Your Heart Forgets Me* | $10 | ■ | Smash 2171 |
| 4/26/69 | 107 | 4 | 2 Change Your Mind ........................................................ *Are You Ready For This* | $10 | | Smash 2217 |

## JAYE, Jerry   C&W/HOT
Born Gerald Jaye Hatley on 10/19/37 in Manila, Arkansas. Pop/country singer.

| 7/29/67 | 107 | 3 | Let The Four Winds Blow ........................................................ *Singing The Blues* | $8 | | Hi 2128 |
| | | | #15 hit for **Fats Domino** in 1961 | | | |

## JAYNETTS, The   HOT/R&B
Female R&B group from the Bronx, New York: Ethel Davis, Mary Sue Wells, Yvonne Bushnell and Ada Ray.

| 11/16/63 | 120 | 2 | Keep An Eye On Her ........................................................ *(instrumental)* | $12 | | Tuff 371 |

## J.B.'s — see A.A.B.B. / WESLEY, Fred

## JEFFERSON AIRPLANE   HOT/ROK/AC
Influential psychedelic rock group from San Francisco featuring **Grace Slick**, **Marty Balin**, Paul Kantner, Jorma Kaukonen and Jack Casady. Many personnel changes and group name changes. Inducted into the Rock and Roll Hall of Fame in 1996. *Top Pop Singles:* 36.

| 2/4/67 | 103 | 5 | 1 My Best Friend ........................................................ *How Do You Feel* | $15 | | RCA Victor 9063 |
| 9/30/67 | 124 | 3 | 2 Two Heads ........................................................ *Ballad Of You & Me & Pooneil (Hot #42)* | $12 | | RCA Victor 9297 |
| 5/31/69 | 133 | 1 | 3 Plastic Fantastic Lover ........................................................ *Other Side Of This Life* | $12 | ■ | RCA Victor 0150 |
| | | | "live" version of their original 1967 recording | | | |
| 7/4/70 | 102 | 2 | 4 Mexico/ | | | |
| | | 2 | 5 Have You Seen The Saucers ........................................................ | $12 | ■ | RCA Victor 0343 |
| 10/7/72 | 104 | 2 | 6 Long John Silver ........................................................ *Milk Train* | $8 | ■ | Grunt 0506 |
| 10/31/81 | 104 | 2 | 7 Save Your Love ........................................ ROK:49 *Wild Eyes* | $5 | | Grunt 12332 |
| | | | **JEFFERSON STARSHIP** | | | |

## JEFFREY, Joe   HOT

| 10/11/69 | 108 | 3 | 1 Dreamin' Till Then ........................................................ *The Train* | $8 | | Wand 11207 |
| 12/27/69 | 109 | 1 | 2 Hey Hey Woman ........................................................ *The Chance Of Loving You* | $8 | | Wand 11213 |
| 4/11/70 | 115 | 5 | 3 My Baby Loves Lovin' ........................................................ *The Chance Of Loving You* | $8 | | Wand 11219 |
| | | | #13 hit for **White Plains** in 1970 | | | |

## JEFFREYS, Garland   ROK/HOT
Born in Brooklyn in 1944. R&B-rock-reggae singer.

| 1/26/74 | 115 | 2 | 1 Wild In The Streets ........................................................ *Lon Chaney* | $6 | | Atlantic 2981 |
| | | | #87 hit for **British Lions** in 1978 | | | |
| 6/17/78 | 107 | 5 | 2 Reelin' ........................................................ *One-Eyed Jack (Jeffreys)* | $5 | ■ | A&M 2030 |
| | | | **GARLAND JEFFREYS and PHOEBE SNOW** | | | |
| 4/9/83 | 107 | 2 | 3 What Does It Take (To Win Your Love) ........................................................ *Rebel Love* | $4 | | Epic 03687 |
| | | | #4 hit for **Jr. Walker & The All Stars** in 1969 | | | |

## JENKINS, Gus   HOT/R&B
Born on 3/24/31 in Birmingham, Alabama. R&B pianist/vocalist. Made the *Hot 100* as Gus Jinkins in 1956.

| 11/28/64 | 113 | 5 | Chittlins ........................................................ *You'll Be The One* [I] | $15 | | Tower 107 |

## JENNIFER ○
French disco singer.

| 6/18/77 | 110 | 2 | Do It For Me ........................................................ *Boogie Boogie Love* | $5 | ■ | Motown 1417 |

## JENNIFER — see WARNES, Jennifer

## JENNINGS, Waylon   C&W/HOT/AC
Born on 6/15/37 in Littlefield, Texas. **Buddy Holly** produced Jennings's first record "Jole Blon" in 1958. Jennings then joined with Holly's backing band as bass guitarist on the fateful "Winter Dance Party" tour in 1959.

| 7/5/69 | 124 | 2 | 1 Delia's Gone ........................ C&W:37 *The Days Of Sand And Shovels (C&W #20)* | $7 | | RCA Victor 0157 |
| | | | #66 hit for **Pat Boone** in 1960 as "Delia Gone" | | | |
| 3/24/73 | 114 | 4 | 2 You Can Have Her ........................ C&W:7 *Gone To Denver* | $6 | | RCA Victor 0886 |
| | | | #12 hit for **Roy Hamilton** in 1961 | | | |
| 8/16/75 | 110 | 1 | 3 Waymore's Blues ........................ *Dreaming My Dreams With You (C&W #10)* | $6 | | RCA Victor 10270 |
| 7/19/80 | 103 | 2 | 4 Clyde ........................ C&W:7 *I Came Here To Party* | $4 | | RCA 12007 |
| | | | **WAYLON** | | | |
| 10/8/83 | 102 | 4 | 5 Take It To The Limit ........................ C&W:8 / AC:31 *Till I Gain Control Again* | $4 | ■ | Columbia 04131 |
| | | | **WILLIE NELSON & WAYLON JENNINGS** | | | |
| | | | #4 hit for the **Eagles** in 1976 | | | |

## JENSEN, Kris   HOT
Born Peter Jensen on 4/4/42 in New Haven, Connecticut. Pop singer/guitarist.

| 1/12/63 | 112 | 1 | Don't Take Her From Me ........................................................ *Claudette* | $12 | | Hickory 1195 |

## JERMS, The ○
Pop group produced by Dean Mathis of **The Newbeats**.

| 5/31/69 | 129 | 3 | Green Door ........................................................ *I'm A Teardrop* | $12 | | Honor Brigade 1 |
| | | | #1 hit for **Jim Lowe** in 1956 | | | |

## JERU THE DAMAJA   R&B/HOT
Real name: Kendrick Jeru Davis. Male rapper from Brooklyn.

| 10/5/96 | 105 | 9 | 1 Ya Playin' Yaself ........................ R&B:57 *(4 versions)* | $5 | | Payday/FFRR 120100 (T) |
| 4/12/97 | 114 | 3 | 2 Me Or The Papes ........................ R&B:78 *(remix) / Ya Playin' Yaself* | $3 | ▌ | Payday/FFRR 531100 |
| | | | above 2 produced by DJ Premier of **Gang Starr** | | | |

## JESSE ○   R&B
Full name: Jesse Campbell. Born and raised in Maywood, Illinois.

| 5/20/95 | 124 | 1 | When U Cry I Cry ........................ R&B:29 *(extended version)* | $3 | ▌ | Underworld 58329 |

### JESTERS, The
*HOT*
R&B vocal group formed in Harlem: Adam Jackson, Jimmy Smith, Melvin Lewis and Donald Lewis.

| 6/20/60 | 110 | 2 | The Wind ................................................................ *Sally Green* | $50 | | Winley 242 |
|---|---|---|---|---|---|---|

produced by Dave "Baby" Cortez; also see original version by **The Diablos**

### JET ✪
Chicago-based pop group led by vocalist Barbara Barrow.

| 10/17/81 | 105 | 2 | Stranded In The Moonlight ................................ *Love Slave* | $5 | | Third Coast 1806 |
|---|---|---|---|---|---|---|

### JETHRO TULL
*ROK/HOT*
Progressive-rock group formed in 1968 in Blackpool, England. Led by Ian Anderson (vocals, flute) and Martin Barre (guitar).

| 9/29/73 | 105 | 3 | 1 A Passion Play (Edit #10).................................. *(Edit #6)* | $6 | | Chrysalis 2017 |
|---|---|---|---|---|---|---|

"A Passion Play (Edit #8)" made the *Hot 100* (#80) on 5/19/73 on Chrysalis 2012

| 6/12/82 | 108 | 2 | 2 Fallen On Hard Times .................. ROK:20 *Pussy Willow* | $5 | | Chrysalis 2613 |
|---|---|---|---|---|---|---|

### JET STREAM, The ✪

| 6/10/67 | 101[1] | 5 | All's Quiet On West 23rd *Crazy Me* | $12 | | Smash 2095 |
|---|---|---|---|---|---|---|

### JETT, Joan, and the Blackhearts
*ROK/HOT*
Born on 9/22/60 in Philadelphia. Played guitar with the Los Angeles female rock band **The Runaways**, 1975-78.

| 12/15/84 | 105 | 1 | 1 I Love You Love ...................................... *Talkin Bout My Baby* (live) | $4 | ■ | Blackheart/MCA 52472 |
| 5/18/96 | 108 | 1 | 2 Love Is All Around ........................................ *Rubber & Glue* | $3 | ▮ | Blackheart/Warner 17637 |
|---|---|---|---|---|---|---|

theme from TV's *The Mary Tyler Moore Show*; #29 Country hit for **Sonny Curtis** in 1980

### JEWELS, The
*HOT/R&B*
Female R&B vocal quartet from Washington, D.C.: Sandra Bears, Grace Ruffin, Margie Clark and Martha Harvin.

| 6/26/65 | 130 | 1 | But I Do .................................................... *Smokey Joe* | $20 | | Dimension 1048 |
|---|---|---|---|---|---|---|

Charlie Calello (orch.); #4 hit for **Clarence Henry** in 1961

### JIM & JEAN
*HOT*
Husband-and-wife pop duo: Jim and Jean Glover.

| 3/18/67 | 123 | 3 | What's That Got To Do With Me .................. *Stalemate* | $10 | | Verve Folkways 5035 |
|---|---|---|---|---|---|---|

### JIVE FIVE Featuring Eugene Pitt
*R&B/HOT*
R&B vocal group formed in Brooklyn in 1959: Eugene Pitt (b: 11/6/37), Jerome Hanna, Billy Prophet, Richard Harris and Norman Johnson.

| 3/31/62 | 105 | 5 | 1 Hully Gully Callin' Time *No Not Again* | $25 | | Beltone 2019 |
| 4/20/63 | 128 | 1 | 2 Rain .......................................................... *She's My Girl* | $25 | | Beltone 2034 |
| 10/30/65 | 106 | 4 | 3 A Bench In The Park.......... *Please Baby Please (Come on Back To Me)* | $20 | | United Artists 936 |
| 7/29/67 | 127 | 1 | 4 Crying Like A Baby............................ *You'll Fall In Love* | $12 | | Musicor 1250 |
| 6/1/68 | 119 | 3 | 5 Sugar (Don't Take Away My Candy) ........ R&B:34 *Blues In The Ghetto* | $12 | | Musicor 1305 |
|---|---|---|---|---|---|---|

### JIVIN' GENE
*HOT*
Born Gene Bourgeois in Port Arthur, Texas. Singer/songwriter/guitarist.

| 4/25/60 | 101[1] | 1 | Go On, Go On *You're Jealous* | $20 | | Mercury 71561 |
|---|---|---|---|---|---|---|

### JODECI
*R&B/HOT*
R&B vocal group from Tiny Grove, North Carolina: K-Ci and JoJo Hailey, with Dalvin and Donald "DeVante Swing" DeGrate.

| 7/9/94 | 101[1] | 11 | What About Us *Sls:74 /R&B:14 (instrumental)* | $3 | ▮ | Uptown/MCA 54861 |
|---|---|---|---|---|---|---|

samples "Computer Love" by **Zapp**

### JOE & ANN ✪
*R&B*

| 12/31/60 | 108 | 1 | Gee Baby .............................. R&B:14 *Wherever You May Be* | $20 | | Ace 577 |
|---|---|---|---|---|---|---|

#52 hit in 1961 for Mickey & Sylvia as "Baby You're So Fine" (also see **Ben and Bea**)

### JOE & EDDIE ✪
Joe Gilbert and Eddie Brown — black folk duo from Berkeley, California. Joe died on 8/6/66 (age 25).

| 2/22/64 | 101[1] | 4 | There's A Meetin' Here Tonite *Lonesome Traveler* | $10 | | GNP Crescendo 195 |
|---|---|---|---|---|---|---|

### JOEL, Billy — see HASSLES, The

### JOHN, Elton
*HOT/AC/ROK/R&B*
Born Reginald Kenneth Dwight on 3/25/47 in Pinner, Middlesex, England. Elton was the #1 pop artist of the '70s. Inducted into the Rock and Roll Hall of Fame in 1994. *Top Pop Singles*: 67.

| 4/7/79 | 110 | 4 | Song For Guy ........................ AC:37 *Lovesick* [I] | $7 | ■ | MCA 40993 |
|---|---|---|---|---|---|---|

### JOHN, Little Willie
*R&B/HOT*
Born William Edgar John on 11/15/37 in Cullendale, Arkansas. Died in Washington State Prison on 5/26/68. R&B singer. Inducted into the Rock and Roll Hall of Fame in 1996.

| 7/13/59 | 108 | 2 | 1 Let Nobody Love You ...................... *Leave My Kitten Alone* (Hot #60) | $25 | | King 5219 |
| 6/30/62 | 116 | 1 | 2 I Wish I Could Cry ...................... *Every Beat Of My Heart* | $15 | | King 5641 |
|---|---|---|---|---|---|---|

### JOHN, Robert
*HOT/AC*
Born Robert John Pedrick in Brooklyn in 1946. First recorded at age 12 for Big Top Records.

| 10/5/68 | 108 | 2 | 1 Don't Leave Me ........................................ *Children* | $10 | | Columbia 44639 |
|---|---|---|---|---|---|---|

written by Nilsson

| 11/3/79 | 102 | 7 | 2 Only Time ...................... AC:42 *Stay A Little Longer* | $5 | | EMI America 8023 |
|---|---|---|---|---|---|---|

### JOHNNY AND THE HURRICANES
*HOT/R&B*
Rock and roll instrumental band formed in Toledo in 1958 featuring leader Johnny Pocisk "Paris" (saxophone).

| 6/19/61 | 116 | 2 | Old Smokie ........................................ *High Voltage* [I] | $20 | ■ | Big Top 3076 |
|---|---|---|---|---|---|---|

rock and roll adaptation of the folk song "On Top Of Old Smoky"

### JOHNNY & THE TOKENS ✪
After **The Tokens** left Warwick Records, owner Morty Craft formed this entirely new pop group using The Tokens name.

| 8/7/61 | 112 | 1 | The Taste Of A Tear.................................... *Never Till Now* | $25 | | Warwick 658 |
|---|---|---|---|---|---|---|

### JOHNNY Z — see JONNY Z

**JOHNS, Sammy**         HOT/AC/C&W
Born on 2/7/46 in Charlotte, North Carolina. Own band, the Devilles, from 1963-73.

| 10/11/80 | 103 | 3 | Falling For You ................................................ *Six Feet Tall And Handsome* | $5 | | Real World 7307 |

**JOHN'S CHILDREN** ❂
British rock group led by vocalist Andy Ellison. Guitarist Marc Bolan went on to form T. Rex.

| 12/31/66 | 102 | 4 | Smashed! Blocked! ................................................ *Strange Affair* | $15 | | White Whale 239 |

**JOHNSON, Betty**         HOT/MEM
Born on 3/16/32 in Charlotte, North Carolina. Married to musical conductor **Charles Randolph Grean**.

| 7/4/60 | 111 | 1 | 1 There's A Star Spangled Banner Waving Somewhere - 1960................................................ *Take A Little Look (In The Good Book)* | $12 | | Coed 532 |

        **BETTY JOHNSON And The Johnson Family Singers**
        original version was a #17 hit for Elton Britt in 1942; #64 hit for Red River Dave in 1960

| 9/12/60 | 109 | 3 | 2 Slipping Around ................................................ *One Has My Name The Other Has My Heart* | $10 | | Dot 16127 |

        Charles Randolph Grean (orch.) #1 hit for **Margaret Whiting** & Jimmy Wakely in 1949

**JOHNSON, Howard** ❂         R&B
R&B vocalist born in Miami. First recorded with Tornader which became Niteflyte.

| 9/25/82 | 105 | 1 | So Fine ................................................ R&B:6 *This Is Heaven* | $4 | | A&M 2415 |

        written and produced by **Kashif**

**JOHNSON, Jesse**         R&B/HOT
Born on 5/29/60 in Rock Island, Illinois. Lead guitarist of **The Time**.

| 6/1/85 | 110 | 1 | Can You Help Me ................................................ R&B:3 *Free World* | $3 | ■ | A&M 2730 |

        **JESSE JOHNSON'S REVUE**

**JOHNSON, Jimmy** ❂         R&B
Born James Thompson on 11/25/28 in Holly Springs, Mississippi. Blues singer/guitarist. Older brother of **Syl Johnson**.

| 2/13/65 | 128 | 2 | Don't Answer The Door (Part 1)................................................ R&B:16 *(Part 2)* | $15 | | Magnum 719 |

        **JIMMY JOHNSON and His Band Featuring Hank Alexander**
        #72 hit for **B.B. King** in 1966

**JOHNSON, Lou**         HOT/R&B
R&B vocalist.

| 3/7/64 | 117 | 1 | 1 It Ain't No Use................................................ *This Night* | $15 | | Hilltop 551 |
| 10/24/64 | 104 | 4 | 2 Kentucky Bluebird (Send A Message To Martha) ................................................ *The Last One To Be Loved* | $15 | | Big Hill 553 |

        recorded in 1966 by **Dionne Warwick** as "Message To Michael"; above 2 produced by **Burt Bacharach**

**JOHNSON, Mark** ❂
| 2/3/68 | 122 | 1 | Ode To Otis Redding ................................................ *The Beautiful Place* [I] [S] | $12 | | Diamond 237 |

        written and produced by **Teddy Vann**

**JOHNSON, Michael**         C&W/AC/HOT
Born on 8/8/44 in Alamosa, Colorado; raised in Denver. In the Chad Mitchell Trio with **John Denver** in 1968.

| 4/21/73 | 118 | 1 | 1 On The Road................................................ *Old Folks* | $5 | | Atco 6895 |
| 2/2/80 | 101[2] | 5 | 2 The Very First Time    AC:29 *Drops Of Water* | $4 | | EMI America 8031 |

**JOHNSON, Puff**         R&B/HOT
Born in 1973 in Detroit; raised in Los Angeles. Female R&B singer.

| 10/26/96 | 118 | 2 | Over And Over ................................................ *God Sent You* | $3 | ▮ | Work 78430 |

        from the movie *The First Wives Club* starring Bette Midler, Diane Keaton and Goldie Hawn

**JOHNSON, Robert** ❂
White Memphis session guitarist. Member of **John Entwistle**'s group Ox in 1974.

| 1/13/79 | 106 | 3 | I'll Be Waiting ................................................ *Tell Me About It, "Slim"* | $5 | | Infinity 50,000 |

**JOHNSON, Syl**         R&B/HOT
Born Syl Thompson on 7/1/39 in Holly Springs, Mississippi. R&B singer/songwriter/guitarist. Younger brother of **Jimmy Johnson**.

| 7/11/70 | 125 | 2 | One Way Ticket To Nowhere................................................ R&B:24 *Kiss By Kiss* | $10 | | Twinight 134 |

**JOHNSTON, Bruce — see BRUCE AND TERRY**

**JOHNSTONS, The** ❂
Folk-rock trio from Ireland: Adrienne Johnston, Mick Moloney and Paul Brady.

| 11/9/68 | 128 | 1 | Both Sides Now ................................................ *Urge For Going* | $7 | | Tetragrammaton 1507 |

        written by Joni Mitchell; #8 hit for **Judy Collins** in 1968

**JOLI, France**         HOT/R&B/AC
Born in 1963 in Montreal. Female dance singer.

| 7/26/80 | 103 | 2 | This Time (I'm Giving All I've Got) ................................................ *Tough Luck* | $5 | | Prelude 8013 |

**JOLLY, Pete** ❂
Born Peter Ceragioli on 6/5/32 in New Haven, Connecticut. Hollywood-based jazz pianist.

| 5/4/63 | 112 | 6 | Little Bird................................................ *Falling In Love With Love* [I] | $10 | | Ava 116 |

        **THE PETE JOLLY TRIO and friends**

**JOMANDA — see FELIX**         R&B/HOT

**JON & ROBIN**         HOT
Duo of Jon Abnor and Javonne "Robin" Braga (who married Jimmy Wright of **The Five Americans** in 1970).

| 11/4/67 | 108 | 4 | 1 I Want Some More................................................ *Love Me Baby* | $8 | | Abnak 124 |

        **JON & ROBIN AND THE IN CROWD**

| 5/25/68 | 131 | 2 | 2 Hangin' From Your Lovin' Tree ................................................ *Let's Take A Walk* | $8 | | Abnak 129 |

        **THE IN CROWD**

| 7/6/68 | 110 | 5 | 3 You Got Style................................................ *Thursday Morning* | $8 | | Abnak 130 |

**JONES, Davy**         HOT/AC
Born on 12/30/45 in Manchester, England. Member of **The Monkees**.

| 10/23/71 | 107 | 3 | I Really Love You ................................................ *Sitting In The Apple Tree* | $10 | | Bell 45,136 |

### JONES, Etta
HOT/R&B
Born on 11/25/28 in Aiken, South Carolina. Jazz singer with Earl Hines's orchestra from 1949-52.

| 3/27/61 | 115 | 2 | Sweethearts On Parade............................................. *You Call It Madness But I Call It Love* | $10 | | King 5443 |
| | | | #1 hit for Guy Lombardo in 1929 | | | |

### JONES, George
C&W/HOT
Born on 9/12/31 in Saratoga, Texas. Country singer/songwriter/guitarist. Married to **Tammy Wynette** from 1969-75.

| 7/13/63 | 124 | 1 | 1 Ain't It Funny What A Fool Will Do ................................ *You Comb Her Hair* (C&W #5) | $15 | ■ | United Artists 578 |
| 6/26/65 | 115 | 2 | 2 I'm A Fool To Care ...................................................... *Louisiana Man* (C&W #25) | $12 | ■ | Musicor 1097 |
| | | | **GEORGE AND GENE** George Jones & Gene Pitney | | | |
| | | | #24 hit for Joe Barry in 1961 | | | |
| 5/31/69 | 124 | 2 | 3 I'll Share My World With You.................................................C&W:2 *I'll See You While Ago* | $10 | | Musicor 1351 |
| 1/9/71 | 112 | 4 | 4 A Good Year For The Roses...................................... C&W:2 *Let A Little Loving Come In* | $10 | | Musicor 1425 |
| | | | a new version (with **Alan Jackson**) made the Country charts (#56) in 1994 | | | |
| 10/25/97 | 109 | 13 | 5 You Don't Seem To Miss Me .............................................. C&W:14 *Where Are You Boy* | $3 | ▮ | Epic 78704 |
| | | | **PATTY LOVELESS** With George Jones | | | |

### JONES, Gloria ✪
Born on 9/12/38 in Long View, Texas. R&B singer. Seriously injured in a car accident on 9/16/77 which killed her companion Marc Bolan, leader of T. Rex.

| 11/13/65 | 128 | 3 | Heartbeat Part 1...............................................................................*Part 2* | $12 | | Uptown 712 |

### JONES, Grace
R&B/HOT
Born on 5/19/52 in Spanishtown, Jamaica. Model/movie actress/singer.

| 1/14/78 | 109 | 4 | 1 La Vie En Rose ............................................................... *I Need A Man* [F] | $5 | | Island 098 |
| | | | there were 7 Top 30 versions of this tune in 1950 | | | |
| 6/6/81 | 101⁶ | 9 | 2 Pull Up To The Bumper ......................................... R&B:5 *Breakdown* | $4 | | Island 49697 |
| 11/13/82 | 103 | 8 | 3 Nipple To The Bottle ............................................. R&B:17 *Ja Guys (dub)* | $3 | | Island 99963 |

### JONES, Howard
HOT/ROK/AC/R&B
Born on 2/23/55 in Southampton, England. Pop singer/songwriter/synth wizard.

| 8/25/84 | 108 | 3 | Pearl In The Shell................................................ *Don't Always Look At The Rain* | $3 | | Elektra 69705 |

### JONES, Jack
AC/HOT
Born on 1/14/38 in Los Angeles. One of the top Adult Contemporary singers of the '60s. *Top Pop Singles*: 20.

| 6/12/65 | 132 | 1 | 1 Travellin' On ........................................... *Seein' The Right Love Go Wrong* (Hot #46) | $7 | | Kapp 672 |
| | | | same tune as Billy Grammer's 1958 hit "Gotta Travel On" | | | |
| 10/23/65 | 134 | 1 | 2 The True Picture ................................................ AC:27 *Just Yesterday* (Hot #73) | $7 | | Kapp 699 |
| 2/5/66 | 123 | 2 | 3 The Weekend ...................................................... AC:20 *Wildflower* | $7 | | Kapp 736 |
| 10/28/67 | 130 | 2 | 4 Open For Business As Usual ............................... AC:26 *The Mood I'm In* | $7 | | Kapp 860 |
| 5/11/68 | 117 | 4 | 5 Follow Me ........................................................... AC:20 *Without Her* | $6 | | RCA Victor 9510 |
| 12/7/68 | 106 | 5 | 6 L.A. Break Down (And Take Me In) .................... AC:21 *Love Story* | $6 | | RCA Victor 9687 |
| | | | featuring Doug Talbert on piano | | | |

### JONES, Jimmy
HOT/R&B
Born on 6/2/37 in Birmingham, Alabama. Joined the R&B group Sparks Of Rhythm in New York in 1955.

| 9/12/60 | 102 | 4 | 1 Ee-I Ee-I Oh! (Sue MacDonald)/ | | | |
| | | | rock and roll version of the song "Old MacDonald Had A Farm" | | | |
| 10/3/60 | 106 | 1 | 2 Itchin'. | $20 | | Cub 9076 |

### JONES, Ken ✪
| 1/4/64 | 125 | 2 | Chicken Pot Pie.................................................... *Second Helping* [I] | $15 | | Almont 305 |
| | | | **KEN JONES** His Piano & Orchestra | | | |

### JONES, Linda
R&B/HOT
Born on 1/14/44 in Newark, New Jersey. Died of diabetes on 3/14/72. R&B singer.

| 12/21/68 | 116 | 2 | I Who Have Nothing................................ *It Won't Take Much (To Bring Me Back)* | $10 | | Loma/Warner 2105 |
| | | | #14 hit for **Tom Jones** in 1970 | | | |

### JONES, Quincy
R&B/HOT/AC
Born Quincy Delight Jones on 3/14/33 in Chicago; raised in Seattle. Composer/producer/conductor/arranger for hundreds of successful singers and orchestras. Won the Grammy's Trustees Award in 1989. Won Grammy's Living Legends Award in 1990.

| 8/11/73 | 102 | 5 | 1 Summer In The City .................................. AC:30 *Sanford & Son Theme* [I] | $6 | | A&M 1455 |
| | | | includes a 30-second vocal by **Valerie Simpson**; #1 hit for **The Lovin' Spoonful** in 1966 | | | |
| 11/20/76 | 104 | 3 | 2 Midnight Soul Patrol ............................................ R&B:47 *Brown Soft Shoe* [I] | $5 | | A&M 1878 |

### JONES, Thelma ✪
R&B
R&B vocalist from Fayetteville, North Carolina.

| 4/13/68 | 132 | 1 | The House That Jack Built................................*Give It To Me Straight* | $10 | | Barry! 1023 |
| | | | #6 hit for **Aretha Franklin** in 1968 | | | |

### JONES, Tom
HOT/AC/C&W/R&B
Born Thomas Jones Woodward on 6/7/40 in Pontypridd, South Wales. Won the 1965 Best New Artist Grammy Award. Host of own TV musical variety series, 1969-71. *Top Pop Singles*: 30.

| 12/11/65 | 125 | 1 | 1 Chills & Fever ....................................................... *Baby I'm In Love* | $15 | | Tower 190 |
| | | | #72 hit for Ronnie Love in 1961 | | | |
| 9/10/66 | 120 | 2 | 2 What A Party ........................................................ *City Girl* | $7 | | Parrot 40008 |
| 6/18/77 | 101¹ | 4 | 3 Take Me Tonight ................................... AC:32 /C&W:87 *I Hope You'll Understand* | $5 | | Epic/MAM 50382 |
| | | | adapted from Tchaikivsky's *Pathetique Symphony* | | | |
| 4/18/81 | 103 | 6 | 4 Darlin'. ................................. C&W:19 / AC:45 *I Don't Want To Know You That Well* | $4 | | Mercury 76100 |
| | | | originally "Bubbled Under" in 1979 by **Frankie Miller** | | | |
| 8/15/81 | 109 | 1 | 5 What In The World's Come Over You ......... C&W:25 *The Things That Matter Most To Me* | $4 | | Mercury 76115 |
| | | | #5 hit for Jack Scott in 1960 | | | |
| 11/12/94 | 108 | 4 | 6 If I Only Knew ..................................................................... *I'm Ready* | $3 | ▮ | Interscope 98203 |

### JONES, Universal
HOT/AC/R&B
Born Eugene B. McDaniels on 2/12/35 in Kansas City. Made the *Hot 100* as Gene McDaniels.

| 9/2/72 | 115 | 3 | River ................................................................. AC:37 *Feeling That Glow* | $8 | | MGM/Verve 10677 |

| DEBUT | PEAK | WKS | A-side (Chart Hit).................................................................B-side | $ | Pic | Label & Number |
|---|---|---|---|---|---|---|

**JONES BOYS, The ✪**
Pop vocal group.

| 9/3/66 | 101[1] | 4 | Impressions *I Remember Barbara* | $10 | | Atco 6426 |

**JONNY Z**
Latin dance singer/rapper John Zazueta.

| 8/3/96 | 102 | 12 | 1 Latin Swing ................................................................. *(club mix)* | $3 | ▌ | Pump/Amigo 645 |
| | | | backing music is "Que Rico El Mambo" by Perez Prado | | | |
| 12/21/96+ | 103 | 11 | 2 No Señor .................................................................... *(radio edit)* | $3 | ▌ | Pump/Amigo 649 |
| | | | samples "Don Quichotte" by Magazine 60 | | | |

**JONZUN CREW, The ✪**                                              R&B
Electronic instrumentation group formed in Boston by ex-Florida brothers Michael and Soni Johnson.

| 10/30/82 | 108 | 3 | Pack Jam (Look Out For The OVC) ....................... R&B:13 *(instrumental)* [I] | $6 | | Tommy Boy 826 (T) |
| | | | available commercially only as a 12" single (a 7" promotional single is available) | | | |

**JOPLIN, Janis**                                                    HOT/ROK
Born on 1/19/43 in Port Arthur, Texas. Died of a heroin overdose in Hollywood on 10/4/70. White blues-rock singer. Lead singer of **Big Brother & The Holding Company**. Inducted into the Rock and Roll Hall of Fame in 1995.

| 2/7/70 | 103 | 6 | 1 Try (Just A Little Bit Harder) ................................. *One Good Man* | $10 | | Columbia 45080 |
| 4/18/70 | 110 | 1 | 2 Maybe ...................................................................... *Wake Me, Lord* | $10 | | Columbia 45128 |
| | | | #15 hit for The Chantels in 1958 | | | |

**JORDAN, Louis ✪**                                          R&B/MEM/POP/C&W
Born on 7/8/08 in Brinkley, Arkansas. Died of a heart attack on 2/4/75. R&B/big band vocalist/saxophonist. Inducted into the Rock and Roll Hall of Fame in 1987 as a rock 'n' roll forefather.

| 5/4/63 | 128 | 1 | Hard Head ................................... *Never Know When A Woman Changes Her Mind* | $12 | | Tangerine 930 |

**JORDAN, Montell**                                                  R&B/HOT
R&B singer from Los Angeles. Stands 6'8" tall.

| 1/13/96 | 125 | 1 | 1 Daddy's Home ....................................... R&B:74 *Comin' Home* | $3 | ▌ | PMP/RAL 577412 |
| 11/22/97 | 103 | 14 | 2 Showdown .......... *Earthquake / Maddoggin / Welcome To California* | $3 | ▌ | Relativity 1643 |
| | | | E-A-SKI Featuring Montell Jordan | | | |

**JORDAN BROS., The ✪**
Rock and roll group of brothers from Schuylkill, Pennsylvania: Joe, Frank, Bob and Lew Jordan.

| 1/21/67 | 129 | 2 | Gimme Some Lovin' ..................................... *When I'm With Her* | $10 | | Philips 40415 |
| | | | #7 hit for The Spencer Davis Group in 1967 | | | |

**JOSEPH, Margie — see HATHAWAY, Donny**

**JOSSETTE ✪**
Techno-dance female singer.

| 3/22/97 | 109 | 8 | In A Dream ...................................................... *(radio edit)* | $3 | ▌ | Galaxy Freestyle 100 |

**J'S WITH JAMIE, The ✪**
Chicago-based pop vocal quartet led by husband-and-wife team of Joe and Jamie Silvia. Heard on many commercial jingles.

| 8/8/64 | 115 | 3 | Theme From "A Summer Place" ....................... *Popsicles In Paris* | $7 | | Columbia 43068 |
| | | | from the movie *A Summer Place* starring Troy Donahue and Sandra Dee; #1 hit for **Percy Faith** in 1960 | | | |

**JUDD, Wynonna — see WYNONNA**

**JUDY, JOHNNY AND BILLY ✪**

| 1/18/60 | 110 | 3 | Beautiful Brown Eyes ...................................... *Toastin' Marshmallows* | $15 | | Silver 1003 |
| | | | #11 hit for Rosemary Clooney in 1951 | | | |

**JUICY ✪**                                                          R&B
R&B/funk brother-and-sister duo of Jerry and Katreese Barnes.

| 8/18/84 | 107 | 1 | Beat Street Strut ...................................... R&B:76 *(instrumental)* | $4 | ■ | Atlantic 89655 |
| | | | from the movie *Beat Street* starring Rae Dawn Chong; Harry Belafonte (executive producer) | | | |

**JULUKA ✪**
The first South African interracial pop band, led by Johnny Clegg and Sipho Mchunu, formed in 1979.

| 7/16/83 | 106 | 4 | Scatterlings Of Africa ...................................................... *Mad Dog* | $4 | | Warner 29599 |

**JUNIOR ✪**                                                         R&B/HOT
Born Junior Giscombe in England. R&B-funk singer/songwriter.

| 6/12/82 | 102 | 5 | Too Late ............................................ R&B:8 *(instrumental)* | $4 | | Mercury 76150 |

**JUNIOR AND THE CLASSICS ✪**
Milwaukee R&B-rock band led by keyboardist Robert "Junior" Brantley.

| 9/26/64 | 134 | 1 | The Dog ....................................................... *Birmingham* | $15 | | Groove 0043 |
| | | | #87 hit for Rufus Thomas in 1963 | | | |

**JUNIOR M.A.F.I.A.**                                                R&B/HOT
Rap group featuring Lil' Kim, Trife and Klepto.

| 12/2/95 | 103 | 12 | I Need You Tonight ........... Sls:60 /R&B:43 *Realms Of Junior M.A.F.I.A. (Part II)* | $3 | ▌ | Undeas/Big Beat 98097 |
| | | | JUNIOR M.A.F.I.A. featuring Aaliyah | | | |

**JU-PAR UNIVERSAL ORCHESTRA ✪**                                      R&B
A "Juney" Garrett and Richard Parker funk aggregation.

| 7/16/77 | 101[1] | 6 | Funky Music R&B:32 *Time* | $5 | | Ju-Par 8002 |

**JUSTICE, Jimmy ✪**
Pop singer.

| 10/13/62 | 127 | 1 | When My Little Girl Is Smiling ....................... *If I Lost Your Love* | $10 | | Kapp 482 |
| | | | Bob Leaper (orch.); #28 hit for The Drifters in 1962 | | | |

**JUSTIS, Bill**                                                     HOT/R&B/C&W
Born on 10/14/26 in Birmingham, Alabama. Died on 7/15/82 in Nashville. Top session saxophonist/arranger/producer.

| 5/11/63 | 101[1] | 4 | Tamoure' *I'm Gonna Learn To Dance* | $10 | ■ | Smash 1812 |

| DEBUT | PEAK | WKS | A-side (Chart Hit)..................................................................B-side | $ | Pic | Label & Number |
|---|---|---|---|---|---|---|

**JUST US**  `HOT/AC`
Duo of New York City producers **Chip Taylor** and **Al Gorgoni**.

| 10/9/71 | 103 | 4 | Used To Be ................................................... *Oh Woman (I Really Know The Blues)* | $8 | | Atlantic 2831 |

# K

**KAEMPFERT, Bert, And His Orchestra**  `HOT/AC/R&B`
Born on 10/16/23 in Hamburg, Germany. Died on 6/21/80 in Switzerland. Multi-instrumentalist/bandleader/producer/arranger for Polydor
Records in Germany. Composed "Strangers In The Night" and "Spanish Eyes" among others. Produced first **Beatles** recording session.

| 2/3/62 | 108 | 3 | 1 Echo In The Night ........................................ *Afrikaan Beat (Hot #42)* [I] | $8 | | Decca 31350 |
| 5/7/66 | 124 | 2 | 2 Strangers In The Night ........................... AC:8 *But Not Today* [I] | $7 | | Decca 31945 |

theme from the movie *A Man Could Get Killed* starring James Garner; #1 hit for **Frank Sinatra** in 1966

**KAGNY & THE DIRTY RATS**
Detroit-based funk group led by Kerry Gordy (son of Motown chairman, Berry Gordy, Jr.).

| 8/20/83 | 110 | 1 | At 15 ................................................................. *Dirty Rats* | $5 | | Motown 1672 |

**KALIN TWINS, The**  `HOT/R&B/C&W`
Duo of twins Herbert and Harold Kalin. Born on 2/16/34 in Port Jervis, New York.

| 12/5/60 | 112 | 2 | Zing! Went The Strings Of My Heart ........................... *No Money Can Buy* | $15 | | Decca 31169 |

Leroy Kirkland (orch.); #22 hit for Judy Garland in 1943

**KALLEN, Kitty**  `MEM/POP/HOT/AC`
Born on 5/25/22 in Philadelphia. Big band singer with Jack Teagarden, Jimmy Dorsey, Harry James and Artie Shaw.

| 3/3/62 | 101[1] | 4 | 1 It Wasn't God Who Made Honky Tonk Angels *You Are My Sunshine* | $8 | ☐ | Columbia 42247 |

Milton DeLugg (orch.); #1 Country hit for Kitty Wells in 1952

| 3/30/63 | 121 | 2 | 2 Please Don't ............................................... *Star Eyes* | $8 | | RCA Victor 8158 |

Ray Ellis (orch.)

**KALYAN** ☼  `R&B`
Fourteen-man soul/calypso band from Trinidad — Olsop David, lead singer.

| 4/2/77 | 102 | 9 | Disco Reggae (Tony's Groove) Part 1 ........................... R&B:92 *Part 2* | $6 | | MCA 40699 |

recorded in Canada

**KANE, Big Daddy — see ASSORTED PHLAVORS**

**KANE, Eden** ☼
Born Richard Sarstedt on 3/29/42 in India and raised in Britain. Brother of **Peter Sarstedt**.

| 10/2/61 | 119 | 1 | Well, I Ask You ......................................... *Before I Lose My Mind* | $15 | | London 1993 |

**KANE'S COUSINS** ☼
A **Steve Alaimo** production.

| 6/14/69 | 116 | 5 | Take Your Love (And Shove It) ................... *Support Your Local Bands* | $12 | | Shove Love 500 |

**KARAZOV, Alexandrow** ☼

| 5/3/69 | 120 | 4 | Castschok ..................................... AC:24 *Jacobuska* [I] | $10 | | Jamie 1372 |

promo copies show title as "Casatschok (Life Is A Dance)"

**KASEM, Casey** ☼
Born Kemal Kasem on 4/27/32 in Detroit. Created popular radio countdown show *American Top 40* in 1970. Also hosted radio countdown
show *Casey's Top 40* and TV's *America's Top Ten*.

| 10/3/64 | 103 | 2 | Letter From Elaina ................... *Theme For Elaina (The Burbank Strings)* [S] | $20 | | Warner 5474 |

René Hall (orch.); background melody is **The Beatles**' tune "And I Love Her"

**KASENETZ-KATZ SINGING**
**ORCHESTRAL CIRCUS**  `HOT`
Bubblegum rock group assembled by producers Jerry Kasenetz and Jeff Katz.

| 7/13/68 | 124 | 3 | 1 Down In Tennessee ............................................. *Mrs. Green* | $8 | | Buddah 52 |

features: **1910 Fruitgum Co./Ohio Express/Music Explosion/**Teri Nelson Group/1989 Musical Marching Zoo/St. Louis Invisible Marching
Band/Lt. Garcia's Magic Music Box/J.C.W. Ratfinks

| 1/4/69 | 105 | 3 | 2 I'm In Love With You ................................. *To You, With Love* | $8 | | Buddah 82 |

**KASENETZ-KATZ SUPER CIRKUS**
Joey Levine (lead singer, above 2)

**KASHIF**  `R&B/HOT`
Born Michael Jones in Brooklyn in 1959. Techno-funk musician/vocalist.

| 3/26/83 | 103 | 6 | 1 I Just Gotta Have You (Lover Turn Me On) ........................ R&B:5 *(instrumental)* | $4 | | Arista 1042 |
| 8/4/84 | 108 | 4 | 2 Baby Don't Break Your Baby's Heart ...................... R&B:6 *(instrumental)* | $3 | | Arista 9200 |

**KAUSION** ☼  `R&B`
Rap trio from Los Angeles: Gonzoe, Cel and Kaydo.

| 9/16/95 | 106 | 9 | What You Wanna Do? ............... R&B:72 *(radio version) / Bounce, Rock, Skate (2 versions)* | $3 | ▌ | Lench Mob 2001 |

samples **Parliament**'s "Aqua Boogie" and "Theme From The Black Hole"

**KAY, John**  `HOT`
Born Joachim Krauledat on 4/12/44 in East Germany. Leader of **Steppenwolf**.

| 6/2/73 | 105 | 5 | 1 Moonshine (Friend of Mine) ......................... *Nobody Lives Here Anymore* | $5 | | Dunhill/ABC 4351 |
| 8/25/73 | 102 | 8 | 2 Easy Evil ............................................. *Dance To My Song* | $5 | | Dunhill/ABC 4360 |

**KAZAN, Lainie** ☼  `AC`
Born Lainie Levine on 5/16/40 in New York City. Movie actress.

| 1/28/67 | 123 | 2 | Kiss Tomorrow Goodbye ............................ AC:29 *Sweet Talk* | $7 | | MGM 13657 |

Herb Bernstein (orch.)

**KC And The SUNSHINE BAND**     R&B/HOT/AC
Disco band formed in Florida in 1973 by lead singer/keyboardist Harry "KC" Casey (b: 1/31/51) and bassist Richard Finch (b: 1/25/54).

| DEBUT | PEAK | WKS | A-side | $ | Pic | Label & Number |
|-------|------|-----|---|---|---|---|
| 4/2/83 | 103 | 4 | 1 **Don't Run (Come Back To Me)**..............................................AC:12 *On The One* | $4 | | Epic 03688 |
| | | | KC & THE SUNSHINE BAND (with Teri DeSario) originally released in 1982 on Epic 03556 | | | |
| 5/5/84 | 104 | 4 | 2 **Are You Ready**.............................................................................*(Part 2)* | $4 | | Meca 1002 |
| | | | KC | | | |

**K DOE, Ernie**     HOT/R&B
Born Ernest Kador on 2/22/36 in New Orleans. R&B singer/songwriter. Recorded with the Blue Diamonds on Savoy in 1954.

| | | | | | | |
|-------|------|-----|---|---|---|---|
| 4/15/67 | 122 | 2 | **Later For Tomorrow**.........................................R&B:37 *Dancin' Man* | $10 | | Duke 411 |

**KEITH**     HOT
Born James Barry Keefer on 5/7/49 in Philadelphia. First recorded as Keith & The Admirations on Columbia in 1965.

| | | | | | | |
|-------|------|-----|---|---|---|---|
| 11/11/67 | 135 | 1 | **I'm So Proud**..............................................................*Candy Candy* | $8 | ■ | Mercury 72746 |

**KEITH, Toby**     C&W/HOT
Born Toby Keith Covel on 7/8/61 in Clinton, Oklahoma. Country singer. Former rodeo hand, oil field worker and semi-pro football player.

| | | | | | | |
|-------|------|-----|---|---|---|---|
| 10/9/93 | 107 | 8 | 1 **He Ain't Worth Missing**.......................C&W:5 *A Little Less Talk And A Lot More Action* | $3 | ▮ | Mercury 862262 |
| | | | B-side was a #2 Country hit in 1993 on Mercury 862844 | | | |
| 9/3/94 | 102 | 11 | 2 **Who's That Man**........................................Sls:50 /C&W:❶¹ *(3 album snippets)* | $3 | ▮ | Polydor 853358 |
| 5/4/96 | 112 | 9 | 3 **Does That Blue Moon Ever Shine On You**...............C&W:2 *(3 album snippets)* | $3 | ▮ | Polydor 576140 |
| 8/30/97 | 116 | 6 | 4 **We Were In Love**.........................................................C&W:2 *Tired* | $3 | ▮ | Mercury 574636 |

**KELLER, Jerry**     HOT
Born on 6/20/37 in Fort Smith, Arkansas; raised in Tulsa, Oklahoma.

| | | | | | | |
|-------|------|-----|---|---|---|---|
| 10/23/61 | 112 | 2 | **Be Careful How You Drive Young Joey**....................*Never Wake Up* | $15 | | Capitol 4630 |
| | | | Richard Wolfe (orch.) | | | |

**KELLY, Casey**     HOT
Born Daniel Cohen in Baton Rouge, Louisiana. Singer/songwriter/pianist/guitarist.

| | | | | | | |
|-------|------|-----|---|---|---|---|
| 1/6/73 | 110 | 3 | **You Can't Get There From Here**.............................*Making Believe* | $6 | | Elektra 45826 |

**KELLY, Paul**     R&B/HOT
Born on 6/19/40 in Miami. With R&B vocal groups The Spades and The Valadiers.

| | | | | | | |
|-------|------|-----|---|---|---|---|
| 12/11/65 | 123 | 1 | 1 **Chills And Fever**................................................*Only Your Love* | $15 | | Dial 4021 |
| 6/24/67 | 126 | 2 | 2 **Sweet Sweet Lovin'**.......................................*Cryin' For My Baby* | $15 | | Philips 40457 |

**KELLY, R. — see MR. LEE**

**KELLY, Wynton** ☺
Born on 12/2/31 in Brooklyn. Jazz pianist.

| | | | | | | |
|-------|------|-----|---|---|---|---|
| 5/9/64 | 113 | 3 | **Little Tracy**..................................................*It's All Right* [I] | $10 | | Verve 10316 |

**KENDRICKS, Eddie**     R&B/HOT/AC
Born on 12/17/39 in Union Springs, Alabama. Died on 10/5/92. Lead singer of **The Temptations**, 1960-71.

| | | | | | | |
|-------|------|-----|---|---|---|---|
| 11/20/71 | 101¹ | 3 | **Can I**........................................................R&B:37 *I Did It All For You* | $6 | | Tamla 54210 |

**KENJOLAIRS, The** ☺
Male pop vocal trio whose name was taken from their first names: Ken, Joe and Larry.

| | | | | | | |
|-------|------|-----|---|---|---|---|
| 12/29/62 | 116 | 3 | **Little White Lies**...................................*The Story Of An Evergreen Tree* | $10 | | A&M 704 |
| | | | #1 hit for Fred Waring's Pennsylvanians in 1930; #25 hit for **Betty Johnson** in 1957 | | | |

**KENNEDY, Ray**     HOT
Pop-rock singer/songwriter. Member of KGB (Kennedy, Rick Grech, Mike Bloomfield).

| | | | | | | |
|-------|------|-----|---|---|---|---|
| 8/30/80 | 109 | 2 | **Starlight**...............................................*Let Me Sing You A Love Letter* | $4 | | ARC 11298 |

**KENNER, Chris**     HOT/R&B
Born on 12/25/29 in Kenner, Louisiana. Died on 1/28/76. Male R&B singer/songwriter. First recorded for Baton in 1956.

| | | | | | | |
|-------|------|-----|---|---|---|---|
| 9/4/61 | 103 | 4 | **A Very True Story**.......................................................*Packin' Up* | $20 | | Instant 3234 |

**KENNY G**     AC/R&B/HOT
Born Kenny Gorelick on 7/6/56 in Seattle. Fusion saxophonist. Joined **Barry White's Love Unlimited Orchestra** at age 17.

| | | | | | | |
|-------|------|-----|---|---|---|---|
| 6/25/94 | 122 | 3 | **Even If My Heart Would Break**........................AC:28 *The Joy Of Life* (Kenny G) | $3 | ▮ | Arista 12674 |
| | | | KENNY G with Aaron Neville | | | |

**KERR, Anita, Quartet**     AC/HOT
Born Anita Jean Grob on 10/13/27 in Memphis. Also recorded as Anita & Th' So-And-So's.

| | | | | | | |
|-------|------|-----|---|---|---|---|
| 12/14/63 | 125 | 3 | **Waitin' For The Evening Train**....................*Guitar Country* (w/Chet Atkins) | $8 | | RCA Victor 8246 |
| | | | from the Broadway musical *Jennie* starring Mary Martin | | | |

**KERR, George** ☺     R&B
Singer/producer for Motown, All Platinum/Stang and many Philadelphia soul records.

| | | | | | | |
|-------|------|-----|---|---|---|---|
| 5/9/70 | 124 | 1 | **3 Minutes 2 - Hey Girl**.............................R&B:15 *Back Lash* (G. Kerr Orch.) | $7 | | All Platinum 2316 |
| | | | recitation, followed by Kerr's version of **Freddie Scott**'s 1963 hit "Hey Girl" | | | |

**KERSH, David**     C&W/HOT
Born on 12/9/70 in Humble, Texas. Country singer/songwriter.

| | | | | | | |
|-------|------|-----|---|---|---|---|
| 11/16/96 | 113 | 10 | **Goodnight Sweetheart**....................C&W:6 *Breaking Hearts And Taking Names* (C&W #65) | $3 | ▮ | Curb 76990 |

**KERSHAW, Nik**     HOT/ROK
Born on 3/1/58 in Bristol, England. Pop singer/songwriter/multi-instrumentalist.

| | | | | | | |
|-------|------|-----|---|---|---|---|
| 4/13/85 | 107 | 2 | **The Riddle**....................................................................*Progress* | $4 | ■ | MCA 52544 |

**KERSHAW, Sammy**     C&W/HOT
Born Samuel Cashat on 2/24/58 in Abbeville, Louisiana. Country singer.

| | | | | | | |
|-------|------|-----|---|---|---|---|
| 3/27/93 | 119 | 6 | 1 **She Don't Know She's Beautiful**........................C&W:❶¹ *I Buy Her Roses* | $3 | ▮ | Mercury 864854 |
| 10/15/94 | 105 | 6 | 2 **Third Rate Romance**.............................Sls:66 /C&W:2 *Paradise From Nine To One* | $3 | ▮ | Mercury 858922 |
| | | | #14 hit for **The Amazing Rhythm Aces** in 1975 | | | |

| DEBUT | PEAK | WKS | A-side (Chart Hit)..........................................................................................................B-side | $ | Pic | Label & Number |
|---|---|---|---|---|---|---|

**KETCHUM, Hal ○**                 C&W
Born on 4/9/53 in Greenwich, New York. Country singer/guitarist.

| 6/3/95 | 124 | 1 | Stay Forever ...................................... **C&W:8** *Every Little Word* | $3 | ▌ | Curb 76929 |

B-side was a #49 Country hit in 1995 on Curb 76965

**KEY, Scott ○**
Scott Key is actually producer Frank Sciarra.

| 7/4/76 | 110 | 1 | Town Cryer ...................................... *Part Two (How 'Bout A Draft)* [N] | $8 | | Pyramid 8002 |

a Dickie Goodman "cut-in" type record

**KEYES, Bert ○**
Top R&B arranger/producer. Wrote "Love On A Two-Way Street."

| 1/30/65 | 132 | 1 | Do-Do Do Bah-Ah ...................................... *Lady In My Heart* [I] | $15 | | Clock 1048 |

**KEYSTONE ○**             R&B
Rap duo from Brooklyn: Will Gardner and Tyrone Taylor.

| 9/6/97 | 107 | 6 | If It Ain't Love ...................................... **R&B:49** *I Can't Live Without You* | $3 | ▌ | Qwest 17375 |

from the movie *Sprung* starring Tisha Campbell

**KHAN, Chaka (Rufus)**         R&B/HOT/AC
Born Yvette Marie Stevens on 3/23/53 in Great Lakes, Illinois. Became lead singer of **Rufus** in 1972. Recorded solo and with Rufus since 1978. *Top Pop Singles:* 24.

| 4/21/73 | 110 | 4 | 1 Slip 'N Slide ...................................... *I Finally Found You* | $7 | | ABC 11356 |
| 8/26/78 | 105 | 3 | 2 Blue Love ...................................... **R&B:34** *Turn* | $5 | | ABC 12390 |

      RUFUS featuring CHAKA KHAN

| 2/17/79 | 109 | 2 | 3 Keep It Together (Declaration Of Love) ...................................... **R&B:16** *Red Hot Poker* | $5 | | ABC 12444 |

      RUFUS (#1 & 3)

| 3/8/80 | 102 | 3 | 4 Any Love ...................................... **R&B:24** *What Am I Missing?* | $4 | | MCA 41191 |

      RUFUS AND CHAKA

| 5/17/80 | 103 | 2 | 5 Clouds ...................................... **R&B:10** *What You Did* | $4 | ■ | Warner 49216 |

      CHAKA KHAN
      written by Ashford & Simpson

| 2/11/84 | 102 | 3 | 6 One Million Kisses ...................................... **R&B:37** *Stay* | $4 | | Warner 29406 |

      RUFUS AND CHAKA KHAN

| 11/23/96 | 102 | 14 | 7 Never Miss The Water    **R&B:36** *(remix) / Papillon (aka Hot Butterfly)* | $3 | ▌ | Reprise 17503 |

      CHAKA KHAN Featuring Me'Shell NdegéOcello

**KHAN, Sajid ○**             AC
Indian youth who starred in the TV series *Maya* as Raji.

| 10/12/68 | 108 | 5 | 1 Getting To Know You ...................................... *Há Ram* | $5 | | Colgems 1026 |

      from the Oscar Hammerstein, Richard Rodgers 1951 musical *The King And I*

| 2/1/69 | 119 | 2 | 2 Dream ...................................... **AC:29** *Someday* | $5 | ■ | Colgems 1034 |

      #1 hit for the Pied Pipers in 1945; #19 hit for **Betty Johnson** in 1958

**KID CREOLE & THE COCONUTS**       R&B/HOT
Born Thomas Augustus Darnell Browder on 8/12/50 in Montreal. Singer/songwriter/producer. Formed The Coconuts with his wife, Adriana "Addy" Kaegi, and Andy "Coati Mundi" Hernandez.

| 8/27/83 | 108 | 2 | 1 If I Only Had A Brain ...................................... *Indiscreet* | $3 | ■ | EMI America 8173 |

      THE COCONUTS
      sung in the 1939 movie *The Wizard Of Oz*

| 7/7/84 | 110 | 2 | 2 My Male Curiosity ...................................... *The Race (Larry Carlton)* | $3 | | Atlantic 89664 |

      from the movie *Against All Odds* starring Rachel Ward and Jeff Bridges

**KIHN, Greg**         ROK/HOT/R&B
Born in Baltimore in 1952. Formed band in 1975 in Berkeley, California.

| 11/4/78+ | 105 | 12 | 1 Remember ...................................... *Politics* | $6 | | Beserkley 5749 |
| 5/2/81 | 102 | 1 | 2 Sheila ...................................... **ROK:39** *When The Music Starts* | $5 | | Beserkley 47131 |

      #1 hit for **Tommy Roe** in 1962

| 10/3/81 | 104 | 4 | 3 The Girl Most Likely ...................................... **ROK:57** *True Confessions* | $5 | | Beserkley 47206 |
| 6/9/84 | 101[1] | 3 | 4 Reunited    **ROK:9** *Work, Work, Work* | $4 | | Beserkley 69736 |
| 8/4/84 | 107 | 1 | 5 Rock ...................................... *Stand Together* | $4 | | Beserkley 69710 |

      GREG KIHN BAND (#1, 4 & 5)

| 6/8/85 | 110 | 1 | 6 Boys Won't (Leave The Girls Alone) ...................................... *Good Life* | $4 | ■ | EMI America 8272 |

**KILGORE, Theola**        HOT/R&B
Born in Shreveport, Louisiana; raised in Oakland. Female gospel-blues singer.

| 7/25/64 | 108 | 4 | 1 I'll Keep Trying/ | | | |
| 6/27/64 | 133 | 1 | 2    He's Coming Back To Me ...................................... | $15 | | KT 501 |

**KILLARMY ○**         R&B
Male rap group from New York City: Killa Sin, Shogun Assassin, Ninth Prince, Baretta Nine, Islord and Dom Pachino.

| 3/29/97 | 101[2] | 14 | Wu-Renegades    **Sls:69** /**R&B:69** *(same version)* | $3 | ▌ | Wu-Tang/Priority 53267 |

      produced by Robert Diggs ("RZA") of **Wu-Tang Clan**

**KILO ○**         R&B
Kilo (pronounced: ky-lo) Ali. Male rapper from Atlanta.

| 3/23/96 | 115 | 10 | Nasty Dancer ...................................... **R&B:67** *White Horse (R&B #67)* | $3 | ▌ | Wrap/Ichiban 349 |

**KIM, Andy**         HOT/AC
Born Andrew Joachim on 12/5/46 in Montreal. His parents were from Lebanon. Pop singer/songwriter.

| 3/22/69 | 110 | 3 | 1 Tricia Tell Your Daddy ...................................... *Foundation Of My Soul* | $7 | | Steed 715 |
| 8/12/72 | 111 | 1 | 2 Who Has The Answers? ...................................... *Shady Hollow Dreamers* | $7 | | Uni 55332 |

**KING, Albert**        R&B/HOT
Born Albert Nelson on 4/25/23 in Indianola, Mississippi. Died on 12/21/92. Noted blues singer/guitarist.

| 3/8/69 | 132 | 2 | 1 As The Years Go Passing By ...................................... *The Hunter* | $8 | | Atlantic 2604 |
| 7/18/70 | 127 | 1 | 2 Can't You See What You're Doing To Me ...................................... **R&B:50** *Cold Sweat* | $7 | | Stax 0069 |
| 10/23/71 | 103 | 2 | 3 Everybody Wants To Go To Heaven ...................................... **R&B:38** *Lovejoy, Ill.* | $7 | | Stax 0101 |

113

| DEBUT | PEAK | WKS | A-side (Chart Hit)............................................................................B-side | $ | Pic | Label & Number |
|---|---|---|---|---|---|---|

## KING, B.B.     R&B/HOT

Born Riley B. King on 9/16/25 in Itta Bena, Mississippi. The most famous blues singer/guitarist in the world today. Inducted into the Rock and Roll Hall of Fame in 1987. Won Grammy's Lifetime Achievement Award in 1987. *Top Pop Singles:* 36.

| DEBUT | PEAK | WKS | A-side | $ | Pic | Label & Number |
|---|---|---|---|---|---|---|
| 6/26/61 | 119 | 1 | 1 Peace Of Mind ........................ R&B:7 *Someday* (R&B #16) | $15 | | Kent 360 |
| 11/10/62 | 106 | 2 | 2 Tomorrow Night .................................. *Mother's Love* | $12 | | ABC-Paramount 10367 |
| 8/8/64 | 107 | 5 | 3 You're Gonna Miss Me/ | | | Kent 396 |
| 8/15/64 | 110 | 4 | 4   Let Me Love You ..................................... | $12 | | Kent 396 |
| 1/14/67 | 112 | 4 | 5 Waitin' On You ............................................. *Night Life* | $10 | | ABC 10889 |
| 11/30/68 | 102 | 6 | 6 Please Send Me Someone To Love ....... *Dance With Me* | $7 | | BluesWay 61021 |
| | | | #1 R&B hit for Percy Mayfield in 1950 | | | |
| 2/1/69 | 113 | 3 | 7 Don't Waste My Time ................ *Get Myself Somebody* | $7 | | BluesWay 61022 |
| 8/9/69 | 127 | 3 | 8 I Want You So Bad .......... R&B:34 *Get Off My Back Woman* (Hot #74) | $7 | | BluesWay 61026 |
| 7/24/76 | 101[1] | 2 | 9 Let The Good Times Roll   R&B:20 *Strange Things* | $5 | | ABC Impulse 31006 |

**BOBBY BLAND & B.B. KING**
"live" recording; #2 R&B hit for Louis Jordan in 1947

| DEBUT | PEAK | WKS | A-side | $ | Pic | Label & Number |
|---|---|---|---|---|---|---|
| 8/12/78 | 102 | 3 | 10 Never Make A Move Too Soon .......... R&B:19 *Let Me Make You Cry A Little Longer* | $5 | | ABC 12380 |
| 9/15/79 | 110 | 1 | 11 Better Not Look Down ...................... R&B:30 *Happy Birthday Blues* | $5 | | MCA 41062 |
| | | | above 2 feature backing and production by The Crusaders | | | |
| 5/11/85 | 107 | 1 | 12 Into The Night .............. R&B:15 *Century City Chase or J.B. In Teheran* [I] | $4 | ■ | MCA 52530 |
| | | | title song from the movie starring Jeff Goldblum and Michelle Pfeiffer | | | |

## KING, Ben E.     R&B/HOT/AC

Born Benjamin Earl Nelson on 9/23/38 in Henderson, North Carolina. Worked with The Moonglows for six months while still in high school. Lead singer of The Drifters, 1959-60. *Top Pop Singles:* 22.

| DEBUT | PEAK | WKS | A-side | $ | Pic | Label & Number |
|---|---|---|---|---|---|---|
| 11/3/62 | 111 | 5 | 1 I'm Standing By ................. *Walking In The Footsteps Of A Fool* | $15 | | Atco 6237 |
| | | | tune is similar to his 1961 hit "Stand By Me" | | | |
| 1/19/63 | 122 | 1 | 2 Tell Daddy ............................. R&B:29 *Auf Weidersehn, My Dear* | $15 | | Atco 6246 |
| 1/25/64 | 102 | 4 | 3 What Now My Love ................................... *Groovin'* | $12 | | Atco 6284 |
| | | | #14 hit for Sonny & Cher in 1966 | | | |
| 3/21/64 | 125 | 1 | 4 Around The Corner ....................... *That's When It Hurts* (Hot #63) | $12 | | Atco 6288 |
| 7/4/64 | 113 | 2 | 5 What Can A Man Do ................................ *Si Senor* | $12 | | Atco 6303 |
| 6/5/65 | 128 | 1 | 6 She's Gone Again ................ *Not Now (I'll Tell You When)* | $12 | | Atco 6357 |
| 3/2/68 | 127 | 2 | 7 We Got A Thing Going On ........... *What'cha Gonna Do About It* | $10 | | Atco 6557 |
| | | | **BEN E. KING & DEE DEE SHARP** | | | |
| 4/27/68 | 117 | 4 | 8 Don't Take Your Love From Me ....... R&B:44 *Forgive This Fool* | $10 | | Atco 6571 |
| 12/21/68 | 134 | 1 | 9 Til I Can't Take It Anymore .......... R&B:37 *It Ain't Fair* | $10 | | Atco 6637 |

## KING, Carole     AC/HOT

Born Carole Klein on 2/9/42 in Brooklyn. Singer/songwriter/pianist. Neil Sedaka wrote his 1959 hit "Oh! Carol" about her. Married to lyricist Gerry Goffin (1958-68). In 1971, won four Grammys. King and Goffin were inducted as a songwriting team into the Rock and Roll Hall of Fame in 1990.

| DEBUT | PEAK | WKS | A-side | $ | Pic | Label & Number |
|---|---|---|---|---|---|---|
| 11/17/62 | 123 | 3 | School Bells Are Ringing ........................ *I Didn't Have Any Summer Romance* | $25 | | Dimension 1004 |

## KING, Claude     C&W/HOT/AC

Born on 2/5/33 in Shreveport, Louisiana. Country singer/songwriter/guitarist.

| DEBUT | PEAK | WKS | A-side | $ | Pic | Label & Number |
|---|---|---|---|---|---|---|
| 12/8/62 | 111 | 1 | 1 I've Got The World By The Tail ........................ C&W:11 *Shopping Center* | $8 | ■ | Columbia 42630 |
| 7/10/65 | 110 | 4 | 2 Tiger Woman ................... C&W:6 *When You Gotta Go (You Gotta Go)* | $7 | | Columbia 43298 |

## KING, Evelyn "Champagne"     R&B/HOT/AC

Born on 6/29/60 in the Bronx, New York. To Philadelphia in 1970. Employed as a cleaning woman at Sigma Sound Studios when discovered.

| DEBUT | PEAK | WKS | A-side | $ | Pic | Label & Number |
|---|---|---|---|---|---|---|
| 4/21/84 | 107 | 2 | 1 Shake Down ........................... R&B:12 *Tell Me Something Good* | $4 | | RCA 13748 |
| 12/1/84 | 107 | 3 | 2 Just For The Night ................... R&B:16 *So In Love* | $4 | ■ | RCA 13914 |

## KING, Freddy     R&B/HOT

Born Freddie Christian on 9/3/34 in Gilmer, Texas. Died on 12/28/76 of a hepatitis-related heart attack. Blues vocalist/guitarist.

| DEBUT | PEAK | WKS | A-side | $ | Pic | Label & Number |
|---|---|---|---|---|---|---|
| 2/2/63 | 103 | 2 | 1 The Bossa Nova Watusi Twist ............ *Look, Ma I'm Cryin'* [I] | $20 | | Federal 12482 |
| 1/4/69 | 127 | 1 | 2 Play It Cool.................................... *Funky* | $8 | | Cotillion 44015 |

## KING, Jonathan     HOT/AC

Born Kenneth King on 12/6/44 in London. Singer/songwriter/producer. Produced Hedgehoppers Anonymous.

| DEBUT | PEAK | WKS | A-side | $ | Pic | Label & Number |
|---|---|---|---|---|---|---|
| 5/13/67 | 122 | 4 | Round, Round ........................... *Time And Motion* | $8 | | Parrot 3011 |

## KING, Pete ○

Born on 8/8/14 in Greenville, Ohio. Died on 9/21/82. Composer/conductor for several movies and TV shows.

| DEBUT | PEAK | WKS | A-side | $ | Pic | Label & Number |
|---|---|---|---|---|---|---|
| 2/27/61 | 108 | 3 | Hey! Look Me Over ................................. *Tall Hope* | $8 | | Kapp 367 |

**THE PETE KING CHORALE AND ORCHESTRA**
from the Broadway musical *Wildcat* starring Lucille Ball

## KING, Solomon ○

Pop vocalist with a style similar to Tom Jones.

| DEBUT | PEAK | WKS | A-side | $ | Pic | Label & Number |
|---|---|---|---|---|---|---|
| 4/6/68 | 117 | 3 | She Wears My Ring ................... *I Get That Feeling Over You* | $8 | | Capitol 2114 |

Charles Blackwell (orch.); #24 R&B hit for Jimmy Sweeney in 1962

## KING CURTIS     HOT/R&B/AC

Born Curtis Ousley on 2/7/34 in Fort Worth, Texas. Stabbed to death on 8/13/71 in New York City. R&B saxophonist. Played on sessions for hundreds of top recording artists.

| DEBUT | PEAK | WKS | A-side | $ | Pic | Label & Number |
|---|---|---|---|---|---|---|
| 8/11/62 | 119 | 1 | 1 Wobble Twist .......................... *Twistin' With The King* [I] | $15 | | Enjoy 1001 |
| | | | **KING CURTIS and THE NOBLE KNIGHTS** | | | |
| 10/24/64 | 112 | 4 | 2 Hide Away .......................... *Stranger On The Shore* [I] | $10 | | Capitol 5270 |
| | | | #29 hit for Freddy King in 1961 | | | |
| 1/2/65 | 130 | 1 | 3 Tanya .......................... *Sister Sadie* [I] | $10 | | Capitol 5324 |
| | | | #3 R&B hit for Joe Liggins in 1946 | | | |
| 7/1/67 | 105 | 6 | 4 You Don't Miss Your Water   *Green Onions* [I] | $8 | | Atco 6496 |
| | | | #95 hit for William Bell in 1962 | | | |

**KING CURTIS — Cont'd**

| DEBUT | PEAK | WKS | A-side / B-side | $ | Pic | Label & Number |
|---|---|---|---|---|---|---|
| 3/22/69 | 116 | 2 | 5 Games People Play/ | | | |
| | | | #12 hit for Joe South in 1969 | | | |
| 4/12/69 | 123 | 2 | 6 Foot Pattin', Part II ...........................................................[I] | $8 | | Atco 6664 |
| 4/12/69 | 132 | 2 | 7 Sing A Simple Song ........................................ Movin' Part IV [I] | $8 | | Cotillion 44030 |
| | | | **THE NOBLE KNIGHTS** | | | |
| | | | #89 hit for Sly & The Family Stone in 1969 | | | |
| 5/31/69 | 127 | 3 | 8 Instant Groove ................................. R&B:35 Sweet Inspiration | $8 | | Atco 6680 |
| | | | **KING CURTIS & THE KINGPINS** (#5, 6 & 8) | | | |
| 8/9/69 | 128 | 2 | 9 La Jeanne .......................................... Little Green Apples [I] | $8 | | Atco 6695 |
| 4/11/70 | 128 | 1 | 10 Teasin' ......................................... Soulin' (Curtis) [I] | $8 | | Atco 6738 |
| | | | **KING CURTIS With Delaney Bramlett, Eric Clapton & Friends** | | | |

## KING FLOYD — see FLOYD, King

## KING HANNIBAL — see MIGHTY HANNIBAL

## KING JUST
HOT/R&B

Male rapper from Staten Island, New York.

| 7/8/95 | 125 | 1 | No Flow On The Rodeo ................ (dub version) / Escape From The Zoo / Warrior's Drum | $3 | ∎ | Black Fist/Select 27492 |

## KING RICHARD'S FLUEGEL KNIGHTS ☉
AC

Instrumental troupe led by Dick (King Richard) Behrke.

| 5/13/67 | 126 | 4 | 1 Everybody Loves My Baby ....................... AC:11 Two Different Worlds [I] | $6 | | MTA 120 |
| | | | #5 hit for Aileen Stanley in 1925 | | | |
| 1/13/68 | 107 | 2 | 2 Camelot ........................................... AC:12 Bye, Bye Blues [I] | $6 | | MTA 138 |
| | | | title song from the Lerner/Lowe musical | | | |

## KINGS, The
HOT

Rock band from Toronto: David Diamond (vocals, bass), Aryan Zero (guitar), Sonny Keyes (keyboards) and Max Styles (drums).

| 3/21/81 | 109 | 1 | Don't Let Me Know .......................................... Partyitis | $5 | | Elektra 47110 |

## KINGSMEN, The
HOT/R&B

Rock band formed in 1957 in Portland, Oregon: Jack Ely (vocals, guitar), Mike Mitchell (guitar), Don Gallucci (piano), Bob Nordby (bass) and Lynn Easton (vocals, drums).

| 12/25/65 | 122 | 1 | 1 (You Got) The Gamma Goochee.......................... It's Only The Dog | $15 | | Wand 1107 |
| 10/21/67 | 128 | 3 | 2 Bo Diddley Bach ......................... Just Before The Break Of Day | $10 | | Wand 1164 |

## KINGSTON TRIO, The
HOT/AC/R&B

Folk trio formed in San Francisco in 1957: Dave Guard (banjo; d: 3/22/91, age 56), **Bob Shane** and Nick Reynolds (guitars). Guard replaced by John Stewart in 1961.

| 2/8/60 | 102 | 3 | 1 Home From The Hill                    El Matador (Hot #32) | $12 | | Capitol 4338 |
| | | | title song from the movie starring Robert Mitchum | | | |
| 9/1/62 | 113 | 1 | 2 Old Joe Clark.......................................... C'mon Betty Home | $10 | | Capitol 4808 |
| | | | traditional folk/bluegrass tune | | | |
| 2/29/64 | 124 | 3 | 3 Last Night I Had The Strangest Dream .............. The Patriot Game | $10 | | Capitol 5132 |
| 5/23/64 | 123 | 1 | 4 If You Don't Look Around ...................... Seasons In The Sun | $10 | | Capitol 5166 |
| | | | B-side is the group's version of **Terry Jacks'** #1 hit in 1974 | | | |
| 1/16/65 | 104 | 1 | 5 I'm Going Home .................................... Little Play Soldiers | $10 | | Decca 31730 |
| 3/23/68 | 104 | 6 | 6 Honey ..................................... I Don't Think Of You Anymore | $10 | | Decca 32275 |
| | | | **BOB SHANE** | | | |
| | | | #1 hit for Bobby Goldsboro in 1968 | | | |
| 5/3/69 | 124 | 2 | 7 Scotch And Soda ........................ One Too Many Mornings [R] | $10 | | Tetragrammaton 1526 |
| | | | "live" version of group's #81 Hot 100 hit in 1962 on Capitol 4740 (originally on their 1958 debut album) | | | |

## KINKS, The
HOT/ROK/AC

Rock group formed in London in 1963 by Ray Davies (lead vocals, guitar) and his brother Dave Davies (lead guitar, vocals). Inducted into the Rock and Roll Hall of Fame in 1990. Top Pop Singles: 23.

| 1/9/65 | 129 | 2 | 1 Long Tall Sally ............................... I Took My Baby Home | $200 | | Cameo 345 |
| | | | originally released in 1964 on Cameo 308 ($400); #6 hit for **Little Richard** in 1956 | | | |
| 10/16/65 | 111 | 4 | 2 See My Friends ...................... Never Met A Girl Like You Before | $15 | | Reprise 0409 |
| 2/12/72 | 106 | 4 | 3 20th Century Man ..................................... Skin And Bone | $10 | | RCA Victor 0620 |
| 10/14/72 | 111 | 2 | 4 Supersonic Rocket Ship ...................... You Don't Know My Name | $10 | | RCA Victor 0807 |
| 6/2/73 | 108 | 1 | 5 One Of The Survivors .............................. Scrapheap City | $10 | | RCA Victor 0940 |

## KINSMAN DAZZ — see DAZZ BAND

## KISS
HOT/ROK/AC

Hard-rock band formed in New York City in 1973: Gene Simmons (bass), Paul Stanley (guitar), Ace Frehley (lead guitar) and Peter Criss (drums). Criss replaced by Eric Carr (d: 11/25/91 of cancer, age 41) in 1981. Frehley replaced by Vinnie Vincent in 1982. Top Pop Singles: 26.

| 1/22/83 | 102 | 8 | I Love It Loud .......................................ROK:22 Danger | $6 | ∎ | Casablanca 2365 |

## KIT AND THE OUTLAWS ☉

Dallas-based teen rock band.

| 1/21/67 | 131 | 1 | Midnight Hour ............................. Don't Tread On Me | $15 | | Philips 40420 |
| | | | #21 hit for **Wilson Pickett** in 1965 | | | |

## KIT KATS, The ☉

Group charted on the Hot 100 in 1970 as The New Hope.

| 11/26/66 | 119 | 1 | 1 Let's Get Lost On A Country Road ........ Find Someone (Who'll Make You Happy) | $12 | | Jamie 1326 |
| 10/7/67 | 130 | 3 | 2 Sea Of Love ........................................ Cold Walls | $12 | | Jamie 1343 |
| | | | #2 hit for Phil Phillips in 1959 | | | |

## KIX
ROK/HOT

Hard-rock quintet formed in 1981 in Hagerstown, Maryland: Steve Whiteman (vocals), Ronnie Younkins and Brian Forsythe (guitars), Donnie Purnell (bass), and Jimmy Chalfant (drums).

| 5/14/83 | 104 | 5 | Body Talk.......................................... Bobby Talk | $4 | | Atlantic 89852 |

**KLEEER** ✪     R&B
R&B/disco group formed in New York City in 1972 as Pipeline; recorded and toured as the Universal Robot Band in 1977.

| | | | | | |
|---|---|---|---|---|---|
| 3/17/79 | 101[1] | 7 | **Keeep Your Body Workin'**             R&B:60 *To Groove You* | $4 | Atlantic 3559 |

**KLUGH, Earl** ✪     R&B/AC
Born on 9/16/53 in Detroit. Jazz acoustic guitarist/pianist. First solo recording for Blue Note in 1976.

| | | | | | |
|---|---|---|---|---|---|
| 8/16/80 | 105 | 1 | **Doc** .......................................................... AC:36 *Cry A Little While* [I] | $4 | United Artists 1355 |

**KLYMAXX**     R&B/HOT/AC
Female R&B group formed in Los Angeles in 1979 featuring Lorena "Lungs" Porter and Joyce "Fenderella" Irby.

| | | | | | |
|---|---|---|---|---|---|
| 2/2/85 | 105 | 2 | **The Men All Pause** ...........................R&B:5 *Don't Hide Your Love* <br> made the Hot 100 on 2/15/86 (#80) | $3 ■ | Constellation 52486 |

**KNICKERBOCKERS, The**     HOT
Rock band from Bergenfield, New Jersey: Buddy Randell (vocals, sax), brothers Beau (guitar) and Johnny (bass) Charles, and Jimmy Walker (drums).

| | | | | | |
|---|---|---|---|---|---|
| 8/13/66 | 106 | 2 | 1 Chapel In The Fields ................................................ *Just One Girl* | $15 | Challenge 59335 |
| 10/22/66 | 133 | 1 | 2 Love Is A Bird .......................... *Rumors, Gossip, Words Untrue* | $15 | Challenge 59341 |

**KNIEVEL, Evel — see MAHONEY, John Culliton**

**KNIGHT, Curtis** ✪
Backing vocalist for **Jimi Hendrix** in 1964.

| | | | | | |
|---|---|---|---|---|---|
| 8/28/61 | 109 | 3 | **That's Why** ..........................................*Voodoo Woman* <br> Jimi Hendrix (guitar) | $40 | Gulf 45-031 |

**KNIGHT, Frederick**     R&B/HOT
Born on 8/15/44 in Alabama. R&B singer/producer.

| | | | | | |
|---|---|---|---|---|---|
| 9/16/72 | 102 | 4 | **Trouble** ........................................................... *Friend* | $6 | Stax 0139 |

**KNIGHT, Gladys, & The Pips**     R&B/HOT/AC
R&B family group from Atlanta featuring Gladys (b: 5/28/44), her brother Merald "Bubba" Knight, and cousins William Guest and Edward Patten. Group inducted into the Rock and Roll Hall of Fame in 1996. *Top Pop Singles: 42.*

| | | | | | |
|---|---|---|---|---|---|
| 11/7/64 | 119 | 5 | 1 Either Way I Lose ..................................... *Go Away, Stay Away* | $20 | Maxx 331 |
| 3/13/65 | 123 | 3 | 2 Stop And Get A Hold Of Myself/ | | |
| 4/24/65 | 129 | 1 | 3   Who Knows ................................. *Stepping Closer To Your Heart* | $20 | Maxx 334 |
| 7/16/66 | 129 | 1 | 4 Just Walk In My Shoes ..................... *Stepping Closer To Your Heart* | $12 | Soul 35023 |
| 12/3/83 | 104 | 7 | 5 Hero .................................. AC:23 /R&B:64 *Seconds* <br> #1 hit in 1989 for Bette Midler as "Wind Beneath My Wings" | $4 | Columbia 04219 |
| 2/16/85 | 102 | 3 | 6 My Time     R&B:16 *(instrumental)* | $4 ■ | Columbia 04761 |
| 9/10/94 | 113 | 5 | 7 I Don't Want To Know ..................... R&B:32 *(album version)* <br> **GLADYS KNIGHT** <br> written and produced by **Babyface** | $3 ▌ | MCA 54919 |

**KNIGHT, Jerry** ✪     R&B
Born and raised in Los Angeles. Bass player, founding member (with **Ray Parker**) of **Raydio**.

| | | | | | |
|---|---|---|---|---|---|
| 5/3/80 | 103 | 5 | **Overnight Sensation** ............................ R&B:17 *Freek Show* | $4 | A&M 2215 |

**KNIGHT, Marie** ✪     R&B
Born on 6/1/25 in Brooklyn. Teamed with Rosetta Tharpe on gospel records from 1947-54.

| | | | | | |
|---|---|---|---|---|---|
| 4/10/65 | 124 | 3 | **Cry Me A River**................................... R&B:35 *Comes The Night* <br> #9 hit for **Julie London** in 1955 | $20 | Musicor 1076 |

**KNIGHT, Terry, and The Pack**     HOT
Rock quintet from Flint, Michigan featuring Terry Knight who produced **Grand Funk Railroad**.

| | | | | | |
|---|---|---|---|---|---|
| 4/16/66 | 125 | 3 | 1 Better Man Than I ................................................. *Got Love* | $20 | Lucky Eleven 226 |
| 8/13/66 | 111 | 4 | 2 A Change On The Way ...................... *What's On Your Mind* | $15 | Lucky Eleven 229 |
| 2/11/67 | 120 | 1 | 3 This Precious Time/ | | |
| 5/27/67 | 117 | 2 | 4   Love, Love, Love, Love, Love............................... <br> "Love, Love..." reissued as the A-side, coupled with "The Train" | $15 | Lucky Eleven 235 |
| 6/28/69 | 114 | 2 | 5 Saint Paul .................................. *(The Legend Of) William And Mary* <br> **TERRY KNIGHT** <br> a **Beatles** tribute - the last 2:15 is the tune "Hey Jude" (sung as "Hey Paul") | $12 | Capitol 2506 |

**KNOBLOCK, Fred**     C&W/AC/HOT
Born in Jackson, Mississippi. Member of the country trio Schuyler, Knobloch & Overstreet (SKO).

| | | | | | |
|---|---|---|---|---|---|
| 8/15/81 | 102 | 8 | **Memphis**.............................. C&W:10 / AC:28 *Love Isn't Easy* <br> #2 hit for **Johnny Rivers** in 1964 | $4 | Scotti Brothers 02434 |

**KNOX, Buddy, And The Rhythm Orchids**     HOT/R&B/C&W
Born Buddy Wayne Knox on 7/20/33 in Happy, Texas. Group includes: Knox and Don Lanier (guitars), Jimmy Bowen (bass) and Dave "Dicky Doo" Alldred (drums).

| | | | | | |
|---|---|---|---|---|---|
| 2/22/64 | 114 | 1 | **Hitchike Back To Georgia**............................... *Thanks A Lot* <br> written by **Joe South** | $15 | Liberty 55650 |

**KOFFMAN, Moe**     HOT
Born Morris Koffman on 12/28/28 in Toronto. Saxophonist with several U.S. big bands from 1950-55.

| | | | | | |
|---|---|---|---|---|---|
| 4/28/62 | 110 | 3 | **Swingin' Shepherd Blues Twist**............... *Train Whistle Twist* [I-R] <br> twist version of his #23 hit in 1958 | $8 | Ascot 2100 |

**KOKOMO** ✪     R&B
English jazz-rock, nine-member band.

| | | | | | |
|---|---|---|---|---|---|
| 8/16/75 | 101[1] | 1 | **I Can Understand It**        *Feeling This Way* <br> written by **Bobby Womack** | $5 | Columbia 10145 |

**KONGOS, John**     HOT
Pop-rock singer from South Africa. Produced by **Elton John**'s producer, Gus Dudgeon.

| | | | | | |
|---|---|---|---|---|---|
| 2/19/72 | 111 | 2 | **Tokoloshe Man** ............... *Can Someone Please Direct Me Back To Earth* | $6 | Elektra 45760 |

| DEBUT | PEAK | WKS | A-side (Chart Hit) ... B-side | $ | Pic | Label & Number |
|---|---|---|---|---|---|---|
| | | | **KOOL & THE GANG**     R&B/HOT/AC | | | |
| | | | R&B group formed in 1964 in Jersey City, New Jersey featuring Robert "Kool" Bell (bass) and his brother Ronald Bell (sax). Added lead singer James "J.T." Taylor in 1978. *Top Pop Singles:* 33. | | | |
| 1/16/71 | 113 | 7 | 1 Who's Gonna Take The Weight (Part One) .................... R&B:28 *(Part Two)* [I] | $6 | | De-Lite 538 |
| 6/19/71 | 105 | 3 | 2 I Want To Take You Higher ........................... R&B:35 *Pneumonia* | $6 | | De-Lite 540 |
| | | | #38 hit for **Sly & The Family Stone** in 1970 | | | |
| 2/26/72 | 107 | 3 | 3 Love The Life You Live Part I ........................ R&B:31 *Part II* | $6 | | De-Lite 546 |
| 7/4/76 | 101[1] | 3 | 4 Universal Sound ........................ R&B:71 *Ancestral Ceremony* | $5 | | De-Lite 1583 |
| 5/7/77 | 101[1] | 6 | 5 Super Band ........................ R&B:17 *Sunshine* | $5 | | De-Lite 1590 |
| 4/29/78 | 102 | 3 | 6 Slick Superchick ........................ R&B:19 *Life's A Song* | $4 | | De-Lite 901 |
| 5/17/80 | 103 | 3 | 7 Hangin' Out ........................ R&B:36 *Got You Into My Life* | $4 | | De-Lite 804 |
| 6/30/84 | 103 | 3 | 8 Straight Ahead ........................ R&B:49 *September Love* | $4 | | De-Lite 831 |
| | | | **KOOL G RAP**     R&B/HOT | | | |
| | | | Born Nathaniel Wilson on 7/20/68 in Elmhurst, Queens, New York. Name is short for Kool Genius of Rap. | | | |
| 9/2/95 | 123 | 1 | It's A Shame ........................................... *(2 versions)* | $6 | ■ | Cold Chillin' 77992 (T) |
| | | | Sean Brown (vocal); samples "Love Is For Fools" by **South Side Movement** | | | |
| | | | **KORN** ○ | | | |
| | | | Techno-rock band from Huntington Beach, California: Jonathan Davis (vocals), Brian Welch and James Munkey (guitars), Fieldy (bass) and David (drums). | | | |
| 4/5/97 | 113 | 4 | A.D.I.D.A.S. ........................... *(2 versions) / Wicked* | $6 | | Immortal/Epic 78530 (CD) |
| | | | **KOZ, Dave** ○     AC | | | |
| | | | Born on 3/27/63 in Los Angeles. Saxophonist. Touring member of Jeff Lorber's band. | | | |
| 10/23/93 | 111 | 4 | You Make Me Smile ....................... AC:20 *Saxman* [I] | $3 | ▌ | Capitol 44947 |
| | | | **KRACKER** ○ | | | |
| | | | Pop-rock group — Michael Stim, lead singer. | | | |
| 12/2/72 | 104 | 6 | Because Of You (The Sun Don't Set)....................... *City Blues* | $6 | | Dunhill/ABC 4329 |
| | | | **KRAFTWERK**     HOT/R&B/AC | | | |
| | | | Synthesizer band formed in 1970 in Dusseldorf, Germany, by Ralf Hutter and Florian Schneider. | | | |
| 6/6/81 | 102 | 6 | 1 Pocket Calculator ........................... *Dentaku* | $5 | ■ | Warner 49723 |
| | | | issued on a special lime-green colored vinyl record | | | |
| 12/12/81 | 103 | 5 | 2 Numbers ........................... R&B:22 *Computer Love* | $4 | | Warner 49795 |
| | | | **KRANZ, George** ○     R&B | | | |
| | | | Singer/percussionist from Germany. | | | |
| 2/25/84 | 110 | 1 | Trommeltanz (Din Daa Daa) .................... R&B:61 *(dub version)* | $5 | | Personal 19804 |
| | | | title translates to "Drum Dance" | | | |
| | | | **KRIS KROSS**     R&B/HOT | | | |
| | | | Teenage male rap duo from Atlanta: Chris "Mack Daddy" Kelly (b: 5/1/78) and Chris "Daddy Mack" Smith (b: 1/10/79). | | | |
| 2/20/93 | 120 | 2 | 1 It's A Shame........................... R&B:55 *(3 versions) / The Way Of The Rhyme* | $5 | ▌ | Ruffhouse 74836 * |
| | | | samples "More Bounce To The Ounce" by **Zapp** | | | |
| 3/19/94 | 121 | 4 | 2 Da Bomb ........................... R&B:74 *Freak Da Funk* | $3 | ▌ | Ruffhouse 77379 |
| | | | Da Brat (guest vocal) | | | |
| | | | **KRS-ONE**     R&B/HOT | | | |
| | | | Born Lawrence "Kris" Parker in 1966 in New York City. Co-founder of Boogie Down Productions. | | | |
| 10/9/93 | 106 | 5 | 1 Outta Here ........................... R&B:61 *I Can't Wake Up* | $3 | ▌ | Jive 42147 |
| 2/1/97 | 118 | 2 | 2 The MC ........................... R&B:67 *Can't Stop, Won't Stop / Word Perfect* | $6 | ■ | Jive 42425 (T) |
| 8/2/97 | 114 | 1 | 3 A Friend ........................... R&B:70 *Heartbeat (2 versions) / Step Into A World* | $6 | | Jive 42474 (CD) |
| | | | samples "Round Midnight" by Luchi DeJesus | | | |
| | | | **K7**     HOT/R&B | | | |
| | | | Male rapper Louis "Kayel" Sharpe, from New York City. Former member of TKA. Also see **Cynthia**. | | | |
| 5/14/94 | 123 | 1 | Hi De Ho.......................... *(4 versions) / Beep Me* | $5 | ▌ | Tommy Boy 616 * |
| | | | **K7 and the swing kids** | | | |
| | | | new rap version of Cab Calloway's 1931 #1 hit "Minnie The Moocher" | | | |
| | | | **KURIOUS** ○ | | | |
| | | | Jorge Antonio Alvarez — Manhattan rapper. Once worked as a messenger and an A&R rep for Def Jam records. | | | |
| 3/12/94 | 123 | 2 | Uptown *Hit ........................... *Spell It Wit A "J"* | $3 | ▌ | Columbia 77206 |
| | | | **KURIOUS** featuring the **Constipated Monkeys** | | | |

# L

| DEBUT | PEAK | WKS | A-side (Chart Hit) ... B-side | $ | Pic | Label & Number |
|---|---|---|---|---|---|---|
| | | | **LaBELLE, Patti, & The Blue Belles**     R&B/HOT/AC | | | |
| | | | Born Patricia Holt on 5/24/44 in Philadelphia. Began singing career as leader of the Ordettes which evolved into **The Blue Belles**. The quartet, formed in Philadelphia in 1962, included Nona Hendryx, Sarah Dash and Cindy Birdsong. Birdsong left in 1967 to join **The Supremes**. Group continued as a trio. In 1971, group shortened its name to **LaBELLE**. | | | |
| 10/13/62 | 122 | 2 | 1 I Found A New Love .......................... *Go On (This Is Goodby)* | $25 | | Newtown 5006 |
| | | | also released with "Pitter Patter" on the B-side ($25) | | | |
| 1/26/63 | 127 | 1 | 2 Cool Water.......................... *When Johnny Comes Marching Home* | $25 | | Newtown 5009 |
| | | | **THE BLUE BELLES** (above 2) | | | |
| | | | first recorded by the **Sons Of The Pioneers** in 1936 | | | |
| 4/1/67 | 125 | 1 | 3 Always Something There To Remind Me .......................... *Tender Words* | $15 | | Atlantic 2390 |
| | | | #8 hit for Naked Eyes in 1983 | | | |
| 10/16/76 | 102 | 7 | 4 Get You Somebody New    R&B:50 *Who's Watching The Watcher?* | $6 | | Epic 50262 |
| | | | **LaBELLE** | | | |

**LaBELLE, Patti — Cont'd**

| DEBUT | PEAK | WKS | A-side / B-side | $ | Pic | Label & Number |
|-------|------|-----|------|---|-----|-----|
| 12/25/82 | 104 | 4 | 5 The Best Is Yet To Come ......................... R&B:14 *More Than Meets The Eye* (Washington) | $4 | | Elektra 69887 |
| | | | GROVER WASHINGTON, JR. with PATTI LaBELLE | | | |

**L.A. BOPPERS** ☉      R&B
*R&B-bop quartet led by Vance Tenort (vocals, percussion). Formed in Los Angeles as backup band for Side Effect.*

| | | | | | | |
|---|---|---|---|---|---|---|
| 3/8/80 | 103 | 8 | Is This The Best (Bop-Doo-Wah) ................................R&B:28 *Life Is What You Make It* | $4 | | Mercury 76038 |

**LA BOUCHE**      HOT
*Male/female dance duo: Melanie Thornton and Lane McCray. La Bouche is French for "mouth."*

| | | | | | | |
|---|---|---|---|---|---|---|
| 7/22/95 | 111 | 5 | 1 Fallin' In Love ................................................. *(club mix)* | $3 | ▮ | Logic 59018 |
| | | | #1 hit for **Hamilton, Joe Frank & Reynolds** in 1975 | | | |
| 3/15/97 | 114 | 3 | 2 Fallin' In Love ................................................. *(club mix)* [R] | $3 | ▮ | Logic 59018 |
| | | | also made *Billboard's* Airplay chart (#35) on 10/19/96 | | | |

**LaBOUNTY, Bill**      AC/HOT
*Pop singer/songwriter/pianist from Los Angeles. Co-wrote* **Steve Wariner**'s #1 Country hit "Lynda."

| | | | | | | |
|---|---|---|---|---|---|---|
| 6/19/76 | 109 | 1 | 1 Lie To Me ...................................................... *Together* | $5 | | 20th Century 2290 |
| 6/26/82 | 110 | 1 | 2 Never Gonna Look Back ........................ AC:22 *Secrets* | $4 | | Warner/Curb 50065 |

**LACE, Patty — see PATTY LACE**

**LADAE!** ☉      R&B
*Male vocal quartet from New York City: Lil Bee, Bobby D, Boogie and Li'l Tone.*

| | | | | | | |
|---|---|---|---|---|---|---|
| 5/25/96 | 107 | 9 | Party 2 Nite.................................... R&B:44 *(remix)* (w/Grand Puba) | $3 | ▮ | Motown 0514 |
| | | | samples "Show You The Way To Go" by The Jacksons | | | |

**LAINE, Denny** ☉
*Born Brian Hines on 10/29/44 in Jersey Coast, England. Lead singer/guitarist of* **The Moody Blues**, *1964-66. Joined* **Paul McCartney**'s *Wings as guitarist in 1971; left in 1981.*

| | | | | | | |
|---|---|---|---|---|---|---|
| 11/6/76 | 108 | 3 | It's So Easy/Listen To Me ........................... *I'm Lookin' For Someone To Love* | $8 | | Capitol 4340 |
| | | | Buddy Holly medley; produced by Paul McCartney | | | |

**LAINE, Frankie**      MEM/POP/HOT/AC
*Born Frank Paul LoVecchio on 3/30/13 in Chicago. First recorded for Exclusive in 1945. Signed to the Mercury label in 1947. Pop Hits & Top Pop Singles: 59.*

| | | | | | | |
|---|---|---|---|---|---|---|
| 4/6/68 | 118 | 3 | 1 I Found You ................ AC:19 *I Don't Want To Set The World On Fire* (AC #26) | $6 | | ABC/TRC 11057 |
| 7/6/68 | 115 | 4 | 2 Take Me Back ............................................. AC:18 *Forsaking All Others* | $6 | | ABC 11097 |

**LAKESIDE**      R&B/HOT
*R&B/funk group formed in 1969 in Dayton, Ohio.*

| | | | | | | |
|---|---|---|---|---|---|---|
| 4/28/79 | 102 | 1 | 1 It's All The Way Live (Part 1).........................R&B:4 *(Part 2)* | $5 | | Solar 11380 |
| 2/13/82 | 102 | 4 | 2 I Want To Hold Your Hand...........................R&B:5 *Magic Moments* | $4 | ▮ | Solar 47954 |
| | | | #1 hit for **The Beatles** in 1964 | | | |
| 5/22/82 | 110 | 1 | 3 Something About That Woman ...................R&B:25 *The Songwriter* | $4 | | Solar 48009 |
| 7/28/84 | 101[1] | 5 | 4 Outrageous ........................................... R&B:7 *So Let's Love* | $4 | | Solar 69716 |

**LaMOND, George**      HOT
*Born George Garcia on 2/25/67 in Washington, D.C. With his cousin Joey Kid, formed New York City club band, Loose Touch.*

| | | | | | | |
|---|---|---|---|---|---|---|
| 2/11/95 | 122 | 2 | It's Always You ................................................. *(5 versions)* | $5 | ▮ | Tommy Boy 655 * |

**LAMP OF CHILDHOOD, The** ☉
*New York-based, folk-rock group led by James Hendricks who had co-founded* **The Mugwumps** *with then-wife* **Mama Cass Elliot**.

| | | | | | | |
|---|---|---|---|---|---|---|
| 6/10/67 | 116 | 2 | No More Running Around ...............................*Two O'Clock Morning* | $8 | | Dunhill 4089 |

**LANCE, Major**      R&B/HOT
*Born on 4/4/42 in Chicago. Died on 9/3/94 of heart disease. R&B singer. First recorded for Mercury in 1959.*

| | | | | | | |
|---|---|---|---|---|---|---|
| 11/13/65 | 109 | 5 | 1 Everybody Loves A Good Time ............................*I Just Can't Help It* | $15 | | Okeh 7233 |
| 6/18/66 | 132 | 2 | 2 Investigate............................................... *Little Young Lover* | $15 | ▮ | Okeh 7250 |
| 8/27/66 | 128 | 2 | 3 It's The Beat ...................................R&B:37 *You'll Want Me Back* | $15 | | Okeh 7255 |
| 6/21/69 | 125 | 1 | 4 Follow The Leader...........................R&B:28 *Since You've Been Gone* | $8 | | Dakar 608 |
| 1/23/71 | 119 | 1 | 5 Must Be Love Coming Down .................R&B:31 *Little Young Lover* | $6 | | Curtom 1956 |
| | | | written and produced by Curtis Mayfield | | | |

**LANDIS, Richard** ☉      AC
*Pop singer/songwriter. Former movie editor. Produced several hits for Juice Newton.*

| | | | | | | |
|---|---|---|---|---|---|---|
| 2/26/72 | 102 | 2 | A Man Who Sings .......................AC:35 *Freedom Is The Name Of The Man* | $6 | | Dunhill/ABC 4300 |

**LANDS, Hoagy** ☉
*R&B vocalist.*

| | | | | | | |
|---|---|---|---|---|---|---|
| 2/15/64 | 125 | 2 | Baby Come On Home ...............................*Baby Let Me Hold Your Hand* | $12 | | Atlantic 2217 |

**LANG, k.d.**      C&W/AC/HOT
*Born Kathryn Dawn Lang on 11/2/61 in Consort, Alberta, Canada.*

| | | | | | | |
|---|---|---|---|---|---|---|
| 11/25/95 | 115 | 3 | If I Were You ................................................. *Get Some* | $3 | ▮ | Warner 17747 |

**LARKIN, Billy, And The Delegates** ☉
*R&B-funk quartet led by Billy on organ.*

| | | | | | | |
|---|---|---|---|---|---|---|
| 9/10/66 | 130 | 3 | Hold On! I'm A Comin' ..................................*Dirty Water* [I] | $10 | | World Pacific 77844 |
| | | | #21 hit for **Sam & Dave** in 1966 | | | |

**LARKS, The**      HOT/R&B
*R&B vocal group from Los Angeles. Originally named Don Julian & The Meadowlarks: Don Julian, Ted Walters and Charles Morrison.*

| | | | | | | |
|---|---|---|---|---|---|---|
| 3/20/65 | 132 | 1 | Mickey's East Coast Jerk ...................................*Soul Jerk* | $15 | | Money 110 |
| | | | follow-up to the group's early 1965 hit "The Jerk" | | | |

**LARSON, Nicolette**      C&W/AC/HOT/R&B
*Born on 7/17/52 in Helena, Montana. Died on 12/16/97 from a cerebral edema. Session vocalist with* **Neil Young**, **Emmylou Harris**, **Linda Ronstadt**, **Van Halen** *and many others.*

| | | | | | | |
|---|---|---|---|---|---|---|
| 8/25/79 | 104 | 5 | 1 Give A Little ............................................ AC:19 *Mexican Divorce* | $4 | | Warner 8851 |

| DEBUT | PEAK | WKS | A-side (Chart Hit)..................................................................................................B-side | $ | Pic | Label & Number |
|-------|------|-----|------------------------------|----|-----|----------------|

**LARSON, Nicolette — Cont'd**

| | | | | | | |
|-------|------|-----|------------------------------|----|-----|----------------|
| 2/28/81 | 110 | 2 | 2 Ooo-eee ......................................................... *Straight From The Heart* | $4 | | Warner 49666 |
| | | | Linda Ronstadt & Ted Templeman (backing vocals, above 2) | | | |
| 11/21/81 | 105 | 3 | 3 Fool Me Again ................................................... *Arthur's Theme* | $4 | | Warner 49820 |
| | | | from the movie *Arthur* starring Dudley Moore | | | |

**LaSALLE, Denise**   R&B/HOT
Born Denise Craig on 7/16/39 in LeFlore County, Mississippi. R&B singer/songwriter.

| | | | | | | |
|-------|------|-----|------------------------------|----|-----|----------------|
| 6/19/76 | 102 | 5 | Married, But Not To Each Other ........................... R&B:16 *Who's The Fool* | $6 | | Westbound 5019 |

**LAST, James**   AC/HOT
Born on 4/17/29 in Bremen, Germany. Producer/arranger/conductor of big cabaret band.

| | | | | | | |
|-------|------|-----|------------------------------|----|-----|----------------|
| 7/19/75 | 106 | 9 | Love For Sale ................................................... *Summertime* [I] | $5 | | Polydor 15108 |
| | | | written by Cole Porter; #5 hit for Libby Holman in 1931; #43 hit for **Arthur Lyman Group** in 1963 | | | |

**L.A. STYLE**   HOT
Techno-rave creation of Dutch producer/musician Denzil Slemming.

| | | | | | | |
|-------|------|-----|------------------------------|----|-----|----------------|
| 4/24/93 | 120 | 7 | I'm Raving ......................................................... *Balloony* | $3 | ▌ | Arista 12524 |
| | | | Nicolette (featured vocalist) | | | |

**LAST WORDS, The**   HOT
Rock group from Miami: Johnny Lombardo (vocals), Mike Byrnes (guitar), Steve Sechak (keyboards) and Ricky Cook (drums).

| | | | | | | |
|-------|------|-----|------------------------------|----|-----|----------------|
| 12/30/67 | 105 | 4 | I Wish I Had Time ............................................. *One More Time* | $8 | | Atco 6542 |

**LATIMORE**   R&B/HOT
Born Benjamin Latimore on 9/7/39 in Charleston, Tennessee. R&B singer. With **Steve Alaimo** in the '60s.

| | | | | | | |
|-------|------|-----|------------------------------|----|-----|----------------|
| 1/26/74 | 102 | 3 | 1 Stormy Monday ................................. R&B:27 *There's No End* | $6 | | Glades 1716 |
| | | | #1 R&B hit for Earl Hines with Billy Eckstine in 1942 | | | |
| 7/16/77 | 104 | 4 | 2 I Get Lifted ................................. R&B:30 *All The Way Lover* | $6 | | Glades 1742 |
| | | | #37 hit for **George McCrae** in 1975; above 2 produced by **Steve Alaimo** | | | |

**LATTISAW, Stacy**   R&B/HOT/AC
Born on 11/25/66 in Washington, D.C. R&B singer. Recorded her first album at age 12.

| | | | | | | |
|-------|------|-----|------------------------------|----|-----|----------------|
| 7/31/82 | 101[2] | 6 | 1 Don't Throw It All Away ........................... R&B:9 *Down For You* | $5 | | Cotillion 47011 |
| 12/25/82 | 108 | 3 | 2 Hey There Lonely Boy ............... R&B:71 *Tonight I'm Gonna Make You Mine* | $5 | | Cotillion 99943 |
| | | | #2 hit for Eddie Holman in 1970 as "Hey There Lonely Girl" | | | |
| 5/26/84 | 102 | 4 | 3 Baby It's You ................................. R&B:37 *50/50 Love* | $4 | | Cotillion 99750 |
| | | | **STACY LATTISAW & JOHNNY GILL** | | | |
| | | | #8 hit for **The Shirelles** in 1962 | | | |

**LAUPER, Cyndi**   HOT/AC/ROK/R&B
Born on 6/20/53 in Queens, New York. Won the 1984 Best New Artist Grammy Award.

| | | | | | | |
|-------|------|-----|------------------------------|----|-----|----------------|
| 5/3/97 | 111 | 2 | You Don't Know ......................................................... *(remix)* | $3 | ▌ | Epic 78535 |

**LAURIE, Annie**   R&B/HOT
R&B singer from Atlanta. Sang with Dallas Brockley, Snookum Russell bands before joining Paul Gayten in 1947.

| | | | | | | |
|-------|------|-----|------------------------------|----|-----|----------------|
| 7/18/60 | 104 | 4 | If You're Lonely ................. R&B:17 *It's Gonna Come Out In The Wash Someday* | $20 | | DeLuxe 6189 |

**LAURNEÁ** ☉   R&B
Born Laurnea Wilkinson in Omaha, Nebraska; raised in Los Angeles. Female R&B singer.

| | | | | | | |
|-------|------|-----|------------------------------|----|-----|----------------|
| 11/15/97 | 107 | 12 | Infatuation ................................. R&B:37 *(remix)* | $3 | ▌ | Yab Yum 78708 |

**LAVETTE, Betty** ☉   R&B
Born Betty Haskin in 1946 in Muskegon, Michigan. R&B singer/actress.

| | | | | | | |
|-------|------|-----|------------------------------|----|-----|----------------|
| 11/24/62 | 101[1] | 6 | 1 My Man - He's A Lovin' Man ........... R&B:7 *Shut Your Mouth* | $15 | | Atlantic 2160 |
| | | | **BETTY LAVETT** | | | |
| 4/24/65 | 103 | 6 | 2 Let Me Down Easy ............... R&B:20 *What I Don't Know (Won't Hurt Me)* | $12 | | Calla 102 |
| 2/6/82 | 103 | 7 | 3 Right In The Middle (Of Falling In Love) ........ R&B:35 *You Seen One You Seen 'Em All* | $5 | | Motown 1532 |
| | | | **BETTYE LAVETTE** | | | |

**LAWRENCE, Steve**   AC/HOT/MEM/POP
Born Sidney Leibowitz on 7/8/35 in Brooklyn. Regular performer on **Steve Allen's** *Tonight Show* for five years. Married singer **Eydie Gorme** on 12/29/57. *Pop Hits & Top Pop Singles*: 25.

| | | | | | | |
|-------|------|-----|------------------------------|----|-----|----------------|
| 2/3/62 | 107 | 5 | 1 Our Concerto .................................................... *Send Someone To Love Me* | $10 | | United Artists 403 |
| 5/19/62 | 120 | 1 | 2 The Lady Wants To Twist ........................... *Tell Her I Said Hello* | $8 | ■ | Columbia 42396 |
| 6/22/63 | 117 | 5 | 3 More (Theme from the Film "Mondo Cane") ........................... *Poor Little Rich Girl* (Hot #27) | $7 | | Columbia 42795 |
| | | | #8 hit for **Kai Winding** in 1963 | | | |
| 1/4/64 | 106 | 3 | 4 My Home Town/ | | | |
| 1/18/64 | 120 | 4 | 5 A Room Without Windows ......................................................... | $7 | ☐ | Columbia 42952 |
| | | | above 2 from the musical *What Makes Sammy Run?* starring Lawrence; Marion Evans (orch., above 3) | | | |
| 1/9/65 | 103 | 2 | 6 Bewitched/ | | | |
| | | | theme from the TV series starring Elizabeth Montgomery | | | |
| 1/9/65 | 113 | 4 | 7 I Will Wait For You ......................................................... | $7 | ☐ | Columbia 43192 |
| | | | love theme from the movie *The Umbrellas Of Cherbourg* starring Catherine Deneuve; Joe Guercio (orch., above 2) | | | |
| 6/5/65 | 126 | 6 | 8 Last Night I Made A Little Girl Cry ........................... *Where Can I Go* | $7 | | Columbia 43303 |
| | | | Robert Mersey (orch.) | | | |
| 8/28/65 | 106 | 6 | 9 Millions Of Roses ................................. AC:11 *The Sounds Of Summer* | $7 | | Columbia 43362 |
| 2/19/66 | 131 | 1 | 10 The Week-End ................................. AC:24 *Only The Young* | $7 | | Columbia 43487 |
| | | | Don Costa (orch.: #2, 9 & 10) | | | |
| 4/26/69 | 119 | 4 | 11 Real True Lovin' ................................. AC:20 *Chapter One* | $6 | | RCA Victor 0123 |
| | | | **STEVE & EYDIE** | | | |
| | | | Marty Manning (orch.) | | | |

**LAWRENCE, Tony** ☉

| | | | | | | |
|-------|------|-----|------------------------------|----|-----|----------------|
| 6/5/61 | 114 | 2 | You Got To Show Me ......................................................... *If Only* | $20 | | Silver Bid 1025 |

| DEBUT | PEAK | WKS | A-side / B-side | $ | Pic | Label & Number |
|---|---|---|---|---|---|---|
| | | | **LAWRENCE, Tracy**     C&W/HOT | | | |
| | | | Born on 1/27/68 in Atlanta, Texas. Male country singer. In 1991, he was shot four times in an attempted holdup in Nashville; fully recovered. | | | |
| 1/11/97 | 104 | 10 | 1 Is That A Tear ..................................... C&W:2 *(3 album snippets)* | $3 | ■ | Atlantic 87020 |
| 4/19/97 | 108 | 10 | 2 Better Man, Better Off .......................... C&W:2 *(3 album snippets)* | $3 | ■ | Atlantic 83004 |
| | | | **LAWSON, Janet** ☺     AC/C&W | | | |
| 7/11/70 | 124 | 1 | Two Little Rooms ........................ AC:35 /C&W:74 *Dindi* | $6 | | United Artists 50671 |
| | | | **LAWTON, Lou** ☺ | | | |
| | | | R&B singer nicknamed "Moondog." | | | |
| 4/9/66 | 133 | 1 | Doing The Philly Dog ............. *I Am Searching (For My Baby)* | $8 | | Capitol 5613 |
| | | | **LEAVILL, Otis**     R&B/HOT | | | |
| | | | Born Otis Leavill Cobb on 2/8/41 in Atlanta. R&B singer/songwriter. Own Chi-Sound label in 1976. | | | |
| 2/27/65 | 116 | 1 | 1 Let Her Love Me ................................ R&B:31 *When The Music Grooves* | $15 | ■ | Blue Rock 4002 |
| | | | produced by **Major Lance** | | | |
| 5/8/65 | 128 | 1 | 2 To Be Or Not To Be ............................................ *Boomerang* | $15 | | Blue Rock 4015 |
| | | | **LEE, Brenda**     HOT/C&W/AC | | | |
| | | | Born Brenda Mae Tarpley on 12/11/44 in Lithonia, Georgia. Professional singer since age six. Signed to Decca Records in 1956. Became known as "Little Miss Dynamite." Successful country singer from 1971-85. Lee ranks as the #1 female singer of the '60s (as designated in *Joel Whitburn's Pop Annual 1955-1994*). Inducted into the Country Music Hall of Fame in 1997. *Top Pop Singles*: 55. | | | |
| 5/1/61 | 101[1] | 1 | 1 It's Never Too Late     *You Can Depend On Me* (Hot #6) | $12 | ■ | Decca 31231 |
| | | | written by Jimmy Seals of **Seals & Crofts** | | | |
| 3/7/64 | 101[3] | 6 | 2 The Waiting Game     *Think* (Hot #25) | $10 | ■ | Decca 31599 |
| 8/15/64 | 135 | 1 | 3 He's Sure To Remember Me..............*When You Loved Me* (Hot #47) | $10 | ■ | Decca 31654 |
| | | | written by **Jackie DeShannon** | | | |
| 3/26/66 | 123 | 2 | 4 Too Little Time/ | | | |
| | | | written by **Marvin Hamlisch** | | | |
| 3/12/66 | 126 | 2 | 5 Time And Time Again | $10 | | Decca 31917 |
| | | | written by **Dorsey Burnette** | | | |
| 4/8/67 | 126 | 4 | 6 Take Me/ | | | |
| | | | #8 Country hit for **George Jones** in 1966 | | | |
| 4/22/67 | 134 | 1 | 7 Born To Be By Your Side | $10 | | Decca 32119 |
| | | | written by **Jerry Reed**; #52 Country hit for **Jimmy Dean** in 1968 | | | |
| 8/12/67 | 134 | 2 | 8 Where Love Is ........................... *My Heart Keeps Hangin' On* | $10 | | Decca 32161 |
| 11/4/67 | 105 | 4 | 9 Where's The Melody? ............. *Save Me For A Rainy Day* | $10 | | Decca 32213 |
| 1/27/68 | 118 | 1 | 10 That's All Right ............................................... *Fantasy* | $10 | | Decca 32248 |
| | | | **LEE, Curtis**     HOT | | | |
| | | | Born on 10/28/41 in Yuma, Arizona. Pop singer/songwriter. | | | |
| 2/6/61 | 110 | 4 | 1 Pledge Of Love ...................................... *Then I'll Know* | $25 | ■ | Dunes 2003 |
| | | | #12 hit for **Ken Copeland** in 1957 | | | |
| 4/7/62 | 110 | 2 | 2 Just Another Fool ........................... *A Night At Daddy Gee's* | $20 | | Dunes 2012 |
| | | | written by **Carole King** & **Gerry Goffin** | | | |
| | | | **LEE, Dickey**     C&W/HOT/R&B | | | |
| | | | Born Dickey Lipscomb on 9/21/36 in Memphis. Pop-country singer/songwriter. First recorded for Tampa Bay Records and then Sun Records in 1957. | | | |
| 9/21/63 | 104 | 2 | 1 The Day The Saw-Mill Closed Down .............. *She Wants To Be Bobby's Girl* | $12 | | Smash 1844 |
| 11/21/64 | 101[2] | 9 | 2 Big Brother     *She's Walking Away* | $20 | | Hall 1924 |
| 1/27/68 | 107 | 7 | 3 Red, Green, Yellow And Blue........................... *Run Right Back* | $10 | | Atco 6546 |
| | | | **LEE, Jackie**     R&B/HOT | | | |
| | | | Born on 9/8/28 in Lake Charles, Louisiana. Earl Nelson, of **Bob & Earl**. Sang lead on Hollywood Flames' "Buzz-Buzz-Buzz." | | | |
| 3/5/66 | 111 | 4 | 1 Your P-E-R-S-O-N-A-L-I-T-Y .............................. *Try My Method* | $15 | | Mirwood 5509 |
| 4/23/66 | 113 | 3 | 2 Do The Temptation Walk ................. *The Shotgun And The Duck* | $15 | | Mirwood 5510 |
| 3/23/68 | 121 | 3 | 3 African Boo-Ga-Loo ............................. R&B:43 *Bring It Home* | $15 | | Keymen 114 |
| | | | **LEE, Johnny**     C&W/HOT/AC | | | |
| | | | Born John Lee Ham on 7/3/46 in Texas City, Texas. Country singer/songwriter. | | | |
| 11/22/80 | 102 | 3 | One In A Million ............................ C&W:❶[2] *Anni* | $4 | | Asylum 47076 |
| | | | **LEE, Laura**     R&B/HOT | | | |
| | | | Born Laura Lee Rundless on 3/9/45 in Chicago. R&B singer/songwriter. In Meditation Singers gospel group, in Detroit, until 1965. | | | |
| 4/27/68 | 123 | 5 | 1 As Long As I Got You ....................... R&B:31 *A Man With Some Backbone* | $15 | | Chess 2041 |
| 12/23/72 | 107 | 3 | 2 Crumbs Off The Table ................. R&B:40 *You've Got To Save Me* | $8 | | Hot Wax 7210 |
| | | | #59 hit for **The Glass House** in 1969 | | | |
| | | | **LEE, Peggy**     MEM/POP/AC/HOT | | | |
| | | | Born Norma Jean Egstrom on 5/26/20 in Jamestown, North Dakota. Jazz singer with Jack Wardlow band (1936-40), Will Osborne (1940-41) and Benny Goodman (1941-43). Went solo in March 1943. Won Grammy's Lifetime Achievement Award in 1995. *Pop Hits* & *Top Pop Singles*: 34. | | | |
| 8/29/64 | 132 | 1 | 1 In The Name Of Love ........................................ *My Sin* | $8 | | Capitol 5241 |
| 1/31/70 | 105 | 2 | 2 Love Story.............................. AC:26 *My Old Flame* | $6 | | Capitol 2721 |
| | | | Mundell Lowe (orch.); written by **Randy Newman** | | | |
| | | | **LEEDS, Hank** ☺ | | | |
| | | | Pop vocalist. | | | |
| 1/4/60 | 103 | 4 | One More For The Road ............................. *(instrumental)* | $12 | | Jaro International 77007 |
| | | | **LEFEVRE, Raymond, And His Orchestra**     HOT/AC | | | |
| | | | Conductor/pianist/flutist from Paris. | | | |
| 5/18/68 | 110 | 4 | La La La (He Gives Me Love) ................. AC:23 *C'est La Rose* [I] | $6 | | 4 Corners 149 |

**LEFT BANKE, The**     HOT
Rock quintet from New York: Steve Martin (vocals), Rick Brand (guitar), Mike Brown (piano; **Stories**), Tom Finn (bass) and George Cameron (drums).

| DEBUT | PEAK | WKS | A-side | $ | Pic | Label & Number |
|-------|------|-----|--------|---|-----|----------------|
| 5/6/67 | 119 | 4 | 1 Ivy, Ivy.................................................................................................And Suddenly | $12 | | Smash 2089 |
| 6/24/67 | 120 | 1 | 2 She May Call You Up Tonight.......................................Barterers And Their Wives | $12 | | Smash 2097 |

**LEIGHTON, Bernie, Piano & Orchestra** ○
Born on 1/30/21 in West Haven, Connecticut. Conductor/pianist.

| | | | | | | |
|-------|------|-----|--------|---|-----|----------------|
| 7/28/62 | 101[1] | 6 | Don't Break The Heart That Loves You     Till You Return [I] | $10 | | Colpix 645 |

arranged and produced by **Don Costa**; #1 hit for **Connie Francis** earlier in 1962

**LEMONHEADS**     ROK/HOT
Rock band from Boston fronted by Evan Dando (vocals, guitar). **Juliana Hatfield** was a member in 1993.

| | | | | | | |
|-------|------|-----|--------|---|-----|----------------|
| 1/23/93 | 118 | 2 | Mrs. Robinson.................................................... ROK:8   Rudderless | $3 | ▌ | Atlantic 87412 |

#1 hit for **Simon & Garfunkel** in 1968

**LEMON PIPERS, The**     HOT
Bubblegum rock quintet from Oxford, Ohio: Ivan Browne (vocals, guitar), Bill Bartlett (guitar), R.G. Nave (organ), Steve Walmsley (bass) and Bill Albaugh (drums).

| | | | | | | |
|-------|------|-----|--------|---|-----|----------------|
| 10/7/67 | 132 | 1 | Turn Around And Take A Look ............................................ Danger | $12 | | Buddah 11 |

**LENNON, John**     HOT/ROK/AC
Born on 10/9/40 in Woolton, Liverpool, England. Shot to death on 12/8/80 in New York City. Founding member of **The Beatles**. Won Grammy's Lifetime Achievement Award in 1991. Inducted into the Rock and Roll Hall of Fame in 1994.

| | | | | | | |
|-------|------|-----|--------|---|-----|----------------|
| 6/9/84 | 108 | 1 | Borrowed Time............................................. Your Hands (Yoko Ono) | $4 | ■ | Polydor 821204 |

**LENNOX, Annie**     HOT/AC/ROK
Born on 12/25/54 in Aberdeen, Scotland. Lead singer of the Eurythmics.

| | | | | | | |
|-------|------|-----|--------|---|-----|----------------|
| 8/19/95 | 101[1] | 8 | A Whiter Shade Of Pale     Sls:66   No More "I Love You's" (remix) | $3 | ▌ | Arista 12850 |

#5 hit for **Procol Harum** in 1967

**LEO & LIBRA** ○

| | | | | | | |
|-------|------|-----|--------|---|-----|----------------|
| 12/20/75 | 109 | 1 | Get It While The Gettin' Is Good............................................................ | $8 | | Sound Bird 5003 |

     **LEO & LIBRA with The Mystic Moods**

**LEONETTI, Tommy**     AC/HOT/MEM
Born on 9/10/29 in Bergen, New Jersey. Died on 9/15/79. Vocalist with Charlie Spivak and other bands.

| | | | | | | |
|-------|------|-----|--------|---|-----|----------------|
| 1/4/64 | 105 | 5 | Soul Dance .............................................. Somebody Loves You | $10 | | RCA Victor 8251 |

**LE ROUX**     HOT/ROK
Rock band from Louisiana: Jeff Pollard (vocals), Tony Haseldon (guitar), Rod Roddy (piano), Bobby Campo (horns), Leon Medica (bass) and David Peters (drums).

| | | | | | | |
|-------|------|-----|--------|---|-----|----------------|
| 12/2/78 | 109 | 3 | 1 Take A Ride On A Riverboat.................................... Backslider | $6 | | Capitol 4651 |
| | | |      **LOUISIANA'S LE ROUX** | | | |
| 9/27/80 | 105 | 1 | 2 Let Me Be Your Fantasy ................. I Know Trouble When I See It | $5 | | Capitol 4928 |

**LESTER, John, & Mello-Queens** ○

| | | | | | | |
|-------|------|-----|--------|---|-----|----------------|
| 6/1/59 | 105 | 3 | Getting Nearer..................................................................At Last | $25 | | C & M 500 |

**LESTER, Ketty**     HOT/R&B/AC
Born Revoyda Frierson on 8/16/34 in Hope, Arkansas. R&B singer/actress.

| | | | | | | |
|-------|------|-----|--------|---|-----|----------------|
| 4/4/64 | 127 | 3 | Some Things Are Better Left | | | |
| | | | Unsaid ..........................The House Is Haunted (By the Echo of Your Last Good-Bye) | $10 | | RCA Victor 8331 |
| | | |      Sammy Lowe (orch.) | | | |

**LESTER, Robie** ○
Female vocalist with a style similar to that of Gogi Grant. Narrator for several Walt Disney storybook records.

| | | | | | | |
|-------|------|-----|--------|---|-----|----------------|
| 4/25/60 | 107 | 1 | The Miracle Of Life.................................... The Ballad Of Cheatin' John | $20 | | Lute 5904 |
| | | |      Don Ralke Music (orch.) | | | |

**LETTERMEN, The**     AC/HOT
Harmonic vocal trio formed in Los Angeles in 1958: Tony Butala (b: 11/20/40), Jim Pike (b: 11/6/38) and Bob Engemann (b: 2/19/36). Engemann replaced by Gary Pike (Jim's brother) in 1968. *Top Pop Singles: 20.*

| | | | | | | |
|-------|------|-----|--------|---|-----|----------------|
| 6/2/62 | 105 | 3 | 1 Turn Around, Look At Me .................................. How Is Julie? (Hot #42) | $7 | ■ | Capitol 4746 |
| | | |      #7 hit for **The Vogues** in 1968 | | | |
| 11/10/62 | 120 | 2 | 2 Again ..................................................... A Tree In The Meadow | $7 | ■ | Capitol 4851 |
| | | |      there were 6 Top 10 versions of this tune in 1949 (from the movie *Road House* starring Ida Lupino) | | | |
| 3/2/63 | 122 | 1 | 3 Heartache Oh Heartache ....................................... No Other Love | $7 | | Capitol 4914 |
| 6/22/63 | 123 | 2 | 4 Allentown Jail............................................... Two Brothers | $7 | | Capitol 4976 |
| | | |      folk song recorded by **Jo Stafford** in 1951 on Columbia 39389 | | | |
| 8/15/64 | 132 | 1 | 5 Put Away Your Tear Drops .............................. Seventh Dawn Theme | $7 | | Capitol 5218 |
| 4/10/65 | 135 | 1 | 6 Girl With A Little Tin Heart ........................................ It's Over | $7 | ■ | Capitol 5370 |
| | | |      written by The Addrisi Brothers | | | |
| 1/8/66 | 114 | 2 | 7 Sweet September ................................... AC:24   I Believe | $7 | | Capitol 5544 |
| 11/5/66 | 112 | 2 | 8 Chanson D'Amour ........................ AC:8   She Don't Want Me Now | $7 | | Capitol 5749 |
| | | |      #6 hit for Art & Dotty Todd in 1958 | | | |
| 6/8/68 | 109 | 2 | 9 All The Grey Haired Men ....................... Anyone Who Had A Heart | $6 | | Capitol 2196 |
| 3/1/69 | 129 | 2 | 10 I Have Dreamed ................ AC:16   The Pendulum Swings Both Ways | $6 | | Capitol 2414 |
| | | |      from the musical *The King And I*; #91 hit for **Chad & Jeremy** in 1965 | | | |
| 11/7/70 | 104 | 1 | 11 Hey, Girl ....................................... AC:17   Worlds | $6 | | Capitol 2938 |
| | | |      #10 hit for **Freddie Scott** in 1963; #9 hit for **Donny Osmond** in 1972 | | | |

**LEVERT**     R&B/HOT
R&B vocal trio from Ohio: Sean and Gerald Levert (sons of **The O'Jays'** Eddie Levert), and Marc Gordon.

| | | | | | | |
|-------|------|-----|--------|---|-----|----------------|
| 3/11/95 | 105 | 11 | 1 Answering Service.................... Sls:65 /R&B:12   Nice & Wet | $3 | ▌ | EastWest 64458 |
| | | |      **GERALD LEVERT** | | | |
| 6/10/95 | 119 | 5 | 2 Put Your Body Where Your Mouth Is........... R&B:40   (3 album snippets) | $3 | ▌ | Atlantic 87165 |
| | | |      **SEAN LEVERT** | | | |

**LEVERT — Cont'd**

| | | | | | | |
|-------|------|-----|----|---|---|---|
| 3/2/96 | 103 | 8 | 3 **Wind Beneath My Wings**       Sls:71 /R&B:30 *Get Your Thing Off* | $3 | ■ | EastWest 64306 |
| | | |     **GERALD LEVERT & EDDIE LEVERT, SR.** | | | |
| | | |     #1 hit for Bette Midler in 1989 | | | |
| 3/1/97 | 107 | 8 | 4 **True Dat** .........................................................*R&B:52 (remix)* | $3 | ■ | Atlantic 84869 |
| | | |     **LEVERT Featuring Yo Yo & Queen Pen** | | | |
| 6/21/97 | 113 | 3 | 5 **Sorry Is** ...............................................*R&B:33 Mama's House* | $3 | ■ | Atlantic 84003 |

**LEWIS, Barbara**      HOT/R&B/AC
Born on 2/9/43 in South Lyon, Michigan. R&B singer/multi-instrumentalist/songwriter (since age nine).

| | | | | | | |
|-------|------|-----|----|---|---|---|
| 8/24/63 | 131 | 1 | 1 **If You Love Her** .............................*Straighten Up Your Heart (Hot #43)* | $15 | | Atlantic 2200 |
| 5/23/64 | 119 | 4 | 2 **Spend A Little Time/** | $15 | | Atlantic 2227 |
| 5/9/64 | 124 | 2 | 3     **Someday We're Gonna Love Again** .................................... | $15 | | Atlantic 2227 |
| 10/31/64 | 113 | 3 | 4 **Pushin' A Good Thing Too Far** ...........................*Come Home* | $15 | | Atlantic 2255 |
| | | |     The Dells (backing vocals, above 3); Riley Hampton (orch., all of above) | | | |

**LEWIS, Bobby**      HOT/R&B
Born on 2/17/33 in Indianapolis. R&B singer. Grew up in an orphanage, adopted by a Detroit family at age 12.

| | | | | | | |
|-------|------|-----|----|---|---|---|
| 1/27/62 | 110 | 3 | **Mamie In The Afternoon** ...........................*Yes, Oh Yes, It Did* | $20 | | Beltone 1016 |
| | | |     twist dance from the Broadway musical *A Family Affair* | | | |

**LEWIS, Gary, And The Playboys**      HOT/AC
Pop group formed in Los Angeles in 1964 featuring Gary Lewis (vocals, drums). Lewis (b: Cary Levitch on 7/31/45) is the son of comedian Jerry Lewis.

| | | | | | | |
|-------|------|-----|----|---|---|---|
| 3/4/67 | 121 | 3 | 1 **Ice Melts In The Sun** ............................*The Loser (With A Broken Heart) (Hot #43)* | $8 | ■ | Liberty 55949 |
| 11/2/68 | 101³ | 5 | 2 **Main Street** ...........................................*C. C. Rider* | $8 | | Liberty 56075 |

**LEWIS, Jerry Lee**      C&W/HOT/R&B/AC
Born on 9/29/35 in Ferriday, Louisiana. Rock and roll singer/pianist. First recorded for Sun in 1956. Made comeback in country music beginning in 1968. Inducted into the Rock and Roll Hall of Fame in 1986.

| | | | | | | |
|-------|------|-----|----|---|---|---|
| 9/22/62 | 114 | 1 | 1 **How's My Ex Treating You** ...........................*Sweet Little Sixteen (Hot #95)* | $25 | | Sun 379 |
| 11/23/63 | 103 | 5 | 2 **Hit The Road Jack** ...........................*Pen And Paper (C&W #36)* | $20 | | Smash 1857 |
| | | |     #1 hit for Ray Charles in 1961 | | | |
| 2/27/65 | 129 | 3 | 3 **Baby, Hold Me Close** ...........................*I Believe In You* | $15 | | Smash 1969 |
| 5/22/71 | 110 | 4 | 4 **Touching Home** ...............*C&W:3 Woman, Woman (Get Out Of My Way)* | $6 | | Mercury 73192 |
| 8/11/73 | 104 | 3 | 5 **No Headstone On My Grave** ...........*C&W:60 Jack Daniels (Old No. 7)* | $6 | | Mercury 73402 |
| | | |     written by Charlie Rich | | | |
| 5/5/79 | 101¹ | 7 | 6 **Rockin' My Life Away**      C&W:18 *I Wish I Was Eighteen Again* | $5 | | Elektra 46030 |

**LEWIS, Linda** ☺      R&B
R&B singer/actress from London. Appeared in the movies *Taste Of Honey* and *A Hard Day's Night*.

| | | | | | | |
|-------|------|-----|----|---|---|---|
| 7/26/75 | 107 | 1 | **It's In His Kiss** ...........................*R&B:96 Walk About* | $5 | | Arista 0129 |
| | | |     #6 hit for Betty Everett in 1964 | | | |

**LEWIS, Ramsey**      R&B/HOT/AC
Born on 5/27/35 in Chicago. R&B/jazz-oriented pianist.

| | | | | | | |
|-------|------|-----|----|---|---|---|
| 7/9/66 | 129 | 1 | 1 **Ain't That Peculiar** ...........................*Wade In The Water (Hot #19)* [I] | $7 | | Cadet 5541 |
| | | |     #8 hit for Marvin Gaye in 1965 | | | |
| 2/24/68 | 123 | 2 | 2 **Bear Mash** ...........................*The Look Of Love* [I] | $6 | | Cadet 5593 |
| 7/22/72 | 101² | 5 | 3 **Slipping Into Darkness**      R&B:44 *Collage* [I] | $5 | | Columbia 45634 |
| | | |     #16 hit for War in 1972 | | | |

**LEWIS, Webster** ☺      R&B
Keyboardist from Baltimore. Toured with Dionne Warwick, Sonny Rollins and Dizzy Gillespie. Former conductor for Lola Falana.

| | | | | | | |
|-------|------|-----|----|---|---|---|
| 5/3/80 | 107 | 3 | **Give Me Some Emotion** ...........................*R&B:41 I Want To Blow (My Horn)* | $4 | | Epic 50832 |
| | | |     produced by Herbie Hancock | | | |

**LEWIS & CLARKE EXPEDITION, The**      HOT
Folk duo: Travis Lewis (Michael Martin Murphey) and Boomer Clarke (Boomer Castleman).

| | | | | | | |
|-------|------|-----|----|---|---|---|
| 5/4/68 | 131 | 3 | **Chain Around The Flowers** ...............................*Why Need They Pretend?* | $10 | | Colgems 1022 |

**LIFE** ☺
Canadian pop group produced by Neil Sheppard. Consisted of four men and one woman.

| | | | | | | |
|-------|------|-----|----|---|---|---|
| 7/19/69 | 120 | 2 | **Hands Of The Clock** ...........................*Ain't I Told You Before* | $8 | | Polydor 15003 |

**LIFE** ☺
Country-flavored pop group led by Kitty Woodson.

| | | | | | | |
|-------|------|-----|----|---|---|---|
| 5/2/81 | 106 | 3 | **Cool Down** ...........................*Whatever It Takes* | $5 | | Elektra 47128 |

**LIGHTER SHADE OF BROWN**      HOT/R&B
Hispanic rap duo of ODM ("One Dope Mexican," Robert Gutierrez) and DTTX ("Don't Try To Xerox," Bobby Ramirez), from Riverside, California.

| | | | | | | |
|-------|------|-----|----|---|---|---|
| 7/9/94 | 107 | 8 | 1 **If You Wanna Groove** ...........................*(remix)* | $3 | ■ | Mercury 858748 |
| 12/6/97 | 118 | 4 | 2 **Whatever U Want** ...........................*(remix)* | $3 | ■ | Thump 2247 |
| | | |     samples "Whatever You Want" by Tony! Toni! Toné! | | | |

**LIGHTFOOT, Gordon**      AC/HOT/C&W
Born on 11/17/38 in Orillia, Ontario, Canada. Folk-pop singer/songwriter/guitarist. First recorded for Chateau in 1962.

| | | | | | | |
|-------|------|-----|----|---|---|---|
| 4/3/71 | 111 | 5 | 1 **If I Could** ...........................*Softly* | $7 | | United Artists 50765 |
| 2/24/73 | 101² | 2 | 2 **You Are What I Am/**      AC:32 | | | |
| 12/2/72 | 102 | 4 | 3     **That Same Old Obsession** ...................................................... | $6 | | Reprise 1128 |

**LIGHTHOUSE**      HOT/AC
Rock band from Toronto which featured a fluctuating lineup of at least 10 members. Lead singer Bob McBride died on 2/20/98 (age 51).

| | | | | | | |
|-------|------|-----|----|---|---|---|
| 2/17/73 | 114 | 3 | **You Girl** ...........................*Merlin* | $6 | | Evolution 1072 |

| DEBUT | PEAK | WKS | A-side (Chart Hit)..........................................................................................................B-side | $ | Pic | Label & Number |
|---|---|---|---|---|---|---|

**LIL BUD & TIZONE** ⊘       R&B
Male rap duo from New York City.

| | | | | | | |
|---|---|---|---|---|---|---|
| 4/12/97 | 101[1] | 11 | Gonna Let U Know      R&B:47 (remix) / (Instrumental) | $3 | ■ | Island 854914 |

        **LIL BUD & TIZONE** featuring Keith Sweat
        Marinna Teal (additional vocal)

**LIL' SHAWN** ⊘      R&B

| | | | | | | |
|---|---|---|---|---|---|---|
| 8/19/95 | 105 | 6 | Dom Perignon ............ R&B:87 Check It Out Y'all | $3 | ■ | Uptown/MCA 55042 |

**LIND, Bob**      HOT
Born on 11/25/44 in Baltimore. Folk-rock singer/songwriter.

| | | | | | | |
|---|---|---|---|---|---|---|
| 7/16/66 | 123 | 1 | 1 I Just Let It Take Me ............ We've Never Spoken | $8 | | World Pacific 77830 |
| 9/10/66 | 135 | 1 | 2 San Francisco Woman ............ Oh Babe Take Me Home | $8 | | World Pacific 77839 |

        above 2 produced and arranged by Jack Nitzsche

**LINDSEY, Theresa** ⊘
R&B vocalist.

| | | | | | | |
|---|---|---|---|---|---|---|
| 2/1/64 | 129 | 2 | Gotta Find A Way ............ Wonderful One | $20 | | Correc-Tone 5840 |

        written and produced by Richard "Popcorn" Wylie

**LIPTON, Peggy** ⊘
Born on 8/30/47 in New York City. Played "Julie Barnes" on TV's *Mod Squad*. Later on *Twin Peaks*. Married to **Quincy Jones** for 12 years.

| | | | | | | |
|---|---|---|---|---|---|---|
| 12/28/68 | 121 | 1 | 1 Stoney End ............ San Francisco Glide | $8 | ■ | Ode 114 |

        #6 hit for **Barbra Streisand** in 1971

| | | | | | | |
|---|---|---|---|---|---|---|
| 2/7/70 | 102 | 2 | 2 Lu ............ Let Me Pass By | $8 | ■ | Ode 124 |
| 6/20/70 | 108 | 3 | 3 Wear Your Love Like Heaven ............ Honey Won't Let Me | $8 | ■ | Ode 66001 |

        #23 hit for **Donovan** in 1967

**LISA LISA**      R&B/HOT/AC
Born Lisa Velez on 1/15/67 in Harlem. Charted several hits with Cult Jam.

| | | | | | | |
|---|---|---|---|---|---|---|
| 1/1/94 | 105 | 8 | Skip To My Lu ............ R&B:38 (instrumental) | $3 | ■ | Pendulum 58094 |

**LITTLE, Rich** ⊘      R&B
Born on 11/26/38 in Ottawa, Canada. Comedian/impressionist. Made first U.S. television appearance on *The Judy Garland Show* in 1964.

| | | | | | | |
|---|---|---|---|---|---|---|
| 6/26/82 | 105 | 1 | President Rap's ............ R&B:39 (same version) [C] | $8 | | Boardwalk 99901 (T) |

        9:07 of Little impersonating President Reagan to a funky musical background

**LITTLE ANTHONY AND THE IMPERIALS**      HOT/R&B
R&B vocal group formed in 1957 in Brooklyn featuring Anthony Gourdine (b: 1/8/40).

| | | | | | | |
|---|---|---|---|---|---|---|
| 3/6/61 | 104 | 4 | 1 Please Say You Want Me ............ So Near Yet So Far | $25 | | End 1086 |
| 8/20/66 | 125 | 1 | 2 You Better Take It Easy Baby ............ Gonna Fix You Good (Every Time You're Bad) | $15 | | Veep 1233 |
| 3/4/67 | 123 | 3 | 3 Don't Tie Me Down ............ Where There's A Will There's A Way To Forget You | $15 | | Veep 1255 |

        above 2 written and produced by Teddy Randazzo

| | | | | | | |
|---|---|---|---|---|---|---|
| 2/14/70 | 116 | 3 | 4 Don't Get Close ............ It'll Never Be The Same Again | $8 | | United Artists 50625 |
| 6/20/70 | 121 | 1 | 5 World Of Darkness ............ The Change | $8 | | United Artists 50677 |
| 4/12/75 | 106 | 1 | 6 Hold On (Just A Little Bit Longer) ............ R&B:79 I've Got To Let You Go (Part 1) | $7 | | Avco 4651 |

        **ANTHONY & THE IMPERIALS** (#3 & 6)

**LITTLE CAESAR and The Romans**      HOT/R&B
R&B vocal group from Los Angeles: Carl "Little Caesar" Burnett, David Johnson, Early Harris, Leroy Sanders and Johnny Simmons.

| | | | | | | |
|---|---|---|---|---|---|---|
| 9/18/61 | 101[1] | 2 | Memories of those Oldies But Goodies ............ Fever | $50 | | Del-Fi 4166 |

        featuring a medley of a dozen classic R&B songs; follow-up to their #9 hit "Those Oldies But Goodies"

**LITTLE EVA**      HOT/R&B
Born Eva Narcissus Boyd on 6/29/43 in Belhaven, North Carolina.

| | | | | | | |
|---|---|---|---|---|---|---|
| 7/27/63 | 101[1] | 6 | 1 What I Gotta Do (To Make You Jealous) ............ The Trouble With Boys | $20 | | Dimension 1013 |
| 11/16/63 | 123 | 3 | 2 Let's Start The Party Again ............ Please Hurt Me | $20 | | Dimension 1019 |

        above 2 written by **Carole King** & **Gerry Goffin**

**LITTLE JOE BLUE** ⊘      R&B
Born Joseph Valery, Jr. on 9/23/34 in Vicksburg, Mississippi. Blues singer/guitarist. With **James Brown** Revue in 1975.

| | | | | | | |
|---|---|---|---|---|---|---|
| 7/30/66 | 111 | 2 | Dirty Work Going On ............ R&B:40 Pretty Woman | $12 | | Checker 1141 |

**LITTLE MILTON**      R&B/HOT
Born Milton Campbell, Jr. on 9/7/34 in Inverness, Mississippi. Blues singer/guitarist. Recorded with **Ike Turner** at Sun Records, 1953-54.

| | | | | | | |
|---|---|---|---|---|---|---|
| 12/18/65 | 106 | 4 | 1 Your People ............ My Baby's Something Else | $12 | | Checker 1128 |
| 8/13/66 | 127 | 4 | 2 Man Loves Two ............ R&B:45 Believe In Me | $12 | | Checker 1149 |
| 10/11/69 | 103 | 5 | 3 Poor Man ............ R&B:18 So Blue (Without You) | $10 | | Checker 1221 |

**LITTLE RICHARD**      R&B/HOT
Born Richard Wayne Penniman on 12/5/32 in Macon, Georgia. R&B-rock and roll singer/pianist. Inducted into the Rock and Roll Hall of Fame in 1986. Won Grammy's Lifetime Achievement Award in 1993. *Top Pop Singles*: 21.

| | | | | | | |
|---|---|---|---|---|---|---|
| 12/18/61 | 113 | 2 | 1 He's Not Just A Soldier ............ Joy, Joy, Joy | $20 | | Mercury 71884 |

        with the Howard Roberts Singers; billed on the label as "King of the Gospel Singers"

| | | | | | | |
|---|---|---|---|---|---|---|
| 4/6/63 | 119 | 4 | 2 Crying In The Chapel ............ Hole In The Wall | $20 | | Atlantic 2181 |

        #6 hit for **Darrell Glenn** in 1953; #3 hit for **Elvis Presley** in 1965

| | | | | | | |
|---|---|---|---|---|---|---|
| 9/5/64 | 126 | 2 | 3 Whole Lotta Shakin' Goin' On/ | | | |

        #3 hit for **Jerry Lee Lewis** in 1957

| | | | | | | |
|---|---|---|---|---|---|---|
| 9/5/64 | 128 | 1 | 4 Goodnight Irene ............ | $20 | | Vee-Jay 612 |

        #1 hit for The Weavers in 1950

| | | | | | | |
|---|---|---|---|---|---|---|
| 7/23/66 | 121 | 3 | 5 Poor Dog (Who Can't Wag His Own Tail) ............ R&B:41 Well | $15 | ■ | Okeh 7251 |
| 1/10/76 | 106 | 1 | 6 Call My Name ............ Steal Miss Liza (Steal Liza Jane) | $8 | | Manticore 7007 |

**LITTLE TEXAS**       C&W/HOT/AC
Country group from Texas: Tim Rushlow (vocals), Porter Howell and Dwayne O'Brien (guitars), Brady Seals (keyboards), Duane Propes (bass) and Del Gray (drums). Seals was replaced by Jeff Huskins in 1995.

| 10/8/94 | 108 | 8 | 1 Kick A Little.............................................................. Sls:68 /C&W:5 *Hit Country Song* | $3 | ▮ | Warner 18103 |
| 8/12/95 | 101² | 9 | 2 **Party All Night**...................................... Sls:60 /C&W:53 *Southern Accent* [N] | $3 | ▮ | Warner 17806 |

**JEFF FOXWORTHY With Little Texas and Scott Rouse**

**LITTLE WALTER and his Jukes** ○      R&B
Born Marion Walter Jacobs on 5/1/30 in Marksville, Louisiana. Died on 2/15/68. Blues vocalist/guitarist/harmonica player.

| 6/27/60 | 106 | 3 | My Babe ........................................................................ *Blue Midnight* [R] | $25 | | Checker 955 |

new version of Little Walter's #1 R&B hit in 1955 on Checker 811 ($50); based on the spiritual tune "This Train"

**L.L. COOL J**      R&B/HOT
Born James Todd Smith on 8/16/68 in Queens, New York. Rapper.

| 12/11/93 | 116 | 3 | Stand By Your Man ..................................... R&B:67 *(5 mixes) / Soul Survivor* | $5 | ▮ | Def Jam 77097 * |

samples "Fool's Paradise" by Meli'sa Morgan and "La Di Da Di" by Doug E. Fresh

**LLOYD, Linda** ○
New York-based songstress.

| 4/4/64 | 122 | 2 | I'm Gonna Love That Guy (Like He's Never Been Loved Before)................................................ *A Cock-Eyed Optimist* | $10 | | Columbia 42990 |

#9 hit for Benny Goodman with Dottie Reid in 1945

**LOCKLIN, Hank**      C&W/HOT
Born Lawrence Hankins Locklin on 2/15/18 in McLellan, Florida. Country singer/songwriter/guitarist.

| 9/4/61 | 107 | 2 | You're The Reason.................... C&W:14 *Happy Birthday To Me* (C&W #7) | $12 | | RCA Victor 7921 |

#11 hit for Bobby Edwards in 1961

**LOEB, Lisa, & Nine Stories**      HOT/ROK/AC
New York-based band featuring Dallas native Loeb.

| 2/17/96 | 112 | 3 | Taffy ................................................................................. *Sandalwood* | $3 | ▮ | Geffen 19393 |

**LOFGREN, Nils** ○      ROK
Born on 6/21/51 in Chicago. Pop-rock singer/guitarist/pianist. Leader of Grin, 1969-74. Member of Bruce Springsteen's E Street Band, 1984-85.

| 10/24/81 | 109 | 2 | Night Fades Away ........................................................ *Ancient History* | $5 | | Backstreet 51191 |

**LOGAN, Betty** ○
Full name: Betty Logan Chotas. Pop singer/songwriter.

| 9/7/63 | 132 | 1 | Are You Sure ............................................................... *Teen Age Party* | $15 | | Academy 102 |

also released on ABC-Paramount 10479 in 1963 ($12)

**LOGGINS, Dave — see MURRAY, Anne**

**LOLITA**      HOT
Full name: Lolita Ditta. Born in St. Poelten, Austria.

| 2/6/61 | 112 | 1 | Theme From "A Summer Place" (Wenn Der Sommer Kommt)........................................... *Cowboy Jimmy Joe* (Hot #94) [F] | $10 | ▮ | Kapp 370 |

German vocal version of Percy Faith's #1 hit in 1960

**LOMAX, Jackie** ○
Born on 5/10/44 in Liverpool, England. Male rock singer/songwriter.

| 9/28/68 | 117 | 2 | 1 Sour Milk Sea/ | | | |
| 10/26/68 | 125 | 3 | 2   The Eagle Laughs At You ................................................................ | $20 | | Apple 1802 |

above 2 written and produced by George Harrison

**LONDON, Joe** ○
Pop singer.

| 11/2/59 | 112 | 1 | It Might Have Been .................................................... *Lonesome Whistle* | $15 | | Liberty 55209 |

**LONDON, Julie**      HOT
Born on 9/26/26 in Santa Rosa, California. Singer/actress. Played "Dixie McCall" on the TV series *Emergency*.

| 10/27/62 | 110 | 5 | 1 Slightly Out Of Tune (Desafinado).................................. *Where Did The Gentleman Go* | $10 | | Liberty 55512 |

#15 hit for Stan Getz/Charlie Byrd in 1962

| 8/31/63 | 118 | 3 | 2 I'm Coming Back To You.................... *When Snow Flakes Fall In The Summer* | $10 | | Liberty 55605 |

Ernie Freeman (orch., above 2)

| 11/23/68 | 125 | 1 | 3 Yummy, Yummy, Yummy .......................................... *Come To Me Slowly* | $8 | | Liberty 56074 |

Tommy Oliver (orch.); #4 hit for Ohio Express in 1968

**LONESTAR**      C&W/HOT
Nashville-based country band: Richie McDonald (vocals, guitar), John Rich (vocals, bass), Michael Britt (guitar), Dean Sams (keyboards) and Keech Rainwater (drums). Also see Mindy McCready.

| 3/23/96 | 122 | 4 | 1 No News/ | C&W:❶³ | | |
| | | 4 | 2   Tequila Talkin'.................................................................... C&W:8 | $3 | ▮ | BNA 64386 |

**LONG, Shorty**      HOT/R&B
Born Frederick Earl Long on 5/20/40 in Birmingham, Alabama. Drowned on 6/29/69 in Ontario, Canada. R&B singer/songwriter.

| 5/30/64 | 125 | 4 | Devil With The Blue Dress ....................................................... *Wind It Up* | $25 | | Soul 35001 |

#4 hit for Mitch Ryder & The Detroit Wheels in 1966

**LONGET, Claudine**      AC/HOT
Born on 1/29/42 in France. Singer/actress. Formerly married to Andy Williams.

| 3/4/67 | 126 | 3 | Here, There And Everywhere ................................ AC:19 *A Man And A Woman* | $8 | | A&M 832 |

originally recorded by The Beatles on their 1966 album *Revolver*; #65 hit for Emmylou Harris in 1976

**LOOKING GLASS**      AC/HOT
Rock group formed at Rutgers University in New Jersey: Elliot Lurie (vocals), Larry Gonsky, Piet Sweval and Jeff Grob.

| 3/3/73 | 104 | 3 | Rainbow Man .............................................................. *Sweet Somethin'* | $6 | | Epic 10953 |

| DEBUT | PEAK | WKS | A-side (Chart Hit) / B-side | $ | Pic | Label & Number |
|---|---|---|---|---|---|---|
| | | | **LOONEY, Shelley ○** | | | |
| | | | Eight-year-old girl from Trenton, Michigan. | | | |
| 3/15/80 | 109 | 1 | **This Is My Country, Thank You Canada** ........................ *Oakwood-It's Nice To Believe* [S] | $5 | | Mercury 76050 |
| | | | Shelley reads a letter thanking Canada for helping the U.S. in Iran; backing song: "This Is My Country" | | | |
| | | | **LOPEZ, Trini**    AC/HOT/R&B | | | |
| | | | Born Trinidad Lopez, III on 5/15/37 in Dallas. Pop-folk singer/guitarist. | | | |
| 1/11/64 | 103 | 2 | 1 **Sinner Not A Saint**    *If* | $10 | | United/Modern 106 |
| 2/5/66 | 113 | 5 | 2 **Made In Paris**........................................... AC:36 *Pretty Little Girl* | $7 | ■ | Reprise 0435 |
| | | | title song from the movie starring **Ann-Margret** | | | |
| 5/27/67 | 123 | 2 | 3 **Up To Now**........................................*In The Land Of Plenty* | $7 | | Reprise 0574 |
| 3/22/69 | 121 | 2 | 4 **Come A Little Bit Closer**........................*My Baby Loves Sad Songs* | $6 | | Reprise 0814 |
| | | | #3 hit for Jay & The Americans in 1964 | | | |
| 5/31/69 | 133 | 3 | 5 **Don't Let The Sun Catch You Cryin'** ...............*My Baby Loves Sad Songs* | $6 | | Reprise 0825 |
| | | | #4 hit for Gerry & The Pacemakers in 1964; above 2 produced by **Tommy Boyce & Bobby Hart** | | | |
| | | | **LORBER, Jeff**    R&B/HOT | | | |
| | | | Born and raised in Philadelphia. Jazz fusion keyboardist. | | | |
| 4/6/85 | 105 | 2 | **Step By Step** ..........................R&B:31 *Pacific Coast Highway* (Lorber) | $4 | | Arista 9307 |
| | | | **JEFF LORBER** featuring Audrey Wheeler | | | |
| | | | **LORDS OF THE UNDERGROUND**    R&B/HOT | | | |
| | | | Rap trio: Mr. Funke, DoItAll and DJ Lord Jazz. Met at North Carolina's Shaw University. | | | |
| 3/18/95 | 111 | 6 | **What I'm After** .........................................*(extended mix)* | $3 | ■ | Pendulum 58321 |
| | | | samples "Tonight's Da Night" by **Redman** and "Pump Me Up" by **Trouble Funk** | | | |
| | | | **LOREN, Bryan ○**    R&B | | | |
| | | | R&B singer/songwriter/producer from Long Island, New York. Wrote and produced several of Vesta Williams's hits. | | | |
| 4/7/84 | 105 | 4 | **Lollipop Luv** ..........................................R&B:23 *(instrumental)* | $4 | | Philly World 99760 |
| | | | **LORENZ, Trey**    R&B/HOT/AC | | | |
| | | | Born on 1/19/69 in Florence, South Carolina. Sang backup on Mariah Carey's #1 hit in 1992 "I'll Be There." | | | |
| 2/6/93 | 118 | 3 | 1 **Photograph Of Mary** ...........................R&B:46 *(radio remix)* | $3 | ■ | Epic 74783 |
| 5/15/93 | 103 | 9 | 2 **Just To Be Close To You** ......................R&B:66 *(2 mixes)* | $3 | ■ | Epic 74934 |
| | | | above 2 produced by Mariah Carey | | | |
| | | | **LORENZO ○**    R&B | | | |
| | | | Full name: Lorenzo Smith. | | | |
| 12/19/92+ | 103 | 12 | 1 **Make Love 2 Me** ...............................Sls:57 /R&B:21 *(3 versions)* | $3 | ■ | Alpha International 787001 |
| 6/3/95 | 118 | 7 | 2 **If It's Alright With You** ......................R&B:41 *(album snippets)* | $3 | ■ | Luke 184 |
| | | | **LORENZO** Featuring Keith Sweat | | | |
| | | | **LOST GENERATION, The**    R&B/HOT | | | |
| | | | Chicago R&B quartet: Lowrell Simon (lead), his brother Fred Simon, Larry Brownlee (of **The C.O.D.'s**; d: 1978) and Jesse Dean. | | | |
| 11/21/70 | 127 | 1 | **Wait A Minute** ..........................R&B:25 *Wasting Time* | $8 | | Brunswick 55441 |
| | | | **LOUCHIE LOU & MICHIE ONE ○** | | | |
| 12/3/94 | 112 | 11 | **Rich Girl** ..........................................*(dance mix)* | $3 | ■ | Fashion/V.P. 7221 |
| | | | rap/reggae version of "If I Were A Rich Man" from the musical *Fiddler On The Roof* | | | |
| | | | **LOUDERMILK, John D.**    HOT/C&W | | | |
| | | | Born on 3/31/34 in Durham, North Carolina. Pop-country singer/songwriter/multi-instrumentalist. | | | |
| 4/11/64 | 132 | 1 | **Blue Train (Of the Heartbreak Line)** ..............C&W:44 *Rhythm And Blues* | $12 | | RCA Victor 8308 |
| | | | **LOUISIANA RED ○** | | | |
| | | | Blues singer Iverson Minter — married to Odetta. | | | |
| 9/12/64 | 117 | 3 | **I'm Too Poor To Die** ...................................*Sugar Hips* | $15 | | Glover 3002 |
| | | | **LOUISIANA'S LE ROUX — see LE ROUX** | | | |
| | | | **LOVE**    HOT | | | |
| | | | Rock band from Los Angeles featuring lead singer Arthur Lee. | | | |
| 5/4/68 | 123 | 2 | **Alone Again Or** ..........................*A House Is Not A Motel* | $10 | | Elektra 45629 |
| | | | an "enhanced" version made the *Hot 100* (#99) on 9/12/70 on Elektra 45700 | | | |
| | | | **LOVE, Marian ○** | | | |
| | | | Songstress from New York City. | | | |
| 3/6/71 | 111 | 3 | **I Believe In Music** ...........................AC:27 *He's Not You* | $12 | | A&R 7100/505 |
| | | | Harold Wheeler (orch.); written by **Mac Davis**; #22 hit for **Gallery** in 1972 | | | |
| | | | **LOVE, Mary ○**    R&B | | | |
| | | | Born Mary Ann Varney on 7/27/43 in Sacramento, California. | | | |
| 5/29/65 | 133 | 1 | **You Turned My Bitter Into Sweet** ...................*I'm In Your Hands* | $20 | | Modern 1006 |
| | | | song is similar in style to **The Supremes**' "Come See About Me" | | | |
| | | | **LOVE AFFAIR ○** | | | |
| | | | Cleveland-based rock quintet led by Rich Spina (vocals/keyboards). | | | |
| 9/27/80 | 109 | 1 | **Mama Sez** ..........................................*Can't Get Enough* | $6 | | Radio 421 |
| | | | **LOVELESS, Patty ○**    C&W | | | |
| | | | Born Patricia Ramey on 1/4/57 in Pikeville, Kentucky. Country singer. Married producer Emory Gordy Jr. in February 1989. | | | |
| 6/26/93 | 112 | 7 | 1 **Blame It On Your Heart** ................C&W:❶² *What's A Broken Heart* | $3 | ■ | Epic 74906 |
| 9/3/94 | 115 | 9 | 2 **I Try To Think About Elvis** ..............C&W:3 *Ships* | $3 | ■ | Epic 77609 |
| 5/13/95 | 117 | 8 | 3 **You Don't Even Know Who I Am**.............C&W:5 *Over My Shoulder* | $3 | ■ | Epic 77856 |
| 10/25/97 | 109 | 13 | 4 **You Don't Seem To Miss Me**................C&W:14 *Where Are You Boy* | $3 | ■ | Epic 78704 |
| | | | **PATTY LOVELESS** With George Jones | | | |

| DEBUT | PEAK | WKS | A-side (Chart Hit)..................................................................................................B-side | $ | Pic | Label & Number |
|---|---|---|---|---|---|---|

**LOVERBOY** ROK/HOT/AC
Rock quintet from Vancouver, Canada featuring Mike Reno (vocals) and Paul Dean (guitar).

| 12/11/82 | 101[4] | 9 | Jump                                                    *Take Me To The Top* | $4 | ■ | Columbia 03346 |
co-written by Bryan Adams

**LOVE SOCIETY** ☉
Pop/rock quintet from Plymouth, Wisconsin: Dave Steffen, Keith Abler, Mike Holdridge, Steve Gilles and Mike Dellger.

| 8/10/68 | 108 | 6 | Do You Wanna Dance ................................................................... *Without You* | $10 | | Scepter 12223 |
#5 hit for **Bobby Freeman** in 1958

**LOVE UNLIMITED** R&B/HOT
Female R&B vocal trio from San Pedro, California: sisters Glodean and Linda James, with Diane Taylor.

| 8/19/72 | 101[1] | 2 | 1 Is It Really True Boy-Is It Really Me                      *Another Chance* | $6 | | Uni 55342 |
| 8/18/73 | 101[2] | 6 | 2 Yes, We Finally Made It         *Oh Love, Well We Finally Made It (R&B #70)* [I] | $5 | | 20th Century 2025 |
above 2 written, produced and arranged by **Barry White**

**LOVE UNLIMITED ORCHESTRA** R&B/HOT/AC
Forty-piece studio orchestra conducted and arranged by Barry White.

| 12/21/74 | 102 | 4 | 1 Baby Blues.................................................................. *What A Groove* [I] | $5 | | 20th Century 2145 |
opening monologue by **Barry White**
| 5/8/76 | 108 | 2 | 2 Midnight Groove .................................... *R&B:91 It's Only What I Feel* [I] | $5 | | 20th Century 2281 |

**LOVIN' SPOONFUL, The** HOT
Jug-band rock group formed in New York City in 1965: John Sebastian (lead vocals), **Zalman Yanovsky** (lead guitar), Steve Boone (bass) and Joe Butler (drums). Also see **The Mugwumps**.

| 9/21/68 | 128 | 2 | (Till I) Run With You .............................. *Revelation: Revolution '69* | $8 | | Kama Sutra 251 |
THE LOVIN' SPOONFUL Featuring Joe Butler

**LOWE, Jim** HOT/R&B/C&W/MEM
Born on 5/7/27 in Springfield, Missouri. DJ/vocalist/pianist/composer. DJ in New York City when he recorded "The Green Door" in 1956.

| 9/21/63 | 103 | 2 | Hootenanny Granny............................... *These Bones Gonna Rise Again* [N] | $10 | | 20th Century Fox 426 |

**LOWE, Nick** HOT/ROK/AC
Born on 3/25/49 in Woodbridge, Suffolk, England. With Brinsley Schwarz (1970-75) and Rockpile. Produced albums for **Elvis Costello**, **Graham Parker** and others.

| 7/22/78 | 109 | 1 | 1 So It Goes............................. *Heart Of The City (live)* (w/Rockpile) | $5 | | Columbia 10734 |
| 11/24/79 | 107 | 2 | 2 Switch Board Susan .......................................... *Basing Street* | $5 | | Columbia 11131 |
| 8/4/84 | 110 | 1 | 3 Half A Boy And Half A Man ................................ *Awesome* | $5 | | Columbia 04486 |

**L.T.D.** R&B/HOT
R&B-funk band from Greensboro, North Carolina featuring Jeffrey Osborne (vocals, drums).

| 1/20/79 | 107 | 1 | 1 We Both Deserve Each Other's Love .......................... *R&B:19 It's Time To Be Real* | $5 | | A&M 2095 |
| 12/5/81 | 102 | 8 | 2 Kickin' Back ............................................ *R&B:10 Now* | $4 | | A&M 2382 |

**LUBA** ☉
Born Luba Kowalchyk in 1958 in Montreal. Female rock singer/songwriter.

| 9/22/84 | 105 | 2 | Everytime I See Your Picture .......................... *Private Wars* | $4 | ■ | Capitol 5378 |

**LUKE — see 2 LIVE CREW**

**LULU** HOT/AC/R&B
Born Marie Lawrie on 11/3/48 near Glasgow, Scotland. Married to Maurice Gibb (**Bee Gees**) from 1969-73.

| 12/26/64 | 105 | 7 | 1 I'll Come Running                                    *Here Comes The Night* | $20 | | Parrot 9714 |
| 7/1/67 | 115 | 3 | 2 The Boat That I Row ................................ *To Sir With Love (Hot #1)* | $10 | | Epic 10187 |
written by Neil Diamond
| 6/29/68 | 108 | 3 | 3 Boy................................................ *Sad Memories* | $8 | | Epic 10346 |
| 7/4/70 | 117 | 2 | 4 After The Feeling Is Gone ................ *AC:20 Good Day Sunshine* | $7 | | Atco 6761 |
LULU with The Dixie Flyers
#89 hit in 1970 for Five Flights Up
| 4/10/82 | 106 | 1 | 5 Who's Foolin' Who ............................ *You Win, I Lose* | $5 | | Alfa 7021 |

**LUMAN, Bob** C&W/HOT
Born on 4/15/37 in Nacogdoches, Texas. Died on 12/27/78. Country-rockabilly singer/songwriter/guitarist.

| 12/5/60 | 105 | 3 | 1 Oh, Lonesome Me/ | | | |
#7 hit for **Don Gibson** in 1958
| 12/19/60 | 106 | 2 | 2 Why, Why, Bye, Bye | $20 | ■ | Warner 5184 |

**LUNIZ** R&B/HOT
Rap duo from Oakland: Yukmouth and Knumskull.

| 11/11/95 | 102 | 11 | Playa Hata .................. *Sls:65 /R&B:51 (2 versions) / Pimps, Playas & Hustlas (2 versions)* | $3 | ▌ | Noo Trybe 38517 |

**LUREX, Larry** ☉
Larry Lurex is actually **Queen's** Freddie Mercury.

| 9/8/73 | 115 | 3 | I Can Hear Music ................................................ *Going Back* | $100 | | Anthem 204 |
#24 hit for **The Beach Boys** in 1969

**LYMAN, Arthur, Group** HOT/AC
Born on 2/2/32 in Kauai, Hawaii. Plays vibraphone, guitar, piano and drums. Formerly with **Martin Denny**.

| 4/20/63 | 129 | 1 | Cotton Fields (The Cotton Song) ........................ *Limbo Rock (Bossa Nova)* [I] | $10 | | Hi Fi 5071 |
#13 hit for The Highwaymen in 1963

**LYNN, Barbara** HOT/R&B
Born Barbara Lynn Ozen on 1/16/42 in Beaumont, Texas. R&B singer/songwriter/guitarist.

| 6/15/63 | 135 | 1 | 1 To Love Or Not To Love ................................ *Promises* | $15 | | Jamie 1251 |
| 7/23/66 | 129 | 2 | 2 I'm A Good Woman .................................... *Running Back* | $20 | | Tribe 8316 |
| 10/8/66 | 110 | 3 | 3 You Left The Water Running ................ *R&B:42 Until I'm Free* | $15 | | Tribe 8319 |

### LYNN, Cheryl                                                     R&B/HOT/AC
Born on 3/11/57 in Los Angeles. R&B-dance singer. Discovered on TV's *Gong Show*.

| 7/24/82 | 105 | 1 | 1 Instant Love................................................................R&B:16 *I Just Wanna Be Your Fantasy* | $4 | | Columbia 02905 |
| 10/16/82 | 101[1] | 10 | 2 If This World Were Mine    R&B:4 *I Just Wanna Be Your Fantasy* (Lynn) | $4 | | Columbia 03204 |

CHERYL LYNN (With Luther Vandross)
#68 hit for **Marvin Gaye** & **Tammi Terrell** in 1968

### LYNN, Donna                                                     HOT
Teenage pop singer.

| 5/2/64 | 129 | 1 | Java Jones (Java).......................................................*The Things That I Feel* | $15 | | Capitol 5156 |

vocal version of **Al Hirt**'s #4 hit in 1964

### LYNN, Judy ○                                                    C&W/AC
Born Judy Lynn Voiten on 4/12/36 in Boise, Idaho. Country singer.

| 4/24/71 | 104 | 3 | Married To A Memory........................AC:18 /C&W:74 *So Natural Is My Love* | $7 | | Amaret 131 |

### LYNN, Loretta                                                   C&W/HOT
Born Loretta Webb on 4/14/34 in Butcher Holler, Kentucky. Country singer/songwriter/guitarist.

| 9/8/73 | 102 | 6 | Love Is The Foundation........................C&W:❶[2] *What Sundown Does To You* | $6 | | MCA 40058 |

### LYNNE, Gloria                                                   HOT/R&B/AC
Born Gloria Alleyne on 11/23/31 in New York City. Jazz-styled vocalist.

| 1/30/61 | 109 | 2 | 1 The Jazz In You..................................................*Love I've Found You* | $12 | | Everest 19390 |

with The Earl May Trio

| 5/8/61 | 111 | 2 | 2 He Needs Me..........................................................*The Lamp Is Low* | $12 | | Everest 19409 |

### LYNYRD SKYNYRD                                                  ROK/HOT
Southern-rock band formed by Ronnie Van Zant (b: 1/15/49; lead singer), Gary Rossington (guitar) and Allen Collins (guitar; d: 1/23/90, age 37) while they were in junior high in Jacksonville, Florida in 1965. Plane crash on 10/20/77 in Gillsburg, Mississippi killed Van Zant and 2 other members.

| 11/4/78 | 103 | 7 | Down South Jukin'.....................................................*Wino* | $5 | | MCA 40957 |

originally released as the B-side of their 1974 *Hot 100* hit "Free Bird"

### LYONS, Ricky ○

| 10/17/60 | 104 | 3 | Shim Sham Shuffle.....................................................*Have No Fear* | $20 | | Federal 12381 |

same melody as **Freddy Cannon**'s 1965 hit "Action"

# M

### MACEO AND THE MACKS                                            R&B/HOT
The JB's spin-off funk group led by Maceo Parker (tenor sax; member of **Parliament/Funkadelic**). Also see **A.A.B.B.** and **Fred Wesley**.

| 1/19/74 | 109 | 3 | Soul Power 74 - Part I......................................R&B:20 *Part II* [I] | $6 | | People 631 |

written, arranged and produced by **James Brown**

### MacISAAC, Ashley ○
Born on 2/24/75 in Cape Breton, Nova Scotia, Canada, of Scottish heritage. Male fiddler.

| 2/15/97 | 102 | 4 | Sleepy Maggie..............................................*(radio edit)* [F] | $3 | ▪ | A&M 2062 |

ASHLEY MacISAAC with Mary Jane Lamond

### MACK, Craig                                                     R&B/HOT
Rapper from Long Island, New York. Was a roadie for EPMD. Discovered by producer Sean "Puff Daddy" Combs.

| 5/3/97 | 102 | 8 | 1 Spirit..........................................Sls:70 /R&B:29 *(remix)* | $3 | ▪ | Perspective 7574 |

SOUNDS OF BLACKNESS Featuring Craig Mack

| 11/8/97 | 103 | 5 | 2 What I Need.............................................R&B:55 *Jockin' My Style* | $3 | ▪ | Street Life 78149 |

### MACK, Lonnie                                                    HOT/R&B
Born Lonnie McIntosh on 7/18/41 in Aurora, Indiana. Rockabilly guitarist/R&B-styled singer.

| 11/30/63 | 113 | 6 | 1 Where There's A Will............................*Baby, What's Wrong* (Hot #93) | $12 | | Fraternity 918 |
| 3/7/64 | 117 | 3 | 2 Lonnie On The Move....................................*Say Something Nice To Me* [I] | $12 | | Fraternity 920 |
| 5/2/64 | 128 | 1 | 3 I've Had It............................................................*Nashville* | $12 | | Fraternity 925 |

#6 hit for The Bell Notes in 1959

### MACK 10                                                         R&B/HOT
Born on 8/9/71 in Inglewood, California. Male rapper. Discovered by **Ice Cube**.

| 9/30/95 | 105 | 6 | On Them Thangs........................................R&B:74 *(radio edit)* | $3 | ▪ | Priority 53220 |

samples "Mary Jane" by **Rick James**

### MAD COBRA                                                       R&B/HOT
Born Ewart Everton Brown on 3/31/68 in Kingston; raised in St. Mary's, Jamaica. Reggae rapper.

| 9/7/96 | 117 | 3 | Big Long John.........................................R&B:79 *(2 versions) / Plant It* | $3 | ▪ | EMI 58573 |

samples "Money" by **Jimmy Spicer**

### MAD LION                                                        R&B/HOT
Born in London; raised in Jamaica. Male dancehall rapper. Based in Brooklyn.

| 1/29/94 | 104 | 7 | 1 Shoot To Kill......................................*(2 mixes) / Girlzz* | $5 | ▪ | Weeded 20072 * |
| 5/20/95 | 112 | 10 | 2 Own Destiny...........................................*(KRS-One remix)* | $3 | ▪ | Weeded 20147 |

from the movie *New Jersey Drive* starring Sharron Corley; samples "It's Ecstasy When You Lay Down Next To Me" by **Barry White**

| 5/11/96 | 113 | 2 | 3 Double Trouble.........................R&B:69 *(Third World remix)* (w/KRS-One) | $3 | ▪ | Weeded 20189 |

MAD LION featuring Brenda K. Starr

### MADONNA                                                         HOT/AC/R&B
Born Madonna Louise Ciccone on 8/16/58 in Bay City, Michigan. Acted in the movies *Desperately Seeking Susan*, *Dick Tracy*, *A League Of Their Own*, *Body Of Evidence* and *Evita*, among others. *Top Pop Singles*: 39.

| 12/25/82 | 107 | 8 | Everybody..............................................................*Part 2* | $10 | | Sire 29841 |

**MAGIC DISCO MACHINE** ☉
Group of Motown session musicians.

| 8/30/75 | 106 | 2 | Control Tower...........................................................................*Scratchin* [I] | $6 | | Motown 1362 |

**MAGIC LANTERNS, The**　　　　　　　　　　　　　　　　HOT
Rock quintet from Lancashire, England. Albert Hammond was a member in 1971.

| 4/24/71 | 103 | 2 | Let The Sun Shine In...........................................................*Old Pa Bradley* | $7 | | Big Tree 113 |

**MAGIC TOUCH, The** ☉
Female R&B group led by Diana Tyler.

| 7/3/71 | 114 | 2 | Step Into My World (Part 2) ...............................R&B:36　*(Part 1)* | $7 | | Black Falcon 19102 |

**MAGNA CARTA** ☉　　　　　　　　　　　　　　　　　　　　　　AC
British pop group. Member Davey Johnstone went on to join Elton John's band in 1972.

| 12/12/70 | 111 | 2 | Airport Song ...........................................AC:39　*Ring Of Stones* | $6 | | Dunhill/ABC 4257 |

**MAGNIFICENT MEN, The**　　　　　　　　　　　　　　　HOT
White R&B-styled group from Harrisburg, Pennsylvania featuring David Bupp (vocals).

| 2/25/67 | 133 | 1 | Stormy Weather.......................*Much Much More Of Your Love* | $8 | | Capitol 5812 |

Sonny Sanders (orch.); #1 hit for both Ethel Waters and Leo Reisman in 1933.

**MAHARIS, George**　　　　　　　　　　　　　　　　　　　HOT/AC
Born on 9/1/28 in New York City. Movie/TV actor. Played "Buz Murdock" on TV's *Route 66*.

| 5/5/62 | 104 | 3 | 1 After The Lights Go Down Low............................*Teach Me Tonight* (Hot #25) | $8 | ■ | Epic 9504 |

#10 hit for Al Hibbler in 1956.

| 7/14/62 | 111 | 2 | 2 They Knew About You ....................*Love Me As I Love You* (Hot #54) | $8 | ■ | Epic 9522 |
| 6/29/63 | 102 | 2 | 3 Where Can You Go (For a Broken Heart)..............................*Kiss Me* | $8 | ■ | Epic 9600 |

**MAHOANEY, Skip — see McHONEY, Skip**

**MAHONEY, John Culliton** ☉

| 9/14/74 | 105 | 2 | The Ballad Of Evel Knievel.............................*Why* (Evel Knievel) | $7 | ■ | Amherst 701 |

released prior to the daredevil's Snake River Canyon "jump" on 9/8/74

**MAIN INGREDIENT, The**　　　　　　　　　　　　R&B/HOT/AC
New York R&B vocal trio formed as the Poets in 1964: Donald McPherson (d: 7/4/71), Luther Simmons, Jr. and Tony Sylvester.

| 5/26/73 | 101[2] | 8 | 1 You Can Call Me Rover　　　　R&B:34　*I'm Better Off Without You* | $6 | | RCA Victor 0939 |
| 9/22/73 | 119 | 1 | 2 Girl Blue ...........................................R&B:51　*Movin' On* | $6 | | RCA Victor 0046 |

written by Stevie Wonder

**MAI TAI**　　　　　　　　　　　　　　　　　　　　　　　R&B/HOT
Black Dutch trio: Jettie Wells, Carolien De Windt and Mildred Douglas.

| 8/10/85 | 109 | 1 | History ...........................................R&B:37　*What Goes On* | $4 | | Critique 715 |

**MAJORS, The**　　　　　　　　　　　　　　　　　　HOT/R&B
R&B vocal group from Philadelphia: Ricky Cordo (lead), Eugene Glass, Frank Troutt, Ronald Gathers and Idella Morris.

| 2/23/63 | 117 | 1 | 1 Anything You Can Do ...............................*What In The World* | $20 | | Imperial 5914 |

from the 1946 Irving Berlin musical *Annie Get Your Gun*

| 9/28/63 | 125 | 1 | 2 Your Life Begins (At Sweet 16) .................*Which Way Did She Go* | $20 | | Imperial 5991 |
| 2/8/64 | 113 | 3 | 3 I'll Be There (To Bring You Love) ...............................*Ooh Wee Baby* | $20 | | Imperial 66009 |

**MAKEBA, Miriam**　　　　　　　　　　　　　　　　HOT/R&B/AC
Born Zensi Miriam Makeba on 3/4/32 in Johannesburg, South Africa. Folk singer.

| 3/23/68 | 123 | 3 | What Is Love ...........................................*Ha Po Zamani* | $7 | | Reprise 0671 |

**MAL** ☉
Italian rock singer.

| 5/13/72 | 108 | 4 | Mighty Mighty And Roly Poly.......................*Nowhere Left To Play* | $7 | | RCA Victor 0682 |

**MALAIKA** ☉　　　　　　　　　　　　　　　　　　　　　R&B
Female singer born in Seattle. Raised in Kansas City, Rochester, New York, and Phoenix. Background vocalist for CeCe Peniston.

| 12/5/92 | 102 | 3 | 1 So Much Love ...........................................Air:55　*(radio mix)* | $3 | ■ | A&M 0071 |
| 6/12/93 | 120 | 2 | 2 Gotta Know (Your Name)...............Air:74 /R&B:68　*("CD" mix)* | $3 | ■ | A&M 0254 |

Chantay Savage (backing vocal)

**MALIBU'S, The** ☉

| 1/25/69 | 121 | 3 | A Broken Man ...........................*It's All Over But The Shouting* | $8 | | White Whale 289 |

**MALO**　　　　　　　　　　　　　　　　　　　　　　　HOT/AC
Latin-rock band featuring Arcelio Garcia (vocals) and Jorge Santana (guitar; brother of Carlos Santana).

| 7/8/72 | 101[1] | 2 | 1 Cafe　　　　　　　　　　　　　　　　*Peace* [F] | $7 | | Warner 7605 |
| 12/2/72 | 103 | 3 | 2 Latin Bugaloo ...........................................*Midnight Thoughts* | $7 | | Warner 7677 |

**MAMAS & THE PAPAS, The**　　　　　　　　　HOT/AC
Quartet formed in Los Angeles in 1965: John Phillips (b: 8/30/35, Paris Island, South Carolina); Holly Michelle Gilliam Phillips (b: 6/4/45, Long Beach, California); Dennis Doherty (b: 11/29/41, Halifax, Nova Scotia, Canada) and Mama Cass Elliot (b: Ellen Cohen on 9/19/41 in Baltimore; d: 7/29/74). Also see The Mugwumps.

| 9/2/67 | 130 | 2 | 1 Straight Shooter ..............*Twelve Thirty (Young Girls Are Coming To The Canyon)* (Hot #20) | $8 | | Dunhill 4099 |
| 10/28/67 | 134 | 1 | 2 Hey Girl ...........................*Glad To Be Unhappy* (Hot #26) | $8 | | Dunhill 4107 |
| 10/24/70 | 104 | 2 | 3 The Good Times Are Coming .................AC:19　*Welcome To The World* | $6 | ■ | Dunhill/ABC 4253 |

from the movie *Monte Walsh* starring Lee Marvin

| 12/19/70 | 110 | 2 | 4 Don't Let The Good Life Pass You By..................AC:34　*A Song That Never Comes* | $6 | | Dunhill/ABC 4264 |

MAMA CASS ELLIOT (above 2)
B-side was a #99 hit in 1970 on Dunhill/ABC 4244

**MANCHESTER, Melissa**　　　　　　　　　　　　　AC/HOT
Born on 2/15/51 in the Bronx, New York. Vocalist/pianist/composer. Former backup singer for Bette Midler.

| 10/18/80 | 102 | 2 | If This Is Love ...........................................AC:19　*Talk* | $4 | | Arista 0551 |

| DEBUT | PEAK | WKS | A-side (Chart Hit)............................................................................B-side | $ | Pic | Label & Number |
|---|---|---|---|---|---|---|

**MANCINI, Henry, And His Orchestra**  AC/HOT
Born on 4/16/24 in Cleveland. Died of cancer on 6/14/94. Leading movie and TV composer/arranger/conductor. Winner of four Oscars and 20 Grammys, plus Grammy's Lifetime Achievement Award (1995).

| DEBUT | PEAK | WKS | A-side / B-side | $ | Pic | Label & Number |
|---|---|---|---|---|---|---|
| 7/17/65 | 117 | 5 | 1 The Sweetheart Tree ........................... AC:23  *Pie-In-The Face Polka* | $8 | ■ | RCA Victor 8624 |
| | | | from the movie *The Great Race* starring Tony Curtis and Natalie Wood | | | |
| 3/7/70 | 115 | 3 | 2 Theme From "Z" (Life Goes On) ............ AC:17  *Theme From The Molly Maguires* [I] | $6 | | RCA Victor 0315 |
| | | | from the movie *Z* starring Yves Montand and Irene Papas | | | |
| 2/9/80 | 101[1] | 1 | 3 Ravel's Bolero  *It's Easy To Say (Julie Andrews & Dudley Moore)* [I] | $4 | ■ | Warner 49139 |
| | | | from the movie *10* starring Bo Derek and Dudley Moore; picture sleeve is a fold-out poster | | | |

**MANDRELL, Barbara**  C&W/AC/HOT
Born on 12/25/48 in Houston. Country singer. Host of own TV variety series *Barbara Mandrell & The Mandrell Sisters*, 1980-82.

| DEBUT | PEAK | WKS | A-side / B-side | $ | Pic | Label & Number |
|---|---|---|---|---|---|---|
| 3/20/71 | 128 | 2 | 1 Do Right Woman - Do Right Man ................ C&W:17  *The Letter* | $8 | | Columbia 45307 |
| 7/22/78 | 103 | 3 | 2 Tonight ................................................ C&W:5  *If I Were A River* | $5 | | ABC 12362 |
| 11/18/78 | 102 | 4 | 3 Sleeping Single In A Double Bed  C&W:❶³  *Just One More Of Your Goodbyes* | $5 | | ABC 12403 |
| 3/1/80 | 102 | 4 | 4 Years  C&W:❶¹ / AC:38  *Darlin'* | $4 | ■ | MCA 41162 |
| 7/12/80 | 105 | 2 | 5 Crackers  C&W:3  *Using Him To Get To You* | $4 | | MCA 41263 |

**MANDRILL**  R&B/HOT
Brooklyn Latin jazz-rock-funk septet formed in 1968 by the Wilson brothers.

| DEBUT | PEAK | WKS | A-side / B-side | $ | Pic | Label & Number |
|---|---|---|---|---|---|---|
| 11/17/73 | 107 | 6 | Mango Meat .......................................... R&B:40  *Afrikus Retrospectus* | $5 | | Polydor 14200 |

**MANFRED MANN**  HOT/ROK
Rock group formed in England in 1964 featuring Manfred Mann (b: Michael Lubowitz, 10/21/40, Johannesburg, South Africa; keyboards) and Paul Jones (vocals). Manfred Mann formed his new Earth Band in 1971 featuring Mick Rogers (vocals). Rogers replaced by Chris Thompson (vocals, guitar) in 1976.

| DEBUT | PEAK | WKS | A-side / B-side | $ | Pic | Label & Number |
|---|---|---|---|---|---|---|
| 6/26/65 | 124 | 2 | 1 My Little Red Book .................................. *What Am I Doing Wrong* | $12 | | Ascot 2184 |
| | | | from the movie *What's New Pussycat* starring Peter Sellers; #52 hit for **Love** in 1966 | | | |
| 8/20/66 | 101[1] | 6 | 2 Just Like A Woman  *I Wanna Be Rich* | $10 | ■ | Mercury 72607 |
| | | | #33 hit for **Bob Dylan** in 1966 | | | |
| 7/13/68 | 104 | 4 | 3 My Name Is Jack .................................. *There Is A Man* | $10 | ■ | Mercury 72822 |
| 10/30/71 | 108 | 1 | 4 Please Mrs. Henry ................................ *Prayer* | $8 | | Polydor 14097 |
| | | | written by Bob Dylan | | | |
| | | | **MANFRED MANN'S EARTH BAND:** | | | |
| 7/22/72 | 112 | 2 | 5 I'm Up And I'm Leaving ........................ *Part Time Man* | $7 | | Polydor 14130 |
| 3/21/81 | 106 | 1 | 6 For You ................................................ ROK:15  *Fool I Am* | $5 | | Warner 49678 |
| | | | written by Bruce Springsteen | | | |

**MANGIONE, Chuck**  AC/HOT/R&B
Born on 11/29/40 in Rochester, New York. Jazz flugelhorn player/bandleader/composer.

| DEBUT | PEAK | WKS | A-side / B-side | $ | Pic | Label & Number |
|---|---|---|---|---|---|---|
| 11/11/78 | 104 | 12 | Children Of Sanchez ........................... AC:44  *Doin' Everything With You* [I] | $4 | ■ | A&M 2088 |
| | | | title song from the movie starring Anthony Quinn | | | |

**MANHATTANS, The**  R&B/HOT/AC
R&B vocal group from Jersey City, New Jersey featuring George "Smitty" Smith (lead vocals; d: 12/16/70; replaced by Gerald Alston). First recorded for Piney in 1962.

| DEBUT | PEAK | WKS | A-side / B-side | $ | Pic | Label & Number |
|---|---|---|---|---|---|---|
| 5/22/65 | 135 | 1 | 1 Searchin' For My Baby/  R&B:20 | | | |
| 7/24/65 | 135 | 1 | 2  I'm The One That Love Forgot | $15 | | Carnival 509 |
| 11/19/66 | 128 | 4 | 3 I Bet'cha (Couldn't Love Me) ................ R&B:23  *Sweet Little Girl* | $15 | | Carnival 522 |
| 11/7/70 | 113 | 1 | 4 From Atlanta To Goodbye ..................... R&B:48  *Fantastic Journey* | $10 | | DeLuxe 129 |
| 5/27/72 | 114 | 3 | 5 A Million To One ................................... R&B:47  *Cry If You Wanna Cry* | $10 | | DeLuxe 137 |
| 10/21/72 | 102 | 6 | 6 One Life To Live ................................... R&B:3  *It's The Only Way* | $10 | | DeLuxe 139 |
| 2/24/73 | 107 | 3 | 7 Back Up .............................................. R&B:19  *Fever* | $10 | | DeLuxe 144 |
| 3/4/78 | 101[5] | 9 | 8 Am I Losing You  R&B:6  *Movin'* | $5 | | Columbia 10674 |
| 12/13/80 | 109 | 1 | 9 I'll Never Find Another (Find Another Like You) ......... R&B:12  *Rendezvous* | $5 | | Columbia 11398 |

**MANHATTAN TRANSFER, The**  AC/HOT/R&B
Versatile vocal harmony quartet formed in New York City in 1972: Tim Hauser, Alan Paul, Janis Siegel and Cheryl Bentyne.

| DEBUT | PEAK | WKS | A-side / B-side | $ | Pic | Label & Number |
|---|---|---|---|---|---|---|
| 1/16/82 | 103 | 6 | 1 Spies In The Night ............................... *Kafka* | $4 | | Atlantic 3877 |
| | | | samples opening riff of "The James Bond Theme" | | | |
| 4/28/84 | 102 | 6 | 2 Mystery ........................... AC:6 /R&B:80  *Goodbye Love* | $4 | | Atlantic 89695 |

**MANLEY, Cynthia** ◌
| DEBUT | PEAK | WKS | A-side / B-side | $ | Pic | Label & Number |
|---|---|---|---|---|---|---|
| 1/15/83 | 109 | 2 | Back In My Arms Again ......................... *That's What I Want* | $4 | | Atlantic 89920 |
| | | | #1 hit for **The Supremes** in 1965 | | | |

**MANN, Barry**  HOT/AC
Born Barry Iberman on 2/9/39 in Brooklyn. One of pop music's most prolific songwriters with his wife, Cynthia Weil.

| DEBUT | PEAK | WKS | A-side / B-side | $ | Pic | Label & Number |
|---|---|---|---|---|---|---|
| 11/13/61 | 109 | 2 | 1 Little Miss U.S.A. ................................. *Find Another Fool* | $20 | | ABC-Paramount 10263 |
| 7/30/66 | 111 | 5 | 2 Angelica ............................................. *Looking At Tomorrow* | $12 | | Capitol 5695 |
| 1/15/72 | 105 | 5 | 3 When You Get Right Down To It ............ AC:40  *Don't Give Up On Me* | $6 | | New Design 1005 |

**MANN, Herbie**  HOT/R&B/AC
Born Herbert Jay Solomon on 4/16/30 in Brooklyn. Renowned jazz flutist.

| DEBUT | PEAK | WKS | A-side / B-side | $ | Pic | Label & Number |
|---|---|---|---|---|---|---|
| 8/18/62 | 101[1] | 6 | 1 Comin' Home Baby  *Summertime* [I] | $10 | | Atlantic 5020 |
| | | | #36 hit for **Mel Torme** in 1962; #80 hit for **Travis Wammack** in 1964 as "Scratchy" | | | |
| 10/13/62 | 111 | 2 | 2 Right Now ........................................... *Boroquinho* [I] | $10 | | Atlantic 5023 |
| 11/18/67 | 101[2] | 4 | 3 Live For Life  AC:33  *Cottage For Sale* | $8 | | Atlantic 2451 |
| | | | **CARMEN McRAE & HERBIE MANN** | | | |
| | | | title song from the movie starring Yves Montand; #99 hit for **Jack Jones** in 1967 | | | |

**MANN, Johnny, Singers**  AC/HOT
Born on 8/30/28 in Baltimore. Mann was musical director for Joey Bishop's TV talk show. Also see **Molly Bee** and **Bobby Vee**.

| DEBUT | PEAK | WKS | A-side / B-side | $ | Pic | Label & Number |
|---|---|---|---|---|---|---|
| 4/23/66 | 126 | 2 | Cinnamint Shuffle (Mexican Shuffle) ............ *Rovin' Gambler* [I] | $6 | | Liberty 55871 |
| | | | #85 hit for **Herb Alpert's Tijuana Brass** in 1964 | | | |

**MANN, Manfred — see MANFRED MANN**

**MANTOVANI AND HIS ORCHESTRA**     MEM/HOT/POP/AC
Born Annunzio Paolo Mantovani on 11/15/05 in Venice, Italy. Died on 3/29/80. Orchestra conductor.

| | | | | | | |
| --- | --- | --- | --- | --- | --- | --- |
| 11/12/66 | 122 | 2 | Games That Lovers Play ............................................... Ebb Tide [I] | $6 | | London 20015 |
| | | |    #45 hit for **Eddie Fisher** in 1966 | | | |

**MARCELS, The**     HOT/R&B
R&B doo-wop group from Pittsburgh featuring Cornelius "Nini" Harp (lead singer).

| | | | | | | |
| --- | --- | --- | --- | --- | --- | --- |
| 3/31/62 | 103 | 1 | Twistin' Fever ............................................... Footprints In The Sand | $50 | | Colpix 629 |

**MARCHAN, Bobby**     R&B/HOT
Born on 4/30/30 in Youngstown, Ohio. Vocalist with Huey "Piano" Smith & The Clowns.

| | | | | | | |
| --- | --- | --- | --- | --- | --- | --- |
| 8/15/64 | 116 | 3 | I've Got A Thing Going On ............................... I Gotta Sit Down And Cry | $15 | | Dial 3022 |

**MARCY JOE**     HOT
Born Marcy Rae Sockel on 1/4/44 in Pittsburgh.

| | | | | | | |
| --- | --- | --- | --- | --- | --- | --- |
| 8/17/63 | 132 | 1 | Lover's Medley "The More I See You"/"When I Fall In Love" ............................... The Car Hop And The Hard Top | $20 | | Swan 4145 |
| | | |    **MARCY JO AND EDDIE RAMBEAU** | | | |
| | | |    #7 hit for **The Lettermen** in 1962; #16 hit for **Chris Montez** in 1966 | | | |

**MARDONES, Benny**     HOT/AC
Born on 11/9/48 in Cleveland. Pop singer/songwriter.

| | | | | | | |
| --- | --- | --- | --- | --- | --- | --- |
| 11/1/80 | 103 | 1 | Hometown Girls ............................................... Crazy Boy | $4 | | Polydor 2131 |

**MARIACHI BRASS — see BAKER, Chet**

**MARIE, Teena**     R&B/HOT
Born Mary Christine Brockert on 3/5/56 in Santa Monica. White funk singer/composer/keyboardist/producer/actress.

| | | | | | | |
| --- | --- | --- | --- | --- | --- | --- |
| 8/4/79 | 102 | 3 | I'm A Sucker For Your Love ............ R&B:8 De Ja Vu (I've Been Here Before) | $4 | | Gordy 7169 |
| | | |    written, produced, arranged and backing vocals by **Rick James** | | | |

**MARION** ☉
Male pianist Marion Carpenter.

| | | | | | | |
| --- | --- | --- | --- | --- | --- | --- |
| 7/27/59 | 102 | 5 | Happy Lonesome ............................... Let The Rest Of The World Go By [I] | $15 | | Sandy 1021 |

**MARJOE** ☉
Born Marjoe Gortner on 1/14/44 in Long Beach, California. Actor/singer. Cast member of TV's Falcon Crest.

| | | | | | | |
| --- | --- | --- | --- | --- | --- | --- |
| 11/25/72 | 109 | 2 | Lo And Behold! ............................................... Hoe-Bus | $6 | ■ | Chelsea 0107 |
| | | |    written by **Bob Dylan** | | | |

**MAR-KEYS, The**     HOT/R&B
Instrumental R&B group formed in Memphis in 1958 featuring Steve Cropper (guitar) and Donald "Duck" Dunn (bass) of **Booker T. & The MG's.**

| | | | | | | |
| --- | --- | --- | --- | --- | --- | --- |
| 4/3/65 | 121 | 1 | 1 Banana Juice ............................................... The Shovel [I] | $12 | | Stax 166 |
| 12/4/65 | 111 | 3 | 2 Grab This Thing, Part 1 ............................................... Part 2 [I] | $12 | | Stax 181 |

**MARKHAM, Pigmeat**     HOT/R&B
Born Dewey Markham on 4/18/06 in Durham, North Carolina. Died on 12/13/81. Stage and TV comedian.

| | | | | | | |
| --- | --- | --- | --- | --- | --- | --- |
| 11/16/68 | 103 | 3 | Sock It To 'Em Judge ............................................... The Hip Judge | $8 | | Chess 2059 |
| | | |    follow-up song to his #19 1968 hit "Here Comes The Judge" | | | |

**MARKS, Larry** ☉
Pop singer/songwriter/producer based in Los Angeles.

| | | | | | | |
| --- | --- | --- | --- | --- | --- | --- |
| 10/5/68 | 129 | 1 | L.A. Break Down (And Take Me In) ............................... Country Woman | $6 | | A&M 969 |

**MARKY MARK And The Funky Bunch**     HOT/R&B
Marky Mark is Mark Wahlberg, the younger brother of Donnie Wahlberg of New Kids On The Block. Born on 6/5/71 in Boston.

| | | | | | | |
| --- | --- | --- | --- | --- | --- | --- |
| 12/5/92 | 104 | 7 | Gonna Have A Good Time ............ Air:72 Don't Ya Sleep | $3 | ■ | Interscope 98493 |

**MARLEY, Bob, And The Wailers**     R&B/HOT/ROK
Born on 2/6/45 in Rhoden Hall, Jamaica. Died of brain cancer on 5/11/81. Reggae singer/guitarist. Celebrated as the master of reggae. Inducted into the Rock and Roll Hall of Fame in 1994.

| | | | | | | |
| --- | --- | --- | --- | --- | --- | --- |
| 8/13/77 | 103 | 5 | Exodus ............................... R&B:19 (instrumental) | $8 | | Island 089 |

**MARLEY, Ziggy, & The Melody Makers**     ROK/R&B/HOT
Family reggae group from Kingston, Jamaica. Children of the late reggae master **Bob Marley.**

| | | | | | | |
| --- | --- | --- | --- | --- | --- | --- |
| 7/12/97 | 118 | 4 | People Get Ready ............................................... (album edit) | $3 | ■ | Elektra 64164 |
| | | |    #14 hit for **The Impressions** in 1965 | | | |

**MARMALADE, The**     AC/HOT
Pop group from Scotland featuring Thomas "Dean Ford" McAleese (vocals).

| | | | | | | |
| --- | --- | --- | --- | --- | --- | --- |
| 5/1/71 | 123 | 1 | My Little One ............ AC:31 Is Your Life Your Own? | $6 | | London 20066 |

**MARR, Hank** ☉
R&B organist.

| | | | | | | |
| --- | --- | --- | --- | --- | --- | --- |
| 1/18/64 | 101[2] | 5 | 1 The Greasy Spoon ............ I Can't Go On (Without You) [I] | $10 | | Federal 12508 |
| 3/27/65 | 134 | 1 | 2 Silver Spoon ............................................... No Rough Stuff [I] | $10 | | Federal 12538 |

**MARSHALL TUCKER BAND, The**     C&W/HOT/ROK/AC
Southern-rock band formed in South Carolina in 1971 featuring Doug Gray (lead vocals) and brothers Toy (lead guitar; d: 2/25/93, age 45) and Tommy Caldwell (bass; d: 4/28/80, age 30).

| | | | | | | |
| --- | --- | --- | --- | --- | --- | --- |
| 9/1/73 | 108 | 2 | 1 Can't You See ............................... See You Later, I'm Gone | $6 | | Capricorn 0021 |
| | | |    a "live" version made the Hot 100 (#75) on 8/20/77 on Capricorn 0278 | | | |
| 2/28/76 | 104 | 3 | 2 Searchin' For A Rainbow ............ C&W:82 Walkin' And Talkin' | $5 | | Capricorn 0251 |
| 5/30/81 | 106 | 1 | 3 This Time I Believe ............ Tell The Blues To Take Off The Night | $4 | | Warner 49724 |

**MARTERIE, Ralph**     MEM/POP/HOT
Born on 12/24/14 in Naples, Italy; raised in Chicago. Died on 10/8/78. Very popular early '50s bandleader.

| | | | | | | |
| --- | --- | --- | --- | --- | --- | --- |
| 5/22/61 | 115 | 2 | Bacardi ............................................... The Shuck [I] | $8 | | United Artists 315 |
| | | |    tune is similar in arrangement to **The Champs'** "Tequila" | | | |

## MARTHA & THE VANDELLAS          R&B/HOT

R&B vocal trio from Detroit, organized by Martha Reeves (b: 7/18/41, Alabama) in 1962 with Annette Beard and Rosalind Ashford. Beard left in 1964, replaced by Betty Kelly. Group re-formed with Martha and sister Lois Reeves, and Sandra Tilley in 1971. Group inducted into the Rock and Roll Hall of Fame in 1995. *Top Pop Singles:* 24.

### MARTHA REEVES & THE VANDELLAS:

| 9/13/69 | 102 | 4 | 1 Taking My Love (And Leaving Me).............................................. **R&B:44** *Heartless* | $10 | | Gordy 7094 |
| 2/19/72 | 102 | 6 | 2 In And Out Of My Life.................................**R&B:22** *Your Love Makes It All Worthwhile* | $10 | | Gordy 7113 |
| 6/17/72 | 103 | 3 | 3 Tear It On Down.........................................................**R&B:37** *I Want You Back* | $10 | | Gordy 7118 |
| | | | written and produced by **Ashford & Simpson** | | | |

## MARTIN, Bobbi          AC/HOT/C&W

Born Barbara Anne Martin on 11/29/43 in Brooklyn; raised in Baltimore. Toured the Far East with Bob Hope's Christmas shows.

| 7/31/65 | 115 | 5 | 1 I Don't Want To Live (Without Your Love) ...................... **AC:21** *Holding Back The Tears* | $7 | | Coral 62457 |
| 2/5/66 | 119 | 3 | 2 Don't Take It Out On Me ........................................*Something On My Mind* | $7 | | Coral 62475 |
| 9/3/66 | 134 | 1 | 3 Oh, Lonesome Me.....................................**C&W:64** *It's A Sin To Tell A Lie* | $7 | | Coral 62488 |
| | | | #7 hit for **Don Gibson** in 1958 | | | |
| 8/31/68 | 114 | 4 | 4 Harper Valley P.T.A.                           *He Called Me Baby* | $6 | | United Artists 50443 |
| | | | #1 hit for **Jeannie C. Riley** in 1968 | | | |
| 3/6/71 | 123 | 1 | 5 No Love At All .............................................*A Place For Me* | $5 | | Buddah 217 |
| | | | #16 hit for **B.J. Thomas** in 1971 | | | |

## MARTIN, Dean          HOT/AC/MEM/POP/C&W

Born Dino Crocetti on 6/7/17 in Steubenville, Ohio. Died on 12/25/95. Vocalist/actor. Teamed with comedian Jerry Lewis for 16 movies. Own TV series from 1965-74. *Pop Hits & Top Pop Singles:* 37.

| 1/18/60 | 107 | 4 | 1 Love Me, My Love .....................................*Who Was That Lady?* | $12 | | Capitol 4328 |
| 3/30/63 | 128 | 1 | 2 Face In A Crowd...............................................*Ain't Gonna Try Anymore* | $10 | | Reprise 20,150 |
| 10/10/64 | 123 | 2 | 3 Every Minute Every Hour ...........................*The Door Is Still Open To My Heart* (Hot #6) | $8 | | Reprise 0307 |
| 8/10/68 | 104 | 2 | 4 That Old Time Feelin'/          **AC:19** | | | |
| 8/10/68 | 105 | 4 | 5    April Again          **AC:9** | $6 | | Reprise 0761 |
| 9/14/68 | 107 | 1 | 6 5 Card Stud .............................................*One Lonely Boy* | $6 | | Reprise 0765 |
| | | | title song from the movie starring Martin and Robert Mitchum | | | |
| 2/22/69 | 103 | 3 | 7 Gentle On My Mind ...........................**AC:9** *That's When I See The Blues* | $6 | | Reprise 0812 |
| | | | #39 hit for **Glen Campbell** in 1968 | | | |
| 10/25/69 | 107 | 3 | 8 One Cup Of Happiness (And One Peace Of Mind) ..............**AC:15** *Crying Time* | $6 | | Reprise 0857 |
| 7/4/70 | 123 | 1 | 9 For The Love Of A Woman ...........................*The Tracks Of My Tears* | $6 | | Reprise 0915 |
| | | | written and produced by Dino Martin, Jr. & Billy Hinsche of **Dino, Desi & Billy** | | | |
| 8/1/70 | 110 | 3 | 10 My Woman, My Woman, My Wife ...........................*Here We Go Again* | $6 | | Reprise 0934 |
| | | | #42 hit for **Marty Robbins** in 1970 | | | |
| 10/31/70 | 101[1] | 2 | 11 Detroit City          **AC:36** *Turn The World Around* | $6 | | Reprise 0955 |
| | | | #16 hit for **Bobby Bare** in 1963 | | | |
| 1/23/71 | 118 | 1 | 12 Georgia Sunshine .......................................*For The Good Times* | $6 | | Reprise 0973 |
| | | | #16 Country hit for **Jerry Reed** in 1970 | | | |

## MARTIN, George, And His Orch.          HOT/AC

Born on 1/3/26 in London. The Beatles' producer from 1962-70. Knighted by Queen Elizabeth II in 1996.

| 8/1/64 | 105 | 4 | 1 And I Love Her ...........................*Ringo's Theme (This Boy)* (Hot #53) [I] | $25 | ■ | United Artists 745 |
| 10/3/64 | 111 | 2 | 2 I Should Have Known Better/          [I] | | | |
| 10/3/64 | 122 | 1 | 3    A Hard Day's Night............................................[I] | $125 | ■ | United Artists 750 |
| | | | all of above from **The Beatles'** movie and album *A Hard Day's Night* | | | |

## MARTIN, Millicent ☺

Born on 6/8/34 in Romford, England. Popular TV and film actress.

| 12/28/63 | 104 | 3 | In The Summer Of His Years ...........................*If I Can Help Somebody* | $12 | | ABC-Paramount 10514 |
| | | | from the BBC-TV tribute to slain President John F. Kennedy; #46 hit for **Connie Francis** in 1964 | | | |

## MARTIN, Moon          HOT/AC

Real name: John Martin. Pop-rock singer/songwriter/guitarist from Oklahoma. Wrote **Robert Palmer's** hit "Bad Case Of Loving You." Lead guitarist of group **Southwind**.

| 1/31/81 | 105 | 1 | Love Gone Bad ...........................*Stranded* | $4 | | Capitol 4963 |

## MARTIN, Rodge ☺

R&B vocalist.

| 4/9/66 | 131 | 1 | When She Touches Me "Nothing Else Matters"...........................*Lovin' Machine* | $12 | | Bragg 227 |

## MARTIN, Tony          MEM/POP/HOT/AC

Born Alvin Morris, Jr. on 12/25/12 in Oakland. Vocalist/actor. *Pop Hits & Top Pop Singles:* 33.

| 1/16/65 | 133 | 1 | Talkin' To Your Picture...........................*Our Rhapsody* | $10 | | Motown 1071 |

## MARTIN, Trade          HOT

Born on 11/19/43 in Union City, New Jersey.

| 1/8/72 | 106 | 2 | I Can't Do It For You ...........................*To Know The Girl* | $10 | | Buddah 266 |

## MARTINDALE, Wink          HOT/C&W

Born Winston Martindale on 12/4/33 in Jackson, Tennessee. DJ since 1950. Host of many TV game shows.

| 3/12/66 | 114 | 4 | Giddyup Go ...........................*The Working Man's Prayer* [S] | $8 | | Dot 16821 |
| | | | Billy Vaughn (orch.); #82 hit for **Red Sovine** in 1966 | | | |

## MARTINEZ, Laura ☺

| 5/4/96 | 124 | 1 | Ritmo Latino ...........................*(house mix)* | $3 | ▌ | Thump 2226 |
| | | | title is Spanish for "Latin Rhythm" | | | |

## MARTINO, Al          AC/HOT/MEM/POP/C&W/R&B

Born Alfred Cini on 10/7/27 in Philadelphia. Portrayed singer Johnny Fontane in the 1972 movie *The Godfather*. *Pop Hits & Top Pop Singles:* 37.

| 3/13/61 | 109 | 5 | 1 Little Girl, Little Boy          *My Side Of The Story* | $10 | ■ | 20th Fox 237 |
| | | | Aldo Provenzano (orch.) | | | |
| 5/26/62 | 119 | 1 | 2 Love, Where Are You Now (Toselli Serenade) ...........................*Exodus* | $8 | | Capitol 4710 |

| DEBUT | PEAK | WKS | A-side (Chart Hit)........................................................................................................B-side | $ | Pic | Label & Number |
|---|---|---|---|---|---|---|

**MARTINO, Al — Cont'd**

| 8/29/64 | 118 | 2 | 3 Thank You For Loving Me .................................................... *Always Together* (Hot #33) | $7 | | Capitol 5239 |
| 3/13/65 | 122 | 1 | 4 With All My Heart............................................... *Somebody Else Is Taking My Place* (Hot #53) | $7 | | Capitol 5384 |
| | | | #15 hit for Jodie Sands in 1957 | | | |
| 10/19/68 | 120 | 2 | 5 Wake Up To Me Gentle ........................................ AC:21 *If You Must Leave My Life* | $6 | | Capitol 2285 |
| | | | from the new rock musical *Alison* | | | |
| 6/20/70 | 123 | 2 | 6 Walking In The Sand ................................... AC:9 *One More Mile (And Darlin', I'll Be Home)* | $6 | | Capitol 2830 |

**MARVELETTES, The**        HOT/R&B

R&B group from Inkster, Michigan. Formed in 1960 by Gladys Horton, with Georgeanna Marie Tillman, Wanda Young, Katherine Anderson and Juanita Cowart. Cowart left in 1962. Gordon left in 1965; died on 1/6/80 of lupus. Horton left in 1967, replaced by Anne Bogan. Also recorded as **The Darnells**. *Top Pop Singles*: 23.

| 11/23/63 | 117 | 2 | 1 Too Hurt To Cry, Too Much In Love To Say Goodbye ................. *Come On Home* | $75 | | Gordy 7024 |
| | | | THE DARNELLS | | | |
| 9/21/68 | 114 | 2 | 2 What's Easy For Two Is Hard For One......................... *Destination: Anywhere* (Hot #63) | $12 | | Tamla 54171 |
| | | | written and produced by **Smokey Robinson**; #29 hit for **Mary Wells** in 1964 | | | |

**MAR . VELLS, The** ☉

Female R&B vocal group.

| 1/25/64 | 115 | 2 | Go On And Have Yourself A Ball ...................................*How Do I Keep The Girls Away* | $25 | | Butane 778 |
| | | | with D. Jones & The Continentals | | | |

**MARVELOWS — see MIGHTY MARVELOWS**

**MARY CHORAL GROUP — see MEDICAL MISSIONARIES OF**

**MARY JANE GIRLS**        R&B/HOT

Female "funk & roll" quartet: Joanne McDuffie, Candice Ghant, Kim Wuletich and Yvette Marina. Formed and produced by **Rick James**.

| 6/4/83 | 101² | 6 | 1 Candy Man | R&B:23 *(instrumental)* | $4 | | Gordy 1670 |
| 8/13/83 | 101¹ | 8 | 2 All Night Long | R&B:11 *Musical Love* | $4 | | Gordy 1690 |
| 10/29/83 | 102 | 9 | 3 Boys | R&B:29 *(instrumental)* | $4 | | Gordy 1704 |
| 2/18/84 | 106 | 1 | 4 Jealousy .................................................................. * R&B:84 *You Are My Heaven* | $4 | | Gordy 1721 |
| | | | all of above written, arranged and produced by **Rick James** | | | |

**MASCOLO, Tony** ☉

Singer from Long Island, New York.

| 10/11/97 | 123 | 1 | I Want Love .................................................................................. *(3 mixes)* | $5 | | Modern Voices 002 * |

**MASEKELA, Hugh**        R&B/HOT/AC

Born Hugh Ramapolo Masekela on 4/4/39 in Wilbank, South Africa. Trumpeter/bandleader/arranger.

| 4/12/69 | 107 | 2 | A Long Ways From Home .......................................................... *Home Boy* [I] | $6 | | Uni 55116 |

**MASKED MARAUDERS, The** ☉

Canadian group masquerading as **Bob Dylan**, **Mick Jagger**, **John Lennon** and **Paul McCartney**.

| 11/29/69 | 123 | 1 | Cow Pie ....................................................................... *I Can't Get No Nookie* [I] | $15 | | Deity 0870 |

**MASON, Barbara**        R&B/HOT

Born on 8/9/47 in Philadelphia. R&B vocalist. First recorded for Crusader in 1964.

| 5/23/70 | 112 | 3 | 1 Raindrops Keep Fallin' On My Head/ | R&B:38 | | | |
| | | | #1 hit for **B.J. Thomas** in 1970 | | | | |
| | | 2 | 2 If You Knew Him Like I Do .................................................... R&B:flip | $8 | | National General 005 |
| 6/9/73 | 125 | 1 | 3 Yes, I'm Ready ........................................... *Who Will You Hurt Next* [R] | $6 | | Buddah 355 |
| | | | new version of her #5 1965 ~~Hot 100~~ hit on Arctic 105 | | | |

**MASON, Dave**        HOT/AC/ROK/R&B

Born on 5/10/46 in Worcester, England. Vocalist/composer/guitarist. Original member of **Traffic**.

| 4/29/72 | 121 | 1 | To Be Free ...................................................................... *Pearly Queen* | $6 | | Blue Thumb 209 |

**MASON, Tony** ☉

R&B vocalist.

| 11/26/66 | 125 | 1 | (We're Gonna) Bring The Country To The City ................................. *Lovely Weekend* | $8 | | RCA Victor 8938 |

**MASON PROFFIT** ☉

Chicago country-rock band led by brothers Terry and John Talbot (now inspirational artists).

| 11/27/71 | 108 | 5 | Hope ........................................................................................*Jewel* | $6 | | Ampex 11048 |

**MASQUERADERS, The**        R&B/HOT

R&B group from Texas: Lee Hatim, Robert Wrightsil, David Sanders, Harold Thomas and Sammy Hutchinson.

| 2/7/76 | 101² | 13 | (Call Me) The Traveling Man | R&B:32 *Sweet Sweeting* | $7 | | HBS/ABC 12157 |
| | | | produced and arranged by **Isaac Hayes** | | | |

**MASTER P**        R&B/HOT

Real name: Percy Miller. Male rapper from Los Angeles. Leader of the rap group Tru.

| 8/17/96 | 109 | 4 | No More Tears ................................. R&B:78 *(2 versions) / The Shocker* | $3 | ▌ | No Limit 53237 |
| | | | MASTER P Featuring Silkk & Mo B. Dick | | | |
| | | | samples "In The Rain" by **The Dramatics** | | | |

**MATHIS, Johnny**        AC/HOT/R&B

Born on 9/30/35 in San Francisco. One of the top love ballad artists of the rock era. *Top Pop Singles*: 45.

| 6/15/59 | 109 | 2 | 1 You Are Everything To Me ............................................ *Small World* (Hot #20) | $10 | | Columbia 41410 |
| 4/10/61 | 107 | 2 | 2 You Set My Heart To Music/ | | $10 | | |
| | | | from the Broadway musical *Thirteen Daughters* | | | |
| 4/10/61 | 118 | 1 | 3   Jenny ..................................................................................... | $10 | ▌ | Columbia 41980 |
| | | | Ray Ellis (orch., above 3) | | | |
| 4/18/64 | 120 | 1 | 4 The Fall Of Love ............................................................ *No More* | $8 | | Mercury 72263 |
| | | | Don Costa (orch.); from the movie *The Fall Of The Roman Empire* starring Sophia Loren | | | |
| 6/12/65 | 104 | 3 | 5 Take The Time ........................................................ AC:32 *Dianacita* | $7 | ▌ | Mercury 72432 |
| 8/7/65 | 108 | 6 | 6 Sweetheart Tree........................................................ AC:21 *Mirage* | $7 | ▌ | Mercury 72464 |
| | | | from the movie *The Great Race* starring Tony Curtis; also released on Mercury 72568 | | | |

| DEBUT | PEAK | WKS | A-side (Chart Hit).................................................................B-side | $ | Pic | Label & Number |
|---|---|---|---|---|---|---|
| | | | **MATHIS, Johnny — Cont'd** | | | |
| 6/22/68 | 111 | 1 | 7 Venus ........................................... AC:23 *Don't Go Breakin' My Heart* | $6 | | Columbia 44517 |
| | | | #1 hit for **Frankie Avalon** in 1959 | | | |
| 8/5/72 | 103 | 4 | 8 Make It Easy On Yourself .......................... AC:16 *Sometimes* | $5 | | Columbia 45635 |
| | | | #20 hit for **Jerry Butler** in 1962 | | | |
| 3/31/84 | 106 | 2 | 9 Love Won't Let Me Wait ..................... AC:14 /R&B:32 *Lead Me To Your Love* (Mathis) | $4 | | Columbia 04379 |
| | | | **JOHNNY MATHIS (with Deniece Williams)** | | | |
| | | | #5 hit for **Major Harris** in 1975 | | | |
| | | | **MATTHEWS, Dave, Band**      ROK/HOT/AC | | | |
| | | | Rock group led by Dave Matthews (vocals, guitar; b: 1/9/67 in Johannesburg, South Africa), with Leroi Moore (sax), Boyd Tinsley (violin), Stefan Lessard (bass) and Carter Beauford (drums). | | | |
| 3/4/95 | 115 | 1 | What Would You Say .......................... Air:22 /ROK:5 / AC:30 | $15 | | RCA 62994 (CD) |
| | | | released only as a CD promo single; no commercial single was issued | | | |
| | | | **MATTHEWS, David** ☉ | | | |
| | | | Born on 4/3/42 in Sonora, Kentucky. Jazz arranger/songwriter/pianist. | | | |
| 7/16/77 | 102 | 7 | theme from Star Wars ........................................... *Princess Leia's theme (from Star Wars)* [I] | $6 | ■ | CTI 039 |
| | | | #1 hit for **Meco** in 1977 | | | |
| | | | **MATTHEWS, Shirley, And The Big Town Girls** ☉ | | | |
| | | | R&B singer from Harrow, Ontario, Canada. | | | |
| 1/11/64 | 104 | 7 | Big-Town Boy............................................ *(You Can) Count On That* | $15 | | Atlantic 2210 |
| | | | **MAUDS, The**      HOT | | | |
| | | | Pop/rock group from Chicago: Jimmy Rogers, Billy Winter, Fuzzy Fuscaldo, Timmy Coniglio and Phil Weinberg. | | | |
| 7/29/67 | 114 | 4 | Hold On ................................................ *C'mon And Move* | $8 | | Mercury 72694 |
| | | | same tune as **Sam & Dave**'s 1966 hit "Hold On! I'm A Comin'" | | | |
| | | | **MAURIAT, Paul, and His Orchestra**      AC/HOT | | | |
| | | | Born in France in 1925. Moved to Paris at age 10. Formed own touring orchestra at age 17. | | | |
| 8/10/68 | 103 | 6 | 1 San Francisco (Wear Some Flowers In Your Hair) ........ AC:16 *I Waited For You (Ce Soir Je T'Attendais)* [I] | $6 | | Philips 40550 |
| | | | #4 hit for **Scott McKenzie** in 1967 | | | |
| 3/15/69 | 119 | 2 | 2 Hey Jude .......................................... AC:24 *Those Were The Days* [I] | $6 | | Philips 40594 |
| | | | #1 hit for **The Beatles** in 1968 | | | |
| 1/22/77 | 109 | 1 | 3 Love Is Still Blue .......................................... *Tattoo Bay* [I] | $6 | | Free Spirit 3001 |
| | | | jazzy version of his 1968 #1 hit | | | |
| | | | **MAXTED, Billy, and his Manhattan Jazz Band** ☉ | | | |
| | | | Pianist/arranger of the dance band era. Wrote "Manhattan Spiritual." | | | |
| 9/25/61 | 117 | 1 | Satin Doll ...................................... *How Long Has This Been Going On* [I] | $20 | | K&H 501 |
| | | | #27 hit for **Duke Ellington** in 1953 | | | |
| | | | **MAXUS** ☉ | | | |
| | | | Rock quintet: Jay Gruska (vocals), Robbie Buchanan (piano), Michael Landau (guitar), Mark Leonard (bass) and Doane Perry (drums). | | | |
| 3/13/82 | 109 | 1 | Nobody's Business ................................................ *What You Give* | $4 | | Warner 50015 |
| | | | **MAXWELL**      R&B/HOT | | | |
| | | | Born in Brooklyn in 1974. R&B singer/songwriter/producer. | | | |
| 2/15/97 | 108 | 11 | Sumthin' Sumthin' ................................... R&B:23 *(4 versions)* | $6 | ■ | Columbia 78477 (T) |
| | | | **MAYALL, John**      HOT | | | |
| | | | Born on 11/29/33 in Macclesfield, Cheshire, England. Bluesman John Mayall's band spawned many of Britain's leading rock musicians. | | | |
| 1/10/70 | 102 | 1 | Room To Move ............................................ *Saw Mill Gulch Road* | $7 | | Polydor 14010 |
| | | | "live" recording | | | |
| | | | **MAYFIELD, Curtis**      R&B/HOT | | | |
| | | | Born on 6/3/42 in Chicago. Soul singer/songwriter/producer. With **Jerry Butler** in the gospel group Northern Jubilee Singers. Joined **The Impressions** in 1957; wrote most of their hits. Own labels: Windy C, Mayfield and Curtom. Won Grammy's Lifetime Achievement Award in 1995. | | | |
| 2/19/72 | 115 | 3 | 1 We Got To Have Peace ........................................ R&B:32 *Love To Keep You In My Mind* | $6 | ■ | Curtom 1968 |
| 10/31/81 | 103 | 2 | 2 She Don't Let Nobody (But Me)............................R&B:15 *You Get All My Love* | $5 | | Boardwalk 122 |
| | | | **MAZE Featuring Frankie Beverly**      R&B/HOT | | | |
| | | | R&B group formed in Philadelphia: Frankie Beverly (vocals), Wayne Thomas, Sam Porter, Robin Duhe, Roame Lowry and McKinley Williams. | | | |
| 8/13/77 | 108 | 1 | 1 Lady Of Magic ..........................................R&B:13 *Time Is On My Side* | $4 | | Capitol 4456 |
| 6/15/85 | 103 | 4 | 2 Too Many Games ...........................................R&B:5 *Twilight* | $3 | ■ | Capitol 5474 |
| 11/27/93 | 115 | 7 | 3 The Morning After ..........................................R&B:19 *Laid Back Girl* | $3 | ▌ | Warner 18349 |

# MC/M.C.:

**MC EIHT — see SPICE 1**

**M.C. HAMMER**      R&B/HOT/AC
Born Stanley Kirk Burrell on 3/30/63 in Oakland. Rapper/producer/founder/leader of The Posse.

| DEBUT | PEAK | WKS | | $ | Pic | Label & Number |
|---|---|---|---|---|---|---|
| 8/6/94 | 115 | 3 | 1 Don't Stop............................................ R&B:63 *(instrumental)* | $3 | ▌ | Giant 18136 |
| | | | **HAMMER** | | | |
| | | | samples "Shake" by **The Gap Band** | | | |
| 8/26/95 | 102 | 10 | 2 Sultry Funk ...................................Sls:64 /R&B:59 *I Need That Number* | $3 | ▌ | Giant 17791 |
| | | | **M.C. HAMMER Featuring VMF** | | | |
| 12/30/95+ | 101[1] | 13 | 3 Goin' Up Yonder .......................... Sls:70 /R&B:38 *Keep On* | $3 | ▌ | Giant 17717 |
| | | | featuring Angel Burgess and the San Jose Community Choir | | | |
| | | | **MC LYTE**      R&B/HOT | | | |
| | | | Born Lana Moorer on 10/11/71 in Queens; raised in Brooklyn. Female rapper. | | | |
| 2/5/94 | 115 | 3 | I Go On ................................................ R&B:68 *(midnight mix)* | $3 | ▌ | First Priority 98356 |

# Mc:

### McCALL, Cash ✪
Real name: Maurice Dollison. R&B singer/guitarist. With Gospel Songbirds vocal group in the early 1960s.  **R&B**

| 7/23/66 | 102 | 5 | When You Wake Up ................................................ R&B:19 *You Ain't Too Cool* | $10 | | Thomas 307 |
| | | | tune's arrangement is similar to the **Four Tops'** "I Can't Help Myself" |

### McCALL, C.W.
Born William Fries on 11/15/28 in Audubon, Iowa. Elected mayor of Ouray, Colorado in the early '80s.  **C&W/HOT/AC**

| 6/28/75 | 101[1] | 3 | 1 Classified ............................................ C&W:13 *I've Trucked All Over This Land* [N] | $5 | | MGM 14801 |
| 12/18/76 | 101[1] | 5 | 2 'Round The World With The Rubber Duck ........... C&W:40 *Night Rider* [N] | $5 | | Polydor 14365 |
| | | | sequel to his #1 hit in 1976, "Convoy" |

### McCALLUM, David ✪
Born on 9/19/33 in Glasgow, Scotland. Portrayed secret agent "Illya Kuryakin" on TV's *The Man From U.N.C.L.E.*

| 2/19/66 | 117 | 5 | Communication ...................................................... *My Carousel* [S-N] | $8 | ■ | Capitol 5571 |
| | | | a female chorus backs McCallum's narration |

### McCANN, Denise ✪
Disco singer from New York City.

| 4/9/77 | 106 | 1 | Tattoo Man .......................................................................... *Either Way* | $5 | | Polydor 14374 |

### McCANN, Les
Born on 9/23/35 in Lexington, Kentucky. Jazz keyboardist/vocalist.  **HOT/R&B**

| 4/20/63 | 122 | 4 | The Shampoo ............................................................. *Kathleen's Theme* [I] | $10 | | Pacific Jazz 350 |

### McCANNON, George III ✪

| 6/6/70 | 111 | 2 | Birds Of All Nations ...................................................... *I Fall To Pieces* | $6 | | Amos 135 |

### McCARTNEY, Paul
Born James Paul McCartney on 6/18/42 in Allerton, Liverpool, England. Founding member/bass guitarist of **The Beatles**. Won Grammy's Lifetime Achievement Award in 1990. Knighted by Queen Elizabeth II in 1997. *Top Pop Singles*: 45.  **HOT/AC/ROK/R&B/C&W**

| 8/30/80 | 106 | 1 | Waterfalls ........................................................................ *Check My Machine* | $6 | ■ | Columbia 11335 |

### McCLINTON, Delbert
Born on 11/4/40 in Lubbock, Texas. Played harmonica on **Bruce Channel's** hit "Hey Baby." Leader of The Ron-Dels.  **HOT/C&W/ROK/AC**

| 11/21/81 | 101[3] | 7 | Sandy Beaches .......................................................... *I Wanna Thank You Baby* | $4 | | Capitol/MSS 5069 |

### McCOY, Charlie
Born on 3/28/41 in Oak Hill, West Virginia. Top Nashville harmonica player and session musician.  **C&W/HOT**

| 4/21/73 | 101[1] | 4 | Orange Blossom Special ............................................ C&W:26 *Hangin' On* [I] | $6 | | Monument 8566 |
| | | | #63 hit for **Billy Vaughn** in 1961 |

### McCOY, Neal
Born Hubert Neal McGauhey on 7/30/58 in Jacksonville, Texas. Country singer.  **C&W/HOT**

| 2/18/95 | 108 | 11 | 1 For A Change................................................ Sls:60 /C&W:3 *(3 album snippets)* | $3 | ▮ | Atlantic 87176 |
| 7/13/96 | 107 | 11 | 2 Then You Can Tell Me Goodbye ...................................... C&W:4 *(3 album snippets)* | $3 | ▮ | Atlantic 87053 |
| | | | #6 hit for **The Casinos** in 1967 |

### McCOY, Van
Born on 1/6/44 in Washington, D.C.  Died on 7/6/79. R&B pianist/producer/songwriter/singer.  **R&B/HOT/AC**

| 9/25/61 | 104 | 4 | 1 Mr. D. J. ............................................................... *Never Trust A Friend* | $25 | | Rock'n 101 |
| 1/22/77 | 105 | 4 | 2 The Shuffle ............................................... R&B:79 *That's The Joint* [I] | $5 | | H&L 4677 |

### McCRACKLIN, Jimmy
Born James David Walker on 8/13/21 in Helena, Arkansas. R&B singer/harmonica player.  **R&B**

| 7/24/65 | 132 | 1 | 1 Arkansas (Part 1) .............................................................. *(Part 2)* | $12 | | Imperial 66116 |
| 7/1/67 | 112 | 1 | 2 Dog (Part I) ................................................................... *(Part II)* | $10 | | Minit 32022 |
| 1/27/68 | 114 | 1 | 3 Get Together ..................................................... *How Do You Like Your Love* | $10 | | Minit 32033 |

### McCRAE, George
Born on 10/19/44 in West Palm Beach, Florida. Duets with wife **Gwen McCrae**; became her manager.  **R&B/HOT/AC**

| 11/19/77 | 110 | 2 | Kiss Me (The Way I Like It) ............................................. R&B:57 *(Pt. 2)* | $5 | | T.K. 1024 |

### McCRAE, Gwen
Born on 12/21/43 in Pensacola, Florida. Married **George McCrae**, who later became her manager.  **R&B/HOT**

| 11/14/70 | 102 | 3 | Lead Me On ....................................... R&B:32 *Like Yesterday Our Love Is Gone* | $8 | | Columbia 45214 |

### McCREA, Darlene ✪

| 8/24/59 | 103 | 3 | You............................................................... *You Made A Fool Of Me* | $15 | | Roulette 4173 |
| | | | **Teddy Vann** (male voice) |

### McCREADY, Mindy
Born on 11/30/75 in Fort Myers, Florida. Country singer.  **C&W/HOT**

| 6/15/96 | 124 | 1 | 1 Ten Thousand Angels ........................................ C&W:6 *Not Somebody's Fool* | $3 | ▮ | BNA 64470 |
| 2/1/97 | 102 | 13 | 2 Maybe He'll Notice Her Now/ | | | |
| | | | **MINDY McCREADY** (Featuring Lonestar's Richie McDonald)  C&W:18 |
| 3/8/97 | 105 | 8 | 3 A Girl's Gotta Do (What A Girl's Gotta Do) ............................. C&W:4 | $3 | ▮ | BNA 64757 |
| 11/1/97 | 102 | 15 | 4 What If I Do ........................................ Sls:72 /C&W:26 *If I Don't Stay The Night* | $3 | ▮ | BNA 64990 |

### McDANIELS, Gene — see JONES, Universal

### McDONALD, Michael
Born on 12/2/52 in St. Louis. Vocalist/keyboardist. Formerly with **Steely Dan** and **The Doobie Brothers**.  **AC/HOT/R&B/ROK**

| 8/21/93 | 114 | 8 | I Stand For You ....................................................... AC:21 *East Of Eden* | $3 | ▮ | Reprise 18469 |

| DEBUT | PEAK | WKS | A-side (Chart Hit)..........................................................................B-side | $ | Pic | Label & Number |
|-------|------|-----|-----------------------------------------------------------------|-----|-----|----------------|

**McDUFF, Brother Jack**       R&B/HOT

Born Eugene McDuffy on 9/17/26 in Champaign, Illinois. R&B/jazz-styled organist. First recorded for Prestige in 1960.

| 11/2/63 | 109 | 8 | 1 Rock Candy ............................................... *A Real Good Yn'* [l] | $10 | | Prestige 273 |
| | | | **JACK McDUFF** | | | |
| 3/28/64 | 116 | 5 | 2 Grease Monkey .......................................... *Wink's Blues* [l] | $10 | | Prestige 299 |
| | | | above 2 are "live" recordings | | | |

**McENTIRE, Reba**       C&W/HOT

Born on 3/28/54 in Chockie, Oklahoma. Country singer. Acted in the movie *Tremors* and several TV movies.

| 7/10/93 | 110 | 8 | 1 It's Your Call ..........................................C&W:5 *For Herself* | $3 | ■ | MCA 54496 |
| 5/7/94 | 101[2] | 12 | 2 Why Haven't I Heard From You    Sls:50 /C&W:5 *If I Had Only Known* | $3 | ■ | MCA 54823 |
| 8/20/94 | 101[2] | 13 | 3 She Thinks His Name Was John    Sls:65 /C&W:15 *I Wish That I Could Tell You* | $3 | ■ | MCA 54899 |

**McGHEE, Jacci**       R&B/HOT

Session singer from the Bronx, New York. Worked with **Keith Sweat**, **Toto**, **Al Green**, **Salt-N-Pepa** and others.

| 2/20/93 | 109 | 8 | It Hurts Me .......................................Sls:70 /R&B:36 *The Other Woman* | $3 | ■ | MCA 54528 |
| | | | written and produced by **Keith Sweat** | | | |

**McGOVERN, Maureen**       AC/HOT/C&W

Born on 7/27/49 in Youngstown, Ohio. Sang theme of TV show *Angie*. Starred in Broadway's *Pirates Of Penzance*.

| 3/23/74 | 101[4] | 6 | Nice To Be Around .................................AC:28 *If I Wrote You A Song* | $5 | | 20th Century 2072 |
| | | | from the movie *Cinderella Liberty* starring James Caan and Marsha Mason | | | |

**McGRAW, Tim**       C&W/HOT

Born on 5/1/67 in Delhi, Louisiana. Country singer. Son of ex-professional baseball player Tug McGraw. Married **Faith Hill** on 10/6/96.

| 3/25/95 | 106 | 12 | Refried Dreams ...........................Sls:69 /C&W:5 *Not A Moment Too Soon* (C&W #1) | $3 | ■ | Curb 76931 |

**McGRIFF, Jimmy**       HOT/R&B

Born on 4/3/36 in Philadelphia. Jazz-R&B organist/multi-instrumentalist.

| 11/14/64 | 133 | 2 | 1 Topkapi ................................... *The Theme from The Man With The Golden Arm* [l] | $10 | | Sue 112 |
| | | | title song from the movie starring Peter Ustinov and Melina Mercouri | | | |
| 9/17/66 | 135 | 1 | 2 I Cover The Waterfront ........................... *Slow But Sure* [l] | $8 | | Solid State 2501 |
| | | | title song from the 1933 movie starring Claudette Colbert and Ben Lyon | | | |
| 5/20/67 | 130 | 2 | 3 I Can't Get No Satisfaction.......... *I Can't Give You Anything But Love, Baby* [l] | $8 | | Solid State 2510 |
| | | | #1 hit for **The Rolling Stones** in 1965 | | | |

**McGUINN, Roger** ✪       ROK

Born James McGuinn on 7/13/42 in Chicago. Founder/lead singer/guitarist of **The Byrds**.

| 8/21/76 | 110 | 1 | Take Me Away ...................................... *Friend* | $6 | | Columbia 10385 |

**McGUINN, CLARK & HILLMAN**       AC/HOT

Roger McGuinn (vocals, guitar), Gene Clark (guitar; d: 5/24/91) and Chris Hillman (bass). All were founding members of **The Byrds**.

| 7/7/79 | 104 | 4 | Surrender To Me .....................................AC:45 *Little Mama* | $4 | | Capitol 4739 |

**McGUIRE, Barry**       HOT

Born on 10/15/37 in Oklahoma City. Member of **The New Christy Minstrels** (1962-65).

| 10/30/65 | 117 | 2 | Upon A Painted Ocean ............... *Child Of Our Times* (Hot #72) | $8 | ■ | Dunhill 4014 |

**McGUIRE SISTERS, The**       HOT/MEM/POP/AC

Sisters Phyllis (b: 2/14/31), Christine (b: 7/30/29) and Dorothy (b: 2/13/30) from Middletown, Ohio. *Pop Hits & Top Pop Singles*: 34.

| 4/7/62 | 107 | 1 | Sugartime Twist.................. *More Hearts Are Broken That Way* [R] | $8 | | Coral 62305 |
| | | | Dick Jacobs (orch.); twist version of their #1 hit from 1958 | | | |

**McHONEY, Skip, and The Casuals** ✪       R&B

Artist later made the R&B charts as Skip Mahoaney & The Casuals.

| 3/16/74 | 113 | 2 | Your Funny Moods ...............................R&B:80 *Struggling Man* | $8 | | D.C. International 5003 |

**McKENDREE SPRING** ✪

Folk-pop quintet led by Fran McKendree.

| 1/16/71 | 105 | 4 | 1 Because It's Time .............................. *Oh Now My Friend* | $6 | | Decca 32773 |
| 3/27/76 | 110 | 3 | 2 Too Young To Feel This Old .................. *I'm Gonna Lose That Game Again* | $5 | | Pye 71060 |

**McKENZIE, Scott**       HOT

Born Philip Blondheim on 1/10/39 in Jacksonville, Florida. Co-wrote **The Beach Boys'** 1988 #1 hit "Kokomo."

| 8/5/67 | 111 | 4 | 1 Look In Your Eyes .................................*All I Want Is You* | $8 | | Capitol 5961 |
| | | | **SCOTT MAC KENZIE** | | | |
| 4/20/68 | 126 | 1 | 2 Holy Man............................ *What's The Difference (Chapter Three)* | $8 | | Ode 107 |
| | | | written and produced by John Phillips (**The Mamas & The Papas**) | | | |

**McKNIGHT, Brian**       R&B/HOT/AC

Born on 6/5/69 in Buffalo, New York. R&B singer/composer. His older brother is Claude McKnight of **Take 6**.

| 11/25/95+ | 103 | 15 | Still In Love.............................................R&B:24 *Marilie* | $3 | ■ | Mercury 856896 |

**McLEAN, Don**       AC/HOT/C&W

Born on 10/2/45 in New Rochelle, New York. Singer/songwriter/poet. The hit "Killing Me Softly" was inspired by Don.

| 2/16/74 | 107 | 3 | Fool's Paradise ....................................AC:25 *Happy Trails* | $5 | | United Artists 363 |
| | | | #58 hit for **The Crickets** in 1958 | | | |

**McLEAN, Penny**       HOT/R&B

Born on 11/4/48 in Klagenfurt, Austria. Member of **Silver Convention**.

| 5/22/76 | 108 | 2 | Smoke Gets In Your Eyes ....................... *1-2-3-4...Fire!* | $5 | | Atco 7048 |
| | | | disco version of Paul Whiteman's 1934 #1 hit and **The Platters'** 1959 #1 hit | | | |

**McNAIR, Barbara** ✪

Born on 3/4/39 in Racine, Wisconsin. R&B vocalist. First recorded for Coral in 1958.

| 5/13/67 | 125 | 5 | Here I Am Baby ................................ *My World Is Empty Without You* | $25 | | Motown 1106 |
| | | | written and produced by Smokey Robinson; #44 hit for **The Marvelettes** in 1968 | | | |

**McNAUGHTON, Byron, & His All News Orchestra** ✪
Studio group from Philadelphia.

| | | | | | | |
|---|---|---|---|---|---|---|
| 9/13/75 | 106 | 3 | **Right From The Shark's Jaws (The Jaws Interview)**......... Jaws Jam (The Chief) [N] | $8 | | Jamie 1427 |

a Dickie Goodman "cut-in" type record

**McPHATTER, Clyde**     HOT/R&B
Born Clyde Lensley McPhatter on 11/15/32 in Durham, North Carolina. Died on 6/13/72. Lead singer of The Dominoes (1950-53) and The Drifters (1953-55). Inducted into the Rock and Roll Hall of Fame in 1987. *Top Pop Singles:* 21.

| | | | | | | |
|---|---|---|---|---|---|---|
| 2/20/61 | 103 | 2 | 1 **Tomorrow Is A-Comin'**/ | | | |
| | | | written by **Gene Pitney** | | | |
| 3/6/61 | 110 | 1 | 2 **I'll Love You Til The Cows Come Home** ..................................... | $15 | ■ | Mercury 71783 |
| 11/3/62 | 118 | 5 | 3 **The Best Man Cried** .................................................... Stop | $15 | ■ | Mercury 72051 |
| 9/21/63 | 127 | 1 | 4 **From One To One** .......................... So Close To Being In Love | $15 | ■ | Mercury 72166 |
| 5/1/65 | 117 | 3 | 5 **Crying Won't Help You Now** ............................. R&B:22 I Found My Love | $12 | ■ | Mercury 72407 |

**McRAE, Carmen**     AC/HOT
Born on 4/8/20 in New York City. Died on 11/10/94. Jazz singer/pianist.

| | | | | | | |
|---|---|---|---|---|---|---|
| 11/18/67 | 101[2] | 4 | **Live For Life**     AC:33 Cottage For Sale | $8 | | Atlantic 2451 |
| | | | **CARMEN McRAE & HERBIE MANN** | | | |
| | | | title song from the movie starring Yves Montand; #99 hit for **Jack Jones** in 1967 | | | |

**McWILLIAMS, David** ✪

| | | | | | | |
|---|---|---|---|---|---|---|
| 6/1/68 | 134 | 1 | **Days Of Pearly Spencer** ..................... There's No Lock Upon My Door | $8 | ■ | Kapp 896 |

**MECO**     HOT/AC/R&B
Born Meco Monardo on 11/29/39 in Johnsonburg, Pennsylvania. Disco producer.

| | | | | | | |
|---|---|---|---|---|---|---|
| 9/19/81 | 106 | 3 | 1 **Blue Moon** ................................................... You Gotta Hurt Me | $5 | | Casablanca 2339 |
| | | | tune featured in the movie *An American Werewolf In London* starring David Naughton; #1 hit for **The Marcels** in 1961 | | | |
| 6/12/82 | 101[2] | 5 | 2 **Big Band Medley** ...................................... AC:18 Part 2 [I] | $4 | | Arista 0686 |
| | | | Pennsylvania 6-5000/String Of Pearls/In The Mood/Don't Be That Way/I've Got A Girl In Kalamazoo/Moonlight Serenade/ Opus No. 1/Two O'Clock Jump | | | |

**MEDICAL MISSIONARIES OF MARY CHORAL GROUP** ✪     AC

| | | | | | | |
|---|---|---|---|---|---|---|
| 2/5/66 | 117 | 2 | **Angels (Watching Over Me)** ............................. AC:31 Spring | $8 | | Kapp 731 |

**MEDLEY, Bill**     HOT/C&W/AC/R&B
Born on 9/19/40 in Santa Ana, California. Baritone of **The Righteous Brothers** duo.

| | | | | | | |
|---|---|---|---|---|---|---|
| 2/22/69 | 112 | 2 | **This Is A Love Song** ..................................... Something's So Wrong | $8 | | MGM 14025 |

**MEISNER, Randy**     HOT/ROK
Born on 3/8/46 in Scottsbluff, Nebraska. Bassist/vocalist of **Poco**, **Rick Nelson**'s Stone Canyon Band and the Eagles.

| | | | | | | |
|---|---|---|---|---|---|---|
| 5/30/81 | 104 | 5 | **Gotta Get Away** ...................................... Trouble Ahead | $4 | | Epic 02059 |

**MEL AND TIM**     R&B/HOT
R&B duo of cousins Mel Hardin and Tim McPherson, from Holly Springs, Mississippi.

| | | | | | | |
|---|---|---|---|---|---|---|
| 5/9/70 | 106 | 2 | 1 **Feeling Bad** ......................................................... I've Got Puredee | $7 | | Bamboo 112 |
| 3/3/73 | 113 | 4 | 2 **I May Not Be What You Want** ....................... R&B:33 Too Much Wheelin' And Dealin' | $6 | | Stax 0154 |
| | | | featured in the 1972 concert movie *Wattstax* | | | |

**MELANIE**     HOT/AC
Born Melanie Safka on 2/3/47 in Queens, New York. Neighborhood Records formed by Melanie and her husband/producer Peter Schekeryk.

| | | | | | | |
|---|---|---|---|---|---|---|
| 10/17/70 | 112 | 1 | 1 **Stop! I Don't Wanna' Hear It Anymore** .......... Peace Will Come (According To Plan) (Hot #32) | $8 | | Buddah 186 |
| | | | from the movie *RPM* starring Anthony Quinn; above title replaced "Close To It All" as the B-side | | | |
| 5/27/72 | 106 | 3 | 2 **Some Day I'll Be A Farmer** ..................................... Steppin' | $6 | ■ | Neighborhood 4204 |
| 1/13/73 | 115 | 3 | 3 **Do You Believe** ..................................... Bitter Bad (Hot #36) | $6 | ■ | Neighborhood 4210 |
| 8/17/74 | 109 | 1 | 4 **Lover's Cross** ..................................................... Holding Out | $6 | | Neighborhood 4215 |
| 3/21/81 | 110 | 1 | 5 **One More Try** ............................................................ Apathy | $5 | | Portrait 51001 |

**MELENDEZ, Lisette**     HOT/R&B
Dance singer from East Harlem, New York.

| | | | | | | |
|---|---|---|---|---|---|---|
| 4/23/94 | 110 | 4 | **Will You Ever Save Me** ..................................... Honestly | $3 | ▌ | Fever/RAL/Chaos 77089 |

**MELLE MEL — see GRANDMASTER**

**MELLENCAMP, John Cougar**     ROK/HOT/AC/C&W
Born on 10/7/51 in Seymour, Indiana. Rock singer/songwriter/producer. *Top Pop Singles:* 28.

| | | | | | | |
|---|---|---|---|---|---|---|
| 4/19/80 | 105 | 3 | **A Little Night Dancin'** .............................................. Pray For Me | $5 | | Riva 204 |
| | | | **JOHN COUGAR** | | | |

**MELLO-QUEENS — see LESTER, John**

**MELVIN, Harold, And The Blue Notes**     R&B/HOT/AC
R&B vocal group formed in Philadelphia in 1954 by Harold Melvin (d: 3/24/97, age 57). **Teddy Pendergrass**, lead singer, 1970-76; replaced by David Ebo.

| | | | | | | |
|---|---|---|---|---|---|---|
| 1/30/65 | 125 | 1 | 1 **Get Out (And Let Me Cry)** ............................. R&B:38 You May Not Love Me | $40 | | Landa 703 |
| | | | John Atkins (lead vocal) | | | |
| 6/11/77 | 102 | 4 | 2 **After You Love Me, Why Do You Leave Me** ................. R&B:15 Big Singing Star | $5 | | ABC 12268 |
| | | | **HAROLD MELVIN & THE BLUE NOTES, Featuring SHARON PAGE** | | | |

**MEMOS, The** ✪
Brooklyn R&B vocal quintet: Henry Alston, James Brown, Eugene Williams, Vernon Britton and Walter Rodes.

| | | | | | | |
|---|---|---|---|---|---|---|
| 10/19/59 | 105 | 2 | **My Type Of Girl** ..................................................... The Biddy Leg | $30 | | Memo 34891 |

**MEMPHIS HORNS, The** ✪     R&B
R&B studio group. Member Wayne Jackson was with **The Mar-Keys**.

| | | | | | | |
|---|---|---|---|---|---|---|
| 2/26/77 | 108 | 1 | 1 **Get Up And Dance** ..................................... R&B:61 Don't Abuse It | $5 | | RCA 10836 |
| 10/1/77 | 101[6] | 15 | 2 **Just For Your Love** ..................................... R&B:17 Keep On Smilin' | $5 | | RCA 11064 |

**MEN AT LARGE**      R&B/HOT
Cleveland R&B duo: David Tolliver and Jason Champion. Both weigh over 300 pounds.

| 1/7/95 | 122 | 1 | Let's Talk About It..........................................R&B:16 *(3 album snippets)* | $3 | ▌ | EastWest 98221 |

written, produced and arranged by **Gerald Levert**

**MENDES, Sergio, & Brasil '66**      AC/HOT/R&B
Born on 2/11/41 in Niteroi, Brazil. Pianist/leader of Latin-styled group originating from Brazil. Member **Lani Hall** (vocals) married **Herb Alpert**.

| 9/23/67 | 126 | 4 | 1 The Frog ..........................................AC:21 *Watch What Happens* [F] | $6 | ▌ | A&M 872 |
| 1/27/68 | 106 | 2 | 2 Say A Little Prayer ..........................................AC:21 *Comin' Home Baby* [I] | $6 | | Atlantic 2472 |

    **SERGIO MENDES**
    #4 hit for Dionne Warwick in 1967

| 2/21/70 | 107 | 1 | 3 Norwegian Wood ..........................................AC:32 *Masquerade* | $6 | ▌ | A&M 1164 |

originally recorded by **The Beatles** for their 1966 album *Rubber Soul*

| 8/29/70 | 101[2] | 6 | 4 For What It's Worth     AC:10 *Viramundo* | $5 | | A&M 1209 |

    #7 hit for **The Buffalo Springfield** in 1967

| 4/14/73 | 113 | 3 | 5 Love Music ..........................................AC:24 *Walk The Way You Talk* | $5 | | Bell 45,335 |

    **SERGIO MENDES & BRASIL '77**

**MENUDO**      R&B/HOT
Puerto Rican teen quintet. The superstar group of Latin America; members must retire at age 16.

| 5/5/84 | 102 | 6 | 1 If You're Not Here (By My Side)..........................R&B:36 *That's What You Do* | $3 | ▌ | RCA 13771 |
| 7/27/85 | 104 | 5 | 2 Please Be Good To Me ..........................................*Chocolate Candy* | $3 | | RCA 14154 |

**MESSENGERS, The**      HOT
Milwaukee rock band led by Greg Jursek and Michael Morgan. After original Messengers left the U.S.A. label, a Chicago group toured as Michael & The Messengers.

| 4/22/67 | 116 | 3 | 1 Midnight Hour ..........................................*Hard Hard Year* | $15 | | U.S.A. 866 |

    #21 hit for **Wilson Pickett** in 1965; first released on U.S.A. 866 as by Michael & The Mesengers with "Up Til News" as the B-side

| 7/22/67 | 129 | 2 | 2 Romeo & Juliet ..........................................*Lies (Don't Mean Nothin)* | $15 | | U.S.A. 874 |

    **MICHAEL & THE MESSENGERS**
    #6 hit for **The Reflections** in 1964

| 10/14/67 | 132 | 2 | 3 Window Shopping ..........................................*California Soul* | $10 | | Soul 35037 |

    written and produced by **R. Dean Taylor**

**MESSIAH** ✪      ROK

| 1/30/93 | 117 | 4 | Temple Of Dreams ..........................................ROK:17 *You're Going Insane* | $3 | ▌ | Def American 18697 |

**MESSINA, Jimmy**      HOT/AC
Born on 12/5/47 in Maywood, California. In duo with Kenny Loggins from 1970-75. Also a member of **Buffalo Springfield** and **Poco**.

| 1/19/80 | 110 | 3 | 1 Do You Want To Dance ..........................................*Seeing You (For The First Time)* | $4 | | Columbia 11182 |
| 8/29/81 | 110 | 3 | 2 Stay The Night..........................................*Move Into Your Heart* | $4 | | Warner 49784 |

    **JIM MESSINA with Pauline Wilson**

**MESSINA, Jo Dee** ✪      C&W
Born in Holliston, Massachusetts. Country singer.

| 5/4/96 | 111 | 5 | Heads Carolina, Tails California..........................C&W:2 *Walk To The Light* | $3 | ▌ | Curb 76982 |

**METALLICS, The** ✪
R&B vocal group.

| 4/14/62 | 101[1] | 5 | Need Your Love     *Itchy Twitchy Too* | $40 | | Baronet 2 |

**METHOD MAN — see O'NEAL, Shaquille**

**ME-2-U** ✪      R&B
Male vocal group from Baltimore-Washington, D.C. area: Jerry Lattisaw, DeVaughn Howard, Eric Sanders, Damon Dunnock and Tony Dumas. Lattisaw is the younger brother of **Stacy Lattisaw**.

| 8/28/93 | 112 | 5 | Want U Back..........................................R&B:45 *(2 versions)* | $3 | ▌ | RCA 62565 |

**METROPOLIS** ✪
Disco studio group from New York City.

| 5/6/78 | 105 | 4 | I Love New York ..........................................*(instrumental)* | $5 | | Salsoul 2060 |

**MIAMI** ✪      R&B
Florida-based disco act: Robert Moore (vocals), Freddie Scott, Warren Thompson, Bobby Williams and Willie Jackson.

| 8/7/76 | 102 | 13 | Kill That Roach..........................................R&B:42 *Mr. Notorious* | $5 | | Drive 6251 |

**MICHAEL, George**      HOT/AC/R&B
Born Georgios Kyriacos Panayiotou on 6/25/63 in Bushey, England. In duo with Andrew Ridgeley as Wham! *Top Pop Singles*: 27.

| 4/5/97 | 101[1] | 6 | Star People     *(2 versions) / The Strangest Thing (live)* | $3 | ▌ | DreamWorks 59005 |

**MICHAEL & THE MESSENGERS — see MESSENGERS, The**

**MICHAELS, Lee**      HOT
Born on 11/24/45 in Los Angeles. Rock organist/vocalist.

| 9/6/69 | 106 | 5 | Heighty Hi ..........................................*Want My Baby* | $7 | | A&M 1095 |

**MICHAELS, Marilyn** ✪      AC
Pop singer. Went on to become a successful comedienne/impressionist in the 1970s.

| 9/5/60 | 110 | 2 | Tell Tommy I Miss Him..........................................*Everyone Was There But You* | $20 | | RCA Victor 7771 |

    Billy Mure (orch.); answer song to **Ray Peterson**'s "Tell Laura I Love Her"

**MIDNIGHT OIL**      ROK/HOT
Rock group formed in 1976 in Sydney, Australia featuring Peter Garrett (vocals).

| 9/25/93 | 108 | 4 | Outbreak Of Love..........................................ROK:9 *Ships Of Freedom* | $3 | ▌ | Columbia 77090 |

**MIDNIGHT STAR**      R&B/HOT
R&B-funk group formed in 1976 at Kentucky State University featuring brothers Reggie (trumpet) and Vincent (trombone) Calloway.

| 9/18/82 | 108 | 2 | Hot Spot..........................................R&B:35 *I Won't Let You Be Lonely* | $4 | | Solar 48012 |

**MIGHTY CLOUDS OF JOY**  R&B/HOT
Gospel group formed in Los Angeles in 1960. Nucleus consisted of Willie Joe Ligon and Johnny Martin (leads).

| | | | | | | |
|---|---|---|---|---|---|---|
| 10/5/74 | 102 | 4 | Time .......................................... R&B:32  *(You Think) "You're Doin' It On Your Own* | $5 | | Dunhill/ABC 15012 |

**MIGHTY HANNIBAL, The ☉**  R&B
Real name is James T. Shaw. Native of Columbus, Georgia. First recorded in 1959.

| | | | | | | |
|---|---|---|---|---|---|---|
| 11/19/66 | 115 | 2 | 1 Hymn No. 5 ................................... R&B:21  *Fishin' Pole* | $15 | | Josie 964 |
| | | | also released on Shurfine 021 in 1966 ($12) | | | |
| 1/13/73 | 105 | 7 | 2 The Truth Shall Make You Free (St. John 8:32) ................... R&B:37  *It's What You Do* | $7 | | Aware 027 |
| | | | **KING HANNIBAL** | | | |

**MIGHTY MARVELOWS, The**  R&B/HOT
R&B group from Chicago Heights, Illinois. First known as the Mystics. Included Melvin Mason (lead), Willie "Sonny" Stevenson, Frank Paden and Johnny Paden. Added Jesse Smith in 1964; became The Marvelows.

| | | | | | | |
|---|---|---|---|---|---|---|
| 3/30/68 | 105 | 6 | In The Morning ......................................... R&B:24  *Talkin' Bout Ya, Baby* | $8 | | ABC 11011 |

**MIGHTY SAM ☉**
Born Sam McClain on 4/15/43 in Monroe, Louisiana. R&B singer.

| | | | | | | |
|---|---|---|---|---|---|---|
| 9/24/66 | 120 | 2 | Fannie Mae............................................................*Badmouthin'* | $12 | | Amy 963 |
| | | | #38 hit for **Buster Brown** in 1960 | | | |

**MiiLKBONE ☉**  R&B
White male rapper from Orange, New Jersey.

| | | | | | | |
|---|---|---|---|---|---|---|
| 9/23/95 | 123 | 1 | Where'z Da' Party At? ................................. R&B:86  *Kids On The Ave* | $3 | ▌ | Set It Off/Capitol 58446 |
| | | | samples "Too Hot" by **Kool & The Gang** | | | |

**MIJANGOS ☉**
Born Andres Mijangos in Acapulco, Mexico. Male dance producer/DJ/remixer.

| | | | | | | |
|---|---|---|---|---|---|---|
| 6/28/97 | 119 | 1 | SaXmania ......................................................... *(3 mixes)* [I] | $6 | | Aqua Boogie 036 (T) |
| | | | John Rekevics (saxophone) | | | |

**MILES, Buddy**  HOT/R&B
Born George Miles on 9/5/46 in Omaha. R&B vocalist/drummer. In **Jimi Hendrix**'s Band Of Gypsys, 1969-70.

| | | | | | | |
|---|---|---|---|---|---|---|
| 11/23/74 | 108 | 1 | We Got Love ........................................................ *Pain* | $5 | | Columbia 10030 |

**MILES, Dick ☉**  C&W

| | | | | | | |
|---|---|---|---|---|---|---|
| 3/30/68 | 114 | 2 | The Last Goodbye................................ C&W:17  *Candle-Lighted World* [S] | $8 | | Capitol 2113 |

**MILLER, Frankie**  HOT
Born in Glasgow, Scotland, circa 1950. Blues-tinged rock singer. Suffered a brain aneurysm on 8/25/94.

| | | | | | | |
|---|---|---|---|---|---|---|
| 3/3/79 | 103 | 3 | Darlin' ........................................................ *Drunken Nights In The City* | $5 | | Chrysalis 2255 |
| | | | "Bubbled Under" in 1981 by **Tom Jones** | | | |

**MILLER, Jody**  C&W/AC/HOT
Born on 11/29/41 in Phoenix; raised in Blanchard, Oklahoma. Pop-country singer.

| | | | | | | |
|---|---|---|---|---|---|---|
| 12/4/65 | 125 | 1 | 1 Magic Town ........................................................ *A Lonely Queen* | $10 | | Capitol 5541 |
| | | | #21 hit for **The Vogues** in 1966 | | | |
| 7/1/72 | 115 | 1 | 2 There's A Party Goin' On................. C&W:4 / AC:23  *Love's The Answer* | $8 | | Epic 10878 |

**MILLER, Lesley ☉**

| | | | | | | |
|---|---|---|---|---|---|---|
| 3/19/66 | 101[1] | 3 | He Wore The Green Beret       *You Got A Way Of Bringing Out My Tears* | $8 | | RCA Victor 8786 |
| | | | answer song to Ssgt. Barry Sadler's #1 hit "The Ballad Of The Green Berets" | | | |

**MILLER, Mitch**  HOT/MEM/POP
Born on 7/4/11 in Rochester, New York. Producer/conductor/arranger. A&R executive for both Columbia and Mercury Records.

| | | | | | | |
|---|---|---|---|---|---|---|
| 12/1/62 | 109 | 3 | The Longest Day ........................................................ *(instrumental)* | $8 | ■ | Columbia 42585 |
| | | | written by **Paul Anka**; title song from the movie starring John Wayne | | | |

**MILLER, Ned**  C&W/HOT/AC
Born Henry Ned Miller on 4/12/25 in Rains, Utah. Country singer/songwriter.

| | | | | | | |
|---|---|---|---|---|---|---|
| 4/25/64 | 131 | 2 | Invisible Tears ................................. C&W:13  *Old Restless Ocean* | $10 | | Fabor 128 |
| | | | #57 hit for **The Ray Conniff Singers** in 1964 | | | |

**MILLER, Roger**  C&W/HOT/AC
Born on 1/2/36 in Fort Worth, Texas. Died of cancer on 10/25/92. Country vocalist/humorist/guitarist/composer.

| | | | | | | |
|---|---|---|---|---|---|---|
| 7/17/65 | 105 | 3 | 1 It Happened Just That Way .............................. AC:26  *One Dyin' And A Buryin'* (Hot #34) | $8 | ■ | Smash 1994 |
| 2/19/66 | 103 | 3 | 2 I've Been A Long Time Leavin' (But I'll Be A Long | | | |
| | | | Time Gone)................................. C&W:13  *Husbands And Wives* (Hot #26) | $8 | | Smash 2024 |
| 10/21/67 | 102 | 5 | 3 The Ballad Of Waterhole #3 (Code Of The West)  C&W:27  *Rainbow Valley* | $8 | ■ | Smash 2121 |
| | | | from the movie *Waterhole #3* starring James Coburn | | | |
| 7/5/69 | 122 | 3 | 4 Me And Bobby McGee ............ C&W:12  *I'm Gonna Teach My Heart To Bend (Instead of Break)* | $7 | | Smash 2230 |
| | | | #1 hit for **Janis Joplin** in 1971 | | | |
| 8/18/73 | 105 | 9 | 5 Open Up Your Heart................................. C&W:14 / AC:20  *Qua La Linta* | $5 | | Columbia 45873 |

**MILLER, Steve, Band**  HOT/ROK/AC/R&B
Born on 10/5/43 in Milwaukee. Blues-rock singer/songwriter/guitarist. *Top Pop Singles*: 20.

| | | | | | | |
|---|---|---|---|---|---|---|
| 7/12/69 | 126 | 2 | 1 My Dark Hour................................................ *Song For Our Ancestors* | $8 | | Capitol 2520 |
| 11/7/70 | 117 | 1 | 2 Steve Miller's Midnight Tango ................................. *Going To Mexico* | $8 | | Capitol 2945 |

**MILLS, Frank**  AC/HOT/C&W
Born in Toronto in 1943. Pianist/composer/producer/arranger.

| | | | | | | |
|---|---|---|---|---|---|---|
| 5/27/72 | 106 | 5 | Poor Little Fool................................. *What Do You Think Of Love* | $5 | | Sunflower 122 |
| | | | #1 hit for **Ricky Nelson** in 1958 | | | |

**MILLS, Hayley**  HOT
Born on 4/18/46 in London. Daughter of English actor John Mills. Disney teen movie star.

| | | | | | | |
|---|---|---|---|---|---|---|
| 7/7/62 | 118 | 1 | Ching-Ching and a Ding Ding Ding ................................. *Side By Side* | $15 | ■ | Buena Vista 401 |

### MILLS, Stephanie
Born on 3/26/56 in Brooklyn. Appeared in the Broadway musicals *Maggie Flynn* and *The Wiz*.  **R&B/HOT/AC**

| DEBUT | PEAK | WKS | A-side / B-side | $ | Pic | Label & Number |
|---|---|---|---|---|---|---|
| 11/17/79 | 101² | 12 | 1 You Can Get Over     R&B:55   *Better Than Ever* | $4 | | 20th Century 2427 |
| 7/31/82 | 101¹ | 6 | 2 Last Night     R&B:14   *Wailin'* | $3 | | Casablanca 2352 |

### MILSAP, Ronnie
Born on 1/16/46 in Robbinsville, North Carolina. Country singer/pianist/guitarist. Blind since birth.  **C&W/AC/HOT/R&B**

| DEBUT | PEAK | WKS | A-side / B-side | $ | Pic | Label & Number |
|---|---|---|---|---|---|---|
| 10/16/65 | 106 | 7 | 1 Never Had It So Good .......................... R&B:19   *Let's Go Get Stoned* | $20 | | Scepter 12109 |
| | | |     written by Ashford & Simpson | | | |
| 5/10/69 | 123 | 3 | 2 Denver ...................... *Nothing Is As Good As It Used To Be* | $20 | | Scepter 12246 |
| 12/19/70 | 125 | 2 | 3 A Rose By Any Other Name (Is Still A Rose) ..................... *Sermonette* | $10 | | Chips 2987 |
| | | |     made the Country charts (#77) on 12/27/75 on Warner 8160 | | | |
| 6/14/75 | 101¹ | 3 | 4 Too Late To Worry, Too Blue To Cry    C&W:6   *Country Cookin'* | $5 | | RCA Victor 10228 |
| | | |     #1 Country hit for Al Dexter in 1944; #76 hit for Glen Campbell in 1962 | | | |
| 8/9/80 | 103 | 4 | 5 Cowboys And Clowns ..................... C&W:❶¹   *Misery Loves Company* (C&W flip) | $4 | ■ | RCA 12006 |
| | | |     from the movie *Bronco Billy* starring Clint Eastwood | | | |
| 1/7/84 | 103 | 3 | 6 Show Her ..................... C&W:❶¹ / AC:17   *Watch Out For The Other Guy* | $3 | | RCA 13658 |

### MIMMS, Garnet
Born Garrett Mimms on 11/16/33 in Ashland, West Virginia. Formed The Enchanters in 1961.  **R&B/HOT**

| DEBUT | PEAK | WKS | A-side / B-side | $ | Pic | Label & Number |
|---|---|---|---|---|---|---|
| 4/24/65 | 124 | 2 | 1 It Was Easier To Hurt Her ................................. *So Close* | $15 | | United Artists 848 |
| 7/17/65 | 115 | 1 | 2 That Goes To Show You ........................... *Everytime* | $15 | | United Artists 887 |
| 7/16/66 | 125 | 3 | 3 It's Been Such A Long Way Home .................... *Thinkin'* | $10 | | Veep 1232 |
| 10/1/66 | 132 | 1 | 4 My Baby ................................ *Keep On Smilin'* | $10 | | Veep 1234 |

### MINISTRY ✪
An assemblage of musicians formed by Chicago-based producer/performer Alain Jourgensen.  **ROK**

| DEBUT | PEAK | WKS | A-side / B-side | $ | Pic | Label & Number |
|---|---|---|---|---|---|---|
| 8/20/83 | 106 | 3 | 1 I Wanted To Tell Her ............................ *A Walk In The Park* | $4 | | Arista 9068 |
| 12/23/95 | 115 | 1 | 2 The Fall ............................ *Reload / TVIII* | $6 | | Warner 43630 (CD) |

### MINKIN, Bill — see SENATOR BOBBY

### MINNELLI, Liza ✪
Born on 3/12/46 in Los Angeles. Singer and Broadway/movie actress. Daughter of Judy Garland.

| DEBUT | PEAK | WKS | A-side / B-side | $ | Pic | Label & Number |
|---|---|---|---|---|---|---|
| 8/13/77 | 104 | 1 | Theme from "New York, New York" ........................... *Hazoy* | $5 | | United Artists 1014 |
| | | |     from the movie *New York, New York* starring Minnelli and Robert DeNiro | | | |

### MINT CONDITION
Funk sextet from Minneapolis: Stokley Williams (vocals), Homer O'Dell, Larry Waddell, Jeffrey Allen, Keri Lewis and Ricky Kinchen.  **R&B/HOT**

| DEBUT | PEAK | WKS | A-side / B-side | $ | Pic | Label & Number |
|---|---|---|---|---|---|---|
| 4/22/95 | 118 | 3 | So Fine ................................ R&B:29   (2 versions) / *Harmony* | $3 | ■ | Perspective 7478 |

### MIRACLES, The
R&B group formed in Detroit featuring **Smokey Robinson** with Bobby Rogers, Ronnie White (d: 8/26/95) and Pete Moore. Billy Griffin replaced Smokey in 1973. *Top Pop Singles*: 46.  **R&B/HOT**

| DEBUT | PEAK | WKS | A-side / B-side | $ | Pic | Label & Number |
|---|---|---|---|---|---|---|
| 4/14/62 | 103 | 4 | 1 I've Been Good To You ........................ *What's So Good About Good-by* (Hot #35) | $25 | ■ | Tamla 54053 |
| 3/30/63 | 107 | 5 | 2 I Can Take A Hint ........................ *A Love She Can Count On* (Hot #31) | $15 | | Tamla 54078 |
| 12/22/73 | 111 | 1 | 3 Give Me Just Another Day ..................... R&B:47   *I Wanna Be With You* | $6 | | Tamla 54240 |
| 5/10/75 | 101² | 4 | 4 Gemini     R&B:43   *You Are Love* | $6 | | Tamla 54259 |
| 2/5/77 | 104 | 4 | 5 Spy For Brotherhood ..................... R&B:37   *The Bird Must Fly Away* | $5 | | Columbia 10464 |
| | | |     THE MIRACLES Featuring Billy Griffin | | | |

### MIRAN, Wayne, And Rush Release ✪
**R&B**

| DEBUT | PEAK | WKS | A-side / B-side | $ | Pic | Label & Number |
|---|---|---|---|---|---|---|
| 10/11/75 | 104 | 4 | Oh Baby ........................... R&B:68   (long version) | $5 | | Roulette 7176 |

### MIRANDA
Female dance singer/songwriter from Burbank. Eighteen years old in 1994.  **HOT**

| DEBUT | PEAK | WKS | A-side / B-side | $ | Pic | Label & Number |
|---|---|---|---|---|---|---|
| 11/12/94 | 110 | 12 | Round & Round ................................ (freestyle mix) | $3 | ■ | Sunshine 7823 |

### MISSION, The ✪
**AC/R&B**

| DEBUT | PEAK | WKS | A-side / B-side | $ | Pic | Label & Number |
|---|---|---|---|---|---|---|
| 10/20/73 | 108 | 7 | Together (Body And Soulin') ........................... AC:36   *Temple Turning Time* | $6 | ■ | Paramount 0213 |
| | | |     Dorothy Lerner (lead vocal) | | | |

### MR. LEE ✪
Producer/remixer/multi-instrumentalist Leroy Haggard. Chicago native.  **R&B**

| DEBUT | PEAK | WKS | A-side / B-side | $ | Pic | Label & Number |
|---|---|---|---|---|---|---|
| 12/5/92+ | 101⁴ | 14 | Hey Love (Can I Have A Word)     R&B:15   *Jazzy Lee* | $3 | ■ | Jive 42017 |
| | | |     MR. LEE Featuring R. Kelly | | | |
| | | |     #90 hit for Stevie Wonder in 1967 | | | |

### MR. MIRAINGA ✪
Pronounced: Mer-ain-gay. Rock-salsa quartet from California: Potz Poturalski (vocals), Stevoreno (guitar), Hedge (bass) and Drt (drums).

| DEBUT | PEAK | WKS | A-side / B-side | $ | Pic | Label & Number |
|---|---|---|---|---|---|---|
| 1/27/96 | 122 | 1 | Burnin' Rubber ................................ *Chili* | $3 | ■ | Way Cool/MCA 55165 |

### MR. MONEY LOC ✪
Male rapper from Long Beach, California.  **R&B**

| DEBUT | PEAK | WKS | A-side / B-side | $ | Pic | Label & Number |
|---|---|---|---|---|---|---|
| 10/18/97 | 121 | 2 | Imma Rolla ........................... R&B:61   (instrumental) | $3 | ■ | Loc-N-Up 70310 |

### MITCHELL, Billy, Group ✪
Born on 11/3/26 in Kansas City, Missouri. Jazz saxophonist/composer.  **R&B**

| DEBUT | PEAK | WKS | A-side / B-side | $ | Pic | Label & Number |
|---|---|---|---|---|---|---|
| 6/28/69 | 115 | 3 | Oh Happy Day ........................... R&B:41   *The Chokin' Kind* [I] | $10 | | Calla 165 |
| | | |     #4 hit for The Edwin Hawkins' Singers in 1969 | | | |

### MITCHELL, Guy
Born Al Cernik on 2/27/27 in Detroit. Pop/country vocalist. Appeared in several movies and TV series. *Pop Hits & Top Pop Singles*: 26.  **MEM/POP/HOT/C&W**

| DEBUT | PEAK | WKS | A-side / B-side | $ | Pic | Label & Number |
|---|---|---|---|---|---|---|
| 3/20/61 | 106 | 4 | 1 Your Goodnight Kiss (Ain't What It Used To Be) ............*Follow Me* (I'll Show You The Way) | $10 | | Columbia 41970 |
| | | |     based on the 1915 tune "The Old Grey Mare (She Ain't What She Used To Be)" | | | |
| 6/30/62 | 110 | 1 | 2 Charlie's Shoes ........................... *Rusty Old Halo* | $8 | | Joy 264 |
| | | |     #1 Country hit for Billy Walker in 1962 | | | |
| 12/1/62 | 101¹ | 3 | 3 Go Tiger, Go!     *If You Ever Go Away* | $8 | | Joy 270 |

| DEBUT | PEAK | WKS | A-side (Chart Hit) ........................................................................B-side | $ | Pic | Label & Number |
|---|---|---|---|---|---|---|

**MITCHELL, Joni**      HOT/AC/ROK
Born Roberta Joan Anderson on 11/7/43 in Fort McLeod, Alberta, Canada. Singer/songwriter/guitarist/pianist. Recipient of *Billboard's* "The Century Award" in 1995. Inducted into the Rock and Roll Hall of Fame in 1997.

| 10/4/80 | 102 | 4 | Why Do Fools Fall In Love ...................................................... *Black Crow* | $5 | | Asylum 47038 |

"live" recording; The Persuasions (R&B backing vocal group); #6 hit for Frankie Lymon & The Teenagers in 1956

**MITCHELL, McKinley ○**      R&B
Born on 12/25/34 in Jackson, Mississippi. Died on 1/18/86. In gospel group, Hearts Of Harmony, in 1950.

| 3/31/62 | 115 | 1 | The Town I Live In ............................................... R&B:8 *No Love (Like My Love)* | $15 | | one-derful! 2030 |

**MITCHELL, Willie**      HOT/R&B/AC
Born on 1/3/28 in Ashland, Mississippi. R&B trumpeter/keyboardist/composer/arranger/producer. President of Hi Records.

| 11/6/65 | 126 | 6 | 1 Everything Is Gonna Be Alright ........................................... *That Driving Beat* | $7 | | Hi 2097 |
| 10/15/66 | 127 | 1 | 2 Mercy ............................................... *Sticks And Stones* [I] | $7 | | Hi 2112 |
| 6/7/69 | 120 | 1 | 3 Young People ............................................... *Kitten Korner* [I] | $7 | | Hi 2158 |
| 11/8/69 | 115 | 1 | 4 My Babe ............................................... R&B:37 *Teenie's Dream* [I] | $7 | | Hi 2167 |

#1 R&B hit for **Little Walter** in 1955

**MOBB DEEP**      R&B/HOT
Rap duo from New York City: Havoc and Prodigy.

| 11/23/96 | 109 | 5 | 1 Front Lines (Hell On Earth) ........................................... R&B:57 *(instrumental)* | $6 | ■ | Loud/RCA 64693 (T) |
| 5/3/97 | 101[2] | 7 | 2 G.O.D. Pt. III ........................ Sls:72 /R&B:64 *The After Hours G.O.D. Pt. III* | $3 | ■ | Loud/RCA 64833 |

samples "Play This Only At Night" by **Doug E. Fresh**

**MOBY GRAPE**      HOT
Rock group from San Francisco: Alexander "Skip" Spence (vocals, guitar; **Jefferson Airplane**), Jerry Miller and Peter Lewis (guitars), Bob Mosley (bass) and Don Stevenson (drums).

| 7/15/67 | 127 | 1 | Hey Grandma ........................................... *Come In The Morning* | $10 | ■ | Columbia 44174 |

one in a series of five singles released simultaneously

**MODERN FOLK QUINTET ○**
Formed in Honolulu in 1962: brothers Jim & Jerry Yester, Chip Douglas, Cyrus Faryar and Henry Diltz. Jim left to join **The Association**. Chip produced several hits for **The Monkees**.

| 4/9/66 | 122 | 2 | Night Time Girl ........................................... *Lifetime* | $8 | | Dunhill 4025 |

**MOKENSTEF**      R&B/HOT
Female R&B vocal trio from Los Angeles: Monifa, Kenya and Stephanie.

| 11/18/95 | 110 | 9 | Sex In The Rain ........................... R&B:63 *I Got Him All The Time* (w/Grand Puba) | $3 | ▮ | OutBurst 577194 |

**MOLLY HATCHET**      ROK/HOT
Southern-rock band formed in 1975 in Jacksonville, Florida featuring Danny Joe Brown (vocals).

| 6/16/79 | 106 | 3 | 1 Dreams I'll Never See ........................................... *The Creeper* | $5 | ■ | Epic 50669 |

written by **Gregg Allman**

| 11/1/80 | 107 | 2 | 2 Beatin' The Odds ........................................... *Few & Far Between* | $5 | | Epic 50943 |

**MOM AND DADS, The ○**
Polka band from Spokane, Washington: Quentin Ratliff, Harold Hendren, Les Welch and Doris Crow.

| 12/11/71+ | 101[1] | 5 | The Rangers Waltz ........................................... *Quentin's E Flat Boogie* [I] | $5 | | GNP Crescendo 439 |

**MOMENTS, The**      R&B/HOT
Soul trio from Hackensack, New Jersey: William Brown (lead), Al Goodman and Harry Ray (d: 10/1/92, age 45). Became Ray, Goodman & Brown in 1978.

| 1/24/70 | 120 | 3 | 1 Lovely Way She Loves ........................... R&B:14 *I've Got to Keep on Loving You* | $7 | | Stang 5009 |
| 2/20/71 | 108 | 5 | 2 I Can't Help It ........................... R&B:27 *To You With Love* | $7 | | Stang 5020 |
| 6/5/71 | 115 | 3 | 3 That's How It Feels ........................... R&B:34 *(long version)* | $7 | | Stang 5024 |
| 12/11/71 | 107 | 1 | 4 To You With Love ........................... R&B:36 *Key To My Happiness* | $7 | | Stang 5033 |

new version of the B-side of #2 above

**MONAHAN, Stephen ○**

| 7/1/67 | 101[1] | 5 | City Of Windows ........................................... *Lost People* | $7 | ■ | Kapp 835 |

**MONA LISA**      R&B/HOT
Born in New York City in 1979. R&B songstress.

| 1/11/97 | 112 | 8 | Just Wanna Please U ........................................... R&B:65 *(2 versions)* | $3 | ▮ | Island 854834 |

samples "What You Won't Do For Love" by **Bobby Caldwell**

**MON a Q ○**
Dance sextet from Tampa, Florida: Monique, George Boulahanis, Bobby Daflos, Emmanuel Gonatos, Mike Koursiotis and Sam Toney.

| 10/18/97 | 120 | 5 | Stay In Love ........................................... *(4 versions)* | $6 | | Matrix 4080 (CD) |

**MONCLAIRS, The ○**
R&B vocal/instrumental group.

| 7/10/65 | 108 | 5 | Happy Feet Time ........................................... *Wait For Me* [I] | $15 | | Sunburst 106 |

**MONDAY AFTER ○**      R&B
R&B vocal group assembled by producer **John Davis**.

| 3/6/76 | 106 | 5 | Merry-Go-Round Pt. I ........................................... R&B:20 *Pt. II* | $6 | | Buddah 512 |

**MONEY, Eddie**      HOT/ROK/AC
Born Edward Mahoney on 3/2/49 in Brooklyn, New York. Rock singer managed by the late West Coast promoter Bill Graham. *Top Pop Singles*: 23.

| 1/16/93 | 102 | 5 | Save A Little Room In Your Heart For Me ........................................... | $15 | | Columbia 4887 (CD) |

"live" recording; released only as a CD promo single; no commercial single was issued; original version released on his 1978 debut album

**MONIFAH**      R&B/HOT
Female R&B singer/actress from New York City. Sang backup for **Maxi Priest**.

| 7/5/97 | 121 | 4 | I Still Love You ........................................... R&B:55 *(instrumental)* | $3 | ▮ | Qwest 17378 |

written and produced by **Heavy D**; from the movie *Sprung* starring Tisha Campbell

**MONITORS, The**            R&B/HOT
R&B vocal group consisting of Sandra and John "Maurice" Fagin, Warren Harris and Richard Street.

| 2/11/67 | 117 | 2 | Since I Lost You Girl.............................. *Don't Put Off 'Til Tomorrow What You Can Do Today* | $20 | | V.I.P. 25039 |

**MONKEES, The**            HOT/AC
Pop band formed in Los Angeles in 1965: Davy Jones (b: 12/30/45, Manchester, England; vocals), Michael Nesmith (b: 12/30/42, Houston; guitar, vocals), Peter Tork (b: 2/13/44, Washington, D.C.; bass, vocals) and Micky Dolenz (b: 3/8/45, Tarzana, California; drums, vocals). Group starred in 58 episodes of *The Monkees* TV show, 1966-68. *Top Pop Singles*: 21.

| 11/18/67 | 104 | 2 | 1 Goin' Down ...............................................................*Daydream Believer* (Hot #1) | $15 | ■ | Colgems 1012 |
| 10/12/68 | 106 | 3 | 2 As We Go Along .......................................................*Porpoise Song* (Hot #62) | $20 | ■ | Colgems 1031 |
| | | | from the movie *Head* starring The Monkees | | | |
| 9/20/69 | 109 | 2 | 3 Mommy And Daddy ..................................................... *Good Clean Fun* (Hot #82) | $30 | ■ | Colgems 5005 |

**MONRO, Matt**            AC/HOT
Born Terrence Parsons on 12/1/32 in London. Died of liver cancer on 2/7/85. Sang with Cyril Stapleton's Orchestra before going solo.

| 7/14/62 | 116 | 4 | 1 Softly As I Leave You .........................................*Is There Anything I Can Do* | $8 | | Liberty 55449 |
| | | | #27 hit for Frank Sinatra in 1964 | | | |
| 9/12/64 | 121 | 3 | 2 Softly As I Leave You ........................................ *I Love You Too* [R] | $8 | | Liberty 55725 |
| | | | same version as #1 above, except 1:20 shorter | | | |
| 2/27/65 | 135 | 1 | 3 For Mama ....................................................... *Going Places* | $8 | | Liberty 55763 |
| | | | #48 hit for Connie Francis in 1965 | | | |
| 5/1/65 | 101[2] | 3 | 4 Without You (I Cannot Live) ........................... *Start Living* | $8 | | Liberty 55786 |
| | | | all of above produced by George Martin | | | |
| 11/26/66 | 126 | 1 | 5 Born Free ....................................... AC:35 *Other People* | $7 | | Capitol 5623 |
| | | | title song from the movie starring Virginia McKenna; #7 hit for Roger Williams in 1966 | | | |

**MONROE, Vaughn**            MEM/POP/HOT
Born on 10/7/11 in Akron, Ohio. Died on 5/21/73. Big-voiced baritone/trumpeter/bandleader. *Pop Hits* & *Top Pop Singles*: 56.

| 5/15/65 | 132 | 1 | Queen Of The Senior Prom ..................................... *Blue Lady* | $8 | | Kapp 669 |
| | | | #39 hit for The Mills Brothers in 1957 | | | |

**MONTAN, Chris** ✪            AC
New Jersey native. Pop keyboardist/guitarist with Karla Bonoff from 1977-79.

| 2/28/81 | 106 | 3 | Let's Pick It Up (Where We Left Off) ..................... AC:17 *Empty Bed Blues* | $4 | | 20th Century 2480 |

**MONTANAS, The**            HOT
British pop/rock group.

| 10/26/68 | 121 | 4 | Run To Me ....................................................*You're Making A Big Mistake* | $10 | | Independence 89 |

**MONTE, Lou**            HOT/MEM/POP
Born on 4/2/17 in Lyndhurst, New Jersey. Vocalist/guitarist.

| 12/26/60 | 114 | 1 | 1 Dominick The Donkey (The Italian Christmas Donkey) .................................................. *Christmas At Our House* [X-N] | $12 | | Roulette 4308 |
| 6/9/62 | 109 | 3 | 2 Please Mr. Columbus (Turn The Ship Around) ................. *Addio, Addio (Good-Bye)* [N] | $10 | | Reprise 20,085 |
| 6/1/63 | 128 | 1 | 3 Bossa Nova Italiano ...................................................*Limbo Italiano* | $10 | | Reprise 20,171 |
| 6/20/64 | 131 | 1 | 4 Hello, Dolly! (Italian Style)............................ *Jungle Louie (The Italian Tarzan)* [F-N] | $10 | | Reprise 0284 |
| | | | #1 hit for Louis Armstrong in 1964 | | | |

**MONTECO** ✪            R&B
Born Monteco Turner on 9/16/78 in Mississippi; raised in New Orleans.

| 2/25/95 | 103 | 14 | Is It Me? ............................................. R&B:32 *(smooth edit)* | $3 | ▌ | MCA 54990 |
| | | | MONTECO featuring Immature | | | |

**MONTENEGRO, Hugo, His Orchestra And Chorus**            AC/HOT
Born in 1925; raised in New York City. Died on 2/6/81. Conductor/composer.

| 11/4/67 | 102 | 5 | 1 For A Few Dollars More .............................. *The Gentle Rain* [I] | $8 | | RCA Victor 9224 |
| | | | title song from the movie starring Clint Eastwood | | | |
| 2/15/69 | 112 | 4 | 2 Good Vibrations ........................................ *Tony's Theme* | $6 | | RCA Victor 9712 |
| | | | #1 hit for The Beach Boys in 1966 | | | |
| 5/31/69 | 112 | 9 | 3 Happy Together .................................... AC:29 *Lady In Cement* | $6 | | RCA Victor 0160 |
| | | | #1 hit for The Turtles in 1967 | | | |

**MONTEZ, Chris**            HOT/AC/R&B
Born Ezekiel Christopher Montanez on 1/17/43 in Los Angeles. Protege of Ritchie Valens.

| 4/7/62 | 108 | 1 | 1 All You Had To Do (Was Tell Me)......................*Love Me* | $15 | | Monogram 500 |
| 8/24/63 | 129 | 1 | 2 My Baby Loves To Dance ............................. *In An English Towne* | $15 | | Monogram 513 |
| | | | tune is similar to "Twist And Shout" | | | |
| 4/11/64 | 125 | 1 | 3 All You Had To Do (Was Tell Me)..................... *You're The One* [R] | $15 | | Monogram 517 |
| | | | CHRIS and KATHY (Chris Montez) (Kathy Young) | | | |
| 7/29/67 | 135 | 1 | 4 Foolin' Around ..................................................*Dindi (Jin-jee)* | $8 | | A&M 855 |

**MONTGOMERY, John Michael**            C&W/HOT
Born on 1/20/65 in Danville, Kentucky. Country singer/guitarist.

| 10/23/93 | 123 | 1 | 1 Beer And Bones ................................. C&W:21 *(3 album snippets)* | $3 | ▌ | Atlantic 87326 |
| 5/14/94 | 115 | 7 | 2 Rope The Moon.............................. Sls:63 /C&W:4 *(3 album snippets)* | $3 | ▌ | Atlantic 87248 |
| 10/7/95 | 112 | 7 | 3 No Man's Land ................................... C&W:3 *(3 album snippets)* | $3 | ▌ | Atlantic 87105 |
| 11/2/96 | 115 | 3 | 4 Ain't Got Nothin' On Us ................... C&W:15 *(3 album snippets)* | $3 | ▌ | Atlantic 87044 |
| 3/29/97 | 109 | 11 | 5 I Miss You A Little ............................. C&W:6 *(3 album snippets)* | $3 | ▌ | Atlantic 84865 |

**MONTGOMERY, Wes**            AC/HOT/R&B
Born John Leslie Montgomery on 3/6/25 in Indianapolis. Died on 6/15/68. Jazz guitarist.

| 3/30/68 | 103 | 5 | 1 Wind Song ................................... AC:36 *Goin' On To Detroit* [I] | $6 | | A&M/CTI 916 |
| 1/25/69 | 119 | 2 | 2 Where Have All The Flowers Gone? ......... AC:39 *Fly Me To The Moon* [I] | $6 | | A&M/CTI 1008 |
| | | | #21 hit for The Kingston Trio in 1962 | | | |

**MOODS, The** ⊘
R&B vocal group.

| 9/12/70 | 113 | 1 | Rainmaker .............................................................................*Lady Rain* $12 | | | Wand 11224 |

**MOODY BLUES, The**      HOT/ROK/AC
Rock band formed in 1964 in Birmingham, England. Main lineup featured Justin Hayward and John Lodge. *Top Pop Singles*: 21.

| 7/9/66 | 119 | 3 | 1 This Is My House (But Nobody Calls) ....................... *Boulevard De La Madeleine* $15 | | | London 1005 |
| 2/10/68 | 103 | 5 | 2 Nights In White Satin ............................................................... *Cities* $8 | | | Deram 85023 |

    a longer edit made the *Hot 100* (#2) on 8/5/72

**MOONEY, Art, And His Orchestra**      MEM/POP/HOT
Born in Lowell, Massachusetts. Leader of a Detroit-based dance band from the mid-1930s to 1940s.

| 6/8/59 | 107 | 2 | 1 Smile .................................................. *Art Mooney Theme (Sunset To Sunrise)* [I] $10 | | | MGM 12802 |

    #10 hit for **Nat King Cole** in 1954

| 12/31/60 | 108 | 2 | 2 I Ain't Down Yet ............................................................... *'Till Tomorrow* [I] $8 | | | MGM 12957 |

    from Broadway's *The Unsinkable Molly Brown* starring Tammy Grimes

**MOONGLOWS — see HARVEY**

**MOORE, Bob, And His Orchestra**      AC/HOT/R&B
Born on 11/30/32 in Nashville. Top session bass player. Led the band on Roy Orbison's sessions for Monument Records.

| 6/8/63 | 101[1] | 6 | Kentucky .......................................................... *The Flower Of Florence* [I] $10 | | | Monument 814 |

**MOORE, Chanté**      R&B/HOT
Female R&B singer. Native of San Francisco. Moved to San Diego at age 12.

| 4/17/93 | 108 | 10 | It's Alright ................................................ R&B:13 *(3 album snippets)* $3 | ■ | | Silas/MCA 54558 |

**MOORE, Dorothy**      R&B/HOT/AC
Born in 1946 in Jackson, Mississippi. Lead singer of The Poppies. Also a popular gospel artist.

| 1/21/78 | 101[2] | 10 | With Pen In Hand     R&B:12 *Too Blind To See* $6 | | | Malaco 1047 |

    written by **Bobby Goldsboro**; #35 hit for **Vikki Carr** in 1969

**MOORE, Gary**      ROK/HOT/AC
Born on 4/4/52 in Belfast, Ireland. Rock guitarist with Thin Lizzy (1974, 1978-79).

| 5/28/83 | 103 | 5 | 1 Always Gonna' Love You ...................................................... *Rockin Every Night* $4 | | | Mirage 99896 |
| 7/23/83 | 110 | 1 | 2 Falling In Love With You ................................................................ *Gonna Break* $4 | | | Mirage 99856 |

**MOORE, Jackie**      R&B/HOT
Female R&B singer from Jacksonville, Florida.

| 3/25/72 | 106 | 5 | 1 Darling Baby ............................................... R&B:22 *Something In A Look* $6 | | | Atlantic 2861 |

    #72 hit for **The Elgins** in 1966

| 11/17/73 | 102 | 13 | 2 Both Ends Against The Middle .................. R&B:28 *Clean Up Your Own Yard* $6 | | | Atlantic 2989 |

**MOORE, Melba**      R&B/HOT
Born Melba Hill on 10/29/45 in New York City. Soul singer/actress.

| 5/30/70 | 111 | 4 | 1 I Got Love ............................................................ *I Love Making Love To You* $7 | | | Mercury 73072 |
| 3/5/77 | 108 | 1 | 2 The Way You Make Me Feel ...................... R&B:62 *So Many Mountains* $5 | | | Buddah 562 |
| 4/28/79 | 103 | 5 | 3 Pick Me Up, I'll Dance     R&B:85 *Where Did You Ever Go* $4 | | | Epic 50663 |
| 11/6/82 | 104 | 4 | 4 Love's Comin' At Ya ...................................... R&B:5 *(instrumental)* $4 | | | EMI America 8126 |
| 3/17/84 | 108 | 3 | 5 Livin' For Your Love ........................... R&B:6 *Got To Have Your Love* $3 | ■ | | Capitol 5308 |
| 4/13/85 | 104 | 5 | 6 Read My Lips ..................................... R&B:12 *Got To Have Your Love* $3 | ■ | | Capitol 5437 |
| 6/29/85 | 106 | 3 | 7 When You Love Me Like This................... R&B:14 *Winner* [I] $3 | ■ | | Capitol 5484 |

**MOORE, Tina** ⊘      R&B
Born and raised in Milwaukee. Attended the Wisconsin Conservatory Of Music.

| 7/29/95 | 112 | 5 | Never Gonna Let You Go................... R&B:27 *Color Me Blue (R&B #73/'94)* $3 | ■ | | Scotti Brothers 78019 |

**MOREING, Jody** ⊘

| 8/15/81 | 103 | 1 | All Girls Want It ............................................ *Make Love, Don't Break Love* $4 | | | Boardwalk 113 |

**MORGAN, Jane**      AC/HOT/C&W
Born Jane Currier in Boston in 1920; raised in Florida. Died in 1974. Popular nightclub entertainer.

| 7/27/59 | 113 | 1 | 1 I Can't Begin To Tell You     *With Open Arms (Hot #39)* $10 | ■ | | Kapp 284 |

    #1 hit for **Bing Crosby** in 1945

| 2/6/61 | 115 | 2 | 2 In Jerusalem ................................................................. *(French version)* $8 | ■ | | Kapp 369 |
| 12/28/63 | 131 | 1 | 3 Bless 'Em All ................................... *Does Goodnight Mean Goodbye* $8 | ■ | | Colpix 713 |

    from the movie *The Victors* starring George Hamilton; #25 hit for Barry Wood & The King Sisters in 1941

| 6/18/66 | 135 | 1 | 4 1-2-3 ........................................................ AC:16 *Kiss Away* $7 | ☐ | | Epic 10032 |

    #2 hit for **Len Barry** in 1965

| 1/28/67 | 121 | 2 | 5 Kiss Tomorrow Goodbye (Capri C'est Fini)........................... AC:30 *Now And Forever* $7 | | | Epic 10113 |

**MORGAN, Jaye P.**      HOT/MEM/AC
Born Mary Margaret Morgan on 12/3/31 in Mancos, Colorado. Sang with Frank DeVol's band from 1950-53. *Top Pop Singles*: 20.

| 6/16/62 | 119 | 1 | 1 A Heartache Named Johnny .......................................... *He Thinks I Still Care* $8 | | | MGM 13076 |
| 8/21/71 | 105 | 3 | 2 A Song For You ............................................... *Do You Really Have A Heart* $7 | | | Beverly Hills 9367 |

    written by **Leon Russell**; #82 hit for **Andy Williams** in 1971

**MORGAN, Lorrie**      C&W/HOT
Born Loretta Lynn Morgan on 6/27/59. Country singer. Youngest daughter of George Morgan. Married Jon Randall on 11/16/96.

| 6/22/96 | 110 | 8 | By My Side ................................................. C&W:18 *Candy Kisses* $3 | ■ | | BNA 64512 |

    LORRIE MORGAN & JON RANDALL

**MORODER, Giorgio — see GIORGIO**

**MORRIS, Russell** ⊘
Pop/rock singer from Australia.

| 8/9/69 | 107 | 2 | The Real Thing (Part I) ..................................................................... *(Part II)* $12 | | | Diamond 263 |

| DEBUT | PEAK | WKS | A-side (Chart Hit)..........................................................................................B-side | $ | Pic | Label & Number |
|---|---|---|---|---|---|---|

**MORRISON, Dorothy** — HOT/R&B
Born in 1945 in Longview, Texas. Former lead vocalist with **The Edwin Hawkins' Singers.**

| 8/15/70 | 114 | 1 | Border Song (Holy Moses) .......................... R&B:43 *Brand New Day* | $7 | | Buddah 184 |

written by Elton John; #37 hit for **Aretha Franklin** in 1970

**MORRISON, Mark** — R&B/HOT
Born in Hanover, Germany; raised in Leicester, England. R&B singer.

| 9/6/97 | 102 | 10 | Crazy ..................................................... R&B:67 *(instrumental)* | $3 | ▪ | Atlantic 84032 |

**MORRISON, Van** — HOT/ROK/AC
Born George Ivan on 8/31/45 in Belfast, Ireland. Blue-eyed soul singer/songwriter. Leader of **Them.** Wrote the classic hit "Gloria." Inducted into the Rock and Roll Hall of Fame in 1993.

| 11/4/67 | 107 | 2 | 1 Ro Ro Rosey ........................................ *Chick - A - Boom* | $10 | | Bang 552 |
| 4/1/72 | 119 | 2 | 2 (Straight to Your Heart) Like A Cannonball .................. *Old Old Woodstock* | $6 | | Warner 7573 |
| 1/13/73 | 101² | 4 | 3 Gypsy ................................................. *Saint Dominic's Preview* | $6 | | Warner 7665 |
| 11/3/79 | 110 | 1 | 4 Bright Side Of The Road .................................... *Rolling Hills* | $5 | | Warner 49086 |
| 3/30/85 | 101¹ | 4 | 5 Tore Down A La Rimbaud         ROK:19 *Haunts Of Ancient Peace* | $4 | | Mercury 880669 |

**MORRISSEY** — ROK/HOT
Born Stephen Morrissey on 5/22/59 in Davyhulme, Lancashire, England. Former lead singer/songwriter of The Smiths.

| 2/18/95 | 118 | 2 | 1 Boxers ............... *Have-A-Go Merchant / Whatever Happens, I Love You* | $6 | | Sire/Reprise 41914 (CD) |
| 8/23/97 | 109 | 2 | 2 Alma Matters ................... *Heir Apparent / I Can Have Both* | $6 | | Mercury 574757 (CD) |

**MOTELS** — HOT/ROK/AC
Pop-rock group formed in Los Angeles in 1978 featuring Martha Davis (vocals).

| 12/8/79 | 109 | 1 | Total Control ...................................... *Love Don't Help* | $5 | | Capitol 4796 |

**MOTHERLODE** ☉ — HOT
Pop quartet from Canada featuring William "Smitty" Smith (vocals, keyboards; d: 12/1/97, age 53).

| 11/29/69 | 111 | 1 | 1 What Does It Take (To Win Your Love)/ | | | |

#4 hit for **Jr. Walker & The All Stars** in 1969

| 11/8/69 | 116 | 2 | 2   Memories Of A Broken Promise ...................................... | $8 | | Buddah 144 |

**MOULTRIE, Mattie** ☉
R&B songstress.

| 1/21/67 | 132 | 2 | That's How Strong My Love Is ............... *The Saddest Story Ever Told* | $12 | | Columbia 43857 |

#74 hit for **Otis Redding** in 1965

**MOUNTAIN** — HOT
New York power-rock group led by Leslie West (b: 10/22/45) and Felix Pappalardi (b: 1939; d: 4/17/83).

| 9/12/70 | 107 | 6 | For Yasgur's Farm ...................................... *To My Friend* | $7 | | Windfall 533 |

Yasgur: man whose land hosted the Woodstock rock festival

**MOUSE** ☉
Mouse is Texas-bred singer Ronnie Weiss who later joined country band Rio Grande.

| 2/26/66 | 121 | 4 | 1 A Public Execution ...................................... *All For You* | $25 | | Fraternity 956 |

tune is similar to **Bob Dylan's** "Like A Rolling Stone"

| 6/8/68 | 125 | 1 | 2 Sometimes You Just Can't Win ........................... *Cryin' Inside* | $20 | ☐ | Fraternity 1005 |

**MOUSE And The Traps**

**MOVERS, The** ☉

| 9/14/68 | 116 | 5 | Birmingham ...................................... *Leave Me Loose* | $20 | | 1-2-3 1700 |

written by Tommy Roe

**M PEOPLE** — HOT
Dance trio: Michael Pickering (from Manchester, England), Heather Small and Paul Heard (both from London).

| 9/17/94 | 125 | 1 | 1 One Night In Heaven................................... *(radio mix)* | $3 | ▪ | Epic 77616 |
| 5/20/95 | 125 | 1 | 2 Open Your Heart ...................................... *(radio edit)* | $3 | ▪ | Epic 77884 |

**MTS**
Dance trio: Melissa Hamm, Tonia Lee and Tony Delaney.

| 4/27/96 | 102 | 26 | I'll Be Alright................................... *(3 album snippets)* | $3 | ▪ | Summit 5454 |

**MTUME** — R&B/HOT
Progressive funk band, led by Philadelphian James Mtume (pronounced: EM-too-may), featuring female vocalist Tawatha Agee.

| 11/17/84 | 104 | 2 | C.O.D. (I'll Deliver) ............................. R&B:20 *(instrumental)* | $4 | | Epic 04657 |

**MUGWUMPS, The** ☉
Group which both formed and disbanded in 1964 included John Sebastian and **Zalman Yanovsky** of **The Lovin' Spoonful** and Cass Elliot and Denny Doherty of **The Mamas & The Papas.**

| 9/3/66 | 127 | 3 | Jug Band Music ...................................... *Bald Headed Woman* | $25 | | Sidewalk 900 |

recorded in 1964

**MUHAMMAD, Idris** — R&B/HOT
Born Leo Morris in New Orleans in 1939. Prolific R&B session drummer since the early '60s.

| 8/27/77 | 102 | 5 | Turn This Mutha Out (Part 1) ........................... R&B:21 *(Part 2)* | $5 | | Kudu 940 |

**MULLINS, Dee** ☉ — C&W
Born on 4/7/37 in Gafford, Texas. Died on 3/13/91. Male country vocalist. Sang in duo with his sister.

| 11/23/68 | 111 | 2 | The Continuing Story Of Harper Valley P.T.A. ................ *Satisfied Old Man* | $7 | | SSS International 749 |

follow-up tune to **Jeannie C. Riley's** #1 hit in 1968

**MURMAIDS, The** — HOT/AC
Los Angeles pop teenage trio: sisters Carol and Terry Fischer, with Sally Gordon.

| 3/14/64 | 116 | 2 | Heartbreak Ahead ...................................... *He's Good To Me* | $12 | | Chattahoochee 636 |

written by David Gates of Bread

**MURPHEY, Michael** — C&W/AC/HOT
Born Michael Martin Murphey on 5/5/38 in Dallas. Country singer/songwriter. Toured as Travis Lewis of **The Lewis & Clarke Expedition.**

| 10/22/83 | 106 | 2 | Don't Count The Rainy Days ............... C&W:9 / AC:16 *The Heart Never Lies* | $4 | ▪ | Liberty 1505 |

**MURPHY, Eddie**                                                                                    R&B/HOT
Born on 4/3/61 in Hempstead, New York. Comedian/actor. Former cast member of TV's *Saturday Night Live*. Starred in numerous movies.

| 5/8/93 | 121 | 2 | Whatzupwitu .............................................................. R&B:74 *(instrumental)* | $3 | ▌ | Motown 2205 |

Michael Jackson (guest vocal)

**MURPHY, Mark ☺**
Born on 3/14/32 in Syracuse, New York. Settled in London in the early 1960's. Jazz singer/actor discovered in 1952 by **Sammy Davis, Jr.**

| 1/19/63 | 123 | 1 | Fly Me To The Moon (In Other Words) ...................................... *Why Don't You Do Right?* | $10 | | Riverside 4526 |

#14 hit for Joe Harnell in 1963

**MURPHY, Walter**                                                                                    AC/HOT/R&B
Born in 1952 in New York City. Former arranger for **Doc Severinsen** and *The Tonight Show* orchestra.

| 4/30/77 | 102 | 9 | Rhapsody In Blue................................................... AC:36 *Fish Legs* [I] | $5 | | Private Stock 45,146 |

#3 hit for Paul Whiteman with George Gershwin in 1924

**MURRAY, Anne**                                                                                    C&W/AC/HOT
Born Morna Anne Murray on 6/20/45 in Springhill, Nova Scotia, Canada. Regular on **Glen Campbell**'s *Goodtime Hour* TV series.
*Top Pop Singles*: 28.

| 3/6/71 | 122 | 2 | 1 A Stranger In My Place ......................................... C&W:27 *Sycamore Slick* | $6 | | Capitol 3059 |
| | | | written by **Kenny Rogers**; re-entered the Country charts (#79) in 1975 on Capitol 4072 | | | |
| 4/1/78 | 103 | 4 | 2 Walk Right Back ..................................................... C&W:4 / AC:15 *A Million More* | $5 | | Capitol 4527 |
| | | | #7 hit for **The Everly Brothers** in 1961 | | | |
| 3/10/84 | 106 | 2 | 3 That's Not The Way (It's S'posed To Be) ..................... AC:12 /C&W:46 *The More We Try* | $4 | | Capitol 5305 |
| 10/13/84 | 103 | 6 | 4 Nobody Loves Me Like You Do ......... C&W:❶[1] / AC:10 *Love You Out Of Your Mind* (Murray) | $4 | ■ | Capitol 5401 |

**ANNE MURRAY (WITH DAVE LOGGINS)**

**MURRAY, Keith**                                                                                    R&B/HOT
Born in 1972 in Long Island, New York. Male rapper. Also see **Erick Sermon**.

| 10/19/96 | 114 | 6 | The Rhyme................................................. R&B:59 *(3 versions) / Yeah* | $6 | ■ | Jive 42405 (T) |

samples "Before I Let You Go" by **Maze** and "Sucker MC's" by **Run-D.M.C.**

**MUSCLE SHOALS HORNS ☺**                                                              R&B
Studio band from Muscle Shoals, Alabama.

| 3/20/76 | 105 | 1 | Born To Get Down (Born To Mess Around) ...................... R&B:8 *Hustle To The Music* | $5 | | Bang 721 |

**MUSIC EXPLOSION, The**                                                              HOT
Pop-rock group from Mansfield, Ohio: James Lyons (vocals), Don Atkins and Richard Nesta (guitars), Burton Sahl (bass) and Bob Avery (drums).

| 10/14/67 | 103 | 6 | 1 We Gotta Go Home ............................................. *Hearts And Flowers* | $12 | | Laurie 3414 |
| 2/10/68 | 119 | 2 | 2 What You Want (Baby I Want You) ........................................ *Road Runner* | $12 | | Laurie 3429 |
| 7/6/68 | 120 | 2 | 3 Yes Sir ..................................................................... *Dazzling* | $12 | | Laurie 3454 |

**MUSIC MACHINE, The**                                                              HOT
Rock quintet from Los Angeles: Sean Bonniwell (vocals, guitar), Mark Landon (guitar), Doug Rhodes (organ), Keith Olsen (bass) and Ron Edgar (drums).

| 5/13/67 | 111 | 2 | Double Yellow Line ................................................ *Absolutley Positively* | $12 | | Original Sound 71 |

**MYERS, Alicia ☺**                                                                  R&B
Former lead singer of One Way.

| 10/6/84 | 105 | 3 | You Get The Best From Me (say, say, say) ................... R&B:5 *I Want To Thank You* | $4 | | MCA 52425 |

**MYRICK, Gary ☺**
Rock guitarist from Texas. Joined British group Havana 3 A.M. in 1991.

| 8/6/83 | 103 | 2 | Message Is You ...................................................... *Glamorous* | $4 | | Epic 04009 |

**MYSTERY TOUR, The ☺**
| 11/29/69 | 104 | 1 | The Ballad Of Paul ........................... *The Ballad Of Paul (Follow The Bouncing Ball)* | $20 | | MGM 14097 |

a story about the rumored death of **Paul McCartney**

**MYSTIC MOODS ORCHESTRA, The**                                                    AC/HOT/R&B
Hollywood studio group produced by Brad Miller. Had a series of "mood music" charted albums. Also see **Leo & Libra**.

| 12/25/71 | 106 | 1 | Sensuous Woman ...................................... AC:21 *Another Dawn (with you)* [I] | $6 | | Warner 7534 |

melody is similar to **Sergio Mendes**' "The Look Of Love"

**MYSTICS, The**                                                                    HOT
Quintet from Brooklyn: Phil Cracolici (lead), Bob Ferrante & George Galfo (tenors), Albee Cracolici (baritone) and Allie Contrera (bass).

| 2/29/60 | 107 | 2 | All Through The Night ...................................... *(I Begin) To Think Again Of You* | $25 | | Laurie 3047 |

**Paul Simon** (guest vocalist); traditional tune written in 1784

**MYSTICS, The ☺**
Seven-man rock band.

| 8/23/69 | 116 | 2 | Pain.................................................................. *But It's Alright* | $10 | | Metromedia 130 |

**MYSTIKAL ☺**                                                                      R&B
Male rapper from New Orleans. Also see **RBL Posse**.

| 9/30/95 | 106 | 15 | Y'all Ain't Ready Yet ........................................ R&B:41 *(2 versions) / Beware* | $3 | ▌ | Big Boy/Jive 42331 |

# N

**NADANUF** ☉      R&B
Female rap duo from Cincinnati: Skwert Diggety and Phor-One-One.

| DEBUT | PEAK | WKS | A-side / B-side | $ | Pic | Label & Number |
|---|---|---|---|---|---|---|
| 11/15/97 | **115** | 4 | The Breaks .................................................... R&B:58 *Many Emcees (Madd Drama)* | $3 | ▌ | Reprise 17310 |

NADANUF featuring Kurtis Blow
new version of Kurtis Blow's #87 hit in 1980

**NAPOLI & GLASSON** ☉
Jeanne Napoli and Barbara Glasson, formerly known as the PJ's.

| | | | | | | |
|---|---|---|---|---|---|---|
| 10/4/75 | **106** | 2 | Il Est Toujours Temps Pour Partir (Never Can Say Goodbye)........................................... *Tired Of Writing Songs* [F] | $6 | | Vigor 1725 |

#9 hit for Gloria Gaynor in 1975

**NAS**      R&B/HOT
Born Nasir Jones. Male rapper. Native of Long Island City, New York. Also known as Nasty Nas.

| | | | | | | |
|---|---|---|---|---|---|---|
| 6/18/94 | **114** | 7 | The World Is Yours ............................................ R&B:67 *(instrumental)* | $3 | ▌ | Columbia 77514 |

samples "It's Yours" by T La Rock

**NASH, Graham**      HOT/ROK
Born on 2/2/42 in Blackpool, England. Co-founding member/guitarist of **The Hollies**. Formed Crosby, Stills & Nash in 1970.

| | | | | | | |
|---|---|---|---|---|---|---|
| 11/27/71 | **111** | 2 | 1 Used To Be A King ............................................ *Wounded Bird* | $6 | | Atlantic 2840 |
| 10/9/76 | **109** | 1 | 2 Spotlight ...................................................... *Foolish Man* | $5 | | ABC 12217 |

DAVID CROSBY/GRAHAM NASH

**NASH, Johnny**      HOT/R&B/AC
Born on 8/19/40 in Houston. Vocalist/guitarist/actor. Own JoDa label in 1965.

| | | | | | | |
|---|---|---|---|---|---|---|
| 2/13/61 | **104** | 4 | 1 Some Of Your Lovin' ...................................... *World Of Tears* | $15 | | ABC-Paramount 10181 |

written and produced by Phil Spector

| | | | | | | |
|---|---|---|---|---|---|---|
| 9/15/62 | **120** | 1 | 2 Ol' Man River ............................................... *My Dear Little Sweetheart* | $12 | | Warner 5301 |

from the 1927 musical *Show Boat*

| | | | | | | |
|---|---|---|---|---|---|---|
| 3/28/64 | **120** | 2 | 3 I'm Leaving ................................................... *Oh Mary Don't You Weep* | $10 | | Groove 0030 |
| 5/21/66 | **120** | 2 | 4 Somewhere ............................................... R&B:35 *Big City* | $10 | | Joda 106 |

from the 1957 musical *West Side Story*

| | | | | | | |
|---|---|---|---|---|---|---|
| 2/15/69 | **130** | 2 | 5 Lovey Dovey .................................................. *You Got Soul* | $10 | | JAD 214 |

B-side made the Hot 100 (#58) on 12/14/68 on JAD 209; #25 hit for **Buddy Knox** in 1961

| | | | | | | |
|---|---|---|---|---|---|---|
| 5/10/69 | **135** | 1 | 6 We Try Harder ............................................... *My Time* | $10 | | Banyan Tree 1001 |

KIM WESTON JOHNNY NASH

| | | | | | | |
|---|---|---|---|---|---|---|
| 8/9/69 | **132** | 2 | 7 Love And Peace ............................................. *People In Love* | $8 | | JAD 218 |
| 3/28/70 | **102** | 5 | 8 (What A) Groovey Feeling          *You Got Soul-Pt 1* | $8 | | JAD 223 |
| 9/29/73 | **103** | 11 | 9 Ooh What A Feeling ...................................... AC:38 *Yellow House* [R] | $6 | | Epic 11034 |

above 2 are different versions of the same song

| | | | | | | |
|---|---|---|---|---|---|---|
| 11/9/74 | **105** | 1 | 10 You Can't Go Halfway ..................................... R&B:38 *The Very First Time* | $6 | | Epic 50021 |
| 5/15/76 | **103** | 4 | 11 (What A) Wonderful World ............... AC:34 /R&B:66 *Rock It Baby (Baby We've Got A Date)* | $6 | | Epic 50219 |

#12 hit for **Sam Cooke** in 1960

**NASHVILLE BRASS — see DAVIS, Danny**

**NASHVILLE TEENS, The**      HOT
Rock group from Weybridge, Surrey, England featuring Arthur Sharp (vocals).

| | | | | | | |
|---|---|---|---|---|---|---|
| 12/12/64 | **117** | 3 | 1 Google Eye .................................................... *T. N. T.* | $12 | | London 9712 |
| 6/12/65 | **123** | 3 | 2 The Little Bird............................................... *Whatcha Gonna Do* | $10 | | MGM 13357 |

above 2 written by John D. Loudermilk

**NASTYBOY KLICK** ☉      R&B
Latin rap group from Phoenix: Marco "MC Magic" Cadenas and his son Li'l Mischief, Sly, Zig Zag, Dos and Bookie-Loc.

| | | | | | | |
|---|---|---|---|---|---|---|
| 12/13/97+ | **103** | 7 | AZ Side ........................................................ *(album version)* | $3 | ▌ | Glass Note 568248 |

NASTYBOY KLICK featuring Mandi
samples "Everybody" by **Madonna**

**NATÉ, Ultra**      HOT
Pronounced: Na-TAY. Female dance singer from Baltimore.

| | | | | | | |
|---|---|---|---|---|---|---|
| 12/11/93 | **122** | 2 | Show Me ........................................................ *Joy* | $3 | ▌ | Warner 18285 |

**NAUGHTY BY NATURE**      R&B/HOT
Rap trio from East Orange, New Jersey: Anthony "Treach" Criss, Vincent Brown and Kier "dj KG" Gist.

| | | | | | | |
|---|---|---|---|---|---|---|
| 9/23/95 | **105** | 8 | Clap Yo Hands ............................................... R&B:70 *(remix)* | $3 | ▌ | Tommy Boy 7703 |

samples "Eric B. Is President" by Eric B. & **Rakim** and "I Thank You" by **Sam & Dave**

**NAZARETH**      HOT/ROK
Hard-rock group formed in Scotland in 1969 featuring Dan McCafferty (lead singer).

| | | | | | | |
|---|---|---|---|---|---|---|
| 7/31/82 | **105** | 2 | Love Leads To Madness ................................... ROK:19 *Take The Rap* | $4 | | A&M 2421 |

**NAZZ**      HOT
Rock quartet from Philadelphia: **Todd Rundgren** (guitar), Robert "Stewkey" Antoni (vocals), Carson Van Osten (bass) and Thom Mooney (drums).

| | | | | | | |
|---|---|---|---|---|---|---|
| 9/21/68 | **112** | 1 | Open My Eyes ................................................ *Hello It's Me* (Hot #66) | $12 | ■ | SGC 001 |

**NDEGÉOCELLO, Me'Shell**      R&B/HOT/AC
Born on 8/29/69 in Berlin; raised in Oxon Hill, Maryland. Female singer/bassist. Last name (pronounced: Nuh-DAY-gay-O-CHEL-lo).

| | | | | | | |
|---|---|---|---|---|---|---|
| 5/21/94 | **113** | 3 | 1 Outside Your Door .......................................... R&B:41 *(remix)* | $3 | ▌ | Maverick/Sire 18176 |
| 11/23/96 | **102** | 14 | 2 Never Miss The Water .................... R&B:36 *(remix) / Papillon (aka Hot Butterfly)* | $3 | ▌ | Reprise 17503 |

CHAKA KHAN Featuring Me'Shell NdegéOcello

**NEELEY, Ted** ☉
Singer/actor. Starred in the movie version of *Jesus Christ Superstar*.

| | | | | | | |
|---|---|---|---|---|---|---|
| 6/14/75 | **102** | 4 | Paradise ....................................................... *Don't Let It Mess Your Mind* | $5 | ☐ | United Artists 644 |

| DEBUT | PEAK | WKS | A-side (Chart Hit).................................................................................B-side | $ | Pic | Label & Number |
|---|---|---|---|---|---|---|
| | | | **NEELY, Sam**  C&W/HOT/AC | | | |
| | | | Born on 8/22/48 in Cuero, Texas. Pop/country singer/songwriter. | | | |
| 5/25/74 | 103 | 5 | Sadie Take A Lover .................................................. *Come A Little Bit Closer* | $5 | | A&M 1523 |
| | | | **NEIGHBORHOOD, The**  HOT/AC | | | |
| | | | Seven-man, two-woman pop vocal group. | | | |
| 10/3/70 | 104 | 3 | Laugh .................................................... *Now's The Time For Love* | $7 | | Big Tree 106 |
| | | | **NELSON**  HOT/ROK | | | |
| | | | Gunnar (vocals, bass) and Matthew Nelson (vocals, rhythm guitar), the identical twin sons (b: 9/20/67) of the late **Rick Nelson**. | | | |
| 6/3/95 | 102 | 9 | (You Got Me) All Shook Up ....................................... *After The Rain '95* | $3 | ▌ | DGC 19386 |
| | | | **NELSON, Rick**  HOT/R&B/AC/C&W | | | |
| | | | Born Eric Hilliard Nelson on 5/8/40 in Teaneck, New Jersey. Died on 12/31/85 in a plane crash in DeKalb, Texas. Son of bandleader Ozzie Nelson and vocalist Harriet Hilliard. Rick appeared on Ozzie's radio and TV series from 1949-66. Inducted into the Rock and Roll Hall of Fame in 1987. *Top Pop Singles:* 54. | | | |
| 8/25/62 | 105 | 2 | 1 I've Got My Eyes On You (And I Like What I See)..................... *Teen Age Idol* (Hot #5) | $20 | ▌ | Imperial 5864 |
| 6/29/63 | 120 | 4 | 2 A Long Vacation..................................................... *Mad Mad World* | $20 | | Imperial 5958 |
| | | | originally released on the 1959 album *Songs By Ricky*; written by **Dorsey Burnette** (also #6 below) | | | |
| 9/7/63 | 127 | 1 | 3 There's Not A Minute ............................................... *Time After Time* | $20 | | Imperial 5985 |
| 10/19/63 | 126 | 1 | 4 Down Home ......................................................... *Fools Rush In* (Hot #12) | $15 | ▌ | Decca 31533 |
| 7/4/64 | 127 | 1 | 5 Lucky Star............................................................ *Everybody But Me* | $15 | | Imperial 66039 |
| | | | originally released on the 1961 album *Rick Is 21* | | | |
| 8/29/64 | 113 | 1 | 6 Lonely Corner.......................................... *There's Nothing I Can Say* (Hot #47) | $12 | ▌ | Decca 31656 |
| 7/3/65 | 130 | 1 | 7 Come Out Dancin'.................................................... *Yesterday's Love* | $12 | ▌ | Decca 31800 |
| 6/18/66 | 108 | 5 | 8 You Just Can't Quit ................................................. *Louisiana Man* | $12 | ▌ | Decca 31956 |
| 5/16/70 | 102 | 2 | 9 I Shall Be Released .............................................. *If You Gotta Go, Go Now* | $10 | | Decca 32676 |
| | | | written by **Bob Dylan**; #67 hit for the Box Tops in 1969 | | | |
| 2/27/71 | 109 | 1 | 10 Life ........................................................ AC:15  *California* | $10 | | Decca 32779 |
| | | | **RICK NELSON and The Stone Canyon Band** | | | |
| | | | **NELSON, Sandy**  HOT/R&B | | | |
| | | | Born Sander Nelson on 12/1/38 in Santa Monica, California. Rock and roll drummer. | | | |
| 9/15/62 | 101[1] | 2 | 1 Live It Up .................................. *...And Then There Were Drums* (Hot #65) [I] | $12 | | Imperial 5870 |
| 12/29/62 | 107 | 2 | 2 Let The Four Winds Blow....................................... *Be Bop Baby* [I] | $12 | | Imperial 5904 |
| | | | #15 hit for Fats Domino in 1961 | | | |
| 3/13/65 | 133 | 2 | 3 Reach For A Star ...................................................... *Chop-Chop* [I] | $10 | | Imperial 66093 |
| 5/22/65 | 120 | 3 | 4 Let There Be Drums '66.................................... *Land Of 1000 Dances* [I-R] | $10 | | Imperial 66107 |
| | | | "live" version of Nelson's #7 hit in 1961 on Imperial 5775 | | | |
| 9/18/65 | 124 | 1 | 5 Drums A Go-Go ........................................................ *Casbah* [I] | $10 | | Imperial 66127 |
| 6/7/69 | 119 | 2 | 6 Manhattan Spiritual .................................................. *The Stripper* [I] | $8 | | Imperial 66375 |
| | | | #10 hit for Reg Owen in 1959 | | | |
| | | | **NELSON, Shara** ⊙ | | | |
| 5/20/95 | 109 | 5 | Down That Road ..................................................... *(remix)* | $3 | ▌ | Chrysalis/EMI 58404 |
| | | | **NELSON, Willie**  C&W/AC/HOT | | | |
| | | | Born on 4/30/33 in Ft. Worth, Texas. Prolific country singer/songwriter/actor. Pioneered the "outlaw" country movement. Won Grammy's Living Legends Award in 1989. Elected to the Country Music Hall of Fame in 1993. | | | |
| 6/23/62 | 109 | 2 | 1 Touch Me .............................................. C&W:7  *Where My House Lives* | $15 | | Liberty 55439 |
| 3/30/63 | 129 | 1 | 2 Half A Man............................................... C&W:25  *The Last Letter* | $15 | | Liberty 55532 |
| 4/17/76 | 101[2] | 4 | 3 I Gotta Get Drunk .................................... C&W:55  *Summer Of Roses* | $7 | | RCA Victor 10591 |
| | | | "live" recording | | | |
| 4/1/78 | 104 | 3 | 4 If You Can Touch Her At All ............................ C&W:5  *Rainy Day Blues* | $5 | | RCA 11235 |
| 2/12/83 | 102 | 4 | 5 Everything's Beautiful (In It's Own Way).......... C&W:7 / AC:19  *Put It Off Until Tomorrow* (**Dolly Parton** Kris Kristofferson) | $5 | | Monument 03408 |
| | | | **DOLLY PARTON  WILLIE NELSON** | | | |
| 10/8/83 | 102 | 4 | 6 Take It To The Limit...................... C&W:8 / AC:31  *Till I Gain Control Again* | $4 | ▌ | Columbia 04131 |
| | | | **WILLIE NELSON & WAYLON JENNINGS** | | | |
| | | | #4 hit for the Eagles in 1976 | | | |
| | | | **NENA**  HOT/ROK/AC | | | |
| | | | Rock quintet formed in 1980 in Berlin, Germany featuring Gabriele "Nena" Kerner (vocals). | | | |
| 5/5/84 | 102 | 1 | Just A Dream ....................................................... *Rette Mich* | $4 | | Epic 04440 |
| | | | **NEON PHILHARMONIC, The**  HOT/AC | | | |
| | | | Chamber-sized orchestra of Nashville Symphony Orchestra musicians. | | | |
| 8/9/69 | 120 | 3 | No One Is Going To Hurt You ......................................... *You Lied* | $6 | | Warner 7311 |
| | | | featuring Don Gant (vocal) and Tupper Saussy (conductor) | | | |
| | | | **NERO, Peter**  AC/HOT | | | |
| | | | Born on 5/22/34 in Brooklyn. Pop-jazz-classical pianist. Won the 1961 Best New Artist Grammy Award. | | | |
| 2/19/72 | 105 | 4 | Brian's Song ............................................ AC:30  *Just For Her* [I] | $4 | | Columbia 45544 |
| | | | theme from the TV movie *Brian's Song* starring James Caan; #56 hit for Michel LeGrand in 1972 | | | |
| | | | **NEVILLE, Aaron**  AC/HOT/R&B/C&W | | | |
| | | | Born on 1/24/41 in New Orleans. Member of the New Orleans family group, The Neville Brothers. Brother Art was keyboardist of The Meters. Bassist/singer Ivan Neville is his son. | | | |
| 8/15/60 | 111 | 2 | 1 Over You ............................................... R&B:21  *Every Day* | $20 | | Minit 612 |
| | | | label misspelled first name as: Arron | | | |
| 6/25/94 | 122 | 3 | 2 Even If My Heart Would Break .................... AC:28  *The Joy of Life* (Kenny G) | $3 | ▌ | Arista 12674 |
| | | | **KENNY G with Aaron Neville** | | | |

| | | | | | | |
|---|---|---|---|---|---|---|

**NEWBEATS, The**  *HOT*
Pop trio: Larry Henley (b: 6/30/41; lead singer) with brothers Dean (b: 3/17/39) and Marc (b: 2/9/42) Mathis.

| DEBUT | PEAK | WKS | A-side / B-side | $ | Pic | Label & Number |
|---|---|---|---|---|---|---|
| 1/23/65 | 118 | 1 | 1 Hey-O-Daddy-O ........................................... *Break Away (From That Boy)* (Hot #40) | $10 | | Hickory 1290 |
| 6/28/69 | 128 | 2 | 2 Thou Shalt Not Steal .......................................................... *Great Balls Of Fire* | $10 | | Hickory 1539 |
| | | | #13 hit for **Dick & DeeDee** in 1965 | | | |
| 3/7/70 | 115 | 2 | 3 Laura (What's He Got That I Ain't Got) ....................... *Break Away (From That Boy)* | $10 | | Hickory 1562 |
| | | | #1 Country hit for **Leon Ashley** in 1967 | | | |

**NEWBURY, Mickey**  *C&W/HOT/AC*
Born Milton S. Newbury, Jr. on 5/19/40 in Houston. Worked as a staff writer for Acuff-Rose in Nashville.

| | | | | | | |
|---|---|---|---|---|---|---|
| 3/3/73 | 103 | 4 | Heaven Help The Child ................................................... *Good Morning Dear* | $5 | | Elektra 45840 |

**NEW CHRISTY MINSTRELS, The**  *HOT/AC*
Folk/balladeer troupe named after the Christy Minstrels (formed in 1842 by Edwin "Pop" Christy). Group founded and led by **Randy Sparks**. Also see **Back Porch Majority**.

| | | | | | | |
|---|---|---|---|---|---|---|
| 3/2/63 | 127 | 2 | 1 Denver ................................................................................ *Liza Lee* | $8 | | Columbia 42673 |
| 1/2/65 | 111 | 2 | 2 Gotta Get A'Goin' ............................................................ *Down The Road I Go* | $6 | | Columbia 43178 |
| 2/8/69 | 114 | 3 | 3 Chitty Chitty Bang Bang ................................................ *Me Old Bam-Boo* | $6 | | Columbia 44631 |
| | | | title song from the movie starring **Dick Van Dyke**; #76 hit for **Paul Mauriat** in 1969 | | | |

**NEW COLONY SIX**  *HOT/AC*
Soft-rock group from Chicago: Patrick McBride, Ronnie Rice, Gerry Van Kollenburg, Les Kummel (d: 12/18/78, age 33), Chuck Jobes, William Herman and Ray Graffia.

| | | | | | | |
|---|---|---|---|---|---|---|
| 4/16/66 | 111 | 4 | 1 I Lie Awake ......................................................... *At The River's Edge* | $15 | | Centaur 1202 |
| 4/8/67 | 108 | 4 | 2 You're Gonna Be Mine ............................................................. *Woman* | $15 | | Sentar 1206 |
| 7/22/67 | 128 | 2 | 3 I'm Just Waitin' (Anticipatin' For Her To Show Up) ....................... *Hello Lonely* | $15 | | Sentar 1207 |
| | | | written by **Tony Orlando** | | | |
| 5/23/70 | 116 | 2 | 4 People And Me ....................................................... *Ride The Wicked Wind* | $10 | | Mercury 73063 |
| | | | written by **Brian Wilson** of **The Beach Boys** | | | |
| 4/15/72 | 109 | 2 | 5 Someone, Sometime ............................................... *Come On Down* | $6 | | Sunlight 1005 |

**NEW EDITION**  *R&B/HOT*
Boston R&B vocal quintet: Ralph Tresvant, Ronald DeVoe, Michael Bivins, Ricky Bell and Bobby Brown. **Johnny Gill** joined in 1988. Bell, Bivins and DeVoe recorded as **Bell Biv DeVoe**.

| | | | | | | |
|---|---|---|---|---|---|---|
| 1/21/84 | 101[1] | 5 | 1 Popcorn Love/ *R&B:25* | | | |
| | | 5 | 2 Jealous Girl ............................................................. *R&B:flip* | $8 | | StreetWise 1116 |
| 8/3/85 | 103 | 4 | 3 My Secret (Didja Gitit Yet?) ............. *R&B:27  I'm Leaving You Again* | $4 | ■ | MCA 52627 |
| 2/15/97 | 116 | 4 | 4 Siempre Tu ........................................ *I'm Still In Love With You* [F] | $3 | ■ | MCA 55316 |

**NEW HAPPINESS, The** ☉
Vocal group led by "Smooth" Lundvall.

| | | | | | | |
|---|---|---|---|---|---|---|
| 10/29/66 | 112 | 4 | Winchester Cathedral ............................... *I'm Gonna Spoil You Baby* | $7 | | Columbia 43851 |
| | | | #1 hit for **The New Vaudeville Band** in 1966 | | | |

**NEW JERSEY MASS CHOIR, The** ☉  *R&B*
Gospel choir directed by Donnie Harper.

| | | | | | | |
|---|---|---|---|---|---|---|
| 2/23/85 | 101[1] | 2 | I Want To Know What Love Is  *R&B:37  Jesus Is Right On Time* | $8 | | Savoy 0004 (T) |
| | | | THE NEW JERSEY MASS CHOIR FEATURING DONNIE HARPER AND SHERRY McGEE | | | |
| | | | #1 hit for **Foreigner** in 1985 (New Jersey Mass Choir backed Foreigner on their hit) | | | |

**NEWLEY, Anthony**  *HOT/AC*
Born on 9/24/31 in London. Actor/singer/composer/comedian.

| | | | | | | |
|---|---|---|---|---|---|---|
| 1/4/64 | 105 | 2 | Tribute ................................................................... *Lament For A Hero* | $10 | | Acappella 778 |
| | | | tribute to slain President John F. Kennedy | | | |

**NEWMAN, Randy**  *HOT/AC/C&W/ROK*
Born on 11/28/43 in New Orleans. Singer/composer/pianist. Scored the movies *Ragtime*, *The Natural* and *Avalon*.

| | | | | | | |
|---|---|---|---|---|---|---|
| 4/16/83 | 110 | 2 | I Love L.A. ................................................................ *Song For The Dead* | $4 | | Warner 29687 |

**NEW ORDER**  *HOT/ROK/R&B*
Techno-dance group from Manchester, England: Bernard Sumner (guitar, vocals), Peter Hook (bass), Stephen Morris (drums) and Gillian Gilbert (keyboards).

| | | | | | | |
|---|---|---|---|---|---|---|
| 7/27/85 | 109 | 1 | The Perfect Kiss ............................................................... *(instrumental)* | $5 | ■ | Qwest 28968 |

**NEW RIDERS OF THE PURPLE SAGE**  *HOT*
Country-rock band formed in San Francsico in 1970 featuring John Dawson (vocals, guitar).

| | | | | | | |
|---|---|---|---|---|---|---|
| 8/21/76 | 105 | 3 | Dead Flowers ....................................... *She's Looking Better Every Beer* | $6 | | MCA 40591 |
| | | | written and recorded by **The Rolling Stones** for their 1971 album *Sticky Fingers* | | | |

**NEWTON, Clif** ☉

| | | | | | | |
|---|---|---|---|---|---|---|
| 9/6/80 | 101[2] | 4 | The Rest Of The Night ........................................... *Two Time Lover* | $4 | | Scotti Brothers 602 |

**NEWTON, Wayne**  *AC/HOT/C&W*
Born on 4/3/42 in Roanoke, Virginia. Top Las Vegas entertainer.

| | | | | | | |
|---|---|---|---|---|---|---|
| 2/22/64 | 123 | 2 | 1 I'm Looking Over A Four Leaf Clover ............................... *Dream Baby* | $8 | | Capitol 5124 |
| | | | #1 hit for **Art Mooney** in 1948 | | | |
| 8/8/64 | 122 | 3 | 2 Only You ....................... *Too Late To Meet (Once Upon A Time)* | $8 | | Capitol 5203 |
| | | | #5 hit for **The Platters** in 1955 | | | |
| 12/25/65 | 123 | 2 | 3 Some Sunday Morning ................... *AC:23  A Little Bit Of Heaven* | $8 | | Capitol 5553 |
| | | | #4 hit for Ada Jones & M.J. O'Connell in 1917; #9 hit for Dick Haymes & Helen Forrest in 1945 | | | |
| 5/28/66 | 113 | 4 | 4 Stagecoach To Cheyenne ................. *AC:23  Somebody To Love* | $8 | ■ | Capitol 5643 |
| | | | from the movie *Stagecoach* starring **Ann-Margret** | | | |
| 10/28/67 | 106 | 5 | 5 Love Of The Common People ................. *AC:33  It's Still Loving You* | $8 | | Capitol 2016 |
| | | | arranged by **Leon Russell**; #54 hit for **The Winstons** in 1969 | | | |
| 3/31/73 | 107 | 3 | 6 While We're Still Young ........................................... *Just Yesterday* | $5 | | Chelsea 0116 |
| | | | written by **Paul Anka** | | | |
| 11/16/74 | 101[1] | 3 | 7 Lady Lay  *AC:47  Walking In The Sand* | $5 | | Chelsea 3003 |

### NEWTON-JOHN, Olivia    HOT/AC/C&W/R&B
Born on 9/26/48 in Cambridge, England. To Australia in 1953. In movies *Grease*, *Xanadu* and *Two Of A Kind*. *Top Pop Singles*: 39.

| 5/26/73 | 119 | 1 | Take Me Home, Country Roads .....................................*Sail Into Tomorrow* | $10 | | MCA 40043 |

#2 hit for **John Denver** in 1971

### NEW VAUDEVILLE BAND, The    AC/HOT
Creation of British record producer Geoff Stephens (b: 10/1/34, London). Arrangements similar to Rudy Vallee's hits during the 1930s.

| 6/3/67 | 102 | 3 | 1 Finchley Central ..............................................**AC:24** *Sadie Moonshine* | $7 | ■ | Fontana 1589 |

featuring **Tristam VII**

| 4/6/68 | 122 | 3 | 2 The Bonnie And Clyde.......................................*Anniversary Song* | $7 | | Fontana 1612 |

a new dance inspired by the movie

### NEW YORK CITI PEECH BOYS ☉    R&B
Percussive funk-rock band formed at the Paradise Garage club in New York City.

| 2/19/83 | 108 | 3 | Life Is Something Special.....................................**R&B:74** *(instrumental)* | $4 | | Island 99926 |

### NEW YORK CITY    R&B/HOT/AC
New York City R&B quartet: Tim McQueen, John Brown, Ed Shell and Claude Johnston.

| 1/11/75 | 104 | 3 | 1 Love Is What You Make It ...................**R&B:41** *Do You Remember Yesterday* | $5 | | Chelsea 3008 |
| 4/5/75 | 105 | 4 | 2 Got To Get You Back In My Life.................**R&B:76** *Reach Out* | $5 | | Chelsea 3010 |

### NEW YORK ROCK ENSEMBLE, The ☉
Classical baroque rock group — Mike Kamen, lead singer.

| 1/23/71 | 123 | 1 | Beside You.................................................*The King Is Dead* | $8 | | Columbia 45288 |

### NEW YOUNG HEARTS, The — see YOUNG HEARTS

### NICHOLS, Roger, Trio ☉
Born on 9/17/40 in Missoula, Montana. Wrote "We've Only Just Begun" and "Rainy Days And Mondays."

| 1/28/67 | 129 | 3 | Snow Queen .................................................*Love Song, Love Song* | $7 | | A&M 830 |

### NIELSEN/PEARSON    HOT/AC
Sacramento pop quartet fronted by lead vocalists/guitarists Reed Nielsen and Mark Pearson.

| 1/31/81 | 110 | 1 | Two Lonely Nights .........................................*Love Me Tonight* | $4 | | Capitol 4965 |

### NIGHTCRAWLERS, The    HOT
Garage-rock band from Daytona Beach, Florida featuring Chuck Conlon (vocals, bass) and Robbie Rouse (vocals).

| 12/18/65 | 135 | 1 | The Little Black Egg .......................................*You're Running Wild* | $15 | | Kapp 709 |

made the *Hot 100* (#85) on 1/21/67; first released on Lee 1012 in 1965 ($50)

### NIGHTINGALE, Ollie    R&B/HOT
Born Ollie Hoskins in Memphis. Formed gospel group, the Dixie Nightingales, in 1950; became Ollie & The Nightingales in 1968. Also see The Ovations.

| 5/29/71 | 121 | 3 | It's A Sad Thing ...........................................**R&B:23** *Standing On Your Promise* | $6 | | Memphis 104 |

### NIGHT RANGER    ROK/HOT
Rock group from California featuring lead singers Kelly Keagy (drums) and Jack Blades (bass).

| 8/16/97 | 102 | 7 | Forever All Over Again ...................................*Anything For You* | $3 | ▌ | Legacy 78617 |

### NIKITA THE K ☉
| 3/25/67 | 105 | 3 | Go Go Radio Moscow ........................................*The Spoiler* [N] | $15 | | Warner 7005 |

**NIKITA THE K And The Friends Of Ed Labunski**
parodies of "Tell It To The Rain," "Georgy Girl" and "We Ain't Got Nothin' Yet"

### NILE, Willie ☉    ROK
Real name: Robert Noonan. Rock singer/songwriter from Buffalo, New York.

| 6/7/80 | 106 | 1 | It's All Over ..............................................*Old Men Sleeping On The Bowery* | $4 | | Arista 0508 |

### NILSSON    HOT/AC
Born Harry Edward Nelson, III on 6/15/41 in Brooklyn. Died on 1/15/94. Close friend of **John Lennon** and Ringo Starr.

| 8/26/67 | 122 | 2 | 1 You Can't Do That .......................................*Ten Little Indians* | $12 | | RCA Victor 9298 |

includes bits of other Beatles' hits; #48 hit for **The Beatles** in 1964

| 8/10/68 | 113 | 5 | 2 Everybody's Talkin' .....................................*Don't Leave Me* | $12 | | RCA Victor 9544 |

made the *Hot 100* (#6) on 8/16/69 on RCA Victor 0161 ($8)

| 8/3/74 | 109 | 3 | 3 Many Rivers To Cross ...................................*Don't Forget Me* | $7 | | RCA Victor 10001 |

written by **Jimmy Cliff**; arranged and produced by **John Lennon**

### NIMBLE, Jack B. — see JACK B. NIMBLE

### NIMOY, Leonard ☉
Born on 3/26/31 in Boston. TV and movie actor/director. Portrayed "Mr. Spock" on *Star Trek*.

| 9/23/67 | 121 | 2 | A Visit To A Sad Planet..............................*Theme From "Star Trek"* [I] [S] | $12 | ■ | Dot 17038 |

narration with orchestral backing by **Charles Grean**

### NINE    R&B/HOT
Born on 9/19/69 in New York City. Male rapper. Formerly known as Nine Double M.

| 4/22/95 | 115 | 3 | Any Emcee .................................................**R&B:82** *Tha Cypha* | $3 | ▌ | Profile 5435 |

samples "I'll Be Around" by the **Spinners**

### NINE INCH NAILS    ROK/HOT
One-man industrial rock band formed in 1988 by Trent Reznor (b: 5/17/65 in Mercer, Pennsylvania).

| 1/21/95 | 109 | 15 | Head Like A Hole..............**ROK:28** *(3 mixes) / Terrible Lie (2 mixes) / You Know Who You Are / Down In It (3 mixes)* | $6 | | TVT 2615 **(CD)** |

### 911 ☉
Male vocal trio from England: Lee Brenan, Jimmy Constable and Simon "Spike" Dawbarn.

| 9/13/97 | 103 | 8 | Love Sensation .............................................*(2 versions)* | $3 | ▌ | Saban/Virgin 38612 |

from the movie *Casper, A Spirited Beginning* starring Steve Guttenberg

### 1910 FRUITGUM CO.    HOT
New Jersey bubblegum rock quintet: Mark Gutkowski (lead singer), Floyd Marcus, Pat Karwan, Steve Mortkowitz and Frank Jeckell.

| 11/22/69 | 118 | 2 | When We Get Married .....................................*Baby Bret* | $8 | | Buddah 146 |

**95 SOUTH**              R&B/HOT

Hip-hop outfit based in Miami: Church's, Black, C.C. Lemonhead, Bootyman and K-Knock. Lemonhead later joined **Quad City DJ's**.

| 9/18/93 | 121 | 1 | 1 Whoot, Here It Is! (The Answer) ........................................................ *(instrumental)* | $3 | ▌ | Epic 77152 |

         **DIS 'N' DAT (featuring 95 South)**
         answer song to "Whoot, There It Is" by 95 South earlier in 1993

| 12/11/93+ | 122 | 2 | 2 Hump Wit It ..............................................................R&B:83 *(ultimix radio)* | $3 | ▌ | Wrap/Toy 187 |
| 2/17/96 | 121 | 5 | 3 Heiny Heiny ...............................................R&B:87 *Freak Ya Down* | $3 | ▌ | Rip-It 9521 |

         samples "Message II (Survival)" by **Melle Mel** & Duke Bootee and "Electric Kingdom" by Twilight 22

**NINO & APRIL — see TEMPO, Nino / STEVENS, April**

**NITTY GRITTY DIRT BAND**        C&W/HOT/AC

Country-folk-rock group from Long Beach, California led by Jeff Hanna (b: 7/11/47; vocals, guitar) and John McEuen (b: 12/19/45; banjo).

| 10/18/69 | 106 | 6 | 1 Some Of Shelly's Blues ............................................ *Yukon Railroad* | $7 | | Liberty 56134 |

         made the *Hot 100* (#64) on 9/11/71 on United Artists 50817 ($5)

| 6/30/73 | 123 | 2 | 2 Cosmic Cowboy - Part 1 ................................................ *Fish Song* | $6 | | United Artists 263 |

         written by **Michael Murphey**

| 10/18/80 | 107 | 1 | 3 Badlands ...............................................*Too Good To Be True* | $4 | | United Artists 1378 |

         **THE DIRT BAND**

**NITZSCHE, Jack, Orchestra**        HOT

Born Bernard Nitzsche on 4/22/37 in Chicago. Arranger/producer/composer/keyboardist. Arranger for many of Phil Spector's productions.

| 5/15/76 | 109 | 1 | Theme From One Flew Over The Cuckoo's Nest ................ *The Last Dance* [I] | $7 | ▌ | Fantasy 760 |

         theme from the movie starring Jack Nicholson

**NO AUTHORITY** ☉

Vocal group from California: Ricky Felix, Danny Zavatsky, Josh Keaton and Eric Stretch.

| 11/15/97 | 101[1] | 11 | Don't Stop                    *(remix)* | $3 | ▌ | MJJ Music 78661 |

         samples "Don't Stop" by M.C. Hammer

**NOBLE KNIGHTS, The — see KING CURTIS**

**NOMADS, The** ☉

Rock and roll instrumental band.

| 3/27/61 | 116 | 2 | Bounty Hunter ...................................... *Desert Tramp* [I] | $20 | | Rust 5028 |

**NOONE, Peter — see HERMAN'S HERMITS**

**NORMA JEAN — see WRIGHT, Norma Jean**

**NORMA JEAN** ☉        C&W

Born Norma Jean Beasler on 1/30/38 in Wellston, Oklahoma. On **Porter Wagoner**'s TV series from 1960-67.

| 10/3/64 | 134 | 1 | Go Cat Go ...............................C&W:8 *Lonesome Number One* | $12 | | RCA Victor 8433 |

         produced by **Chet Atkins**

**NORTH, Freddie**        R&B/HOT

R&B vocalist from Nashville. Worked in sales and promotion for Nashboro Records. DJ on *Night Train*, WLAC-Nashville.

| 2/12/72 | 116 | 1 | You And Me Together Forever .. R&B:26 *Did I Come Back Too Soon (Or Stay Away Too Long)* | $7 | | Mankind 12009 |

**NORTHCOTT, Tom**        HOT

Canadian folk singer. Hosted TV show in Canada.

| 7/29/67 | 123 | 1 | Sunny Goodge Street ...................... *Who Planted Thorns In Miss Alice's Garden* | $8 | | Warner 7051 |

         written by **Donovan**; arranged by Leon Russell

**NOVA, Aldo**        ROK/HOT

Born Aldo Scarporuscio in Montreal. Rock singer/songwriter/guitarist/keyboardist.

| 12/3/83 | 107 | 3 | Always Be Mine ..................................*Race Cars / Armageddon* | $4 | ■ | Portrait 04207 |

**NOVO COMBO** ☉        ROK

New York-based rock quartet: Pete Hewlett (vocals), Jack Griffith (guitar), Stephen Dees (bass) and Michael Shrieve (drums).

| 2/6/82 | 103 | 4 | Tattoo ..............................................ROK:42 *Don't Do That* | $4 | | Polydor 2194 |

**N-PHASE** ☉        R&B

Vocal quintet from Rock Hill, South Carolina: Melvin Baxter, Al Boyd, Tevlin Williamson, Donnie Mayes and Marlon Davis.

| 7/30/94 | 105 | 10 | Spend The Night ..............................R&B:23 *(remix)* | $3 | ▌ | Maverick/Sire 18194 |

         written and produced by R. Kelly

**NRBQ**        HOT

Multi-styled group formed as the New Rhythm & Blues Quartet in Miami in 1967. Numerous personnel changes. Also see **Al Anderson**.

| 6/28/69 | 122 | 2 | Stomp .......................................... *I Didn't Know Myself* | $8 | | Columbia 44865 |

**NUGENT, Ted**        HOT/ROK

Born on 12/13/48 in Detroit. Heavy-metal rock guitarist. Member of **The Amboy Dukes** and Damn Yankees.

| 3/3/84 | 107 | 3 | Tied Up In Love ..............................ROK:41 *Lean Mean R&R Machine* | $4 | ■ | Atlantic 89705 |

**NUMAN, Gary**        HOT

Born Gary Webb on 3/8/58 in Hammersmith, England. Synthesized techno-rock artist.

| 6/28/80 | 105 | 3 | 1 Are 'Friends' Electric? ..............................*You Are In My Vision* | $5 | | Atco 7206 |

         **GARY NUMAN & TUBEWAY ARMY**

| 9/27/80 | 102 | 2 | 2 I Die: You Die ..................................... *Sleep By Windows* | $5 | | Atco 7308 |

**NUNN, Bobby** ☉        R&B

R&B vocalist/keyboardist from Buffalo, New York.

| 10/2/82 | 104 | 9 | She's Just A Groupie .........................R&B:15 *Never Seen Anything Like You* | $4 | | Motown 1643 |

**NUNNERY, Stu** ☉

| 11/10/73 | 101[1] | 7 | 1 Sally From Syracuse         *Madelaine* | $6 | | Evolution 1084 |
| 3/16/74 | 107 | 6 | 2 Madelaine .......................................... *Sally From Syracuse* | $6 | | Evolution 1088 |

         above 2 titles released together on both Evolution 1084 and 1088

**N.V. — see GARCIA, Tony**

**NYRO, Laura**                            HOT/AC
Born Laura Nigro on 10/18/47 in the Bronx, New York. Died on 4/8/97 of ovarian cancer. White soul-gospel singer/songwriter.

| 10/22/66+ | 103 | 12 | 1 Wedding Bell Blues................................................................................ *Stoney End* | $15 | | Verve Folkways 5024 |
| | | | #1 hit for **The 5th Dimension** in 1969 | | | |
| 2/12/72 | 103 | 3 | 2 It's Gonna Take A Miracle ................................................................... *Desiree* | $7 | | Columbia 45537 |
| | | | #10 hit for **Deniece Williams** in 1982 | | | |

**OAK**                        HOT
Pop/rock group from New Hampshire: Rick Pinette (vocals), Scott Weatherspoon (guitar), David Stone (keyboards), John Foster (bass) and Daniel Caron (drums).

| 1/5/80 | 108 | 1 | Draw The Line................................................................................... *Friends* | $4 | | Mercury 76014 |

**OAK RIDGE BOYS**        C&W/AC/HOT
Country vocal group: Duane Allen (lead), Joe Bonsall (tenor), Richard Sterban (bass) and Bill Golden (baritone).

| 7/22/78 | 102 | 3 | 1 I'll Be True To You.................................... C&W:❶[1] *An Old Time Family Bluegrass Band* | $5 | | ABC 12350 |
| 10/7/78 | 107 | 2 | 2 Cryin' Again ......................................................... C&W:3 *I Can Love You* | $5 | | ABC 12397 |
| 9/20/80 | 105 | 1 | 3 Heart Of Mine ................................................ C&W:3 / AC:49 *Love Takes Two* | $4 | | MCA 41280 |
| 10/3/81 | 104 | 2 | 4 Fancy Free ............................................ C&W:❶[1] / AC:17 *How Long Has It Been* | $4 | | MCA 51169 |

**O'BRYAN**                  R&B/HOT
Born O'Bryan Burnett II. R&B singer from Sneads Ferry, North Carolina.

| 6/9/84 | 101[2] | 8 | Lovelite ....................................................... R&B:❶[1] *(instrumental)* | $4 | ■ | Capitol 5329 |

**OCEAN, Billy**           R&B/HOT/AC
Born Leslie Sebastian Charles on 1/21/50 in Trinidad. Raised in England. Moved to the U.S. in the late '70s.

| 8/14/76 | 106 | 5 | 1 L.O.D. (Love On Delivery)................................. R&B:55 *Mr. Business Man* | $5 | | Ariola America 7630 |
| 6/20/81 | 103 | 6 | 2 Night (Feel Like Getting Down)............................ R&B:7 *Stay The Night* | $4 | | Epic 02053 |

**OCEAN BLUE, The** ✪         ROK
Pop-rock band formed in Hershey, Pennsylvania in 1986: Dave Schelzel (vocals, guitar), Steve Lau (keyboards), Bobby Mittan (bass) and Rob Minnig (drums).

| 10/23/93 | 121 | 2 | Sublime ............................................................. ROK:3 *Crash* | $3 | ▌ | Sire/Reprise 18383 |

**OCHS, Phil** ✪
Born on 12/19/40 in El Paso, Texas. Hanged himself on 4/9/76. Folk-protest singer/songwriter.

| 2/24/68 | 118 | 3 | Outside Of A Small Circle Of Friends........................................ *Miranda* | $10 | | A&M 891 |

**OCTOBER, Johnny** ✪
Real name: Johnny Ottobre. Native of Philadelphia. Lead singer of The Four Dates.

| 10/26/59 | 106 | 3 | Growin' Prettier ..................................................... *Young And In Love* | $20 | ■ | Capitol 4267 |
| | | | Jesse Stone (orch.) | | | |

**ODDS** ✪
Rock quartet from Vancouver: Doug Elliot, Craig Northey, Steven Drake and Pat Steward.

| 4/5/97 | 120 | 2 | Someone Who's Cool ................................................ *Family Cauldron* | $3 | ▌ | Elektra 64183 |

**O'DELL, Kenny**          C&W/HOT
Born Kenneth Gist, Jr. in Oklahoma (early 1940s). Singer/songwriter/guitarist. Worked with **Duane Eddy**.

| 5/18/68 | 118 | 1 | 1 Happy With You............................................... *I Could Love You* | $7 | | Vegas 724 |
| 6/21/75 | 105 | 1 | 2 My Honky Tonk Ways ....................................... C&W:37 *Behind Closed Doors* | $5 | | Capricorn 0233 |

**ODOM, Joe** ✪

| 5/31/69 | 109 | 3 | It's In Your Power ..................................................... *Big Love* | $7 | | 1-2-3 1710 |

**ODYSSEY**              R&B/HOT/AC
New York R&B-disco trio: Manila-born Tony Reynolds, and sisters Lillian and Louise Lopez, originally from the Virgin Islands.

| 11/4/78 | 107 | 2 | 1 Single Again/What Time Does The Balloon Go Up................................ *Pride* | $4 | | RCA 11399 |
| 6/28/80 | 105 | 2 | 2 Don't Tell Me, Tell Her.................................. R&B:44 *Use It Up And Wear It Out* | $4 | | RCA 11962 |
| 8/7/82 | 104 | 7 | 3 Inside Out.......................................................... R&B:12 *Love's Alright* | $4 | | RCA 13217 |

**OHIO EXPRESS**         HOT
Bubblegum rock group from Mansfield, Ohio featuring Joey Levine (b: 5/29/47).

| 11/22/69 | 101[1] | 4 | Cowboy Convention ............................... *The Race (That Took Place)* [N] | $7 | | Buddah 147 |

**OHIO PLAYERS**        R&B/HOT
R&B/funk band featuring Clarence "Satch" Satchell (vocals, sax) and Leroy "Sugarfoot" Bonner (vocals, guitar).

| 1/7/78 | 101[1] | 7 | 1 Good Luck Charm (Part I) ................................... R&B:51 *(Part II)* | $5 | | Mercury 73974 |
| | | | from the movie *Mr. Mean* starring Fred Williamson | | | |
| 9/23/78 | 105 | 3 | 2 Funk-O-Nots .......................................... R&B:27 *Sleepwalkin'* | $5 | | Mercury 74014 |

**OHTA, Herb (Ohta-San)** ✪     AC
Guitar player.

| 8/3/74 | 104 | 2 | Song For Anna (Chanson D' Anna) ............... AC:26 *Keeping You Company* [I] | $5 | | A&M 1505 |

**O'JAYS, The**           R&B/HOT/AC
R&B vocal trio from Canton, Ohio: **Eddie Levert**, Walter Williams and William Powell (d: 5/26/77; replaced by Sammy Strain). Levert's sons Gerald and Sean are members of the trio **Levert**. *Top Pop Singles*: 30.

| 2/1/64 | 131 | 1 | 1 Stand Tall................................................... *The Storm Is Over* | $15 | | Imperial 66007 |
| 10/27/79 | 102 | 1 | 2 Sing A Happy Song....................................... R&B:7 *One In A Million (Girl)* | $5 | | Philadelphia Int'l. 3707 |
| 5/8/82 | 101[1] | 4 | 3 I Just Want To Satisfy ............................. R&B:15 *Don't Walk Away Mad* | $5 | | Philadelphia Int'l. 02834 |
| 7/31/93 | 104 | 10 | 4 Somebody Else Will ......................... R&B:27 *(radio edit) / Decisions* | $3 | ■ | EMI/ERG 50462 |

| DEBUT | PEAK | WKS | A-side (Chart Hit)..........B-side | $ | Pic | Label & Number |
|---|---|---|---|---|---|---|

**O'KEEFE, Danny**　　　　　　　　　HOT/AC/C&W
Born in Spokane, Washington. Pop singer/songwriter.

| | | | | | | |
|---|---|---|---|---|---|---|
| 12/30/72 | 102 | 3 | 1 The Road ..........*I'm Sober Now* | $6 | | Signpost 70012 |
| 10/20/73 | 110 | 2 | 2 Angel Spread Your Wings ..........*Mad Ruth The Babe* | $5 | | Atlantic 2978 |

**OLD SCHOOL JUNKIES** ☻

| | | | | | | |
|---|---|---|---|---|---|---|
| 9/21/96 | 102 | 12 | The Funk Phenomena ..........(2 versions) [I] | $3 | ∎ | Henry Street 5005 |

ARMAND VAN HELDEN Presents OLD SCHOOL JUNKIES

**OLIVER**　　　　　　　　　AC/HOT
Born William Oliver Swofford on 2/22/45 in North Wilkesboro, North Carolina.

| | | | | | | |
|---|---|---|---|---|---|---|
| 5/1/71 | 124 | 1 | Early Mornin' Rain　　AC:38 *Catch Me If You Can* | $6 | | United Artists 50762 |

written by Gordon Lightfoot; #91 hit for Peter, Paul & Mary in 1965

**OLIVOR, Jane**　　　　　　　　　AC/HOT
Lyrical stylist from New York City.

| | | | | | | |
|---|---|---|---|---|---|---|
| 4/5/80 | 108 | 3 | Don't Let Go Of Me ..........*Vagabond* | $4 | | Columbia 11223 |

**OLLIE & THE NIGHTINGALES — see NIGHTINGALE, Ollie**

**OLSSON, Nigel**　　　　　　　　　HOT/AC
Born on 2/10/49 in Merseyside, England. Drummer for Elton John's band from 1971-76.

| | | | | | | |
|---|---|---|---|---|---|---|
| 1/24/76 | 107 | 2 | A Girl Like You ..........*Girl, We've Got To Keep On* | $6 | | Rocket 40491 |

#10 hit for The Young Rascals in 1967

**OLYMPIC RUNNERS** ☻　　　　　　　　　R&B
English group: Pete Wingfield, Joe Jammer, DeLisle Harper, Glen LeFleur and George Chandler (vocals).

| | | | | | | |
|---|---|---|---|---|---|---|
| 8/24/74 | 103 | 3 | 1 Put The Music Where Your Mouth Is/　　R&B:72 [I] | | | |
| 7/20/74 | 107 | 1 | 2 　Do It Over　　R&B:72 | $6 | | London 202 |
| 1/11/75 | 103 | 6 | 3 Grab It ..........R&B:73 *Let Your Fingers Do The Talking* [I] | $6 | | London 216 |
| 8/16/75 | 109 | 1 | 4 Drag It Over Here　　R&B:92 *Mac B. Coolie* | $6 | | London 219 |

**O'NEAL, Alexander**　　　　　　　　　R&B/HOT
Born on 11/15/53 in Natchez, Mississippi. Minneapolis-based R&B vocalist.

| | | | | | | |
|---|---|---|---|---|---|---|
| 3/30/85 | 101[2] | 8 | 1 Innocent　　R&B:11 *Are You The One?* | $4 | ∎ | Tabu 04718 |
| 2/13/93 | 108 | 5 | 2 Love Makes No Sense ..........R&B:13 *(album version)* | $3 | ∎ | Tabu 7706 |

**O'NEAL, Shaquille**　　　　　　　　　R&B/HOT
Born on 3/6/72 in Newark, New Jersey. NBA all-star center. Stands 7-foot-1-inch. Starred in the movies *Blue Chips*, *Kazaam* and *Steel*.

| | | | | | | |
|---|---|---|---|---|---|---|
| 2/25/95 | 103 | 5 | No Hook ..........Sls:54 /R&B:66 (2 remixes) / (So U Wanna Be) *Hardcore* | $3 | ∎ | Jive 42284 |

SHAQUILLE O'NEAL (featuring Prince Rakeem The RZA and Method Man)

**ONE G PLUS THREE** ☻　　　　　　　　　AC
Latino band based in Los Angeles.

| | | | | | | |
|---|---|---|---|---|---|---|
| 10/24/70 | 122 | 2 | Poquito Soul..........AC:38 *Summertime* [I] | $8 | | Gordo 705 |

also released in 1970 on Paramount 0054 ($6); Poquito is Spanish for Little

**100 PROOF (Aged In Soul)**　　　　　　　　　R&B/HOT
R&B group from Detroit: Clyde Wilson ("Steve Mancha"), lead; Joe Stubbs and Eddie Anderson ("Eddie Holiday").

| | | | | | | |
|---|---|---|---|---|---|---|
| 6/26/71 | 121 | 2 | Driveway ..........R&B:33 *Love Is Sweeter (The Second Time Around)* | $7 | | Hot Wax 7104 |

**100 STRINGS — see JAMES, Joni**

**ONES, The** ☻

| | | | | | | |
|---|---|---|---|---|---|---|
| 2/10/68 | 117 | 1 | You Haven't Seen My Love ..........*Happy Day* | $20 | | Motown 1117 |

originally released on Fenton 2514 in 1967 ($75)

**ONYX**　　　　　　　　　R&B/HOT
Rap foursome based in Jamaica, New York: Sticky Fingaz, Big D.S., Fredro Star and Suave Sonny Caesar.

| | | | | | | |
|---|---|---|---|---|---|---|
| 8/5/95 | 102 | 5 | Live!!! ..........Sls:65 /R&B:81 *Kill Dem All* (Kali Ranks) | $3 | ∎ | Def Jam 579620 |

from the rap concert movie *The Show!*; samples "Wherever You Are" by Isaac Hayes

**ORBISON, Roy**　　　　　　　　　HOT/AC/C&W/R&B/ROK
Born on 4/23/36 in Vernon, Texas. Died of a heart attack on 12/6/88 in Madison, Tennessee. Member of the supergroup Traveling Wilburys in 1988. Inducted into the Rock and Roll Hall of Fame in 1987. *Top Pop Singles*: 32.

| | | | | | | |
|---|---|---|---|---|---|---|
| 3/25/67 | 132 | 1 | 1 So Good ..........*Memories* | $15 | | MGM 13685 |
| 10/28/67 | 119 | 2 | 2 She ..........*Here Comes The Rain Baby* | $15 | | MGM 13817 |
| 7/6/68 | 121 | 2 | 3 Walk On ..........*Flowers* | $15 | | MGM 13950 |
| 10/19/68 | 104 | 1 | 4 Heartache　　*Sugar Man* | $12 | | MGM 13991 |
| 9/13/69 | 133 | 1 | 5 Penny Arcade ..........*Tennessee Owns My Soul* | $12 | | MGM 14079 |
| 5/2/70 | 122 | 1 | 6 So Young ..........*If I Had A Woman Like You* | $12 | | MGM 14121 |

love theme from the movie *Zabriskie Point* starring Harrison Ford

| | | | | | | |
|---|---|---|---|---|---|---|
| 6/30/79 | 109 | 3 | 7 Easy Way Out..........*Tears* | $6 | | Asylum 46048 |

**ORBITAL** ☻
Electronic-dance duo from London: brothers Phil and Paul Hartnoll.

| | | | | | | |
|---|---|---|---|---|---|---|
| 4/12/97 | 104 | 9 | The Saint ..........*The Box / The Sinner* [I] | $3 | ∎ | Internal/FFRR 531102 |

from the movie *The Saint* starring Val Kilmer

**ORCHESTRAL MANOEUVRES IN THE DARK**　　　　　　　　　HOT/ROK/AC
English electro-pop outfit formed in 1978 and fronted by keyboardists/vocalists Andrew McCluskey and Paul Humphreys.

| | | | | | | |
|---|---|---|---|---|---|---|
| 7/17/93 | 111 | 2 | Stand Above Me ..........Air:75 /ROK:5 *Can I Believe You* | $3 | ∎ | Virgin 12666 |

**ORGANIZED NOIZE** ☻　　　　　　　　　R&B
Rap production team. Production work for TLC, Outkast and Goodie Mob.

| | | | | | | |
|---|---|---|---|---|---|---|
| 9/14/96 | 105 | 14 | Set It Off ..........R&B:51 *(instrumental)* | $3 | ∎ | EastWest 64253 |

ORGANIZED NOIZE featuring Andrea Martin & Queen Latifah
title song from the movie starring Jada Pinkett and Queen Latifah

## ORIGINAL CASTE, The  —  HOT/AC
Canadian pop quintet: Dixie Lee Innes (lead vocals), Bruce Innes, Graham Bruce, Joseph Cavender and Bliss Mackie.

| DEBUT | PEAK | WKS | A-side | B-side | $ | Pic | Label & Number |
|---|---|---|---|---|---|---|---|
| 4/25/70 | 119 | 1 | 1 Mr. Monday | Highway | $8 | | T•A 192 |
| 7/11/70 | 114 | 1 | 2 Nothing Can Touch Me (Don't Worry Baby, It's Alright) | Country Song | $8 | | T•A 197 |
| 10/3/70 | 117 | 1 | 3 Ain't That Tellin' You People | Sweet Chicago | $8 | | T•A 204 |

## ORIGINALS, The  —  R&B/HOT
R&B group formed in Detroit in 1966: Freddie Gorman, Henry Dixon, Walter Gaines and **Ty Hunter**.

| | | | | | | | |
|---|---|---|---|---|---|---|---|
| 3/4/72 | 113 | 1 | I'm Someone Who Cares | Once I Have You (I Will Never Let Go) | $8 | | Soul 35093 |

## ORIGINOO GUNN CLAPPAZ ☉  —  R&B
Male rap trio: Starang Wondah, Louieville Sluggah and Top Dog.

| | | | | | | | |
|---|---|---|---|---|---|---|---|
| 1/13/96 | 103 | 3 | 1 Blah .......... R&B:62 LeFlaur LeFlah Eshkoshka (Hot #75) | | $3 | ■ | Priority 53223 |
| | | | THE FABULOUS FIVE FEATURING: HELTAH SKELTAH AND ORIGINOO GUNN CLAPPAZ | | | | |
| 10/5/96 | 115 | 5 | 2 NoFear .......... R&B:63 Da Storm | | $3 | ■ | Priority 53243 |

## ORLANDO, Tony  —  HOT/AC
Born Michael Anthony Orlando Cassavitis on 4/3/44 in New York City. In 1971, teamed with session singers Telma Hopkins (from Louisville) and Joyce Vincent (from Detroit) to form Dawn. Hosted TV variety show *Tony Orlando & Dawn* from 1974-76. *Top Pop Singles:* 25.

| | | | | | | | |
|---|---|---|---|---|---|---|---|
| 9/8/62 | 109 | 2 | 1 Chills | At The Edge Of Tears | $15 | ■ | Epic 9519 |
| 2/23/63 | 133 | 1 | 2 Shirley | Joanie | $15 | | Epic 9570 |
| 11/9/63 | 124 | 1 | 3 I'll Be There | What Am I Gonna Do | $15 | | Epic 9622 |
| | | | #79 hit for **Bobby Darin** in 1960 | | | | |
| 4/12/69 | 109 | 3 | 4 I Was A Boy (When You Needed A Man) | Moments From Now Tomorrow | $25 | | Harbour 304 |
| | | | BILLY SHIELDS | | | | |

## ORLEANS  —  HOT/AC/C&W
Rock group formed in New York City in 1972 featuring **John Hall**.

| | | | | | | | |
|---|---|---|---|---|---|---|---|
| 9/18/82 | 110 | 1 | One Of A Kind | Beatin' Around The Bush | $4 | | Radio 99981 |

## ORLONS, The  —  HOT/R&B
R&B group from Philadelphia featuring lead singer Rosetta Hightower.

| | | | | | | | |
|---|---|---|---|---|---|---|---|
| 2/6/65 | 129 | 1 | I Ain't Comin' Back | Come On Down Baby Baby | $15 | ■ | Cameo 352 |

## ORPHEUS  —  HOT
Boston soft-rock quartet: Bruce Arnold, Jack McKenes, John Eric Gulliksen and Harry Sandler.

| | | | | | | | |
|---|---|---|---|---|---|---|---|
| 3/9/68 | 111 | 7 | Can't Find The Time | Lesley's World | $7 | | MGM 13882 |
| | | | made the *Hot 100* (#80) on 8/23/69 | | | | |

## OSBOURNE, Ozzy  —  ROK/HOT
Born John Michael Osbourne on 12/3/48 in Birmingham, England. Heavy-metal artist; former lead singer of Black Sabbath.

| | | | | | | | |
|---|---|---|---|---|---|---|---|
| 7/4/81 | 106 | 5 | 1 Crazy Train .......... ROK:9 Steal Away (The Night) | | $5 | | Jet 02079 |
| 2/11/84 | 109 | 1 | 2 Bark At The Moon .......... ROK:12 Spiders | | $4 | | CBS Associated 04318 |
| 3/10/84 | 104 | 3 | 3 So Tired .......... "B" Side | | $4 | | CBS Associated 04383 |

## O'SHEA, Shad, & The 18 Wheelers ☉  —  C&W
Shad was the president of Fraternity Records.

| | | | | | | | |
|---|---|---|---|---|---|---|---|
| 3/20/76 | 110 | 1 | Colorado Call .......... C&W:85 Bub-Bub-Bub-Boo [N] | | $5 | | Private Stock 45,071 |

## OSIBISA ☉  —  R&B
Britain-based R&B band founded by Ghanaian Teddy Osei (reeds, percussion).

| | | | | | | | |
|---|---|---|---|---|---|---|---|
| 4/24/76 | 108 | 1 | Sunshine Day .......... R&B:61 Bum To Bum | | $5 | | Island 053 |

## OSMOND, Donny  —  HOT/AC
Born on 12/9/57 in Ogden, Utah. Became a member of The Osmonds in 1963. Starred with sister, **Marie Osmond**, in musical/variety show *Donny & Marie*, 1976-78. *Top Pop Singles:* 27.

| | | | | | | | |
|---|---|---|---|---|---|---|---|
| 9/10/77 | 109 | 2 | You've Got Me Dangling On A String | I'm Sorry | $5 | | Polydor/Kolob 14417 |
| | | | #38 hit for **Chairmen Of The Board** in 1970 | | | | |

## OSMOND, Little Jimmy  —  HOT
Born on 4/16/63 in Canoga Park, California. Youngest member of the Osmond family.

| | | | | | | | |
|---|---|---|---|---|---|---|---|
| 4/15/72 | 101[1] | 1 | Mother Of Mine | Long Haired Lover From Liverpool (Hot #38) | $5 | | MGM 14376 |

## OSMOND, Marie  —  C&W/HOT/AC
Born Olive Marie Osmond on 10/13/59 in Ogden, Utah. Co-hosted musical/variety series *Donny & Marie* with her brother **Donny Osmond**, 1976-78.

| | | | | | | | |
|---|---|---|---|---|---|---|---|
| 9/21/74 | 102 | 3 | In My Little Corner Of The World .......... C&W:33 It's Just The Other Way Around | | $5 | | MGM/Kolob 14694 |
| | | | arranged and produced by **Sonny James**; #10 hit for **Anita Bryant** in 1960 | | | | |

## O'SULLIVAN, Gilbert  —  AC/HOT
Born Raymond O'Sullivan on 12/1/46 in Waterford, Ireland.

| | | | | | | | |
|---|---|---|---|---|---|---|---|
| 3/6/71 | 114 | 1 | Nothing Rhymed | Everybody Knows | $7 | | MAM 3602 |

## OTIS & CARLA — see REDDING, Otis / THOMAS, Carla

## OUTKAST  —  R&B/HOT
Atlanta-based male rap duo: Andre "Dre" Benjamin and Antoine "Big Boi" Patton.

| | | | | | | | |
|---|---|---|---|---|---|---|---|
| 11/12/94 | 109 | 7 | Git Up, Git Out .......... Sls:75 /R&B:59 (instrumental) | | $3 | ■ | LaFace 24085 |
| | | | The Goodie Mob (backing vocals) | | | | |

## OUTLAWS  —  HOT/ROK
Southern-rock band formed in Tampa in 1974 featuring guitarists Hughie Thomasson, Billy Jones (d: 2/7/95, age 45) and **Henry Paul**.

| | | | | | | | |
|---|---|---|---|---|---|---|---|
| 4/18/81 | 102 | 2 | I Can't Stop Loving You | Wishing Well | $5 | | Arista 0597 |

## OUTSIDERS, The  —  HOT
Cleveland rock quintet: Sonny Geraci (lead singer), Tom King (guitar), Bill Bruno (lead guitar), Mert Madsen (bass) and Rick Baker (drums). Geraci later led band Climax.

| | | | | | | | |
|---|---|---|---|---|---|---|---|
| 3/4/67 | 118 | 3 | 1 I'll Give You Time (To Think It Over) | I'm Not Tryin' To Hurt You | $10 | ■ | Capitol 5843 |
| 5/6/67 | 121 | 4 | 2 Gotta Leave Us Alone | I Just Can't See You Anymore | $10 | | Capitol 5892 |

| DEBUT | PEAK | WKS | A-side (Chart Hit) / B-side | $ | Pic | Label & Number |
|---|---|---|---|---|---|---|
| | | | **OUTSIDERS, The — Cont'd** | | | |
| 12/9/67 | 117 | 1 | 3 Little Bit Of Lovin'.........................................................................*I Will Love You* | $10 | | Capitol 2055 |
| 9/5/70 | 107 | 1 | 4 Changes.......................................................................................*Lost In My World* | $7 | | Bell/Carousel 904 |
| | | | THE OUTSIDERS Featuring Sonny Geraci (#1 & 4) | | | |
| | | | **OVATIONS, The**     R&B/HOT | | | |
| | | | R&B group led by Louis Williams. Re-formed in 1972 with former members of Ollie & The Nightingales. | | | |
| 8/19/72 | 104 | 3 | Touching Me................................................R&B:19 *Don't Break Your Promise* | $8 | | Sounds Of Memphis 708 |
| | | | **OVERSTREET, Tommy ✪**     C&W | | | |
| | | | Born on 9/10/37 in Oklahoma City. Country singer/songwriter. | | | |
| 6/26/71 | 123 | 1 | 1 Gwen (Congratulations) ...............C&W:5 *One Love, Two Hearts, Three Lives* | $6 | | Dot 17375 |
| 1/20/73 | 102 | 3 | 2 Heaven Is My Woman's Love .......................C&W:3 *Baby's Gone* | $6 | | Dot 17428 |
| | | | **OWENS, Buck**     C&W/HOT/AC | | | |
| | | | Born Alvis Edgar Owens on 8/12/29 in Sherman, Texas. Country singer/guitarist/songwriter. Co-host of TV's *Hee Haw*, 1969-86. | | | |
| 3/13/61 | 113 | 1 | 1 Foolin' Around...........................C&W:2 *High As The Mountains (C&W #27)* | $12 | | Capitol 4496 |
| 8/22/64 | 130 | 1 | 2 Don't Let Her Know .................C&W:33 *I Don't Care (Just as Long as You Love Me)* (Hot #92) | $8 | | Capitol 5240 |
| 7/31/65 | 120 | 1 | 3 Only You (Can Break My Heart)...........................C&W:❶¹ *Gonna Have Love (C&W #10)* | $8 | ■ | Capitol 5465 |
| | | | **BUCK OWENS And The Buckaroos:** | | | |
| 2/18/67 | 114 | 3 | 4 Where Does The Good Times Go ...........................C&W:❶⁴ *The Way That I Love You* | $8 | ■ | Capitol 5811 |
| 10/28/67 | 114 | 4 | 5 It Takes People Like You (To Make People Like Me).........................C&W:2 *You Left Her Lonely Too Long* | $8 | ■ | Capitol 2001 |
| 2/8/69 | 106 | 5 | 6 Who's Gonna Mow Your Grass     C&W:❶² *There's Gotta Be Some Changes Made* | $7 | ■ | Capitol 2377 |
| 5/24/69 | 114 | 3 | 7 Johnny B. Goode .............................C&W:❶² *Maybe If I Close My Eyes (It'll Go Away)* | $7 | ■ | Capitol 2485 |
| | | | recorded live at the London Palladium; #8 hit for Chuck Berry in 1958 | | | |
| 12/5/70 | 110 | 2 | 8 I Wouldn't Live In New York City (If They Gave Me The Whole Dang Town).........................C&W:9 *No Milk And Honey In Baltimore* | $6 | ■ | Capitol 2947 |
| 3/20/71 | 119 | 3 | 9 Bridge Over Troubled Water.............................C&W:9 *(I'm Goin') Home* | $6 | ■ | Capitol 3023 |
| | | | #1 hit for Simon & Garfunkel in 1970 | | | |
| 6/12/71 | 106 | 4 | 10 Ruby (Are You Mad).....................C&W:3 *Heartbreak Mountain* | $6 | | Capitol 3096 |
| | | | **OZARK MOUNTAIN DAREDEVILS**     HOT/C&W/AC | | | |
| | | | Country-rock group from Springfield, Missouri: Larry Lee (vocals, drums), John Dillon (guitar), Steve Cash (harmonica) and Michael "Supe" Granda (bass). | | | |
| 10/5/74 | 101¹ | 5 | Look Away     *It Probably Always Will* | $6 | | A&M 1623 |
| | | | **OZONE ✪**     R&B | | | |
| | | | Nashville-based band produced by Teena Marie: Thomas Bumpass, William White, Ray Woodard, Greg Hargrove, Benny Wallace, Jimmy Stewart, Charles Glenn and Paul Hines. | | | |
| 8/28/82 | 109 | 3 | Li'l Suzy ..............................................R&B:59 *I'm Not Easy* | $4 | | Motown 1627 |

# P

| DEBUT | PEAK | WKS | A-side (Chart Hit) / B-side | $ | Pic | Label & Number |
|---|---|---|---|---|---|---|
| | | | **PABLO CRUISE**     HOT/AC/R&B/ROK | | | |
| | | | San Francisco pop-rock quartet formed in 1973 featuring Dave Jenkins (vocals, guitar). | | | |
| 7/26/75 | 104 | 2 | 1 Island Woman .............................................*Denny* | $6 | | A&M 1695 |
| 10/1/83 | 107 | 1 | 2 Will You, Won't You.....................................*Another World* | $4 | | A&M 2570 |
| | | | **PAGAN, Ralfi**     R&B/HOT | | | |
| 7/24/71 | 104 | 3 | Make It With You ........................R&B:32 *Stray Woman* | $6 | | Wand 11236 |
| | | | originally released on Fania 11236 in 1971 ($8); #1 hit for Bread in 1970 | | | |
| | | | **PAGE, Gene ✪**     R&B/AC | | | |
| | | | Keyboardist/arranger/conductor from Los Angeles. Staff arranger with Reprise and Motown Records. | | | |
| 2/8/75 | 104 | 2 | All Our Dreams Are Coming True .........................AC:37 *Satin Soul* [I] | $5 | | Atlantic 3247 |
| | | | produced by Barry White | | | |
| | | | **PAGE, Patti**     HOT/MEM/POP/C&W/AC | | | |
| | | | Born Clara Ann Fowler on 11/8/27 in Muskogee, Oklahoma. Own TV series *The Patti Page Show*, 1955-58, and *The Big Record*, 1957-58. Pop Hits & Top Pop Singles: 81. | | | |
| 2/23/63 | 114 | 3 | 1 Just A Simple Melody .........................*Pretty Boy Lonely* (Hot #98) | $8 | ☐ | Columbia 42671 |
| 6/1/63 | 127 | 2 | 2 I'm Walkin' ..............................*Invitation To The Blues* | $8 | ■ | Mercury 72123 |
| | | | #4 hit for both Fats Domino and Ricky Nelson in 1957 | | | |
| 2/29/64 | 131 | 1 | 3 I Adore You .........................*I Wonder, I Wonder, I Wonder* | $6 | | Columbia 42963 |
| 2/26/66 | 126 | 1 | 4 Custody/     AC:26 | | | |
| 2/26/66 | 130 | 1 | 5 Till You Come Back To Me ......................................... | $6 | | Columbia 43517 |
| 10/8/66 | 113 | 3 | 6 Almost Persuaded     AC:20 *It's The World Outside* | $6 | | Columbia 43794 |
| | | | #24 hit for David Houston in 1966 | | | |
| 11/9/68 | 121 | 1 | 7 Stand By Your Man.........................AC:20 *Red Summer Roses* | $6 | | Columbia 44666 |
| | | | #19 hit for Tammy Wynette in 1969 | | | |
| 6/13/70 | 114 | 3 | 8 I Wish I Had A Mommy Like You .......C&W:22 *He'll Never Take The Place Of You* | $5 | | Columbia 45159 |
| | | | **PALEY BROTHERS, The ✪** | | | |
| | | | Twins Andy and Jonathan Paley. Andy produced the 1990 *Dick Tracy* soundtrack. | | | |
| 5/20/78 | 109 | 2 | You're The Best ................................................*Magic Power* | $5 | ■ | Sire 1021 |

| DEBUT | PEAK | WKS | A-side (Chart Hit) / B-side | $ | Pic | Label & Number |
|---|---|---|---|---|---|---|
| | | | **PALM BEACH BAND BOYS, The** ☺     AC | | | |
| | | | A Danny Davis production; similar to The New Vaudeville Band. | | | |
| 12/24/66 | 117 | 2 | I'm Gonna Sit Right Down And Write Myself A Letter ............ AC:25 *I Don't Want To Set The World On Fire* | $6 | | RCA Victor 9026 |
| | | | #3 hit for Billy Williams in 1957 | | | |
| | | | **PALMER, Robert**     HOT/ROK/AC/R&B | | | |
| | | | Born Alan Palmer on 1/19/49 in Batley, England. Lead singer of short-lived supergroup The Power Station. | | | |
| 1/3/76 | 105 | 2 | 1 Get Outside ....................................... *Which Of Us Is The Fool* | $6 | | Island 042 |
| 1/17/76 | 106 | 2 | 2 Give Me An Inch Girl .............................. *Pressure Drop* | $6 | | Island 049 |
| 11/17/79 | 106 | 1 | 3 Jealous ........................................... *In Walks Love Again* | $5 | | Island 49094 |
| 11/29/80 | 105 | 8 | 4 Looking For Clues ................................. *Woke Up Laughing* | $5 | | Island 49620 |
| | | | **PALUMBO, John** ☺ | | | |
| | | | Born on 1/13/51 in Steubenville, Ohio. Lead singer of Crack The Sky. | | | |
| 3/30/85 | 109 | 1 | Blowing Up Detroit ................................ *Hurt Me* | $4 | ■ | HME 04706 |
| | | | **PANHANDLE** ☺ | | | |
| 11/22/69 | 122 | 1 | Hey Girl .......................................... *All The Time Now* | $8 | | Happy Tiger 523 |
| | | | **PANTHER Soundtrack**     R&B/HOT | | | |
| | | | Featured on the soundtrack from the movie *Panther* starring Kadeem Hardison. | | | |
| 6/10/95 | 106 | 6 | The Points ........................................ R&B:80 *(5 remixes)* | $5 | ■ | Mercury 856937 * |
| | | | performed by: Big Mike, Bone Thugs-N-Harmony, Buckshot, Busta Rhymes, **Coolio**, Doodlebug of **Digable Planets**, Helter Skelter, **Ill Al Skratch**, **Jamal**, Menace Clan, The Notorious B.I.G. and **Redman**; Shatasha Williams (female vocal) | | | |
| | | | **PAPERBOY**     R&B/HOT | | | |
| | | | Male rapper from Los Angeles. | | | |
| 6/26/93 | 120 | 3 | Bumpin' (Adaptation Of Humpin') .................. R&B:90 *Jack Move* | $3 | ■ | Next Plateau 357021 |
| | | | rap version of "Humpin'" by The Gap Band | | | |
| | | | **PARADE, The**     HOT | | | |
| | | | Los Angeles pop-rock trio led by Jerry Riopelle, with Murray MacLeod and Smokey Roberds. | | | |
| 2/24/68 | 127 | 1 | The Radio Song ................................... *I Can See Love* | $8 | | A&M 904 |
| | | | tune is similar to The Beach Boys' "I Can Hear Music" | | | |
| | | | **PARAGONS, The**     HOT | | | |
| | | | Doo-wop group from Brooklyn — Julian McMichael, lead singer. McMichael later joined The Olympics. | | | |
| 9/19/60 | 103 | 3 | Blue Velvet ....................................... *Wedding Bells* | $50 | | Musicraft 1102 |
| | | | reissued on Musictone 1102 in 1961 ($30); #1 hit for **Bobby Vinton** in 1963 | | | |
| | | | **PARIS** ☺     R&B | | | |
| | | | Born Oscar Jackson on 10/29/67 in San Francisco. Rapper. | | | |
| 11/5/94 | 119 | 2 | Guerrilla Funk .................................... R&B:90 *(2 remixes)* | $3 | ■ | Priority 53169 |
| | | | Da Old Skool (guest vocals) | | | |
| | | | **PARIS, Bobby** ☺ | | | |
| 1/18/64 | 128 | 1 | 1 Who Needs You ................................. *Little Miss Dreamer* | $20 | | Chattahoochee 631 |
| 9/21/68 | 129 | 2 | 2 Per-so-nal-ly .................................. *Tragedy* | $12 | | Tetragrammaton 1504 |
| | | | melody is similar to **Lloyd Price**'s 1957 hit "Just Because" | | | |
| | | | **PARKER, Graham**     ROK/HOT/AC | | | |
| | | | Born on 11/18/50 in East London. Pub-rock vocalist/guitarist/songwriter. | | | |
| 4/2/77 | 107 | 1 | 1 (Let Me Get) Sweet On You ........... *Hold Back The Night* (Hot #58) / *White Honey* / *Soul Shoes* | $8 | ■ | Mercury 74000 |
| | | | **GRAHAM PARKER AND THE RUMOUR** 4-track pink vinyl E.P. | | | |
| 7/28/79 | 103 | 5 | 2 I Want You Back (Alive) .......................... *Local Girls* | $5 | ■ | Arista 0420 |
| | | | #1 hit for The Jackson 5 in 1970 | | | |
| | | | **PARKER, Junior**     R&B/HOT | | | |
| | | | Born Herman Parker, Jr. on 3/3/27 in West Memphis, Arkansas. Died on 11/8/71. Blues singer/harmonica player. | | | |
| 5/4/63 | 101[1] | 3 | 1 If You Don't Love Me ........................... *I Can't Forget About You* | $15 | | Duke 364 |
| 5/28/66 | 128 | 2 | 2 Goodbye Little Girl ............................. *Walking The Floor Over You* | $15 | | Duke 398 |
| 2/6/71 | 114 | 2 | 3 Drownin' On Dry Land ........................... R&B:48 *Rivers Invitation* | $7 | | Capitol 2997 |
| | | | **PARKER, Ray Jr./Raydio**     R&B/HOT/AC | | | |
| | | | Born on 5/1/54 in Detroit. Prominent session guitarist in California. Formed and led band Raydio. | | | |
| 8/12/78 | 102 | 6 | 1 Honey I'm Rich ................................. R&B:43 *Betcha You Can't Love Me Just Once* | $5 | | Arista 0353 |
| 10/20/79 | 103 | 3 | 2 More Than One Way To Love A Woman ......... R&B:25 *Hot Stuff* | $5 | | Arista 0441 |
| | | | **RAYDIO** (above 2) | | | |
| 10/23/82 | 106 | 3 | 3 It's Our Own Affair ............................. R&B:44 *Just Havin' Fun* | $4 | | Arista 1014 |
| | | | **RAY PARKER JR.** | | | |
| | | | **PARKER, Robert**     HOT/R&B | | | |
| | | | Born on 10/14/30 in Crescent City, Louisiana. R&B saxophonist/vocalist/bandleader. | | | |
| 10/19/59 | 113 | 1 | 1 All Nite Long (Part 1) ........................... *(Part 2)* [I] | $20 | | Ron 327 |
| 9/17/66 | 128 | 2 | 2 The Scratch ..................................... *Happy Feet* | $10 | | Nola 726 |
| | | | **PARKS, Michael**     HOT/AC/C&W | | | |
| | | | Born on 4/4/38 in Corona, California. Movie and TV actor/singer. Starred in the 1969 TV series *Then Came Bronson*. | | | |
| 1/3/70 | 117 | 2 | Tie Me To Your Apron Strings Again ............. *Won't You Ride In My Little Red Wagon* | $6 | | MGM 14092 |
| | | | **PARLIAMENT/FUNKADELIC**     R&B/HOT | | | |
| | | | Highly influential and prolific funk aggregation of nearly 40 musicians spearheaded by **George Clinton** who founded the doo-wop group **The Parliaments** in 1955 in Newark, New Jersey. Parliament and Funkadelic shared the same personnel which included various offshoots: **Bootsy's Rubber Band** and **The Brides Of Funkenstein**. Parliament/Funkadelic were inducted into the Rock and Roll Hall of Fame in 1997. | | | |
| 4/13/68 | 104 | 4 | 1 Look At What I Almost Missed ................... *What You Been Growing* | $20 | | Revilot 217 |
| | | | **THE PARLIAMENTS** | | | |
| 8/14/71 | 107 | 2 | 2 Breakdown ...................................... R&B:30 *Little Ole Country Boy* | $10 | | Invictus 9095 |
| 3/17/73 | 118 | 2 | 3 Loose Booty ..................................... R&B:49 *A Joyful Process* (R&B #38) | $8 | | Westbound 205 |

| DEBUT | PEAK | WKS | A-side (Chart Hit)..............................................................................B-side | $ | Pic | Label & Number |
|---|---|---|---|---|---|---|

**PARLIAMENT/FUNKADELIC — Cont'd**

| DEBUT | PEAK | WKS | A-side B-side | $ | Pic | Label & Number |
|---|---|---|---|---|---|---|
| 10/6/73 | 102 | 12 | 4 Cosmic Slop ............................ *If You Don't Like The Effects, Don't Produce The Cause* | $8 | | Westbound 218 |
| 10/23/76 | 102 | 4 | 5 Undisco Kidd .................................... R&B:30 *How Do Yeaw View You?* | $7 | | Westbound 5029 |
| | | | **FUNKADELIC** (above 3) | | | |
| 12/25/76 | 104 | 6 | 6 Psychoticbumpschool ................................... R&B:69 *Vanish In Our Sleep* | $6 | | Warner 8291 |
| 3/5/77 | 102 | 2 | 7 Dr. Funkenstein ...................................... R&B:43 *Children Of Production* | $6 | | Casablanca 875 |
| 7/9/77 | 104 | 4 | 8 Can't Stay Away .................................... R&B:19 *Another Point Of View* | $6 | | Warner 8403 |
| | | | **BOOTSY'S RUBBER BAND** (#6 & 8) | | | |
| 12/3/77 | 102 | 9 | 9 Bop Gun (Endangered Species) ...........R&B:14 *I've Been Watching You (Move Your Sexy Body)* | $6 | | Casablanca 900 |
| | | | **PARLIAMENT** (#2, 7 & 9) | | | |
| 12/23/78+ | 101[1] | 12 | 10 Disco To Go .......................................... R&B:7 *When You're Gone* | $5 | | Atlantic 3498 |
| | | | **THE BRIDES OF FUNKENSTEIN** | | | |
| 5/1/82 | 103 | 2 | 11 Take A Lickin' And Keep On Kickin' ...................................... R&B:29 *Shine-O-Myte* | $4 | | Warner 50044 |
| | | | **WILLIAM "BOOTSY" COLLINS** | | | |
| 3/5/83 | 101[3] | 9 | 12 Atomic Dog ............................................. R&B:0[4] *(instrumental)* | $4 | ■ | Capitol 5201 |
| 6/15/85 | 101[1] | 5 | 13 Double Oh-Oh .............................................. R&B:32 *Bangladesh* | $4 | ■ | Capitol 5473 |
| 10/2/93 | 106 | 6 | 14 Paint The White House Black ........................... R&B:62 *(instrumental)* | $3 | ■ | Paisley Park 18382 |
| | | | **GEORGE CLINTON** (above 3) | | | |
| | | | samples "Smiling Faces Sometimes" by **The Undisputed Truth** | | | |

**PARSONS, Alan, Project**     HOT/ROK/AC

Duo formed in London in 1975: producer Alan Parsons (guitar, keyboards) and lyricist Eric Woolfson (vocals, keyboards).

| DEBUT | PEAK | WKS | A-side B-side | $ | Pic | Label & Number |
|---|---|---|---|---|---|---|
| 3/26/77 | 108 | 1 | 1 To One In Paradise ........................... *Cask Of Amontillado* | $5 | | 20th Century 2333 |
| 2/9/80 | 105 | 4 | 2 You Won't Be There .................................... *Secret Garden* | $4 | | Arista 0491 |

**PARTON, David** ⊘

| 4/23/77 | 105 | 6 | Isn't She Lovely ........................... *Love And Peace Of Mind* | $5 | | Private Stock 45,139 |
|---|---|---|---|---|---|---|
| | | | written by **Stevie Wonder** | | | |

**PARTON, Dolly** ⊘     C&W/AC/HOT

Born on 1/19/46 in Sevier County, Tennessee. Leading female artist of the Country charts. Starred in several movies. *Top Pop Singles*: 20.

| DEBUT | PEAK | WKS | A-side B-side | $ | Pic | Label & Number |
|---|---|---|---|---|---|---|
| 10/2/65 | 108 | 3 | 1 Happy, Happy Birthday Baby ........................... *Old Enough To Know Better* | $15 | | Monument 897 |
| | | | produced by **Ray Stevens**; #5 hit for **The Tune Weavers** in 1957 | | | |
| 1/9/71 | 108 | 7 | 2 Joshua ............................ C&W:0[1] *I'm Doing This For Your Sake* | $8 | | RCA Victor 9928 |
| 8/21/71 | 106 | 1 | 3 The Right Combination ................... C&W:14 *The Pain Of Loving You* | $8 | | RCA Victor 9994 |
| | | | **PORTER WAGONER AND DOLLY PARTON** | | | |
| 9/28/74 | 105 | 2 | 4 Love Is Like A Butterfly ................... C&W:0[1] / AC:38 *Sacred Memories* | $7 | | RCA Victor 10031 |
| 8/23/75 | 105 | 1 | 5 The Seeker ....................................... C&W:2 *Love With Feeling* | $6 | | RCA Victor 10310 |
| | | | produced by **Porter Wagoner** | | | |
| 2/12/83 | 102 | 4 | 6 Everything's Beautiful (In It's Own Way)   C&W:7 / AC:19 *Put It Off Until Tomorrow* (**Dolly Parton** Kris Kristofferson) | $5 | | Monument 03408 |
| | | | **DOLLY PARTON  WILLIE NELSON** | | | |
| 7/19/97 | 119 | 3 | 7 Peace Train ........................... *(2 versions)* | $4 | ■ | Flip It 44000 |
| | | | **Ladysmith Black Mambazo** (backing vocals); #7 hit for **Cat Stevens** in 1971 | | | |

**PASSION** ⊘     R&B

Born in Oakland in 1974. Female rapper.

| 6/8/96 | 108 | 3 | Where I'm From ................... R&B:88 *(instrumental)* | $3 | ■ | MCA 55096 |
|---|---|---|---|---|---|---|
| | | | samples "I'm A Player" by **Too $hort**; from the movie *Bulletproof* starring Damon Wayans | | | |

**PASSIONS, The**     HOT

Brooklyn pop vocal quartet: Jimmy Gallagher (lead), Tony Armato, Albee Galione and Vinnie Acierno.

| 3/14/60 | 113 | 2 | I Only Want You ........................... *This Is My Love* | $40 | | Audicon 105 |
|---|---|---|---|---|---|---|

**PATTERSON, Rahsaan** ⊘     R&B

R&B singer/songwriter from New York City. Son of jazz saxophonist Rahsaan Roland Kirk. Co-wrote Brandy's "Baby."

| 8/9/97 | 122 | 1 | Where You Are ................... R&B:53 *One More Night* | $3 | ■ | MCA 55355 |
|---|---|---|---|---|---|---|

**PATTY LACE AND THE PETTICOATS** ⊘

| 12/28/63 | 104 | 1 | Sneaky Sue ........................... *The Back* [I] | $15 | | Kapp 563 |
|---|---|---|---|---|---|---|
| | | | arrangement is similar to **The Shangri-Las**' 1964 hit "Leader Of The Pack" | | | |

**PAUL, Henry, Band**     HOT/ROK

Southern-rock band featuring Henry Paul (vocals, guitar). Paul was lead guitarist of the **Outlaws** from 1974-80; formed country trio **BlackHawk** in 1993.

| DEBUT | PEAK | WKS | A-side B-side | $ | Pic | Label & Number |
|---|---|---|---|---|---|---|
| 9/13/80 | 103 | 4 | 1 Longshot ........................... *I Can See It* | $4 | | Atlantic 3755 |
| 3/6/82 | 105 | 3 | 2 Brown Eyed Girl ........................... *Crazy Eyes* | $4 | | Atlantic 4020 |
| | | | #10 hit for **Van Morrison** in 1967 | | | |

**PAUL, Les, And Mary Ford**     MEM/POP/HOT/C&W

Paul was born Lester Polsfuss on 6/9/16 in Waukesha, Wisconsin. Ford was born Colleen Summers on 7/7/28 in Pasadena; died on 9/30/77. Paul is a self-taught guitarist and innovator in electric guitar and multi-track recordings. Married vocalist Mary Ford on 12/29/49; divorced in 1963. Les was inducted into the Rock and Roll Hall of Fame in 1988. *Pop Hits* & *Top Pop Singles*: 42.

| 4/17/61 | 105 | 3 | It's Been A Long, Long Time ........................... *Jura (I Swear I Love You)* (Hot #37) | $8 | ■ | Columbia 41994 |
|---|---|---|---|---|---|---|
| | | | **Les Paul And His Trio** accompanied **Bing Crosby**'s #1 version in 1945 | | | |

**PAUL AND PAULA**     HOT/R&B/AC

Real names: Ray Hildebrand (b: 12/21/40, Joshua, Texas) and Jill Jackson (b: 5/20/42, McCaney, Texas).

| DEBUT | PEAK | WKS | A-side B-side | $ | Pic | Label & Number |
|---|---|---|---|---|---|---|
| 8/24/63 | 108 | 3 | 1 Flipped Over You ........................... *Something Old, Something New* (Hot #77) | $12 | | Philips 40130 |
| 9/28/63 | 105 | 3 | 2 A Perfect Pair ........................... *First Day Back At School* (Hot #60) | $12 | | Philips 40142 |
| 4/4/64 | 105 | 3 | 3 We'll Never Break Up For Good ........................... *Crazy Little Things* | $12 | | Philips 40168 |

**PAVONE, Rita**     HOT

Pop singer from Torino, Italy.

| 6/27/64 | 123 | 1 | 1 Just Once More ........................... *Remember Me* (Hot #26) | $8 | ■ | RCA Victor 8365 |
|---|---|---|---|---|---|---|
| 10/3/64 | *104* | 3 | 2 Wait For Me ........................... *It's Not Easy* | $8 | ■ | RCA Victor 8420 |

## PEACHES & HERB     R&B/HOT/AC

R&B duo from Washington, D.C.: Herb Fame (born Herbert Feemster, 1942) and Francine Barker (born Francine Hurd, 1947). Re-formed with Fame and Linda Green in 1977.

| DEBUT | PEAK | WKS | A-side | B-side | $ | Pic | Label & Number |
|---|---|---|---|---|---|---|---|
| 1/4/69 | 126 | 1 | 1 So True .......................................... *We've Got To Love One Another* | *Satisfy My Hunger* | $8 | | Date 1633 |
| | | | billed on the label as "The Sweethearts Of Soul" | | | | |
| 5/23/70 | 110 | 2 | 2 It's Just A Game, Love ........................... R&B:50 | *Satisfy My Hunger* | $8 | | Date 1669 |
| | | | from the movie *The Split* starring Jim Brown | | | | |
| 4/9/77 | 107 | 2 | 3 We're Still Together ............................. R&B:98 | *Love Is Here Beside Us* | $5 | | MCA 40701 |

## PEANUT BUTTER CONSPIRACY, The     HOT

California psychedelic rock quintet: Sandi Robinson (vocals), Lance Fent and John Merrill (guitars), Al Brackett (bass) and Jim Voight (drums).

| DEBUT | PEAK | WKS | A-side | B-side | $ | Pic | Label & Number |
|---|---|---|---|---|---|---|---|
| 11/16/68 | 125 | 1 | I'm A Fool .......................................... *It's So Hard* | | $12 | | Columbia 44667 |

## PEARL HARBOR & THE EXPLOSIONS ☺

San Francisco-based rock group, led by German-born Pearl E. Gates.

| DEBUT | PEAK | WKS | A-side | B-side | $ | Pic | Label & Number |
|---|---|---|---|---|---|---|---|
| 2/16/80 | 108 | 2 | You Got It (Release It) .......................... *Busy Little B Side* | | $5 | | Warner 49143 |

## PEARL JAM     ROK/HOT

Seattle-based grunge rock band: vocalist Eddie Vedder (b: Eddie Mueller), guitarists Stone Gossard and Mike McCready, bassist Jeff Ament and drummer Dave Abbruzzese. All recorded with Temple Of The Dog. Abbruzzese left band in August 1994. Drummer Jack Irons (**Red Hot Chili Peppers**) joined in late 1994.

| DEBUT | PEAK | WKS | A-side | B-side | $ | Pic | Label & Number |
|---|---|---|---|---|---|---|---|
| 4/8/95 | 102 | 9 | 1 Not For You ........................... ROK:12 *Out Of My Mind (live)* | | $4 | ▮ | Epic 77772 |
| 6/24/95 | 102 | 15 | 2 Immortality     ROK:10 *Rearviewmirror* | | $4 | ▮ | Epic 77873 |
| | | | above 2 from their 1994 album *Vitality* | | | | |
| 7/15/95 | 118 | 6 | 3 Dissident ............. ROK:3 *Release / Rearviewmirror / Even Flow / Dissident / Why Go / Deep (all live)* | | $6 | | Epic 77939 (CD) |
| 2/3/96 | 120 | 5 | 4 Alive ............................................ *Once / Wash* | | $6 | | Epic 77933 (CD) |
| | | | #16 Album Rock hit and #18 Modern Rock hit in 1992 | | | | |
| 5/18/96 | 123 | 1 | 5 Even Flow ....................................... *Dirty Frank / Oceans* | | $6 | | Epic 77934 (CD) |
| | | | #3 Album Rock hit and #21 Modern Rock hit in 1992 | | | | |
| 1/11/97 | 110 | 37 | 6 Alive ............................................ *Once / Wash* [R] | | $6 | | Epic 77933 (CD) |
| 1/18/97 | 108 | 34 | 7 Even Flow ....................................... *Dirty Frank / Oceans* [R] | | $6 | | Epic 77934 (CD) |
| | | | above 4 from their 1992 album *Ten* | | | | |
| 1/25/97 | 120 | 2 | 8 Dissident .................. *Release / Rearviewmirror / Even Flow / Dissident / Why Go / Deep (all live)* [R] | | $6 | | Epic 77939 (CD) |
| | | | #3 & 8: from their 1993 album *Vs.* | | | | |

## PEARLY GATE, The ☺

Studio group led by **Ron Dante** (**The Archies**).

| DEBUT | PEAK | WKS | A-side | B-side | $ | Pic | Label & Number |
|---|---|---|---|---|---|---|---|
| 12/6/69 | 104 | 2 | Free .............................................. *Carole's Epic Song* | | $8 | | Decca 732573 |

## PEARSON, Mr. Danny ☺     R&B

Born in Racine, Wisconsin. Moved to California in 1974; discovered by **Barry White**.

| DEBUT | PEAK | WKS | A-side | B-side | $ | Pic | Label & Number |
|---|---|---|---|---|---|---|---|
| 4/14/79 | 106 | 4 | What's Your Sign Girl? ........................... R&B:16 *Is It Really True Girl* | | $5 | | Unlimited Gold 1400 |
| | | | arranged and produced by **Barry White** | | | | |

## PEEBLES, Ann     R&B/HOT

Born on 4/27/47 in East St. Louis. Sang in family gospel group, the Peebles Choir, from age eight.

| DEBUT | PEAK | WKS | A-side | B-side | $ | Pic | Label & Number |
|---|---|---|---|---|---|---|---|
| 9/25/71 | 113 | 1 | 1 Slipped, Tripped And Fell In Love .................... R&B:42 *99 Lbs.* | | $7 | | Hi 2198 |
| | | | #84 hit for **Clarence Carter** in 1971 | | | | |
| 2/26/72 | 101[2] | 12 | 2 Breaking Up Somebody's Home     R&B:13 *Trouble, Heartaches & Sadness* | | $7 | | Hi 2205 |
| | | | #91 hit for **Albert King** in 1973 | | | | |
| 8/26/72 | 117 | 2 | 3 Somebody's On Your Case ......................... R&B:32 *I've Been There Before* | | $7 | | Hi 2219 |
| 2/3/73 | 111 | 4 | 4 I'm Gonna Tear Your Playhouse Down ........... R&B:31 *One Way Street* | | $7 | | Hi 2232 |
| | | | #13 hit for **Paul Young** in 1985 | | | | |
| 5/4/74 | 102 | 6 | 5 (You Keep Me) Hangin' On ....................... R&B:37 *Heartaches, Heartaches* | | $7 | | Hi 2265 |
| | | | #25 hit for **Joe Simon** in 1968 | | | | |

## PEELS, Leon ☺

R&B singer from Los Angeles. Former lead singer of The Blue Jays.

| DEBUT | PEAK | WKS | A-side | B-side | $ | Pic | Label & Number |
|---|---|---|---|---|---|---|---|
| 7/25/64 | 135 | 1 | A Casual Kiss .................................... *Cottonhead Joe* | | $30 | | Whirlybird 2002 |

## PENDERGRASS, Teddy     R&B/HOT/AC

Born on 3/26/50 in Philadelphia. Lead singer of **Harold Melvin's Blue Notes**.

| DEBUT | PEAK | WKS | A-side | B-side | $ | Pic | Label & Number |
|---|---|---|---|---|---|---|---|
| 9/10/77 | 102 | 12 | 1 The Whole Town's Laughing At Me ........... R&B:16 *The More I Get The More I Want* | | $5 | | Philadelphia Int'l. 3633 |
| 1/6/79 | 106 | 2 | 2 Only You ........................................ R&B:22 *It Don't Hurt Now* | | $5 | | Philadelphia Int'l. 3657 |
| 9/5/81 | 103 | 5 | 3 I Can't Live Without Your Love ............... R&B:10 *You Must Live On* | | $5 | | Philadelphia Int'l. 02462 |
| 3/26/94 | 105 | 13 | 4 Believe In Love ................................. Sls:58 /R&B:14 *Say It* | | $3 | ▮ | Elektra 64574 |
| 8/16/97 | 105 | 8 | 5 Give It To Me ................................... R&B:57 *(3 versions)* | | $3 | ▮ | Surefire 18003 |

## PENFIELD, Holly ☺

Female singer/songwriter/pianist.

| DEBUT | PEAK | WKS | A-side | B-side | $ | Pic | Label & Number |
|---|---|---|---|---|---|---|---|
| 8/16/80 | 105 | 8 | Only His Name .................................. *Eyes Behind Your Eyes* | | $4 | ■ | Dreamland 102 |

## PENGUINS, The     R&B/HOT

R&B vocal group formed in Los Angeles in 1954: Cleveland Duncan, Dexter Tisby, Bruce Tate and Curtis Williams.

| DEBUT | PEAK | WKS | A-side | B-side | $ | Pic | Label & Number |
|---|---|---|---|---|---|---|---|
| 12/28/59+ | 101[2] | 7 | Earth Angel .......................... *Hey Senorita* [R] | | $60 | | Dooto 348 |
| | | | same version that made the pop charts (#8) on 12/25/54 on DooTone 348; above reissue is on a yellow label | | | | |

## PENISTON, CeCe     HOT/R&B

Born on 9/6/69 in Dayton, Ohio. Moved to Phoenix in 1977. In 1989, crowned Miss Black Arizona.

| DEBUT | PEAK | WKS | A-side | B-side | $ | Pic | Label & Number |
|---|---|---|---|---|---|---|---|
| 2/25/95 | 101[1] | 4 | 1 Keep Givin' Me Your Love *(remix)* | | $3 | ▮ | Columbia 77795 |
| | | | from the movie *Ready To Wear (Pret-A-Porter)* starring Julia Roberts | | | | |
| 11/30/96+ | 120 | 11 | 2 Before I Lay (You Drive Me Crazy) ................ R&B:52 *Movin' On* | | $3 | ▮ | A&M 2004 |
| | | | JoJo Hailey of **Jodeci** (male vocal) | | | | |

## PENNINGTON, Barbara ☺

British disco singer.

| DEBUT | PEAK | WKS | A-side | B-side | $ | Pic | Label & Number |
|---|---|---|---|---|---|---|---|
| 4/30/77 | 107 | 1 | Twenty-Four Hours A Day ....................... *I Can't Erase The Thoughts Of You* | | $5 | | United Artists 928 |

| DEBUT | PEAK | WKS | A-side (Chart Hit)...............................................................................................B-side | $ | Pic | Label & Number |
|---|---|---|---|---|---|---|

**PEOPLE**     HOT
Rock sextet from San Jose, California featuring Gene Mason and Larry Norman (vocals).

| 9/7/68 | 111 | 3 | Apple Cider.................................................................................................*Ashes Of Me* | $10 | | Capitol 2251 |

from the rock musical *Alison*

**PERREY, Jean Jacques** ○     AC
French synthesizer player.

| 6/27/70 | 106 | 1 | Passport To The Future ..................................... AC:20 *Country Rock Polka* [I] | $10 | | Vanguard 35105 |

arrangement is similar to **The Tornadoes'** "Telstar"

**PERRY, Jeff** ○     R&B
Born on 10/23/51 in Chicago. R&B vocalist, formerly in Three Of A Kind.

| 9/13/75 | 108 | 1 | Love Don't Come No Stronger (Than Yours And Mine)....................................................... R&B:19 *I've Got To See You Right Away* | $5 | | Arista 0133 |

**PERRY, Joe, Project** ○     ROK
Born on 9/10/50 in Lawrence, Massachusetts. Lead guitarist of Aerosmith.

| 5/17/80 | 110 | 1 | Let The Music Do The Talking ........................................... *Bone To Bone* | $5 | | Columbia 11250 |

**PERSIANS** ○     R&B
R&B vocal group: James Gill, Leroy Priester, Freddie Lewis, James Harlee and Jim Brown.

| 2/12/72 | 108 | 2 | Your Love ....................................................... R&B:39 *Keep On Moving* | $10 | | Capitol 3230 |

**PERSUADERS, The**     R&B/HOT
R&B group formed in New York City in 1969: Douglas "Smokey" Scott, Willie Holland, James "B.J." Barnes and Charles Stodghill.

| 11/11/72 | 104 | 3 | 1 Peace In The Valley Of Love ............................ R&B:21 *What Is The Definition Of Love* | $10 | | Win Or Lose 225 |
| 5/26/73 | 105 | 4 | 2 Bad, Bold And Beautiful, Girl ........................... R&B:24 *Please Stay* | $8 | | Atco 6919 |

**PETER AND GORDON**     HOT/AC
Pop duo formed in London in 1963: Peter Asher (b: 6/22/44, London) and Gordon Waller (b: 6/4/45, Braemar, Scotland).

| 5/14/66 | 130 | 1 | 1 Stranger With A Black Dove ...................... *There's No Living Without Your Loving* (Hot #50) | $10 | ■ | Capitol 5650 |
| 8/31/68 | 118 | 1 | 2 You've Had Better Times ................................... *Sipping My Wine* | $10 | | Capitol 2214 |

**PETER, PAUL & MARY**     HOT/AC
Folk trio formed in New York City in 1961: **Mary Travers** (b: 11/7/37, Louisville); **Peter Yarrow** (b: 5/31/38, New York City); and **Paul Stookey** (b: 12/30/37, Baltimore). Top Pop Singles: 20.

| 1/7/67 | 123 | 3 | 1 Hurry Sundown ................................... AC:37 *For Baby (For Bobbie)* | $8 | | Warner 5883 |
| 10/19/68 | 113 | 2 | 2 Love City (Postcards To Duluth) ...................... *Yesterday's Tomorrow* | $7 | | Warner 7232 |

**PETERS AND LEE** ○     AC/C&W
British duo: Lennie Peters (who was blind; d: 10/10/92, age 59) and Dianne Lee.

| 9/1/73 | 119 | 2 | Welcome Home ................................... AC:26 /C&W:79 *Can't Keep My Mind On The Game* | $6 | | Philips 40729 |

**PETERSON, Lucky, Blues Band** ○     R&B
Born on 12/13/64 in Buffalo, New York. Lead singer/organist of Chicago band formed by Willie Dixon.

| 8/21/71 | 102 | 3 | 1-2-3-4 ....................................................... R&B:40 *Good Old Candy* | $8 | | Today 1503 |

**PETERSON, Oscar, Trio** ○     R&B
Jazz trio: Oscar (b: 8/15/25 in Montreal; piano), Ray Brown (bass) and Ed Thigpen (drums).

| 9/28/63 | 109 | 2 | 1 Hymn To Freedom ..................................... *Hallelujah Time* | $8 | | Verve 10302 |

with the Malcolm Dodds Singers

| 10/24/64 | 101[1] | 7 | 2 Mumbles .................................................... *Incoherent Blues* | $8 | | Mercury 72342 |

'mumbled' vocal by Clark Terry

**PETERSON, Ray**     HOT/AC
Born on 4/23/39 in Denton, Texas. Formed own Dunes label in 1960.

| 2/29/60 | 104 | 6 | 1 What Do You Want To Make Those Eyes At Me For? *Answer Me My Love* | $20 | | RCA Victor 7703 |

#3 hit for Ada Jones & Billy Murray in 1917; #15 hit for Betty Hutton in 1945

| 2/6/61 | 104 | 4 | 2 I'm Tired ................................................... *My Blue Angel* | $20 | | RCA Victor 7845 |

#3 Country hit for **Webb Pierce** in 1957

| 1/11/64 | 108 | 2 | 3 Promises (You Made Now Are Broken) ................. *Sweet Little Kathy* | $20 | | Dunes 2030 |
| 9/12/64 | 128 | 2 | 4 Oh No! .................................................. *If You Were Here* | $15 | ■ | MGM 13269 |
| 12/19/64 | 106 | 5 | 5 Across The Street (Is A Million Miles Away) ........... *When I Stop Dreaming* | $15 | | MGM 13299 |

written by **Gene Pitney**; arranged by **Ray Stevens**

**PET SHOP BOYS**     HOT/ROK/AC/R&B
British duo formed in 1981: Neil Tennant (vocals) and Chris Lowe (keyboards).

| 8/28/93 | 109 | 7 | 1 Can You Forgive Her? ................................... ROK:10 *(remix)* | $3 | ■ | EMI/ERG 50461 |
| 11/20/93 | 106 | 11 | 2 Go West ................................................. *(album version)* | $3 | ■ | EMI/ERG 58084 |

#45 hit for the **Village People** in 1979

| 7/27/96 | 107 | 4 | 3 Before ................................. *The Truck-Driver And His Mate / Hit and Miss* | $3 | ■ | Atlantic 87049 |
| 11/15/97 | 125 | 1 | 4 Somewhere.............. *A Red Letter Day / The View From Your Balcony / Delusions Of Grandeur* | $6 | ■ | Atlantic 84033 (CD) |

from the Broadway musical *West Side Story*; #26 hit for **Len Barry** in 1966

**PETTY, Tom, & The Heartbreakers**     ROK/HOT/AC
Rock group formed in Los Angeles in 1975 featuring Petty (b: 10/20/53, Gainesville, Florida; vocals, guitar). Member of the supergroup Traveling Wilburys. Top Pop Singles: 26.

| 5/21/94 | 109 | 5 | American Girl ......................................... *Think About Me* | $3 | ■ | MCA 54843 |

first released on Shelter 62007 ($8) in 1977 (didn't chart)

**PHAJJA** ○     R&B
Female R&B vocal trio from Chicago: sisters Kena and Nakia Epps, with Karen Johnson.

| 7/5/97 | 112 | 3 | What Are You Waiting For? ............................ R&B:38 *(instrumental)* | $3 | ■ | Warner 17372 |

**PHILLIP and LLOYD (The Blues Busters)** ○     R&B
Duo of Phillip James and Lloyd Campbell.

| 1/17/76 | 105 | 4 | Baby I'm Sorry ..................................... *Just Don't Want To Be Lonely* | $10 | | Scepter 12413 |

## PHILLIPS, Esther                                                  R&B/HOT/AC

Born Esther Mae Jones on 12/23/35 in Galveston, Texas. Died on 8/7/84. One of the first female superstars of R&B. Recorded and toured with The Johnny Otis Orchestra as "Little Esther," 1948-54.

| DEBUT | PEAK | WKS | A-side / B-side | $ | Pic | Label & Number |
|---|---|---|---|---|---|---|
| 2/9/63 | 112 | 4 | 1 Am I That Easy To Forget ...................................*I Really Don't Want To Know* (Hot #61) | $15 | | Lenox 5560 |
| | | | "LITTLE ESTHER" PHILLIPS | | | |
| | | | #25 hit for Debbie Reynolds in 1960 | | | |
| 3/30/63 | 129 | 2 | 2 If You Want It (I've Got It) ..............*You Never Miss Your Water (Till The Well Runs Dry)* (Hot #73) | $15 | | Lenox 5565 |
| | | | "LITTLE ESTHER" PHILLIPS & "BIG AL" DOWNING | | | |
| 7/24/65 | *115* | 3 | 3 Moonglow & Theme From Picnic ..................................... AC:28 *Makin' Whoopee* | $12 | | Atlantic 2294 |
| | | | Ray Ellis (orch.); #1 hit for Morris Stoloff and orchestra in 1956 | | | |
| 10/30/65 | 129 | 1 | 4 Let Me Know When It's Over.................................................*I Saw Me* | $12 | | Atlantic 2304 |
| 2/15/69 | 121 | 7 | 5 Too Late To Worry, Too Blue To Cry ...................... R&B:35 *I'm In The Mood For Love* | $10 | | Roulette 7031 |
| | | | Ernie Freeman (orch.); #76 hit for Glen Campbell in 1962 | | | |
| 7/25/70 | 118 | 1 | 6 Set Me Free ............................................R&B:39 *Brand New Day* | $8 | | Atlantic 2745 |
| | | | ESTHER PHILLIPS With The Dixie Flyers | | | |
| | | | #67 Country hit for Curly Putman in 1967 | | | |
| 4/22/72 | 122 | 2 | 7 Home Is Where The Hatred Is ............................ R&B:40 *'Til My Back Ain't Got No Bone* | $8 | | Kudu 904 |
| 12/9/72 | 106 | 6 | 8 I've Never Found A Man (To Love Me Like You Do) R&B:17 *Cherry Red* | $8 | | Kudu 910 |
| | | | #40 hit for Eddie Floyd in 1968 as "I've Never Found A Girl" | | | |

## PHILLIPS, Phil                                                  HOT/R&B

Born John Phillip Baptiste on 3/14/31. Black vocalist from Lake Charles, Louisiana.

| 4/18/60 | 108 | 2 | What Will I Tell My Heart...................................*Your True Love Once More* | $20 | | Mercury 71611 |
|---|---|---|---|---|---|---|
| | | | Belford Hendricks (orch.); #2 hit for Andy Kirk with Pha Terrell in 1937; #64 hit for Fats Domino in 1957 | | | |

## PHILLIPS, Shawn                                                  HOT/AC

Born on 2/3/43 in Fort Worth, Texas. Soft-rock vocalist.

| 6/2/73 | 112 | 1 | 1 Anello (Where Are You) ....................................*Hey Miss Lonely* | $6 | | A&M 1435 |
|---|---|---|---|---|---|---|
| 10/25/75 | 106 | 4 | 2 Do You Wonder .......................................*Summer Vignette* | $5 | | A&M 1750 |

## PHILLY DEVOTIONS                                                  R&B/HOT

Philadelphia R&B/disco group: Ellis "Butch" Hill, Ernest "Chucky" Gibson, Morris Taylor and Matthew Coginton.

| 9/20/75 | 106 | 3 | I Just Can't Make It (Without You) ...........................*(long version)* | $5 | | Columbia 10191 |
|---|---|---|---|---|---|---|

## PHOTOGLO                                                  AC/HOT

| 8/9/80 | 106 | 1 | When Love Is Gone..............................AC:44 *Faded Blue* | $4 | | 20th Century 2458 |
|---|---|---|---|---|---|---|

## PIAF, Edith                                                  MEM/POP/HOT

Born Edith Giovanna Gassion on 12/19/15 in Belleville, Paris. Died on 10/11/63. Legendary French chanteuse.

| 5/15/61 | 116 | 3 | Exodus ..........................*No Regrets (Non, Je Ne Regrette Rien)* [F] | $12 | | Capitol 4564 |
|---|---|---|---|---|---|---|
| | | | from the Otto Preminger movie starring Paul Newman; #2 hit for Ferrante & Teicher in 1961; lyrics by Pat Boone | | | |

## PICKETT, Bobby                                                  HOT/R&B

Born on 2/11/40 in Somerville, Massachusetts. Recorded his "Monster Mash" hit as Bobby "Boris" Pickett & The Crypt-Kickers.

| 11/28/64 | 135 | 1 | 1 The Monster Swim ..............................*The Werewolf Watusi* [N] | $20 | | RCA Victor 8459 |
|---|---|---|---|---|---|---|
| | | | BOBBY PICKETT and the Rolling Bones | | | |
| | | | arrangement is nearly identical to Pickett's "Monster Mash" hit in 1962 | | | |
| 12/18/76 | 107 | 6 | 2 King Kong (Your Song) ...........................*Disco Kong* [N] | $6 | | Polydor 14361 |
| | | | BOBBY PICKETT AND PETER FERRARA | | | |

## PICKETT, Wilson                                                  R&B/HOT

Born on 3/18/41 in Prattville, Alabama. Soul singer/songwriter. With The Falcons, 1961-63. Inducted into the Rock and Roll Hall of Fame in 1991. *Top Pop Singles*: 38.

| 7/11/64 | 124 | 1 | 1 I'm Gonna Cry.................................*For Better Or Worse* | $12 | | Atlantic 2233 |
|---|---|---|---|---|---|---|
| 12/25/65 | 109 | 2 | 2 My Heart Belongs To You..................................*Let Me Be Your Boy* | $20 | | Verve 10378 |
| | | | originally released on Correc-Tone 501 ($60) and on Cub 9113 ($40) in 1962 | | | |
| 3/23/68 | 101[3] | 3 | 3 I've Come A Long Way                       R&B:46 *Jealous Love* (Hot #50) | $10 | | Atlantic 2484 |
| | | | written by Bobby Womack | | | |
| 5/19/73 | 104 | 5 | 4 International Playboy......................R&B:30 *Come Right Here* | $7 | | Atlantic 2961 |
| 12/8/73+ | 103 | 10 | 5 Soft Soul Boogie Woogie ...................R&B:20 *Take That Pollution Out Your Throat* | $6 | | RCA Victor 0174 |

## PIECES OF A DREAM ☺                                                  R&B

R&B trio from Philadelphia, formed in 1975 as Touch Of Class.

| 2/18/84 | 107 | 2 | Fo-Fi-Fo ..................................R&B:15 *The Shadow Of Your Smile* | $4 | | Elektra 69771 |
|---|---|---|---|---|---|---|
| | | | title refers to number of playoff games (4-5-4) won by the NBA champs, Philadelphia 76ers | | | |

## PIERCE, Webb                                                  C&W/HOT/MEM

Born on 8/8/21 in West Monroe, Louisiana. Died on 2/24/91. A leading country singer, from 1952-58.

| 8/15/60 | 108 | 4 | 1 Drifting Texas Sand .................................C&W:11 *All I Need Is You* | $10 | | Decca 31118 |
|---|---|---|---|---|---|---|
| 1/9/61 | 118 | 2 | 2 There's More Pretty Girls Than One..............................*Let Forgiveness In* (C&W #5) | $10 | | Decca 31197 |
| 6/29/63 | 118 | 2 | 3 Sands Of Gold .......................C&W:7 *Nobody's Darlin' But Mine* | $10 | | Decca 31488 |
| 5/23/64 | 126 | 3 | 4 French Riviera ..........................................*Memory #1* (C&W #2) | $10 | | Decca 31617 |

## PING-PONG ☺

| 5/1/61 | 103 | 3 | Sucu Sucu.............................*Maria Della Montana* [F] | $10 | | Kapp 377 |
|---|---|---|---|---|---|---|
| | | | with the Al Verlane Orchestra | | | |

## PINK FLOYD                                                  ROK/HOT

English progressive-rock band formed in 1965: David Gilmour (guitar; replaced Syd Barrett in 1968), Roger Waters (bass), Nick Mason (drums) and Rick Wright (keyboards). Inducted into the Rock and Roll Hall of Fame in 1996.

| 9/16/67 | 134 | 1 | 1 See Emily Play......................................*Scarecrow* | $200 | ☐ | Tower 356 |
|---|---|---|---|---|---|---|
| | | | THE PINK FLOYD | | | |
| 3/2/74 | 101[3] | 6 | 2 Us And Them                                      *Time* | $15 | | Harvest 3832 |

## PINUPS, The ☺

| 6/19/82 | 110 | 1 | Song On The Radio..............................*It's Only Love* | $4 | ■ | Columbia 02739 |
|---|---|---|---|---|---|---|

## PITNEY, Gene
HOT/C&W/AC/R&B

Born on 2/17/41 in Hartford, Connecticut. Recorded for Decca in 1959 with **Ginny Arnell** as: Jamie & Jane. Recorded for Blaze in 1960 as Billy Bryan. First recorded under own name for Festival in 1960. Wrote "Hello Mary Lou," "He's A Rebel" and "Rubber Ball." *Top Pop Singles*: 24.

| DEBUT | PEAK | WKS | A-side / B-side | $ | Pic | Label & Number |
|---|---|---|---|---|---|---|
| 3/30/63 | 130 | 1 | 1 Teardrop By Teardrop ..................... *Mecca* (Hot #12) | $15 | ■ | Musicor 1028 |
| 2/1/64 | 131 | 2 | 2 Who Needs It ......... *That Girl Belongs To Yesterday* (Hot #49) | $15 | ■ | Musicor 1036 |
| 6/26/65 | 115 | 2 | 3 I'm A Fool To Care ................... *Louisiana Man* (C&W #25) | $12 | ■ | Musicor 1097 |
| | | | **GEORGE AND GENE** George Jones & Gene Pitney | | | |
| | | | #24 hit for Joe Barry in 1961 | | | |
| 3/19/66 | 115 | 3 | 4 Nessuno Mi Puo' Giudcare ............................ *Lei Mi Aspetta* [F] | $12 | | Musicor 1155 |
| 9/10/66 | 115 | 4 | 5 (In The) Cold Light Of Day ............ *The Boss's Daughter* | $12 | ■ | Musicor 1200 |
| 3/11/67 | 106 | 4 | 6 Animal Crackers (In Cellophane Boxes) *Don't Mean To Be A Preacher* | $12 | | Musicor 1235 |
| 10/7/67 | 130 | 2 | 7 Something's Gotten Hold Of My Heart ......... *Building Up My Dream World* | $12 | | Musicor 1252 |

## PIXIES THREE, The
HOT

White teenage female trio (ages 14-16 in 1963) from Hanover, Pennsylvania: Midge Bollinger (lead), Debbie Swisher and Kaye McColl.

| 7/4/64 | 116 | 3 | It's Summer Time U.S.A. ................................ *The Hootch* | $15 | ■ | Mercury 72288 |
|---|---|---|---|---|---|---|

## PLANT, Robert
ROK/HOT

Born on 8/20/48 in West Bromwich, England. Lead singer of Led Zeppelin and The Honeydrippers.

| 8/3/85 | 108 | 2 | 1 Too Loud .............................................. *Kallalou Kallalou* | $4 | ■ | Es Paranza 99622 |
|---|---|---|---|---|---|---|
| 8/14/93 | 111 | 4 | 2 29 Palms .................. ROK:4 *Whole Lotta Love (acoustic)* | $3 | I | Es Paranza 98388 |

## PLASTIC COW GOES MOOOOOOg, The ☻

Jazz pianist/studio musician Mike Melvoin performs on the Moog Synthesizer. Wendy Melvoin (**Prince's Revolution**, Wendy & Lisa) and Susannah Melvoin (The Family) are his twin daughters.

| 11/1/69 | 113 | 2 | Lady Jane ................................ *One Man, One Volt* [I] | $6 | | Dot 17300 |
|---|---|---|---|---|---|---|
| | | | #24 hit for **The Rolling Stones** in 1966 | | | |

## PLATTERS, The
HOT/R&B/AC

R&B group formed in Los Angeles in 1953: Tony Williams (lead; d: 8/14/92), David Lynch (tenor; 1/2/81), Paul Robi (baritone; d: 2/1/89), Herb Reed (bass) and Zola Taylor. Williams left to go solo, replaced by Sonny Turner in 1961. Group inducted into the Rock and Roll Hall of Fame in 1990. *Top Pop Singles*: 40.

| 5/30/60 | 102 | 1 | 1 (I'll Be With You In) Apple Blossom Time *Ebb Tide* (Hot #56) | $15 | | Mercury 71624 |
|---|---|---|---|---|---|---|
| | | | **THE PLATTERS Featuring TONY WILLIAMS** | | | |
| | | | #2 hit for Charles Harrison in 1920; #31 hit for Tab Hunter in 1959 | | | |
| 12/11/61 | 109 | 2 | 2 You'll Never Know/ | | | |
| | | | #1 hit for Dick Haymes in 1943 | | | |
| 11/27/61 | 115 | 3 | 3 Song For The Lonely ................................ | $12 | ■ | Mercury 71904 |
| 9/10/66 | 111 | 1 | 4 Devri ................... *Alone In The Night (Without You)* | $10 | | Musicor 1195 |
| 8/24/68 | 125 | 2 | 5 Hard To Get A Thing Called Love ............ *Why* | $10 | | Musicor 1322 |

## PLAYA PONCHO featuring L.A. SNO ☻
R&B

| 8/12/95 | 110 | 17 | Whatz Up, Whatz Up ....... R&B:63 *(B-Rock remix)* | $3 | I | So So Def 77958 |
|---|---|---|---|---|---|---|

## PLAYBOYS OF EDINBURG, The ☻

Texas-based teen rock band: Michael Williams, Jim Williams, Val Curl and Jerry McCord.

| 7/16/66 | 108 | 7 | Look At Me Girl ................... *News Sure Travels Fast* | $15 | | Columbia 43716 |
|---|---|---|---|---|---|---|
| | | | #52 hit for **Bobby Vee** in 1966 | | | |

## PLAYER
HOT/AC/R&B

Pop-rock group formed in Los Angeles featuring Peter Beckett (vocals, guitar). Beckett joined Little River Band by 1992.

| 9/6/80 | 105 | 3 | Givin' It All ................................ *Tip Of The Iceberg* | $4 | | Casablanca 2295 |
|---|---|---|---|---|---|---|

## PLAYERS, The ☻
R&B

R&B vocal group led by Herbert Butler.

| 9/10/66 | 107 | 3 | 1 He'll Be Back ............. R&B:24 *I Wanna Be Free* | $10 | | Minit 32001 |
|---|---|---|---|---|---|---|
| 12/10/66 | 130 | 2 | 2 I'm Glad I Waited ............. R&B:32 *Why Did I Lie* | $10 | | Minit 32012 |

## PLEASURE FAIR, The ☻

Los Angeles-based folk group that later evolved into Bread.

| 7/22/67 | 134 | 1 | Morning Glory Days ................... *Fade In Fade Out* | $8 | | Uni 55016 |
|---|---|---|---|---|---|---|
| | | | arranged and conducted by David Gates of Bread | | | |

## PM DAWN
HOT/R&B/ROK/AC

Jersey City, New Jersey dance/rap duo of brothers Attrell (b: 5/15/70) and Jarrett (b: 7/17/71) Cordes.

| 12/18/93 | 115 | 4 | You Got Me Floatin' ................... *When Midnight Sighs* | $3 | I | Gee Street 858056 |
|---|---|---|---|---|---|---|
| | | | written and recorded by **Jimi Hendrix** on his 1968 album *Axis: Bold As Love* | | | |

## POCKETS
R&B/HOT

R&B group from Baltimore featuring Larry Jacobs (vocals).

| 11/18/78 | 106 | 1 | Take It On Up ........................ R&B:24 *Sphinx* | $5 | | Columbia 10755 |
|---|---|---|---|---|---|---|

## POCO
HOT/AC/ROK/C&W

Country-rock band formed in Los Angeles by Rusty Young (pedal steel guitar) and **Buffalo Springfield** members **Richie Furay** (rhythm guitar) and **Jim Messina** (lead guitar). **Randy Meisner** (later of the Eagles) left in 1969, replaced by bassist Timothy B. Schmit.

| 11/13/71 | 110 | 3 | 1 Just For Me And You ........................ *Ol' Forgiver* | $7 | | Epic 10804 |
|---|---|---|---|---|---|---|
| 9/15/79 | 103 | 2 | 2 Legend ........................ *Indian Summer* | $5 | | MCA 41103 |
| 4/10/82 | 109 | 1 | 3 Sea Of Heartbreak ............ AC:35 *Feudin'* [I] | $4 | | MCA 52001 |
| | | | #21 hit for **Don Gibson** in 1961 | | | |
| 10/9/82 | 108 | 2 | 4 Ghost Town ................................ *High Sierra* | $4 | ■ | Atlantic 89970 |

## POE
ROK/HOT

Real name: Annie Danielewski. Female alternative rock singer/songwriter from New York City.

| 1/27/96 | 106 | 3 | 1 Trigger Happy Jack (Drive By a Go-Go) ...... ROK:27 *(2 mixes) / That Day / Padre Fear* | $6 | | Modern 95722 (CD) |
|---|---|---|---|---|---|---|
| 3/1/97 | 104 | 5 | 2 Hello ................... Air:65 /ROK:13 *(album version)* | $3 | I | Modern 98028 |

### POINT BLANK
ROK/HOT

Rock sextet from Texas: Bubba Keith (vocals), Rusty Burns and Kim Davis (guitars), Mike Hamilton (keyboards), Bill Randolph (bass) and Buzzy Gruen (drums).

| | | | | | | |
|---|---|---|---|---|---|---|
| 4/11/81 | 107 | 9 | 1 Let Me Stay With You Tonight .......................................... ROK:38 *Walk Across The Fire* | $4 | | MCA 51083 |
| 5/1/82 | 109 | 1 | 2 Let Her Go................................................................................. *Love On Fire* | $4 | | MCA 52029 |

### POINTER SISTERS
R&B/HOT/AC/C&W

R&B group formed in Oakland in 1971: sisters Ruth, Anita, June and Bonnie Pointer. Bonnie went solo in 1978; group continued as a trio. *Top Pop Singles:* 27.

| | | | | | | |
|---|---|---|---|---|---|---|
| 4/6/74 | 108 | 5 | 1 Steam Heat................................................................ *Shaky Flat Blues* | $6 | | Blue Thumb 248 |
| | | | from the musical *The Pajama Game*; #8 hit for **Patti Page** in 1954 | | | |
| 12/11/76 | 103 | 1 | 2 You Gotta Believe ............................................... R&B:14 *Shaky Flat Blues* | $5 | | ABC/Blue Thumb 271 |
| 11/3/79 | 107 | 1 | 3 Blind Faith.......................................................... *The Shape I'm In* | $4 | | Planet 45906 |
| | | | written by **Gerry Rafferty** and **Joe Egan** of Stealers Wheel | | | |
| 11/24/79 | 106 | 4 | 4 Who Do You Love ........................................................................ | $4 | | Planet 45908 |
| | | | originally recorded by **Ian Hunter** in 1975 on his debut album | | | |

### POISON
HOT/ROK

Hard-rock quartet formed in Harrisburg, Pennsylvania featuring Bret Michaels (vocals).

| | | | | | | |
|---|---|---|---|---|---|---|
| 5/22/93 | 104 | 4 | Until You Suffer Some (Fire And Ice) .......................... *Bastard Son Of A Thousand Blues* | $3 | ▐ | Capitol 44919 |

### POLITICIANS, The ✪
R&B

R&B band formed by writer/producer McKinley Jackson.

| | | | | | | |
|---|---|---|---|---|---|---|
| 4/29/72 | 110 | 1 | Free Your Mind .................................................. R&B:33 *Love Machine* [I] [I] | $7 | | Hot Wax 7114 |

### PONDEROSA TWINS + ONE
R&B/HOT

Cleveland teenage R&B group, consisting of two sets of twins: Alvin & Alfred Pelham and Keith & Kirk Gardner, plus Ricky Spencer.

| | | | | | | |
|---|---|---|---|---|---|---|
| 1/15/72 | 102 | 5 | 1 Bound ........................................................ R&B:41 *I Remember You* | $10 | | Astroscope 103 |
| 6/10/72 | 102 | 3 | 2 Why Do Fools Fall In Love .......................... R&B:40 *Bitter With The Sweet* | $10 | | Astroscope 104 |
| | | | **PONDEROSA TWINS** | | | |
| | | | #6 hit for **Frankie Lymon & The Teenagers** in 1956 | | | |

### PONTY, Jean-Luc ✪

Born on 9/29/42 in Normandy, France. Emigrated to the U.S. in 1973. Classically-trained, jazz-rock violinist.

| | | | | | | |
|---|---|---|---|---|---|---|
| 3/6/82 | 108 | 4 | As ...................................................................................... *Jig* [I] | $4 | | Atlantic 4009 |
| | | | #36 hit for **Stevie Wonder** in 1978 | | | |

### POOR, The ✪

Country-pop group led by **Randy Meisner** (Poco, Eagles) with Allen Kemp, Randy Naylor and Pat Shanahan.

| | | | | | | |
|---|---|---|---|---|---|---|
| 4/8/67 | 133 | 2 | She's Got The Time (She's Got The Changes)............................ *Love Is Real* | $25 | | York 402 |

### POORBOYS, The ✪
ROK

Rock band from Claremont, California: Dennis Hill (vocals, guitar), Rik Sanchez (guitar), Joey Phillipy (bass) and Andre Bonter (drums).

| | | | | | | |
|---|---|---|---|---|---|---|
| 3/13/93 | 122 | 3 | Guilty ............................................................. ROK:16 *Do You Know What I Mean* | $3 | ▐ | Hollywood 64668 |

### POPPIES, The
HOT

Black female vocal trio: **Dorothy Moore** (lead), Petsye McCune and Rosemary Taylor.

| | | | | | | |
|---|---|---|---|---|---|---|
| 5/28/66 | 106 | 4 | He's Ready .................................................................... *He's Got Real Love* | $10 | ▐ | Epic 10019 |

### POPPY FAMILY, The — see JACKS, Susan

### PORRELLO, Joey ✪

| | | | | | | |
|---|---|---|---|---|---|---|
| 1/17/76 | 108 | 1 | Fools Rush In ........................................................ *Those Were The Good Old Days* | $6 | | Drive 6243 |
| | | | #3 hit for **Glenn Miller** in 1940; #12 hit for **Rick Nelson** in 1963 | | | |

### PORTER, Billy ✪
R&B

Born in Pittsburgh in 1973. Singer/actor. Appeared on Broadway in *Grease* and *Smokey Joe's Cafe*.

| | | | | | | |
|---|---|---|---|---|---|---|
| 8/23/97 | 109 | 8 | Show Me.................................................... R&B:44 *Medley: True Love/I Am A Spy/Lullaby* | $3 | ▐ | DV8/A&M 2282 |

### PORTER, David
R&B/HOT

Born on 11/21/41 in Memphis. Singer/songwriter.

| | | | | | | |
|---|---|---|---|---|---|---|
| 6/6/70 | 105 | 4 | Can't See You When I Want To .................................... R&B:29 *One Part-Two Parts* | $6 | | Enterprise 9014 |
| | | | produced by **Isaac Hayes** | | | |

### PORTRAIT
R&B/HOT

Male R&B vocal quartet: Eric Kirkland, Michael Angelo Saulsberry, Irving Washington III and Phillip Johnson.

| | | | | | | |
|---|---|---|---|---|---|---|
| 3/20/93 | 102 | 10 | 1 Honey Dip ...................................... Sls:71 /R&B:18 *(2 mixes)* / *(3 album snippets)* | $3 | ▐ | Capitol 44870 |
| 4/29/95 | 119 | 1 | 2 I Can Call You ........................................... R&B:22 *(3 mixes)* | $3 | ▐ | Capitol 58264 |

### POSEY, Sandy
C&W/HOT

Born on 6/18/44 in Jasper, Alabama. Worked as a session singer in Nashville and Memphis in the early '60s.

| | | | | | | |
|---|---|---|---|---|---|---|
| 2/17/68 | 102 | 4 | Something I'll Remember ......................................... *Silly Girl, Silly Boy* | $8 | | MGM 13892 |

### POSITIVE K
R&B/HOT

Darryl Gibson, rapper from the Bronx, New York. Became a Muslim in 1982, adopted the name Positive Knowledge Allah.

| | | | | | | |
|---|---|---|---|---|---|---|
| 12/5/92 | 101[1] | 1 | Night Shift ................................... R&B:flip *I Got A Man (Hot #14)* / *(3 album snippets)* | $3 | ▐ | Island 864305 |

### POSSUM DIXON ✪
ROK

Rock quartet: Rob Zabrecky (vocals, bass), Celso Chavez (guitar), Robert O'Sullivan (keyboards) and Richard Treuel (drums).

| | | | | | | |
|---|---|---|---|---|---|---|
| 2/26/94 | 110 | 7 | Watch The Girl Destroy Me ................................. ROK:9 *For Your Love* / *John Struck Lucy* | $3 | ▐ | Interscope 98308 |

### POURCEL, Franck, And His Orchestra
AC/HOT/R&B

Born on 1/1/15 in Marseilles, France. String orchestra leader/composer/arranger/violinist.

| | | | | | | |
|---|---|---|---|---|---|---|
| 3/6/61 | 112 | 3 | Milord ......................................................... *Milord (Edith Piaf-Hot #88)* [I] | $12 | | Capitol 4493 |
| | | | #45 hit for **Bobby Darin** in 1964 | | | |

### P.O.V. ✪
R&B

Quartet formed at Seton Hall Prep School in New Jersey: Hakim Bell (son of Robert "Kool" Bell, leader of **Kool & The Gang**), Lincoln DeVlugt, Mark Sherman and Ewarner Mills.

| | | | | | | |
|---|---|---|---|---|---|---|
| 10/23/93 | 120 | 4 | All Thru The Nite ........................................................ R&B:31 *(instrumental)* | $3 | ▐ | Giant 18414 |
| | | | **P.O.V. with Jade** | | | |

### POWELL, Bobby
R&B/HOT

Blind southern soul singer from Baton Rouge. Attended Southern University for the Blind.

| 4/23/66 | 120 | 2 | Do Something For Yourself .................... R&B:39 *It's Getting Late In The Evening* | $15 | | Whit 715 |

### POWELL, Jesse ✪
R&B

R&B singer/songwriter from Gary, Indiana.

| 3/23/96 | 113 | 8 | 1 All I Need ............................................ R&B:32 *(Instrumental)* | $3 | ▌ | Silas/MCA 55136 |
| 8/17/96 | 119 | 2 | 2 Gloria .................................................. R&B:51 *It's You That I Need* | $3 | ▌ | Silas/MCA 55208 |

#25 hit for **Enchantment** in 1977

### POWER PLANT, The ✪
Pop vocal group.

| 10/7/67 | 134 | 1 | I Can't Happen Without You ................. *She's So Far Out She's In* | $10 | | Diamond 229 |

### POZO-SECO SINGERS
HOT/AC

Native Texan trio: Susan Taylor, Lofton Kline and country star **Don Williams** (lead singer).

| 3/11/67 | 102 | 5 | 1 Excuse Me Dear Martha ....................... *I Believed It All* (Hot #96) | $7 | | Columbia 44041 |
| 11/28/70 | 115 | 1 | 2 Strawberry Fields/Something ............... *There's Never Been A Time* | $7 | | Certron 10020 |

**POZO SECO**
medley of **Beatles'** hits: #8/'67 and #3/'69, respectively

### PREPARATIONS, The ✪
R&B

New York City R&B trio: Frank McLeod, Gregory Reel and Henry Sollis. First worked as the Spiders.

| 4/13/68 | 134 | 1 | Get-E-Up (The Horse) ......................... R&B:30 *It Won't Be A Dance (If You're Not There)* | $12 | | Heart & Soul 201 |

### PRESLEY, Elvis
HOT/C&W/AC/R&B

"The King of Rock & Roll." Born on 1/8/35 in Tupelo, Mississippi. Died on 8/16/77 (age 42). First recorded for Sun in 1954. Signed to RCA Records on 11/22/55. Starred in 31 feature movies (beginning with *Love Me Tender* in 1956). In U.S. Army from 3/24/58 to 3/5/60. Married Priscilla Beaulieu on 5/1/67; divorced on 10/11/73. Their only child, Lisa Marie, (b: 2/1/68) married **Michael Jackson** on 5/26/94; divorced in 1996. Won Grammy's Lifetime Achievement Award in 1971. Inducted into the Rock and Roll Hall of Fame in 1986. *Top Pop Singles*: 151.

| 5/9/64 | 103 | 2 | 1 Suspicion............................................. *Kiss Me Quick* (Hot #34) | $15 | ▆ | RCA Victor 447-0639 |

recorded March 19, 1962 (on the *Pot Luck* album); #3 hit for **Terry Stafford** in 1964

| 7/25/64 | 111 | 2 | 2 Never Ending........................................ *Such A Night* (Hot #16) | $15 | ▆ | RCA Victor 47-8400 |

released in 1967 as a bonus song on the soundtrack album *Double Trouble*

| 12/5/64 | 107 | 4 | 3 Wooden Heart....................................... *Blue Christmas* (Xmas #1) | $20 | ▆ | RCA Victor 447-0720 |

from the 1960 movie and album *G.I. Blues*; #1 hit for **Joe Dowell** in 1961; also see #6 below

| 3/6/65 | 121 | 1 | 4 You'll Be Gone...................................... *Do The Clam* (Hot #21) | $12 | ▆ | RCA Victor 47-8500 |

released as a bonus song on the soundtrack album *Girl Happy*

| 8/28/65 | 112 | 2 | 5 (It's A) Long Lonely Highway................. *I'm Yours* (Hot #11) | $12 | ▆ | RCA Victor 47-8657 |

released as a bonus song on the soundtrack album *Kissin' Cousins*

| 11/13/65 | 110 | 2 | 6 Wooden Heart....................................... *Puppet On A String* (Hot #14) [R] | $12 | ▆ | RCA Victor 447-0650 |

also see #3 above; #1, 3 & 6: issued on RCA's "Gold Standard Series"

| 7/2/66 | 109 | 1 | 7 Come What May.................................... *Love Letters* (Hot #19) | $12 | ▆ | RCA Victor 47-8870 |

#43 hit for **Clyde McPhatter** in 1958

| 1/28/67 | 102 | 5 | 8 Fools Fall In Love................................. *Indescribably Blue* (Hot #33) | $12 | ▆ | RCA Victor 47-9056 |

released in 1971 on the album *I Got Lucky*; #69 hit for **The Drifters** in 1957

| 4/20/68 | 106 | 1 | 9 We Call On Him..................................... *You'll Never Walk Alone* (Hot #90) | $20 | ▆ | RCA Victor 47-9600 |

released in 1971 on the album *You'll Never Walk Alone*

| 11/30/68 | 112 | 1 | 10 Edge Of Reality.................................... *If I Can Dream* (Hot #12) | $10 | ▆ | RCA Victor 47-9670 |

from the movie *Live A Little, Love A Little*; released in 1970 on the album *Almost In Love*

| 4/26/69 | 101[1] | 2 | 11 How Great Thou Art | *His Hand In Mine* | $25 | ▆ | RCA Victor 74-0130 |

**ELVIS PRESLEY With The Jordanaires and The Imperials Quartet**
from Elvis' 1967 album of the same title

| 5/20/78 | 109 | 2 | 12 Softly, As I Leave You ......................... C&W:flip *Unchained Melody* (C&W #6) [S] | $5 | ▆ | RCA PB-11212 |

"live" recording; Elvis narrates, with vocal by Sherrill Nielsen; released in 1980 on the box set *Elvis Aron Presley*; #27 hit for **Frank Sinatra** in 1964

| 8/26/78 | 105 | 2 | 13 (Let Me Be Your) Teddy Bear .............. C&W:flip *Puppet On A String* (C&W #78) [R] | $5 | ▆ | RCA PB-11320 |

**ELVIS PRESLEY with The Jordanaires** (#1, 2, 4, 5, 7-9 & 13)
originally made the pop charts (#1) on 6/24/57 on RCA Victor 47-7000

### PRESTON, Billy
R&B/HOT/AC

Born on 9/9/46 in Houston. R&B vocalist/keyboardist. Recorded with **The Beatles** on "Get Back" and "Don't Let Me Down."

| 3/21/70 | 108 | 2 | 1 All That I've Got (I'm Gonna Give It To You)........................... *As I Get Older* | $12 | ▆ | Apple 1817 |

produced by **George Harrison**

| 5/12/79 | 108 | 1 | 2 Go For It............................................... *With You I'm Born Again* [I] | $5 | | Motown 1460 |

from the movie *Fast Break* starring Gabe Kaplan

| 8/15/81 | 106 | 1 | 3 Searchin'.............................................. *Hey You* | $5 | | Motown 1520 |

**BILLY PRESTON & SYREETA** (above 2)

### PRESTON, Johnny
HOT/R&B

Born John Preston Courville on 8/18/39 in Port Arthur, Texas. Discovered by J.P. "Big Bopper" Richardson.

| 10/24/60 | 105 | 2 | Charming Billy....................................... *Up In The Air* | $15 | ▆ | Mercury 71691 |

inspired by the traditional folk song from 1824 "Billy Boy"

### PRETENDERS
ROK/HOT/AC

Rock quartet featuring lead singer/songwriter/guitarist Chrissie Hynde (b: 9/7/51, Akron, Ohio).

| 10/17/81 | 110 | 1 | Louie Louie............................................ *In The Sticks* | $5 | ▆ | Sire 49819 |

### PREVIN, Andre
HOT

| 5/30/60 | 108 | 2 | Like Love.............................................. *Love Me Or Leave Me* [I] | $8 | | Columbia 41683 |

sequel to Andre Previn & David Rose's 1959 hit "Like Young"

### PRICE, Kenny ✪
C&W

Born on 5/27/31 in Florence, Kentucky. Died on 8/4/87. Country singer. Known as "The Round Mound Of Sound."

| 1/30/71 | 119 | 1 | The Sheriff Of Boone County ................. C&W:8 *Six String Guitar* | $7 | | RCA Victor 9932 |

## PRICE, Lloyd — R&B/HOT
Born on 3/9/33 in Kenner, Louisiana. R&B vocalist/pianist/composer. Owned KRC, Double-L, and Turntable record labels.

| DEBUT | PEAK | WKS | A-side (Chart Hit) ........B-side | $ | Pic | Label & Number |
|---|---|---|---|---|---|---|
| 9/5/60 | 103 | 4 | 1 Who Coulda' Told You (They Lied) ............... *Just Call Me (And I'll Understand)* (Hot #79) | $15 | | ABC-Paramount 10139 |
| 6/12/61 | 110 | 1 | 2 Mary And Man-O .................... *I Ain't Givin' Up Nothin'* | $15 | | ABC-Paramount 10221 |
| 11/17/62 | 123 | 1 | 3 Under Your Spell Again ...................*Happy Birthday, Mama* | $15 | | ABC-Paramount 10372 |
| | | | #4 Country hit for **Buck Owens** in 1959; #35 hit for **Johnny Rivers** in 1966 | | | |
| 10/31/64 | 123 | 1 | 4 I Love You (I Just Love You) ...................*Don't Cry* | $10 | | Monument 856 |
| 12/26/64 | 124 | 1 | 5 Amen ...................*I'd Fight The World* | $10 | | Monument 865 |
| | | | Erma Franklin (female vocal); from the movie *Lilies of The Fields* starring Sidney Poiter; #7 hit for **The Impressions** in 1965 | | | |
| 7/10/65 | 107 | 4 | 6 If I Had My Life To Live Over ...................*Two For Love* | $10 | | Monument 887 |
| 4/21/73 | 102 | 2 | 7 Love Music                        *Just For Baby* | $7 | | GSF 6894 |
| | | | #97 hit for **The Raiders** in 1973 | | | |

## PRICE, Ray — C&W/HOT/AC
Born on 1/12/26 in Perryville, Texas. Country singer.

| DEBUT | PEAK | WKS | A-side | $ | Pic | Label & Number |
|---|---|---|---|---|---|---|
| 10/2/61 | 115 | 1 | 1 Soft Rain ...................C&W:3 *Here We Are Again* (C&W #26) | $12 | | Columbia 42132 |
| 4/29/72 | 109 | 3 | 2 The Lonesomest Lonesome ...............C&W:2 *That's What Leaving's About* (C&W #66) | $6 | | Columbia 45583 |
| | | | written by **Mac Davis** | | | |

## PRIDE, Charley — C&W/HOT/AC
Born on 3/18/38 in Sledge, Mississippi. The most successful black country performer.

| DEBUT | PEAK | WKS | A-side | $ | Pic | Label & Number |
|---|---|---|---|---|---|---|
| 2/15/69 | 120 | 4 | 1 Kaw-Liga ...................C&W:3 *The Little Folks* | $7 | | RCA Victor 9716 |
| | | | "live" recording; #1 Country hit for **Hank Williams** in 1953 | | | |
| 5/29/71 | 104 | 1 | 2 Let Me Live ...................C&W:21 *Did You Think To Pray* (C&W #70) | $7 | | RCA Victor 9974 |
| 8/5/72 | 102 | 1 | 3 It's Gonna Take A Little Bit Longer ........C&W:❶³ *You're Wanting Me To Stop Loving You* | $6 | ■ | RCA Victor 0707 |
| 3/10/73 | 101¹ | 2 | 4 A Shoulder To Cry On ...................C&W:❶ *I'm Learning To Love Her* | $6 | | RCA Victor 0884 |
| | | | written by **Merle Haggard** | | | |
| 7/7/73 | 101¹ | 6 | 5 Don't Fight The Feelings Of Love ...................C&W:❶ *Tennessee Girl* | $6 | | RCA Victor 0942 |
| 5/31/75 | 101¹ | 2 | 6 I Ain't All Bad ...................C&W:6 *The Hard Times Will Be The Best Times* | $5 | | RCA Victor 10236 |

## PRIEST, Maxi — R&B/HOT/AC
Born Max Elliott on 6/10/60 in London to Jamaican parents. Dancehall reggae singer.

| DEBUT | PEAK | WKS | A-side | $ | Pic | Label & Number |
|---|---|---|---|---|---|---|
| 11/30/96 | 105 | 9 | Watching The World Go By ...................*All The Way / Lion In The Jungle* | $3 | ■ | Virgin 38570 |

## PRIMA, Louis, & Keely Smith — MEM/POP/HOT/R&B
Prima was born on 12/7/11 in New Orleans. Died on 8/24/78. Vocalist/trumpeter/composer/bandleader. First recorded for Bluebird in 1933. Own band in 1934. Married to jazz-styled vocalist Dorothy Keely Smith (b: 3/9/32 in Norfolk, Virginia) from 1952-61. Popular Las Vegas duo.

| DEBUT | PEAK | WKS | A-side | $ | Pic | Label & Number |
|---|---|---|---|---|---|---|
| 8/31/59 | 115 | 1 | I'm Confessin' (That I Love You) ...................*Night And Day* | $10 | ■ | Dot 15978 |
| | | | #2 hit for Guy Lombardo in 1930; #58 hit for **Frank Ifield** in 1963 | | | |

## PRIMAL SCREAM ✪
Rock-funk group from Glasgow, Scotland: Bobby Gillespie (vocals), Andrew Innes and Robert Young (guitars), Henry Raycock (bass) and Toby Toman (drums).

| DEBUT | PEAK | WKS | A-side | $ | Pic | Label & Number |
|---|---|---|---|---|---|---|
| 5/7/94 | 107 | 7 | Rocks ...................ROK:16 *Everybody Needs Somebody* | $3 | ■ | Sire 18189 |

## PRINCE — R&B/HOT/ROK/AC
Born Prince Roger Nelson on 6/7/58 in Minneapolis. Vocalist/multi-instrumentalist/composer/producer. Starred in the movies *Purple Rain*, *Under The Cherry Moon*, *Sign 'O' The Times* and *Graffiti Bridge*. Founded own label, Paisley Park. Changed his name on 6/7/93 to a combination male/female symbol. *Top Pop Singles*: 48.

| DEBUT | PEAK | WKS | A-side | $ | Pic | Label & Number |
|---|---|---|---|---|---|---|
| 10/25/80 | 101¹ | 6 | 1 Uptown ...................R&B:5 *Crazy You* | $15 | ■ | Warner 49559 |
| 1/30/82 | 104 | 3 | 2 Let's Work ...................R&B:9 *Ronnie, Talk To Russia* | $15 | | Warner 50002 |
| 1/2/93 | 108 | 8 | 3 Damn U ...................R&B:32 *2 Whom It May Concern* | $3 | ■ | Paisley Park 18700 |
| | | | **PRINCE AND THE NEW POWER GENERATION** | | | |
| 12/11/93 | 107 | 4 | 4 Peach ...................*Nothing Compares 2 U* (R&B #62) | $3 | ■ | Paisley Park 18372 |

## PRINCE HAROLD ✪ — R&B
R&B vocalist from Lexington, Kentucky. Raised in New York.

| DEBUT | PEAK | WKS | A-side | $ | Pic | Label & Number |
|---|---|---|---|---|---|---|
| 12/10/66 | 114 | 2 | Forget About Me ...................R&B:25 *Baby, You've Got Me* | $10 | | Mercury 72621 |

## PRINCE LA LA ✪ — R&B
Born Lawrence Nelson in New Orleans. R&B singer/guitarist. Brother of guitarist Walter "Papoose" Nelson.

| DEBUT | PEAK | WKS | A-side | $ | Pic | Label & Number |
|---|---|---|---|---|---|---|
| 11/20/61 | 119 | 1 | She Put The Hurt On Me ...................R&B:28 *Don't You Know Little Girl (I'm In Love)* | $15 | | A.F.O. 301 |

## PROBY, P. J. — HOT
Born James Marcus Smith on 11/6/38 in Houston. To Los Angeles in 1957 and performed as Jet Powers.

| DEBUT | PEAK | WKS | A-side | $ | Pic | Label & Number |
|---|---|---|---|---|---|---|
| 12/5/64 | 117 | 1 | 1 Together ...................*Sweet And Tender Romance* | $15 | | London 9705 |
| | | | #1 hit for Paul Whiteman in 1928; #6 hit for **Connie Francis** in 1961 | | | |
| 11/12/66 | 131 | 1 | 2 I Can't Make It Alone ...................*If I Ruled The World* | $12 | ■ | Liberty 55915 |
| | | | #63 hit for **Lou Rawls** in 1969 | | | |
| 6/10/67 | 119 | 2 | 3 Work With Me Annie ...................*You Can't Come Home Again (If You Leave Me Now)* | $12 | ■ | Liberty 55974 |
| | | | #1 R&B hit for **Hank Ballard's Midnighters** in 1954 (pop version known as "Dance With Me Henry") | | | |
| 9/23/67 | 130 | 2 | 4 Just Holding On ...................*Butterfly High* | $12 | | Liberty 55989 |
| 5/18/68 | 135 | 1 | 5 I Apologize Baby ...................*It's Your Day Today* | $12 | | Liberty 56031 |
| | | | Proby released a different tune in 1965 titled "I Apologize" | | | |

## PROCOL HARUM — HOT/R&B/ROK
British rock group formed in 1967 by Gary Brooker (vocals, piano) and lyricist Keith Reid. **Robin Trower** was lead guitarist from 1968-71.

| DEBUT | PEAK | WKS | A-side | $ | Pic | Label & Number |
|---|---|---|---|---|---|---|
| 6/16/73 | 117 | 3 | Grand Hotel ...................*Fires (Which Burnt Brightly)* | $7 | ■ | Chrysalis 2013 |

## PRODUCERS, The — HOT/ROK
Pop-rock quartet formed in Atlanta in 1979: Van Temple (vocals, guitar), Wayne Famous (keyboards), Kyle Henderson (bass) and Bryan Holmes (drums).

| DEBUT | PEAK | WKS | A-side | $ | Pic | Label & Number |
|---|---|---|---|---|---|---|
| 8/22/81 | 108 | 4 | What's He Got? ...................*Boys Say When/Girls Say Why* | $5 | | Portrait 02445 |

## PROYECTO UNO ✪
Hip-hop group from Puerto Rico: Magic Juan, Erik Morales, Johnny Salgado and Nelson Zapata.

| DEBUT | PEAK | WKS | A-side | $ | Pic | Label & Number |
|---|---|---|---|---|---|---|
| 1/18/97 | 112 | 6 | Pumpin' ...................*(Spanish edit)* | $3 | ■ | H.O.L.A. 341009 |

| DEBUT | PEAK | WKS | A-side (Chart Hit)..............................................................................................B-side | $ | Pic | Label & Number |
|---|---|---|---|---|---|---|

### PRYSOCK, Arthur     R&B/HOT/AC/C&W
Born on 1/2/29 in Spartanburg, South Carolina. Died on 6/14/97. First recorded with Buddy Johnson, 1944.

| DEBUT | PEAK | WKS | A-side / B-side | $ | Pic | Label & Number |
|---|---|---|---|---|---|---|
| 3/2/63 | **128** | 1 | 1 Our Love Will Last .............................................................. *Come And See This Old Fool* | $12 | | Old Town 1132 |
| 6/27/64 | **124** | 5 | 2 Close Your Eyes ................................................................... *My Everlasting Love* | $12 | | Old Town 1163 |
| | | | written in 1932; #4 R&B hit for Herb Lance in 1949 | | | |
| 10/3/64 | **126** | 2 | 3 Without The One You Love..................................................... *Fly Me To The Moon* | $12 | | Old Town 1170 |
| 10/9/65 | **125** | 2 | 4 Only A Fool Breaks His Own Heart....................................... *Open Up Your Heart* | $10 | | Old Town 1185 |
| 7/2/66 | **124** | 4 | 5 Let It Be Me (Je t'appartiens) .......................... AC:28 *Because* | $10 | | Old Town 1196 |
| | | | #7 hit for The Everly Brothers in 1960 | | | |
| 1/28/67 | **120** | 2 | 6 You Don't Have To Say You Love Me ............. *Ten Thousand Kisses, Ten Thousand Hugs* | $10 | | Verve 10470 |
| | | | #4 hit for Dusty Springfield in 1966 | | | |
| 4/27/68 | **134** | 2 | 7 Mamam ................................................................... *No Sun Today* | $10 | | Verve 10592 |
| 11/3/73 | **110** | 6 | 8 In The Rain    R&B:36 *Thank Heaven For You* | $6 | | Old Town 100 |
| | | | #5 hit for The Dramatics in 1972 | | | |

### PULVER, Judi ○
Pop/rock singer/songwriter based in Southern California.

| 10/6/73 | **118** | 2 | Dancing On The Moon ........................................................ *Be Long (She Don't Know)* | $6 | ■ | MGM 14615 |
|---|---|---|---|---|---|---|

### PUNCH ○
Pop/rock vocal group from Los Angeles: Kathy, Dee, Charlie & Steve.

| 10/2/71 | **110** | 1 | Fallin', Lady ...................................................................... *Travelin' Boy* | $7 | | A&M 1288 |
|---|---|---|---|---|---|---|

### PURE LOVE & PLEASURE ○
Pop/rock quintet featuring lead vocalists David McAnally and Pegge Ann May.

| 4/4/70 | **104** | 4 | All In My Mind..................................................................... *What'cha Gonna Do* | $7 | | Dunhill/ABC 4232 |
|---|---|---|---|---|---|---|

### PURE PRAIRIE LEAGUE     HOT/AC/C&W
Country-rock group formed in Cincinnati in 1971. Country singer **Vince Gill** was lead singer from late 1979-83.

| 6/12/76 | **106** | 1 | That'll Be The Day.................................................C&W:96 *I Can Only Think Of You* | $5 | | RCA Victor 10679 |
|---|---|---|---|---|---|---|
| | | | #1 hit for Buddy Holly & The Crickets in 1957 | | | |

### PURE SOUL     R&B/HOT
Female R&B vocal quartet from Washington, D.C.: Shawn Allen, Heather Perkins, Keitha Shepherd and Kirstin Hall.

| 11/11/95 | **101**[2] | 8 | I Want You Back    R&B:26 *(acapella version)* | $3 | ▮ | StepSun/Interscope 98108 |
|---|---|---|---|---|---|---|

### PURIFY, James And Bobby     R&B/HOT
R&B duo: cousins James Purify (b: 5/12/44, Pensacola, Florida) and Robert Lee Dickey (b: 9/2/39, Tallahassee, Florida). Dickey replaced by Ben Moore in 1974.

| 1/4/75 | **101**[2] | 4 | Do Your Thing    R&B:30 *Why Love* | $6 | | Casablanca 812 |
|---|---|---|---|---|---|---|
| | | | #30 hit for Isaac Hayes in 1972 | | | |

### PURSELL, Bill     HOT/AC/R&B
Pianist from Tulare, California. Appeared with the Nashville Symphony Orchestra.

| 5/25/63 | **121** | 1 | Loved ................................................................................ *Stranger* [!] | $8 | | Columbia 42780 |
|---|---|---|---|---|---|---|
| | | | Grady Martin (orch.) | | | |

### PUTMAN, Curly ○     C&W
Born Claude Putman, Jr. on 11/20/30 in Princeton, Alabama. Country singer and prolific songwriter.

| 7/8/67 | **134** | 3 | My Elusive Dreams ...........................................C&W:41 *Hurtin' Like A Heartache* | $7 | | ABC 10934 |
|---|---|---|---|---|---|---|
| | | | #1 Country hit for David Houston & Tammy Wynette in 1967 | | | |

# Q

### Q     HOT
Pop quartet from Beaver Falls, Pennsylvania: Don Garvin (guitar), Robert Peckman (bass), Bill Thomas (keyboards) and Bill Vogel (drums). Garvin and Peckman were members of The Jaggerz.

| 7/16/77 | **108** | 1 | Sweet Summertime.............................................*If It Ain't One Thing, It's Another* | $5 | ■ | Epic/Sweet City 50404 |
|---|---|---|---|---|---|---|

### Q-FEEL     HOT
U.K. techno dance duo.

| 3/26/83 | **110** | 2 | Dancing In Heaven (Orbital Be-Bop)................... *At The Top (All The Way To St. Tropez)* | $4 | | Jive 2001 |
|---|---|---|---|---|---|---|
| | | | made the Hot 100 (#75) on 6/17/89 on Jive 1220 | | | |

### QUAD CITY DJ'S     R&B/HOT
Studio dance group from Orlando, Florida: Nathaniel "C.C. Lemonhead" Orange, Johnny "Jay Ski" McGowan and Lana.

| 8/2/97 | **105** | 6 | Summer Jam ........................................................ R&B:95 *(album version)* | $3 | ▮ | Big Beat 98016 |
|---|---|---|---|---|---|---|

### QUATRO, Mike, Jam Band ○
Keyboard player from Detroit. Brother of Suzi Quatro.

| 7/8/72 | **108** | 4 | Circus................................................................................ *Time Spent In Dreams* | $7 | | Evolution 1062 |
|---|---|---|---|---|---|---|

### QUEEN     HOT/ROK/AC/R&B
Rock group formed in England in 1972: Freddie Mercury (vocals; d: 11/24/91), Brian May (guitar), John Deacon (bass) and Roger Taylor (drums). *Top Pop Singles*: 27.

| 1/20/96 | **118** | 2 | Too Much Love Will Kill You ......................................... *Rock In Rio Blues* | $3 | ▮ | Hollywood 64005 |
|---|---|---|---|---|---|---|

### QUEENSRYCHE     ROK/HOT
Heavy-metal quintet formed in 1981, in Bellevue, Washington: Geoff Tate (vocals), Chris DeGarmo and Michael Wilton (guitars), Eddie Jackson (bass) and Scott Rockenfield (drums).

| 7/24/93 | **111** | 4 | Real World.............................................................ROK:3 *Last Time In Paris* | $3 | ▮ | Columbia 77077 |
|---|---|---|---|---|---|---|
| | | | from the movie Last Action Hero starring Arnold Schwarzenegger | | | |

### ? AND THE MYSTERIANS     HOT

Punk-rock quintet from Saginaw, Michigan: Mexican-born Rudy "?" Martinez (vocals), Bobby Balderrama (guitar), Frank Rodriguez (organ), Frank Lugo (bass) and Eddie Serrato (drums).

| 8/26/67 | 110 | 3 | Do Something To Me ........................................................................*Love Me Baby* | $15 | | Cameo 496 |
|---|---|---|---|---|---|---|
| | | | #38 hit for Tommy James & The Shondells in 1968 | | | |

### QUESTIONMARK ASYLUM ☺     R&B

Rap quartet: Kenny "Mistafiss" Jones, Marcell "Rostaswan" Gadson, Dominick "Digge Dom" Warren and Douglas "Ding Ding" Francis.

| 5/6/95 | 104 | 12 | Hey Lookaway ...............................**R&B:56** *(Erick Sermon remix) / Got Dem Joints* | $3 | ▌ | Kaper/RCA 64305 |
|---|---|---|---|---|---|---|
| | | | samples "Thoughts Of Old Flames" by Pleasure | | | |

### QUICKSILVER MESSENGER SERVICE     HOT

San Francisco rock group: Gary Duncan (vocals, guitar), John Cipollina (guitar; d: 5/29/89), David Freiberg (bass) and Greg Elmore (drums).

| 11/23/68 | 110 | 2 | Stand By Me ...................................................................................*Bears* | $10 | | Capitol 2320 |
|---|---|---|---|---|---|---|

### QUINTEROS, Eddie ☺

| 3/28/60 | 101[1] | 5 | Come Dance With Me .........................................................*Vivian* | $30 | | Brent 7009 |
|---|---|---|---|---|---|---|
| | | | imitation of Ritchie Valens' 1958 hit "Come On, Let's Go" | | | |

### QUOTATIONS, The ☺

Doo-wop vocal group from Brooklyn, New York.

| 1/27/62 | 105 | 5 | Imagination ..............................................................................*Ala-Men-Sy* | $30 | | Verve 10245 |
|---|---|---|---|---|---|---|
| | | | doo-wop version of Glenn Miller's #1 hit in 1940 | | | |

# R

### RADIANTS, The     R&B/HOT

R&B vocal group formed in Chicago in 1960: Maurice McAlister, Jerome Brookes, Green "Mac" McLaurin, Wallace Sampson and Elzie Butler.

| 11/23/63 | 104 | 5 | 1 Shy Guy ...........................................................................*I'm In Love* | $15 | | Chess 1872 |
|---|---|---|---|---|---|---|
| | | | **Maurice McAlister & THE RADIANTS** | | | |
| 9/4/65 | 116 | 1 | 2 Whole Lot Of Woman ......................................................*Tomorrow* | $12 | | Chess 1939 |

### RADICE, Mark ☺     R&B

Born on 11/23/57 in Newark, New Jersey. R&B singer/pianist/composer. First recorded at age nine.

| 9/18/76 | 110 | 1 | If You Can't Beat 'Em, Join 'Em .......**R&B:55** *The Whole Wide World Ain't Nothin' But A Party* | $6 | | United Artists 840 |
|---|---|---|---|---|---|---|

### RAELETTS, The     R&B/HOT

Originally formed as The Cookies, later became the backup group for Ray Charles. Lineup in 1971: Mable John, Susaye Green, Vernita Moss and Estella Yarbrough. Also called **Sisters Love**.

| 7/31/71 | 101[1] | 2 | Here I Go Again .................*Leave My Man (Woman) Alone (w/Vernita Moss)* | $8 | | Tangerine 1017 |
|---|---|---|---|---|---|---|
| | | | **THE RAELETTS Featuring Estella Yarbrough** | | | |

### RAGE ☺

| 1/23/93 | 118 | 1 | Run To You ...................................................................*Ease The Pain* | $3 | ▌ | Critique 15494 |
|---|---|---|---|---|---|---|
| | | | #6 hit for Bryan Adams in 1985 | | | |

### RAIDERS — see REVERE, Paul

### RAINBOW ☺

Pop vocal group.

| 4/15/72 | 114 | 3 | Open Up Your Heart...........................*Your Love Keeps Comin' On* | $7 | | Evolution 1056 |
|---|---|---|---|---|---|---|

### RAINBOW     ROK/HOT

Hard-rock band led by British guitarist Ritchie Blackmore and bassist **Roger Glover**, both members of **Deep Purple**.

| 3/8/80 | 110 | 1 | 1 All Night Long........................................................*Danger Zone* | $5 | | Polydor 2060 |
|---|---|---|---|---|---|---|
| 4/18/81 | 105 | 2 | 2 I Surrender .............**ROK:19** *Vielleicht Das Nachster Zeit (Maybe Next Time)* | $5 | | Polydor 2163 |

### RAINDROPS, The     HOT/R&B

Songwriting team of Ellie Greenwich (b: 10/23/40) and husband Jeff Barry (b: 4/3/38). Their song hits were celebrated in the 1985 Broadway musical *Leader Of The Pack*.

| 5/30/64 | 109 | 5 | Let's Go Together ...................................*You Got What I Like* | $20 | | Jubilee 5475 |
|---|---|---|---|---|---|---|

### RAINWATER, Marvin     C&W/HOT

Born Marvin Karlton Percy on 7/2/25 in Wichita, Kansas. Country singer of Cherokee Indian heritage.

| 9/18/61 | 119 | 1 | I Can't Forget .................................................................*Boo Hoo* | $15 | | Warwick 666 |
|---|---|---|---|---|---|---|

### RAITT, Bonnie     AC/HOT/ROK/C&W

Born on 11/8/49 in Burbank, California. Veteran blues-rock singer/guitarist. Daughter of Broadway actor/singer John Raitt.

| 3/13/82 | 104 | 9 | 1 Keep This Heart In Mind .......................**ROK:39** *Can't Get Enough* | $4 | | Warner 50022 |
|---|---|---|---|---|---|---|
| 6/5/82 | 109 | 2 | 2 Me And The Boys ......................................*River Of Tears* | $4 | | Warner 29992 |

### RAJA-NEÉ ☺     R&B

Female vocalist.

| 1/14/95 | 114 | 5 | Turn It Up ....................................................**R&B:31** *Bitchism* | $3 | ▌ | Perspective 7472 |
|---|---|---|---|---|---|---|
| | | | samples "Make Me Say It Again, Girl" by The Isley Brothers | | | |

### RAKIM     R&B/HOT

Born William Griffin on 1/28/68 in Long Island, New York. Male rapper. Former partner of Eric B.

| 11/20/93 | 118 | 2 | Heat It Up.....................................................**R&B:92** *(The Wiz mix)* | $3 | ▌ | MCA 54743 |
|---|---|---|---|---|---|---|
| | | | from the movie *Gunmen* starring Christopher Lambert | | | |

**RAMBEAU, Eddie**　　　　　　　　　　　　　　　　AC/HOT
Born Edward Flurie on 6/30/43 in Hazleton, Pennsylvania. Pop singer/songwriter.

| | | | | | | |
|---|---|---|---|---|---|---|
| 8/17/63 | 132 | 1 | 1 Lover's Medley "The More I See You"/"When I Fall In Love"...............................................*The Car Hop And The Hard Top* | $20 | | Swan 4145 |

　　　　MARCY JO AND EDDIE RAMBEAU
　　　　#7 hit for The Lettermen in 1962; #16 hit for Chris Montez in 1966

| | | | | | | |
|---|---|---|---|---|---|---|
| 7/17/65 | 112 | 4 | 2 My Name Is Mud...................................................AC:30 *I Just Need Your Love* | $10 | | DynoVoice 207 |
| 11/6/65 | 129 | 1 | 3 The Train........................................................*Yesterday's Newspapers* | $10 | | DynoVoice 211 |
| 10/22/66 | 122 | 3 | 4 Clock...............................................................................*If I Were You* | $10 | | DynoVoice 225 |

**RAMPAGE**　　　　　　　　　　　　　　　　R&B/HOT
Male rapper from New York City.

| | | | | | | |
|---|---|---|---|---|---|---|
| 12/27/97+ | 106 | 8 | Wegetzdown...................................R&B:67 *(remix) / Get The Money & Dip* | $3 | ■ | Elektra 64137 |

　　　　samples "She's Strange" by Cameo

**RANDALL, Jon — see MORGAN, Lorrie**

**RANDAZZO, Teddy**　　　　　　　　　　　　　　　　HOT
Born on 5/20/37 in New York City. Pop singer/songwriter/producer. Member of The Three Chuckles.

| | | | | | | |
|---|---|---|---|---|---|---|
| 11/7/64 | 130 | 2 | Lost Without You..................................................*Less Than Tomorrow* | $10 | | DCP 1108 |

**RANDI, Don** ☉
Prolific Hollywood session pianist. Played piano on many Phil Spector-produced hits.

| | | | | | | |
|---|---|---|---|---|---|---|
| 4/3/65 | 113 | 3 | Mexican Pearls...........................................*I Don't Wanna Be Kissed* [I] | $7 | | Palomar 2203 |

　　　　Camarata (orch.); #94 hit for Billy Vaughn in 1965

**RANDOLPH, Barbara** ☉
R&B vocalist.

| | | | | | | |
|---|---|---|---|---|---|---|
| 10/14/67 | 116 | 4 | I Got A Feeling.........................................*You Got Me Hurtin' All Over* | $20 | | Soul 35038 |

**RANDOLPH, Boots**　　　　　　　　　　　　　　　　AC/HOT/R&B
Born Homer Louis Randolph, III on 6/3/27 in Paducah, Kentucky. Premier Nashville session saxophonist.

| | | | | | | |
|---|---|---|---|---|---|---|
| 12/30/67 | 105 | 4 | 1 Big Daddy.........................................................*Love Letters* | $6 | | Monument 1038 |

　　　　written by John D. Loudermilk; original version by Boots issued in 1961 on RCA Victor 7835

| | | | | | | |
|---|---|---|---|---|---|---|
| 5/16/70 | 111 | 1 | 2 Anna...................................................AC:40 *Spanish Harlem* | $6 | | Monument 1199 |

　　　　#5 hit for Silvana Mangano in 1953; #54 hit for Jorgen Ingmann in 1961

**RANDOLPH, Luther, & Johnny Stiles** ☉

| | | | | | | |
|---|---|---|---|---|---|---|
| 7/6/63 | 109 | 10 | Cross Roads (Part 1).........................................*(Part 2)* [I] | $12 | | Cameo 253 |

**RANDY and THE RAINBOWS**　　　　　　　　　　　　HOT/R&B
White doo-wop group from Queens, New York: Dominick "Randy" Safuto (lead) and brother Frank Safuto, brothers Mike and Sal Zero, and Ken Arcipowski.

| | | | | | | |
|---|---|---|---|---|---|---|
| 12/19/64 | 133 | 1 | Little Star............................................................*Sharin'* | $20 | | Rust 5091 |

　　　　#1 hit for The Elegants in 1958

**RANEY, Sue** ☉　　　　　　　　　　　　　　　　AC
Pop singer from New York City. Founder of Rayel Records production company.

| | | | | | | |
|---|---|---|---|---|---|---|
| 5/9/60 | 109 | 2 | Biology...............................................................*Too Soon* | $12 | | Capitol 4360 |

　　　　Bill Holman (orch.)

**RANJI** ☉

| | | | | | | |
|---|---|---|---|---|---|---|
| 5/20/72 | 109 | 4 | It's So Easy (To Be Bad).........................*When You Find Out Where You're Going* | $7 | ■ | Anthem 51007 |

**RANKIN, Kenny** ☉
Singer/songwriter/acoustic guitarist. First recorded on Groove as Kenneth Rankins & The Spars in 1956.

| | | | | | | |
|---|---|---|---|---|---|---|
| 5/21/77 | 110 | 2 | On And On.......................................*Through The Eye Of The Eagle* | $6 | | Little David 735 |

　　　　Don Costa (orch.); #11 hit for Stephen Bishop in 1977

**RAPPIN' 4-TAY**　　　　　　　　　　　　　　　　R&B/HOT
Born Anthony Forte in San Francisco in 1969. Male rapper. Served time in San Quentin prison.

| | | | | | | |
|---|---|---|---|---|---|---|
| 8/3/96 | 117 | 2 | A Lil' Some'em Some'em..........................R&B:74 *(2 versions) / Off Parole* | $3 | ■ | Chrysalis/EMI 58575 |

　　　　samples "I Wanta' Do Something Freaky To You" by Leon Haywood

**RARE BIRD** ☉
British rock group — Steve Gould, lead singer. Gould later formed the group Runner.

| | | | | | | |
|---|---|---|---|---|---|---|
| 4/11/70 | 121 | 3 | 1 Sympathy.................................................*Beautiful Scarlet* | $7 | | Probe/ABC 477 |
| 9/1/73 | 122 | 1 | 2 Birdman - Part One (Title No. 1 Again).......................*(Part Two)* | $6 | | Polydor 15079 |

**RARE EARTH**　　　　　　　　　　　　　　　　HOT/R&B
Nucleus of Detroit rock group: Gil Bridges (saxophone, flute), John Persh (trombone, bass) and Pete Rivera (drums).

| | | | | | | |
|---|---|---|---|---|---|---|
| 4/14/73 | 108 | 3 | 1 "Ma".................................................................*(instrumental)* | $6 | | Rare Earth 5053 |
| 9/29/73 | 110 | 8 | 2 Hum Along And Dance.................................R&B:95 *Come With Me* | $6 | | Rare Earth 5054 |
| 11/8/75 | 106 | 3 | 3 It Makes You Happy (But It Ain't Gonna Last Too Long)............................*Boogie With Me Children* | $6 | | Rare Earth 5058 |

**RASCALS, The**　　　　　　　　　　　　　　　　HOT/R&B
Blue-eyed, soul-pop quartet formed in New York City in 1964: Felix Cavaliere (vocals, organ), Gene Cornish (vocals, guitar), Eddie Brigati (vocals, percussion) and Dino Danelli (drums). Inducted into the Rock and Roll Hall of Fame in 1997.

| | | | | | | |
|---|---|---|---|---|---|---|
| 1/2/71 | 119 | 2 | Right On.............................................................*Almost Home* | $6 | | Atlantic 2773 |

**RAWLS, Lou**　　　　　　　　　　　　　　　　R&B/HOT
Born on 12/1/35 in Chicago. Silky soul singer/actor. With the Pilgrim Travelers gospel group, 1957-59.

| | | | | | | |
|---|---|---|---|---|---|---|
| 2/17/68 | 113 | 4 | 1 My Ancestors..........................................................*Evil Woman* | $8 | | Capitol 2084 |
| 5/11/68 | 103 | 5 | 2 You're Good For Me *Soul Serenade* | $8 | | Capitol 2172 |
| 11/23/68 | 123 | 2 | 3 The Split.........................................................*Why Can't I Speak* | $7 | | Capitol 2348 |

　　　　title song from the movie starring Jim Brown

| | | | | | | |
|---|---|---|---|---|---|---|
| 2/12/72 | 105 | 4 | 4 His Song Shall Be Sung......................R&B:44 *Believe In Me* | $6 | | MGM 14349 |

　　　　written by Bobby Hebb

| DEBUT | PEAK | WKS | A-side (Chart Hit) ... B-side | $ | Pic | Label & Number |
|---|---|---|---|---|---|---|
| | | | **RAWLS, Lou — Cont'd** | | | |
| 11/4/72 | 106 | 4 | 5 Walk On In ............... AC:34 *The Politician* | $6 | | MGM 14428 |
| | | | written by **Carole King** | | | |
| | | | **RAYDIO — see PARKER, Ray Jr.** | | | |
| | | | **RAYE, Collin** C&W/HOT/AC | | | |
| | | | Born on 8/22/59 in DeQueen, Arkansas. Country singer. | | | |
| 1/27/96 | 114 | 6 | Not That Different ............... C&W:3 *Sweet Miss Behavin'* | $3 | ■ | Epic 78189 |
| | | | **RBL POSSE** ☉ R&B | | | |
| | | | Rap duo from San Francisco: Christian Mathews and Kyle Church. RBL stands for Ruthless By Law. | | | |
| 8/2/97 | 122 | 6 | How We Comin' ............... R&B:90 *(remix)* | $3 | ■ | Big Beat 98017 |
| | | | featuring **Mystikal** & Big Lurch | | | |
| | | | **RCR** HOT/R&B | | | |
| | | | Pop trio: Donna and Sandra Rhodes and Charles Chalmers. Backed **Frank Sinatra** on his 1975 hit "Anytime." | | | |
| 7/26/80 | 108 | 2 | Give It To You ............... R&B:89 *Moments of Magic* | $4 | | Radio 712 |
| | | | **READY FOR THE WORLD** R&B/HOT/AC | | | |
| | | | R&B funk sextet formed in 1982 in Flint, Michigan featuring Melvin Riley (vocals). | | | |
| 2/23/85 | 103 | 5 | Tonight ............... R&B:6 *(same version)* | $4 | | MCA 52507 |
| | | | **REAL LIVE** ☉ R&B | | | |
| | | | New Jersey-based rap duo: producer K-Def and rapper Larry-O. | | | |
| 2/3/96 | 106 | 5 | Real Live Sh*t ............... R&B:72 *Crime Is Money* | $3 | ■ | Big Beat 98113 |
| | | | **REAL LIVE featuring K-Def & Larry-O** | | | |
| | | | samples "It Ain't Hard To Tell" by **Nas**; remix later released on Big Beat 98069 featuring Ghostface Killa, Cappadonna, Lord Tariq and Killa Sin | | | |
| | | | **REAL McCOY** HOT/AC | | | |
| | | | Dance trio: German rapper/songwriter Olaf "O-Jay" Jeglitza with American singers Vanessa Mason and Lisa Cork. | | | |
| 2/17/96 | 101[1] | 18 | 1 Sleeping With An Angel/ | | | |
| 5/18/96 | 102 | 7 | 2 Ooh Boy | $3 | ■ | Arista 12964 |
| | | | #72 hit for **Rose Royce** in 1978 | | | |
| 6/28/97 | 105 | 7 | 3 I Wanna Come (With You) ............... *Silly* | $3 | ■ | Arista 13385 |
| 10/11/97 | 102 | 5 | 4 (If You're Not In It For Love) I'm Outta Here ............... *(album version) / Party* | $3 | ■ | Arista 13403 |
| | | | #1 Country hit for **Shania Twain** in 1995 | | | |
| | | | **REDBONE** HOT/R&B | | | |
| | | | Native American "swamp-rock" group formed in Los Angeles in 1968 featuring brothers Lolly and Pat Vegas. | | | |
| 4/1/72 | 111 | 3 | 1 When You Got Trouble ............... *Jerico* | $6 | | Epic 10839 |
| 7/6/74 | 101[1] | 1 | 2 Wovoka ............... *Clouds In My Sunshine* | $5 | | Epic 11131 |
| 8/31/74 | 108 | 3 | 3 Suzie Girl ............... *Interstate Highway 101* | $5 | | Epic 50015 |
| | | | **REDDING, Otis** R&B/HOT | | | |
| | | | Born in Dawson, Georgia. Killed in a plane crash on 12/10/67. Soul singer/songwriter/producer/pianist. Inducted into the Rock and Roll Hall of Fame in 1989. *Top Pop Singles*: 30. | | | |
| 4/26/69 | 109 | 3 | 1 When Something Is Wrong With My Baby ............... *Ooh Carla, Ooh Otis* | $10 | | Atco 6665 |
| | | | **OTIS & CARLA** | | | |
| | | | #42 hit for **Sam & Dave** in 1967 | | | |
| 8/2/69 | 103 | 5 | 2 Free Me/ R&B:30 | | | |
| 8/16/69 | 110 | 2 | 3 (Your Love Has Lifted Me) Higher & Higher | $10 | | Atco 6700 |
| | | | #6 hit for **Jackie Wilson** in 1967 | | | |
| 4/4/70 | 105 | 4 | 4 Demonstration ............... *Johnny's Heartbreak* | $10 | | Atco 6742 |
| 2/6/71 | 110 | 2 | 5 I've Been Loving You Too Long ............... *Try A Little Tenderness* [R] | $10 | | Atco 6802 |
| | | | recorded at the Monterey International Pop Festival, June 1967; studio version made the *Hot 100* (#21) on 5/15/65 on Volt 126 | | | |
| | | | **RED HOT CHILI PEPPERS** ROK/HOT | | | |
| | | | Los Angeles-based, rap-styled rock foursome featuring Anthony Kiedis (vocals). Kiedis appeared in the movie *Point Break*. | | | |
| 12/26/92 | 124 | 2 | Behind The Sun ............... ROK:7 *Higher Ground* | $3 | ■ | EMI 50412 |
| | | | recorded in 1987 (on their album *The Uplift Mofo Party Plan*) | | | |
| | | | **REDMAN** R&B/HOT | | | |
| | | | Rapper from Newark, New Jersey. Discovered by **Erick Sermon** of EPMD. Also see **Frankie Cutlass**. | | | |
| 12/19/92 | 124 | 2 | 1 Blow Your Mind ............... R&B:33 *(3 versions) / How To Roll A Blunt* | $5 | ■ | RAL/Chaos 74424 * |
| | | | samples "The Show" by **Doug E. Fresh**, "Dance Floor" by **Zapp** and "Theme From The Black Hole" by **Parliament** | | | |
| 2/20/93 | 109 | 5 | 2 Time 4 Sum Aksion ............... R&B:63 *(3 versions)* | $5 | ■ | RAL/Chaos 74794 * |
| | | | samples "How I Could Just Kill A Man" by **Cypress Hill** and "Playin' Kinda Ruff" by **Zapp** | | | |
| 11/19/94 | 105 | 8 | 3 Rockafella ............... Sls:67 / R&B:62 *(remix version)* | $3 | ■ | RAL 853966 |
| | | | samples "I Want'a Do Something Freaky To You" by **Leon Haywood** and "Flashlight" by **Parliament** | | | |
| | | | **RED RIDER** HOT | | | |
| | | | Canadian rock group led by singer/songwriter **Tom Cochrane**. | | | |
| 6/7/80 | 103 | 3 | Don't Fight It ............... *Look Out Again* | $4 | | Capitol 4868 |
| | | | **REDWING** ☉ | | | |
| | | | Pop-rock quartet from Sacramento, California: Ron Flogel, Andrew Samuels, George Hullin and Tom Phillips. | | | |
| 4/17/71 | 108 | 4 | California Blues ............... *Dark Thursday* | $8 | | Fantasy 657 |
| | | | written by the legendary Jimmie Rodgers in 1929 as "Blue Yodel No. 4" | | | |
| | | | **REED, Jerry** C&W/HOT/AC | | | |
| | | | Born Jerry Reed Hubbard on 3/20/37 in Atlanta. Country singer/guitarist/songwriter/actor. | | | |
| 7/27/59 | 115 | 1 | 1 Soldier's Joy ............... *Little Lovin' Liza* | $15 | | NRC 5008 |
| | | | #15 hit for **Hawkshaw Hawkins** in 1959 | | | |
| 7/31/61 | 117 | 1 | 2 Love And War (Ain't Much Difference In The Two) ............... *Love Is The Cause Of It All* | $12 | | Columbia 42047 |
| 10/4/75 | 104 | 2 | 3 You Got A Lock On Me ............... C&W:60 *Reedology* | $5 | | RCA Victor 10389 |
| 9/17/77 | 103 | 16 | 4 East Bound And Down ............ C&W:2 *(I'm Just A) Redneck In A Rock And Roll Bar* (C&W flip) | $5 | | RCA 11056 |
| | | | from the movie *Smokey and the Bandit* starring Reed and Burt Reynolds | | | |

### REED, Jimmy
R&B/HOT

Born Mathis James Reed on 9/6/25 in Dunleith, Mississippi. Died on 8/29/76. Distinctive, influential blues singer/guitarist/harmonica player/songwriter. Inducted into the Rock and Roll Hall of Fame in 1991.

| | | | | | | |
|---|---|---|---|---|---|---|
| 9/19/60 | 104 | 3 | 1 Going By The River (Part II)...............................*Hush-Hush* (Hot #75) | $20 | | Vee-Jay 357 |
| 9/21/63 | 119 | 3 | 2 Mary-Mary..................................*I'm Gonna Help You* | $20 | | Vee-Jay 552 |
| 1/14/67 | 125 | 3 | 3 Two Ways To Skin (A Cat)..............................*Got No Where To Go* | $8 | | ABC 10887 |

### REED, Lou
ROK/HOT

Born Lewis Alan Reed on 3/2/42 in Freeport, Long Island, New York. Lead singer/songwriter of the New York seminal rock band Velvet Underground; regarded as the godfather of punk rock.

| | | | | | | |
|---|---|---|---|---|---|---|
| 6/9/73 | 119 | 1 | 1 Satellite Of Love.........................................*Walk And Talk It* | $7 | | RCA Victor 0964 |
| | | | arranged and produced by **David Bowie** and Mick Ronson | | | |
| 11/9/74 | 103 | 2 | 2 Sally Can't Dance..........................................*Ennui* | $6 | | RCA Victor 10081 |

### REED, Vivian ✪
R&B

Born in Pittsburgh. Sang with the Good Hope Baptist Choir; studied opera for five years.

| | | | | | | |
|---|---|---|---|---|---|---|
| 6/15/68 | 113 | 4 | 1 Yours Until Tomorrow...............................R&B:44 *I Wanna Be Free* | $8 | | Epic 10319 |
| 9/14/68 | 115 | 2 | 2 You've Lost That Lovin' Feeling/(You're My) Soul And Inspiration..........................*Mama Open The Door* | $8 | | Epic 10382 |
| | | | **Righteous Brothers** medley: #1/'65 and #1/'66 | | | |

### REESE, Della
HOT/R&B/AC

Born Delloreese Patricia Early on 7/6/31 in Detroit. With **Mahalia Jackson** gospel troupe from 1945-49; with Erskine Hawkins in the early '50s. Regular on TV's *Touched By An Angel*.

| | | | | | | |
|---|---|---|---|---|---|---|
| 8/14/61 | 115 | 1 | 1 A Far Far Better Thing.........................................*I Possess* | $10 | ■ | RCA Victor 7884 |
| 1/10/70 | 121 | 4 | 2 Games People Play/ | | | |
| | | | #12 hit for **Joe South** in 1969 | | | |
| 1/3/70 | 128 | 5 | 3 Compared To What | $7 | ■ | Avco Embassy 4515 |
| | | | #85 hit for **Les McCann & Eddie Harris** in 1970 | | | |

### REEVES, Jim
C&W/HOT/AC/MEM

Born James Travis Reeves on 8/20/24 in Panola County, Texas. Killed in a plane crash on 7/31/64 in Nashville. Elected to the Country Music Hall of Fame in 1967. *Top Pop Singles*: 23.

| | | | | | | |
|---|---|---|---|---|---|---|
| 2/2/63 | 103 | 9 | 1 Is This Me?...............................C&W:3 *Missing Angel* | $10 | ■ | RCA Victor 8127 |
| | | | written by **Dottie West** | | | |
| 1/25/64 | 102 | 9 | 2 Welcome To My World .............C&W:2 *Good Morning Self* (C&W #43) | $10 | | RCA Victor 8289 |
| 4/4/64 | 115 | 1 | 3 Love Is No Excuse/ | C&W:7 | | |
| 3/21/64 | 121 | 1 | 4 Look Who's Talking | $10 | | RCA Victor 8324 |
| | | | **JIM REEVES & DOTTIE WEST** (above 2) | | | |
| 1/21/67 | 112 | 6 | 5 I Won't Come In While He's There ......................C&W:❶¹ *Maureen* | $8 | | RCA Victor 9057 |

### REEVES, Martha — see MARTHA & THE VANDELLAS

### REFLECTIONS, The
HOT

Rock and roll band from Detroit: Tony "Spaghetti" Micale (lead vocals), Danny Bennie, Phil "Parrot" Castrodale, Johnny Dean and Ray "Razor" Steinberg.

| | | | | | | |
|---|---|---|---|---|---|---|
| 9/12/64 | 124 | 1 | 1 (I'm Just) A Henpecked Guy....................*Don't Do That To Me* | $15 | | Golden World 16 |
| 1/2/65 | 121 | 3 | 2 Shabby Little Hut ...............*You're My Baby (And Don't You Forget It)* | $15 | | Golden World 19 |

### REGOR, Dennis ✪

| | | | | | | |
|---|---|---|---|---|---|---|
| 10/12/63 | 115 | 3 | Toys In The Attic.................*Toys In The Attic* (w/The Paulette Sisters) [I] | $10 | | Contempo 904 |
| | | | title song from the movie starring **Dean Martin**; #85 hit for Joe Sherman in 1963 | | | |

### REID, Clarence
R&B/HOT

Born on 2/14/45 in Cochran, Georgia. Soul singer/composer/arranger/producer. Also recorded as Blowfly.

| | | | | | | |
|---|---|---|---|---|---|---|
| 11/8/69 | 120 | 2 | I'm Gonna Tear You A New Heart ......................*I'm A Man Of My Word* | $8 | | Alston 4578 |

### REIVERS, The ✪

Austin, Texas band, originally known as Zeitgeist. Took present name from William Faulkner novel.

| | | | | | | |
|---|---|---|---|---|---|---|
| 9/5/70 | 112 | 3 | Revolution In My Soul ...........................................*Constantly* | $7 | | White Whale 360 |
| | | | written and produced by **Paul Davis** | | | |

### REJOICE!
HOT/AC

Husband-wife pop duo of Tom and Nancy Brown from Sausalito, California.

| | | | | | | |
|---|---|---|---|---|---|---|
| 3/8/69 | 126 | 3 | November Snow..............................AC:31 *Quick Draw Man* | $7 | | Dunhill/ABC 4176 |

### R.E.M.
ROK/HOT/AC

Alternative rock quartet formed in 1980 in Athens, Georgia: Michael Stipe (vocals), Peter Buck (guitar), Mike Mills (bass) and Bill Berry (drums).

| | | | | | | |
|---|---|---|---|---|---|---|
| 8/17/85 | 110 | 1 | 1 Can't Get There From Here ......................ROK:14 *Bandwagon* | $8 | ■ | I.R.S. 52642 |
| 8/26/95 | 113 | 5 | 2 Crush With Eyeliner.............ROK:20 *Fall On Me / Me In Honey / Finest Worksong* (all live) | $6 | | Warner 41904 (CD) |

### REMAINS, The ✪

Rock quartet formed at Boston University in 1964: Barry Tashian (guitar), Vern Miller (bass), Bill Briggs (keyboards) and Chip Damiani (drums).

| | | | | | | |
|---|---|---|---|---|---|---|
| 4/23/66 | 129 | 2 | Diddy Wah Diddy ...........................................*Once Before* | $60 | ☐ | Epic 10001 |

### RENAY, Diane
HOT/AC

Born Renee Diane Kushner in Philadelphia.

| | | | | | | |
|---|---|---|---|---|---|---|
| 6/20/64 | 124 | 5 | 1 Growin' Up Too Fast ...........................................*Waitin' For Joey* | $15 | | 20th Century Fox 514 |
| 8/22/64 | 131 | 2 | 2 It's In Your Hands ................................*A Present From Eddie* | $15 | | 20th Century Fox 533 |
| 11/28/64 | 101² | 3 | 3 Watch Out Sally | *Billy Blue Eyes* | $15 | | MGM 13296 |

### RENE, Googie
R&B/HOT

Born Raphael Rene. Bandleader/keyboardist. Son of songwriter/producer Leon Rene. First recorded for Class in 1956.

| | | | | | | |
|---|---|---|---|---|---|---|
| 12/26/60 | 105 | 1 | The Slide (Part I) ...............................R&B:20 *Part II* | $15 | ■ | Rendezvous 134 |

### RENE, Wendy ✪

R&B singer from Memphis.

| | | | | | | |
|---|---|---|---|---|---|---|
| 10/10/64 | 134 | 1 | After Laughter .........................................*What Will Tomorrow Bring* | $12 | | Stax 154 |

**RENE & ANGELA**  R&B/HOT
Los Angeles-based R&B duo: Rene Moore and **Angela Winbush**. Formed in 1978.

| 6/29/85 | 101[1] | 1 | Save Your Love (For #1)  R&B:**O**[2] (instrumental) | $4 | | Mercury 880731 |

**RENE & RENE**  HOT/AC
Mexican-American male duo from Laredo, Texas: Rene Ornelas (b: 8/26/36) and Rene Herrera (b: 10/2/35).

| 3/15/69 | 128 | 2 | Las Cosas ........................................ You Will Cry | $6 | | White Whale 298 |

translation of Spanish title: The Things; sung in English and Spanish

**REO SPEEDWAGON**  HOT/ROK/AC
Rock quintet formed in 1968 in Champaign, Illinois: Mike Murphy (vocals), Gary Richrath (guitar), Neal Doughty (keyboards), Gregg Philbin (bass) and Alan Gratzer (drums).

| 3/4/72 | 122 | 1 | Sophisticated Lady ......................................................... Prison Women | $12 | | Epic 10827 |

**REPARATA AND THE DELRONS**  HOT
Brooklyn pop vocal trio: Mary "Reparata" Aiese, Sheila Reillie and Carol Drobnicki.

| 2/3/68 | 127 | 1 | Captain Of Your Ship .................................... Toom Toom (Is A Little Boy) | $12 | | Mala 589 |

**REUNION**  HOT/AC
Studio group from New York City: Joey Levine (lead vocals; **Ohio Express**), Marc Bellack, Paul DiFranco and Norman Dolph.

| 2/1/75 | 101[1] | 3 | Disco-Tekin  Goodstuff | $5 | | RCA Victor 10150 |

**REVERE, Paul, AND The Raiders**  HOT/AC
Rock and roll band formed in 1960 in Caldwell, Idaho. Group featured Paul Revere (b: 1/7/42, Boise, Idaho; keyboards) and Mark Lindsay (lead singer). On daily ABC-TV show *Where The Action Is* in 1965. Own TV show *Happening* in 1968. *Top Pop Singles*: 24.

| 11/2/63 | 103 | 3 | 1 Louie, Louie .........................................................Night Train | $30 | | Columbia 42814 |

#2 hit for **The Kingsmen** in 1963; first released on Sande 101 in 1963 ($150)

| 5/2/64 | 118 | 3 | 2 Louie - Go Home ........................................ Have Love, Will Travel | $20 | | Columbia 43008 |
| 10/3/64 | 133 | 1 | 3 Over You ......................................................... Swim | $20 | | Columbia 43114 |
| 5/15/65 | 131 | 1 | 4 Sometimes ....................................... Oo Poo Pah Doo | $20 | | Columbia 43273 |

#53 hit for Gene Thomas in 1961 as "Sometime"

| 12/2/67 | 102 | 4 | 5 Do Unto Others  Peace Of Mind (Hot #42) | $10 | ■ | Columbia 44335 |
| 5/9/70 | 120 | 1 | 6 Gone Movin' On .................................... Interlude (To Be Forgotten) | $7 | | Columbia 45150 |

**RAIDERS**

**REYNOLDS, L.J. — see CHOCOLATE SYRUP**

**RHINOCEROS**  HOT
Rock group from Los Angeles featuring John Finley (vocals).

| 8/8/70 | 109 | 3 | Better Times ......................................................... It's A Groovy World | $8 | | Elektra 45694 |

**RHODES KIDS, The ✪**
Family pop group from Houston: Paul, Ron, Gary, Patricia, Marsha, Brett and Mark Rhodes.

| 2/22/75 | 107 | 1 | Runaway ...................................... (instrumental) | $6 | | GRC 2052 |

#1 hit for **Del Shannon** in 1961

**RHYTHMCENTRIC ✪**

| 5/4/96 | 113 | 5 | You Don't Have To Worry ......................................... (Philly side) | $3 | ▮ | Tazmania 811 |

**RHYTHM HERITAGE**  R&B/AC/HOT
Los Angeles studio group assembled by prolific producers Steve Barri and Michael Omartian.

| 8/14/76 | 101[1] | 3 | Disco-Fied  R&B:80 (It's Time To) Boogie Down | $4 | | ABC 12205 |

**RIBEIRO, Alfonso ✪**  R&B
Born on 9/21/71 in New York City. Cast member of TV's *Silver Spoons* and *The Fresh Prince Of Bel-Air*.

| 9/8/84 | 104 | 2 | Dance Baby ......................................................... (dub version) | $4 | ■ | Prism 99723 |

**RICE, Sir Mack ✪**  R&B
Real name: Bonny Rice. R&B singer from Detroit. In **The Falcons** from 1957-63.

| 5/15/65 | 108 | 5 | 1 Mustang Sally ......................... R&B:15 Daddy's Home To Stay | $10 | | Blue Rock 4014 |

#23 hit for **Wilson Pickett** in 1966

| 2/22/69 | 135 | 2 | 2 Coal Man ......................... R&B:48 Love's A Mother Brother | $8 | | Atco 6645 |

**MACK RICE**

**RICH, Charlie**  C&W/AC/HOT
Born on 12/14/32 in Colt, Arkansas. Died on 7/25/95. Rockabilly-country singer/pianist/songwriter.

| 11/13/61 | 111 | 2 | 1 Just A Little Bit Sweet ......................................... It's Too Late | $25 | | Phillips 3572 |
| 11/30/63 | 108 | 7 | 2 Big Boss Man ........................ Let Me Go My Merry Way | $15 | | Groove 0025 |

#13 R&B hit for **Jimmy Reed** in 1961; #38 hit for **Elvis Presley** in 1967

| 9/12/64 | 131 | 1 | 3 Nice And Easy ......................... Turn Around And Face Me | $15 | | Groove 0041 |

#60 hit for Frank Sinatra in 1960

| 12/11/65 | 132 | 2 | 4 I Can't Go On ......................................................... Dance Of Love | $10 | | Smash 2012 |
| 3/12/66 | 125 | 3 | 5 Hawg Jaw ........................ Something Just Came Over Me | $10 | | Smash 2022 |
| 7/30/77 | 101[5] | 14 | 6 Rollin' With The Flow  C&W:**O**[2] / AC:32 To Sing A Love Song | $5 | | Epic 50392 |

**RICHARD, Cliff**  HOT/AC
Born Harry Rodger Webb on 10/14/40 in Lucknow, India, of British parentage. Vocalist/actor/guitarist. To England in 1948. Knighted by Queen Elizabeth II in 1995.

| 4/18/64 | 109 | 6 | 1 I Only Have Eyes For You ......................... I'm The Lonely One (Hot #92) | $15 | ■ | Epic 9670 |

#11 hit for **The Flamingos** in 1959

| 5/19/73 | 109 | 3 | 2 Power To All Our Friends ......................... Come Back Billie Joe | $6 | | Sire 707 |

**RICHIE, Lionel**  AC/R&B/HOT/C&W
Born on 6/20/49 in Tuskegee, Alabama. Former lead singer of the Commodores.

| 8/17/96 | 101[1] | 15 | Ordinary Girl  AC:9 /R&B:76 (edit) / Say You, Say Me | $3 | ▮ | Mercury 578374 |

written by Richie and **Babyface**

| DEBUG | PEAK | WKS | A-side (Chart Hit)....................................B-side | $ | Pic | Label & Number |
|---|---|---|---|---|---|---|
| | | | **RICKS, Jimmy** HOT | | | |
| 1/16/61 | 103 | 4 | 1 I'll Never Be Free............................ You're The Boss (Hot #81) | $20 | | Atlantic 2090 |
| | | | LaVERN BAKER & JIMMY RICKS | | | |
| | | | #3 hit for Kay Starr & Tennessee Ernie Ford in 1950 | | | |
| 9/5/64 | 115 | 3 | 2 Trouble In Mind................................ Romance In The Dark | $15 | | Atlantic 2246 |
| | | | blues standard written in 1926; #86 hit for **Aretha Franklin** in 1963 | | | |
| | | | **RIDDLE, Nelson** HOT/AC/MEM | | | |
| | | | Born on 6/1/21 in Oradell, New Jersey. Died on 10/6/85. One of the most in-demand of all arranger/conductors for many top artists. | | | |
| 10/20/62 | 130 | 2 | Naked City Theme............................ The Defenders Theme [I] | $10 | | Capitol 4843 |
| | | | written by Billy May; from the ABC-TV series starring James Franciscus | | | |
| | | | **RIGHTEOUS BROTHERS, The** HOT/R&B/AC | | | |
| | | | Blue-eyed soul duo: **Bill Medley** (b: 9/19/40, Santa Ana, California; baritone) and Bobby Hatfield (b: 8/10/40, Beaver Dam, Wisconsin; tenor). First recorded as the Paramours for Smash in 1962. Top Pop Singles: 23. | | | |
| 5/2/64 | 119 | 3 | 1 Try To Find Another Man................ I Still Love You | $20 | | Moonglow 231 |
| 10/24/64 | 114 | 1 | 2 This Little Girl Of Mine.......... If You're Lying You'll Be Crying | $20 | | Moonglow 235 |
| | | | #9 R&B hit for **Ray Charles** in 1955; #26 hit for **The Everly Brothers** in 1958 | | | |
| 2/6/65 | 101[2] | 3 | 3 <u>My Babe</u> Fee-Fi-Fidily-I-Oh (Dinah Blow Your Horn) [R] | $20 | | Moonglow 223 |
| | | | originally made the Hot 100 (#75) on 9/7/63 | | | |
| 2/13/65 | 117 | 3 | 4 Fannie Mae................................ Bring Your Love To Me (Hot #83) | $15 | | Moonglow 238 |
| | | | #38 hit for **Buster Brown** in 1960 | | | |
| 10/9/65 | 103 | 4 | 5 For Your Love................................ Gotta Tell You How I Feel | $15 | | Moonglow 243 |
| | | | #13 hit for Ed Townsend in 1958 | | | |
| 10/15/66 | 118 | 3 | 6 The White Cliffs Of Dover................ She's Mine, All Mine | $15 | ■ | Philles 132 |
| | | | #6 hit for Glenn Miller in 1942 | | | |
| 2/11/67 | 108 | 5 | 7 Along Came Jones................................ Jimmy's Blues [N] | $10 | | Verve 10479 |
| | | | from the TV series Please Don't Eat The Daisies starring Patricia Crowley; #9 hit for The Coasters in 1959 | | | |
| 9/30/67 | 128 | 4 | 8 Been So Nice.......... Stranded In The Middle Of Noplace (Hot #72) | $10 | ■ | Verve 10551 |
| 2/3/68 | 121 | 1 | 9 Here I Am................................ So Many Lonely Nights Ahead | $10 | | Verve 10577 |
| | | | **RILEY, Jeannie C.** C&W/HOT/AC | | | |
| | | | Born Jeanne Carolyn Stephenson on 10/19/45 in Anson, Texas. Country singer. | | | |
| 7/5/69 | 111 | 5 | 1 The Rib................................ C&W:32 I'm The Woman | $6 | | Plantation 22 |
| 10/4/69 | 111 | 2 | 2 Things Go Better With Love...... C&W:34 The Back Side Of Dallas (C&W #33) | $6 | | Plantation 29 |
| 2/7/70 | 106 | 3 | 3 Country Girl................................ C&W:7 We Were Raised On Love | $6 | | Plantation 44 |
| | | | **RILEY, Teddy — see BLACKstreet** | | | |
| | | | **RIPPLE** R&B/HOT | | | |
| | | | Chicago-based interracial progressive R&B septet originally from Kalamazoo, Michigan. | | | |
| 3/9/74 | 108 | 8 | Willie Pass The Water.................. R&B:27 Git Owf | $6 | | GRC 1013 |
| | | | **RIPPY, Rodney Allen** ☉ | | | |
| | | | Born on 7/29/68 in Shelby, North Carolina. Black child actor. | | | |
| 10/20/73 | 112 | 4 | Take Life A Little Easier................ World Of Love | $5 | ■ | Bell 45,403 |
| | | | **RITCHIE FAMILY, The** R&B/HOT/AC | | | |
| | | | Philadelphia disco group named for arranger/producer Ritchie Rome. Group featured various session singers and musicians. | | | |
| 3/19/77 | 102 | 4 | Life Is Music................................ R&B:74 Lady Luck | $5 | | Marlin 3309 |
| | | | **RIVERA, Hector** ☉ R&B | | | |
| 12/31/66 | 104 | 7 | At The Party................................ R&B:26 Do It To Me | $10 | | Barry! 1011 |
| | | | **RIVERS, Johnny** HOT/AC/C&W | | | |
| | | | Born John Ramistella on 11/7/42 in New York City. Rock and roll singer/guitarist/songwriter/producer. Top Pop Singles: 29. | | | |
| 7/11/64 | 120 | 2 | 1 Oh What A Kiss................................ Knock Three Times | $12 | | United Artists 741 |
| 7/21/73 | 113 | 2 | 2 Searchin'/So Fine................................ New Year Dues | $6 | | United Artists 226 |
| | | | medley: "Searchin'" #3 hit in 1957 for The Coasters/"So Fine" #11 hit in 1959 for **The Fiestas** | | | |
| 6/15/74 | 106 | 1 | 3 Six Days On The Road................ C&W:58 Artists & Poets | $6 | | Atlantic 3028 |
| | | | #32 hit for **Dave Dudley** in 1963 | | | |
| | | | **RIVIERAS, The** HOT | | | |
| | | | Northern New Jersey R&B quartet: Homer Dunn (lead), Charles Allen (bass), Ronald Cook (tenor) and Andrew Jones (baritone). | | | |
| 7/27/59 | 103 | 4 | 1 Our Love................................ Midnight Flyer | $35 | | Coed 513 |
| | | | also released with "True Love Is Hard To Find" on the B-side ($35); #1 hit for Tommy Dorsey in 1939 | | | |
| 6/13/60 | 103 | 3 | 2 Moonlight Cocktails................................ Blessing Of Love | $35 | | Coed 529 |
| | | | #1 hit for Glenn Miller in 1942 ("Moonlight Cocktail") | | | |
| | | | **RIVINGTONS, The** HOT/R&B | | | |
| | | | Los Angeles R&B quartet: Carl White (lead; d: 1/7/80), Sonny Harris, Rocky Wilson, Jr. and Al Frazier. | | | |
| 1/12/63 | 106 | 1 | Mama-Oom-Mow-Mow (The Bird)................ Waiting | $25 | | Liberty 55528 |
| | | | sequel to The Rivingtons' 1962 hit "Papa-Oom-Mow-Mow" | | | |
| | | | **R.J.'S LATEST ARRIVAL** ☉ R&B | | | |
| | | | Seven-member R&B/funk group led by keyboardist Ralph James Rice from Detroit. | | | |
| 7/20/85 | 107 | 1 | Swing Low................................ R&B:27 (instrumental) | $4 | | Atlantic 89551 |
| | | | **ROACHES, The** ☉ | | | |
| 4/11/64 | 117 | 1 | Beatle Mania Blues................................ Angel Of Angels | $20 | | Crossway 447 |
| | | | **ROAD, The** ☉ | | | |
| | | | Rock band led by brothers Jerry and Phil Hudson. | | | |
| 2/1/69 | 114 | 3 | She's Not There................................ A Bummer | $10 | | Kama Sutra 256 |
| | | | #2 hit for **The Zombies** in 1964 | | | |
| | | | **ROAD APPLES, The** HOT | | | |
| | | | Boston-based pop group led by singer/guitarist David Finnerty. | | | |
| 3/13/76 | 110 | 1 | Holding On................................ Good Lovin' Woman | $6 | | Polydor 14307 |

| DEBUT | PEAK | WKS | A-side (Chart Hit)................B-side | $ | Pic | Label & Number |
|---|---|---|---|---|---|---|
| | | | **ROAD HOME, The ✪** | | | |
| 9/25/71 | 120 | 1 | Keep It In The Family .................................... *Comin' Back Home* | $7 | | Dunhill/ABC 4285 |
| | | | **ROBBINS, Marty**         C&W/HOT/AC | | | |
| | | | Born Martin David Robinson on 9/26/25 in Glendale, Arizona. Died on 12/8/82. Country singer/guitarist/songwriter. *Top Pop Singles:* 24. | | | |
| 1/13/62 | 109 | 2 | 1 Sometimes I'm Tempted ....................C&W:12 *I Told The Brook* (Hot #81) | $15 | ■ | Columbia 42246 |
| 9/21/63 | 115 | 4 | 2 Not So Long Ago ....................C&W:13 *I Hope You Learn A Lot* | $12 | | Columbia 42831 |
| 2/22/64 | 106 | 5 | 3 Girl From Spanish Town ....................C&W:15 *Kingston Girl* | $12 | | Columbia 42968 |
| 6/27/64 | 103 | 4 | 4 The Cowboy In The Continental Suit    C&W:3 *Man Walks Among Us* | $10 | | Columbia 43049 |
| 11/14/64 | 105 | 3 | 5 One Of These Days ....................C&W:8 *Up In The Air* | $10 | | Columbia 43134 |
| 5/15/65 | 103 | 2 | 6 Ribbon Of Darkness ....................C&W:❶ *Little Robin* | $10 | | Columbia 43258 |
| | | | written by **Gordon Lightfoot** | | | |
| 6/3/67 | 114 | 3 | 7 Tonight Carmen....................C&W:❶ *Waiting In Reno* | $8 | | Columbia 44128 |
| 10/24/70 | 108 | 1 | 8 Jolie Girl ....................C&W:7 *The City* | $6 | | Columbia 45215 |
| 1/9/71 | 113 | 4 | 9 Padre ....................C&W:5 *At Times* | $6 | | Columbia 45273 |
| | | | #13 hit for Toni Arden in 1958 | | | |
| 7/3/71 | 121 | 2 | 10 The Chair....................C&W:7 *Seventeen Years* | $6 | | Columbia 45377 |
| 6/25/77 | 108 | 1 | 11 I Don't Know Why (I Just Do) ....................C&W:10 *Inspiration For A Song* | $5 | | Columbia 10536 |
| | | | #2 hit for Wayne King in 1931; #12 hit for **Linda Scott** in 1961 | | | |
| | | | **ROBBS, The ✪** | | | |
| | | | Rock quartet of brothers from Oconomowoc, Wisconsin: Dee (lead vocals), Craig, Joe and Bruce Donaldson. To West Coast in the late '60s, replaced **Paul Revere & The Raiders** as house band for TV show *Where The Action Is.* | | | |
| 6/11/66 | 103 | 7 | 1 Race With The Wind     *In A Funny Sort Of Way* | $10 | | Mercury 72579 |
| 5/6/67 | 123 | 2 | 2 Rapid Transit ....................*Cynthia Loves* | $10 | | Mercury 72678 |
| 10/25/69 | 131 | 1 | 3 Movin' ....................*Write To You* | $8 | | Dunhill/ABC 4208 |
| 5/2/70 | 114 | 2 | 4 Last Of The Wine ....................*Written In The Dust* | $8 | | Dunhill/ABC 4233 |
| 9/12/70 | 106 | 3 | 5 I'll Never Get Enough....................*It All Comes Back* | $7 | ■ | ABC 11270 |
| 8/7/71 | 116 | 2 | 6 Girl, I've Got News For You ....................*All The Way Home* | $7 | | ABC 11304 |
| | | | **CHEROKEE** | | | |
| | | | **ROBERT & JOHNNY**      HOT/R&B | | | |
| | | | R&B duo from the Bronx, New York: Robert Carr (d: 5/18/93) and Johnny Mitchell. | | | |
| 1/23/61 | 104 | 3 | We Belong Together ....................*In The Rain* [R] | $25 | | Old Town 1086 |
| | | | originally made the *Hot 100* (#32) on 2/24/58 on Old Town 1047 ($35) | | | |
| | | | **ROBERTS, Austin**      HOT/AC | | | |
| | | | Born on 9/19/45 in Newport News, Virginia. Pop singer/songwriter. | | | |
| 6/2/73 | 120 | 1 | The Last Thing On My Mind ....................*Losing You Is More Than I Can Stand* | $5 | | Chelsea 0123 |
| | | | **ROBERTS, Bruce ✪** | | | |
| | | | Born in New York City. Supplied the singing voice for Danny Bonaduce on TV's *The Partridge Family.* | | | |
| 12/7/96 | 109 | 4 | Whenever There Is Love ....................*(instrumental)* | $3 | ▮ | Universal 56034 |
| | | | **BRUCE ROBERTS AND DONNA SUMMER** | | | |
| | | | from the movie *Daylight* starring Sylvester Stallone | | | |
| | | | **ROBERTS, Derrik**      HOT | | | |
| 1/15/66 | 105 | 1 | There Won't Be Any Snow (Christmas In The Jungle)....................*A World Without Sunshine* [X-S] | $20 | | Roulette 4656 |
| | | | #8 hit on *Billboard's* 1965 Christmas Singles chart | | | |
| | | | **ROBERTS, Lea**      R&B/HOT | | | |
| | | | Leatha Roberta Hicks from Dayton. Moved to Newark in 1968, discovered by producer George Butler. | | | |
| 11/2/74 | 109 | 1 | Laughter In The Rain ....................R&B:69 *She Will Break Your Heart* | $5 | | United Artists 539 |
| | | | #1 hit for **Neil Sedaka** in 1975 | | | |
| | | | **ROBERTS, Renee ✪** | | | |
| 4/7/62 | 112 | 1 | I Want To Love You (So Much It Hurts Me) ....................*Aching Heart* | $15 | | New Phoenix 6198 |
| | | | Billy Mure (orch.) | | | |
| | | | **ROBERTSON, Don**      HOT | | | |
| | | | Born on 12/5/22 in Peking, China; moved to Chicago at age four. Pianist/composer. Created the Nashville piano style. | | | |
| 7/24/61 | 117 | 2 | Tennessee Waltz ....................*Feather In The Wind* [I] | $10 | | RCA Victor 7909 |
| | | | #1 hit for **Patti Page** in 1950 | | | |
| | | | **ROBIN S**      R&B/HOT | | | |
| | | | Robin Stone. R&B female singer from Jamaica, New York. | | | |
| 11/27/93 | 112 | 4 | 1 What I Do Best....................R&B:52 *Show Me Love* (radio mix) | $3 | ▮ | Big Beat 98355 |
| 3/26/94 | 103 | 8 | 2 I Want To Thank You....................*(album version)* | $3 | ▮ | Big Beat 98325 |
| | | | **ROBINS, Jimmy ✪**      R&B | | | |
| | | | Born James Robbins in Chicago. R&B vocalist. First recorded for Federal in 1963. | | | |
| 12/24/66 | 131 | 2 | I Can't Please You ....................R&B:21 *I Made It Over* | $20 | | Jerhart 207 |
| | | | originally released as by James Robbins on Mica 2016 in 1965 ($35) | | | |
| | | | **ROBINS, The ✪** | | | |
| | | | R&B vocal group (not the "Smokey Joe's Cafe" group). | | | |
| 4/24/61 | 108 | 3 | White Cliffs Of Dover ....................*How Many More Times* | $50 | | Lavender 001 |
| | | | #6 hit for Glenn Miller in 1942 | | | |
| | | | **ROBINSON, Alvin**      HOT/R&B | | | |
| | | | Born in New Orleans in 1937. Died on 1/24/89 of a heart attack. R&B session guitarist/vocalist. Worked with Joe Jones and **Dr. John**. | | | |
| 9/19/64 | 108 | 4 | Fever ....................*Down Home Girl* | $20 | | Red Bird 10-010 |
| | | | #1 R&B hit for **Little Willie John** in 1956; #8 hit for **Peggy Lee** in 1958 | | | |
| | | | **ROBINSON, Bill, and The Quails ✪** | | | |
| 1/18/64 | 103 | 2 | The Cow ....................*Take Me Back, Baby* | $20 | | American 1023 |

**ROBINSON, Roscoe**　　　　　　　　　R&B/HOT
Born on 5/22/28 in Dumont, Arkansas. R&B singer/producer.

| 11/12/66 | 125 | 1 | How Much Pressure (Do You Think I Can Stand) ................ R&B:39 *Do It Right Now (R&B #40)* | $15 | | Wand 1143 |

**ROBINSON, Smokey**　　　　　　　　R&B/HOT/AC
Born William Robinson on 2/19/40 in Detroit. Lead singer of **The Miracles**, 1958-72. Wrote dozens of hit songs for Motown artists. Vice President of Motown Records, 1985-88. Inducted into the Rock and Roll Hall of Fame in 1987. Won Grammy's Living Legends Award in 1989. *Top Pop Singles:* 25.

| 8/6/77 | 101[1] | 3 | 1 Vitamin U ........................................ R&B:18 *Holly* | $5 | | Tamla 54284 |
| 7/31/82 | 107 | 2 | 2 Yes It's You Lady ................................ *Are You Still Here* | $4 | | Tamla 1630 |
| 3/12/83 | 101[2] | 4 | 3 I've Made Love To You A Thousand Times　R&B:8　*Into Each Rain Some Life Must Fall* | $4 | | Tamla 1655 |
| 5/14/83 | 110 | 1 | 4 Touch The Sky ................................ R&B:68 *All My Life's A Lie* | $4 | | Tamla 1678 |
| 12/3/83 | 103 | 1 | 5 Don't Play Another Love Song ... AC:36 /R&B:75 *Wouldn't You Like To Know* | $4 | | Tamla 1700 |
| 5/19/84 | 106 | 6 | 6 And I Don't Love You ......................... R&B:33 *Dynamite* | $4 | | Tamla 1735 |
| 10/6/84 | 109 | 2 | 7 I Can't Find ................................ R&B:41 *Gimme What You Want* | $4 | | Tamla 1756 |

**ROBINSON, Sylvia — see SYLVIA**

**ROBI ROB'S CLUBWORLD — see C + C MUSIC FACTORY**

**ROBINSON, Vicki Sue**　　　　　　　HOT/R&B
Born in Philadelphia in 1955. Disco vocalist. Appeared in the original Broadway productions of *Hair* and *Jesus Christ Superstar*.

| 1/22/77 | 104 | 2 | 1 Should I Stay/I Won't Let You Go ............ *When You're Lovin' Me* | $5 | | RCA 10863 |
| | | | **VICKI SUE ROBINSON with The New York Community Choir** | | | |
| 4/22/78 | 110 | 1 | 2 Trust In Me ................................ *Don't Try To Win Me Back Again* | $4 | | RCA 11227 |
| 3/31/79 | 102 | 9 | 3 Nightime Fantasy ......................... *Feels So Good It Must Be Wrong* | $4 | | RCA 11441 |
| | | | from the movie *Nocturna* starring Yvonne de Carlo | | | |

**ROCK, Pete, & C.L. Smooth**　　　　　R&B/HOT
Producer/DJ Pete Rock and rapper C.L. Smooth are from Mt. Vernon, New York. Worked with **Johnny Gill**. Also see **Ini**.

| 3/20/93 | 108 | 8 | 1 Lots Of Lovin ................................ R&B:66 *It's Not A Game* | $3 | ■ | Elektra 64662 |
| 10/1/94 | 117 | 2 | 2 I Got A Love ................................ R&B:69 *The Main Ingredient* | $3 | ■ | Elektra 64513 |
| | | | samples "Groovy Situation" by **Mel And Tim** and "Ain't Got The Love" by **The Ambassadors** | | | |

**ROCKINGHAM, David, Trio**　　　　　HOT
Organist Rockingham with guitarist/producer R.C. "Bobby" Robinson and drummer Shante Hamilton

| 3/7/64 | 119 | 1 | Midnight ................................ *Bee Dee* [I] | $10 | | Josie 917 |
| | | | sequel to Rockingham's 1963 #62 hit "Dawn" on Josie 913 | | | |

**ROCKIN' HORSE** ☉

| 7/12/75 | 104 | 5 | Love Do Me Right ......................... *You're So Good For Me* | $6 | | RCA Victor 10265 |

**ROCK MASTER SCOTT and THE DYNAMIC THREE** ☉　　R&B

| 1/19/85 | 103 | 4 | Request Line ................................ R&B:21 *(dub version)* | $5 | | Reality 951 |
| | | | also released as a 12" single on Reality 230 | | | |

**ROCKWELL**　　　　　　　　　R&B/HOT/ROK
Born Kennedy Gordy on 3/15/64 in Detroit. Son of Motown chairman, Berry Gordy, Jr.

| 2/23/85 | 108 | 1 | He's A Cobra ................................ R&B:65 *Change Your Ways* | $4 | ■ | Motown 1772 |

**RODGERS, Jimmie**　　　　　　　　HOT/AC/C&W/R&B
Born James Frederick Rodgers on 9/18/33 in Camas, Washington. Pop vocalist/guitarist. Own NBC-TV variety series in 1959. *Top Pop Singles:* 25.

| 12/21/59 | 112 | 1 | 1 Wistful Willie ................................ *It's Christmas Once Again* [X] | $20 | | Roulette 4205 |
| 2/23/63 | 129 | 1 | 2 Face In A Crowd ......................... *Lonely Tears* | $10 | | Dot 16450 |
| 12/21/63 | 131 | 1 | 3 Mama Was A Cotton Picker ............ *Together* | $10 | | Dot 16561 |
| 10/26/68 | 104 | 7 | 4 Today ................................ AC:19 *The Lovers* | $7 | | A&M 976 |
| | | | #17 hit for **The New Christy Minstrels** in 1964 | | | |
| 5/3/69 | 123 | 2 | 5 The Windmills Of Your Mind ......... *L.A. Break Down (And Take Me In)* | $7 | | A&M 1055 |
| | | | theme from the movie *The Thomas Crown Affair* starring Steve McQueen; #31 hit for **Dusty Springfield** in 1969 | | | |

**RODGERS, Paul** ☉　　　　　　　　ROK
Born in Middlesbrough, Cleveland, England on 12/17/49. Lead singer of **Free** (1969-73), Bad Company (1974-82) and The Firm (1984-86).

| 11/26/83 | 102 | 6 | Cut Loose ................................ ROK:15 *Talking Guitar Blues* | $4 | ■ | Atlantic 89749 |

**RODNEY O & JOE COOLEY**　　　　　R&B/HOT
Los Angeles rap trio: Rodney Oliver, Joe Cooley and "General" Jeff Page.

| 11/8/97 | 123 | 1 | What U Gotta Say ......................... R&B:90 *Mega Mix* | $3 | ■ | New Quest 54224 |
| | | | samples "Flirt" by **Cameo** | | | |

**ROE, Tommy**　　　　　　　　　HOT/C&W/AC/R&B
Born on 5/9/42 in Atlanta. Pop-rock singer/guitarist/composer. *Top Pop Singles:* 22.

| 11/3/62 | 108 | 1 | 1 Piddle de Pat ................................ *Susie Darlin'* (Hot #35) | $12 | ■ | ABC-Paramount 10362 |
| 2/10/68 | 114 | 4 | 2 Dottie I Like It ......................... *Soft Words* | $8 | | ABC 11039 |
| 11/14/70 | 117 | 3 | 3 Brush A Little Sunshine ................ *King Of Fools* | $8 | | ABC 11281 |
| 1/23/71 | 104 | 3 | 4 Little Miss Goodie Two Shoes ..... *Traffic Jam* | $8 | | ABC 11287 |
| 4/17/71 | 124 | 1 | 5 Pistol Legged Mama ................... *King Of Fools* | $8 | | ABC 11293 |

**ROGER — see ZAPP**

**ROGERS, Kenny/First Edition**　　　　C&W/AC/HOT/R&B
Born Kenneth Donald Rogers on 8/21/38 in Houston. Formed and fronted **The First Edition** in 1967. Rogers split from group in 1973. Starred in movie *Six Pack* and several TV movies including *The Gambler I, II & III* miniseries. *Top Pop Singles:* 40.

| 5/11/68 | 133 | 3 | 1 Only Me ................................ *Dream On* | $8 | | Reprise 0683 |
| 10/12/68 | 119 | 2 | 2 Are My Thoughts With You ........... *If I Could Only Change Your Mind* | $8 | | Reprise 0773 |
| | | | written by **Mickey Newbury** | | | |

| DEBUT | PEAK | WKS | A-side (Chart Hit).........................................................................................................B-side | $ | Pic | Label & Number |
|-------|------|-----|-------------------------------------------------------------------------------------------------|---|-----|----------------|

**ROGERS, Kenny/First Edition — Cont'd**

| DEBUT | PEAK | WKS | A-side / B-side | $ | Pic | Label & Number |
|-------|------|-----|------|---|-----|----------------|
| 5/17/69 | 126 | 1 | 3 Once Again She's All Alone ....................................................*Good Time Liberator* | $8 | | Reprise 0822 |
| | | | **THE FIRST EDITION** (above 3) | | | |
| 12/2/72 | 105 | 5 | 4 Lady, Play Your Symphony ............................*There's An Old Man In Our Town* | $7 | | Jolly Rogers 1001 |
| | | | **KENNY ROGERS AND THE FIRST EDITION** | | | |
| 3/18/78 | 101[2] | 8 | 5 Every Time Two Fools Collide        C&W:❶[2] / AC:44  *We Love Each Other* | $5 | | United Artists 1137 |
| 5/19/79 | 102 | 8 | 6 All I Ever Need Is You .......... C&W:❶[1] / AC:38  (Hey Won't You Play) Another Somebody Done Somebody Wrong Song | $5 | | United Artists 1276 |
| | | | **KENNY ROGERS & DOTTIE WEST** (above 2) | | | |
| | | | #7 hit for **Sonny & Cher** in 1971 | | | |

**ROGERS, Lee ☉**          R&B
Born in 1942 in Detroit. R&B singer. Once fronted a doo-wop group called The Peppermints.

| DEBUT | PEAK | WKS | A-side / B-side | $ | Pic | Label & Number |
|-------|------|-----|------|---|-----|----------------|
| 11/28/64 | 114 | 4 | I Want You To Have Everything ..........................*R&B:17 Our Love Is More* | $20 | | D-Town 1035 |

**ROGUE ☉**

| DEBUT | PEAK | WKS | A-side / B-side | $ | Pic | Label & Number |
|-------|------|-----|------|---|-----|----------------|
| 5/1/76 | 108 | 1 | Fallen Angel ...................................................................*Run For Shelter* | $6 | | Epic 50209 |

**ROGUES, The — see BRUCE AND TERRY**

**ROLLING STONES, The**          HOT/ROK/R&B/AC
R&B-influenced rock group formed in London in January 1963: Mick Jagger (b: 7/26/43; vocals), Keith Richards (b: 12/18/43; lead guitar), Brian Jones (b: 2/28/42; d: 7/3/69; guitar), Bill Wyman (b: 10/24/36; bass) and Charlie Watts (b: 6/2/41; drums). Jones left group shortly before drowning; replaced by Mick Taylor (b: 1/17/48). In 1975, Ron Wood (ex-**Jeff Beck Group**, ex-**Faces**) replaced Taylor. Won Grammy's Lifetime Achievement Award in 1986. Group inducted into the Rock and Roll Hall of Fame in 1989. Revered as the world's all-time greatest rock and roll band. *Top Pop Singles*: 56.

| DEBUT | PEAK | WKS | A-side / B-side | $ | Pic | Label & Number |
|-------|------|-----|------|---|-----|----------------|
| 1/30/65 | 124 | 1 | 1 What A Shame ........................................*Heart Of Stone* (Hot #19) | $25 | ■ | London 9725 |
| 1/21/95 | 113 | 2 | 2 You Got Me Rocking ....................*ROK:2 (2 versions) / Jump On Top Of Me* | $3 | ▌ | Virgin 38468 |
| 12/2/95 | 109 | 1 | 3 Like A Rolling Stone ..............*ROK:16 Black Limousine / All Down The Line* | $3 | ▌ | Virgin 38523 |
| | | | #2 hit for **Bob Dylan** in 1965 | | | |

**ROLLINS BAND ☉**          ROK
Henry Rollins (b: Henry Garfield on 2/13/61 in Washington, D.C.) formed Rollins Band in April 1987 with guitarist Chris Haskett, bassist Andrew Weiss, drummer Sim Cain and soundman Theo Van Rock. By 1994, Melvin Gibbs replaced Weiss.

| DEBUT | PEAK | WKS | A-side / B-side | $ | Pic | Label & Number |
|-------|------|-----|------|---|-----|----------------|
| 7/9/94 | 109 | 2 | Liar ..........................................*ROK:26 Too Much Right Now* | $3 | ▌ | Imago 25072 |

**ROME & PARIS — see STRANGELOVES, The**

**RONETTES, The**          HOT/R&B
Classic '60s girl group featuring lead singer Veronica Bennett (Ronnie Spector) and Phil Spector's "Wall of Sound" production.

| DEBUT | PEAK | WKS | A-side / B-side | $ | Pic | Label & Number |
|-------|------|-----|------|---|-----|----------------|
| 4/5/69 | 108 | 4 | You Came, You Saw, You Conquered! ............................*Oh, I Love You* | $15 | | A&M 1040 |
| | | | **THE RONETTES Featuring the voice of VERONICA** | | | |

**RONNIE and THE HI-LITES**          HOT
R&B vocal quintet from Jersey City featuring Ronnie Goodson (13 years old in 1962), who died of a brain tumor on 11/4/80.

| DEBUT | PEAK | WKS | A-side / B-side | $ | Pic | Label & Number |
|-------|------|-----|------|---|-----|----------------|
| 7/21/62 | 120 | 1 | 1 Be Kind....................................*Send My Love (Special Delivery)* | $25 | | Joy 265 |
| 8/10/63 | 116 | 5 | 2 A Slow Dance .........................................:*...What The Next Day May Bring* | $25 | | Win 250 |

**RONNY AND THE DAYTONAS**          HOT
White vocal group featuring Bucky (Ronny) Wilkin and James (Buzz) Cason.

| DEBUT | PEAK | WKS | A-side / B-side | $ | Pic | Label & Number |
|-------|------|-----|------|---|-----|----------------|
| 5/1/65 | 107 | 4 | 1 Tiger-A-Go-Go ....................................................*Bay City* | $20 | | Amy 924 |
| | | | **BUZZ and BUCKY** | | | |
| 3/26/66 | 115 | 3 | 2 Somebody To Love Me ....................................*Goodbye Baby* | $20 | | Mala 525 |
| 11/19/66 | 133 | 1 | 3 I'll Think Of Summer ........................................*Little Scrambler* | $20 | | Mala 542 |

**RONSTADT, Linda**          AC/HOT/C&W/ROK/R&B
Born on 7/15/46 in Tucson, Arizona. To Los Angeles in 1964. Formed the Stone Poneys in 1966. Went solo in 1968. *Top Pop Singles*: 35.

| DEBUT | PEAK | WKS | A-side / B-side | $ | Pic | Label & Number |
|-------|------|-----|------|---|-----|----------------|
| 4/4/70 | 111 | 2 | 1 Will You Love Me Tomorrow? .............................*Lovesick Blues* | $8 | | Capitol 2767 |
| | | | #1 hit for **The Shirelles** in 1961 | | | |
| 7/20/74 | 108 | 1 | 2 Colorado ....................................................*Desperado* | $6 | | Asylum 11039 |
| 12/22/84+ | 101[1] | 6 | 3 Skylark        AC:12  *Lush Life* | $5 | | Asylum 69671 |
| | | | **Nelson Riddle** (orch.); #7 hit for **Glenn Miller** in 1942 | | | |
| 12/4/93 | 112 | 8 | 4 Heartbeats Accelerating ..........................*AC:31 Winter Light* | $3 | ▌ | Elektra 64584 |
| 10/21/95 | 101[1] | 5 | 5 A Dream Is A Wish Your Heart Makes        Sls:60 *Un Precioso Sueño* | $3 | ▌ | Walt Disney 60344 |
| | | | from the Disney animated movie *Cinderella* | | | |

**ROOMATES, The**          HOT
White vocal group from Queens, New York featuring lead singer Steve Susskind.

| DEBUT | PEAK | WKS | A-side / B-side | $ | Pic | Label & Number |
|-------|------|-----|------|---|-----|----------------|
| 7/31/61 | 119 | 1 | Band Of Gold ...................................*O Baby Love* | $20 | | Valmor 10 |
| | | | #4 hit for **Don Cherry** in 1956 | | | |

**ROOSTERS, The ☉**

| DEBUT | PEAK | WKS | A-side / B-side | $ | Pic | Label & Number |
|-------|------|-----|------|---|-----|----------------|
| 4/20/68 | 106 | 4 | Love Machine ...................................................*I'm Suspectin'* | $8 | | Philips 40504 |

**ROOTS, The**          R&B/HOT
Hip-hop quartet from Philadelphia: Tariq Trotter, Ahmir-Khalib Thompson, Malik Abdul-Basit and Leonard Hubbard.

| DEBUT | PEAK | WKS | A-side / B-side | $ | Pic | Label & Number |
|-------|------|-----|------|---|-----|----------------|
| 2/11/95 | 123 | 1 | 1 Proceed (part 1)........................*R&B:79 (album version) / Proceed III / What Goes On Pt. 7* | $3 | ▌ | DGC 19380 |
| 7/27/96 | 101[1] | 8 | 2 Clones        Sls:72 /R&B:62  *(instrumental) / Section (2 versions)* | $3 | ▌ | DGC 19402 |

**ROSELLI, Jimmy**          AC/HOT
Italian singer.

| DEBUT | PEAK | WKS | A-side / B-side | $ | Pic | Label & Number |
|-------|------|-----|------|---|-----|----------------|
| 8/10/63 | 135 | 1 | Mala Femmina ...................................*Her Eyes Shone Like Diamonds* [F] | $10 | | Lenox 5571 |

**ROSE ROYCE**          R&B/HOT/AC
R&B group from Los Angeles featuring Gwen "Rose" Dickey (vocals). Did soundtrack for the movie *Car Wash*.

| DEBUT | PEAK | WKS | A-side / B-side | $ | Pic | Label & Number |
|-------|------|-----|------|---|-----|----------------|
| 3/4/78 | 101[1] | 6 | 1 Wishing On A Star ..................................*R&B:52 Love, More Love* | $5 | | Whitfield 8531 |
| 9/29/79 | 105 | 7 | 2 Is It Love You're After ........................*R&B:31 You Can't Run From Yourself* | $5 | | Whitfield 49049 |

### ROSS, Diana     R&B/HOT/AC
Born Diane Earle on 3/26/44 in Detroit. Lead singer of The Supremes from 1961-69. Went solo in late 1969. *Top Pop Singles*: 41.

| DEBUT | PEAK | WKS | A-side / B-side | $ | Pic | Label & Number |
| --- | --- | --- | --- | --- | --- | --- |
| 1/16/82 | 109 | 2 | 1 My Old Piano ............................................................ *Now That You're Gone* | $4 | ☐ | Motown 1531 |
| 9/30/95 | 114 | 7 | 2 Take Me Higher ...................................... R&B:77 *Don't Stop* | $3 | ■ | Motown 0432 |

### ROSS, Jackie     HOT/R&B
Born on 1/30/46 in St. Louis. Sang gospel on her parents' radio show at age three. Moved to Chicago in 1954.

| | | | | | | |
| --- | --- | --- | --- | --- | --- | --- |
| 12/5/64 | 126 | 2 | Haste Makes Waste ................................................ *Wasting Time* | $10 | | Chess 1915 |

### ROSS, Jerry, Symposium ۵     AC
Studio group assembled by producer Jerry Ross (executive with the Colossus record label).

| | | | | | | |
| --- | --- | --- | --- | --- | --- | --- |
| 7/11/70 | 123 | 1 | Let Me Love You One More Time (Un Poquito Mas)........................ *Little Green Bag* | $6 | | Colossus 119 |

### ROSSO, Nini ۵     AC
Born Celeste Rosso on 9/19/26 in Turin, Italy. Jazz trumpeter.

| | | | | | | |
| --- | --- | --- | --- | --- | --- | --- |
| 10/16/65+ | 101[1] | 10 | Il Silenzio     AC:32 *Via Caracciola* [I] | $7 | | Columbia 43363 |
| | | | Willy Brezza (orch.); #96 hit for **Al Hirt** in 1965 | | | |

### ROTARY CONNECTION     HOT
Canadian rock-R&B sextet — Minnie Riperton, lead singer.

| | | | | | | |
| --- | --- | --- | --- | --- | --- | --- |
| 10/12/68 | 132 | 1 | 1 Paper Castle ........................................ *Teach Me How To Fly* | $8 | | Cadet Concept 7007 |
| 11/16/68 | 113 | 1 | 2 Aladdin ...................................................... *Magical World* | $8 | | Cadet Concept 7008 |

### ROTTIN RAZKALS ۵     R&B
Rap trio from East Orange, New Jersey: Diesel, Chap and FAM.

| | | | | | | |
| --- | --- | --- | --- | --- | --- | --- |
| 2/11/95 | 103 | 13 | Oh Yeah! ........................................ R&B:63 *A-Yo* | $3 | ■ | Illtown 0260 |
| | | | samples "Say Yeah" by The Commodores | | | |

### ROULETTES, The ۵
Rock quartet — Bart Bishop, lead singer.

| | | | | | | |
| --- | --- | --- | --- | --- | --- | --- |
| 6/6/81 | 105 | 1 | Only Heaven Knows ........................................ *Turn, Look Away* | $7 | | Takoma 8002 |

### ROUND ROBIN     HOT

| | | | | | | |
| --- | --- | --- | --- | --- | --- | --- |
| 4/3/65 | 135 | 1 | Land Of A Thousand Dances "The Na Na Song" ........................ *Yea Yea* | $12 | | Domain 1420 |
| | | | "live" recording; #6 hit for **Wilson Pickett** in 1966 | | | |

### ROUTERS, The     HOT
Rock and roll instrumental quintet led by Mike Gordon. Member Scott Engel joined The Walker Bros.

| | | | | | | |
| --- | --- | --- | --- | --- | --- | --- |
| 2/16/63 | 115 | 2 | Half Time ...................................................... *Make It Snappy* [I] | $15 | | Warner 5332 |

### ROWAN BROTHERS, The     HOT
Brothers Lorin, Chris and Peter Rowan. Originally from the Boston area. Peter was a member of Earth Opera and **Seatrain**.

| | | | | | | |
| --- | --- | --- | --- | --- | --- | --- |
| 12/2/72 | 112 | 3 | All Together ........................................ *Lady Of Laughter* | $6 | | Columbia 45728 |

### ROX ۵
Rock group led by vocalist Mike Rox.

| | | | | | | |
| --- | --- | --- | --- | --- | --- | --- |
| 4/11/81 | 109 | 3 | Ddddddance .................................... *You Don't Know What I Caught* | $5 | | Boardwalk 70059 |

### ROXY MUSIC     HOT/ROK/AC
English art-rock band. Nucleus consisted of **Bryan Ferry** (vocals, keyboards), Phil Manzanera (guitar) and Andy MacKay (horns).

| | | | | | | |
| --- | --- | --- | --- | --- | --- | --- |
| 10/4/80 | 102 | 3 | 1 Oh Yeah (On The Radio) ........................................ *(long version)* | $5 | | Atco 7310 |
| 11/8/80 | 106 | 1 | 2 In The Midnight Hour........................... *Flesh And Blood* | $5 | | Atco 7315 |
| | | | #21 hit for **Wilson Pickett** in 1965 | | | |
| 7/10/82 | 104 | 3 | 3 Take A Chance With Me ........................................ *India* | $4 | ■ | Warner 29978 |
| 6/4/83 | 102 | 3 | 4 More Than This ............................ ROK:58 *Always Unknowing* | $4 | | Warner 29912 |
| | | | #25 hit for 10,000 Maniacs in 1997 | | | |

### ROYAL, Billy Joe     C&W/HOT
Born on 4/3/42 in Valdosta, Georgia. Guitarist/pianist/drummer. First recorded for Fairlane in 1961.

| | | | | | | |
| --- | --- | --- | --- | --- | --- | --- |
| 2/26/66 | 104 | 4 | 1 It's A Good Time     *Don't Wait Up For Me Mama* | $8 | | Columbia 43538 |
| 12/10/66 | 117 | 2 | 2 Yo-Yo ............................................ *We Tried* | $8 | | Columbia 43883 |
| | | | #3 hit for The Osmonds in 1971 | | | |
| 6/3/67 | 113 | 1 | 3 These Are Not My People/ | | | |
| | | | #55 hit for **Johnny Rivers** in 1969 | | | |
| 6/10/67 | 117 | 2 | 4   The Greatest Love............................................ | $8 | | Columbia 44103 |
| | | | #67 hit for **Dorsey Burnette** in 1969; all of above written and produced by **Joe South** | | | |
| 8/10/68 | 117 | 2 | 5 Storybook Children ............................ *Just Between Me And You* | $8 | | Columbia 44574 |
| | | | #54 hit for **Billy Vera & Judy Clay** in 1968 | | | |
| 9/26/70 | 113 | 2 | 6 Every Night.................................................. *Burning A Hole* | $6 | | Columbia 45220 |
| | | | written and recorded by Paul McCartney on his debut album in 1970 | | | |
| 7/10/71 | 111 | 1 | 7 Poor Little Pearl ........................................ *The Lady Lives To Love* | $6 | | Columbia 45406 |
| | | | written by **Mac Davis**; produced by **The Tokens** | | | |

### ROYALETTES, The     HOT/R&B
R&B female quartet from Baltimore: sisters Anita and Sheila Ross, Terry Jones and Ronnie Brown.

| | | | | | | |
| --- | --- | --- | --- | --- | --- | --- |
| 9/7/63 | 121 | 2 | 1 Blue Summer ........................................ *Willie The Wolf* | $15 | | Chancellor 1140 |
| 4/17/65 | 113 | 2 | 2 Poor Boy.......................................... *Watch What Happens* | $12 | | MGM 13327 |
| 2/5/66 | 116 | 5 | 3 You Bring Me Down ................................ *Only When You're Lonely* | $12 | ■ | MGM 13451 |
| | | | above 2 written and produced by Teddy Randazzo | | | |

### ROYAL GUARDSMEN, The     HOT
Novelty-pop sextet from Ocala, Florida featuring Barry Winslow (vocals, guitar) and Chris Nunley (vocals).

| | | | | | | |
| --- | --- | --- | --- | --- | --- | --- |
| 4/12/69 | 112 | 2 | Mother Where's Your Daughter........................................ *Magic Window* | $10 | | Laurie 3494 |

### ROYALTONES, The     HOT
Rock and roll instrumental group from Dearborn, Michigan. Formed in 1957 as the Paragons. Featuring tenor saxophonist George Katsakis.

| | | | | | | |
| --- | --- | --- | --- | --- | --- | --- |
| 4/11/64 | 103 | 6 | Our Faded Love ........................................ *Holy Smokes* [I] | $15 | | Mala 473 |

## ROZALLA
HOT
Born Rozalla Miller on 3/18/64 in Ndola, Zambia. Dance vocalist.

| 12/12/92 | 106 | 8 | Are You Ready To Fly?.....................................................................Air:63 (remix) | $3 | ∎ | Epic 74728 |

## RUBERT'S PEOPLE ✪
British pop/rock band.

| 10/7/67 | 111 | 1 | Reflections Of Charles Brown .................................................................Hold On | $15 | | Bell 684 |

## RUBY AND THE PARTY GANG ✪
R&B
| 12/25/71 | 105 | 3 | Hey Ruby (Shut Your Mouth) ................R&B:29 Ruby's House Party [N] | $10 | | Law-ton 1554 |

## RUBY AND THE ROMANTICS
HOT/R&B/AC
R&B quintet from Akron, Ohio: Ruby Nash Curtis (b: 11/12/39, New York City; lead), Ed Roberts (d: 8/10/93, age 57) and George Lee (tenors), Ronald Mosley (baritone) and Leroy Fann (bass; d: 1973).

| 6/26/65 | 108 | 2 | 1 Your Baby Doesn't Love You Anymore ...................................We'll Meet Again | $12 | | Kapp 665 |
| 8/6/66 | 120 | 3 | 2 We Can Make It .............................................................Remember Me | $12 | | Kapp 759 |
| 4/12/69 | 113 | 2 | 3 Hurting Each Other ...................Baby I Could Be So Good At Lovin' You | $10 | | A&M 1042 |
| | | | #2 hit for the Carpenters in 1972 |

## RUFFA Featuring Tasha ✪
R&B
Ruffa is a male rapper from Jamaica. Tasha Holiday was born in Atlantic City, New Jersey.

| 6/1/96 | 124 | 1 | Don't You Worry ...........................................R&B:66 Representin' | $3 | ∎ | MCA 55094 |
| | | | samples "Piece Of My Love" by Guy |

## RUFFIN, David
R&B/HOT/AC
Born Davis Eli Ruffin on 1/18/41 in Meridian, Mississippi. Died on 6/1/91. Brother of Jimmy Ruffin. Lead singer of The Temptations, 1963-68.

| 3/6/71 | 112 | 1 | 1 Don't Stop Loving Me ...........................................Each Day Is A Lifetime | $6 | | Motown 1178 |
| 10/1/77 | 108 | 6 | 2 Just Let Me Hold You For A Night ................R&B:18 Rode By The Place (Where We Used To Stay) | $5 | | Motown 1420 |

## RUFFIN, Jimmy
HOT/R&B/AC
Born on 5/7/39 in Collinsville, Mississippi. Brother of David Ruffin. Backup work at Motown in the early '60s.

| 1/1/66 | 120 | 3 | 1 As Long As There Is L-O-V-E Love.....................How Can I Say I'm Sorry | $12 | | Soul 35016 |
| | | | written and produced by Smokey Robinson |
| 8/31/68 | 113 | 3 | 2 Don't Let Him Take Your Love From Me...........Lonely Lonely Man Am I | $8 | | Soul 35046 |
| 12/13/69 | 104 | 2 | 3 Farewell Is A Lonely Sound ...........If You Will Let Me, I Know I Can | $8 | | Soul 35060 |

## RUFUS — see KHAN, Chaka

## RUHNKE, Craig ✪
Born in 1949 in Canada. Pop singer/songwriter/pianist.

| 8/24/74 | 107 | 2 | Summer Girl ...........................................Turn The Lights Down Low | $6 | | United Artists 506 |

## RUNAWAYS, The ✪
Los Angeles female teen hard-rock band led by vocalists Joan Jett and Cherie Currie. Varying personnel included Lita Ford and Micki Steele (Bangles).

| 8/7/76 | 106 | 1 | 1 Cherry Bomb ...........................................Blackmail | $10 | | Mercury 73819 |
| 3/12/77 | 110 | 1 | 2 Heartbeat ...........................Neon Angels On The Road To Ruin | $10 | | Mercury 73890 |

## RUNDGREN, Todd
HOT/ROK/AC
Born on 6/22/48 in Upper Darby, Pennsylvania. Virtuoso musician/songwriter/producer/engineer. Leader of groups Nazz and Utopia. Produced Meat Loaf's Bat Out Of Hell album and albums for Badfinger, Grand Funk Railroad, The Tubes, XTC, Patti Smith and many others.

| 1/18/75 | 105 | 4 | 1 Wolfman Jack ...........................................Breathless | $6 | | Bearsville 0301 |
| | | | TODD RUNDGREN (featuring Wolfman Jack) |
| 3/28/81 | 107 | 1 | 2 Time Heals ...........................ROK:18 Tiny Demon | $5 | | Bearsville 49696 |

## RUN-D.M.C.
R&B/HOT
Rap trio from Queens, New York: rappers Joseph Simmons (Run) and Darryl McDaniels (DMC) with DJ Jason Mizell (Jam Master Jay).

| 3/23/85 | 108 | 1 | 1 King Of Rock ...........................R&B:14 (instrumental) | $4 | | Profile 5064 |
| 6/8/85 | 107 | 5 | 2 You Talk Too Much ...........R&B:19 Daryll & Joe (Krush-Groove 3) | $4 | | Profile 5069 |
| 8/7/93 | 106 | 5 | 3 Ooh, Whatcha Gonna Do ...........R&B:78 (instrumental) | $3 | ∎ | Profile 5400 |

## RuPAUL
HOT
Born RuPaul Andre Charles on 11/17/60 in San Diego. Black male transvestite. Host of own talk show on VH-1.

| 6/5/93 | 106 | 4 | 1 Back To My Roots ............(4 versions) / Supermodel / Strudelmodel | $5 | ∎ | Tommy Boy 565 * |
| 1/1/94 | 113 | 2 | 2 Little Drummer Boy.....................(album medley) [X] | $4 | ∎ | Tommy Boy 7593 |
| | | | #13 hit for The Harry Simeone Chorale in 1958 |
| 3/15/97 | 119 | 3 | 3 A Little Bit Of Love ...........................(funk edit) | $3 | ∎ | Rhino 74455 |
| | | | guest appearance by Vicki Sue Robinson |

## RUSH
ROK/HOT
Canadian power-rock trio formed in Toronto in 1969: Geddy Lee (vocals, bass), Alex Lifeson (guitar) and Neil Peart (drums).

| 5/24/80 | 110 | 1 | 1 Entre Nous ...........................Different Strings | $6 | | Mercury 76060 |
| 1/15/83 | 105 | 4 | 2 Subdivisions ...........................ROK:8 Countdown | $6 | | Mercury 76196 |
| 7/21/84 | 105 | 2 | 3 Body Electric ...........ROK:23 Between The Wheels | $5 | | Mercury 880050 |

## RUSH, Merrilee
HOT/AC
Pop songstress from Seattle, Washington. Discovered by fellow Northwesterners Paul Revere & The Raiders.

| 5/24/69 | 130 | 2 | 1 Everyday Livin' Days ...........................Your Loving Eyes Are Blind | $8 | | AGP 112 |
| 10/4/69 | 125 | 1 | 2 Sign On For The Good Times ...........................Robin McCarver | $8 | | AGP 121 |
| | | | written by Eddie Rabbitt |
| 1/10/70 | 122 | 1 | 3 Angel On My Shoulder.....................It's Worth It All | $8 | | AGP 126 |
| | | | similar to Merrilee's #5 1968 hit "Angel Of The Morning" |

## RUSH, Tom ✪
Born on 2/8/41 in Portsmouth, New Hampshire. Singer/songwriter. Attended Harvard College.

| 2/27/71 | 105 | 5 | 1 Who Do You Love ...........Something In The Way She Moves | $8 | | Elektra 45718 |
| | | | written and recorded by Bo Diddley in 1956; #95 hit for The Woolies in 1967 |
| 6/3/72 | 111 | 4 | 2 Mother Earth ...........................Wind On The Water | $7 | | Columbia 45584 |

| DEBUT | PEAK | WKS | A-side (Chart Hit) | B-side | $ | Pic | Label & Number |
|---|---|---|---|---|---|---|---|

**RUSHEN, Patrice**     R&B/HOT
Born on 9/30/54 in Los Angeles. Jazz-R&B vocalist/pianist/songwriter.

| 1/24/81 | 102 | 6 | Look Up .................................................. **R&B:13** *The Dream* | $4 | | Elektra 47067 |

**RUSSELL, Andy** ☺     MEM/POP/AC
Born Andres Rabajos to Mexican-Spanish parents in Los Angeles. Died on 4/16/92 (age 72). Replaced **Frank Sinatra** as lead singer on radio's *Your Hit Parade* in 1947.

| 7/8/67 | 119 | 5 | It's Such A Pretty World Today ............ **AC:❶**[1] *Summer Roses* | $7 | | Capitol 5917 |

Perry Botkin, Jr. (orch.); #1 Country hit for Wynn Stewart in 1967

**RUSSELL, Bobby**     C&W/AC/HOT
Born on 4/19/41 in Nashville. Died on 11/19/92. Wrote "The Night The Lights Went Out In Georgia," "Honey" and "Little Green Apples."

| 1/25/69 | 115 | 2 | Carlie .................................................. **C&W:66** *Ain't Society Great?* | $7 | | Elf 90,023 |

**RUSSELL, Harvey, & The Rogues** ☺
White pop/rock and roll band.

| 9/24/66 | 131 | 2 | Shake Sherry ........................... *I'm Still In Love With You* | $12 | | Roulette 4697 |

#43 hit for The Contours in 1963

**RUSSELL, Leon**     HOT/C&W/AC/ROK
Born on 4/2/41 in Lawton, Oklahoma. Rock singer/songwriter/multi-instrumentalist sessionman. Regular with Phil Spector's "Wall of Sound" session group. Own labels: Shelter and Paradise.

| 6/20/70 | 109 | 4 | 1 Roll Away The Stone ................................ *Hummingbird* | $7 | | Shelter 301 |
| 9/25/71 | 105 | 2 | 2 A Hard Rain's A Gonna Fall ............ *Me And Baby Jane* | $7 | | Shelter 7305 |

written and recorded by **Bob Dylan** on his 1963 album *The Freewheelin' Bob Dylan*

| 1/8/72 | 115 | 1 | 3 Tryin' To Stay 'Live ........................... *Straight Brother* | $7 | | Shelter 7313 |

THE ASYLUM CHOIR **lead vocal: Leon Russell**

**RUSTY & DOUG** ☺     C&W
Cajun duo of brothers Russell Lee "Rusty" (b: 2/2/38) and Doug Kershaw (b: 1/24/36). Both from Tiel Ridge, Louisiana.

| 3/13/61 | 104 | 3 | Louisiana Man ............................... **C&W:10** *Make Me Realize* | $20 | | Hickory 1137 |

#97 hit for Pozo-Seco Singers in 1967

**RYDELL, Bobby**     HOT/AC/R&B
Born Robert Ridarelli on 4/26/42 in Philadelphia. Late '50s-early '60s teen idol. *Top Pop Singles*: 30.

| 5/5/62 | 109 | 3 | 1 Teach Me To Twist ............... *Swingin' Together* [N] | $15 | ■ | Cameo 214 |

**BOBBY RYDELL CHUBBY CHECKER**

| 5/26/62 | 109 | 3 | 2 Gee, It's Wonderful ....................... *I'll Never Dance Again* (Hot #14) | $15 | ■ | Cameo 217 |
| 6/1/63 | 114 | 1 | 3 Will You Be My Baby ....................... *Wildwood Days* (Hot #17) | $12 | ■ | Cameo 252 |

**RYDER, Mitch**     HOT
Born William Levise, Jr. on 2/26/45 in Detroit. Leader of white R&B-rock group, The Detroit Wheels. Formed new rock group, Detroit, in 1971.

| 12/16/67 | 113 | 1 | 1 Come See About Me ....................... *A Face In The Crowd* | $10 | | New Voice 828 |

**MITCH RYDER And The Detroit Wheels**
#1 hit for **The Supremes** in 1964

| 5/18/68 | 106 | 2 | 2 Ruby Baby & Peaches On A Cherry Tree ....... *You Get Your Kicks* | $10 | | New Voice 830 |

medley featuring **Dion's** #2 hit in 1963, "Ruby Baby" ("Peaches On A Cherry Tree" written by **Bob Crewe**)

| 6/15/68 | 122 | 2 | 3 The Lights Of Night ....................... *I Need Loving You* | $8 | | DynoVoice 916 |
| 1/4/69 | 125 | 1 | 4 Ring Your Bell ............... *Baby I Need Your Loving & Theme For Mitch* | $8 | | DynoVoice 934 |

**MITCH RYDER And The Spirit Feel**

| 1/1/72 | 107 | 5 | 5 Rock 'N Roll ....................... *Box Of Old Roses* | $7 | | Paramount 0133 |

**DETROIT featuring MITCH RYDER**
written by Lou Reed and recorded by The Velvet Underground in 1970

# S

**SAAD, Sue, And The Next** ☺
Rock quintet: Sue Saad (vocals), James Lance, Tony Riparetti, Billy Anstatt and Bobby Manzer.

| 3/1/80 | 107 | 2 | 1 Won't Give It Up ....................... *Kamonbaybeh* | $4 | ■ | Planet 45912 |
| 12/12/81 | 104 | 5 | 2 Looker ....................... *(instrumental)* (Barry DeVorzon & Michael Towers) | $4 | | Warner 49851 |

**SUE SAAD**
title song from the movie starring Albert Finney

**SABELLE** ☺     R&B
Born on 7/26/67 in New York City. Female dance singer.

| 2/15/97 | 106 | 7 | One O'Clock ....................... *On The Line* | $3 | ▌ | Work 78435 |

**SAD CAFÉ**     HOT
Pop-rock group from Manchester, England featuring Paul Young (vocals; Mike + The Mechanics).

| 10/6/79 | 108 | 2 | Emptiness ....................... *Cottage Love* | $4 | | A&M 2181 |

**SADE**     R&B/AC/HOT
Born Helen Folasade Adu on 1/16/59 in Ibadan, Nigeria. Won the 1985 Best New Artist Grammy Award.

| 12/8/84+ | 102 | 10 | 1 Hang On To Your Love ....................... **R&B:14** *Cherry Pie* | $4 | ■ | Portrait 04664 |
| 9/11/93 | 116 | 4 | 2 Cherish The Day ....................... **R&B:45** *(2 remixes)* | $3 | ▌ | Epic 74980 |

**SAFARIS** ☺
Rock and roll instrumental group.

| 10/12/63 | 120 | 2 | Kick Out ....................... *Lonely Surf Guitar* [I] | $30 | | Valiant 6036 |

tune is similar to **The Surfaris'** 1963 hit "Wipe Out"

## SAGITTARIUS (Featuring Gary Usher)　HOT
Studio band. At various times included Bruce Johnston and Terry Melcher (**Bruce And Terry**), Gary Usher (d: 5/25/90, age 51), Kurt Boettcher (d: 1987) and **Glen Campbell**. The latter three also recorded in **The Hondells**.

| | | | | | |
|---|---|---|---|---|---|
| 10/25/69 | 135 | 1 | I Guess The Lord Must Be In New York City ..................... *I Still Can See Your Face* | $12 | Together 122 |

#34 hit for **Nilsson** in 1969

## SAHM, Doug — see SIR DOUGLAS QUINTET

## SAIGON KICK　ROK/HOT
Hard-rock quartet formed in Miami in 1988 featuring Matt Kramer (vocals).

| 2/6/93 | 111 | 6 | All I Want...................................................................... ROK:15 *Chanel* | $3 | ■ Third Stone 98531 |
|---|---|---|---|---|---|

## SAILCAT　HOT/AC
Pop duo: Court Pickett (vocals) and John Wyker (vocals, guitar).

| 4/28/73 | 115 | 2 | She Showed Me ......................................................... *Sweet Little Jenny* | $6 | Elektra 45844 |
|---|---|---|---|---|---|

## SAILOR ○
Rock group from London: sibling vocalists Gavin and Virginia David with Henry Marsh (guitar) and Phil Pickett (keyboards).

| 11/15/80 | 103 | 2 | Runaway ..................................................................... *Starlight* | $5 | Caribou 9035 |
|---|---|---|---|---|---|

## SAIN, Oliver ○　R&B
Born on 3/1/32 in Dundee, Mississippi. To St. Louis in 1960. First band featured **Little Milton** (vocals).

| 3/27/76 | 103 | 6 | 1 She's A Disco Queen/ | | |
|---|---|---|---|---|---|
| | | 6 | 2　Party Hearty ............................................................. R&B:16 [I] | $6 | Abet 9463 |

## SAINTE-MARIE, Buffy　HOT/AC
Born on 2/20/41 of Cree Indian parents on Piapot Reserve, Saskatchewan, Canada. Folk singer/songwriter.

| 8/15/70 | 109 | 5 | The Circle Game ................................................. *Better To Find Out For Yourself* | $8 | Vanguard 35108 |
|---|---|---|---|---|---|

written by **Joni Mitchell**; from the movie *Strawberry Statement* starring Kim Darby

## ST. JAMES, Jon ○　R&B
British techno-pop singer.

| 3/3/84 | 105 | 4 | Oogity Boogity ........................................ R&B:89 *Two Girls Dancing* | $4 | EMI America 8198 |
|---|---|---|---|---|---|

## S'AINT JOHN ○
Dance studio group assembled by producers Jose Nunez and Keith Litman. Features singer Herman Olivera.

| 7/27/96 | 108 | 3 | Agua ............................................................ *(remix)* [F] | $3 | ■ Gossip 1003 |
|---|---|---|---|---|---|

title is Spanish for "Water"

## ST. PETERS, Crispian　HOT
Born Peter Smith on 4/5/44 in Swanley, Kent, England. Pop singer/guitarist.

| 11/26/66 | 106 | 3 | 1 Your Ever Changin' Mind ........................................ *But She's Untrue* | $10 | Jamie 1328 |
|---|---|---|---|---|---|
| 10/5/68 | 133 | 2 | 2 Look Into My Teardrops ....................................... *Please Take Me Back* | $8 | Jamie 1359 |

## SAINT TROPEZ　R&B/HOT
Name pronounced: san tro-pay. Female disco trio: Teresa Burton, Kathy Deckard and Phyllis Rhodes.

| 7/7/79 | 102 | 4 | Fill My Life With Love ........................................... *When You Are Gone* | $5 | Butterfly 41081 |
|---|---|---|---|---|---|

## SALSOUL ORCHESTRA, The　R&B/HOT/AC
Disco orchestra conducted by Philadelphia producer/arranger Vincent Montana, Jr.

| 6/25/77 | 106 | 3 | 1 Short Shorts ........................................................... *It's A New Day* | $5 | Salsoul 2037 |
|---|---|---|---|---|---|

#3 hit for the Royal Teens in 1958

| 7/30/77 | 105 | 2 | 2 Getaway/ | R&B:33 [I] | | |
|---|---|---|---|---|---|
| | | 2 | 3　Magic Bird Of Fire ...................................................... [I] | $ | Salsoul 2038 |
| 1/28/78 | 104 | 3 | 4 Dance A Little Bit Closer | *Cuchi-Cuchi* | $5 | Salsoul 2048 |

**CHARO With The Salsoul Orchestra**

| 11/10/79 | 105 | 10 | 5 How High............................................ R&B:66 *Nothing Can Change This Love* | $5 | Salsoul 2096 |
|---|---|---|---|---|---|

**THE SALSOUL ORCHESTRA featuring COGNAC**

## SALT WATER TAFFY ○
Bubblegum group led by Rod McBrien and John Giametta.

| 5/11/68 | 105 | 4 | Finders Keepers ..................................................... *He'll Pay* | $10 | Buddah 37 |
|---|---|---|---|---|---|

arranged and conducted by **Meco**

## SAM & DAVE　R&B/HOT
Soul duo: Samuel Moore (b: 10/12/35, Miami) and David Prater (b: 5/9/37, Ocilla, Georgia). Prater was killed in a car crash on 4/9/88. Duo inducted into the Rock and Roll Hall of Fame in 1992.

| 3/7/70 | 117 | 3 | 1 Baby-Baby Don't Stop Now.......................................... *I'm Not An Indian Giver* | $6 | Atlantic 2714 |
|---|---|---|---|---|---|
| 4/25/70 | 123 | 3 | 2 One Part Love-Two Parts Pain ......... *When You Steal From Me (You're Only Cheating Yourself)* | $6 | Atlantic 2728 |

**SAM & DAVE with The Dixie Flyers**

| 11/27/71 | 102 | 1 | 3 Don't Pull Your Love ........................................... R&B:36 *Jody Ryder Got Killed* | $6 | Atlantic 2839 |
|---|---|---|---|---|---|

#4 hit for **Hamilton, Joe Frank & Reynolds** in 1971

## SAM THE SHAM　HOT/R&B
Dallas rock and roll group formed in the early 1960s, featuring lead singer Domingo "Sam" Samudio (b: 1940, Dallas).

| 9/23/67 | 117 | 2 | 1 Banned In Boston .............................................. *Money's My Problem* | $10 | MGM 13803 |
|---|---|---|---|---|---|
| 12/16/67 | 110 | 5 | 2 Yakety Yak....................................... *Let Our Love Light Shine* [N] | $10 | MGM 13863 |

#1 hit for The Coasters in 1958

| 10/5/68 | 120 | 2 | 3 I Couldn't Spell !!*@!........................................ *The Down Home Strut* [N] | $15 | MGM 13972 |
|---|---|---|---|---|---|

## SANBORN, David　R&B/AC/HOT
Born on 7/30/45 in Tampa, Florida. Saxophonist/flutist. Stricken with polio as a child.

| 3/23/85 | 103 | 2 | Love & Happiness .................................................. R&B:66 *Lisa* | $4 | ■ Warner 29087 |
|---|---|---|---|---|---|

Hamish Stuart (of AWB; vocal); #58 hit for Earnest Jackson in 1973

## SANDALWOOD ○　AC

| 6/23/73 | 111 | 3 | Lovin' Naturally ........................................... AC:19 *Elevator Operator* | $6 | Bell 45,348 |
|---|---|---|---|---|---|

| DEBUT | PEAK | WKS | A-side (Chart Hit)........................................................................................B-side | $ | Pic | Label & Number |
|---|---|---|---|---|---|---|

**SANDPEBBLES, The** — R&B/HOT
R&B vocal trio: Calvin White, Andrea Bolden and Lonzine Wright. Changed name to C And The Shells in 1969.

| 4/6/68 | 122 | 1 | If You Didn't Hear Me The First Time (I'll Say It Again)............ R&B:42 *Flower Power* | $10 | | Calla 148 |

**SANDPIPERS, The** — AC/HOT
Pop vocal trio: Jim Brady (b: 8/24/44), Michael Piano (b: 10/26/44) and Richard Shoff (b: 4/30/44). Met while in the Mitchell Boys Choir.

| 5/20/67 | 112 | 2 | 1 Glass ...................................................................................... *It's Over* | $6 | | A&M 851 |
| 6/15/68 | 124 | 1 | 2 Quando M'Innamoro.......................................... AC:16 *Wooden Heart* [F] | $6 | | A&M 939 |

Italian version of **Engelbert Humperdinck**'s 1968 hit "A Man Without Love"

**SANDS, Evie** — HOT/AC
Born in New York City. Hit the New York charts as a teenage rocker, 1965-68.

| 8/14/65 | 114 | 5 | 1 Take Me For A Little While................................ *Run Home To Your Mama* | $12 | | Blue Cat 118 |

written by **Trade Martin**; #38 hit for **Vanilla Fudge** in 1968

| 4/27/68 | 133 | 2 | 2 Billy Sunshine............................................................ *It Makes Me Laugh* | $10 | | Cameo 2002 |
| 1/3/70 | 116 | 5 | 3 Crazy Annie.....................................................................*Maybe Tomorrow* | $7 | | A&M 1157 |

inspired by the movie *Midnight Cowboy* starring Dustin Hoffman

| 3/21/70 | 110 | 3 | 4 But You Know I Love You.................................. AC:30 *Maybe Tomorrow* | $7 | | A&M 1175 |

#19 hit for **The First Edition** in 1969

**SANDY B** ✪
Female dance singer from New York City.

| 4/26/97 | 109 | 4 | Make The World Go Round .................................................. *(5 versions)* | $6 | | Champion 327 **(CD)** |

**SAN FRANCISCO SYMPHONY ORCHESTRA — see SIEGEL-SCHWALL BAND**

**SANS, Billy** — HOT
Pop female vocalist.

| 2/9/74 | 103 | 5 | Bicycle Morning ...................................................................... *For Ever* | $5 | | Atco 6945 |

**SANTAMARIA, Mongo** — HOT/R&B/AC
Born Ramon Santamaria on 4/7/22 in Havana, Cuba. Bandleader/conga, bongo and percussion player.

| 10/18/69 | 132 | 1 | We Got Latin Soul ............................... R&B:40 *Getting It Out Of My System* [I] | $6 | | Columbia 44998 |

**SANTANA** — HOT/ROK/AC/R&B
Latin-rock group formed in San Francisco in 1966 featuring Devadip **Carlos Santana** (b: 7/20/47, Autlan de Navarro, Mexico; vocals, guitar). Members Neal Schon and Gregg Rolie formed Journey in 1973.

| 2/16/74 | 102 | 7 | 1 When I Look In Your Eyes ....................................... *Samba De Sausalito* | $5 | | Columbia 45999 |
| 3/19/77 | 102 | 1 | 2 Let The Children Play ..................................................................... *Carnaval* | $5 | | Columbia 10481 |
| 6/11/83 | 107 | 1 | 3 Watch Your Step ................................................... *Tales Of Kilimanjaro* | $4 | | Columbia 03925 |

**CARLOS SANTANA**

| 5/25/85 | 102 | 1 | 4 I'm The One Who Loves You ................................................... *Right Now* | $4 | | Columbia 04912 |

#73 hit for **The Impressions** in 1963

**SANTO & JOHNNY** — HOT/R&B/AC
Brooklyn-born guitar duo: Santo Farina (b: 10/24/37; steel guitar) and his brother Johnny (b: 4/30/41; rhythm guitar).

| 5/30/60 | 109 | 2 | 1 The Breeze And I ...................................................................... *Lazy Day* [I] | $15 | | Canadian American 115 |

#1 hit for Jimmy Dorsey in 1940; #8 hit for Caterina Valente in 1955

| 4/21/62 | 101¹ | 3 | 2 Spanish Harlem ........................................... *Stage To Cimarron* [I] | $12 | | Canadian American 137 |

#10 hit for **Ben E. King** in 1961

| 4/4/64 | 122 | 4 | 3 A Thousand Miles Away ............................................. *Road Block* [I] | $12 | ■ | Canadian American 167 |

#5 R&B hit for The Heartbeats in 1957

**SANTOS, Larry** — AC/HOT
Born on 6/2/41 in Oneonta, New York. Wrote "Candy Girl" by the **The 4 Seasons**. First recorded with The Tones in 1959 on Baton.

| 1/2/71 | 114 | 3 | 1 Now That I Have Found You ........................................... *Wandering Man* | $7 | | Evolution 1029 |
| 12/11/76 | 109 | 2 | 2 Long, Long Time............................................ AC:38 *You Are Everything I Need* | $5 | | Casablanca 869 |

#25 hit for **Linda Ronstadt** in 1970

**SAPPHIRES, The** — HOT/R&B
Philadelphia R&B trio: Carol Jackson (lead singer), George Garner and Joe Livingston.

| 8/10/63 | 133 | 2 | 1 Where Is Johnny Now ............................................................. *Your True Love* | $20 | | Swan 4143 |
| 10/10/64 | 106 | 5 | 2 Thank You For Loving Me....................................... *Our Love Is Everywhere* | $20 | | ABC-Paramount 10590 |

**SARSTEDT, Peter** — HOT/AC
British singer. Brother of **Eden Kane** (Richard Sarstedt).

| 7/12/69 | 116 | 2 | Frozen Orange Juice ........................................................... *Aretusa Loser* | $7 | ■ | World Pacific 77919 |

**SASH!** ✪
Techno-rave dance trio from Germany: DJ Sascha, Thomas Ludke and Ralf Kappmeier.

| 11/22/97 | 112 | 1 | Encore Une Fois .............................................. *(edited version) / Ecuador* [I] | $3 | ■ | FFRR 573284 |

**SATTIN, Lonnie** ✪
Pop singer. Born in Jacksonville, Florida and raised in Philadelphia.

| 7/4/60 | 103 | 4 | I'll Fly Away.................................................................... *Any More Than I* | $15 | | Warner 5158 |

famous Albert Brumley gospel song

**SAVAGE, Chantay** — R&B/HOT
Female R&B singer/songwriter from Chicago. Also see **Malaika**.

| 7/2/94 | 108 | 8 | 1 Don't Let It Go To Your Head/ | | | |
| 7/2/94 | 120 | 2 | 2     Give It To Ya .................................................................. R&B:flip | $3 | ■ | RCA 62788 |
| 9/6/97 | 101¹ | 8 | 3 Reminding Me (Of Sef) ............. R&B:57 *(3 versions) / 1'2 Many (2 versions)* | $3 | ■ | Relativity 1627 |

**COMMON Featuring Chantay Savage**
samples "Mellow, Mellow Right On" by Lowrell

**SAVAGE GRACE** ✪
Detroit-based rock quartet: Ron Koss (vocals, guitar), Al Jacquez, John Seanor and Larry Zack.

| 7/25/70 | 104 | 2 | Come On Down ............................................................. *Hymn To Freedom* | $7 | | Reprise 0924 |

**SAVE FERRIS ☉**  ROK
Ska-rock group from California: Monique Powell (vocals), Brian Mashburn (vocals, guitar), Eric Zamora, T-Bone Willy and Jose Castellanos (horns), Bill Uechi (bass) and Marc Harismendy (drums).

| 11/22/97 | 104 | 11 | Come On Eileen ........................................ ROK:26  For You | $3 | ▌ | Starpool/Epic 78729 |

#1 hit for Dexys Midnight Runners in 1983

**SAVOY BROWN**  HOT
British blues-rock band formed in 1966 featuring Chris Youlden (vocals), Lonesome Dave Peverett (vocals, guitar; of **Foghat**) and Kim Simmonds (guitar).

| 7/18/81 | 107 | 4 | Lay Back In The Arms Of Someone ....................... Don't Tell Me I Told You | $5 | ■ | Town House 1054 |

**SAWYER BROWN ☉**  C&W/AC
Group formed in Nashville in the late '70s featuring Mark Miller (lead singer). CMA Award: 1985 Horizon Award.

| 9/4/93 | 117 | 3 | 1 Thank God For You ..................... C&W:❶² Cafe On The Corner (C&W #5) / (3 album snippets) | $3 | ▌ | Curb 76914 |
| 5/17/97 | 117 | 11 | 2 Six Days On The Road/  C&W:13 | | | |

#32 Pop and #2 Country hit for Dave Dudley in 1963

| 8/9/97 | 109 | 7 | 3 This Night Won't Last Forever ............................................ C&W:6 | $3 | ▌ | Curb 73016 |

#19 hit for **Michael Johnson** in 1979

**SAYER, Leo**  HOT/AC/R&B/C&W
Born Gerard Sayer on 5/21/48 in Shoreham, England. Songwriting team with David Courtney, 1972-75.

| 7/13/74 | 103 | 1 | One Man Band ........................................................... Drop Back | $6 | | Warner 7824 |

made the *Hot 100* (#96) on 6/28/75 on Warner 8097

**SCAGGS, Boz**  HOT/AC/R&B
Born William Royce Scaggs on 6/8/44 in Ohio. Joined **Steve Miller**'s band, The Marksmen, in 1959 in Dallas.

| 4/12/75 | 107 | 3 | You Make It So Hard (To Say No) ....................... There Is Someone Else | $6 | | Columbia 10124 |

originally released on Columbia 46025 in 1974

**SCARFACE**  R&B/HOT
Born Brad Jordan on 11/9/69 in Houston. Member of rap group **The Geto Boys**.

| 11/27/93 | 112 | 3 | 1 Now I Feel Ya ................................................ R&B:79 (instrumental) | $3 | ▌ | Rap-A-Lot 53841 |
| 5/20/95 | 115 | 2 | 2 Among The Walking Dead ........................ R&B:91 (radio edit) | $3 | ▌ | Motown 0302 |

from the movie *The Walking Dead* starring Allen Payne

**SCHMIT, Timothy B.**  HOT/AC/ROK
Born on 10/30/47 in Sacramento. Member of **Poco**, 1970-77, and the Eagles, 1977-82.

| 10/27/84 | 101[1] | 5 | Playin' It Cool  ROK:48  Wrong Number | $4 | | Asylum 69690 |

**SCOTT, Freddie**  R&B/HOT
Born on 4/24/33 in Providence, Rhode Island. Recorded first hit while working as a songwriter for Columbia Music.

| 8/12/67 | 120 | 2 | He Will Break Your Heart ........................................ I'll Be Gone | $8 | | Shout 216 |

#7 hit for **Jerry Butler** in 1960

**SCOTT, George ☉**
Mexican "Ranchero"-styled acoustic guitarist.

| 6/12/61 | 104 | 3 | The Matador ................................................. Twilight [I] | $12 | | Fairlane 701 |

with the Bud Mote Orchestra

**SCOTT, Linda**  HOT/AC/R&B
Born Linda Joy Sampson on 6/1/45 in Queens, New York. Vocalist on Arthur Godfrey's CBS radio show, late 1950s.

| 2/17/62 | 116 | 1 | 1 Town Crier .......................................... Yessiree (Hot #60) | $20 | | Congress 101 |
| 9/7/63 | 108 | 3 | 2 Let's Fall In Love .................................. I Know It You Know It | $20 | | Congress 200 |

#1 hit for Eddy Duchin in 1934; Hutch Davie (orch., above 2)

| 2/13/65 | 135 | 1 | 3 Patch It Up ........................................... If I Love Again | $12 | | Kapp 641 |

written by **Bob Crewe**; Charles Calello (orch.)

**SCOTT, Peggy**  HOT/R&B
Born Peggy Stoutmeyer on 6/25/48 in Opp, Alabama. Half of soul duo Peggy Scott & Jo Jo Benson.

| 4/12/69 | 126 | 2 | Every Little Bit Hurts ........................ You Can Never Get Something For Nothing | $8 | | SSS International 767 |

#13 hit for **Brenda Holloway** in 1964

**SCOTT, Simon ☉**
Rock and roll singer.

| 10/24/64 | 128 | 1 | Move It Baby ........................................ What Kind Of Woman | $15 | | Imperial 66066 |

The LeRoys (backing band and vocals)

**SCOTT BROS. ☉**

| 4/18/60 | 110 | 2 | Stolen Angel .......................................... Keep Laughin' | $20 | | Ribbon 6905 |

Jerry Field (orch.)

**SCOTTI, Tony**  HOT/AC

| 3/16/68 | 126 | 1 | 1 Come Live With Me ..................... Theme From 'Valley Of The Dolls' | $6 | | Liberty 56006 |

from the movie *Valley Of The Dolls* starring Sharon Tate and Scotti

| 5/3/69 | 117 | 2 | 2 Devil Or Angel ........................................ A Thing Called Love | $6 | | Liberty 56101 |

#6 hit for **Bobby Vee** in 1960

| 6/12/71 | 118 | 2 | 3 It Won't Hurt To Try It ............................... Somebody Like Me | $6 | | Sunflower 109 |
| 7/1/72 | 101[1] | 5 | 4 Breaking Up Is Hard To Do  Come Run With Me | $6 | | MGM 14412 |

**HEAVEN BOUND with Tony Scotti**
#1 hit for **Neil Sedaka** in 1962; Tommy Oliver (orch., all of above)

**SCUFFY SHEW ☉**

| 11/10/73 | 112 | 6 | Reason To Feel ........................................... Moody | $6 | | Metromedia 0043 |

**SEA, Johnny**  C&W/HOT
Born on 7/15/40 in Gulfport, Mississippi. Joined the *Louisiana Hayride* while still in high school. Real last name: Seay.

| 5/9/64 | 121 | 4 | My Baby Walks All Over Me ........................ C&W:27 There's Another Man | $8 | | Philips 40164 |

Johnny Cash sound-a-like song

**SEAL**  HOT/AC/ROK/R&B
Born Sealhenry Samuel on 2/19/63 in Paddington, England, of Nigerian/Brazilian descent. Male singer.

| 11/12/94 | 109 | 5 | Newborn Friend ................................................................................ *Blues In 'E'* | $3 | ▮ | ZTT/Sire 18053 |

**SEA LEVEL**  HOT/R&B
Jazzy blues-rock band: Chuck Leavell (vocals, keyboards), Jimmy Nails and Davis Causey (guitars), Randall Bramblett (piano), Lamar Williams (bass), Jai Johanny Johanson and George Weaver (drums). Leavell, Williams and Johanson were members of **The Allman Brothers Band**.

| 2/10/79 | 101³ | 8 | Living In A Dream       *Sneakers (Fifty-Four)* (R&B #91) | $5 | | Capricorn 0312 |

**SEALS, Dan**  C&W/HOT/AC
Born on 2/8/48 in McCamey, Texas. Half of the duo **England Dan & John Ford Coley**. Brother of Jim Seals of **Seals & Crofts**.

| 4/3/82 | 110 | 1 | Can't Get You Out Of My Mind ................................................ *Harbinger* | $4 | | Atlantic 4015 |

**SEALS & CROFTS**  AC/HOT
Pop duo: Jim Seals (b: 10/17/41, Sidney, Texas) and Dash Crofts (b: 8/14/40, Cisco, Texas). With **The Champs** from 1958-65. Jim is the brother of **Dan Seals**.

| 12/18/71 | 104 | 4 | When I Meet Them ..................................................................... *Irish Linen* | $7 | | Warner 7536 |

**SEASHELLS, The** ☉
Female rock and roll band.

| 1/27/73 | 115 | 2 | (The Best Part Of) Breakin' Up ............................................. *Play That Song* | $8 | | Columbia 45760 |
| | | | #39 hit for **The Ronettes** in 1964 | | | |

**SEATRAIN**  HOT
Fusion-rock band from Marin County, California featuring John Gregory (vocals, guitar).

| 11/13/71 | 108 | 3 | Marblehead Messenger ............................................................ *Despair Tire* | $7 | | Capitol 3201 |

**SECADA, Jon**  AC/HOT
Born Juan Secada on 10/4/63 in Havana, Cuba; raised in Hialeah, Florida. Earned a Master's degree in jazz at the University of Miami. Co-wrote six songs on **Gloria Estefan**'s album *Into The Light* and a backing vocalist for that tour. Legally changed first name from Juan to Jon in 1990.

| 6/10/95 | 112 | 7 | 1 Where Do I Go From You ................................ AC:36 *(3 versions)* | $3 | ▮ | SBK/EMI 58401 |
| 10/7/95 | 108 | 13 | 2 If I Never Knew You ........................................... *(Spanish version)* | $3 | ▮ | Hollywood 64002 |
| | | |     JON SECADA & SHANICE | | | |
| | | |     love theme from the Walt Disney animated movie *Pocahontas* | | | |

**SEDAKA, Neil**  HOT/AC/R&B
Born on 3/13/39 in Brooklyn. Pop singer/songwriter/pianist. Formed songwriting team with lyricist Howard Greenfield. Recorded with **The Tokens** on Melba in 1956. *Top Pop Singles*: 30.

| 6/1/59 | 111 | 4 | 1 Crying My Heart Out For You ........................... *You Gotta Learn Your Rhythm And Blues* | $20 | | RCA Victor 7530 |
| 4/25/64 | 107 | 2 | 2 The Closest Thing To Heaven ............................ *Without A Song* | $12 | ▮ | RCA Victor 8341 |
| 10/31/64 | 104 | 4 | 3 I Hope He Breaks Your Heart ............................ *Too Late* | $12 | | RCA Victor 8453 |
| 3/13/65 | 107 | 3 | 4 Let The People Talk ............................................ *In The Chapel With You* | $12 | ▮ | RCA Victor 8511 |
| 1/7/67 | 121 | 1 | 5 We Can Make It If We Try ................................. *Too Late* | $10 | | RCA Victor 9004 |
| 8/27/77 | 104 | 3 | 6 Alone At Last.......................................... AC:17 *Sleazy Love* | $4 | | Elektra 45421 |
| 9/6/80 | 107 | 1 | 7 Letting Go ................................................. *It's Good To Be Alive Again* | $4 | | Elektra 47017 |

**SEEKERS, The**  AC/HOT
Australian-born, pop-folk quartet: Judith Durham (b: 7/3/43; lead singer), Keith Potger (guitar), Bruce Woodley (Spanish guitar) and Athol Guy (standup bass). Potger formed The New Seekers in 1970.

| 5/1/65 | 122 | 2 | 1 Chilly Wind .............................................. *The Light From The Lighthouse* | $15 | | Marvel 1060 |
| | | |     variation of the same folk song as **The Serendipity Singers'** "Down Where The Winds Blow" | | | |
| 11/20/65 | 105 | 3 | 2 The Carnival Is Over ............................ AC:27 *We Shall Not Be Moved* | $10 | | Capitol 5531 |
| 8/26/67 | 115 | 4 | 3 On The Other Side ............................. *I Wish You Could Be Here* | $10 | | Capitol 5974 |
| 3/16/68 | 135 | 1 | 4 Love Is Kind, Love Is Wine ................. AC:21 *All I Can Remember* | $10 | | Capitol 2122 |

**SEGER, Bob**  HOT/ROK/AC/C&W
Born on 5/6/45 in Dearborn, Michigan; raised in Detroit. Rock singer/songwriter/guitarist. *Top Pop Singles*: 32.

| 9/9/67 | 103 | 5 | 1 Heavy Music (Part 1) .......................................... *(Part 2)* | $20 | | Cameo 494 |
| | | |     BOB SEGER & THE LAST HEARD | | | |
| 8/23/69 | 103 | 4 | 2 Noah ......................................................... *Lennie Johnson* | $8 | | Capitol 2576 |
| | | |     THE BOB SEGER SYSTEM | | | |
| 5/24/75 | 103 | 4 | 3 Beautiful Loser........................................... *Fine Memory* | $5 | | Capitol 4062 |

**SELENA**  AC/HOT
Born Selena Quintanilla on 4/16/71 in Corpus Christi, Texas. Shot to death by Yolanda Saldivar (founder of Selena's fan club) on 3/31/95.

| 4/13/96 | 107 | 4 | I'm Getting Used To You ...................... AC:23 *(3 mixes)* | $5 | ▮ | EMI Latin 58554 (T) |

**SENATOR BOBBY**  HOT
Senator Bobby is Bill Minkin of a comedy troupe called The Hardly-Worthit Players.

| 6/15/68 | 128 | 1 | Sock It To Me, Baby.......................................... *(instrumental)* [N] | $10 | | RCA Victor 9522 |
| | | |     Bill Minkin as SENATOR BOBBY | | | |
| | | |     #6 hit for **Mitch Ryder & The Detroit Wheels** in 1967 | | | |

**SENAY, Eddy** ☉  R&B
Born in Detroit. R&B guitar instrumentalist.

| 4/8/72 | 104 | 3 | Hot Thang ...................................... R&B:39 *Ain't No Sunshine* [I] | $6 | | Sussex 230 |

**SERENDIPITY SINGERS, The**  HOT/AC
Pop-folk group organized at the University of Colorado.

| 8/1/64 | 112 | 3 | 1 Down Where The Winds Blow (Chilly Winds) ............ *The New Frankie And Johnny Song* | $7 | | Philips 40215 |
| | | |     originally recorded by **The Kingston Trio** on their 1962 album *College Concert* | | | |
| 1/9/65 | 124 | 1 | 2 Little Brown Jug............................................. *High North Star* [N] | $7 | ▮ | Philips 40246 |
| | | |     includes a chorus of **The New Christy Minstrels'** "Green, Green"; #10 hit for Glenn Miller in 1939 | | | |
| 12/4/65 | 118 | 4 | 3 Plastic .................................... *When Peaches Grow On Lilac Trees* [N] | $7 | | Philips 40331 |

**SERMON, Erick**  R&B/HOT
Erick is the 'E' in the Long Island rap duo EPMD.

| 2/10/96 | 103 | 6 | Welcome ...................................... R&B:41 *Do Your Thing* | $3 | ▮ | Def Jam/RAL 577790 |
| | | |     Keith Murray (guest vocal) | | | |

| DEBUT | PEAK | WKS | A-side (Chart Hit)..............................................................B-side | $ | Pic | Label & Number |
|---|---|---|---|---|---|---|

**SEVEN SEAS ☺**        R&B
Miami-based studio R&B/disco group assembled by producer Willie Clarke.

| 9/27/75 | 104 | 1 | Super "Jaws" ............................................ R&B:48 *Pat's Jam* [I] | $6 | | Glades 1728 |

inspired by the 1975 movie *Jaws* starring Roy Scheider

**SEVERINSEN, Doc ☺**        AC/R&B
Born Carl H. Severinsen on 7/7/27 in Arlington, Oregon. Trumpet virtuoso — leader of the *Tonight Show* band (1967-92).

| 3/24/73 | 106 | 4 | The Last Tango In Paris ...................... AC:33 *Alone Again (Naturally)* [I] | $5 | | RCA Victor 0904 |

title song from the movie starring Marlon Brando

**SEX-O-LETTES, The**        HOT/R&B
Female backing group for Disco Tex.

| 11/6/76 | 105 | 1 | Ride A Wild Horse ............................................ *Hey There Little Firefly* | $5 | | Chelsea 3053 |

**SEYMOUR, Phil**        HOT/AC/ROK
Born on 5/15/52 in Tulsa, Oklahoma. Died of lymphoma on 8/17/93. Vocalist/drummer/bassist. Formerly with the **Dwight Twilley Band**.

| 5/16/81 | 110 | 3 | Let Her Dance ............................................ *We Don't Get Along* | $5 | | Boardwalk 02056 |

written and recorded by the **Bobby Fuller Four** in 1966

**SF SPANISH FLY**        HOT
San Francisco-based vocal duo: John "Milo" Pro and Octaviano Silva.

| 2/11/95 | 105 | 15 | 1 Daddy's Home ............................................ *(1995 radio remix)* | $3 | ▌ | Upstairs/Warner 17876 |

    **SPANISH FLY**
charted first 6 weeks on Upstairs 108; #2 hit for **Shep And The Limelites** in 1961

| 2/22/97 | 102 | 11 | 2 I Can See ............................................ *(remix)* | $3 | ▌ | Upstairs/Warner 17398 |

**SHACK ☺**        R&B
Memphis R&B duo: William Shack and Patricia Becton.

| 2/13/71 | 118 | 4 | Too Many Lovers .............................. R&B:23 *A Love Affair That Bears No Pain* | $8 | | Volt 4051 |

**SHACKELFORDS, The**        HOT
Pop singing group put together by producers **Lee Hazlewood** and Marty Cooper. Named after Lee's first wife, Naomi Shackleford.

| 6/3/67 | 115 | 1 | California Sunshine Girl ............................................ *(instrumental)* | $10 | | LHI 17008 |

**SHAGGY**        R&B/HOT
Born Orville Richard Burrell on 10/22/68 in Kingston, Jamaica. Reggae dancehall vocalist.

| 2/17/96 | 108 | 13 | Why You Treat Me So Bad ........... R&B:52 *(club mix)* / *The Train Is Coming* / *Demand The Ride* | $3 | ▌ | Virgin 38529 |

    **SHAGGY Featuring Grand Puba**
samples "Mr. Brown" by **Bob Marley**

**SHALAMAR**        R&B/HOT/AC
R&B/dance vocal trio formed in 1978: Jody Watley, Jeffrey Daniels and Howard Hewett.

| 7/24/82 | 102 | 1 | 1 I Can Make You Feel Good .................... R&B:33 *I Just Stopped By Because I Had To* | $4 | | Solar 48013 |
| 1/28/84 | 101[1] | 7 | 2 You Can Count On Me .............................. R&B:77 *The Look* | $4 | | Solar 69765 |
| 3/23/85 | 106 | 1 | 3 My Girl Loves Me .............................. R&B:22 *Right Here* | $4 | | Solar 69660 |

**SHA NA NA**        HOT/R&B
Fifties rock and roll specialists led by John "Bowzer" Baumann (b: 9/14/47, Queens, New York). Own TV variety show, 1977-81.

| 5/15/71 | 110 | 7 | Only One Song ............................................ *Yakity Yak/Jail House Rock (Medley)* | $6 | | Kama Sutra 522 |

**SHANE, Bob — see KINGSTON TRIO, The**

**SHANE, Jackie ☺**
Female R&B vocalist.

| 1/19/63 | 124 | 2 | Any Other Way ............................................ *Sticks And Stones* | $12 | | Sue 776 |

Frank Motley (orch.); #81 hit for **Chuck Jackson** in 1963

**SHANGO**        HOT/AC
Quartet member Tommy Reynolds was later part of **Hamilton, Joe Frank & Reynolds**.

| 7/11/70 | 107 | 5 | Some Things A Man's Gotta Do............................ *Walking In The Sunshine* | $6 | | Dunhill/ABC 4242 |

**SHANGRI-LAS, The**        HOT/R&B
"Girl group" formed in Queens, New York: sisters Mary (lead singer) and Betty Weiss, and twins Mary Ann (d: 1971) and Marge Ganser (d: 7/28/96).

| 1/7/67 | 123 | 2 | The Sweet Sounds Of Summer ............................................ *I'll Never Learn* | $15 | | Mercury 72645 |

**SHANICE**        R&B/HOT/AC
Born Shanice Wilson on 5/14/73 in Pittsburgh. R&B singer/songwriter.

| 7/30/94 | 122 | 1 | 1 Somewhere .............................. R&B:28 *(6 album snippets)* | $3 | ▌ | Motown 2240 |
| 10/8/94 | 114 | 3 | 2 Turn Down The Lights .............................. R&B:21 *(instrumental)* | $3 | ▌ | Motown 2255 |
| 10/7/95 | 108 | 13 | 3 If I Never Knew You ............................................ *(Spanish version)* | $3 | ▌ | Hollywood 64002 |

    **JON SECADA & SHANICE**
love theme from the Walt Disney animated movie *Pocahontas*

**SHANNON**        R&B/HOT
Brenda Shannon Greene from Washington, D.C. R&B/dance singer.

| 8/17/85 | 103 | 2 | Stronger Together.............................. R&B:26 *Let Me See Your Body Move* | $4 | ■ | Mirage 99631 |

**SHANNON, Del**        HOT/AC/R&B/C&W
Born Charles Westover on 12/30/34 in Coopersville, Michigan. Died on 2/8/90 of a self-inflicted gunshot wound. Formed own Berlee label in 1963.

| 3/17/62 | 113 | 2 | 1 I Won't Be There/ | | | |
| 3/17/62 | 117 | 1 | 2 Ginny In The Mirror | $20 | | Big Top 3098 |
| 3/14/64 | 133 | 1 | 3 That's The Way Love Is ............................................ *Time Of The Day* | $20 | | Berlee 502 |
| 8/28/65 | 128 | 2 | 4 Move It On Over ............................................ *She Still Remembers Tony* | $15 | | Amy 937 |
| 9/10/66 | 128 | 3 | 5 Under My Thumb ............................................ *She Was Mine* | $15 | | Liberty 55904 |

    recorded by **The Rolling Stones** on their 1966 album *Aftermath*

| 2/11/67 | 131 | 2 | 6 She............................................ *What Makes You Run* | $12 | | Liberty 55939 |

    recorded by **The Monkees** on their 1967 album *More Of The Monkees*

**SHANNON, Del — Cont'd**

| 9/9/67 | 112 | 7 | 7 Runaway         *He Cheated* [R] | $15 | | Liberty 55993 |
| | | | "live" version of Del's #1 hit from 1961 | | | |
| 6/21/69 | 127 | 3 | 8 Comin' Back To Me .................................................... *Sweet Mary Lou* | $12 | | Dunhill/ABC 4193 |
| | | | written by Del Shannon and **Brian Hyland** | | | |

**SHANNON, Pat** ☉
Male pop vocalist.

| 1/24/70 | 103 | 3 | Back To Dreamin' Again ....................................................... *Moody* | $6 | | Uni 55191 |

**SHANTE, Roxanne** ☉      **R&B**
Born Lolita Gooden on 3/8/70 in Long Island, New York. Female rapper.

| 3/9/85 | 109 | 1 | Roxanne's Revenge..................................... **R&B:22** *(instrumental)* | $5 | | Pop Art 7546 |
| | | | also released as a 12" single on Pop Art 1406; answer song to "Roxanne, Roxanne" by UTFO; | | | |

**SHARP, Dee Dee**      **R&B/HOT**
Born Dione LaRue on 9/9/45 in Philadelphia. Backing vocalist at Cameo Records in 1961. Married record producer Kenny Gamble in 1967.

| 8/8/64 | 131 | 1 | 1 Never Pick A Pretty Boy.................................. *He's No Ordinary Guy* | $15 | ■ | Cameo 329 |
| | | | answer song to **Jimmy Soul's** "If You Wanna Be Happy" | | | |
| 3/19/66 | 126 | 3 | 2 It's A Funny Situation ................... *There Ain't Nothin' I Wouldn't Do For You* | $12 | | Cameo 382 |
| 3/2/68 | 127 | 2 | 3 We Got A Thing Going On ........................ *What'cha Gonna Do About It* | $10 | | Atco 6557 |
| | | | **BEN E. KING & DEE DEE SHARP** | | | |

**SHARPEES**      **HOT**
R&B group from St. Louis: Benny Sharp, Herbert Reeves (lead), Vernon Guy and Horise O'Toole.

| 7/17/65 | 117 | 5 | 1 Do The "45"........................................... *Make Up Your Mind* | $15 | | One-derful! 4835 |
| 5/7/66 | 133 | 2 | 2 I've Got A Secret ..................................... *Make Up Your Mind* | $15 | | One-derful! 4843 |

**SHAW, Carol** ☉

| 12/28/63 | 132 | 1 | Jimmy Boy............................................................. *Please Don't* | $20 | | Atco 6278 |

**SHAW, Marlena**      **R&B/HOT**
Born Marlena Burgess in 1944 in New Rochelle, New York. Band vocalist with Count Basie from 1967-72.

| 5/22/76 | 103 | 6 | It's Better Than Walkin' Out................**R&B:74** *Be For Real (R&B flip)* | $5 | | Blue Note 790 |

**SHAW, Sandie**      **HOT**
Born Sandra Goodrich on 2/26/47 in Dagenham, England. Pop songstress.

| 8/14/65 | 123 | 3 | 1 I'll Stop At Nothing ........................... *Stop Feeling Sorry For Yourself* | $10 | | Reprise 0394 |
| 12/25/65 | 131 | 1 | 2 How Can You Tell ....................................... *If Ever You Need Me* | $10 | | Reprise 0427 |

**SHAW•BLADES**      **HOT/ROK**
Also see **Jude Cole**.

| 5/27/95 | 120 | 1 | I'll Always Be With You ................................ *Straight Down The Line* | $3 | ▌ | Warner 17879 |

**SHAWN, Damon** ☉      **R&B**
Male R&B singer from Detroit.

| 4/22/72 | 105 | 4 | Feel The Need ............................................. **R&B:42** *I'm Wishing* | $8 | | Westbound 193 |
| | | | "Bubbled Under" on 11/11/72 by the **Detroit Emeralds** as "Feel The Need In Me" | | | |

**SHEEP, The**      **HOT**
Jack Rasca, John Shine, Richie Lauro and Joey Richards — rock group produced by The Strangeloves.

| 5/28/66 | 130 | 2 | I Feel Good ........................................................... *Dynamite* | $20 | | Boom 60,007 |
| | | | #38 hit for Shirley & Lee in 1957 | | | |

**SHEILA E.**      **R&B/HOT/AC**
Born Sheila Escovedo on 12/12/59 in San Francisco. R&B singer/percussionist. Toured and recorded with **Prince**.

| 8/3/85 | 102 | 1 | Sister Fate ......................................... **R&B:36** *(instrumental)* | $4 | ■ | Paisley Park 28955 |

**SHELTON, Roscoe** ☉      **R&B**
Born on 8/22/31 in Lynchburg, Tennessee. Blues vocalist.

| 1/30/65 | 109 | 4 | 1 Strain On My Heart ................................... **R&B:25** *Question* | $12 | | Sims 217 |
| 10/30/65 | 135 | 1 | 2 I Know Your Heart Has Been Broken.............. *You're Such A Good Thing* | $10 | | Sound Stage 7 2549 |
| 1/29/66 | 102 | 3 | 3 Easy Going Fellow ............................. **R&B:32** *Roll With The Punch* | $10 | | Sound Stage 7 2555 |

**SHEP AND THE LIMELITES**      **HOT/R&B**
R&B vocal trio from New York City featuring James "Shep" Sheppard (d: 1/24/70).

| 1/25/64 | 125 | 3 | Why, Why, Won't You Believe Me ..............*Easy To Remember (When You Want To Forget)* | $20 | | Hull 761 |

**SHEPPARD, T.G.**      **C&W/HOT/AC**
Born William Browder on 7/20/42 in Alamo, Tennessee. Country singer.

| 2/7/76 | 102 | 2 | Motels And Memories ................................ **C&W:7** *Pigskin Charade* | $5 | | Melodyland 6028 |

**SHEPPARDS, The** ☉
Chicago-based R&B vocal group: Millard Edwards, Murrie Eskridge, O.C. Perkins, James Allen, James Isaac and Kermit Chandler.

| 8/24/59 | 109 | 1 | Island Of Love ............................................................ *Loving You* | $50 | | Apex 7750 |

**SHEPSTONE & DIBBENS** ☉
Pop vocal duo.

| 9/15/73 | 111 | 8 | Shady Lady .............................................................. *China Heart* | $6 | | Buddah 379 |

**SHERMAN, Allan**      **HOT/AC**
Born Allan Copelon on 11/30/24 in Chicago. Died on 11/21/73. Creator/producer of TV's *I've Got A Secret*.

| 9/26/64 | 113 | 2 | The End Of A Symphone - Part 1 ...........................*Part 2* [N] | $10 | ■ | RCA Victor 8412 |
| | | | **ALLAN SHERMAN BOSTON POPS ORCHESTRA ARTHUR FIEDLER, Conductor** | | | |
| | | | recorded "live" at Tanglewood in the Berkshire Mountains of Massachusetts | | | |

**SHERMAN, Bobby**      **HOT**
Born on 7/22/43 in Santa Monica, California. Regular on TV's *Shindig*; played "Jeremy Bolt" on TV's *Here Come The Brides*.

| 3/6/65 | 118 | 3 | 1 It Hurts Me ......................................... *Give Me Your Word* | $15 | ■ | Decca 31741 |
| 4/14/73 | 113 | 1 | 2 Early In The Morning ............. *Unborn Lullabye (Let Your Mind Be Your Captain)* | $5 | | Metromedia 0100 |
| | | | #61 hit for **The Tokens** in 1970 as "She Lets Her Hair Down"; also see **Don Young's** version | | | |

**SHERMAN, Garry, & His Orchestra** ⊙
Studio orchestra leader for **Bobby Goldsboro** and **Gene Pitney**, among others.

| 12/13/69 | 112 | 1 | Alice's Restaurant Massacree ......................................................... *The Let Down* | $6 | | United Artists 50589 |
|---|---|---|---|---|---|---|

vocals by a chorus; #97 hit for **Arlo Guthrie** in 1969 as "*Alice's Rock & Roll Restaurant*"

**SHERRYS, The**                                    HOT/R&B
Female R&B vocal group from Philadelphia.

| 5/11/63 | 116 | 3 | Saturday Night....................................................................*I've Got No One* | $20 | | Guyden 2084 |
|---|---|---|---|---|---|---|

**SHERWOOD, Holly** ⊙                              AC
Female singer/actress. Member of the original cast of Broadway's *Godspell*.

| 9/18/71 | 104 | 2 | 1 Day By Day (Godspell Medley) .......................................... *Great Golden Day* | $7 | | Carousel 30,057 |
|---|---|---|---|---|---|---|

Tony Orlando (co-producer); #13 hit for Godspell in 1972

| 5/19/73 | 117 | 2 | 2 Yesterday And You ....................................... AC:30  *Time Of Our Lives* | $6 | | Rocky Road 30068 |
|---|---|---|---|---|---|---|

**SHEVELLES, The** ⊙
British pop/rock and roll band.

| 9/5/64 | 104 | 7 | I Could Conquer The World ..................................*How Would You Like Me To Love You* | $15 | | World Artists 1025 |
|---|---|---|---|---|---|---|

written by Paul Evans

**SHEW, Scuffy — see SCUFFY SHEW**

**SHIEKS, The** ⊙
Rock and roll instrumental band.

| 12/14/59 | 111 | 1 | Baghdad Rock (Part 1) ..................................................... *(Part 2)* [I] | $40 | | Trine 1101 |
|---|---|---|---|---|---|---|

**SHIELDS, Billy — see ORLANDO, Tony**

**SHIRELLES, The**                                  HOT/R&B
R&B female vocal group of teenagers from Passaic, New Jersey: Shirley Owens Alston, Beverly Lee, Doris Kenner and Addie "Micki" Harris (d: 6/10/82, age 42). Inducted into the Rock and Roll Hall of Fame in 1996. *Top Pop Singles*: 26.

| 12/11/61 | 107 | 2 | 1 The Things I Want To Hear (Pretty Words) ..............................*Baby It's You* (Hot #8) | $15 | | Scepter 1227 |
|---|---|---|---|---|---|---|
| 4/7/62 | 109 | 2 | 2 Love Is A Swingin' Thing.............................................. *Soldier Boy* (Hot #1) | $15 | | Scepter 1228 |
| 7/14/62 | 104 | 2 | 3 Mama, Here Comes The Bride .............................*Welcome Home Baby* (Hot #22) | $15 | | Scepter 1234 |
| 9/29/62 | 102 | 2 | 4 It's Love That Really Counts (in the long run) ......................*Stop The Music* (Hot #36) | $15 | | Scepter 1237 |
| 10/10/64 | 125 | 2 | 5 Lost Love .............................................................*Maybe Tonight* (Hot #88) | $12 | | Scepter 1284 |
| 7/3/65 | 108 | 2 | 6 March (You'll Be Sorry) ..................................*Everybody's Goin' Mad* | $12 | | Scepter 12101 |
|  |  |  | written by The Tokens |  |  |  |
| 10/16/65 | 125 | 2 | 7 My Heart Belongs To You............................................ *Love That Man* | $12 | | Scepter 12114 |
| 10/8/66 | 122 | 4 | 8 Shades Of Blue................................*When The Boys Talk About The Girls* | $12 | | Scepter 12162 |
|  |  |  | also released with "Looking Around" as the B-side |  |  |  |
| 1/28/67 | 110 | 3 | 9 Don't Go Home (My Little Darlin')............................... *Nobody Baby After You* | $12 | | Scepter 12185 |
|  |  |  | #22 hit for The Playmates in 1958 |  |  |  |

**SHIRLEY, Don**                                    HOT/AC
Born on 1/27/27 in Kingston, Jamaica. Pianist/organist.

| 12/25/61 | 116 | 1 | Lonesome Road ...........................*Drown In My Own Tears* (Hot #100) [I] | $10 | | Cadence 1408 |
|---|---|---|---|---|---|---|

traditional black American spiritual

**SHOCKING BLUE**                                   HOT
Dutch rock quartet: Mariska Veres (lead singer), Robbie van Leeuwen (guitar), Cor van Beek (drums) and Klaasje van der Wal (bass).

| 12/26/70 | 102 | 9 | 1 Never Marry A Railroad Man .............................. *Never Love A Railroad Man* | $6 | | Colossus 123 |
|---|---|---|---|---|---|---|
| 10/30/71 | 110 | 1 | 2 Serenade ...................................................... *Sleepless At Midnight* | $6 | | Buddah 258 |

**SHONDELL, Troy**                                  HOT/C&W
Born on 5/14/44 in Fort Wayne, Indiana. Pop-country singer/songwriter.

| 6/2/62 | 107 | 2 | 1 Na-Ne-No .............................................................. *Just Because* | $15 | | Liberty 55445 |
|---|---|---|---|---|---|---|
|  |  |  | written by Paul Dino; produced by Phil Spector |  |  |  |
| 1/4/69 | 129 | 1 | 2 Let's Go All The Way ....................................................*Let Me Love You* | $10 | | TRX 5015 |

**SHONDELLS, The** ⊙
Female R&B vocal group featuring Novella Simmons & Shirlee Brooks.

| 10/13/62 | 116 | 3 | Wonderful One ...................................................... *I Gotta Tell It* | $25 | | King 5656 |
|---|---|---|---|---|---|---|

**SHORE, Dinah**                                    MEM/POP/HOT
Born Frances Rose Shore on 3/1/17 in Winchester, Tennessee. Died on 2/24/94. One of the most popular female vocalists of the 1940 to mid-1950s era. Hosted many TV variety shows from 1951-80. *Pop Hits & Top Pop Singles*: 69.

| 12/26/60 | 103 | 3 | I Ain't Down Yet ....................................................*I Gotta Love You* | $10 | | Capitol 4476 |
|---|---|---|---|---|---|---|

Dick Reynolds (orch.); from Broadway's *The Unsinkable Molly Brown* starring Tammy Grimes; no vocals other than "doo's and daa's"

**SHOR PATROL** ⊙
Rock band from Baltimore featuring lead singer Alana Shor.

| 7/16/83 | 108 | 3 | Loverboy ........................................................... *Can I Do It?* | $4 | | Arista 9024 |
|---|---|---|---|---|---|---|

**SHORT-KUTS, The** ⊙
R&B group from Memphis: Eddie Harrison, lead singer.

| 9/13/69 | 109 | 2 | Born On The Bayou ........................................ *Thank You Number One* | $8 | | Pepper 445 |
|---|---|---|---|---|---|---|

recorded by Creedence Clearwater Revival on their 1969 album *Bayou Country*

**SHOWMEN, The**                                    HOT/R&B
R&B group from Norfolk, Virginia, led by General Norman Johnson (**Chairmen Of The Board**).

| 6/17/67 | 101[2] | 7 | 39-21-46 ...................................................*Swish Fish* | $12 | | Minit 32007 |
|---|---|---|---|---|---|---|

first released on Minit 662 in 1963 ($25)

**SHOW STOPPERS, The**                              HOT
R&B quartet of two sets of brothers from Philadelphia: Laddie and Alec Burke (**Solomon Burke**'s brothers) and Earl and Timmy Smith.

| 5/27/67 | 118 | 1 | Ain't Nothin' But A House Party .............................*What Can A Man Do??* | $10 | | Showtime 101 |
|---|---|---|---|---|---|---|

made the *Hot 100* (#87) on 6/1/68 on Heritage 800

**SHUT DOWNS, The** ☺
A Kirby St. Romain, Scotty McKay "hot-rod" rock and roll instrumental production.

| 11/9/63 | 131 | 1 | Four In The Floor ........................................................ *Beach Buggy* [I] | $30 | Dimension 1016 |

**SICKNIKS, The** ☺
Comedy troupe led by Will Jordan and Sandy Baron. *Sicknik* was a magazine aimed at teenagers (similar to *Mad*).

| 6/26/61 | 105 | 1 | The Presidential Press Conference (Parts 1 & 2) ........................[N] | $25 | ■ Amy 824 |

President Kennedy (Sandy Baron) questioned by Elvis, Fats, Duane, Everlys, etc. to a rock and roll beat

**SIDEKICKS, The**           HOT
Pop quartet: Jon Spirt, Mike Burke, brothers Zack (vocals) and Randy Bocelle.

| 10/29/66 | 115 | 4 | Fifi The Flea ........................................................ *Not Now* | $10 | RCA Victor 8969 |

**SIEGEL-SCHWALL BAND** ☺
Chicago-based, blues-rock band formed by keyboardist Corky Siegel and guitarist Jim Schwall.

| 5/12/73 | 105 | 2 | Blues Band, Opus 50, Part 1 ........................................ *Part 2* [I] | $10 | ■ Deutsche Gramm. 15068 |

SIEGEL-SCHWALL BAND and SAN FRANCISCO SYMPHONY ORCHESTRA, SEIJI OZAWA, Conductor
The Third Movement of "Three Pieces For Blues Band And Symphony Orchestra" by William Russo

**SIERRAS, The** ☺

| 9/14/63 | 108 | 2 | I'll Believe It When I See It ........................... *I Should Have Loved You* | $30 | Goldisc 4 |

answer song to The Essex' 1963 #1 hit "Easier Said Than Done"

**SIGLER, Bunny**           R&B/HOT
Born Walter Sigler on 3/27/41 in Philadelphia. R&B vocalist/multi-instrumentalist/composer/producer.

| 9/27/75 | 102 | 4 | That's How Long I'll Be Loving You ........................... *Somebody Free* | $8 | Philadelphia Int'l. 3575 |

**SILK** ☺           R&B
Disco group produced by David Porter (Isaac Hayes' songwriting partner).

| 7/9/77 | 107 | 1 | Party - Pt. 1 ........................... R&B:81 *Pt. 2* | $7 | Prelude 71084 |

**SILK**           R&B/HOT
Atlanta R&B male vocal quintet: Timothy Cameron, Jimmy Gates, Jr., Johnathen Rasboro, Gary Jenkins and Gary Glenn.

| 10/16/93 | 109 | 3 | It Had To Be You ........................... R&B:45 *Give Me What I Want (w/Keith Sweat)* | $3 | ▮ Keia/Elektra 64599 |

written and produced by Keith Sweat

**SILKIE, The**           HOT
Folk quartet formed in 1963 in Hull, England: Silvia Tatler (vocals), Ivor Aylesbury and Mike Ramsden (guitars), and Kevin Cunningham (bass).

| 1/22/66 | 124 | 2 | 1 The Keys To My Soul ........................... *Leave Me To Cry* | $10 | Fontana 1536 |
| 8/6/66 | 133 | 1 | 2 Born To Be With You ........................... *I'm So Sorry* | $10 | Fontana 1551 |

written by Don Robertson; #5 hit for The Chordettes in 1956

**SILVER CONVENTION**           R&B/HOT/AC
German studio disco act assembled by producer Michael Kunze and writer/arranger Silvester Levay.

| 4/5/75 | 103 | 6 | 1 Save Me ........................... *Save Me Again* | $5 | Midland Int'l. 10212 |
| 12/11/76 | 102 | 6 | 2 Dancing In The Aisles (Take Me Higher) ...........R&B:80 *Thank You Mister D.J.* | $5 | Midland Int'l. 10849 |
| 6/18/77 | 103 | 2 | 3 Telegram ........................... *Midnight Lady* | $5 | ■ Midsong Int'l. 10972 |

**SILVER HAWK** ☺

| 5/22/71 | 108 | 3 | Awaiting On You All ........................... *All I Can Do* | $8 | Westbound 178 |

written and recorded by George Harrison on his 1970 album *All Things Must Pass*

**SILVERSTEIN, Shel** ☺
Satirical songwriter/poet/author/cartoonist. Born in Chicago in 1932. Wrote Johnny Cash's 1969 hit "A Boy Named Sue."

| 2/3/73 | 107 | 7 | Sarah Cynthia Sylvia Stout (Would Not Take The Garbage Out) ........................... *Stacy Brown Got Two* [N] | $7 | Columbia 45772 |

**SIMEONE, Harry, Chorale**           HOT/AC
Born on 5/9/11 in Newark, New Jersey. Arranger/conductor for movies and TV shows. Began career as staff music arranger for CBS radio, followed by 14 years as an arranger for Fred Waring.

| 1/9/65 | 105 | 1 | 1 O' Bambino (One Cold And Blessed Winter) ................. *Sing Of A Merry Christmas* [X] | $7 | ■ Kapp 628 |

#9 hit on *Billboard's* special Christmas charts in 1964

| 8/21/65 | 109 | 4 | 2 Summer Wind ........................AC:20 *Sailor (Your Home Is The Sea)* (Williams) | $7 | Kapp 55 |

ROGER WILLIAMS & The HARRY SIMEONE CHORALE
released on Kapp's "Winners Circle Series" label; #25 hit for Frank Sinatra in 1966

**SIMMONS, Fay** ☺

| 3/27/61 | 107 | 2 | Everybody's Doin' The Pony ........................... *I Won't Stop Lovin' You* | $20 | Senca 125 |

**SIMON, Carly**           AC/HOT/C&W
Born on 6/25/45 in New York City. Pop vocalist/songwriter. Won the 1971 Best New Artist Grammy Award. *Top Pop Singles*: 23.

| 12/13/80 | 102 | 6 | 1 Take Me As I Am ........................... *James* | $4 | Warner 49630 |
| 12/19/81 | 106 | 4 | 2 Hurt ........................... *From The Heart* | $4 | Warner 49880 |

#8 R&B hit for Roy Hamilton in 1955; #4 hit for Timi Yuro in 1961

**SIMON, Joe**           R&B/HOT
Born on 9/2/43 in Simmesport, Louisiana. R&B singer. First recorded with the vocal group the Golden Tones for Hush in 1960. *Top Pop Singles*: 31.

| 9/12/64 | 102 | 9 | 1 My Adorable One ........................... *Say (That Your Love Is True)* | $12 | Vee-Jay 609 |
| 8/5/67 | 129 | 3 | 2 Put Your Trust In Me (Depend On Me) ...................R&B:47 *Just A Dream* | $7 | Sound Stage 7 2583 |
| 4/24/71 | 117 | 2 | 3 To Lay Down Beside You ...............R&B:flip *Help Me Make It Through The Night (Hot #69)* | $5 | ■ Spring 113 |
| 9/11/76 | 102 | 3 | 4 Come To This ........................... R&B:22 *Let The Good Times Roll* | $5 | Spring 166 |

**SIMON & GARFUNKEL**           HOT/AC
Folk-rock duo from New York City: Paul Simon and Art Garfunkel. Recorded as Tom & Jerry in 1957. Duo inducted into the Rock and Roll Hall of Fame in 1990.

| 4/23/66 | 123 | 4 | 1 That's My Story ...... *(Uncle Simon's) Tia-Juana Blues* (Paul Simon & Lou Simon & The Ace Trumpets) | $20 | ABC 10788 |

PAUL SIMON & ARTHUR GARFUNKEL (label shows Carfunkel)
first released on Big 618 ($50) in 1958 and then on Hunt 319 ($50) in 1958 (both as Tom & Jerry)

| 4/12/69 | 101[3] | 7 | 2 Baby Driver ........................... *The Boxer (Hot #7)* | $8 | ■ Columbia 44785 |

| DEBUT | PEAK | WKS | A-side (Chart Hit) ... B-side | $ | Pic | Label & Number |
|---|---|---|---|---|---|---|

### SIMONE, Nina        R&B/HOT
Born Eunice Waymon on 2/21/33 in Tryon, South Carolina. Jazz-influenced vocalist/pianist/composer.

| 9/11/61 | 113 | 3 | 1 Gin House Blues ................................................ *You Can Have Him* | $12 | | Colpix 608 |
| 12/5/64 | 131 | 1 | 2 Don't Let Me Be Misunderstood ................................ *A Monster* | $8 | | Philips 40232 |
| | | | #15 hit for The Animals in 1965 | | | |
| 6/26/65 | 120 | 4 | 3 I Put A Spell On You ............................ R&B:23 *Gimme Some* | $8 | | Philips 40286 |
| | | | written and recorded by Screamin' Jay Hawkins in 1956 on Okeh 7072 ($40) | | | |
| 11/4/67 | 133 | 1 | 4 (You'll) Go To Hell ............................ *It Be's That Way Sometime* | $8 | | RCA Victor 9286 |

### SIMPLY RED        AC/HOT/R&B
Blue-eyed soul group formed in Manchester, England, featuring vocalist Mick "Red" Hucknall (b: 6/8/60).

| 11/11/95 | 114 | 12 | Fairground ............................................ (3 album snippets) | $3 | ▌ | EastWest 64356 |
| | | | samples "Fanfarra" by Sergio Mendes and "Give It Up" by The Goodmen | | | |

### SIMTEC & WYLIE ○        R&B
R&B duo from Chicago: Walter "Simtec" Simmons and Wylie Dixon.

| 9/11/71 | 101[1] | 1 | Gotta' Get Over The Hump ......... R&B:29 *Nine Times Out Of Ten* | $8 | | Mister Chand 8005 |
| | | | Mister Chand label pictures owner and producer Gene Chandler | | | |

### SINATRA, Frank        MEM/POP/HOT/AC/R&B
Born Francis Albert Sinatra on 12/12/15 in Hoboken, New Jersey. Died of a heart attack on 5/14/98. With Harry James in 1939-40; with Tommy Dorsey, 1940-42. Starred in many movies. Won an Oscar for the movie *From Here To Eternity* in 1953. Own Reprise record company in 1961. Won Grammy's Lifetime Achievement Award in 1965. Regarded by many as the greatest popular singer of the 20th century. Pop Hits & Top Pop Singles: 146.

| 6/20/60 | 111 | 1 | 1 It's Over, It's Over, It's Over ............... *River, Stay 'Way From My Door* (Hot #82) | $12 | | Capitol 4376 |
| 11/3/62 | 101[1] | 2 | 2 The Look Of Love ............................ *Indiscreet* | $10 | | Reprise 20,107 |
| | | | also released with "I Left My Heart In San Francisco" on the B-side ($50) | | | |
| 6/15/63 | 108 | 4 | 3 Come Blow Your Horn ............................ *I Have Dreamed* | $10 | | Reprise 20,184 |
| | | | above 2 from the movie *Come Blow Your Horn* starring Sinatra | | | |
| 10/26/63 | 111 | 1 | 4 Love Isn't Just For The Young ........ *(You Brought) A New Kind Of Love (To Me)* | $10 | ▌ | Reprise 20,209 |
| | | | Marty Paich (orch.) | | | |
| 6/13/64 | 110 | 5 | 5 My Kind Of Town ............................ *I Like To Lead When I Dance* | $12 | | Reprise 0279 |
| | | | from the movie *Robin And The 7 Hoods* starring Sinatra | | | |
| 9/4/65 | 102 | 5 | 6 When Somebody Loves You ......... AC:10 *When I'm Not Near The Girl I Love* | $8 | | Reprise 0398 |
| | | | Ernie Freeman (orch.) | | | |
| 11/6/65 | 131 | 1 | 7 Everybody Has The Right To Be Wrong! (At Least Once) ......... AC:25 *I'll Only Miss Her When I Think Of Her* (AC #18) | $8 | | Reprise 0410 |
| | | | Torrie Zito (orch.); from the Broadway musical *Skyscraper* starring Julie Harris | | | |
| 12/25/65 | 115 | 2 | 8 Moment To Moment ............................ AC:18 *It Was A Very Good Year* (Hot #28) | $8 | ▌ | Reprise 0429 |
| | | | title song from the movie starring Jean Seberg; Nelson Riddle (orch.: #1, 3, 5 & 8) | | | |
| 6/13/70 | 123 | 1 | 9 What's Now Is Now ............................ AC:31 *The Train* | $6 | | Reprise 0920 |
| | | | Bob Gaudio (orch.) | | | |

### SINATRA, Nancy, & Lee Hazelwood        HOT/AC
Nancy was born on 6/8/40 in Jersey City, New Jersey. First child of Nancy and Frank Sinatra. Starred with Elvis Presley in the 1968 movie *Speedway*. Top Pop Singles: 21.

| 10/28/67 | 107 | 3 | 1 Sand ............................ *Lady Bird* (Hot #20) | $10 | | Reprise 0629 |
| 2/19/72 | 120 | 2 | 2 Down From Dover ............................ *Paris Summer* | $10 | | RCA Victor 0614 |
| | | | written by Dolly Parton | | | |

### SINGING NUN, The        HOT/AC
Sister Luc-Gabrielle (real name: Jeanine Deckers) from the Fichermont, Belgium convent. Committed suicide on 3/31/85 (age 52).

| 2/8/64 | 115 | 1 | Tous Les Chemins (All The Roads) ......... *Frere "Tout L' Monde"* [F] | $8 | ▌ | Philips 40165 |
| | | | SOEUR SOURIRE (The Singing Nun) | | | |

### SINGLETON, Margie ○        C&W
Born on 10/5/35 in Coushatta, Louisiana. Country singer. Worked on the *Louisiana Hayride* from 1957-59.

| 1/26/63 | 124 | 1 | Magic Star (Tel-Star) ............................ *Only Your Shadow Knows* | $10 | | Mercury 72079 |
| | | | The Merry Melody Singers (backing vocals); #1 hit for The Tornadoes in 1962 (as "Telstar") | | | |

### SIOUXSIE & THE BANSHEES        ROK/HOT
Avant-punk band formed in 1976 by vocalist Siouxsie Sioux (Susan Dallion) and bassist Steve Severin (Steve Havoc).

| 3/25/95 | 125 | 1 | O Baby ............................ ROK:21 *B Side Ourselves* | $3 | ▌ | Geffen 19383 |
| | | | produced by John Cale of The Velvet Underground | | | |

### SIR DOUGLAS QUINTET        HOT
Tex-Mex rock band: Doug Sahm, Augie Myers, Harvey Regan, Frank Morin and John Perez.

| 7/24/65 | 105 | 4 | 1 The Tracker ............................ *Blue Norther* | $10 | | Tribe 8310 |
| 5/21/66 | 129 | 1 | 2 Quarter To Three ............................ *She's Gotta Be Boss* | $10 | | Tribe 8317 |
| | | | #1 hit for U.S. Bonds in 1961 | | | |
| 10/29/66 | 132 | 1 | 3 She Digs My Love ............................ *When I Sing The Blues* | $10 | | Tribe 8321 |
| 5/17/69 | 108 | 3 | 4 It Didn't Even Bring Me Down ........ *Lawd I'm Just A Country Boy In This Great Big Freaky City* | $8 | | Smash 2222 |
| 12/20/69 | 104 | 1 | 5 At The Crossroads ............................ *Texas Me* | $8 | | Smash 2253 |
| 3/3/73 | 115 | 3 | 6 (Is Anybody Going To) San Antone ............................ *Don't Turn Around* | $8 | | Atlantic 2946 |
| | | | DOUG SAHM and BAND | | | |
| | | | Bob Dylan (guest vocals); #70 hit for Charley Pride in 1970 | | | |

### SISTER AND BROTHERS, The ○        R&B
Mixed male-female R&B vocal group from Chicago.

| 7/18/70 | 131 | 1 | Dear Ike (Remember I'm John's Girl) ......... R&B:28 *Yeah, You Right* [S] | $7 | | Uni 55238 |

### SISTER SLEDGE        R&B/HOT/AC
Sisters Debra, Joni, Kim and Kathy Sledge from North Philadelphia. First recorded as Sisters Sledge for Money Back label in 1971.

| 4/19/80 | 101[1] | 3 | Reach Your Peak ............................ R&B:21 *You Fooled Around* | $4 | | Cotillion 45013 |

**SISTERS LOVE** ○          R&B
R&B group consisting of **Merry Clayton**, Odia Coates, Gwen Berry and Lillian Fort. All except Fort had been in **The Raeletts**.

| 6/5/71 | 108 | 7 | Are You Lonely? .................................................... R&B:20 *Ring Once* | $8 | | A&M 1259 |

written and produced by **Gene Chandler**

**SKEE-LO**     R&B/HOT
Male rapper from Riverside, California.

| 12/9/95+ | 112 | 2 | Top Of The Stairs .................................................... R&B:73 *(street mix)* | $3 | ▮ | Sunshine/Scotti 78057 |

from the movie *Money Train* starring Wesley Snipes

**SKELLERN, Peter**     HOT/AC
British singer/pianist. Had a bit part in the movie *Lassiter*.

| 10/18/75 | 106 | 1 | Hold On To Love ........................................................ | $5 | | Private Stock 45,028 |

**SKIP AND FLIP**     HOT/R&B
Gary "Flip" Paxton and Clyde "Skip" Battin. Paxton formed the Hollywood Argyles, and later started own Garpax record label.

| 8/8/60 | 109 | 1 | Hully Gully Cha Cha Cha .................................... *Teenage Honeymoon* | $20 | | Brent 7013 |

## SKIP & THE CASUALS — see McHONEY, Skip

**SKIPWORTH & TURNER** ○     R&B
R&B duo of Rodney Skipworth (from Syracuse, keyboards) and Phil Turner (from Memphis; vocals).

| 5/18/85 | 104 | 2 | Thinking About Your Love.................................... R&B:10 *(instrumental)* | $4 | ▮ | 4th & B'Way 7414 |

from the movie *Pumping Iron II: The Women* starring female bodybuilders

**SKYLARK**     AC/HOT/R&B
Interracial group from Vancouver, Canada, featuring lead singers **Donny Gerrard**, B.J. (Bonnie Jean) Cook and **Carl Graves**.

| 9/1/73 | 106 | 7 | I'll Have To Go Away .................................... AC:39 *Twenty-Six Years* | $5 | ▮ | Capitol 3661 |

**SKYLINERS, The**     HOT/R&B
Pittsburgh white vocal quintet: **Jimmy Beaumont** (lead), Janet Vogel (d: 2/21/80), Wally Lester, Joe VerScharen and Jackie Taylor.

| 12/18/61 | 105 | 4 | 1 Close Your Eyes .................................... *Our Love Will Last* | $40 | | Colpix 613 |

written by Chuck Willis; #5 R&B hit for The Five Keys in 1955; #8 hit for **Peaches & Herb** in 1967

| 2/16/63 | 128 | 1 | 2 Comes Love .................................... *Tell Me* | $30 | | Viscount 104 |

**SKYY**     R&B/HOT
Brooklyn R&B-funk octet featuring sisters Denise, Delores and Bonnie Dunning (vocals).

| 5/10/80 | 102 | 3 | High.................................... R&B:13 *Who's Gonna Love Me* | $4 | | Salsoul 2113 |

**SLADE**     HOT/ROK
Hard-rock quartet formed in 1966 in Wolverhampton, England: Noddy Holder (vocals), David Hill (guitar), Jim Lea (bass, keyboards) and Don Powell (drums).

| 9/1/73 | 114 | 1 | Let The Good Times Roll/Feel So Fine .................................... *I Don' Mind* | $8 | | Polydor 15080 |

medley of Shirley & Lee R&B hits: #1'56 and #2'55

**SLATKIN, Felix**     HOT
St. Louis native. Virtuoso violinist/conductor/composer/arranger. Worked with many movie and record companies. Died on 2/9/63 (age 47).

| 11/20/61 | 120 | 1 | Theme From King Of Kings .................................... *Mandolino* [I] | $10 | | Liberty 55372 |

from the movie *King Of Kings* starring Jeffrey Hunter

**SLAVE**     R&B/HOT
Funk band from Dayton, Ohio, formed by Steve Washington in 1975. Washington and members Starleana Young and Tom Lockett, Jr. left to form Aurra in 1979. **Steve Arrington** was a member from 1979-82. Young and member Curt Jones later formed Deja.

| 2/25/78 | 110 | 1 | 1 The Party Song .................................... R&B:22 *We Can Make Love* | $4 | | Cotillion 44231 |
| 2/3/79 | 110 | 1 | 2 Just Freak .................................... R&B:64 *The Way You Love Is Heaven* | $4 | | Cotillion 44242 |
| 1/16/82 | 103 | 7 | 3 Wait For Me .................................... R&B:20 *Steal Your Heart* | $4 | | Cotillion 46028 |

**SLEDGE, Percy**     HOT/R&B
Born on 11/25/40 in Leighton, Alabama. R&B singer.

| 10/19/68 | 109 | 3 | 1 You're All Around Me .................................... *Self Preservation* | $10 | | Atlantic 2563 |
| 5/31/69 | 126 | 2 | 2 The Angels Listened In .................................... *Any Day Now* (Hot #86) | $10 | | Atlantic 2616 |

#22 hit for **The Crests** in 1959

| 8/9/69 | 116 | 2 | 3 Kind Woman .................................... *Woman Of The Night* | $10 | | Atlantic 2646 |

written by **Richie Furay** (Poco/Buffalo Springfield)

**SLICK, Grace**     HOT/ROK
Born Grace Wing on 10/30/39 in Chicago. Female lead singer of **Jefferson Airplane/Starship**.

| 7/26/80 | 104 | 2 | Dreams .................................... *Do It The Hard Way* | $4 | ▮ | RCA 12041 |

**SLICK RICK**     R&B/HOT
Rapper Ricky Walters, born to Jamaican parents on 1/14/65 in South Wimbledon, London. Teamed with **Doug E. Fresh**, 1984-85.

| 3/4/95 | 101[1] | 11 | Sittin' In My Car .................................... Sls:54 /R&B:56 *(remix)* | $3 | ▮ | Def Jam 853992 |

**SLICK RICK** Featuring Doug E. Fresh On The Beatbox
samples "For The Love Of You" by **The Isley Brothers**

**SLOAN, P.F.**     HOT
Los Angeles native Phillip "Flip" Sloan. Vocalist/guitarist/songwriter. Wrote "Eve Of Destruction" and many others.

| 4/2/66 | 109 | 1 | From A Distance .................................... *Patterns, Seg. 4* | $15 | | Dunhill 4024 |

**SLOW PAIN** ○
| 2/17/96 | 103 | 6 | Money Maid (Fallin' In Love).................................... *(remix version)* | $3 | ▮ | Thump 2225 |

rap version of "Could It Be I'm Falling In Love" by the **Spinners**

**SLY & THE FAMILY STONE**     HOT/R&B/AC
San Francisco interracial "psychedelic soul" group fronted by Sylvester "Sly Stone" Stewart (b: 3/15/44; lead singer, keyboards). Member Larry Graham formed Graham Central Station in 1973. Group inducted into the Rock and Roll Hall of Fame in 1993. *Top Pop Singles*: 20.

| 11/3/79 | 104 | 2 | Remember Who You Are .................................... R&B:38 *Sheer Energy* | $5 | | Warner 49062 |

**SMACK** ○
Group of studio musicians from New Jersey that "cover" unavailable singles, led by producer Adam Marano.

| 12/13/97+ | 114 | 11 | Walkin' On The Sun .................................... *(remix)* | $3 | ▮ | Under The Cover 976 |

#2 *Hot 100 Airplay* hit for Smash Mouth in 1997

### SMITH, Karen ☉        R&B
R&B vocalist.

| 6/11/66 | 123 | 3 | Boys Are Made To Love ...................................... R&B:37 *Hey Love* | $15 | | Venus 1066 |

written by Don Julian of **The Larks**

### SMALL FACES        HOT
British rock band: Steve Marriott (guitar; d: 4/20/91), Ronnie Lane (bass; d: 6/4/97), Ian McLagen (organ) and Kenney Jones (drums). In 1968, Marriott formed **Humble Pie**. In 1969, remaining members formed Faces with former **Jeff Beck** Group members **Rod Stewart** (vocals) and Ronnie Wood (bass).

| 5/4/68 | 114 | 2 | Lazy Sunday ...................................... *Rollin' Over (Part II of Happiness Stan)* | $15 | | Immediate 5007 |

### SMASHING PUMPKINS        ROK/HOT
Rock quartet formed in Chicago in 1989: Billy Corgan (vocals), James Iha (guitar), D'Arcy Wretzky (bass) and Jimmy Chamberlin (drums).

| 12/18/93 | 103 | 1 | Today ...................................... Air:69 /ROK:4 | | | album cut |

from the album *Siamese Dream* on Virgin 88267; no U.S. commercial single was issued

### SMIF-N-WESSUN        R&B/HOT
Brooklyn, New York rap duo: Tek and Steele.

| 5/6/95 | 116 | 3 | Wontime ...................................... *(instrumental)* | $3 | ▮ | Wreck/Nervous 20110 |

### SMITH        HOT
Los Angeles-based rock group featuring Gayle McCormick (vocals).

| 8/15/70 | 101[1] | 4 | Comin' Back To Me (Ooh Baby)     *Minus-Plus* | $7 | | Dunhill/ABC 4246 |

### SMITH, Adrian ☉
Female pop/country singer.

| 5/26/73 | 114 | 2 | Wild About My Lovin' ...................................... *Steer Clear* | $6 | | MCA 40045 |

### SMITH, Carl        C&W/HOT
Born on 3/15/27 in Maynardsville, Tennessee. Country singer.

| 7/18/60 | 107 | 3 | If The World Don't End Tomorrow I'm Comin' After You .............. *Lonely Old Room* | $12 | | Columbia 41729 |

### SMITH, Connie ☉        C&W
Born Constance June Meadows on 8/14/41 in Elkhart, Indiana. Country singer. Member of the *Grand Ole Opry* since 1971.

| 10/3/64 | 101[1] | 10 | 1 Once A Day     C&W:❶[8] *The Threshold* | $10 | | RCA Victor 8416 |
| 1/16/65 | 116 | 3 | 2 Then And Only Then ...................................... C&W:4 *Tiny Blue Transistor Radio (C&W #25)* | $10 | | RCA Victor 8489 |
| 4/24/65 | 130 | 2 | 3 I Can't Remember ...................................... C&W:9 *Senses* | $10 | | RCA Victor 8551 |

above 3 written by Bill Anderson

| 6/26/71 | 119 | 3 | 4 Just One Time ...................................... C&W:2 *Don't Walk Away* | $7 | | RCA Victor 9981 |

#29 hit for **Don Gibson** in 1960

### SMITH, Helene ☉        R&B
R&B vocalist from Miami, produced by Willie Clark and **Clarence Reid**.

| 6/24/67 | 128 | 1 | A Woman Will Do Wrong ...................................... R&B:20 *Like A Baby* | $12 | | Phil-L.A. of Soul 300 |

### SMITH, Jerry        C&W/AC/HOT
Session pianist. Wrote and performed on **The Dixiebelles**' "(Down At) Papa Joe's" as Cornbread & Jerry.

| 7/4/70 | 125 | 2 | Drivin' Home ...................................... C&W:44 *Louisiana Blues* [I] | $6 | | Decca 32679 |

### SMITH, Jimmy        HOT/R&B
Born on 12/8/25 in Norristown, Pennsylvania. Pioneer jazz organist. First recorded with own trio for Blue Note in 1956.

| 5/26/62 | 103 | 2 | 1 One O'clock Jump ...................................... *Jumpin' The Blues* [I] | $10 | | Blue Note 1820 |

Count Basie's theme song — written by Basie in 1937

| 9/15/62 | 107 | 1 | 2 Everybody Loves My Baby ...................................... *Ain't She Sweet* [I] | $10 | | Blue Note 1851 |

#5 hit for Aileen Stanley in 1925; also popularized by Fats Waller

| 9/21/63 | 113 | 1 | 3 What'd I Say? ...................................... *Theme From "Any Number Can Win"* (Smith-Hot #96) [I] | $8 | | Verve 10299 |

**KENNY BURRELL and JIMMY SMITH**
#6 hit for **Ray Charles** in 1959

| 3/6/65 | 105 | 5 | 4 Goldfinger (Part I) ...................................... *(Part II)* [I] | $8 | | Verve 10346 |

from the James Bond movie *Goldfinger* starring Sean Connery; #8 hit for **Shirley Bassey** in 1965

### SMITH, Keely — see PRIMA, Louis

### SMITH, Margo ☉        C&W/AC
Born Betty Lou Miller on 4/9/42 in Dayton, Ohio. Country singer.

| 3/11/78 | 104 | 3 | Don't Break The Heart That Loves You ...................................... C&W:❶[2] / AC:40 *Apt. #4, Sixth Street In Cincinnati* | $5 | | Warner 8508 |

#1 hit for **Connie Francis** in 1962

### SMITH, Michael W.        HOT/AC
Contemporary Christian singer/keyboardist/songwriter from Kenova, West Virginia.

| 7/17/93 | 116 | 3 | Picture Perfect ...................................... *Cross Of Gold* | $3 | ▮ | Reunion/RCA 62554 |

### SMITH, O.C.        R&B/AC/HOT
Born Ocie Lee Smith on 6/21/36 in Mansfield, Louisiana. First recorded for Cadence in 1956. With Count Basie from 1961-63.

| 1/21/67 | 127 | 1 | 1 That's Life ...................................... *I'm Your Man* | $7 | | Columbia 43525 |

#4 hit for **Frank Sinatra** in 1966

| 7/27/68 | 105 | 1 | 2 Main Street Mission ...................................... *Gas, Food, Lodging* | $6 | | Columbia 44555 |
| 11/22/69 | 103 | 5 | 3 Me And You ...................................... R&B:38 *Can't Take My Eyes Off You* | $6 | | Columbia 45038 |
| 2/21/70 | 114 | 1 | 4 Moody ...................................... AC:38 *Isn't Life Beautiful* | $6 | | Columbia 45098 |
| 11/18/72 | 102 | 6 | 5 Don't Misunderstand ...................................... *If You Touch Me (You've Got To Love Me)* | $6 | | Columbia 45655 |

from the movie *Shaft's Big Score* starring Richard Roundtree

### SMITH, Ray        HOT
Born on 10/31/34 in Melber, Kentucky. Committed suicide on 11/29/79. Recorded for Sun Records, 1958-62.

| 8/8/60 | 103 | 1 | One Wonderful Love ...................................... *Makes Me Feel Good* | $25 | | Judd 1019 |

| DEBUT | PEAK | WKS | A-side (Chart Hit)..........................................................................B-side | $ | Pic | Label & Number |
|---|---|---|---|---|---|---|

**SMITH, Rex**       AC/HOT
Born on 9/19/56 in Jacksonville, Florida. Vocalist/actor. Starred in several Broadway musicals.

| 10/20/79 | 109 | 2 | Sooner Or Later ........................................ *Never Gonna Give You Up* | $4 | ■ | Columbia 11105 |

        introduced by Smith on 3/25/79 in the TV movie *Sooner Or Later*

**SMITH, Sammi**       C&W/AC/HOT
Born on 8/5/43 in Orange, California. Female country singer.

| 5/15/71 | 118 | 3 | Then You Walk In........................... C&W:10 / AC:30  *Willie* | $5 | | Mega 0026 |

**SMOKEY AND HIS SISTER** ⊙

| 5/13/67 | 121 | 1 | Creators Of Rain ................................ *In A Dream Of Silent Seas* | $8 | ■ | Columbia 43995 |

**SMOOTH**       R&B/HOT
Female rapper.

| 9/18/93 | 115 | 2 | 1 You Been Played............................ R&B:54  *Smooth Medley* | $3 | ❚ | TNT/Jive 42140 |

        samples "Sunny" by Wes Montgomery; from the movie *Menace II Society* starring Tyrin Turner

| 8/31/96 | 120 | 1 | 2 Love & Happiness........................... R&B:66  *(instrumental)* | $3 | ❚ | Perspective 7546 |

        co-written by Al Green; #58 hit for Earnest Jackson in 1973

**SMOOTHEDAHUSTLER** ⊙       R&B
Male rapper from New York City. Brother of Trigger The Gambler.

| 11/25/95+ | 102 | 11 | 1 Broken Language ............................ R&B:65  *Hustlin' (R&B flip)* | $3 | ❚ | Profile 5440 |

        featuring rap artist Trigger

| 4/27/96 | 112 | 3 | 2 Hustler's Theme ............................. R&B:74  *Murdafest* | $3 | ❚ | Profile 5449 |

**SMYTH, Patty**       HOT/ROK/AC
Born on 6/26/57 in New York City. Lead singer of Scandal. In the 1980s, was married to punk rocker Richard Hell (Television).

| 2/4/95 | 106 | 7 | Look What Love Has Done (Theme From Junior) ......... AC:23  *(instrumental)* | $3 | ❚ | MCA 54971 |

        from the movie *Junior* starring Arnold Schwarzenegger

**SNELL, Annette** ⊙       R&B
Female R&B singer from Nashville.

| 10/20/73 | 102 | 9 | You Oughta' Be Here With Me ................ R&B:19  *Footprints On My Mind* | $15 | | Dial 1023 |

**SNIFF 'n' the TEARS**       HOT
British rock group featuring Paul Roberts (vocals) and Loz Netto (guitar).

| 12/15/79 | 108 | 3 | New Lines On Love................................ *Fight For Love* | $5 | | Atlantic 3626 |

**SNOW, Hank**       C&W/HOT/MEM
Born Clarence Snow on 5/9/14 in Brooklyn, Nova Scotia, Canada. Country singer.

| 6/27/60 | 101² | 4 | 1 Miller's Cave ........................ C&W:9  *The Change Of The Tide* | $12 | | RCA Victor 7748 |

        #33 hit for Bobby Bare in 1964

| 10/5/63 | 124 | 4 | 2 Ninety Miles An Hour (Down a Dead End Street)............ C&W:2  *Blue Roses* | $10 | | RCA Victor 8239 |

**SNOW, Phoebe — see JEFFREYS, Garland**

**SOBER, Errol**       HOT
Los Angeles-based pop session singer.

| 5/30/70 | 106 | 1 | 1 What Do You Say To A Naked Lady ................. *I'll Come Running To You* | $6 | | Abnak 148 |
| 10/12/74 | 108 | 2 | 2 I Did What I Did For Maria ................... *I'm Movin' To Happy* | $5 | | ABC 12016 |

**SOCCIO, Gino**       R&B/HOT
Born in 1955 in Montreal. Techno-disco producer/multi-instrumentalist.

| 5/30/81 | 103 | 5 | 1 Try It Out ........................... R&B:22  *Closer* | $4 | | RFC/Atlantic 3813 |
| 7/3/82 | 108 | 2 | 2 It's Alright .......................... R&B:60  *Look At Yourself* | $4 | | RFC/Atlantic 4052 |

**SOEUR SOURIRE — see SINGING NUN, The**

**SOFT CELL**       HOT/ROK
British electro-rock duo: Marc Almond (vocals) and David Ball (synthesizer).

| 9/18/82 | 101² | 7 | What! ................................ *Memorabilia* | $4 | ■ | Sire 29976 |

**SOLO**       R&B/HOT
R&B vocal quartet from New York: Eunique Mack, Darnell Chavis, Daniele Stokes and Robert Anderson.

| 6/15/96 | 121 | 3 | He's Not Good Enough .......................... R&B:50  *Holdin' On* | $3 | ❚ | Perspective 7526 |

**SOMETHIN' FOR THE PEOPLE**       R&B/HOT
R&B vocal trio from Oakland: Jeff "Fuzzy" Young, Curtis "Sauce" Wilson and Rochad "Cat Daddy" Holiday.

| 2/10/96 | 105 | 9 | You Want This Party Started ................ R&B:29  *Still The Man* | $3 | ❚ | Warner 17753 |

**SOMMERS, Joanie**       HOT/AC
Born on 2/24/41 in Buffalo; moved to California in 1954. Sang Pepsi-Cola jingles in the early and mid-1960s.

| 8/24/63 | 132 | 1 | Little Girl Bad ................................ *Wishing Well* | $12 | | Warner 5374 |

**SONNY & CHER — see CHER**

**SONOMA** ⊙       AC
Mixed pop vocal quartet.

| 12/15/73 | 112 | 4 | Love For You................ AC:33  *Thank You Just The Same* | $5 | | Dunhill/ABC 4365 |

**SONS OF CHAMPLIN**       HOT/R&B
Pop/rock band from San Francisco featuring Bill Champlin (vocals, guitar). Champlin joined Chicago in 1982. Also see **Tim Weisberg**.

| 6/3/67 | 124 | 1 | 1 Sing Me A Rainbow ................................ *Fat City* | $10 | | Verve 10500 |
| 10/11/75 | 103 | 6 | 2 Lookout................................ *Queen Of The Rain* | $5 | | Ariola America 7606 |
| 9/25/76 | 107 | 1 | 3 Imagination's Sake ................................ *You* | $5 | | Ariola America 7633 |

**SORROWS, The** ⊙
British rock group — Don ("Indian Reservation") Fardon, lead singer.

| 12/4/65 | 129 | 1 | Take A Heart ...................... *We Should Get Along Fine* | $15 | | Warner 5662 |

| DEBUT | PEAK | WKS | A-side / B-side | $ | Pic | Label & Number |
|---|---|---|---|---|---|---|
| | | | **S.O.S. BAND, The**     R&B/HOT | | | |
| | | | Funk-R&B band from Atlanta. Lead singer/keyboardist Mary Davis went solo in 1986, various personnel changes since. | | | |
| 11/10/84 | 102 | 9 | No One's Gonna Love You ..................... R&B:15 *I Don't Want Nobody Else* | $4 | | Tabu 04665 |
| | | | **SOUL, Jimmy**     HOT/R&B | | | |
| | | | Born James McCleese in New York City in 1942. Died of a heart attack on 6/25/88. | | | |
| 7/27/63 | 108 | 4 | Treat 'Em Tough ................................... *Church Street In The Summertime* | $15 | ■ | S.P.Q.R. 3310 |
| | | | **SOUL BROTHERS SIX**     HOT | | | |
| | | | R&B group from Rochester, New York: John Ellison, Von Elle Benjamin, Lester Peleman, Joe Johnson, and Charles and Harry Armstrong. | | | |
| 1/27/68 | 107 | 2 | What Can You Do When You Ain't Got Nobody ................. *You Better Check Yourself* | $20 | | Atlantic 2456 |
| | | | **SOUL CHILDREN, The**     R&B/HOT | | | |
| | | | R&B group formed by songwriters **Isaac Hayes** and **David Porter**: Anita Louis, Shelbra Bennett, John Colbert and Norman West. | | | |
| 8/19/72 | 102 | 4 | 1 Don't Take My Kindness For Weakness ...................... R&B:14 *Just The One (I've Been Looking For)* | $8 | | Stax 0132 |
| 3/10/73 | 105 | 3 | 2 It Ain't Always What You Do (It's Who You Let See You Do It) ...................... R&B:11 *All That Shines Ain't Gold* | $8 | | Stax 0152 |
| | | | **SOUL FOR REAL**     R&B/HOT | | | |
| | | | R&B vocal quartet of the Dalyrimple brothers from Long Island: Chris, Andre, Brian and Jason. | | | |
| 9/2/95 | 102 | 7 | 1 If You Want It ...................... R&B:53 *(instrumental)* | $3 | ▌ | Uptown/MCA 55005 |
| | | | written and produced by **Heavy D** | | | |
| 1/4/97 | 117 | 3 | 2 Love You So ...................... R&B:64 *(instrumental/remix w/Heavy D) / Never Felt This Way* | $3 | ▌ | Uptown/Universal 56035 |
| | | | samples "Blues & Pants" by **James Brown** | | | |
| | | | **SOUL GENERATION ✪**     R&B | | | |
| | | | R&B studio group assembled by Tony Camillo. | | | |
| 5/27/72 | 115 | 1 | That's The Way It's Got To Be (Body And Soul) ............. R&B:27 *Mandingo Woman* | $10 | | Ebony Sounds 175 |
| | | | **SOUL RUNNERS — see WRIGHT, Charles** | | | |
| | | | **SOUL SISTERS**     HOT/R&B | | | |
| | | | R&B vocal duo: Thresia Cleveland and Ann Gissendanner. | | | |
| 8/29/64 | 107 | 2 | Loop De Loop ...................... *Long Gone* | $15 | | Sue 107 |
| | | | #4 hit for **Johnny Thunder** in 1963 | | | |
| | | | **SOUL SURVIVORS, The**     HOT/R&B | | | |
| | | | White-soul band from New York City and Philadelphia: vocals by Kenny Jeremiah and brothers Charles and Richard Ingui. | | | |
| 5/10/69 | 115 | 1 | Mama Soul ...................... *Tell Daddy* | $10 | | Atco 6650 |
| | | | **SOUL TRAIN GANG**     R&B/HOT | | | |
| | | | Studio singers from the syndicated TV show *Soul Train*. | | | |
| 12/4/76 | 107 | 1 | Ooh Cha ...................... R&B:62 *Country Girl* | $5 | | Soul Train 10792 |
| | | | **SOUL TWINS, The ✪** | | | |
| | | | R&B duo: Richard Greene and Johnny Griffith. | | | |
| 6/24/67 | 123 | 1 | Just One Look ...................... *It's Not What You Do, It's The Way That You Do It* | $20 | | Karen 1535 |
| | | | #10 hit for **Doris Troy** in 1963 | | | |
| | | | **SOUND FACTORY**     HOT | | | |
| | | | Swedish dance production featuring vocalist St. James. | | | |
| 7/31/93 | 111 | 2 | 1 To The Rhythm ...................... *(edit)* | $3 | ▌ | Logic/RCA 62543 |
| | | | **SOUND FACTORY featuring St. James.** | | | |
| 6/11/94 | 112 | 6 | 2 Good Time ...................... *(edit)* | $3 | ▌ | Logic/RCA 62840 |
| | | | **SOUND FOUNDATION ✪** | | | |
| 11/29/69 | 118 | 1 | Morning Dew (Walk Me Out In The) ...................... *Magic Carpet Ride* | $8 | | Smobro 401 |
| | | | #52 hit for **Lulu** in 1968 | | | |
| | | | **SOUNDS OF BLACKNESS**     R&B/HOT | | | |
| | | | Thirty-member choir and 10-piece orchestra formed out of the Macalester College Black Choir in 1971. Directed by Gary Hines. | | | |
| 5/3/97 | 102 | 8 | Spirit ...................... Sls:70 /R&B:29 *(remix)* | $3 | ▌ | Perspective 7574 |
| | | | **SOUNDS OF BLACKNESS Featuring Craig Mack** | | | |
| | | | **SOUNDS ORCHESTRAL**     AC/HOT | | | |
| | | | British studio project produced by John Schroeder. Included arranger/producer Johnny Pearson on piano. | | | |
| 12/4/65 | 104 | 1 | A Boy And A Girl ...................... AC:30 *Go Home Girl* [I] | $10 | | Parkway 968 |
| | | | **SOUTH, Joe**     HOT/AC/C&W | | | |
| | | | Born Joe Souter on 2/28/40 in Atlanta. Successful Nashville session guitarist/songwriter in the mid-1960s. | | | |
| 1/13/68 | 106 | 6 | 1 Birds Of A Feather ...................... *It Got Away* | $8 | | Capitol 2060 |
| | | | a new version with a "Games People Play" ending made the *Hot 100* (#96) on 7/12/69 on Capitol 2532 | | | |
| 5/17/69 | 104 | 3 | 2 Leanin' On You ...................... *Don't You Be Ashamed* | $6 | | Capitol 2491 |
| 10/3/70 | 118 | 3 | 3 Why Does A Man Do What He Has To Do ...................... *Be A Believer* | $6 | | Capitol 2916 |
| | | | theme from the movie *The Racing Scene* | | | |
| | | | **SOUTH CENTRAL CARTEL ✪**     R&B | | | |
| | | | Rap outfit: Havoc da Mouthpiece (son of an original member of **The Chi-Lites**), Prodeje, Havikk da Rymeson, L.V., Kaos #1 and Gripp. | | | |
| 4/16/94 | 110 | 4 | Gang Stories ...................... Sls:70 /R&B:63 *(instrumental) / Servin' 'Em Heat (2 versions)* | $4 | ▌ | DJ West/Chaos 77367 * |
| | | | samples "The Hood Took Me Under" by MC Eiht | | | |
| | | | **SOUTHER, J.D.**     HOT/AC/C&W | | | |
| | | | Born John David Souther in Detroit. Teamed with Chris Hillman and **Richie Furay** as The Souther, Hillman, Furay Band in 1974. | | | |
| 2/9/80 | 105 | 3 | 1 White Rhythm And Blues ...................... AC:46 *The Last In Love* | $4 | | Columbia 11196 |
| 7/21/84 | 104 | 6 | 2 Go Ahead And Rain ...................... *All I Want* | $4 | ■ | Warner 29289 |
| | | | **SOUTHSIDE JOHNNY & THE JUKES**     ROK/HOT/R&B | | | |
| | | | Rock band formed in Asbury Park, New Jersey; led by vocalist/harmonica player Johnny Lyon (b: 12/4/48, Neptune, New Jersey). | | | |
| 8/7/76 | 105 | 1 | 1 I Don't Want To Go Home ...................... *The Fever* | $5 | | Epic 50238 |
| | | | **SOUTHSIDE JOHNNY & THE ASBURY JUKES** | | | |

| DEBUT | PEAK | WKS | A-side (Chart Hit) ...B-side | $ | Pic | Label & Number |
|---|---|---|---|---|---|---|
| | | | **SOUTHSIDE JOHNNY & THE JUKES — Cont'd** | | | |
| 11/5/83 | 108 | 1 | 2 Trash It Up ................................................. *Ms. Park Avenue* | $4 | | Mirage 99839 |
| 8/11/84 | 103 | 6 | 3 New Romeo ................................... ROK:43 *Tell Me Lies* | $4 | | Mirage 99732 |
| | | | **SOUTHWEST F.O.B.**  HOT | | | |
| | | | Dallas-based group featuring "England" Dan Seals (saxophone) and John Ford Coley (organ). | | | |
| 1/17/70 | 115 | 2 | Feelin' Groovy .................................................. *Beggar Man* | $10 | | HIP 8022 |
| | | | #13 hit for Harpers Bizarre in 1967 | | | |
| | | | **SOUTHWIND** ☉ | | | |
| | | | Los Angeles rock group featuring lead guitarist Moon Martin. | | | |
| 12/13/69 | 127 | 2 | 1 Ready To Ride ............................... *Cool Green Hills Of Earth* | $8 | | Blue Thumb 108 |
| 5/2/70 | 105 | 4 | 2 Boogie Woogie Country Girl ................... *Honky Tonkin'* | $8 | | Blue Thumb 111 |
| | | | charted as the B-side of Joe Turner's #2 R&B hit "Corrine Corrina" in 1956 | | | |
| | | | **SOVINE, Red**  C&W/HOT | | | |
| | | | Born Woodrow Wilson Sovine on 7/17/18 in Charleston, West Virginia. Died on 4/4/80. Country singer/songwriter/guitarist. | | | |
| 9/25/76 | 102 | 9 | Little Joe ...................... C&W:45 *Cold Love To Go* [S] | $5 | | Starday 144 |
| | | | **SPACEK, Sissy** ☉  C&W | | | |
| | | | Born Mary Elizabeth Spacek in Quitman, Texas on 12/25/49. Singer/actress. Won Academy Award portraying Loretta Lynn in the movie *Coal Miner's Daughter*. | | | |
| 8/27/83 | 110 | 1 | Lonely But Only For You ............... C&W:15 *Old Home Town* | $4 | ■ | Atlantic America 99847 |
| | | | **SPANDAU BALLET**  HOT/AC/ROK/R&B | | | |
| | | | Pop quintet formed in London in 1979: Tony Hadley (vocals), brothers Gary (guitar) and Martin (bass) Kemp, Steve Norman (sax) and John Keeble (drums). | | | |
| 6/4/83 | 108 | 2 | Lifeline ..................................................... *Live And Let Live* | $4 | | Chrysalis 42686 |
| | | | **SPARKS**  HOT | | | |
| | | | Rock duo of brothers Ron (keyboards; b: 8/12/50) and Russell (vocals; b: 10/5/55) Mael. | | | |
| 11/4/72 | 112 | 3 | 1 Wonder Girl ......................... *(No More) Mr. Nice Guys* | $6 | | Bearsville 0006 |
| | | | produced by Todd Rundgren | | | |
| 7/28/84 | 104 | 1 | 2 With All My Might ........................... *Sparks In The Dark* | $4 | ■ | Atlantic 89645 |
| | | | **SPARKS, Randy** ☉ | | | |
| | | | Leader of The New Christy Minstrels and Back Porch Majority. | | | |
| 12/5/64 | 126 | 1 | Julie Knows .......................... *At The End Of The Rainbow* | $7 | ■ | Columbia 43138 |
| | | | **SPECIAL DELIVERY**  R&B/HOT | | | |
| | | | R&B vocal group featuring Terry Huff. | | | |
| 8/20/77 | 107 | 1 | Oh Let Me Know It (pt. 1) ............... R&B:22 *(pt. 2)* | $5 | | Shield 6307 |
| | | | **SPECIAL ED** ☉  R&B | | | |
| | | | Edward Archer — rapper from Brooklyn. Member of The Crooklyn Dodgers. | | | |
| 6/10/95 | 109 | 7 | Neva Go Back .......... Sls:75 /R&B:68 *Just A Killa (w/Bounty Killer)* | $3 | ▌ | Profile 5433 |
| | | | **SPELLBINDERS, The**  HOT/R&B | | | |
| | | | R&B vocal group from Jersey City: Bob Shivers, Jimmy Wright, Ben Grant, McArthur Munford and Elouise Pennington. | | | |
| 3/19/66 | 118 | 2 | 1 Chain Reaction ....................... *A Little On The Blue Side* | $10 | | Columbia 43522 |
| 6/4/66 | 130 | 3 | 2 We're Acting Like Lovers ..................... *Long Lost Love* | $10 | ☐ | Columbia 43611 |
| | | | **SPENCER, Richard — see WINSTONS, The** | | | |
| | | | **SPHERIS, Jimmy** ☉ | | | |
| | | | Pop singer/songwriter/guitarist. Born in Greece; raised in California. | | | |
| 8/2/80 | 110 | 2 | Hold Tight ........................................................ *It Is You* | $4 | | Curb/Warner 49527 |
| | | | **SPICE 1** ☉  R&B | | | |
| | | | Rapper born in Bryan, Texas; raised in Hayward and Oakland, California. Discovered by Too $hort. | | | |
| 10/22/94 | 111 | 7 | 1 Strap On The Side ............ R&B:74 *(street remix) / Jealous Got Me Strapped (w/2 Pac)* | $3 | ▌ | Jive 42232 |
| | | | samples "I Don't Believe You Want To Get Up & Dance (Oops!)" by The Gap Band | | | |
| 11/25/95 | 122 | 4 | 2 1990-Sick (Kill 'Em All) ............ R&B:91 *(solo version) / Sucka Ass Niggas* | $3 | ▌ | Jive 42350 |
| | | | SPICE 1 (featuring MC Eiht) | | | |
| | | | **SPIN DOCTORS**  ROK/HOT/AC | | | |
| | | | Rock quartet from New York: Christopher Barron (vocals), Eric Schenkman (guitar), Mark White (bass) and Aaron Comess (drums). | | | |
| 8/14/93 | 102 | 6 | How Could You Want Him (When You Know You Could Have Me?) ................................... ROK:28 *Hard To Exist* | $3 | ▌ | Epic Associated 74910 |
| | | | **SPINNERS**  R&B/HOT/AC | | | |
| | | | R&B vocal group from Ferndale High School near Detroit. First recorded on Harvey Fuqua's Tri-Phi label. Many personnel changes. 1972 lineup included Philippe Wynne (d: 7/14/84), Bobbie Smith, Billy Henderson, Henry Fambrough and Pervis Jackson. Wynne left group in 1977 and toured with Parliament/Funkadelic; replaced by John Edwards. Top Pop Singles: 30. | | | |
| 5/21/66 | 111 | 5 | 1 Truly Yours ............................... R&B:16 *Where Is That Girl* | $15 | | Motown 1093 |
| 11/3/79 | 103 | 6 | 2 Body Language .......................... R&B:35 *With My Eyes* | $5 | | Atlantic 3619 |
| 10/31/81 | 110 | 3 | 3 You Go Your Way (I'll Go Mine) ...... R&B:39 *Got To Be Love* | $4 | | Atlantic 3865 |
| 1/9/82 | 107 | 1 | 4 Love Connection (Raise The Window Down) ....... R&B:68 *Love Is Such A Crazy Feeling* | $4 | | Atlantic 3882 |
| 4/14/84 | 104 | 8 | 5 Right Or Wrong ......................... R&B:22 *Love Is In Season* | $4 | | Atlantic 89689 |
| | | | **SPIRAL STARECASE, The**  HOT | | | |
| | | | Pop-rock quintet from Sacramento: Pat Upton (vocals, guitar), Harvey Kaplan (organ), Dick Lopes (sax), Bobby Raymond (bass) and Vinny Parello (drums). | | | |
| 3/2/68 | 111 | 2 | Baby What I Mean ............................. *Makin' My Mind Up* | $8 | | Columbia 44442 |
| | | | #62 hit for The Drifters in 1966 | | | |

| DEBUT | PEAK | WKS | A-side (Chart Hit) / B-side | $ | Pic | Label & Number |
|---|---|---|---|---|---|---|
| | | | **SPIRIT**     HOT/ROK | | | |
| | | | Los Angeles eclectic rock group featuring Jay Ferguson (lead singer). Ferguson left to form Jo Jo Gunne in mid-1971. | | | |
| 5/18/68 | 123 | 2 | 1 Mechanical World .......................................................... *Uncle Jack* | $10 | | Ode 108 |
| 9/27/69 | 118 | 2 | 2 Dark Eyed Woman .................................................... *New Dope In Town* | $10 | | Ode 122 |
| 3/20/71 | 111 | 3 | 3 Nature's Way ........................................................ *Mr. Skin* (Hot #92) | $7 | | Epic 10701 |
| | | | **SPIRIT OF US** ☺ | | | |
| 8/15/70 | 106 | 3 | Simple Song Of Freedom ......................... *He Ain't Heavy - He's My Brother* | $6 | | Viva 641 |
| | | | written by **Bobby Darin**; #50 hit for Tim Hardin in 1969 | | | |
| | | | **SPLIT ENZ**     HOT/ROK | | | |
| | | | Pop-rock group from New Zealand featuring brothers Tim (vocals) and Neil (guitar, vocals) Finn, who were later members of **Crowded House**. | | | |
| 6/27/81 | 104 | 3 | 1 One Step Ahead ........................................................ *In The Wars* | $6 | ■ | A&M 2339 |
| | | | issued as a laser-etched vinyl single | | | |
| 6/5/82 | 104 | 3 | 2 Six Months In A Leaky Boat ................................... *Make Sense Of It* | $5 | ■ | A&M 2411 |
| | | | **SPOKESMEN, The**     HOT | | | |
| | | | Johnny Madara, David White and Roy Gilmore. White was with Danny & The Juniors. | | | |
| 1/15/66 | 106 | 4 | Michelle ............................................ *Better Days Are Yet To Come* | $10 | | Decca 31895 |
| | | | originally recorded by **The Beatles** on their 1966 album *Rubber Soul*; #18 hit for **David & Jonathan** in 1966 | | | |
| | | | **SPOOKY TOOTH** ☺ | | | |
| | | | British hard-rock group led by **Gary Wright** and Mike Harrison. | | | |
| 10/4/69 | 132 | 1 | Feelin' Bad ..................................... *I've Got Enough Heartaches* | $7 | | A&M 1110 |
| | | | **SPOTLIGHTS, The** ☺ | | | |
| 2/19/66 | 111 | 4 | Batman And Robin ..................................... *Dayflower* [N] | $12 | | Smash 2020 |
| | | | **SPRINGFIELD, Dusty**     HOT/AC | | | |
| | | | Born Mary O'Brien on 4/16/39 in London. Pop vocalist/guitarist. With brother Tom Springfield in folk trio **The Springfields**, 1960-63. | | | |
| 12/26/64 | 109 | 4 | 1 Guess Who?/ | | | |
| 1/9/65 | 128 | 1 | 2   Live It Up | $10 | ■ | Philips 40245 |
| 7/10/65 | 108 | 4 | 3 In The Middle Of Nowhere ................................. *Baby, Don't You Know* | $10 | ■ | Philips 40303 |
| 9/28/68 | 122 | 2 | 4 I Close My Eyes And Count To Ten ................................. *La Bamba* | $8 | | Philips 40553 |
| 4/26/69 | 105 | 1 | 5 I Don't Want To Hear It Anymore ................*The Windmills Of Your Mind* (Hot #31) | $7 | | Atlantic 2623 |
| | | | written by **Randy Newman** | | | |
| 10/4/69 | 113 | 1 | 6 In The Land Of Make Believe ...................... AC:27 *So Much Love* | $7 | | Atlantic 2673 |
| 5/16/70 | 105 | 3 | 7 I Wanna Be A Free Girl ....................... AC:25 *Let Me In Your Way* | $7 | | Atlantic 2729 |
| 3/24/73 | 121 | 1 | 8 Who Gets Your Love ................................... *Of All The Things* | $6 | | Dunhill/ABC 4341 |
| 5/19/73 | 118 | 3 | 9 Mama's Little Girl ........................... AC:33 *Learn To Say Goodbye* (AC #33) | $6 | | Dunhill/ABC 4344 |
| | | | also released on Dunhill/ABC 4357 | | | |
| 7/9/77 | 110 | 1 | 10 Let Me Love You Once Before You Go ...................... *I'm Your Child* | $5 | | United Artists 1006 |
| | | | **SPRINGFIELDS, The**     HOT/C&W | | | |
| | | | English folk trio: **Dusty Springfield** and brother Tom Springfield and Tim Feild. | | | |
| 11/17/62 | 114 | 1 | 1 Gotta Travel On ......................... *Dear Hearts And Gentle People* (Hot #95) | $12 | | Philips 40072 |
| | | | #4 hit for Billy Grammer in 1959; based on a 19th-century tune from the British Isles | | | |
| 4/27/63 | 129 | 1 | 2 Island Of Dreams ................................... *Foggy Mountain Top* | $12 | | Philips 40099 |
| | | | **SPYRO GYRA**     AC/HOT/R&B | | | |
| | | | Jazz-pop band formed in 1975 in Buffalo, New York. Led by saxophonist Jay Beckenstein (b: 5/14/51). | | | |
| 7/26/80 | 105 | 5 | 1 Percolator ................................... AC:48 *Philly* [I] | $4 | | MCA 41275 |
| 11/7/81 | 108 | 1 | 2 Summer Strut ................................... *Amber Dream* [I] | $4 | | MCA 51200 |
| | | | **SQUEEZE**     ROK/HOT/AC | | | |
| | | | English pop-rock group formed in 1974 and led by vocalists/guitarists Chris Difford and Glenn Tilbrook. | | | |
| 7/10/82 | 103 | 3 | Black Coffee In Bed ................................... ROK:26 *The Hunt* | $5 | ■ | A&M 2424 |
| | | | **STAFFORD, Jim**     HOT/C&W/AC | | | |
| | | | Born on 1/16/44 in Eloise, Florida. Pop-novelty singer/songwriter/guitarist. Own summer variety TV show in 1975. | | | |
| 2/7/81 | 102 | 2 | Cow Patti .......................... C&W:65 *Texas Guitar Swing* [N] | $4 | | Viva/Warner 49611 |
| | | | from the Clint Eastwood movie *Any Which Way You Can* | | | |
| | | | **STAFFORD, Jo**     MEM/POP/HOT | | | |
| | | | Born on 11/12/20 in Coalinga, California. Sang with Tommy Dorsey's band. The #1 solo female vocalist of the pre-rock era. *Pop Hits & Top Pop Singles*: 77. | | | |
| 9/14/59 | 105 | 3 | Pine Top's Boogie ................................... *All Yours* (Tua) | $12 | | Columbia 41413 |
| | | | Frank DeVol (orch.); #20 hit for Pine Top Smith in 1929; recorded by Tommy Dorsey in 1938 as "Boogie Woogie" | | | |
| | | | **STAFFORD, Terry**     C&W/HOT/AC | | | |
| | | | Born in Hollis, Oklahoma; raised in Amarillo, Texas. Died on 3/17/96. **Elvis Presley** sound-alike. | | | |
| 8/22/64 | 101[1] | 5 | Follow The Rainbow ............................ *Are You A Fool Like Me?* | $12 | | Crusader 109 |
| | | | **STAIRSTEPS — see FIVE STAIRSTEPS** | | | |
| | | | **STAKKA BO** ☺     ROK | | | |
| | | | Dance-rap duo from Sweden: Stakka Bo (real name: Johan Renck) and Oscar Franzen. | | | |
| 6/25/94 | 109 | 7 | Here We Go ................................... ROK:20 *(12" version)* | $3 | ▌ | Polydor 855800 |
| | | | **STALLION**     HOT | | | |
| | | | Denver-based quintet: Buddy Stephens (vocals), Danny O'Neil (guitar), Wally Damrick (keyboards), Jorg Gonzalez (bass) and Larry Thompson (drums). | | | |
| 7/9/77 | 108 | 1 | Magic Of The Music ................................... *Glad That I Found You* | $5 | | Casablanca 886 |
| | | | **STALLONE, Frank**     HOT/AC | | | |
| | | | Born on 7/30/50 in Philadelphia. Singer/actor. Brother of Sylvester Stallone. | | | |
| 9/15/84 | 105 | 3 | If We Ever Get Back ................................... *Love Is Like A Light* | $4 | | Polydor 881142 |

### STAMPEDERS     HOT/AC
Pop-rock trio from Calgary: Rich Dodson (guitar), Ronnie King (bass) and Kim Berly (drums). All share vocals.

| | | | | | | |
| --- | --- | --- | --- | --- | --- | --- |
| 3/24/73 | 115 | 4 | Oh My Lady ......................................................................... *Wild Eyes* | $6 | | Bell 45,331 |

### STANDELLS, The     HOT
Los Angeles-area, early punk-rock quartet: Dick Dodd (lead singer, drums), Larry Tamblyn and Tony Valentino (guitars) and Gary Lane (bass).

| | | | | | | |
| --- | --- | --- | --- | --- | --- | --- |
| 2/6/65 | 102 | 3 | 1 The Boy Next Door ..................................................... *B. J. Quetzal* | $20 | ■ | Vee-Jay 643 |
| | | |    written, arranged and produced by Sonny Bono of **Sonny & Cher** | | | |
| 3/25/67 | 133 | 1 | 2 Riot On Sunset Strip .............................................. *Black Hearted Woman* | $15 | ■ | Tower 314 |
| | | |    title song from the movie starring Aldo Ray | | | |

### STANLEY, Pamala ◌
Dance/disco singer.

| | | | | | | |
| --- | --- | --- | --- | --- | --- | --- |
| 11/10/79 | 108 | 1 | 1 This Is Hot ................................................. *Only You Can Reach Me* | $5 | | EMI America 9183 |
| 6/16/84 | 106 | 5 | 2 Coming Out Of Hiding ...................... *I Don't Want To Talk About It* | $5 | ■ | TSR 105 |
| | | |    also available as a 12" single on TSR 830 | | | |

### STANSFIELD, Lisa — see BABYFACE

### STAPLES, Mavis     R&B/HOT
Born in 1940 in Chicago. Leader of **The Staple Singers**. Appeared in the 1990 movie *Graffiti Bridge*.

| | | | | | | |
| --- | --- | --- | --- | --- | --- | --- |
| 7/12/69 | 107 | 4 | 1 Never, Never Let You Go.................................... *Ain't That Good* | $7 | | Stax 0041 |
| | | |    **EDDIE FLOYD, MAVIS STAPLES** | | | |
| 10/28/72 | 109 | 3 | 2 Endlessly ................................. R&B:30 *Don't Change Me Now* | $6 | | Volt 4086 |
| | | |    #12 hit for **Brook Benton** in 1959 | | | |

### STAPLE SINGERS, The     R&B/HOT/AC
Family R&B group featuring Cleotha, Yvonne and lead singer **Mavis Staples**.

| | | | | | | |
| --- | --- | --- | --- | --- | --- | --- |
| 10/27/84 | 109 | 1 | Slippery People ......................... R&B:22 *On My Own Again* | $4 | | Private I 04583 |

### STARCASTLE ◌
Six-man progressive rock group — Terry Luttrell, lead singer.

| | | | | | | |
| --- | --- | --- | --- | --- | --- | --- |
| 5/22/76 | 101[1] | 5 | Lady Of The Lake      *Nova* | $5 | | Epic 50226 |

### STARCHER, Buddy     C&W/HOT
Born Oby Edgar Starcher on 3/16/06 near Ripley, West Virginia. Country singer/disc jockey.

| | | | | | | |
| --- | --- | --- | --- | --- | --- | --- |
| 6/18/66 | 131 | 1 | Day Of Decision .................................. *A Taxpayer's Letter* [S] | $7 | | Decca 31975 |
| | | |    answer song to Barry McGuire's "Eve Of Destruction"; #35 hit for **Johnny Sea** in 1966 | | | |

### STARCLUB ◌     ROK
British pop band: Owen Vyse (vocals, guitar), Steve French (guitar), Julian Taylor (bass) and Alan White (drums).

| | | | | | | |
| --- | --- | --- | --- | --- | --- | --- |
| 2/20/93 | 119 | 3 | Hard To Get ............................... ROK:10 *(3 album snippets)* | $3 | ▮ | Island 864788 |

### STARLETS, The — see ANGELS, The

### STARPOINT     R&B/HOT
R&B dance sextet from Maryland. Did session work for Motown and All-Platinum Records.

| | | | | | | |
| --- | --- | --- | --- | --- | --- | --- |
| 7/2/83 | 107 | 2 | Don't Be So Serious ................................... R&B:14 *Let Go* | $4 | | Boardwalk 178 |

### STARR, Brenda K. — see MAD LION

### STARR, Edwin     R&B/HOT
Born Charles Hatcher on 1/21/42 in Nashville. R&B vocalist. With Bill Doggett Combo from 1963-65.

| | | | | | | |
| --- | --- | --- | --- | --- | --- | --- |
| 11/4/67 | 120 | 3 | 1 I Want My Baby Back.......................... *Gonna Keep On Tryin' Till I Win Your Love* | $7 | | Gordy 7066 |
| 4/20/68 | 112 | 3 | 2 I Am The Man For You Baby ........................ R&B:45 *My Weakness Is You* | $7 | | Gordy 7071 |
| 11/16/68 | 119 | 1 | 3 Way Over There ......................... *If My Heart Could Tell The Story* | $7 | | Gordy 7078 |
| | | |    #94 hit for **The Miracles** in 1962 | | | |
| 3/7/70 | 117 | 1 | 4 Time ........................... R&B:39 *Running Back And Forth* | $7 | | Gordy 7097 |
| 3/23/74 | 110 | 1 | 5 Ain't It Hell Up In Harlem *Don't It Feel Good To Be Free* | $5 | | Motown 1284 |
| | | |    from the movie *Hell Up In Harlem* starring Fred Williamson | | | |

### STARS ON 45     HOT/AC/R&B
Dutch session vocalists and musicians assembled by producer Jaap Eggermont.

| | | | | | | |
| --- | --- | --- | --- | --- | --- | --- |
| 8/6/83 | 107 | 1 | The Star Sisters Medley ........................... *Stars Serenade* | $4 | | 21 Records 110 |
| | | |    **STARS ON 45 proudly presents THE STAR SISTERS**<br>   Andrews Sisters medley: Boogie Woogie Bugle Boy/South American Way/Bei Mir Bist Du Schoen/In The Mood/Rum And Coca Cola/<br>   Tico Tico/Say Si Si (Para Vigo Me Voy) | | | |

### STARZ     HOT
New York-based rock quintet featuring Michael Lee Smith (brother of **Rex Smith**; lead singer).

| | | | | | | |
| --- | --- | --- | --- | --- | --- | --- |
| 3/3/79 | 104 | 4 | Last Night I Wrote A Letter ......................... *Coliseum Rock* | $5 | | Capitol 4671 |

### STATLER BROTHERS, The     C&W/HOT/AC
Country vocal quartet from Staunton, Virginia: brothers Harold and Don Reid, Phil Balsley and Lew DeWitt (d: 8/15/90). Currently host their own Nashville Network cable TV variety show.

| | | | | | | |
| --- | --- | --- | --- | --- | --- | --- |
| 2/26/66 | 110 | 5 | 1 My Darling Hildegarde........................ *The Doodlin' Song* | $8 | | Columbia 43526 |
| 4/22/72 | 105 | 5 | 2 Do You Remember These .................... C&W:2 / AC:18 *Since Then* | $6 | | Mercury 73275 |

### STATON, Candi     R&B/HOT/AC
Born in Hanceville, Alabama. Sang with the Jewel Gospel Trio from age 10. Went solo in 1968. Married for a time to **Clarence Carter**.

| | | | | | | |
| --- | --- | --- | --- | --- | --- | --- |
| 9/20/69 | 124 | 2 | 1 Never In Public............................ R&B:22 *You Don't Love Me No More* | $7 | | Fame 1459 |
| 4/24/71 | 109 | 7 | 2 Mr. And Mrs. Untrue ..................... R&B:20 *Too Hurt To Cry* (R&B flip) | $7 | | Fame 1478 |
| 9/3/77 | 102 | 2 | 3 Nights On Broadway .......................... R&B:16 *You Are* | $5 | | Warner 8387 |
| | | |    #7 hit for the **Bee Gees** in 1975 | | | |

### STEEL RIVER ◌
Canadian rock band.

| | | | | | | |
| --- | --- | --- | --- | --- | --- | --- |
| 11/14/70 | 109 | 3 | 1 Ten Pound Note................................... *Momma Pie Blues* | $6 | | Evolution 1030 |
| 7/24/71 | 106 | 2 | 2 Southbound Train.................................................. *A Lie* | $6 | | Evolution 1044 |

## STEELY DAN
HOT/AC/ROK/R&B

Los Angeles-based, pop/jazz-styled duo: **Donald Fagen** (b: 1/10/48, Passaic, New Jersey; keyboards, vocals) and Walter Becker (b: 2/20/50, New York City; bass, vocals).

| | | | | | | |
|---|---|---|---|---|---|---|
| 9/20/75 | 103 | 1 | Bad Sneakers .................................................................... *Chain Lightning* | $5 | | ABC 12128 |

## STEFF ✪
Male pop/rock vocalist Steff Sulke from Switzerland.

| 1/22/66 | 124 | 1 | Where Did She Go.................................................................. *Others* | $8 | | Epic 9870 |

## STEPPENWOLF
HOT/ROK

Hard-rock quintet formed in Los Angeles in 1967 featuring Joachim **"John Kay"** Krauledat (vocals, guitar).

| 3/22/75 | 108 | 3 | Smokey Factory Blues.......................................................... *Fool's Fantasy* | $6 | | Mums 6036 |

## STEVENS, April — see TEMPO, Nino

## STEVENS, Cat
HOT/AC/R&B

Born Steven Georgiou on 7/21/47 in London. Converted to Muslim religion in 1979, took name Yusef Islam.

| | | | | | | |
|---|---|---|---|---|---|---|
| 12/17/66 | 118 | 2 | 1 I Love My Dog .............................................................*Portobello Road* | $10 | | Deram 7501 |
| 3/11/67 | 115 | 6 | 2 Matthew And Son ................................................................ *Granny* | $10 | | Deram 7505 |

## STEVENS, Connie
HOT/R&B

Born Concetta Ingolia on 8/8/38 in Brooklyn. TV and movie star. Married for a time to **Eddie Fisher**.

| 11/24/62 | 104 | 2 | Hey, Good Lookin'......................................*Nobody's Lonesome For Me* | $12 | | Warner 5318 |

Perry Botkin, Jr. (orch.); #1 Country hit for **Hank Williams** in 1951

## STEVENS, Dodie
HOT/C&W/R&B

Born Geraldine Ann Pasquale on 2/17/46 in Chicago. First recorded as Geri Pace on Gold Star in 1954; also recorded as **Geraldine Stevens**.

| 8/24/59 | 111 | 1 | 1 Miss Lonely Hearts .......................................................*Poor Butterfly* | $15 | | Dot 15975 |

Milt Rogers (orch.)

| 8/23/69 | 117 | 4 | 2 Billy, I've Got To Go To Town ...........*C&W:57 It's Not Their Heartache, It's Mine* | $8 | | World Pacific 77927 |

**GERALDINE STEVENS**
answer song to **Kenny Rogers'** "Ruby, Don't Take Your Love To Town" (new lyrics by **Vic Dana**)

## STEVENS, Ray
C&W/HOT/AC/R&B

Born Harold Ray Ragsdale on 1/24/39 in Clarkdale, Georgia. First recorded for Prep Records in 1957. One of the top novelty artists of the rock era. *Top Pop Singles: 27.*

| | | | | | | |
|---|---|---|---|---|---|---|
| 8/8/60 | 108 | 1 | 1 Sergeant Preston Of The Yukon ............................ *Who Do You Love* [N] | $25 | | NRC 057 |
| 12/18/65 | 130 | 1 | 2 Party People.................................................................. *A-B-C* | $10 | | Monument 911 |
| | | | written by **Joe South** | | | |
| 7/20/68 | 122 | 1 | 3 Funny Man ........................... *Just One Of Life's Little Tragedies* [R] | $10 | | Mercury 72816 |
| | | | originally made the *Hot 100* (#81) on 3/30/63 on Mercury 72098 | | | |
| 11/2/68 | 114 | 3 | 4 The Great Escape ................................ *Isn't It Lonely Together* | $8 | | Monument 1099 |
| 12/13/69 | 123 | 2 | 5 Have A Little Talk With Myself ..................*C&W:63 The Little Woman* | $8 | | Monument 1171 |
| 3/7/70 | 112 | 2 | 6 I'll Be Your Baby Tonight ...........................*Fool On The Hill* | $8 | | Monument 1187 |
| | | | written and recorded by **Bob Dylan** on his 1968 album *John Wesley Harding* | | | |
| 5/22/76 | 101[1] | 2 | 7 You Are So Beautiful *C&W:16 One Man Band* | $5 | | Warner 8198 |
| | | | #5 hit for **Joe Cocker** in 1975 | | | |
| 7/24/76 | 108 | 1 | 8 Lady Of Spain ................................................... *Mockingbird Hill* | $5 | | Barnaby 619 |
| | | | arranged in the style of **Fats Domino**; #5 hit for Ray Noble in 1931; #6 hit for **Eddie Fisher** in 1952 | | | |
| 3/1/80 | 101[2] | 8 | 9 Shriner's Convention *C&W:7 You're Never Goin' To Tampa With Me* [N] | $4 | | RCA 11911 |

## STEVENSON, B.W.
AC/HOT

Born Louis Stevenson on 10/5/49 in Dallas. Died on 4/28/88 after heart surgery. B.W. is short for Buck Wheat.

| 7/1/72 | 114 | 2 | Say What I Feel .......................................*AC:38 Lonesome Song* | $6 | | RCA Victor 0728 |

## STEWART, James ✪
AC

Born on 5/20/08 in Indiana, Pennsylvania. Died on 7/2/97. One of America's all-time leading actors.

| 7/10/65 | 133 | 2 | The Legend Of Shenandoah ........ *AC:33 We're Ridin' Out Tonight* (Charles "Bud" Dant) [S] | $12 | ■ | Decca 31795 |

Charles "Bud" Dant (orch.); inspired by the movie *Shenandoah* starring Stewart

## STEWART, Rod
HOT/ROK/AC/R&B

Born Roderick Stewart on 1/10/45 in London. With the Hoochie Coochie Men, Steampacket and Shotgun Express. Joined **Jeff Beck** Group, 1967-69. With Faces from 1969-75. Won Grammy's Living Legends Award in 1989. Inducted into the Rock and Roll Hall of Fame in 1994. *Top Pop Singles: 53.*

| 7/18/70 | 126 | 1 | 1 It's All Over Now.......................................................... *Jo's Lament* | $10 | | Mercury 73095 |
| | | | written by **Bobby Womack**; #26 hit for **The Rolling Stones** in 1964 | | | |
| 9/16/95 | 119 | 5 | 2 This ...........................*AC:33 The Groom's Still Waiting At The Altar* | $3 | ■ | Warner 17854 |

## STEWART, Sandy
HOT

Background vocalist and session musician for Stevie Nicks.

| 4/14/84 | 105 | 2 | Saddest Victory ..................................................... *Mind Over Matter* | $4 | ■ | Modern 99774 |

## STIGERS, Curtis
AC/HOT

Born in Boise, Idaho. Adult Contemporary vocalist/saxophonist.

| 12/5/92 | 107 | 8 | Never Saw A Miracle ......................*AC:5 I Guess It Wasn't Mine* | $3 | ■ | Arista 12459 |

## STILES, Johnny — see RANDOLPH, Luther

## STILLS-YOUNG BAND, The
HOT/AC/ROK

Six-man band led by Stephen Stills and **Neil Young**.

| 12/18/76 | 105 | 4 | Midnight On The Bay ....................................................... *Black Coral* | $5 | | Reprise 1378 |

## STITES, Gary
HOT

Born on 7/23/40 in Denver. Pop singer/songwriter/guitarist.

| 10/8/66 | 123 | 1 | Hurting ....................................................................... *Thinking Of You* | $12 | | Epic 10064 |

## STOMPERS, The
HOT

Rock group from Boston: Sal Baglio (vocals, guitar), Dave Friedman (keyboards), Stephen Gilligan (bass) and Mark Cuccinello (drums).

| 9/29/84 | 110 | 2 | One Heart For Sale .................................................... *Leave It In Motion* | $5 | | Mercury 880174 |

**STONE, Kirby, Four — see TOKENS, The**

**STORIES**           HOT/R&B
New York rock quartet featuring Ian Lloyd (vocals, bass).

| | | | | | | |
|---|---|---|---|---|---|---|
| 2/10/73 | **111** | 4 | Darling ......................... *Take Cover* | $6 | | Kama Sutra 566 |

**STORM** ☼      AC/R&B

| | | | | | | |
|---|---|---|---|---|---|---|
| 9/11/71 | **105** | 5 | Bend Me, Shape Me ........................................... *I'm A Man (Give Me Good Loving)* | $7 | | Sunflower 113 |

**STORM, Billy**     HOT
Born William Jones on 6/29/38 in Dayton, Ohio. Lead singer of the R&B group The Valiants.

| | | | | | | |
|---|---|---|---|---|---|---|
| 2/24/62 | **105** | 8 | Love Theme From "El Cid" ........................................... *Don't Let Go* | $20 | | Infinity 013 |
| | | | Hank Levine (orch.); from the movie *El Cid* starring Charlton Heston | | | |

**STRAIT, George**     C&W/HOT
Born on 5/18/52 in Poteet, Texas. Country singer. Starred in the movie *Pure Country*.

| | | | | | | |
|---|---|---|---|---|---|---|
| 1/1/94 | **109** | 10 | 1 I'd Like To Have That One Back ........ Sls:72 /C&W:3 *That's Where My Baby Feels At Home* | $3 | ▮ | MCA 54767 |
| 4/16/94 | **114** | 7 | 2 Lovebug ........................... Sls:69 /C&W:8 *Just Look At Me* | $3 | ▮ | MCA 54819 |
| | | | #6 Country hit for George Jones in 1965 | | | |
| 8/6/94 | **112** | 8 | 3 The Man In Love With You ........................... Sls:73 /C&W:4 *We Must Be Loving Right* | $3 | ▮ | MCA 54854 |
| 2/4/95 | **111** | 9 | 4 You Can't Make A Heart Love Somebody ........ Sls:61 /C&W:❶¹ *What Am I Waiting For* | $3 | ▮ | MCA 54964 |

**STRANGELOVES, The**     HOT
Writers/producers Bob Feldman, Jerry Goldstein and Richard Gottehrer. Team wrote/produced **The Angels'** "My Boyfriend's Back" and produced The McCoys' "Hang On Sloopy." Gottehrer produced the **Go-Go's'** first two albums.

| | | | | | | |
|---|---|---|---|---|---|---|
| 12/19/64 | **122** | 1 | 1 Love, Love (That's All I Want From You)........................... *I'm On Fire* | $20 | | Swan 4192 |
| | | | **STRANGE LOVES** | | | |
| | | | #3 hit for Jaye P. Morgan in 1955 | | | |
| 7/31/65 | **106** | 5 | 2 Out In The Sun (Hey-O) ........................... *Someday Soon* | $30 | | Bang 504 |
| | | | **THE BEACH-NUTS** (The Strangeloves & The Angels) | | | |
| | | | loosely based on Harry Belafonte's "Banana Boat (Day-O)" | | | |
| 7/2/66 | **104** | 3 | 3 Because Of You ........................... *Why Oh Why* | $12 | | Roulette 4681 |
| | | | **ROME & PARIS** (Bob Feldman & Jerry Goldstein) | | | |
| | | | #1 hit for Tony Bennett in 1951 | | | |
| 11/23/68 | **120** | 5 | 4 Honey Do ........................... *I Wanna Do It* | $10 | | Sire 4102 |

**STRASSMAN, Marcia** ☼
Born on 4/28/48 in New York City. TV/movie actress. Played "Julie Kotter" on TV's *Welcome Back, Kotter*.

| | | | | | | |
|---|---|---|---|---|---|---|
| 4/22/67 | **105** | 9 | The Flower Children ........................... *Out Of the Picture* | $8 | | Uni 55006 |

**STRATFORDS, The** ☼
Pop/rock and roll group.

| | | | | | | |
|---|---|---|---|---|---|---|
| 2/22/64 | **124** | 4 | Never Leave Me ........................... *Enaj* [I] | $15 | | O'Dell 100 |

**STRAWBS** ☼
Progressive rock band formed in 1967 in Leicester, England, and led by David Cousins (vocals, guitar).

| | | | | | | |
|---|---|---|---|---|---|---|
| 4/21/73 | **111** | 3 | Part Of The Union ........................... *Tomorrow* | $8 | | A&M 1419 |

**STREAMLINERS WITH JOANNE, The** ☼     AC

| | | | | | | |
|---|---|---|---|---|---|---|
| 7/3/65 | **117** | 1 | Frankfurter Sandwiches........................... AC:40 *Pachalafaka* [N] | $8 | | United Artists 880 |
| | | | 1920's-styled novelty tune | | | |

**STREET PEOPLE** ☼     R&B
R&B/disco group led by singer/songwriter/producer Ray Dahrouge.

| | | | | | | |
|---|---|---|---|---|---|---|
| 9/25/76 | **109** | 2 | I Wanna Spend My Whole Life With You .......... R&B:57 *Never Get Enough Of Your Love* | $6 | | Vigor 1732 |

**STREISAND, Barbra**     AC/HOT
Born Barbara Joan Streisand on 4/24/42 in Brooklyn. Broadway/movie star. One of America's top vocalists of the past four decades. Won Grammy's Living Legends Award (1991) and Grammy's Lifetime Achievement Award (1995). *Top Pop Singles*: 43.

| | | | | | | |
|---|---|---|---|---|---|---|
| 3/28/64 | **114** | 2 | 1 I Am Woman ........................... *People* (Hot #5) | $8 | | Columbia 42965 |
| | | | from the Broadway musical *Funny Girl* starring Streisand (as "You Are Woman, I Am Man") | | | |
| 9/26/64 | **123** | 1 | 2 Absent Minded Me ........................... *Funny Girl* (Hot #44) | $7 | | Columbia 43127 |
| 3/16/68 | **107** | 5 | 3 Our Corner Of The Night........................... AC:19 *He Could Show Me* | $7 | | Columbia 44474 |
| 12/18/71 | **105** | 1 | 4 Space Captain ........................... *One Less Bell To Answer/A House Is Not A Home* | $6 | | Columbia 45511 |
| | | | backed by the female group Fanny | | | |

**STRING-A-LONGS, The**     HOT/AC/R&B
Guitar instrumental quintet: Keith McCormack, Aubrey Cordova, Richard Stephens and Jimmy Torres (guitars) and Don Allen (drums).

| | | | | | | |
|---|---|---|---|---|---|---|
| 12/15/62 | **133** | 1 | Matilda ........................... *Replica* [I] | $10 | | Dot 16393 |
| | | | #47 hit for Cookie & His Cupcakes in 1959; calypso song popularized by Harry Belafonte in 1953 | | | |

**STRONG, Nolan — see DIABLOS, The**

**STUART, Chad — see CHAD & JEREMY**

**STYX**     HOT/ROK/AC
Chicago-based rock quintet featuring Dennis DeYoung (vocals, keyboards) and **Tommy Shaw** (lead guitar). *Top Pop Singles*: 23.

| | | | | | | |
|---|---|---|---|---|---|---|
| 5/14/77 | **109** | 1 | Crystal Ball ........................... *Put Me On* | $6 | | A&M 1931 |

**SUGAR** ☼     ROK
Rock trio formed in Athens, Georgia, in 1992: Bob Mould (vocals, guitar), David Barbe (bass) and Malcolm Travis (drums).

| | | | | | | |
|---|---|---|---|---|---|---|
| 9/3/94 | **120** | 4 | Your Favorite Thing........................... ROK:14 *Mind Is An Island / Frustration / And You Tell Me* | $6 | | Rykodisc 1038 (CD) |

**SUGARLOAF/JERRY CORBETTA**     HOT
Rock quartet from Denver featuring Jerry Corbetta (lead singer, keyboards).

| | | | | | | |
|---|---|---|---|---|---|---|
| 11/1/75 | **110** | 1 | I Got A Song ........................... *Boogie Man* | $6 | | Claridge 408 |
| | | | first released on Brut 815 in 1973 ($8) with a picture sleeve | | | |

### SULLIVAN, Tom ☉       AC
Born on 3/27/47 in West Roxbury, Massachusetts. Singer/songwriter/actor; blind since birth.

| 5/1/76 | 103 | 6 | Yes, I'm Ready ..................................... AC:44 *This Is Not My Town* | $5 | ■ | ABC 12174 |

#5 hit for **Barbara Mason** in 1965

### SUMMER, Donna — see ROBERTS, Bruce

### SUMMER JUNKIES ☉
Techno-dance outfit.

| 2/15/97 | 118 | 1 | I'm Gonna Luv U .............................................(2 versions) | $4 | ▮ | Panic 001 |

### SUMMERS, Bill, And Summers Heat ☉       R&B
Bill is an R&B percussionist; formerly with **Herbie Hancock**'s Head Hunters.

| 5/23/81 | 103 | 5 | Call It What You Want ........................... R&B:16 *Your Style Ain't The Way* | $4 | | MCA 51073 |

### SUMMERS, Bob ☉

| 1/23/71 | 118 | 2 | When I'm Dead And Gone ...................................... *Lucy Lou* | $6 | | MGM 14206 |

#47 hit for **McGuinness Flint** in 1971

### SUMMER WINE ☉

| 2/17/73 | 103 | 3 | Why Do Fools Fall In Love ................... *Ode To The Steel Guitar* | $6 | | Sire 701 |

#6 hit for **The Teenagers Featuring Frankie Lymon** in 1956

### SUNNY & The Sunliners       HOT/R&B/AC
Group from San Antonio, Texas, formed in 1959 featuring Sunny Ozuna. Originally known as Sunny & The Sunglows.

| 1/23/65 | 128 | 1 | Something's Got A Hold On Me ................ *I'm Not A Fool Anymore* | $12 | | Tear Drop 3045 |

#37 hit for **Etta James** in 1962

### SUNSHINE COMPANY, The       HOT/AC
Pop quintet from Southern California: Mary Nance (vocals), Doug Mark and Maury Manseau (guitars), Larry Sims (bass) and Merle Brigante (drums).

| 5/18/68 | 112 | 3 | 1 Let's Get Together .................... *Sunday Brought The Rain* | $8 | | Imperial 66298 |

#5 hit for **The Youngbloods** in 1969 as "Get Together"

| 7/27/68 | 106 | 2 | 2 On A Beautiful Day ............................ AC:31 *Darcy Farrow* | $8 | | Imperial 66308 |
| 10/19/68 | 111 | 3 | 3 Willie Jean ................................................. *Love Poem* | $8 | | Imperial 66324 |

written by **Hoyt Axton**

### SUPER CAT       R&B/HOT
Born William Maragh on 6/25/63 of East Indian heritage in Kingston, Jamaica. Dance-hall reggae singer.

| 8/21/93 | 105 | 6 | Dolly My Baby ................................... R&B:64 *South Central* | $3 | ▮ | Columbia 77211 |

Trevor Sparks (backing vocal)

### SUPREMES, The       HOT/R&B/AC
R&B vocal trio from Detroit: Diana Ross (b: 3/26/44), Mary Wilson (b: 3/6/44) and Florence Ballard (b: 6/30/43; d: 2/22/76 of cardiac arrest). Ballard discharged from group in 1967, replaced by Cindy Birdsong. Ross left in 1969 for solo career, replaced by Jean Terrell. Group inducted into the Rock and Roll Hall of Fame in 1988. *Top Pop Singles*: 47.

| 4/6/63 | 129 | 2 | My Heart Can't Take It No More ............. *You Bring Back Memories* | $40 | | Motown 1040 |

### SURFARIS, The       HOT/R&B
Surf band from Glendora, California featuring Ron Wilson (drummer; d: May 1989) and Jim Fuller (lead guitar).

| 8/8/70 | 110 | 5 | Wipe Out ............................................. *Surfer Joe* [I-R] | $8 | | Dot/Paramount 144 |

originally made the *Hot 100* (#2) on 6/22/63 on Dot 16479; re-charted (#16) on 7/30/66 on Dot 144

### SURFER GIRLS, The ☉

| 5/2/64 | 134 | 1 | Draggin' Wagon ................................. *One Boy Tells Another* | $30 | | Columbia 43001 |

melody taken from **Chuck Berry**'s "Johnny B. Goode"

### SURVIVOR       HOT/ROK/AC
Rock group formed in Chicago in 1978 featuring Dave Bickler (vocals) and Jim Peterik (keyboards; former lead singer of **Ides Of March**).

| 6/14/80 | 103 | 3 | 1 Rebel Girl ...................................................... *Freelance* | $5 | | Scotti Brothers 517 |
| 2/18/84 | 104 | 5 | 2 I Never Stopped Loving You .................. *Ready For The Real Thing* | $4 | | Scotti Brothers 04347 |

### SWAMP DOGG — see WILLIAMS, Little Jerry

### SWAMPSEEDS, The ☉
Rock group.

| 5/11/68 | 124 | 2 | Can I Carry Your Balloon ..................... *Coney Island Parade* | $12 | | Epic 10281 |

### SWANN, Bettye       R&B/HOT
Born Betty Jean Champion on 10/24/44 in Shreveport, Louisiana. In vocal group the Fawns, recorded for Money in 1964.

| 4/3/65 | 131 | 1 | 1 Don't Wait Too Long ................ R&B:27 *What Is My Life Coming To* | $12 | | Money 108 |
| 6/21/69 | 109 | 5 | 2 Angel Of The Morning ................................ *No Faith No Love* | $8 | | Capitol 2515 |

#7 hit for **Merrilee Rush** in 1968

| 11/15/69 | 102 | 2 | 3 Don't You Ever Get Tired (Of Hurting Me) ........ *Willie & Laura Mae Jones* | $8 | | Capitol 2606 |

#1 Country hit for **Ronnie Milsap** in 1989

| 2/7/70 | 114 | 2 | 4 Little Things Mean A Lot .............. *Just Because You Can't Be Mine* | $8 | | Capitol 2723 |

#1 hit for **Kitty Kallen** in 1954

### SWE-DANES, The ☉
Alice Babs, Ulrich Neumann and Svend Asmussen.

| 2/22/60 | 101[1] | 4 | Scandinavian Shuffle ...................................... *Hot Toddy* | $12 | | Warner 5144 |

no vocals other than la-da-daa's

### SWEAT, Keith       R&B/HOT
Born on 7/22/61 in New York City. R&B singer/songwriter. Also see **Silk**.

| 12/5/92 | 117 | 1 | 1 I Want To Love You Down ..................... R&B:20 *Let Me Love You* | $3 | ▮ | Elektra 64694 |
| 6/3/95 | 118 | 7 | 2 If It's Alright With You ..................... R&B:41 *(album snippets)* | $3 | ▮ | Luke 184 |

**LORENZO** Featuring Keith Sweat

| 4/12/97 | 101[1] | 11 | 3 Gonna Let U Know ............... R&B:47 *(remix) / (instrumental)* | $3 | ▮ | Island 854914 |

**LIL BUD & TIZONE** featuring Keith Sweat
Marinna Teal (additional vocal)

**SWEET, Matthew**               ROK/HOT

Born on 10/6/64 in Lincoln, Nebraska. Rock bassist/drummer/singer. Toured as guitarist with Lloyd Cole.

| 8/19/95 | 113 | 5 | We're The Same ........................................................... ROK:34 *Speed Racer* $3 | ▌ Zoo 14234 |

**SWEET, Rachel**             HOT/C&W

Born in 1963 in Akron, Ohio. Performed in the musicals *The Music Man*, *Fiddler On The Roof* and *The Sound Of Music*.

| 6/7/80 | 107 | 1 | Spellbound ........................................................................ *Tonight* $5 | Stiff/Columbia 11272 |

**SWEETBACK** ⊙           R&B

Trio consisting of the musicians from **Sade**'s band: Stuart Matthewman (guitar, sax), Andrew Hale (keyboards) and Paul S. Denman (bass).

| 2/15/97 | 112 | 5 | You Will Rise ................................................... R&B:42 (edit) $3 | ▌ Epic 78509 |

SWEETBACK Featuring **Amel Larrieux** (of Groove Theory)

**SWEET INSPIRATIONS, The**         R&B/HOT

R&B vocal quartet: Cissy Houston, Estelle Brown, Sylvia Shemwell and Myrna Smith. Backing vocalists for **Aretha Franklin** and Elvis Presley.

| 9/9/67 | 123 | 2 | 1 That's How Strong My Love Is ................................ *I've Been Loving You Too Long* $8 | Atlantic 2436 |

#74 hit for **Otis Redding** in 1965

| 11/30/68 | 128 | 1 | 2 What The World Needs Now Is Love ........................... *You Really Didn't Mean It* $8 | Atlantic 2571 |

#7 hit for **Jackie DeShannon** in 1965

| 4/19/69 | 112 | 4 | 3 Crying In The Rain ............................ R&B:42 *Everyday Will Be Like A Holiday* $8 | Atlantic 2620 |

#6 hit for **The Everly Brothers** in 1962

| 12/20/69 | 117 | 4 | 4 (Gotta Find) A Brand New Lover-Part 1 ..................... R&B:25 *Part 2* $8 | ☐ Atlantic 2686 |
| 10/31/70 | 123 | 2 | 5 This World ........................................ R&B:45 *Light Sings* $7 | Atlantic 2750 |

from the musical *The Me Nobody Knows*; #38 hit for **The Staple Singers** in 1972

| 8/25/79 | 104 | 5 | 6 Love Is On The Way             (instrumental) $5 | RSO 932 |

**SWEET MARIE, The** ⊙

Pop/rock vocal group.

| 2/3/73 | 123 | 1 | Stella's Candy Store ................................................ *Another Feelin'* $8 | ▪ Yardbird 8013 |

a longer version issued in 1972 on a red vinyl Yard Bird 8013 record ($12)

**SWINGING BLUE JEANS, The**         HOT

Rock quartet from Liverpool, England: Ray Ennis and Ralph Ellis (guitars), Norman Kuhlke (drums) and Les Braid (bass).

| 10/3/64 | 130 | 1 | 1 Promise You'll Tell Her........................................... *Tutti Frutti* $12 | Imperial 66059 |
| 3/19/66 | 116 | 2 | 2 Don't Make Me Over ......................................... *What Can I Do Today* $12 | Imperial 66154 |

#21 hit for **Dionne Warwick** in 1963

**SWINGIN' MEDALLIONS, The**         HOT

Rock band from Greenwood, South Carolina. Members Brent Fortson and Steven Caldwell formed Pieces Of Eight.

| 4/29/67 | 107 | 4 | I Found A Rainbow ................................................. *Don't Cry No More* $12 | Smash 2084 |

**SWV — see AZ**

**SYKES, Keith** ⊙

Rockabilly singer from Memphis.

| 12/6/80 | 108 | 4 | Love To Ride .................................... *I'm Not Strange (I'm Just Like You)* $5 | Backstreet 51028 |

**SYLVIA**              R&B/HOT/AC

Born Sylvia Vanderpool on 5/6/36 in New York City. Half of Mickey & Sylvia duo. Owner of All Platinum/Vibration/Sugar Hill labels.

| 8/22/70 | 102 | 1 | 1 Have You Had Any Lately? ............................... *Anytime* (Sylvia and Al) $6 | Stang 5015 |

SYLVIA ROBINSON

first pressings show title as "Had Any Lately?"

| 3/30/74 | 103 | 11 | 2 Sweet Stuff ...................................... R&B:16 *Had Any Lately* $5 | Vibration 529 |

**SYREETA — see PRESTON, Billy**

**SYSTEM, The**            R&B/HOT/AC

New York City-based, techno-funk duo: Mic Murphy (vocals, guitar) and David Frank (synthesizer).

| 8/10/85 | 108 | 1 | The Pleasure Seekers ........................................ R&B:21 (dub version) $4 | ▪ Mirage 99639 |

# T

**TAKE 6** ⊙            R&B

Contemporary Christian, acappella, pop-jazz sextet: Claude McKnight, Mark Kibble, Mervyn Warren, Cedric Dent, David Thomas and Alvin Chea.

| 7/23/94 | 112 | 4 | Biggest Part Of Me................................. R&B:36 *My Friend* (w/Ray Charles) $3 | ▌ Reprise 18122 |

#3 hit for **Ambrosia** in 1980

**TALKING HEADS**            ROK/HOT

New York City-based new wave band: David Byrne (lead singer, guitar), Jerry Harrison (keyboards, guitar), Tina Weymouth (bass) and husband Chris Frantz (drums). Weymouth and Frantz also formed **Tom Tom Club**.

| 2/7/81 | 103 | 1 | 1 Once In A Lifetime ............................................. *Seen & Not Seen* $5 | Sire 49649 |

a "live" version made the *Hot 100* (#91) on 4/19/86 on Sire 29163

| 6/22/85 | 105 | 1 | 2 Road To Nowhere ...................................... ROK:25 *Give Me Back My Name* $4 | ▪ Sire 28987 |

**TAMS, The**            HOT/R&B

Atlanta R&B quintet: brothers Charles and Joseph (lead singer; d: 3/16/96) Pope, with Robert Smith, Floyd Ashton and Horace Key.

| 11/7/64 | 129 | 3 | 1 Find Another Love ............................... *My Baby Loves Me* (w/Little Floyd) $20 | G/A 714 |
| 9/28/68 | 118 | 2 | 2 Trouble Maker .............................................. *Laugh At The World* $10 | ABC 11128 |

**TANEGA, Norma**            HOT

Born on 1/30/39 in Vallejo, California. Singer/songwriter/pianist/guitarist.

| 5/21/66 | 129 | 2 | A Street That Rhymes At Six A.M. ........................... *Treat Me Right* $12 | New Voice 810 |

**TAPP, Demetriss ☉**                                       C&W
Country/pop singer from North Carolina with a style similar to **Brenda Lee**.

| 11/16/63 | 118 | 5 | Lipstick Paint A Smile On Me....................................................... *If You Find Love* | $12 | | Brunswick 55251 |

Dick Jacobs (orch.)

**TASSO, Vicki ☉**
Pop songstress.

| 6/16/62 | 118 | 1 | The Sound Of The Hammer.................................................................*Foolish Me* | $15 | | Colpix 638 |

Don Costa (orch.)

**TATE, Howard**                                            R&B/HOT
R&B singer from Macon, Georgia. Moved to Philadelphia at age seven.

| 4/8/67 | 134 | 1 | 1 Get It While You Can..................................................... *Glad I Knew Better* | $10 | | Verve 10496 |
| 9/20/69 | 120 | 3 | 2 These Are The Things That Make Me Know You're Gone.........................................**R&B:28** *That's What Happens* | $10 | | Turntable 505 |

produced by **Lloyd Price** (owner of the Turntable label)

**TAYLOR, B.E., Group**                                     HOT/ROK
Pop-rock group from Pittsburgh led by vocalist Taylor. Includes three former **Crack The Sky** members.

| 4/20/85 | 102 | 4 | Reggae Rock N Roll ................................................................. *Dangerous Rhythm* | $4 | | Epic 04862 |

**TAYLOR, Chip ☉**                                          C&W
Born James Wesley Voigt in New York in 1940. Brother of actor Jon Voigt. Wrote "Angel of The Morning" and "Wild Thing." Also see **Just Us**.

| 11/17/62 | 113 | 1 | Here I Am ..............................................................*I Love You But I Know* | $10 | | Warner 5314 |

Stan Applebaum (orch.)

**TAYLOR, James**                                           AC/HOT/C&W/ROK
Born on 3/12/48 in Boston. Singer/songwriter/guitarist. Married **Carly Simon** on 11/3/72; divorced in 1983. *Top Pop Singles*: 22.

| 4/12/69 | 118 | 2 | Carolina In My Mind ....................................................*Something's Wrong* | $10 | | Apple 1805 |

made the *Hot 100* (#67) on 11/14/70; also released with "Taking It In" on the B-side ($300)

**TAYLOR, Johnnie**                                         R&B/HOT
Born on 5/5/38 in Crawfordsville, Arkansas. In the Soul Stirrers gospel group before going solo. Known as The Soul Philosopher. *Top Pop Singles*: 21.

| 6/23/62 | 112 | 2 | 1 Rome (Wasn't Built In A Day) ..........................................*Never, Never* | $30 | | SAR 131 |

written by **Sam Cooke**

| 8/2/69 | 115 | 2 | 2 Just Keep On Loving Me ...................................................*My Life* | $10 | | Stax 0042 |

**JOHNNIE TAYLOR, CARLA THOMAS**

| 4/8/72 | 109 | 5 | 3 Doing My Own Thing (Part I).................................**R&B:16** *(Part II)* | $7 | | Stax 0122 |
| 9/30/72 | 101² | 5 | 4 Stop Doggin' Me ..........................................**R&B:13** *Stop Teasin' Me* | $6 | | Stax 0142 |
| 4/22/78 | 101² | 4 | 5 Keep On Dancing ........................**R&B:32** *I Love To Make Love When It's Raining* | $4 | | Columbia 10709 |
| 8/17/96 | 102 | 14 | 6 Good Love ...................................................**R&B:39** *(3 mixes)* | $3 | ▌ | Malaco 2525 |

**TAYLOR, Little Johnny**                                   R&B/HOT
Born Johnny Young on 2/11/43 in Memphis. Blues singer/harmonica player.

| 5/4/63 | 125 | 2 | 1 You'll Need Another Favor ....................**R&B:27** *What You Need Is A Ball* | $15 | | Galaxy 718 |
| 4/11/64 | 101¹ | 6 | 2 If You Love Me (Like You Say)/ | | | |
| 4/11/64 | 107 | 2 | 3    First Class Love ...................................................... | $15 | | Galaxy 729 |
| 7/18/64 | 109 | 3 | 4 Nightingale Melody ..........................................*You Win, I Lose* | $15 | | Galaxy 731 |

**TAYLOR, R. Dean**                                         HOT/AC/C&W
Born in Toronto in 1939. First recorded for Barry in 1960. Co-wrote **The Supremes'** hit "Love Child."

| 7/31/71 | 104 | 4 | Candy Apple Red ....................................................*Woman Alive* | $6 | | Rare Earth 5030 |

**TAYLOR, Ted**                                             R&B/HOT
Born Austin Taylor on 2/16/37 in Okmulgee, Oklahoma. Killed in an automobile accident on 10/22/87. R&B singer/songwriter.

| 12/31/60 | 105 | 2 | 1 Look Out ..................................................*Darling Take Me Back* | $25 | | Top Rank 2076 |
| 2/23/63 | 134 | 1 | 2 I'll Release You .........................................*Can't Take No More* | $12 | | Okeh 7165 |

answer song to **Esther Phillips'** 1962 hit "Release Me"

| 5/4/63 | 123 | 3 | 3 Be Ever Wonderful ......................................*That's Life I Guess* | $12 | | Okeh 7171 |
| 9/14/63 | 104 | 1 | 4 You Give Me Nothing To Go On ....................*Him Instead Of Me* | $12 | | Okeh 7176 |
| 7/3/65 | 132 | 1 | 5 (Love Is Like A) Ramblin' Rose ................................*I'm So Satisfied* | $12 | | Okeh 7222 |
| 3/26/66 | 129 | 2 | 6 Daddy's Baby ...........................................*Mercy Have Pity* | $12 | | Okeh 7240 |
| 8/30/69 | 118 | 3 | 7 It's Too Late .........................................**R&B:30** *The Road Of Love* | $10 | | Ronn 34 |

#3 R&B hit for Chuck Willis in 1956

**TCHAIKOVSKY, Bram — see BRAM TCHAIKOVSKY**

**T-CONNECTION**                                            R&B/HOT
Disco group from Nassau, Bahamas featuring Theophilus "T" Coakley (vocals, keyboards).

| 12/17/77 | 103 | 14 | On Fire .............................................**R&B:27** *Go Back Home* | $5 | | Dash 5041 |

**TEARS FOR FEARS**                                         HOT/ROK/AC/R&B
British duo: Roland Orzabal (b: 8/22/61; vocals, guitar, keyboards) and Curt Smith (b: 6/24/61; vocals, bass). Smith left in 1992.

| 12/4/93 | 125 | 1 | 1 Goodnight Song ................................................*New Star* | $3 | ▌ | Mercury 862804 |
| 10/21/95 | 102 | 5 | 2 God's Mistake ............................................*Creep (live)* | $3 | ▌ | Epic 78064 |

**TEDDY and The CONTINENTALS ☉**
R&B vocal group led by Teddy Henry.

| 9/18/61 | 101¹ | 1 | Ev'rybody Pony ............................................*Tick Tick Tock* | $40 | | Pik 234/5 |

first released on Richie 1001 in 1961 ($75)

**TEDDY and the Pandas ☉**
Pop/rock quintet from Boston led by guitarist Teddy Dewart.

| 4/30/66 | 134 | 1 | 1 Once Upon A Time (This World Was Mine)..........*(Bye Bye) Out The Window* | $15 | | Musicor 1176 |
| 8/20/66 | 103 | 5 | 2 We Can't Go On This Way ....................................*Smokey Fire* | $15 | | Musicor 1190 |

**TEMPESTS, The ☉**
Vocal group led by brothers Roger and Mike Branch.

| DEBUT | PEAK | WKS | A-side | B-side | $ | Pic | Label & Number |
|---|---|---|---|---|---|---|---|
| 8/5/67 | 127 | 3 | Would You Believe | You (Are The Star I Wish On) | $15 | | Smash 2094 |

**TEMPO, Nino, & April Stevens**　　　　　　　HOT/AC/R&B
Nino (born Antonio Lo Tempio on 1/6/35) and sister April Stevens (born Carol Lo Tempio on 4/29/36) from Niagara Falls, New York.

| DEBUT | PEAK | WKS | A-side | B-side | $ | Pic | Label & Number |
|---|---|---|---|---|---|---|---|
| 3/30/63 | 126 | 1 | 1 Paradise | Indian Love Call | $10 | | Atco 6248 |

APRIL STEVENS & NINO TEMPO
#1 hit for both Guy Lombardo and Leo Reisman in 1932; #48 hit for Sammy Turner in 1960

| | | | | | | | |
|---|---|---|---|---|---|---|---|
| 9/12/64 | 113 | 1 | 2 Ooh La La | Melancholy Baby | $10 | | Atco 6314 |
| 6/5/65 | 127 | 1 | 3 Swing Me | Tomorrow Is Soon A Memory | $10 | | Atco 6350 |
| 1/21/67 | 133 | 2 | 4 You'll Be Needing Me Baby | The Habit Of Lovin' You Baby | $8 | | White Whale 241 |

written by David Gates of Bread

| | | | | | | | |
|---|---|---|---|---|---|---|---|
| 4/15/67 | 101[2] | 5 | 5 My Old Flame | Wings Of Love | $8 | | White Whale 246 |

#7 hit for Guy Lombardo in 1934

| | | | | | | | |
|---|---|---|---|---|---|---|---|
| 5/25/68 | 127 | 2 | 6 Let It Be Me | Wings Of Love | $8 | | White Whale 268 |

#7 hit for The Everly Brothers in 1960

| | | | | | | | |
|---|---|---|---|---|---|---|---|
| 12/9/72 | 113 | 3 | 7 Love Story | Hoochy Coochy-Wing Dang Doo | $6 | | A&M 1394 |

title song from the movie starring Ali McGraw; #9 hit for Andy Williams in 1971

| | | | | | | | |
|---|---|---|---|---|---|---|---|
| 7/7/73 | 122 | 2 | 8 Put It Where You Want It | I Can't Get Over You Baby | $6 | | A&M 1443 |

NINO & APRIL
#52 hit for The Crusaders in 1972

**TEMPTATIONS, The**　　　　　　　R&B/HOT/AC
Detroit R&B group formed in 1960: **Eddie Kendricks** (d: 10/5/92), **Paul Williams** (d: 8/17/73), **Melvin Franklin** (d: 2/23/95), **Otis Williams** and **Elbridge Bryant**, who was replaced by **David Ruffin** (d: 6/1/91) in 1964. Many personnel changes from 1968-on. Inducted into the Rock and Roll Hall of Fame in 1989. *Top Pop Singles:* 55.

| DEBUT | PEAK | WKS | A-side | B-side | $ | Pic | Label & Number |
|---|---|---|---|---|---|---|---|
| 12/1/62 | 122 | 1 | 1 Paradise | Slow Down Heart | $35 | | Gordy 7010 |
| 5/23/64 | 102 | 8 | 2 The Girl's Alright With Me | I'll Be In Trouble (Hot #33) | $15 | | Gordy 7032 |
| 7/31/65 | 123 | 2 | 3 You've Got To Earn It......R&B:22 | Since I Lost My Baby (Hot #17) | $15 | | Gordy 7043 |
| 8/5/67 | 124 | 1 | 4 I've Been Good To You | You're My Everything (Hot #6) | $12 | | Gordy 7063 |

above 2 written and produced by **Smokey Robinson**

| | | | | | | | |
|---|---|---|---|---|---|---|---|
| 3/30/68 | 116 | 2 | 5 I Truly, Truly Believe......R&B:41 | I Wish It Would Rain (Hot #4) | $12 | | Gordy 7068 |
| 11/28/81 | 104 | 4 | 6 Oh, What A Night | Isn't The Night Fantastic | $5 | | Gordy 7213 |

**10CC**　　　　　　　HOT/AC
English art-rock group that evolved from Hotlegs. Consisted of Eric Stewart, Graham Gouldman, Lol Creme and Kevin Godley. Stewart and Gouldman were members of The Mindbenders. Godley & Creme left in 1976.

| DEBUT | PEAK | WKS | A-side | B-side | $ | Pic | Label & Number |
|---|---|---|---|---|---|---|---|
| 7/13/74 | 103 | 2 | 1 The Wall Street Shuffle | Gismo My Way | $6 | | UK 49023 |
| 7/31/76 | 104 | 2 | 2 Lazy Ways/ | | | | |
| | | 2 | 3   Life Is A Minestrone | | $5 | | Mercury 73805 |

**TERMINATOR X ☉**　　　　　　　R&B
Born Norman Lee Rogers on 8/25/66 in New York City. Member of rap group Public Enemy.

| DEBUT | PEAK | WKS | A-side | B-side | $ | Pic | Label & Number |
|---|---|---|---|---|---|---|---|
| 3/5/94 | 104 | 9 | It All Comes Down To The Money...R&B:72 | Ruff E Nuff | $3 | ▌ | P.R.O. Division 77168 |

TERMINATOR X And The Godfathers Of Threatt featuring Whodini
Khadejia Bass (female vocal); samples "I Got My Mind Made Up" by **Instant Funk**

**TEX, Joe**　　　　　　　R&B/HOT
Born Joseph Arrington, Jr. on 8/8/33 in Rogers, Texas. Died of a heart attack on 8/13/82. R&B singer/songwriter. *Top Pop Singles:* 28.

| DEBUT | PEAK | WKS | A-side | B-side | $ | Pic | Label & Number |
|---|---|---|---|---|---|---|---|
| 8/15/60 | 102 | 3 | 1 All I Could Do Was Cry (Part 1) | (Part 2) | $30 | | Anna 1119 |

#33 hit for **Etta James** in 1960

| | | | | | | | |
|---|---|---|---|---|---|---|---|
| 10/4/69 | 117 | 3 | 2 It Ain't Sanitary | We Can't Sit Down Now | $8 | | Dial 4094 |
| 11/15/69 | 105 | 3 | 3 (When Johnny Comes Marching Home Again) I Can't See You | | | | |
| | | | No More | Sure Is Good | $8 | | Dial 4095 |
| 10/9/71 | 102 | 2 | 4 Give The Baby Anything The Baby Wants...R&B:20 | Takin' A Chance | $6 | | Dial 1008 |
| 3/3/73 | 103 | 5 | 5 Woman Stealer...R&B:41 | Cat's Got Her Tongue | $6 | ▌ | Dial 1020 |

**TEXTONES, The ☉**
Rock quintet led by singer/guitarist Carla Olson. Drummer **Phil Seymour** was with **Dwight Twilley**, 1974-80.

| DEBUT | PEAK | WKS | A-side | B-side | $ | Pic | Label & Number |
|---|---|---|---|---|---|---|---|
| 6/29/85 | 109 | 2 | Midnight Mission | Upset Me | $4 | ▌ | Gold Mountain 82016 |

Don Henley (backing vocal)

**TEXTOR, Keith, Singers ☉**　　　　　　　AC
Born on 7/21/21 in Coon Rapids, Iowa. Leader of vocal chorus. Composed many commercials.

| DEBUT | PEAK | WKS | A-side | B-side | $ | Pic | Label & Number |
|---|---|---|---|---|---|---|---|
| 10/10/70 | 112 | 1 | Measure The Valleys...AC:26 | We're Together | $6 | | A&R 500 |

**THEE MIDNITERS**
Los Angeles Mexican-American group featuring lead singer Willie Garcia.

| DEBUT | PEAK | WKS | A-side | B-side | $ | Pic | Label & Number |
|---|---|---|---|---|---|---|---|
| 9/4/65 | 127 | 2 | Whittier Blvd. | Evil Love [I] | $15 | | Chattahoochee 684 |

**THEE PROPHETS**　　　　　　　HOT
Pop-rock quartet from Milwaukee: Brian Lake (lead singer), Jim Anderson, Dave Leslie and Chris Michaels.

| DEBUT | PEAK | WKS | A-side | B-side | $ | Pic | Label & Number |
|---|---|---|---|---|---|---|---|
| 5/17/69 | 111 | 4 | Some Kind-A Wonderful | They Call Her Sorrow | $8 | | Kapp 997 |

#32 hit for **The Drifters** in 1961

**THEM**　　　　　　　HOT
Rock band from Belfast, Northern Ireland, featuring **Van Morrison** (vocals).

| DEBUT | PEAK | WKS | A-side | B-side | $ | Pic | Label & Number |
|---|---|---|---|---|---|---|---|
| 3/13/65 | 102 | 8 | Baby, Please Don't Go | Gloria (Hot #71/'66) | $20 | | Parrot 9727 |

#106 hit for **The Amboy Dukes** in 1968

**THIRD RAIL, The**　　　　　　　HOT
Studio project featuring lead singer Joey Levine (**Ohio Express** and **Reunion**).

| DEBUT | PEAK | WKS | A-side | B-side | $ | Pic | Label & Number |
|---|---|---|---|---|---|---|---|
| 3/16/68 | 113 | 2 | It's Time To Say Goodbye | Overdose Of Love | $10 | | Epic 10285 |

### THIRD WORLD                                                                R&B/HOT
Reggae fusion band from Jamaica featuring William "Bunny Rugs" Clarke (vocals).

| 3/27/82 | 101[1] | 10 | Try Jah Love                              R&B:23  *Inna Time Like This* | $5 | | Columbia 02744 |

written, arranged and produced by Stevie Wonder

### THIRTEENTH FLOOR ELEVATORS, The                                            HOT
Rock group from Austin, Texas: Roky Erickson (vocals), Stacy Sutherland, Tommy Hall, Dan Galindo and Danny Thomas.

| 11/26/66 | 129 | 1 | Reverbaration (Doubt) ............................................ *Fire Engine* | $25 | | IA 111 |

### THOMAS, B.J.                                                    HOT/AC/C&W
Born Billy Joe Thomas on 8/7/42 in Hugo, Oklahoma. Joined band, The Triumphs, while in high school. *Top Pop Singles*: 26.

| 12/17/66 | 129 | 3 | Plain Jane .................................................. *My Home Town* | $8 | | Scepter 12179 |

### THOMAS, Carla                                                         R&B/HOT
Born on 12/21/42 in Memphis. Daughter of **Rufus Thomas**. *Top Pop Singles*: 22.

| 5/18/68 | 114 | 2 | 1 A Dime A Dozen ............................................ *I Want You Back* | $12 | | Stax 251 |
| 4/26/69 | 109 | 3 | 2 When Something Is Wrong With My Baby............... *Ooh Carla, Ooh Otis* | $10 | | Atco 6665 |

**OTIS & CARLA**
#42 hit for **Sam & Dave** in 1967

| 7/12/69 | 106 | 4 | 3 I Need You Woman                              *I Can't Stop* | $10 | | Stax 0044 |

**WILLIAM BELL, CARLA THOMAS**

| 8/2/69 | 115 | 2 | 4 Just Keep On Loving Me ................................ *My Life* | $10 | | Stax 0042 |

**JOHNNIE TAYLOR, CARLA THOMAS**

| 8/23/69 | 117 | 2 | 5 I've Fallen In Love .............. R&B:36  *Where Do I Go (Hot #86/'68)* | $10 | | Stax 0011 |
| 6/6/70 | 107 | 3 | 6 Guide Me Well.............. R&B:41  *Some Other Man (Is Beating Your Time)* | $8 | | Stax 0056 |

### THOMAS, Irma                                                         R&B/HOT
Born Irma Lee on 2/18/41 in Ponchatoula, Louisiana. Nicknamed "The Soul Queen of New Orleans."

| 3/6/65 | 109 | 4 | 1 You Don't Miss A Good Thing (Until It's Gone) ...... *Some Things You Never Get Used To* | $12 | | Imperial 66095 |
| 5/15/65 | 130 | 1 | 2 I'm Gonna Cry Till My Tears Run Dry.......... *Nobody Wants To Hear Nobody's Troubles* | $12 | | Imperial 66106 |
| 11/13/65 | 118 | 3 | 3 Take A Look ........................................ *What Are You Trying To Do* | $12 | | Imperial 66137 |
| 6/18/66 | 119 | 3 | 4 It's A Man's--Woman's World - Part I ........................ *Part II* | $10 | | Imperial 66178 |

answer song to Percy Sledge's #1 1966 hit "When A Man Loves A Woman"

### THOMAS, Lillo ○                                                         R&B
Brooklyn R&B vocalist. At age 16, set a world record for the 200-meter dash.

| 8/18/84 | 102 | 4 | Your Love's Got A Hold On Me................... R&B:11  *Trust Me* | $4 | ■ | Capitol 5357 |

### THOMAS, Nolan                                                       R&B/HOT
R&B singer/songwriter from New Jersey.

| 6/15/85 | 105 | 1 | One Bad Apple ...............................R&B:48  *(dub version)* | $4 | | Mirage 99651 |

#1 hit for The Osmonds in 1971

### THOMAS, Rufus                                                       R&B/HOT
Born on 3/26/17 in Cayce, Mississippi. R&B singer/songwriter/choreographer. Father of singers Vaneese and **Carla Thomas**.

| 6/17/72 | 114 | 1 | 1 Love Trap ............................................... *6-3-8* | $7 | | Stax 0129 |
| 9/23/72 | 103 | 4 | 2 Itch And Scratch (Part I) .................................... *(Part II)* | $7 | | Stax 0140 |

### THOMAS, Timmy                                                       R&B/HOT
Born on 11/13/44 in Evansville, Indiana. R&B singer/songwriter/keyboardist.

| 7/21/73 | 107 | 5 | 1 Let Me Be Your Eyes.........................R&B:48  *Cold Cold People* | $6 | | Glades 1712 |
| 11/17/73 | 102 | 13 | 2 What Can I Tell Her ........................... R&B:19  *Opportunity* | $6 | | Glades 1717 |

### THOMPSON, Gina                                                      R&B/HOT
Born in 1974 in Vineland, New Jersey. R&B singer.

| 3/22/97 | 122 | 1 | You Bring The Sunshine ......... R&B:53  *The Things That You Do (w/Raekwon & Craig Mack)* | $3 | ▮ | Mercury 574138 |

### THOMPSON, Hank                                                     C&W/MEM/HOT
Born on 9/3/25 in Waco, Texas. Country singer.

| 3/21/60 | 102 | 6 | 1 A Six Pack To Go ......................C&W:10  *What Made Her Change* | $12 | | Capitol 4334 |

**HANK THOMPSON And The Brazos Valley Boys**

| 4/23/66 | 134 | 1 | 2 Pick Me Up On Your Way Down .......................... *You Nearly Lose Your Mind* | $10 | | Capitol 5599 |

#2 Country hit for Charlie Walker in 1958

### THOMPSON, Marc Anthony ○
Punk-funk singer born in Panama, raised in Watts, Los Angeles.

| 10/13/84 | 101[2] | 4 | So Fine                                      *Alot Of Girls (Would Turn)* | $4 | ■ | Warner 29175 |

### THOMPSON, Sue                                                     C&W/HOT/AC
Born Eva Sue McKee on 7/19/26 in Nevada, Missouri. Became a popular country singer in the '70s; charted 9 hits with **Don Gibson**.

| 6/9/62 | 112 | 4 | 1 If The Boy Only Knew ................ *Have A Good Time (Hot #31)* | $12 | | Hickory 1174 |
| 3/30/63 | 135 | 1 | 2 What's Wrong Bill ........................................ *I Need A Harbor* | $12 | ■ | Hickory 1204 |
| 2/22/64 | 132 | 1 | 3 Big Daddy ............................................. *I'd Like To Know You Better* | $12 | | Hickory 1240 |
| 5/8/65 | 115 | 5 | 4 Stop Th' Music................................... *What I'm Needin' Is You* | $12 | | Hickory 1308 |

all of above written by John D. Loudermilk

| 8/6/66 | 131 | 1 | 5 Put It Back (Where You Found It) ............. *I Can't Help It (If I'm Still In Love With You)* | $12 | | Hickory 1403 |

### THOMSON, Ali                                                         AC/HOT
Pop singer/songwriter from Glasgow, Scotland. Younger brother of Supertramp's Dougie Thomson.

| 3/14/81 | 105 | 7 | Foolish Child ........................................ *Secrets Hide Inside* | $4 | | A&M 2314 |

### THORNDIKE PICKLEDISH CHOIR, The ○
Novelty production by Robert Oh Smith.

| 2/4/67 | 131 | 1 | Ballad Of Walter Wart (Brrriggett) ...............*It's Warts On The Flip Side That Counts* [N] | $10 | | MTA 114 |

| DEBUT | PEAK | WKS | A-side (Chart Hit) / B-side | $ | Pic | Label & Number |
|---|---|---|---|---|---|---|
| | | | **THOROGOOD, George, & The Destroyers**    ROK/HOT | | | |
| | | | Rock and roll guitarist/vocalist Thorogood was born on 12/31/52 in Wilmington, Delaware. | | | |
| 9/11/82 | 106 | 2 | 1 Nobody But Me .............................................ROK:32   *That Philly Thing* | $5 | ■ | EMI America 8123 |
| | | | #8 hit for The Human Beinz in 1968 | | | |
| 9/18/93 | 124 | 1 | 2 Get A Haircut ..............................................ROK:2   *Gone Dead Train* | $3 | ▌ | EMI/ERG 50458 |
| | | | **THORPE, Billy, And The Aztecs**    HOT | | | |
| | | | England-born rock and roll singer/guitarist; raised in Australia. Member of Mick Fleetwood's (of **Fleetwood Mac**) Zoo. | | | |
| 5/1/65 | 130 | 2 | Over The Rainbow ...........................................*That I Love* | $15 | | GNP Crescendo 340 |
| | | | #16 hit for The Demensions in 1960; first sung by Judy Garland in the 1939 movie *The Wizard Of Oz* | | | |
| | | | **THP ORCHESTRA** ✪    R&B | | | |
| | | | Canadian disco production: Barbara Fry (vocals) and W. Michael Lewis (synthesizer). | | | |
| 2/25/78 | 103 | 11 | Two Hot For Love ...........................................R&B:46   *Dawn Patrol* | $5 | | Butterfly 1206 |
| | | | **3° DEGREES, The**    R&B/HOT/AC | | | |
| | | | Philadelphia R&B trio discovered by Richard Barrett: Fayette Pinkney, Linda Turner and Shirley Porter. | | | |
| 10/2/65 | 126 | 2 | Close Your Eyes ...........................................*Gotta Draw The Line* | $15 | | Swan 4224 |
| | | | written by Chuck Willis; #5 R&B hit for The Five Keys in 1955; #8 hit for **Peaches & Herb** in 1967 | | | |
| | | | **THREE DIMENSIONS, The** ✪ | | | |
| 12/4/65 | 113 | 8 | Look At Me ...........................................*Act Like A Baby* | $10 | | RCA Victor 8709 |
| | | | THE THREE DIMENSIONS (with the thing) | | | |
| | | | **THREE DOG NIGHT**    HOT/AC/R&B | | | |
| | | | Los Angeles rock trio formed in 1968: **Danny Hutton** (b: 9/10/42), Cory Wells (b: 2/5/42) and Chuck Negron (b: 6/8/42). *Top Pop Singles*: 21. | | | |
| 1/25/69 | 116 | 1 | Nobody ...........................................*It's For You* | $10 | ☐ | Dunhill/ABC 4168 |
| | | | **3T**    R&B/HOT | | | |
| | | | R&B vocal trio of brothers Taryll, TJ and Taj Jackson. Sons of Tito Jackson (The Jacksons). | | | |
| 6/15/96 | 103 | 6 | 1 Tease Me..........................................R&B:90   *(radio edit) / Anything (acoustic)* | $3 | ▌ | MJJ Music 78291 |
| 9/14/96 | 112 | 5 | 2 Why ..........................................R&B:71   *Didn't Mean To Hurt You ('96)* | $3 | ▌ | MJJ Music 78366 |
| | | | 3T Featuring MICHAEL JACKSON | | | |
| | | | **3XKRAZY** ✪    R&B | | | |
| | | | Rap trio from Oakland: Bart, Keek Tha Sneek and Agerman. | | | |
| 5/10/97 | 101[1] | 14 | Keep It On The Real      R&B:60   *Can't F*ck With This* | $3 | ▌ | Noo Trybe 38584 |
| | | | **THROWING MUSES** ✪    ROK | | | |
| | | | Boston-based duo: Kristin Hersh (guitarist/vocalist) and David Narcizo (drummer). | | | |
| 3/11/95 | 120 | 2 | Bright Yellow Gun ...........................................ROK:20   *Like A Dog* | $3 | ▌ | Sire/Reprise 17937 |
| | | | **THUNDER, Johnny**    HOT/R&B | | | |
| | | | Born Gil Hamilton on 8/15/41 in Leesburg, Florida. R&B singer discovered by producer **Teddy Vann**. | | | |
| 3/30/63 | 122 | 3 | 1 The Rosy Dance..........................................*Rock-A-Bye My Darling* | $12 | ■ | Diamond 132 |
| | | | inspired by the children's game "Ring Around The Rosie" | | | |
| 10/26/63 | 118 | 2 | 2 Hey Child ..........................................*Darling Je Vous Aime Beau Coup* | $12 | | Diamond 148 |
| 12/12/64 | 121 | 4 | 3 Send Her To Me ..........................................*Shout It To The World* | $12 | | Diamond 175 |
| 3/12/66 | 106 | 4 | 4 My Prayer ..........................................*A Broken Heart* | $12 | | Diamond 196 |
| | | | #2 hit for Glenn Miller in 1939; #1 hit for **The Platters** in 1956 | | | |
| 4/5/69 | 122 | 2 | 5 I'm Alive ..........................................*Verbal Expressions Of T.V.* | $10 | | Calla 161 |
| | | | written and arranged by **Tommy James** | | | |
| | | | **THUNDERCLAP NEWMAN**    HOT | | | |
| | | | British rock trio: Andy Newman (keyboards), John "Speedy" Keene (vocals) and Jimmy McCulloch (guitarist with **Paul McCartney**'s Wings, 1975-77; d: 9/27/79). Group assembled by **Pete Townshend**. | | | |
| 10/24/70 | 120 | 1 | Something In The Air ...........................................*Wilhemina* [R] | $10 | | Track 2769 |
| | | | originally made the *Hot 100* (#37) on 9/6/69 on Track 2656; revived due to inclusion in the movie *The Strawberry Statement* starring Kim Darby | | | |
| | | | **THUNDERMUG** ✪ | | | |
| | | | Rock quartet from Toronto: Joe De Angelis (vocals), Bill Durst, Jim Corbett and Ed Pranskus. | | | |
| 12/16/72 | 110 | 4 | Africa ...........................................*Will They Ever* | $8 | | Big Tree 154 |
| | | | **TIDAL WAVES** ✪ | | | |
| | | | Garage-rock band from Sanford, Maine. | | | |
| 7/2/66 | 123 | 2 | Farmer John ...........................................*She Left Me All Alone* | $15 | | HBR 482 |
| | | | #19 hit for The Premiers in 1964 | | | |
| | | | **TIGERS, The** ✪ | | | |
| | | | Rock and roll quintet from Los Angeles led by Danny Peil. | | | |
| 6/5/65 | 119 | 2 | GeeTO Tiger ...........................................*The GeeTO Prowl* | $40 | ■ | Colpix 773 |
| | | | title refers to Pontiac's 1965 G.T.O. muscle car | | | |
| | | | **TILLIS, Mel** ✪    C&W/AC | | | |
| | | | Born Lonnie Melvin Tillis on 8/8/32 in Tampa, Florida. Wrote "Detroit City" and "Ruby Don't Take Your Love To Town." | | | |
| 6/3/67 | 128 | 1 | 1 Life Turned Her That Way ...........................................C&W:11   *If I Could Only Start Over* | $8 | ■ | Kapp 804 |
| 3/13/71 | 114 | 3 | 2 The Arms Of A Fool ...........................................C&W:4   *Veil Of White Lace* | $6 | | MGM 14211 |
| | | | MEL TILLIS AND THE STATESIDERS | | | |
| 7/17/71 | 110 | 3 | 3 Take My Hand ...........................................C&W:8   *Life's Little Surprises* | $6 | | MGM 14255 |
| | | | MEL TILLIS AND SHERRY BRYCE with The Statesiders | | | |
| | | | **TILLOTSON, Johnny**    HOT/AC/C&W/R&B | | | |
| | | | Born on 4/20/39 in Jacksonville, Florida. Signed by Cadence Records in 1958. In the movie *Just For Fun*. *Top Pop Singles*: 26. | | | |
| 9/29/62 | 106 | 2 | 1 What'll I Do ...........................................*Send Me The Pillow You Dream On* (Hot #17) | $12 | | Cadence 1424 |
| | | | written by Irving Berlin; #1 hit for Paul Whiteman in 1924 | | | |
| 2/8/64 | 112 | 2 | 2 Please Don't Go Away...........................................*Worried Guy* (Hot #37) | $10 | ■ | MGM 13193 |
| 2/5/66 | 128 | 1 | 3 Hello Enemy ...........................................*I Never Loved You Anyway* | $10 | ■ | MGM 13445 |

| DEBUT | PEAK | WKS | A-side (Chart Hit) ... B-side | $ | Pic | Label & Number |
|---|---|---|---|---|---|---|
| | | | **TILLOTSON, Johnny — Cont'd** | | | |
| 6/7/69 | 119 | 5 | 4 Tears On My Pillow ........................ *Remember When* | $7 | | Amos 117 |
| | | | Jimmy Bowen (orch.); #4 hit for **Little Anthony & The Imperials** in 1958 | | | |
| 6/19/71 | 127 | 2 | 5 Apple Bend ........................ *Star Spangled Bus* | $6 | | Buddah 232 |
| | | | **TIME, The**        **R&B/HOT** | | | |
| | | | Funk group formed in Minneapolis by **Prince** and lead singer Morris Day in 1981. Group featured in the movie *Purple Rain*. | | | |
| 12/18/82 | 104 | 1 | 1 The Walk ........................ **R&B:24** *OneDayI'mGonnaBeSomebody* | $4 | | Warner 29856 |
| 8/18/84 | 106 | 3 | 2 Ice Cream Castles ........................ **R&B:11** *Tricky* | $4 | | Warner 29247 |
| | | | **TIME TONES, The**        **HOT** | | | |
| | | | Interracial vocal quintet from Long Island: Rodgers LaRue (lead), Glenn Williams, Claude "Sonny" Smith, Tom DeGeorge and Tom Glozek. | | | |
| 7/31/61 | 106 | 3 | Pretty, Pretty Girl (The New Beat) ........................ *I've Got A Feeling* | $30 | | Atco 6201 |
| | | | **TINO, Babs** ⊙ | | | |
| | | | Female blue-eyed soul singer. | | | |
| 8/25/62 | 117 | 1 | Forgive Me (For Giving You Such A Bad Time) ........................ *If I Didn't Love You So Much* | $12 | | Kapp 472 |
| | | | Chuck Sagle (orch.); written and produced by **Burt Bacharach** | | | |
| | | | **TINY TIM**        **HOT/C&W** | | | |
| | | | Born Herbert Khaury on 4/12/30 in New York City. Died on 11/30/96. Novelty singer/ukulele player. | | | |
| 9/21/68 | 122 | 2 | Hello, Hello ........................ *The Other Side* | $7 | | Reprise 0769 |
| | | | #26 hit for Sopwith "Camel" in 1967 | | | |
| | | | **TIPPIN, Aaron** ⊙        **C&W** | | | |
| | | | Born on 7/3/58 in Pensacola, Florida. Country singer/songwriter. | | | |
| 11/11/95+ | 101[2] | 13 | That's As Close As I'll Get To Loving You   **Sls:70** */C&W:*❶[2] *She Feels Like A Brand New Man Tonight* | $3 | ■ | RCA 64392 |
| | | | **TIPTON, John** ⊙ | | | |
| | | | Pop singer/songwriter. | | | |
| 6/7/69 | 118 | 1 | Spring ........................ *Two Lonely Lips* | $7 | | Date 1641 |
| | | | **TISHA** ⊙        **R&B** | | | |
| | | | Born Tisha Campbell on 10/13/70 in Oklahoma City. Singer/actress. Acted in movies *House Party*, *House Party II* and *School Daze*. Cast member of TV show *Martin*. | | | |
| 1/23/93 | 104 | 7 | Push ........................ **R&B:31** *(2 mixes)* | $3 | ■ | Capitol 44850 |
| | | | **TNT BAND** ⊙        **R&B** | | | |
| 1/25/69 | 117 | 4 | The Meditation ........................ **R&B:32** *Mr. Slick* | $7 | | Cotique 136 |
| | | | Tito Ramos (vocal) | | | |
| | | | **TOBY BEAU**        **HOT/AC** | | | |
| | | | Pop quintet from Texas: Balde Silva (vocals, harmonica), Danny McKenna (guitar), Ron Rose (banjo), Steve Zipper (bass) and Rob Young (drums). | | | |
| 10/28/78 | 108 | 1 | Into The Night ........................ *Wink Of An Eye* | $5 | | RCA 11388 |
| | | | **TOKENS, The**        **HOT/AC/R&B** | | | |
| | | | Pop vocal group from Brooklyn: brothers Phil and Mitch Margo, Hank Medress, Jay Siegel and Joseph Venneri. Formed own label, B.T. Puppy, in 1964. Produced **The Chiffons** and **The Happenings**. | | | |
| 9/18/61 | 120 | 1 | 1 Sincerely ........................ *When Summer Is Through* | $20 | | RCA Victor 7925 |
| | | | #1 R&B hit for **The Moonglows** in 1955 | | | |
| 3/23/63 | 126 | 1 | 2 Tonight I Met An Angel ........................ *Hindi Lullabye* | $15 | ■ | RCA Victor 8148 |
| 10/12/63 | 108 | 1 | 3 Please Write ........................ *I'll Always Love You* | $20 | | Laurie 3180 |
| 5/2/64 | 105 | 5 | 4 Swing ........................ *A Girl Named Arlene* | $12 | | B.T. Puppy 500 |
| 11/13/65 | 120 | 5 | 5 The Three Bells (The Jimmy Brown Song) ........................ *A Message To The World* | $12 | | B.T. Puppy 516 |
| | | | #1 hit for **The Browns** in 1959 | | | |
| 5/28/66 | 102 | 10 | 6 Greatest Moments In A Girl's Life ........................ *Breezy* | $12 | ■ | B.T. Puppy 519 |
| 1/28/67 | 110 | 2 | 7 Life Is Groovy ........................ **AC:23** *Split* | $12 | | B.T. Puppy 524 |
| | | | **UNITED STATES DOUBLE QUARTET: THE TOKENS   THE KIRBY STONE FOUR** | | | |
| 4/26/69 | 118 | 3 | 8 Go Away Little Girl/Young Girl ........................ *I Want To Make Love To You* | $8 | | Warner 7280 |
| | | | medley: **Steve Lawrence** #1/'63 and Union Gap #2/'68 | | | |
| | | | **TO KOOL CHRIS** ⊙ | | | |
| | | | Male DJ/producer from Mexico. | | | |
| 4/5/97 | 122 | 1 | Esta Loca ........................ *(3 versions)* | $3 | ■ | Scotti Brothers 78112 |
| | | | Anastasia Gomez (female vocal); title is Spanish for "She's Crazy" | | | |
| | | | **TOM & JERRIO**        **HOT/R&B** | | | |
| | | | R&B dance duo: Robert "Tommy Dark" Tharp and Jerry "Jerryo" Murray. Tharp was a baritone in **The Ideals** vocal group from 1952-65. | | | |
| 8/14/65 | 123 | 1 | Great Goo-Ga-Moo-Ga ........................ *Come On And Love Me* | $8 | | ABC-Paramount 10704 |
| | | | **TOMMY TUTONE**        **HOT/ROK** | | | |
| | | | Rock band formed in San Francisco in 1978: Tommy Heath (vocals), Jim Keller (guitar), Jon Lyons (bass) and Victor Carberry (drums). | | | |
| 7/24/82 | 101[1] | 5 | Which Man Are You ........................ *Only One* | $4 | | Columbia 03002 |
| | | | **TOMPALL — see GLASER, Tompall** | | | |
| | | | **TOMS, Gary**        **R&B/HOT** | | | |
| | | | Leader of a disco band formed in 1973 in New York City. | | | |
| 10/16/76 | 109 | 1 | Stand Up And Shout ........................ **R&B:53** *Party Hardy* | $5 | | p.i.p. 6524 |
| | | | **TOM TOM CLUB**        **ROK/R&B/HOT** | | | |
| | | | Studio project formed by **Talking Heads** members/husband-and-wife Chris Frantz and Tina Weymouth. | | | |
| 5/15/82 | 105 | 3 | 1 Wordy Rappinghood ........................ *(You Don't Stop) Wordy Rappinghood* [N] | $5 | | Sire 50067 |
| 9/17/83 | 106 | 3 | 2 The Man With The 4-Way Hips ........................ *(dub version)* | $5 | ■ | Sire 29549 |

| DEBUT | PEAK | WKS | A-side (Chart Hit)..........................................................................................................B-side | $ | Pic | Label & Number |
|---|---|---|---|---|---|---|

**TONEY, Oscar Jr.** HOT/R&B
Born on 5/26/39 in Selma, Alabama. Own R&B group, The Searchers, first recorded for Max in 1957.

| 10/14/67 | 120 | 3 | You Can Lead Your Woman To The Altar ......................................... *Unlucky Guy* | $10 | | Bell 688 |

**TONYA** ○ R&B
Born LaTonya Youngblood in Prentiss, Mississippi. Female R&B singer.

| 7/26/97 | 106 | 5 | I've Been Having An Affair............................................................**R&B:38** *(Part 2)* | $3 | ■ | J-Town/Malaco 2318 |

**TONY TONI TONÉ** R&B/HOT
R&B-funk trio from Oakland: Brothers Dwayne and Raphael (Saadiq) Wiggins, with cousin Timothy Christian.

| 8/20/94 | 107 | 8 | Slow Wine........................................ **R&B:21** *(edit) / It Never Rains (In Southern California)* | $3 | ■ | Wing 853476 |

**TOO DOWN** ○
White rap duo: Kid K and Rock G.

| 4/10/93 | 111 | 6 | The Oceanfront ................................................................... *(instrumental)* | $3 | ■ | Danzalot 13887 |
| | | | samples "I'm Your Puppet" by **James & Bobby Purify** | | | |

**TORNADOES, The** HOT/R&B
British surf-rock instrumental quintet featuring Alan Caddy (lead guitar), George Bellamy (rhythm guitar) and Roger Jackson (keyboards).

| 2/23/63 | 119 | 1 | Like Locomotion ............................................................... *Globetrottin'* [I] | $20 | | London 9579 |

**TORNADOES, The** ○
Instrumental surf-rock group formed in Redlands, California in 1959 featuring brothers Gerald and Norman Sanders.

| 10/13/62 | 102 | 6 | Bustin' Surfboards .................................................... *Beyond The Surf* [I] | $25 | | Aertaun 100 |

**TOROK, Mitchell** HOT/C&W/MEM/R&B
Born on 10/28/29 in Houston. Country singer/songwriter/guitarist. First recorded in 1948.

| 11/2/59 | 102 | 3 | Mexican Joe ................................................................. *You Are The One* | $15 | | Guyden 2028 |
| | | | #1 Country hit for **Jim Reeves** in 1953 | | | |

**TORONTO**
Rock quartet from Toronto: Holly Woods (vocals), Sheron Alton and Brian Allen (guitars), and Scott Kreyer (keyboards).

| 9/13/80 | 104 | 2 | Even The Score ................................................................ *Tie Me Down* | $5 | | A&M 2255 |

**TOTAL DEVASTATION** ○ R&B
San Francisco rap trio: Tuff Cut Tim, Tone and Freakin' Puertrican B-Fresh.

| 8/7/93 | 103 | 15 | Many Clouds Of Smoke ................... **Sls:75 /R&B:95** *(instrumental)* | $3 | ■ | PGA/Arista 12624 |
| | | | first released on PGA 005 in 1993 | | | |

**TOTO** HOT/AC/ROK/R&B
Rock group formed in Los Angeles in 1978: Bobby Kimball (vocals), Steve Lukather (guitar), David Paich and Steve Porcaro (keyboards), David Hungate (bass) and Jeff Porcaro (drums; d: 8/5/92).

| 3/7/81 | 107 | 1 | Goodbye Elenore ................................................................. *Turn Back* | $5 | | Columbia 11437 |

**TOWER OF POWER** R&B/HOT/AC
Interracial R&B-funk band formed in 1968 in Oakland featuring vocalist Lenny Williams.

| 9/1/73 | 107 | 3 | 1 Sparkling In The Sand ..................................... *Back On The Streets Again* | $8 | | San Francisco 64 |
| 3/1/75 | 102 | 2 | 2 Only So Much Oil In The Ground ..........................**R&B:85** *Give Me The Proof* | $5 | | Warner 8055 |
| 7/22/78 | 106 | 3 | 3 Lovin' You Is Gonna See Me Thru ...........................**R&B:98** *I Am A Fool* | $5 | | Columbia 10718 |

**TOWNES, Carol Lynn** R&B/HOT
New York-based disco singer. Lead singer of Fifth Avenue.

| 3/16/85 | 109 | 1 | 1 Believe In The Beat.............................**R&B:65** *E. Latin Boogie* (Ollie E. Brown) | $4 | | Polydor 881413 |
| | | | from the movie *Breakin' 2: Electric Boogaloo* starring Lucinda Dickey | | | |
| 7/27/85 | 106 | 1 | 2 I Freak For You ............................................... *I Want A Man Like You* | $4 | | Polydor 881953 |

**TOWNSEND, Ed** HOT/R&B
Born on 4/16/29 in Fayetteville, Tennessee. R&B singer/songwriter. Wrote **Marvin Gaye's** "Let's Get It On."

| 8/3/59 | 106 | 3 | 1 Hold On.......................................................... *This Little Love Of Mine* | $20 | | Capitol 4240 |
| 10/24/60 | 101[1] | 4 | 2 Stay With Me (A Little While Longer) ............ *I Love Everything About You* | $20 | | Warner 5174 |
| | | | **ED TOWNSEND With The Townsmen** | | | |
| | | | René Hall (orch.) | | | |
| 12/18/61 | 114 | 1 | 3 And Then Came Love ........................................ *Little Bitty Dave* | $20 | | Challenge 9129 |

**TOWNSHEND, Pete** ROK/HOT
Born on 5/19/45 in London. Lead guitarist/songwriter of The Who.

| 8/7/82 | 105 | 5 | Face Dances Part Two.......................................**ROK:15** *Man Watching* | $4 | ■ | Atco 99989 |

**TOYS, The** HOT/R&B
Female R&B vocal trio from Jamaica, New York: Barbara Harris, June Montiero and Barbara Parritt.

| 5/7/66 | 111 | 2 | 1 Silver Spoon ..................................................*Can't Get Enough Of You Baby* | $15 | | DynoVoice 219 |
| | | | adaptation of Beethoven's *Piano Sonata No. 8* | | | |
| 7/6/68 | 112 | 3 | 2 Sealed With A Kiss ...............................**R&B:43** *I Got My Heart Set On You* | $12 | | Musicor 1319 |
| | | | #3 hit for **Brian Hyland** in 1962 | | | |

**TRACEY, Norma, And The Cinderella Kids** ○
Born in 1955 in Philadelphia. Discovered by **Bobby Rydell**.

| 1/30/65 | 107 | 4 | Leroy ............................................*Harpsichord Blues* (Big J.J.) [N] | $15 | | Day Dell 1005 |
| | | | based on the "Ken-L Ration" dog food jingle "My Dog's Better Than Your Dog" | | | |

**TRADE WINDS, The** HOT
New York City pop singing/songwriting/production duo: Pete Anders (Andreoli) and Vinnie Poncia.

| 5/1/65 | 129 | 1 | 1 The Girl From Greenwich Village .................... *There's A Rock & Roll Show In Town* | $25 | | Red Bird 10-028 |
| 12/24/66 | 132 | 1 | 2 Catch Me In The Meadow ..........................................*I Believe In Her* | $15 | | Kama Sutra 218 |

**TRAFFIC** HOT/ROK
British rock band: Steve Winwood (keyboards, guitar), Dave Mason (guitar), Jim Capaldi (drums) and Chris Wood (sax; d: 7/12/83).

| 10/26/68 | 123 | 3 | Feelin' Alright?.......................................................... *Withering Tree* | $10 | | United Artists 50460 |
| | | | #33 hit for **Joe Cocker** in 1972 | | | |

| DEBUT | PEAK | WKS | | A-side (Chart Hit)............................................................................B-side | $ | Pic | Label & Number |
|---|---|---|---|---|---|---|---|
| | | | | **TRAMMPS, The**     R&B/HOT | | | |
| | | | | Philadelphia disco group. Key members: Jimmy Ellis (lead tenor), Earl Young (lead bass), Harold and Stanley Wade (tenors) and Robert Upchurch (baritone). Own Golden Fleece label in 1973. | | | |
| 10/7/72 | 108 | 2 | 1 | Sixty Minute Man .................................................. *Scrub Board* | $8 | | Buddah 321 |
| | | | | #1 R&B hit for The Dominoes in 1951 | | | |
| 11/16/74 | 101[1] | 1 | 2 | Trusting Heart     R&B:72 *Down Three Dark Streets* | $8 | | Golden Fleece 3255 |
| 11/20/76 | 105 | 7 | 3 | Ninety-Nine And A Half.......................R&B:76 *Can We Come Together* | $5 | | Atlantic 3365 |
| | | | | #53 hit for **Wilson Pickett** in 1966 | | | |
| 7/2/77 | 105 | 4 | 4 | I Feel Like I've Been Livin' (On The Dark Side Of The Moon)....................................R&B:52 *Don't Burn Your Bridges* | $5 | | Atlantic 3403 |
| 12/24/77 | 104 | 4 | 5 | The Night The Lights Went Out ...........R&B:80 *I'm So Glad You Came Along* | $5 | | Atlantic 3442 |
| | | | | **TRASH** ✪ | | | |
| | | | | Scottish rock group originally known as White Trash. | | | |
| 11/15/69 | 112 | 1 | | Golden Slumbers/Carry That Weight ....................... *Trash Can* | $20 | | Apple 1811 |
| | | | | originally recorded by **The Beatles** on their 1969 *Abbey Road* album | | | |
| | | | | **TRASHMEN, The**     HOT | | | |
| | | | | Surf-rock quartet from Minneapolis: Tony Andreason, Dal Winslow, Bob Reed and Steve Wahrer (d: 1/21/89). | | | |
| 5/16/64 | 124 | 2 | | Bad News ................................................. *On The Move* [I] | $20 | | Garrett 4005 |
| | | | | **TRASK, Diana** ✪     C&W | | | |
| | | | | Born on 6/23/40 in Melbourne, Australia. Country singer. Moved to the U.S. in 1959. | | | |
| 12/6/69 | 114 | 2 | 1 | I Fall To Pieces ................................C&W:37 *Long Ago Is Gone* | $6 | | Dot 17316 |
| | | | | #12 hit for **Patsy Cline** in 1961 | | | |
| 6/1/74 | 101[2] | 5 | 2 | Lean It All On Me     C&W:13 *The King* | $5 | | Dot 17496 |
| | | | | **TRAVERS, Mary**     AC/HOT | | | |
| | | | | Born on 11/7/37 in Louisville. Member of the folk trio **Peter, Paul & Mary**. | | | |
| 3/10/73 | 122 | 3 | | Too Many Mondays ....................... *That Year There Was No Winter* | $5 | | Warner 7675 |
| | | | | **TRAVIS & BOB**     HOT/R&B | | | |
| | | | | Travis Pritchett and Bob Weaver from Jackson, Alabama. | | | |
| 7/13/59 | 114 | 1 | | Little Bitty Johnny ...................................... *Teenage Vision* | $20 | | Sandy 1019 |
| | | | | **TRAVOLTA, John**     HOT/AC | | | |
| | | | | Born on 2/18/54 in Englewood, New Jersey. Actor/singer. Starred in the 1970's movies *Saturday Night Fever* and *Grease*. Huge comeback in the 1994 movie *Pulp Fiction*. | | | |
| 9/3/77 | 106 | 2 | | (Feel So Good) Slow Dancing ....................... *Moonlight Lady* | $4 | ■ | Midsong Int'l. 10977 |
| | | | | **TREMELOES, The**     HOT | | | |
| | | | | British pop-rock quartet: Alan Blakely and Ricky West (guitars), Len "Chip" Hawkes (bass) and Dave Munden (drums). | | | |
| 6/1/68 | 122 | 2 | 1 | Helule Helule ....................................... *Girl From Nowhere* | $8 | | Epic 10328 |
| 10/26/68 | 127 | 1 | 2 | My Little Lady .................................... *All The World To Me* | $8 | | Epic 10376 |
| | | | | **TRENT, Jackie** ✪ | | | |
| | | | | British female vocalist. Married to record producer Tony Hatch, with whom she co-wrote several of Petula Clark's hits. | | | |
| 4/25/64 | 106 | 4 | | If You Love Me, Really Love Me.......................... *Only One Such As You* | $12 | | Kapp 583 |
| | | | | a Phil Spector-styled production; #4 hit for Kay Starr in 1954 | | | |
| | | | | **TRIBE** ✪ | | | |
| | | | | Dance trio featuring female vocalist Cinzia Mella. | | | |
| 12/16/95 | 123 | 1 | | So In Love ................................................ *Just You & I* | $3 | ■ | Ti Amo 909 |
| | | | | **TRIBE CALLED QUEST, A**     R&B/HOT | | | |
| | | | | New York rap outfit: Jonathan "Q-Tip" Davis, Ali Shaheed Muhammad and Malik "Phife" Taylor. | | | |
| 6/25/94 | 102 | 6 | 1 | Oh My God ....................R&B:69 *Lyrics To Go / One Two S**t* (w/Busta Rhymes) | $3 | ■ | Jive 42212 |
| | | | | samples "Who's Gonna Take The Weight" by **Kool & The Gang** and "Absolutions" by Lee Morgan | | | |
| 12/28/96+ | 108 | 6 | 2 | Stressed Out.............................R&B:56 *(4 versions)* (w/Raphael Saadiq and Björk) | $6 | | Jive 42420 (**CD**) |
| | | | | **A TRIBE CALLED QUEST featuring Faith Evans** | | | |
| | | | | **TRILOGY**     HOT | | | |
| | | | | Hip-hop trio from the Bronx, New York: Duran Ramos, Angel DeLeon and Darrin Dewitt Henson. | | | |
| 12/5/92 | 118 | 6 | 1 | Good Time ........................................ *(Pop radio edit)* | $3 | ■ | Atco 98512 |
| 12/3/94 | 104 | 5 | 2 | Take A Toke ...........................................R&B:48 *(remix)* | $3 | ■ | Columbia 77741 |
| | | | | **C+C MUSIC FACTORY "featuring" Trilogy** | | | |
| | | | | **TRITT, Travis** ✪     C&W | | | |
| | | | | Born James Travis Tritt on 2/9/63 in Marietta, Georgia. Country singer. Joined the *Grand Ole Opry* in 1992. | | | |
| 6/12/93 | 108 | 6 | 1 | T-R-O-U-B-L-E.............................Sls:72 /C&W:13 *(single version)* | $3 | ■ | Warner 18496 |
| | | | | #35 hit for **Elvis Presley** in 1975 | | | |
| 5/21/94 | 112 | 12 | 2 | Foolish Pride .........................Sls:72 /C&W:❶[1] *No Vacation From The Blues* | $3 | ■ | Warner 18180 |
| 9/14/96 | 110 | 10 | 3 | More Than You'll Ever Know....................C&W:3 *Still In Love With You* (C&W #23/'98) | $3 | ■ | Warner 17606 |
| | | | | **TRIUMPH**     ROK/HOT | | | |
| | | | | Hard-rock trio from Toronto: Rik Emmett (guitar, vocals), Gil Moore (drums, vocals) and Mike Levine (keyboards, bass). | | | |
| 2/13/82 | 102 | 6 | | Say Goodbye .........................................ROK:50 *Allied Forces* | $4 | | RCA 13035 |
| | | | | **TROCCOLI, Kathy**     AC/HOT | | | |
| | | | | New York City native. Grammy-nominated Contemporary Christian artist. Backing singer with **Taylor Dayne**. | | | |
| 12/3/94 | 120 | 2 | | If I'm Not In Love ...................................AC:22 *Mission Of Love* | $3 | ■ | Reunion/RCA 64216 |
| | | | | **TROGGS, The**     HOT | | | |
| | | | | British rock quartet from Andover, England featuring Reg Presley (real name: Reg Ball; lead singer). | | | |
| 7/6/68 | 120 | 4 | 1 | You Can Cry If You Want To ...................... *There's Something About You* | $10 | | Fontana 1622 |
| 4/19/75 | 102 | 5 | 2 | Good Vibrations ...................................... *Push It Up To Me* | $6 | | Pye 71015 |
| | | | | #1 hit for **The Beach Boys** in 1966 | | | |

| DEBUT | PEAK | WKS | A-side (Chart Hit) / B-side | $ | Pic | Label & Number |
|---|---|---|---|---|---|---|
| | | | **TROLLS, The**      HOT | | | |
| | | | Four-man rock band from Illinois: Richard Clark, Richard Gallagher, Max Jordan Jr. and Kenneth Cortese (died in the same plane crash that killed **Jim Croce**). | | | |
| 6/15/68 | 129 | 1 | **I Got To Have Ya** ...................................................... *Don't Come Around* | $20 | | U.S.A. 905 |
| | | | **TROWER, Robin**      ROK/HOT | | | |
| | | | Born on 3/9/45 in London. Rock guitarist. Original member of **Procol Harum**. | | | |
| 4/21/73 | 109 | 4 | 1 **Man Of The World** ...................................................... *Take A Fast Train* | $6 | | Chrysalis 2009 |
| 1/13/79 | 110 | 1 | 2 **My Love (Burning Love)** ...................................................... *Sail On* | $5 | | Chrysalis 2238 |
| | | | **TROY, Doris**      HOT/R&B | | | |
| | | | Born Doris Higginson on 1/6/37 in New York City. R&B vocalist/songwriter. The off-Broadway musical *Mama, I Want To Sing* is based on her life. | | | |
| 11/2/63 | 102 | 6 | 1 **What'cha Gonna Do About It/** | | | |
| 10/19/63 | 118 | 2 | 2    **Tomorrow Is Another Day** ...................................................... | $12 | | Atlantic 2206 |
| 3/28/64 | 128 | 2 | 3 **Please Little Angel** ...................................................... *One More Chance* | $12 | | Atlantic 2222 |
| | | | written by **Ashford & Simpson** | | | |
| | | | **TUBES**      HOT/ROK | | | |
| | | | Rock troupe formed in San Francisco featuring Fee Waybill (vocals). | | | |
| 10/10/81 | 101[2] | 5 | **Talk To Ya Later**      ROK:7 *Power Tools* | $4 | | Capitol 5016 |
| | | | **TUCKER, Marshall — see MARSHALL** | | | |
| | | | **TUCKER, Tanya**      C&W/HOT/AC | | | |
| | | | Born on 10/10/58 in Seminole, Texas; raised in Wilcox, Arizona. Country singer. | | | |
| 7/1/78 | 105 | 2 | 1 **Save Me**      C&W:86 *Slippin' Away* | $5 | ■ | MCA 40902 |
| | | | Tucker's plea to "save the seals" from slaughter | | | |
| 4/7/79 | 103 | 6 | 2 **Lover Goodbye** ...................................................... *I'm The Singer, You're The Song* (C&W #18) | $4 | | MCA 41005 |
| | | | written by Phil Everly of **The Everly Brothers** | | | |
| 3/27/93 | 112 | 5 | 3 **It's A Little Too Late** .................. C&W:2 *Cadillac Ranch* (Chris Ledoux-C&W #18) | $3 | ▌ | Liberty 44915 |
| 5/17/97 | 114 | 5 | 4 **Little Things** ...................................................... C&W:9 *Two Sparrows In A Hurricane* (C&W #2/'92) | $3 | ▌ | Capitol 58630 |
| | | | **TUCKER, Tommy**      HOT/R&B | | | |
| | | | Born Robert Higginbotham on 3/5/39 in Springfield, Ohio. Died of poisoning on 1/22/82. R&B vocalist/pianist. First recorded for Hi in 1959. | | | |
| 7/17/65 | 103 | 3 | **Alimony** ...................................................... *All About Melanie* | $12 | | Checker 1112 |
| | | | **TURALÉ, Nick** ☻ | | | |
| | | | R&B singer/keyboardist from Dallas. | | | |
| 8/10/96 | 107 | 1 | **Another Day** ...................................................... *(3 mixes)* | $3 | ▌ | D-Town 1001 |
| | | | **TURBANS, The**      R&B/HOT | | | |
| | | | Philadelphia R&B quartet: Al Banks (lead), Matthew Platt (tenor), Charles Williams (baritone) and Andrew "Chet" Jones (bass). | | | |
| 4/17/61 | 114 | 2 | **When You Dance** ...................................................... *Golden Rings* [R] | $30 | | Parkway 820 |
| | | | new version of tune that made the *Hot 100* (#33) on 11/12/55 on Herald 458 | | | |
| | | | **TURNER, Ike & Tina**      R&B/HOT | | | |
| | | | Husband-and-wife R&B duo: guitarist Ike Turner (b: 11/5/31 in Clarksdale, Mississippi) and vocalist Tina Turner. Married from 1958-76. Ike did prolific session, production and guitar work during the 1950s. In 1960, developed a dynamic stage show around Tina; "The Ike & Tina Turner Revue" featuring her backing vocalists, **The Ikettes**, and Ike's Kings Of Rhythm. Duo inducted into the Rock and Roll Hall of Fame in 1991. *Top Pop Singles:* 20. | | | |
| 2/27/61 | 117 | 1 | 1 **I'm Jealous** ...................................................... *You're My Baby* | $20 | | Sue 740 |
| 2/8/64 | 122 | 2 | 2 **You Can't Miss Nothing That You Never Had** ...................... *God Gave Me You* | $15 | | Sonja 2005 |
| | | | charted for 1 week on 2/8/64 and 1 week on 5/9/64 | | | |
| 2/27/65 | 108 | 6 | 3 **Tell Her I'm Not Home** ...................................................... R&B:33 *I'm Thru With Love* | $15 | | Loma 2011 |
| | | | female version of **Chuck Jackson**'s 1963 hit "Tell Him I'm Not Home" | | | |
| 6/5/65 | 107 | 6 | 4 **Good Bye, So Long** ...................................................... R&B:32 *Hurt Is All You Gave Me* | $15 | | Modern 1007 |
| 8/7/65 | 134 | 1 | 5 **I Don't Need** ...................................................... *Gonna Have Fun* | $15 | | Modern 1012 |
| 7/1/67 | 114 | 5 | 6 **I'll Never Need More Than This** ...................... *The Cash Box Blues or (Oops, We Printed The Wrong Story Again)* | $15 | | Philles 135 |
| 3/30/68 | 117 | 4 | 7 **So Fine** ...................................................... R&B:50 *So Blue Over You* | $15 | | Innis 6667 |
| | | | **IKE AND TINA And THE IKETTES** | | | |
| | | | #11 hit for **The Fiestas** in 1959 | | | |
| 10/18/69 | 112 | 3 | 8 **River Deep-Mountain High** ...................................................... *I'll Keep You Happy* [R] | $12 | | A&M 1118 |
| | | | originally made the *Hot 100* (#88) on 5/28/66 on Philles 131; #6 & 8: produced by Phil Spector | | | |
| 10/18/69 | 126 | 2 | 9 **I Know** ...................................................... *Bold Soul Sister* (Hot #59) | $7 | | Blue Thumb 104 |
| | | | #3 hit for **Barbara George** in 1962 | | | |
| 11/7/70 | 105 | 4 | 10 **Workin' Together** ...................................................... R&B:41 *The Way You Love Me* | $7 | | Liberty 56207 |
| 7/31/71 | 120 | 1 | 11 **I've Been Loving You Too Long** ...................................................... *Crazy 'Bout You Baby* [R] | $7 | | Blue Thumb 202 |
| | | | originally made the *Hot 100* (#68) on 4/26/69 on Blue Thumb 101; #21 hit for **Otis Redding** in 1965 | | | |
| 11/13/71 | 104 | 3 | 12 **I'm Yours (Use Me Anyway You Wanna)** ...................................................... R&B:47 *Doin' It* | $6 | | United Artists 50837 |
| 5/4/74 | 106 | 1 | 13 **Sweet Rhode Island Red** ...................................................... R&B:43 *Get It Out Of Your Mind* | $6 | | United Artists 409 |
| | | | **TURNER, Joe**      R&B/MEM/HOT | | | |
| | | | Born on 5/18/11 in Kansas City, Missouri. Died of a heart attack on 11/24/85. Blues/R&B vocalist known as "Big Joe." Appeared in the movie *Shake, Rattle And Rock!* in 1957. Inducted into the Rock and Roll Hall of Fame in 1987 as a blues pioneer. | | | |
| 5/2/60 | 102 | 3 | **My Little Honey Dripper** ...................................................... *Chains Of Love* | $20 | | Atlantic 2054 |
| | | | inspired by Joe Liggins #1 1945 R&B hit "The Honeydripper" | | | |
| | | | **TURNER, Tina**      HOT/R&B/AC/ROK | | | |
| | | | Born Anna Mae Bullock on 11/26/38 in Brownsville, Tennessee. R&B-rock vocalist/actress. Half of **Ike & Tina Turner** duo. In movies *Tommy* and *Mad Max-Beyond Thunderdome*. | | | |
| 11/25/95 | 102 | 10 | 1 **Goldeneye** ...................................................... Sls:71 /R&B:89 *(3 mixes)* | $3 | ▌ | Virgin 38524 |
| | | | title song from the James Bond movie starring Pierce Brosnan; written by Bono & The Edge of **U2** | | | |
| 12/21/96+ | 101[2] | 15 | 2 **In Your Wildest Dreams**      R&B:34 *(3 mixes)* | $3 | ▌ | Virgin 38578 |
| | | | **TINA TURNER Featuring BARRY WHITE** | | | |

### TURNER, Titus
**HOT/R&B**
Born on 5/11/33 in Atlanta. Died on 9/13/84. R&B vocalist/songwriter. First recorded for Okeh in 1951.

| 4/10/61 | 115 | 1 | Pony Train ........................................................ *Bla, Bla, Bla Cha Cha Cha* | $15 | | Jamie 1177 |

Mort Garson (orch.); tune is similar to **Chubby Checker**'s #1 1961 hit "Pony Time"

### TURRENTINE, Stanley ☉
**R&B**
Born on 4/5/34 in Pittsburgh. Jazz fusion tenor saxophonist. Married for a time to Shirley Scott.

| 7/26/75 | 105 | 2 | Naked As The Day I Was Born ................................................. *Spaced* | $6 | | Fantasy 745 |

### TURTLES, The
Pop-folk-rock group formed in Los Angeles in 1961. Led by Mark Volman (b: 4/19/47, Los Angeles) and Howard Kaylan (born Howard Kaplan on 6/22/47, New York City). Many personnel changes except for Volman and Kaylan (also known as Flo & Eddie).

| 11/7/70 | 105 | 3 | Me About You ................................................... *Think I'll Run Away* | $8 | | White Whale 364 |

#83 hit for The Mojo Men in 1967

### TUXEDO JUNCTION
**AC/HOT**
Disco studio outfit of female vocalists assembled by producers W. Michael Lewis and Laurin Rinder.

| 8/12/78 | 103 | 3 | Moonlight Serenade ......................... **AC:42** *Volga Boatman* | $5 | | Butterfly 1210 |

#3 hit for Glenn Miller in 1939 (Miller's theme song)

### TWAIN, Shania
**C&W/HOT**
Born Eileen Regina Edwards on 8/28/65 in Windsor, Ontario. Country singer.

| 3/16/96 | 108 | 12 | You Win My Love ............... **C&W:❶²** *Home Ain't Where His Heart Is (Anymore)* (C&W #28) | $3 | ■ | Mercury 852138 |

### TWENNYNINE WITH LENNY WHITE
**R&B/HOT**
R&B-funk band from New York featuring Lenny White (drums; Return To Forever) and Donald Blackman (vocals).

| 11/29/80 | 106 | 1 | Kid Stuff ................................................ **R&B:19** *Slip Away* [N] | $4 | ■ | Elektra 47043 |

### TWICE AS MUCH ☉
British folk duo.

| 7/9/66 | 122 | 2 | Sittin' On A Fence .................................................. *Baby I Want You* | $15 | ■ | MGM 13530 |

written by Mick Jagger and Keith Richards (on **The Rolling Stones'** *Flowers* album)

### TWILLEY, Dwight
**HOT/ROK**
Born on 6/6/51 in Tulsa, Oklahoma. Rock singer/songwriter. Formed the Dwight Twilley Band with **Phil Seymour** (d: 8/17/93) in 1974.

| 11/1/75 | 103 | 2 | 1 You Were So Warm ................................................ *Sincerely* | $5 | ■ | Shelter 40450 |

**DWIGHT TWILLEY BAND**

| 3/27/82 | 106 | 2 | 2 Somebody To Love ................................. **ROK:14** *Later That Night* | $4 | | EMI America 8109 |

### TWINKLE ☉
British female vocalist. Real name: Lynn Annette Ripley.

| 1/23/65 | *110* | 4 | Terry .................................................... *The Boy Of My Dreams* | $15 | ☐ | Tollie 9040 |

### TWISTA
**R&B/HOT**
Twista is a male rapper from Chicago. Known as Tung Twista in 1992 when he was recognized as the world's fastest rapper by the Guinness Book of World Records.

| 4/26/97 | 101[1] | 17 | Emotions ................................. **Sls:69 /R&B:50** *(album version)* | $3 | ■ | Big Beat 98025 |

### TWISTED SISTER
**ROK/HOT**
Hard-rock group from Long Island, New York featuring Dee Snider (vocals).

| 1/5/85 | 107 | 2 | The Price ............................................ **ROK:19** *S.M.F.* | $4 | | Atlantic 89591 |

### TWITTY, Conway
**C&W/HOT/R&B/AC**
Born Harold Lloyd Jenkins on 9/1/33 in Friars Point, Mississippi. Died of an abdominal aneurysm on 6/5/93. Superstar country singer.
*Top Pop Singles:* 20.

| 9/12/60 | 106 | 3 | 1 What A Dream ................................... *Tell Me One More Time* | $20 | | MGM 12918 |

made the Country charts (#50) on 9/11/71 on MGM 14274; written by Chuck Willis; #1 R&B hit for Ruth Brown in 1954

| 10/16/61 | 107 | 1 | 2 Sweet Sorrow ..................................... *It's Drivin' Me Wild* | $15 | ■ | MGM 13034 |
| 4/17/71 | 105 | 8 | 3 How Much More Can She Stand ......... **C&W:❶¹** *Just Like A Stranger* | $7 | | Decca 32801 |
| 7/31/71 | 112 | 3 | 4 I Wonder What She'll Think About Me Leaving ................................... **C&W:4** *Heartache Just Walked In* | $7 | | Decca 32842 |

written by **Merle Haggard**

| 5/27/72 | 112 | 2 | 5 (Lost Her Love) On Our Last Date ......... **C&W:❶¹** *I'll Never Make It Home Tonight* | $7 | | Decca 32945 |

vocal version of **Floyd Cramer**'s #2 1960 hit "Last Date"

### 2 BAD MICE ☉
Techno-dance outfit.

| 12/10/94 | 123 | 1 | Bombscare ............................................ *(original version)* | $3 | ■ | Sm:)e 9003 |

### II D EXTREME
**R&B/HOT**
R&B trio from Washington, D.C.: D'Extra Wiley, Randy Gill (brother of **Johnny Gill**) and his cousin Jermaine Mickey.

| 10/23/93 | 103 | 16 | 1 Up On The Roof .............................. **Sls:69 /R&B:33** *(radio edit)* | $3 | ■ | Gasoline Alley 54738 |

#5 hit for The Drifters in 1963

| 6/8/96 | 117 | 3 | 2 If I Knew Then (What I Know Now) ............... **R&B:52** *Farewell...Love, D'Extra* | $3 | ■ | Gasoline Alley 55140 |

### 2 LIVE CREW, The
**R&B/HOT**
Miami-based rap outfit featuring Luther "**Luke Skyywalker**" Campbell (owner of Luke Records).

| 7/3/93 | 107 | 9 | 1 Work It Out! ................................. **Sls:74 /R&B:58** *(dirty version)* | $3 | ■ | Luke 162 |

**LUKE**

| 3/1/97 | 107 | 10 | 2 Do The Damn Thing ................... **R&B:75** *(4 versions) / (album snippets)* | $3 | ■ | Lil' Joe 893 |

### 2 OF CLUBS
**HOT**
Duo of Patti Valantine and Linda Parrish (former wife of Carl Edmonson, leader of The Dolphins).

| 10/8/66 | 125 | 2 | Heart ...................................................... *My First Heart Break* | $12 | | Fraternity 972 |

### 2 UNLIMITED
**HOT**
Techno-house duo from Amsterdam: Ray "Kid Ray" Slijngaard (b: 6/28/71) and Anita Dells (b: 12/25/71).

| 8/14/93 | 104 | 9 | Tribal Dance ............................................ *(no rap edit)* | $3 | ■ | Critique 15508 |

## TWO — also see TO KOOL / TOO DOWN

## TYLER, Bonnie
HOT/AC/C&W/ROK

Born Gaynor Hopkins on 6/8/53 in Swansea, Wales. Worked local clubs until the mid-1970s.

| 8/19/78 | 103 | 4 | 1 If I Sing You A Love Song ..........................................................................*Heaven* | $5 | ■ | RCA 11349 |
| 2/24/79 | 107 | 1 | 2 My Guns Are Loaded ........................................................ C&W:86 *Baby I Just Love You* | $5 | | RCA 11468 |

## TYMES, The
HOT/R&B/AC

R&B group formed in Philadelphia in 1956: George Williams (lead), George Hilliard, Donald Banks, Albert Berry and Norman Burnett.

| 3/21/64 | 124 | 1 | Wonderland Of Love ................................................... *To Each His Own* (Hot #78) | $15 | ■ | Parkway 908 |

## TYPICALLY TROPICAL ⊘
Group of British session musicians assembled by Jeffrey Calvert and Max West.

| 10/11/75 | 108 | 1 | Barbados ............................................................................................... *Sandy* | $10 | | Gull 6004 |

## TYSON, Roy ⊘
Twelve-year-old R&B singer.

| 12/7/63 | 106 | 2 | Oh What A Night For Love ........................................ *Not Too Young To Sing The Blues* | $75 | | Double-L 723 |

written by Lloyd Price

## TZUKE, Judie ⊘
Pronounced: ZOOK. British pop singer/songwriter.

| 12/22/79+ | 101[1] | 8 | Stay With Me Till Dawn               AC:47 *New Friends Again* | $5 | | Rocket/MCA 41133 |

# U

## UFO ⊘
ROK

British hard-rock group led by Phil Mogg (vocals) and Michael Schenker (guitar; left by 1980 to form own group).

| 8/20/77 | 106 | 3 | Too Hot To Handle.......................................................................... *Electric Phase* | $6 | ■ | Chrysalis 2157 |

## ULTRA ⊘

| 1/1/94 | 125 | 1 | Believe Me Baby .......................................................................................*Swingline* | $3 | ▌ | Urge 741003 |

## ULTRAVOX
ROK/HOT

British electronic-rock quartet: Midge Ure (vocals, guitar), Billy Currie (synthesizer, piano), Chris Cross (bass) and Warren Cann (drums).

| 7/7/84 | 108 | 2 | Dancing With Tears In My Eyes .................................................................. *Building* | $4 | ■ | Chrysalis 42781 |

## UNCHAINED MYNDS, The ⊘
Rock band from La Crosse, Wisconsin — Randy Purdy, lead singer.

| 4/12/69 | 115 | 3 | We Can't Go On This Way ........................................... *Going Back To Miami* | $10 | | Buddah 111 |

originally released on Teen Town 109 in 1969 ($25)

## UNDERDOGS, The ⊘
Rock and roll band.

| 2/4/67 | 122 | 4 | Love's Gone Bad ........................................................................ *Mo Jo Hanna* | $20 | | V.I.P. 25040 |

## UNDERGROUND SUNSHINE
HOT

Rock quartet based in Montello, Wisconsin featuring brothers Egbert "Berty" (vocals, bass) and Frank (drums) Kohl.

| 10/11/69 | 102 | 3 | Don't Shut Me Out ................................................................ *Take Me, Break Me* | $10 | | Intrepid 75012 |

written by David Gates of Bread

## UNDISPUTED TRUTH, The
R&B/HOT/AC

R&B vocal group consisting of Joe Harris, Billie Calvin and Brenda Evans. Many personnel changes from 1973-on.

| 11/18/72 | 107 | 3 | 1 Girl You're Alright.................................... R&B:43 *With A Little Help From My Friends* | $6 | | Gordy 7122 |
| 3/24/73 | 109 | 3 | 2 Mama I Got A Brand New Thing (Don't Say No).................................................... R&B:46 *Gonna Keep On Tryin' Till I Win Your Love* | $6 | | Gordy 7124 |
| 11/23/74 | 106 | 2 | 3 Lil' Red Ridin' Hood ......................................................... *Big John Is My Name* | $6 | | Gordy 7140 |
| 7/23/77 | 109 | 1 | 4 Sunshine........................................................................... *Hole In The Wall* | $5 | | Whitfield 8362 |

## UNIQUES, The
HOT

Southern pop quintet featuring country star Joe Stampley.

| 10/8/66 | 126 | 1 | 1 Run And Hide .................................................................. *Good Bye, So Long* | $10 | | Paula 245 |
| 10/12/68 | 115 | 3 | 2 How Lucky (Can One Man Be)...........................................*You Don't Miss Your Water* | $8 | | Paula 313 |

produced by Ray Stevens

| 8/2/69 | 105 | 3 | 3 Toys Are Made For Children............................................................. *My Babe* | $8 | | Paula 324 |
| 9/12/70 | 112 | 1 | 4 All These Things ...........................................*You Know That I Love You* [R] | $8 | | Paula 332 |

originally made the *Hot 100* (#97) on 7/2/66 on Paula 238; #1 Country hit for Joe Stampley in 1976

## UNITED STATES DOUBLE QUARTET — see TOKENS, The

## UNIT FOUR plus TWO
HOT/AC

British pop-rock sextet featuring Peter "The Count" Moules (vocals).

| 10/9/65 | 131 | 2 | Hark ..................................................................... *Stop Wasting Your Time* | $10 | | London 9790 |

## UNTOUCHABLES, The ⊘
R&B vocal quartet — Billy Storm, leader.

| 11/7/60 | 104 | 4 | 60 Minute Man ............................................................. *Everybody's Laughing* | $30 | | Madison 139 |

#1 R&B hit for The Dominoes in 1951

## UNV
R&B/HOT

Detroit R&B vocal quartet: brothers John and Shawn Powe, John Clay and Demetrius Peete.

| 10/9/93 | 102 | 9 | Straight From My Heart ...................... R&B:36 *Something's Goin' On* (remix) | $3 | ▌ | Maverick/Sire 18353 |

## UPROAR ⊘
Pop/rock band.

| 6/24/78 | 105 | 3 | Drifting Away (I've Been Drifting Away) ......................................... *One Of The Boys* | $10 | | East Coast 1065 |

| DEBUT | PEAK | WKS | A-side (Chart Hit)........B-side | $ | Pic | Label & Number |
|---|---|---|---|---|---|---|
| | | | **URIAH HEEP**        HOT/ROK | | | |
| | | | British hard-rock band featuring David Byron (vocals; d: 2/28/85), Mick Box (guitar) and Ken Hensley (keyboards; later with **Blackfoot**). | | | |
| 9/25/82 | 106 | 4 | That's The Way That It Is ................................ROK:25 *Son Of A Bitch* | $5 | ■ | Mercury 76177 |
| | | | **USHER**        R&B/HOT | | | |
| | | | Born Usher Raymond on 10/14/78 in Chattanooga, Tennessee. Male vocal protege of producers/songwriters L.A. Reid and **Babyface**. | | | |
| 7/1/95 | 109 | 10 | The Many Ways ............................... Sls:73 /R&B:42 *(instrumental)* | $3 | ▮ | LaFace 24105 |
| | | | Al B. Sure! (backing vocal) | | | |
| | | | **U2**        ROK/HOT/AC | | | |
| | | | Rock band formed in 1976 in Dublin, Ireland: Paul "Bono" Hewson (vocals), Dave "The Edge" Evans (guitar), Adam Clayton (bass) and Larry Mullen, Jr. (drums). *Top Pop Singles*: 24. | | | |
| 7/2/83 | 101² | 4 | 1 Two Hearts Beat As One ................ROK:12 *Endless Deep* | $6 | ■ | Island 99861 |
| 11/13/93 | 103 | 3 | 2 Lemon ........................ Air:71 /ROK:3 *(4 versions)* | $6 | ■ | Island 862957 (T) |
| 12/13/97 | 103 | 11 | 3 Please ....................ROK:31 *Please / Where The Streets Have No Name / With Or Without You / Staring At The Sun (all live versions)* | $6 | | Island 572195 (CD) |

# V

| DEBUT | PEAK | WKS | A-side (Chart Hit)........B-side | $ | Pic | Label & Number |
|---|---|---|---|---|---|---|
| | | | **VALE, Jerry**        AC/HOT/MEM/POP | | | |
| | | | Born Genaro Vitaliano on 7/8/32 in the Bronx, New York. Pop ballad singer. | | | |
| 8/10/63 | 118 | 2 | 1 Old Cape Cod ............................. *Theme For Young Lovers (Where Is My Someone)* | $7 | | Columbia 42826 |
| | | | #3 hit for **Patti Page** in 1957 | | | |
| 2/15/64 | 123 | 1 | 2 On And On ...................... *The Peking Theme (So Little Time)* | $7 | | Columbia 42951 |
| | | | adapted from Offenbach's classical piece "Barcarolle"; also see **Eddy Arnold**'s "Please Don't Go" | | | |
| 10/16/65 | 118 | 4 | 3 Deep In Your Heart     AC:16 *If It Isn't In Your Heart* | $6 | | Columbia 43413 |
| | | | from the musical *Drat! The Cat!* | | | |
| 7/23/66 | 120 | 1 | 4 It'll Take A Little Time ................ AC:14 *Palermo* | $6 | | Columbia 43696 |
| 1/7/67 | 132 | 1 | 5 I've Lost My Heart Again .............. AC:32 *Somewhere* | $6 | | Columbia 43895 |
| 4/22/67 | 126 | 4 | 6 Time Alone Will Tell (Non Pensare A Me) ........ AC:6 *So Near...Yet So Far* | $6 | | Columbia 44087 |
| | | | #94 hit for **Connie Francis** in 1967 | | | |
| | | | **VALENTINOS**        HOT/R&B | | | |
| | | | Cleveland family R&B group: **Bobby Womack** and his brothers Cecil, Curtis, Friendly Jr. and Harris. | | | |
| 4/14/73 | 109 | 1 | I Can Understand It-Part I ................................ *Part II* | $10 | | Clean 60005 |
| | | | #35 hit for **The New Birth** in 1973 | | | |
| | | | **VALERIE & NICK — see ASHFORD & SIMPSON** | | | |
| | | | **VALLEY, Jim** ☺ | | | |
| | | | Guitarist with **The Viceroys**, **Paul Revere And The Raiders**, and Don and The Goodtimes. | | | |
| 8/12/67 | 106 | 4 | Try, Try, Try ................................ *Invitation* | $10 | ■ | Dunhill 4096 |
| | | | **VALLI, Frankie**        HOT/AC/R&B | | | |
| | | | Born Francis Castellucio on 5/3/37 in Newark, New Jersey. Lead singer of **The 4 Seasons**. | | | |
| 10/30/65 | 128 | 2 | 1 The Sun Ain't Gonna Shine (Anymore) ............... *This Is Goodbye* | $12 | | Smash 1995 |
| | | | #13 hit for The Walker Bros. in 1966 | | | |
| 4/30/66 | 112 | 4 | 2 You're Ready Now .................... *Cry For Me* | $12 | | Smash 2037 |
| 4/30/77 | 108 | 2 | 3 Easily ....................... AC:26 *What Good Am I Without You* | $6 | | Private Stock 45,140 |
| | | | **VALRAYS, The** ☺ | | | |
| 5/9/64 | 121 | 1 | Yo Me Pregunto (I Ask Myself) .................... *Tonky* [F] | $20 | | Parkway 904 |
| | | | **VANCE, Vince, & The Valiants** ☺        C&W | | | |
| | | | Vocal and novelty group from New Orleans. Lead vocals by Vance, Kate Carlin, Gerra Adkins, Chrislynn Lee and Lisa Layne. | | | |
| 11/1/80 | 101³ | 3 | Bomb Iran     *Bye-Bye, Baby* [N] | $7 | | Paid 109 |
| | | | parody of **The Beach Boys**' "Barbara-Ann"; first released on Towel 1000 in 1980 ($15) | | | |
| | | | **VANDROSS, Luther**        R&B/HOT/AC | | | |
| | | | Born on 4/20/51 in New York City. R&B singer/producer/songwriter. Much songwriting and production work for other artists. *Top Pop Singles*: 23. | | | |
| 5/29/76 | 102 | 5 | 1 It's Good For The Soul - Pt. I ................ R&B:28 *Pt. II* | $6 | | Cotillion 44200 |
| | | | LUTHER | | | |
| 1/16/82 | 107 | 2 | 2 Don't You Know That? ....................R&B:10 *I've Been Working* | $4 | | Epic 02658 |
| 10/16/82 | 101¹ | 10 | 3 If This World Were Mine    R&B:4 *I Just Wanna Be Your Fantasy (Lynn)* | $4 | | Columbia 03204 |
| | | | CHERYL LYNN (With Luther Vandross) | | | |
| | | | #68 hit for **Marvin Gaye** & Tammi Terrell in 1968 | | | |
| 1/14/84 | 102 | 3 | 4 I'll Let You Slide ...................... R&B:9 *(instrumental)* | $4 | ■ | Epic 04231 |
| 6/29/85 | 101⁵ | 9 | 5 It's Over Now     R&B:4 *(instrumental)* | $4 | ■ | Epic 04944 |
| | | | **VAN DYKE, Dick**        HOT/AC | | | |
| 5/22/65 | 123 | 1 | Chim Chim Cheree ........................ *Step In Time* | $7 | ■ | Buena Vista 441 |
| | | | DICK VAN DYKE with THE JACK HALLORAN SINGERS | | | |
| | | | from the Walt Disney movie "Mary Poppins" starring Van Dyke; #81 hit for **The New Christy Minstrels** in 1965 | | | |
| | | | **VAN DYKE, Earl** ☺ | | | |
| | | | Born in 1929. Died on 9/18/92 (age 62). R&B keyboardist. Leader of Motown's studio band in the 1960s. | | | |
| 5/3/69 | 114 | 2 | Runaway Child, Running Wild ..................... *Gonna Give Her All The Love I've Got* [I] | $15 | | Soul 35059 |
| | | | #6 hit for **The Temptations** in 1969 | | | |

## VAN DYKE, Leroy
**C&W/HOT**
Born on 10/4/29 in Spring Fork, Missouri. Country singer. Former livestock auctioneer.

| 4/30/66 | 120 | 3 | You Couldn't Get My Love Back (If You Tried) ...................................(Now And Then There's) A Fool Such As I | $8 | | Warner 5807 |

## VAN DYKES, The
**R&B/HOT**
R&B trio formed in 1964 in Fort Worth, Texas: Rondalis Tandy (lead), Wenzon Mosley (tenor) and James May (baritone).

| 6/25/66 | 109 | 5 | I've Got To Go On Without You ..........................R&B:28 What Will I Do (If I Lose You) | $15 | | Mala 530 |

## VAN HALEN
**ROK/HOT**
Hard-rock band formed in 1974 in Pasadena, California: David Lee Roth (vocals), Eddie Van Halen (guitar), Michael Anthony (bass) and Alex Van Halen (drums). Sammy Hagar replaced Roth as lead singer in 1985. Top Pop Singles: 22.

| 8/1/81 | 110 | 1 | 1 So This Is Love? .........................................ROK:15 Hear About It Later | $4 | ■ | Warner 49751 |
| 5/15/93 | 111 | 6 | 2 Dreams...................................................Judgement Day | $3 | ▌ | Warner 18592 |

"live" version of #22 hit for Van Halen in 1986 on Warner 28702

## VAN HELDEN, Armand — see OLD SCHOOL JUNKIES

## VANILLA FUDGE
**HOT**
Psychedelic-rock quartet formed in New York in 1966: Mark Stein (lead singer, keyboards), Vinnie Martell (guitar), Tim Bogert (bassist) and Carmine Appice (drummer).

| 5/24/69 | 103 | 4 | 1 Some Velvet Morning ...................................................People | $8 | | Atco 6679 |

#26 hit for Nancy Sinatra & Lee Hazlewood in 1968

| 8/23/69 | 111 | 2 | 2 Need Love.......................................I Can't Make It Alone | $8 | | Atco 6703 |

## VANITY
**R&B/HOT**
Born Denise Mathews on 1/3/63 in Niagara, Canada. Lead singer of Vanity 6 (assembled by **Prince**). Model/actress.

| 10/2/82 | 101[7] | 15 | 1 Nasty Girl ........................................R&B:7 Drive Me Wild | $4 | | Warner 29908 |

**VANITY 6**

| 1/12/85 | 107 | 3 | 2 Mechanical Emotion ...............................R&B:23 Crazy Maybe | $4 | ■ | Motown 1767 |

Morris Day (backing vocal)

## VANN, Teddy
**HOT**
Pop-R&B singer/songwriter/producer. Also see **Darlene McCrea** and **The Wheels**.

| 3/7/60 | 104 | 7 | Cindy ...................................................I'm Waiting | $25 | | Triple-X 101 |

Abie Baker (orch.); #39 hit for **Trini Lopez** in 1966

## VANN, Tommy, and The Echoes ☉
Pop group from Baltimore.

| 3/12/66 | 103 | 5 | 1 Too Young ...........................................Give A Little Bit | $15 | | Academy 118 |

#1 hit for Nat "King" Cole in 1951; #13 hit for Donny Osmond in 1972

| 7/2/66 | 125 | 2 | 2 Pretty Flamingo...................................I'll Forget Her Tomorrow | $15 | | Academy 120 |

#29 hit for **Manfred Mann** in 1966

## VAN ZANT, Johnny, Band ☉
**ROK**
The younger brother of Ronnie (Lynyrd Skynyrd) and Donnie Van Zant (38 Special). Formed hard-rock quintet Van-Zant by 1985.

| 10/25/80 | 105 | 3 | 1 634-5789 .........................................Put My Trust In You | $4 | | Polydor 2126 |

#13 hit for **Wilson Pickett** in 1966

| 6/8/85 | 102 | 4 | 2 You've Got To Believe In Love ....................ROK:27 Lonely Girls | $4 | ■ | Geffen 29037 |

**VAN-ZANT**

## VAUGHAN, Sarah
**HOT/MEM/POP/R&B/AC**
Born on 3/27/24 in Newark, New Jersey. Died on 4/3/90. Jazz singer. Dubbed "The Divine One." With Billy Eckstine from 1944-45. Won Grammy's Lifetime Achievement Award in 1989. Pop Hits & Top Pop Singles: 33.

| 7/20/59 | 106 | 1 | 1 Misty ................................Broken-Hearted Melody (Hot #7) | $10 | | Mercury 71477 |

introduced by the Errol Garner Trio in 1954 on Mercury 70442; #12 hit for **Johnny Mathis** in 1959

| 4/18/60 | 103 | 4 | 2 Our Waltz ............................................Some Other Spring | $10 | | Mercury 71610 |

written and first recorded by David Rose in 1942 on Victor 27853

| 5/30/60 | 111 | 2 | 3 Ooh! What A Day! ..............................My Dear Little Sweetheart | $10 | | Roulette 4256 |
| 4/18/64 | 131 | 2 | 4 Bluesette .............................................You Got It Made | $8 | | Mercury 72249 |

introduced by Toots Thielemans in 1963 on ABC Paramount 10500

## VAUGHN, Billy, and His Orchestra
**HOT/AC**
Born Richard Vaughn on 4/12/19 in Glasgow, Kentucky. Died on 9/26/91. Organized The Hilltoppers vocal group in 1952. Music director (arranger/conductor) for Dot Records. Pop Hits & Top Pop Singles: 29.

| 7/6/59 | 102 | 4 | 1 All Nite Long .................................Blues Stay Away From Me [I] | $8 | | Dot 15960 |

tune is actually "Night Train"; #1 R&B hit for Jimmy Forest in 1952 (riff borrowed from Duke Ellington's 1946 tune "Happy-Go-Lucky Local")

| 11/16/59 | 105 | 2 | 2 (It's No) Sin .............................................After Hours [I] | $8 | | Dot 15993 |

#1 hit for Eddy Howard in 1951

| 2/1/60 | 103 | 4 | 3 Chop Sticks/ | [I] | | | |

traditional piano novelty tune written in 1877

| 1/18/60 | 110 | 2 | 4 You're The Only Star (In My Blue Heaven) ........................[I] | $8 | | Dot 16021 |

written in 1938 by Gene Autry

| 9/19/60 | 111 | 1 | 5 Old Cape Cod ........................The Sundowners (Hot #51) [I] | $8 | | Dot 16133 |

#3 hit for Patti Page in 1957

| 12/11/61 | 119 | 1 | 6 Everybody's Twisting Down In Mexico .............Melody In The Night [I] | $8 | | Dot 16295 |
| 10/27/62 | 107 | 2 | 7 Blue Flame/ | [I] | | | |

#5 hit for Woody Herman in 1941

| 11/3/62 | 115 | 2 | 8 Someone ......................................................[I] | $7 | | Dot 16397 |
| 6/22/63 | 131 | 1 | 9 Happy Cowboy .......................................Broken Doll [I] | $7 | | Dot 16477 |
| 1/2/65 | 120 | 6 | 10 Pearly Shells (Popo O Ewa) .........................Maybe [I] | $6 | | Dot 16664 |

#60 hit for Burl Ives in 1964

| 11/5/66 | 131 | 1 | 11 Tiny Bubbles ...............................Too Many Hot Tacos [I] | $6 | | Dot 16957 |

#57 hit for Don Ho in 1967

| 1/28/67 | 105 | 6 | 12 Sweet Maria ..........................AC:6 There Goes My Everything | $6 | | Dot 16985 |

**THE BILLY VAUGHN SINGERS**
#8 & 12: written by Bert Kaempfert

## VEE, Bobby
**HOT/AC/R&B**

Born Robert Velline on 4/30/43 in Fargo, North Dakota. One of America's top teen-idols of the early '60s. First recorded for Soma in 1959. *Top Pop Singles:* 38.

| DEBUT | PEAK | WKS | A-side | B-side | $ | Pic | Label & Number |
|---|---|---|---|---|---|---|---|
| 5/23/60 | 112 | 1 | 1 **One Last Kiss** ....................................... *Laurie* | | $20 | | Liberty 55251 |
| | | | from the Broadway musical *Bye Bye Birdie* starring Chita Rivera | | | | |
| 5/8/61 | 119 | 1 | 2 **Baby Face** ........................ *How Many Tears* (Hot #63) | | $15 | ■ | Liberty 55325 |
| | | | #1 hit for Jan Garber in 1926; #42 hit for **Bobby Darin** in 1962 | | | | |
| 1/12/63 | 110 | 2 | 3 **Anonymous Phone Call** *The Night Has A Thousand Eyes* (Hot #3) | | $15 | | Liberty 55521 |
| | | | above 2 with The Johnny Mann Singers | | | | |
| 9/12/64 | 120 | 1 | 4 **Where Is She?** .......................... *How To Make A Farewell* | | $15 | | Liberty 55726 |
| | | | The Eligibles (backing vocals) | | | | |
| 9/25/65 | 124 | 2 | 5 **Run Like The Devil** .................... *Take A Look Around Me* | | $12 | | Liberty 55828 |
| 2/26/66 | 133 | 2 | 6 **A Girl I Used To Know** ............................. *Gone* | | $12 | | Liberty 55854 |
| | | | #3 Country hit for **George Jones** in 1962 | | | | |
| 2/28/70 | 111 | 2 | 7 **In And Out Of Love** .............. *Electric Trains And You* | | $8 | | Liberty 56149 |

## VEGA, Tata ○
**R&B**

Born Carmen Rosa Vega on 10/7/51 in Queens, New York. R&B/gospel singer.

| DEBUT | PEAK | WKS | A-side | B-side | $ | Pic | Label & Number |
|---|---|---|---|---|---|---|---|
| 7/16/77 | 108 | 2 | 1 **You'll Never Rock Alone** ...... *Just When Things Are Getting Good* | | $5 | | Tamla 54282 |
| 7/28/79 | 107 | 2 | 2 **I Need You Now** .......................... *In The Morning* | | $5 | | Tamla 54304 |

## VEJTABLES, The
**HOT**

San Francisco rock group: Bob Bailey, Ned Hollis, Ron Edwards and Reese Sheets with female drummer Jan Errico.

| DEBUT | PEAK | WKS | A-side | B-side | $ | Pic | Label & Number |
|---|---|---|---|---|---|---|---|
| 11/27/65 | 117 | 3 | **The Last Thing On My Mind** ............. *Mansion Of Tears* | | $12 | | Autumn 23 |
| | | | #56 hit for Neil Diamond in 1973 | | | | |

## VELVA BLU ○

Studio group assembled by dance producers Lawrence Fordyce, Joe Stone and Paul Klein.

| DEBUT | PEAK | WKS | A-side | B-side | $ | Pic | Label & Number |
|---|---|---|---|---|---|---|---|
| 11/8/97 | 108 | 12 | **Barbie Girl** ............................... *I Like Plastic* | | $3 | ■ | Groove 5051 |
| | | | #7 hit for Aqua in 1997 | | | | |

## VELVELETTES, The
**R&B/HOT**

Female R&B group formed at Western Michigan State University in the early '60s.

| DEBUT | PEAK | WKS | A-side | B-side | $ | Pic | Label & Number |
|---|---|---|---|---|---|---|---|
| 10/1/66 | 102 | 2 | **These Things Will Keep Me Loving You** ........... R&B:43 *Since You've Been Loving Me* | | $20 | | Soul 35025 |

## VELVET, Jimmy
**HOT/AC**

Memphis native. Based in Jacksonville, Florida. Pop singer.

| DEBUT | PEAK | WKS | A-side | B-side | $ | Pic | Label & Number |
|---|---|---|---|---|---|---|---|
| 3/28/64 | 118 | 2 | **To The Aisle** .............................. *Lonely, Lonely Night* | | $20 | | ABC-Paramount 10528 |
| | | | #25 hit for **The Five Satins** in 1957 | | | | |

## VELVETS, The
**HOT**

R&B doo-wop quintet from Odessa, Texas featuring Virgil Johnson (lead).

| DEBUT | PEAK | WKS | A-side | B-side | $ | Pic | Label & Number |
|---|---|---|---|---|---|---|---|
| 8/25/62 | 102 | 1 | **Let The Good Times Roll** ........ *The Lights Go On, The Lights Go Off* | | $25 | | Monument 464 |
| | | | #1 R&B hit for Shirley & Lee in 1956 | | | | |

## VENTURES, The
**HOT/AC/R&B**

Guitar-based instrumental rock and roll band formed in the Seattle/Tacoma, Washington, area: guitarists Nokie Edwards (b: 5/9/39; bass), Bob Bogle (b: 1/16/37; lead) and Don Wilson (b: 2/10/37; rhythm), and drummer Howie Johnson (d: 1988). Johnson replaced by Mel Taylor (d: 8/11/96) in 1961.

| DEBUT | PEAK | WKS | A-side | B-side | $ | Pic | Label & Number |
|---|---|---|---|---|---|---|---|
| 6/9/62 | 104 | 2 | 1 **Instant Mashed** | *My Bonnie Lies* [I] | $20 | | Dolton 55 |
| 3/30/63 | 114 | 1 | 2 **Skip To M' Limbo** ..................... *El Cumbanchero* [I] | | $20 | | Dolton 68 |
| 6/15/63 | 122 | 3 | 3 **The Ninth Wave** ....................... *Damaged Goods* [I] | | $20 | | Dolton 78 |
| 5/2/64 | 126 | 5 | 4 **Fugitive** ..................................... *Scratchin'* [I] | | $20 | | Dolton 94 |
| 11/21/64 | 135 | 1 | 5 **Rap City** ............... *Slaughter On Tenth Avenue* (Hot #35) [I] | | $15 | ■ | Dolton 300 |
| | | | adaptation of Brahm's *Hungarian Dance No. 5* | | | | |
| 6/11/66 | 120 | 3 | 6 **Blue Star** .............................. *Comin' Home Baby* [I] | | $15 | ■ | Dolton 320 |
| | | | theme from the TV series *Medic* starring Richard Boone; #29 hit for Felicia Sanders in 1955 | | | | |
| 9/3/66 | 116 | 3 | 7 **Green Hornet Theme** ..................... *Fuzzy And Wild* [I] | | $15 | ■ | Dolton 323 |
| | | | theme from the TV series *The Green Hornet* starring Van Williams | | | | |
| 10/29/66 | 116 | 2 | 8 **Wild Thing** ................................ *Penetration* [I] | | $15 | ■ | Dolton 325 |
| | | | #1 hit for **The Troggs** in 1966 | | | | |
| 12/24/66 | 110 | 9 | 9 **Theme From "The Wild Angels"** ..................... *Kickstand* [I] | | $15 | | Dolton 327 |
| | | | title song from the movie starring Peter Fonda; #99 hit for Davie Allan & The Arrows in 1966 | | | | |
| 7/1/67 | 106 | 6 | 10 **Theme From Endless Summer** ......... *Strawberry Fields Forever* [I] | | $10 | | Liberty 55977 |
| | | | from the Bruce Brown surfing documentary movie *The Endless Summer* | | | | |
| 12/25/71 | 109 | 2 | 11 **Joy** .......................... *Cherries Jubilee* [I] | | $8 | | United Artists 50872 |
| | | | based upon Bach's "Jesu, Joy Of Man's Desiring"; #6 hit for Apollo 100 in 1972 | | | | |

## VERA, Billy
**HOT/R&B/AC/C&W/ROK**

Born William McCord on 5/28/44 in Riverside, California; raised in Westchester County, New York. Wrote hit songs for many pop, country and R&B artists. In the movies *Buckaroo Banzai* and *The Doors*, and the HBO movie *Baja Oklahoma*. Formed The Beaters (an R&B-based, 10-piece band) in Los Angeles in 1979.

| DEBUT | PEAK | WKS | A-side | B-side | $ | Pic | Label & Number |
|---|---|---|---|---|---|---|---|
| 6/8/68 | 107 | 2 | 1 **When Do We Go** ............................... *Even Since* | | $10 | | Atlantic 2515 |
| | | | **BILLY VERA & JUDY CLAY** | | | | |
| 9/28/68 | 121 | 2 | 2 **I've Been Loving You Too Long** ........... *Are You Coming To My Party* | | $10 | | Atlantic 2555 |
| | | | #21 hit for **Otis Redding** in 1965 | | | | |
| 5/17/69 | 112 | 3 | 3 **The Bible Salesman** ............. *Are You Coming To My Party* | | $10 | ■ | Atlantic 2628 |
| | | | inspired by the movie *Salesman* | | | | |

## VERNE, Larry
**HOT/R&B**

Born on 2/8/36 in Minneapolis. Photo studio worker-turned-novelty singer.

| DEBUT | PEAK | WKS | A-side | B-side | $ | Pic | Label & Number |
|---|---|---|---|---|---|---|---|
| 5/8/61 | 113 | 2 | **Abdul's Party** ........................... *Tubby Tilly* [N] | | $10 | | Era 3044 |

## VERONICA
**R&B/HOT**

Born in New York City in 1975 to Puerto Rican parents. Female R&B singer.

| DEBUT | PEAK | WKS | A-side | B-side | $ | Pic | Label & Number |
|---|---|---|---|---|---|---|---|
| 10/25/97 | 102 | 10 | **Rise** ................................. R&B:38 *Rise* (w/Fat Joe) | | $3 | ■ | H.O.L.A. 341031 |

**VERTICAL HOLD** ✪                                 R&B
R&B vocal trio: Willie Bruno, David Bright and Angie B. Stone (former member of Sequence).

| | | | | | | |
|---|---|---|---|---|---|---|
| 6/19/93 | 108 | 9 | Seems You're Much Too Busy .......................... Air:73 /R&B:17 (remix) | $3 | ▌ | A&M 0140 |

**VIBRATIONS, The**                R&B/HOT
Los Angeles R&B vocal group. Originally recorded as The Jayhawks. Consisted of James Johnson, Carlton Fisher, Richard Owens, Dave Govan and Don Bradley. Also recorded the hit "Peanut Butter" as The Marathons.

| | | | | | | |
|---|---|---|---|---|---|---|
| 6/6/60 | 110 | 3 | 1 So Blue ................................................ Love Me Like You Should | $50 | | Checker 954 |
| 4/24/61 | 112 | 3 | 2 The Junkernoo ................................ Continental With Me, Baby | $25 | | Checker 974 |
| | | |     tune is similar to **Hank Ballard & The Midnighters'** "Finger Poppin' Time" | | | |
| 7/3/61 | 117 | 1 | 3 Stranded In The Jungle ........................ Don't Say Goodbye [N-R] | $25 | | Checker 982 |
| | | |     new version of #18 hit in 1956 on Flash 109 (recorded by The Vibrations as The Jayhawks) | | | |
| 10/31/64 | 109 | 5 | 4 Sloop Dance | $20 | | Okeh 7205 |
| | | |                                   Watusi Time | | | |
| | | |     sequel to The Vibrations' 1964 #26 hit "My Girl Sloopy" on Atlantic 2221 | | | |
| 2/13/65 | 118 | 1 | 5 Keep On Keeping On .................................... Hello Happiness | $15 | | Okeh 7212 |
| 5/29/65 | 130 | 1 | 6 End Up Crying ............................................ Ain't Love That Way | $15 | | Okeh 7220 |
| 10/15/66 | 118 | 3 | 7 And I Love Her ................................ R&B:47 Soul A Go-Go | $15 | | Okeh 7257 |
| | | |     #12 hit for **The Beatles** in 1964 | | | |

**VICEROYS, The** ✪
Instrumental rock and roll band from Seattle led by guitarist **Jim Valley**.

| | | | | | | |
|---|---|---|---|---|---|---|
| 3/30/63 | 127 | 3 | Seagrams ........................................ Moasin' [I] | $25 | | Bethlehem 3045 |
| | | |     because of a legal conflict, title later changed to "Seagreen" ($20) | | | |

**VICTORIANS, The** ✪
Female vocal group.

| | | | | | | |
|---|---|---|---|---|---|---|
| 7/27/63 | 120 | 3 | What Makes Little Girls Cry ........................ Climb Every Mountain | $20 | | Liberty 55574 |

**VILLAGE PEOPLE**                  HOT/R&B
New York City campy, disco group formed by French producer Jacques Morali (d: 11/15/91) featuring Victor Willis (lead singer).

| | | | | | | |
|---|---|---|---|---|---|---|
| 10/15/77+ | 102 | 30 | San Francisco (You've Got Me) ........................ Village People | $6 | | Casablanca 896 |

**VILLAGE STOMPERS, The**            HOT/AC/R&B
Dixieland-styled band from Greenwich Village, New York City.

| | | | | | | |
|---|---|---|---|---|---|---|
| 2/1/64 | 104 | 6 | 1 The La-Dee-Da Song ........................................ Blue Grass [I] | $7 | ■ | Epic 9655 |
| 10/3/64 | 132 | 3 | 2 Oh! Marie .................................... Limehouse Blues [I] | $7 | | Epic 9718 |
| | | |     #12 hit for Horace Heidt in 1937; #25 hit for **Louis Prima** in 1944 | | | |
| 7/17/65 | 130 | 1 | 3 Those Magnificent Men In Their Flying Machines ........ AC:35 Sweet Water Bay [I] | $7 | | Epic 9824 |
| | | |     title song from the movie starring Stuart Whitman | | | |

**VINCENT, Kyle** ✪
Born in Berkeley, California. Pop/rock singer/songwriter.

| | | | | | | |
|---|---|---|---|---|---|---|
| 5/31/97 | 101³ | 12 | Wake Me Up (When The World's Worth Waking Up For)    It Wasn't Supposed To Happen | $3 | ▌ | Hollywood 64015 |

**VINTON, Bobby**                  HOT/AC/C&W
Born Stanley Robert Vinton on 4/16/35 in Canonsburg, Pennsylvania. Leader of the backing band for Dick Clark's "Caravan of Stars" in 1960. Own musical variety TV series from 1975-78. *Top Pop Singles: 47.*

| | | | | | | |
|---|---|---|---|---|---|---|
| 12/25/65 | 111 | 2 | 1 Careless ........................................ Satin Pillows (Hot #23) | $7 | ■ | Epic 9869 |
| | | |     #2 hit for Glenn Miller in 1940 | | | |
| 9/19/70 | 109 | 4 | 2 Why Don't They Understand ........ AC:23 Where Is Love? | $6 | ■ | Epic 10651 |
| | | |     #10 hit for **George Hamilton IV** in 1958 | | | |
| 4/3/71 | 101¹ | 2 | 3 I'll Make You My Baby ........................ AC:30 She Loves Me | $6 | | Epic 10711 |
| | | |     answer song to "Make Me Your Baby" by **Barbara Lewis** | | | |
| 6/9/73 | 106 | 1 | 4 Hurt ........................ AC:40 I Love You The Way You Are | $6 | | Epic 10980 |
| | | |     #8 R&B hit for **Roy Hamilton** in 1955; #4 hit for **Timi Yuro** in 1961 | | | |
| 3/28/81 | 108 | 1 | 5 Let Me Love You Goodbye ........................ AC:45 You Are Love | $4 | | Tapestry 006 |

**VIOLINAIRES, The** ✪
Male R&B/gospel vocal group.

| | | | | | | |
|---|---|---|---|---|---|---|
| 4/6/68 | 121 | 3 | I Don't Know ........................................ Call On Him | $12 | | Checker 5043 |

**V.I.P.'S, The** ✪
R&B vocal group.

| | | | | | | |
|---|---|---|---|---|---|---|
| 8/15/64 | 117 | 4 | You Pulled A Fast One ........................................ Flashback | $20 | | Big Top 518 |
| | | |     Leroy Glover (orch.) | | | |

**VISCOUNTS, The**                 HOT/R&B
New Jersey jazzy rock and roll instrumental quintet featuring Harry Haller (tenor saxophone).

| | | | | | | |
|---|---|---|---|---|---|---|
| 2/19/66 | 122 | 1 | Night Train ........................ When The Saints Go Marching In [I-R] | $15 | | Amy 949 |
| | | |     originally made the *Hot 100* (#82) on 7/18/60 on Madison 133; #1 R&B hit for Jimmy Forest in 1952 | | | |

**VOGGUE** ✪
Female disco duo from Canada: Chantal Condor and Angela Songui.

| | | | | | | |
|---|---|---|---|---|---|---|
| 8/22/81 | 109 | 1 | Dancin' The Night Away ........................................ Roller Boggie | $4 | | Atlantic 3847 |

**VOGUES, The**                 AC/HOT
Vocal group formed in Turtle Creek, Pennsylvania: Bill Burkette (lead), Hugh Geyer and Chuck Blasko (tenors), and Don Miller (baritone).

| | | | | | | |
|---|---|---|---|---|---|---|
| 1/31/70 | 101² | 3 | 1 God Only Knows ........................ AC:21 Moody | $6 | | Reprise 0887 |
| | | |     #39 hit for **The Beach Boys** in 1966 | | | |
| 5/2/70 | 101¹ | 3 | 2 Hey, That's No Way To Say Goodbye ........ AC:18 Over The Rainbow | $6 | | Reprise 0909 |
| | | |     written and recorded by Leonard Cohen on his 1968 album *Songs Of Leonard Cohen* | | | |
| 6/12/71 | 118 | 3 | 3 Love Song ........................................ AC:23 We're On Our Way | $5 | | Bell 991 |
| | | |     written, produced and arranged by **Teddy Randazzo** | | | |

## VOLUMES, The

HOT

R&B vocal quintet from Detroit: Ed Union (lead), Elijah Davis, Larry Wright, Joe Travillion and Ernest Newsom.

| DEBUT | PEAK | WKS | A-side | B-side | $ | Pic | Label & Number |
|---|---|---|---|---|---|---|---|
| 8/11/62 | 118 | 1 | 1 **Come Back Into My Heart**............................................. *The Bell* | $40 | | Chex 1005 |
| 10/24/64 | 117 | 6 | 2 **Gotta Give Her Love**............................... *I Can't Live Without You* | $30 | | American Arts 6 |

## VONNAIR SISTERS, The ☉

| | | | | | | |
|---|---|---|---|---|---|---|
| 11/13/61 | 106 | 2 | 1 **Dreamin' About You**.............................................. *Strummin' Song* | $25 | ■ | Buena Vista 388 |
| | | | **ANNETTE and the Vonnair Sisters** | | | |
| 1/13/62 | 115 | 2 | 2 **Goodbye To Toyland**........................ *I Don't Wanna Play In Your Yard* | $15 | | Buena Vista 390 |
| | | | adapted from the 1903 Victor Herbert tune "Toyland" | | | |

## VOYAGE

R&B/HOT

European disco group: Sylvia Mason (vocals), Slim Pezin (guitar), Marc Chantereau (keyboards), Sauver Mallin (bass) and Pierre-Alain Dahan (drums).

| | | | | | | |
|---|---|---|---|---|---|---|
| 5/26/79 | 105 | 1 | **Let's Fly Away**......................................... *Gone With The Music* | $5 | | Marlin 3334 |

## VYBE

R&B/HOT

Female R&B vocal quartet from Los Angeles: Pam, Tanya, Debbie and Dove.

| | | | | | | |
|---|---|---|---|---|---|---|
| 4/29/95 | 112 | 3 | **Take It To The Front**............................ **R&B:42** *All My Love* | $3 | ▮ | Island 851616 |
| | | | produced by **Somethin' For The People** | | | |

## WACKERS, The

HOT

Pop/rock quintet from California and based in Montreal, Canada. Led by singer/guitarist Randy Bishop.

| | | | | | | |
|---|---|---|---|---|---|---|
| 3/24/73 | 124 | 1 | **Hey Lawdy Lawdy**.............................................. *I'm In Love* | $6 | | Elektra 45841 |

## WADE, Adam

HOT/AC/R&B

Born on 3/17/37 in Pittsburgh. Black Adult Contemporary vocalist. TV actor/host of the 1975 game show *Musical Chairs*.

| | | | | | | |
|---|---|---|---|---|---|---|
| 11/20/61 | 108 | 3 | 1 **Preview Of Paradise**.................................. *Cold Cold Winter* | $10 | | Coed 560 |
| 2/3/62 | 109 | 3 | 2 **It's Good To Have You Back With Me/** | $10 | | Coed 565 |
| 2/3/62 | 114 | 2 | 3   **How Are Things In Lovers Lane**................................ | $10 | | |
| 4/28/62 | 118 | 1 | 4 **For The First Time In My Life**...................... *Little Miss Lovely* | $10 | | Coed 567 |
| 12/8/62 | 104 | 4 | 5 **There'll Be No Teardrops Tonight** *Here Comes The Pain* | $8 | ■ | Epic 9557 |
| | | | written in 1949 by Hank Williams | | | |
| 2/16/63 | 117 | 4 | 6 **Don't Let Me Cross Over**......................... *Rain From The Skies* | $8 | | Epic 9566 |
| | | | #1 Country hit for Carl Butler & Pearl in 1962 | | | |

## WADE, Brandon ☉

| | | | | | | |
|---|---|---|---|---|---|---|
| 12/16/67 | 120 | 1 | **Letter From A Teenage Son**.................... *(mono version)* [S] | $6 | ■ | Philips 40503 |

answer to Victor Lundberg's "An Open Letter To My Teenage Son"; backed by 21 members of the Chicago Symphony Orchestra playing Ravel's "Pavane"

## WAGNER, Jack

HOT/AC

Born on 10/3/59 in Washington, Missouri. TV actor/singer. Played "Frisco Jones" on the TV soap opera *General Hospital*, 1983-87; joined the cast of *Melrose Place* in 1994.

| | | | | | | |
|---|---|---|---|---|---|---|
| 3/2/85 | 101[1] | 2 | **Premonition** *Lady Of My Heart (Hot #76)* | $3 | ■ | Qwest 29085 |

## WAGONER, Porter

C&W/HOT

Born on 8/12/27 in West Plains, Missouri. Country singer.

| | | | | | | |
|---|---|---|---|---|---|---|
| 7/3/71 | 116 | 1 | 1 **Charley's Picture**.......................... **C&W:15** *Simple As I Am* | $8 | | RCA Victor 9979 |
| 8/21/71 | 106 | 1 | 2 **The Right Combination**.......... **C&W:14** *The Pain Of Loving You* | $8 | | RCA Victor 9994 |
| | | | **PORTER WAGONER AND DOLLY PARTON** | | | |

## WAILERS, The

HOT/R&B

Teenage rock and roll instrumental quintet from Tacoma, Washington, formed in 1958 by rhythm guitarist John Greek.

| | | | | | | |
|---|---|---|---|---|---|---|
| 6/11/66 | 118 | 4 | **It's You Alone**............................................................ *Tears* | $12 | | United Artists 50026 |
| | | | written by Ray Davies of **The Kinks** | | | |

## WAITE, John

HOT/ROK/AC

Born on 7/4/55 in Lancashire, England. Lead singer of The Babys and Bad English.

| | | | | | | |
|---|---|---|---|---|---|---|
| 10/9/93 | 103 | 6 | **In Dreams**............................................................ *(2 versions)* | $3 | ▮ | Imago 25050 |
| | | | from the movie *True Romance* starring Christian Slater | | | |

## WALDEN, Narada Michael

R&B/HOT

Born Michael Walden on 4/23/52 in Kalamazoo, Michigan. R&B singer/songwriter/drummer/producer.

| | | | | | | |
|---|---|---|---|---|---|---|
| 2/23/85 | 106 | 2 | **Gimme, Gimme, Gimme**.................... **R&B:39** *Wear Your Love* (Walden) | $4 | | Warner 29077 |
| | | | **NARADA MICHAEL WALDEN (with Patti Austin)** | | | |

## WALKER, Billy

C&W/HOT

Born on 1/14/29 in Ralls, Texas. Country singer.

| | | | | | | |
|---|---|---|---|---|---|---|
| 1/30/65 | 128 | 1 | **Cross The Brazos At Waco**................. **C&W:2** *Down To My Last Cigarette* | $8 | ☐ | Columbia 43120 |

## WALKER, Clay

C&W/HOT

Born on 8/19/69 in Beaumont, Texas. Country singer. Diagnosed with multiple sclerosis in April 1996.

| | | | | | | |
|---|---|---|---|---|---|---|
| 1/1/94 | 107 | 6 | 1 **Live Until I Die**.................. **C&W:❶**[1] *The Silence Speaks For Itself* | $3 | ▮ | Giant 18332 |
| 1/7/95 | 121 | 1 | 2 **If I Could Make A Living**.................. **C&W:❶**[1] *Down By The Riverside* | $3 | ▮ | Giant 18068 |
| 10/28/95 | 120 | 6 | 3 **Who Needs You Baby**........................ **C&W:2** *Where Were You* | $3 | ▮ | Giant 17771 |
| 2/10/96 | 105 | 16 | 4 **Hypnotize The Moon**.................. **C&W:2** *A Cowboy's Toughest Ride* | $3 | ▮ | Giant 17704 |

| DEBUT | PEAK | WKS | A-side (Chart Hit) / B-side | $ | Pic | Label & Number |
|---|---|---|---|---|---|---|
| | | | **WALKER, David T.** ✪     R&B | | | |
| | | | Born in Los Angeles. Guitarist/composer. With The Olympics and **The Midnighters**. Band director at Motown in Detroit. | | | |
| 12/20/69 | 128 | 1 | 1 My Baby Loves Me................................... R&B:46 *Can I Change My Mind* [I] | $7 | | Revue 11060 |
| 1/9/71 | 117 | 1 | 2 Love Vibrations....................................... R&B:35 *Doo Doo* [I] | $7 | | Zea 50005 |
| 7/1/72 | 104 | 3 | 3 Hot Fun In The Summertime................... *I Want To Talk To You* | $6 | | Ode 66025 |
| | | | #2 hit for **Sly & The Family Stone** in 1969 | | | |
| | | | **WALKER, Gary** ✪ | | | |
| | | | Born Gary Leeds on 9/3/44 in Los Angeles. Member of The Walker Bros. | | | |
| 5/28/66 | 129 | 2 | You Don't Love Me...................................... *Get It Right* | $10 | | Date 1506 |
| | | | **WALKER, Jr., & The All Stars**     R&B/HOT | | | |
| | | | R&B band formed in South Bend, Indiana, in 1961 by saxophonist/vocalist Walker (b: Oscar G. Mixon on 6/14/31 in Blytheville, Arkansas; d: 11/23/95; known as Autry DeWalt II). *Top Pop Singles:* 21. | | | |
| 2/20/71 | 117 | 3 | 1 Carry Your Own Load.............................. R&B:50 *Holly Holy* (Hot #75) | $8 | | Soul 35081 |
| 2/24/73 | 101[1] | 4 | 2 Gimme That Beat (Part 1)      R&B:50 *(Part 2)* | $8 | | Soul 35104 |
| | | | **WALKER, Ronnie** ✪ | | | |
| | | | R&B vocalist. | | | |
| 10/7/67 | 128 | 1 | Really, Really Love You ........................... *Ain't It Funny* | $12 | | Philips 40470 |
| | | | **WALLACE, Jerry**     C&W/HOT/AC/R&B/MEM | | | |
| | | | Born on 12/15/28 in Guilford, Missouri. Pop-country singer/guitarist. First recorded for Allied in 1951. | | | |
| 5/2/60 | 115 | 1 | 1 You're Singing Our Love Song To Somebody Else ..............*King Of The Mountain* | $15 | | Challenge 59072 |
| 10/16/61 | 110 | 2 | 2 Lonesome............................... *Eyes (Don't Give My Secret Away)* | $15 | | Challenge 9117 |
| 10/31/64 | 114 | 2 | 3 Even The Bad Times Are Good/ | $15 | | Challenge 59265 |
| | | | a new version made the Country charts (#74) in 1970 on Liberty 56155 | | | |
| 10/17/64 | 132 | 2 | 4 Spanish Guitars ..................................................... | $15 | | Challenge 59265 |
| | | | **WALLACE BROTHERS**     HOT/R&B | | | |
| | | | R&B duo: Ervin and Johnny Wallace. Member Johnny Simon later joined The Naturals. | | | |
| 5/16/64 | 107 | 11 | Precious Words .............................. *You're Mine* | $15 | | Sims 174 |
| | | | **WALSH, James, Gypsy Band**     HOT | | | |
| 6/9/79 | 103 | 4 | Love Is For The Best In Us ................. *Don't Look Back* | $5 | | RCA 11480 |
| | | | **WALSH, Joe**     ROK/HOT | | | |
| | | | Born on 11/20/47 in Wichita, Kansas. Rock singer/songwriter/guitarist. Member of **The James Gang** and the Eagles. | | | |
| 6/5/76 | 105 | 1 | 1 Walk Away ................................. *Help Me Thru The Night* | $5 | | ABC 12187 |
| | | | "live" version of song which made the *Hot 100* (#51) by Joe's group, **The James Gang**, on 5/29/71 on ABC 11301 | | | |
| 11/11/78 | 106 | 1 | 2 Over And Over ........................................ *At The Station* | $4 | | Asylum 45536 |
| 1/13/79 | 109 | 1 | 3 Turn To Stone ..................... *Rocky Mountain Way* [R] | $4 | | ABC 12426 |
| | | | originally made the *Hot 100* (#93) on 3/1/75 on Dunhill/ABC 15026 | | | |
| | | | **WALTERS, Jamie**     HOT/AC | | | |
| | | | Male singer/actor. Former lead singer of The Heights. Cast member of TV's *Beverly Hills 90210*. | | | |
| 8/12/95 | 105 | 5 | Why ................................................. *The Distance* | $3 | ■ | Atlantic 87159 |
| | | | **WAMMACK, Travis**     HOT | | | |
| | | | Born in 1946 in Walnut, Mississippi; raised in Memphis. Prolific session guitarist of the FAME studios in Muscle Shoals, Alabama. | | | |
| 4/9/66 | 128 | 1 | Louie Louie.................................................... *Upset* [I] | $10 | | Atlantic 2322 |
| | | | #2 hit for **The Kingsmen** in 1963 | | | |
| | | | **WANDERERS, The**     HOT | | | |
| | | | R&B vocal quartet — Ray Pollard, lead singer. First recorded for Savoy in 1953. | | | |
| 8/7/61 | 107 | 2 | I'll Never Smile Again ........................... *A Little Too Long* | $30 | | Cub 9094 |
| | | | #1 hit for Tommy Dorsey in 1940; #25 hit for **The Platters** in 1961 | | | |
| | | | **WANG CHUNG**     HOT/ROK | | | |
| | | | British pop-rock group: Jack Hues (lead singer, guitar, keyboards), Nick Feldman (bass, keyboards) and Darren Costin (drums). | | | |
| 5/11/85 | 110 | 1 | 1 Fire In The Twilight.............................. *The Reggae* [I] (Keith Forsey) | $4 | ■ | A&M 2728 |
| | | | from the movie *The Breakfast Club* starring Molly Ringwald and Emilio Estevez | | | |
| 7/12/97+ | 107 | 23 | 2 Dance Hall Days ..................................... *(3 mixes) / Let's Go* [R] | $6 | ■ | Geffen 22301 (T) |
| | | | 12" remix of their #16 hit in 1984 on Geffen 29310 | | | |
| | | | **WANTED, The** ✪ | | | |
| | | | Rock and roll band. | | | |
| 4/8/67 | 118 | 3 | In The Midnight Hour.............................. *Here To Stay* | $10 | | A&M 844 |
| | | | #21 hit for **Wilson Pickett** in 1965 | | | |
| | | | **WAR**     R&B/HOT/AC | | | |
| | | | Latin-style R&B band formed in 1969 in Long Beach, California featuring Lonnie Jordan (keyboards) and Lee Oskar (harmonica). Eric Burdon's backup band until 1971. | | | |
| 4/3/71 | 107 | 4 | 1 Lonely Feelin'........................... R&B:38 *Sun Oh Son* | $6 | ■ | United Artists 50746 |
| 4/10/71 | 108 | 2 | 2 Home Cookin'...................... *They Can't Take Away Our Music* (Hot #50) | $8 | | MGM 14196 |
| | | | **ERIC BURDON AND WAR** | | | |
| 4/28/79 | 101[5] | 9 | 3 Good, Good Feelin'      R&B:12 *Baby Face (She Said Do Do Do Do)* | $5 | | MCA 40995 |
| | | | **WARD, Jacky** ✪     C&W/AC | | | |
| | | | Born on 11/18/46 in Groveton, Texas. Male country singer. | | | |
| 4/29/78 | 106 | 3 | A Lover's Question............... C&W:3 / AC:32 *She Belongs To Me* | $5 | | Mercury 55018 |
| | | | #6 hit for **Clyde McPhatter** in 1959 | | | |
| | | | **WARD, Robin**     HOT/R&B | | | |
| | | | Born Jacqueline Eloise McDonnell in Hawaii. Pop singer from Nebraska. | | | |
| 3/14/64 | 123 | 1 | Winter's Here ........................................ *Bobby* | $12 | | Dot 16578 |
| | | | Perry Botkin, Jr. (orch.) | | | |

### WARINER, Steve      C&W/HOT/AC
Born Steve Noel Wariner on 12/25/54 in Noblesville, Indiana. Country singer/songwriter/bassist.

| 11/14/81 | 107 | 4 | All Roads Lead To You ........................... C&W:❶[1] *Here We Are* | $4 | | RCA 12307 |

### WARNES, Jennifer      AC/HOT/C&W
Born on 3/3/47 in Seattle. Adult Contemporary vocalist. Lead actress in the Los Angeles production of *Hair*.

| 5/10/69 | 128 | 2 | 1 Easy To Be Hard.......................... *Let The Sunshine In (The Flesh Failures)* | $8 | | Parrot 336 |

**JENNIFER**
from the rock musical *Hair*; #4 hit for **Three Dog Night** in 1969

| 4/3/82 | 107 | 3 | 2 Come To Me ........................................ AC:40 *I'm Restless* | $4 | | Arista 0670 |
| 7/2/83 | 105 | 4 | 3 Nights Are Forever ............................. AC:8 *Kick The Can* | $4 | | Warner 29593 |

from the movie *Twilight Zone-The Movie* starring John Lithgow

### WARREN, Doug, and the Rays ⊘
Rock and roll band.

| 7/11/60 | 107 | 4 | If The World Don't End Tomorrow (I'm Comin' After You) ............... *Around Midnight* | $30 | | Image/NRC 1011 |

### WARWICK, Dee Dee      R&B/HOT
Born in 1945. R&B singer. Younger sister of **Dionne Warwick**; cousin of Whitney Houston.

| 11/9/63 | 117 | 2 | 1 You're No Good ................................... *Don't Call Me Any More* | $15 | | Jubilee 5459 |

#1 hit for **Linda Ronstadt** in 1975

| 3/13/65 | 124 | 3 | 2 Do It With All Your Heart ............................... *Happiness* | $10 | | Blue Rock 4008 |
| 5/31/69 | 106 | 4 | 3 That's Not Love .................................. R&B:42 *It's Not Fair* | $8 | | Mercury 72927 |
| 7/19/69 | 113 | 3 | 4 Ring Of Bright Water ........................ *Next Time (You Fall In Love)* | $8 | ■ | Mercury 72940 |

title song from the British movie starring Bill Travers and Virginia McKenna

### WARWICK, Dionne      R&B/HOT/AC
Born Marie Dionne Warwick on 12/12/40 in East Orange, New Jersey. Cousin of Whitney Houston. Was **Burt Bacharach**'s main "voice" for the songs he composed. Since the early '90s, hosted TV infomercials for the Psychic Friends Network. *Top Pop Singles*: 55.

| 12/11/71 | 107 | 2 | 1 The Love Of My Man .................................. *Hurts So Bad* | $6 | | Scepter 12336 |

#21 hit for **Theola Kilgore** in 1963

| 8/26/72 | 113 | 4 | 2 I'm Your Puppet ................................ *Don't Make Me Over* | $6 | | Scepter 12352 |

**DIONNE WARWICKE** (above 2)
#6 hit for **James & Bobby Purify** in 1966

| 4/16/77 | 109 | 2 | 3 Only Love Can Break A Heart ................... AC:46 *If I Ruled The World* | $5 | | Musicor 6303 |

#2 hit for **Gene Pitney** in 1962

| 7/16/83 | 101[1] | 3 | 4 All The Love In The World    AC:16 *You Are My Love* | $4 | | Arista 9032 |

Barry Gibb (backing vocal); written by the **Bee Gees**

### WASHINGTON, Baby      R&B/HOT
Born Jeanette Washington (aka: **Justine Washington**) on 11/13/40 in Bamberg, South Carolina; raised in Harlem. R&B vocalist/pianist.

| 2/15/60 | 105 | 2 | 1 Work Out .......................... *Let's Love In The Moonlight* | $25 | | Neptune 107 |
| 8/25/62 | 116 | 3 | 2 Handful Of Memories .......................... R&B:16 *Careless Hands* | $20 | | Sue 767 |
| 12/15/62 | 102 | 2 | 3 Hush Heart ..................................... *I've Got A Feeling* | $20 | | Sue 769 |
| 2/29/64 | 125 | 2 | 4 Who's Going To Take Care Of Me ........ *I Can't Wait Until I See My Baby* (Hot #93) | $15 | | Sue 797 |

**JUSTINE WASHINGTON**

| 1/30/65 | 121 | 2 | 5 Run My Heart ......................................... *Your Fool* | $15 | | Sue 119 |
| 11/27/65 | 125 | 4 | 6 No Time For Pity .................................... *There He Is* | $15 | | Sue 137 |
| 7/7/73 | 119 | 2 | 7 Forever ................................. R&B:30 *Baby Let Me Get Close To You* | $10 | | Master Five 9103 |

**BABY WASHINGTON & DON GARDNER**

### WASHINGTON, Gino ⊘
R&B vocalist.

| 3/7/64 | 120 | 2 | 1 Out Of This World ........................ *Come Monkey With Me* | $20 | | Wand 147 |

**GINO WASHINGTON And The Rochelles With The Atlantics**

| 7/11/64 | 121 | 1 | 2 Gino Is A Coward ........................... *Puppet On A String* | $15 | | Ric-Tic 100 |

first released in 1964 on SonBert 3770 ($20)

### WASHINGTON, Grover Jr.      R&B/HOT/AC
Born on 12/12/43 in Buffalo. Jazz-R&B saxophonist. Own band, the Four Clefs, at age 16.

| 3/18/72 | 120 | 1 | 1 Inner City Blues ................................ R&B:42 *Ain't No Sunshine* [I] | $6 | | Kudu 902 |

#9 hit for **Marvin Gaye** in 1971

| 4/10/82 | 102 | 3 | 2 Jamming ...................................... R&B:65 *East River Drive* | $4 | | Elektra 47425 |

written by Bob Marley

| 12/25/82 | 104 | 4 | 3 The Best Is Yet To Come ............. R&B:14 *More Than Meets The Eye* (Washington) | $4 | | Elektra 69887 |

**GROVER WASHINGTON, JR. with PATTI LaBELLE**

### WASHINGTON, Jerry ⊘      R&B
R&B vocalist from South Carolina.

| 2/24/73 | 120 | 2 | Right Here Is Where You Belong ................... R&B:48 *In My Life I've Loved* | $8 | | Excello 2327 |

### WASHRAG ⊘
Studio group from Memphis.

| 10/21/72 | 112 | 2 | Bang! ............................................ *The Gang* [I] | $7 | | TMI 0107 |

### WAS (NOT WAS)      HOT/R&B/ROK/AC
Detroit R&B ensemble fronted by composer/bassist Don Fagenson ("Don Was") and lyricist/flutist David Weiss ("David Was").

| 11/12/83 | 106 | 1 | 1 Smile ......................................... *The Party Broke Up* | $4 | | Geffen 29477 |

Doug Fieger of The Knack (guest vocalist)

| 1/21/84 | 109 | 1 | 2 Knocked Down, Made Small (Treated Like A Rubber Ball) ............. *Man Vs. The Empire Brain Building* | $4 | | Geffen 29407 |

### WATERS, Crystal      HOT/R&B
Female R&B-dance singer from South New Jersey. Niece of Ethel Waters. Also see **Bad Yard Club**.

| 8/12/95 | 106 | 5 | Relax ........................................... *(radio mix)* | $3 | ▌ | Mercury 852060 |

**WATERS, Roger ☺**          ROK
Born George Roger Waters on 9/6/44 in Cambridgeshire, England. Former leader/bassist of **Pink Floyd**.

| 6/2/84 | 110 | 1 | 5:01AM (The Pros And Cons Of Hitch Hiking).........................ROK:17 *4:30AM (Apparently They Were Travelling Abroad)* $4 | | | Columbia 04455 |

**WATLEY, Jody**        R&B/HOT/AC
Born on 1/30/59 in Chicago. Female vocalist of **Shalamar** (1977-84). Goddaughter of **Jackie Wilson**. Won the 1987 Best New Artist Grammy Award.

| 3/19/94 | 115 | 4 | 1 When A Man Loves A Woman.....................................R&B:11 *(instrumental)* $3 | ▐ | MCA 54793 |
| 7/29/95 | 118 | 2 | 2 Affection...................................................................R&B:28 *(instrumental)* $5 | ▐ | Avitone/Bellmark 74506 * |

**WATSON, Johnny "Guitar"**        R&B/HOT
Born on 2/3/35 in Houston. Died on 5/17/96 of a heart attack while performing at the Yokohama Blues Cafe in Japan. Influential funk-R&B vocalist/guitarist/pianist. First recorded for Federal in 1952.

| 8/14/76 | 101[3] | 9 | 1 I Need It        R&B:40 *Since I Met You Baby* $6 | | | DJM 1013 |
| 11/13/76 | 101[2] | 7 | 2 Superman Lover        R&B:19 *We're No Exception* $6 | | | DJM 1019 |

**WATSON, Kino ☺**        R&B
Born in Dallas, North Carolina. Male R&B singer/songwriter.

| 6/8/96 | 120 | 2 | Bring It On .............................................................R&B:50 *(remix)* $3 | ▐ | Columbia 78273 |

Wild Al-Diggity (rap); samples "Float On" by **The Floaters**

## WATTS 103rd STREET RHYTHM BAND — see WRIGHT, Charles

**WC AND THE MAAD CIRCLE**        R&B/HOT
Los Angeles-born rapper WC was a member of Low Profile. **Coolio** was a member until early 1994.

| 5/4/96 | 109 | 5 | The One ..................................................................R&B:76 *(remix)* $3 | ▐ | Payday/London 854518 |

samples "Girl Callin'" by **Chocolate Milk**

**WEATHER GIRLS, The**        R&B/HOT
San Francisco R&B-disco duo: Martha Wash and Izora Redman. Formerly "Two Tons O' Fun."

| 8/3/85 | 107 | 2 | Well-A-Wiggy...........................................................R&B:76 *You Can Do It* $4 | | | Entertainment Co. 05428 |

**WEATHERLY, Jim**        C&W/AC/HOT
Born on 3/17/43 in Pontotoc, Mississippi. Pop-country singer/songwriter. Wrote several of **Gladys Knight**'s hits.

| 1/6/73 | 116 | 2 | Loving You Is Just An Old Habit......................*Between His Goodbye And My Hello* $5 | | | RCA Victor 0822 |

**WEATHERS, Oscar ☺**        R&B
R&B vocalist.

| 3/20/71 | 125 | 2 | 1 You Wants To Play ...............................................R&B:35 *The Spoiler* $10 | | | Top & Bottom 405 |
| 7/28/73 | 113 | 1 | 2 Tell It Like It Is-Part 1..........................................R&B:51 *Part 2* $10 | | | Blue Candle 1498 |

#2 hit for **Aaron Neville** in 1967

**WEBS, The ☺**        R&B
R&B vocal group.

| 12/2/67 | 102 | 5 | This Thing Called Love .........................................R&B:37 *Tomorrow* $15 | | | Pop-Side 4593 |

**WEBSTER, Chase ☺**        C&W
Pop singer/songwriter. Born on a farm near Franklin, Tennessee. Wrote **Pat Boone**'s "Moody River."

| 12/4/61 | 116 | 1 | Sweethearts In Heaven...........................................*Could This Be Magic* $10 | | | Dot 16270 |

#19 Country hit for **Buck Owens** & Rose Maddox in 1963

## WECHTER, Julius — see BAJA MARIMBA BAND

**WE FIVE**        HOT/AC
California pop vocal quintet featuring Beverly Bivens (lead singer) and Mike Stewart (brother of John Stewart).

| 5/28/66 | 116 | 4 | There Stands The Door .........................................*Somewhere* $8 | | | A&M 800 |

**WEISBERG, Tim**        AC/HOT
Born in 1943 in Hollywood. Flautist; studied classical music as an adolescent.

| 9/20/80 | 106 | 2 | I'm The Lucky One.................................................*Magic Lady* $4 | | | MCA 41307 |

Bill Champlin of **Sons Of Champlin** (vocal)

**WELCH, Bob**        HOT/AC/ROK
Born on 7/31/46 in Los Angeles. Guitarist/vocalist with **Fleetwood Mac** (1971-74).

| 11/28/81 | 107 | 2 | Two To Do .............................................................*Imaginary Fool* $4 | | | RCA 12356 |

**WELCH, Lenny**        HOT/AC/R&B
Born on 5/15/38 in Asbury Park, New Jersey. Black Adult Contemporary vocalist.

| 3/12/66 | 102 | 5 | 1 Rags To Riches        *I Want You To Worry (About Me)* $12 | | | Kapp 740 |

#1 hit for **Tony Bennett** in 1953

| 3/18/67 | 134 | 1 | 2 Since I Fell For You .............................................*A Taste Of Honey* [R] $10 | | | Columbia 44007 |

same version as his #4 *Hot 100* hit in 1963; #3 R&B hit for **Annie Laurie** & Paul Gayten in 1947

| 3/25/67 | 128 | 1 | 3 The Right To Cry....................................................*Until The Real Thing Comes Along* $10 | | | Kapp 808 |
| 2/17/68 | 112 | 1 | 4 Darling Stay With Me ...........................................*Wait Awhile Longer* $8 | | | Mercury 72777 |
| 4/18/70 | 110 | 3 | 5 To Be Loved/Glory Of Love ..................................*My Heart Won't Let Me* $7 | | | Common. United 3011 |

medley: **Jackie Wilson** (#7/'58 R&B) and The Five Keys (#1/'51 R&B)

**WELK, Lawrence, and His Orchestra**        HOT/MEM/POP/AC/C&W
Born on 3/11/03 in Strasburg, North Dakota. Died on 5/17/92 of pneumonia. Accordion player and polka/sweet bandleader since the mid-1920s. Own national TV musical variety show debuted in 1955. *Pop Hits & Top Pop Singles: 28.*

| 12/4/61 | 117 | 1 | 1 A-One A-Two A-Cha Cha Cha.................................*You Gave Me Wings* [I] $8 | | | Dot 16285 |
| 9/28/63 | 103 | 3 | 2 Blue Velvet/        [I] | | | |

#1 hit for **Bobby Vinton** in 1963

| 10/5/63 | 106 | 3 | 3 Fiesta...................................................................[I] $6 | | | Dot 16526 |
| 4/8/67 | 104 | 4 | 4 The Beat Goes On.................................................*Then You Can Tell Me Goodbye* [I] $6 | | | Dot 17001 |

#6 hit for **Sonny & Cher** in 1967

### WELLER, Freddy ○                                                    C&W
Born on 9/9/47 in Atlanta. Worked with **Paul Revere & The Raiders** from 1967-71.

| | | | | | | |
|---|---|---|---|---|---|---|
| 7/26/69 | 113 | 1 | 1 **These Are Not My People** ....................................... C&W:5 *You Never Knew Julie* | $6 | | Columbia 44916 |
| | | | written by **Joe South**; produced by Mark Lindsay; #55 hit for **Johnny Rivers** in 1969 | | | |
| 3/13/71 | 125 | 1 | 2 **The Promised Land** ..........................................C&W:3 *Goodnight Sandy* | $6 | | Columbia 45276 |
| | | | written by **Chuck Berry**; #14 hit for **Elvis Presley** in 1974 | | | |
| 7/17/71 | 108 | 4 | 3 **Indian Lake** ...............................................C&W:3 *(I'd Do It All) Over You* | $6 | | Columbia 45388 |
| | | | #10 hit for **The Cowsills** in 1968 | | | |

### WELLS, Mary                                                        HOT/R&B
Born on 5/13/43 in Detroit. Died on 7/26/92. R&B vocalist. Married for a time to Cecil Womack (brother of **Bobby Womack**). *Top Pop Singles*: 23.

| | | | | | | |
|---|---|---|---|---|---|---|
| 3/6/65 | 107 | 3 | 1 **Why Don't You Let Yourself Go** ............................. *Never, Never Leave Me* (Hot #54) | $15 | | 20th Century Fox 570 |
| 4/1/67 | 122 | 1 | 2 **(Hey You) Set My Soul On Fire** ............................*Coming Home* | $15 | | Atco 6469 |
| 2/7/70 | 115 | 1 | 3 **Dig The Way I Feel** ........................................R&B:35 *Love Shooting Bandit* | $12 | | Jubilee 5684 |

### WERNER, David ○
Rock singer/guitarist from Pittsburgh.

| | | | | | | |
|---|---|---|---|---|---|---|
| 10/6/79 | 104 | 2 | **What's Right** ...................................................*Eye To Eye* | $5 | | Epic 50756 |

### WESLEY, Fred, & The J.B.'s                                         R&B/HOT
James Brown's super-funk backup band led by trombonist/keyboardist Fred Wesley. He and other JB members were members of the **Parliament/Funkadelic** organization. Also see **Maceo & The Macks**.

| | | | | | | |
|---|---|---|---|---|---|---|
| 11/17/73 | 104 | 10 | **If You Don't Get It The First Time, Back Up And Try It Again, Party** ..........R&B:24 *You Can Have Watergate Just Gimme Some Bucks And I'll Be Straight* | $6 | | People 627 |
| | | | written, produced, arranged and vocal by James Brown | | | |

### WEST, Dottie ○                                                     C&W/AC/HOT
Born Dorothy Marsh on 10/11/32 in McMinnville, Tennessee. Died on 9/4/91 from injuries suffered in a car accident. Country singer.

| | | | | | | |
|---|---|---|---|---|---|---|
| 4/4/64 | 115 | 1 | 1 **Love Is No Excuse** .......................................... C&W:7 | | | |
| 3/21/64 | 121 | 1 | 2 **Look Who's Talking** ..............................................................| $10 | | RCA Victor 8324 |
| | | | **JIM REEVES & DOTTIE WEST** (above 2) | | | |
| 3/18/78 | 101[2] | 8 | 3 **Every Time Two Fools Collide** ........ C&W:❶[2] / AC:44 *We Love Each Other* | $5 | | United Artists 1137 |
| 5/19/79 | 102 | 8 | 4 **All I Ever Need Is You** .......... C&W:❶[1] / AC:38 *(Hey Won't You Play) Another Somebody Done Somebody Wrong Song* | $5 | | United Artists 1276 |
| | | | **KENNY ROGERS & DOTTIE WEST** (above 2) | | | |
| | | | #7 hit for **Sonny & Cher** in 1971 | | | |

### WEST, Keith ○
Lead singer/guitarist of the British group, Tomorrow.

| | | | | | | |
|---|---|---|---|---|---|---|
| 10/21/67 | 109 | 3 | **Exerpt from "A Teenage Opera" (Grocer Jack)** ..................*Theme from "A Teenage Opera"* (Mark Wirtz Orchestra) | $10 | | New Voice 825 |

### WESTON, Kim                                                        R&B/HOT
Born Agatha Natalie Weston in Detroit. R&B vocalist, previously sang in gospel groups.

| | | | | | | |
|---|---|---|---|---|---|---|
| 5/10/69 | 135 | 1 | 1 **We Try Harder** .............................................*My Time* | $10 | | Banyan Tree 1001 |
| | | | **KIM WESTON JOHNNY NASH** | | | |
| 5/30/70 | 120 | 2 | 2 **Lift Ev'ry Voice And Sing** ................................*This Is America* | $8 | | Pride 1 |
| | | | original version released on MGM 13927 in 1969 | | | |

### WHA-KOO ○
Pop-rock group: David Palmer (vocals), Danny Douma and Nick van Maarth (guitars), Richard Kosinski (keyboards), Don Francisco (percussion), Peter Freiberger (bass) and Claude Pepper (drums).

| | | | | | | |
|---|---|---|---|---|---|---|
| 5/13/78 | 101[1] | 5 | **(You're Such A) Fabulous Dancer** *Fat Love* | $5 | | ABC 12354 |

### WHALE ○                                                            ROK
Grunge/hip-hop trio from Sweden: Henrik Schyffert, Cia Berg and Gordon Cyrus.

| | | | | | | |
|---|---|---|---|---|---|---|
| 6/4/94 | 102 | 9 | **Hobo Humpin Slobo Babe** ...................................ROK:24 *Eye 842* | $3 | ▌ | EastWest 98281 |

### WHEELER, Audrey — see LORBER, Jeff

### WHEELS, The ○
Group is actually pop-R&B singer/producer **Teddy Vann**.

| | | | | | | |
|---|---|---|---|---|---|---|
| 1/4/60 | 102 | 7 | **Clap Your Hands - Part 1** ...................................*Part 2* | $25 | | Folly 800 |
| | | | **THE WHEELS with the Teddy Vann Chorus & Orch.** | | | |

### WHIRLING DERVISHES ○
Rock sextet featuring Don Dazzo (vocals).

| | | | | | | |
|---|---|---|---|---|---|---|
| 1/7/95 | 120 | 1 | **You're A Mean One Mr. Grinch** ................... *Chill / Winter Kills / Sinning And Skating* [X-N] | $7 | ▌ | Continuum 12421 * |
| | | | remake of the song from the Dr. Seuss animated holiday TV program *How The Grinch Stole Christmas* | | | |

### WHISPERS, The                                                     R&B/HOT/AC
Los Angeles R&B group formed in 1964: Gordy Harmon, twin brothers Walter and Wallace "Scotty" Scott, Marcus Hutson and Nicholas Cardwell. The Scotts also recorded as Walter & Scotty since 1993.

| | | | | | | |
|---|---|---|---|---|---|---|
| 12/26/70 | 116 | 1 | 1 **There's A Love For Everyone** ............. R&B:31 *It Sure Ain't Pretty (Hard Core Unemployed)* | $7 | | Janus 140 |
| | | | written by Sugar Pie DeSanto | | | |
| 2/19/72 | 114 | 1 | 2 **Can't Help But Love You** ...................................R&B:35 *A Hopeless Situation* | $7 | | Janus 174 |
| | | | written by Robert John | | | |
| 10/30/76 | 101[3] | 6 | 3 **Living Together (In Sin)** R&B:21 *I've Got A Feeling* | $6 | | Soul Train 10773 |
| 6/3/78 | 101[2] | 11 | 4 **(Let's Go) All The Way** R&B:10 *Chocolate Girl* | $5 | | Solar 11246 |
| 5/16/81 | 105 | 3 | 5 **I Can Make It Better** ......................................R&B:40 *Say You (Would Love For Me Too)* | $4 | | Solar 12232 |
| 2/13/82 | 103 | 4 | 6 **In The Raw** ................................................R&B:8 *Small Talkin'* | $4 | | Solar 47961 |
| 10/1/83 | 110 | 1 | 7 **This Time** .................................................R&B:32 *Love For Love* | $4 | | Solar 69809 |
| 12/8/84 | 105 | 4 | 8 **Contagious** ...............................................R&B:10 *Keep Your Love Around* | $4 | | Solar 69683 |
| 3/23/85 | 106 | 4 | 9 **Some Kinda Lover** .........................................R&B:17 *Never Too Late* | $4 | | Solar 69658 |

| DEBUT | PEAK | WKS | A-side (Chart Hit).................................................................................B-side | $ | Pic | Label & Number |
|---|---|---|---|---|---|---|

**WHISTLE**     R&B/HOT
R&B vocal group from Brooklyn: Brian Faust, Rickford Bennett, Kerry "Kraze" Hodge and Tarek Stevens.

| | | | | | | |
|---|---|---|---|---|---|---|
| 2/3/96 | **115** | 4 | Chance For Our Love ...............................................(acapella version) / Please Love Me | $3 | ▇ | Select 25044 |

**WHITCOMB, Ian**     HOT
Born on 7/10/41 in Woking, England. Pop singer/songwriter/author. Currently resides in California.

| | | | | | | |
|---|---|---|---|---|---|---|
| 11/26/66 | **101**[1] | 3 | Where Did Robinson Crusoe Go With Friday On Saturday Night?     *Poor Little Bird* [N] | $12 | ▇ | Tower 274 |

IAN WHITCOMB and His Seaside Syncopators
#6 hit for Al Jolson in 1916

**WHITE, Barry**     R&B/HOT/AC
Born on 9/12/44 in Galveston, Texas. Soul singer/songwriter/keyboardist/producer/arranger. Formed **Love Unlimited** and **Love Unlimited Orchestra**.

| | | | | | | |
|---|---|---|---|---|---|---|
| 1/29/77 | **105** | 1 | 1 Don't Make Me Wait Too Long ...................... R&B:20 *Can't You See It's Only You I Want* | $5 | | 20th Century 2309 |
| 2/11/78 | **101**[3] | 5 | 2 Playing Your Game, Baby     R&B:8 *Of All The Guys In The World* | $5 | | 20th Century 2361 |
| 2/3/79 | **102** | 8 | 3 Just The Way You Are...................................... R&B:45 *Now I'm Gonna Make Love To You* | $5 | | 20th Century 2395 |
| | | | #3 hit for Billy Joel in 1978 | | | |
| 12/21/96+ | **101**[2] | 15 | 4 In Your Wildest Dreams     R&B:34 *(3 mixes)* | $3 | ▇ | Virgin 38578 |
| | | | TINA TURNER Featuring BARRY WHITE | | | |

**WHITE, Bryan** ✪     C&W
Born on 2/17/74 in Lawton, Oklahoma; raised in Oklahoma City. Country singer/songwriter.

| | | | | | | |
|---|---|---|---|---|---|---|
| 9/9/95 | **112** | 9 | 1 Someone Else's Star .................................. C&W:❶[1] *This Town* | $3 | ▇ | Asylum 64435 |
| 12/30/95+ | **114** | 4 | 2 Rebecca Lynn ............................................ C&W:❶[1] *Nothing Less Than Love* | $3 | ▇ | Asylum 64360 |
| 3/30/96 | **101**[2] | 18 | 3 I'm Not Supposed To Love You Anymore     Sls:72 /C&W:4 *Blindhearted* | $3 | ▇ | Asylum 64313 |
| 8/31/96 | **119** | 2 | 4 So Much For Pretending ........................... C&W:❶[2] *On Any Given Night* | $3 | ▇ | Asylum 64267 |
| 8/30/97 | **101**[1] | 14 | 5 Love Is The Right Place     C&W:4 *Between Now And Forever* | $3 | ▇ | Asylum 64152 |

**WHITE, Danny** ✪
Born Joseph Daniel White on 7/6/31 in New Orleans. Died on 1/5/96. R&B singer.

| | | | | | | |
|---|---|---|---|---|---|---|
| 11/10/62 | **120** | 1 | Kiss Tomorrow Goodbye ................................ *The Little Bitty Things* | $25 | | Frisco 104 |

**WHITE, Karyn**     R&B/HOT/AC
Born on 10/14/65 in Los Angeles. Prominent R&B session singer. Touring vocalist with **O'Bryan** in 1984. Recorded with jazz-fusion keyboardist **Jeff Lorber** in 1986. Married to superproducer Terry Lewis. Also see **Johnny Gill**.

| | | | | | | |
|---|---|---|---|---|---|---|
| 6/17/95 | **120** | 2 | I'd Rather Be Alone............................................ R&B:50 *Nobody But My Baby* | $3 | ▇ | Warner 17922 |

**WHITE, Lenny — see TWENNYNINE**

**WHITE, Roger** ✪

| | | | | | | |
|---|---|---|---|---|---|---|
| 10/7/67 | **123** | 4 | Mystery Of Tallahatchie Bridge................................ C&W:57 *Wild Roses* | $12 | | Big A 103 |
| | | | answer song to **Bobbie Gentry**'s "Ode To Billie Joe" | | | |

**WHITE, Tony Joe**     HOT/C&W
Born on 7/23/43 in Goodwill, Louisiana. Bayou rock singer/songwriter. Wrote **Brook Benton**'s hit "Rainy Night In Georgia."

| | | | | | | |
|---|---|---|---|---|---|---|
| 4/4/70 | **112** | 2 | 1 High Sheriff Of Calhoun Parrish ............................................ *Groupy Girl* | $7 | | Monument 1193 |
| 11/28/70 | **117** | 1 | 2 Scratch My Back .................................................. *Old Man Willis* | $7 | | Monument 1227 |
| 7/10/76 | **108** | 2 | 3 It Must Be Love .................................................. *Susie-Q* | $5 | | 20th Century 2276 |

**WHITEHEAD, Charlie** ✪

| | | | | | | |
|---|---|---|---|---|---|---|
| 7/12/75 | **106** | 2 | Love Being Your Fool ................................ R&B:24 *Now That I Can Dance* | $6 | | Island 007 |
| | | | #38 hit for **Travis Wammack** in 1975 | | | |

**WHITESNAKE**     ROK/HOT/AC
Ex-**Deep Purple** vocalist David **Coverdale** formed British heavy-metal band in 1978. Coverdale fronted everchanging lineup.

| | | | | | | |
|---|---|---|---|---|---|---|
| 2/14/81 | **109** | 3 | Ain't No Love In The Heart Of The City ............................ *Come On* | $5 | | Mirage 3794 |
| | | | #91 hit in 1974 for **Bobby Bland** | | | |

**WHITING, Margaret**     MEM/POP/AC/C&W/HOT
Born on 7/22/24 in Detroit; raised in Hollywood. One of the top female vocalists of the '40s. *Pop Hits* & *Top Pop Singles*: 36.

| | | | | | | |
|---|---|---|---|---|---|---|
| 3/4/67 | **132** | 1 | 1 Just Like A Man ............................................ AC:29 *The World Inside Your Arms* | $6 | | London 106 |
| 10/21/67 | **108** | 6 | 2 I Almost Called Your Name     AC:4 *Let's Pretend* | $6 | | London 115 |
| 2/24/68 | **115** | 3 | 3 It Keeps Right On A Hurtin'/     AC:28 | | | |
| | | | #3 hit for **Johnny Tillotson** in 1962 | | | |
| 3/9/68 | **127** | 2 | 4 I Hate To See Me Go................................ AC:27 | $6 | | London 119 |
| 5/18/68 | **117** | 2 | 5 Faithfully .................................................. AC:19 *Am I Losing You?* | $6 | | London 122 |
| 9/28/68 | **124** | 3 | 6 Can't Get You Out Of My Mind ...................... AC:11 *Maybe Just One More* | $6 | | London 124 |
| | | | written by **Paul Anka** | | | |

**WHITMAN, Slim**     C&W/MEM/POP/HOT
Born Otis Whitman, Jr. on 1/20/24 in Tampa. Country balladeer/yodeller.

| | | | | | | |
|---|---|---|---|---|---|---|
| 9/17/66 | **134** | 1 | 1 I Remember You ............................................ C&W:49 *A Travelin' Man* | $10 | | Imperial 66181 |
| | | | #9 hit for Jimmy Dorsey in 1942; #5 hit for **Frank Ifield** in 1962; new version by Whitman made the Country charts (#44) in 1981 | | | |
| 1/23/71 | **121** | 1 | 2 Guess Who ............................................ C&W:7 *From Heaven To Heartache* | $8 | | United Artists 50731 |
| | | | #31 hit for Jesse Belvin in 1959 | | | |

**WHITNEY, Marva**     R&B/HOT
Soul songstress.

| | | | | | | |
|---|---|---|---|---|---|---|
| 8/23/69 | **110** | 4 | Things Got To Get Better (Get Together)...................... R&B:22 *Get Out Of My Life* | $10 | | King 6249 |
| | | | written and produced by **James Brown** | | | |

### WHO, The     HOT/ROK

Rock group formed in London in 1964: **Roger Daltrey** (b: 3/1/44, lead singer), **Pete Townshend** (b: 5/19/45; guitar, vocals), **John Entwistle** (b: 10/9/44; bass) and Keith Moon (b: 8/23/47; drums). Their 1969 rock opera album *Tommy* became a movie in 1975. Moon died of a drug overdose on 9/7/78, replaced by Kenney Jones (formerly with **Small Faces**). Group inducted into the Rock and Roll Hall of Fame in 1990. *Top Pop Singles: 26.*

| 8/13/66 | 106 | 3 | 1 The Kids Are Alright ........................................................... *A Legal Matter* | $30 | | Decca 31988 |
| | | | title of their biographical movie released in 1979 | | | |
| 1/13/79 | 107 | 1 | 2 Trick Of The Light ................................................................................... *905* | $6 | | MCA 40978 |

### WHODINI     R&B/HOT

New York rap group. Began as a duo of Jalil "Whodini" Hutchins and John "Ecstacy" Fletcher. Grandmaster Dee joined in 1986.

| 1/26/85 | 104 | 5 | 1 Freaks Come Out At Night .............................. R&B:43 *(instrumental)* | $4 | | Jive 9302 |
| 3/5/94 | 104 | 9 | 2 It All Comes Down To The Money ................. R&B:72 *Ruff E Nuff* | $3 | ■ | P.R.O. Division 77168 |
| | | | **TERMINATOR X And The Godfathers Of Threatt featuring Whodini** | | | |
| | | | Khadejia Bass (female vocal); samples "I Got My Mind Made Up" by Instant Funk | | | |

### WHORIDAS, The ☺     R&B

Rap duo from Oakland: Mr. Taylor and King Sann.

| 8/10/96 | 121 | 4 | 1 Shot Callin' & Big Ballin' ................. *(2 versions) / Town S#!t* | $3 | ■ | Southpaw 97005 |
| | | | samples "Bounce, Rock, Skate, Roll" by Vaughan Mason and Crew | | | |
| 7/5/97 | 102 | 12 | 2 Talkin' Bout' Bank ................................................ R&B:54 *Taxin'* | $3 | ■ | Southpaw 4007 |

### WIGGINS, Jay ☺     R&B

R&B vocalist from Philadelphia.

| 9/21/63 | 116 | 1 | Sad Girl ................................................................................ *No Not Me* | $25 | | I.P.G. 1008 |

### WIGHTMAN, Steve ☺

Pop vocalist.

| 5/15/76 | 110 | 1 | You Know The Feelin' ....................................................... *Misty Morning* | $6 | | Farr 003 |

### WILBURN BROTHERS, The ☺     C&W

Country duo from Hardy, Arkansas: brothers Virgil Doyle (b: 7/7/30; d: 10/16/82) and Thurman Theodore "Teddy" Wilburn (b: 11/30/31). Own TV series featuring **Loretta Lynn**.

| 6/30/62 | 101[1] | 1 | Trouble's Back In Town     C&W:4 *Young But True Love* | $10 | | Decca 31363 |

### WILD, Jack     HOT

Born in 1952. British juvenile actor. Played "The Artful Dodger" in the movie *Oliver* and "Jimmy" on TV's *H.R. Pufnstuf.*

| 8/15/70 | 115 | 2 | 1 Wait For Summer ................................................................. *Melody* | $6 | | Capitol 2868 |
| 8/28/71 | 107 | 1 | 2 (Holy Moses!) Everything's Coming Up Roses .......... *Bring Yourself Back To Me* | $6 | | Buddah 241 |

### WILDWEEDS     HOT

Rock group from Connecticut featuring Al Anderson (guitar; **NRBQ**).

| 7/10/71 | 113 | 4 | And When She Smiles ........................ *Paint And Powder Ladies* | $8 | | Vanguard 35134 |

### WILLIAMS, Andy     HOT/AC/R&B

Born Howard Andrew Williams on 12/3/28 in Wall Lake, Iowa. On **Steve Allen's** *Tonight Show* from 1952-55. Own NBC-TV variety series from 1962-67, 1969-71. *Top Pop Singles: 47.*

| 6/15/63 | 115 | 3 | 1 The Peking Theme (So Little Time) ......................... *Hopeless* (Hot #13) | $8 | | Columbia 42784 |
| | | | from the movie *55 Days At Peking* starring Charlton Heston | | | |
| 8/8/64 | 121 | 2 | 2 Under Paris Skies ................................................... *Let It Be Me* | $8 | | Cadence 1447 |
| | | | title song from the 1953 French movie; #26 hit for **Mitch Miller** in 1953 | | | |
| 2/19/66 | 127 | 2 | 3 Bye Bye Blues ............................... AC:18 *You're Gonna Hear From Me!* (AC #13) | $7 | | Columbia 43519 |
| | | | #5 hit for **Les Paul & Mary Ford** in 1953; #5 hit for **Bert Kaempfert** in 1966 | | | |
| 6/11/66 | 109 | 5 | 4 How Can I Tell Her It's Over ................... AC:17 *The Summer Of Our Love* | $7 | | Columbia 43650 |
| 11/18/67 | 113 | 3 | 5 Holly ........................................... AC:4 *When I Look In Your Eyes* | $7 | ■ | Columbia 44325 |
| 8/9/69 | 119 | 2 | 6 Live And Learn ................................................ AC:12 *You Are* | $7 | | Columbia 44929 |
| 11/1/69 | 109 | 3 | 7 A Woman's Way .............................. AC:4 *What Am I Living For* | $7 | | Columbia 45003 |
| 8/5/72 | 102 | 4 | 8 MacArthur Park ........................... AC:26 *Amazing Grace* | $6 | | Columbia 45647 |
| | | | #2 hit for **Richard Harris** in 1968 | | | |

### WILLIAMS, Carol ☺     R&B

Dance/disco singer from London.

| 3/27/76 | 102 | 3 | More ........................................................ R&B:98 *More Of More* | $5 | | Salsoul 2006 |
| | | | music by **The Salsoul Orchestra**; theme from the Italian documentary movie *Mondo Cane*; #8 hit for **Kai Winding** in 1963 | | | |

### WILLIAMS, Christopher     R&B/HOT

Harlem native. Nephew of jazz great **Ella Fitzgerald**.

| 12/19/92+ | 104 | 13 | All I See .......................... Sls:72 /R&B:19 *(instrumental)* | $3 | ■ | Uptown/MCA 54508 |

### WILLIAMS, Danny     HOT/R&B/AC

Born on 1/7/42 in Port Elizabeth, South Africa. Moved to England in 1960.

| 7/4/64 | 110 | 5 | More ......................................................................... *Rhapsody* | $10 | | United Artists 601 |
| | | | theme from the Italian documentary movie *Mondo Cane*; #8 hit for **Kai Winding** in 1963 | | | |

### WILLIAMS, Deniece     R&B/HOT/AC

Born Deniece Chandler on 6/3/51 in Gary, Indiana. R&B vocalist/songwriter.

| 8/13/77 | 103 | 2 | 1 That's What Friends Are For .................... R&B:65 *It's Important To Me* | $5 | | Columbia 10556 |
| 10/27/79 | 105 | 3 | 2 I Found Love ........................... R&B:32 *Are You Thinking?* | $4 | | ARC 11063 |
| 7/31/82 | 103 | 5 | 3 Waiting By The Hotline ........................... R&B:29 *Love Notes* | $4 | | ARC 03015 |
| 6/25/83 | 102 | 4 | 4 Do What You Feel    R&B:9 *Love, Peace And Unity* | $4 | ■ | Columbia 03807 |
| 3/31/84 | 106 | 2 | 5 Love Won't Let Me Wait ................ AC:14 /R&B:32 *Lead Me To Your Love* (Mathis) | $4 | | Columbia 04379 |
| | | | **JOHNNY MATHIS (with Deniece Williams)** | | | |
| | | | #5 hit for Major Harris in 1975 | | | |

### WILLIAMS, Don     C&W/AC/HOT

Born on 5/27/39 in Floydada, Texas. Country singer/songwriter/guitarist. Leader of the **Pozo-Seco Singers**.

| 10/30/76 | 103 | 5 | 1 She Never Knew Me .................................. C&W:2 *Ramblin'* [I] | $5 | | ABC/Dot 17658 |
| 5/14/77 | 108 | 1 | 2 Some Broken Hearts Never Mend ........... C&W:❶[1] *I'll Forgive But I'll Never Forget* | $5 | | ABC/Dot 17683 |

## WILLIAMS, Don — Cont'd
| DEBUT | PEAK | WKS | | | | |
|---|---|---|---|---|---|---|
| 9/17/77 | 110 | 1 | 3 **I'm Just A Country Boy** .................................... C&W:❶[1] *It's Gotta Be Magic* | $5 | | ABC/Dot 17717 |
| | | | #55 hit for **George McCurn** in 1963 | | | |
| 1/20/79 | 106 | 1 | 4 **Tulsa Time** ............................................ C&W:❶[1] *When I'm With You* | $5 | | ABC 12425 |
| | | | #30 hit for **Eric Clapton** in 1980 | | | |

## WILLIAMS, Hank ☉                    C&W
Born Hiram King Williams on 9/17/23 in Mount Olive, Alabama. Died on 1/1/53. Won Grammy's Lifetime Achievement Award in 1987. Inducted into the Rock and Roll Hall of Fame in 1987 as a forefather of rock 'n' roll.

| DEBUT | PEAK | WKS | | | | |
|---|---|---|---|---|---|---|
| 4/23/66 | 109 | 3 | **I'm So Lonesome I Could Cry** ................................................ C&W:43 *You Win Again* | $10 | | MGM 13489 |
| | | | new backing vocals and orchestration added to his original 1949 recording; #8 hit for **B.J. Thomas** in 1966 | | | |

## WILLIAMS, Hank Jr.                    C&W/HOT
Born Randall Hank Williams on 5/26/49 in Shreveport, Louisiana. Country singer/songwriter/guitarist. Son of country music's first superstar, Hank Williams.

| DEBUT | PEAK | WKS | | | | |
|---|---|---|---|---|---|---|
| 5/24/69 | 107 | 2 | 1 **Cajun Baby** ................................................ C&W:3 *My Heart Won't Let Me Go* | $7 | | MGM 14047 |
| | | | co-written by **Hank Williams**; new version by Hank and Doug Kershaw made the Country charts (#52) in 1988 | | | |
| 1/16/71 | 108 | 8 | 2 **Rainin' In My Heart** ...................................... C&W:3 *A-eee* (Williams) | $6 | | MGM 14194 |
| | | | **HANK WILLIAMS, JR. With THE MIKE CURB CONGREGATION** | | | |
| | | | #34 hit for **Slim Harpo** in 1961 | | | |
| 6/12/71 | 102 | 2 | 3 **I've Got A Right To Cry** .. C&W:6 *Jesus Loved The Devil Out Of Me* (w/Mike Curb Congregation) | $6 | | MGM 14240 |
| | | | #2 R&B hit for **Joe Liggins** in 1946 | | | |
| 9/15/79 | 104 | 5 | 4 **Family Tradition** ............................................ C&W:4 *Paying On Time* | $4 | | Elektra 46046 |

## WILLIAMS, John                    HOT/AC
Born on 2/8/32 in New York City. Noted composer/conductor of many top box-office movie hits. Succeeded Arthur Fiedler as conductor of the **Boston Pops Orchestra** in 1980; resigned in 1993 but continued as music adviser. Winner of 15 Grammys.

| DEBUT | PEAK | WKS | | | | |
|---|---|---|---|---|---|---|
| 7/17/82 | 103 | 2 | 1 **Theme From E.T. (The Extra-Terrestrial)** ............................ *Over The Moon* [I] | $4 | ■ | MCA 52072 |
| | | | from the Steven Spielberg movie starring Henry Thomas | | | |
| 9/13/97 | 118 | 1 | 2 **The Imperial March (Darth Vader's Theme)** ............................ *(no B-side)* [I] | $25 | | RCA Victor 68821 (CD) |
| | | | special issue die-cut CD (in the shape of Darth Vader's head); performed by The London Symphony Orchestra (1980); from the reissue of the movie *The Empire Strikes Back* | | | |

## WILLIAMS, Johnny ☉                    C&W
Country singer. Featured performer at Gilley's nightclub during the late '70s and early '80s.

| DEBUT | PEAK | WKS | | | | |
|---|---|---|---|---|---|---|
| 4/22/72 | 104 | 6 | **He Will Break Your Heart** ...................................... C&W:68 *If Loving You Means Anything* | $7 | | Epic 10845 |
| | | | #7 hit for **Jerry Butler** in 1960 | | | |

## WILLIAMS, Lenny ☉                    R&B
Born in February 1945, in Little Rock, Arkansas. First recorded for Fantasy in the early '60s. Lead vocalist of **Tower Of Power** from 1972-75.

| DEBUT | PEAK | WKS | | | | |
|---|---|---|---|---|---|---|
| 9/17/77 | 105 | 5 | 1 **Shoo Doo Fu Fu Ooh!** ............................................ R&B:31 *Trust In Me* | $5 | | ABC 12300 |
| 1/14/78 | 108 | 1 | 2 **Choosing You** ............................................ R&B:62 *Problem Solver* | $5 | | ABC 12289 |
| 8/19/78 | 104 | 12 | 3 **You Got Me Running** ............................................ R&B:40 *Come Reap My Love* | $5 | | ABC 12387 |
| 11/25/78 | 102 | 9 | 4 **Midnight Girl** ............................... R&B:20 *I Still Reach Out To You* | $5 | | ABC 12423 |
| 10/4/80 | 109 | 1 | 5 **Ooh Child** ............................................ R&B:34 *Let's Do It Today* | $4 | | MCA 41306 |
| | | | #8 hit for **The Five Stairsteps** in 1970 | | | |

## WILLIAMS, Little Jerry ☉                    R&B
Born in 1942 in Portsmouth, Virginia. R&B singer/producer. Assumed name **Swamp Dogg** in 1970.

| DEBUT | PEAK | WKS | | | | |
|---|---|---|---|---|---|---|
| 11/21/64 | 102 | 6 | 1 **I'm The Lover Man** ...................................... *The Push Push Push* | $12 | | Loma 2005 |
| 1/15/66 | 122 | 1 | 2 **Baby, You're My Everything** .............. R&B:32 *Just What Do You Plan To Do About It* | $12 | | Calla 105 |
| 5/30/70 | 113 | 2 | 3 **Mama's Baby - Daddy's Maybe** .............................. R&B:33 *Sal-A-Faster* | $8 | | Canyon 30 |
| | | | **SWAMP DOGG** | | | |

## WILLIAMS, Mason                    AC/HOT
Born on 8/24/38 in Abilene, Texas. Folk guitarist/songwriter/author/photographer/TV comedy writer.

| DEBUT | PEAK | WKS | | | | |
|---|---|---|---|---|---|---|
| 7/26/69 | 118 | 2 | **A Gift Of Song** ............................................ AC:33 *A Major Thang* | $6 | | Warner 7301 |
| | | | accompanied by the Choir of St. Mark's Presbyterian Church, Van Nuys, California | | | |

## WILLIAMS, Paul                    AC/HOT/C&W
Born on 9/19/40 in Omaha. Singer/songwriter/actor. Wrote "We've Only Just Begun" and "Rainy Days & Mondays."

| DEBUT | PEAK | WKS | | | | |
|---|---|---|---|---|---|---|
| 3/10/73 | 106 | 5 | 1 **I Won't Last A Day Without You** ............................................ AC:40 *Little Girl* | $5 | | A&M 1409 |
| | | | #11 hit for the **Carpenters** in 1974 | | | |
| 12/8/73+ | 108 | 10 | 2 **Inspiration** ............................................ AC:18 *What Would They Say* | $5 | | A&M 1479 |

## WILLIAMS, Robin ☉
Born on 7/21/52 in Chicago. Leading actor/comedian since 1978.

| DEBUT | PEAK | WKS | | | | |
|---|---|---|---|---|---|---|
| 12/27/80 | 104 | 4 | **I Yam What I Am** ...................................... *He Needs Me* (Shelley Duvall) [N] | $5 | ■ | Boardwalk 5701 |
| | | | written and produced by **Nilsson**; from the movie *Popeye* starring Williams and Shelley Duvall | | | |

## WILLIAMS, Roger                    HOT/AC
Born Louis Weertz on 10/1/24 in Omaha. Top popular pianist since his #1 hit "Autumn Leaves" in 1955. *Top Pop Singles*: 23.

| DEBUT | PEAK | WKS | | | | |
|---|---|---|---|---|---|---|
| 10/19/59 | 106 | 4 | 1 **Sunrise Serenade** ...................................... *Cool Water* [I] | $10 | ■ | Kapp 301 |
| | | | #1 hit for **Glen Gray** with pianist **Frankie Carle** in 1939 | | | |
| 5/4/63 | 113 | 3 | 2 **On The Trail** ............................................ *Walking Alone* [I] | $8 | | Kapp 522 |
| | | | from Ferde Grofe's *Grand Canyon Suite*; #13 hit for **Paul Whiteman** in 1932 | | | |
| 12/21/63 | 109 | 3 | 3 **Theme From "The Cardinal"** ............................................ *Walking Alone* [I] | $8 | ■ | Kapp 560 |
| | | | from the movie *The Cardinal* starring Tom Tryon | | | |
| 8/21/65 | 109 | 4 | 4 **Summer Wind** ............................ AC:20 *Sailor (Your Home Is The Sea)* (Williams) | $7 | | Kapp 55 |
| | | | **ROGER WILLIAMS & The HARRY SIMEONE CHORALE** | | | |
| | | | released on Kapp's "Winners Circle Series" label; #25 hit for **Frank Sinatra** in 1966 | | | |
| 10/14/67 | 108 | 4 | 5 **More Than A Miracle** ............................................ AC:2 *Tiny Bubbles* | $6 | ■ | Kapp 843 |
| | | | title song from the movie starring Sophia Loren | | | |
| 12/7/68 | 119 | 2 | 6 **Only For Lovers** ...................................... *Theme For "Elvira"* [I] | $6 | | Kapp 949 |
| 4/1/72 | 116 | 5 | 7 **Love Theme From The Godfather** ............ *Theme From Kotch (Life Is What You Make It)* [I] | $5 | | Kapp 2165 |
| | | | from the movie *The Godfather* starring Marlon Brando; #34 hit for **Andy Williams** in 1972 | | | |

**WILLIAMS, Terry** ☉        AC
Former member of **Kenny Rogers and The First Edition**.

| 11/25/72 | 112 | 5 | Melanie Makes Me Smile .................................................. *Baby Believe Me* | $5 | ☐ | MGM/Verve 10686 |

#87 hit for Tony Burrows in 1970

**WILLIES, The** ☉
Pop vocal group.

| 10/8/66 | 113 | 5 | The Willy ............................................................................. *Say You're Mine Again* | $10 | | Co & Ce 239 |

**WILLIS, Hal** ☉        C&W
Born Leonard Francis Gauthier in Roslyn, Quebec. Moved to Nashville in 1958. Country singer.

| 10/31/64 | 120 | 6 | The Lumberjack................................................... C&W:5 *Dig Me A Hole* | $12 | | Sims 207 |

**WILLIS, Timmy** ☉        R&B

| 2/3/68 | 120 | 3 | Mr. Soul Satisfaction............................................ R&B:39 *I'm Wondering* | $12 | | Veep 1279 |

originally released on Sidra 9013 in 1967 ($15)

**WILLOWS**        HOT/R&B
R&B doo-wop group formed in New York City in 1952 as the Five Willows featuring Tony Middleton (lead). Also see **Sammy Ambrose**.

| 3/6/61 | 114 | 1 | Church Bells May Ring ................................................. *Baby Tell Me* [R] | $75 | | Melba 102 |

Neil Sedaka (chimes); originally made the *Hot 100* (#62) on 4/7/56

**WILLS, Nikki** ☉
Pop vocalist with her husband's group, the Johnny Average Band.

| 12/19/81 | 109 | 3 | Some Guys Have All The Luck ................................... *Picture Of You* | $5 | | Bearsville 49868 |

#39 hit for **The Persuaders** in 1973; #10 hit for **Rod Stewart** in 1984

**WILMER & THE DUKES**        HOT
R&B-rock quintet led by Wilmer Alexander, Jr.

| 8/23/69 | 114 | 2 | Living In The U.S.A. ......................................................... *Count On Me* | $8 | | Aphrodisiac 262 |

#49 hit for the **Steve Miller Band** in 1974 (originally charted by Miller in 1968-#94)

**WILSON, Al**        R&B/HOT/AC
Born on 6/19/39 in Meridian, Mississippi. R&B singer/drummer. Member of The Rollers from 1960-62.

| 1/6/68 | 102 | 4 | 1 Do What You Gotta Do............................. R&B:39 *Now I Know What Love Is* | $8 | | Soul City 761 |

#83 hit for **Nina Simone** and **Bobby Vee** in 1968

| 4/12/69 | 106 | 3 | 2 I Stand Accused ................................... *Shake Me, Wake Me (When It's Over)* | $8 | | Soul City 773 |

#61 hit for **Jerry Butler** in 1964; above 2 produced by **Johnny Rivers**

**WILSON, Carl**        AC/HOT
Born on 6/21/46 in Hawthorne, California. Died of cancer on 2/6/98. Guitarist of **The Beach Boys**.

| 8/22/81 | 107 | 4 | Heaven................................................................. AC:20 *Hurry Love* | $7 | | Caribou 02136 |

**WILSON, Carnie & Wendy — see WILSON PHILLIPS**

**WILSON, J. Frank**        HOT
Born on 12/11/41 in Lufkin, Texas. Died on 10/4/91. Band, The Cavaliers, formed in San Angelo, Texas.

| 1/23/65 | 101[1] | 4 | Six Boys      *Say It Now* | $10 | | Josie 929 |

**WILSON, Jackie**        HOT/R&B
Born on 6/9/34 in Detroit. Died on 1/21/84. Joined Billy Ward's Dominoes as **Clyde McPhatter**'s replacement in 1953. Solo since 1957. Inducted into the Rock and Roll Hall of Fame in 1987. *Top Pop Singles*: 54.

| 10/6/62 | 119 | 1 | 1 Baby, That's All ...................................... *Forever And A Day* (Hot #82) | $20 | | Brunswick 55233 |
| 1/5/63 | 121 | 1 | 2 What Good Am I Without You?.................. *A Girl Named Tamiko* | $20 | ■ | Brunswick 55236 |
| 2/29/64 | 123 | 2 | 3 I'm Travelin' On ...................................................... *Haunted House* | $15 | | Brunswick 55260 |
| 4/18/64 | 110 | 1 | 4 Call Her Up ................................................................ *The Kickapoo* | $15 | | Brunswick 55263 |
| 10/10/64 | 102 | 6 | 5 She's All Right | *Watch Out* | $15 | | Brunswick 55273 |
| 1/1/66 | 128 | 1 | 6 Please Don't Hurt Me (I've Never Been In Love Before)................. *Think Twice* (Hot #93) | $15 | | Brunswick 55287 |

JACKIE WILSON And LaVERN BAKER

| 3/22/69 | 105 | 3 | 7 I Still Love You .......................................... R&B:39 *Hum De Dum De Do* | $12 | | Brunswick 55402 |
| 9/13/69 | 108 | 4 | 8 Helpless........................................................ R&B:21 *Do It The Right Way* | $12 | | Brunswick 55418 |

**WILSON, Nancy**        R&B/AC/HOT
Born on 2/20/37 in Chillicothe; raised in Columbus, Ohio. Jazz stylist with Rusty Bryant's Carolyn Club Band in Columbus.

| 11/21/64 | 106 | 4 | 1 And Satisfy | *Take What I Have* | $7 | | Capitol 5319 |
| 5/8/65 | 125 | 1 | 2 Welcome, Welcome.................................... *The Best Is Yet To Come* | $7 | | Capitol 5408 |
| 12/14/68 | 117 | 3 | 3 In A Long White Room................................ AC:31 *Only Love* | $6 | | Capitol 2361 |
| 3/15/69 | 111 | 4 | 4 You'd Better Go .......................................... R&B:44 *I'm Your Special Fool* | $6 | | Capitol 2422 |
| 8/2/69 | 114 | 2 | 5 Got It Together ............................................... *One Soft Night* | $6 | | Capitol 2555 |

**WILSON, Pat** ☉
Female pop/rock vocalist.

| 4/7/84 | 104 | 1 | Bop Girl .......................................................................... *Tacky* | $4 | | Warner 29361 |

**WILSON PHILLIPS**        AC/HOT
Pop vocal/songwriting trio of sisters **Carnie and Wendy Wilson**, with Chynna Phillips. Carnie and Wendy's father is Brian Wilson (**The Beach Boys**). Chynna is the daughter of Michelle and John Phillips (**The Mamas & The Papas**).

| 12/5/92 | 119 | 3 | 1 Flesh & Blood ...................................... AC:17 *Silent Night* | $3 | ■ | SBK 50415 |
| 1/1/94 | 101[1] | 2 | 2 Hey Santa!    AC:22 *Have Yourself A Merry Little Christmas* [X] | $3 | ■ | SBK/ERG 58047 |

CARNIE and WENDY WILSON

**WINANS, Mario** ☉        R&B
Born in Detroit. Singer/session drummer. Brother of BeBe and CeCe Winans.

| 7/5/97 | 108 | 7 | Don't Know ................................................... R&B:48 *(remix)* (w/Allure and Mase) | $3 | ■ | Motown 0618 |

samples "With You In Mind" by Acoustic Alchemy

**WINBUSH, Angela**        R&B/HOT
Composer/producer/vocalist. In Rene & Angela duo with Rene Moore from 1980-86. Married Ronald Isley of **The Isley Brothers** on 6/26/93.

| 4/23/94 | 117 | 5 | Treat U Rite ........................................................ R&B:6 *Dream Lover* | $3 | ■ | Elektra 64562 |

**WINDING, Kai**  AC/HOT
Born on 5/18/22 in Aarhus, Denmark. Died on 5/6/83. Jazz trombonist. Moved to U.S. in 1934.

| 3/14/64 | 120 | 2 | Mondo Cane #2 .......................................................... *Portrait Of My Love* [I] | $8 | ■ | Verve 10313 |

music from the sequel to the Italian shockumentary movie

**WINGFIELD, Pete**  HOT/R&B
Born on 5/7/48 in England. Keyboardist. Worked with **Freddy King**, Jimmy Witherspoon and Van Morrison.

| 2/14/76 | 108 | 2 | Lovin' As You Wanna Be ..................................................... *Please* | $5 | | Island 051 |

**WINSTONS, The**  HOT/AC/R&B
R&B septet from Washington, D.C. featuring Richard Spencer (vocals).

| 1/3/70 | 107 | 3 | Say Goodbye To Daddy ........................................ *Mama's Song* | $7 | | Metromedia 166 |

RICHARD SPENCER & THE WINSTONS

**WINTER, Edgar**  HOT
Born on 12/28/46 in Beaumont, Texas. Albino rock singer/keyboardist/saxophonist. Younger brother of **Johnny Winter**.

| 6/26/71 | 128 | 2 | Where Would I Be (Without You) .............................. *Good Morning Music* | $7 | | Epic 10740 |

EDGAR WINTER'S WHITE TRASH Featuring Jerry La Croix

**WINTER, Johnny**  HOT/ROK
Born on 2/23/44 in Leland, Mississippi. Albino blues-rock guitarist/vocalist. Older brother of **Edgar Winter**.

| 5/3/69 | 129 | 2 | 1 Rollin' And Tumblin' ...................................................... *Forty-Four* | $10 | | Imperial 66376 |

written and recorded by Muddy Waters in 1949 on Aristocrat 412 ($60)

| 1/25/75 | 108 | 2 | 2 Raised On Rock ............................................. *Pick Up On My Mojo* | $6 | | Blue Sky 2754 |

#41 hit for Elvis Presley in 1973

**WINTERS, Robert, & Fall** ✪  R&B
Winters is an R&B vocalist/keyboardist from Detroit. Stricken with polio at age five; confined to a wheelchair.

| 5/9/81 | 101[1] | 7 | Magic Man                      R&B:11 *One More Year* | $4 | | Buddah 624 |

**WINTERS, Ruby**  R&B/HOT
Born in Louisville; raised in Cincinnati. R&B vocalist.

| 10/28/67 | 109 | 3 | 1 I Want Action ...................................... R&B:47 *Better* | $15 | | Diamond 230 |
| 10/4/69 | 121 | 3 | 2 Always David ................... R&B:23 *We're Living To Give (To Give To Each Other)* | $15 | | Diamond 265 |

**WINWOOD, Steve**  ROK/HOT/AC/R&B
Born on 5/12/48 in Birmingham, England. Rock singer/keyboardist/guitarist. Lead singer of **Spencer Davis Group**, Blind Faith and **Traffic**.

| 8/8/81 | 104 | 2 | Night Train ................................................... *(instrumental)* | $4 | | Island 49773 |

**WITHERS, Bill**  R&B/HOT/AC
Born on 7/4/38 in Slab Fork, West Virginia. R&B vocalist/guitarist/composer. Moved to California in 1967 and made demo records of his songs. Married to actress Denise Nicholas.

| 5/25/85 | 106 | 2 | Oh Yeah! ............................ R&B:22 / AC:40 *Just Like The First Time* | $4 | | Columbia 04841 |

**WOLFMAN JACK**  HOT
Born Robert Weston Smith on 1/21/38 in Brooklyn. Died of a heart attack on 7/1/95. Legendary DJ.

| 9/23/72 | 106 | 6 | 1 I Ain't Never Seen A White Man ........................................ *Gallop* [S] | $6 | ■ | Wooden Nickel 0108 |
| 1/18/75 | 105 | 4 | 2 Wolfman Jack ........................................................ *Breathless* | $6 | | Bearsville 0301 |

TODD RUNDGREN (featuring Wolfman Jack)

**WOMACK, Bobby**  R&B/HOT
Born on 3/4/44 in Cleveland. R&B vocalist/guitarist/songwriter. Recorded with his brothers as the **Valentinos** and The Lovers, 1962-64. Married for a time to **Sam Cooke**'s widow, Barbara. His brother, Cecil, and Sam Cooke's daughter, Linda, recorded as Womack & Womack.

| 3/15/69 | 119 | 3 | 1 I Left My Heart In San Francisco .................. R&B:48 *Love, The Time Is Now* | $8 | | Minit 32059 |

#19 hit for Tony Bennett in 1962

| 5/29/71 | 111 | 4 | 2 The Preacher (Part 2)/More Than I Can Stand ............. R&B:30 *The Preacher (Part 1)* | $7 | | United Artists 50773 |

monologue intro to "More Than I Can Stand" which made the Hot 100 (#90) on 4/25/70 on Minit 32093

| 10/20/73 | 101[3] | 10 | 3 I'm Through Trying To Prove My Love To You    R&B:80 *Nobody Wants You When You're Down And Out* (Hot #29) | $6 | | United Artists 255 |
| 3/6/82 | 101[3] | 3 | 4 If You Think You're Lonely Now                R&B:3 *Secrets* (R&B #55) | $4 | | Beverly Glen 2000 |
| 2/16/85 | 102 | 6 | 5 (No Matter How High I Get) I'll Still Be Lookin' Up To You ................. R&B:2 *La Luz* | $4 | ■ | MCA 52467 |

WILTON FELDER Featuring Bobby Womack and Introducing Alltrinna Grayson

**WOMACK, Lee Ann** ✪  C&W
Country singer from Jacksonville, Texas.

| 5/24/97 | 124 | 2 | Never Again, Again .................................... C&W:23 *(3 album snippets)* | $3 | ▮ | Decca 55320 |

**WOMENFOLK, The**  HOT
Pasadena female folk quintet: Elaine Gealer, Joyce James, Leni Ashmore, Babs Cooper and Judy Fine.

| 5/7/66 | 105 | 3 | The Last Thing On My Mind ....................... *Meditation (Meditacao)* | $7 | | RCA Victor 8784 |

Billy Mure (orch.); #56 hit for Neil Diamond in 1973

**WONDER, Stevie**  R&B/HOT/AC
Born Steveland Morris on 5/13/50 in Saginaw, Michigan. R&B singer/songwriter/multi-instrumentalist/producer. Blind since birth. Winner of 17 Grammy Awards. Inducted into the Rock and Roll Hall of Fame in 1989. Won Grammy's Lifetime Achievement Award in 1996. *Top Pop Singles*: 65.

| 8/31/63 | 101[1] | 1 | 1 I Call It Pretty Music, But The Old People Call It The Blues Pt 1    *Pt 2* | $40 | ■ | Tamla 54061 |

LITTLE STEVIE WONDER
Stevie's first record release from 1962

| 7/16/66 | 131 | 1 | 2 With A Child's Heart ................................. R&B:8 *Nothing's Too Good For My Baby* (Hot #20) | $15 | | Tamla 54130 |

#50 hit for Michael Jackson in 1973

**WOOD, Bobby**  HOT/C&W
Pop/country singer/pianist. Session work in Memphis.

| 10/17/64 | 130 | 3 | 1 That's All I Need To Know ....................... C&W:46 *This Time* | $10 | | Joy 288 |
| 1/6/68 | 110 | 5 | 2 Break My Mind ..................................... *This Thing Called Love* | $7 | | MGM 13797 |

#6 Country hit for George Hamilton IV in 1967

**WOOD, Brenton**      R&B/HOT
Born Alfred Smith on 7/26/41 in Shreveport, Louisiana. R&B singer/songwriter/pianist.

| | | | | | | |
|---|---|---|---|---|---|---|
| 8/10/68 | 121 | 2 | 1 Me And You ........................................... *Some Got It, Some Don't* (R&B #42) | $8 | | Double Shot 130 |
| 3/15/69 | 131 | 2 | 2 A Change Is Gonna Come ................................ *Where Were You* | $8 | | Double Shot 137 |
| | | | #31 hit for **Sam Cooke** in 1965 | | | |

**WOOD, Chuck** ✪
R&B vocalist.

| | | | | | | |
|---|---|---|---|---|---|---|
| 9/23/67 | 119 | 3 | Seven Days Too Long ................................... *Soul Shing-A-Ling* | $8 | | Roulette 4754 |

**WOODS, Rev. Maceo** ✪      R&B
Director/pianist for his church choir in Chicago.

| | | | | | | |
|---|---|---|---|---|---|---|
| 12/20/69 | 121 | 2 | Hello Sunshine ....................... R&B:28 *Amazing Grace* | $8 | | Volt 4025 |
| | | | **REV. MACEO WOODS AND THE CHRISTIAN TABERNACLE BAPTIST CHURCH CHOIR** | | | |

**WOOLEY, Sheb — see COLDER, Ben**

**WORL-A-GIRL** ✪
Female reggae foursome.

| | | | | | | |
|---|---|---|---|---|---|---|
| 4/2/94 | 120 | 3 | No Gunshot (Put Down The Gun) ........................... *(remix)* | $3 | ▌ | Chaos/Columbia 77413 |

**WORLD OF OZ** ✪
British pop-rock quartet.

| | | | | | | |
|---|---|---|---|---|---|---|
| 11/30/68 | 126 | 1 | King Croesus .......................................... *Jack* | $8 | | Deram 85034 |
| | | | Croesus: last wealthy king of Lydia (560-546 B.C.) | | | |

**WORLD WIDE MESSAGE TRIBE, The** ✪
Techno-dance/rap outfit from Manchester, England.

| | | | | | | |
|---|---|---|---|---|---|---|
| 11/9/96 | 109 | 4 | The Real Thing ....................................... *Sweet Salvation* | $3 | ▌ | Warner Alliance 17496 |

**WRECKX-N-EFFECT**      R&B/HOT
Male rap group: Aqil Davidson, Markell Riley and Brandon Mitchell (d: in 1990 of gunshot fire). Riley is the brother of producer **Teddy Riley**.

| | | | | | | |
|---|---|---|---|---|---|---|
| 3/27/93 | 101[1] | 12 | Wreckx Shop    Sls:54 /R&B:46 *(album version)* | $3 | ▌ | MCA 54531 |

**WRIGHT, Betty**      R&B/HOT
Born on 12/21/53 in Miami. R&B singer. In family gospel group, Echoes Of Joy, from 1956.

| | | | | | | |
|---|---|---|---|---|---|---|
| 11/9/68 | 103 | 5 | 1 He's Bad Bad Bad ................................... *Watch Out Love* | $10 | | Alston 4571 |
| 8/14/71 | 109 | 1 | 2 I Love The Way You Love ................... R&B:44 *When We Get Together Again* | $8 | | Alston 4594 |
| 4/22/72 | 104 | 2 | 3 If You Love Me Like You Say You Love Me/    R&B:21 | | | |
| 4/8/72 | 121 | 2 | 4   I'm Gettin' Tired Baby ............................. R&B:42 | $8 | | Alston 4609 |
| 6/17/72 | 101[1] | 3 | 5 Is It You Girl    R&B:18 *Cryin' In My Sleep* | $8 | | Alston 4611 |

**WRIGHT, Charles**      R&B/HOT
Born in 1942 in Clarksdale, Mississippi. Vocalist/pianist/guitarist/producer/leader of an eight-man, R&B-funk band from the Watts section of Los Angeles. Evolved from the **Soul Runners**.

| | | | | | | |
|---|---|---|---|---|---|---|
| 1/14/67 | 103 | 9 | 1 Grits 'N Corn Bread ............................ R&B:33 *Spreadin' Honey* [I] | $25 | | MoSoul 101 |
| | | | **SOUL RUNNERS** | | | |
| | | | B-side charted later in 1967 (#73) on Keymen 108 as by The Watts 103rd St. Rhythm Band | | | |
| 11/22/69 | 103 | 2 | 2 Must Be Your Thing/    R&B:35 | | | |
| 10/11/69 | 109 | 2 | 3   Comment ....................................... | $7 | | Warner 7338 |
| | | | **CHARLES WRIGHT AND THE WATTS 103RD STREET RHYTHM BAND** (above 2) | | | |

**WRIGHT, Chely** ✪      C&W
Born on 10/25/70 in Kansas City. Female country singer/guitarist.

| | | | | | | |
|---|---|---|---|---|---|---|
| 9/20/97 | 112 | 10 | Shut Up And Drive ............................. C&W:14 *(3 album snippets)* | $3 | ▌ | MCA 72012 |

**WRIGHT, Gary**      HOT/AC/ROK/R&B
Born on 4/26/43 in Creskill, New Jersey. Pop-rock singer/songwriter/keyboardist. Co-leader of the rock group **Spooky Tooth**.

| | | | | | | |
|---|---|---|---|---|---|---|
| 10/31/81 | 107 | 3 | Heartbeat............................................. *Comin' Apart* | $4 | | Warner 49836 |

**WRIGHT, Norma Jean** ✪      R&B
R&B/dance vocalist. Original member of **Chic**. Born in Elyria, Ohio. Not to be confused with the country artist Norma Jean.

| | | | | | | |
|---|---|---|---|---|---|---|
| 9/9/78 | 103 | 5 | Saturday ...................................... R&B:15 *This Is The Love* | $4 | | Bearsville 0326 |

**WRIGHT, O.V.**      R&B/HOT
Born Overton Vertis Wright on 10/9/39 in Leno, Tennessee. Died on 11/16/80. R&B singer.

| | | | | | | |
|---|---|---|---|---|---|---|
| 8/29/64 | 109 | 8 | 1 That's How Strong My Love Is ............... *There Goes My Used To Be* | $15 | | Goldwax 106 |
| | | | **O.V. WRIGHT WITH THE KEYS** | | | |
| | | | #74 hit for **Otis Redding** in 1965 | | | |
| 3/6/71 | 118 | 4 | 2 When You Took Your Love From Me ........ R&B:21 *I Was Born All Over* | $8 | | Back Beat 620 |
| 9/25/71 | 103 | 3 | 3 A Nickel And A Nail........................ R&B:19 *Pledging My Love* | $8 | | Back Beat 622 |

**WRIGHT, Ruby** ✪      C&W
Born on 10/27/39 in Nashville. Daughter of country singers Kitty Wells and Johnny Wright. Member of Nita, Rita & Ruby.

| | | | | | | |
|---|---|---|---|---|---|---|
| 9/12/64 | 103 | 5 | Dern Ya ........................ C&W:13 *Such A Silly Notion* [N] | $12 | | RIC 126-64 |
| | | | answer song to **Roger Miller**'s "Dang Me" | | | |

**WU-TANG CLAN**      R&B/HOT
Rap group from Staten Island, New York featuring arrangements by Prince Rakeem The RZA. Also see **Genius/GZA** and **Method Man**.

| | | | | | | |
|---|---|---|---|---|---|---|
| 9/25/93 | 105 | 2 | 1 Protect Ya Neck ...................... R&B:86 *Method Man* (Hot #69) | $3 | ▌ | Loud/RCA 62544 |
| 7/16/94 | 116 | 2 | 2 Can It Be All So Simple............ R&B:82 *Wu-Tang Clan Ain't Nuthing Ta F' Wit* | $3 | ▌ | Loud/RCA 62891 |
| | | | samples "The Way We Were" by **Gladys Knight & The Pips** | | | |

**WYLIE, Popcorn** ✪      R&B
Born Richard Wylie on 6/6/39 in Detroit. R&B musician/songwriter/arranger/producer.

| | | | | | | |
|---|---|---|---|---|---|---|
| 12/29/62 | 109 | 3 | 1 Come To Me .................................... *Weddin' Bells* | $25 | ▌ | Epic 9543 |
| | | | **RICHARD "POPCORN" WYLIE** | | | |
| 10/23/71 | 109 | 1 | 2 Funky Rubber Band ........................ R&B:40 *(instrumental)* | $10 | | Soul 35087 |

**WYNETTE, Tammy**      C&W/HOT/AC
Born Virginia Wynette Pugh on 5/5/42 in Itawamba County, Mississippi. Died of a blood clot on 4/6/98. Dubbed "The First Lady of Country Music." Married to **George Jones** from 1969-75.

| | | | | | | |
|-------|------|-----|------|---|-----|----------------|
| 12/5/70 | 104 | 3 | 1 The Wonders You Perform ........................................ C&W:5 *Gentle Shepherd* | $8 | | Epic 10687 |
| 3/20/71 | 103 | 10 | 2 We Sure Can Love Each Other ................................... C&W:2 *Fun* | $8 | | Epic 10707 |
| 7/31/71 | 111 | 2 | 3 Good Lovin' (Makes It Right) .................................. C&W:❶² *I Love You, Mr. Jones* | $8 | | Epic 10759 |
| 1/20/73 | 106 | 4 | 4 'Til I Get It Right ............................................. C&W:❶¹ *The Bridge Of Love* | $7 | | Epic 10940 |
| 10/23/76 | 101¹ | 2 | 5 You And Me    C&W:❶² / AC:28 *When Love Was All We Had* | $6 | | Epic 50264 |

**WYNONNA**      C&W/AC/HOT
Born Christina Ciminella on 5/30/64 in Ashland, Kentucky. Country singer. Half of The Judds duo with her mother, Naomi (The Judds - *Top Country Singles:* 23.)

| | | | | | | |
|-------|------|-----|------|---|-----|----------------|
| 2/13/93 | 119 | 3 | 1 My Strongest Weakness ............................................. C&W:4 *What It Takes* | $3 | ▌ | Curb/MCA 54516 |
| 9/4/93 | 102 | 11 | 2 Only Love .................................... Sls:63 /C&W:3 *Just Like New* | $3 | ▌ | Curb/MCA 54689 |
| 1/21/95 | 120 | 4 | 3 Healing ....................................................... *(same version)* | $3 | ▌ | Curb 76928 |

     **WYNONNA & MICHAEL ENGLISH**
     from the movie *Silent Fall* starring Richard Dreyfuss

# X

**XAVIER** ✪      R&B
Eight-member R&B/funk group — lead vocals by Xavier Smith and Ayanna Little.

| | | | | | | |
|-------|------|-----|------|---|-----|----------------|
| 4/24/82 | 104 | 1 | Work That Sucker To Death ............................... R&B:6 *Love Is On The One* | $4 | | Liberty 1445 |

**XAVION** ✪      R&B
R&B sextet from Memphis.

| | | | | | | |
|-------|------|-----|------|---|-----|----------------|
| 9/8/84 | 103 | 2 | Eat Your Heart Out ........................................ | $4 | | Asylum 69707 |

**XTC**      ROK/HOT
British rock group formed in 1977: Andy Partridge (guitar), Dave Gregory (keyboards), Colin Moulding (bass) and Terry Chambers (drums).

| | | | | | | |
|-------|------|-----|------|---|-----|----------------|
| 1/24/81 | 104 | 3 | Generals And Majors ........................................ ROK:28 *Living Through Another Cuba* | $4 | | RSO/Virgin 300 |

**XZIBIT**      R&B/HOT
Born in Detroit; raised in New Mexico. Male rapper. Affilated with, but not a member of, **Tha Alkaholiks**.

| | | | | | | |
|-------|------|-----|------|---|-----|----------------|
| 11/30/96+ | 101³ | 13 | The Foundation    R&B:58 *Eyes May Shine* | $3 | ▌ | Loud/RCA 64708 |

# Y

**YANKOVIC, "Weird Al"**      HOT/ROK/R&B
Born on 10/24/59 in Lynwood, California. Novelty singer/accordionist. Specializes in song parodies.

| | | | | | | |
|-------|------|-----|------|---|-----|----------------|
| 3/21/81 | 104 | 2 | 1 Another One Rides The Bus ................................ *Gotta Boogie* [N] | $5 | | T.K. 1043 |
| | | |    parody of **Queen**'s #1 1980 hit "Another One Bites The Dust" | | | |
| 8/6/83 | 106 | 2 | 2 I Love Rocky Road ........................................ *Happy Birthday* [N] | $4 | | Rock 'N' Roll 03998 |
| | | |    parody of **Joan Jett & The Blackhearts**' #1 1982 hit "I Love Rock 'N Roll" | | | |
| 10/29/94 | 104 | 8 | 3 Headline News ........................................ *Christmas At Ground Zero* [N] | $3 | ▌ | Scotti Brothers 78011 |
| | | |    parody of the **Crash Test Dummies**' #4 1994 hit "Mmm Mmm Mmm Mmm" | | | |
| 5/25/96 | 102 | 9 | 4 Gump ........................................ Sls:71 *Spy Hard* [N] | $3 | ▌ | Rock 'N' Roll 78073 |
| | | |    parody of **The Presidents Of The United States Of America**'s #1 1995 Modern Rock hit "Lump" | | | |

**YANOVSKY, Zalman (Zally)** ✪
Born on 2/19/44 in Toronto. Original member of **The Lovin' Spoonful** and **The Mugwumps**.

| | | | | | | |
|-------|------|-----|------|---|-----|----------------|
| 10/7/67 | 101² | 5 | As Long As You're Here    *Ereh Er'ouy Sa Gnol Sa* | $10 | ■ | Buddah 12 |

**YARBROUGH & PEOPLES**      R&B/HOT
Dallas R&B duo: Cavin Yarbrough and Alisa Peoples. Discovered by **The Gap Band**.

| | | | | | | |
|-------|------|-----|------|---|-----|----------------|
| 1/15/83 | 101⁵ | 10 | Heartbeats    R&B:10 *(instrumental)* | $4 | | Total Experience 8204 |

**YARDBIRDS, The**      HOT
Legendary rock group formed in 1963 in Surrey, England, which featured guitarists **Eric Clapton** (1963-65), **Jeff Beck** (1965-66) and Jimmy Page (1966-68). Page formed the New Yardbirds in October 1968, which evolved into Led Zeppelin.

| | | | | | | |
|-------|------|-----|------|---|-----|----------------|
| 5/18/68 | 127 | 1 | Goodnight Sweet Josephine ........................................ *Think About It* | $50 | | Epic 10303 |

**YARROW, Peter**      AC/HOT
Born on 5/31/38 in New York City. Folk singer/songwriter/guitarist. Peter of **Peter, Paul & Mary**.

| | | | | | | |
|-------|------|-----|------|---|-----|----------------|
| 5/27/72 | 110 | 2 | Weave Me The Sunshine ........................................ AC:25 *Wings Of Time* | $5 | | Warner 7587 |

**YEARWOOD, Trisha**      C&W/HOT
Born on 9/19/64 in Monticello, Georgia. Country singer. Backing singer on Garth Brooks's first album.

| | | | | | | |
|-------|------|-----|------|---|-----|----------------|
| 8/20/94 | 114 | 9 | 1 XXX's And OOO's (An American Girl) ................ C&W:❶² *One In A Row* | $3 | ▌ | MCA 54898 |
| | | |    title song from the made-for-TV movie | | | |
| 4/1/95 | 120 | 3 | 2 Thinkin' About You ........................................ C&W:❶² *Fairytale* | $3 | ▌ | MCA 54973 |

**YELLO**      HOT
Computer/synthesizer trio from Zurich, Switzerland: Dieter Meier, Boris Blank and Carlos Peron.

| | | | | | | |
|-------|------|-----|------|---|-----|----------------|
| 7/16/83 | 103 | 4 | I Love You ........................................ *Rubber West* | $4 | ■ | Elektra 69824 |

| DEBUT | PEAK | WKS | A-side (Chart Hit).................................................................................B-side | $ | Pic | Label & Number |
|---|---|---|---|---|---|---|

**YELLOW BALLOON, The**      HOT
Studio group from Oregon featuring lead singer Alex Valdez with Don Grady of TV's *My Three Sons*.

| 6/24/67 | 101² | 6 | Good Feelin' Time     *I've Got A Feeling For Love* | $12 | | Canterbury 513 |

**YELLOW HAND** ◑
Pop-rock group led by Jerry Tawney (vocals) and Pat Flynn (guitar).

| 12/5/70 | 120 | 1 | Down To The Wire.................................... *God Knows I Love You* | $8 | | Capitol 2957 |

written by **Neil Young**

**YELLOW PAYGES, The** ◑
Rock quartet: Dan Hortter (lead vocals), Bill Ham (guitar), Bob Barnes (bass) and Dan Gorman (drums).

| 5/23/70 | 102 | 3 | I'm A Man ........................................................ *Home Again* | $15 | | Uni 55225 |

written and recorded by **Bo Diddley** in 1955; #17 hit for **The Yardbirds** in 1965

**YELLOWSTONE & VOICE** ◑

| 5/5/73 | 117 | 2 | Well Hello .................................................. *Memories* | $7 | | Verve 10708 |

**YES**      ROK/HOT/R&B
Progressive-rock group formed in London in 1968 which featured **Jon Anderson** (vocals), Steve Howe (guitar) and Rick Wakeman (keyboards) in an everchanging lineup.

| 10/25/80 | 104 | 2 | Into The Lens (I Am A Camera).................. *Does It Really Happen?* | $4 | | Atlantic 3767 |

**Y?N-VEE** ◑      R&B
Name pronounced: "why envy." Female rap/vocal quartet: Sonshine (Natasha Walker), Vayne (Tescia Harris), Nic-Nam (Nicole Chaney) and Yesz (Yenan Ragsdale).

| 9/24/94 | 101¹ | 8 | Chocolate     R&B:44 *(club remix)* | $3 | ▌ | RAL/PMP 853502 |

**YOAKAM, Dwight**      C&W/HOT
Born on 10/23/56 in Pikeville, Kentucky. Country singer/songwriter. First recorded for Oak Records. Acted in the 1996 movie *Sling Blade*.

| 5/15/93 | 101¹ | 15 | Ain't That Lonely Yet     Sls:58 /C&W:2 *A Thousand Miles From Nowhere* (C&W #2) | $3 | ▌ | Reprise 18528 |

**YONAH** ◑

| 9/15/79 | 102 | 2 | After The First One............................................... *Cats In California* | $5 | | Free Flight 11696 |

**YOUNG, Barry**      AC/HOT
Adult Contemporary vocalist.

| 2/5/66 | 130 | 1 | Since You Have Gone From Me ......................... *Nashville, Tennessee* | $7 | | Dot 16819 |

**Ernie Freeman** (orch.)

**YOUNG, Don** ◑
Pop/rock singer.

| 12/27/69 | 104 | 4 | She Let Her Hair Down (Early In The Morning)................... *Movin* | $7 | | Bang 574 |

tune originated as a TV jingle for a shampoo; #61 hit for **The Tokens** in 1970

**YOUNG, Faron**      C&W/HOT/AC
Born on 2/25/32 in Shreveport, Louisiana. Died on 12/10/96 of a self-inflicted gunshot wound. Country singer.

| 3/2/63 | 114 | 3 | The Yellow Bandana ................. C&W:4 *How Much I Must Have Loved You* | $12 | | Mercury 72085 |

The Merry Melody Singers (backing vocals)

**YOUNG, Kathy — see MONTEZ, Chris**

**YOUNG, Neil**      ROK/HOT/AC/C&W
Born on 11/12/45 in Toronto, Canada. Rock singer/songwriter/guitarist. Formed rock band the Mynah Birds, featuring lead singer **Rick James**, early '60s. Formed **Buffalo Springfield** in 1966. Joined with Crosby, Stills & Nash, 1970-71. Inducted into the Rock and Roll Hall of Fame in 1995.

| 12/22/73 | 108 | 6 | 1 Time Fades Away ............................................ *The Last Trip To Tulsa* | $7 | | Reprise 1184 |
| 12/18/76 | 105 | 4 | 2 Midnight On The Bay ........................................ *Black Coral* | $5 | | Reprise 1378 |

**THE STILLS-YOUNG BAND**

**YOUNGBLOODS, The**      HOT/AC
Folk-rock group formed in Boston in 1965 featuring **Jesse Colin Young** (vocals, bass).

| 5/10/69 | 124 | 3 | 1 Darkness, Darkness .......................................... *On Sir Francis Drake* | $7 | | RCA Victor 0129 |

made the Hot 100 (#86) on 5/2/70 on RCA Victor 0342

| 11/8/69 | 114 | 2 | 2 Sunlight .................................................................. *Trillium* | $7 | | RCA Victor 0270 |
| 6/12/71 | 123 | 1 | 3 Sunlight ....................................................... *Reason To Believe* [R] | $7 | | RCA Victor 0465 |

above 2 are the same version

| 7/2/77 | 109 | 1 | 4 Higher & Higher ...................................................... *Fool* | $5 | | Warner 8398 |

**JESSE COLIN YOUNG**

**YOUNG HEARTS**      R&B/HOT
R&B vocal group from Los Angeles: Ronald Preyer, Charles Ingersoll, Earl Carter and James Moore.

| 4/27/68 | 109 | 3 | 1 Oh, I'll Never Be The Same........................... R&B:29 *Get Yourself Together* | $10 | | Minit 32039 |
| 11/14/70 | 123 | 2 | 2 The Young Hearts Get Lonely Too .......................... R&B:40 *Why Do You Have To Go?* | $10 | | Zea 50001 |

**THE NEW YOUNG HEARTS**
written by Richard "Dimples" Fields

**YOUNG-HOLT UNLIMITED**      AC/R&B/HOT
Chicago R&B instrumental group: Eldee Young (bass), Isaac "Red" Holt (drums; both of the **Ramsey Lewis Trio**) and Don Walker (piano).

| 8/2/69 | 110 | 3 | 1 Straight Ahead.................................. AC:32 *California Montage* [I] | $7 | | Brunswick 755417 |
| 11/1/69 | 115 | 1 | 2 Horoscope ........................................................ *Soulful Samba* [S] | $7 | | Brunswick 755420 |
| 9/26/70 | 106 | 4 | 3 Mellow Dreaming.................................. AC:18 *Black And White* [I] | $6 | | Cotillion 44092 |

**YOUNG M.C.**      R&B/HOT
Born Marvin Young on 5/10/67 in London; raised in Queens, New York. Rapper. Co-writer of Tone Loc's "Wild Thing."

| 7/10/93 | 120 | 1 | What's The Flavor? .................................. R&B:86 *(2 remixes)* | $3 | ▌ | Capitol 44928 |

**YOUNGSTA'S — see DA YOUNGSTA'S**

**YOUNG WORLD SINGERS, The ○**
Group of young female singers produced by Bud Granoff.

| 8/22/64 | 132 | 1 | Ringo For President ...................................................................... A Boy Like That [N] | $15 | | Decca 31660 |
|---|---|---|---|---|---|---|

a tribute to **The Beatles**' Ringo Starr

**YURO, Timi**  HOT/AC/R&B
Born Rosemarie Timothy Aurro Yuro on 8/4/40 in Chicago. First recorded for Liberty in 1959.

| 4/4/64 | 130 | 1 | 1 Permanently Lonely................................................................... Call Me | $12 | | Liberty 55665 |
|---|---|---|---|---|---|---|
| | | | written by **Willie Nelson** | | | |
| 8/22/64 | 120 | 4 | 2 If................................................................. (I'm Afraid) The Masquerade Is Over | $10 | | Mercury 72316 |
| | | | #1 hit for **Perry Como** in 1951; #82 hit for **The Paragons** in 1961 | | | |
| 1/8/66 | 118 | 4 | 3 Once A Day.................................................................................Pretend | $10 | | Mercury 72515 |
| | | | #1 Country hit for **Connie Smith** in 1964 | | | |
| 10/18/75 | 108 | 1 | 4 Southern Lady.................................................... Lovin' You Is All I Ever Had | $6 | | Playboy 6050 |

# Z

**ZADORA, Pia**  C&W/HOT/R&B
Born Pia Schipani on 5/4/56 in New York City. Movie and stage actress/singer.

| 11/5/83 | 110 | 1 | Rock It Out..................................................... Give Me Back My Heart | $4 | ■ | Curb/MCA 52294 |
|---|---|---|---|---|---|---|

**ZAGER & EVANS**  HOT/AC
Pop-folk duo from Lincoln, Nebraska: Denny Zager and Rick Evans (both sing and play guitar).

| 10/11/69 | 106 | 3 | Mr. Turnkey ............................................................ Cary Lynn Javes | $6 | | RCA Victor 0246 |
|---|---|---|---|---|---|---|

**ZANG, Tommy ○**
Born in Kansas City; raised on a farm near Independence, Missouri. Pop singer.

| 8/15/60 | 108 | 2 | I Can't Stop Loving You ................................................... Truly, Truly | $12 | | Hickory 1122 |
|---|---|---|---|---|---|---|
| | | | written by **Don Gibson** in 1958; #1 hit for **Ray Charles** in 1962 | | | |

**ZAPP/ROGER**  R&B/HOT
Dayton, Ohio electro-funk band formed by the Troutman brothers: **Roger** ("Zapp"), Lester, Larry and Tony Troutman.

| 7/17/82 | 101[3] | 6 | 1 Dance Floor (Part I) .......................................... R&B:❶[2] (Part II) | $4 | | Warner 29961 |
|---|---|---|---|---|---|---|
| 11/6/82 | 103 | 7 | 2 Doo Wa Ditty (Blow That Thing)....................... R&B:10 Come On | $4 | | Warner 29891 |
| 8/20/83 | 102 | 4 | 3 I Can Make You Dance (Part I) .......................R&B:4 (Part II) | $4 | | Warner 29553 |
| 11/12/83 | 107 | 2 | 4 Heartbreaker (Part I) .......................................R&B:15 (Part II) | $4 | | Warner 29462 |
| | | | **ZAPP** (all of above) | | | |
| 4/23/94 | 108 | 6 | 5 Computer Love ....................... R&B:65 Slow And Easy (edit) [R] | $3 | ■ | Reprise 18251 |
| | | | **ZAPP & ROGER Featuring Shirley Murdock and Charlie Wilson** | | | |
| | | | remix of Zapp's #8 R&B hit in 1986 on Warner 28805 | | | |
| 2/8/97 | 120 | 1 | 6 Living For The City ............................. R&B:57 (instrumental) | $3 | ■ | Reprise 17510 |
| | | | **ROGER & ZAPP** | | | |
| | | | Shirley Murdock and Ronnie Diamond Hoard (backing vocals); #8 hit for **Stevie Wonder** in 1974 | | | |

**ZAPPA, Frank**  HOT/ROK
Born Francis Vincent Zappa Jr. on 12/21/40 in Baltimore, Maryland. Died on 12/4/93. Rock music's leading satirist. Singer/songwriter/guitarist/activist. Formed The Mothers Of Invention in 1965. Inducted into the Rock and Roll Hall of Fame in 1995.

| 3/19/77 | 105 | 4 | 1 Disco Boy ................................................................. Miss Pinky | $20 | | Warner 8342 |
|---|---|---|---|---|---|---|
| 5/24/80 | 103 | 6 | 2 I Don't Wanna Get Drafted ......................... Ancient Armaments | $6 | ■ | Zappa 1001 |

**ZEBRA**  ROK/HOT
Rock trio from New Orleans: Randy Jackson (vocals, guitar), Felix Hanemann (bass) and Guy Gelso (drums).

| 9/10/83 | 107 | 1 | Tell Me What You Want ...................................ROK:29 When You Get There | $4 | | Atlantic 89781 |
|---|---|---|---|---|---|---|

**ZEPHYRS, The ○**
Rock group from England.

| 4/17/65 | 109 | 4 | She's Lost You ............................................ There's Something About You | $15 | | Rotate 5006 |
|---|---|---|---|---|---|---|

**ZHANÉ**  R&B/HOT
Pronounced: Jah-Nay. Female R&B vocal duo from Philadelphia: Reneé Neufville and Jean Norris.

| 9/17/94 | 119 | 6 | 1 Vibe ............................................................ R&B:33 (LP version) | $3 | ■ | Illtown/Motown 2261 |
|---|---|---|---|---|---|---|
| | | | co-written and produced by **Naughty By Nature**; samples "Love X Love" by **George Benson** | | | |
| 6/7/97 | 106 | 12 | 2 Crush ......................................................... R&B:24 Saturday Night | $3 | ■ | Illtown/Motown 0640 |

**ZOMBIES, The**  HOT
British rock quintet featuring Rod Argent (keyboards) and Colin Blunstone (vocals). Rod formed **Argent** in 1969.

| 9/4/65 | 110 | 4 | 1 Whenever You're Ready ................................................ I Love You | $12 | | Parrot 9786 |
|---|---|---|---|---|---|---|
| 11/6/65 | 113 | 3 | 2 Just Out Of Reach ...................................................... Remember You | $12 | | Parrot 9797 |
| | | | from the Otto Preminger movie Bunny Lake Is Missing starring Laurence Olivier and The Zombies | | | |
| 5/17/69 | 109 | 3 | 3 Imagine The Swan ............................... Conversation Of Floral Street | $10 | | Date 1644 |

**ZORRO ○**
Male R&B vocalist.

| 8/14/61 | 118 | 2 | Somebody Cares .............................................. Come On Fish With Me | $40 | | Maske 702 |
|---|---|---|---|---|---|---|
| | | | answer song to **Baby Washington**'s "Nobody Cares" | | | |

**ZZ TOP**  ROK/HOT
Boogie-rock trio formed in Houston in 1969: Billy Gibbons (vocals, guitar), Dusty Hill (vocals, bass) and Frank Beard (drums).

| 6/4/77 | 105 | 4 | 1 Enjoy And Get It On........................................................ El Diablo | $6 | | London 252 |
|---|---|---|---|---|---|---|
| 12/26/81 | 103 | 6 | 2 Tube Snake Boogie ........................ROK:4 Heaven, Hell Or Houston | $4 | | Warner 49865 |
| 3/5/94 | 124 | 1 | 3 Pincushion ......................................ROK:❶[4] (3 album snippets) | $3 | ■ | RCA 62741 |

# SONG TITLE SECTION

Lists, alphabetically, all A-side titles from the *Bubbling Under The Hot 100* artist section. The artist's name is listed with each title along with the highest position attained and the year the song peaked.

Some titles show the letter **F** as a position, indicating that the title was listed on the charts as a flip side and did not make it on its own.

A song with more than one charted version is listed once, with the artists' names listed below in chronological order. Many songs that have the same title, but are different tunes, are listed separately, with the most popular title listed first. This will make it easy to determine which songs are the same composition, the number of charted versions of a particular song, and which of these were the most popular.

Cross references have been used throughout to aid in finding a title.

Please keep the following in mind when searching for titles:

Titles such a "I.O.U." and "S.O.S." will be found at the beginning of their respective letters; however, titles such as "L-O-V-E" and "Per-so-nal-ly" which are spellings of words, are listed with their regular spellings.

Titles which are identical, except for an apostrophized word in one of the titles, are shown together. ("Darlin'" appears immediately above "Darling")

# A

| | |
|---|---|
| 117/61 | **A-One A-Two A-Cha Cha Cha** *Lawrence Welk* |
| 103/97 | **AZ Side** *Nastyboy Klick* |
| 113/61 | **Abdul's Party** *Larry Verne* |
| 117/62 | **Abigail** *Embers* |
| 104/93 | **Above The Rim** *Bell Biv DeVoe* |
| 123/64 | **Absent Minded Me** *Barbra Streisand* |
| 101/93 | **Accidents Will Happen** *Elvis Costello* |
| 106/64 | **Across The Street (Is A Million Miles Away)** *Ray Peterson* |
| 113/97 | **A.D.I.D.A.S.** *Korn* |
| 118/95 | **Affection** *Jody Watley* |
| 110/72 | **Africa** *Thundermug* |
| 121/68 | **African Boo-Ga-Loo** *Jackie Lee* |
| 101/61 | **African Waltz** *Johnny Dankworth* |
| 102/61 | **After All We've Been Through** *Maxine Brown* |
| 111/64 | **After It's Too Late** *Bobby Bland* |
| 134/64 | **After Laughter** *Wendy Rene* |
| 112/62 | **After Loving You** *Eddy Arnold* |
| 126/67 | **After The Ball** *Bob Crewe* |
| 117/70 | **After The Feeling Is Gone** *Lulu* |
| 102/79 | **After The First One** *Yonah* |
| 104/62 | **After The Lights Go Down Low** *George Maharis* |
| 102/77 | **After You Love Me, Why Do You Leave Me** *Harold Melvin/Blue Notes Feat. Sharon Page* |
| 130/66 | **After You There Can Be Nothing** *Walter Jackson* |
| 117/62 | **After You've Gone** *Frankie Avalon* |
| | **Again** |
| 120/62 | *Lettermen* |
| 107/64 | *James Brown* (also see: Don't Ever Touch Me) |
| 119/69 | **Age (Where I Started Again)** *Horatio* |
| 125/67 | **Agnes English** *John Fred* |
| 108/96 | **Agua** *S'Aint John* |
| 131/69 | **Ah, Ha, Ha, Do Your Thing** *Hit Parade* |
| 115/96 | **Ain't Got Nothin' On Us** *John Michael Montgomery* |
| 124/63 | **Ain't It Funny What A Fool Will Do** *George Jones* |
| 110/74 | **Ain't It Hell Up In Harlem** *Edwin Starr* |
| 101/69 | **Ain't It Like Him** *Edwin Hawkins' Singers* |
| 112/96 | **Ain't Never Gonna Give You Up** *Paula Abdul* |
| 109/81 | **Ain't No Love In The Heart Of The City** *Whitesnake* |
| 101/94 | **Ain't Nobody** *Jaki Graham* |
| 118/67 | **Ain't Nothin' But A House Party** *Show Stoppers* |
| 113/71 | **Ain't Nothing Gonna Change Me** *Betty Everett* |
| 114/73 | **Ain't Nothing You Can Do** *Z.Z. Hill* |
| 101/93 | **Ain't That Lonely Yet** *Dwight Yoakam* |
| | **Ain't That Loving You Baby** |
| 108/64 | *Betty Everett & Jerry Butler* |
| 133/64 | *Everly Brothers* |
| 129/66 | **Ain't That Peculiar** *Ramsey Lewis* |
| 117/70 | **Ain't That Tellin' You People** *Original Caste* |
| 102/79 | **Ain't We Funkin' Now** *Brothers Johnson* |
| 111/70 | **Airport Song** *Magna Carta* |
| 113/68 | **Aladdin** *Rotary Connection* |
| 104/69 | **Albatross** *Fleetwood Mac* |
| 112/69 | **Alice's Restaurant Massacree** *Garry Sherman* |
| 103/65 | **Alimony** *Tommy Tucker* |
| | **Alive** |
| 120/96 | *Pearl Jam* |
| 110/97 | *Pearl Jam* |
| 101/75 | **All Cried Out** *Lamont Dozier* |
| 103/81 | **All Girls Want It** *Jody Moreing* |
| 112/95 | **All Glocks Down** *Heather B.* |
| 102/60 | **All I Could Do Was Cry** *Joe Tex* |
| 102/79 | **All I Ever Need Is You** *Kenny Rogers & Dottie West* |

| | |
|---|---|
| 110/81 | **All I Need** *Dan Hartman* |
| 113/96 | **All I Need** *Jesse Powell* |
| 104/92 | **All I See** *Christopher Williams* |
| 111/93 | **All I Want** *Saigon Kick* |
| 108/70 | **All I Want To Be Is Your Woman** *Carolyn Franklin* |
| 126/63 | **All I Want To Do Is Run** *Elektras* |
| 104/70 | **All In My Mind** *Pure Love & Pleasure* |
| 116/71 | **All Kinds Of People** *Burt Bacharach* |
| 122/68 | **All My Love's Laughter** *Ed Ames* |
| | **All My Loving** |
| 118/64 | *Jimmy Griffin* |
| 134/64 | *Chipmunks* |
| 101/83 | **All Night Long** *Mary Jane Girls* |
| 110/80 | **All Night Long** *Rainbow* |
| 102/59 | **All Nite Long** *Billy Vaughn* |
| 113/59 | **All Nite Long** *Robert Parker* |
| 121/94 | **All Nite Long** *A.L.T.* |
| 103/84 | **All Night Passion** *Alisha* |
| 104/75 | **All Our Dreams Are Coming True** *Gene Page* |
| 107/81 | **All Roads Lead To You** *Steve Wariner* |
| | **All Shook Up** ..see: (You Got Me) |
| 108/70 | **All That I've Got (I'm Gonna Give It To You)** *Billy Preston* |
| 109/68 | **All The Grey Haired Men** *Lettermen* |
| 101/83 | **All The Love In The World** *Dionne Warwick* |
| | **(All The Roads)** ..see: Tous Les Chemins |
| 103/67 | **All The Time** *Jack Greene* |
| 125/69 | **All The Waiting Is Not In Vain** *Tyrone Davis* |
| 106/80 | **All The Way** *Brick* (also see: Let's Go) |
| 101/73 | **All The Way Down** *Etta James* |
| 102/78 | **All The Way Lover** *Millie Jackson* |
| 112/70 | **All These Things** *Uniques* |
| 107/60 | **All Through The Night** *Mystics* |
| 120/93 | **All Thru The Nite** *P.O.V. with Jade* |
| 112/72 | **All Together** *Rowans* |
| | **All You Had To Do (Was Tell Me)** |
| 108/62 | *Chris Montez* |
| 125/64 | *Chris & Kathy* |
| 101/67 | **All's Quiet On West 23rd** *Jet Stream* |
| 123/63 | **Allentown Jail** *Lettermen* |
| 109/97 | **Alma Matters** *Morrissey* |
| 103/78 | **Almighty Fire (Woman Of The Future)** *Aretha Franklin* |
| 113/66 | **Almost Persuaded** *Patti Page* |
| 123/68 | **Alone Again Or** *Love* |
| 104/77 | **Alone At Last** *Neil Sedaka* |
| 108/67 | **Along Came Jones** *Righteous Brothers* |
| 118/62 | **Along Came Linda** *Tommy Boyce* |
| 107/83 | **Always Be Mine** *Aldo Nova* |
| 121/69 | **Always David** *Ruby Winters* |
| 103/83 | **Always Gonna' Love You** *Gary Moore* |
| 111/71 | **Always Remember** *Bill Anderson* |
| 125/67 | **Always Something There To Remind Me** *Patti LaBelle & The Bluebelles* |
| 101/66 | **Am I A Loser (From The Start)** *Eddie Holman* |
| 111/73 | **Am I Blue** *Cher* |
| 101/78 | **Am I Losing You** *Manhattans* |
| 112/63 | **Am I That Easy To Forget** *"Little Esther" Phillips* |
| | **Amarillo** ..see: (Is This The Way To) |
| 124/64 | **Amen** *Lloyd Price* |
| 110/69 | **Amen (1970)** *Impressions* |
| 101/74 | **America** *David Essex* |
| 109/94 | **American Girl** *Tom Petty* (also see: XXX's And OOO's) |
| 115/95 | **Among The Walking Dead** *Scarface* |
| 105/83 | **Amor** *Julio Iglesias* |
| | **(Amore, Scusame)** ..see: My Love, Forgive Me |
| 106/84 | **And I Don't Love You** *Smokey Robinson* |
| | **And I Love Her** |
| 105/64 | *George Martin* |
| 118/66 | *Vibrations* |
| 106/64 | **And Satisfy** *Nancy Wilson* |
| 114/61 | **And Then Came Love** *Ed Townsend* |
| 113/71 | **And When She Smiles** *Wildweeds* |
| 116/70 | **And You Do** *Charade* |

| | |
|---|---|
| 112/73 | **Anello (Where Are You)** *Shawn Phillips* |
| 109/69 | **Angel Of The Morning** *Bettye Swann* |
| 122/70 | **Angel On My Shoulder** *Merrilee Rush* |
| 110/73 | **Angel Spread Your Wings** *Danny O'Keefe* |
| 111/66 | **Angelica** *Barry Mann* |
| 122/96 | **Angels Among Us** *Alabama* |
| 126/69 | **Angels Listened In** *Percy Sledge* |
| 117/66 | **Angels (Watching Over Me)** *Medical Missionaries Of Mary Choral Group* |
| 106/67 | **Animal Crackers (In Cellophane Boxes)** *Gene Pitney* |
| 111/70 | **Anna** *Boots Randolph* |
| 110/63 | **Anonymous Phone Call** *Bobby Vee* |
| 107/96 | **Another Day** *Nick Turalé* |
| 109/76 | **Another Night** *Camel* |
| 104/81 | **Another One Rides The Bus** *"Weird Al" Yankovic* |
| 121/67 | **Another Page** *Connie Francis* |
| 115/70 | **Answer Me, My Love** *Happenings* |
| 105/95 | **Answering Service** *Gerald Levert* (also see: Call Me 'Mr. Telephone') |
| 115/95 | **Any Emcee** *Nine* |
| 102/80 | **Any Love** *Rufus & Chaka* |
| | **Any Other Way** |
| 131/62 | *William Bell* |
| 124/63 | *Jackie Shane* |
| 131/63 | **Any Way You Wanta** *Harvey* |
| 105/79 | **Anybody Wanna Party?** *Gloria Gaynor* |
| 117/63 | **Anything You Can Do** *Majors* |
| 103/71 | **Anytime Sunshine** *Crazy Paving* |
| 110/83 | **Anytime You Want Me** *Amy Holland* |
| 111/69 | **Anyway That You Want Me** *Walter Jackson* |
| 107/72 | **Anyway The Wind Blows** *Grass Roots* |
| 109/79 | **Anyway You Want It** *Enchantment* |
| | **(Ape Man)** ..see: Luther The Anthropoid |
| 127/71 | **Apple Bend** *Johnny Tillotson* |
| | **Apple Cider** |
| 111/68 | *People* |
| 133/69 | *Five By Five* |
| 102/74 | **Apple Of My Eye** *Badfinger* |
| 106/64 | **Apple Of My Eye** *4 Seasons* |
| 105/68 | **April Again** *Dean Martin* |
| 126/69 | **Aquarius** *Dick Hyman Trio* |
| 111/63 | **Arabia** *Delcos* |
| 117/62 | **Archie's Melody** *By Liners* |
| 105/80 | **Are 'Friends' Electric?** *Gary Numan & Tubeway Army* |
| 119/68 | **Are My Thoughts With You** *First Edition* |
| 108/71 | **Are You Lonely?** *Sisters Love* |
| 107/69 | **Are You Lonely For Me Baby** *Chuck Jackson* |
| 104/84 | **Are You Ready** *KC* |
| 113/69 | **Are You Ready** *Chambers Brothers* |
| 106/92 | **Are You Ready To Fly?** *Rozalla* |
| 112/73 | **Are You Really Happy Together** *Bulldog* |
| 102/59 | **Are You Sorry?** *Joni James* |
| 102/61 | **Are You Sure** *Allisons* |
| 132/63 | **Are You Sure** *Betty Logan* |
| 129/66 | **Arena, The** *Al Hirt* |
| 132/65 | **Arkansas** *Jimmy McCracklin* |
| 114/71 | **Arms Of A Fool** *Mel Tillis/Statesiders* |
| 125/64 | **Around The Corner** *Ben E. King* |
| 109/61 | **Around The World** *Buddy Greco* (also see: 'Round The World) |
| 112/62 | **Arrivederci, Roma** *Eddie Fisher* |
| 108/82 | **As** *Jean-Luc Ponty* |
| 123/68 | **(As, I Went Down To) Jerusalem** *Hello People* |
| 123/68 | **As Long As I Got You** *Laura Lee* |
| 120/66 | **As Long As There Is L-O-V-E Love** *Jimmy Ruffin* |
| 101/67 | **As Long As You're Here** *Zalman Yanovsky* |
| 132/69 | **As The Years Go Passing By** *Albert King* |
| 111/67 | **As Time Goes By** *Mel Carter* |
| 106/68 | **As We Go Along** *Monkees* |
| 101/80 | **Ashes To Ashes** *David Bowie* |
| 110/83 | **At 15** *Kagny & The Dirty Rats* |
| 104/69 | **At The Crossroads** *Sir Douglas Quintet* |
| 104/66 | **At The Party** *Hector Rivera* |
| 120/68 | **Atlanta Georgia Stray** *Sonny Curtis* |

227

104/82 **Blue Moon With Heartache**
 *Rosanne Cash*
107/61 **Blue Muu Muu** *Annette*
120/66 **Blue Star** *Ventures*
121/63 **Blue Summer** *Royalettes*
132/64 **Blue Train (Of the Heartbreak Line)**
 *John D. Loudermilk*
**Blue Velvet**
103/60 *Paragons*
103/63 *Lawrence Welk*
112/62 **Bluebirds Over The Mountain** *Echoes*
105/73 **Blues Band, Opus 50**
 *Siegel-Schwall Band*
109/59 **Blues Get Off My Shoulder** *Dee Clark*
131/64 **Bluesette** *Sarah Vaughan*
**Bo Diddley**
116/63 *Buddy Holly*
117/63 *Ronnie Hawkins*
128/67 **Bo Diddley Bach** *Kingsmen*
107/66 **Boa Constrictor** *Johnny Cash*
115/67 **Boat That I Row** *Lulu*
**(Body And Soul) ..see: That's The Way**
 **It's Got To Be**
**(Body And Soulin') ..see: Together**
105/84 **Body Electric** *Rush*
103/79 **Body Language** *Spinners*
104/83 **Body Talk** *Kix*
103/80 **Bodyshine** *Instant Funk*
**Bolero: see: Ravel's Bolero**
101/80 **Bomb Iran** *Vince Vance*
123/94 **Bombscare** *2 Bad Mice*
113/73 **Bondi Junction** *Peter Foldy*
110/80 **Boney Moronie** *Cheeks*
122/68 **Bonnie And Clyde** *New Vaudeville Band*
**(Boo-Ga-Loo) ..see: New Breed**
103/74 **Boobs A Lot** *Holy Modal Rounders*
110/79 **Boogie Motion** *Beautiful Bend*
105/82 **Boogie Woogie Country Girl** *Southwind*
106/61 **Book Of Love** *Bobby Bare*
104/84 **Bop Girl** *Pat Wilson*
102/77 **Bop Gun (Endangered Species)**
 *Parliament*
114/70 **Border Song (Holy Moses)**
 *Dorothy Morrison*
126/66 **Born Free** *Matt Monro*
109/69 **Born On The Bayou** *Short-Kuts*
134/67 **Born To Be By Your Side** *Brenda Lee*
**Born To Be With You**
101/60 *Echoes*
126/65 *Capitol Showband*
133/66 *Silkie*
108/76 *Dion*
105/76 **Born To Get Down (Born To Mess**
 **Around)** *Muscle Shoals Horns*
108/84 **Borrowed Time** *John Lennon*
128/63 **Bossa Nova Italiano** *Lou Monte*
103/63 **Bossa Nova Watusi Twist** *Freddy King*
102/73 **Both Ends Against The Middle**
 *Jackie Moore*
**Both Sides Now**
123/68 *Harpers Bizarre*
128/68 *Johnstons*
102/75 **Bottle (La Botella)** *Bataan*
102/72 **Bound** *Ponderosa Twins + One*
116/61 **Bounty Hunter** *Nomads*
118/95 **Boxers** *Morrissey*
108/68 **Boy** *Lulu*
104/65 **Boy And A Girl** *Sounds Orchestral*
**(Boy Meets Girl) ..see: Favourite Shirts**
102/65 **Boy Next Door** *Standells*
102/65 **Boys** *Beatles*
102/83 **Boys** *Mary Jane Girls*
123/66 **Boys Are Made To Love** *Karen Small*
105/59 **Boys Do Cry** *Joe Bennett*
110/85 **Boys Won't (Leave The Girls Alone)**
 *Greg Kihn*
102/73 **Bra** *Cymande*
109/60 **Brand New Heartache** *Everly Brothers*
116/73 **Brand New Kind Of Love**
 *Bobby Goldsboro*
**Brand New Lover ..see: (Gotta Find)**
109/69 **Brand New Me** *Jerry Butler*

**Break My Mind**
106/68 *Sammy Davis, Jr.*
110/68 *Bobby Wood*
126/67 **Break On Through (To The Other Side)**
 *Doors*
110/73 **Breakaway** *Millie Jackson*
107/71 **Breakdown** *Parliament*
115/68 **Breakin' Down The Walls Of Heartache**
 *Bandwagon*
**Breakin' Up ..see: (Best Part Of)**
101/72 **Breaking Up Is Hard To Do** *Heaven*
 *Bound with Tony Scotti*
101/72 **Breaking Up Somebody's Home**
 *Ann Peebles*
115/97 **Breaks, The** *Nadanuf*
105/94 **Breathless** *All-4-One*
109/60 **Breeze And I** *Santo & Johnny*
105/72 **Brian's Song** *Peter Nero*
119/71 **Bridge Over Troubled Water**
 *Buck Owens/Buckaroos*
117/95 **Bright As Yellow** *Innocence Mission*
110/79 **Bright Side Of The Road** *Van Morrison*
120/95 **Bright Yellow Gun** *Throwing Muses*
101/61 **Bring Back Your Heart** *Del Vikings*
111/97 **Bring Back Your Love** *Christión*
120/96 **Bring It On** *Kino Watson*
101/76 **Bring It On Home To Me** *Mickey Gilley*
**Bring The Country To The City ..see:**
 **(We're Gonna)**
108/59 **Broken Arrow** *Chuck Berry*
102/95 **Broken Language** *Smoothedahustler*
121/69 **Broken Man** *Malibu's*
102/60 **Broken Vow** *Chordettes*
105/82 **Brown Eyed Girl** *Henry Paul Band*
113/63 **Brown-Eyed Handsome Man**
 *Buddy Holly*
101/66 **Brown Paper Sack** *Gentrys*
117/70 **Brush A Little Sunshine** *Tommy Roe*
102/95 **Bubba Hyde** *Diamond Rio*
121/92 **Bubba Shot The Jukebox**
 *Mark Chesnutt*
124/94 **Buck Em Down** *Black Moon*
120/93 **Bumpin' (Adaptation Of Humpin')**
 *Paperboy*
105/74 **Burn** *Deep Purple*
122/96 **Burnin' Rubber** *Mr. Mirainga*
102/62 **Bustin' Surfboards** *Tornadoes*
125/69 **But For Love** *Eddy Arnold*
130/65 **But I Do** *Jewels*
110/70 **But You Know I Love You** *Evie Sands*
101/76 **Butterfly For Bucky** *Bobby Goldsboro*
103/97 **Butterfly Kisses** *Jeff Carson*
104/62 **Buttons And Bows** *Browns*
121/66 **Buzzzzzz** *Jimmy Gordon*
110/96 **By My Side** *Lorrie Morgan*
**By The Time I Get To Phoenix**
110/68 *Ace Cannon*
114/68 *Dee Irwin & Mamie Galore (medley)*
113/61 **Bye Bye Baby** *Bob Conrad*
118/67 **Bye, Bye Baby** *Big Brother & The*
 *Holding Company*
115/59 **Bye Bye Baby Goodbye** *Teresa Brewer*
127/66 **Bye Bye Blues** *Andy Williams*

# C

104/84 **C.O.D. (I'll Deliver)** *Mtume*
**Cabaret**
129/66 *Mike Douglas*
118/67 *Ray Conniff*
101/72 **Cafe** *Malo*
101/96 **Café Con Leché** *El Presidente*
118/95 **Cain's Blood** *4 Runner*
107/69 **Cajun Baby** *Hank Williams, Jr.*
115/96 **Caliente** *Bayside Boys*
108/71 **California Blues** *Redwing*

110/67 **California My Way** *Committee*
115/67 **California On My Mind** *Coastliners*
115/67 **California Sunshine Girl** *Shackelfords*
108/72 **California Wine** *Bobby Goldsboro*
110/64 **Call Her Up** *Jackie Wilson*
103/81 **Call It What You Want**
 *Bill Summers & Summers Heat*
102/61 **Call Me Anytime** *Frankie Avalon*
106/85 **Call Me Mr. 'Telephone' (Answering**
 **Service)** *Cheyne*
101/76 **(Call Me) The Traveling Man**
 *Masqueraders*
106/76 **Call My Name** *Little Richard*
**(Calling Your Name) ..see: Gentle**
107/65 **Camel Walk** *Ikettes*
107/68 **Camelot** *King Richard's Fluegel Knights*
103/93 **Can He Love U Like This** *After 7*
**Can I**
101/71 *Eddie Kendricks*
107/73 *Vee Allen*
124/68 **Can I Carry Your Balloon** *Swampseeds*
**(Can I Have A Word) ..see: Hey Love**
116/94 **Can It Be All So Simple** *Wu-Tang Clan*
115/69 **Can You Dance To It?** *Cat Mother/All*
 *Night Newsboys*
101/85 **Can You Feel It** *Fat Boys*
109/93 **Can You Forgive Her?** *Pet Shop Boys*
110/85 **Can You Help Me**
 *Jesse Johnson's Revue*
105/93 **Can't Do A Thing (To Stop Me)**
 *Chris Isaak*
111/68 **Can't Find The Time** *Orpheus*
112/94 **Can't Get Enough** *El DeBarge*
110/85 **Can't Get There From Here** *R.E.M.*
110/82 **Can't Get You Out Of My Mind**
 *Dan Seals*
124/68 **Can't Get You Out Of My Mind**
 *Margaret Whiting*
123/63 **Can't Go On Without You** *Fats Domino*
114/72 **Can't Help But Love You** *Whispers*
102/76 **Can't Let A Woman** *Ambrosia*
130/64 **Can't Live Without Her** *Billy Butler*
103/79 **Can't Say Goodbye** *Bobby Caldwell*
105/70 **Can't See You When I Want To**
 *David Porter*
104/77 **Can't Stay Away** *Bootsy's Rubber Band*
105/79 **Can't Take It With You**
 *Allman Brothers Band*
108/75 **Can't Take My Eyes Off You**
 *Gerri Granger*
118/70 **Can't You** *Paul Davis*
108/73 **Can't You See** *Marshall Tucker Band*
127/70 **Can't You See What You're Doing To**
 **Me** *Albert King*
104/71 **Candy Apple Red** *R. Dean Taylor*
118/68 **Candy Kid** *Cowsills*
101/83 **Candy Man** *Mary Jane Girls*
115/61 **Cappuccina** *Nat King Cole*
128/69 **Capt. Groovy And His Bubblegum**
 **Army** *Capt. Groovy*
127/68 **Captain Of Your Ship**
 *Reparata & The Delrons*
113/95 **Car** *Jeff Carson*
107/59 **Car Trouble** *Eligibles*
108/76 **Cara Mia** *Paul Delicato*
**Cardinal, The ..see: Theme From**
109/74 **Careful Man** *John Edwards*
111/65 **Careless** *Bobby Vinton*
115/69 **Carlie** *Bobby Russell*
107/65 **Carmen** *Bruce & Terry*
105/65 **Carnival Is Over** *Seekers*
118/69 **Carolina In My Mind** *James Taylor*
**Carry That Weight ..see: Golden**
 **Slumbers**
117/71 **Carry Your Own Load**
 *Jr. Walker & The All Stars*
124/62 **Cast Your Fate To The Wind**
 *Martin Denny*
120/69 **Castschok** *Alexandrow Karazov*
135/64 **Casual Kiss** *Leon Peels*
102/59 **Cat Walk** *Lee Allen*
132/66 **Catch Me In The Meadow** *Trade Winds*
120/95 **Caught Up In The Game** *Bushwackas*

# E

# F

**Fallin' In Love**
111/95  *La Bouche*
114/97  *La Bouche*
    (also see: Money Maid)
109/80  **Fallin' In Love (Bein' Friends)**
    *Rocky Burnette*
110/71  **Fallin', Lady** *Punch*
103/80  **Falling For You** *Sammy Johns*
110/83  **Falling In Love With You** *Gary Moore*
104/79  **Family Tradition** *Hank Williams, Jr.*
104/81  **Fancy Free** *Oak Ridge Boys*
117/65  **Fannie Mae** *Righteous Brothers*
120/66  **Fannie Mae** *Mighty Sam*
106/97  **Fantasy** *Acid Factor*
115/61  **Far Far Better Thing** *Della Reese*
104/69  **Farewell Is A Lonely Sound**
    *Jimmy Ruffin*
123/66  **Farmer John** *Tidal Waves*
120/68  **Fat Albert (Hey, Hey, Hey)** *Fat Albert Orchestra & Chorus*
112/95  **Fat Cats-Bigga Fish (Get Down, Get Down)** *Coup*
101/82  **Favourite Shirts (Boy Meets Girl)** *Haircut One Hundred*
106/67  **February Sunshine** *Giant Sunflower*
106/96  **Feel Good** *B-Code*
106/77  **(Feel So Good) Slow Dancing**
    *John Travolta*
    (also see: Slow Dancing)
104/85  **Feel So Real** *Steve Arrington*
**Feel The Need**
105/72  *Damon Shawn*
110/72  *Detroit Emeralds*
123/68  **Feelin' Alright?** *Traffic*
115/70  **Feelin' Groovy** *Southwest F.O.B.*
113/63  **Feelin' Sad** *Ray Charles*
**Feeling Bad**
132/69  *Spooky Tooth*
106/70  *Mel & Tim*
134/69  **Feelings** *Cherry People*
117/96  **Feels Like The First Time** *Intro*
109/70  **Feet Start Walking** *Doris Duke*
117/61  **Feminine Touch** *Dorsey Burnette*
107/97  **Femininity** *Eric Benét*
**Fever**
105/61  *Pete Bennett & The Embers*
108/64  *Alvin Robinson*
104/77  **Fiesta** *Gato Barbieri*
106/63  **Fiesta** *Lawrence Welk*
115/66  **Fifi The Flea** *Sidekicks*
123/68  **Fifty Two Per Cent**
    *Max Frost & The Troopers*
102/79  **Fill My Life With Love** *Saint Tropez*
102/67  **Finchley Central** *New Vaudeville Band*
129/64  **Find Another Love** *Tams*
105/68  **Finders Keepers** *Salt Water Taffy*
**Fine, Fine, Fine ..see: (He's Gonna Be)**
101/84  **Fine, Fine Line** *Andy Fraser*
110/85  **Fire In The Twilight** *Wang Chung*
105/85  **Fire Still Burns** *Russ Ballard*
107/64  **First Class Love** *Little Johnny Taylor*
103/74  **First Time We Met** *Independents*
107/68  **5 Card Stud** *Dean Martin*
112/66  **Five Card Stud** *Lorne Greene*
118/64  **Five Little Fingers** *Bill Anderson*
127/66  **Five Miles From Home (Soon I'll See Mary)** *Pat Boone*
110/84  **5:01AM (The Pros And Cons Of Hitch Hiking)** *Roger Waters*
119/92  **Flesh & Blood** *Wilson Phillips*
108/63  **Flipped Over You** *Paul & Paula*
105/67  **Flower Children** *Marcia Strassman*
115/66  **Flowers On The Wall**
    *Chet Baker/Mariachi Brass*
102/85  **Fly Girl** *Boogie Boys*
123/63  **Fly Me To The Moon (In Other Words)**
    *Mark Murphy*
130/68  **Fly With Me** *Avant Garde*
125/69  **Flyin' High** *Baja Marimba Band*
108/61  **Flying Blue Angels**
    *George, Johnny & The Pilots*
108/78  **Flying Over America** *Fresh Aire*
107/84  **Fo-Fi-Fo** *Pieces Of A Dream*
117/68  **Follow Me** *Jack Jones*

125/69  **Follow The Leader** *Major Lance*
101/64  **Follow The Rainbow** *Terry Stafford*
101/72  **Fool Me** *Lynn Anderson*
105/81  **Fool Me Again** *Nicolette Larson*
119/68  **Fool Of Fools** *Tony Bennett*
107/74  **Fool's Paradise** *Don McLean*
113/61  **Foolin' Around** *Buck Owens*
135/67  **Foolin' Around** *Chris Montez*
105/81  **Foolish Child** *Ali Thomson*
112/94  **Foolish Pride** *Travis Tritt*
102/67  **Fools Fall In Love** *Elvis Presley*
103/62  **Fools Hall Of Fame** *Paul Anka*
108/76  **Fools Rush In** *Joey Porrello*
123/69  **Foot Pattin'** *King Curtis & The Kingpins*
108/95  **For A Change** *Neal McCoy*
102/67  **For A Few Dollars More**
    *Hugo Montenegro*
128/70  **For A Friend** *Bugaloos*
120/62  **For All We Know** *Caslons*
135/65  **For Mama** *Matt Monro*
118/62  **For The First Time In My Life**
    *Adam Wade*
123/70  **For The Love Of A Woman** *Dean Martin*
118/95  **For The Love Of You**
    *Doctor Dre & Ed Lover*
**For What It's Worth**
125/69  *Cher*
101/70  *Sergio Mendes*
109/94  **For Whom The Bell Tolls** *Bee Gees*
107/70  **For Yasgur's Farm** *Mountain*
106/81  **For You** *Manfred Mann's Earth Band*
106/80  **For You, For Love** *Average White Band*
103/65  **For Your Love** *Righteous Brothers*
108/79  **For Your Love** *Chilly*
119/73  **Forever** *Baby Washington & Don Gardner*
102/97  **Forever All Over Again** *Night Ranger*
114/66  **Forget About Me** *Prince Harold*
117/62  **Forgive Me (For Giving You Such A Bad Time)** *Babs Tino*
105/68  **46 Drums - 1 Guitar** *Little Carl Carlton*
134/63  **Found True Love** *Billy Butler*
101/96  **Foundation** *Xzibit*
**Four-Five-Four ..see: Fo-Fi-Fo**
131/63  **Four In The Floor** *Shut Downs*
121/63  **Four Letter Man** *Freddy Cannon*
114/63  **Four Strong Winds** *Brothers Four*
123/67  **Four Walls (Three Windows and Two Doors)** *J.J. Jackson*
117/65  **Frankfurter Sandwiches**
    *Streamliners With Joanne*
127/63  **Fraulein** *Bobby Helms*
101/94  **Freaks** *Doug E. Fresh & The Get Fresh Crew*
104/85  **Freaks Come Out At Night** *Whodini*
102/81  **Freaky Dancin'** *Cameo*
104/69  **Free** *Pearly Gate*
104/74  **Free** *Fresh Start*
110/61  **Free** *Ty Hunter*
103/77  **Free And Single** *Brothers Johnson*
109/70  **Free As The Wind** *Brooklyn Bridge*
103/69  **Free Me** *Otis Redding*
110/72  **Free Your Mind** *Politicians*
103/80  **Freedom Of Choice** *Devo*
101/70  **Freight Train** *Duane Eddy*
126/64  **French Riviera** *Webb Pierce*
114/97  **Friend, A** *KRS-One*
**(Friend of Mine) ..see: Moonshine**
133/64  **Friendliest Thing** *Eydie Gorme*
123/66  **Friends And Lovers Forever**
    *Nancy Ames*
101/73  **Friends Or Lovers** *Act I*
126/67  **Frog, The** *Sergio Mendes*
109/66  **From A Distance** *P.F. Sloan*
113/70  **From Atlanta To Goodbye** *Manhattans*
109/77  **From Here To Eternity** *Giorgio*
116/63  **From Me To You** *Beatles*
132/66  **From Nashville With Love** *Chet Atkins*
104/78  **From Now On** *Bobby Arvon*
127/63  **From One To One** *Clyde McPhatter*
120/64  **From Russia With Love** *Al Caiola*
105/70  **From The Very Start** *Children*
112/73  **From Toys To Boys** *Emotions*
102/76  **From Us To You** *Stairsteps*

109/96  **Front Lines (Hell On Earth)** *Mobb Deep*
116/69  **Frozen Orange Juice** *Peter Sarstedt*
**Fugitive**
126/64  *Ventures*
129/64  *Jan Davis*
109/73  **Full Circle** *Byrds*
104/77  **Funk Funk** *Cameo*
126/69  **Funk No. 48** *James Gang*
105/78  **Funk-O-Nots** *Ohio Players*
102/96  **Funk Phenomena** *Old School Junkies*
106/70  **Funky** *Chambers Brothers*
102/68  **Funky Bull** *Dyke & The Blazers*
109/71  **Funky L.A.** *Paul Humphrey*
101/77  **Funky Music** *Ju-Par Universal Orchestra*
109/71  **Funky Rubber Band** *Popcorn Wylie*
106/79  **Funky Space Reincarnation**
    *Marvin Gaye*
120/66  **Funny How Love Can Be** *Danny Hutton*
102/66  **Funny (How Time Slips Away)**
    *Ace Cannon*
122/68  **Funny Man** *Ray Stevens*
103/66  **Funny (Not Much)** *Walter Jackson*
119/65  **Funny Thing About It** *Nancy Ames*


# G

103/64  **Gale Winds** *Egyptian Combo*
124/96  **Gamers** *Conscious Daughters*
**Games People Play**
116/69  *King Curtis & The Kingpins*
121/70  *Della Reese*
122/66  **Games That Lovers Play** *Mantovani*
**Gamma Goochie ..see: (You Got) The**
110/94  **Gang Stories** *South Central Cartel*
110/80  **Gangsters Of The Groove** *Heatwave*
134/65  **(Gary, Please Don't Sell) My Diamond Ring** *Wendy Hill*
**Gee Baby**
108/60  *Joe & Ann*
119/62  *Ben & Bea*
106/60  **Gee, But I'm Lonesome** *Ron Holden*
109/62  **Gee, It's Wonderful** *Bobby Rydell*
112/61  **Gee Oh Gee** *Echoes*
102/65  **Gee The Moon Is Shining Bright**
    *Dixie Cups*
115/63  **Gee What A Guy** *Yvonne Caroll*
103/60  **Gee Whiz** *Bobby Day*
119/65  **GeeTO Tiger** *Tigers*
101/75  **Gemini** *Miracles*
104/81  **Generals and Majors** *XTC*
108/85  **Gentle (Calling Your Name)** *Frederick*
103/69  **Gentle On My Mind** *Dean Martin*
118/71  **Georgia Sunshine** *Dean Martin*
113/93  **Gepetto** *Belly*
124/93  **Get A Haircut** *George Thorogood*
**Get-E-Up ..also see: Giddyup**
134/68  **Get-E-Up (The Horse)** *Preparations*
101/94  **Get It Together** *Beastie Boys*
109/75  **Get It While The Gettin' Is Good**
    *Leo & Libra*
134/67  **Get It While You Can** *Howard Tate*
118/64  **Get My Hands On Some Lovin'** *Artistics*
104/84  **Get Nekked** *Rick Dees*
102/94  **Get Off This** *Cracker*
102/78  **Get On Up (Disco)** *Tyrone Davis*
125/65  **Get Out (And Let Me Cry)**
    *Harold Melvin/Blue Notes*
105/76  **Get Outside** *Robert Palmer*
126/69  **Get Ready** *Ella Fitzgerald*
114/68  **Get Together** *Jimmy McCracklin*
108/77  **Get Up And Dance** *Memphis Horns*
102/76  **Get You Somebody New** *LaBelle*
**Get Your Lie Straight**
105/71  *Bill Coday*
120/71  *Bill Coday*
105/77  **Getaway** *Salsoul Orchestra*

| | | |
|---|---|---|
| 129/63 | **Half A Man** *Willie Nelson* | |
| 116/70 | **Half As Much** *Sonny Charles* | |
| 115/63 | **Half Time** *Routers* | |
| 118/63 | **Halfway** *Eddie Hodges* | |
| 111/65 | **Hallelujah** *Invitations* | |
| 108/69 | **Hallelujah (I Am The Preacher)** | |
| | *Deep Purple* | |
| 102/96 | **Halo** *Deep Blue Something* | |
| 116/62 | **Handful Of Memories** *Baby Washington* | |
| 120/69 | **Hands Of The Clock** *Life* | |
| 115/70 | **Handsome Johnny** *Richie Havens* | |
| 102/84 | **Hang On To Your Love** *Sade* | |
| | **Hang Up My Rock And Roll Shoes** | |
| | **..see: (I Don't Want To)** | |
| 131/68 | **Hangin' From Your Lovin' Tree** | |
| | *In Crowd* | |
| | **Hangin' On ..see: (You Keep Me)** | |
| 107/64 | **Hangin' On To My Baby** *Tracey Dey* | |
| 103/80 | **Hangin' Out** *Kool & The Gang* | |
| 111/71 | **Hanging On (To) A Memory** | |
| | *Chairmen Of The Board* | |
| 129/69 | **Happy** *William Bell* | |
| 131/63 | **Happy Cowboy** *Billy Vaughn* | |
| 108/65 | **Happy Feet Time** *Monclairs* | |
| 108/65 | **Happy, Happy Birthday Baby** | |
| | *Dolly Parton* | |
| 126/64 | **Happy I Long To Be** *Betty Everett* | |
| 104/62 | **Happy Jose** *Dave Appell* | |
| 102/59 | **Happy Lonesome** *Marion* | |
| 134/68 | **Happy Man** *Perry Como* | |
| 102/63 | **Happy Puppy** *Bent Fabric* | |
| 112/69 | **Happy Together** *Hugo Montenegro* | |
| 118/68 | **Happy With You** *Kenny O'Dell* | |
| 122/64 | **Hard Day's Night** *George Martin* | |
| 128/63 | **Hard Head** *Louis Jordan* | |
| 103/72 | **Hard Life, Hard Times (Prisoners)** | |
| | *John Denver* | |
| 105/71 | **Hard Rain's A Gonna Fall** *Leon Russell* | |
| 119/93 | **Hard To Get** *Starclub* | |
| 125/68 | **Hard To Get A Thing Called Love** | |
| | *Platters* | |
| 104/82 | **Harder Than Diamond** *Chubby Checker* | |
| 125/64 | **Harem, The** *Mr. Acker Bilk* | |
| 131/65 | **Hark** *Unit Four plus Two* | |
| 106/69 | **Harlan County** *Jim Ford* | |
| 127/65 | **Harlem Shuffle** *Wayne Cochran* | |
| 114/68 | **Harper Valley P.T.A.** *Bobbi Martin* | |
| | *(also see: Continuing Story Of)* | |
| 126/64 | **Haste Makes Waste** *Jackie Ross* | |
| 123/69 | **Have A Little Talk With Myself** | |
| | *Ray Stevens* | |
| 135/64 | **Have You Ever Been Lonely** | |
| | *Clarence "Frogman" Henry* | |
| 102/70 | **Have You Had Any Lately?** | |
| | *Sylvia Robinson* | |
| F/70 | **Have You Seen The Saucers** | |
| | *Jefferson Airplane* | |
| 132/64 | **Hawaii Tattoo** *Martin Denny* | |
| 125/66 | **Hawg Jaw** *Charlie Rich* | |
| 107/93 | **He Ain't Worth Missing** *Toby Keith* | |
| | **(He Gives Me Love) ..see: La La La** | |
| 111/61 | **He Needs Me** *Gloria Lynne* | |
| 130/63 | **He Understands Me** *Teresa Brewer* | |
| 126/63 | **He Was A Friend Of Mine** | |
| | *Briarwood Singers* | |
| 134/64 | **He Was A Friend Of Mine** *Bobby Bare* | |
| 108/82 | **He Was Really Sayin' Somethin'** | |
| | *Bananarama* | |
| | **He Will Break Your Heart** | |
| 120/67 | *Freddie Scott* | |
| 104/72 | *Johnny Williams* | |
| 101/66 | **He Wore The Green Beret** *Lesley Miller* | |
| 107/66 | **He'll Be Back** *Players* | |
| 116/70 | **He'll Never Love You** *Gentrys* | |
| 108/85 | **He's A Cobra** *Rockwell* | |
| 115/62 | **He's A Rebel** *Vikki Carr* | |
| 103/68 | **He's Bad Bad Bad** *Betty Wright* | |
| 133/64 | **He's Coming Back To Me** | |
| | *Theola Kilgore* | |
| 125/65 | **(He's Gonna Be) Fine, Fine, Fine** *Ikettes* | |
| 115/64 | **He's Just A Playboy** *Drifters* | |
| 121/96 | **He's Not Good Enough** *Solo* | |
| 113/61 | **He's Not Just A Soldier** *Little Richard* | |

| | | |
|---|---|---|
| 105/61 | **He's Old Enough To Know Better** | |
| | *Crickets* | |
| 106/66 | **He's Ready** *Poppies* | |
| 135/64 | **He's Sure To Remember Me** | |
| | *Brenda Lee* | |
| 113/63 | **He's The One You Love** *Inez Foxx* | |
| 109/94 | **Head Like A Hole** *Nine Inch Nails* | |
| 104/94 | **Headline News** *"Weird Al" Yankovic* | |
| 110/78 | **Headliner** *Fandango* | |
| 111/96 | **Heads Carolina, Tails California** | |
| | *Jo Dee Messina* | |
| 120/95 | **Healing** *Wynonna & Michael English* | |
| 119/62 | **(Hear My Song) Violetta** *Ray Adams* | |
| 125/66 | **Heart** *2 Of Clubs* | |
| 102/81 | **Heart & Soul** *Exile* | |
| 122/67 | **Heart And Soul** *Incredibles* | |
| | **(Heart In Distress) ..see: S.O.S.** | |
| 105/80 | **Heart Of Mine** *Oak Ridge Boys* | |
| 104/68 | **Heartache** *Roy Orbison* | |
| 119/62 | **Heartache Named Johnny** | |
| | *Jaye P. Morgan* | |
| 122/63 | **Heartache Oh Heartache** *Lettermen* | |
| 119/63 | **Heartaches** *Kenny Ball* | |
| 107/81 | **Heartbeat** *Gary Wright* | |
| 110/77 | **Heartbeat** *Runaways* | |
| 110/85 | **Heartbeat** *Dazz Band* | |
| 128/65 | **Heartbeat** *Gloria Jones* | |
| 101/83 | **Heartbeats** *Yarbrough & Peoples* | |
| 112/93 | **Heartbeats Accelerating** *Linda Ronstadt* | |
| 119/64 | **Heartbreak** *Dee Clark* | |
| 116/64 | **Heartbreak Ahead** *Murmaids* | |
| 107/83 | **Heartbreaker** *Zapp* | |
| 124/63 | **Heartless Heart** *Floyd Cramer* | |
| 108/85 | **Hearts On Fire** *Sam Harris* | |
| 109/83 | **Heat In The Street** *Axe* | |
| 118/93 | **Heat It Up** *Rakim* | |
| 125/96 | **Heathen Rage** *Capleton* | |
| 107/81 | **Heaven** *Carl Wilson* | |
| 103/73 | **Heaven Help The Child** *Mickey Newbury* | |
| 110/72 | **Heaven Help Us All** *Beverly Bremers* | |
| 102/73 | **Heaven Is My Woman's Love** | |
| | *Tommy Overstreet* | |
| 103/67 | **Heavy Music** *Bob Seger* | |
| 106/69 | **Heighty Hi** *Lee Michaels* | |
| 121/96 | **Heiny Heiny** *95 South* | |
| | **(Hell On Earth) ..see: Front Lines** | |
| 104/97 | **Hello** *Poe* | |
| 125/64 | **Hello, Dolly!** *Ella Fitzgerald* | |
| 131/64 | **Hello, Dolly! (Italian Style)** *Lou Monte* | |
| 128/66 | **Hello Enemy** *Johnny Tillotson* | |
| 122/68 | **Hello, Hello** *Tiny Tim* | |
| 109/76 | **Hello, Operator** *Gerard* | |
| 120/62 | **Hello Out There** *Carl Belew* | |
| 121/69 | **Hello Sunshine** *Rev. Maceo Woods* | |
| 131/63 | **Hello Wall No. 2** *Ben Colder* | |
| 108/69 | **Helpless** *Jackie Wilson* | |
| 122/68 | **Helule Helule** *Tremeloes* | |
| | **Henpecked Guy ..see: (I'm Just) A** | |
| | **Here Come The Tears** | |
| 102/65 | *Gene Chandler* | |
| 124/67 | *Darrell Banks* | |
| 124/67 | **Here Comes My Baby** *Perry Como* | |
| 108/95 | **Here For You** *Firehouse* | |
| 113/62 | **Here I Am** *Chip Taylor* | |
| 121/68 | **Here I Am** *Righteous Brothers* | |
| 125/67 | **Here I Am Baby** *Barbara McNair* | |
| 101/71 | **Here I Go Again** *Raeletts* | |
| 106/69 | **Here I Go Again** *Country Joe & The Fish* | |
| 107/64 | **Here I Go Again** *Hollies* | |
| 112/70 | **Here I Go Again** *Archie Bell* | |
| 115/70 | **Here I Stand** *Crossroads* | |
| 107/81 | **Here Is My Love** *Tommy Dee* | |
| 118/62 | **Here It Comes Again** *Chantels* | |
| | **Here, There And Everywhere** | |
| 120/66 | *Fourmost* | |
| 126/67 | *Claudine Longet* | |
| 109/94 | **Here We Go** *Stakka Bo* | |
| 102/83 | **Here We'll Stay** *Frida* | |
| 101/97 | **Here's The Deal** *Jeff Carson* | |
| 129/64 | **Here's To Our Love** *Brian Hyland* | |
| 125/63 | **Here's Where I Came In (Here's Where I** | |
| | **Walk Out)** *Aretha Franklin* | |
| | **Hero ..see: Wind Beneath My Wings** | |

| | | |
|---|---|---|
| 117/97 | **Hey AZ** *AZ* | |
| 105/70 | **Hey America** *James Brown* | |
| 128/65 | **Hey Baby** *Hi-Lites* | |
| 118/63 | **Hey Child** *Johnny Thunder* | |
| 112/71 | **Hey, Does Somebody Care** | |
| | *God's Children* | |
| 104/70 | **Hey, Girl** *Lettermen* | |
| 122/69 | **Hey Girl** *Panhandle* | |
| 134/67 | **Hey Girl** *Mamas & The Papas* | |
| | **Hey, Good Lookin'** | |
| 104/62 | *Connie Stevens* | |
| 124/66 | *Bill Black's Combo* | |
| 127/67 | **Hey Grandma** *Moby Grape* | |
| | **(Hey, Hey, Hey) ..see: Fat Albert** | |
| 109/69 | **Hey Hey Woman** *Joe Jeffrey Group* | |
| 125/65 | **Hey Ho What You Do To Me** | |
| | *Guess Who* | |
| 119/69 | **Hey Jude** *Paul Mauriat* | |
| 124/73 | **Hey Lawdy Lawdy** *Wackers* | |
| 134/65 | **Hey Little Girl** *Z.Z. Hill* | |
| 103/61 | **Hey Little One** *Bruce Bruno* | |
| 108/61 | **Hey! Look Me Over** *Pete King* | |
| 104/95 | **Hey Lookaway** *Questionmark Asylum* | |
| 101/92 | **Hey Love (Can I Have A Word)** | |
| | *Mr. Lee Featuring R. Kelly* | |
| 115/72 | **Hey Mister** *Ray Charles* | |
| 130/68 | **Hey Mister** *Four Jacks & A Jill* | |
| | **(Hey-O) ..see: Out In The Sun** | |
| 118/65 | **Hey-O-Daddy-O** *Newbeats* | |
| 105/71 | **Hey Ruby (Shut Your Mouth)** | |
| | *Ruby & The Party Gang* | |
| 101/94 | **Hey Santa!** *Carnie & Wendy Wilson* | |
| 101/70 | **Hey, That's No Way To Say Goodbye** | |
| | *Vogues* | |
| 108/82 | **Hey There Lonely Boy** *Stacy Lattisaw* | |
| 107/76 | **Hey, What's That Dance You're Doing** | |
| | *Choice Four* | |
| 110/71 | **Hey Willy** *Hollies* | |
| 122/67 | **(Hey You) Set My Soul On Fire** | |
| | *Mary Wells* | |
| 121/61 | **Hey You, What Are You, Some Kind Of** | |
| | **Nut?** *Andy Cory* | |
| 123/94 | **Hi De Ho** *K7* | |
| 123/67 | **Hi-Ho Silver Lining** *Jeff Beck* | |
| 104/75 | **Hi-Jack** *Barrabas* | |
| 112/64 | **Hide Away** *King Curtis* | |
| 102/80 | **High** *Skyy* | |
| 112/70 | **High Sheriff Of Calhoun Parrish** | |
| | *Tony Joe White* | |
| 109/77 | **Higher & Higher** *Jesse Colin Young* | |
| | *(also see: Your Love Has Lifted Me and* | |
| | *Your Love Keeps Liftin' Me)* | |
| 124/70 | **Hikky Burr** *Bill Cosby* | |
| 123/64 | **His Lips Get In The Way** | |
| | *Bernadette Castro* | |
| 105/72 | **His Song Shall Be Sung** *Lou Rawls* | |
| 109/85 | **History** *Mai Tai* | |
| 101/81 | **Hit And Run** *Bar-Kays* | |
| 103/63 | **Hit The Road Jack** *Jerry Lee Lewis* | |
| 114/64 | **Hitchike Back To Georgia** *Buddy Knox* | |
| 102/94 | **Hobo Humpin Slobo Babe** *Whale* | |
| 109/61 | **Hold It** *James Brown* | |
| 106/59 | **Hold On** *Ed Townsend* | |
| 133/65 | **Hold On Baby** *Sam Hawkins* | |
| 103/81 | **Hold On, Hold Out** *Jackson Browne* | |
| | **Hold On! I'm A Comin'** | |
| 130/66 | *Billy Larkin & The Delegates* | |
| 114/67 | *Mauds* | |
| 106/75 | **Hold On (Just A Little Bit Longer)** | |
| | *Anthony & The Imperials* | |
| 106/75 | **Hold On To Love** *Peter Skellern* | |
| 110/80 | **Hold Tight** *Jimmy Spheeris* | |
| 110/76 | **Holding On** *Road Apples* | |
| 123/97 | **Hole In My Heart** *BlackHawk* | |
| 103/68 | **Hole In My Pocket** | |
| | *Barry Goldberg Reunion* | |
| 113/67 | **Holly** *Andy Williams* | |
| 104/70 | **Holly Go Softly** *Cornerstone* | |
| 126/68 | **Holy Man** *Scott McKenzie* | |
| | **(Holy Moses) ..see: Border Song** | |
| 107/71 | **(Holy Moses!) Everything's Coming Up** | |
| | **Roses** *Jack Wild* | |
| 107/60 | **Holy One** *Freddie Fender* | |
| 120/96 | **Home** *4U* | |

115/94　**I Go On** *MC Lyte*
116/67　**I Got A Feeling** *Barbara Randolph*
104/62　**I Got A Funny Kind Of Feeling**
　　　　*Maxine Brown*
117/94　**I Got A Love** *Pete Rock & C.L. Smooth*
110/75　**I Got A Song** *Sugarloaf/Jerry Corbetta*
124/63　**I Got Burned** *Ral Donner*
106/97　**I Got Dat Feelin'** *DJ Kool*
111/70　**I Got Love** *Melba Moore*
123/96　**I Got Somebody Else** *Changing Faces*
129/68　**I Got To Have Ya** *Trolls*
108/93　**I Got You Babe**
　　　　*Cher with Beavis & Butt-head*
122/94　**I Gotcha' Back** *Genius*
101/76　**I Gotta Get Drunk** *Willie Nelson*
101/60　**I Gotta Go ('Cause I Love You)**
　　　　*Brian Hyland*
135/69　**I Guess The Lord Must Be In New York City** *Sagittarius*
127/68　**I Hate To See Me Go** *Margaret Whiting*
119/69　**I Have But One Life To Live**
　　　　*Sammy Davis, Jr.*
129/69　**I Have Dreamed** *Lettermen*
104/64　**I Hope He Breaks Your Heart**
　　　　*Neil Sedaka*
106/75　**I Just Can't Make It (Without You)**
　　　　*Philly Devotions*
104/73　**I Just Can't Stop Loving You** *Cornelius Brothers & Sister Rose*
119/64　**I Just Don't Know What To Do With Myself** *Tommy Hunt*
103/83　**I Just Gotta Have You (Lover Turn Me On)** *Kashif*
123/66　**I Just Let It Take Me** *Bob Lind*
102/85　**I Just Wanna Hang Around You**
　　　　*George Benson*
113/72　**I Just Want To Be There** *Independents*
103/78　**I Just Want To Be With You** *Floaters*
101/82　**I Just Want To Satisfy** *O'Jays*
104/74　**I Keep On Lovin' You** *Z.Z. Hill*
126/69　**I Know** *Ike & Tina Turner*
107/63　**I Know Better** *Flamingos*
117/65　**I Know It's All Right** *Sam Hawkins*
103/59　**I Know It's Hard But It's Fair**
　　　　*"5" Royales*
117/71　**I Know You Got Soul** *Bobby Byrd*
135/65　**I Know Your Heart Has Been Broken**
　　　　*Roscoe Shelton*
108/59　**I Laughed At Love** *Joni James*
119/69　**I Left My Heart In San Francisco**
　　　　*Bobby Womack*
111/66　**I Lie Awake** *New Colony Six*
101/78　**I Like Girls** *Fatback*
108/80　**(I Like) The Way You Play** *Glass Moon*
108/77　**I Love A Mellow Groove**
　　　　*Jimmy Castor Bunch*
102/83　**I Love It Loud** *Kiss*
110/83　**I Love L.A.** *Randy Newman*
118/66　**I Love My Dog** *Cat Stevens*
105/78　**I Love New York** *Metropolis*
106/83　**I Love Rocky Road** *"Weird Al" Yankovic*
109/71　**I Love The Way You Love** *Betty Wright*
107/76　**I Love To Love** *Al Downing*
103/83　**I Love You** *Yello*
　　　　*(also see: S.O.S.)*
115/72　**I Love You - Stop** *Stairsteps*
124/67　**(I Love You Babe But) Give Me My Freedom** *Glories*
126/65　**I Love You Baby** *Dottie & Ray*
112/66　**I Love You Drops** *Don Cherry*
123/64　**I Love You (I Just Love You)** *Lloyd Price*
105/84　**I Love You Love**
　　　　*Joan Jett & the Blackhearts*
113/73　**I May Not Be What You Want** *Mel & Tim*
104/79　**I Might As Well Forget About Loving You** *Kinsman Dazz*
115/62　**I Miss You** *Dreamlovers*
109/97　**I Miss You A Little**
　　　　*John Michael Montgomery*
117/62　**I Misunderstood** *Wanda Jackson*
114/96　**I Must Stand** *Ice-T*
101/76　**I Need It** *Johnny Guitar Watson*
108/74　**I Need Time** *Bloodstone*
107/79　**I Need You Now** *Tata Vega*

103/95　**I Need You Tonight** *Junior M.A.F.I.A. Featuring Aaliyah*
106/69　**I Need You Woman**
　　　　*William Bell, Carla Thomas*
122/70　**I Never Picked Cotton** *Roy Clark*
104/84　**I Never Stopped Loving You** *Survivor*
117/73　**I Only Get This Feeling** *Chuck Jackson*
　　　　**I Only Have Eyes For You**
109/64　　*Cliff Richard*
104/74　　*Mel Carter*
122/71　**I Only Want To Say (Gethsemane)**
　　　　*Jose Feliciano*
113/60　**I Only Want You** *Passions*
106/84　**I Promise (I Do Love You)** *Dreamboy*
　　　　**I Put A Spell On You**
120/65　　*Nina Simone*
111/68　　*Crazy World Of Arthur Brown*
107/71　**I Really Love You** *Davy Jones*
123/69　**I Really Love You** *Ambassadors*
107/94　**I Remember** *Coolio*
102/60　**I Remember (In The Still Of The Night)**
　　　　*Crests*
116/94　**I Remember You** *Denine*
134/66　**I Remember You** *Slim Whitman*
129/69　**I Saw The Light** *Nashville Brass feat. Danny Davis*
　　　　**I Say A Little Prayer ..see: Say A Little Prayer**
102/70　**I Shall Be Released** *Rick Nelson*
111/64　**I Should Have Known Better**
　　　　*George Martin*
　　　　**I Stand Accused**
127/67　　*Inez & Charlie Foxx*
106/69　　*Al Wilson*
114/93　**I Stand For You** *Michael McDonald*
105/69　**I Still Love You** *Jackie Wilson*
121/97　**I Still Love You** *Monifah*
　　　　*(also see: Baby, Baby)*
105/81　**I Surrender** *Rainbow*
101/74　**I Told You So** *Delfonics*
104/93　**I Totally Miss You** *Bad Boys Blue*
101/77　**I Tried To Tell Myself** *Al Green*
116/68　**I Truly, Truly Believe** *Temptations*
115/94　**I Try To Think About Elvis**
　　　　*Patty Loveless*
105/70　**I Wanna Be A Free Girl** *Dusty Springfield*
133/67　**I Wanna Be There** *Blues Magoos*
112/93　**I Wanna Be Your Man**
　　　　*Chaka Demus & Pliers*
105/97　**I Wanna Come (With You)** *Real McCoy*
132/67　**I Wanna Help Hurry My Brothers Home**
　　　　*Jimmy Holiday*
101/78　**I Wanna Live Again** *Carillo*
103/70　**I Wanna Love You**
　　　　*George Baker Selection*
109/76　**I Wanna Spend My Whole Life With You** *Street People*
133/64　**I Wanna Swim With Him** *Daisies*
117/62　**I Wanna Thank Your Folks**
　　　　*Johnny Burnette*
132/65　**I Want A Little Girl** *Joe Hinton*
109/67　**I Want Action** *Ruby Winters*
123/97　**I Want Love** *Tony Mascolo*
120/67　**I Want My Baby Back** *Edwin Starr*
108/67　**I Want Some More**
　　　　*Jon & Robin & The In Crowd*
120/65　**I Want To Get Married** *Delicates*
114/67　**I Want To Go Back There Again**
　　　　*Chris Clark*
102/82　**I Want To Hold Your Hand** *Lakeside*
101/85　**I Want To Know What Love Is**
　　　　*New Jersey Mass Choir*
117/92　**I Want To Love You Down** *Keith Sweat*
112/62　**I Want To Love You (So Much It Hurts Me)** *Renee Roberts*
105/71　**I Want To Take You Higher**
　　　　*Kool & The Gang*
103/94　**I Want To Thank You** *Robin S*
110/76　**I Want You** *Gato Barbieri*
101/95　**I Want You Back** *Pure Soul*
103/79　**I Want You Back (Alive)** *Graham Parker*
127/69　**I Want You So Bad** *B.B. King*
114/64　**I Want You To Have Everything**
　　　　*Lee Rogers*

106/83　**I Wanted To Tell Her** *Ministry*
109/69　**I Was A Boy (When You Needed A Man)** *Billy Shields*
116/68　**I Who Have Nothing** *Linda Jones*
110/63　**I Will Never Turn My Back On You**
　　　　*Chuck Jackson*
113/65　**I Will Wait For You** *Steve Lawrence*
121/96　**I Wish** *Barrio Boyzz*
116/62　**I Wish I Could Cry** *Little Willie John*
114/70　**I Wish I Had A Mommy Like You**
　　　　*Patti Page*
105/67　**I Wish I Had Time** *Last Words*
130/64　**I Wish I Knew What Dress To Wear**
　　　　*Ginny Arnell*
101/95　**I Wish You Well** *Tom Cochrane*
113/62　**I Won't Be There** *Del Shannon*
112/67　**I Won't Come In While He's There**
　　　　*Jim Reeves*
106/73　**I Won't Last A Day Without You**
　　　　*Paul Williams*
　　　　**I Won't Let You Go ..see: Should I Stay**
117/65　**I Wonder** *Butterflys*
112/71　**I Wonder What She'll Think About Me Leaving** *Conway Twitty*
118/63　**I Worry Bout You** *Etta James*
128/69　**I Wouldn't Change The Man He Is**
　　　　*Blinky*
102/74　**I Wouldn't Give You Up**
　　　　*Ecstasy, Passion & Pain*
110/70　**I Wouldn't Live In New York City (If They Gave Me The Whole Dang Town)** *Buck Owens/Buckaroos*
104/80　**I Yam What I Yam** *Robin Williams*
　　　　*(also see: I Am What I Am)*
116/73　**(I'd Be) A Legend In My Time**
　　　　*Sammy Davis, Jr.*
120/97　**I'd Be With You** *Kippi Brannon*
109/94　**I'd Like To Have That One Back**
　　　　*George Strait*
106/62　**I'd Never Find Another You** *Paul Anka*
120/95　**I'd Rather Be Alone** *Karyn White*
　　　　**I'd Rather Be Rich**
131/64　　*Robert Goulet*
132/64　　*Pearl Bailey*
120/95　**I'll Always Be With You** *Shaw/Blades*
102/96　**I'll Be Alright** *MTS*
102/60　**I'll Be Home For Christmas (If Only In My Dreams)** *Bing Crosby*
115/70　**I'll Be There** *Eddie Holman*
　　　　**I'll Be There**
124/63　　*Tony Orlando*
125/70　　*Cissy Houston*
113/64　**I'll Be There (To Bring You Love)**
　　　　*Majors*
102/78　**I'll Be True To You** *Oak Ridge Boys*
106/79　**I'll Be Waiting** *Robert Johnson*
102/60　**(I'll Be With You In) Apple Blossom Time** *Platters*
　　　　**I'll Be Your Baby Tonight**
133/68　　*Burl Ives*
112/70　　*Ray Stevens*
108/63　**I'll Believe It When I See It** *Sierras*
105/64　**I'll Come Running** *Lulu*
110/62　**I'll Come Running Back To You**
　　　　*Roy Hamilton*
108/65　**I'll Cry Alone** *Gale Garnett*
　　　　**(I'll Deliver) ..see: C.O.D.**
103/65　**I'll Find A Whole Lot Better** *Byrds*
117/64　**I'll Find You** *Valerie & Nick*
103/60　**I'll Fly Away** *Lonnie Sattin*
118/67　**I'll Give You Time (To Think It Over)**
　　　　*Outsiders*
112/66　**I'll Go Crazy** *Buckinghams*
106/73　**I'll Have To Go Away** *Skylark*
106/84　**I'll Keep Holding On** *Jim Capaldi*
116/65　**I'll Keep Holding On (Just To Your Love)** *Sonny James*
120/65　**I'll Keep On Trying** *Walter Jackson*
108/64　**I'll Keep Trying** *Theola Kilgore*
102/84　**I'll Let You Slide** *Luther Vandross*
110/61　**I'll Love You Til The Cows Come Home**
　　　　*Clyde McPhatter*
108/66　**I'll Make It Easy (If You'll Come On Home)** *Incredibles*

**237**

# J

109/60 **Jaguar And Thunderbird** *Chuck Berry*
105/84 **Jail House Rap** *Fat Boys*
105/82 **Jamaica** *Bobby Caldwell*
102/82 **Jamming** *Grover Washington, Jr.*
129/64 **Java Jones (Java)** *Donna Lynn*
 **Jaws ..see: Super "Jaws"**
109/61 **Jazz In You** *Gloria Lynne*
106/79 **Jealous** *Robert Palmer*
F/84 **Jealous Girl** *New Edition*
106/84 **Jealousy** *Mary Jane Girls*
118/61 **Jenny** *Johnny Mathis*
111/65 **Jerk It** *Gypsies*
 **Jerusalem ..see: (As, I Went Down To)**
109/72 **Jesahel** *English Congregation*
109/95 **Jesus Freak** *DC Talk*
107/70 **Jesus, Take A Hold** *Merle Haggard*
112/69 **Jet Song (When The Weekend's Over)**
 *Groop*
132/63 **Jimmy Boy** *Carol Shaw*
 **(Jimmy Brown Song) ..see: Three Bells**
106/61 **Jingle-Bell Rock** *Chet Atkins*
111/69 **Jive** *Bob Darin*
111/67 **Jo Jo's Place** *Bobby Goldsboro*
114/62 **Joey's Song** *Bill Black's Combo*
105/60 **John Henry (The Steel Driving Man)**
 *Buster Brown*
114/69 **Johnny B. Goode**
 *Buck Owens/Buckaroos*
121/64 **Johnny Loves Me** *Florraine Darlin*
108/70 **Jolie Girl** *Marty Robbins*
108/71 **Joshua** *Dolly Parton*
109/71 **Joy** *Ventures*
127/66 **Jug Band Music** *Mugwumps*
102/76 **Juicy Fruit (Disco Freak)** *Isaac Hayes*
126/64 **Julie Knows** *Randy Sparks*
104/83 **Juliet** *Robin Gibb*
116/64 **Juliet** *Four Pennies*
101/82 **Jump** *Loverboy*
 **(Junior, Theme From) ..see: Look What Love Has Made**
112/61 **Junkernoo, The** *Vibrations*
102/84 **Just A Dream** *Nena*
108/60 **Just A Little Bit Of You** *Dallas Frazier*
111/61 **Just A Little Bit Sweet** *Charlie Rich*
128/69 **Just A Little Closer** *Archie Bell*
108/63 **Just A Lonely Man** *Fats Domino*
114/63 **Just A Simple Melody** *Patti Page*
106/70 **Just About The Same** *Association*
102/82 **Just An Illusion** *Imagination*
110/62 **Just Another Fool** *Curtis Lee*
101/83 **Just Another Saturday Night** *Alex Call*
101/82 **Just Be Yourself** *Cameo*
124/65 **Just Dance On By** *Eydie Gorme*
111/62 **Just For A Thrill** *Aretha Franklin*
110/71 **Just For Me And You** *Poco*
107/84 **Just For The Night**
 *Evelyn "Champagne" King*
101/77 **Just For Your Love** *Memphis Horns*
110/79 **Just Freak** *Slave*
105/85 **Just Got Lucky** *Dokken*
130/67 **Just Holding On** *P.J. Proby*
115/69 **Just Keep On Loving Me**
 *Johnnie Taylor, Carla Thomas*
113/67 **Just Let It Happen** *Arbors*
 **Just Let Me Dream ..see: (If I'm Dreaming)**
108/77 **Just Let Me Hold You For A Night**
 *David Ruffin*
103/83 **Just Let Me Wait** *Jennifer Holliday*
132/67 **Just Like A Man** *Margaret Whiting*
101/66 **Just Like A Woman** *Manfred Mann*
 **Just Like Romeo And Juliet ..see: Romeo & Juliet**
120/67 **Just Loving You** *Anita Harris*
123/64 **Just Once More** *Rita Pavone*
123/67 **Just One Look** *Soul Twins*
119/71 **Just One Time** *Connie Smith*
113/65 **Just Out Of Reach** *Zombies*

102/79 **Just The Way You Are** *Barry White*
103/93 **Just To Be Close To You** *Trey Lorenz*
129/66 **Just Walk In My Shoes**
 *Gladys Knight & The Pips*
112/97 **Just Wanna Please U** *Mona Lisa*
102/76 **Just Your Fool** *Leon Haywood*

# K

120/69 **Kaw-Liga** *Charley Pride*
101/79 **Keeep Your Body Workin'** *Kleeer*
120/63 **Keep An Eye On Her** *Jaynetts*
101/95 **Keep Givin' Me Your Love**
 *Ce Ce Peniston*
120/71 **Keep It In The Family** *Road Home*
101/97 **Keep It On The Real** *3XKrazy*
109/79 **Keep It Together (Declaration Of Love)**
 *Rufus*
109/66 **Keep Looking** *Solomon Burke*
104/73 **Keep Me In Mind** *Lynn Anderson*
101/78 **Keep On Dancing** *Johnnie Taylor*
118/65 **Keep On Keeping On** *Vibrations*
104/82 **Keep This Heart In Mind** *Bonnie Raitt*
 **(Keep Your Eye On The Sparrow) ..see: Baretta's Theme**
107/83 **Kelly's Eyes** *Andre Cymone*
101/63 **Kentucky** *Bob Moore*
104/64 **Kentucky Bluebird (Send A Message To Martha)** *Lou Johnson*
114/62 **Kentucky Means Paradise**
 *Green River Boys featuring Glen Campbell*
124/66 **Keys To My Soul** *Silkie*
108/94 **Kick A Little** *Little Texas*
120/63 **Kick Out** *Safaris*
102/81 **Kickin' Back** *L.T.D.*
106/80 **Kid Stuff** *Twennynine with Lenny White*
106/66 **Kids Are Alright** *Who*
 **(Kill 'Em All) ..see: 1990-Sick**
102/76 **Kill That Roach** *Miami*
127/67 **Kind Of Hush** *Gary & The Hornets*
116/69 **Kind Woman** *Percy Sledge*
126/68 **King Croesus** *World Of Oz*
107/76 **King Kong (Your Song)**
 *Bobby Pickett & Peter Ferrara*
 **King Of Kings ..see: Theme From**
108/85 **King Of Rock** *Run-D.M.C.*
124/63 **King Of The Surf Guitar** *Dick Dale*
102/97 **Kiss And Tell** *Brownstone*
110/61 **Kiss For Christmas (O Tannenbaum)**
 *Joe Dowell*
 **Kiss Him Goodbye ..see: Na Na Hey Hey**
105/73 **Kiss It And Make It Better** *Mac Davis*
110/77 **Kiss Me (The Way I Like It)**
 *George McCrae*
120/62 **Kiss Tomorrow Goodbye**
 *Danny White*
 **Kiss Tomorrow Goodbye**
121/67 *Jane Morgan*
123/67 *Lainie Kazan*
118/66 **Kissin' My Life Away** *Hondells*
107/94 **Kite** *Nick Heyward*
114/67 **Kites Are Fun** *Free Design*
108/67 **Kitty Doyle** *Dino, Desi & Billy*
113/71 **Knock Three Times**
 *Billy "Crash" Craddock*
109/84 **Knocked Down, Made Small (Treated Like A Rubber Ball)** *Was (Not Was)*

# L

 **L.A. Break Down**
106/68 *Jack Jones*
129/68 *Larry Marks*
106/76 **L.O.D. (Love On Delivery)** *Billy Ocean*
124/64 **La De Da I Love You** *Inez & Charlie Foxx*
104/64 **La-Dee-Da Song** *Village Stompers*
128/69 **La Jeanne** *King Curtis*
 **La La La (He Gives Me Love)**
110/68 *Raymond Lefevre*
119/68 *Lesley Gore*
109/78 **La Vie En Rose** *Grace Jones*
106/94 **Labour Of Love** *Frente!*
113/69 **Lady Jane** *Plastic Cow Goes Mooooog*
101/74 **Lady Lay** *Wayne Newton*
108/77 **Lady Of Magic** *Maze*
108/76 **Lady Of Spain** *Ray Stevens*
101/76 **Lady Of The Lake** *Starcastle*
105/72 **Lady, Play Your Symphony**
 *Kenny Rogers/First Edition*
120/62 **Lady Wants To Twist** *Steve Lawrence*
 **Land Of A Thousand Dances**
135/65 *Round Robin*
106/66 *Cannibal & The Headhunters*
126/66 **Lara's Theme** *Brass Ring*
128/69 **Las Cosas** *Rene & Rene*
 **Last Date ..see: (Lost Her Love)**
125/63 **Last Day In The Mines** *Dave Dudley*
109/76 **Last Day Of December** *Chilliwack*
129/65 **Last Exit To Brooklyn**
 *Scott Bedford Four*
114/68 **Last Goodbye** *Dick Miles*
101/82 **Last Night** *Stephanie Mills*
101/83 **Last Night A D.J. Saved My Life** *Indeep*
124/64 **Last Night I Had The Strangest Dream**
 *Kingston Trio*
126/65 **Last Night I Made A Little Girl Cry**
 *Steve Lawrence*
104/79 **Last Night I Wrote A Letter** *Starz*
114/70 **Last Of The Wine** *Robbs*
106/73 **Last Tango In Paris** *Doc Severinsen*
 **Last Thing On My Mind**
117/65 *Vejtables*
105/66 *Womenfolk*
120/73 **Last Thing On My Mind** *Austin Roberts*
106/69 **Last Time** *Buchanan Brothers*
122/67 **Later For Tomorrow** *Ernie K Doe*
103/72 **Latin Bugaloo** *Malo*
102/96 **Latin Swing** *Jonny Z*
104/70 **Laugh** *Neighborhood*
111/66 **Laughing Song** *Freddy Cannon*
109/74 **Laughter In The Rain** *Lea Roberts*
 **Laura (What's He Got That I Ain't Got)**
120/67 *Leon Ashley*
115/70 *Newbeats*
 **Lavender Blue ..see: (We Wear)**
107/81 **Lay Back In The Arms Of Someone**
 *Savoy Brown*
107/95 **Lay Down Your Love**
 *4 P.M. (for positive music)*
132/69 **Lay Lady Lay** *Byrds*
114/68 **Lazy Sunday** *Small Faces*
104/76 **Lazy Ways** *10CC*
102/70 **Lead Me On** *Gwen McCrae*
101/74 **Lean It All On Me** *Diana Trask*
104/69 **Leanin' On You** *Joe South*
121/65 **Learning The Game** *Hullaballoos*
102/75 **Leave It Alone** *Dynamic Superiors*
104/75 **Leave My World** *Johnny Bristol*
110/72 **Leavin' It's Over** *Hudson Brothers*
103/79 **Legend** *Poco*
 **Legend In My Time ..see: (I'd Be) A**
133/65 **Legend Of Shenandoah** *James Stewart*
123/68 **Legend Of Xanadu** *Dave Dee, Dozy, Beaky, Mick & Tich*
103/93 **Lemon** *U2*
113/97 **Lemon Tree** *Fool's Garden*
107/65 **Leroy** *Norma Tracey*
129/63 **Let Go** *Roy Hamilton*

108/63 **Mama Didn't Lie** *Fasinations*
104/62 **Mama, Here Comes The Bride** *Shirelles*
109/73 **Mama I Got A Brand New Thing (Don't Say No)** *Undisputed Truth*
119/95 **Mama, I'm In Love** *Coolio*
110/81 **Mama Lied** *Phil Gentili*
106/70 **Mama Mama** *James Anderson*
106/63 **Mama-Oom-Mow-Mow (The Bird)** *Rivingtons*
109/80 **Mama Sez** *Love Affair*
115/69 **Mama Soul** *Soul Survivors*
131/63 **Mama Was A Cotton Picker** *Jimmie Rodgers*
124/66 **Mama (When My Dollies Have Babies)** *Cher*
107/76 **Mama You're All Right With Me** *Four Tops*
113/70 **Mama's Baby - Daddy's Maybe** *Swamp Dogg*
118/73 **Mama's Little Girl** *Dusty Springfield*
104/59 **Mama's Place** *Bing Day*
134/68 **Mamam** *Arthur Prysock*
110/62 **Mamie In The Afternoon** *Bobby Lewis*
107/71 **Mammy Blue** *James Darren*
112/94 **Man In Love With You** *George Strait*
127/66 **Man Loves Two** *Little Milton*
109/73 **Man Of The World** *Robin Trower*
106/70 **Man, The Wife, & The Little Baby Daughter** *Phil Flowers*
124/97 **Man This Lonely** *Brooks & Dunn*
102/72 **Man Who Sings** *Richard Landis*
106/83 **Man With The 4-Way Hips** *Tom Tom Club*
**Man Without Love** ..see: Quando M'Innamoro
104/74 **Man You Are In Me** *Janis Ian*
107/73 **Mango Meat** *Mandrill*
114/72 **Manhattan Kansas** *Glen Campbell*
119/69 **Manhattan Spiritual** *Sandy Nelson*
103/93 **Many Clouds Of Smoke** *Total Devastation*
109/74 **Many Rivers To Cross** *Nilsson*
109/95 **Many Ways** *Usher*
108/71 **Marblehead Messenger** *Seatrain*
110/72 **Marcella** *Beach Boys*
108/65 **March (You'll Be Sorry)** *Shirelles*
115/72 **Margie, Who's Watching The Baby** *R.B. Greaves*
110/62 **Maria** *George Chakiris*
112/61 **Married** *Frankie Avalon*
102/76 **Married, But Not To Each Other** *Denise LaSalle*
104/71 **Married To A Memory** *Judy Lynn*
111/67 **Marryin' Kind Of Love** *Critters*
109/80 **Marseilles** *Angel City*
110/61 **Mary And Man-O** *Lloyd Price*
119/63 **Mary-Mary** *Jimmy Reed*
127/64 **Mary, Oh Mary** *Fats Domino*
102/84 **Mask, The** *Roger Glover*
102/62 **Masquerade Is Over** *Five Satins*
104/61 **Matador, The** *George Scott*
101/85 **Material Thangz** *Deele*
133/62 **Matilda** *String-A-Longs*
(also see: Waltzing Matilda)
115/67 **Matthew And Son** *Cat Stevens*
**Maybe**
116/69 *Chantels*
110/70 *Janis Joplin*
116/69 **Maybe** *Betty Everett*
118/73 **Maybe Baby** *Gallery*
102/97 **Maybe He'll Notice Her Now** *Mindy McCready*
122/73 **Maybe I Know** *Ellie Greenwich*
107/64 **Maybe The Last Time** *James Brown*
117/63 **Maybe You'll Be There** *Billy & The Essentials*
**Me About You**
119/68 *Jackie DeShannon*
105/70 *Turtles*
122/69 **Me And Bobby McGee** *Roger Miller*
123/69 **Me & Mr. Hohner** *Bobby Darin*
109/82 **Me And The Boys** *Bonnie Raitt*
104/77 **Me And The Elephants** *Bobby Goldsboro*

103/69 **Me And You** *O.C. Smith*
112/96 **Me And You** *Kenny Chesney*
121/68 **Me And You** *Brenton Wood*
114/97 **Me Or The Papes** *Jeru The Damaja*
112/70 **Measure The Valleys** *Keith Textor Singers*
107/85 **Mechanical Emotion** *Vanity*
123/68 **Mechanical World** *Spirit*
117/69 **Meditation, The** *TNT Band*
101/74 **Meet Me On The Corner Down At Joe's Cafe** *Peter Noone*
105/84 **Mega-Mix** *Herbie Hancock*
112/72 **Melanie Makes Me Smile** *Terry Williams*
106/70 **Mellow Dreaming** *Young-Holt Unlimited*
104/84 **Melody** *Boys Brigade*
122/70 **Melody** *Ides Of March*
123/68 **Melody For You** *Grass Roots*
114/69 **Memories Are Made Of This** *Gene & Debbe*
116/69 **Memories Of A Broken Promise** *Motherlode*
101/61 **Memories of those Oldies But Goodies** *Little Caesar/Romans*
102/81 **Memphis** *Fred Knoblock*
105/85 **Men All Pause** *Klymaxx*
104/71 **Men Are Getting Scarce** *Chairmen Of The Board*
127/66 **Mercy** *Willie Mitchell*
106/76 **Merry-Go-Round** *Monday After*
103/83 **Message Is You** *Gary Myrick*
**Message To Michael** ..see: Kentucky Bluebird
102/59 **Mexican Joe** *Mitchell Torok*
113/65 **Mexican Pearls** *Don Randi*
**(Mexican Shuffle)** ..see: Cinnamint Shuffle
102/70 **Mexico** *Jefferson Airplane*
106/66 **Michelle** *Spokesmen*
132/65 **Mickey's East Coast Jerk** *Larks*
119/64 **Midnight** *David Rockingham Trio*
109/81 **Midnight Confession** *Karla DeVito*
116/69 **Midnight Cowboy** *John Barry*
102/78 **Midnight Girl** *Lenny Williams*
108/76 **Midnight Groove** *Love Unlimited Orchestra*
**Midnight Hour**
116/67 *Messengers*
118/67 *Wanted*
131/67 *Kit & The Outlaws*
106/80 *Roxy Music*
111/62 **Midnight In Moscow** *Jan Burgens*
102/77 **Midnight Love Affair** *Carol Douglas*
109/85 **Midnight Mission** *Textones*
105/76 **Midnight On The Bay** *Stills-Young Band*
104/76 **Midnight Soul Patrol** *Quincy Jones*
115/62 **Midnight Sun** *Five Whispers*
108/72 **Mighty Mighty And Roly Poly** *Mal*
106/96 **Milk** *Garbage*
101/60 **Miller's Cave** *Hank Snow*
114/72 **Million To One** *Manhattans*
106/65 **Millions Of Roses** *Steve Lawrence*
112/61 **Milord** *Franck Pourcel*
112/62 **Mind Over Matter (I'm Gonna Make You Mine)** *Nolan Strong*
129/67 **Miniskirts In Moscow or...** *Bob Crewe Generation*
113/62 **Minstrel And Queen** *Impressions*
107/60 **Miracle Of Life** *Robie Lester*
116/61 **Misfits, The** *Don Costa*
111/59 **Miss Lonely Hearts** *Dodie Stevens*
108/72 **Missing You** *Luther Ingram*
120/68 **Mission: Impossible (medley)** *Alan Copeland*
**(Mission On The Bowery)** ..see: Candy Kid
110/76 **Mississippi Lady** *Jim Croce*
114/72 **Mississippi Lady** *Griffin*
**Mister** ..see: Mr.
106/59 **Misty** *Sarah Vaughan*
104/73 **Mom** *Earth, Wind & Fire*
127/63 **Moment Of Truth** *Tony Bennett*
115/65 **Moment To Moment** *Frank Sinatra*
109/69 **Mommy And Daddy** *Monkees*
101/61 **Monday To Sunday** *Alan Dale*

120/64 **Mondo Cane #2** *Kai Winding*
(also see: More)
103/96 **Money Maid (Fallin' In Love)** *Slow Pain*
103/70 **Money Music** *Boys In The Band*
133/63 **Monkey Walk** *Flares*
135/64 **Monster Swim** *Bobby Pickett*
107/81 **Mony Mony** *Billy Idol*
114/70 **Moody** *O.C. Smith*
**Moonglow/Picnic Theme**
121/64 *Baja Marimba Band*
115/65 *Esther Phillips*
103/60 **Moonlight Cocktails** *Rivieras*
102/84 **Moonlight Lady** *Julio Iglesias*
103/78 **Moonlight Serenade** *Tuxedo Junction*
105/73 **Moonshine (Friend of Mine)** *John Kay*
**More**
117/63 *Steve Lawrence*
110/64 *Danny Williams*
102/76 *Carol Williams*
(also see: Mondo Cane #2)
102/64 **More And More Of Your Amor** *Nat King Cole*
**More I See You**
132/63 *Marcy Jo & Eddie Rambeau (medley)*
131/66 *"Groove" Holmes*
108/76 *Peter Allen*
104/67 **More, More, More Of Your Love** *Bob Brady*
108/67 **More Than A Miracle** *Roger Williams*
121/97 **More Than Everything** *Rhett Akins*
**More Than I Can Stand** ..see: Preacher
103/79 **More Than One Way To Love A Woman** *Raydio*
102/83 **More Than This** *Roxy Music*
110/96 **More Than You'll Ever Know** *Travis Tritt*
104/96 **More To Love** *Case*
115/93 **Morning After** *Maze Featuring Frankie Beverly*
118/69 **Morning Dew (Walk Me Out In The)** *Sound Foundation*
134/67 **Morning Glory Days** *Pleasure Fair*
118/95 **Mortal Kombat** *Immortals*
131/68 **Most Beautiful Thing In My Life** *Herman's Hermits*
118/66 **Most Of All** *Cowsills*
102/76 **Motels And Memories** *T.G. Sheppard*
111/72 **Mother Earth** *Tom Rush*
101/72 **Mother Of Mine** *Little Jimmy Osmond*
112/69 **Mother Where's Your Daughter** *Royal Guardsmen*
114/94 **Motherless Child** *Eric Clapton*
101/82 **Mountain Music** *Alabama*
132/63 **Mountain Of Love** *David Houston*
128/64 **Move It Baby** *Simon Scott*
128/65 **Move It On Over** *Del Shannon*
131/69 **Movin'** *Robbs*
124/67 **Moving Finger Writes** *Len Barry*
109/71 **Mr. And Mrs. Untrue** *Candi Staton*
111/63 **Mr. Cool** *Champs*
104/61 **Mr. D. J.** *Van McCoy*
120/61 **Mr. Johnny Q** *Bobbettes*
121/65 **Mr. Jones (A Ballad Of A Thin Man)** *Grass Roots*
101/96 **Mr. Kirk** *4 Hero*
119/70 **Mr. Monday** *Original Caste*
114/66 **Mr. Moon** *Coachmen*
103/61 **Mr. Paganini (You'll Have To Swing It)** *Ella Fitzgerald*
113/64 **Mr. Sandman** *Fleetwoods*
120/68 **Mr. Soul Satisfaction** *Timmy Willis*
106/69 **Mr. Turnkey** *Zager & Evans*
127/67 **Mr. Unreliable** *Cryan' Shames*
118/93 **Mrs. Robinson** *Lemonheads*
105/60 **Mule Skinner Blues** *Rusty Draper*
104/64 **Mumbles** *Oscar Peterson Trio*
130/66 **Music** *Festivals*
109/73 **Music, Music, Music** *Teresa Brewer*
119/67 **Music To Watch Girls By** *Al Hirt*
119/71 **Must Be Love Coming Down** *Major Lance*
103/69 **Must Be Your Thing** *Charles Wright*
108/65 **Mustang Sally** *Sir Mack Rice*
117/64 **Mustang 2 + 2 (Big Mule)** *Casuals*
102/64 **My Adorable One** *Joe Simon*

110/77 **Painting My Love Song** *Henry Gross*
108/96 **Pants R Saggin'** *DJ Trajic*
104/71 **Papa Was A Good Man** *Johnny Cash*
132/68 **Paper Castle** *Rotary Connection*
108/92 **Paper Doll** *Fleetwood Mac*
110/97 **Papi Chulo** *Funkdoobiest*
102/75 **Paradise** *Ted Neeley*
110/72 **Paradise** *Jackie DeShannon*
122/62 **Paradise** *Temptations*
126/63 **Paradise** *April Stevens & Nino Tempo*
102/60 **Pardon Me** *Billy Bland*
111/73 **Part Of The Union** *Strawbs*
102/94 **Party** *Dis 'N' Dat*
107/77 **Party** *Silk*
101/95 **Party All Night** *Jeff Foxworthy With Little Texas & Scott Rouse*
101/83 **Party Animal** *James Ingram*
F/76 **Party Hearty** *Oliver Sain*
112/68 **Party People** *Solomon Burke*
130/65 **Party People** *Ray Stevens*
110/78 **Party Song** *Slave*
107/96 **Party 2 Nite** *Ladae*
101/83 **Party Train** *Gap Band*
105/73 **Passion Play (Edit #10)** *Jethro Tull*
106/70 **Passport To The Future** *Jean Jacques Perrey*
135/65 **Patch It Up** *Linda Scott*
132/68 **Path Of Love** *John Cowsill*
125/67 **Patty Cake** *Capitols*
**Paul** ..see: Ballad Of
128/68 **Paul's Midnight Ride** *Delights Orchestra*
118/92 **Peace & Love Inc.** *Information Society*
104/72 **Peace In The Valley Of Love** *Persuaders*
119/61 **Peace Of Mind** *B.B. King*
125/66 **Peace Of Mind** *Count Five*
119/97 **Peace Train** *Dolly Parton*
107/93 **Peach** *Prince*
**Peaches On A Cherry Tree** ..see: Ruby Baby
108/63 **Peanuts** *4 Seasons*
108/84 **Pearl In The Shell** *Howard Jones*
113/63 **Pearl Pearl Pearl** *Flatt & Scruggs*
120/65 **Pearly Shells (Popo O Ewa)** *Billy Vaughn*
106/82 **Peek-A-Boo!** *Devo*
115/63 **Peking Theme (So Little Time)** *Andy Williams*
107/71 **Pencil Marks On The Wall** *Herschel Bernardi*
101/74 **Pencil Thin Mustache** *Jimmy Buffett*
133/69 **Penny Arcade** *Roy Orbison*
116/70 **People And Me** *New Colony Six*
118/97 **People Get Ready** *Ziggy Marley*
126/68 **People Make The World** *Roosevelt Grier*
103/80 **People Who Died** *Jim Carroll Band*
105/80 **Percolator** *Spyro Gyra*
106/73 **Percolator** *Hot Butter*
101/95 **Perfect Day** *Duran Duran*
109/85 **Perfect Kiss** *New Order*
105/63 **Perfect Pair** *Paul & Paula*
111/60 **Perfect Understanding** *Doris Day*
130/64 **Permanently Lonely** *Timi Yuro*
129/68 **Per-so-nal-ly** *Bobby Paris*
108/70 **Peter And The Wolf** *Charles Randolph Grean Sounde*
**Philly Dog** ..see: Doing The
118/93 **Photograph Of Mary** *Trey Lorenz*
103/59 **Piano Shuffle** *Dave "Baby" Cortez*
103/79 **Pick Me Up, I'll Dance** *Melba Moore*
134/66 **Pick Me Up On Your Way Down** *Hank Thompson*
108/75 **Pick Up The Pieces One By One** *A.A.B.B.*
**Picnic Theme** ..see: Moonglow
116/93 **Picture Perfect** *Michael W. Smith*
108/62 **Piddle de Pat** *Tommy Roe*
115/94 **Piece Of My Heart** *Faith Hill*
124/94 **Pincushion** *ZZ Top*
105/59 **Pine Top's Boogie** *Jo Stafford*
**Pipeline**
106/66 *Chantay's*
109/77 *Bruce Johnston*
101/75 **Pirate Looks At Forty** *Jimmy Buffett*

124/71 **Pistol Legged Mama** *Tommy Roe*
109/71 **Plain And Simple Girl** *Garland Green*
129/66 **Plain Jane** *B.J. Thomas*
118/65 **Plastic** *Serendipity Singers*
133/69 **Plastic Fantastic Lover** *Jefferson Airplane*
127/69 **Play It Cool** *Freddy King*
102/95 **Playa Hata** *Luniz*
101/84 **Playin' It Cool** *Timothy B. Schmit*
101/78 **Playing Your Game, Baby** *Barry White*
103/97 **Please** *U2*
104/85 **Please Be Good To Me** *Menudo*
108/62 **Please Come Home For Christmas** *Charles Brown*
121/63 **Please Don't** *Kitty Kallen*
102/60 **Please Don't Eat The Daisies** *Doris Day*
129/69 **Please Don't Go** *Eddy Arnold*
112/64 **Please Don't Go Away** *Johnny Tillotson*
128/66 **Please Don't Hurt Me (I've Never Been In Love Before)** *Jackie Wilson & LaVern Baker*
101/60 **Please Help Me, I'm Falling** *Homer & Jethro*
128/64 **Please Little Angel** *Doris Troy*
109/62 **Please Mr. Columbus (Turn The Ship Around)** *Lou Monte*
108/71 **Please Mrs. Henry** *Manfred Mann*
119/64 **Please, Please Make It Easy** *Brook Benton*
**Please, Please, Please**
105/60 *James Brown*
114/60 *"5" Royales*
104/61 **Please Say You Want Me** *Little Anthony & The Imperials*
102/68 **Please Send Me Someone To Love** *B.B. King*
115/68 **Please Stay** *Dave Clark Five*
108/63 **Please Write** *Tokens*
108/85 **Pleasure Seekers** *System*
110/61 **Pledge Of Love** *Curtis Lee*
118/67 **Pledge Of Love** *Bobby Goldsboro*
102/81 **Pocket Calculator** *Kraftwerk*
106/95 **Points** *Panther Soundtrack*
106/66 **Pollyanna** *Classics*
115/61 **Pony Train** *Titus Turner*
113/65 **Poor Boy** *Royalettes*
124/63 **Poor Boy** *Jimmy Holiday*
121/66 **Poor Dog (Who Can't Wag His Own Tail)** *Little Richard*
106/72 **Poor Little Fool** *Frank Mills*
111/71 **Poor Little Pearl** *Billy Joe Royal*
103/69 **Poor Man** *Little Milton*
119/69 **Poor Moon** *Canned Heat*
109/96 **Poor, Poor Pitiful Me** *Terri Clark*
104/84 **Pop Goes My Love** *Freeez*
109/96 **Pop Goz The 9** *Gripsta*
101/84 **Popcorn Love** *New Edition*
132/65 **Popping Popcorn** *Dave "Baby" Cortez*
122/70 **Poquito Soul** *One G Plus Three*
126/66 **Portuguese Washerwomen** *Baja Marimba Band*
**(Postcards To Duluth)** ..see: Love City
106/76 **Power Of Love** *Dells*
109/73 **Power To All Our Friends** *Cliff Richard*
101/81 **Praise** *Marvin Gaye*
105/71 **Pray For Me** *Intruders*
111/71 **Preacher/More Than I Can Stand** *Bobby Womack*
107/64 **Precious Words** *Wallace Brothers*
101/85 **Premonition** *Jack Wagner*
105/82 **President Rap's** *Rich Little*
105/61 **Presidential Press Conference** *Sickniks*
125/66 **Pretty Flamingo** *Tommy Vann & The Echoes*
118/63 **Pretty Girls Everywhere** *Arthur Alexander*
106/61 **Pretty, Pretty Girl (The New Beat)** *Time Tones*
**(Pretty Words)** ..see: Things I Want To Hear
108/61 **Preview Of Paradise** *Adam Wade*
107/85 **Price, The** *Twisted Sister*
104/65 **Price Of Love** *Everly Brothers*
103/63 **Prima Donna** *Glen Campbell*

108/62 **Prince, The** *Jackie DeShannon*
**(Prisoner In Love)** ..see: No Bail In This Jail
**(Prisoners)** ..see: Hard Life, Hard Times
114/65 **Private John Q** *Glen Campbell*
123/95 **Proceed** *Roots*
**Professional Widow**
108/96 *Tori Amos*
122/97 *Tori Amos*
123/63 **Promise Me Anything** *Annette*
130/64 **Promise You'll Tell Her** *Swinging Blue Jeans*
125/71 **Promised Land** *Freddy Weller*
108/64 **Promises (You Made Now Are Broken)** *Ray Peterson*
122/93 **Prop Me Up Beside The Jukebox (If I Die)** *Joe Diffie*
**(Pros And Cons Of Hitch Hiking)** ..see: 5:01 AM
105/93 **Protect Ya Neck** *Wu-Tang Clan*
121/70 **Proud Woman** *Johnny Adams*
104/76 **Psychoticbumpschool** *Bootsy's Rubber Band*
121/66 **Public Execution** *Mouse*
121/94 **Puerto Rico** *Frankie Cutlass*
101/81 **Pull Up To The Bumper** *Grace Jones*
112/97 **Pumpin'** *Proyecto Uno*
111/64 **Puppet On A String** *Bob & Earl*
129/67 **Puppet On A String** *Al Hirt*
107/59 **Pure Love** *Sonny James*
119/73 **Purple People Eater** *Dickie Goodman*
104/93 **Push** *Tisha Campbell*
113/64 **Pushin' A Good Thing Too Far** *Barbara Lewis*
103/75 **Put Another Log On The Fire** *Tompall*
132/64 **Put Away Your Tear Drops** *Lettermen*
131/66 **Put It Back (Where You Found It)** *Sue Thompson*
122/73 **Put It Where You Want It** *Nino & April*
112/73 **Put On Your Shoes And Walk** *Clarence Carter*
103/74 **Put The Music Where Your Mouth Is** *Olympic Runners*
119/95 **Put Your Body Where Your Mouth Is** *Sean Levert*
129/67 **Put Your Trust In Me (Depend On Me)** *Joe Simon*
104/80 **Pyramid Song** *J.C. Cunningham*

# Q

124/68 **Quando M'Innamoro** *Sandpipers*
129/66 **Quarter To Three** *Sir Douglas Quintet*
132/65 **Queen Of The Senior Prom** *Vaughn Monroe*
**(Quentin's Theme)** ..see: Shadows Of The Night
122/63 **Queridita Mia (Little Darlin')** *Keith Colley*
111/94 **Quiet Time To Play** *Johnny Gill*

# R

103/66 **Race With The Wind** *Robbs*
127/68 **Radio Song** *Parade*
109/82 **Ragin' Cajun** *Charlie Daniels Band*
102/66 **Rags To Riches** *Lenny Welch*
128/63 **Rain** *Jive Five*
101/82 **Rain Is Falling** *ELO*
105/67 **Rain Rain Go Away** *Lee Dorsey*

104/73 **Rainbow Man** *Looking Glass*
121/94 **Rainbow's Cadillac** *Bruce Hornsby*
112/70 **Raindrops Keep Fallin' On My Head**
 *Barbara Mason*
108/71 **Rainin' In My Heart** *Hank Williams,*
 *Jr./Mike Curb Congregation*
113/70 **Rainmaker** *Moods*
108/75 **Raised On Rock** *Johnny Winter*
 **Ramblin' Rose ..see: (Love Is Like A)**
118/68 **Randy** *Happenings*
101/71 **Rangers Waltz** *Mom & Dads*
135/64 **Rap City** *Ventures*
123/67 **Rapid Transit** *Robbs*
118/64 **Raunchy** *Bill Black's Combo*
101/80 **Ravel's Bolero** *Henry Mancini*
133/65 **Reach For A Star** *Sandy Nelson*
120/61 **Reach For The Stars** *Shirley Bassey*
101/80 **Reach Your Peak** *Sister Sledge*
102/78 **Reaching For The Sky** *Peabo Bryson*
104/85 **Read My Lips** *Melba Moore*
102/79 **Ready 'N' Steady** *D.A.*
127/69 **Ready To Ride** *Southwind*
106/96 **Real Live Sh*t** *Real Live featuring K-Def*
 *& Larry-O*
103/65 **Real Thing** *Tina Britt*
107/69 **Real Thing** *Russell Morris*
109/96 **Real Thing** *World Wide Message Tribe*
119/69 **Real True Lovin'** *Steve & Eydie*
111/93 **Real World** *Queensryche*
128/67 **Really, Really Love You** *Ronnie Walker*
112/73 **Reason To Feel** *Scuffy Shew*
114/95 **Rebecca Lynn** *Bryan White*
103/80 **Rebel Girl** *Survivor*
108/61 **Rebel - Johnny Yuma** *Johnny Cash*
118/93 **Recipe Of A Hoe** *Boss*
123/93 **Reckless** *Alabama*
124/94 **Recognized Thresholds Of Negative**
 **Stress** *Boogiemonsters*
115/95 **Record Jock** *Dana Dane*
115/63 **Red Don't Go With Blue** *Jimmy Clanton*
107/68 **Red, Green, Yellow And Blue**
 *Dickey Lee*
127/69 **Red Red Wine** *Jimmy James*
101/83 **Red Skies** *Fixx*
107/78 **Reelin'** *Garland Jeffreys & Phoebe Snow*
111/67 **Reflections Of Charles Brown**
 *Rubert's People*
106/95 **Refried Dreams** *Tim McGraw*
102/85 **Reggae Rock N Roll** *B.E. Taylor Group*
106/95 **Relax** *Crystal Waters*
 **(Release It) ..see: You Got It**
104/80 **Relight My Fire** *Dan Hartman*
105/78 **Remember** *Greg Kihn Band*
102/95 **Remember We** *Da Bush Babees*
104/79 **Remember Who You Are**
 *Sly & The Family Stone*
101/97 **Reminding Me (Of Sef)** *Common Sense*
103/85 **Request Line** *Rock Master Scott & The*
 *Dynamic Three*
101/84 **Rescue Me** *Duke Jupiter*
101/61 **Respectable** *Chants*
101/80 **Rest Of The Night** *Clif Newton*
102/95 **Resurrection** *Common Sense*
111/90 **Return Of Da Livin' Dead** *D.O.C.*
101/84 **Reunited** *Greg Kihn Band*
129/66 **Reverbaration (Doubt)**
 *Thirteenth Floor Elevators*
112/70 **Revolution In My Soul** *Reivers*
102/77 **Rhapsody In Blue** *Walter Murphy*
114/96 **Rhyme** *Keith Murray*
124/69 **Rhythm Of Life** *Sammy Davis, Jr.*
111/69 **Rib, The** *Jeannie C. Riley*
105/94 **Ribbon In The Sky** *Intro*
103/65 **Ribbon Of Darkness** *Marty Robbins*
112/94 **Rich Girl** *Louchie Lou & Michie One*
122/67 **Richard & Me** *Gene & Tommy*
104/65 **Richest Man Alive** *Mel Carter*
115/62 **Richie** *Gloria Dennis*
118/97 **Richter Scale** *EPMD*
107/65 **Riddle, The** *Nik Kershaw*
105/76 **Ride A Wild Horse** *Sex-O-Lettes*
104/78 **Ride-O-Rocket** *Brothers Johnson*
106/71 **Right Combination** *Porter Wagoner &*
 *Dolly Parton*

106/75 **Right From The Shark's Jaws**
 *Byron McNaughton*
120/73 **Right Here Is Where You Belong**
 *Jerry Washington*
103/82 **Right In The Middle (Of Falling In Love)**
 *Bettye LaVette*
111/62 **Right Now** *Herbie Mann*
119/71 **Right On** *Rascals*
123/69 **Right Or Left At Oak Street** *Roy Clark*
104/84 **Right Or Wrong** *Spinners*
110/62 **Right Thing To Say** *Nat King Cole*
112/96 **Right Time** *Corrs*
128/67 **Right To Cry** *Lenny Welch*
103/77 **Rigor Mortis** *Cameo*
132/65 **Rindercella** *Archie Campbell*
 (also see: Cinderella)
113/69 **Ring Of Bright Water** *Dee Dee Warwick*
125/69 **Ring Your Bell** *Mitch Ryder/Spirit Feel*
127/65 **Ringo Beat** *Ella Fitzgerald*
132/64 **Ringo For President**
 *Young World Singers*
133/67 **Riot On Sunset Strip** *Standells*
102/97 **Rise** *Veronica*
122/65 **Rising Sun** *Deep Six*
110/77 **Rita May** *Bob Dylan*
124/96 **Ritmo Latino** *Laura Martinez*
115/72 **River** *Universal Jones*
112/69 **River Deep-Mountain High**
 *Ike & Tina Turner*
107/67 **Ro Ro Rosey** *Van Morrison*
117/61 **Roach, The** *Gene & Wendell*
102/72 **Road, The** *Danny O'Keefe*
105/85 **Road To Nowhere** *Talking Heads*
127/64 **Roberta** *Barry & The Tamerlanes*
102/95 **Robi-Rob's Boriqua Anthem**
 *C & C Music Factory*
107/84 **Rock** *Greg Kihn Band*
 **Rock And Roll ..also see: Rock 'N' Roll**
105/70 **Rock And Roll Music** *Frost*
105/75 **Rock And Roll Music** *Humble Pie*
 **Rock Around The Clock ..see: (We're**
 **Gonna)**
106/80 **Rock Brigade** *Def Leppard*
109/63 **Rock Candy** *Jack McDuff*
110/83 **Rock It Out** *Pia Zadora*
107/72 **Rock 'N Roll** *Detroit feat. Mitch Ryder*
109/82 **Rock 'N' Roll Party In The Streets** *Axe*
101/84 **Rock You** *Helix*
105/94 **Rockafella** *Redman*
101/79 **Rockin' My Life Away** *Jerry Lee Lewis*
106/60 **Rockin' Red Wing** *Ernie Freeman*
107/94 **Rocks** *Primal Scream*
109/70 **Roll Away The Stone** *Leon Russell*
104/60 **Roll Call Company "J"** *Balladeers*
 **Rollin' and Tumblin'**
115/67 *Canned Heat*
129/69 *Johnny Winter*
118/95 **Rollin' Wit Dane** *Dana Dane*
101/77 **Rollin' With The Flow** *Charlie Rich*
104/73 **Rolling Down A Mountainside**
 *Isaac Hayes*
112/62 **Rome (Wasn't Built In A Day)**
 *Johnnie Taylor*
105/59 **Romeo** *Cadillacs*
 **Romeo & Juliet**
129/67 *Michael & The Messengers*
106/75 *Fallen Angels*
105/59 **Ronnie Is My Lover** *Delicates*
102/70 **Room To Move** *John Mayall*
120/64 **Room Without Windows**
 *Steve Lawrence*
115/94 **Rope The Moon**
 *John Michael Montgomery*
115/66 **Rosanna** *Capreez*
105/75 **Rosanne** *Guess Who*
125/70 **Rose By Any Other Name (Is Still A**
 **Rose)** *Ronnie Milsap*
119/69 **Rose Garden** *Dobie Gray*
129/64 **Rosemarie** *Pat Boone*
 **Rosemary's Baby ..see: Lullaby From**
116/64 **Rosie** *Chubby Checker*
122/63 **Rosy Dance** *Johnny Thunder*
106/59 **Roulette** *Russ Conway*
110/94 **Round & Round** *Miranda*

115/60 **Round Robin** *Donnie Brooks*
122/67 **Round, Round** *Jonathan King*
101/76 **'Round The World With The Rubber**
 **Duck** *C.W. McCall*
109/85 **Roxanne's Revenge** *Roxanne Shante*
106/71 **Ruby (Are You Mad)**
 *Buck Owens/Buckaroos*
106/68 **Ruby Baby & Peaches On A Cherry**
 **Tree** *Mitch Ryder*
134/64 **Ruby Red, Baby Blue** *Fleetwoods*
104/60 **Rudolph, The Red-Nosed Reindeer**
 *Paul Anka*
104/80 **Rumours Of Glory** *Bruce Cockburn*
126/66 **Run And Hide** *Uniques*
124/65 **Run Like The Devil** *Bobby Vee*
130/64 **Run Little Girl** *Donnie Elbert*
121/65 **Run My Heart** *Baby Washington*
115/69 **Run On** *Arthur Conley*
121/68 **Run To Me** *Montanas*
121/95 **Run To Me** *Double You*
124/94 **Run To The Sun** *Erasure*
118/93 **Run To You** *Rage*
 **Run With You ..see: (Till I)**
103/80 **Runaway** *Sailor*
 **Runaway**
112/67 *Del Shannon*
107/75 *Rhodes Kids*
114/69 **Runaway Child, Running Wild**
 *Earl Van Dyke*
103/83 **Runaway Love** *Firefall*
119/70 **Runaway People** *Dyke & The Blazers*
107/78 **Runnin' For Your Lovin'**
 *Brothers Johnson*
105/84 **Rush, Rush** *Debbie Harry*

# S

101/66 **S.O.S. (Heart In Distress)**
 *Christine Cooper*
108/61 **S.O.S. (I Love You)** *Ronnie Hayden*
115/94 **Sabotage** *Beastie Boys*
116/63 **Sad Girl** *Jay Wiggins*
105/84 **Saddest Victory** *Sandy Stewart*
103/74 **Sadie Take A Lover** *Sam Neely*
103/62 **Sailor Boy** *Cathy Carr*
104/97 **Saint, The** *Orbital*
110/61 **St. Louis Blues** *Cousins*
114/69 **Saint Paul** *Terry Knight*
109/94 **Saints** *Breeders*
103/74 **Sally Can't Dance** *Lou Reed*
101/73 **Sally From Syracuse** *Stu Nunnery*
105/93 **Sally Got A One Track Mind** *Diamond &*
 *The Psychotic Neurotics*
118/67 **Sally Sayin' Somethin'** *Billy Harner*
118/73 **Salty Tears** *Mara Lynn Brown*
 **San Antone ..see: (Is Anybody Going**
 **To)**
103/68 **San Francisco (Wear Some Flowers In**
 **Your Hair)** *Paul Mauriat*
135/66 **San Francisco Woman** *Bob Lind*
102/77 **San Francisco (You've Got Me)**
 *Village People*
101/85 **Sanctified Lady** *Marvin Gaye*
103/71 **Sanctuary** *Dion*
107/67 **Sand** *Nancy Sinatra/Lee Hazlewood*
102/97 **Sand And Water** *Beth Nielsen Chapman*
118/63 **Sands Of Gold** *Webb Pierce*
108/64 **Sandy** *Johnny Crawford*
101/81 **Sandy Beaches** *Delbert McClinton*
107/73 **Sarah Cynthia Sylvia Stout (Would Not**
 **Take The Garbage Out)**
 *Shel Silverstein*
119/73 **Satellite Of Love** *Lou Reed*
117/61 **Satin Doll** *Billy Maxted*
103/78 **Saturday** *Norma Jean Wright*
116/63 **Saturday Night** *Sherrys*

247

| | |
|---|---|
| 110/73 | **Slip 'N Slide** *Rufus* |
| 113/71 | **Slipped, Tripped And Fell In Love** |
| | *Ann Peebles* |
| 109/84 | **Slippery People** *Staple Singers* |
| 109/60 | **Slipping Around** *Betty Johnson* |
| 101/72 | **Slipping Into Darkness** *Ramsey Lewis* |
| 109/64 | **Sloop Dance** *Vibrations* |
| 116/63 | **Slow Dance** *Ronnie & The Hi-Lites* |
| 106/84 | **Slow Dancing** *Lindsey Buckingham* |
| | (also see: Feel So Good) |
| 103/70 | **Slow Down** *Crow* |
| 106/82 | **Slow Down** *Lacy J. Dalton* |
| 101/59 | **Slow Motion** *Wade Flemons* |
| 102/76 | **Slow Motion** *Dells* |
| 107/94 | **Slow Wine** *Tony! Toni! Toné!* |
| 124/68 | **Small Talk** *Lesley Gore* |
| 102/66 | **Smashed! Blocked!** *John's Children* |
| 102/78 | **Smile** *Emotions* |
| 106/83 | **Smile** *Was (Not Was)* |
| 107/59 | **Smile** *Art Mooney* |
| 110/60 | **Smiling Bill McCall** *Johnny Cash* |
| 119/96 | **Smoke And Ashes** *Tracy Chapman* |
| 108/76 | **Smoke Gets In Your Eyes** |
| | *Penny McLean* |
| 108/75 | **Smokey Factory Blues** *Steppenwolf* |
| 104/63 | **Sneaky Sue** *Patty Lace* |
| 129/67 | **Snow Queen** *Roger Nichols Trio* |
| 110/60 | **So Blue** *Vibrations* |
| 114/72 | **So Far Away** *Crusaders* |
| 101/84 | **So Fine** *Marc Anthony Thompson* |
| 105/82 | **So Fine** *Howard Johnson* |
| | **So Fine** |
| 117/68 | Ike & Tina Turner |
| 113/73 | Johnny Rivers (medley) |
| 118/95 | **So Fine** *Mint Condition* |
| 112/96 | **So Fly** *Domino* |
| 132/67 | **So Good** *Roy Orbison* |
| 123/95 | **So In Love** *Tribe* |
| 109/78 | **So It Goes** *Nick Lowe* |
| 116/63 | **(So It Was...So It Is) So It Always Will Be** *Everly Brothers* |
| | **(So Little Time) ..see: Peking Theme** |
| 132/64 | **So Long** *James Brown* |
| 120/71 | **So Long, Marianne** *Brian Hyland* |
| 107/83 | **So Many Men, So Little Time** |
| | *Miquel Brown* |
| 119/96 | **So Much For Pretending** *Bryan White* |
| 131/65 | **So Much In Love With You** |
| | *Ian & The Zodiacs* |
| 102/92 | **So Much Love** *Malaika* |
| 130/67 | **So Sharp** *Dyke & The Blazers* |
| 110/81 | **So This Is Love?** *Van Halen* |
| 104/84 | **So Tired** *Ozzy Osbourne* |
| 126/69 | **So True** *Peaches & Herb* |
| 122/70 | **So Young** *Roy Orbison* |
| 110/66 | **Sock It To 'Em J.B.** *Rex Garvin* |
| 103/68 | **Sock It To 'Em Judge** *Pigmeat Markham* |
| 121/68 | **Sock It To Me** *Deacons* |
| 128/68 | **Sock It To Me, Baby** *Senator Bobby* |
| 116/68 | **Sock It To Me Sunshine** *Curtain Calls* |
| 102/78 | **Soft And Easy** *Blackbyrds* |
| 115/61 | **Soft Rain** *Ray Price* |
| 103/73 | **Soft Soul Boogie Woogie** *Wilson Pickett* |
| | **Softly As I Leave You** |
| 116/62 | Matt Monro |
| 121/64 | Matt Monro |
| 117/67 | Eydie Gorme |
| 109/78 | Elvis Presley |
| 115/59 | **Soldier's Joy** *Jerry Reed* |
| 103/61 | **Solitaire** *Embers* |
| 109/81 | **Some Are Born** *Jon Anderson* |
| 108/77 | **Some Broken Hearts Never Mend** |
| | *Don Williams* |
| | **Some Day ..see: Someday** |
| 109/81 | **Some Guys Have All The Luck** |
| | *Nikki Wills* |
| 106/85 | **Some Kinda Lover** *Whispers* |
| 111/69 | **Some Kind-A Wonderful** *Thee Prophets* |
| 106/69 | **Some Of Shelly's Blues** |
| | *Nitty Gritty Dirt Band* |
| 104/61 | **Some Of Your Lovin'** *Johnny Nash* |
| 123/65 | **Some Sunday Morning** *Wayne Newton* |
| 107/70 | **Some Things A Man's Gotta Do** *Shango* |

| | |
|---|---|
| 127/64 | **Some Things Are Better Left Unsaid** |
| | *Ketty Lester* |
| 103/69 | **Some Velvet Morning** *Vanilla Fudge* |
| 118/61 | **Somebody Cares** *Zorro* |
| 115/65 | **(Somebody) Ease My Troublin' Mind** |
| | *Sam Cooke* |
| 119/97 | **Somebody Else** *Hurricane G* |
| 104/93 | **Somebody Else Will** *O'Jays* |
| 104/93 | **Somebody New** *Billy Ray Cyrus* |
| 103/61 | **Somebody Nobody Wants** *Dion* |
| 105/67 | **Somebody Ought To Write A Book About It** *Ray Charles* |
| 115/97 | **Somebody Slap Me** *John Anderson* |
| 106/82 | **Somebody To Love** *Dwight Twilley* |
| 115/66 | **Somebody To Love Me** |
| | *Ronny & The Daytonas* |
| 109/80 | **Somebody Wants You** *Aussie Band* |
| 109/84 | **Somebody's Eyes** *Karla Bonoff* |
| 127/66 | **Somebody's Got To Love You** |
| | *Don Covay/Goodtimers* |
| 102/78 | **Somebody's Gotta Win, Somebody's Gotta Lose** *Controllers* |
| 117/72 | **Somebody's On Your Case** |
| | *Ann Peebles* |
| 106/72 | **Some Day I'll Be A Farmer** *Melanie* |
| 119/71 | **Someday We'll Look Back** |
| | *Merle Haggard* |
| 124/64 | **Someday We're Gonna Love Again** |
| | *Barbara Lewis* |
| 123/64 | **Someday You'll Want Me To Want You** |
| | *Patsy Cline* |
| 115/62 | **Someone** *Billy Vaughn* |
| 112/95 | **Someone Else's Star** *Bryan White* |
| 109/72 | **Someone, Sometime** *New Colony Six* |
| 120/97 | **Someone Who's Cool** *Odds* |
| | **Something ..see: Strawberry Fields** |
| 110/82 | **Something About That Woman** |
| | *Lakeside* |
| 102/68 | **Something I'll Remember** *Sandy Posey* |
| 120/70 | **Something In The Air** |
| | *Thunderclap Newman* |
| 112/67 | **Something Inside Me** *Ray Charles* |
| 102/71 | **Something Old, Something New** |
| | *Fantastics* |
| 107/74 | **Something There Is About You** |
| | *Bob Dylan* |
| | **Something's Got A Hold Of Me** |
| 117/64 | Don & Alleyne Cole |
| 128/65 | Sunny & The Sunliners |
| 130/67 | **Something's Gotten Hold Of My Heart** |
| | *Gene Pitney* |
| 130/69 | **Something's Happening** |
| | *Herman's Hermits* |
| 131/65 | **Sometimes** *Paul Revere & The Raiders* |
| 109/62 | **Sometimes I'm Tempted** *Marty Robbins* |
| 110/67 | **Sometimes She's A Little Girl** |
| | *Tommy Boyce & Bobby Hart* |
| 125/68 | **Sometimes You Just Can't Win** |
| | *Mouse & The Traps* |
| | **Somewhere** |
| 131/65 | Brothers Four |
| 120/66 | Johnny Nash |
| 125/67 | Pet Shop Boys |
| 122/94 | **Somewhere** *Shanice* |
| 117/62 | **Somewhere In This Town** |
| | *Bruce Channel* |
| | **Somewhere My Love ..see: Lara's Theme** |
| 104/74 | **Song For Anna (Chanson D' Anna)** |
| | *Ohta-San* |
| 110/79 | **Song For Guy** *Elton John* |
| 115/61 | **Song For The Lonely** *Platters* |
| | **Song For You** |
| 105/71 | Jaye P. Morgan |
| 104/93 | Ray Charles |
| 104/66 | **Song From The Oscar** *Tony Bennett* |
| 105/77 | **Song In The Night** *Johnny Duncan* |
| 114/61 | **Song Of The Nairobi Trio** |
| | *Fortune Tellers* |
| 110/82 | **Song On The Radio** *Pinups* |
| 111/60 | **Sons And Lovers** *Percy Faith* |
| 119/65 | **Sons Of Katie Elder** *Johnny Cash* |
| 109/79 | **Sooner Or Later** *Rex Smith* |

| | |
|---|---|
| 110/82 | **Sooner Or Later** *Larry Graham* |
| | (also see: One Of Us Must Know) |
| 122/72 | **Sophisticated Lady** *REO Speedwagon* |
| 109/79 | **Sorry** *Natalie Cole* |
| 113/97 | **Sorry Is** *Levert* |
| | **Soul And Inspiration ..see: You've Lost That Lovin' Feeling** |
| 126/68 | **Soul Clappin** *Buena Vistas* |
| 105/64 | **Soul Dance** *Tommy Leonetti* |
| 109/74 | **Soul Power 74** *Maceo & The Macks* |
| 117/69 | **Soul Pride** *James Brown* |
| 133/66 | **Soul Sister** *Four Gents* |
| 125/67 | **Soulsation** *Capreez* |
| 121/64 | **Soulville** *Aretha Franklin* |
| 118/94 | **Sound Boy Killing** *Mega Banton* |
| 111/63 | **Sound Of Surf** *Percy Faith* |
| 118/62 | **Sound Of The Hammer** *Vicki Tasso* |
| 117/68 | **Sour Milk Sea** *Jackie Lomax* |
| 111/69 | **South Carolina** *Flirtations* |
| 106/71 | **Southbound Train** *Steel River* |
| 133/65 | **Southern Country Boy** *Carter Brothers* |
| 108/75 | **Southern Lady** *Timi Yuro* |
| 111/59 | **Souvenirs** *Barbara Evans* |
| 101/77 | **Space Age** *Jimmy Castor Bunch* |
| 110/96 | **Space Age** *Eightball & MJG Featuring Nina Creque* |
| 105/71 | **Space Captain** *Barbra Streisand* |
| 124/69 | **Space Oddity** *David Bowie* |
| 117/93 | **Spaceman** *4 Non Blondes* |
| 132/64 | **Spanish Guitars** *Jerry Wallace* |
| 101/62 | **Spanish Harlem** *Santo & Johnny* |
| 101/76 | **Spanish Hustle** *Fatback Band* |
| 107/61 | **Sparkle And Shine** *Four Coquettes* |
| 107/73 | **Sparkling In The Sand** *Tower Of Power* |
| 109/66 | **Speak Her Name** *David & Jonathan* |
| 107/68 | **Special Care** *Buffalo Springfield* |
| 106/84 | **Special Kind** *America* |
| 103/93 | **Special Kind Of Love** *Dina Carroll* |
| 109/70 | **Special Memory** *Jerry Butler* |
| 129/65 | **Special Years** *Brook Benton* |
| 105/75 | **Speed Trap** *Hoyt Axton* |
| 107/80 | **Spellbound** *Rachel Sweet* |
| 119/64 | **Spend A Little Time** *Barbara Lewis* |
| 105/94 | **Spend The Night** *N-Phase* |
| 103/82 | **Spies In The Night** *Manhattan Transfer* |
| 102/97 | **Spirit** *Sounds Of Blackness* |
| 113/67 | **Splash 1** *Clique* |
| 123/68 | **Split, The** *Lou Rawls* |
| 135/65 | **Spootin'** *Bill Black's Combo* |
| 109/76 | **Spotlight** *David Crosby/Graham Nash* |
| 118/69 | **Spring** *John Tipton* |
| 104/77 | **Spy For Brotherhood** *Miracles* |
| | **St. Louis Blues ..see: Saint** |
| 105/82 | **Stage Fright** *Chic* |
| 113/66 | **Stagecoach To Cheyenne** |
| | *Wayne Newton* |
| F/96 | **Stakes Is High** *De La Soul* |
| 111/93 | **Stand Above Me** *O.M.D.* |
| 108/79 | **Stand By** *Natalie Cole* |
| 102/64 | **Stand By Me** *Cassius Clay* |
| 110/68 | **Stand By Me** *Quicksilver Messenger Service* |
| 116/93 | **Stand By Your Man** *L.L. Cool J* |
| 121/68 | **Stand By Your Man** *Patti Page* |
| 131/64 | **Stand Tall** *O'Jays* |
| 109/76 | **Stand Up And Shout** *Gary Toms* |
| 109/61 | **Standing In The Need Of Love** |
| | *Clarence Henry* |
| 101/74 | **Standing In The Rain** *James Gang* |
| 107/66 | **Standing On Guard** *Falcons* |
| 131/68 | **Standing On The Outside** |
| | *Brenda Jo Harris* |
| 102/79 | **Star Cruiser** *Gregg Diamond* |
| 101/97 | **Star People** *George Michael* |
| 107/83 | **Star Sisters Medley** *Stars on 45* |
| | **Star Wars ..see: Theme from** |
| 129/62 | **Stardust Bossa Nova** *Ella Fitzgerald* |
| 102/59 | **Starlight** *Lee Greenlee* |
| 109/80 | **Starlight** *Ray Kennedy* |
| 105/81 | **Stars On The Water** *Rodney Crowell* |
| 102/93 | **State Of Mind** *Clint Black* |
| 124/95 | **Stay Forever** *Hal Ketchum* |
| 120/97 | **Stay In Love** *Mon a q* |

122/65 **Stay In My Corner** *Dells*
110/81 **Stay The Night**
 *Jim Messina/Pauline Wilson*
121/65 **Stay Together Young Lovers** *Ben Aiken*
101/60 **Stay With Me (A Little While Longer)**
 *Ed Townsend*
101/79 **Stay With Me Till Dawn** *Judie Tzuke*
108/76 **Staying Power** *Barbi Benton*
121/70 **Stealing Moments From Another**
 **Woman's Life** *Glass House*
108/74 **Steam Heat** *Pointer Sisters*
123/73 **Stella's Candy Store** *Sweet Marie*
105/85 **Step By Step** *Jeff Lorber*
106/62 **Step By Step, Little By Little**
 *Anita Bryant*
114/71 **Step Into My World** *Magic Touch*
106/62 **Step Right Up (And Say You Love Me)**
 *Nat King Cole*
103/80 **Steppin' (Out)** *Gap Band*
117/70 **Steve Miller's Midnight Tango**
 *Steve Miller Band*
101/66 **Sticky, Sticky** *Bobby Harris*
111/68 **Still Burning In My Heart** *Drifters*
103/95 **Still In Love** *Brian McKnight*
110/60 **Stolen Angel** *Scott Bros.*
122/69 **Stomp** *NRBQ*
102/75 **Stomp And Buck Dance** *Crusaders*
130/69 **Stone Free** *Jimi Hendrix Experience*
129/68 **Stone Good Lover** *Jo Armstead*
121/68 **Stoney End** *Peggy Lipton*
113/72 **Stoney Ground** *Foundations*
112/68 **Stop Along The Way** *Timothy Carr*
123/65 **Stop And Get A Hold Of Myself**
 *Gladys Knight & The Pips*
112/73 **Stop And Start It All Again**
 *Jonathan Edwards*
101/72 **Stop Doggin' Me** *Johnnie Taylor*
108/63 **Stop Foolin'** *Brook Benton & Damita Jo*
112/70 **Stop! I Don't Wanna' Hear It Anymore**
 *Melanie*
132/67 **Stop Light** *Five Americans*
134/63 **Stop Pretending** *Clovers*
115/65 **Stop Th' Music** *Sue Thompson*
103/62 **Stop The Clock** *Fats Domino*
101/71 **Stop The World And Let Me Off**
 *Flaming Ember*
108/94 **Storm In The Heartland** *Billy Ray Cyrus*
102/74 **Stormy Monday** *Latimore*
133/67 **Stormy Weather** *Magnificent Men*
107/60 **Story Of A Broken Heart** *Johnny Cash*
105/81 **Story Of A Life** *Harry Chapin*
117/62 **Story Of My Life** *"Big" Al Downing*
110/63 **Story Untold** *Emotions*
117/68 **Storybook Children** *Billy Joe Royal*
103/84 **Straight Ahead** *Kool & The Gang*
110/69 **Straight Ahead** *Young-Holt Unlimited*
102/93 **Straight From My Heart** *UNV*
106/92 **Straight Out The Sewer** *DAS EFX*
130/67 **Straight Shooter** *Mamas & The Papas*
119/72 **(Straight to Your Heart) Like A**
 **Cannonball** *Van Morrison*
109/65 **Strain On My Heart** *Roscoe Shelton*
117/61 **Stranded In The Jungle** *Vibrations*
105/81 **Stranded In The Moonlight** *Jet*
105/83 **Stranger** *ELO*
122/71 **Stranger In My Place** *Anne Murray*
130/66 **Stranger With A Black Dove**
 *Peter & Gordon*
124/66 **Strangers In The Night** *Bert Kaempfert*
111/94 **Strap On The Side** *Spice 1*
115/70 **Strawberry Fields/Something**
 *Pozo Seco*
105/84 **Street Dance** *Break Machine*
104/80 **Street Life** *Herb Alpert*
124/70 **Street Singer** *Merle Haggard*
129/66 **Street That Rhymes At Six A.M.**
 *Norma Tanega*
124/66 **Streets Of Baltimore** *Bobby Bare*
124/65 **Streets Of Laredo** *Johnny Cash*
107/76 **Streets Will Love You To Death**
 *Leon Haywood*
108/96 **Stressed Out** *Tribe Called Quest*
 *featuring Faith Evans*

101/76 **Strokin'** *Leon Haywood*
103/85 **Stronger Together** *Shannon*
102/63 **Struttin' With Maria** *Herb Alpert*
110/75 **Stuck In A Hole** *Caravan*
108/81 **Stuck In The Middle**
 *Grand Funk Railroad*
F/77 **Stuck Inside Of Mobile With The**
 **Memphis Blues Again** *Bob Dylan*
105/83 **Subdivisions** *Rush*
121/93 **Sublime** *Ocean Blue*
107/78 **Substitute** *Gloria Gaynor*
103/61 **Sucu Sucu** *Ping-Pong*
112/62 **Sugar Blues** *Don Costa*
119/68 **Sugar (Don't Take Away My Candy)**
 *Jive Five*
108/74 **Sugar Lump** *Leon Haywood*
107/62 **Sugartime Twist** *McGuire Sisters*
102/95 **Sultry Funk**
 *M.C. Hammer Featuring VMF*
135/67 **Summer Day Reflection Song** *Donovan*
107/74 **Summer Girl** *Craig Ruhnke*
102/73 **Summer In The City** *Quincy Jones*
105/97 **Summer Jam** *Quad City DJ's*
101/74 **Summer Love** *Blackbyrds*
**Summer Place ..see: Theme From A**
104/60 **Summer Set** *Mr. Acker Bilk*
108/81 **Summer Strut** *Spyro Gyra*
109/65 **Summer Wind** *Roger Williams/Harry*
 *Simeone Chorale*
129/63 **Summer's Come And Gone**
 *Brandywine Singers*
**Summertime**
106/59  *Sam Cooke*
114/71  *Herb Alpert*
104/94 **Summertime Blues** *Alan Jackson*
108/97 **Sumthin' Sumthin'** *Maxwell*
**Sun Ain't Gonna Shine (Anymore)**
128/65  *Frankie Valli*
115/68  *Fuzzy Bunnies*
120/65 **Sun Glasses** *Skeeter Davis*
132/66 **Sunday, The Day Before Monday**
 *Tommy Boyce*
**Sunlight**
114/69  *Youngbloods*
123/71  *Youngbloods*
123/67 **Sunny Goodge Street** *Tom Northcott*
106/59 **Sunrise Serenade** *Roger Williams*
119/65 **Sunrise, Sunset** *Eddie Fisher*
109/77 **Sunshine** *Undisputed Truth*
117/71 **Sunshine** *Flaming Ember*
117/68 **Sunshine Among Us** *Eternity's Children*
108/76 **Sunshine Day** *Osibisa*
101/68 **Sunshine Girl** *Herman's Hermits*
104/69 **Sunshine, Red Wine** *Crazy Elephant*
107/66 **Sunshine Superman** *Willie Bobo*
101/77 **Super Band** *Kool & The Gang*
108/74 **Super Cool** *Kiki Dee*
104/75 **Super "Jaws"** *Seven Seas*
108/78 **Super Woman** *Dells*
101/76 **Superman Lover** *Johnny Guitar Watson*
102/78 **Supernatural Feeling** *Blackbyrds*
105/75 **Supership** *George Benson*
111/72 **Supersonic Rocket Ship** *Kinks*
104/79 **Surrender To Me**
 *McGuinn, Clark & Hillman*
103/64 **Suspicion** *Elvis Presley*
108/74 **Suzie Girl** *Redbone*
103/63 **Swanee River** *Ace Cannon*
115/71 **Sweet Gingerbread Man**
 *Mike Curb Congregation*
114/93 **Sweet Harmony** *Beloved*
110/81 **Sweet Home Alabama**
 *Charlie Daniels Band*
105/67 **Sweet Maria** *Billy Vaughn Singers*
102/71 **Sweet Mary** *Argent*
**Sweet On You ..see: (Let Me Get)**
106/74 **Sweet Rhode Island Red**
 *Ike & Tina Turner*
114/66 **Sweet September** *Lettermen*
107/61 **Sweet Sorrow** *Conway Twitty*
123/67 **Sweet Sounds Of Summer** *Shangri-Las*
103/74 **Sweet Stuff** *Sylvia*
108/77 **Sweet Summertime** *Q*

126/67 **Sweet Sweet Lovin'** *Paul Kelly*
**Sweetheart Tree**
108/65  *Johnny Mathis*
117/65  *Henry Mancini*
116/61 **Sweethearts In Heaven** *Chase Webster*
115/61 **Sweethearts On Parade** *Etta Jones*
111/59 **Sweetie Pie** *Bob Crewe*
105/64 **Swing** *Tokens*
107/85 **Swing Low** *R.J.'s Latest Arrival*
110/62 **Swing Low** *Floyd Cramer*
127/65 **Swing Me** *Nino Tempo & April Stevens*
110/62 **Swingin' Shepherd Blues Twist**
 *Moe Koffman*
107/79 **Switch Board Susan** *Nick Lowe*
121/70 **Sympathy** *Rare Bird*

# T

132/65 **T.C.B.** *Dee Clark*
103/97 **T.O.N.Y. (Top Of New York)**
 *Capone-N-Noreaga*
112/96 **Taffy** *Lisa Loeb & Nine Stories*
**Take A Chance ..see: Make It With You**
104/82 **Take A Chance With Me** *Roxy Music*
129/65 **Take A Heart** *Sorrows*
103/82 **Take A Lickin' And Keep On Kickin'**
 *William "Bootsy" Collins*
118/65 **Take A Look** *Irma Thomas*
109/78 **Take A Ride On A Riverboat**
 *Louisiana's Le Roux*
104/94 **Take A Toke** *C+C Music Factory*
 *"featuring" Trilogy*
119/70 **Take Her Back** *Gemini*
102/78 **Take It Off The Top** *Dixie Dregs*
106/78 **Take It On Up** *Pockets*
112/95 **Take It To The Front** *Vybe*
102/83 **Take It To The Limit** *Willie Nelson &*
 *Waylon Jennings*
112/73 **Take Life A Little Easier**
 *Rodney Allen Rippy*
126/67 **Take Me** *Brenda Lee*
102/80 **Take Me As I Am** *Carly Simon*
110/76 **Take Me Away** *Roger McGuinn*
111/97 **Take Me Away** *Culture Beat*
115/68 **Take Me Back** *Frankie Laine*
121/66 **Take Me Back To New Orleans**
 *Gary (U.S.) Bonds*
102/80 **Take Me Down** *Exile*
114/65 **Take Me For A Little While** *Evie Sands*
115/93 **Take Me For A Little While**
 *Coverdale•Page*
103/96 **Take Me Higher** *Energy*
114/95 **Take Me Higher** *Diana Ross*
 *(also see: Dancing In The Aisles)*
119/73 **Take Me Home, Country Roads**
 *Olivia Newton-John*
121/68 **Take Me In Your Arms (Rock Me A**
 **Little While)** *Isley Brothers*
115/60 **Take Me To Your Ladder (I'll See Your**
 **Leader Later)** *Buddy Clinton*
101/77 **Take Me Tonight** *Tom Jones*
108/70 **Take Me With You** *Honey Cone*
110/71 **Take My Hand** *Mel Tillis & Sherry Bryce*
104/65 **Take The Time** *Johnny Mathis*
114/66 **Take Your Love** *Bobby Goldsboro*
116/69 **Take Your Love (And Shove It)**
 *Kane's Cousins*
102/69 **Taking My Love (And Leaving Me)**
 *Martha Reeves/Vandellas*
108/80 **Taking Somebody With Me When I Fall**
 *Larry Gatlin/Gatlin Brothers Band*
103/95 **Tales From The Hood** *Domino*
101/63 **Talk Back Trembling Lips**
 *Ernest Ashworth*

251

# U

104/93 **Until You Suffer Some (Fire And Ice)**
*Poison*
134/65 **Un-Wind The Twine**
*Alvin Cash & The Crawlers*
103/93 **Up On The Roof** *Il D Extreme*
116/69 **Up Tight Good Woman** *Solomon Burke*
123/67 **Up To Now** *Trini Lopez*
**Up-Up And Away ..see: We Can Fly**
117/65 **Upon A Painted Ocean** *Barry McGuire*
101/80 **Uptown** *Prince*
126/67 **Uptown** *Chambers Brothers*
123/94 **Uptown *Hit** *Kurious Featuring The Constipated Monkeys*
101/74 **Us And Them** *Pink Floyd*
103/84 **Use It Or Lose It** *Michael Furlong*
103/71 **Used To Be** *Just Us*
111/71 **Used To Be A King** *Graham Nash*
110/75 **Using The Power** *Climax Blues Band*

# V

101/59 **Vacation Days Are Over** *Argyles*
102/70 **Valley To Pray** *Arlo Guthrie*
133/65 **Venice Blue** *Bobby Darin*
111/68 **Venus** *Johnny Mathis*
101/80 **Very First Time** *Michael Johnson*
103/59 **Very Precious Love** *Hernando*
103/61 **Very True Story** *Chris Kenner*
119/94 **Vibe** *Zhané*
127/66 **Viet Nam Blues** *Dave Dudley*
**Violetta ..see: (Hear My Song)**
133/69 **Virginia Girl** *Five Americans*
121/67 **Visit To A Sad Planet** *Leonard Nimoy*
101/77 **Vitamin U** *Smokey Robinson*
108/94 **Vocab** *Fugees (Tranzlator Crew)*
110/84 **Voices** *Russ Ballard*
107/62 **Volare** *Ace Cannon*
101/61 **Voyage To The Bottom Of The Sea**
*Frankie Avalon*

# W

131/70 **Wabash Cannon Ball**
*Danny Davis/Nashville Brass*
113/62 **Waddle, Waddle** *Bracelets*
127/70 **Wait A Minute** *Lost Generation*
103/82 **Wait For Me** *Slave*
104/64 **Wait For Me** *Rita Pavone*
115/70 **Wait For Summer** *Jack Wild*
125/63 **Waitin' For The Evening Train**
*Anita Kerr Quartet*
112/67 **Waitin' On You** *B.B. King*
103/82 **Waiting By The Hotline**
*Deniece Williams*
104/81 **Waiting For A Friend** *Roger Daltrey*
127/63 **Waiting For Billy** *Connie Francis*
101/64 **Waiting Game** *Brenda Lee*
101/97 **Wake Me Up (When The World's Worth Waking Up For)** *Kyle Vincent*
120/68 **Wake Up To Me Gentle** *Al Martino*
104/82 **Walk, The** *Time*
107/80 **Walk, The** *Inmates*
107/70 **Walk A Mile In My Shoes**
*Willie Hightower*
105/76 **Walk Away** *Joe Walsh*
103/65 **Walk Hand In Hand**
*Gerry & The Pacemakers*
121/68 **Walk On** *Roy Orbison*
106/72 **Walk On In** *Lou Rawls*

102/62 **Walk On The Wild Side** *Elmer Bernstein*
103/78 **Walk Right Back** *Anne Murray*
109/76 **Walk Right In** *Yvonne Elliman*
121/93 **Walk Through The World** *Marc Cohn*
119/64 **Walk, Walk** *Freewheelers*
103/64 **Walkin'** *Al Hirt*
114/97 **Walkin' On The Sun** *Smack*
108/63 **Walking After Midnight** *Patsy Cline*
120/62 **Walking Cane** *Billy Duke*
123/70 **Walking In The Sand** *Al Martino*
115/73 **Walking On Back** *Edward Bear*
103/74 **Wall Street Shuffle** *10 C.C.*
**Walter Wart ..see: Ballad Of**
112/60 **Waltzing Matilda** *David Carroll*
*(also see: Matilda)*
112/93 **Want U Back** *Me-2-U*
104/61 **Wanted, One Girl** *Jan & Dean*
110/74 **Warmin' Up The Band** *Don Everly*
111/71 **Warpath** *Isley Brothers*
108/70 **Wash, Mama, Wash**
*Dr. John The Night Tripper*
129/63 **Washington Square** *Ames Brothers*
107/74 **Watch Out For Lucy** *Dobie Gray*
101/64 **Watch Out Sally** *Diane Renay*
110/94 **Watch The Girl Destroy Me**
*Possum Dixon*
119/70 **Watch What Happens** *Lena Horne*
107/83 **Watch Your Step** *Carlos Santana*
108/78 **Watching The Detectives** *Elvis Costello*
101/66 **Watching The Late Late Show**
*Don Covay & The Goodtimers*
105/96 **Watching The World Go By** *Maxi Priest*
113/72 **Water, Paper & Clay** *Mary Hopkin*
108/61 **Water Was Red** *Johnny Cymbal*
106/80 **Waterfalls** *Paul McCartney*
101/73 **Watergate Blues** *Tom T. Hall*
**Waterhole #3 ..see: Ballad Of**
121/63 **Watermelon Man** *Herbie Hancock*
128/65 **Watusi '64** *Jay Bentley*
119/68 **Way Over There** *Edwin Starr*
108/77 **Way You Make Me Feel** *Melba Moore*
**Way You Play ..see: (I Like) The**
110/75 **Waymore's Blues** *Waylon Jennings*
104/63 **Wayward Wind** *Frank Ifield*
108/70 **We All Sung Together** *Grin*
120/65 **We Are In Love** *Bobby Byrd*
**We Belong Together**
104/61 **Robert & Johnny**
108/61 **Belmonts**
107/79 **We Both Deserve Each Other's Love**
*L.T.D.*
101/76 **We Both Need Each Other**
*Norman Connors*
106/68 **We Call On Him** *Elvis Presley*
129/68 **We Can Fly/Up-Up And Away** *Al Hirt*
101/69 **We Can Make It** *Ray Charles*
120/66 **We Can Make It** *Ruby & The Romantics*
121/67 **We Can Make It If We Try** *Neil Sedaka*
107/65 **We Can't Believe You're Gone**
*Bobby Harris*
**We Can't Go On This Way**
103/66 **Teddy & the Pandas**
115/69 **Unchained Mynds**
117/65 **We Didn't Ask To Be Brought Here**
*Bobby Darin*
108/77 **We Do It** *Carol Douglas*
108/76 **(We Don't Want Your Money) We Want Mine** *Crack The Sky*
127/68 **We Got A Thing Going On**
*Ben E. King & Dee Dee Sharp*
132/69 **We Got Latin Soul** *Mongo Santamaria*
108/74 **We Got Love** *Buddy Miles*
104/75 **We Got To Get Our Thing Together**
*Dells*
115/72 **We Got To Have Peace** *Curtis Mayfield*
108/80 **We Gotta' Get Out Of Here** *Ian Hunter*
103/67 **We Gotta Go Home** *Music Explosion*
128/64 **We Have Something More (Than A Summer Love)** *Connie Francis*
102/83 **We Live So Fast** *Heaven 17*
130/68 **We Played Games** *John Fred*
116/94 **We Run Things (It's Like Dat)**
*Da Bush Babees*

103/71 **We Sure Can Love Each Other**
*Tammy Wynette*
135/69 **We Try Harder**
*Kim Weston / Johnny Nash*
125/94 **We Wait And We Wonder** *Phil Collins*
123/66 **(We Wear) Lavender Blue**
*Finders Keepers*
116/97 **We Were In Love** *Toby Keith*
101/73 **We'll Make Love** *Al Anderson*
131/67 **(We'll Meet In The) Yellow Forest**
*Jay & The Americans*
105/64 **We'll Never Break Up For Good**
*Paul & Paula*
130/66 **We're Acting Like Lovers** *Spellbinders*
123/68 **We're All Going To The Same Place**
*Tommy Boyce & Bobby Hart*
125/66 **(We're Gonna) Bring The Country To The City** *Tony Mason*
**(We're Gonna) Rock Around The Clock**
118/68 **Bill Haley**
121/68 **Freddy Cannon**
107/77 **We're Still Together** *Peaches & Herb*
113/95 **We're The Same** *Matthew Sweet*
108/70 **Wear Your Love Like Heaven**
*Peggy Lipton*
110/72 **Weave Me The Sunshine** *Peter Yarrow*
103/66 **Wedding Bell Blues** *Laura Nyro*
**Weekend, The**
123/66 **Jack Jones**
131/66 **Steve Lawrence**
106/97 **Wegetzdown** *Rampage*
103/96 **Welcome** *Erick Sermon*
119/73 **Welcome Home** *Peters & Lee*
**Welcome Home**
129/62 **Frankie Avalon**
130/64 **Anita Bryant**
102/64 **Welcome To My World** *Jim Reeves*
125/65 **Welcome, Welcome** *Nancy Wilson*
**Welcome, Welcome Home ..see: Welcome Home**
107/85 **Well-A-Wiggy** *Weather Girls*
117/73 **Well Hello** *Yellowstone & Voice*
119/61 **Well, I Ask You** *Eden Kane*
101/82 **What!** *Soft Cell*
133/69 **What A Beautiful Feeling**
*California Earthquake*
120/68 **What A Day** *Contrasts*
106/60 **What A Dream** *Conway Twitty*
**(What A) Groovey Feeling**
102/70 **Johnny Nash**
103/73 **Johnny Nash**
120/66 **What A Party** *Tom Jones*
124/65 **What A Shame** *Rolling Stones*
110/77 **What A Sound** *Henry Gross*
103/76 **(What A) Wonderful World** *Johnny Nash*
116/68 **What A Wonderful World**
*Louis Armstrong*
101/94 **What About Us** *Jodeci*
123/64 **What Am I Gonna Do With You**
*Skeeter Davis*
117/97 **What Am I To You** *Jana*
107/60 **What Are You Doing New Year's Eve**
*Danté & the Evergreens*
112/97 **What Are You Waiting For?** *Phajja*
113/64 **What Can A Man Do** *Ben E. King*
102/73 **What Can I Tell Her** *Timmy Thomas*
107/68 **What Can You Do When You Ain't Got Nobody** *Soul Brothers Six*
113/96 **What Did I Do To You?** *Terry Ellis*
106/70 **What Do You Say To A Naked Lady**
*Errol Sober*
104/60 **What Do You Want To Make Those Eyes At Me For?** *Ray Peterson*
121/67 **What Does It Take (To Keep a Man Like You Satisfied)** *Skeeter Davis*
**What Does It Take (To Win Your Love)**
111/69 **Motherlode**
107/83 **Garland Jeffreys**
121/63 **What Good Am I Without You?**
*Jackie Wilson*
110/59 **What Good Is Graduation** *Graduates*
112/93 **What I Do Best** *Robin S*
101/63 **What I Gotta Do (To Make You Jealous)**
*Little Eva*

# FACTS AND FEATS

**Top *Bubbling Under* Artists**

**Top Artist Achievements**
    **Most Charted *Bubbling Under* Singles**
    **Most #101 Hits**
    **Most Weeks At The #101 Position**

***Bubbling Under* Singles Of Longevity**

**The MVPs (Most Valuable Platters)**

**1. Parliament/Funkadelic**
189 points

**2. Pearl Jam**
151 points

**3. Ray Charles**
126 points

**4. Aretha Franklin**
109 points

**5. Bobby Goldsboro**
107 points

**6. James Brown**
106 points

**7. Elvis Presley**
105 points

**8. The Everly Brothers**
104 points

**9. B.B. King**
101 points

**10. Ike & Tina Turner**
99 points

**11. The Whispers**
99 points

**12. Billy Vaughn**
96 points

**13. Dean Martin**
95 points

**14. Johnny Cash**
95 points

**15. Johnny Nash**
93 points

**16. Marty Robbins**
93 points

**17. Kool & The Gang**
93 points

**18. Steve Lawrence**
91 points

**19. The Ventures**
85 points

**20. Chaka Khan (Rufus)**
83 points

**21. Sammy Davis, Jr.**
82 points

**22. Bryan White**
79 points

**23. Teddy Pendergrass**
78 points

**24. Johnny Mathis**
74 points

|      | Points |                            |      | Points |                            |
|------|--------|----------------------------|------|--------|----------------------------|
| 25.  | 74     | Johnnie Taylor             | 63.  | 61     | Roger Williams             |
| 26.  | 73     | The Manhattans             | 64.  | 61     | Dion                       |
| 27.  | 72     | The Isley Brothers         | 65.  | 61     | Jerry Lee Lewis            |
| 28.  | 71     | Buck Owens                 | 66.  | 61     | Kenny Rogers/First Edition |
| 29.  | 71     | The Righteous Brothers     | 67.  | 60     | Andy Williams              |
| 30.  | 71     | Melba Moore                | 68.  | 60     | The Dells                  |
| 31.  | 71     | Smokey Robinson            | 69.  | 60     | Willie Nelson              |
| 32.  | 71     | Luther Vandross            | 70.  | 59     | Glen Campbell              |
| 33.  | 71     | Real McCoy                 | 71.  | 59     | Jimmy Buffett              |
| 34.  | 70     | The Tokens                 | 72.  | 59     | Reba McEntire              |
| 35.  | 69     | Fats Domino                | 73.  | 58     | Sonny James                |
| 36.  | 69     | Dusty Springfield          | 74.  | 58     | Neil Sedaka                |
| 37.  | 68     | Brenda Lee                 | 75.  | 58     | Ronnie Milsap              |
| 38.  | 68     | Frank Sinatra              | 76.  | 58     | Devo                       |
| 39.  | 68     | Herb Alpert/Tijuana Brass  | 77.  | 58     | The Trammps                |
| 40.  | 68     | Greg Kihn                  | 78.  | 58     | Cameo                      |
| 41.  | 68     | Zapp/Roger                 | 79.  | 58     | Mary Jane Girls            |
| 42.  | 68     | Doug E. Fresh              | 80.  | 57     | Jackie Wilson              |
| 43.  | 67     | The Shirelles              | 81.  | 57     | Ace Cannon                 |
| 44.  | 67     | Ray Stevens                | 82.  | 57     | The 4 Seasons              |
| 45.  | 67     | Jackie DeShannon           | 83.  | 57     | Roger Miller               |
| 46.  | 67     | Dolly Parton               | 84.  | 57     | Tammy Wynette              |
| 47.  | 66     | Connie Francis             | 85.  | 56     | King Curtis                |
| 48.  | 66     | Nat "King" Cole            | 86.  | 56     | Jerry Butler               |
| 49.  | 66     | Charley Pride              | 87.  | 56     | Al Green                   |
| 50.  | 66     | The Gap Band               | 88.  | 56     | Linda Ronstadt             |
| 51.  | 65     | Gene Chandler              | 89.  | 56     | Toby Keith                 |
| 52.  | 65     | Levert                     | 90.  | 55     | Gladys Knight & The Pips   |
| 53.  | 65     | Barry White                | 91.  | 55     | Charlie Rich               |
| 54.  | 64     | Lenny Williams             | 92.  | 55     | Ann Peebles                |
| 55.  | 63     | The Lettermen              | 93.  | 55     | Wilson Pickett             |
| 56.  | 63     | Rick Nelson                | 94.  | 55     | Spinners                   |
| 57.  | 63     | Mindy McCready             | 95.  | 55     | Patty Loveless             |
| 58.  | 62     | Paul Anka                  | 96.  | 54     | Wayne Newton               |
| 59.  | 62     | Bobby Bland                | 97.  | 54     | Tom Jones                  |
| 60.  | 62     | The Beach Boys             | 98.  | 54     | The Brothers Johnson       |
| 61.  | 62     | Bobby Womack               | 99.  | 54     | The Miracles               |
| 62.  | 61     | Brook Benton               | 100. | 54     | Deniece Williams           |

## POINT SYSTEM

Points are awarded according to the following formula:

1.  Each artist's charted singles are given points based on their highest charted position:

| #101     | = | 10 points |
|----------|---|-----------|
| #102-105 | = | 8 points  |
| #106-110 | = | 6 points  |
| #111-120 | = | 4 points  |
| #121-135 | = | 2 points  |

2.  Total weeks charted are added in.

In the case of a tie, the artist with the most charted *Bubbling Under* singles is listed first.
If artists are still tied, then the artists are listed alphabetically.

## MOST CHART HITS

1. Ray Charles .............................14
2. The Everly Brothers ................14
3. Parliament/Funkadelic............14
4. James Brown ..........................13
5. Elvis Presley ..........................13
6. Ike & Tina Turner ...................13
7. Aretha Franklin ......................12
8. B.B. King ...............................12
9. Dean Martin ...........................12
10. Billy Vaughn ...........................12
11. Johnny Cash ...........................11
12. Fats Domino ...........................11
13. Connie Francis........................11
14. Bobby Goldsboro ....................11
15. Steve Lawrence.......................11
16. The Lettermen ........................11
17. Johnny Nash ...........................11
18. Marty Robbins.........................11
19. The Ventures ..........................11
20. Sammy Davis, Jr. ....................10
21. King Curtis ..............................10
22. Brenda Lee ..............................10
23. Ricky Nelson ...........................10
24. Buck Owens ............................10
25. Dusty Springfield ....................10
26. Brook Benton ............................9
27. The Isley Brothers ....................9
28. Ben E. King ...............................9
29. The Manhattans ........................9
30. Johnny Mathis...........................9
31. The Righteous Brothers ...........9
32. The Shirelles ............................9
33. Frank Sinatra ...........................9
34. Ray Stevens .............................9
35. The Whispers ...........................9

## MOST #101 HITS

1. Parliament/Funkadelic..............3
2. Charley Pride ...........................3
3. Atlanta Rhythm Section ...........2
4. The Beach Boys........................2
5. Jimmy Buffett...........................2
6. Clarence Carter ........................2
7. Common Sense ........................2
8. The Delfonics ...........................2
9. Doug E. Fresh & The Get
   Fresh Crew ............................2
10. Duane Eddy...............................2
11. Fatback ....................................2
12. The Gap Band ...........................2
13. Marvin Gaye .............................2
14. Mickey Gilley ............................2
15. Herman's Hermits .....................2
16. Kool & The Gang ......................2
17. Brenda Lee ...............................2
18. Love Unlimited..........................2
19. Herbie Mann .............................2
20. Mary Jane Girls ........................2
21. C.W. McCall ..............................2
22. Reba McEntire ..........................2
23. Stephanie Mills ........................2
24. Van Morrison............................2
25. Smokey Robinson .....................2
26. Linda Ronstadt .........................2
27. Ray Stevens .............................2
28. Johnnie Taylor ..........................2
29. Luther Vandross .......................2
30. The Vogues ..............................2
31. Johnny "Guitar" Watson ...........2
32. The Whispers ...........................2
33. Barry White ..............................2
34. Bryan White ..............................2
35. Bobby Womack..........................2

## MOST WEEKS AT #101

1. Vanity 6 ...................................7
2. Atlanta Rhythm Section ...........6
3. Michael Henderson...................6
4. Al Hudson/The Soul Partners ...6
5. Grace Jones.............................6
6. The Memphis Horns .................6
7. Luther Vandross .......................6
8. Bobby Womack..........................6
9. Atlantic Starr ...........................5
10. The Manhattans ........................5
11. Parliament/Funkadelic..............5
12. Charlie Rich .............................5
13. War ..........................................5
14. Johnny "Guitar" Watson ...........5
15. The Whispers ...........................5
16. Barry White ..............................5
17. Yarbrough & Peoples ...............5
18. Clarence Carter ........................4
19. The Delfonics ...........................4
20. Doug E. Fresh & The Get
    Fresh Crew ...........................4
21. The Gap Band ...........................4
22. Herman's Hermits ....................4
23. Jimmy "Bo" Horne ...................4
24. Brenda Lee ...............................4
25. Loverboy ..................................4
26. Reba McEntire...........................4
27. Maureen McGovern ..................4
28. Mr. Lee.....................................4
29. Johnnie Taylor ..........................4

# RECORDS OF LONGEVITY — Singles

Singles with 14 or more total weeks charted.

| PK YR | PK WKS | PK POS | WKS CHR | RANK | TITLE | ARTIST |
|---|---|---|---|---|---|---|
| 97 | 4 | 110 | 42* | 1. Alive | Pearl Jam |
| 97 | 1 | 108 | 35* | 2. Even Flow | Pearl Jam |
| 78 | 1 | 102 | 30 | 3. San Francisco (You've Got Me) | Village People |
| 97 | 2 | 105 | 27 | 4. Block Rockin' Beats | The Chemical Brothers |
| 96 | 1 | 102 | 26 | 5. I'll Be Alright | MTS |
| 98 | 1 | 107 | 23 | 6. Dance Hall Days | Wang Chung |
| 96 | 1 | 102 | 22 | 7. I Do | Paul Brandt |
| 96 | 1 | 103 | 20 | 8. Change My Mind | John Berry |
| 96 | 2 | 101 | 18 | 9. I'm Not Supposed To Love You Anymore | Bryan White |
| 96 | 1 | 101 | 18 | 10. Sleeping With An Angel | Real McCoy |
| 97 | 1 | 101 | 17 | 11. Emotions | Twista |
| 95 | 4 | 110 | 17 | 12. Whatz Up, Whatz Up | Playa Poncho featuring L.A. Sno |
| 77 | 3 | 103 | 16 | 13. East Bound And Down | Jerry Reed |
| 96 | 1 | 103 | 16 | 14. Take Me Higher | Energy |
| 93 | 1 | 103 | 16 | 15. Up On The Roof | II D Extreme |
| 96 | 1 | 105 | 16 | 16. Your Love Amazes Me | Michael English |
| 96 | 1 | 105 | 16 | 17. Hypnotize The Moon | Clay Walker |
| 82 | 7 | 101 | 15 | 18. Nasty Girl | Vanity 6 |
| 77 | 6 | 101 | 15 | 19. Just For Your Love | The Memphis Horns |
| 97 | 2 | 101 | 15 | 20. In Your Wildest Dreams | Tina Turner |
| 96 | 1 | 101 | 15 | 21. Ordinary Girl | Lionel Richie |
| 93 | 1 | 101 | 15 | 22. Ain't That Lonely Yet | Dwight Yoakam |
| 95 | 2 | 102 | 15 | 23. Immortality | Pearl Jam |
| 97 | 1 | 102 | 15 | 24. What If I Do | Mindy McCready |
| 93 | 2 | 103 | 15 | 25. Many Clouds Of Smoke | Total Devastation |
| 96 | 1 | 103 | 15 | 26. Still In Love | Brian McKnight |
| 95 | 1 | 105 | 15 | 27. Daddy's Home | Spanish Fly |
| 95 | 1 | 106 | 15 | 28. Y'all Ain't Ready Yet | Mystikal |
| 95 | 1 | 109 | 15 | 29. Head Like A Hole | Nine Inch Nails |
| 77 | 5 | 101 | 14 | 30. Rollin' With The Flow | Charlie Rich |
| 93 | 4 | 101 | 14 | 31. Hey Love (Can I Have A Word) | Mr. Lee Featuring R. Kelly |
| 97 | 2 | 101 | 14 | 32. Wu-Renegades | Killarmy |
| 94 | 1 | 101 | 14 | 33. Ain't Nobody | Jaki Graham |
| 97 | 1 | 101 | 14 | 34. Keep It On The Real | 3XKrazy |
| 97 | 1 | 101 | 14 | 35. Love Is The Right Place | Bryan White |
| 78 | 4 | 102 | 14 | 36. Smile | The Emotions |
| 98 | 1 | 102 | 14 | 37. Sand And Water | Beth Nielsen Chapman |
| 96 | 1 | 102 | 14 | 38. Never Miss The Water | Chaka Khan Featuring Me'Shell Ndegéocello |
| 96 | 1 | 102 | 14 | 39. Good Love | Johnnie Taylor |
| 77 | 4 | 103 | 14 | 40. On Fire | T-Connection |
| 95 | 2 | 103 | 14 | 41. Is It Me? | Monteco Featuring Immature |
| 97 | 1 | 103 | 14 | 42. Showdown | E-A-Ski |
| 96 | 1 | 104 | 14 | 43. You Could Be My Boo | The Almighty RSO featuring Faith Evans |
| 96 | 3 | 105 | 14 | 44. Set It Off | Organized Noize |

\* Singles which charted more than once (at least 6 months apart).
  To qualify, the recharted hit must be the original recording (or remix of original recording) and not a re-recording.

# MVP'S (Most Valuable Platters)

Following is a list of all records in the singles section valued at $40 or more.

| Year | Value | Title | Artist | Label & Number |
|------|-------|-------|--------|----------------|
| 63 | $900 | 1. From Me To You | The Beatles... | Vee-Jay 522 |
| 65 | $200 | 2. Long Tall Sally | The Kinks... | Cameo 345 |
| 67 | $200 | 3. See Emily Play | The Pink Floyd... | Tower 356 |
| 61 | $150 | 4. Life Is But A Dream | The Earls... | Rome 101 |
| 65 | $125 | 5. Boys | The Beatles... | Capitol 6066 |
| 64 | $125 | 6. I Should Have Known Better / A Hard Day's Night | George Martin... | United Artists 750 |
| 73 | $100 | 7. I Can Hear Music | Larry Lurex... | Anthem 204 |
| 60 | $75 | 8. Please, Please, Please | James Brown... | Federal 12258 |
| 60 | $75 | 9. Cinderella | Classics... | Dart 1015 |
| 63 | $75 | 10. Too Hurt To Cry, Too Much In Love To Say Goodbye | Darnells... | Gordy 7024 |
| 63 | $75 | 11. Oh What A Night For Love | Roy Tyson... | Double-L 723 |
| 61 | $75 | 12. Church Bells May Ring | Willows... | Melba 102 |
| 69 | $60 | 13. Space Oddity | David Bowie... | Mercury 72949 |
| 59 | $60 | 14. How Will It End? | Barry Darvell... | Colt 45 107 |
| 63 | $60 | 15. Arabia | The Delcos... | Showcase 2501 |
| 59 | $60 | 16. Earth Angel | The Penguins... | Dooto 348 |
| 66 | $60 | 17. Diddy Wah Diddy | The Remains... | Epic 10001 |
| 63 | $50 | 18. Lovers | The Blendtones... | Success 101 |
| 60 | $50 | 19. If I Knew | The Cruisers... | V-Tone 207 |
| 61 | $50 | 20. Lullaby Of The Bells | The Deltairs... | Ivy 101 |
| 60 | $50 | 21. The Wind | The Diablos... | Fortune 511 |
| 63 | $50 | 22. Peanuts | The 4 Seasons... | Vee-Jay EP 1-901 |
| 63 | $50 | 23. Since I Don't Have You | The 4 Seasons... | Vee-Jay EP 1-902 |
| 63 | $50 | 24. Bo Diddley | Buddy Holly... | Coral 62352 |
| 60 | $50 | 25. The Wind | The Jesters... | Winley 242 |
| 61 | $50 | 26. Memories of those Oldies But Goodies | Little Caesar and The Romans... | Del-Fi 4166 |
| 62 | $50 | 27. Twistin' Fever | The Marcels... | Colpix 629 |
| 60 | $50 | 28. Blue Velvet | The Paragons... | Musicraft 1102 |
| 61 | $50 | 29. White Cliffs Of Dover | The Robins... | Lavender 001 |
| 59 | $50 | 30. Island Of Love | The Sheppards... | Apex 7750 |
| 60 | $50 | 31. So Blue | The Vibrations... | Checker 954 |
| 68 | $50 | 32. Goodnight Sweet Josephine | The Yardbirds... | Epic 10303 |
| 59 | $40 | 33. Romeo | The Cadillacs... | Josie 866 |
| 62 | $40 | 34. If You Want To | The Carousels... | Gone 5118 |
| 64 | $40 | 35. Baby, Baby (I Still Love You) | The Cinderellas... | Dimension 1026 |
| 61 | $40 | 36. Life Is But A Dream Sweetheart | The Classics... | Mercury 71829 |
| 79 | $40 | 37. Ready 'N' Steady | D.A. ... | Rascal 102 |
| 59 | $40 | 38. When Your Love Comes Along | The Five Satins... | Another First 104 |
| 60 | $40 | 39. Lonely Guy | The Gallahads... | Del-Fi 4137 |
| 63 | $40 | 40. Any Way You Wanta | Harvey... | Tri-Phi 1017 |
| 65 | $40 | 41. Hey Baby | The Hi-Lites... | Wassel 701 |
| 63 | $40 | 42. Brown-Eyed Handsome Man | Buddy Holly... | Coral 62369 |
| 61 | $40 | 43. That's Why | Curtis Knight... | Gulf 45-031 |
| 65 | $40 | 44. Get Out (And Let Me Cry) | Harold Melvin & The Blue Notes... | Landa 703 |
| 62 | $40 | 45. Need Your Love | The Metallics... | Baronet 2 |
| 60 | $40 | 46. I Only Want You | The Passions... | Audicon 105 |
| 59 | $40 | 47. Baghdad Rock (Part 1) | The Shieks... | Trine 1101 |
| 61 | $40 | 48. Close Your Eyes | The Skyliners... | Colpix 613 |
| 60 | $40 | 49. P.S. I Love You | The Starlets... | Astro 202 |
| 62 | $40 | 50. Mind Over Matter (I'm Gonna Make You Mine) | Nolan Strong... | Fortune 546 |
| 63 | $40 | 51. My Heart Can't Take It No More | The Supremes... | Motown 1040 |
| 61 | $40 | 52. Ev'rybody Pony | Teddy & The Continentals... | Pik 234/5 |
| 65 | $40 | 53. GeeTO Tiger | The Tigers... | Colpix 773 |
| 62 | $40 | 54. Come Back Into My Heart | The Volumes... | Chex 1005 |
| 63 | $40 | 55. I Call It Pretty Music, But The Old People Call It The Blues Pt. 1 | Little Stevie Wonder... | Tamla 54061 |
| 61 | $40 | 56. Somebody Cares | Zorro... | Maske 702 |

# #101 SINGLES

This section lists, in chronological order, all 369 singles that hit the #101 position on *Billboard's Bubbling Under The Hot 100* chart but <u>did not</u> go on to make the *Hot 100* chart.

No #101 hits are listed for the period that Billboard discontinued the *Bubbling Under The Hot 100* chart, from August 1985 through November 1992.

**DATE:** Date single first peaked at the #101 position

**WKS:** Total weeks single held the #101 position

↕: Indicates single hit #101, dropped down, and then returned to the #101 spot

# #101 SINGLES

## 1959

| | DATE | WKS | |
|---|---|---|---|
| 1. | 8/3 | 1 | **Slow Motion** *Wade Flemons* |
| 2. | 10/12 | 1 | **Vacation Days Are Over** *The Argyles* |

## 1960

| | DATE | WKS | |
|---|---|---|---|
| 1. | 2/1 | 2 | **Earth Angel** *The Penguins* |
| 2. | 3/7 | 1 | **Scandinavian Shuffle** *The Swe-Danes* |
| 3. | 3/14 | 1 | **Tamiami** *Bill Haley & His Comets* |
| 4. | 4/4 | 2 | **You Belong To Me** |
| | | | *100 Strings & Joni James* |
| 5. | 4/18 | 1 | **Come Dance With Me** *Eddie Quinteros* |
| 6. | 4/25 | 1 | **Go On, Go On** *Jivin' Gene* |
| 7. | 5/2 | 1 | **That's You** *Nat King Cole* |
| 8. | 6/13 | 1 | **Born To Be With You** *The Echoes* |
| 9. | 6/27 | 2 | **Miller's Cave** *Hank Snow* |
| 10. | 10/10 | 1 | **Please Help Me, I'm Falling** |
| | | | *Homer & Jethro* |
| 11. | 11/7 | 1 | **Theme From "The Dark At The Top Of The Stairs"** *Percy Faith* |
| 12. | 11/14 | 1 | **Stay With Me (A Little While Longer)** |
| | | | *Ed Townsend* |

## 1961

| | DATE | WKS | |
|---|---|---|---|
| 1. | 1/9 | 1 | **I Gotta Go ('Cause I Love You)** |
| | | | *Brian Hyland* |
| 2. | 2/27 | 1 | **Little Sad Eyes** *The Castells* |
| 3. | 3/13 | 1 | **Banned In Boston** *Merv Griffin* |
| 4. | 4/10 | 1 | **Gidget Goes Hawaiian** *Duane Eddy* |
| 5. | 4/17 | 2 | **African Waltz** *Johnny Dankworth* |
| 6. | 5/1 | 1 | **It's Never Too Late** *Brenda Lee* |
| 7. | 5/29 | 1 | **Respectable** *The Chants* |
| 8. | 6/5 | 1 | **Bring Back Your Heart** *The Del Vikings* |
| 9. | 7/3 | 1 | **Monday To Sunday** *Alan Dale* |
| 10. | 7/10 | 2 | **Voyage To The Bottom Of The Sea** |
| | | | *Frankie Avalon* |
| 11. | 9/18 | 1 | **Ev'rybody Pony** *Teddy & The Continentals* |
| 12. | 9/25 | 1 | **Memories of those Oldies But Goodies** |
| | | | *Little Caesar and The Romans* |
| 13. | 11/20 | 1 | **Trade Winds, Trade Winds** *Aki Aleong* |

## 1962

| | DATE | WKS | |
|---|---|---|---|
| 1. | 1/13 | 1 | **The Avenger** *Duane Eddy & The Rebels* |
| 2. | 3/3 | 1 | **It Wasn't God Who Made Honky Tonk Angels** *Kitty Kallen* |
| 3. | 4/28 | 1 | **Need Your Love** *The Metallics* |
| 4. | 5/5 | 1 | **Spanish Harlem** *Santo & Johnny* |
| 5. | 6/30 | 1 | **Trouble's Back In Town** |
| | | | *The Wilburn Brothers* |
| 6. | 9/1 | 1 | **Comin' Home Baby** *Herbie Mann* |
| 7. | 9/15 | 1 | **Don't Break The Heart That Loves You** |
| | | | *Bernie Leighton* |
| 8. | 9/22 | 1 | **Live It Up** *Sandy Nelson* |
| 9. | 11/3 | 1 | **The Look Of Love** *Frank Sinatra* |
| 10. | 11/10 | 1 | **I Dig This Station** *Gary (U.S.) Bonds* |
| 11. | 12/1 | 1 | **Go Tiger, Go!** *Guy Mitchell* |
| 12. | 12/22 | 1 | **My Man - He's A Lovin' Man** *Betty LaVett* |

## 1963

| | DATE | WKS | |
|---|---|---|---|
| 1. | 3/23 | 2 | **The Bird** *The Dutones* |
| 2. | 5/25 | 1 | **If You Don't Love Me** *Junior Parker* |
| 3. | 6/8 | 1 | **Kentucky** *Bob Moore* |
| 4. | 6/15 | 1 | **It's Been Nice (Goodnight)** |
| | | | *The Everly Brothers* |
| 5. | 6/29 | 1 | **Tamoure'** *Bill Justis* |
| 6. | 7/20 | 1 | **If You Don't Come Back** *The Drifters* |
| 7. | 8/10 | 1 | **What I Gotta Do (To Make You Jealous)** *Little Eva* |
| 8. | 8/24 | 1 | **Lonely World** *Dion* |
| 9. | 8/31 | 1 | **I Call It Pretty Music, But The Old People Call It The Blues Pt 1** |
| | | | *Little Stevie Wonder* |
| 10. | 10/12 | 2 | **Talk Back Trembling Lips** |
| | | | *Ernest Ashworth* |

## 1964

| | DATE | WKS | |
|---|---|---|---|
| 1. | 2/1 | 2 | **The Greasy Spoon** *Hank Marr* |
| 2. | 2/22 | 1 | **There's A Meetin' Here Tonite** |
| | | | *Joe & Eddie* |
| 3. | 3/21 | 3 | **The Waiting Game** *Brenda Lee* |
| 4. | 5/2 | 1 | **If You Love Me (Like You Say)** |
| | | | *Little Johnny Taylor* |
| 5. | 5/23 | 2 | **Gotta Get Away** |
| | | | *Billy Butler & The Enchanters* |
| 6. | 9/12 | 1 | **Follow The Rainbow** *Terry Stafford* |
| 7. | 9/19 | 1 | **She Knows Me Too Well** *The Beach Boys* |
| 8. | 11/14 | 1 | **Once A Day** *Connie Smith* |
| 9. | 11/28 | 1 | **Mumbles** *Oscar Peterson Trio* |
| 10. | 12/5 | 2 | **Watch Out Sally** *Diane Renay* |
| 11. | 12/19 | 2 | **Big Brother** *Dickey Lee* |

## 1965

| | DATE | WKS | |
|---|---|---|---|
| 1. | 1/23 | 1 | **Everyday** *The Rogues* |
| 2. | 1/30 | 1 | **Six Boys** *J. Frank Wilson* |
| 3. | 2/13 | 2 | **My Babe** *The Righteous Brothers* |
| 4. | 3/20 | 2 | **The Greatest Story Ever Told** |
| | | | *Ferrante & Teicher* |
| 5. | 5/1 | 2 | **Without You (I Cannot Live)** *Matt Monro* |
| 6. | 9/11 | 1 | **I'm Down** *The Beatles* |
| 7. | 11/27 | 2 | **Goodbye Babe** *The Castaways* |

## 1966

| | DATE | WKS | |
|---|---|---|---|
| 1. | 1/1 | 1 | **Il Silenzio** *Nini Rosso* |
| 2. | 1/8 | 2 | **Brown Paper Sack** *The Gentrys* |
| 3. | 2/19 | 1 | **S.O.S. (Heart In Distress)** |
| | | | *Christine (Carol) Cooper* |
| 4. | 3/19 | 1 | **He Wore The Green Beret** *Lesley Miller* |
| 5. | 3/26 | 1 | **Watching The Late Late Show** |
| | | | *Don Covay & The Goodtimers* |
| 6. | 4/9 | 1 | **Good, Good Lovin'** *The Blossoms* |
| 7. | 6/4 | 2↕ | **Look Before You Leap** |
| | | | *The Dave Clark Five* |
| 8. | 9/10 | 1 | **Sticky, Sticky** *Bobby Harris* |
| 9. | 9/17 | 1 | **Just Like A Woman** *Manfred Mann* |
| 10. | 9/24 | 1 | **Impressions** *The Jones Boys* |

# #101 SINGLES

## 1966 (cont'd)

11. 11/26  1  **Where Did Robinson Crusoe Go With Friday On Saturday Night?**
*Ian Whitcomb & His Seaside Syncopators*
12. 12/3  1  **Am I A Loser (From The Start)**
*Eddie Holman*

| | DATE | WKS | 1967 |
|---|---|---|---|
| 1. | 3/25 | 2 | **She's Looking Good** *Rodger Collins* |
| 2. | 4/29 | 2 | **My Old Flame** *Nino Tempo & April Stevens* |
| 3. | 6/24 | 2↕ | **39-21-46** *The Showmen* |
| 4. | 7/1 | 1 | **All's Quiet On West 23rd** *The Jet Stream* |
| 5. | 7/8 | 2 | **Good Feelin' Time** *The Yellow Balloon* |
| 6. | 7/29 | 1 | **City Of Windows** *Stephen Monahan* |
| 7. | 8/26 | 1 | **Lovin' Sound** *Ian & Sylvia* |
| 8. | 10/21 | 2 | **As Long As You're Here** *Zalman (Zally) Yanovsky* |
| 9. | 12/2 | 2 | **Live For Life** *Carmen McRae & Herbie Mann* |

| | DATE | WKS | 1968 |
|---|---|---|---|
| 1. | 3/23 | 3 | **I've Come A Long Way** *Wilson Pickett* |
| 2. | 8/17 | 3 | **Sunshine Girl** *Herman's Hermits* |
| 3. | 11/16 | 3 | **Main Street** *Gary Lewis & The Playboys* |

| | DATE | WKS | 1969 |
|---|---|---|---|
| 1. | 3/1 | 1 | **Baby Make Me Feel So Good** *Five Stairsteps & Cubie* |
| 2. | 4/19 | 3↕ | **Baby Driver** *Simon & Garfunkel* |
| 3. | 5/3 | 1 | **How Great Thou Art** *Elvis Presley* |
| 4. | 6/28 | 1 | **Lollipop (I Like You)** *The Intruders* |
| 5. | 8/9 | 1 | **Ain't It Like Him** *Edwin Hawkins' Singers* |
| 6. | 9/6 | 2 | **One Woman** *Steve Alaimo* |
| 7. | 9/27 | 1 | **The Best Part Of A Love Affair** *The Emotions* |
| 8. | 10/4 | 1 | **We Can Make It** *Ray Charles* |
| 9. | 11/1 | 1 | **Today I Sing The Blues** *Aretha Franklin* |
| 10. | 11/8 | 1 | **Love And Let Love** *The Hardy Boys* |
| 11. | 12/6 | 1 | **Cowboy Convention** *Ohio Express* |

| | DATE | WKS | 1970 |
|---|---|---|---|
| 1. | 1/31 | 2 | **God Only Knows** *The Vogues* |
| 2. | 5/16 | 1 | **Hey, That's No Way To Say Goodbye** *The Vogues* |
| 3. | 8/22 | 1 | **Comin' Back To Me (Ooh Baby)** *Smith* |
| 4. | 9/12 | 2 | **For What It's Worth** *Sergio Mendes* |
| 5. | 10/31 | 1 | **Detroit City** *Dean Martin* |

| | DATE | WKS | 1971 |
|---|---|---|---|
| 1. | 2/13 | 1 | **Stop The World And Let Me Off** *The Flaming Ember* |
| 2. | 4/3 | 1 | **I'll Make You My Baby** *Bobby Vinton* |
| 3. | 7/31 | 1 | **Here I Go Again** *The Raeletts* |
| 4. | 8/14 | 1 | **Got To Have Your Lovin'** *King Floyd* |
| 5. | 9/11 | 1 | **Gotta' Get Over The Hump** *Simtec & Wylie* |

## 1971 (cont'd)

6. 11/6  1  **Look What We've Done To Love**
*The Glass House*
7. 11/20  1  **Can I** *Eddie Kendricks*
8. 12/18  2  **Scratch My Back (And Mumble In My Ear)** *Clarence Carter*

| | DATE | WKS | 1972 |
|---|---|---|---|
| 1. | 1/1 | 1 | **The Rangers Waltz** *The Mom & Dads* |
| 2. | 1/29 | 1 | **See What You Done, Done (Hymn #9)** *Delia Gartrell* |
| 3. | 4/1 | 1 | **Train Of Glory** *Jonathan Edwards* |
| 4. | 4/15 | 1 | **Mother Of Mine** *Little Jimmy Osmond* |
| 5. | 4/29 | 2 | **Breaking Up Somebody's Home** *Ann Peebles* |
| 6. | 6/24 | 1 | **Is It You Girl** *Betty Wright* |
| 7. | 7/15 | 1 | **Cafe** *Malo* |
| 8. | 7/29 | 1 | **Breaking Up Is Hard To Do** *Heaven Bound with Tony Scotti* |
| 9. | 8/5 | 2 | **Slipping Into Darkness** *Ramsey Lewis* |
| 10. | 8/19 | 1 | **Is It Really True Boy-Is It Really Me** *Love Unlimited* |
| 11. | 10/7 | 1 | **Innocent Til Proven Guilty** *The Honey Cone* |
| 12. | 10/21 | 2 | **Stop Doggin' Me** *Johnnie Taylor* |
| 13. | 11/18 | 1 | **Oney** *Johnny Cash* |
| 14. | 11/25 | 1 | **Fool Me** *Lynn Anderson* |

| | DATE | WKS | 1973 |
|---|---|---|---|
| 1. | 1/27 | 2 | **Gypsy** *Van Morrison* |
| 2. | 2/10 | 2 | **Think It Over** *The Delfonics* |
| 3. | 2/24 | 2 | **You Are What I Am** *Gordon Lightfoot* |
| 4. | 3/10 | 1 | **Gimme That Beat (Part 1)** *Jr. Walker & The All Stars* |
| 5. | 3/17 | 1 | **A Shoulder To Cry On** *Charley Pride* |
| 6. | 3/24 | 2 | **We'll Make Love** *Al Anderson* |
| 7. | 4/7 | 1 | **Friends Or Lovers** *Act I* |
| 8. | 5/12 | 1 | **Orange Blossom Special** *Charlie McCoy* |
| 9. | 6/9 | 2 | **You Can Call Me Rover** *The Main Ingredient* |
| 10. | 7/14 | 2 | **Lovin' On Borrowed Time** *William Bell* |
| 11. | 7/28 | 1 | **You're Gettin' A Little Too Smart** *Detroit Emeralds* |
| 12. | 8/11 | 1 | **Don't Fight The Feelings Of Love** *Charley Pride* |
| 13. | 8/18 | 2 | **Watergate Blues** *Tom T. Hall* |
| 14. | 9/1 | 2 | **Yes, We Finally Made It** *Love Unlimited* |
| 15. | 10/13 | 1 | **I Can't Believe That It's All Over** *Skeeter Davis* |
| 16. | 10/27 | 2↕ | **All The Way Down** *Etta James* |
| 17. | 11/3 | 3 | **I'm Through Trying To Prove My Love To You** *Bobby Womack* |
| 18. | 12/1 | 1 | **Sally From Syracuse** *Stu Nunnery* |
| 19. | 12/22 | 2↕ | **I'm The Midnight Special** *Clarence Carter* |

# #101 SINGLES

## 1974

| | DATE | WKS | | |
|---|---|---|---|---|
| 1. | 1/26 | 1 | **Biff, The Friendly Purple Bear** | *Dick Feller* |
| 2. | 3/9 | 3 | **Us And Them** *Pink Floyd* | |
| 3. | 3/30 | 4 | **Nice To Be Around** *Maureen McGovern* | |
| 4. | 4/27 | 2 | **I Told You So** *The Delfonics* | |
| 5. | 5/25 | 1 | **Standing In The Rain** *The James Gang* | |
| 6. | 6/1 | 2 | **Lean It All On Me** *Diana Trask* | |
| 7. | 7/6 | 1 | **Wovoka** *Redbone* | |
| 8. | 8/24 | 1 | **Summer Love** *The Blackbyrds* | |
| 9. | 9/14 | 1 | **America** *David Essex* | |
| 10. | 9/21 | 1 | **Meet Me On The Corner Down At Joe's Cafe** *Peter Noone* | |
| 11. | 10/12 | 1 | **Pencil Thin Mustache** *Jimmy Buffett* | |
| 12. | 11/2 | 1 | **Look Away** *Ozark Mountain Daredevils* | |
| 13. | 11/16 | 1 | **Trusting Heart** *The Trammps* | |
| 14. | 11/30 | 1 | **Lady Lay** *Wayne Newton* | |

## 1975

| | DATE | WKS | | |
|---|---|---|---|---|
| 1. | 1/11 | 2↕ | **Do Your Thing** *James & Bobby Purify* | |
| 2. | 2/8 | 1 | **Changes (Messin' With My Mind)** *Vernon Burch* | |
| 3. | 2/15 | 1 | **Disco-Tekin** *Reunion* | |
| 4. | 4/19 | 1 | **A Pirate Looks At Forty** *Jimmy Buffett* | |
| 5. | 5/17 | 2 | **Gemini** *The Miracles* | |
| 6. | 5/31 | 1 | **All Cried Out** *Lamont Dozier* | |
| 7. | 6/7 | 1 | **I Ain't All Bad** *Charley Pride* | |
| 8. | 6/28 | 1 | **Too Late To Worry, Too Blue To Cry** *Ronnie Milsap* | |
| 9. | 7/5 | 1 | **Classified** *C.W. McCall* | |
| 10. | 8/9 | 1 | **Barbara Ann** *The Beach Boys* | |
| 11. | 8/16 | 1 | **I Can Understand It** *Kokomo* | |
| 12. | 12/6 | 2 | **Birmingham Blues** *The Charlie Daniels Band* | |

## 1976

| | DATE | WKS | | |
|---|---|---|---|---|
| 1. | 4/10 | 2 | **(Call Me) The Traveling Man** *The Masqueraders* | |
| 2. | 4/24 | 1 | **Spanish Hustle** *The Fatback Band* | |
| 3. | 5/1 | 2 | **I Gotta Get Drunk** *Willie Nelson* | |
| 4. | 5/22 | 1 | **Baretta's Theme** *Sammy Davis, Jr.* | |
| 5. | 5/29 | 1 | **You Are So Beautiful** *Ray Stevens* | |
| 6. | 6/5 | 1 | **Do You Wanna Do A Thing** *Bloodstone* | |
| 7. | 6/12 | 1 | **Lady Of The Lake** *Starcastle* | |
| 8. | 7/4 | 1 | **Strokin' (Pt. II)** *Leon Haywood* | |
| 9. | 7/10 | 1 | **A Butterfly For Bucky** *Bobby Goldsboro* | |
| 10. | 7/17 | 1 | **Universal Sound** *Kool & The Gang* | |
| 11. | 7/31 | 1 | **Let The Good Times Roll** *Bobby Bland & B.B. King* | |
| 12. | 8/14 | 2 | **We Both Need Each Other** *Norman Connors* | |
| 13. | 8/28 | 1 | **Disco-Fied** *Rhythm Heritage* | |
| 14. | 9/4 | 1 | **Bring It On Home To Me** *Mickey Gilley* | |
| 15. | 9/18 | 3↕ | **I Need It** *Johnny Guitar Watson* | |
| 16. | 10/30 | 1 | **You And Me** *Tammy Wynette* | |
| 17. | 11/6 | 3 | **Living Together (In Sin)** *The Whispers* | |
| 18. | 12/18 | 1 | **'Round The World With The Rubber Duck** *C.W. McCall* | |
| 19. | 12/25 | 2 | **Superman Lover** *Johnny Guitar Watson* | |

## 1977

| | DATE | WKS | | |
|---|---|---|---|---|
| 1. | 1/8 | 6↕ | **Be My Girl** *Michael Henderson* | |
| 2. | 1/15 | 1 | **A Love Of Your Own** *AWB* | |
| 3. | 3/12 | 2 | **I Tried To Tell Myself** *Al Green* | |
| 4. | 3/26 | 1 | **Space Age** *Jimmy Castor Bunch* | |
| 5. | 5/21 | 1 | **Super Band** *Kool & The Gang* | |
| 6. | 5/28 | 1 | **I Can't Get Over You** *The Dramatics* | |
| 7. | 7/9 | 1 | **Take Me Tonight** *Tom Jones* | |
| 8. | 8/13 | 1 | **Vitamin U** *Smokey Robinson* | |
| 9. | 8/20 | 1 | **Funky Music** *Ju-Par Universal Orchestra* | |
| 10. | 8/27 | 5 | **Rollin' With The Flow** *Charlie Rich* | |
| 11. | 11/12 | 6↕ | **Just For Your Love** *The Memphis Horns* | |

## 1978

| | DATE | WKS | | |
|---|---|---|---|---|
| 1. | 1/28 | 1 | **Good Luck Charm (Part I)** *Ohio Players* | |
| 2. | 2/4 | 2 | **With Pen In Hand** *Dorothy Moore* | |
| 3. | 2/18 | 3 | **Playing Your Game, Baby** *Barry White* | |
| 4. | 3/11 | 1 | **Wishing On A Star** *Rose Royce* | |
| 5. | 3/18 | 5↕ | **Am I Losing You** *The Manhattans* | |
| 6. | 4/15 | 2 | **Every Time Two Fools Collide** *Kenny Rogers & Dottie West* | |
| 7. | 5/6 | 2 | **Keep On Dancing** *Johnnie Taylor* | |
| 8. | 5/27 | 1 | **(You're Such A) Fabulous Dancer** *Wha-Koo* | |
| 9. | 7/1 | 3 | **This Magic Moment** *Richie Furay* | |
| 10. | 7/22 | 2 | **(Let's Go) All The Way** *The Whispers* | |
| 11. | 8/19 | 1 | **I Wanna Live Again** *Carillo* | |
| 12. | 9/16 | 1 | **I Like Girls** *Fatback* | |
| 13. | 11/4 | 3 | **Let's Start The Dance** *Hamilton Bohannon* | |

## 1979

| | DATE | WKS | | |
|---|---|---|---|---|
| 1. | 1/6 | 3↕ | **Long Stroke** *ADC Band* | |
| 2. | 1/13 | 1 | **Disco To Go** *The Brides Of Funkenstein* | |
| 3. | 3/10 | 3 | **Living In A Dream** *Sea Level* | |
| 4. | 4/7 | 1 | **Keeep Your Body Workin'** *Kleeer* | |
| 5. | 4/14 | 1 | **Accidents Will Happen** *Elvis Costello* | |
| 6. | 4/28 | 5 | **Good, Good Feelin'** *War* | |
| 7. | 6/16 | 3 | **Baby Fat** *Robert Byrne* | |
| 8. | 7/7 | 1 | **Rockin' My Life Away** *Jerry Lee Lewis* | |
| 9. | 7/14 | 3↕ | **Shake** *The Gap Band* | |
| 10. | 7/28 | 1 | **Shoulda Gone Dancin'** *High Inergy* | |
| 11. | 9/1 | 6↕ | **You Can Do It** *Al Hudson & The Partners* | |
| 12. | 11/3 | 4↕ | **You Get Me Hot** *Jimmy "Bo" Horne* | |
| 13. | 12/8 | 2 | **It's Different For Girls** *Joe Jackson* | |
| 14. | 12/22 | 2 | **You Can Get Over** *Stephanie Mills* | |

## 1980

| | DATE | WKS | | |
|---|---|---|---|---|
| 1. | 1/5 | 1 | **When You Walk In The Room** *Karla Bonoff* | |
| 2. | 1/12 | 1 | **My Feet Keep Dancing** *Chic* | |
| 3. | 1/19 | 1 | **Stay With Me Till Dawn** *Judie Tzuke* | |
| 4. | 2/2 | 1 | **You Know How To Love Me** *Phyllis Hyman* | |
| 5. | 2/9 | 1 | **Ravel's Bolero** *Henry Mancini* | |
| 6. | 2/16 | 2 | **The Very First Time** *Michael Johnson* | |
| 7. | 3/22 | 2 | **Shriner's Convention** *Ray Stevens* | |
| 8. | 4/26 | 1 | **Reach Your Peak** *Sister Sledge* | |

# #101 SINGLES

## 1980 (cont'd)

| | | | | |
|---|---|---|---|---|
| 9. | 5/10 | 2 | **Got To Be Enough** | Con Funk Shun |
| 10. | 6/14 | 1 | **You Got Me** | Tommy James |
| 11. | 6/21 | 2 | **Sitting In The Park** | GQ |
| 12. | 7/19 | 1 | **Does She Have A Friend?** | Gene Chandler |
| 13. | 9/20 | 2 | **The Rest Of The Night** | Clif Newton |
| 14. | 10/4 | 1 | **You May Be Right** | The Chipmunks |
| 15. | 10/11 | 2 | **I Ain't Much** | Atlanta Rhythm Section |
| 16. | 10/25 | 1 | **Ashes To Ashes** | David Bowie |
| 17. | 11/1 | 3 | **Bomb Iran** | Vince Vance & The Valiants |
| 18. | 11/29 | 1 | **Uptown** | Prince |
| 19. | 12/6 | 1 | **That's All That Matters** | Mickey Gilley |
| 20. | 12/27 | 4 | **Silver Eagle** | Atlanta Rhythm Section |

## 1981

| | DATE | WKS | | |
|---|---|---|---|---|
| 1. | 3/21 | 1 | **Praise** | Marvin Gaye |
| 2. | 4/18 | 5 | **When Love Calls** | Atlantic Starr |
| 3. | 5/30 | 1 | **Magic Man** | Robert Winters & Fall |
| 4. | 6/20 | 6 | **Pull Up To The Bumper** | Grace Jones |
| 5. | 10/10 | 2 | **Talk To Ya Later** | The Tubes |
| 6. | 10/24 | 1 | **It's Over** | Teddy Baker |
| 7. | 11/14 | 1 | **Too Late The Hero** | John Entwistle |
| 8. | 12/5 | 3 | **Sandy Beaches** | Delbert McClinton |
| 9. | 12/26 | 3 | **Hit And Run** | Bar-Kays |

## 1982

| | DATE | WKS | | |
|---|---|---|---|---|
| 1. | 2/13 | 3 | **Rain Is Falling** | ELO |
| 2. | 3/6 | 3 | **If You Think You're Lonely Now** | Bobby Womack |
| 3. | 3/27 | 1 | **Mountain Music** | Alabama |
| 4. | 5/1 | 1 | **Try Jah Love** | Third World |
| 5. | 5/8 | 1 | **Just Be Yourself** | Cameo |
| 6. | 5/15 | 1 | **I Just Want To Satisfy** | The O'Jays |
| 7. | 6/12 | 2 | **Big Band Medley** | Meco |
| 8. | 7/24 | 3↕ | **Dance Floor (Part I)** | Zapp |
| 9. | 8/7 | 1 | **Last Night** | Stephanie Mills |
| 10. | 8/14 | 1 | **Which Man Are You** | Tommy Tutone |
| 11. | 8/21 | 2 | **Don't Throw It All Away** | Stacy Lattisaw |
| 12. | 9/18 | 2 | **What!** | Soft Cell |
| 13. | 10/16 | 1 | **Favourite Shirts (Boy Meets Girl)** | Haircut One Hundred |
| 14. | 10/23 | 1 | **If This World Were Mine** | Cheryl Lynn (With Luther Vandross) |
| 15. | 10/30 | 7 | **Nasty Girl** | Vanity 6 |
| 16. | 12/18 | 4 | **Jump** | Loverboy |

## 1983

| | DATE | WKS | | |
|---|---|---|---|---|
| 1. | 2/5 | 5 | **Heartbeats** | Yarbrough & Peoples |
| 2. | 3/12 | 2 | **I've Made Love To You A Thousand Times** | Smokey Robinson |
| 3. | 3/26 | 2 | **Last Night A D.J. Saved My Life** | Indeep |
| 4. | 4/9 | 1 | **Red Skies** | The Fixx |
| 5. | 4/16 | 3 | **Atomic Dog** | George Clinton |
| 6. | 5/14 | 2 | **Na Na Hey Hey Kiss Him Goodbye** | Bananarama |
| 7. | 6/4 | 1 | **Just Another Saturday Night** | Alex Call |
| 8. | 6/11 | 2 | **Candy Man** | Mary Jane Girls |

## 1983 (cont'd)

| | | | | |
|---|---|---|---|---|
| 9. | 6/25 | 1 | **Between The Sheets** | The Isley Brothers |
| 10. | 7/9 | 2 | **Two Hearts Beat As One** | U2 |
| 11. | 7/30 | 1 | **All The Love In The World** | Dionne Warwick |
| 12. | 8/20 | 1 | **All Night Long** | Mary Jane Girls |
| 13. | 10/1 | 1 | **Party Train** | The Gap Band |
| 14. | 10/29 | 1 | **Party Animal** | James Ingram |
| 15. | 11/19 | 1 | **U Bring The Freak Out** | Rick James |
| 16. | 12/10 | 1 | **Make Believe It's Your First Time** | Carpenters |
| 17. | 12/17 | 2↕ | **White Lines (Don't Don't Do It)** | Grandmaster & Melle Mel |

## 1984

| | DATE | WKS | | |
|---|---|---|---|---|
| 1. | 1/21 | 1 | **Popcorn Love** | New Edition |
| 2. | 2/11 | 1 | **You Can Count On Me** | Shalamar |
| 3. | 4/28 | 2 | **Beat Box** | Art Of Noise |
| 4. | 6/16 | 1 | **Reunited** | Greg Kihn Band |
| 5. | 7/7 | 2 | **Lovelite** | O'Bryan |
| 6. | 8/4 | 1 | **Fine, Fine Line** | Andy Fraser |
| 7. | 8/11 | 1 | **Outrageous** | Lakeside |
| 8. | 8/18 | 1 | **Rescue Me** | Duke Jupiter |
| 9. | 8/25 | 1 | **Young Hearts** | Commuter |
| 10. | 9/15 | 1 | **Rock You** | Helix |
| 11. | 9/22 | 2 | **Don't Stand Another Chance** | Janet Jackson |
| 12. | 10/20 | 2 | **So Fine** | Marc Anthony Thompson |
| 13. | 11/10 | 1 | **Playin' It Cool** | Timothy B. Schmit |

## 1985

| | DATE | WKS | | |
|---|---|---|---|---|
| 1. | 1/12 | 1 | **Skylark** | Linda Ronstadt |
| 2. | 2/23 | 1 | **I Want To Know What Love Is** | The New Jersey Mass Choir |
| 3. | 3/2 | 1 | **Premonition** | Jack Wagner |
| 4. | 3/30 | 2↕ | **Bad Habits** | Jenny Burton |
| 5. | 4/6 | 1 | **Tore Down A La Rimbaud** | Van Morrison |
| 6. | 4/20 | 1 | **Can You Feel It** | Fat Boys |
| 7. | 4/27 | 2↕ | **Innocent** | Alexander O'Neal |
| 8. | 5/25 | 2↕ | **Sanctified Lady** | Marvin Gaye |
| 9. | 6/15 | 1 | **Material Thangz** | The Deele |
| 10. | 6/29 | 1 | **Save Your Love (For #1)** | Rene & Angela |
| 11. | 7/6 | 1 | **Double Oh-Oh** | George Clinton |
| 12. | 7/20 | 5 | **It's Over Now** | Luther Vandross |

> *Chart discontinued from August 31,1985 through November 25.1992*

## 1992

| | DATE | WKS | | |
|---|---|---|---|---|
| 1. | 12/5 | 1 | **Night Shift** | Positive K |
| 2. | 12/26 | 1 | **Taste It** | INXS |

# #101 SINGLES

# BEST SELLING POP EP'S

## THE HISTORY OF *BILLBOARD'S*
## *BEST SELLING POP EP'S* CHART

EP is the abbreviation for 7" Extended Play 45-r.p.m. vinyl singles. The EP format, now nearly forgotten, was popular in the 1950s. An EP single typically contained four songs packaged in a cardboard picture sleeve. Often the songs were culled from the artist's LP (12" Long Play vinyl album). One LP commonly spawned multiple EP volumes. In the 1950s, an EP usually sold at retail for $1.49, a single for 89¢ and an LP for $3.98.

On October 7, 1957, *Billboard* began regular weekly publication of a Top 10 *Best Selling Popular EP's* chart that ran through October 10, 1960. The chart was compiled from retail sales reports. This three-year period covered the heyday of the short-lived EP format.

From a collector's standpoint, EP's are more difficult to find than singles or albums by the same artist. The "rock and roll" EP's of this era are highly collectable.

# EP
# PHOTO
# SECTION

This section is a photo gallery of EP's, arranged alphabetically by artist name, of every EP that hit *Billboard's Best Selling Pop EP's* chart from October 7, 1957 through October 10, 1960.

The following is listed below each photo:

**Artist Name**...*EP Title*
Track Titles
**Debut Date - Peak Position / Weeks Charted**
Label and Number...Current value of a near-mint commercial copy

A number in square brackets following the label number indicates the total number of records in a multiple disc set.

**The Ames Bros.** ...*There'll Always Be a Christmas, Vol. I*
Silver Bells • The Christmas Song • Jingle Bells • There'll Always Be A Christmas
**12/9/57 - #7 / 2** wks.
RCA Victor EPA 1-1541...$25

**Chet Atkins**...*Chet Atkins At Home*
Say "Si Si" • Vilia • Yankee Doodle Dixie • You're Just In Love
**7/21/58 - #8 / 2** wks.
RCA Victor EPA-4194...$25

**Harry Belafonte**...*An Evening with Belafonte, Vol. I*
Merci Bon Dieu • The Drummer And The Cook • Danny Boy
**5/26/58 - #8 / 1** wk.
RCA Victor EPA 1-1402...$25

**Harry Belafonte**...*Calypso*
Day O • I Do Adore Her • Jamaica Farewell • Will His Love Be Like His Rum? • Star O • Hosanna • Brown Skin Girl • Dolly Dawn
**6/16/58 - #10 / 1** wk.
RCA Victor EPB-1248 [2]...$35

**Harry Belafonte**...*Belafonte, Act 1*
Take My Mother Home • Unchained Melody • Matilda
**1/12/59 - #4 / 3** wks.
RCA Victor EPA-693...$25

**Pat Boone**...*Four By Pat*
Technique • Cathedral In The Pines • Louella • Without My Love
**10/7/57 - #2⁴ / 29** wks.
Dot DEP 1057...$40

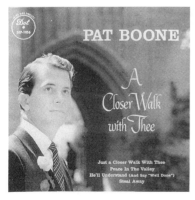

**Pat Boone**...*A Closer Walk with Thee*
Just A Closer Walk With Thee • Peace In The Valley • He'll Understand (And Say "Well Done") • Steal Away
**10/7/57 - #5 / 19** wks.
Dot DEP 1056...$40

**Pat Boone**... ...*and a very Merry Christmas to you...*
White Christmas • Silent Night • Jingle Bells • Santa Claus Is Comin' To Town
**12/9/57 - #3 / 8** wks.
re-charted at #3 on 12/29/58
Dot DEP 1062...$35

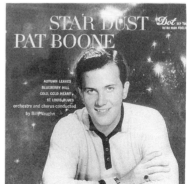

**Pat Boone**...*Star Dust*
Autumn Leaves • Blueberry Hill • Cold, Cold Heart • St. Louis Blues
**10/6/58 - #4 / 16** wks.
Dot DEP 1069...$35

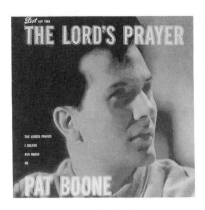

**Pat Boone**...*The Lord's Prayer*
The Lord's Prayer • I Believe •
Ave Maria • He
**10/27/58 - #5 / 5** wks.
Dot DEP 1068...$35

**Pat Boone**...*Mardi Gras*
Bourbon Street Blues • Loyalty •
Bigger Than Texas • A Fiddle, A Rifle, An Axe,
And A Bible
**2/2/59 - #3 / 5** wks.
Dot DEP 1075...$40

**Pat & Shirley Boone**...*Side By Side*
You Can't Be True, Dear • My Happiness •
Now Is The Hour • Side By Side
**\* 6/22/59 - #1⁸ / 29** wks.
Dot DEP 1076...$25

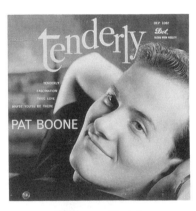

**Pat Boone**...*Tenderly*
Tenderly • Fascination •
True Love • Maybe You'll Be There
**6/29/59 - #5 / 20** wks.
Dot DEP 1082...$25

**Johnny Cash**...*Johnny Cash sings Hank
Williams*
I Can't Help It • You Win Again •
Hey, Good Lookin' • I Could Never Be Ashamed
**10/13/58 - #3 / 11** wks.
Sun EPA-111...$150

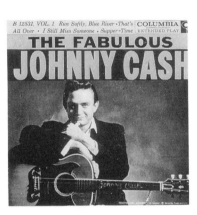

**Johnny Cash**...*The Fabulous Johnny Cash,
Vol. 1*
Run Softly, Blue River • That's All Over •
I Still Miss Someone • Supper-Time
**12/1/58 - #7 / 4** wks.
Columbia B-12531...$60

**Johnny Cash**...*The Fabulous Johnny Cash,
Vol. 2*
Frankie's Man, Johnny • The Troubadour •
Don't Take Your Guns To Town • That's Enough
**2/9/59 - #2⁴ / 23** wks.
Columbia B-12532...$60

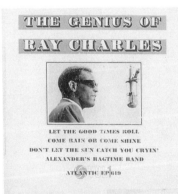

**Ray Charles**...*The Genius Of Ray Charles, Vol. 1*
Let The Good Times Roll • Come Rain Or Come
Shine • Don't Let The Sun Catch You Cryin' •
Alexander's Ragtime Band
**2/15/60 - #3 / 8** wks.
Atlantic EP 619...$125

**Nat "King" Cole**...*Around The World*
Around The World • Fascination • An Affair
To Remember • There's A Gold Mine In The Sky
**10/7/57 - #3 / 8** wks.
Capitol EAP 1-813...$30

**Nat "King" Cole...***Love is the Thing, Part 1*
Love Is The Thing • Stay As Sweet As You Are •
When I Fall In Love • Where Can I Go Without You?
**10/7/57 - #6 / 12** wks.
Capitol EAP 1-824...$25

**Nat "King" Cole...***St. Louis Blues, Part 1*
Overture (Introducing "Love Theme" and
"Hesitating Blues") • Harlem Blues •
Yellow Dog Blues • St. Louis Blues
**7/14/58 - #8 / 2** wks.
Capitol EAP 1-993...$30

**Nat "King" Cole...***Cole Español, Part 1*
Cachito • Maria Elena •
Las Mañanitas • Quizas, Quizas, Quizas
**10/27/58 - #9 / 3** wks.
Capitol EAP 1-1031...$25

**Perry Como...***Perry Como Sings Merry
Christmas Music*
Santa Claus Is Comin' To Town • Frosty The Snow
Man • Winter Wonderland •
Rudolph The Red-Nosed Reindeer • Jingle Bells
**12/9/57 - #9 / 2** wks.
RCA Victor EPA-920...$20

**Perry Como...***Perry Como Sings Merry
Christmas Music*
Joy To The World! • White Christmas •
God Rest Ye Merry, Gentlemen • The Christmas Song
• I'll Be Home For Christmas • C-H-R-I-S-T-M-A-S •
O Come, All Ye Faithful • Silent Night
**12/22/58 - #5 / 2** wks.
RCA Victor EPB-1243 [2]...$25

**Perry Como...***Como's Golden Records*
Don't Let The Stars Get In Your Eyes • Wanted •
Papa Loves Mambo • Hot Diggity (Dog Ziggity Boom)
**9/29/58 - #4 / 11** wks.
RCA Victor EPA-5012...$20

**Ray Conniff...***'S Wonderful*
'S Wonderful • Dancing In The Dark •
Speak Low • Begin The Beguine
**10/6/58 - #5 / 6** wks.
Columbia B-9251...$15

**Ray Conniff...***Concert In Rhythm*
Favorite Theme From Tchaikovsky's First Piano Concerto •
Favorite Theme From Tchaikovsky's Swan Lake Ballet •
Favorite Theme From Rachmaninoff's Second Piano Concerto
• Favorite Theme From Tchaikovsky's Fifth Symphony
**11/16/59 - #10 / 1** wk.
Columbia B-11631...$10

**Sam Cooke...***songs by Sam Cooke (Vol. 2)*
You Send Me • The Lonesome Road •
That Lucky Old Sun • Canadian Sunset
**3/10/58 - #5 / 3** wks.
Keen B-2002...$125

**Dave "Baby" Cortez**...*The Happy Organ*
The Happy Organ • Love Me As I Love You •
Dave's Special • You're The Girl
**6/29/59 - #8 / 8 wks.**
RCA Victor EPA-4342...$60

**Bing Crosby**...*Merry Christmas*
Silent Night • Adeste Fideles • White Christmas •
God Rest Ye Merry Gentlemen • I'll Be Home For
Christmas • Faith Of Our Fathers • Jingle Bells •
Santa Claus Is Comin' To Town
**12/23/57 - #9 / 2 wks.**
re-charted at #10 on 1/5/59
Decca ED-547 [2]...$25

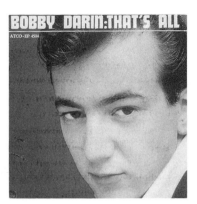

**Bobby Darin**...*Bobby Darin: That's All*
Mack The Knife • That's The Way Love Is •
Beyond The Sea • That's All
**1/25/60 - #5 / 7 wks.**
Atco EP 4504...$75

**Bobby Darin**...*This Is Darin*
Clementine • My Gal Sal •
Guys And Dolls • Down With Love
**3/28/60 - #3 / 8 wks.**
Atco EP 4508...$50

**Martin Denny**...*Exotica (Part One)*
Quiet Village • Return To Paradise •
Stone God • Jungle Flower
**10/19/59 - #3 / 10 wks.**
Liberty LEP 1-3034...$20

**Fats Domino**...*Here Comes Fats*
The Rooster Song • My Happiness •
As Time Goes By • Hey La Bas
**10/21/57 - #6 / 2 wks.**
Imperial EP 147...$175

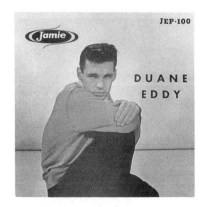

**Duane Eddy**...*Duane Eddy*
Cannonball • Moovin' N' Groovin' •
Mason-Dixon Lion • The Lonely One
**2/2/59 - #2[3] / 23 wks.**
Jamie JEP-100...$100

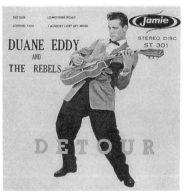

**Duane Eddy And The Rebels**...*Detour*
Lonesome Road • I Almost Lost My Mind •
Detour • Loving You
**2/9/59 - #2[4] / 12 wks.**
Jamie JEP-301...$80

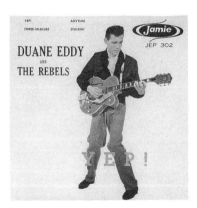

**Duane Eddy And The Rebels**...*Yep!*
"Yep!" • Three-3C-Blues •
Anytime • Stalkin'
**6/1/59 - #9 / 4 wks.**
Jamie JEP-302...$80

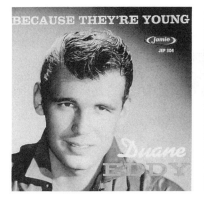

**Duane Eddy And The Rebels**...*Because They're Young*
Because They're Young • Easy •
Rebel Walk • The Battle
**5/23/60 - #1⁸ / 21** wks.
Jamie JEP-304...$80

**Tommy Edwards**...*It's All In The Game, Vol. 1.*
It's All In The Game • My Sugar My Sweet •
I'll Always Be With You • That's All
**11/2/59 - #6 / 4** wks.
MGM X1614...$40

**The Everly Brothers**...*Everly Bros. (Vol. 1)*
Wake Up Little Susie • Maybe Tomorrow •
Bye Bye Love • I Wonder If I Care As Much
**1/27/58 - #3 / 22** wks.
Cadence CEP 104...$100

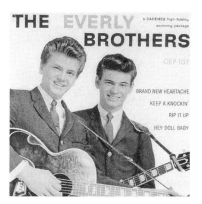

**The Everly Brothers**...*The Everly Brothers (Vol. 3)*
Brand New Heartache • Keep A Knockin' •
Rip It Up • Hey Doll Baby
**11/3/58 - #4 / 11** wks.
Cadence CEP 107...$100

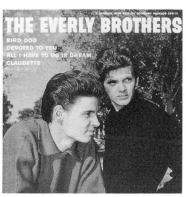

**The Everly Brothers**...*The Everly Brothers*
Bird Dog • Devoted To You •
All I Have To Do Is Dream • Claudette
**4/13/59 - #8 / 2** wks.
Cadence CEP 111...$80

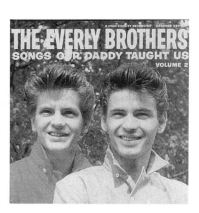

**The Everly Brothers**...*Songs Our Daddy Taught Us, Volume 2*
Barbara Allen • Long Time Gone • Lightning Express •
Who's Gonna Shoe Your Pretty Little Feet
**6/8/59 - #8 / 1** wk.
Cadence CEP 109...$80

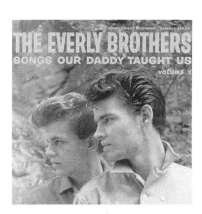

**The Everly Brothers**...*Songs Our Daddy Taught Us, Volume 3*
Down In The Willow Garden • Kentucky •
I'm Here To Get My Baby Out Of Jail •
Rockin' Alone In My Old Rockin' Chair
**6/22/59 - #4 / 16** wks.
Cadence CEP 110...$80

**Fabian**...*Hold That Tiger! (Vol. 1)*
Hold Me (In Your Arms) • Just One More Time •
Please Don't Stop • Ooh, What You Do!
**6/29/59 - #5 / 12** wks.
Chancellor A-5003...$75

**"Tennessee" Ernie Ford**...*Hymns, Part 1*
The Ninety And Nine • Softly And Tenderly •
Who At My Door Is Standing • Rock Of Ages
**10/7/57 - #1⁸ / 123** wks.
Capitol EAP 1-756...$15

**"Tennessee" Ernie Ford**...*Spirituals, Part 1*
Just A Closer Walk With Thee • Peace In The
Valley • Wayfaring Pilgrim • Were You There?
**10/28/57 - #1[1] / 101 wks.**
Capitol EAP 1-818...$15

**"Tennessee" Ernie Ford**...*Nearer The
Cross, Part 1*
What A Friend We Have In Jesus • Jesus, Savior,
Pilot Me • His Eye Is On The Sparrow •
Beautiful Isle Of Somewhere
**6/9/58 - #1[1] / 68 wks.**
Capitol EAP 1-1005...$15

**"Tennessee" Ernie Ford**...*The Star Carol,
Part 1*
Joy To The World • O Little Town Of Bethlehem •
The Star Carol • Hark! The Herald Angels Sing
**12/15/58 - #1[2] / 4 wks.**
Capitol EAP 1-1071...$15

**The Four Freshmen**...*Four Freshmen and
Five Saxes, Part 1*
Liza • You've Got Me Cryin' Again • This Love
Of Mine • I Get Along Without You Very Well
**11/4/57 - #8 / 2 wks.**
Capitol EAP 1-844...$20

**The Four Freshmen**...*4 Freshmen and 5
Trumpets, Part 1*
After You've Gone • Ev'ry Time We Say Goodbye •
Easy Street • Good Night Sweetheart
**2/24/58 - #6 / 2 wks.**
Capitol EAP 1-763...$20

**The Four Freshmen**...*Freshmen Favorites,
Part 3*
Love Turns Winter To Spring • The Day Isn't Long
Enough • In This Whole Wide World • Charmaine
**8/25/58 - #10 / 1 wk.**
Capitol EAP 3-743...$25

**Jackie Gleason**...*To A Sleeping Beauty*
To A Sleeping Beauty • Apology At Bedtime
**10/7/57 - #7 / 2 wks.**
Capitol EAP 1-871...$30

**Buddy Holly**...*The Buddy Holly Story*
It Doesn't Matter Anymore • Heartbeat •
Raining In My Heart • Early In The Morning
**5/18/59 - #9 / 5 wks.**
Coral EC 81182...$500

**The Jonah Jones Quartet**...*Swingin' On
Broadway, Part 1*
Baubles, Bangles And Beads • The Party's Over •
Till There Was You • Seventy Six Trombones
**6/16/58 - #9 / 1 wk.**
Capitol EAP 1-963...$15

**Jonah Jones**...*Muted Jazz*
Rose Room • Mack The Knife •
My Blue Heaven • Royal Garden Blues
**9/1/58 - #6 / 2** wks.
Capitol EAP 1-839...$15

**The Kingston Trio**...*The Kingston Trio At Large, Part 1*
M.T.A. • All My Sorrows •
Scarlet Ribbons • Remember The Alamo
**11/30/59 - #2**[1] **/ 34** wks.
Capitol EAP 1-1199...$30

**The Kingston Trio**...*Here We Go Again!, Part 1*
Molly Dee • Across The Wide Missouri •
Goober Peas • A Worried Man
**1/11/60 - #6 / 14** wks.
Capitol EAP 1-1258...$30

**The Kingston Trio**...*The Kingston Trio*
Three Jolly Coachmen • Wreck Of The "John B" •
Bay Of Mexico • Saro Jane
**6/6/60 - #7 / 3** wks.
Capitol EAP 1-996...$35

**Mario Lanza**...*Seven Hills Of Rome*
Seven Hills Of Rome • Arrivederci Roma •
Come Dance With Me • Lolita
**3/24/58 - #5 / 4** wks.
RCA Victor EPA-4222...$30

**Mario Lanza**...*The Student Prince*
Orchestral Introduction • Serenade • Golden Days •
Drink, Drink, Drink • Summertime In Heidelberg •
Beloved • Gaudeamus Igitur • Deep In My Heart,
Dear • I'll Walk With God
**5/26/58 - #7 / 1** wk.
RCA Victor ERB 1837 [2]...$35

**Mario Lanza**...*For The First Time*
Come Prima • Pineapple Pickers •
O, Mon Amour • O Sole Mio • Hofbrauhaus Song
**1/11/60 - #2**[1] **/ 18** wks.
RCA Victor EPA-4344...$25

**Jerry Lee Lewis**...*The Great Ball of Fire*
Mean Woman Blues • I'm Feelin' Sorry •
Whole Lot Of Shakin' Going On • Turn Around
**4/7/58 - #10 / 1** wk.
Sun EPA-107...$150

**Little Richard**...*Here's Little Richard*
Tutti-Frutti • True, Fine Mama •
Rip It Up • Jenny, Jenny
**10/7/57 - #7 / 4** wks.
Specialty SEP-402...$150

**Julie London**...*Lonely Girl, Part One*
Lonely Girl • Fools Rush In •
How Deep Is The Ocean • Mean To Me
**11/11/57 - #10 / 1** wk.
Liberty LEP 1-3012...$25

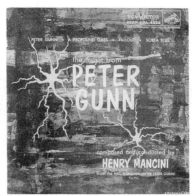

**Henry Mancini**...*the music from Peter Gunn*
Peter Gunn • A Profound Gass •
Fallout! • Sorta Blue
**2/23/59 - #1**[9] **/ 46** wks.
RCA Victor EPA-4333...$25

**Henry Mancini**...<u>*more*</u> *music from Peter Gunn*
Walkin' Bass • Spook! • The Little
Man Theme • Goofin' At The Coffee House
**9/14/59 - #9 / 3** wks.
RCA Victor EPA-4339...$20

**Mantovani**...*Mantovani Film Encores, Vol. 1*
September Song • Intermezzo •
Over The Rainbow • Laura
**7/28/58 - #7 / 1** wk.
London BEP 6320...$15

**Johnny Mathis**...*Johnny Mathis*
Autumn In Rome • Love, Your Spell Is Everywhere
• Cabin In The Sky • In Other Words
**2/17/58 - #1**[1] **/ 22** wks.
Columbia B-8871...$30

**Johnny Mathis**...*Warm*
Warm • A Handful Of Stars •
My One And Only Love • While We're Young
**2/24/58 - #3 / 18** wks.
Columbia B-10781...$20

**Johnny Mathis**...*Swing Softly*
To Be In Love • You'd Be So Nice To Come Home To
• It's De-Lovely • I've Got The World On A String
**9/22/58 - #9 / 1** wk.
Columbia B-11651...$20

**Johnny Mathis**...*Merry Christmas, Vol. I*
Winter Wonderland • Blue Christmas •
White Christmas • Sleigh Ride
**12/29/58 - #2**[2] **/ 4** wks.
re-charted at #7 on 12/28/59
Columbia B-11951...$20

**Johnny Mathis**...*Heavenly, Vol. I*
Heavenly • Misty •
Hello, Young Lovers • I'll Be Easy To Find
**10/5/59 - #1**[9] **/ 36** wks.
Columbia B-13511...$25

**Johnny Mathis**...*Open Fire, Two Guitars,*
*Vol. I*
An Open Fire • Please Be Kind •
Bye Bye Blackbird • Tenderly
**4/4/60 - #6 / 7** wks.
Columbia B-12701...$20

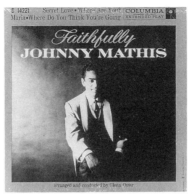

**Johnny Mathis**...*Faithfully*
Secret Love • Where Are You! •
Maria • Where Do You Think You're Going
**4/11/60 - #3 / 27** wks.
Columbia B-14221...$20

**Glenn Miller and the Army Air Force
Band**...*Marvelous Miller Moods, Vol. I*
Star Dust • A Lovely Way To Spend An Evening •
Long Ago And Far Away • My Ideal
**11/4/57 - #7 / 2** wks.
recorded in 1943; vocals on last 3 by Johnny Desmond
RCA Victor EPA 1-1494...$20

**Glenn Miller**...*Glenn Miller*
In The Mood • Little Brown Jug •
American Patrol • Song Of The Volga Boatmen
**5/12/58 - #8 / 2** wks.
RCA Victor EPA-148...$25

**Mitch Miller And The Gang**...*Sing Along
With Mitch, Vol. 1*
That Old Gang Of Mine • Down By The Old Mill
Stream • You Are My Sunshine • By The Light Of
The Silvery Moon
**8/11/58 - #1[6] / 34** wks.
Columbia B-11601...$10

**Mitch Miller And The Gang**...*More Sing
Along With Mitch, Vol. 1*
Pretty Baby/Be My Little Baby Bumble Bee •
Moonlight And Roses • Sweet Adeline/Let Me Call
You Sweetheart • The Whiffenpoof Song
**2/9/59 - #7 / 5** wks.
Columbia B-12431...$10

**Mitch Miller And The Gang**...*Still More!
Sing Along With Mitch*
In A Shanty In Old Shanty Town • Smiles •
Beer Barrel Polka • Hinky Dinky Parlez-Vous/She'll
Be Coming 'Round The Mountain
**3/30/59 - #5 / 8** wks.
Columbia B-12831...$10

**Mitch Miller And The Gang**...*Christmas
Sing-Along With Mitch*
Joy To The World • We Three Kings Of The
Orient Are • Hark! The Herald Angels Sing •
It Came Upon The Midnight Clear
**12/28/59 - #2[1] / 2** wks.
Columbia B-12051...$10

**Mitch Miller And The Gang**...*Fireside Sing
Along With Mitch, Vol. I*
Polly Wolly Doodle/Wait For The Wagon/The Old Grey
Mare • Juanita/Sweet Genevieve • Drink To Me Only
With Thine Eyes/Vive L'Amour • Drunk Last Night
**2/8/60 - #4 / 8** wks.
Columbia B-13891...$10

**Mitch Miller And The Gang**...*Party Sing Along With Mitch, Volume I*
I Love You Truly • Meet Me Tonight In Dreamland •
The Sweetest Story Ever Told • I Wonder Who's
Kissing Her Now
**5/2/60 - #1$^4$ / 11 wks.**
Columbia B-13311...$10

**Domenico Modugno**...*Nel Blu Dipinto Di Blu (Volare) and other Italian favorites*
Nel Blu Dipinto Di Blu (Volare) • Mariti In Citta •
A Pizza C' 'A Pummarola • Ventu D'Estati
**11/3/58 - #8 / 2 wks.**
Decca ED 2633...$30

**Ricky Nelson**...*Ricky (Honeycomb)*
Honeycomb • Boppin' The Blues • Be-Bop Baby •
Have I Told You Lately That I Love You
**11/25/57 - #1$^1$ / 41 wks.**
Imperial IMP-153...$150

**Ricky Nelson**...*Ricky Nelson (Unchained Melody)*
Unchained Melody • I'll Walk Alone •
There Goes My Baby • Poor Little Fool
**6/30/58 - #1$^3$ / 13 wks.**
Imperial IMP-158...$150

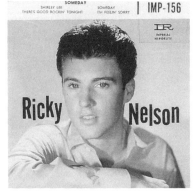

**Ricky Nelson**...*Ricky Nelson (Someday)*
Someday • I'm Feelin' Sorry •
Shirley Lee • There's Good Rockin' Tonight
**8/4/58 - #3 / 8 wks.**
Imperial IMP-156...$150

**Ricky Nelson**...*Ricky Sings Again (Be True To Me)*
Be True To Me • One Of These Mornings •
Lonesome Town • It's Late
**1/12/59 - #1$^{11}$ / 55 wks.**
Imperial IMP-159...$150

**Ricky Nelson**...*Songs By Ricky (Don't Leave Me)*
Don't Leave Me • That's All •
Sweeter Than You • A Long Vacation
**9/21/59 - #1$^7$ / 28 wks.**
Imperial IMP-164...$150

**Knuckles O'Toole**...*Knuckles O'Toole plays Honky Tonk Piano*
If You Knew Susie • Paper Doll • Peg O' My Heart •
Shine On Harvest Moon/Bicycle Built For Two/The
Bowery/The Sidewalks Of New York
**5/5/58 - #6 / 4 wks.**
Grand Award EP 2001...$15

**Elvis Presley**...*Loving You, Vol. I*
Loving You • Party •
(Let Me Be Your) Teddy Bear • True Love
**10/7/57 - #1$^5$ / 32 wks.**
RCA Victor EPA 1-1515...$100

**Elvis Presley**...*Loving You, Vol. II*
Lonesome Cowboy • Hot Dog •
Mean Woman Blues • Got A Lot O'Livin' To Do
**10/7/57 - #4 / 7** wks.
RCA Victor EPA 2-1515...$100

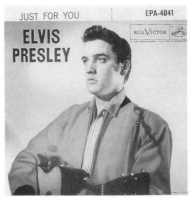

**Elvis Presley**...*Just For You*
I Need You So • Have I Told You Lately That I Love
You? • Blueberry Hill • Is It So Strange
**10/7/57 - #2**[1] / **17** wks.
RCA Victor EPA-4041...$125

**Elvis Presley**...*Peace In The Valley*
(There'll Be) Peace In The Valley (For Me) •
It Is No Secret (What God Can Do) •
I Believe • Take My Hand, Precious Lord
**10/7/57 - #3 / 14** wks.
RCA Victor EPA-4054...$100

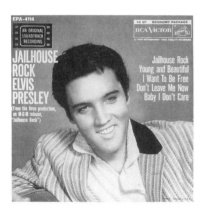

**Elvis Presley**...*Jailhouse Rock*
Jailhouse Rock • Young And Beautiful •
I Want To Be Free • Don't Leave Me Now •
(You're So Square) Baby I Don't Care
**11/11/57 - #1**[28] / **50** wks.
RCA Victor EPA-4114...$100

**Elvis Presley**...*Elvis, Volume I*
Rip It Up • Love Me • When My Blue Moon
Turns To Gold Again • Paralyzed
**11/18/57 - #1**[2] / **36** wks.
RCA Victor EPA-992...$100

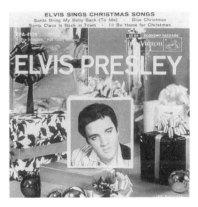

**Elvis Presley**...*Elvis Sings Christmas Songs*
Santa Bring My Baby Back (To Me) •
Blue Christmas • Santa Claus Is Back In Town •
I'll Be Home For Christmas
**12/2/57 - #1**[2] / **9** wks.
first charted at #2 in 1957; re-charted at #1 on 12/28/59
RCA Victor EPA-4108...$100

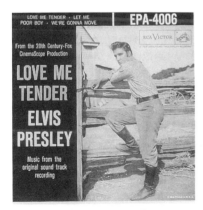

**Elvis Presley**...*Love Me Tender*
Love Me Tender • Let Me •
Poor Boy • We're Gonna Move
**1/13/58 - #9 / 4** wks.
RCA Victor EPA-4006...$100

**Elvis Presley**...*Elvis Presley*
Blue Suede Shoes • I'm Counting On You • I Got A
Woman • One-Sided Love Affair • Tutti Frutti •
Tryin' To Get To You • I'm Gonna Sit Right Down
And Cry • I'll Never Let You Go
**1/20/58 - #9 / 3** wks.
RCA Victor EPB-1254 [2]...$400

**Elvis Presley**...*Elvis Presley*
Blue Suede Shoes • Tutti Frutti •
I Got A Woman • Just Because
**5/26/58 - #6 / 2** wks.
RCA Victor EPA-747...$125

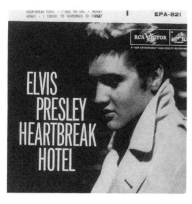

**Elvis Presley**...*Heartbreak Hotel*
Heartbreak Hotel • I Was The One •
Money Honey • I Forgot To Remember To Forget
**4/21/58 - #5 / 3 wks.**
RCA Victor EPA-821...$125

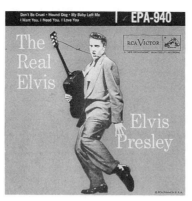

**Elvis Presley**...*The Real Elvis*
Don't Be Cruel • I Want You, I Need You, I Love
You • Hound Dog • My Baby Left Me
**6/16/58 - #5 / 5 wks.**
RCA Victor EPA-940...$125

**Elvis Presley**...*King Creole, Vol. 1*
King Creole • New Orleans •
As Long As I Have You • Lover Doll
**7/21/58 - #1[30] / 55 wks.**
RCA Victor EPA-4319...$100

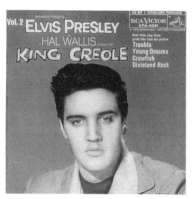

**Elvis Presley**...*King Creole, Vol. 2*
Trouble • Young Dreams •
Crawfish • Dixieland Rock
**8/25/58 - #2[18] / 22 wks.**
RCA Victor EPA-4321...$100

**Elvis Presley**...*Elvis Sails*
Press Interview With Elvis Presley • Elvis Presley's
Newsreel Interview • Pat Hernon Interviews Elvis
In The Library Of The U.S.S. Randall At Sailing
on 9/22/58
**1/12/59 - #2[1] / 12 wks.**
RCA Victor EPA-4325...$125

**Elvis Presley**...*A Touch Of Gold, Volume I*
Hard Headed Woman • Good Rockin' Tonight •
Don't • I Beg Of You
**6/29/59 - #1[16] / 28 wks.**
RCA Victor EPA-5088...$100

**Louis Prima, Keely Smith with Sam
Butera**...*The Wildest Show At Tahoe, Part 1*
On The Sunny Side Of The Street/Exactly Like You
• Robin Hood/Oh Babe
**10/12/59 - #9 / 1 wk.**
Capitol EAP 1-908...$25

**Jim Reeves**...*He'll Have To Go*
He'll Have To Go • Wishful Thinking •
Please Come Home • After Awhile
**4/18/60 - #2[10] / 26 wks.**
RCA Victor EPA-4357...$40

**Marty Robbins**...*Gunfighter Ballads And
Trail Songs, Vol. I*
El Paso • A Hundred And Sixty Acres • They're
Hanging Me Tonight • The Strawberry Roan
**1/11/60 - #1[6] / 32 wks.**
Columbia B-13491...$35

**Jimmie Rodgers**...*Jimmie Rodgers*
Woman From Liberia • The Mating Call •
Hey Little Baby • Water Boy
**1/27/58 - #10 / 1** wk.
Roulette EPR 1-303...$50

**Tommy Sands**...*Sing Boy Sing, Part 1*
I'm Gonna Walk And Talk With My Lord •
Who Baby • Rock Of Ages • Sing Boy Sing
**3/17/58 - #8 / 2** wks.
Capitol EAP 1-929...$60

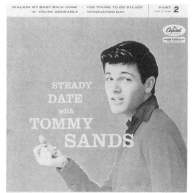

**Tommy Sands**...*Steady Date with Tommy
Sands, Part 2*
Walkin' My Baby Back Home • Too Young To Go
Steady • "A" You're Adorable • Graduation Day
**5/5/58 - #8 / 1** wk.
Capitol EAP 2-848...$60

**The Robert Shaw Chorale**...*Christmas
Hymns And Carols*
Silent Night • O Come, All Ye Faithful • Hark! The
Herald Angels Sing • Deck The Halls With Boughs Of
Holly • We Three Kings • O Little Town Of Bethlehem
**12/29/58 - #4 / 2** wks.
RCA Victor ERA 1-2139...$10

**Frank Sinatra**...*a Swingin' Affair!, Part 1*
From This Moment On • Nice Work If You Can
Get It • The Lonesome Road • You'd Be So
Nice To Come Home To
**11/18/57 - #8 / 2** wks.
Capitol EAP 1-803...$35

**Frank Sinatra**...*Come Fly With Me, Part 1*
Come Fly With Me • Isle Of Capri •
It's Nice To Go Trav'ling
**3/3/58 - #3 / 17** wks.
Capitol EAP 1-920...$35

**Frank Sinatra**...*This Is Sinatra
Volume Two, Part 1*
Hey! Jealous Lover • Everybody Loves Somebody •
I Believe • Put Your Dreams Away
**6/2/58 - #7 / 1** wk.
Capitol EAP 1-982...$35

**Frank Sinatra**...*Frank Sinatra!*
The Lady Is A Tramp • Witchcraft •
Come Fly With Me • Tell Her You Love Her
**12/22/58 - #10 / 1** wk.
Capitol EAP 1-1013...$40

**Frank Sinatra**...*Come Dance With Me!,
Part 1*
Come Dance With Me • Something's Gotta Give •
The Song Is You • The Last Dance
**7/13/59 - #8 / 9** wks.
Capitol EAP 1-1069...$35

**Frank Sinatra**...*No One Cares, Part 1*
When No One Cares • I'll Never Smile Again •
A Cottage For Sale • None But The Lonely Heart
**10/12/59 - #9 / 10** wks.
Capitol EAP 1-1221...$35

**Dakota Staton**...*The Late, Late Show, Part 1*
Broadway • Trust In Me •
Moonray • Ain't No Use
**7/14/58 - #5 / 13** wks.
Capitol EAP 1-876...$25

**Dakota Staton**...*Crazy He Calls Me, Part 1*
Crazy He Calls Me • Idaho •
How Does It Feel? • How High The Moon
**7/20/59 - #2$^1$ / 8** wks.
Capitol EAP 1-1170...$25

**The Twin-Tones**...*Jim and John THE
TWIN-TONES*
Jo-Ann • Before You Go •
My Dancing Lady • One Mail A Day
**2/10/58 - #4 / 2** wks.
RCA Victor EPA-4107...$30

**Fred Waring and the Pennsylvanians**...
*now is the Caroling Season, Part 1*
Now Is The Caroling Season • We Three Kings •
Winter Wonderland • It Was A Night Of Wonder •
White Christmas
**12/30/57 - #7 / 2** wks.
Capitol EAP 1-896...$10

**Hank Williams**...*The Unforgettable Hank
Williams, Vol. I*
I Can't Get You Off My Mind • I Don't Care
(If Tomorrow Never Comes) • Dear John •
My Love For You (Has Turned To Hate)
**6/1/59 - #2$^8$ / 32** wks.
MGM X1637...$50

**Roger Williams**...*Roger Williams Plays,
Vol. 1*
Autumn Leaves • Take Care •
Summertime • 'Til Roses Cry
**4/21/58 - #6 / 7** wks.
Kapp KE-708...$15

**Roger Williams**...*Roger Williams*
Till • Marcheta • Always •
The Merry Widow Waltz
**7/28/58 - #9 / 3** wks.
Kapp KE-751...$15

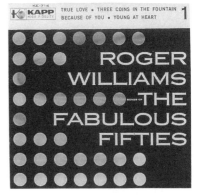

**Roger Williams**...*songs of The Fabulous
Fifties, Vol. 1*
True Love • Because Of You •
Young At Heart • Three Coins In The Fountain
**3/24/58 - #7 / 1** wk.
Kapp KE-714...$10

**Roger Williams**...*songs of The Fabulous Fifties, Vol. 4*
Tennessee Waltz • High Noon •
Blue Tango • Hey There
**12/1/58 - #8 / 1** wk.
Kapp KE-717...$10

**Roger Williams**...*songs of The Fabulous Forties, Vol. 1*
Holiday For Strings • The Last Time I Saw Paris •
Anniversary Song • Some Enchanted Evening
**6/23/58 - #7 / 2** wks.
Kapp KE-737...$10

**My Fair Lady** (Original Cast)
Overture • Why Can't The English? • Wouldn't It Be
Loverly • With A Little Bit Of Luck • I'm An Ordinary
Man • Just You Wait • The Rain In Spain • I Could
Have Danced All Night • Ascot Gavotte • On The
Street Where You Live • You Did It • Show Me •
Get Me To The Church On Time • A Hymn To Him •
Without You • I've Grown Accustomed To Her Face
**11/24/58 - #9 / 1** wk.
Columbia A-5090 [4]...$25

**South Pacific** (Original Cast)
Overture • Dites Moi • A Cock-Eyed Optimist •
Twin Soliloquies • Some Enchanted Evening •
Bloody Mary • There Is Nothin' Like A Dame •
Bali Ha'i • I'm Gonna Wash That Man Right Outa
My Hair • A Wonderful Guy • Younger Than
Springtime • Happy Talk • Honey Bun • Carefully
Taught • This Nearly Was Mine • Finale
**12/8/58 - #1[1] / 16** wks.
Columbia A-850 [7]...$40

**South Pacific** (Soundtrack)
Bali Ha'i • Dites Moi • Cock-Eyed Optimist •
Twin Soliloquies/Some Enchanted Evening •
Carefully Taught • Bloody Mary • My Girl Back
Home • Honey Bun • There Is Nothing Like
A Dame • I'm Gonna Wash That Man Right
Outa My Hair • Happy Talk • I'm In Love With
A Wonderful Guy • Younger Than Springtime •
This Nearly Was Mine
**9/7/59 - #3 / 8** wks.
RCA Victor EOC-1032 [3]...$40

# BUBBLING UNDER THE TOP POP ALBUMS

## THE HISTORY OF *BILLBOARD'S* *BUBBLING UNDER THE TOP POP ALBUMS* CHART

The *Bubbling Under The Top Pop Albums* chart began on December 26, 1970 and ended on August 24, 1985.  The chart listed albums that were on the rise in sales, but did not quite achieve the sales necessary to make *Billboard's* 200-position *Top LPs* chart.  The *Bubbling Under* chart was compiled from data provided by national retail stores.

The following is synopsis of the *Bubbling Under The Top Pop Albums* chart:

| Chart Title | Dates Researched | # of Positions |
|---|---|---|
| Bubbling Under The Top LP's | 12/26/70 - 7/6/74 | 4 to 35 |
| Bubbling Under The Top LP's | 7/13/74 - 10/13/84 | 10 |
| Bubbling Under The Top 200 Albums | 10/20/84 - 2/2/85 | 10 |
| Bubbling Under The Top Pop Albums | 2/9/85 - 8/24/85 | 10 |
| Bubbling Under The Top Pop Albums | 8/24/85 | final chart |

The smallest of all the *Bubbling Under The Top Pop Albums* charts was four positions (July 29, 1972) and the largest equaled 35 (March 27, 1971).

*Billboard* did not publish an issue for the last week of the year since 1976.  For the years 1976 through 1984, *Billboard* considered the charts listed in the last published issue of each year to be "frozen" and all chart positions remained the same for the unpublished week. This frozen chart data is included in our tabulations.

For reasons unexplained, *Billboard* did not publish a *Bubbling Under The Top Pop Albums* chart in the following issues:

January 1, 1972
July 7, 1973
January 5, 1974
January 12, 1974
April 13, 1974
June 29, 1974
July 27, 1974
July 15, 1978

These unpublished weeks were treated as frozen weeks.

This is a guide to the *Bubbling Under The Top Pop Albums* artist section. The artist section is organized alphabetically by artist name and lists all *Bubbling Under* albums that did not chart on *Billboard's* Top 200 *Top Pop Albums* chart. The albums are listed in chronological order and sequentially numbered (if an artist had more than one charted album).

## EXPLANATION OF COLUMNAR HEADINGS

| | |
|---:|:---|
| **DEBUT:** | Date album first charted |
| **PEAK:** | Highest charted *Bubbling Under* position (highlighted in bold type) |
| **WKS:** | Total weeks charted |
| **$:** | Current value of near-mint commercial copy |
| **LABEL & NUMBER:** | Original label and number of album when charted |

## EXPLANATION OF SYMBOLS

✪ indicates that the artist never hit *Billboard's Top Pop Albums* chart (appears to the right of the artist name)

[1] Superior number to the right of a #201 peak position is the <u>total weeks</u> the album held that position

+ Indicates album peaked in the <u>year after</u> it first charted

## LETTER(S) IN BRACKETS AFTER ALBUM TITLES

C - Comedy
E - Earlier Recordings/Releases
F - Foreign Language
G - Greatest Hits
I - Instrumental Recording
K - Compilation
L - Live Recording
M - Mini Album (12" album with four to six tracks)

N - Novelty
R - Reissue or re-release with a new label number of a previously charted album
S - Movie Soundtrack
T - Talk/Spoken Word Recording
TV - Television Program Soundtrack
X - Christmas

## ARTIST'S #201 ALBUMS

All #201 albums are shaded with a light gray background for immediate identification.

## ARTIST NOTES

Below every artist name are brief biographical notes about the artist. Names of artists mentioned in the artist notes of other *Bubbling Under* album artists are highlighted in bold type if they have their own discography elsewhere in this artist section. A name is only shown bold the first time it appears in an artist's biography. To conserve space in some artist biographies, the abbreviation "b:" for "born on" and the abbreviation "d:" for "died on" are used. If an artist charted 20 or more albums in our *Top Pop Albums 1955-1996* (+1997) book, the total is shown at the end of their biographies (ex.: *Top Pop Albums*: 23).

# TITLE NOTES

Directly under some album titles are notes indicating guest artists, the location of live recordings, the names of famous producers, etc. Duets and other significant artist name variations are shown in bold capital letters. Names of artists mentioned in the title notes of other *Bubbling Under* album artists are highlighted in bold type if they have their own discography elsewhere in this artist section. All movie, TV and album titles, and other major works, are shown in italics.

As always, we gladly welcome any corrections/updates to our artist biographies or title notes (please include verification).

# LISTING OF TRACKS

Below each album is a listing of its tracks in order of their appearance on the album. If a track's spelling on the album label and album jacket conflict, the spelling on the label is usually shown unless the label spelling is proven incorrect.

# ALBUM PRICE GUIDE

The dollar amounts listed in the price column are estimates of the dealer-asking prices for *near-mint* commercial copies. Please keep in mind that this book is not intended to be an all-purpose album price guide but a novice's tool to album pricing.

Early limited pressings or variations from the original commercial release, such as promotional copies, mistakes or differentiations on the label, colored vinyl, etc. can vastly increase or, in <u>very</u> rare cases, decrease the price of the record. The price listed in this book is for the widely distributed pressing of an album during its chart run. The prices do not apply to promotional copies which can be priced anywhere from slightly to significantly higher than the commercial releases. When evaluating the more common albums, the age of the record is a major determining factor. Generally, older albums are more scarce and more difficult to find in good condition and thus command a higher value.

Remember that pricing is very subjective and varies greatly from dealer to dealer and region to region. It is not unusual for prices of the same record of identical grade to fluctuate widely. An album's true value is dependent on its demand, condition and availability.

# A

## ABBA

Pop quartet from Stockholm, Sweden: Anni-Frid "Frida" Lyngstad and Agnetha Fältskog (vocals), Bjorn Ulvaeus (guitar) and Benny Andersson (keyboards). Bjorn and Agnetha were married from 1971-79. Benny and Frida were married from 1978-81.

| 4/28/84 | 208 | 2 | I Love Abba ......................................... [K] $10 | Atlantic 80142 |
|---------|-----|---|------|------|

Cassandra • The Name Of The Game • Should I Laugh Or Cry • Our Last Summer • I Do, I Do, I Do, I Do, I Do • Chiquitita • Andante, Andante • I Have A Dream • My Love, My Life • I Wonder (Departure) • One Man, One Woman • Slipping Through My Fingers • Fernando • Eagle

## ACE SPECTRUM

R&B vocal group from New York City: Ed "Easy" Zant, Aubrey "Troy" Johnson, Elliot Isaac and Rudy Gay.

| 7/13/74 | 209 | 1 | Inner Spectrum ......................................... $12 | Atlantic 7299 |
|---------|-----|---|------|------|

Don't Send Nobody Else • Don't Let Me Be Lonely Tonight • If You Were There • Moving On • Pickup • Me And My Love • Easy • I Don't Want To Play Around

## ADAMS, Jay Boy ☉

Country-rock singer/guitarist.

| 10/1/77 | 210 | 1 | Jay Boy Adams ......................................... $12 | Atlantic 18221 |
|---------|-----|---|------|------|

Nine Hard Years • Mitchell County Sunset • The Legend Of Jack Diamond • Sew A Sail • You Don't Miss Things (When They're Gone) • Ladies 'Round The River • Mountains And Airplanes • Cactus Cafe • In Rain In Spring • Copper Mountain

## ADRENALIN ☉

Rock group: Marc Gilbert (vocals), Michael Romeo and Flash (guitars), Bruce Schafer (bass), Jimmy Romeo (saxophone), Mark Pastoria (keyboards) and Brian Pastoria (drums).

| 8/11/84 | 203 | 8 | American Heart ......................................... $10 | Rocshire 9517 |
|---------|-----|---|------|------|

Faraway Eyes • Broken Hearted Bound • Northern Shores • Photograph (Time Passes On) • The Kid's Got A Will To Live • Baby I'm Back • Gimme Your Heart • The Pressure's On • Michael • Freedom Road

## AFRO-CUBAN BAND

Disco studio group based in New York and produced by Michael Zager. Previously known as Love Childs Afro Cuban Blues Band.

| 9/16/78 | 204 | 4 | Rhythm Of Life ......................................... $10 | Arista 4188 |
|---------|-----|---|------|------|

Rhythm Of Life • Black Widow Woman • Baila • The Moon Is The Daughter Of The Devil • You're Like • Delicado

## AIRTO

Born Airto Moreira on 8/5/41 in Itaiopolis, Brazil. Male jazz percussionist/singer. Married to jazz vocalist **Flora Purim**.

| 11/29/75 | 207 | 1 | Identity ......................................... $12 | Arista 4068 |
|----------|-----|---|------|------|

produced by **Herbie Hancock**

The Magicians (Bruxos) • Tales From Home (Lendas) • Identity • Encounter (Encontro No Bar) • Medley: Wake Up Song (Baião Do Acordar)/Café • Mãe Cambina • Flora On My Mind

## AIRWAVES ☉

Pop-rock trio from Wales: Ray Martinez (vocals, guitar), John David (vocals, bass) and Dave Charles (drums).

| 5/13/78 | 204 | 3 | New Day ......................................... $10 | A&M 4689 |
|---------|-----|---|------|------|

Love Stop • Let Me In • The Cat • Keep Away The Blues • Hope You Won't • You Are The New Day • So Hard Living Without You • Nobody Is • Hideaway • Don't Let The Daylight In • Go Getter

## ALABAMA STATE TROUPERS, The ☉

Concert revue featuring vocalists **Don Nix** and Jeanie Greene (backing vocalist with **Elvis Presley**, Ronnie Hawkins and **Carl Perkins**) with legendary 1920s blues guitarist/vocalist Walter "Furry" Lewis (d: 1981). Backed by the Mt. Zion Band and the Mt. Zion Choir.

| 2/26/72 | 218 | 2 | Road Show ......................................... [L] $20 | Elektra 75022 [2] |
|---------|-----|---|------|------|

recorded on 10/15/71 in Long Beach, California, and on 10/17/71 in Pasadena

Furry's Blues • Brownsville • I'm Black • A Chicken Ain't Nothin' But A Bird • Will The Circle Be Unbroken • Amos Burke • Mighty Time • Jesus On The Mainline • Mary Louise • Yes, I Do Understand • Opening • Living In The Country • Joa-Bim • Dixie • Heavy Makes You Happy • Iuka • Furry's Rap • Asphalt Outlaw Hero • Olena • My Father's House • Going Down

## ALBERT, Morris

Born Morris Albert Kaisermann in Brazil. Singer/songwriter.

| 6/18/77 | 201 | 6 | Love And Life | $12 | RCA Victor 2070 |
|---------|-----|---|------|---|------|

Conversation • You • Flight Theme • Midnight • I Love You • So Good To Me • Part Of Me • Never Let You Go • Mornings • Someone, Somehow

## ALDA RESERVE ☉

Rock group: Brad Ellis (vocals, keyboards), Mark Suall (guitar), Tony Shanahan (bass) and Matthew "Chips" Patuto (drums).

| 11/24/79 | 210 | 4 | Love Goes On ......................................... $10 | Sire 6079 |
|----------|-----|---|------|------|

Some Get Away • Dressed For Love • Cure Me • Pain Is Mine • Overnite Jets • Ancient Lies • That Was Summertime • Whiter Than White • Love Goes On

## ALESSI ☉

Identical twin brothers Billy and Bobby Alessi. Born on 7/12/53 in West Hampstead, New York.

| 2/4/78 | 210 | 1 | All For A Reason ......................................... $10 | A&M 4657 |
|--------|-----|---|------|------|

All For A Reason • Love To Have Your Love • Farewell • Avalon • Air Cushion • London • Hate To Be In Love • You Can Crowd Me • Make It Last • Here Again

## ALLEN, Peter

Born Peter Allen Woolnough on 2/10/44 in Tenterfield, Australia. Died of AIDS on 6/18/92. Cabaret-style performer. Married to **Liza Minnelli** from 1967-73.

| 12/10/77 | 209 | 1 | It's Time For Peter Allen ......................................... [L] $15 | A&M 3706 [2] |
|----------|-----|---|------|------|

recorded at Avery Fischer Hall and The Bottom Line in New York City and The Roxy in Los Angeles

Love Crazy • She Loves To Hear The Music • Everything Old Is New Again • Interesting Changes • I Honestly Love You • Continental American • The Natural Thing To Do • The More I See You • As Time Goes By • Intermission/I Honestly Love You • Don't Wish Too Hard • Don't Cry Out Loud • Tenterfield Saddler • Medley: Puttin' Out Roots/The Sideshow's Leaving Town • I Go To Rio • Quiet Please, There's A Lady On Stage • Audience

### ALPERT, Herb, & The T.J.B.
Born on 3/31/35 in Los Angeles. Producer/composer/trumpeter/bandleader. Founded A&M Records with Jerry Moss in 1962.
*Top Pop Albums: 27.*

| | | | | | |
|---|---|---|---|---|---|
| 8/16/80 | 206 | 1 | Greatest Hits Vol. 2 ................................................................................... [G] $10 | | A&M 4627 |

What Now My Love • The Work Song • Brasilia • Jerusalem • So What's New • Last Tango In Paris • My Favorite Things • This Guy's In Love With You • A Banda • Flamingo • Cabaret • Zazueira • Bittersweet Samba • Wade In The Water

### AMANT ⊙
Disco studio group assembled by producer Ray Martinez.

| | | | | | |
|---|---|---|---|---|---|
| 3/31/79 | 203 | 4 | Amant .................................................................................................... $10 | | Marlin 2227 |

If There's Love • Hazy Shades Of Love

### AMAZING BLONDEL ⊙
Medieval-styled trio from Scunthorpe, England: John David Gladwin (lute, oboe), Terry Wincott (pipe organ, flute) and Edward Baird (guitar, percussion). Named for Richard the Lionhearted's legendary favorite minstrel.

| | | | | | |
|---|---|---|---|---|---|
| 2/17/73 | 210 | 3 | England ................................................................................................ $15 | | Island 9327 |

Seascape • Landscape • Afterglow • A Spring Air • Cantus Firmus To Counterpoint • Sinfonia For Guitar And Strings • Dolor Dulcis (Sweet Sorrow) • Lament To The Earl Of Bottesford Beck

### AMAZING SPIDER-MAN, The — see CHILDREN'S ALBUMS

### AMERICAN STANDARD BAND ⊙
Pop-rock group: Kevin Falvey (vocals, keyboards), Cliff Goodwin (guitar), Deric Dyer (sax), Howard Hersh (bass) and John Riley (drums).

| | | | | | |
|---|---|---|---|---|---|
| 4/28/79 | 201 | 3 | American Standard Band | $10 | Island 9540 |

Got What It Takes • You Never Get Over Heartbreak • Questions And Answers • Make It Last • So Far Away • Fallin' In Love Again • Take It Easy On Me • Dance With Me Forever • Take Me Away My Friend • Children's Island

### ANDERSEN, Eric
Born on 2/14/43 in Pittsburgh. Folk singer/songwriter.

| | | | | | |
|---|---|---|---|---|---|
| 6/12/76 | 208 | 4 | Sweet Surprise ...................................................................................... $12 | | Arista 4075 |

Lost In A Song • How It Goes • Dreams Of Mexico • San Diego Serenade • Sweet Surprise • Down At The Cantina • Crazy River • Love Will Meet Again

### ANDERSON, Ian ⊙
Born on 8/10/47 in Edinburgh, Scotland. Lead vocalist/flutist of progressive-rock band Jethro Tull.

| | | | | | |
|---|---|---|---|---|---|
| 1/21/84 | 202 | 4 | Walk Into Light ..................................................................................... $10 | | Chrysalis 41443 |

Fly By Night • Made In England • Walk Into Light • Trains • End Game • Black And White Television • Toad In The Hole • Looking For Eden • User-Friendly • Different Germany

### ANDERSON, John
Born on 12/13/54 in Orlando; raised in Apopka, Florida. Country singer/guitarist.

| | | | | | |
|---|---|---|---|---|---|
| 10/6/84 | 202 | 3 ● | Greatest Hits ................................................................................... [G] $10 | | Warner 25169 |

Swingin' • I Just Came Home To Count The Memories • She Just Started Liking Cheatin' Songs • 1959 • Chicken Truck • I'm Just An Old Chunk Of Coal (But I'm Gonna Be A Diamond Some Day) • Would You Catch A Falling Star • Wild And Blue • Your Lying Blue Eyes • Black Sheep

### ANDERSON, Laurie
Born on 6/5/47 in Chicago. Avant-garde performance artist.

| | | | | | |
|---|---|---|---|---|---|
| 2/6/82 | 203 | 3 | O Superman ...................................................................................... [M] $10 | | Warner 49888 |

O Superman • Walk The Dog

### ANDERSON, Lynn
Born on 9/26/47 in Grand Forks, North Dakota; raised in Sacramento, California. Country singer. Daughter of country singer Liz Anderson.

| | | | | | |
|---|---|---|---|---|---|
| 3/17/73 | 201 | 3 | Keep Me In Mind | $12 | Columbia 32078 |

Keep Me In Mind • Pass Me By (If You're Only Passing Through) • I Believe In Music • Just Between The Two Of Us • All Or Nothing With Me • The City Of New Orleans • Home Is Where I Hang My Head • A Perfect Match *[w/Glenn Sutton]* • Who Could I Turn To • Half A Dozen Tricycle Motors • Rodeo Cowboy

### ANGEL CITY
Hard-rock group from Australia: Doc Neeson (vocals), brothers Rick and John Brewster (guitars), Jim Hilbun (bass) and Brent Eccles (drums).

| | | | | | |
|---|---|---|---|---|---|
| 2/9/85 | 201 | 8 | Two Minute Warning | $10 | MCA 5509 |

Underground • Look The Other Way • Between The Eyes • Front Page News • Be With You • Small Price • Poem/Walking To Babylon • Sticky Little Bitch • Razor's Edge • Gonna Leave You

### ANIMALYMICS — see GOULDMAN, Graham

### APRIL WINE
Rock group from Montreal: Myles Goodwyn (vocals, guitar), David Henman (guitar), Jim Clench (bass) and Ritchie Henman (drums).

| | | | | | |
|---|---|---|---|---|---|
| 10/28/72 | 205 | 2 | April Wine ........................................................................................... $15 | | Big Tree 2012 |

Farkus • You Could Have Been A Lady • Believe In Me • Work All Day • Drop Your Guns • Bad Side Of The Moon • Refuge • Flow River Flow • Carry On • Didn't You

### ARCHIES, The
Studio group created by Don Kirshner; based on the Saturday morning cartoon television series.

| | | | | | |
|---|---|---|---|---|---|
| 4/24/71 | 207 | 1 | This Is Love ........................................................................................ $25 | | Kirshner 110 |

This Is Love • Don't Need No Bad Girl • Should Anybody Ask • Easy Guy • Maybe I'm Wrong • What Goes On • Carousel Man • Hold On To Lovin' • This Is The Night • Little Green Jacket • Together We Two • Throw A Little Love My Way

### ARMANDO('s), Don, Second Avenue Rhumba Band ⊙
Disco group headed by Don Armando Bonilla, percussionist with Dr. Buzzard's Original "Savannah" Band. Featured lead vocalist Fonda Rae.

| | | | | | |
|---|---|---|---|---|---|
| 2/2/80 | 208 | 1 | Don Armando's Second Avenue Rhumba Band ................................. $10 | | ZE 33005 |

produced and arranged by Andy "Coati Mundi" Hernandez **(Kid Creole & The Coconuts)**
Deputy Of Love • Compliment Your Leading Lady • Winter Love • Goin' To A Showdown • How To Handle A Woman • I'm An Indian Too • Medley: Para Ti/This Is Just For You

## ARTFUL DODGER ✪
Rock band: Billy Paliselli (vocals), Gary Herrewig and Gary Cox (guitars), Steve Cooper (bass), and Steve Brigida (drums). Cox left by 1980.

| | | | | | |
|---|---|---|---|---|---|
| 9/11/76 | 208 | 2 | **1 Honor Among Thieves** ...................................................... $12 | | Columbia 34273 |

Honor Among Thieves • Not Enough • Scream • Keep A-Knockin' • Keep Me Happy • Remember • Dandelion • Hey Boys • Good Fun

| | | | | | |
|---|---|---|---|---|---|
| 8/30/80 | 209 | 1 | **2 Rave On** ............................................................................... $10 | | Ariola America 1503 |

She's Just My Baby • It's A Lie • So Afraid • Get In Line • Now Or Never Mind • Come Close To Me • I Don't Wanna See Her • Forever • A Girl (La La La) • Gone Again

## A's, The
Pop-rock group from Philadelphia: Richard Bush (vocals), Rick DiFonzo (guitar), Rocco Notte (keyboards), Terry Bortman (bass) and Mike Snyder (drums).

| | | | | | |
|---|---|---|---|---|---|
| 9/29/79 | 201 | 3 | **The A's** | $10 | Arista 4238 |

After Last Night • C.I.A. • Five Minutes In A Hero's Life • Words • Parasite • Artificial Love • Who's Gonna Save The World • Teenage Jerk Off • Medley: Grounded/Twist And Shout Interpolation • Nothing Wrong With Falling In Love

## ASLEEP AT THE WHEEL
Western swing band from Paw Paw, West Virginia. Core members: Ray Benson (male vocals, guitar), Chris O'Connell (female voclas, guitar), Reuben "Lucky Oceans" Gosfield (steel guitar), Danny Levin (fiddle, mandolin) and Jim "Floyd Domino" Haber (piano).

| | | | | | |
|---|---|---|---|---|---|
| 8/19/78 | 209 | 2 | **Collision Course** .................................................................. $15 | | Capitol 11726 |

Pipe Dreams • Song Of The Wanderer • Pine Grove Blues • One O'Clock Jump • Louisiana • Texas Me & You • Ruler Of My Heart • Don't Forget The Trains • Ain't Nobody Here But Us Chickens • Ghost Dancer

## ASYLUM CHOIR — see RUSSELL, Leon

## ATLANTA RHYTHM SECTION
Southern-rock group from Doraville, Georgia: Rodney Justo (vocals), Barry Bailey and J.R. Cobb (guitars), Dean Daughtry (keyboards), Paul Goddard (bass) and Robert Nix (drums).

| | | | | | |
|---|---|---|---|---|---|
| 4/15/72 | 210 | 2 | **Atlanta Rhythm Section** ..................................................... $25 | | Decca 75265 |

Love Me Just A Little (Sometime) • Baby No Lie • All In Your Mind • Earnestine • Forty Days And Forty Nights • Another Man's Woman (It's So Hard) • Days Of Our Lives • Yours And Mine • Can't Stand It No More • One More Problem

## ATTITUDES ✪
Los Angeles-based quartet of top sidemen: David Foster (keyboards, composer), Danny Kortchmar (guitar), Paul Stallworth (bass) and Jim Keltner (drums; later with Little Village). Foster, a prolific songwriter, and Kortchmar were lated noted producers.

| | | | | | |
|---|---|---|---|---|---|
| 3/20/76 | 206 | 1 | **Attitudes** ............................................................................... $12 | | Dark Horse 22008 |

Ain't Love Enough • Street Scene • A Moment • You And I Are So In Love • Squank • Lend A Hand • Chump Change Romeo • First Ballad • Honey Don't Leave L.A. • In The Flow Of Love

## AUDIENCE
Rock group from London: Howard Werth (vocals, guitar), Keith Gemmell (sax), Trevor Williams (bass) and Tony Connor (percussion).

| | | | | | |
|---|---|---|---|---|---|
| 9/11/71 | 204 | 1 | **The House On The Hill** ........................................................ $15 | | Elektra 74100 |

Indian Summer • You're Not Smilin' • Jackdaw • It Brings A Tear • Raviole • Nancy • I Had A Dream • I Put A Spell On You • The House On The Hill

## AUGER('s), Brian, Oblivion Express
Born on 7/18/39 in Bihar, India; raised in London. Jazz-rock keyboardist/vocalist. In the mid-'60s, formed Trinity, then Steampacket. His Oblivion Express included Jim Mullen (guitar), Barry Dean (bass) and Robbie McIntosh (drums; **AWB**).

| | | | | | |
|---|---|---|---|---|---|
| 4/17/71 | 209 | 3 | **1 Brian Auger's Oblivion Express** ................................... $15 | | RCA Victor 4462 |

Dragon Song • Total Eclipse • The Light • On The Road • The Sword • Oblivion Express

| | | | | | |
|---|---|---|---|---|---|
| 11/13/71 | 211 | 2 | **2 A Better Land** ................................................................... $15 | | RCA Victor 4540 |

Dawn Of Another Day • Marai's Wedding • Trouble • Women Of The Seasons • Fill Your Head With Laughter • On Thinking It Over • Tomorrow City • All The Time There Is • A Better Land

## AURACLE ✪
Jazz-pop group: Richard Braun (trumpet), Stephen Kujala (woodwinds), Steven Rehbein (percussion), John Serry (keyboards), Bill Staebell (bass) and Ron Wagner (drums).

| | | | | | |
|---|---|---|---|---|---|
| 7/22/78 | 201 | 5 | **Glider** [I] | $10 | Chrysalis 1172 |

Columbian Bubblegum • Tom Thumb • Glider • 'Sno Fun • Sleezy Listening • Kids' Stuff • Chez Amis • Sartori

## AURRA
R&B group from Ohio led by bassist/saxophonist Steve Washington and featuring vocalists Starleana Young and Curt Jones. All three were members of Slave.

| | | | | | |
|---|---|---|---|---|---|
| 3/26/83 | 208 | 1 | **Live And Let Live** ............................................................... $10 | | Salsoul 8559 |

Such A Feeling • Coming To Get You • Live And Let Live • Undercover Lover • Baby Love • You Can't Keep On Walking • One More Time • Positive

## AUSTIN, Patti
Born on 8/10/48 in New York City. R&B singer.

| | | | | | |
|---|---|---|---|---|---|
| 7/19/80 | 208 | 2 | **Body Language** .................................................................... $10 | | CTI 36503 |

Body Language • Another Nail For My Heart • S.O.S. • We've Got Tonight • (Ooh-Wee) He's Killing Me • I Can't Stop • Love Me Again • Soar Me Like An Eagle Flies • People In Love (Do The Strangest Things) • I Want You Tonight

## AWB (AVERAGE WHITE BAND)
Scottish group formed in London: Alan Gorrie (vocals, bass), Onnie McIntyre (guitar, vocals), Hamish Stuart (guitar, vocals), Malcolm Duncan (saxophone), Roger Ball (saxophone, keyboards) and Robbie McIntosh (drums; died of drug poisoning on 9/23/74). Steve Ferrone replaced McIntosh; both were earlier with **Brian Auger's** Oblivion Express.

| | | | | | |
|---|---|---|---|---|---|
| 10/13/73 | 216 | 3 | **1 Show Your Hand** .............................................................. $20 | | MCA 345 |

**THE AVERAGE WHITE BAND**

The Jugglers • This World Has Music • Twilight Zone • Put It Where You Want It • Show Your Hand • Back In '67 • Reach Out • T.L.C.

| | | | | | |
|---|---|---|---|---|---|
| 8/7/82 | 202 | 2 | **2 Cupid's In Fashion** ........................................................... $10 | | Arista 9594 |

You're My Number One • Easier Said Than Done • You Wanna Belong • Cupid's In Fashion • Theatre Of Excess • I Believe • Is It Love That You're Running From • Reach Out I'll Be There • Isn't It Strange • Love's A Heartache

| DEBUT | PEAK | WKS | Album Title | $ | Label & Number |
|-------|------|-----|-------------|---|----------------|

### AXTON, Hoyt
Born on 3/25/38 in Camanche, Oklahoma. Country singer/songwriter/actor. Son of songwriter Mae Axton ("Heartbreak Hotel"). Acted in the movies *The Black Stallion* and *Gremlins*.

| 7/10/71 | 215 | 1 | **Joy To The World** ......... $15 Capitol 788 |
Joy To The World • Alice In Wonderland • Never Been To Spain • The Pusher • Ease Your Pain • Have A Nice Day • Indian Song • California Women • Lightnin' Bar Blues • Medley: Farther Along/Old Time Religion

### AYERS, Roy
Born on 9/10/40 in Los Angeles. Vibraphone player/keyboardist/vocalist.

| 10/23/76 | 206 | 1 | 1 **Daddy Bug & Friends** ......... [I] $12 Atlantic 1692 |
guests include **Ron Carter** (bass), **Herbie Hancock** (piano) and Herbie Mann (flute)
Daddy Bug • I Love You Michelle • Bonita • Slow Motion • Native Dancer • In The Limelight • Virgo Vibes (Outside Blues)

| 7/5/80 | 205 | 2 | 2 **Prime Time** ......... $10 Polydor 6276 |
**ROY AYERS/WAYNE HENDERSON**
trombonist Henderson (b: 9/24/39 in Houston) was an original member of **The Crusaders**
You Make Me Feel Like (Rockin' With Ya) • Thank You Thank You • Weekend Lover • Tell Me What You Want • Can You Dance • It Ain't Your Sign, It's Your Mind • Have Your Way • Million Dollar Baby (Feel So Real)

| 1/12/85 | 201 | 6 | 3 **In The Dark** ......... [I] $10 Columbia 39422 |
guests include Tom Browne (trumpet), **Stanley Clarke** (drum machine), Paulinho da Costa (percussion), Miki Howard (vocals) and Grover Washington Jr. (sax)
In The Dark • Sexy, Sexy, Sexy • I Can't Help It • Compadre • Goree Island • Poo Poo La La • Blast The Box • Love Is In The Feel

### AZTECA
Latin jazz-rock ensemble led by brothers Pete (vocals) and Thomas "Coke" (timbales) Escovedo. Pete is the father of Sheila E.; Coke died on 7/13/86 (age 45).

| 10/27/73 | 209 | 5 | **Pyramid Of The Moon** ......... $15 Columbia 32451 |
guests include Lenny White (drums) and Neal Schon (guitar; Journey)
Someday We'll Get By • Mazatlan • Find Love Today • Whatcha Gonna Do • New Day Is On The Rise • Mexicana • Mexicana • Red Onions • Love Is A Stranger • Night In Nazca

### AZTEC TWO-STEP
Pop/rock duo from Boston: guitarists/vocalists Rex Fowler and Neal Shulman.

| 11/15/75 | 209 | 3 | 1 **Second Step** ......... $12 RCA Victor 1161 |
It's Going On Saturday • Our Lives • I'm In Love Again • Faster Gun • Humpty Dumpty • Move Up To Love • Cosmos Lady • Walking On Air • Lullabye On New York • Hey, Little Mama

| 2/18/78 | 210 | 1 | 2 **Adjoining Suites** ......... $12 RCA Victor 2453 |
I Wonder If We Tried • Brand New • You And I • One Thing I Forgot To Tell You • John Gary • Looking Glass • Hurting • Up In Lilly's Room • Waywarding Day • Born Again

# B

### BABY HUEY ☉
Born James Thomas Ramey in 1954 in Richmond, Indiana. Died of natural causes on 10/28/70 (age 26). Weighed 350 pounds. Took name from the comic strip.

| 5/8/71 | 214 | 2 | **The Baby Huey Story/The Living Legend** ......... $30 Curtom 8007 |
Listen To Me • Mama Get Yourself Together • A Change Is Going To Come • Mighty, Mighty • Hard Times • California Dreamin' • Running • One Dragon Two Dragon

### BAEZ, Joan
Born on 1/9/41 in Staten Island, New York. Leading folk singer/songwriter/political activist. *Top Pop Albums*: 25.

| 4/3/76 | 205 | 6 | **The Joan Baez Lovesong Album** ......... [K] $15 Vanguard 79/80 [2] |
recordings from 1961-70
Come All Ye Fair And Tender Ladies • Love Minus Zero/No Limit • Sweet Sir Galahad • Love Is Just A Four-Letter Word • The Wild Mountain Thyme • The Lass From The Low Country • Sad-Eyed Lady Of The Lowlands • Plaisir D'Amour • House Carpenter • Once I Had A Sweetheart • Danger Waters (Hold Me Tight) • The River In The Pines • Turquoise • The Death Of Queen Jane • All In Green Went My Love Riding • Once I Knew A Pretty Girl • The Unquiet Grave • So We'll Go No More A-Roving

### BAKER, Ginger
Born Peter Baker on 8/19/39 in Lewisham, England. Drummer for **Cream** and Blind Faith. Got start as replacement for Charlie Watts (who left to join The Rolling Stones) in Alexis Korner's Blues Inc. in 1962. Then with the **Graham Bond** Organization. Bond was with Air Force 2.

| 1/9/71 | 211 | 2 | 1 **Ginger Baker's Air Force 2** ......... $15 Atco 343 |
Let Me Ride • Sweet Wine • Do U No Hu Yor Yor Phrenz R? • We Free Kings • I Don't Want To Go On Without You • Toady • 12 Gates Of The City

| 9/2/72 | 205 | 4 | 2 **Live!** ......... [L] $15 Signpost 8401 |
**FELA RANSOME-KUTI and THE AFRICA '70 with GINGER BAKER**
Let's Start • Black Man's Cry • Ye Ye De Smell • Egbe Mi O (Carry Me I Want To Die)

| 9/23/72 | 201 | 5 | 3 **Stratavarious** ......... [I] $15 Atco 7013 |
Ariwo • Tiwa (It's Our Own) • Something Nice • Ju Ju • Blood Brothers 69 • Coda

| 11/4/72 | 205 | 5 | 4 **At His Best** ......... [K] $20 Polydor 3504 [2] |
includes recordings with Blind Faith and **Cream**
Let Me Ride • Had To Cry Today • I Don't Want To Go On Without You • Do What You Like • Da Da Man • Sweet Wine • Well All Right • Can't Find My Way Home • Aiko Biaye

| DEBUT | PEAK | WKS | Album Title | $ | Label & Number |
|-------|------|-----|-------------|---|----------------|

### BANDY, Moe, & Joe Stampley
Country duo. Bandy was born on 2/12/44 in Meridian, Mississippi. Stampley was born on 6/6/43 in Springhill, Louisiana.

| | | | | | |
|-------|------|-----|-------------|---|----------------|
| 7/21/84 | 205 | 3 | The Good Ol' Boys - Alive & Well ............................ $10 | | Columbia 39426 |

Where's The Dress • He's Back In Texas • Honky Tonk Money • Wild And Crazy Guys • We've Got Our Moe-Joe Workin' • The Boy's Night Out • Daddy's Honky Tonk • Wildlife Sanctuary • Alive And Well • Still On A Roll

### BANJO BARONS ✪
Banjo group conducted by Teo Macero.

| | | | | | |
|-------|------|-----|-------------|---|----------------|
| 4/21/73 | 207 | 2 | Dueling Banjos ............................[I] $12 | | Harmony 32214 |

Dueling Banjos • Blowin' In The Wind • Green, Green • Where Have All The Flowers Gone? • You're So Vain • I Can See Clearly Now • The Green Leaves Of Summer • El Paso • Greenfields • Song Sung Blue

### BANKS, Tony
Born on 3/27/51 in East Heathly, Sussex, England. Keyboardist with Genesis.

| | | | | | |
|-------|------|-----|-------------|---|----------------|
| 7/2/83 | 202 | 3 | The Fugitive ............................................ $10 | | Atlantic 80071 |

with Daryl Stuermer (guitar; Genesis)

This Is Love • Man Of Spells • And The Wheels Keep Turning • Say You'll Never Leave Me • Thirty-Threes • By You • At The Edge Of Night • Charm • Moving Under

### BARBIERI, Gato
Born Leandro Barbieri on 11/28/33 in Rosario, Argentina. Jazz tenor saxophonist.

| | | | | | |
|-------|------|-----|-------------|---|----------------|
| 11/24/73 | 203 | 8 | Chapter One: Latin America ............................[I] $12 | | Impulse 9248 |

Encuentros • India • La China Leoncia Arreo La Correntinada Trajo Entre La Muchachada La Flor De La Juventud • Nunca Mas • To Be Continued

### BARE, Bobby
Born on 4/7/35 in Ironton, Ohio. Country singer/songwriter/guitarist.

| | | | | | |
|-------|------|-----|-------------|---|----------------|
| 8/21/76 | 205 | 6 | 1 The Winner And Other Losers ............................ $12 | | RCA Victor 1786 |

author/composer Shel Silverstein wrote/co-wrote half of the tracks and played harmonica

Climbin' The Ladder And Climbin' The Walls • Baby Wants To Boogie • Keeping Rosie Proud Of Me • Bald Headed Woman • Vince • Lost In Austin • Put A Little Lovin' On Me • Yes, Mr. Rodgers • Brian Hennessey • My Better Half • Dropkick Me, Jesus • The Winner

| | | | | | |
|-------|------|-----|-------------|---|----------------|
| 6/27/81 | 204 | 2 | 2 As Is ............................................ $10 | | Columbia 37157 |

produced by Rodney Crowell; guests include Rosanne Cash, Sonny Curtis and Ricky Skaggs

Dollar Pool Fool • Learning To Live Again • Call Me The Breeze • Take Me As I Am (Or Let Me Go) • Let Him Roll • New Cut Road • She Is Gone • Dropping Out Of Sight • Summer Wages • White Freight Liner Blues

### BAR-KAYS, The
Soul-funk group from Memphis: Larry Dodson (vocals), James Alexander (bass), Barry Wilkins (guitar), Harvey Henderson (sax), Winston Stewart (keyboards) and Alvin Hunter (drums). Four of group's earlier members died in plane crash that also killed Otis Redding on 12/10/67 in Madison, Wisconsin.

| | | | | | |
|-------|------|-----|-------------|---|----------------|
| 2/24/73 | 212 | 5 | Do You See What I See? ............................ $20 | | Volt 8001 |

Do You See What I See? • God Is Watching • Be Yourself • You're The Best Thing That Ever Happened To Me • You're Still My Brother • I Was Made To Love Her • Your Good Thing Is About To Come To An End • It Ain't Easy • Love Pollution • People, Unite To Save Humanity

### BARRÈRE, Paul ✪
Born on 7/3/48 in Burbank, California. Former guitarist of Little Feat.

| | | | | | |
|-------|------|-----|-------------|---|----------------|
| 3/5/83 | 204 | 5 | On My Own Two Feet ............................ $10 | | Mirage 90070 |

Sweet Coquette • High Roller • Fool For You • Love Sweet Love • Who Knows For Sure • She Lays Down The Beat • Fortune Cookie • Along This Lane

### BASIL, Toni
Born Antonia Basilotta in Philadelphia in 1950. Choreographer/actress/video director. Worked on TV shows Shindig and Hullabaloo. Choreographed the movie American Grafitti. Appeared in the movie Easy Rider and others.

| | | | | | |
|-------|------|-----|-------------|---|----------------|
| 2/4/84 | 206 | 2 | Toni Basil ............................ $10 | | Chrysalis 41449 |

Over My Head • I Don't Hear You • Easy For You To Say • Suspense • Go For The Burn • Spacewalkin' The Dog • Street Beat • Do You Wanna Dance • Best Performance

### BASSEY, Shirley
Born on 1/8/37 in Cardiff, Wales. Soul singer.

| | | | | | |
|-------|------|-----|-------------|---|----------------|
| 1/22/77 | 205 | 5 | 1 Shirley Bassey's Greatest Hits ............................[G] $12 | | United Artists 715 [2] |

Goldfinger • Feelings • I, Capricorn • What I Did For Love • I'll Be Your Audience • Something • Diamonds Are Forever • The Greatest Performance Of My Life • For All We Know • Yesterday, When I Was Young • Send In The Clowns • I (Who Have Nothing) • (Where Do I Begin) Love Story • What Are You Doing The Rest Of Your Life? • Nobody Does It Like Me • Never, Never, Never • The Ballad Of The Sad Young Men • Big Spender • And I Love You So • This Is My Life (LaVita)

| | | | | | |
|-------|------|-----|-------------|---|----------------|
| 7/23/77 | 204 | 5 | 2 You Take My Heart Away ............................ $10 | | United Artists 751 |

You Take My Heart Away • Perfect Strangers • Sometimes • This One's For You • Silly Love Songs • Stargazer • Can't Help Falling In Love • I Let You Let Me Down • If • Come In From The Rain • I Need To Be In Love • C'est La Vie

### BATDORF & RODNEY
Duo of John Batdorf and Mark Rodney. Batdorf formed the group Silver in 1976.

| | | | | | |
|-------|------|-----|-------------|---|----------------|
| 3/11/72 | 214 | 1 | Off The Shelf ............................ $12 | | Atlantic 8298 |

Oh My Surprise • Me And My Guitar • Can You See Him • Workin' Man, Blind Man • You Are The One • Don't You Hear Me Callin' • Where Were You And I • Never See His Face Again • One Day • Farm • Let Me Go

### BEAU, Toby — see TOBY

## BE-BOP DELUXE
British rock group: Bill Nelson (vocals), Charles Tumahai (bass) and Simon Fox (drums). Andy Clark (keyboards) joined by 1976.

| 9/27/75 | 203 | 6 | 1 Futurama ............................................................................................... | $12 | Harvest 11432 |

Stage Whispers • Love Of The Madman • Maid In Heaven • Sister Seagull • Sound Track • Music In Dreamland • Jean Cocteau • Between The Worlds • Swan Song

| 2/17/79 | 202 | 6 | 2 The Best Of And The Rest Of Be Bop Deluxe ............................................[K] | $15 | Harvest 11870 [2] |

Axe Victim • Maid In Heaven • Music In Dreamland • Sister Seagull • Sleep That Burns • Ships In The Night • Blazing Apostles • Kiss Of Light • Dance Of The Uncle Sam Humanoids • Forbidden Lovers • Panic In The World • Blimps • Autosexual • Lovers Are Mortal • Shine • Quest For The Harvest Of The Stars • Japan • Speed Of The Wind • Lights • Blue As A Jewel • Face In The Rain • Futurist Manifesto

## BECKETT ○
Born Alston Beckett Cyrus on 8/1/49 in Layou, West Indies. Disco singer/songwriter.

| 8/20/77 | 210 | 1 | Disco Calypso ................................................................................... | $12 | Casablanca 7059 |

Coming High • Legalize The Grass • St. Thomas Mas • Disco Calypso • St. Vincent, I Love You • Oppression

## BEDLAM ○
British hard-rock group: Francesco Aiello (vocals), brothers Dave (guitar) and Dennis (bass) Ball, and Cozy Powell (drums; Whitesnake; Emerson, Lake & Powell; Black Sabbath).

| 9/29/73 | 207 | 3 | Bedlam ............................................................................................ | $20 | Chrysalis 1048 |

I Believe In You (Fire In My Body) • Hot Lips • Sarah • Sweet Sister Mary • Seven Long Years • The Beast • Whisky And Wine • Looking Through Love's Eyes (Busy Dreamin') • Putting On The Flesh • Set Me Free

## BELL, William
Born William Yarborough on 7/16/39 in Memphis. R&B singer.

| 5/1/71 | 209 | 2 | Wow... ............................................................................................. | $25 | Stax 2037 |

I Can't Make It (All By Myself) • 'Till My Back Ain't Got No Bone • All For The Love Of A Woman • My Door Is Always Open • A Penny For Your Thoughts • You'll Want Diamonds • Winding, Winding Road • Somebody's Gonna Get Hurt • I Forgot To Be Your Lover • I'll Be Home

## BENNO, Marc — see RUSSELL, Leon

## BENSON, George
Born on 3/22/43 in Pittsburgh. R&B-jazz singer/guitarist.

| 12/25/76 | 206 | 2 | Blue Benson ............................................................................... [I] | $12 | Polydor 6084 |

guests include Ron Carter (bass), Billy Cobham Jr. (drums) and Herbie Hancock (piano)

Billie's Bounce • Low Down And Dirty • That Lucky Old Sun (Just Rolls Around Heaven All Day) • Thunder Walk • Doobie, Doobie Blues • What's New • I Remember Wes

## BENTON, Barbi ○
Born Barbara Klein on 1/28/50 in Sacramento, California. Country singer/actress/model.

| 9/18/76 | 208 | 1 | Something New ............................................................................. | $12 | Playboy 411 |

Something New • Needing You • In The Winter • #1 With A Heartache • Lucky One • Riding On A Rainbow • Staying Power • Ride Baby Ride • San Diego Serenade • He's A Rebel • Thinking Of You

## BETH, Karen
Folk-rock singer.

| 1/9/71 | 201 | 1 | Harvest | $15 | Decca 75247 |

Like Wine To Me • Last Time • Sometimes True • The Way Back • Hard Luck Mama • Hold Tight • Gentle Place (Song For Tom) • I'm No Good For You • No Apologies • Ribbon • Up To My Neck In High Muddy Waters

## BIRDSONG, Edwin ○
R&B singer/later a rapper from Los Angeles. Sang in the LA Community Choir. Attended Juilliard School. Worked with Roy Ayers as manager and writer from 1976-77.

| 8/28/71 | 218 | 1 | What It Is ....................................................................................... | $15 | Polydor 4071 |

The Uncle Tom Game • The Spirit Of Do...Do • My Father Preaches That God Is The Father • It Aint No Fun Being A Welfare Recipient • When A Newborn Baby Is Born, The World Gets One More Chance • Mr. Money Man • Mongoose • The Old Messiah • Pretty Brown Skin • It's Hard To Move When It's Your Move • God's Home

## BIRTHA ○
Female rock group from Glendale, California: Shele Pinizzotto (guitar), Sherry Hagler (keyboards), Rosemary Butler (bass) and Liver Favela (drums). All share vocals.

| 9/30/72 | 209 | 4 | Birtha .............................................................................................. | $15 | Dunhill 50127 |

Free Spirit • Fine Talking Man • Tuesday • Feeling Lonely • She Was Good To Me • Work On A Dream • Too Much Woman (For A Hen Pecked Man) • Judgement Day • Forgotten Soul

## BISHOP, Elvin
Born on 10/21/42 in Tulsa, Oklahoma. Lead guitarist with The Paul Butterfield Blues Band (1965-68). Bishop's Group and Band included Jo Baker (vocals), Stephen Miller (organ, piano, vocals), Kip Maercklein (bass) and Jon Chambers (drums).

| 1/2/71 | 202 | 1 | 1 Feel It! ......................................................................................... | $15 | Fillmore 30239 |

THE ELVIN BISHOP GROUP
guests include The Pointer Sisters and Mike Carabello and Jose Chepito Areas (both of Santana)

Don't Fight It (Feel It) • I Just Can't Go On • So Good • Crazy Bout You Baby • So Fine • Party Till The Cows Come Home • Hogbottom • Be With Me • As The Years Go Passing By

| 12/2/72 | 206 | 3 | 2 Rock My Soul ............................................................................... | $12 | Epic 31563 |

THE ELVIN BISHOP BAND
Rock My Soul • Holler And Shout • Let It Shine • Don't Mind If I Do • Rock Bottom • Last Mile • Have A Good Time • Wings Of A Bird • Old Man Trouble • Out Behind The Barn • Stomp

| 12/16/78 | 201 | 9 | 3 Hog Heaven | $10 | Capricorn 0215 |

with guest Maria Muldaur
It's A Feelin' • Arkansas • True Love • Southern Dreams • Waterfalls • Oh Babe • Let's Break Down • Right Now Is The Hour • Midnight Creeper

### BLACK HEAT ○
Soul group: Bradley Owens (guitar), Johnell Grey (keyboards), Namon "Chip" Jones (bass), Esco Cromer (drums), Raymond Green (percussion), Ray Thompson (sax, flute) and Rodney Edwards (trumpet). The first five share vocals.

| 4/6/74 | 201 | 9 | No Time To Burn | $12 | Atlantic 7294 |

No Time To Burn • You Should've Listened • Check It All Out • Love The Life You Live • Super Cool • M & M's • Things Change • Rapid Fire • Times Have Changed

### BLANCMANGE ○
British techno-rock duo: Neil Arthur (vocals, guitar) and Stephen Luscombe (keyboards).

| 3/26/83 | 206 | 4 | 1 Happy Families | $10 | Island 90053 |

I Can't Explain • Feel Me • I've Seen The Word • Wasted • Living On The Ceiling • Waves • Kind • Sad Day • Cruel • God's Kitchen

| 9/29/84 | 204 | 3 | 2 Mange Tout | $10 | Sire 25172 |

Don't Tell Me • Game Above My Head • Blind Vision • Time Became The Tide • That's Love That It Is • Murder • See The Train • All Things Are Nice • My Baby • The Day Before You Came

### BLAND, Bobby
Born on 1/27/30 in Rosemark, Tennessee. R&B/blues singer. Nicknamed "Blue." Member of legendary blues band the Beale Streeters in 1949. Inducted into the Rock and Roll Hall of Fame in 1992.

| 9/19/81 | 207 | 2 | 1 Try Me, I'm Real | $10 | MCA 5233 |

Try Me, I'm Real • But I Do • What A Difference A Day Makes • That's How I Feel About You • Givin' Up The Streets For Love • Just You, Just Me • A Song For You, My Son • I Cover The Waterfront • Love Is Where It's At

| 7/17/82 | 201 | 8 | 2 Here We Go Again | $10 | MCA 5297 |

Here We Go Again • Recess In Heaven • Never Let Me Go • Country Love • Exactly, Where It's At • You're About To Win • Is This The Blues • Don't Go To Strangers • We've Had A Good Time

### BLOOD, SWEAT AND TEARS
Rock-jazz fusion group from New York City. Numerous personnel changes. **David Clayton-Thomas** was lead singer from 1969-71; returned in 1974.

| 12/3/77 | 205 | 4 | Brand New Day | $12 | ABC 1015 |

with guest Chaka Khan

Somebody I Trusted (Put Out The Light) • Dreaming As One • Same Old Blues • Lady Put Out The Light • Womanizer • Blue Street • Gimme That Wine • Rock & Roll Queen • Don't Explain

### BLOW, Kurtis
Born Kurt Walker on 8/9/59 in New York City. Pioneering rapper. Began as a disco DJ in Harlem. Appeared in the movie *Krush Groove*.

| 9/17/83 | 203 | 3 | Party Time? | $10 | Mercury 812757 |

Party Time • Big Time Hood • Nervous • Got To Dance • One-Two-Five (Main Street, Harlem, USA)

### BLUES IMAGE
Rock group from Tampa, Florida: Dennis Correll (vocals), Kent Henry (guitar), Frank "Skip" Konte (keyboards), Joe Lala (percussion), Malcolm Jones (bass) and Manuel Bertematti (drums).

| 2/27/71 | 204 | 3 | Red White & Blues Image | $20 | Atco 348 |

Rise Up • Behind Every Man • Gas Lamps And Clay • Take Me Back • It Happens All The Time • Good Life • It's The Truth • Let's Take A Ride • Ain't No Rules In California

### BLUES PROJECT, The
Blues-rock group from New York City: Danny Kalb (vocals, guitar), Steve Katz (guitar), Al Kooper (organ), Andy Kulberg (bass) and Roy Blumenfeld (drums).

| 11/10/73 | 219 | 2 | Reunion In Central Park | [L] $20 | MCA 8003 [2] |

**THE ORIGINAL BLUES PROJECT**
recorded on 6/24/73

Louisiana Blues • Steve's Song • I Can't Keep From Cryin' Sometimes • You Can't Catch Me • Fly Away • Caress Me Baby • Catch The Wind • (I Heard Her Say) Wake Me, Shake Me • Two Trains Running

### BLUE STEEL ○
Rock band from Texas: Leonard Arnold (vocals, guitar), Richard Bowden and Howard Burke (guitars), Marc Durham (bass), and Mickey McGee and Michael Huey (drums). Bowden later formed country-novelty duo with Sandy Pinkard.

| 10/6/79 | 203 | 2 | No More Lonely Nights | $10 | Infinity 9018 |

No More Lonely Nights • Bulldog • Guitar Song • Baby, You Can't Dance • Twist One Up • Shark • I Should Be Sleeping • Honey Dew • Take Me • Willie And Waylon • Hoo-Doo-Voo-Doo

### BOHANNON, Hamilton
Born on 3/7/42 in Newnan, Georgia. Drummer for Stevie Wonder from 1965-67.

| 8/27/77 | 203 | 4 | 1 Phase II | $12 | Mercury 1159 |

with guest Ray Parker Jr.

Andrea • But What Is A Dream • Daddy's Little Son • Bohannon Disco Symphony • Isn't It A Beautiful Morning • Just Doing My Thing • Moving Fast

| 8/4/79 | 202 | 3 | 2 Too Hot To Hold | $12 | Mercury 3778 |

The Groove Machine • The Boogie Train • Stop And Go • I'll Be Here For You • The Time Is Now • Andrea • Love Floats

### BOLTON, Michael
Born Michael Bolotin on 2/26/53 in New Haven, Connecticut. Lead singer of Blackjack in the late '70s. Began recording as Michael Bolton in 1983.

| 8/9/75 | 209 | 3 | Michael Bolotin | $15 | RCA Victor 0992 |

Your Love • Give Me A Reason • Dream While You Can • Tell Me How You Feel • It's All Comin' Back To You • It's Just A Feelin' • Everybody Needs A Reason • You're No Good • Time Is On My Side • Take Me As I Am • Lost In The City

### BOND, Graham ○
Born on 10/28/37 in Romford, England. Died on 5/8/74 (discovered under the wheels of a train). British R&B pioneer. Alto saxophonist/organist. Joined Alexis Korner's Blues Inc. in 1962. Formed the Graham Bond Organization in 1963. Joined **Ginger Baker's** Air Force.

| 1/30/71 | 210 | 1 | Holy Magick | $20 | Mercury 61327 |

guests include Rick Grech (bass; **Family**, Traffic, Blind Faith) and Bond's then-wife, Diane Stewart (vocals)

Holy Magick (Suite) • Return Of Arthur • The Magician • The Judgement • My Archangel Mikael

### BONEY M.
Vocal group created in Germany by producer/composer Frank Farian. Consisted of Marcia Barrett, Maizie Williams, Liz Mitchell and Bobby Farrell. All were from the West Indies.

| 12/17/77 | 206 | 3 | Love For Sale ............................................................... $12 Atlantic 19145 |

Ma Baker • Love For Sale • Daddy Cool • Have You Ever Seen The Rain • Gloria, Can You Waddle • Plantation Boy • Motherless Child • Silent Lover • A Woman Can Change A Man • Still I Am Sad

### BONGOS, The ☺
Pop-rock group from Hoboken, New Jersey: Richard Barone (vocals), James Mastro (guitar), Rob Norris (bass) and Frank Giannini (drums).

| 3/16/85 | 209 | 1 | Beat Hotel ............................................................... $10 RCA Victor 8043 |

Space Jungle • Apache Dancing • Brave New World • A Story (Written In The Sky) • The Beat Hotel • Come Back To Me • Splinters • She Starts Shaking • Totem Pole • Blow Up

### BONUS, Jack ☺
Blues-rock singer/guitarist/saxophonist from San Francisco.

| 6/17/72 | 203 | 3 | Jack Bonus ............................................................... $15 Grunt 1005 |

The Hobo Song • St. Louis Missouri Boy • Cold Chicago Wind • Aphro-Kay • Pecan Pie (Extract) • Sweet Mahidabelle • Let The Children Be • The Little Boy Who Flew Away • Mother Dear • Ay Que Lyn

### BOOKER T. & THE MG'S
Interracial R&B band formed by sessionmen from Stax Records in Memphis. Consisted of Booker T. Jones (keyboards; b: 11/12/44), **Steve Cropper** (guitar), Donald "Duck" Dunn and Willie Hall (drums). Group inducted into the Rock & Roll Hall of Fame in 1992.

| 4/2/77 | 209 | 3 | Universal Language ............................................................... $12 Asylum 1093 |

Sticky Stuff • Grab Bag • Space Nuts • Love Wheels • Moto Cross • Last Tango In Memphis • M.G.'s Salsa • Tie Stick • Reincarnation

### BOOMTOWN RATS, The
Post-punk group from Dun Laoghaire, Ireland: Bob Geldof (vocals), Gerry Cott and Garry Roberts (guitars), Johnnie Fingers (keyboards), Pete Briquette (bass) and Simon Crowe (drums). Geldof organized Band Aid.

| 9/25/82 | 201 | 5 | V Deep ............................................................... $10 Columbia 38195 |

Never In A Million Years • The Bitter End • Talking In Code • He Watches It All • A Storm Breaks • Charmed Lives • House On Fire • Whitehall • Skin On Skin • The Little Death • ...House Burned Down

### BOSTON POPS ORCHESTRA
Founded in 1885 by Henry Lee Higginson, conductor of the Boston Symphony Orchestra. Arthur Fiedler (b: 12/17/1894 in Boston; d: 7/10/79) joined the orchestra in 1915 as a violist; began his reign as its conductor in 1930 and remained until his death.

| 7/3/71 | 219 | 1 | Encore (Fiedler's Greatest Hits) ............................................. [G-I] $12 Polydor 5005 |

**BOSTON POPS/ARTHUR FIEDLER**

Love Theme From "Romeo And Juliet" • Raindrops Keep Fallin' On My Head • Theme From "Midnight Cowboy" • Do You Know The Way To San Jose? • Hava Nagila • Aquarius • Malambo • Blue Danube Waltz • Richard Rodgers' Waltzes: Lover/Falling In Love With Love/Oh, What A Beautiful Mornin'/It's A Grand Night For Singing • The Stars And Stripes Forever • Sabre Dance

### BOWIE, David
Born David Robert Jones on 1/8/47 in London. Pop-rock singer/actor. Performed under several personas, "Ziggy Stardust" and "Thin White Duke" among them. Inducted into the Rock and Roll Hall of Fame in 1996. *Top Pop Albums*: 33.

| 6/26/82 | 204 | 2 | Bertolt Brecht's Baal .......................................... [M-TV] $10 RCA Victor 4346 |

songs from BBC-TV production (aired 3/2/82) of play by Bertolt Brecht, composer famous for "Mack The Knife"; Bowie starred as Baal

Baal's Hymm • Remembering Marie A. • Ballad Of The Adventurers • The Drowned Girl • The Dirty Song

### BRADY BUNCH, The
Vocal group consisting of the child actors of TV's *The Brady Bunch*. Barry Williams (Greg), Chris Knight (Peter), Mike Lookinland (Bobby), Maureen McCormick (Marsha), Eve Plumb (Jan) and Susan Olsen (Cindy).

| 1/20/73 | 210 | 4 | 1 The Kids From The Brady Bunch ........................................ $20 Paramount 6037 |

Love Me Do • It's A Sunshine Day • Keep On • Ben • Playin' The Field • Candy (Sugar Shoppe) • In No Hurry • Saturday In The Park • Merry-Go-Round • You Need That Rock 'N Roll • Drummer Man

| 7/28/73 | 218 | 5 | 2 Phonographic Album ........................................ $20 Paramount 6058 |

Zuckerman's Famous Pig • I'd Love You To Want Me • Colorado Snow • Parallel Lines • A Simple Man • Everything I Do • Yo-Yo Man • Summer Breeze • Charlotte's Web • Gonna Find A Rainbow • River Song (Theme From "Tom Sawyer")

### BRAINS, The ☺
New-wave rock group from Atlanta: Tom Gray (vocals), Rick Price (guitar), Bryan Smithwick (bass) and Charles Wolff (drums).

| 4/11/81 | 208 | 1 | Electronic Eden ........................................ $10 Mercury 4012 |

Dream Life • One In A Million • Hypnotized • No Tears Tonite • Eyes Of Ice • Asphalt Wonderland • Little Girl Gone • Ambush • Heart In The Street • House Of Cards • Collision

### BRAINSTORM
R&B-disco band from Detroit: Belita Karen "B.B." Woods (vocals), Charles Overton (sax, vocals), Larry H. "Leap" Sims (horns), Trenita Womack (percussion) and Renell Gonsalves (drums; son of famous Duke Ellington saxman Paul Gonsalves).

| 5/19/79 | 204 | 3 | Funky Entertainment ........................................ $10 Tabu 35749 |

Hot For You • A Case Of The Boogie • Popcorn • Funky Entertainment • You Put A Charge In My Life • Don't Let Me Catch You With Your Groove Down

### BRAMLETT, Bonnie
Half of Delaney & Bonnie. Born Bonnie Lynn O'Farrell on 11/8/44 in Acton, Illinois. Married to Delaney Bramlett from 1967-72. Began acting as Bonnie Sheridan in 1987. Regular on TV's *Roseanne*.

| 6/30/73 | 222 | 2 | Sweet ........................................ $15 Columbia 31786 |

Able, Qualified And Ready • Singer Man • Crazy 'Bout My Baby • Got To Get Down • Good Vibrations • Rollin' • Celebrate Life • The Sorrow Of Love • (You Don't Know) How Glad I Am • Don't Wanna Go Down There

| DEBUT | PEAK | WKS | Album Title | $ | Label & Number |
|-------|------|-----|-------------|---|----------------|

## BRAND X
British jazz-fusion group: Phil Collins (drums; Genesis), John Goodsall (guitar), Robin Lumley (keyboards), Percy Jones (bass), Morris Pert (percussion) and Kenwood Dennard (drums; left by 1980). Peter Robinson (keyboards) and Mike Clarke (drums) joined by 1980.

| 12/17/77 | 204 | 4 | 1 Livestock .................................................................................[I] | $12 | Passport 9824 |

Nightmare Patrol • -Ish • Euthanasia Waltz • Isis Mourning (Part 1 & Part 2) • Malaga Virgen

| 7/19/80 | 204 | 4 | 2 Do They Hurt? ...........................................................................[I] | $10 | Passport 9845 |

Noddy Goes To Sweden • Voidarama • Act Of Will • Fragile! • Cambodia • Triumphant Limp • D.M.Z.

## BREAKS, The ☼
Pop group from Memphis: Susanne Jerome Taylor (vocals), Pat Taylor (guitar), Tom Ward (keyboards), Rob Caudill (bass) and Russ Caudill (drums).

| 9/17/83 | 203 | 5 | The Breaks ................................................................................. | $10 | RCA Victor 4675 |

She Wants You • You Stole My Heart • Don't Mislead Me • Fire In The Wire • Green Eyes • Wishy Washy • I Play The Fool • Lonely Girls • Keepin' The Love Alive • The Last To Know

## BRECKER BROTHERS, The
Horn duo of Philadelphia-born brothers Randy (b: 11/27/45; trumpet) and Michael (b: 3/29/49; reeds) Brecker. Both are prolific sessionmen. The brothers began recording together in their group Dreams, also with Spyro Gyra.

| 11/4/78 | 207 | 1 | 1 Heavy Metal Be-Bop ....................................................................[I] | $10 | Arista 4185 |

East River (La-Di-Da) • Inside Out • Some Skunk Funk • Sponge • Funky Sea, Funky Dew • Squids

| 6/28/80 | 204 | 1 | 2 Detente.......................................................................................[I] | $10 | Arista 4272 |

produced by George Duke; guests include **Airto** (percussion), and Irene Cara and Luther Vandross (background vocals)
You Ga (Ta Give It) • Not Tonight • Don't Get Funny With My Money • Tee'd Off • You Left Something Behind • Squish • Dream Theme • Baffled • I Don't Know Either

## BREWER, Teresa ☼
Born Theresa Breuer on 5/7/31 in Toledo, Ohio. Pop singer.

| 11/10/73 | 220 | 2 | Music, Music, Music ..................................................................... | $15 | Flying Dutchman 12013 |

Music, Music, Music • Ol' Man Mose • Another Useless Day • Playground In My Mind • Give Me Love (Give Me Peace On Earth) • Music To The Man • Bei Mir Bist Du Schon (Means That Your Grand) • Late Night Movie • Delta Dawn • School Days

## BREWER & SHIPLEY
Folk-rock duo formed in Los Angeles: Mike Brewer (b: 1944 in Oklahoma City) and Tom Shipley (b: 1942 in Mineral Ridge, Ohio).

| 8/2/75 | 202 | 1 | Welcome To Riddle Bridge ........................................................... | $12 | Capitol 11402 |

Commercial Success • Indian Summer • On The Road In Kansas City • Brighter Days • So Satisfied • Brain Damage • Crying In The Valley • Rock & Roll Hostage • Don't It Feel Like Heaven • Hearts Overflowing

## BRIGHTER SIDE OF DARKNESS ☼
R&B vocal group from Chicago: Darryl Lamont, Ralph Eskridge, Randolph Murph and Larry Washington.

| 4/14/73 | 202 | 4 | Love Jones ................................................................................. | $12 | 20th Century 405 |

Just A Little Bit • Oh Baby • I Owe You Love • Love Jones • I'm A Loser • Love Jones (instrumental) • Something To Remember You By • Just A Little Bit (instrumental) • Summer Ride • I'm The Guy

## BROADWAY SYMPHONY ORCHESTRA ☼
Studio group assembled by producer Luther Henderson.

| 7/3/82 | 207 | 1 | Turned-On Broadway ...................................................................[I] | $10 | RCA Victor 4327 |

Turned-On Broadway No. 1: Overture/There's No Business Like Show Business/That's Entertainment/Lullaby Of Broadway/Everything's Coming Up Roses/Some People/I Could Have Danced All Night/Hey, Look Me Over/Cabaret/Hello, Dolly!/Don't Cry For Me Argentina/What I Did For Love/Tomorrow/Jellicle Cat/New York, New York/Come, Friends, Who Plough The Sea/There's No Business Like Show Business • Turned-On Broadway No. 2: Another Op'nin', Another Show/Let Me Entertain You/Give My Regards To Broadway/I Got Rhythm/I'm Gonna Wash That Man Right Outa My Hair/Some Enchanted Evening/Shall We Dance?/If Ever I Would Leave You/Just In Time/Don't Rain On My Parade/Sit Down, You're Rockin' The Boat/Once In Love With Amy/I Want To Be Happy/Bali Ha'i/I've Got Your Number/Diamonds Are A Girl's Best Friend/If My Friends Could See Me Now/Let Me Entertain You • Ballads On Broadway: Maria/Tonight/On The Street Where You Live/Corner Of The Sky/Send In The Clowns/I Got It Bad And That Ain't Good/The Impossible Dream/If You Believe • Rock Down Broadway No. 1: Walk Him Up The Stairs/I Got Love/One Last Kiss/We Go Together/Magic To Do/Aquarius/Ease On Down The Road • Rock Down Broadway No. 2: Ease On Down The Road/New Fangled Preacher Man/Merrily We Roll Along/I'll Never Fall In Love Again/Superstar/Song Of The King/Steppin' To The Bad Side/Buenos Aires • Waltzes On Broadway: Carousel Waltz/Could I Leave You?/Wait Till You See Her/The Most Beautiful Girl In The World/Love Makes The World Go 'Round/Sunrise, Sunset/Wunderbar/Night Waltz/Matchmaker, Matchmaker/I'm All Smiles/I Feel Pretty/Look To The Rainbow/A Wonderful Guy/Hello, Young Lovers/Oh, What A Beautiful Mornin'/It's A Grand Night For Singing • Broadway Latin: America/Two Ladies In De Shade Of De Banana Tree/Hernando's Hideaway/Whatever Lola Wants (Lola Gets)/Mu-Cha-Cha/The Rain In Spain/Push De Button/America/Habañera • Henderson And Sullivan: We Sail The Ocean Blue/When I Was A Lad/Never Mind The Why And Wherefore/I Am The Monarch Of The Sea/I'm Called Little Buttercup/Tit-Willow/Three Little Maids From School/Here's A How-De-Do!/I've Got A Little List/Behold The Lord High Executioner/Climbing Over Rocky Mountain/With Cat-Like Tread (Come, Friends, Who Plough The Sea)

## BROOD, Herman, And His Wild Romance
Born on 11/5/46 in Zwolle, Holland. Rock singer.

| 6/28/80 | 207 | 2 | Go Nutz ...................................................................................... | $10 | Ariola America 1500 |

Go Nutz • I Love You Like I Love Myself • I Don't Need You • Easy Pick Up • I'll Be Doggone • You Can't Beat Me • Hot Shot • Old Memories • Stop Messin' Round In My Mind • Born Before My Time • Beauty Is Only Skin Deep • Right On The Money

### BROOKS, Albert ○
Born Albert Einstein on 7/22/47 in Los Angeles. Comedian/director/actor. Son of radio comedian Parkyarkarkus. Acted in the movies *Lost In America*, *Broadcast News*, *Mother* and more. Brother of comedian daredevil Super Dave Osborne.

**1/19/74 · 211 · 3** — **1 Comedy Minus One** ............................................................[C] $12 — ABC 800
Introduction • Memoirs Of An Opening Act - Part 1 • What Do You Think Of The Record? • Memoirs Of An Opening Act - Part 2 • Another Kooky Krazy Kall • Another Introduction And A Stereo Demonstration • Rewriting The National Anthem • Another Kooky Krazy Kall • Comedy Minus One

**7/26/75 · 205 · 3** — **2 A Star Is Bought** ............................................................[C] $12 — Asylum 1035
In The Beginning • Phone Call To Americans • Near The Beginning • Party From Outer Space (Featuring Phony Hits) • In The Middle • Phone Calls From Americans • An End In Sight • Love Song • The End Of The First Beginning • A New Beginning • Promotional Gimmick • Call This Cut Three, Side Two • The Englishman-German-Jew Blues • The Beginning Of The End • The Albert Brooks Show #112 (August 4, 1943) • The End

### BROOM, Bobby ○
Jazz guitarist from New York City.

**8/15/81 · 203 · 7** — **Clean Sweep** ............................................................[I] $10 — Arista/GRP 5504
Clean Sweep • No Bad Vibes • Remember When • She's My Reason • Saturday Night • Niqui • Share My Love • Con Alma

### BROWN, Dennis ○
Born in February 1956 in Kingston, Jamaica. Reggae singer/songwriter.

**5/2/81 · 208 · 2** — **Foul Play** ............................................................ $10 — A&M 4850
On The Rocks • The Existence Of Jah • Come On Baby • The World Is Troubled • I Need Your Love • Foul Play • Your Man • If I Had The World • If I Follow My Heart • The Cheater

### BROWN, James
Born on 5/3/33 in Barnwell, South Carolina; raised in Augusta, Georgia. One of the originators of "Soul" music. Inducted into the Rock and Roll Hall of Fame in 1986. Won Grammy's Lifetime Achievement Award in 1992. *Top Pop Albums*: 49.

**10/6/73 · 202 · 3** — **Soul Classics Vol. II** ............................................................[G] $25 — Polydor 5402
Get On The Good Foot - Part 1 • Honky Tonk - Part 1 • Talking Loud And Saying Nothing - Part 1 • I'm A Greedy Man - Part 1 • I Got Ants In My Pants - Part 1 • There It Is - Part 1 • Talking Loud And Saying Nothing - Part 2 • King Heroin • I Got A Bag Of My Own • Think

### BROWN, Jocelyn ○
Born and raised in North Carolina. Female R&B singer.

**11/24/84 · 208 · 1** — **Somebody Else's Guy** ............................................................ $10 — Vinyl Dreams 1
Somebody Else's Guy • I'm Caught Up (In A One Night Love Affair) • Hot Blood • I Wish You Would • Ain't No Mountain High Enough • Hot Natured Woman • I'm Somebody Else's Guy [rap version by Frederick "M.C. Count" Linton]

### BROWN, Peter
Born on 7/11/53 in Blue Island, Illinois. Disco vocalist/keyboardist/producer.

**1/26/80 · 206 · 4** — **Stargazer** ............................................................ $10 — Drive 108
Crank It Up • It's Alright • Stargazer • Got To Get The Show On The Road • Leadmeon • West Of The North Star • Love In Our Hearts • Penguin

### BROWN, Toni — see TONI & TERRY

### BROWNSVILLE STATION
Rock group from Ann Arbor, Michigan: Michael Lutz (vocals, bass), Michael "Cub" Koda and Bruce Nazarian (guitars) and Henry Weck (drums).

**6/4/77 · 204 · 2** — **Brownsville Station** ............................................................ $12 — Private Stock 2026
Hot Spit • Sleazy Louise • Lady (Put The Light On Me) • Lover • Mr. Johnson Sez • (Throw Me A) Lifeline • Rockers' N' Rollers • My Friend Jack • Ain't That A Shame • The Martian Boogie

### BRUBECK, Dave
Born David Warren on 12/6/20 in Concord, California. His quartet was one of America's all-time most popular jazz groups on college campuses in the '50s and '60s. Two Generations included his sons: Darius (keyboards), Chris (trombone) and Danny (drums). Dave won Grammy's Lifetime Achievement Award in 1996.

**11/9/74 · 206 · 2** — **Brother, The Great Spirit Made Us All** ............................................................[I] $12 — Atlantic 1660
**DAVE BRUBECK: TWO GENERATIONS OF BRUBECK**
Mr. Broadway • Forty Days • The Duke • It's A Raggy Waltz • Sky Scape • Temptation Boogie • Ragaroni • Christopher Columbus

### BRUCE, Jack
Born on 5/14/43 in Lanarkshire, Scotland. Bassist for **Cream**.

**8/14/71 · 202 · 4** — **1 Harmony Row** ............................................................ $15 — Atco 365
Can You Follow? • Escape To The Royal Wood (On Ice) • You Burned The Tables On Me • There's A Forest • Morning Story • Folk Song • Smiles And Grins • Post War • A Letter Of Thanks • Victoria Sage • The Consul At Sunset

**11/11/72 · 204 · 5** — **2 At His Best** ............................................................[K] $20 — Polydor 3505 [2]
Never Tell Your Mother She's Out Of Tune • Morning Story • Theme For An Imaginary Western • Post War • Tickets To Waterfalls • Folk Song • You Burned The Tables On Me • He The Richmond • Victoria Sage • A Letter Of Thanks • The Clearout • Hckhh Blues • Boston Ball Game, 1967 • Rope Ladder To The Moon • Weird Of Hermiston • Smiles And Grins • To Isengard • The Consul At Sunset • Can You Follow?

### BRUCE, Lenny
Born Leonard Alfred Schneider on 10/13/25 in Long Island, New York. Died of a heroin overdose on 8/3/66. Satirical comedian. Dustin Hoffman portrayed Bruce in the 1974 autobiographical movie.

**3/29/75 · 206 · 4** — **The Law, Language And Lenny Bruce** ............................................................[C] $20 — Warner 9101
no track titles listed on this album

**BUCKLEY, Tim**
Born on 2/14/47 in Washington, D.C. Died of a heroin/morphine overdose on 6/29/75. Singer/songwriter. Father of Jeff Buckley.

| | | | | | |
|---|---|---|---|---|---|
| 10/27/73 | 201 | 5 | 1 Sefronia .......................................................... | $15 | DiscReet 2157 |

Dolphins • Honey Man • Because Of You • Peanut Man • Martha • Quicksand • I Know I'd Recognize Your Face • Stone In Love • Sefronia - After Asklepiades, After Kafka • Sefronia - The King's Chain • Sally Go 'Round The Roses

| | | | | | |
|---|---|---|---|---|---|
| 10/19/74 | 208 | 2 | 2 Look At The Fool .............................................. | $15 | DiscReet 2301 |

Look At The Fool • Bring It On Up • Helpless • Freeway Blues • Tijuana Moon • Ain't It Peculiar • Who Could Deny You • Mexicali Voodoo • Down In The Street • Wanda Lu

**BUFFETT, Jimmy**
Born on 12/25/46 in Pascagoula, Mississippi; raised in Mobile, Alabama. Settled in Key West in 1971. *Top Pop Albums*: 23.

| | | | | | |
|---|---|---|---|---|---|
| 7/28/73 | 205 | 2 | A White Sport Coat And A Pink Crustacean ......... | $15 | Dunhill 50150 |

The Great Filling Station Holdup • Railroad Lady • He Went To Paris • Grapefruit - Juicy Fruit • Cuban Crime Of Passion • Why Don't We Get Drunk • Peanut Butter Conspiracy • They Don't Dance Like Carmen No More • I Have Found Me A Home • My Lovely Lady • Death Of An Unpopular Poet

**BULLENS, Cindy ☉**
Born in 1953 in West Newbury, Massachusetts. Pop-rock singer/guitarist.

| | | | | | |
|---|---|---|---|---|---|
| 3/24/79 | 202 | 2 | 1 Desire Wire ..................................................... | $10 | United Artists 933 |

Survivor • Anxious Heart • Desire Wire • Time 'N Charges • High School History • Mean In Your Heart • Hot Tears • Knee Deep In Love • Finally Rockin'

| | | | | | |
|---|---|---|---|---|---|
| 12/15/79+ | 203 | 5 | 2 Steal The Night .............................................. | $10 | Casablanca 7185 |

Full Tilt Rocker • Real To Real • Trust Me • Hurry Up Forever • Steal The Night Away • Too Close To Home • Powerless • Raincheck On Romance • Two-Track Mind • Holding Me Crazy

**BUOYS, The ☉**
Rock group from Wilkes-Barre, Pennsylvania: Bill Kelly (vocals), Carl Siracuse (guitar), Fran Brozena (keyboards), Jerry Hludzik (bass) and Chris Hanlon (drums). **Rupert Holmes** was their composer/arranger.

| | | | | | |
|---|---|---|---|---|---|
| 8/14/71 | 202 | 3 | The Buoys ........................................................ | $20 | Scepter 24001 |

Give Up Your Guns • Castles • Sunny Days • Memories • The Prince Of Thieves • Timothy • Tell Me Heaven Is Here • Bloodknot • Tomorrow • Absent Friend

**BURNETT, T-Bone**
Born John Henry Burnett on 1/14/48 in St. Louis; raised in Fort Worth, Texas. Rock singer/songwriter/guitarist. Married singer Sam (Leslie) Phillips.

| | | | | | |
|---|---|---|---|---|---|
| 10/23/82 | 208 | 1 | Trap Door ......................................................... | $10 | Warner 23691 |

Hold On Tight • Diamonds Are A Girl's Best Friend • I Wish You Could Have Seen Her Dance • A Ridiculous Man • Poetry • Trap Door

**BURNETTE, Billy ☉**
Born on 5/8/53 in Memphis. Son of Dorsey Burnette, nephew of Johnny Burnette, and cousin of Rocky Burnette. Member of Fleetwood Mac from 1987-1993.

| | | | | | |
|---|---|---|---|---|---|
| 11/8/80 | 208 | 2 | Billy Burnette ................................................... | $10 | Columbia 36792 |

In Just A Heartbeat • Oh, Susan • Danger Zone • Don't Say No • Rockin' L.A. • Honey Hush • Rockin' With Somebody New • One Night • Sittin' On Ready • Angeline • Tear It Up

**BURNS & SCHREIBER ☉**
Comedy duo of TV writers/actors/producers Jack Burns (b: New York City) and Avery Schreiber (b: 4/9/35 in Chicago). Had own TV variety series, *The Burns And Schreiber Comedy Hour*, in summer of 1973.

| | | | | | |
|---|---|---|---|---|---|
| 12/1/73 | 215 | 1 | Burns' & Schreiber's Pure B.S.! ....................... [C] | $15 | Little David 1006 |

Dial-A-Friend • Youth Wants To Know • The Faith Healer: Holy Moley/First Phone Call/Giant Communist Frogs/Second Phone Call • The Man From P.R.O.D. • Family Reunion (Homecoming) • Booze • The Cab Driver

**BUSH, Kate**
Born on 7/30/58 in Bexleyheath, Kent, England. Singer/songwriter with influential idiosyncratic style.

| | | | | | |
|---|---|---|---|---|---|
| 2/18/84 | 201 | 7 | Lionheart ......................................................... | $10 | EMI America 17008 |

Symphony In Blue • Medley: In Search Of Peter Pan/When You Wish Upon A Star • Wow • Don't Push Your Foot On The Heartbrake • Oh England My Lionheart • Fullhouse • In The Warm Room • Kashka From Baghdad • Coffee Homeground • Hammer Horror

**BUTLER, Jerry**
Born on 12/8/39 in Sunflower, Mississippi. R&B singer. Known as "The Iceman."

| | | | | | |
|---|---|---|---|---|---|
| 11/4/72 | 212 | 2 | 1 Melinda ........................................................ [S] | $15 | Pride 0006 |

Speak The Truth To The People (Frankie's Theme) • Melinda Title Theme • Part III • Tank's Theme • Love Is • Melinda Latino • I Can't Let You Go • The Blues (Dope Pusher's Theme) • Music For Tank's Boat • Melinda Reprise

| | | | | | |
|---|---|---|---|---|---|
| 7/14/73 | 201 | 11 | 2 The Love We Have, The Love We Had | $12 | Mercury 660 |

**JERRY BUTLER & BRENDA LEE EAGER**
As The Seasons Change • Lean On Me • I Like Your Lovin' • If The World Were Mine • Can't Understand It • How Long Will It Last • Ever Since I Can Remember • The Love We Had Stays On My Mind • Take Me In Your Arms (Rock Me A Little While) • Were We Lovers, Were We Friends

**BYRD, Donald**
Born on 12/9/32 in Detroit. R&B-jazz trumpeter/flugelhorn player. Founded The Blackbyrds in 1973 while teaching jazz at Howard University in Washington, D.C.

| | | | | | |
|---|---|---|---|---|---|
| 11/24/79 | 204 | 1 | Donald Byrd And 125th Street, N.Y.C. ............... | $10 | Elektra 247 |

Pretty Baby • Gold The Moon, White The Sun • Giving It Up • Marilyn • People Suppose To Be Free • Veronica • Morning • I Love You

**B'ZZ, The ☉**
Rock group from Chicago: Tom Holland (vocals), Michael Tafoya (guitar), Anatole Halinkovitch (keyboards), David Angel (bass) and Stephan Riley (drums).

| | | | | | |
|---|---|---|---|---|---|
| 3/12/83 | 210 | 1 | Get Up ............................................................. | $10 | Epic 38230 |

Get Up Get Angry • Too Much To Ask For • Caught In The Middle • Steal My Love • When You Love • Make It Through The Night • I Love The Way • Take Your Time • Not My Girl • Runaway Love Affair

# C

## CAFÉ JACQUES ○
Pop-rock trio: Chris Thomson (vocals), Mike Ogletree (guitar) and Peter Veitch (keyboards).

| 4/1/78 | 210 | 1 | **Round The Back** .................................................... | $10 | Columbia 35294 |

with guest Phil Collins (drums)

Meaningless • Ain't No Love In The Heart Of The City • Sands Of Singapore • Farewell My Lovely • Eberehtel • Dark Eyed Johnny • Sandra's A Phonie • None Of Your Business • Crime Passionelle • Lifeline

## CALE, John
Born on 12/4/40 in Garnant, South Wales. Founding member of **The Velvet Underground**.

| 9/6/75 | 203 | 4 | 1 **Slow Dazzle** .................................................... | $12 | Island 9317 |

Mr. Wilson • Taking It All Away • Dirty-Ass Rock 'N' Roll • Darling I Need You • Rollaroll • Heartbreak Hotel • Ski Patrol • I'm Not The Loving Kind • Guts • The Jeweller

| 2/9/80 | 201 | 3 | 2 **Sabotage/Live** .............................. [L] | $12 | I.R.S. 004 |

recorded at the CBGB club in New York City in June 1979

Mercenaries (Ready For War) • Baby You Know • Evidence • Dr. Mudd • Walkin' The Dog • Captain Hook • Only Time Will Tell • Sabotage • Chorale

## CALL, The
Rock group from California: Michael Been (vocals, guitar), Tom Ferrier (guitar), Jim Goodwin (keyboards), Joe Reed (bass) and Scott Musick (drums).

| 6/16/84 | 204 | 3 | **Scene Beyond Dreams** .................................................... | $10 | Mercury 422818 |

Scene Beyond Dreams • The Burden • Tremble • Delivered • Heavy Hand • Promise And Threat • One Life Leads To Another • Apocalypse • Notified

## CAMEL
Rock group from Surrey, England: Andy Latimer (guitar), Colin Bass (bass), Jan Schelhass and Kit Watkins (keyboards), and Andy Ward (drums).

| 1/12/80 | 208 | 1 | **I Can See Your House From Here** .................................................... | $10 | Arista 4254 |

with guest Phil Collins (drums)

Wait • Your Love Is Stranger Than Mine • Eye Of The Storm • Who We Are • Survival • Hymn To Her • Neon Magic • Remote Romance • Ice

## CAMPBELL, Glen
Born on 4/22/36 in Delight, Arkansas. Country singer/guitarist/actor. Prolific studio musician in the 1960s. Hosted TV's *The Glen Campbell Goodtime Hour* from 1968-72. *Top Pop Albums*: 25.

| 1/19/74 | 205 | 1 | **I Remember Hank Williams** .................................................... | $12 | Capitol 11253 |

I Could Never Be Ashamed Of You • Your Cheatin' Heart • I'm So Lonesome I Could Cry • Half As Much • Wedding Bells • You Win Again • Mansion On The Hill • Take These Chains From My Heart • Cold, Cold Heart • I Can't Help It (If I'm Still In Love With You)

## CANNED HEAT
Blues-rock band from Los Angeles: Bob "The Bear" Hite (vocals, harmonica), Henry Vestine and Richard Hite (guitars), James Shane (bass), Ed Beyer (keyboards) and Adolfo "Fito" de la Parra (drums). Bob Hite died of a drug-related heart attack on 4/6/81 (age 36). Vestine died of heart failure on 10/20/97 (age 52).

| 4/21/73 | 209 | 4 | 1 **The New Age** .................................................... | $15 | United Artists 049 |

Keep It Clean • Harley Davidson Blues • Don't Deceive Me • You Can Run, But You Sure Can't Hide • Lookin' For My Rainbow • Rock & Roll Music • Framed • Election Blues • So Long Wrong

| 2/2/74 | 217 | 5 | 2 **One More River To Cross** .................................................... | $12 | Atlantic 7289 |

One More River To Cross • L.A. Town • I Need Someone • Bagful Of Boogie • I'm A Hog For You Baby • You Am What You Am • Shake, Rattle & Roll • Bright Times Are Comin' • Highway 401 • We Remember Fats (Fats Domino Medley): Introduction/The Fat Man/I'm In Love Again/I'm Walkin'/Whole Lot Of Loving/Let The Four Winds Blow/I'm Ready/So Long

## CAPTAIN BEEFHEART & THE MAGIC BAND
Born Don Van Vliet on 1/15/41 in Glendale, California. Multi-octave rock singer. Backed by various personnel. Retired from music in 1986 to become a professional painter.

| 1/30/71 | 203 | 1 | 1 **Lick My Decals Off, Baby** .................................................... | $50 | Straight 6420 |

Lick My Decals Off, Baby • Doctor Dark • I Love You, You Big Dummy • Peon • Bellerin' Plain • Woe-Is-Uh-Me-Bop • Japan In A Dishpan • I Wanna Find A Woman That'll Hold My Big Toe Till I Have To Go • Petrified Forest • One Red Rose That I Mean • The Buggy Boogie Woogie • The Smithsonian Institute Blues (Or The Big Dig) • Space-Age Couple • The Clouds Are Full Of Wine (Not Whiskey Or Rye) • Flash Gordon's Ape

| 10/25/80 | 203 | 2 | 2 **Doc At The Radar Station** .................................................... | $10 | Virgin 13148 |

Hot Head • Ashtray Heart • A Carrot Is As Close As A Rabbit Gets To A Diamond • Run Paint Run Run • Sue Egypt • Brickbats • Dirty Blue Gene • Best Batch Yet • Telephone • Flavor Bud Living • Sheriff Of Hong Kong • Making Love To A Vampire With A Monkey On My Knee

## CAPTAIN SKY
Born Daryl L. Cameron on 7/10/57 in Chicago. R&B-funk singer/songwriter/producer.

| 10/25/80 | 210 | 1 | **Concerned Party #1** .................................................... | $10 | TEC 1202 |

Elementary School Of Funk • Bubble Gum (I Chewz You) • Sir Jam A Lot • Trace Of Love • Concerned Party #1 • Tootsie Rock • Non Stop (To The Sky) • Let Me Come Inside

| DEBUT | PEAK | WKS | Album Title | $ | Label & Number |
|-------|------|-----|-------------|-----|----------------|

## CARAVAN
Rock group from Canterbury, England: Pye Hastings (vocals, guitar), Dave Sinclair (piano), Geoff Richardson (viola), John G. Perry (bass) and Richard Coughlan (drums).

| | | | | | |
|-------|------|-----|-------------|-----|----------------|
| 10/26/74 | 207 | 1 | Caravan & The New Symphonia...............................................................[L] $15 | | London 650 |

recorded on 10/28/73 at Theatre Royal, Drury Lane; The New Symphonia is a 39-piece orchestra

Introduction • Mirror For The Day • The Love In Your Eye • Virgin On The Ridiculous • For Richard

## CARLOS, Walter
Born in 1939 in Pawtucket, Rhode Island. Classical musician who performs on the Moog Synthesizer. Had a sex change and known as Wendy Carlos by 1982.

| | | | | | |
|-------|------|-----|-------------|-----|----------------|
| 12/13/75 | 201 | 4 | By Request...............................................................[I] $12 | | Columbia 32088 |

Three Dances From "Nutcracker Suite": Russian Dance/Dance Of The Sugar Plum Fairy/Dance Of The Reed-Pipes • Dialogues For Piano And Two Loudspeakers • Episodes For Piano And Electronic Sound • Geodesic Dance • Brandenburg Concerto No. 2 In F Major (First Movement) • "Little" Fugue In G Minor • What's New Pussycat? • Eleanor Rigby • Wedding March (Based On The Bridal Chorus From "Lohengrin") • Pompous Circumstances (Variations & Fantasy on a Theme by Elgar)

## CARN, Jean
Born Sarah Jean Perkins in Columbus, Georgia. R&B singer.

| | | | | | |
|-------|------|-----|-------------|-----|----------------|
| 7/17/82 | 210 | 1 | Trust Me................................................................ $10 | | Motown 6010 |

Steady On My Mind • Don't Let Me Slip Away • Trust Me • Super Explosion • My Baby Loves Me • If You Don't Know Me By Now • Completeness • Better To Me

## CARNES, Kim
Born on 7/20/45 in Los Angeles. Singer/pianist/composer. Member of **The Sugar Bears**.

| | | | | | |
|-------|------|-----|-------------|-----|----------------|
| 3/31/79 | 206 | 3 | St. Vincent's Court............................................................ $10 | | EMI America 17004 |

What Am I Gonna Do • Jamaica Sunday Morning • Stay Away • Lookin' For A Big Night • Paris Without You (St. Vincent's Court) • It Hurts So Bad • Lose In Love • Skeptical Shuffle • Take Me Home To Where My Heart Is • Blinded By Love • Goodnight Moon

## CARR, Vikki
Born Florencia Martinez Cardona on 7/19/41 in El Paso, Texas. Pop singer.

| | | | | | |
|-------|------|-----|-------------|-----|----------------|
| 3/1/75 | 203 | 3 | Hoy (Today)...............................................................[F] $12 | | Columbia 33340 |

Hoy • Sin Saber Por Que "The Way We Were" • Esperame • El Tiempo Que Te Quede Libre • Hasta Que Vuelvas • El Pajaro Herido • Esta Tarde Vi Llover • Voy A Esperar • Te Amo • Que Alegre Va Maria

## CARROLL, Jim
Born in New York City in 1950. Rock singer/poet/novelist. His band included Lenny Kaye and Paul Sanchez (guitars), Steve Linsley (bass) and Wayne Woods (drums). The 1995 movie The Basketball Diaries was based on Carroll's life.

| | | | | | |
|-------|------|-----|-------------|-----|----------------|
| 3/10/84 | 207 | 2 | I Write Your Name............................................................ $10 | | Atlantic 80123 |

**THE JIM CARROLL BAND**

Love's A Crime • (No More) Luxuries • Voices • Sweet Jane • Hold Back The Dream • Freddy's Store • Black Romance • I Write Your Name • Low Rider • Dance The Night Away

## CARTER, Carlene
Born Rebecca Carlene Smith on 9/26/55 in Madison, Tennessee. Country singer. Daughter of June Carter and Carl Smith. Married to Nick Lowe from 1979-90. Later married Howie Epstein of Tom Petty & The Heartbreakers.

| | | | | | |
|-------|------|-----|-------------|-----|----------------|
| 10/20/79 | 204 | 4 | Two Sides To Every Woman............................................................ $10 | | Warner 3375 |

Do It In A Heartbeat • Lies • Swap-Meat Rag • Gold-Hearted Lady • Two Sides To Every Woman • It's No Wonder (Why I Love Him) • One Good Lover • Old Photographs • Radio Sweetheart

## CARTER, Ron
Born on 5/4/37 in Ferndale, Michigan. Jazz bassist.

| | | | | | |
|-------|------|-----|-------------|-----|----------------|
| 7/7/79 | 202 | 6 | Parade...............................................................[I] $10 | | Milestone 9088 |

with guests **Chick Corea** (piano), Joe Henderson (sax) and **Tony Williams** (drums)

Parade • A Theme In 3/4 • Sometimes I Feel Like A Motherless Child • Tinderbox • Gypsy • G.J.T.

## CASH, Johnny
Born J.R. Cash on 2/26/32 in Kingsland, Arkansas. Legendary country singer/songwriter/guitarist. Elected to the Country Music Hall of Fame in 1980. Won Grammy's Living Legends Award in 1990. Inducted into the Rock and Roll Hall of Fame in 1992. Top Pop Albums: 34.

| | | | | | |
|-------|------|-----|-------------|-----|----------------|
| 2/6/71 | 209 | 1 | 1 Little Fauss And Big Halsy...............................................................[S] $20 | | Columbia 30385 |

**JOHNNY CASH with Carl Perkins and The Tennessee Three**

Rollin' Free • Ballad Of Little Fauss And Big Halsy • Ballad Of Little Fauss And Big Halsy (instrumental) • 706 Union (instrumental) • The Little Man • The Little Man (instrumental) • Wanted Man • Rollin' Free (instrumental) • True Love Is Greater Than Friendship [Carl Perkins] • Movin'

| DEBUT | PEAK | WKS | Album Title | $ | Label & Number |
|---|---|---|---|---|---|

**CASH, Johnny — Cont'd**

| | | | | | |
|---|---|---|---|---|---|
| 5/12/73 | 205 | 4 | 2 The Gospel Road .............................................................................................[S] | $20 | Columbia 32253 [2] |

soundtrack to movie about the life of Jesus filmed in Israel; with The Carter Family, Rita Coolidge and **The Statler Brothers**

Praise The Lord • Introduction (narrative) • Gospel Road (Part 1) • Jesus' Early Years (narrative) • Gospel Road (Part 2) • John The Baptist (narrative) • Baptism Of Jesus (narrative) • Wilderness Temptation (narrative) • Follow Me, Jesus (narrative) • Gospel Road (Part 3) • Jesus Announces His Divinity (narrative) • Jesus' Opposition Is Established (narrative) • Jesus' First Miracle (narrative) • He Turned The Water Into Wine (Part 1) • State Of The Nation (narrative) • I See Men As Trees Walking • Jesus Was A Carpenter (Part 1) • Choosing Of Twelve Disciples (narrative) • Jesus' Teachings (narrative) • Parable Of The Good Shepherd (narrative) • The Two Greatest Commandments (narrative) • Greater Love Hath No Man (narrative) • John The Baptist's Imprisonment And Death (narrative) • Jesus Cleanses Temple (narrative) • Jesus Upbraids Scribes And Pharisees (narrative) • Jesus In The Temple (narrative) • Come Unto Me (narrative) • The Adulterous Woman (narrative) • Help (Part 1) *[Kris Kristofferson]* • Jesus And Nicodemus (narrative) • Help (Part 2) *[Kris Kristofferson]* • Sermon On The Mount (narrative) • Blessed Are (narrative) • The Lord's Prayer, Amen Chorus *[Carter Family & Statler Brothers]* • Introducing Mary Magdalene (narrative) • Mary Magdalene Speaks (narrative) • Follow Me *[June Carter Cash]* • Magdalene Speaks Again (narrative) • Crossing The Sea Of Galilee (narrative) • He Turned The Water Into Wine (Part 2) • He Turned The Water Into Wine (Part 3) • Feeding The Multitude (narrative) • He Turned The Water Into Wine (Part 4) • More Jesus Teaching (narrative) • The Living Water And The Bread Of Life (narrative) • Gospel Road (Part 4) • Jesus And Children (narrative) • Children • Four Months To Live (narrative) • Help (Part 3) • Help (Part 4) • Raising Of Lazarus (narrative) • Jesus' Second Coming (narrative) • Jesus' Entry Into Jerusalem (narrative) • Burden Of Freedom • Jesus Wept (narrative) • Burden Of Freedom (Chorus) • Jesus Cleanses Temple Again (narrative) • Feast Of The Passover (nararative) • Lord, Is It I? *[Statler Brothers]* • The Last Supper • John 14: 1-3 (narrative) • And Now He's Alone (narrative) • Agony In Gethsemane (narrative) • Jesus Before Caiaphas, Pilate And Herod (narrative) • Burden Of Freedom • Crucifixion (narrative) • Jesus' Last Words (narrative) • Jesus' Death • Earthquake And Darkness (narrative) • He Is Risen (narrative) • Mary Magdalene Returns To Galilee (narrative) • Jesus Appears To Disciples (narrative) • The Great Commission (narrative) • Ascension, Amen Chorus • Jesus Was A Carpenter (Part 2)

| | | | | | |
|---|---|---|---|---|---|
| 7/4/81 | 201 | 4 | 3 The Baron | $10 | Columbia 37179 |

The Baron • Mobile Bay • The Hard Way • A Ceiling, Four Walls, And A Floor • Hey, Hey Train • The Reverend Mr. Black • The Blues Keep Gettin' Bluer • Chattanooga City Limit Sign • Thanks To You • The Greatest Love Affair

| | | | | | |
|---|---|---|---|---|---|
| 5/22/82 | 205 | 3 | 4 The Survivors ...............................................................................[L] | $10 | Columbia 37961 |

**JOHNNY CASH/JERRY LEE LEWIS/CARL PERKINS**
recorded on 4/23/81 at the Sporthalle Boeblingen in Stuttgart, West Germany

Get Rhythm • I Forgot To Remember To Forget • Goin' Down The Road Feelin' Bad • That Silver Haired Daddy Of Mine • Matchbox • I'll Fly Away • Whole Lot-ta Shakin' Goin' On • Rockin' My Life Away • Blue Suede Shoes • There Will Be Peace In The Valley For Me • Can The Circle Be Unbroken • I Saw The Light

## CASHMAN & WEST

Duo of pop record producers/songwriters/singers Dennis "Terry Cashman" Minogue (b: 7/5/41) and Thomas "Tommy West" Picardo, Jr. (b: 8/17/42). Produced all of Jim Croce's recordings.

| | | | | | |
|---|---|---|---|---|---|
| 11/23/74 | 202 | 2 | Lifesong | $10 | ABC/Dunhill 50179 |

Maury • Rock Me To Your Music • A Man Can't Always Be • I Could Feel The Morning • The Dutchman • New York Woman • Fly Away • Tuna Fish Song • Three Stones From The Sun • Lifesong

## CAT MOTHER

Rock group from New York: Charlie Prichard (guitar), Bob Smith (piano, vocals), Steve Davidson (congas), Roy Michaels (bass, vocals) and Michael Equine (drums). Formerly known as Cat Mother and the All Night News Boys.

| | | | | | |
|---|---|---|---|---|---|
| 5/27/72 | 212 | 2 | Cat Mother | $30 | Polydor 5017 |

Greenwood Shuffle • She Came From A Different World • Ode To Oregon • Three And Me • The Dribbleworks Blues • Trials And Tribulations • Letter To The President • Heebeiejeebies • Love Until Your Heart Breaks

## CAVALIERE, Felix ✪

Born on 11/29/43 in Pelham, New York. Lead singer of The Rascals after a stint with Joey Dee's band.

| | | | | | |
|---|---|---|---|---|---|
| 4/19/80 | 203 | 5 | Castles In The Air | $10 | Epic 35990 |

Good To Have Love Back • Only A Lonely Heart Sees • All Or Nothing • Castles In The Air • People Got To Be Free • Dancin' The Night Away • Love Is The First Day Of Spring • Outside Your Window • Don't Hold Back Your Love • You Turned Me Around

## CHANGE

European-American studio group formed in Italy by producers Jacques Fred Petrus and Mauro Malavasi with varying members. In 1985 featured vocalists were Deborah "Crab" Cooper and Rick Brennan. Led by Paolo Gianolio (guitar) and David Romani (bass).

| | | | | | |
|---|---|---|---|---|---|
| 4/20/85 | 208 | 2 | Turn On Your Radio | $10 | Atlantic 81243 |

Turn On Your Radio • Let's Go Together • Examination • You'll Always Be Part Of Me • Oh What A Feeling • Mutual Attraction • Love The Way You Love Me • If You Want My Love

## CHARLES, Ray

Born Ray Charles Robinson on 9/23/30 in Albany, Georgia. Legendary R&B singer/pianist. Partially blind at age five, completely blind at seven (glaucoma). Formed own band in 1954. Inducted into the Rock and Roll Hall of Fame in 1986. Won Grammy's Lifetime Achievement Award in 1987. Many TV and movie appearances. *Top Pop Albums*: 38.

| | | | | | |
|---|---|---|---|---|---|
| 5/5/73 | 216 | 4 | 1 Genius Live In Concert .......................................................[L-R] | $12 | Bluesway 6053 |

originally released as *Ray Charles Live In Concert* on ABC-Paramount 500 and hit #80 on pop albums chart in 1965; recorded on 9/20/64 at The Shrine Civic Auditorium in Los Angeles

Opening • Swing A Little Taste • I Gotta Woman • Margie • You Don't Know Me • Hide Nor Hair • Baby, Don't You Cry • Makin' Whoopee • Hallelujah I Love Her So • Don't Set Me Free • What'd I Say • Finale

| | | | | | |
|---|---|---|---|---|---|
| 3/9/74 | 206 | 4 | 2 Come Live With Me | $12 | Crossover 9000 |

Till There Was You • If You Go Away • It Takes So Little Time • Come Live With Me • Somebody • Problems, Problems • Where Was He • Louise • Everybody Sing

| | | | | | |
|---|---|---|---|---|---|
| 1/5/80 | 204 | 1 | 3 Ain't It So | $10 | Atlantic 19251 |

Some Enchanted Evening • Blues In The Night • Just Because • What'll I Do • One Of These Days • Love Me Or Set Me Free • Drift Away • (Turn Out The Light And) Love Me Tonight

| | | | | | |
|---|---|---|---|---|---|
| 10/18/80 | 203 | 1 | 4 Brother Ray Is At It Again! | $10 | Atlantic 19281 |

Compared To What • Anyway You Want To • Don't You Love Me Anymore? • A Poor Man's Song • Now That We've Found Each Other • Ophelia • I Can't Change It • Questions

| DEBUT | PEAK | WKS | Album Title | $ | Label & Number |
|---|---|---|---|---|---|

## CHARLIE
British rock group: Terry Thomas and John Verity (guitars, vocals), John Anderson (bass), and Steve Gadd and Bob Henrit (drums). Henrit joined **The Kinks** by 1984.

| 10/17/81 | 201 | 6 | **Good Morning America** | $10 | RCA Victor 4137 |

Good Morning America • I Can't Get Over You • Roll The Dice • Heading For Home • Saturday Night • All My Life • Fool For Your Love • My Perfect Lover • I'm Angry With You • Just One More Chance • The Girl Won't Dance With Me

## CHASE, Chevy ○
Born Cornelius Crane Chase on 10/8/43 in New York City. Comedian/actor/keyboardist. An original cast member of TV's *Saturday Night Live*, 1975-76. Went on to star in several movies. Hosted own late night TV talk show in 1993.

| 9/13/80 | 201 | 5 | **Chevy Chase** [N] | $10 | Arista 9519 |

Nat'l Anthem • Short People • Never Never Gonna Sing For You • I Shot The Sheriff • Let It Be • Love To Have My Baby • Sixteen Tons • Wild Thing • Rappers' Plight

## CHEAP TRICK
Rock group from Rockford, Illinois: Robin Zander (vocals), Rick Nielsen (guitar), Tom Petersson (bass) and Brad "Bun E. Carlos" Carlson (drums).

| 4/9/77 | 207 | 1 | **Cheap Trick** | $12 | Epic 34400 |

Hot Love • Speak Now Or Forever Hold Your Peace • He's A Whore • Mandocello • The Ballad Of T.V. Violence (I'm Not The Only Boy) • ELO Kiddies • Daddy Should Have Stayed In High School • Taxman, Mr. Thief • Cry, Cry • Oh, Candy

## CHEECH & CHONG
Comedians Richard "Cheech" Marin (b: 7/13/46, Watts, California) and Thomas Chong (b: 5/24/38, Edmonton, Alberta, Canada). Starred in movies since 1978.

| 10/24/81 | 201 | 4 | **Cheech & Chong's Greatest Hit** [C-G] | $10 | Warner 3614 |

Dave • Earache My Eye • Lets' Make A Dope Deal • Basketball Jones • Blind Melon Chitlin' • Sister Mary Elephant • Sargent Stadanko • Dave (Cont.) • Cruisin' With Pedro De Pacas • The Continuing Adventures Of Pedro De Pacas And Man • Pedro And Man At The Drive-Inn • Trippin' In Court

## CHERRY, Ava ○
Female R&B-disco singer from Chicago.

| 3/15/80 | 206 | 2 | **Ripe!!!** | $10 | RSO 3072 |

I Just Can't Shake The Feeling • Love Is Good News • You Never Loved Me • I'm Always Ready • Single Woman, Married Man • Gimme Your Lovin' • Where There's Smoke There's Fire

## CHILLIWACK
Rock group from Vancouver led by Bill Henderson (vocals, guitar). Numerous personnel changes through the years.

| 2/26/72 | 210 | 2 | 1 **Chilliwack** | $15 | A&M 3509 [2] |

Lonesome Mary • Eat • Rosie • Ridin' • Ride-Out • Always • Changing Reels • Shine • Claps/Chants • Whistle/Flute Pads • Antiphony • Traveling Music • Sleep Music • Night-Morning

| 11/1/75 | 210 | 1 | 2 **Rockerbox** | $12 | Sire 7511 |

If You Want My Love • I Know, You Know • When You Gonna Tell The Truth • Train's A Comin' Back • Marianne • Treat Me Fine, Treat Me Good • Magnolia • Last Day Of December

## CHINA CRISIS
Rock duo from Liverpool, England: Gary Daly (lead vocals, keyboards) and Eddie Lundon (guitar).

| 3/24/84 | 202 | 4 | **Working With Fire And Steel** | $10 | Warner 25062 |

Working With Fire And Steel • When The Piper Calls • Hanna Hanna • Animals In Jungles • Here Come A Raincloud • Wishful Thinking • Tragedy And Mystery • Papua • The Gates Of Door To Door • The Soul Awakening

## CHOCOLATE MILK
R&B group from New Orleans: Frank Richard (vocals), Mario Tio (guitar), Robert Dabon (keyboards), Amadee Castanell (sax), Joe Foxx (trumpet) and Dwight Richards (drums).

| 10/9/76 | 202 | 6 | **Comin'** | $12 | RCA Victor 1830 |

Comin' • Something New • Do Unto Others • Feel The Need • With All Our Love • Starbright • I Refuse • Island Love

## CISSEL, Chuck ○
R&B singer/actor from Tulsa, Oklahoma. Last name rhymes with "sizzle." Studied with the Joffrey Ballet in New York City. Acted in numerous commercials and Broadway shows.

| 2/23/80 | 204 | 4 | **Just For You** | $10 | Arista 4257 |

Just For You • Emergency • River Of Love • Don't Tell Me You're Sorry • Forever • Cisselin' Hot • Lady In My World • I've Been Needing Love So Long • Do You Believe

## CITY BOY
British rock group: Lol Mason (vocals), Mike Slamer (guitar), Max Thomas (keyboards), Chris Dunn (bass) and Steve Broughton (drums).

| 10/8/77 | 207 | 2 | **Young Men Gone West** | $12 | Mercury 1182 |

Bordello Night • Dear Jean (I'm Nervous) • Honeymooners • She's Got Style • Bad For Business • Young Men Gone West • I've Been Spun • One After Two • The Runaround • The Man Who Ate His Car • Millionaire

## C.J. & CO.
Disco group from Detroit assembled by Dennis Coffey.

| 9/2/78 | 204 | 1 | **Deadeye Dick** | $10 | Westbound 6104 |

Burning Drums Of Fire • Deadeye Dick • Beware The Stranger • Big City Sidewalk • Hear Say • You're Still The Sweetest Thing In My Life

### CLARK, Roy
Born Roy Linwood Clark on 4/15/33 in Meherrin, Virginia. Country singer/songwriter/guitarist/banjo player. Co-hosted TV's *Hee Haw*.

| 12/16/72 | 207 | 3 | 1 Roy Clark Live! ............................................................... [L] | $12 | Dot 26005 |

recorded at the Landmark Hotel in Las Vegas
Alabama Jubilee • Kansas City • Thank God And Greyhound • Under The Double Eagle • Foggy Mountain Breakdown • Orange Blossom Special • Yesterday, When I Was Young • Green Green Grass Of Home • The Lawrence Welk - Hee Haw Counter-Revolution Polka • The Great Pretender Medley: The Great Pretender/High Noon (Do Not Forsake Me)/Loch Lomond/Turkey In The Straw/Somewhere My Love/Honky Tonk

| 2/9/74 | 204 | 5 | 2 Roy Clark's Family Album ................................................. | $12 | Dot 26018 |

guests include Roy's dad, his uncles Dudley and Paul, his cousin Kenneth and his friend Bob Schodt
Rollin' In My Sweet Baby's Arms • Sweet Bunch Of Daisies • Jesse James • Heel And Toe Polka • Lonesome Road Blues • Old Joe Clark • Log Cabin In The Lane • I'll Be All Smiles Tonight • Jimmy Brown, The Newsboy • Rubber Dolly

### CLARKE, Stanley
Born on 6/30/51 in Philadelphia. R&B-jazz bassist/violinist/cellist. His band included Robert Brookins and Sunnie Paxson (keyboards), and Rayford Griffin (drums).

| 7/27/85 | 203 | 4 | Find Out! ................................................................. | $10 | Epic 40040 |

**THE STANLEY CLARKE BAND**
Find Out • What If I Should Fall In Love • Born In The U.S.A. • The Sky's The Limit • Don't Turn The Lights Out • Campo Americano • Stereotypica • Psychedelic • My Life

### CLAYTON-THOMAS, David
Born David Thomsett on 9/13/41 in Surrey, England. Lead singer of **Blood, Sweat & Tears**.

| 10/28/72 | 202 | 2 | Tequila Sunrise ......................................................... | $12 | Columbia 31700 |

I Could Just Boogie All Night Long • Yesterday's Music • Friday The 13th Child • The Face Of Man • One More Time Around • Down Bound Train • Nobody Calls Me Prophet • Last Time That She Cried • Failin' By Degrees • My Song (For Geanenne) • Bread 'N Butter Boogie • I Could Just Boogie All Night Long (Reprise)

### CLIFF, Jimmy
Born James Chambers on 4/1/48 in St. James, Jamaica. Reggae singer/composer. Starred in the movies *The Harder They Come* (1975) and *Club Paradise* (1986).

| 9/22/73 | 214 | 3 | 1 Unlimited ................................................................. | $12 | Reprise 2147 |

Under The Sun, Moon And Stars • Fundamental Reggay • World Of Peace • Black Queen • Be True • Oh Jamaica • Commercialization • The Price Of Peace • On My Life • I See The Light • Rip-Off • Poor Slave • Born To Win

| 1/20/79 | 209 | 1 | 2 Give Thankx ............................................................. | $10 | Warner 3240 |

Bongo Man • Stand Up And Fight Back • She Is A Woman • You Left Me Standing By The Door • Footprints • Meeting In Afrika • Wanted Man • Lonely Streets • Love I Need • Universal Love (Beyond The Boundaries)

| 12/6/80 | 201 | 8 | 3 I Am The Living ....................................................... | $10 | MCA 5153 |

I Am The Living • Another Summer • All The Strength We Got • It's The Beginning Of An End • Gone Clear • Love Again • Satan's Kingdom • Morning Train

| 11/28/81 | 207 | 2 | 4 Give The People What They Want ............................... | $10 | MCA 5217 |

Son Of Man • Give The People What They Want • Experience • Shelter Of Your Love • Majority Rule • Turn The Tables • Material World • World In A Trap • What Are You Doing With Your Life • My Philosophy

| 12/3/83 | 207 | 1 | 5 The Power And The Glory ........................................ | $10 | Columbia 38986 |

We All Are One • Sunshine In The Music • Reggae Night • Piece Of The Pie • American Dream • Roots Woman • Love Solution • Power And The Glory • Journey

### CLIMAX BLUES BAND
Blues-rock band formed in Stafford, England. Nucleus consisted of Colin Cooper (sax, vocals), Peter Haycock (guitar, vocals) and Derek Holt (bass).

| 6/26/71 | 204 | 8 | 1 Climax Blues Band .................................................... | $15 | Sire 4901 |

Country Hat • Everyday • Reap What I've Sowed • Brief Case • Medley: Alright Blue/Country Hat, Reprise • Seventh Son • Please Don't Help Me • Like Uncle Charlie • Louisiana Blues • Cut You Loose

| 2/19/72 | 211 | 5 | 2 Tightly Knit ............................................................. | $15 | Sire 5903 |

Hey Mama • Shoot Her If She Runs • Towards The Sun • Come On In My Kitchen • Who Killed McSwiggin • Little Link • St. Michael's Blues • Bide My Time • That's All

### CLOVER ✪
Country-rock group from San Francisco: Alex Call (vocals, guitar), **Huey Lewis** (vocals, harmonica), John McFee (guitar), Sean Hopper (keyboards), John Ciambotti (bass) and Tony Braunagel (drums). Lewis and Hopper later formed The News. McFee later joined **The Doobie Brothers**.

| 2/25/78 | 207 | 5 | Love On The Wire ...................................................... | $15 | Mercury 3708 |

Hearts Under Fire • Southern Belles • Oh Senorita • Still Alive • Keep On Rolling • California Kid • Easy Love • Ain't Nobody • From Now On • Travelin' Man

### COATES, Odia ✪
Native of Berkeley, California. Died of breast cancer on 5/19/91 (age 49). Member of the gospel group Edwin Hawkins Singers.

| 7/26/75 | 202 | 9 | Odia Coates .............................................................. | $12 | United Artists 228 |

Showdown • Do I Love You (Yes, In Every Way) • One Man Woman/One Woman Man • Heaven And Hell • Don't Leave Me In The Morning • You Come And You Go • The Charmer • The Woman's Song • I'll Just Keep On Loving You • (I'm) Having Your Baby • Thief (In The Night)

### COCKBURN, Bruce
Pronounced: CO-burn. Born on 5/27/45 in Ottawa, Canada. Pop-rock singer/songwriter.

| 1/23/82 | 208 | 2 | Inner City Front .......................................................... | $10 | Millennium 7761 |

You Pay Your Money And You Take Your Chance • The Strong One • All's Quiet On The Inner City Front • Radio Shoes • Wanna Go Walking • And We Dance • Justice • Broken Wheel • Loner

### CODE BLUE ⊙
Rock trio: Dean Chamberlain (guitar), Gary Tibbs (bass) and Randall Marsh (drums). All share vocals.

| | | | | | |
|---|---|---|---|---|---|
| 10/4/80 | 202 | 2 | **Code Blue** ................................................................................ | $10 | Warner 3461 |

album and cover packaged in a large blue plastic bag
Whisper/Touch • Modern Times • Hurt • Face To Face • Burning Bridges • Somebody Knows • Other End Of Town •
Where I Am • Settle For Less • The Need • Paint By Numbers

### COE, David Allan
Born on 9/6/39 in Akron, Ohio. Country singer/actor. Billed as "The Mysterious Rhinestone Cowboy" until 1978.

| | | | | | |
|---|---|---|---|---|---|
| 4/17/76 | 202 | 4 | **Longhaired Redneck** ................................................................... | $12 | Columbia 33916 |

Longhaired Redneck • When She's Got Me (Where She Wants Me) • Revenge • Texas Lullaby • Living On The Run •
Family Reunion • Rock & Roll Holiday • Free Born Rambling Man • Spotlight • Dakota The Dancing Bear, Part II

### COLE, Lloyd, And The Commotions ⊙
Born on 1/31/61 in Buxton, England; raised in Glasgow, Scotland. Backing quartet, The Commotions, with guitarist/vocalist Cole from 1984-89:
Neil Clark (guitar), Blair Cowan (keyboards), Lawrence Donegan (bass) and Steven Irvine (drums).

| | | | | | |
|---|---|---|---|---|---|
| 3/30/85 | 201 | 8 | **Rattlesnakes** | $10 | Geffen 24064 |

Perfect Skin • Speedboat • Rattlesnakes • Down On Mission Street • Forest Fire • Charlotte Street • 2cv • Four Flights
Up • Patience • Are You Ready To Be Heartbroken?

### CONLEY, Earl Thomas ⊙
Born on 10/17/41 in West Portsmouth, Ohio. Country singer/songwriter/guitarist.

| | | | | | |
|---|---|---|---|---|---|
| 11/24/84 | 210 | 1 | **Treadin' Water** ......................................................................... | $10 | RCA Victor 5175 |

Too Hot To Handle • Love Don't Care (Whose Heart It Breaks) • Labor Of Love • Your Love Says All There Is • Love's On
The Move Again • Chance Of Lovin' You • Honor Bound • Treadin' Water • Feels Like A Saturday Night • Turn This Bus
Around (Bad Bob's)

### CONNIFF, Ray
Born on 11/6/16 in Attleboro, Massachusetts. Arranger/conductor. *Top Pop Albums: 51.*

| | | | | | |
|---|---|---|---|---|---|
| 3/29/75 | 204 | 6 | **Laughter In The Rain** ................................................................. | $12 | Columbia 33332 |

Laughter In The Rain • I Honestly Love You • Sundown • Angie Baby • Mandy • Seasons In The Sun • Eres Tu • Cat's In
The Cradle • Feel Like Makin' Love • (You're) Having My Baby

### COODER, Ry
Born on 3/15/47 in Los Angeles. Blues-rock guitarist/singer/songwriter.

| | | | | | |
|---|---|---|---|---|---|
| 2/13/71 | 216 | 1 | **1 Ry Cooder** ............................................................................ | $15 | Reprise 6402 |

Alimony • France Chance • One Meat Ball • Do Re Mi • Old Kentucky Home • How Can A Poor Man Stand Such Times
And Live • Available Space • Pig Meat • Police Dog Blues • Goin' To Brownsville • Dark Is The Night

| | | | | | |
|---|---|---|---|---|---|
| 7/12/80 | 206 | 3 | **2 The Long Riders** ...............................................[I-S] | $10 | Warner 3448 |

The Long Riders • I'm A Good Old Rebel • Seneca Square Dance • Archie's Funeral (Hold To God's Unchanging Hand) • I
Always Knew That You Were The One • Rally 'Round The Flag • Wildwood Boys • Better Things To Think About • My
Grandfather • Cole Younger Polka • Escape From Northfield • Jesse James

| | | | | | |
|---|---|---|---|---|---|
| 3/9/85 | 210 | 1 | **3 Paris, Texas** .....................................................[I-S] | $10 | Warner 25270 |

with David Lindley (banjo) and Jim Dickinson (piano)
Paris, Texas • Brothers • Nothing Out There • Cancion Mixteca • No Safety Zone • Houston In Two Seconds • She's
Leaving The Bank • On The Couch • I Knew These People • Dark Was The Night

### COOK, Barbara ⊙
Born on 10/25/27 in Atlanta. Singer/actress. Appeared in Broadway's *Plain and Fancy, Candide, The Music Man* and *She Loves Me.*

| | | | | | |
|---|---|---|---|---|---|
| 7/4/81 | 209 | 3 | **It's Better With A Band** ...........................................[L] | $10 | MMG 104 |

recorded on 9/14/80 at Carnegie Hall in New York City; with band directed by Wally Harper
I Love A Piano • It's Better With A Band • Medley: Remember/Come In From The Rain • Medley: Chant La Vie/Sing A Song
With Me • Them There Eyes • Bernstein Medley: Simple Song/One Hand, One Heart/Some Other Time/I Can Cook, Too •
Medley: I Never Meant To Hurt You/I Never Knew That Men Cried • The Ingenue • If Love Were All • Sweet Georgia Brown

### COOPER BROTHERS ⊙
Pop-rock band from Ottawa, Canada: brothers Richard (guitar) and Brian (bass) Cooper, Terry King (guitar), Al Serwa (keyboards), Glenn Bell
(drums), Darryl Alguire (guitar) and Charles Robinson III (flute). All but Serwa share vocals.

| | | | | | |
|---|---|---|---|---|---|
| 7/21/79 | 204 | 2 | **Pitfalls Of The Ballroom** ......................................................... | $10 | Capricorn 0226 |

Make The Last One A Fast One • I'll Know Her When I See Her • Show Some Emotion • Ridin' High • Is It The Dancer Or
The Dance • Sweet Forgiver • Mustard The Dog • Heroes

### COPPERHEAD ⊙
Rock group: Gary Philippet (vocals, guitar), John Cipollina (guitar; Quicksilver Messenger Service), Jim McPherson (keyboards), Hutch
Hutchinson (bass) and David Weber (drums). Cipollina died on 5/29/89 (age 45).

| | | | | | |
|---|---|---|---|---|---|
| 6/23/73 | 208 | 5 | **Copperhead** ............................................................................. | $15 | Columbia 32250 |

Roller Derby Star • Kibitzer • A Little Hand • Kamikaze • Spin-Spin • Pawnshop Man • Wing-Dang-Doo • They're Making A
Monster

### COREA, Chick
Born Anthony Armando Corea on 6/11/42 in Chelsea, Massachusetts. Jazz-rock pianist. Formed Return To Forever in 1973.

| | | | | | |
|---|---|---|---|---|---|
| 10/16/82 | 207 | 2 | **Touchstone** ............................................................[I] | $10 | Warner 23699 |

guests include (Stanley Clarke, Al Di Meola and **Lenny White**)
Touchstone: Procession/Ceremony/Departure • The Yellow Nimbus • Duende • Compadres • Estancia • Dance Of Chance

### CORYELL, Larry
Born on 4/2/43 in Galveston, Texas. Jazz/rock guitarist. Founder of Eleventh House.

| | | | | | |
|---|---|---|---|---|---|
| 11/25/72 | 212 | 2 | **1 Offering** ..............................................................[I] | $15 | Vanguard 79319 |

Foreplay • Ruminations • Scotland I • Offering • The Meditation Of November 8th • Beggar's Chant

| | | | | | |
|---|---|---|---|---|---|
| 6/2/73 | 206 | 6 | **2 The Real Great Escape** .......................................................... | $15 | Vanguard 79329 |

vocals by Larry and Julie Coryell
The Real Great Escape • Are You Too Clever • Love Life's Offering • Makes Me Wanna Shout • All My Love's Laughter •
Scotland II • P.F. Sloan

| DEBUT | PEAK | WKS | Album Title | $ | Label & Number |
|-------|------|-----|-------------|---|----------------|

**CORYELL, Larry — Cont'd**

2/12/77 | 209 | 1 | **3 The Lion and the Ram** ............................................................................ [I] $12 | Arista 4108
Larry's Boogie • Stravinsky • Toy Soldiers • Short Time Around • Improvisation Of Bach Lute Prelude • Song For My Friend's Children • Bicentennial Head Fest • The Fifties • Domesticity • The Lion And The Ram

8/27/77 | 205 | 3 | **4 Back Together Again** .................................................................................... $12 | Atlantic 18220
**CORYELL/MOUZON**
Alphonse Mouzon (b: 11/21/48 in Charleston, South Carolina) is a prolific drummer/pianist
Beneath The Earth • The Phonse • Transvested Express • Crystallization • Rock 'N' Roll Lovers • Get On Up (We Gonna Boogie) • Reconciliation • Back Together Again • Mr. C • High Love

**COSBY, Bill**
Born on 7/12/38 in Philadelphia. Top comedian who has starred in several movies and TV shows. *Top Pop Albums:* 22.

3/11/78 | 201 | 4 | **Bill's Best Friend** [C] $10 | Capitol 11731
Roland And The Rollercoaster • Puberty • People Who Drink • Frisbies • Chinese Mustard • Famous People • Let's Make A Deal • Cars • Illegal Drugs • Parents And Grandparents

**COTTON, Gene ☉**
Born on 6/30/44 in Columbus, Ohio. Singer/songwriter/guitarist.

4/8/78 | 202 | 9 | **Save The Dancer** ......................................................................................... $10 | Ariola America 50031
Before My Heart Finds Out • You're A Part Of Me • Like A Sunday In Salem • Going Through The Motions Of Love • Save The Dancer • Only The Lucky • She's Sweet, She's Somebody • Shine On • You Were Right • As Long As There's Laughter

**COULSON, DEAN, McGUINNESS, FLINT ☉**
British folk-rock band: Dennis Coulson (vocals), Dixie Dean (bass), Tom McGuinness (guitar) and Hughie Flint (drums). The latter two were with Manfred Mann and formed quintet McGuinness Flint, in 1971, of which Coulson was a member.

9/1/73 | 203 | 6 | **Lo & Behold** .............................................................................................. $15 | Sire 7405
all songs written by Bob Dylan; produced by Manfred Mann
Eternal Circle • Lo And Behold • Let Me Die In My Footsteps • Open The Door Homer • Lay Down Your Weary Tune • Don't You Tell Henry • Get Your Rocks Off • The Death Of Emmett Till • Odds And Ends • Sign On The Cross

**COVAY, Don ☉**
Born in March 1938 in Orangeburg, South Carolina. R&B singer/songwriter.

8/18/73 | 204 | 4 | **Super Dude I** ............................................................................................. $10 | Mercury 653
Overtime Man • Leave Him (Part I) • I Stayed Away Too Long • I Was Checkin' Out She Was Checkin' In • Hold You To Your Promise • Memphis • The Pinch Hitters • Somebody's Been Enjoying My Home • Bad Mouthing • Leave Him (Part II) • Money (That's What I Want) • Don't Step On A Man When He's Down

**COVEN ☉**
Pop group: Jinx Dawson (female vocals), Oz (male vocals), Christopher Nelson (guitar), John Hobbs (keyboards) and Steve Ross (drums).

2/19/72 | 201 | 2 | **Coven** | $15 | MGM 4801
Nightingale • Shooting Star • Natural Love • What Can I Get Out Of You • Dark Day In Chitown • Jailhouse Rock • Lonely Lover • I Guess It's A Beautiful Day • Washroom Wonder • Nobody's Leavin' Here Tonight • One Tin Soldier (The Legend of Billy Jack)

**COWBOY ☉**
Pop-rock group: Scott Boyer (vocals), Tommy Talton (guitar) and Pete Kowalke (guitars), Bill Pilmore (keyboards), George Clark (bass) and Tomm Wynn (drums). Lineup in 1977: Boyer, Talton, Chip Condon (keyboards), Arch Pearson (bass) and Chip Miller (drums).

1/2/71 | 210 | 1 | **1 Reach For The Sky** ................................................................................... $15 | Atco 351
Opening • Livin' In The Country • Song Of Love And Peace • Amelia's Earache • Pick Your Nose • Pretty Friend • Everything Here • Stick Together • Use Your Situation • It's Time • Honey Ain't Nowhere • Rip & Snort • Josephine, Beyond Compare

12/10/77+ | 204 | 3 | **2 Cowboy** ................................................................................................... $12 | Capricorn 0194
Takin'it All The Way • Now That I Know • Pat's Song • Straight Into Love • Everybody Knows Your Name • What Can I Call It? • Nobody Else's Man • Except For Real • Satisfy • River To The Sea

**COX, Mick, Band ☉**
Rock group: Cox (guitar), Tony O'Malley (vocals), Mick Weaver (keyboards), Chris Stewart (bass) and Andrew Steele (drums).

6/30/73 | 207 | 5 | **The Mick Cox Band** ................................................................................... $12 | Capitol 11175
Stuck On You • This Time Round • Ranger • Queens Avenue • White Lie • Redirecting Mary • Ego Trap • Questions

**COYOTE SISTERS, The ☉**
Female vocal trio: Marty Gwinn, Leah Kunkel (sister of Mama Cass of **The Mamas & The Papas**) and Renee' Armand.

9/8/84 | 201 | 6 | **The Coyote Sisters** $10 | Morocco 6063
I've Got A Radio • Nobody Moves Like Us • Straight From The Heart (Into Your Life) • Floating World • Once You Know • Anybody's Angel • See You Tonight • (Don't Listen To That) Reggae • Echo • I'll Do It

**CRANSTON, Lamont — see LAMONT**

**CRAWFORD, Hank**
Born on 12/21/34 in Memphis. Jazz alto saxophonist.

2/16/74 | 202 | 6 | **1 Wildflower** ............................................................................................... [I] $12 | Kudu 15
Corazon • Wildflower • Mr. Blues • You've Got It Bad Girl • Good Morning Heartache

10/26/74 | 201 | 4 | **2 Don't You Worry 'Bout A Thing** .............................................................. [I] $12 | Kudu 19
above 2 arranged and produced by Bob James, with **Idris Muhammad** (drums)
Don't You Worry 'Bout A Thing • Jana • All In Love Is Fair • Sho Is Funky • Groove Junction

**CRAWLER**
British rock group: Terry Wilson-Slesser (vocals), Geoff Whitehorn (guitar), John Bundrick (keyboards), Terry Wilson (bass) and Tony Braunagel (drums). Formerly known as Back Street Crawler.

10/14/78 | 210 | 1 | **Snake, Rattle & Roll** ................................................................................... $10 | Epic 35482
Sail On • Disc Heroes • How Will You Break My Heart • Muddy Water • First Class Operator • Where Is The Money? • Hold On • Midnight Blues • Liar • One Way Street

| DEBUT | PEAK | WKS | Album Title | $ | Label & Number |
|-------|------|-----|-------------|---|----------------|

### CREAM
British rock supergroup: Eric Clapton (guitar), **Jack Bruce** (bass) and **Ginger Baker** (drums). Inducted into the Rock and Roll Hall of Fame in 1993.

| 6/25/83 | 205 | 1 ▲ | **Strange Brew - The Very Best Of Cream** ........................................[G] $10 | RSO 811639 |
|---------|-----|-----|------|------|

Badge • Sunshine Of Your Love • Crossroads • White Room • Born Under A Bad Sign • Strange Brew • Anyone For Tennis • I Feel Free • Politician • Spoonful

### CREEDENCE CLEARWATER REVIVAL
Rock group from El Cerrito, California: brothers John (vocals, guitar) and Tom (guitar) Fogerty, Stu Cook (keyboards, bass) and Doug Clifford (drums). Tom Fogerty died of repiratory failure on 9/6/90 (age 48). Group inducted into the Rock and Roll Hall of Fame in 1993.

| 10/30/82 | 202 | 7 | **Chooglin'** ..................................................................[K] $10 | Fantasy 9621 |

I Heard It Through The Grapevine • Keep On Chooglin' • Suzie Q • Pagan Baby • Born On The Bayou

### CRISS, Gary ☉
Disco singer.

| 9/9/78 | 201 | 3 | **Rio De Janeiro** | $10 | Salsoul 8504 |

Rio De Janeiro • Medley: The Girl From Ipanema/Brazilian Nights • Amazon Queen • The Lady Is Latin (The Girl Is Bad) • My Rio Lady • The Calm Before The Storm

## CROCKER, Frankie — see HEART AND SOUL ORCHESTRA

### CROPPER, Steve
Born on 10/21/41 in Willow Springs, Missouri. Guitarist of **Booker T. & The MG's**, The Mar-Keys and The Blues Brothers band.

| 2/21/81 | 210 | 2 | **Playin' My Thang** .................................................... $10 | MCA 5171 |

Give 'Em What They Want • Let The Good Times Roll • Playin' My Thang • Fly • Sandy Beaches • With You • Feet • Why Do You Say You Love Me • Ya Da Ya Da

### CROUCH, Andraé ☉
Born on 7/1/42 in Los Angeles. Leading gospel choir leader/songwriter.

| 10/17/81 | 208 | 1 | **Don't Give Up** ........................................................ $10 | Warner 3513 |

Waiting For The Son • Don't Give Up • I Can't Keep It To Myself • Hollywood Scene • Handwriting On The Wall • I Love Walking With You • Save The People • I'll Be Good To You, Baby (A Message To The Silent Victims) • Start All Over Again

### CROW
Rock-blues group from Minneapolis: Dave Waggoner (vocals), Dick Wiegand (guitar), Kink Middlemist (organ), Larry Wiegand (bass) and Denny Craswell (drums; The Castaways).

| 2/27/71 | 207 | 6 | **Mosaic** ........................................................................ $15 | Amaret 5009 |

(Don't Try To Lay No Boogie Woogie On The) "King Of Rock And Roll" • Easy Street • Yellow Dawg • Sky Is Crying • I Need Love • Keeps Me Runnin' • Watching Can Waste Up The Time • Satisfied • Watch That Cat • Let's Not Say Goodbye

### CROWFOOT ☉
Rock trio: Sam McCue (guitar), Russell Dashiell (bass) and Don Francisco (drums). All share vocals.

| 10/23/71 | 211 | 1 | **Find The Sun** ........................................................... $15 | ABC 745 |

Travel In Time • Hollywood • Sailing Girl • Run For Cover • Find The Sun • Got To Fly • Summer's Gone • Sometimes Lovin' You • We're Doin' It Wrong • Feel The Flow

### CROWN HEIGHTS AFFAIR
R&B-disco group from New York City: Phil Thomas (vocals), William Anderson (guitar), Howard Young (keyboards), Bert Reid, James Baynard and Raymond Reid (horn section), Muki Wilson (bass), and Raymond Rock (drums).

| 2/19/77 | 207 | 1 | 1 **Do It Your Way** ..................................................... $10 | De-Lite 2022 |

Searching For Love • Love Me • Dancin' • Music Is The World • Far Out • Sexy Ways • French Way

| 9/9/78 | 205 | 3 | 2 **Dream World** ........................................................ $10 | De-Lite 9506 |

Galaxy Of Love • I Love You • Say A Prayer For Two • Dream World • Things Are Going To Get Better • I'm Gonna Love You Forever • Cherry

| 5/12/79 | 207 | 3 | 3 **Dance Lady Dance** .............................................. $10 | De-Lite 9512 |

Dance Lady Dance • The Rock Is Hot • Number One Woman • Come Fly With Me • You Don't Have To Say You Love Me • Empty Soul Of Mine

### CRUSADERS, The
Instrumental jazz-oriented group formed in Houston. Changed name from The Jazz Crusaders to The Crusaders in 1971. Included Joe Sample (keyboards), Wilton Felder (reeds), Nesbert "Stix" Hooper (drums) and Wayne Henderson (trombone; left in 1975). Larry Carlton was a frequent guest guitarist from 1972-77.

| 10/13/73 | 203 | 8 | **At Their Best** ...............................................[I-K] $15 | Motown 796 |

Jazz! • Listen And You'll See • Papa Hooper's Barrelhouse Groove • Time Has No Ending • Young Rabbits - '71 '72 • Rainy Night In Georgia • Way Back Home • Thank You (Falletin Me Be Mice Elf Agin) • Spanish Harlem

### CRYSTAL GRASS ☉
Disco studio group assembled by producer Lee Hallyday.

| 7/26/75 | 204 | 2 | **Crystal World** ........................................................ $12 | Polydor 6516 |

You're All I Ever Dreamed Of • Love To Dance This One With You • You've Got The Love I Needed So Bad Girl • I've Got The Music In Me • She's Got The Style To Love Me • Heavy Eyes • Crystal World • You're The First, The Last, My Everything • Funny How Love Dies • Pain Sweet Pain ("L'Exorcisme")

### CUMMINGS, Burton
Born on 12/31/47 in Winnipeg, Canada. Lead singer of The Guess Who. Acted in the 1982 movie *Melanie*.

| 8/26/78 | 203 | 2 | **Dream Of A Child** ................................................ $12 | Portrait 35481 |

Break It To Them Gently • Hold On, I'm Comin' • I Will Play A Rhapsody • Wait By The Water • When A Man Loves A Woman • Shiny Stockings • Guns, Guns, Guns • Takes A Fool To Love A Fool • Meanin' So Much • It All Comes Together • Roll With The Punches • Dream Of A Child

### CURB, Mike, Congregation

Curb was born on 12/24/44 in Savannah, Georgia. Pop music mogul and politician. President of MGM Records, 1969-73. Elected lieutenant governor of California in 1978; served as governor of California, 1980. Formed own company, Sidewalk Records in 1964, became Curb Records in 1974. Currently resides in Nashville.

| 7/10/71 | 205 | 6 | 1 Put Your Hand In The Hand | $15 | MGM 4788 |

Joy To The World • Yesterday Today And Tomorrow • Have You Ever Seen The Rain • Ain't Gonna Study War No More • Cotton Fields (The Cotton Song) • Put Your Hand In The Hand • United We Stand • Go The Direction Of Love • Reach Out And Touch (Somebody's Hand) • Hallelujah

| 2/19/72 | 206 | 4 | 2 Softly Whispering I Love You | $15 | MGM 4821 |

Softly Whispering I Love You • Mammy Blue • I'd Like To Teach The World To Sing (In Perfect Harmony) • Butterfly • Forty Days And Forty Nights • Take Up The Hammer Of Hope • Give A Little Laughter • Time To Ride • United We Stand • I Saw The Light

| 7/1/72 | 208 | 1 | 3 The World Of Steve & Eydie | $12 | MGM 4803 |

**STEVE LAWRENCE & EYDIE GORME with The Mike Curb Congregation**
E Fini • Shiretoko • Rose D'Irlande • Un Poquito Mas • We Shall Dance • Bashana Haba-Ah • Du Sollst Nicht Weinen • Lead Me On • We Can Make It Together [w/The Osmonds] • Tristeza

### CZUKAY, Holger — see WOBBLE, Jah

# D

### DADDY DEWDROP ○

Born Richard Monda in Cleveland. Songwriter for the TV cartoon series *Sabrina & The Groovy Ghoulies*.

| 6/26/71 | 211 | 3 | Daddy Dewdrop | [N] $20 | Sunflower 5006 |

Chick-A-Boom (Don't Ya Jes' Love It) • 5-Card Stud • The March Of The White Corpuscles • Strike • John Jacob Jingleheimer Smith • Fox Huntin' (On The Weekend) • Diggin' On Mrs. Jones • Abracadabra Alakazam • Johnny Do It Faster • Migraine Headaches

### DARIN, Bobby

Born Walden Robert Cassotto on 5/14/36 in the Bronx, New York. Died of heart failure on 12/20/73. Pop singer/pianist/guitarist/drummer. Won the 1959 Best New Artist Grammy Award. Married to actress Sandra Dee from 1960-67. Inducted into the Rock and Roll Hall of Fame in 1990.

| 4/6/74 | 204 | 6 | Darin 1936-1973 | $15 | Motown 813 |

I Won't Last A Day Without You • Wondrin' Where It's Gonna End • Sail Away • Another Song On My Mind • Happy (Love Theme From "Lady Sings The Blues") • Blue Monday • Don't Think Twice, It's All Right • The Letter • If I Were A Carpenter • Moritat (Mack The Knife)

### DAVIDSON, Dianne ○

Folk singer/songwriter/guitarist.

| 4/29/72 | 212 | 2 | Back Woods Woman | $12 | Janus 3043 |

Delta Dawn • Rocky Top • The Best I Can • Now That You're A Woman • Country Comfort • Appalachian Boy • Sympathy • All I Wanted (All The Time) • Town And Country Cafe • Where Do The Children Play

### DAVIES, Dave

Born on 2/3/47 in Muswell Hill, London. Lead guitarist of **The Kinks**.

| 9/3/83 | 202 | 3 | Chosen People | $10 | Warner 23917 |

Tapas • Charity • Mean Disposition • Love Gets You • Danger Zone • True Story • Take One More • Freedom Lies • Matter Of Decision • Is It Any Wonder • Fire Burning • Chosen People • Cold Winter

### DAVIS, Betty ○

Female R&B singer. Formerly married to Miles Davis.

| 9/22/73 | 202 | 6 | 1 Betty Davis | $15 | Just Sunshine 5 |

guests include Neal Schon, Larry Graham and The Pointer Sisters
If I'm In Luck I Might Get Picked Up • Walkin Up The Road • Anti Love Song • Your Man My Man • Ooh Yea • Steppin In Her I. Miller Shoes • Game Is My Middle Name • In The Meantime

| 11/22/75 | 202 | 5 | 2 Nasty Girl | $12 | Island 9329 |

Nasty Gal • Talkin Trash • Dedicated To The Press • You And I • Feelins • F.U.N.K • Gettin Kicked Off, Havin Fun • Shut Off The Light • This Is It! • The Lone Ranger

### DAVIS, Danny, and The Nashville Brass

Born George Nowlan on 4/29/25 in Dorchester, Massachusetts. Country trumpet player/bandleader.

| 2/12/72 | 202 | 6 | Nashville Brass Turns To Gold | [I] $12 | RCA Victor 4627 |

Java • Forever • Ol' Red River Valley • Sixteen Tons • January Eighth • Honky Tonk • Melodie d'Amour • Riders In The Sky • El Paso • Flowers On The Wall

### DAVIS, Mac

Born on 1/21/42 in Lubbock, Texas. Country singer/songwriter/guitarist/actor. Hosted own musical variety TV series from 1974-76. Acted in several movies.

| 6/10/78 | 207 | 6 | Fantasy | $10 | Columbia 35284 |

Music In My Life • You Are • I Don't Want To Get Over You • Dreams That Last Forever • Shee Moe Foe • Fantasy • For No Reason At All • Sad Girl • Melting In The Moonlight • If There Were Only Time For Love

### DAVIS, Spencer, Group

Born on 7/14/41 in Swansea, Wales. R&B-styled singer/rhythm guitarist. Group included Ray Fenwick (guitar), Eddie Hardin (keyboards), Charlie McCracken (bass) and Pete York (drums).

| 9/22/73 | 206 | 4 | Gluggo | $15 | Vertigo 1015 |

Catch You On The Rebop • Don't You Let It Bring You Down • Alone • Today Gluggo, Tomorrow The World • Feeling Rude • Legal Eagle Shuffle • Trouble In Mind • Mr. Operator • Tumble Down Tenement Row

| DEBUT | PEAK | WKS | Album Title | $ | Label & Number |
|-------|------|-----|-------------|---|----------------|

**DAZZ BAND — see KINSMAN DAZZ**

### DEAD BOYS
Punk group from Cleveland: Stiv Bators (vocals), Gene "Cheetah Chrome" Connor and Jimmy Zero (guitars), Jeff Magnum (bass) and Johnny Blitz (drums). Bators later formed **The Lords Of The New Church**. Bators died on 6/4/90 (age 40) after being hit by a car in Paris.

| 7/22/78 | 206 | 2 | We Have Come For Your Children ............................................................ | $20 | Sire 6054 |

3rd Generation Nation • I Won't Look Back • (I Don't Wanna Be No) Catholic Boy • Flame Thrower Love • Son Of Sam • Tell Me • Big City • Calling On You • Dead And Alive • Ain't It Fun

### DEAD KENNEDYS ○
Punk group from San Francisco: Eric "Jello Biafra" Boucher (vocals), East Bay Ray (guitar), Klaus Fluoride (bass) and J.H. Pelligro (drums).

| 2/21/81 | 204 | 2 | Fresh Fruit For Rotting Vegetables ........................................................ | $12 | I.R.S. 70014 |

Kill The Poor • Forward To Death • When Ya Get Drafted • Let's Lynch The Landlord • Police Truck • Drug Me • Your Emotions • Chemical Warfare • California Uber Alles • I Kill Children • Stealing Peoples' Mail • Funland At The Beach • Ill In The Head • Holiday In Cambodia • Viva Las Vagas

### DECO ○
R&B duo: Philip Ingram and Zane Giles.

| 3/23/85 | 209 | 2 | Fast Forward .................................................................................... [S] | $10 | Qwest 25263 |

Breakin' Out • Do You Want It Right Now [Siedah Garrett] • Long As We Believe [Siedah Garrett & David Swanson] • Curves • Taste • Showdown [Pulse] • Survive • Fast Forward

### DEE, Kiki
Born Pauline Matthews on 3/6/47 in Yorkshire, England.

| 6/15/74 | 202 | 3 | Loving & Free ...................................................................................... | $12 | Rocket 395 |

produced by Elton John (Elton and his band provide instrumental backing)
Loving And Free • If It Rains • Lonnie And Josie • Travellin' In Style • You Put Something Better Inside Of Me • Super Cool • Rest My Head • Amoureuse • Song For Adam • Sugar On The Floor

### DEEP PURPLE
Heavy-metal group from Hertford, England: Ian Gillan (vocals), Ritchie Blackmore (guitar), Jon Lord (keyboards), Roger Glover (bass) and Ian Paice (drums). *Top Pop Albums:* 20.

| 10/21/78 | 201 | 6 | 1 When We Rock, We Rock And When We Roll, We Roll [G] | $12 | Warner 3223 |

Space Truckin' • Kentucky Woman • Hard Road (Wring That Neck) • Burn • Woman From Tokyo • Hush • Smoke On The Water • Highway Star

| 7/17/82 | 206 | 1 | 2 Deep Purple In Concert .................................................................... [E-L] | $12 | Portrait 38050 [2] |

recorded in 1970 and 1972
Speed King • Wring That Neck • Child In Time • Mandrake Root • Highway Star • Strange Kind Of Woman • Lazy • Never Before • Space Truckin' • Lucille

### DEES, Stephen ○
Singer/songwriter/guitarist from Philadelphia.

| 5/21/77 | 207 | 2 | Hip Shot ............................................................................................ | $10 | RCA Victor 2186 |

produced by Daryl Hall
Counting On You • Wacky Together • Kerry • You Defy The Law Of Gravity • Got My Eyes On You Babe • Too Close for Comfort • Out-A My Skin • Beat The Devil

**DELBERT & GLEN — see McCLINTON, Delbert**

### DELFONICS, The
R&B vocal trio from Philadelphia: William Hart, Wilbert Hart and John Johnson.

| 4/6/74 | 205 | 4 | Alive & Kicking .................................................................................. | $30 | Philly Groove 1501 |

Lying To Myself • I Told You So • First Thing On My Mind • Hey Baby • Think It Over • Pardon Me Girl • Seventeen (And In Love) • I Don't Want To Make You Wait • Love Is • Can't Go On Living • Start All Over Again

### DELILAH ○
Female disco singer.

| 2/24/79 | 209 | 1 | Dancing In The Fire .......................................................................... | $10 | ABC 1131 |

Dancing In The Fire • Are You Ready • Showbiz Medley: Showbiz/The Stripper/Night Train • Give A Little Love

### DEL-LORDS, The ○
Rock group from New York City: Scott Kempner and Eric Ambel (guitars), Manny Caiati (bass) and Frank Funaro (drums). All share vocals.

| 2/2/85 | 203 | 4 | Frontier Days .................................................................................... | $10 | EMI America 17133 |

How Can A Poor Man Stand Such Times And Live • Get Tough • Livin' On Love • Double Life • I Play The Drums • Burning In The Flame Of Love • Pledge Of Love • Shame On You • Mercenary • Feel Like Going Home

### DELLS, The
R&B vocal group from Harvey, Illinois: Johnny Carter, Marvin Junior, Verne Allison, Mickey McGill and Chuck Barksdale.

| 11/3/73 | 202 | 6 | 1 The Dells ...................................................................................... | $25 | Cadet 50046 |

Let The Feeling Talk To You • I Miss You • My Pretending Days Are Over • Let's Make It Last • I Hear Voices • If You Move I'll Fall • Don't Make Me A Storyteller

| 3/1/75 | 210 | 1 | 2 The Dells Greatest Hits Volume 2 .................................................. [G] | $20 | Cadet 60036 |

Learning To Love You Was Easy (It's So Hard Trying To Get Over You) • If It Ain't One Thing It's Another • The Love We Had (Stays On My Mind) • My Pretending Days Are Over • Medley: I Can Sing A Rainbow/Love Is Blue • Bring Back The Love Of Yesterday • Run For Cover • Hi Diddley Dee Dum Dum (It's A Good Good Feelin') • Give Your Baby A Standing Ovation • Good-Bye Mary Ann • Oh, What A Night

| 9/20/75 | 207 | 1 | 3 We Got To Get Our Thing Together ................................................ | $20 | Cadet 60044 |

We Got To Get Our Thing Together • Strike Up The Band • Reminiscing • I'll Be Waiting There For You • Thank God You're My Lady • Love Is Missing From Our Lives • Overnight • Gotta Get Home To My Baby • The Power Of Love • You Don't Care

| 6/25/77 | 208 | 1 | 4 They Said It Couldn't Be Done, But We Did It ................................ | $15 | Mercury 1145 |

Teaser • Our Love • Could It Be • Rich Man, Poor Man (Peace) • They Said It Could't Be Done (But We Did It) • Waiting For You • Get On Down • Betcha Never Been Loved (Like This Before)

| DEBUT | PEAK | WKS | Album Title | $ | Label & Number |
|-------|------|-----|-------------|---|----------------|

**DELLS, The — Cont'd**

| 2/18/78 | 204 | 3 | 5 **Love Connection** | $15 | Mercury 3711 |

Private Property • God Helps Those (Who Help Themselves) • I'm In Love (I Can't Explain What I Feel) • Don't Trick Me, Treat Me • How Can One Man Be So Lucky • Should I Or Should I Not • Love Connection • Wasted Tears

| 3/3/79 | 203 | 4 | 6 **Face To Face** | $10 | ABC 1113 |

Face To Face • Hooked On Loving You • Thought I Could • (You Bring Out) The Best In Me • Changed Man • Love Me • Plastic People • Wrapped Up Tight

**DeLORY, Al ○**
Prolific producer/arranger/conductor.

| 3/13/71 | 220 | 2 | **Love Story** | [I] $15 | Capitol 677 |

Theme From "Love Story" • Make It Easy On Yourself • Rainy Night In Georgia • Love Theme From "Romeo & Juliet" • Theme From "Borsalino" • We've Only Just Begun • A Theme From "Easy Rider" (Wasn't Born To Follow) • Wichita Lineman • Jean • Elegy

**DENNY, Sandy**
Born on 1/6/41 in Wimbledon, England. Died of a brain hemorrhage on 4/21/78. Lead singer of **Fairport Convention**.

| 1/6/73 | 204 | 4 | **Sandy** | $12 | A&M 4371 |

It'll Take A Long Time • Sweet Rosemary • For Nobody To Hear • Tomorrow Is A Long Time • Quiet Joys Of Brotherhood • Listen, Listen • The Lady • Bushes & Briars • It Suits Me Well • The Music Weaver

**DENVER, John**
Born Henry John Deutschendorf on 12/31/43 in Roswell, New Mexico. Died on 10/12/97 at the controls of a light plane which crashed off the California coast. Pop-folk-country singer/songwriter/guitarist. Starred in the 1977 movie *Oh, God. Top Pop Albums:* 28.

| 6/25/83 | 202 | 1 | 1 **Rocky Mountain Holiday** | $10 | RCA Victor 4721 |

**JOHN DENVER & THE MUPPETS**

Hey Old Pal • Grandma's Feather Bed • She'll Be Comin' 'Round The Mountain • Catch Another Butterfly • Down By The Old Mill Stream • Durango Mountain Caballero • Gone Fishin' • Medley: Tumbling Tumbleweeds/Happy Trails • Poems, Prayers and Promises • Take 'Em Away • Going Camping • Home On the Range • No One Like You

| 11/24/84 | 203 | 8 | 2 **Greatest Hits Volume 3** | [G] $10 | RCA Victor 5313 |

How Can I Leave You Again • Some Days Are Diamonds (Some Days Are Stone) • Shanghai Breezes • Seasons Of The Heart • Perhaps Love [w/Plácido Domingo] • Love Again [w/Sylvie Vartan] • Dancing With The Mountains • Wild Montana Skies • I Want To Live • The Gold And Beyond • Autograph

**DEODATO**
Born Eumir De Almeida Deodato on 6/21/42 in Rio de Janeiro, Brazil. Keyboardist/producer/arranger.

| 8/18/73 | 213 | 2 | 1 **DonatoDeodato** | [I] $12 | Muse 5017 |

Deodato with Brazilian keyboardist Joao Donato

Whistle Stop • Where's J.D.? • Capricorn • Nightripper • You Can Go • Batuque

| 8/18/79 | 202 | 5 | 2 **Knights Of Fantasy** | [I] $10 | Warner 3321 |

Medley: Space Dust/Sherlock • Shazam • Bachmania: Jesu, Joy Of Man's Desiring/Love Is Blue/Whistle Bump • Knights Of Fantasy • Lovely Lady

**DEPECHE MODE**
All-synthesized rock band from Basildon, England: singer David Gahan with Martin Gore, Andy Fletcher and Alan Wilder. Group name is French for fast fashion.

| 10/8/83 | 201 | 5 | **Construction Time Again** | $10 | Sire 23900 |

Love, In Itself • More Than A Party • Pipeline • Everything Counts • Two Minute Warning • Shame • The Landscape Is Changing • Told You So • And Then...

**DERRINGER, Rick**
Born Richard Zehringer on 8/5/47 in Celina, Ohio. Former lead singer/guitarist of The McCoys.

| 11/3/79 | 203 | 1 | 1 **Guitars And Women** | $12 | Blue Sky 36092 |

Something Warm • Guitars And Women • Everything • Man In The Middle • It Must Be Love • Desires Of The Heart • Timeless • Hopeless Romantic • Need A Little Girl (Just Like You) • Don't Ever Say Goodbye

| 10/25/80 | 205 | 1 | 2 **Face To Face** | $12 | Blue Sky 36551 |

Runaway • You'll Get Yours • Big City Loneliness • Burn The Midnight Oil • Let The Music Play • Jump, Jump, Jump • I Want A Lover • My My, Hey Hey (Out Of The Blue)

**DeSHANNON, Jackie**
Born Sharon Myers on 8/21/44 in Hazel, Kentucky. Pop singer/songwriter. Acted in the movies *Surf Party*, *C'mon Let's Live A Little* and *Hide And Seek*. Married **Randy Edelman**.

| 12/3/77 | 203 | 5 | **You're The Only Dancer** | $15 | Amherst 1010 |

Don't Let The Flame Burn Out • I Just Can't Say No To You • Just To Feel This Love From You • I Don't Think I Can Wait • To Love Somebody • You're The Only Dancer • Try To Win A Friend • Dorothy • Your Love Has Got A Hold On Me • Tonight You're Doin' It Right

**DESMOND, Paul**
Born on 11/25/24 in San Francisco. Died on 5/30/77. Jazz alto saxophonist with **Dave Brubeck**.

| 3/13/71 | 207 | 2 | **Bridge Over Troubled Water** | [I] $15 | A&M 3032 |

guest musicians include **Airto**, **Ron Carter** and **Herbie Hancock**

El Condor Pasa • So Long, Frank Lloyd Wright • The 59th Bridge Song (Feelin' Groovy) • Mrs. Robinson • Old Friends • America • For Emily Whenever I May Find Her • Medley: Scarborough Fair/Chanticle • Ceclia • Bridge Over Troubled Water

| DEBUT | PEAK | WKS | Album Title | $ | Label & Number |
|-------|------|-----|-------------|---|----------------|

**DE SOUZA, Raul** ○
Born on 8/23/34 in Rio de Janeiro, Brazil. Trombone player.

| 10/8/77 | 207 | 2 | **1 Sweet Lucy** ..............................................................[I] $10 | Capitol 11648 |
|---------|-----|---|---|---|

guest musicians include **Airto** and Patrice Rushen

Sweet Lucy • Wires • Wild And Shy • At Will • Banana Tree • A Song Of Love • New Love (Cancao Do Nosso Amor) • Bottom Heat

| 6/3/78 | 202 | 3 | **2 Don't Ask My Neighbors** ..............................................[I] $10 | Capitol 11774 |
|--------|-----|---|---|---|

above 2 produced by George Duke

Don't Ask My Neighbors • La La Song • Daisy Mae • Beauty And The Beast • Fortune • Overture • At The Concert • I Believe You • Jump Street

**DESTRI, Jimmy** ○
Born on 4/13/54 in New York City. Keyboard player for the new-wave group Blondie.

| 1/30/82 | 201 | 5 | **Heart On A Wall** $10 | Chrysalis 1368 |
|---------|-----|---|---|---|

Bad Dreams • Don't Look Around • Living In Your Heart • My Little World • Little Metal Drummer (Little Metal Drummer) • Numbers Don't Count (On Me) • The King Of Steam • Under The Ice • Heart On A Wall

**DeVILLE, Mink — see MINK**

**DeVITO, Karla** ○
Singer/actress from New York City. Toured with Meat Loaf in 1978. Starred in the Broadway musical *The Pirates Of Penzance*. Married to actor Robby Benson.

| 10/3/81 | 203 | 3 | **Is This A Cool World Or What?** .................................... $10 | Epic 37014 |
|---------|-----|---|---|---|

Cool World • I Can't Stand To Reminisce • Heaven Can Wait • Midnight Confession • Big Idea • Almost Saturday Night • Boy Talk • Just One Smile • I'm Just Using You • Work • Bloody Bess • Just Like You

**DIAMOND, Neil**
Born on 1/24/41 in Brooklyn. Singer/songwriter/guitarist. Starred in and composed the music for the 1980 movie *The Jazz Singer*. Top Pop Albums: 40.

| 9/19/81 | 201 | 4 | ● **Love Songs** [K] $10 | MCA 5239 |
|---------|-----|---|---|---|

Theme (Orchestral) • Stones • If You Go Away • The Last Thing On My Mind • Coldwater Morning • Juliet • Both Sides Now • Play Me • Hurtin' You Don't Come Easy • Husbands And Wives • Until It's Time For You To Go • And The Grass Won't Pay No Mind • A Modern-Day Version Of Love • Suzanne

**DIDDLEY, Bo**
Born Otha Ellas Bates McDaniel on 12/30/28 in McComb, Mississippi. Influential R&B-rock and roll singer/songwriter/guitarist. Name "bo diddley" is a one-stringed African guitar. Inducted into the Rock and Roll Hall of Fame in 1987.

| 5/26/73 | 208 | 5 | **1 The London Bo Diddley Sessions** ............................... $30 | Chess 50029 |
|---------|-----|---|---|---|

Don't Want No Lyin' Woman • Bo Diddley • Going Down • Make A Hit Record • Bo-Jam • Husband-In-Law • Do The Robot • Sneakers On A Rooster • Get Out Of My Life

| 2/14/76 | 207 | 1 | **2 The 20th Anniversary Of Rock 'N' Roll** ...................... $20 | RCA Victor 1229 |
|---------|-----|---|---|---|

Ride The Water (Part 1) • Not Fade Away • Kill My Body • Drag On • Ride The Water (Part 2) • Bo Diddley Jam: I'm A Man/Hey Bo Diddley/Who Do You Love/Bo Diddley's A Gunslinger/I'm A Man

**DILLARDS, The**
Country-rock group from Salem, Missouri: Rodney Dillard (vocals, guitar), Billy Ray Lathum (banjo), Dean Webb (mandolin), Mitch Jayne (bass) and Paul York (drums).

| 1/19/74 | 211 | 1 | **Tribute To The American Duck** ..................................... $12 | Poppy 175 |
|---------|-----|---|---|---|

Music Is Music • Caney Creek • Dooley • Love Has Gone Away • You've Gotta Be Strong • Carry Me Off • Smile For Me • Hot Rod Banjo • Daddy Was A Mover • What's Time To A Hog?

**DINNER, Michael** ○
Born in 1953 in Denver. Singer/songwriter/guitarist. Directed the 1985 movie *Heaven Help Us*.

| 9/21/74 | 206 | 6 | **1 The Great Pretender** ................................................. $10 | Fantasy 9454 |
|---------|-----|---|---|---|

guests include Andrew Gold and Linda Ronstadt

The Great Pretender • Jamaica • Yellow Rose Express • Sunday Morning Fool • Last Dance In Salinas • Tattooed Man From Chelsea • Woman Of Aran • Pentacott Lane • Icarus • Texas Knight

| 8/28/76 | 204 | 4 | **2 Tom Thumb The Dreamer** .......................................... $10 | Fantasy 9512 |
|---------|-----|---|---|---|

Tom Thumb The Dreamer • Julye • The Promised Land • Thrown Out Of The Paradise Ballroom • Swallow • Sitting In Limbo • Apple Annie • Silver Bullets • Pale Fire

**DION**
Born Dion DiMucci on 7/18/39 in the Bronx, New York. Formed vocal group Dion & The Belmonts in the Bronx in 1958. Dion went solo in 1960. Brief reunion with The Belmonts in 1967 and 1972, periodically since then. Inducted into the Rock and Roll Hall of Fame in 1989.

| 3/13/71 | 210 | 2 | **You're Not Alone** ....................................................... $15 | Warner 1872 |
|---------|-----|---|---|---|

Close To It All • Sunniland • Windows • The Visitor • Peaceful Place • Let It Be • The Stuff I Got • Blackbird • Josie • Attraction Works Better Than Promotion

**DIVINYLS**
Rock group from Sydney, Australia: Christina Amphlett (vocals), Mark McEntee (guitar), Bjarne Ohlin (keyboards), Richard Grossman (bass) and Richard Harvey (drums).

| 4/9/83 | 205 | 9 | **Desperate** ................................................................ $10 | Chrysalis 41404 |
|--------|-----|---|---|---|

Boys In Town • Only Lonely • Science Fiction • Siren Song • Elsie • Only You • Ring Me Up • Victoria • Take A Chance • I'll Make You Happy

**DOC HOLLIDAY** ○
Southern-rock group from Raleigh, North Carolina: Bruce Brookshire and Rick Skelton (guitars), Eddie Stone (keyboards), John Samuelson (bass) and Herman Nixon (drums). All share vocals.

| 4/4/81 | 201 | 4 | **1 Doc Holliday** $10 | A&M 4847 |
|--------|-----|---|---|---|

Ain't No Fool • Magic Midnight • A Good Woman's Hard To Find • Round And Round • Moonshine Runner • Keep On Running • Never Another Night • The Way You Do • Somebody Help Me • I'm A Rocker

| 3/6/82 | 204 | 3 | **2 Doc Holliday Rides Again...** ....................................... $10 | A&M 4882 |
|--------|-----|---|---|---|

Last Ride • Good Boy Gone Bad • Don't Go Talkin' • Southern Man • Let Me Be Your Lover • Doin' (It Again) • Don't Stop Loving Me • Hot Rod • Lonesome Guitar

| DEBUT | PEAK | WKS | Album Title | $ | Label & Number |
|-------|------|-----|-------------|---|----------------|

**DR. FEELGOOD** ☉
Rock group from Canvey Island, England: Lee Brilleaux (vocals), Wilko Johnson (guitar), John Sparks (bass) and John "The Figure" Martin (drums). Brilleaux died of cancer on 4/7/94 (age 41).

| 3/27/76 | 203 | 5 | Malpractice | $12 | Columbia 34098 |

I Can Tell • Going Back Home • Back In The Night • Another Man • Rolling And Tumbling • Don't Let Your Daddy Know • Watch Your Step • Don't You Just Know It • Riot In Cell Block No. 9 • Because You're Mine • You Shouldn't Call The Doctor (If You Can't Afford The Bills)

**DR. HOOK**
Pop-rock group from Union City, New Jersey: Ray Sawyer (vocals; dubbed "Dr. Hook" because of eye patch), Dennis Locorriere (vocals, guitar), Rik Elswit (guitar), William Francis (keyboards), Jance Garfat (bass) and John Wolters (drums). Wolters died of cancer on 6/16/97 (age 52).

| 12/5/81 | 202 | 2 | Dr. Hook Live | [L] $10 | Capitol 12114 |

You Make My Pants Want To Get Up And Dance • Sexy Eyes • The Cover Of The Rolling Stone • Carry Me, Carrie • I Got Stoned And I Missed It • When You're In Love With A Beautiful Woman • Ooh Poo Pah Doo • Sylvia's Mother

**DR. JOHN**
Born Malcolm "Mac" Rebennack on 11/20/42 in New Orleans. Pioneer "swamp rock"-styled pianist.

| 12/2/78 | 207 | 3 | City Lights | $10 | Horizon 732 |

Dance The Night Away With You • Street Side • Wild Honey • Rain • Snake Eyes • Fire Of Love • Medley: Sonata/He's A Hero • City Lights

**DR. STRUT** ☉
Jazz group from Los Angeles: Tim Weston (guitar), David Woodford (sax), Everett Bryson (percussion), Kevin Bassinson (keyboards), Peter Freiberger (bass) and Claude Pepper (drums).

| 3/22/80 | 201 | 4 | Struttin' | [I] $10 | Motown 931 |

Struttin' • Acufunkture • Blue Lodge • CMS • Flip City • Commuter Rabbit (For Folon) • After • Nitwit • Nice 'N' Sleazy • No! You Came Here For An Argument

**DOMINGO, Plácido**
Born on 1/21/41 in Madrid. One of the world's leading operatic tenors.

| 8/25/84 | 210 | 1 | Always In My Heart (Siempre En Mi Corazón) - The Songs Of Ernesto Lecuona | [F] $10 | CBS 38828 |

songs of Cuban composer-pianist Lecuona; with the Royal Philharmonic Orchestra, Lee Holdridge, director
Siboney • Noche Azul • Andalucía • Siempre En Mi Corazón • Maria La O • Canto Karabali • Juventud • Malagueña • Damisela Encantadora • La Comparsa

**DONALDSON, Lou**
Born on 11/1/26 in Badin, North Carolina. Jazz alto saxophonist.

| 6/9/73 | 207 | 3 | Sophisticated Lou | [I] $15 | Blue Note 024 |

You've Changed • Stella By Starlight • What Are You Doing The Rest Of Your Life? • The Long Goodbye • You Are The Sunshine Of My Life • Autumn In New York • Blues Walk • Time After Time

**DONATO, Joao** ☉
Male keyboardist from Brazil.

| 8/18/73 | 213 | 2 | DonatoDeodato | [I] $12 | Muse 5017 |

Donato with Brazilian keyboardist/producer/arranger Eumir De Almeida Deodato
Whistle Stop • Where's J.D.? • Capricorn • Nightripper • You Can Go • Batuque

**DONOVAN**
Born Donovan Phillip Leitch on 5/10/46 in Maryhill, Scotland. Singer/songwriter/guitarist. Father of actress Ione Skye. *Top Pop Albums*: 20.

| 4/3/71 | 215 | 3 | Here Me Now | $15 | Janus 3025 |

Oh Deed I Do • You're Gonna Need Somebody On Your Bond • Tangerine Puppet • Car-Car Song • Donna Donna • Do You Hear Me Now • The Ballad Of Geraldine • Circus Of Sour • Cuttin' Out • Goldwatch Blues

**DOOBIE BROTHERS, The**
Rock group from San Jose, California: Tom Johnston (vocals, guitar), Patrick Simmons (vocals, guitar), Dave Shogren (bass) and John Hartman (drums).

| 9/11/71 | 210 | 1 | The Doobie Brothers | $12 | Warner 1919 |

Nobody • Slippery St. Paul • Greenwood Creek • It Won't Be Right • Travelin' Man • Feelin' Down Farther • The Master • Growin' A Little Each Day • Beehive State • Closer Every Day • Chicago

**DORE, Charlie**
Born in London in 1956. Female singer/songwriter.

| 9/12/81 | 204 | 1 | Listen! | $10 | Chrysalis 1325 |

Listen • Do Me A Favour-Don't • You Should Hear (How She Talks About You) • Falling • Don't Say No • Wise To The Lines • I'm Over Here • Like They Do It In America • Sister Revenge • Didn't I Tell You

**DOUCETTE**
Rock group from Montreal: Jerry Doucette (vocals, guitar), Mark Olson (keyboards), Donnie Cummings (bass) and Duris Maxwell (drums).

| 5/26/79 | 202 | 5 | The Douce Is Loose | $10 | Mushroom 5013 |

Run Buddy Run • Rita • Someday • Father Dear Father • Nobody • Before I Die • All Over Me • Further On Up The Road

**DOUG AND THE SLUGS** ☉
Rock group from Vancouver: Doug Bennett (vocals), John Burton and Rick Baker (guitars), Simon Kendall (keyboards), Steve Bosley (bass) and John Wally Watson (drums).

| 2/21/81 | 204 | 2 | Cognac and Bologna | $10 | RCA Victor 3887 |

To Be Laughing • Just Another Case • Soldier Of Fortune • Too Bad • Advice To A Friend • Stay With Me • Chinatown Calculation • Thunder Makes The Noise • Drifting Away • If I Fail • Tropical Rainstorm

### DOZIER, Lamont
Born on 6/16/41 in Detroit. R&B singer/songwriter/producer. With the brothers Brian and Eddie Holland in songwriting/production team for Motown. Trio left Motown in 1968 and formed own Invictus/Hot Wax label. Inducted into the Rock and Roll Hall of Fame in 1990.

| 1/23/82 | 210 | 1 | Lamont .................................................................................... | $10 | M&M 104 |

You Oughta Be In Pictures • Never Had It So Good • I Ain't Playing • I See You • The Pressure Is On • Shout About It • Locked Into You • Ain't No Way • Help Is On The Way

### DRAGON ✪
Pop-rock group from Auckland, New Zealand: Marc Hunter (vocals), Robert Taylor (guitar), Alan Mansfield and Paul Hewson (keyboards), Todd Hunter (bass), and Terry Chambers (drums).

| 9/15/84 | 208 | 3 | Body And The Beat ........................................................... | $10 | Polydor 817874 |

Rain • Promises (So Far Away) • Wilderworld • Cry • Cool Down • Body And The Beat • Witnessing • Magic • What Am I Gonna Do • Fool

### DREAM SYNDICATE, The
Rock group from Los Angeles: Steve Wynn (vocals, guitar), Karl Precoda (guitar), Kendra Smith (bass) and Dennis Duck (drums).

| 4/30/83 | 208 | 1 | The Days Of Wine And Roses ......................................... | $10 | Ruby 23844 |

Tell Me When It's Over • Definitely Clean • That's What You Always Say • Then She Remembers • Halloween • When You Smile • Until Lately • Too Little, Too Late • The Days Of Wine And Roses

### DUDEK, Les
Born on 8/2/57 in Rhode Island. Prolific session guitarist. Formed rock band Black Rose with then-girlfriend Cher.

| 4/17/76 | 204 | 3 | 1 Les Dudek ....................................................................... | $12 | Columbia 33702 |

City Magic • Sad Clown • Don't Stop Now • Each Morning • It Can Do • Take The Time • Cruisin' Groove • What A Sacrifice

| 5/23/81 | 203 | 2 | 2 Gypsy Ride ...................................................................... | $10 | MCA 36798 |

What's Lost Is Truly Gone • Deja Vu (Da Voodoo's In You) • Sacrifice The Fool • Forever Or Never • Too Damn Dizzy • Call Me Later • Gypsy Ride • Hey, Chicky Chicky • Don't Trust That Woman • I'm O.K.

### DUDES ✪
Rock group from Montreal: singers/guitarists Brian Greenway, David Henman and Bob Segarini, bassist "Kootch" Trochim and drummers Ritchie Henman and Wayne Cullen.

| 10/25/75 | 208 | 2 | We're No Angels ............................................................... | $12 | Columbia 33577 |

Saturday Night • Fuel Injection • I Just Wanna Dance • Lylee Lady • Deeper And Deeper • Dancin' Shoes • Got Me Where You Want Me • My Mind's On You • Rock 'N Roll Debutante • We're No Angels

### DUKE JUPITER
Rock group from Rochester, New York: Marshall James Styler (vocals, keyboards), Greg Walker (guitar), George Barajas (bass) and David Corcoran (drums). Barajas died on 8/17/82 (age 33).

| 4/17/82 | 204 | 5 | Duke Jupiter 1 ................................................................... | $10 | Coast To Coast 37912 |

I'll Drink To You • Rockin' In A Motel Room • (You've Gotta Love) The Wrong Ones • Don't Look At Me Like That • Sugar Blues • Rock 'N' Roll Band • Slow, Loud And Dirty • Don't You Walk That Way • Baby, I Do

### DUNLAP, Gene ✪
Born in Detroit. Drummer/guitarist/keyboardist. Member of **Earl Klugh**'s group. The Ridgeways vocal group consisted of sisters Gloria, Esther and Gracie with brother Tommy Ridgeway.

| 3/14/81 | 202 | 9 | It's Just The Way I Feel ..................................................... | $10 | Capitol 12130 |

**GENE DUNLAP Featuring The Ridgeways**
The Intro • Rock Radio • Before You Break My Heart • I Got You • Love Dancin' • It's Just The Way I Feel • Should I Take Her Back, Should I Let Her Go • Surest Things Can Change

### DURY, Ian
Born on 5/12/42 in Upminster, England. Known as "The Poet of Punk." Crippled by polio during childhood. Taught art at the Canterbury Art College. Later wrote music for British TV programs and acted (in movie *The Cook, The Thief, His Wife & Her Lover*).

| 11/21/81 | 208 | 2 | Lord Upminster ................................................................. | $10 | Polydor 6337 |

with Chas Jankel (guitar), Tyrone Downie (keyboards), Robbie Shakespeare (bass) and Sly Dunbar (drums)
Spasticus (Autisticus) • Red (Letter) • The (Body Song) • Lonely (Town) • Trust (Is A Must) • Funky Disco (Pops) • Girls (Watching) • Wait (For Me)

### DYNAMIC SUPERIORS, The
R&B vocal group from Washington, D.C.: Tony Washington (lead), George Spann, George Peterbark, Michael McCalphin and Maurice Washington.

| 4/5/75 | 201 | 8 | The Dynamic Superiors | $12 | Motown 822 |

Shoe Shoe Shine • Soon • Leave It Alone • Don't Send Nobody Else • Romeo • Star Of My Life • Cry When You Want To • I Got Away • One-Nighter • Release Me

# E

### EARLAND, Charles
Born on 5/24/41 in Philadelphia. R&B-jazz keyboard player.

| 10/30/76 | 207 | 3 | 1 The Great Pyramid ........................................................... | $12 | Mercury 1113 |

**CHARLES EARLAND and Oddysey**
The Great Pyramid • Ahead Of Your Time • Mona Lisa • In The Land Of Mu • Upper Atlantis • Drifting

| 4/3/82 | 208 | 3 | 2 Earland's Jam ................................................................[I] | $10 | Columbia 37573 |

The Only One • Guilty • Laser Lips • Never Knew Love Like This Before • Marcia's Waltz (Preview) • Earland's Jam • You Belong To Me • Marcia's Waltz • Animal • Mercy

### ECKSTINE, Billy
Born on 7/8/14 in Pittsburgh. Died of a heart attack on 3/8/93. Singer/guitarist/trumpeter. Nicknamed "Mr. B." His son Ed was the president of Mercury Records.

| DEBUT | PEAK | WKS | Album Title | $ | Label & Number |
|---|---|---|---|---|---|
| 8/7/71 | 213 | 3 | **Feel The Warm** | $12 | Enterprise 1017 |

Make It With You • Think About Things • Don't Leave Me • Mixed Up Girl • Third Child • Feel The Warm • Walk A Mile In My Shoes • Something More • We've Only Just Begun • Love The One You're With

### EDELMAN, Randy ○
Singer/songwriter/pianist. Scored several movies. Married **Jackie DeShannon**.

| 3/22/75 | 208 | 2 | **Prime Cuts** | $12 | 20th Century 448 |
|---|---|---|---|---|---|

Bluebird • Pistol Packin' Melody • I Am A Dancer • Where Did We Go Wrong? • Stan, The Pantsman • You Are The Sunlight - I Am The Moon • The Woman On Your Arm • Isn't It A Shame • Everybody Wants To Call You Sweetheart • June Lullaby

### EDGE, The — see WOBBLE, Jah

### EDMUNDS, Dave
Born on 4/15/44 in Cardiff, Wales. Singer/songwriter/guitarist/producer. Formed rockabilly band Rockpile in 1976.

| 3/4/72 | 212 | 2 | 1 **Rockpile** | $30 | MAM 3 |
|---|---|---|---|---|---|

Down Down Down • I Hear You Knocking • Hell Of A Pain • It Ain't Easy • The Promised Land • Dance, Dance, Dance • (I Am A) Lover Not A Fighter • Egg Or The Hen • Sweet Little Rock & Roller • Outlaw Blues

| 5/21/77 | 209 | 2 | 2 **Get It** | $10 | Swan Song 8418 |
|---|---|---|---|---|---|

Get Out Of Denver • I Knew The Bride • Back To School Days • Here Comes The Weekend • Worn Out Suits, Brand New Pockets • Where Or When • JuJu Man • Git It • Let's Talk About Us • Hey Good Lookin' • What Did I Do Last Night? • Little Darlin' • My Baby Left Me

| 10/14/78 | 202 | 2 | 3 **Tracks On Wax 4** | $10 | Swan Song 8505 |
|---|---|---|---|---|---|

Trouble Boys • Never Been In Love • Not A Woman, Not A Child • Television • What Looks Best On You • Readers Wives • Deborah • Thread Your Needle • On The Jukebox • It's My Own Business • Heart Of The City

### EDWARDS, Dennis
Born on 2/3/43 in Birmingham, Alabama. Lead singer of The Contours until 1968. Lead singer of **The Temptations** from 1968-77, 1980-84 and 1987-present.

| 7/27/85 | 205 | 5 | **Coolin' Out** | $10 | Gordy 6148 |
|---|---|---|---|---|---|

Try A Little Tenderness • State Of Limbo • Amanda • No Such Thing • Why Do People Fall In Love [w/Thelma Houston] • Givin' So Much • Coolin' Out • Breakin' Loose • Wrap You

### EDWARDS, Jonathan
Born on 7/28/46 in Aitkin, Minnesota; raised in Virginia. Singer/songwriter/guitarist.

| 1/19/74 | 205 | 3 | 1 **Have A Good Time For Me** | $12 | Atco 7036 |
|---|---|---|---|---|---|

Have Yourself A Good Time For Me • King Of Hearts • Places I've Been • I'm Alone • Travelin' Blues • Rollin' Along • My Home Ain't In The Hall Of Fame • Angelina • Thirty Miles To Go • Sit Down Rock And Roll Man • When The Roll Is Called Up Yonder

| 1/11/75 | 205 | 2 | 2 **Lucky Day** | [L] $12 | Atco 104 |
|---|---|---|---|---|---|

recorded on 3/22 & 3/23/74 at The Performance Center in Cambridge, Massachusetts
Give Us A Song • Don't Cry Blue • Nova Scotia • Today I Started Loving You Again • Shanty • Have You Seen Her • Everybody Knows Her • Lucky Day • Sometimes • Hit Parade Of Love • Stop And Start It All Again • My Home Ain't In The Hall Of Fame • That's What Our Life Is • Medley: You Are My Sunshine/Sunshine (Go Away Today)

| 4/24/76 | 203 | 3 | 3 **Rockin' Chair** | $10 | Reprise 2238 |
|---|---|---|---|---|---|

How Long • Hearts Overflowing • Favorite Song • White Line • Ain't Got Time • Hello • Song For The Life • Rockin' Chair (Gonna Get You) • The Christian Life • Lady

### EGAN, Walter
Born on 7/12/48 in Jamaica, New York. Singer/guitarist.

| 8/11/79 | 201 | 1 | **Hi Fi** | $10 | Columbia 35796 |
|---|---|---|---|---|---|

I Can't Wait • That's That • Little Miss, It's You • Man B. Goode • I Do • HiFi Love • Hurt Again • Drive Away • Love At Last • Like You Do • You're The One • Bad News T.F.

### 805 ○
Rock group from New York City: Dave Porter (vocals, guitar), Ed Vivenzio (keyboards), Greg Liss (bass) and Frank Briggs (drums).

| 8/14/82 | 203 | 4 | **Stand In Line** | $10 | RCA Victor 8013 |
|---|---|---|---|---|---|

Stand In Line • Young Boys • Fools Parade • Making It All Seem True • Defense • Gimme Everything • Keeping The Spark Alive • Float Away • Out In The Light • Going Nowhere At All

### EL COCO
Disco group from Los Angeles led by producers Laurin Rinder and Michael Lewis.

| 11/11/78 | 208 | 1 | **Dancing In Paradise** | $10 | AVI 6044 |
|---|---|---|---|---|---|

Dancing In Paradise • Love In Your Life • Ugly People • It's Your Last Chance • Afrodesia • Coco Kane

### ELEPHANT'S MEMORY
Rock/jazz group from New York City: Michal Shapiro (female vocals), Stan Bronstein (male vocals, sax), Richard Ayers (guitar), Richard Sussman (piano), Myron Yules (trombone), John Ward (bass) and Rick Frank (drums).

| 10/28/72 | 205 | 3 | **Elephant's Memory** | $20 | Apple 3389 |
|---|---|---|---|---|---|

produced by John Lennon and Yoko Ono
Liberation Special • Baddest Of The Mean • Cryin Blacksheep Blues • Chuck 'N Bo • Gypsy Wolf • Madness • Life • Wind Ridge • Power Boogie • Local Plastic Ono Band

### ELVIS BROTHERS, The ○
Rock trio of brothers from Chicago: Rob (vocals, guitar), Graham (bass) and Brad (drums) Elvis.

| 10/22/83 | 209 | 1 | **Movin' Up** | $10 | Portrait 38865 |
|---|---|---|---|---|---|

(I Know You) Shake It • It's So Hard • Hidden In A Heartbeat • Hey Tina • Red Dress • Fire In The City • Here We Go Again • Movin' Up • Santa Fe • Full Speed Straight Ahead • You Got Me • Long Gone

### ELY, Joe
Born on 9/2/47 in Amarillo, Texas; raised in Lubbock, Texas. Country-rock singer/songwriter/guitarist.

| 5/19/84 | 204 | 4 | **Hi-Res** ........................................................................... | $10 | MCA 5480 |

What's Shakin' Tonight • Cool Rockin' Loretta • Madame Wo • Dream Camera • Letter To Laredo • She Gotta Get The Gettin' • Lipstick In The Night • Imagine Houston • Dame Tu Mano • Locked In A Boxcar With The Queen Of Spain

### ELY, Rick ◎
Singer/actor. Played "Jeremy Larkin" on the TV series *The Young Rebels* (1970-71).

| 12/26/70 | 202 | 1 | **Rick Ely** ........................................................................ | $12 | RCA Victor 4443 |

Circle Game • Up On The Roof • The Other Side Of Life • Something • Make It With You • Morning Girl • Your Song • The Last Thing On My Mind • The Fool On The Hill

### EMOTIONS, The
R&B vocal trio from Chicago: sisters Wanda, Sheila and Pamela Hutchinson.

| 6/23/84 | 206 | 2 | 1 **Sincerely** ................................................................... | $10 | Red Label 001 |

All Things Come In Time • Are You Through With My Heart • You're The One • Can't Blow Out The Candle • Sincerely • You're The Best • You Know I'm The One • Never Let Another • I Can Do Anything

| 5/25/85 | 203 | 2 | 2 **If I Only Knew** ............................................................ | $10 | Motown 6136 |

Supernatural • The Good Times • Miss Your Love • If I Only Knew Then (What I Know Now) • Just A Girl In Love • Shine Your Love On Me • Giving You All I Got • Closer To You • Eternally

### ENCHANTMENT
R&B vocal quintet from Detroit: Ed "Mickey" Clanton, Bobby Green, Davis Banks, Emanuel Johnson and Joe Thomas.

| 12/6/80+ | 202 | 7 | **Soft Lights, Sweet Music** ........................................ | $10 | RCA Victor 3824 |

Settin' It Out • I'm Who You Found (Not Who You Lost) • I Believe In You • Moment Of Weakness • I Can't Fake It • Soft Lights, Sweet Music • Are You Ready For Love • I Can't Be The One • You And Me

### ENGLAND DAN & JOHN FORD COLEY
Soft-rock duo. England Dan Seals was born on 2/8/48 in McCamey, Texas; raised in Rankin, Texas. Brother of Jim Seals of Seals & Crofts. Coley was born on 10/13/48 in Austin, Texas.

| 11/20/76 | 202 | 3 | **I Hear The Music** ........................................... [E] | $10 | A&M 4613 |

recorded in 1973

Used To You • Tell Her Hello • New Jersey • Idolizer • Mud And Stone • I Hear The Music • Legendary Captain • Miss Me • The Pilot • Carry On

### ENGLISH CONGREGATION, The ◎
British vocal group led by Brian Keith (also a member of **The Kingsway Youth Opera Company**).

| 8/26/72 | 209 | 3 | **Jesahel** ......................................................................... | $12 | Signpost 8405 |

Jesahel • Day By Day • Softly Whispering I Love You • Until It's Time For You To Go • Midnight Blue • Will You Love Me Tomorrow • A Friend In Need • Everything I Am • Love Song • Loving Your Neighbour

### ESSEX, David
Born David Cook on 7/23/47 in London. Portrayed Christ in the London production of *Godspell*. Star of British movies since 1970.

| 11/8/75 | 204 | 9 | **All The Fun Of The Fair** ........................................ | $15 | Columbia 33813 |

All The Fun Of The Fair • Hold Me Close • Circles • If I Could • Rolling Stone • Won't Get Burned Again • Coconut Ice • Watch Out (Carolina) • Here It Comes Again • Funfair (Reprise)

### EVERLY BROTHERS, The
Donald (real name: Isaac Donald) was born on 2/1/37 in Brownie, Kentucky; Philip on 1/19/39 in Chicago. Vocal duo/guitarists/songwriters. Duo split up in July 1973 and reunited in September 1983. Inducted into the Rock and Roll Hall of Fame in 1986.

| 2/13/71 | 205 | 1 | 1 **End Of An Era** ................................................... [K] | $20 | Barnaby 30260 [2] |

Take A Message To Mary • Roving Gambler • Claudette • This Little Girl Of Mine • I Wonder If I Care As Much • Kentucky • When Will I Be Loved • Down In The Willow Garden • Barbara Allen • Devoted To You • Oh, What A Feeling • That Silver-Haired Daddy Of Mine • Since You Broke My Heart • I'm Here To Get My Baby Out Of Jail • Put My Little Shoes Away • Oh, So Many Years • Hey, Doll Baby • Who's Gonna Shoe Your Pretty Little Feet

| 4/1/72 | 208 | 4 | 2 **Stories We Could Tell** .................................................. | $12 | RCA Victor 4620 |

All We Really Want To Do • Breakdown • Green River • Mandolin Wind • Up In Mabel's Room • Del Rio Dan • Ridin' High • Christmas Eve Can Kill You • Three-Armed, Poker-Playin' River Rat • I'm Tired Of Singing My Song In Las Vegas • Stories We Could Tell

### EVERYTHING BUT THE GIRL
Pop duo from London: Tracey Thorn (vocals) and Ben Watt (guitar, keyboards, vocals). Group name taken from a furniture store on England's Hull University campus.

| 6/22/85 | 202 | 1 | **Love Not Money** .............................................................. | $10 | Sire 25274 |

When All's Well • Heaven Help Me • Are You Trying To Be Funny? • Ugly Little Dreams • Shoot Me Down • Sean • Ballad Of The Times • Kid • Anytown • This Love (Not For Sale) • Trouble And Strife • Angel

### EXOTIC GUITARS, The
Studio group featuring the lead guitar of Al Casey.

| 5/8/71 | 210 | 2 | **I Can't Stop Loving You** ............................................... | $10 | Ranwood 8085 |

I Can't Stop Loving You • El Condor Pasa • Candida • September Song • My Sweet Lord • Who's Sorry Now • Till Love Touches Your Life • Theme From "Love Story" • Honey • Hava Nagila

### EXUMA ◎
Male R&B singer/guitarist/drummer.

| 10/16/71 | 202 | 5 | **Do Wah Nanny** .............................................................. | $15 | Kama Sutra 2040 |

Do Wah Nanny • Silver City • Eyebrows And Beard • She Looks So Fine • Roweena • The Bowery • 22nd Century • Do Wah Nanny (Pt. 2)

### EYE TO EYE
Pop duo: vocalist Deborah Berg from Seattle and pianist Julian Marshall from England.

| 10/29/83 | 205 | 1 | **Shakespeare Stole My Baby** ..................................... | $10 | Warner 23919 |

Shakespeare Stole My Baby • Tonight Insomnia • Falling For A Funny One • Jabberwokky • Lucky • T.W.A Sari • Something Good • Mermaid Man • Are You Listening?

# F

### FABULOUS RHINESTONES — see RHINESTONES

### FABULOUS THUNDERBIRDS, The
Male blues-rock group from Austin, Texas: Kim Wilson (vocals, harmonica), Jimmie Vaughan (guitar; older brother of Stevie Ray Vaughan), Keith Ferguson (bass) and Fran Christina (drums). Ferguson died of liver failure on 4/29/97 (age 49).

| 5/24/80 | 204 | 4 | **What's The Word** ........ | $10 | Chrysalis 1287 |

Runnin' Shoes • You Ain't Nothin But Fine • Low-Down Woman • Extra Jimmies • Sugar-Coated Love • Last Call For Alcohol • The Crawl • Jumpin' Bad • Learn To Treat Me Right • I'm A Good Man (If You Give Me A Chance) • Dirty Work • That's Enough Of That Stuff • Los Fabulosos Thunderbirds

### FACES
Rock group formed in London by former Small Faces members Ronnie Lane (bass), **Ian McLagan** (organ) and Kenney Jones (drums) with former Jeff Beck Group members **Rod Stewart** (vocals) and Ronnie Wood (bass). Lane left in 1973; replaced by Tetsu Yamauchi (of Free). Disbanded in late 1975. Wood joined The Rolling Stones in 1976. Jones joined The Who in 1978 and formed The Law in 1991. Lane died of multiple sclerosis on 6/4/97 (age 51).

| 12/11/76 | 207 | 1 | **Snakes And Ladders/The Best Of Faces** .......... [G] | $20 | Warner 2897 |

Pool Hall Richard • Cindy Incidentally • Ooh La La • Sweet Lady Mary • Flying • Pineapple And The Monkey • You Can Make Me Dance, Sing Or Anything • Had Me A Real Good Time • Stay With Me • Miss Judy's Farm • Silicone Grown • Around The Plynth

### FAHEY, John ○
Born on 2/28/39 in Cecil County, Maryland. Acoustic guitarist.

| 8/11/73 | 208 | 2 | **After The Ball** .......... [I] | $12 | Reprise 2145 |

Horses • New Orleans Shuffle • Beverly • Om Shanthi Norris • I Wish I Know How It Would Feel To Be Free • When You Wore A Tulip (And I Wore A Big Red Rose) • Hawaiian Two-Step • Bucktown Stomp • Candy Man • After The Ball

### FAIRPORT CONVENTION
Folk-rock group from London featuring lead singer **Sandy Denny** (d: 4/21/78, age 37). Varying membership included vocalist **Ian Matthews** (1967-69) and guitarist **Richard Thompson** (1967-71).

| 5/5/73 | 203 | 3 | 1 **Rosie** ......... | $15 | A&M 4386 |

Rosie • Matthew, Mark, Luke & John • Knights Of The Road • Peggy's Pub • Plainsman • Hungarian Rhapsody • My Girl • Me With You • Hens March Through The Midden • Furs And Feathers

| 5/22/76 | 207 | 1 | 2 **Fairport Chronicles** .......... [K] | $15 | A&M 3530 [2] |

Tale In Hard Time • Who Knows Where The Time Goes • Walk Awhile • Come All Ye • Listen, Listen • Bridge Over The River Ash • I'll Keep It With Mine • My Girl The Month Of May • Million Dollar Bash • The Way I Feel • Learning The Game • Meet On The Ledge • Percy's Song • Now Be Thankful • Tam Lin • Genesis Hall • Fotheringay • Sloth • Farewell, Farewell • End Of A Holiday

### FAITH, Percy
Born on 4/7/08 in Toronto. Died of cancer on 2/9/76. Orchestra leader. *Top Pop Albums*: 30.

| 12/16/72+ | 204 | 7 | 1 **Percy Faith's All-Time Greatest Hits** .......... [G-I] | $15 | Columbia 31588 [2] |

Baubles, Bangles And Beads • Swedish Rhapsody • Angel Of The Morning • Show Me • The Theme From "A Summer Place" • Delicado • Younger Than Springtime • Malaguena • Windy • The Virginian • The Song From Moulin Rouge • Theme For Young Lovers • Bouquet • Mexican Hat Dance (Jarabe Tapatio) • Tara's Theme • I Will Follow You • The Sound Of Music • Love Theme From "Romeo And Juliet" • Yellow Days • MacArthur Park

| 3/24/73 | 213 | 3 | 2 **Clair** .......... [I] | $12 | Columbus 32164 |

Clair • Don't Let Me Be Lonely Tonight • Ben • Sweet Surrender • I Can See Clearly Now • 2001 (Also Sprach Zarathustra) • Nights In White Satin • Summer Breeze • Super Fly • Love Theme From "Lady Sings The Blues" • We Were Havin' Some Fun At The Conservatory, When....... • Dueling Banjos

### FAITH BAND ○
Pop-rock group from Indianapolis: Carl Storie (vocals), David Bennett (guitar), John Cascella (keyboards), Mark Cawley (bass) and David Barnes (drums).

| 7/7/79 | 206 | 4 | **Face To Face** .......... | $10 | Mercury 3770 |

Touchy Situation • You're My Weakness • Big City Lights • Hopeless Romantic • Diamond In The Rough • Leave This Love • Fool's Love • Long Distance Runner • Forever

### FAMILY
British rock group: Roger Chapman (vocals), John Wetton (guitar, keyboards; King Crimson, Uriah Heep, U.K., Asia), Charlie Whitney (guitar), Poli Palmer (keyboards) and Rob Townsend (drums).

| 3/10/73 | 207 | 3 | **Anyway** .......... | $15 | United Artists 5527 |

Good News-Bad News • Willow Tree • Holding The Compass • Strange Band • In My Own Time • Part Of The Load • Anyway • Normans • Lives And Ladies

### FAMILY OF MANN, The ○
Jazz group: Herbie Mann (flute), Sam Brown (guitar), David Newman (sax), Pat Rebillot (keyboards), Armen Halburian (percussion), Tony Levin (bass) and Steve Gadd (drums).

| 11/2/74 | 201 | 4 | **First Light** .......... [I] | $12 | Atlantic 1658 |

Toot Stick • Davey Blue • Daffodil • The Turtle And The Frog • Muh Hoss Knows The Way • Music Is A Game We Play • Sunrise Highs • Thank You Mr. Rushing • Mexicali • Lullaby For Mary Elizabeth

### FANTASY ○
R&B vocal group from New York City: Ken Robeson, Tami Hunt, Rufus Jackson and Carolyn Edwards.

| 5/9/81 | 201 | 2 | **Fantasy** .......... | $10 | Pavillion 37151 |

You're Too Late • Too Much Too Soon • (Hey Who's Gotta) Funky Song • Love Explosion • You Can't Lose What You Never Had • Now I Have Everything • Read Between The Lines

## FARGO, Donna
Born Yvonne Vaughan on 11/10/45 in Mount Airy, North Carolina. Country singer.

| | | | | | |
|---|---|---|---|---|---|
| 1/19/74 | 204 | 6 | **1 All About A Feeling** ........................................ | $12 | Dot 26019 |

It Do Feel Good • I'll Try A Little Bit Harder • Puffy Eyes • Nothing Can Stay • All About A Feeling • Little Girl Gone • Just Call Me • Hot Diggety Dog • Does It Matter • Rotten Little Song • Just A Friend Of Mine

| | | | | | |
|---|---|---|---|---|---|
| 12/7/74 | 207 | 1 | **2 Miss Donna Fargo** ........................................ | $12 | ABC/Dot 2002 |

You Can't Be A Beacon (If Your Light Don't Shine) • U.S. Of A. • If You're Somewhere Listening • Words • Go Straight To Her • It Do Feel Good • Honeychild • Only The Strong • A Woman's Prayer • Send Me Home • Heartbreak Hotel

## FATBACK
R&B-funk group: Michael Walker (vocals), George Victory (guitar), George Williams (trumpet), Fred Demery (sax), Gerry Thomas (keyboards), Johnny Flippin (bass) and Bill Curtis (drums).

| | | | | | |
|---|---|---|---|---|---|
| 7/24/82 | 204 | 6 | **On The Floor** ........................................ | $10 | Spring 6736 |

On The Floor • U.F.O. (Unidentified Funk Object) • Burn Baby Burn • She's My Shining Star • Hip So Slick • Do It To Me Now

## FELLINI, Suzanne ✪
Born on 8/6/55 in New York City. Singer/actress.

| | | | | | |
|---|---|---|---|---|---|
| 5/17/80 | 203 | 4 | **Suzanne Fellini** ........................................ | $10 | Casablanca 7205 |

Double Take • First Kiss • Bad Influence • Love On The Phone • Crazy • Permanent Damage • Give Me The Light • Bad Boy • I'm A Rock • Something's Over

## FENDER, Freddy
Born Baldemar Huerta on 6/4/37 in San Benito, Texas. Mexican-American singer/guitarist. In the movie *The Milagro Beanfield War*. Joined the Texas Tornados in 1990.

| | | | | | |
|---|---|---|---|---|---|
| 11/8/75 | 203 | 1 | **Since I Met You Baby** ........................................ | [E] $12 | GRT 8005 |

new musical tracks behind Fender's original vocals from 1960

Since I Met You Baby • A Man Can Cry • Louisiana Blues • Crazy Baby • I'm Gonna Leave • Little Mama • You're Something Else For Me • Too Late To Remedy • Find Somebody New • Go On Baby (I Can Do Without You) • Wild Side Of Life

## FERRY, Bryan
Born on 9/26/45 in County Durham, England. Lead singer of **Roxy Music**. Married socialite Lucy Helmore on 6/26/82.

| | | | | | |
|---|---|---|---|---|---|
| 9/7/74 | 204 | 5 | **These Foolish Things** ........................................ | $12 | Atlantic 7304 |

A Hard Rain's A-Gonna Fall • River Of Salt • Don't Ever Change • Piece Of My Heart • Baby, I Don't Care • It's My Party • Don't Worry Baby • Sympathy For The Devil • The Tracks Of My Tears • You Won't See Me • I Love How You Love Me • Loving You Is Sweeter Than Ever • These Foolish Things Remind Me Of You

## FEVER ✪
Disco trio from Ohio: Dale Reed (saxophone), Joe Bomback (keyboards) and Dennis Waddington (bass). With vocals by Clydene Jackson.

| | | | | | |
|---|---|---|---|---|---|
| 12/22/79+ | 205 | 5 | **Fever** ........................................ | $10 | Fantasy 9580 |

Beat Of The Night • Work Me • Treat Me Right • Pump It Up • The Fever Rock • Over The Edge

## FIELDS, W.C.
Born on 2/20/1879 in Philadelphia. Died on 12/25/46. Classic comedian of American movies.

| | | | | | |
|---|---|---|---|---|---|
| 4/24/76 | 210 | 2 | **The Best Of W.C. Fields** ........................................ | [C] $10 | Columbia 34144 |

The Temperence Lecture • A Drink Of Water • False Arrest • Other Selected Performances • The Pharmacist • Skunk Trap • Other Selected Performances

## FIESTA ✪
R&B vocal group: Thomas Bullock, Johnny Burton, Wesley Lee, Carl Sims and Thomas Wiley.

| | | | | | |
|---|---|---|---|---|---|
| 2/17/79 | 206 | 2 | **Fiesta** ........................................ | $10 | Arista 4196 |

E.S.P. • Thanks For The Sweet Memories • Hold On • Baby If You Love Me • Everyday Housewife Rap • Everyday Housewife • Quit Funkin' With Me • One More Chance

## 5TH DIMENSION, The
R&B vocal group from Los Angeles: Marilyn McCoo, Billy Davis Jr., Florence LaRue, Lamont McLemore and Ron Townson. McCoo and Davis were married in 1969 and recorded as a duo since 1976.

| | | | | | |
|---|---|---|---|---|---|
| 1/11/75 | 202 | 7 | **Soul & Inspiration** ........................................ | $12 | Bell 1315 |

Soul & Inspiration • Harlem • The Best Of My Love • My Song • Hard Core Poetry • No Love In The Room • House For Sale • Somebody Warm Like Me • Salty Tears • I Don't Know How To Look For Love

## FINGERPRINTZ ✪
British rock group: Jimme O'Neill (vocals), Cha Burnz (guitar), Kenny Alton (bass) and Bogdan Wiczling (drums).

| | | | | | |
|---|---|---|---|---|---|
| 10/4/80 | 206 | 1 | **Distinguishing Marks** ........................................ | $10 | Virgin 13136 |

Yes Eyes • Houdini Love • Criminal Mind • Bullet Proof Heart • Remorse Code • Amnesia • Ringing Tone • Radiation • Jabs • Hide And Seek

## FIRESIGN THEATRE, The
Satirical comedy group: Phil Austin, Peter Bergman, David Ossman and Philip Proctor.

| | | | | | |
|---|---|---|---|---|---|
| 6/2/73 | 211 | 2 | **1 TV Or Not TV** ........................................ | [C] $12 | Columbia 32199 |

**PROCTOR & BERGMAN**

Insert Here • Channel 85 Sign-on • Escaping From The Declining Fall Of The Roaming Umpire, Chapter XIII • Police Lineup • Salute My Boots • The Channel 85 Story • Cirque Internationale • Communist Love Song • Channel 85 Reply • Tobor Radar Robot • The Pills Brothers On Drugs • The MZ Information Show • Bring Us Together • Nasi Goring • Our Lady Of The Torch • Emergency Alert • Emerging Fall Of The Roaming Umpire, Program VII • Give Up This Day • Channel 85 Sign-off • Insert Here

| | | | | | |
|---|---|---|---|---|---|
| 10/25/75 | 201 | 6 | **2 In The Next World, You're On Your Own** ........................................ | [C] $12 | Columbia 33475 |

Police Street • We've Lost Our Big Kabloona

### FIRST CHOICE
Female R&B vocal trio from Philadelphia: Rochelle Fleming, Annette Guest and Joyce Jones.

| 6/5/76 | 204 | 3 | **So Let Us Entertain You** .................................................................................. | $12 | Warner 2934 |

First Choice Theme • Ain't It Bad • I'll Stay Right Here • Yes, Maybe No • Gotta Get Away (From You Baby) • Are You Ready For Me? • Don't Fake It • I Got A Feeling • Let Him Go • If The Sun Shines

### FIRST CLASS, The ✪
British studio group: Tony Burrows (lead vocals), John Carter, Del John and Chas Mills (backing vocals), Spencer James (guitar), Clive Barrett (keyboards), Robin Shaw (bass) and Eddie Richards (drums).

| 11/9/74 | 204 | 1 | **The First Class** ............................................................................................... | $12 | UK 53109 |

Beach Baby • Won't Somebody Help Me • What Became Of Me • Surfer Queen • The First Day Of Your Life • Long Time Gone • Dreams Are Ten A Penny • Bobby Dazzler • The Disco Kid • I Was Always A Joker

### FISHER, Matthew ✪
Born on 3/7/46 in London. Singer/songwriter/keyboardist. Member of **Procol Harum** from 1966-70.

| 11/3/73 | 210 | 5 | **Journey's End** ................................................................................................. | $12 | RCA Victor 0195 |

Suzanne • Going For A Song • Play The Game • Separation • Hard To Be Sure • Marie • Not This Time • Interlude • Journey's End (Part 1) • Journey's End (Part 2)

### FIVE STAIRSTEPS, The — see STAIRSTEPS

### FLACK, Roberta
Born on 2/10/39 in Asheville, North Carolina; raised in Arlington, Virginia. R&B singer/pianist.

| 11/21/81+ | 201 | 11 | **The Best Of Roberta Flack** | [G] $10 | Atlantic 19317 |

Killing Me Softly With His Song • The Closer I Get To You [w/Donny Hathaway] • You've Got A Friend [w/Donny Hathaway] • Feel Like Makin' Love • Will You Still Love Me Tomorrow • Where Is The Love [w/Donny Hathaway] • The First Time Ever I Saw Your Face • Back Together Again [w/Donny Hathaway] • You Are My Heaven [w/Donny Hathaway] • If Ever I See You Again • Jesse

### FLASH CADILLAC AND THE CONTINENTAL KIDS ✪
Fifties-styled rock act from Colorado: Sam "Flash Cadillac" McFadden (vocals, guitar), Lin "Spike" Phillips (guitar), Chris "Angelo" Moe (keyboards), Dwight "Spider" Bement (sax), Warren "Butch" Knight (bass) and Jeff "Wally" Stuart (drums). Group appeared as the prom band in the movie *American Graffiti.*

| 1/13/73 | 205 | 4 | 1 **Flash Cadillac And The Continental Kids** ................................................ | $15 | Epic 31787 |

Muleskinner Blues (Blue Yodel No. 8) • Reputation • Crying In The Rain • Teenage Eyes • Betty Lou • Pipeline • She's So Fine • Tell Him No • Nothin' For Me • You Gotta Rock • Endless Sleep • Up On The Mountain

| 8/16/75 | 205 | 4 | 2 **Sons Of The Beaches** ..................................................................................... | $12 | Private Stock 2012 |

Summer Means Fun • Time Will Tell • Hot Summer Girls • It's A Summer Night • Come On Let's Go • Did You Boogie (With Your Baby) • Good Times, Rock & Roll • I Wish You'd Dance • It's Hard (To Break The Ice) • Rock 'N' Roll Menace

### FLEISCHMAN, Robert ✪
Singer/songwriter/keyboardist from San Francisco.

| 5/19/79 | 205 | 2 | **Perfect Stranger** ............................................................................................ | $10 | Arista 4220 |

All For You • Far Too Long • Southern Lights • Ace In The Hole • One More Time • Part Of Me • Never Never Land • Heartstrings Delight

### FLOYD, Eddie ✪
Born on 6/25/35 in Montgomery, Alabama; raised in Detroit. Soul singer.

| 9/4/71 | 209 | 2 | **Down To Earth** ................................................................................................. | $25 | Stax 2041 |

People Get Ready • Linda Sue Dixon • My Mind Was Messed Around At The Time • When The Sun Goes Down • Salvation • I Only Have Eyes For You • Tears Of Joy • Changing Love

### FLYING BURRITO BROTHERS, The
Country-rock group from Los Angeles: guitarists/vocalists Floyd "Gib" Guilbeau, "Sneaky" Pete Kleinow and Joel Scott Hill, bassist Skip Battin and drummer Gene Parsons.

| 6/26/76 | 204 | 1 | **Airborne** .......................................................................................................... | $12 | Columbia 34222 |

Out Of Control • Waitin' For Love To Begin • Toe Tappin' Music • Quiet Man • Northbound Bus • Big Bayou • Walk On The Water • Linda Lu • Border Town • She's A Sailor • Jesus Broke The Wild Horse

### FM ✪
Pop-rock trio from Toronto: Cameron Hawkins (vocals, keyboards), Nash The Slash (electric violin) and Martin Deller (drums).

| 3/3/79 | 203 | 4 | **Black Noise** ..................................................................................................... | $10 | Visa 7007 |

Phasors On Stun • One O'Clock Tomorrow • Hours • Journey • Dialing For Dharma • Slaughter In Robot Village • Aldeberan • Black Noise

### FOGELBERG, Dan
Born on 8/13/51 in Peoria, Illinois. Soft-rock singer/songwriter.

| 10/20/73 | 210 | 2 | **Home Free** ........................................................................................................ | $15 | Columbia 31751 |

To The Morning • Stars • More Than Ever • Be On Your Way • Hickory Grove • Long Way Home (Live In The Country) • Looking For A Lady • Anyway I Love You • Wysteria • The River

### FONDA, Jane — see AEROBIC ALBUMS

### FOUNTAIN, Pete
Born on 7/3/30 in New Orleans. Jazz clarinet player.

| 7/21/73 | 217 | 3 | **Pete Fountain's Crescent City** ..................................................................... | [I] $12 | MCA 336 |

Tie A Yellow Ribbon Round The Old Oak Tree • Am I Blue • All By Myself • Muskrat Ramble • Nobody's Sweetheart • High Society • Basin Street Blues • Oh Babe, What Would You Say? • Funky Beat • Spain • Dream • At The Jazz Band Ball

### 4 OUT OF 5 DOCTORS ✪
Rock group from Washington, D.C.: George Pittaway (guitar), Jeff Severson (keyboards), Cal Everett (bass) and Tom Ballew (drums).

| 2/28/81 | 202 | 2 | **4 Out Of 5 Doctors** ........................................................................................ | $10 | Nemperor 36575 |

Modern Man • Jeff, Jeff • Waiting For A Change • Elizabeth • Opus 10 • I Want Her • New Wave Girls • Mr. Cool Shoes • Danger Man • Mushroom Boy • Not From Her World

| DEBUT | PEAK | WKS | Album Title | $ | Label & Number |
|-------|------|-----|-------------|---|----------------|

## FOUR TOPS

R&B vocal group from Detroit: Levi Stubbs (lead singer), Renaldo "Obie" Benson, Lawrence Payton and Abdul "Duke" Fakir. Payton died of cancer on 6/20/97 (age 59). Group inducted into the Rock and Roll Hall of Fame in 1990. *Top Pop Albums*: 27.

| | | | | | |
|---|---|---|---|---|---|
| 8/10/74 | 203 | 4 | 1 Anthology ........................................................................................................ [K] | $25 | Motown 809 [3] |

Baby I Need Your Loving • Without The One You Love (Life's Not Worthwhile) • Sad Souvenirs • Ask The Lonely • I Can't Help Myself (Sugar Pie, Honey Bunch) • Helpless • It's The Same Old Song • Something About You • Shake Me, Wake Me (When It's Over) • Loving You Is Sweeter Than Ever • Then • Reach Out I'll Be There • Standing In The Shadows Of Love • I Got A Feeling • Bernadette • 7-Rooms Of Gloom • I'll Turn To Stone • You Keep Running Away • Walk Away Renee • If I Were A Carpenter • Yesterday's Dreams • Mac Arthur Park • Climb Ev'ry Mountain • Everybody's Talking • For Once In My Life • A Place In The Sun • Reflections • I'm In A Different World • Can't Seem To Get You Out Of My Mind • Don't Let Him Take Your Love From Me • It's All In The Game • Still Water (Love) • River Deep-Mountain High [w/The Supremes] • Just Seven Numbers (Can Straighten Out My Life) • In These Changing Times • You Gotta Have Love In Your Heart • I Can't Quit Your Love • (It's The Way) Nature Planned It • Medley: Hey Man/We Got To Get You A Woman

| 11/25/78 | 208 | 2 | 2 At The Top ........................................................................................................ | $12 | ABC 1092 |

H.E.L.P. • Bits And Pieces • Seclusion • Put It On The News • This House • Just In Time • Inside A Brokenhearted Man • When Your Dreams Take Wings And Fly

| 11/5/83 | 202 | 7 | 3 Back Where I Belong ....................................................................................... | $10 | Motown 6066 |

Make Yourself Right At Home • I Just Can't Walk Away • Sail On • Back Where I Belong • What Have We Got To Lose [w/Aretha Franklin] • The Masquerade Is Over • Body And Soul • Hang [w/The Temptations]

## FOXY

Latino dance band from Miami: Ish Ledesma (vocals, guitar), Richie Puente (percussion), Arnold Paseiro (bass) and Joe Galdo (drums). Puente is son of luminary Latin bandleader Tito Puente.

| 1/26/80 | 207 | 3 | Party Boys ........................................................................................................ | $10 | Dash 30015 |

Girls • Let's Be Bad Tonight • Sambamé Rio • I Belong To You • She's So Cool • I Can't Stand The Heat • RRRRRRock • Fantazy • Pensando En Ti • Party Boys

## FRANKLIN, Aretha

Born on 3/25/42 in Memphis; raised in Buffalo and Detroit. Known as "The Queen Of Soul." Daughter of famous gospel preacher Rev. Cecil L. Franklin, pastor of Detroit's New Bethel Baptist Church. Appeared in the 1980 movie *The Blues Brothers*. In 1987, became the first woman to be inducted into the Rock and Roll Hall of Fame. *Top Pop Albums*: 39.

| 10/3/81 | 209 | 2 | The Legendary Queen Of Soul ........................................................... [K] | $12 | Columbia 37377 [2] |

compilation of her Columbia recordings from 1960-66

Mockingbird • How Glad I Am • Walk On By • You'll Lose A Good Thing • Every Little Bit Hurts • I Can't Wait Until I See My Baby's Face • You Made Me Love You • Nobody Like You • Rough Lover • Lee Cross • Runnin' Out Of Fools • Won't Be Long • Until You Were Gone • Blue Holiday • One Room Paradise • Cry Like A Baby • Can't You Just See Me • Two Sides Of Love • I Won't Cry Anymore • I'll Keep On Smiling

## FRANKLIN, Rodney

Born on 9/16/58 in Berkeley, California. Jazz pianist.

| 11/29/80 | 207 | 1 | 1 Rodney Franklin ...................................................................................... [I] | $10 | Columbia 36747 |

Windy City • Life Moves On • In The Center • Awakening • I Like The Music Make It Hot • Theme For Jackie • On The Path • Creation

| 10/17/81 | 204 | 6 | 2 Endless Flight ........................................................................................... | $10 | Columbia 37154 |

Dance Tonight • Cancion Para Mi Mama (Song For My Mother) • Vibrations • Benetta • Morning Light (Reprise From Dance Tonight) • Endless Flight • Mensaje De Dios (Message From God) • Return To The Source • Hill Street Blues • Cancion Para Mi Mama (Epilogue)

## FRASER, Andy ☉

Born on 8/7/52 in London. Rock singer/bassist. Formerly with **John Mayall**'s Bluesbreakers and Free.

| 7/7/84 | 209 | 1 | Fine Fine Line ........................................................................................... | $10 | Island 90153 |

Fine, Fine Line • Branded By The Fire • Chinese Eyes • Knocking At Your Door • Million Miles Away • Do You Love Me • Night To Last Forever • Danger • One Night Love Affair • Living This Eternal Dream

## FRASER & DEBOLT (with Ian Guenther) ☉

Folk duo from Canada: Anthony Fraser and Donna DeBolt. Ian Guenther is their fiddler.

| 2/13/71 | 206 | 1 | Fraser & DeBolt (with Ian Guenther) ........................................... | $12 | Columbia 30381 |

All This Paradise • Gypsy Solitaire • Them Dance Hall Girls • David's Tune • The Waltze Of The Tennis Players • Armstrong Tourest Rest Home • Fraser And DeBolt Theme • Old Man On The Corner • Warmth • Stoney Day • Pure Spring Water • Don't Let Me Down

## FREE BEER ☉

Male rock trio: Sandy Allen (vocals, guitar), Michael Packer (bass) and Caleb Potter (drums).

| 8/30/75 | 203 | 3 | Free Beer ........................................................................................................ | $12 | Southwind 6402 |

I'm In Love • Coupe De Ville • Cruisin' • Brandy & Beer • Out On The Road • Riding Shotgun On A Dream Wagon • The Letdown • We Can Call It Home • Good Times, Sad Times • Zanzibar • River Of Wine • New England Girls

## FRENCH KISS ☉

Disco trio: Lamarr Stevens, Muffi Durham and Yvette Johnson.

| 6/2/79 | 210 | 1 | Panic ........................................................................................................ | $10 | Polydor 6197 |

Panic • We're The Right Combination • You Got Me Groovin' • All Out Of Tears • Mischief

## FULL MOON ☉

Jazz-rock group: Buzz Feiten (vocals, guitar), **Neil Larsen** (keyboards), Willie Weeks (bass) and Art Rodriguez (drums). The first two formed the Larsen-Feiten Band; both are prolific session musicians.

| 2/6/82 | 206 | 6 | Full Moon ........................................................................................................ | $10 | Warner 3585 |

**FULL MOON Featuring Neil Larsen & Buzz Feiten**

Phantom Of The Footlights • The Visitor • Twilight Moon • Sierra • Brown Eyes • Heroe's Welcome • Standing In Line • Little Cowboys

**FUNK INC.** ✪

Jazz-R&B group from Indianapolis: Steve Weakley (guitar), Bobby Watley (organ), Eugene Barr (sax), Cecil Hunt (congas) and Jimmy Munford (drums).

2/26/72 | **211** | 2 | **Funk Inc.** .......................................................................................... [I] $12 | Prestige 10031

Kool Is Back • Bowlegs • Sister Janie • The Thrill Is Gone • The Whipper

# G

**GALE, Arlyn** ✪

Male singer/songwriter/guitarist.

10/7/78 | **206** | 1 | **Back To The Midwest Night** .................................................................... $10 | ABC 1096

Back To The Midwest Night • Take The Night Flight • Tiger On The Lawn • Sunrise On Sunset • Ronee • Suspicious Fires • She's Alright • Halfway To Hell

**GALE, Eric**

Born on 9/20/38 in Brooklyn. Died of cancer on 5/25/94. Jazz-soul session guitarist. Member of **Stuff**.

11/8/80 | **201** | 5 | **Touch Of Silk** [I] $10 | Columbia 36570

You Got My Life In Your Hands • Touch Of Silk • War Paint • Once In A Smile • With You I'm Born Again • Au Privave • Live To Love

**GALLAGHER** ✪

Male comedian.

3/15/80 | **206** | 5 | **Gallagher** .............................................................................................. [C] $10 | United Artists 1019

no track titles listed on this album

**GALLAGHER, Rory**

Born on 3/2/49 in Ballyshannon, Ireland; raised in Cork, Ireland. Died on 6/14/95 from complications following a liver transplant. Blues-rock guitarist/vocalist. Leader of **Taste**.

11/15/80 | **206** | 3 | **Stage Struck** ......................................................................................... [L] $10 | Chrysalis 1280

recorded on his 1979 world tour

Shin Kicker • Wayward Child • Brute Force And Ignorance • Moonchild • Follow Me • Bought And Sold • Last Of The Independants • Shadow Play

**GALLAGHER AND LYLE** ✪

Scottish duo: Benny Gallagher and Graham Lyle. Both formerly with McGuiness Flint.

6/26/76 | **210** | 1 | **Breakaway** ............................................................................................ $10 | A&M 4566

Breakaway • Stay Young • I Wanna Stay With You • Heart On My Sleeve • Fifteen Summers • Sign Of The Times • If I Needed Someone • Storm In My Soul • Rockwriter • Northern Girl

**GAMBLE, Dee Dee Sharp — see SHARP, Dee Dee**

**GANG OF FOUR**

New-wave group from Leeds, England: Jon King (vocals), Andy Gill (guitar), Dave Allen (bass) and Hugo Burnham (drums).

11/29/80 | **201** | 7 | **Gang Of Four** [M] $10 | Warner 3494

Outside The Trains Don't Run On Time • He'd Send In The Army • It's Her Factory • Armalite Rifle

**GARCIA, Jerry — see WALES, Howard**

**GARTHEWAITE, Terry — see TONI & TERRY**

**GATLIN, Larry**

Born on 5/2/48 in Seminole, Texas. Country singer/songwriter/guitarist. Leader of The Gatlin Brothers.

7/5/80 | **204** | 2 | **The Pilgrim** ........................................................................................... [E] $10 | Columbia 36541

recorded and first released in 1974 on Monument 32571 ($15)

Sweet Becky Walker • My Mind's Gone To Memphis • Bitter They Are, Harder They Fall • The Heart • Try To Win A Friend • It Must Have Rained In Heaven • To Make Me Wanna Stay Home • Light At The End Of The Darkness • Dig A Little Deeper • Penny Annie

**GAYE, Marvin**

Born on 4/2/39 in Washington, D.C. Fatally shot by his father after a quarrel on 4/1/84 in Los Angeles. R&B singer/songwriter. Inducted into the Rock and Roll Hall of Fame in 1987. Won Grammy's Lifetime Achievement Award in 1996. *Top Pop Albums: 29.*

5/5/84 | **203** | 2 | 1 **Great Songs And Performances That Inspired The Motown 25th Anniversary Television Special** ...................................................... [G] $10 | Motown 5311

What's Going On • I Want You • Mercy Mercy Me (The Ecology) • Inner City Blues (Make Me Wanna Holler) • My Mistake (Was To Love You) *[w/Diana Ross]* • I Heard It Through The Grapevine • Too Busy Thinging About My Baby • Ain't That Peculiar • Let's Get It On • Got To Give It Up

5/19/84 | **208** | 1 | 2 **Motown Superstar Series Volume 15** ...................................................... [K] $10 | Motown 115

Medley: What's Going On/God Is Love/Mercy Mercy Me (The Ecology)/Inner City Blues (Make Me Wanna Holler) • I Want You • Keep Gettin' It On • After The Dance • I Wish It Would Rain • Come Get To This

**GAYNOR, Gloria**

Born on 9/7/49 in Newark, New Jersey. Disco singer.

7/11/81 | **206** | 5 | 1 **I Kinda Like Me** ................................................................................... $10 | Polydor 6324

I Kinda Like Me • Fingers In The Fire • Let's Mend What's Been Broken • Yesterday We Were Like Buddies • I Can Stand The Pain • I Love You Cause • When You Get Around To It • Chasin' Me Into Somebody Else's Arms • The Story Of The Joneses

1/8/83 | **210** | 1 | 2 **Gloria Gaynor** ..................................................................................... $10 | Atlantic 80033

Stop In The Name Of Love • Runaround Love • Mack-Side • Tease Me • America • For You, My Love • Love Me Real • Even A Fool Would Let Go

### GEILS, J., Band
Rock-blues group from Boston: Jerome Geils (guitar), Peter Wolf (vocals), Magic Dick Salwitz (harmonica), Seth Justman (keyboards), Danny Klein (bass) and Stephen Jo Bladd (drums).

| 12/6/80 | 201 | 5 | Best Of The J. Geils Band Two [K] | $10 | Atlantic 19284 |

First I Look At The Purse • The Lady Makes Demands • Trying To Live My Life Without You • Stoop Down • Givin' It All Up • Love-Itis • Cry One More Time • Monkey Island • Mean Love

### GENTLE GIANT
Progressive-rock group: brothers Derek (vocals) and Ray (bass) Shulman, Gary Green (guitar), Kerry Minnear (keyboards) and John Weathers (drums).

| 4/5/80 | 203 | 2 | Civilian | $10 | Columbia 36341 |

Convenience (Clean And Easy) • All Through The Night • Shadows On The Street • Number One • Underground • I Am A Camera • Inside Out • It's Not Imagination

### GENTRY, Bobbie
Born Roberta Streeter on 7/27/44 in Chickasaw County; raised in Greenwood, Mississippi. Country singer singer/songwriter/guitarist. Won the 1967 Best New Artist Grammy Award. Married Jim Stafford on 10/15/78; since divorced.

| 5/22/71 | 221 | 2 | Patchwork | $15 | Capitol 494 |

Benjamin • Marigolds And Tangerines • Billy The Kid • Beverly • Miss Clara/Azusa Sue • But I Can't Get Back • Jeremiah • Belinda • Mean Stepmama Blues • Your Number One Fan • Somebody Like Me • Lookin' In

### GETZ, Stan
Born Stan Gayetzsky on 2/2/27 in Philadelphia. Died of cancer on 6/6/91. Legendary tenor saxophonist.

| 6/26/76 | 208 | 1 | The Best Of Two Worlds [I] | $12 | Columbia 33703 |

featuring Joao Gilberto (guitar)
Double Rainbow • Aguas De Marco (Waters Of March) • Ligia • Falsa Bahiana • Retrato En Branco E Prieto (Picture In Black And White) • Izaura (You Know I Just Shouldn't Stay) • Eu Vim Da Bahia • Joao Marcello • E. Preciso Perdoar • Just One Of Those Things

### GIBB, Robin ○
Born on 12/22/49 in Manchester, England. Member of the Bee Gees.

| 7/28/84 | 204 | 4 | Secret Agent | $10 | Mirage 90170 |

Boys Do Fall In Love • In Your Diary • Robot • Rebecca • Secret Agent • Livin' In Another World • X-Ray Eyes • King Of Fools • Diamonds

### GIBBONS, Steve, Band ○
British rock group: Steve Gibbons (vocals, guitar), Bob Wilson (guitar), Dave Carroll (steel guitar), Trevor Burton (bass) and Bob Lamb (drums).

| 9/9/78 | 207 | 2 | Down In The Bunker | $10 | Polydor 6154 |

No Spitting On The Bus • Any Road Up • Down In The Bunker • Big J.C. • Mary Ain't Goin' Home • Down In The City • Let's Do It Again • Eddy Vortex • Chelita • When You Get Outside • Grace

### GIBBS, Terri
Born on 6/15/54 in Augusta, Georgia. Female country singer/pianist. Blind since birth.

| 10/24/81 | 202 | 3 | I'm A Lady | $10 | MCA 5255 |

I Wanna Be Around • Papa's No Fool • Too Far Gone • Every Now And Then • That's What Friends Are For • I'm A Lady • Another Place, Another Time • Mis'ry River • Too Long • Georgia On My Mind

### GILLEY, Mickey
Born on 3/9/36 in Natchez, Louisiana; raised in Ferriday, Louisiana. Country singer/pianist. First cousin to both **Jerry Lee Lewis** and Jimmy Swaggart. Co-owner of Gilley's nightclub in Pasadena, Texas, from 1971-89. Gilley and the club were featured in the movie *Urban Cowboy*.

| 9/11/82 | 202 | 6 | Put Your Dreams Away | $10 | Epic 38082 |

Talk To Me • Don't You Be Foolin' With A Fool • I Really Don't Want To Know • If I Can't Hold Her On The Outside • Put Your Dreams Away • Texas Heartache Number One • She Beats All I've Ever Seen • The Beginning Of The End • Honky Tonkin' (I Guess I Done Me Some) • Rocky Road To Romance

### GIRLSCHOOL
Female heavy-metal group from England: guitarists/vocalists Kelly Johnson and Kim McAuliffe, with bassist Gil Weston and drummer Denise Dufort.

| 11/27/82 | 207 | 2 | 1 Screaming Blue Murder | $10 | Mercury 4066 |

Screaming Blue Murder • You Got Me • Live With Me • When Your Blood Runs Cold • Hellrazor • Don't Call It Love • Take It From Me • Wildlife • Flesh And Blood • Tush • It Turns Your Head Around

| 1/14/84 | 207 | 2 | 2 Play Dirty | $10 | Mercury 814689 |

produced by Jim Lea and Noddy Holder of Slade
Going Under • High And Dry • 20th Century Boy • Running For Cover • Breaking All The Rules • Play Dirty • Burning In The Heat • Rock Me Shock Me • Surrender • Breakout (Knob In The Media)

### GLADSTONE ○
Pop group from Tyler, Texas: H.L. Voelker (vocals), Michael Rabon and Doug Rhone (guitars), Jerry Scheff (bass) and Ron Tutt (drums). Rabon was leader of The Five Americans.

| 9/23/72 | 208 | 4 | Gladstone | $12 | ABC 751 |

Marietta Station • A Piece Of Paper • Red Bird • Fade Away • Can't Seem To Find My Way Home • Lady Eyes • Peace In The Valley • Love Me If You Dare • You Got To Me • Livin' In The Country • Don't You Think I Can Love You • Dalarna

### GLASS HARP
Rock trio from Ohio: Phil Keaggy (vocals, guitar), Dan Pecchio (bass) and John Sferra (drums). Keaggy was later a prolific Contemporary Christian artist.

| 2/27/71 | 216 | 7 | 1 Glass Harp | $25 | Decca 75261 |

Can You See Me • Children's Fantasy • Changes (In The Heart Of My Own True Love) • Village Queen • Black Horse • Southbound • Whatever Life Demands • Look In The Sky • Garden • On Our Own

| 9/23/72 | 203 | 4 | 2 It Makes Me Glad | $25 | Decca 75358 |

See Saw • Sailing On A River • La De Da • Colt • Sea And You • David & Goliath • I'm Going Home • Do Lord • Song In The Air • Let's Live Together

## GOLDEN EARRING

Rock group from Amsterdam, Holland: Frans Krassenburg (vocals), George Kooymans (guitar), Rinus Gerritsen (bass) and Jaap Eggermont (drums). Originally known as **The Golden Earrings**. Krassenburg and Eggermont left in 1969, replaced by Barry Hay (vocals) and Cesar Zuiderwijk (drums). Group shortened name to Golden Earring. Eggermont later assembled the Stars on 45 studio group.

| 8/3/74 | 203 | 5 | 1 The Golden Earrings .............................................................[E] | $12 | Capitol 11315 |

recorded in 1967

Smoking Cigarettes • In My House • Don't Wanna Lose That Girl • Impeccable Girl • Tears And Lies • You've Got The Intention To Hurt Me • Dream • You Break My Heart • Baby Don't Make Me Nervous • Call Me • Lionel The Miser • There Will Be A Tomorrow

| 10/22/77 | 203 | 4 | 2 Live ..............................................................................[L] | $15 | MCA 8009 [2] |

Candy's Going Bad • She Flies On Strange Wings • Mad Love's Comin' • Eight Miles High • Vanilla Queen • To The Hilt • Fightin' Windmills • Con Man • Radar Love • Just Like Vince Taylor

| 11/4/78 | 204 | 3 | 3 Grab It For A Second ............................................................. | $12 | MCA 3057 |

Movin' Down Life • Against The Grain • Grab It For A Second • Cell 29 • Roxanne • Leather • Temptin' • U-Turn Time

## GOLDSBORO, Bobby

Born on 1/18/41 in Marianna, Florida. Singer/songwriter/guitarist. Hosted own syndicated TV show from 1972-75.

| 5/27/72 | 214 | 3 | 1 California Wine ................................................................... | $20 | United Artists 5578 |

California Wine • Lizzie And The Rain Man • Southern Fried Singin' Sunday Mornin' • Love The One You're With • Back That Way You Came • The Nights Of Your Life • Born To Make You Happy • Country Feelin's • Somebody Loves Me • Why Don't We Go Somewhere And Love • My Lady Friend • To Be With You

| 3/31/73 | 207 | 2 | 2 Brand New Kind Of Love ......................................................... | $15 | United Artists 019 |

Brand New Kind Of Love • Let Me Love You For Tonight • I Believe In Music • Childhood-1949 • The Guitar Man • A Song For Children • I Can See Clearly Now • By Your Side • Fever • Birmingham Lucy

## GOMM, Ian

Born on 3/17/47 in Ealing, England. Member of London band Brinsley Schwarz from 1972-75.

| 3/21/81 | 210 | 2 | What A Blow ....................................................................... | $10 | Stiff/Epic 36433 |

Man On A Mountain • Do It In Style • Jealousy • It Don't Help • Here It Comes Again (That Feeling) • What A Blow • Nobody's Fool • (Swayin' To The Music) Slow Dancin' • (I'm In A) Heartache • I Like You, I Don't Love You • I Just Wanna Stay Here • Jaguar

## GOODIE — see WHITFIELD, Robert

## GOODMAN, Steve

Born on 7/25/48 in Chicago. Died of leukemia on 9/20/84. Singer/songwriter/guitarist.

| 2/24/73 | 214 | 3 | Somebody Else's Troubles ........................................................ | $15 | Buddah 5121 |

guests include Maria Muldaur

The Dutchman • Six Hours Ahead Of The Sun • Song For David • Chicken Cordon Bleus • Somebody Else's Troubles • The Loving Of The Game • I Ain't Heard You Play No Blues • Don't Do Me Any Favors Anymore • The Vegetable Song (The Barnyard Dance) • Lincoln Park Pirates • The Ballad Of Penny Evans

## GOOD RATS ☉

Rock group from New York City: brothers Peppi (vocals) and Mickey (guitar) Marchello, John Gatto (guitar), Lenny Kotke (bass) and Joe Franco (drums). Franco later joined Twisted Sister.

| 2/10/79 | 210 | 1 | Birth Comes To Us All ........................................................... | $10 | Passport 9830 |

You're Still Doing It • City Liners • Cherry River • Ordinary Man • Man On A Fish • School Days • Juvenile Song • Gino • Bed And A Bottle • Birth Comes To Us All

## GOODY GOODY ☉

Disco studio group from Philadelphia with lead vocals by Denise Montana.

| 11/11/78 | 210 | 1 | Goody Goody ...................................................................... | $10 | Atlantic 19197 |

#1 Dee Jay • Super Jock • Bio-Rhythms • Goody Goody • It Looks Like Love • You Know How Good It Is

## GOOSE CREEK SYMPHONY

Country-rock group: Charlie Gearheart (vocals, guitar), Paul Spradlin (guitar), Bob Henke (keyboards), Ellis Schweid (fiddle), Chris Mostert (sax), Pat Moore (bass) and Dennis Kenmore (drums).

| 11/23/74 | 201 | 7 | Do Your Thing But Don't Touch Mine | $12 | Columbia 32918 |

Plans Of The Lord • Teresa • Do Your Thing But Don't Touch Mine • Saturday Night At The Grange Medley: Saturday Night At The Grange/Li'l Liza Jane/Everybody Wants To Boogie/Black Jack Davy/Plans Of The Lord (Reprise) • Hot Dog Daddy • The World We're Livin' In Today • Pick Up The Tempo • Big Black Hoss

## GORDON, Robert

Born in 1947 in Washington, D.C. Rockabilly singer. Lead singer of the New York punk band Tuff Darts.

| 8/28/82 | 201 | 6 | Too Fast To Live Too Young To Die | $10 | RCA Victor 4380 |

Red Hot • The Way I Walk • Sea Cruise • Black Slacks • Rock Billy Boogie • Fire • Something's Gonna Happen • It's Only Make Believe • Someday, Someway • Wasting My Time • Flyin' Saucers Rock & Roll • Too Fast To Live, Too Young To Die

## GORME, Eydie

Born on 8/16/31 in New York City. Married **Steve Lawrence** on 12/29/57. Steve and Eydie remain a durable nightclub act.

| 7/24/71 | 213 | 3 | 1 It Was A Good Time ............................................................. | $12 | MGM 4780 |

Somebody Waiting • If • Goin' Back • Fire And Rain • To Wait For Love • Sal And Sally • A House Is Not A Home • Oh No Not My Baby • Someone Who Cares • It Was A Good Time

| 7/1/72 | 208 | 1 | 2 The World Of Steve & Eydie ................................................... | $12 | MGM 4803 |

STEVE LAWRENCE & EYDIE GORME with The Mike Curb Congregation

E Fini • Shiretoko • Rose D'Irlande • Un Poquito Mas • We Shall Dance • Bashana Haba-Ah • Du Sollst Nicht Weinen • Lead Me On • We Can Make It Together [w/The Osmonds] • Tristeza

## GOULDMAN, Graham ☉

Born on 5/10/46 in Manchester, England. Singer/songwriter/bassist. Member of **10cc**.

| 8/16/80 | 209 | 1 | Animalympics ...................................................................[S] | $10 | A&M 4810 |

Go For It • Underwater Fantasy • Away From It All • Born To Lose • Kit Mambo • Z.O.O. • Love's Not For Me (Rene's Song) • With You I Can Run Forever • Bionic Boar • We've Made It To The Top

### GRANDMASTER FLASH
Born Joseph Saddler on 1/1/58 in New York City. Pioneering rap DJ/producer. His group consisted of rappers Nathaniel "Kidd Creole" Glover, Guy "Rahiem" Williams, Lavón, Mr. Broadway and Larry Love.

| | | | | | | |
|---|---|---|---|---|---|---|
| 7/13/85 | 201 | 5 | | **They Said It Couldn't Be Done** | $10 | Elektra 60389 |

Girls Love The Way He Spins • The Joint Is Jumpin' • Rock The House • Jailbait • Sign Of The Times • Larry's Dance Theme • Who's That Lady • Alternate Groove • Paradise

### GRASS ROOTS, The
Pop-rock group from Los Angeles: Rob Grill (vocals, bass), Warren Entner, Reed Kailing and Virgil Weber (guitars), and Joel Larson (drums).

| | | | | | | |
|---|---|---|---|---|---|---|
| 5/19/73 | 222 | 2 | | Alotta' Mileage | $15 | Dunhill 50137 |

Where There's Smoke There's Fire • Pick Up Your Feet • You've Got To Bend With The Breeze • Just A Little Tear • Ain't No Way To Go Home • Claudia • Love Is What You Make It • Look But Don't Touch • Ballad Of Billy Joe • We Almost Made It Together • Little Bit Of Love

### GRAY, Dobie
Born Lawrence Darrow Brown on 7/26/40 in Brookshire/Simonton, Texas. Singer/songwriter/actor. Acted in the L.A. production of *Hair*.

| | | | | | | |
|---|---|---|---|---|---|---|
| 11/16/74 | 203 | 1 | | Hey Dixie | $12 | MCA 449 |

Hey Dixie • How Can You Live All Alone • So High (Rock Me Baby & Roll Me Away) • Watch Out For Lucy • Old Time Feeling • Turning On You • Roll On Sweet Mississippi • Can You Feel It • Performance • The Music's Real (Mentor's Song)

### GREEN, Peter
Born Peter Greenbaum on 10/29/46 in London. Blues-rock singer/guitarist. Former member of **John Mayall**'s Bluesbreakers and Fleetwood Mac.

| | | | | | | |
|---|---|---|---|---|---|---|
| 2/20/71 | 205 | 1 | 1 | The End Of The Game | [I] $20 | Reprise 6436 |

Bottoms Up • Timeless Time • Descending Scale • Burnt Foot • Hidden Depth • The End Of The Game

| | | | | | | |
|---|---|---|---|---|---|---|
| 12/8/79 | 201 | 11 | 2 | **In The Skies** | [I] $12 | Sail 0110 |

In The Skies • Slabo Day • A Fool No More • Tribal Dance • Seven Stars • Funky Chunk • Just For You • Proud Pinto • Apostle

### GREENE, Mike ☉
Jazz singer/saxophonist.

| | | | | | | |
|---|---|---|---|---|---|---|
| 9/6/75 | 206 | 3 | | Pale, Pale Moon | $12 | GRC 10013 |

Hermetically Sealed • I Do All I Can • Pale, Pale Moon • It's Hard • With A Knife • Just Me And You • In The Morning • I Wonder Why • Valdez Bailey • Why Must I Be Lonely

### GREENSLADE ☉
Rock group: Dave Greenslade (vocals, guitar), Dave Lawson (keyboards), Tony Reeves (bass) and Andrew McCulloch (drums).

| | | | | | | |
|---|---|---|---|---|---|---|
| 7/28/73 | 218 | 2 | | Greenslade | $12 | Warner 2698 |

Feathered Friends • An English Western • Drowning Man • Temple Song • Melange • What Are You Doin' To Me • Sundance

### GREENWOOD, Lee
Born on 10/27/42 in Los Angeles. Country singer/songwriter/multi-instrumentalist.

| | | | | | | |
|---|---|---|---|---|---|---|
| 6/5/82 | 204 | 5 ● | | Inside And Out | $10 | MCA 5305 |

A Love Song • Ring On Her Finger, Time On Her Hands • I Don't Want To Be A Memory • Ain't No Trick (It Takes Magic) • It Turns Me Inside Out • She's Lying • Home Away From Home • Love Don't Get No Better • Thank You For Changing My Life • Broken Pieces Of My Heart

### GREGGAINS, Joanie — see AEROBIC ALBUMS

### GREY, Joel ☉
Born Joel Katz on 4/11/32 in Cleveland. Singer/actor. Starred in many movies and Broadway shows. Father of actress Jennifer Grey.

| | | | | | | |
|---|---|---|---|---|---|---|
| 6/30/73 | 217 | 3 | | Live! | [L] $12 | Columbia 32252 |

recorded at the Waldorf Astoria Hotel in New York City

Overture • Keeping The Customers Satisfied • Love Is Here To Stay • Rumania, Rumania • Anthony Newley Medley: Once In A Lifetime/Gonna Build A Mountain/Look At That Face/Someone Nice Like You/What Kind Of Fool Am I?/Who Can I Turn To?/Gonna Build A Mountain (Reprise) • George M. Cohan Medley: Give My Regards To Broadway/Harrigan/You're A Grand Old Flag/Yankee Doodle Boy • Lean On Me • Doodle Doo Doo • Happiness Is A Thing Called Joe • "Cabaret" Medley: Willkommen/The Money Song • For All We Know

### GRISMAN, David
Born on 3/23/45 in Hackensack, New Jersey. Jazz-bluegrass mandolin player.

| | | | | | | |
|---|---|---|---|---|---|---|
| 5/7/83 | 204 | 4 | | David Grisman's Dawg Jazz/Dawg Grass | [I] $10 | Warner 23804 |

Dawg Jazz • Steppin' With Stephane • Fumblebee • In A Sentimental Mood • 14 Miles To Barstow • Swamp Dawg • Dawggy Mountain Breakdown • Wayfaring Stranger • Happy Birthday Bill Monroe • Dawg Grass (Op. 12)

### GROOTNA ☉
Rock group from San Francisco: Anna Rizzo (vocals), Vic Smith and Slim Chance (guitars), Richard Sussman (piano), Kelly Bryan (bass) and Dewey DaGrease (drums).

| | | | | | | |
|---|---|---|---|---|---|---|
| 1/29/72 | 213 | 1 | | Grootna | $15 | Columbia 31032 |

produced by Marty Balin

I'm Funky • Road Fever • Going To Canada • Waitin' For My Ship • That's What You Get • Full Time Woman • Young Woman's Blues • Customs (Is It All Over) • Medley: Your Grandmother Loves You/I She It

### GROSS, Henry
Born on 4/1/51 in Brooklyn. Soft-rock singer/guitarist. Former member of Sha-Na-Na.

| | | | | | | |
|---|---|---|---|---|---|---|
| 3/9/74 | 204 | 3 | | Henry Gross | $12 | A&M 4416 |

Simone • Come On Say It • The Ever Lovin' Days • Lay Your Love Down • Meet Me On The Corner • How I'm Gonna Love You • With The Sleep In My Eyes • Fly Away • Skin King • Sweet Sassafras

### GROUNDHOGS ☉
Blues-rock trio from England: Tony McPhee (vocals, guitar), Pete Cruikshank (bass) and Ken Pustelnik (drums).

| | | | | | | |
|---|---|---|---|---|---|---|
| 7/22/72 | 202 | 6 | | Who Will Save The World? - The Mighty Groundhogs | $25 | United Artists 5570 |

Earth Is Not Room Enough • Wages Of Peace • Body In Mind • Music Is The Food Of Thought • Bog Roll Blues • Death Of The Sun • Amazing Grace • The Grey Maze

| DEBUT | PEAK | WKS | Album Title | $ | Label & Number |
|--------|------|-----|-------------|---|----------------|

### GRYPHON ○
Jazz-rock group from England: Graeme Taylor (guitar), Richard Harvey (keyboards), Brian Gulland (bassoon), Philip Nestor (bass) and David Oberlé (drums).

12/14/74 | **201** | 4 | **Red Queen To Gryphon Three** ............................ [I] $20  Bell 1316
Opening Move • Second Spasm • Lament • Checkmate

### GUADALCANAL DIARY
Rock quartet from Marietta, Georgia: Murray Attaway (vocals), Jeff Walls (guitar), Rhett Crowe (bass) and John Poe (drums). Group named after the 1943 movie starring Preston Foster.

8/3/85 | **202** | 3 | **Walking In The Shadow Of The Big Man** .................... $10  Elektra 60429
Trail Of Tears • Fire From Heaven • Sleepers Awake • Gilbert Takes The Wheel • Ghost On The Road • Watusi Rodeo • Why Do The Heathen Rage? • Pillow Talk • Walking In The Shadow Of The Big Man (Part 1) • Kumbayah

### GUTHRIE, Arlo
Born on 7/10/47 in Coney Island, New York. Folk singer/songwriter/guitarist. Son of Woody Guthrie.

1/28/78 | **202** | 3 | **The Best Of Arlo Guthrie** ............................ [G] $10  Warner 3117
Alice's Restaurant Massacree • Gabriel's Mother's Hiway Ballad #16 Blues • Cooper's Lament • Motorcycle (Significance Of The Pickle) Song • Coming Into Los Angeles • Last Train • City Of New Orleans • Darkest Hour • Last To Leave

### GUTHRIE, Gwen
R&B singer/songwriter from Newark, New Jersey. Former session singer.

11/27/82 | **208** | 2 | **Gwen Guthrie** ............................ $10  Island 90004
Peek-A-Boo • Getting Hot • Your Turn To Burn • Dance Fever • For You (With A Melody Too) • It Should Have Been You • Is This Love? • God Don't Like Ugly

# H

### HAGAR, Sammy
Born on 10/13/47 in Monterey, California. Rock singer/songwriter/guitarist. Lead singer of Montrose (1973-75) and Van Halen (1985-96).

11/19/83 | **203** | 4 | **Live 1980** ............................ [L] $10  Capitol 12299
recorded at Hammersmith Odeon in London
Trans Am (Highway Wonderland) • Love Or Money • Plain Jane • 20th Century Man • This Planet's On Fire (Burn In Hell) • In The Night (Entering The Danger Zone) • The Danger Zone • Space Station #5

### HAGEN, Nina
Born on 3/11/55 in East Berlin. Dance-punk singer/actress.

6/15/85 | **201** | 5 | **Nina Hagen In Ekstasy** | $10  Columbia 40004
Universal Radio • Gods Of Aquarius • Russian Reggae • My Way • 1985 Ekstasy Drive • Prima Nina In Ekstasy • Spirit In The Sky • Atomic Flash Deluxe • The Lord's Prayer • Gott Im Himmel

### HALL, Carol ○
Female singer/songwriter.

4/8/72 | **215** | 2 | **Beads And Feathers** ............................ $12  Elektra 75018
Carnival Man • Sandy • Thank You Babe • Hello My Old Friend • Uncle Malcolm • Sunday Lady • Nana • Hard Times Lovin' • My House • Charlie's Waiting For The Snow • I Never Thought Anything This Good Could Happen To Me

### HALL, John
Born on 10/25/47 in Baltimore. Rock singer/guitarist. Founder/leader of Orleans.

5/19/79 | **203** | 4 | **Power** ............................ $10  Columbia 35790
Home At Last • Power • Heartbreaker • So • Run Away With Me • Firefly Lover • Medley: Arms/Half Moon • Cocaine Drain

### HALL, Lani ○
Lead vocalist with Sergio Mendes & Brasil '66. Married to **Herb Alpert**.

11/18/72 | **203** | 12 | **1 Sundown Lady** ............................ $12  A&M 4359
produced by **Herb Alpert**
Love Song • Tiny Dancer • How Can I Tell You • You • Ocean Song • We Could Be Flying • Come Down In Time • Sun Down • Vincent • Wherever I May Find Him

3/14/81 | **206** | 3 | **2 Blush** ............................ $10  A&M 4829
Where's Your Angel? • In The Dark • Come What May • Love Me Again • No Strings • Ain't Got Nothin' For Me • Wish I Would've Stayed • I Don't Want You To Go • Only You

### HALL, Tom T.
Born on 5/25/36 in Olive Hill, Kentucky. Country singer/songwriter/guitarist. Hosted TV's *Pop Goes The Country*.

1/31/76 | **202** | 3 ● | **Greatest Hits-Vol. 2** ............................ $10  Mercury 1044
Country Is • I Love • The Little Lady Preacher • Sneaky Snake • I Like Beer • Ravishing Ruby • Old Dogs - Children And Watermelon Wine • Deal • Who's Gonna Feed Them Hogs • That Song Is Driving Me Crazy • I Care

### HAMMER, Jan
Born on 4/17/48 in Prague, Czechoslovakia. Jazz-rock keyboardist.

7/4/76 | **201** | 7 | **1 Oh, Yeah?** ............................ [I] $12  Nemperor 437
**JAN HAMMER GROUP**
Magical Dog • One To One • Evolove • Oh, Yeah? • Bambu Forest • Twenty One • Let The Children Grow • Red And Orange

3/31/79 | **209** | 1 | **2 Black Sheep** ............................ [I] $10  Asylum 173
**HAMMER**
Jet Stream • Heavy Love • Black Sheep • Light Of Dawn • Hey Girl • Waiting No More • Between The Sheets Of Music • Manic Depression • Silent One

| DEBUT | PEAK | WKS | Album Title | $ | Label & Number |
|-------|------|-----|-------------|---|----------------|

## HANCOCK, Herbie
Born on 4/12/40 in Chicago. Jazz-electronic keyboardist. Scored many movies.

| 1/19/80 | 202 | 2 | 1 **The Best Of Herbie Hancock** .................................................[G-I] $10 | | Columbia 36309 |

Doin' It • I Thought It Was You • Chameleon • Hang Up Your Hang Ups • Ready Or Not • Tell Everybody

| 2/12/83 | 202 | 4 | 2 **Quartet** .............................................................................[I] $12 | | Columbia 38275 [2] |

with **Ron Carter** (bass), Wynton Marsalis (trumpet) and **Tony Williams** (drums)

Well You Needn't • 'Round Midnight • Clear Ways • A Quick Sketch • The Eye Of The Hurricane • Parade • The Sorcerer • Pee Wee • I Fall In Love Too Easily

## HANSEN, Randy ☼
Born on 12/8/54 in Seattle. Rock singer/songwriter.

| 11/22/80 | 210 | 2 | **Randy Hansen** ............................................................... $10 | | Capitol 12119 |

Champagne And Cocaine • Watch What You Say • Time Won't Stop • I Want To Take You Higher • Millonnaire • Dancin' With Me • Don't Pretend

## HARDIN, Tim
Born on 12/23/41 in Eugene, Oregon. Died of a drug overdose on 12/29/80. Folk-blues singer/songwriter. Relative of notorious outlaw John Wesley Hardin.

| 11/25/72 | 209 | 2 | **Painted Head** ............................................................... $20 | | Columbia 31764 |

guests include Peter Frampton

You Can't Judge A Book By The Cover • Midnight Caller • Yankee Lady • Lonesome Valley • Sweet Lady • Do The Do • Perfection • Till We Meet Again • I'll Be Home • Nobody Knows You When You're Down And Out

## HARRIS, Richard
Born on 10/1/30 in Limerick, Ireland. Began prolific acting career in 1958. Portrayed "King Arthur" in the long-running stage production and movie version of *Camelot*.

| 5/12/73 | 203 | 5 | **His Greatest Performances** ...............................[G] $12 | | Dunhill 50139 |

Mac Arthur Park • Didn't We • My Boy • There Are Too Many Saviours On My Cross • Fill The World With Love • A Tramp Shining • The Yard Went On Forever • Lovers Such As I • One Of The Nicer Things • Requiem

## HARTLEY, Keef, Band
Born in 1944 in Preston, England. Drummer with **John Mayall**'s Bluesbreakers and **Vinegar Joe**. His band included Miller Anderson (vocals, guitar), Gary Thain (bass) and Mick Weaver (keyboards).

| 7/10/71 | 203 | 7 | **Overdog** ............................................................... $15 | | Dream 18057 |

You Can Choose • Plain Talking • Medley: Theme Song/En Route/Theme Song (Reprise) • Overdog • Roundabout • Imitations From Home • We Are All The Same

## HARVEY, Alex
Born on 2/5/35 in Glasgow; raised in Britian. Died of a heart attack on 2/4/82. Rock singer. His band included Zal Cleminson (guitar), Hugh McKenna (keyboards), Chris Glen (bass) and Ted McKenna (drums).

| 6/21/75 | 204 | 2 | **Tomorrow Belongs To Me** ............................................. $12 | | Vertigo 2004 |

**THE SENSATIONAL ALEX HARVEY BAND**

Action Strasse • Snake Bite • Soul In Chains • The Tale Of The Giant Stoneater • Ribs And Balls • Give My Compliments To The Chef • Shark's Teeth • Shake That Thing • Tomorrow Belongs to Me • To Be Continued... (Hail Vibrania!)

## HATHAWAY, Donny
Born on 10/1/45 in Chicago; raised in St. Louis. Committed suicide by jumping from the 15th floor of New York City's Essex House hotel on 1/13/79. R&B singer/songwriter/keyboardist/producer/arranger.

| 9/20/80 | 201 | 4 | **In Performance** [L] $10 | | Atlantic 19278 |

recorded at The Bitter End and Carnegie Hall in New York City and at the Troubador in Los Angeles

To Be Young, Gifted And Black • A Song For You • Nu-Po • I Love You More Than You'll Ever Know • We Need You Right Now • Sack Full Of Dreams

## HAWKWIND
Space-rock group from London: Robert Calvert (vocals), Dave Brock (guitar), Simon House (keyboards), Adrian Shaw (bass) and Simon King (drums).

| 2/25/78 | 208 | 5 | **Quark Strangeness And Charm** .................................... $10 | | Sire 6047 |

Spirit Of The Age • Damnation Alley • Fable Of A Failed Race • Quark Strangeness And Charm • Hassan I Sahba • The Forge Of Vulcan • Days Of The Underground • Iron Dream

## HAYES, Bonnie ☼
Female new wave singer/songwriter. The Wild Combo consisted of Kevin Hayes, Hank Manniger and Paul Davis.

| 8/7/82 | 206 | 2 | **Good Clean Fun** .................................................... $10 | | Slash 112 |

**BONNIE HAYES with The Wild Combo**

Girls Like Me • Shelly's Boyfriend • Separating • Dum Fun • Coverage • Inside Doubt • Joyride • Loverboy • Raylene • The Last Word

## HEADS HANDS AND FEET ☼
British rock group: Tony Colton (vocals), Albert Lee and Ray Smith (guitars), Chas Hodges (bass) and Pete Gavin (drums).

| 5/19/73 | 221 | 3 | **Old Soldiers Never Die** ......................................... $20 | | Atco 7025 |

Jack Of All Trades • Meal Ticket • I Won't Let You Down • Soft Word Sunday Morning • One Woman • Just Another Ambush • Stripes • Taking My Music To the Man • Another Useless Day

## HEADSTONE ☼
Rock group: Mark Ashton (vocals), Steve Bolton (guitar), Philip Chen (bass) and Chilli Charles (drums).

| 10/12/74 | 201 | 5 | **Bad Habits** | $12 | ABC/Dunhill 50174 |

Don't Turn Your Back • Take Me Down • High On You • Love You Too • O₃B • Open Your Eyes • Live For Each Other • You've Heard It All Before • Bad Habits • Take A Plane • DMT

## HEART AND SOUL ORCHESTRA, The ☼
Disco studio group assembled by DJ/VJ Frankie Crocker.

| 9/11/76 | 210 | 1 | **Frankie Crocker's Heart And Soul Orchestra Presents The Disco Suite Symphony No. 1 In Rhythm And Excellence** ...............[I] $12 | | Casablanca 7031 [2] |

Poincianna • Friendly Persuasion • I Can't Get Started • The Very Thought Of You • Be My Love • Moonlight In Vermont • Skylark • Flamingo

## HEARTSFIELD
Rock group from Chicago: J.C. Heartsfield (vocals), Fred Dobbs, Perry Jordan and Phil Lucafo (guitars), Greg Biela (bass), and Artie Baldacci (drums).

| 8/10/74 | 202 | 8 | **The Wonder Of It All** | $12 | Mercury 1003 |

The Wonder Of It All • House Of Living • Pass Me By • Shine On • Eight Hours Time • I've Just Fallen • Racin' The Sun • LaFayette County

## HEAT ○
Dance group led by saxophonist/keyboardist Tom Saviano and vocalist Jean Marie Arnold.

| 5/10/80 | 208 | 1 | **Heat** | $10 | MCA 3225 |

Just Like You • It's Up To You • This Love That We've Found • Don't You Walk Away • Pickin' And Choosin' • Whatever It Is • Side Steppin' • Billet Doux (Love Letter)

## HEATH BROTHERS, The
Jazz duo: brothers Jimmy (reeds) and Percy (bass) Heath.

| 5/17/80 | 207 | 1 | 1 **Live At The Public Theater** | [I-L] $10 | Columbia 36374 |

A Sassy Samba • Warm Valley • Cloak And Dagger • For The Public • Watergate Blues • We Need Peace And We Need Love • Artherdoc Blues

| 7/11/81 | 202 | 2 | 2 **Expressions Of Life** | [I] $10 | Columbia 37126 |

Dreamin' • Tender Touch • Ruby, My Dear • Then What • Use It (Don't Abuse It) • No More Weary Blues • Equipoise • Confirmation

## HEAVY PETTIN ○
British rock group: Hamie (vocals), Gordon Bonnar and Punky Mendoza (guitars), Brian Waugh (bass) and Gary Moat (drums).

| 8/10/85 | 209 | 1 | **Rock Ain't Dead** | $10 | Polydor 825897 |

Rock Ain't Dead • Sole Survivor • China Boy • Lost In Love • Northwinds • Angel • Heart Attack • Dream Time • Walkin' With Angels • Throw A Party

## HEDGE & DONNA ○
Husband-and-wife vocal duo of Hedge and Donna Capers.

| 8/7/71 | 212 | 2 | **Evolution** | $12 | Polydor 4063 |

guests include Joe Walsh
Touch Caste On The Water • She Said She Said • Colorado Exile • Free & Easy • Aragon Ballroom • Heavy Ways Of Moving • Collage • May 7th • Sundays Birthday Child • Sail A Schooner • Nickle A Night • Blind Man From Arizona

## HELL, Richard, & The Voidoids ○
Born Richard Myers on 10/2/49 in Lexington, Kentucky. Punk singer/bassist. Formerly married to Patty Smyth. The Voidoids consisted of guitarists Robert Quine and Ivan Julian with drummer Marc Bell.

| 12/3/77 | 208 | 3 | **Blank Generation** | $20 | Sire 6037 |

Love Comes In Spurts • Liars Beware • New Pleasure • Betrayal Takes Two • Down At The Rock And Roll Club • Who Says? • Blank Generation • Walking On The Water • The Plan • Another World

## HELM, Levon
Born on 5/26/43 in Arkansas. Singer/drummer/actor. Member of The Band. Portrayed Loretta Lynn's father in the movie *Coal Miner's Daughter*.

| 10/7/78 | 206 | 2 | **Levon Helm** | $10 | ABC 1089 |

Ain't No Way To Forget You • Driving At Night • Play Something Sweet • Sweet Johanna • I Came Here To Party • Take Me To The River • Standing On A Moutaintop • Let's Do It In Slow Motion • Audience For My Pain

## HENDERSON, Eddie ○
Born on 10/26/40 in New York City. Jazz trumpeter/flugelhorn player.

| 10/15/77 | 207 | 5 | **Comin' Through** | [I] $10 | Capitol 11671 |

guests include Philip Bailey, Lee Ritenour and Patrice Rushen
Say You Will • Open Eyes • Morning Song • Movin' On • Return To The Source • The Funk Surgeon • Beyond Forever • Connie

## HENDERSON, Finis ○
Pronounced: FINE-us. Male R&B singer from Chicago.

| 8/6/83 | 208 | 1 | **Finis** | $10 | Motown 6036 |

Skip To My Lou • Making Love • Lovers • You Owe It All To Love • Blame It On The Night • Call Me • Vina Del Mar • Crush On You • I'd Rather Be Gone • School Girl

## HENDERSON, Luther — see BROADWAY SYMPHONY ORCHESTRA

## HENDERSON, Wayne — see AYERS, Roy

## HENDRIX, Jimi — see ISLEY BROTHERS, The

## HEPTONES, The ○
Reggae vocal trio from Kingston, Jamaica: Barry Llewellyn, Earl Morgan and Leroy Sibbles.

| 8/21/76 | 207 | 1 | **Night Food** | $12 | Island 9381 |

Country Boy • I've Got The Handle • Sweet Talkin' • Book Of Rules • Mama Say • Deceivers • Love Won't Come Easy • Fatty Fatty • Baby I Need Your Lovin' • In The Groove

## HERMAN'S HERMITS
Pop group from Manchester, England: Peter "Herman" Noone (vocals), Derek Leckenby and Keith Hopwood (guitars), Karl Green (bass), and Barry Whitwam (drums). Noone later formed **The Tremblers**. Leckenby died of lymphoma on 6/4/94 (age 48).

| 8/11/73 | 202 | 5 | **Herman's Hermits XX (Their Greatest Hits)** | [G] $15 | Abkco 4227 [2] |

Mrs. Brown You've Got A Lovely Daughter • No Milk Today • End Of The World • This Door Swings Both Ways • Just A Little Bit Better • I'm Henry The VIII, I Am • I'm Into Something Good • There's A Kind Of Hush All Over The World • Silhouettes • Museum • Can't You Hear My Heartbeat • Dandy • Wonderful World • I Can Take Or Leave Your Loving • Hold On • Don't Go Out In The Rain (You're Going To Melt) • Listen People • Leaning On A Lamp Post • East West • A Must To Avoid

| DEBUT | PEAK | WKS | Album Title | $ | Label & Number |
|---|---|---|---|---|---|

### HERON, Mike ☉
Born on 12/12/42 in Glasgow, Scotland. Singer/songwriter/multi-instrumentalist.

| 6/26/71 | 218 | 2 | **Smiling Men With Bad Reputations** ..................................................... | $25 | Elektra 74093 |

guests include **John Cale, Richard Thompson** and Tommy & The Bijoux (actually The Who)

Call Me Diamond • Flowers Of The Forest • Audrey • Brindaban • Feast Of Stephen • Spirit Beautiful • Warm Heart Pastry • Beautiful Stranger • No Turning Back

### HIATT, John
Born on 8/20/52 in Indianapolis. Singer/songwriter/guitarist.

| 7/7/79 | 202 | 4 | 1 **Slug Line**.......................................................................................... | $10 | MCA 3088 |

You Used To Kiss The Girls • The Negros Were Dancing • Slug Line • Madonna Road • (No More) Dancin' In The Streets • Long Night • The Night That Kenny Died • Radio Girl • You're My Love Inrerest • Take Off Your Uniform • Sharon's Got A Drugstore • Washable Ink

| 5/8/82 | 203 | 4 | 2 **All Of A Sudden** ............................................................................ | $10 | Geffen 2009 |

I Look For Love • This Secret Life • Overnight Story • Forever Yours • Some Fun Now • The Walking Dead • I Could Use An Angel • Getting Excited • Doll Hospital • Something Happens • Marianne • My Edge Of The Razor

| 2/16/85 | 210 | 1 | 3 **Warming Up To The Ice Age** ....................................................... | $10 | Geffen 24055 |

guests include Elvis Costello

The Usual • The Crush • When We Ran • She Said The Same Things to Me • Living A Little, Laughing A Little • Zero House • Warming Up To The Ice Age • I'm A Real Man • Number One Honest Game • I Got A Gun

### HIDDEN STRENGTH ☉
Jazz-funk group: Roy Herring (vocals), Grover Underwood and Ken Sullivan (keyboards), Ray Anderson (trombone), Robert Leach (sax), Alvin Brown (bass) and Al Thomas (drums).

| 3/6/76 | 208 | 3 | **Hidden Strength**............................................................................ | $12 | United Artists 555 |

It Didn't Have To Be This Way • Happy Song • Angel Of Love • Hustle On Up (Do The Bump) • Why Does It Feel So Good To Me • I Wanna Be Your Main Man • Hustle On Up (Do The Bump) (Instrumental) • All We Need Is Time

### HIGH INERGY
Female R&B vocal group from Pasadena, California: Barbara Mitchell, Linda Howard and Michelle Rumph.

| 11/10/79 | 205 | 2 | 1 **Frenzy** ......................................................................................... | $10 | Gordy 989 |

Skate To The Rhythm • Main Ingredient • I Love Makin' Love (To The Music) • Will We Ever Love Again • Phantom • Heartbeat • Somebody, Somewhere • Voulez Vous • Time Of Your Life

| 9/27/80 | 208 | 1 | 2 **Hold On**........................................................................................ | $10 | Gordy 996 |

I Just Can't Help Myself • Sweet Man • Make Me Yours • Hold On To My Love • If I Love You Tonight • Boomerang Love • I'm A Believer • It Was You Babe

| 6/13/81 | 203 | 5 | 3 **High Inergy** ................................................................................ | $10 | Gordy 1005 |

Goin' Thru The Motions • All Of You • Heaven's Just A Step Away (Everytime I Hold You) • Fill The Need In Me • Devotion • I Just Wanna Dance With You • Now That There's You • Don't Park Your Loving • Soakin' Wet

| 6/4/83 | 206 | 3 | 4 **Groove Patrol** ............................................................................ | $10 | Motown 6041 |

Dirty Boyz • Rock My Heart • He's A Pretender • Groove Patrol • Blame It On Love *[w/Smokey Robinson]* • Back In My Arms Again • So Right • Just A Touch Away

### HILL, Z.Z.
Born Arzel Hill on 9/30/35 in Naples, Texas. Died of a heart attack on 4/27/84. Blues singer/guitarist.

| 10/2/82 | 209 | 2 | **Down Home** ................................................................................... | $10 | Malaco 7406 |

Down Home Blues • Cheating In The Next Room • Everybody Knows About My Good Thing • Love Me • That Means So Much To Me • When Can We Do This Again • Right Arm For Your Love • When It Rains It Pours • Woman Don't Go Astray • Givin' It Up For Your Love

### HOG HEAVEN ☉
Rock group formerly known as **Tommy James**'s Shondells: Eddie Gray (guitar), Ronnie Rosman (keyboards), Mike Vale (bass) and Pete Lucia (drums). All share vocals.

| 4/17/71 | 210 | 5 | **Hog Heaven** .................................................................................. | $20 | Roulette 42057 |

Wilma Mae • Glass Room • Bumpin' Slapcar Mama • Prayer • Happy • Pennsylvania • Come Away • We All Go Down • Theme From A Thought

### HOLMES, Groove
Born Richard Holmes on 5/2/31 in Camden, New Jersey. Died of cancer on 6/29/91. Jazz organist.

| 7/10/76 | 206 | 2 | **I'm In The Mood For Love** .......................................................... | $12 | Flying Dutchman 1537 |

vocals by Brenda Jones and Breathless

I'm In The Mood For Love • This Is The Me Me (Not The You You) • I've Got Love For You • Non Kulu Leku • Sweet Georgia Brown • Morning Children • Reaching' The Preacher • Caravan

### HOLMES, Rupert
Born on 2/24/47 in Cheshire, England; raised in New York City. Singer/songwriter/producer.

| 12/20/80 | 208 | 1 | **Adventure** ..................................................................................... | $10 | MCA 5129 |

Adventure • The Mask • Blackjack • The O'Brien Girl • Crowd Pleaser • You'll Love Me Again • Cold • Morning Man • I Don't Need You • Special Thanks

### HOODOO GURUS
Pop-rock group from Sydney, Australia: Dave Faulkner (vocals), Brad Shepherd (guitar), Clyde Bramley (bass) and James Baker (drums).

| 12/1/84 | 209 | 1 | **Stoneage Romeos** ........................................................................ | $10 | A&M 5012 |

I Want You Back • Tojo • Leilani • Arthur • Dig It Up • (Let's All) Turn On • Death Ship • In The Echo Chamber • Zanzibar • I Was A Kamikaze Pilot • My Girl

### HOODOO RHYTHM DEVILS ☉
Vocal duo of Joe Crane and Glenn Walters.

| 3/25/78 | 208 | 1 | **All Kidding Aside** ........................................................................ | $10 | Fantasy 9543 |

Workin' In A Coal Mine • Poison • All Night • Teen Tang • Correction In Your Direction • Sweet City Street • Gotta Lot Of Love In My Soul • Far From Over • I Had A Fight With Love (And I Lost) • Cross Roads

### HOOKFOOT ✪
British rock group: Caleb Quaye (vocals), Ian Duck (guitar), Dave Glover (bass) and Roger Pope (drums).

| | | | | | |
| --- | --- | --- | --- | --- | --- |
| 9/25/71 | 205 | 4 | Hookfoot ............................................................................................ | $15 | A&M 4316 |

Bluebird • Mystic Lady • Movies • Nature Changes • Wim-Wom • Don't Let It Bring You Down • Coombe Gallows • Crazy Fool • Golden Eagle

### HOPKIN, Mary
Born on 5/3/50 in Pontardawe, Wales. Pop singer. Married to producer Tony Visconti from 1971-81.

| | | | | | |
| --- | --- | --- | --- | --- | --- |
| 12/4/71 | 204 | 3 | 1 Earth Song/Ocean Song ................................................................. | $30 | Apple 3381 |

International • There's Got To Be More • Silver Birch And Weeping Willow • How Come The Sun • Earth Song • Martha • Streets Of London • The Wind • Water, Paper & Clay • Ocean Song

| | | | | | |
| --- | --- | --- | --- | --- | --- |
| 11/25/72 | 201 | 5 | 2 Those Were The Days ................................................... [G] | $30 | Apple 3595 |

Those Were The Days • Que Sera, Sera (Whatever Will Be, Will Be) • The Fields Of St. Etienne • Kew Gardens • Temma Harbour • Think About Your Children • Knock Knock Who's There • Heritage • Sparrow • Lontano Degli Occhi • Goodbye

### HOTEL ✪
Pop-rock group from Birmingham, Alabama: Marc Phillips (vocals, keyboards), Tommy Calton and Mike Reid (guitars), Lee Bargeron (keyboards), George Creasman (bass) and Michael Cadenhead (drums).

| | | | | | |
| --- | --- | --- | --- | --- | --- |
| 8/18/79 | 204 | 2 | Hotel ................................................................................................. | $10 | MCA 3158 |

You've Got Another Thing Coming • You'll Love Again • Right On Time • One Time Too Many • Old Silver • Not Wise To Say • Losing My Mind • City Lights • Hold On To The Night • Your Green Eyes

### HOUSTON, Cissy ✪
Born Emily Houston in 1933 in Newark, New Jersey. R&B singer. Mother of Whitney Houston.

| | | | | | |
| --- | --- | --- | --- | --- | --- |
| 9/16/78 | 205 | 6 | Think It Over ..................................................................................... | $12 | Private Stock 7015 |

Think It Over • Love Don't Hurt People • Somebody Should Have Told Me • After You • Warning-Danger • I Just Want To Be With You • An Umbrella Song • Sometimes • I Won't Be The One

### HOUSTON, David
Born on 12/9/38 in Bossier City, Louisiana. Died of an aneurysm on 11/30/93. Country singer.

| | | | | | |
| --- | --- | --- | --- | --- | --- |
| 6/12/71 | 218 | 2 | A Woman Always Knows ................................................................. | $15 | Epic 30657 |

A Woman Always Knows • That's Why I Cry • The Rest Of My Life • Let's Build A World Together • You'll Have To Read The Book • I'm Down To My Last "I Love You" • You'll Have Love • Then I'll Know You Care • I Guess I'll Live • Baby Mine • If You Were Never Here

### HOUSTON, Thelma
Born on 5/7/46 in Leland, Mississippi. R&B singer/actress.

| | | | | | |
| --- | --- | --- | --- | --- | --- |
| 7/21/79 | 204 | 3 | 1 Ride To The Rainbow ...................................................................... | $10 | Tamla 365 |

Saturday Night, Sunday Morning • I Wanna Be Back In Love Again • Love Machine • Imaginary Paradise • Just A Little Piece Of You • Ride To The Rainbow • Paying For It With My Heart • Give It To Me

| | | | | | |
| --- | --- | --- | --- | --- | --- |
| 2/2/80 | 201 | 4 | 2 Breakwater Cat ............................................................................... | $10 | RCA Victor 3500 |

Breakwater Cat • Long Lasting Love • Before There Could Be Me • Gone • What Was That Song • Suspicious Minds • Down The Backstairs Of My Life • Understand Your Man • Lost And Found • Something We May Never Know

### HUFF, Leon ✪
Born on 4/8/42 in Camden, New Jersey. R&B keyboardist/producer. Formed Philadelphia International Records with partner Kenny Gamble in 1971.

| | | | | | |
| --- | --- | --- | --- | --- | --- |
| 11/8/80 | 204 | 1 | Here To Create Music ........................................................... [I] | $10 | Philadelphia Int'l. 36758 |

Your Body Won't Move, If You Can't Feel The Groove • I Ain't Jivin', I'm Jammin' • No Greater Love • Tight Money • Low Down, Hard Times Blues • Tasty • This One's For Us • Latin Spirit

### HUMMINGBIRD ✪
Jazz group: Bobby Tench and Bernie Holland (guitars), Max Middleton (keyboards), Clive Chaman (bass) and Bernard Purdie (drums).

| | | | | | |
| --- | --- | --- | --- | --- | --- |
| 9/4/76 | 206 | 5 | We Can't Go On Like This ...................................................... [I] | $12 | A&M 4595 |

Fire And Brimstone • Gypsy Skys • Trouble Maker • Scorpio • We Can't Go On Meeting Like This • The City Mouse • A Friend Forever • Heaven Knows (Where You've Been) • Snake Snack • Let It Burn

### HUMPERDINCK, Engelbert
Born Arnold George Dorsey on 5/2/36 in Madras, India; raised in Leicester, England. Starred in his own musical variety TV series in 1970.

| | | | | | |
| --- | --- | --- | --- | --- | --- |
| 6/4/77 | 201 | 10 | 1 Engelbert Sings For You ........................................... [K] | $15 | London 688 [2] |

Everybody Knows • Misty Blue • Two Different Worlds • From Here To Eternity • The Shadow Of Your Smile • A Time For Us • Gentle On My Mind • Il Mondo • A Place In The Sun • This Is My Song • To The Ends Of The Earth • How Near Is Love • Cafe (Casa Hai Messo Nel Caffe) • By The Time I Get To Phoenix • Wonderland By Night • Up, Up And Away • Can't Take My Eyes Off You • There's A Kind Of Hush • Take My Heart • What A Wonderful World

| | | | | | |
| --- | --- | --- | --- | --- | --- |
| 6/20/81 | 203 | 5 | 2 Don't You Love Me Anymore? ...................................................... | $10 | Epic 37128 |

Don't You Love Me Anymore? • Stay Away • When The Night Ends • I Don't Break Easily • Say Goodnight • Maybe This Time • Baby Me Baby • Heart Don't Fail Me Now • Come Spend The Morning • Till I Get It Right

### HUMPHREY, Bobbi
Born Barbara Ann Humphrey on 4/25/50 in Dallas. Jazz flutist.

| | | | | | |
| --- | --- | --- | --- | --- | --- |
| 11/6/76 | 208 | 4 | Bobbi Humphrey's Best ........................................... [G-I] | $10 | Blue Note 699 |

Chicago, Damn • Uno Esta • Fancy Dancer • Fun House • Harlem River Drive • San Francisco Lights • Satin Doll • You Are The Sunshine Of My Life • Spanish Harlem

### HUNTER, Ian
Born on 6/3/46 in Shrewsbury, England. Singer/guitarist. Leader of **Mott The Hoople** from 1969-74.

| | | | | | |
| --- | --- | --- | --- | --- | --- |
| 11/3/79 | 202 | 6 | Shades Of Ian Hunter (The Ballad Of Ian Hunter & Mott The Hoople) ....... [K] | $15 | Columbia 36251 [2] |

record 1: **Mott The Hoople**; record 2: solo Ian Hunter

All The Young Dudes • One Of The Boys • Sweet Jane • All The Way From Memphis • I Wish I Was Your Mother • The Golden Age Of Rock 'N' Roll • Roll Away The Stone • Marionette • Rose • Foxy Foxy • Where Do You All Come From • Rest In Peace • Saturday Gigs • Once Bitten Twice Shy • 3,000 Miles From Here • I Get So Excited • You Nearly Did Me In • All American Alien Boy • England Rocks • Wild N' Free • Justice Of The Peace • Overnight Angels • Golden Opportunity

### HUNTER, Robert ☉
Born in 1938. Singer/songwriter/guitarist. Non-performing lyricist for the Grateful Dead.

| 7/6/74 | 204 | 4 | **Tales Of The Great Rum Runners** .................................................................. $30 | Round 101 |

backing musicians include members of the Grateful Dead

Lady Simplicity • That Train • Dry Dusty Road • I Heard You Singing • Rum Runners • Children's Lament • Maybe She's A Bluebird • Boys In The Barroom • It Must Have Been The Roses • Arizona Lightning • Standing At Your Door • Mad • Keys To The Rain

### HYDRA ☉
Southern-rock group: Wayne Bruce (vocals), Spencer Kirkpatrick (guitar), Orville Davis (bass) and Steve Pace (drums).

| 9/14/74 | 202 | 5 | 1 **Hydra**.................................................................................................... $12 | Capricorn 0130 |

Glitter Queen • Keep You Around • It's So Hard • Going Down • Feel A Pain • Good Time Man • Let Me Down Easy • Warp 16 • If You Care To Survive • Miriam

| 9/27/75 | 207 | 2 | 2 **Land Of Money** ...................................................................................... $12 | Capricorn 0157 |

Little Miss Rock N' Roll • The Pistol • Makin' Plans • Land Of Money • Get Back To The City • Don't Let Time Pass You By • Let The Show Go On • Slow And Easy • Take Me For My Music

### IAN, Janis
Born Janis Eddy Fink on 4/7/51 in New York City. Singer/songwriter/pianist/guitarist.

| 4/10/71 | 223 | 2 | **Present Company** .................................................................................. $12 | Capitol 683 |

The Seaside • Present Company • See My Grammy Ride • Here In Spain • On The Train • He's A Rainbow • Weary Lady • Nature's At Peace • See The River • Let It Run Free • Alabama • Liberty • My Land • Hello Jerry • Can You Reach Me • The Sunlight

### IAN & SYLVIA
Canadian folk-country duo: Ian Tyson (b: 9/25/33 in Victoria, British Columbia) and wife Sylvia Fricker (b: 9/19/40 in Chatham, Ontario). Began performing together in 1959. Married in 1964.

| 9/11/71 | 201 | 4 | **Ian & Sylvia** | $12 | Columbia 30736 |

with guitarist David Wilcox

More Often Than Not • Creators Of Rain • Summer Wages • Midnight • Barney • Some Kind Of Fool • Shark And The Cockroach • Last Lonely Eagle • Lincoln Freed Me • Needle Of Death • Everybody Has To Say Goodbye

### IDES OF MARCH, The
Rock group from Chicago: Jim Peterik (vocals, guitar), Larry Millas (keyboards), John Larson and Chuck Soumar (horns), Bob Bergland (bass), and Mike Borch (drums). Group named after a line in Shakespeare's *Julius Caesar*. Peterik later played keyboards for Survivor.

| 7/24/71 | 207 | 5 | **Common Bond** .................................................................................. $20 | Warner 1896 |

Friends Of Feeling • Ogre • L.A. Goodbye • Hymn For Her • Mrs. Grayson's Farm • Superman • We Are Pillows • Prelude To Freedom • Freedom Sweet • Tie-Dye Princess

### IF
British jazz-rock group: J.W. Hodgkinson (vocals), Terry Smith (guitar), Dick Morrissey and Dave Quincy (reeds), John Mealing (keyboards), Jim Richardson (bass) and Dennis Elliott (drums).

| 1/30/71 | 203 | 8 | **If 2** ...................................................................................................... $15 | Capitol 676 |

Your City Is Falling • Sunday Sad • Tarmac T. Pirate And The Lonesome Nymphoniac • I Couldn't Write And Tell You • Shadows And Echos • A Song For Elsa, Three Days Before Her 25th Birthday

### IMAGINATION ☉
R&B trio from London: Leee John (vocals), Ashley Ingram (keyboards; bass) and Errol Kennedy (drums).

| 3/31/84 | 205 | 2 | **New Dimension** ...................................................................................... $10 | Elektra 60316 |

New Dimension • State Of Love • Point Of No Return • When I See The Fire • This Means War (Shoobedoodah Dabba Doobee) • Wrong In Love • Looking At Midnight • The Need To Be Free

### IMPACT ☉
R&B vocal group from Baltimore: Damon Otis Harris, John Simms, Charles Timmons and Donald Tilghman. Harris was a member of **The Temptations** from 1971-75.

| 7/10/76 | 205 | 5 | **Impact** ................................................................................................. $12 | Atco 135 |

Happy Man • Taboo • Friends • Give A Broken Heart A Break • One Last Memory • Love Attack • Winning Combination • Man And Woman • It Only Happens In The Movies

### IMPRESSIONS, The
R&B vocal group from Chicago originally lead by Curtis Mayfield. Mayfield left in 1970. The 1973 lineup: Leroy Hutson, Sam Gooden and Fred Cash. Hutson left in late 1973, replaced by Reggie Torian and Ralph Johnson.

| 3/17/73 | 204 | 5 | 1 **Preacher Man** ...................................................................................... $12 | Curtom 8016 |

What It Is • Preacher Man • Simple Message • Find The Way • Thin Line • Color Us All Gray (I'm Lost) • I'm Loving You

| 10/26/74 | 202 | 1 | 2 **Three The Hard Way** ......................................................................... [S] $12 | Curtom 8602 |

Make A Resolution • Wendy • That's What Love Will Do • Something's Mighty, Mighty Wrong • Mister Keyes • Having A Ball • On The Move • Three The Hard Way (Chase & Theme)

### IMUS IN THE MORNING ☉
Born John Donald Imus on 7/23/40 in Riverside, California. Radio talk-show host. DJ at WGAR in Cleveland at the time of album below.

| 5/27/72 | 201 | 3 | **1200 Hamburgers To Go** | [C] $15 | RCA Victor 4699 |

1200 Hamburgers To Go • Reverend Billy Sol Hargis • Rent-A-Car Phone Call • Imus In Washington • Tyde Dyde Diaper Service Phone Call • Colombus School Of 101 Show Biz Careers Live Auditions • Silver Bullet Phone Call • Judge Hanging • Clark Kent Phone Call • Crazy Bob 'Little Red Riding Hood' • Brother Love • Tricky Dick's Sensational Used Cars

### INCREDIBLE STRING BAND
Eclectic folk group from Glasgow, Scotland: multi-instrumentalists **Mike Heron** and Robin Williamson, with Malcolm LeMaistre (vocals), Graham Forbes (guitar), Stan Lee (bass) and Jack Ingram (drums).

| 7/20/74 | 208 | 2 | Hard Rope & Silken Twine................................................... $12 | | Reprise 2198 |

Maker Of Islands • Cold February • Glancing Love • Dreams Of No Return • Dumb Kate • Ithkos

### INDEPENDENTS, The
R&B vocal group: Chuck Jackson, Maurice Jackson, Helen Curry and Eric Thomas. Chuck Jackson, no relation to Maurice and not to be confused with the same-named solo singer, is the brother of civil rights leader Jesse Jackson.

| 12/21/74 | 209 | 1 | Discs Of Gold ........................................... [G] $15 | | Wand 699 |

Leaving Me • It's All Over • I Love You, Yes I Do • In The Valley Of My World • Just As Long As You Need Me • Baby I've Been Missing You • The First Time We Met • Arise And Shine (Let's Get It On) • I Just Want To Be There • Let This Be A Lesson To You

### INDUSTRY ✪
Rock group from Long Island, New York: Jon Carin (vocals), Brian Unger (guitar), Rudy Perrone (bass) and Mercury Caronia (drums).

| 1/21/84 | 207 | 1 | Industry ....................................................... [M] $10 | | Capitol 15011 |

Communication • State Of The Nation • Romantic Dreams • Still Of The Night • Living Alone Too Long

### INMATES, The
British rock group: Bill Hurley (vocals), Peter Gunn and Tony Oliver (guitars), Ben Donnelly (bass) and Jim Russell (drums).

| 11/8/80 | 206 | 1 | Shot In The Dark................................................. $10 | | Polydor 6302 |

(I Thought I Heard A) Heartbeat • Tell Me What's Wrong • So Much In Love • Stop It Baby • Waiting Game • Feelin' Good • Talk Talk • Why When Love Is Gone • Sweet Rain • Crime Don't Pay • (She's) Some Kind Of Wonderful

### INTRUDERS
R&B vocal group from Philadelphia: Sam "Little Sonny" Brown, Eugene "Bird" Daughtry (d: 12/25/94, age 55), Phil Terry and Robert "Big Sonny" Edwards.

| 7/21/73 | 205 | 4 | Super Hits ........................................... [G] $20 | | Gamble 32131 |

Cowboys To Girls • Together • (We'll Be) United • Love Is Like A Baseball Game • Slow Drag • When We Get Married • Sad Girl • A Love That's Real • Friends No More • Gonna Be Strong • Me Tarzan, You Jane • Check Yourself

### IRON BUTTERFLY
Heavy-metal group from San Diego: Erik Braunn (vocals, guitar), Bill DeMartines (keyboards), Phil Kramer (bass) and Ron Bushy (drums). Kramer mysteriously disappeared on 2/12/95.

| 1/3/76 | 207 | 2 | Sun And Steel................................................. $12 | | MCA 2164 |

Sun And Steel • Lightnin' • Beyond The Milky Way • Free • Scion • Get It Out • I'm Right, I'm Wrong • Watch The World Goin' By • Scorching Beauty

### IRON CITY HOUSEROCKERS ✪
Rock group from Pittsburgh: Joe Grushecky (vocals), Gary Scalese (guitar), Marc Reisman (harmonica), Gil Snyder (keyboards), Art Nardini (bass) and Ned Rankin (drums). Ed Britt replaced Scalese in early 1980.

| 6/30/79 | 201 | 6 | 1 Love's So Tough $10 | | MCA 3099 |

I Can't Take It • Hideaway • Turn It Up • Dance With Me • Love So Tough • Veronica • Heroes Are Hard To Find • Stay With Me Tonight • I'm Lucky

| 8/30/80 | 204 | 5 | 2 Have A Good Time (But Get Out Alive) .......................... $10 | | MCA 5111 |

Have A Good Time (But Get Out Alive) • Don't Let Them Push You Around • Pumping Iron • Hypnotized • Price Of Love • Angela • We're Not Dead Yet • Blondie • Old Man Bar • Junior's Bar • Runnin' Scared • Rock Ola

### ISIS ✪
Female R&B-funk group: Stella Bass (vocals, bass), Suzi Ghezzi (guitar), Jeanie Fineberg, Lauren Draper and Lolly Bienenfeld (horns), and Liberty Mata (drums).

| 9/28/74 | 208 | 2 | Isis ....................................................... $12 | | Buddah 5605 |

Waiting For The Sonrise • Everybody Needs A Forever • Servant Saviour • Rubber Boy • April Fool • Bitter Sweet • Do The Football • She Loves Me • Cocaine Elaine

### ISLEY BROTHERS, The
R&B vocal trio of brothers from Cincinnati: O'Kelly, Ronald and Rudolph Isley. O'Kelly died of a heart attack on 3/31/86 (age 48). Ronald married Angela Winbush on 6/26/93. Group inducted into the Rock and Roll Hall of Fame in 1992. *Top Pop Albums*: 27.

| 3/13/71 | 202 | 5 | 1 In The Beginning...........................................[E] $15 | | T-Neck 3007 |

**THE ISLEY BROTHERS & JIMI HENDRIX**
recorded in 1964; all songs feature then-session guitarist Jimi Hendrix
Move Over Let Me Dance Part I • Have You Been Disappointed Part I and Part II • Testify Part I and Part II • Move Over Let Me Dance Part II • Wild Little Tiger • The Last Girl • Simon Says • Looking For A Love

| 11/18/78 | 204 | 4 | 2 Timeless ........................................... [G] $12 | | T-Neck 35650 [2] |

It's Your Thing • Love The One You're With • I Know Who You've Been Socking It To • Get Into Something • I Need You So • Work To Do • Brother, Brother • Keep On Doin' • I Turned You On • Put A Little Love In Your Heart • Pop That Thang • Lay, Lady, Lay • Spill The Wine • Fire And Rain • Freedom • Medley: Ohio/Machine Gun • Nothing To Do But Today • Lay Away • If He Can You Can • It's Too Late

# J

### JACKSON, Millie
Born on 7/15/44 in Thompson, Georgia. R&B singer/songwriter.

| 8/15/81 | 201 | 5 | 1 Just A Lil' Bit Country $10 | | Spring 6732 |

I Can't Stop Loving You • Till I Get It Right • Pick Me Up On Your Way Down • Loving You • I Laughed A Lot • Love On The Rocks • Standing In Your Line • Rose Colored Glasses • It Meant Nothing To Me • Anybody That Don't Like Millie Jackson

| DEBUT | PEAK | WKS | Album Title | $ | Label & Number |
|-------|------|-----|-------------|---|----------------|

**JACKSON, Millie — Cont'd**

12/4/82 | **201** | 11 | 2 Hard Times ...... $10 | Spring 6737

Blufunkes • Special Occasion • I Don't Want To Cry • We're Gonna Make It • Hard Times • The Blues Don't Get Tired Of Me • Mess On Your Hands • Finger Rap • Mess On Your Hands (Reprise) • Finger Rap (Reprise) • Feel Love Comin' On

**JACKSON, Walter**
Born on 3/19/38 in Pensacola, Florida. Died on 6/20/83 of a cerebral hemorrhage. R&B singer.

6/6/81 | **206** | 5 | Tell Me Where It Hurts ...... $10 | Columbia 37132

Tell Me Where It Hurts • When I See You • Never Sing The Song • At Last • Living Without You • Come To Me • What If I Walked Out On You • If It's Magic

**JADE WARRIOR**
British progressive-rock trio: Glyn Havard (vocals, bass), Tony Duhig (guitar) and Jon Field (percussion).

2/24/73 | **211** | 3 | Last Autumn's Dream ...... $12 | Vertigo 1012

A Winter's Tale • Snake • Dark River • Joanne • Obedience • Morning Hymn • May Queen • The Demon Trucker • Lady Of The Lake • Borne On To The Solar Wind

**JAGS, The** ✪
Rock group from Scarborough, England: Nick Watkinson (vocals, guitar), John Alder (guitar), Steve Prudence (bass) and Alex Baird (drums).

5/31/80 | **205** | 3 | Evening Standards ...... $10 | Island 9603

Back Of My Hand • Desert Island Discs • Woman's World • She's So Considerate • Little Boy Lost • Medley: Single Vision/BWM • Evening Standards • Party Games • Tune Into Heaven • Last Picture Show • The Tourist

**JAKE JONES** ✪
Rock group from St. Louis: Phil Jost, Mike Krenski, Joe Marshall and Charles Sabatino.

5/15/71 | **228** | 1 | Jake Jones ...... $12 | Kapp 3648

Ill-Mo Junction • Trippin' Down A Country Road • Mirrored Door • She Must Be Free • In All My Dreams • Breathe Deep • Lost In My Own Back Yard • Feather Bed • Catch The Wind • I'll Be Seeing You

**JAM, The**
New wave trio from Woking, England: Paul Weller (vocals, bass), Bruce Foxton (guitar) and Rick Buckler (drums). Weller later formed The Style Council.

1/28/78 | **201** | 4 | 1 This Is The Modern World ...... $10 | Polydor 6129

The Modern World • All Around The World • I Need You (For Someone) • London Traffic • Standards • Life From A Window • In The Midnight Hour • In The Street, Today • London Girl • Here Comes The Weekend • The Combine • Tonight At Noon • Don't Tell Them You're Sane

5/5/79 | **204** | 2 | 2 All Mod Cons ...... $10 | Polydor 6188

All Mod Cons • To Be Someone (Didn't We Have A Nice Time) • Mr. Clean • David Watts • English Rose • In The Crowd • The Butterfly Collector • It's Too Bad • Fly • The Place I Love • 'A' Bomb In Wardour Street • Down In The Tube Station At Midnight

11/26/83 | **201** | 6 | 3 Snap! [K] $12 | Polydor 815537 [2]

In The City • Away From The Numbers • All Around The World • The Modern World • News Of The World • Billy Hunt • English Rose • Mr. Clean • David Watts • 'A' Bomb In Wardour Street • Down In The Tube Station At Midnight • Strange Town • The Butterfly Collector • When You're Young • Smither-Jones • Thick As Thieves • The Eton Rifles • Going Underground • Dreams Of Children • That's Entertainment • Start! • Man In The Corner Shop • Funeral Pyre • Absolute Beginners • Tales From The Riverbank • Town Called Malice • Precious • The Bitterest Pill (I Ever Had To Swallow) • Beat Surrender

**JAMAL, Ahmad**
Born Fritz Jones on 7/2/30 in Pittsburgh. Jazz pianist.

3/16/74 | **201** | 5 | 1 Jamalca [I] $12 | 20th Century 432

Ghetto Child • Misdemeanor • Along The Nile • Trouble Man • Jamalca • Don't Misunderstand • Theme Bahamas • Children Calling • M*A*S*H Theme

2/15/75 | **203** | 1 | 2 Jamal Plays Jamal ...... [I] $12 | 20th Century 459

Eclipse • Pastures • Dialogue • Spanish Interlude • Death & Resurrection • Swahililand

11/15/80 | **201** | 3 | 3 Night Song [I] $10 | Motown 945

When You Wish Upon A Star • Deja Vu • Need To Smile • Bad Times (Theme From Defiance) • Touch Me In The Morning • Night Song • Theme From M*A*S*H • Something's Missing In My Life

**JAMES, Tommy**
Born Thomas Jackson on 4/29/47 in Dayton, Ohio. Pop-rock singer/songwriter. Also see **Hog Heaven**.

3/4/72 | **216** | 1 | My Head, My Bed & My Red Guitar ...... $20 | Roulette 3007

Nothing To Hide • Tell 'Em Willie Boy's A'Comin' • White Horses • The Last One To Know • Rosalee • Paper Flowers • Walk A Country Mile • Who's Gonna Cry • Forty Days And Forty Nights • Kingston Highway • I Live To Love A Woman • Fortunada • Dark Is The Night

**JAPAN** ✪
New wave group from London: David Sylvian (vocals, guitar), Mick Karn (sax), Richard Barbieri (keyboards) and Steve Jansen (drums). Sylvian and Jansen (real last name: Batt) are brothers.

3/27/82 | **204** | 6 | Japan ...... $10 | Epic 37914

The Art Of Parties • Talking Drum • Ghosts • Gentlemen Take Polaroids • Still Life In Mobile Homes • Visions Of China • Taking Islands In Africa • Swing • Cantonese Boy

**JARREAU, Al**
Born on 3/12/40 in Milwaukee. R&B-jazz vocalist.

9/20/75 | **209** | 1 | We Got By ...... $12 | Reprise 2224

Spirit • We Got By • Susan's Song • You Don't See Me • Lock All The Gates • Raggedy Ann • Letter Perfect • Sweet Potato Pie • Aladdin's Lamp

### JARRETT, Keith
Born on 5/8/45 in Allentown, Pennsylvania. Jazz pianist.

| | | | | | |
|---|---|---|---|---|---|
| 8/24/74 | 208 | 1 | **1 Treasure Island** .................................................................................... [I] $12 | | ABC/Impulse 9274 |

The Rich (And The Poor) • Blue Streak • Fullsuvollivus (Fools Of All Of Us) • Treasure Island • Yaqui Indian Folk Song • Le Mistral • Angles (Without Edges) • Sister Fortune

| 12/13/75+ | 202 | 11 | **2 Backhand** ........................................................................................... [I] $12 | ABC/Impulse 9305 |

Inflight • Kumma • Vapallia • Backhand

| 2/28/76 | 201 | 8 | **3 The Köln Concert** [I-L] $15 | ECM 1064 [2] |

recorded on 1/24/75 in Köln, Germany; no track titles listed on this album

| 11/19/77 | 206 | 1 | **4 The Survivor's Suite** ............................................................................ [I] $10 | ECM 1085 |

no track titles listed on this album

| 5/27/78 | 201 | 15 | **5 Bop-Be** [I] $10 | ABC/Impulse 9334 |

Mushi Mushi • Silence • Bop-Be • Pyramids Moving • Gotta Get Some • Blackberry Winter • Pocket Full Of Cherry

| 10/28/78 | 203 | 1 | **6 The Best Of Keith Jarrett** ................................................................ [G-I] $10 | ABC/Impulse 9348 |

Blackberry Winter • Yaqui Indian Folk Song • Roads Traveled, Roads Veiled • Fantasm • Byablue • Treasure Island • De Drums • Silence

### JELLYBEAN
Born John Benitez on 11/7/57 in New York City. Club DJ/remixer/producer.

| 10/20/84 | 206 | 1 | **Wotupski!?!** ........................................................................................ [M] $10 | EMI America 19011 |

Compromise • Sidewalk Talk • Dancing On The Fire • Was Dog A Doughnut • The Mexican

### JENNINGS, Waylon
Born on 6/15/37 in Littlefield, Texas. Country singer/songwriter/guitarist. Married Jessi Colter on 10/26/69. *Top Pop Albums*: 24.

| 5/26/73 | 214 | 5 | **1 Lonesome, On'ry & Mean** ..................................................................... $15 | RCA Victor 4854 |

Lonesome, On'ry And Mean • Freedom To Stay • Lay It Down • Gone To Denver • Good Time Charlie's Got The Blues • You Can Have Her • Pretend I Never Happened • San Francisco Mabel Joy • Sandy Sends Her Best • Me And Bobby McGee

| 9/29/84 | 208 | 1 | **2 Never Could Toe The Mark** ................................................................... $10 | RCA Victor 5017 |

Never Could Toe The Mark • Talk Good Boogie • People Up In Texas • Sparkling Brown Eyes • If She'll Leave Her Mama • Settin' Me Up • The Gemini Song (When I'm Bad, I'm Bad) • Where Would I Be (Without You) • Whatever Gets You Through The Night • The Entertainer

| 11/24/84 | 202 | 4 | **3 Waylon's Greatest Hits Vol. 2** ......................................................... [G] $10 | RCA Victor 5325 |

Looking For Suzanne • The Conversation • Waltz Me To Heaven • Theme From The Dukes Of Hazzard (Good Ol' Boys) • Don't You Think This Outlaw Bit's Done Got Out Of Hand • I Ain't Living Long Like This • Come With Me • America • Shine • Women Do Know How To Carry On

### JOEL, Billy
Born on 5/9/49 in Hicksville, Long Island, New York. Pop-rock singer/songwriter/pianist. Married supermodel Christie Brinkley on 3/23/85; divorced in 1994. Recipient of Grammy's Living Legends Award in 1990 and *Billboard*'s Century Award in 1994.

| 4/8/72 | 202 | 3 | **Cold Spring Harbor** ............................................................................. $40 | Family 2700 |

album was mastered at the wrong speed; re-issued with the correct speed in 1984 on Columbia 38984 (#158)

She's Got A Way • You Can Make Me Free • Everybody Love You Now • Why Judy Why • Failing Of The Rain • Turn Around • You Look So Good To Me • Tomorrow Is Today • Nocturne • Got To Begin Again

### JOHN, Robert
Born Robert John Pedrick in Brooklyn in 1946. Pop singer.

| 9/13/80 | 205 | 4 | **Back On The Street** ............................................................................ $10 | EMI America 17027 |

(So Long) Since I Felt This Way • Hey There Lonely Girl • Just One More Try • On My Own • Give Up Your Love • Sherry • Winner Take All • Hurtin' Doesn't Go Away • Back On The Street Again • You Could Have Told Me

### JOHNSON, Michael
Born on 8/8/44 in Alamosa, Colorado; raised in Denver. Singer/songwriter/guitarist.

| 9/1/73 | 213 | 1 | **1 There Is A Breeze** ............................................................................ $20 | Atco 7028 |

Pilot Me • In Your Eyes • There Is A Breeze • See You Soon • Old Folks • Rooty Toot Toot For The Moon • My Opening Farewell • I Got You Covered • On The Road • Study In E Minor • Happier Days • You've Got To Be Carefully Taught

| 9/13/80 | 203 | 2 | **2 You Can Call Me Blue** ....................................................................... $10 | EMI America 17035 |

You Can Call Me Blue • After You • Savin' It Up • You, You, You • Blame It On The Rain • Right Through The Heart • Don't Ask Why • Staying With It • You Sure Fooled Me • Empty Hearts

### JONES, Davy
Born on 12/30/45 in Manchester, England. Member of **The Monkees**.

| 10/30/71 | 205 | 1 | **Davy Jones** ....................................................................................... $20 | Bell 6067 |

Road To Love • How About Me • Singin' To The Music • Rainy Jane • Look At Me • Say It Again • I Really Love You • Love Me For A Day • Sitting In The Apple Tree • Take My Love • Pretty Little Girl • Welcome To My Love

### JONES, George
Born on 9/12/31 in Saratoga, Texas. Country singer/songwriter/guitarist. Married to **Tammy Wynette** from 1969-75.

| 1/19/80 | 206 | 4 | **My Very Special Guests** ...................................................................... $10 | Epic 35544 |

Night Life *[w/Waylon Jennings]* • Bartender's Blues *[w/James Taylor]* • Here We Are *[w/Emmylou Harris]* • I've Turned You To Stone *[w/Linda Ronstadt]* • It Sure Was Good *[w/Tammy Wynette]* • I Gotta Get Drunk *[w/Willie Nelson]* • Proud Mary *[w/Johnny Paycheck]* • Stranger In The House *[w/Elvis Costello]* • I Still Hold Her Body (But I Think I've Lost Her Mind) *[w/Dr. Hook]* • Will The Circle Be Unbroken *[w/The Staple Singers]*

### JONES, Jack
Born on 1/14/38 in Los Angeles. Son of actress Irene Hervey and actor Allan Jones. Formerly married to actress Jill St. John.

| 11/20/71 | 201 | 1 | **Song For You** $12 | RCA Victor 4613 |

If • If You Could Read My Mind • It's Too Late • Doesn't Anybody Know • Love Looks So Good On You • A Song For You • What Have They Done To The Moon • Let Me Be The One • Pure Imagination • This Is Your Life • There's Still Time

### JONES, Jake — see JAKE JONES

**JONES, Tamiko** ☺
Born Barbara Tamiko Ferguson in 1945 in Kyle, West Virginia; raised in Detroit. R&B singer.

5/17/75 | **204** | 5 | **Love Trip** ........................................................................... $12    Arista 4040
Touch Me Baby • Everyone Belongs To Someone • I'm The Woman Behind The Man • Just You And Me • Just Sitting Around • Let Me In Your Life • Creepin' • Oh How I Love You • Who Is She (And What Is She To You) • Read Me Right • Chili Dog • A Long Way To Go

**JONESES, The** ☺
R&B vocal group from Pittsburgh: brothers Reggie and Wendall Noble, Harold Taylor, Sam White and Glenn Dorsey.

12/7/74+ | **202** | 12 | **Keepin' Up With The Joneses** ........................................ $12    Mercury 1021
I Can't See What You See In Me • Fire • Our Love Song • Hey Babe (Is The Gettin' Still Good?) Pt. 1 • Hey Babe (Is The Gettin' Still Good?) Pt. 2 • Sugar Pie Guy Pt. 1 • Sugar Pie Guy Pt. 2 • I Promise You • Baby Don't Do It • Please Let Me Stay

**JONES GIRLS, The**
Female R&B vocal trio from Detroit: sisters Shirley, Brenda and Valorie Jones.

5/5/84 | **201** | 1 | **Keep It Comin'**    $10    Philadelphia Int'l. 38555
Keep It Comin' • Won't Let You Take It Back • Why You Wanna Do That To Me • You Can't Have My Love • Better Things To Do • Love Is Comin' At Cha • Ah, Ah, Ah, Ah • (You Got The) Right Stuff

**JUDAS PRIEST**
Heavy-metal group from Birmingham, England: Rob Halford (vocals), K.K. Downing and Glenn Tipton (guitars), Ian Hill (bass) and Simon Phillips (drums). Phillips left in early 1977, replaced by Les Binks.

8/28/76 | **204** | 6 | **1 Sad Wings Of Destiny** ........................................... $15    Ovation 1751
Victim Of Changes • The Ripper • Dreamer Deceiver • Deceiver • Prelude • Tyrant • Genocide • Epitaph • Island Of Domination

7/30/77 | **207** | 1 | ● **2 Sin After Sin** ................................................... $12    Columbia 34787
Sinner • Diamonds And Rust • Starbreaker • Last Rose Of Summer • Let Us Prey • Medley: Call For The Priest/Raw Deal • Here Come The Tears • Dissident Aggressor

**JULUKA**
Interracial pop group from South Africa: Johnny Clegg and Sipho Mchunu (vocals, guitars), Cyril Mnculwane and Glenda Miller (keyboards), Scorpion Madondo (horns), Gary Van Zyl (bass) and Derrick Debeer (drums).

11/3/84 | **209** | 1 | **Stand Your Ground** ................................................. $10    Warner 25155
Kilimanjaro • Look Into The Mirror • December African Rain • Mana Lapho (Stand Your Ground) • Work For All • Fever • Mantombana • Crazy Woman • Bullets For Bafazane • Walima'Mabele

**JUNIE** ☺
Born Walter Morrison in Dayton, Ohio. Former keyboardist with the **Ohio Players**.

6/20/81 | **205** | 1 | **Five** ....................................................................... $10    Columbia 37133
Rappin About Rappin (Uh-Uh-Uh) • I Love You Madly • Cry Me A River • Victim Of Love • 5 • Last One To Know • Jarr The Ground • Taste Of Love

**JUPITER, Duke — see DUKE**

# K

**KAEMPFERT, Bert, And His Orchestra**
Born on 10/16/23 in Hamburg, Germany. Died on 6/21/80. Multi-instrumentalist/bandleader/producer. *Top Pop Albums*: 20.

5/27/72 | **218** | 1 | **6 Plus 6** ...............................................................[I] $12    Decca 75322
Never My Love • Dino's Melody • My Way • Petula's Song • A Tune For Tony • At The Rainbow's End • Stoney End • A Song For Satch • Theme From "Shaft" • All I Ever Need Is You • Melancholy Serenade • Tom's Tune

**KANTNER, Paul**
Born on 3/12/42 in San Francisco. Rock singer/songwriter/guitarist. Founding member of Jefferson Airplane/Starship.

10/29/83 | **201** | 3 | **The Planet Earth Rock And Roll Orchestra**    $10    RCA Victor 4320
guests include several members of Jefferson Starship
The Planet Earth Rock And Roll Orchestra • (She Is A) Telepath • Circle Of Fire • Mount Shasta • Lilith's Song • Transubstantiation: Part I Esperanto/Part II Science Friction • The Mountain Song • Declaration Of Independence • Underground (The Laboratories) • The Sky Is No Limit • Let's Go

**KAPLAN, Gabriel** ☺
Born on 3/31/46 in Brooklyn. Comedian/actor. Star of TV's *Welcome Back Kotter*.

7/20/74 | **210** | 2 | **Holes And Mellow Rolls** .......................................[C] $12    ABC 815
Ling Chow And Grosshopper • Holes And Mellow Rolls • Masturbation • Stand Clear For Nocturnal Emission • Exorcist • E.E.O. • Jim And Margaret • Winky Dink • Artie • Ed Sullivan, Ed Sullivan • Linda • End

**KAY-GEES, The**
Funk group from Jersey City, New Jersey: Kevin Bell (guitar), Peter Duarte, Ray Wright and Dennis White (horns), Wilson Beckett (percussion), Kevin Lassiter (keyboards), Michael Cheek (bass) and Callie Cheek (drums).

7/31/76 | **210** | 2 | **Find A Friend** ........................................................ $12    Gang 102
vocals by Something Sweet and Tomorrow's Edition
Find A Friend • On The Money • Keep On Saying • I Believe In Music • Be Real • Together • Acknowledgement • Waiting At The Bus Stop • Inspiration • Thank You Dear Lord • Mr. Nothin' • S.T.P. (Singing, Teaching & Preaching) • Find A Friend (Conclusion)

| DEBUT | PEAK | WKS | Album Title | $ | Label & Number |
|-------|------|-----|-------------|---|----------------|

### KEATS ☉
Group of veteran British session musicians: Colin Blunstone (**The Zombies**), Pete Bardens, Ian Bairnson, David Paton and Stuart Elliott.

| | | | | | |
|---|---|---|---|---|---|
| 11/3/84 | 209 | 2 | Keats ....................................................................................... $10 EMI America 17136 |

    produced by Alan Parsons
        Heaven Knows • Tragedy • Fight To Win • Walking On Ice • How Can You Walk Away • Turn Your Heart Around •
        Avalanche • Give It Up • Ask No Questions • Night Full Of Voices

### KEEN, Speedy ☉
Born on John Keen on 3/29/45 in London. Former lead singer of Thunderclap Newman.

| 6/16/73 | 206 | 4 | Previous Convictions ............................................................. $12 Track/MCA 331 |

        Old Fashioned Girl • Keep Your Head Down • Let Us In • Somethin' Else • The Flying Wino • Don't You Know He's
        Coming • Positively 4th Street • Forever After • That's The Way It Is • Keep On The Grass • Aires Lady • Lesliana

### KELLY, Casey ☉
Born Daniel Cohen in Baton Rouge, Louisiana. Singer/songwriter/pianist/guitarist.

| 10/14/72 | 201 | 4 | Casey Kelly ............................................................................... $12 Elektra 75040 |

        Silver Meteor • Making Believe • Run Away • Poor Boy • For Miss Julie • A Good Love Is Like A Good Song • You Can't
        Get There From Here • Escaping Reality • Resign Yourself To Me • Visiting An Old Friend

### KELLY, Roberta ☉
Female disco singer.

| 7/31/76 | 209 | 1 | Trouble-Maker ......................................................................... $12 Oasis 5005 |

        Trouble-Maker • Love Power • Think I'm Gonna Break Someone's Heart Tonight • Innocent • The Family

### KENDALLS, The ☉
Country duo from St. Louis: father-and-daughter Royce and Jeannie Kendall. Royce died of a heart attack on 5/22/98 (age 63).

| 1/31/81 | 205 | 5 | The Best Of The Kendalls ................................................ [G] $10 Ovation 1756 |

        Heaven's Just A Sin Away • Don't Let Me Cross Over • Sweet Desire • Just Like Real People • I Had A Lovely Time •
        Pittsburgh Stealers • It Don't Feel Like Sinnin' To Me • Makin' Believe • Put It Off Until Tomorrow • You'd Make An Angel
        Wanna Cheat

### KENDRICKS, Eddie
Born on 12/17/39 in Union Springs, Alabama; raised in Birmingham. Died of cancer on 10/5/92. Lead singer of **The Temptations** from 1960-71.

| 8/22/81 | 207 | 2 | Love Keys ................................................................................ $10 Atlantic 19294 |

        (Oh I) Need Your Lovin' • I'm In Need Of Love • I Don't Need Nobody Else • Old Home Town • Bernadette • You Can't Stop
        My Loving • Never Alone • Hot • Looking For Love • In Love We're One

### KERR, Anita, Singers
Born Anita Jean Grob on 10/13/27 in Memphis. Her vocal group consisted of Dorothy Dillard, William Wright, Thomas Brannon and Phillip Forrest.

| 9/20/75 | 203 | 1 | The Anita Kerr Singers ........................................................ $10 RCA Victor 1166 |

        I'll Play For You • At Seventeen • Love Won't Let Me Wait • I'm Not Lisa • Before The Next Teardrop Falls • (Hey, Won't
        You Play) Another Somebody Done Somebody Wrong Song • Every Time You Touch Me (I Get High) • I Love • Love Will
        Keep Us Together • The Masterpiece • Your Love's Return (Song For Stephen Foster)

### KERSHAW, Doug ☉
Born on 1/24/36 in Tiel Ridge, Louisiana. Cajun singer/songwriter/fiddler.

| 2/19/72 | 206 | 4 | 1 Swamp Grass ......................................................................... $15 Warner 2581 |

        Louisiana Woman • Louisiana Man • Isn't That About The Same • Can't It Wait Till Tomorrow • Swamp Grass • From A
        Little Flirt Comes A Big Hurt • Take Me Back To Mama • Zacharia • (Ain't Gonna Get Me Down) Till I Hit The Ground •
        Cajun Funk

| 9/22/73 | 214 | 2 | 2 Douglas James Kershaw ...................................................... $15 Warner 2725 |

        The Best Years Of My Life • Mardi Gras • Willie's Shades • Play That Old Sweet Song Again • You're Gonna Be
        Impressed • Tricks • You'd Best Believe You've Heard • A Song Called Jeannie • I Had A Good Woman But She Married
        Lawrence • Louisiana Love Song

### KID CREOLE AND THE COCONUTS
Born Thomas Augustus Darnell Browder on 8/12/50 in Montreal. Singer/songwriter/producer. Formed The Coconuts with wife Adriana "Addy" Kaegi and Andy "Coati Mundi" Hernandez.

| 10/22/83 | 204 | 1 | Doppelganger ......................................................................... $10 Sire 23977 |

        The Lifeboat Party • Underachiever • If You Wanna Be Happy • Distractions • Survivors • Call Me The Entertainer •
        There's Something Wrong In Paradise • Its' A Wonderful Life • Bongo Eddie's Lament • Broadway Rhythm • Back In The
        Field Again • The Seven Year Itch

### KIDDO ☉
Funk group from Long Beach, California: Donnie Sterling (vocals), Michael Hampton (guitar), Willie Jenkins (percussion), Leroy Davis (sax), Fred "Juice" Johnson (bass) and Leon "Rock" Goodin (drums).

| 5/21/83 | 206 | 4 | Kiddo ....................................................................................... $10 A&M 4924 |

        Tired Of Looking • What I See, I Like • Try My Loving (Gimme Just Enough) • Thinking About Your Charm • Give It Up •
        Strangers • Suzy's Gone • Cheated, Mistreated

### KING, Evelyn "Champagne"
Born on 6/29/60 in the Bronx, New York; raised in Philadelphia. R&B-disco singer.

| 12/22/84+ | 203 | 8 | So Romantic ............................................................................ $10 RCA Victor 5308 |

        Show Me (Don't Tell Me) • Heartbreaker • Till Midnight • Just For The Night • Give Me One Reason • Out Of Control •
        Talking In My Sleep • I'm So Romantic • So In Love

### KING BISCUIT BOY
King Biscuit Boy is singer/songwriter Richard Newell.

| 2/26/72 | 218 | 3 | Gooduns ................................................................................... $15 Paramount 6023 |

        You Done Tore Your Playhouse Down Again • Boom, Boom Out Goes The Lights • Georgia Rag • Barefoot Rock • Boogie
        Walk Part I • Ranky Tanky • Twenty Nine Ways To My Baby's Door • Bald Head Rhumba Boogie • Lord Pity Us All

## KING HARVEST
Pop-rock group from Olcott, New York: Ron Altbach (vocals, piano), Eddie Tuleja (guitar), Rod Novack (sax), Dave "Doc" Robinson (bass) and Bobby Figueroa (drums).

| 10/4/75 | 209 | 1 | King Harvest ..................................................................................................... | $12 | A&M 4540 |

Borderline • Vaea (Vy-Ya) • Country Pie • Shine On • Little Bit Like Magic • As Soon As We Can Get It Together • Rue Du Four Rag • Fly By • Old Friends • Jumbee

## KINGSWAY YOUTH OPERA COMPANY, The ☉
British vocal group: John Goodison, Brian Keith, Jenny Mason, Norman Smith and Martin Jay. Keith was leader of **The English Congregation**.

| 8/28/71 | 217 | 2 | Jesus Christ Superstar .......................................................................................... | $15 | Deram 18060 |

Medley: Superstar/Heaven On Their Minds • Medley: What's The Buzz/Strange Thing Mystifying • Everything's Alright • Hosana • Medley: Simon Zealotes/Poor Jerusalem • I Don't Know How To Love Him • Superstar • The Last Supper • Gethsemane • Crucifixion

## KINKS, The
Rock group from London: Ray Davies (vocals, guitar) and brother **Dave Davies** (guitar), with Pete Quaife (bass) and Mick Avory (drums). Group inducted into the Rock and Roll Hall of Fame in 1990. *Top Pop Albums*: 33.

| 3/31/84 | 209 | 2 | A Compleat Collection ............................................................................... [K] | $12 | Compleat 2001 [2] |

Stop Your Sobbing • Revenge • I'm Not Like Everybody Else • Where Have All The Good Times Gone? • You Really Got Me • I Took My Baby Home • Long Tall Sally • You Still Want Me • You Do Something To Me • Sittin' On My Sofa • Till The End Of The Day • Come On Now • Who'll Be The Next In Line • Dedicated Follower Of Fashion • Something Better Beginning • Tired Of Waiting For You • See My Friends • Set Me Free • Gotta Move • All Day & All Of The Night

## KINSMAN DAZZ
Funk group from Cleveland led by saxophonist Bobby Harris. Later known as the Dazz Band.

| 12/9/78+ | 203 | 4 | Kinsman Dazz ..................................................................................................... | $12 | 20th Century 574 |

Saturday Night • Get Down With The Feelin' • I Might As Well Forget About Loving You • Makin' Music • Dazzberry Jam • And I Mean • (Don't Want To) Stand In Your Way • Name That Tune • In My Life

## KIRWAN, Danny ☉
Born on 5/13/50 in London. Blues-rock singer/guitarist. Member of Fleetwood Mac from 1968-71.

| 1/17/76 | 207 | 4 | Second Chapter ..................................................................................................... | $12 | DJM 1 |

Ram Jam City • Odds And Ends • Hot Summer's Day • Mary Jane • Skip A Dee Doo • Love Can Always Bring You Happiness • Second Chapter • Lovely Days • Falling In Love With You • Silver Streams • Cascades

## KISSING THE PINK ☉
British synth-pop group: Nick Whitecross (vocals, guitar), Jon Hall and George Stewart (keyboards), Josephine Wells (sax), Pete Barnett (bass) and Steve Cusack (drums). Shortened name to KTP in 1985.

| 8/13/83 | 203 | 6 | Naked ..................................................................................................................... | $10 | Atlantic 80080 |

The Last Film • Frightened In France • Watching Their Eyes • Love Lasts Forever • All For You • The Last Film (Hymn version) • Big Man Restless • Desert Song • Broken Body • Maybe This Day • In Awe Of Industry • Mr. Blunt

## KITTYHAWK ☉
Jazz group from Los Angeles: Daniel Bortz (guitar), Paul Edwards (keyboards), Richard Elliot (sax) and Michael Jochum (drums).

| 5/10/80 | 207 | 2 | 1 Kittyhawk ............................................................................................... [I] | $10 | EMI America 17029 |

Islands • Never Once • Chinese Firedrill • Once Upon A Time • Big City • Wooed But Not Wed • Piper's Romp • Aerial View

| 8/8/81 | 207 | 3 | 2 Race For The Oasis ................................................................................... [I] | $10 | EMI America 17053 |

Race For The Oasis • Wind, Sand And Stars • Bells Of Talieson • King's Crossing • Mo • Arroyo • Kilimanjaro • Mighty Steel, Modern Love

## KIX
Hard-rock group from Hagerstown, Maryland: Steve Whiteman (vocals), Ronnie Younkins and Brian Forsythe (guitars), Donnie Purnell (bass), and Jimmy Chalfant (drums).

| 10/10/81 | 207 | 4 | Kix ....................................................................................................................... | $10 | Atlantic 19307 |

Atomic Bombs • Love At First Sight • Heartache • Poison • The Itch • Kix Are For Kids • Contrary Mary • The Kid • Yeah, Yeah, Yeah

## KLEEER
R&B group from New York City: Isabelle Coles (vocals), Richard Lee (guitar), Paul Crutchfield (percussion), Norman Durham (bass) and Woody Cunningham (drums).

| 7/7/79 | 208 | 4 | I Love To Dance ..................................................................................................... | $10 | Atlantic 19237 |

Tonight's The Night (Good Time) • Keeep Your Body Workin' • Happy Me • I Love To Dance • It's Magic • To Groove You • Amour • Kleeer Sailin'

## KLEIN, Robert
Born on 2/8/42 in New York City. Comedian/actor/writer. Acted in several movies and TV shows.

| 5/18/74 | 205 | 3 | 1 Mind Over Matter ................................................................................... [C] | $12 | Brut 6600 |

The Final Record Offer • Fred Capossela • Feminine/Masculine • 100% Undetectable Hairpiece • Crime & Punishment • Jacques Cousteau • Juergen's Myasthenia • Mysticism • The Borscht Belt • Our Heros • The National Anthem • Oil • On The Road • Test On This • Graffiti • No News News (Milton Lewis) • Wallowing In Watergate • Greed & Jeopardy • The Ted Mack Amateur Hour • In Praise Of The Harmonica • Obligatory Drug Bit: First Time Stoned • Mind Over Matter

| 6/28/75 | 203 | 3 | 2 New Teeth ................................................................................................... [C] | $10 | Epic 33535 |

Mother Isn't Always Right • Six Clean Words You Can Say Anywhere • At The Dentist • Continental Steel • Science Marches On • On Campus • Stranger In A Strange Land • On The Bayou • Animals All • Illusions • Fear Is The Greatest Salesman • Young People's Guide To The Orchestra • Ferrill Cynch • Odd Jobs • Actors' Strike • Scary Story • Babe Ruth Story • Mobutaba

## KLEMMER, John
Born on 7/3/46 in Chicago. Jazz saxophonist/flutist.

| 12/12/81+ | 202 | 8 | Solo Saxophone II - Life ............................................................................... [I] | $10 | Elektra 566 |

Life (Prologue) • Humanesque • The Journey From Life To Death • All I Ever Wanted Was My Life • The Deepest Need Of The Human Heart • The Celebration Of Being Alive • Yes To Life • Finesse (The Art Of Living) • Love Is Life/Life Is Love • The Mystery Of Being • The Rain Is The Tears Of My God For Me • The Struggle To Be Free • Life (Finale)

### KLUGH, Earl

Born on 9/16/53 in Detroit. Jazz guitarist/pianist. *Top Pop Albums*: 20.

| | | | | | |
|-------|------|-----|-------------|---|----------------|
| 1/14/84 | 204 | 2 | 1 Marvin & Tige ......[I-S] $10 | | Capitol 12307 |

composed and conducted by Patrick Williams

Main Title • Momma Dies • Out...Then Back • Tenderness • Romance • Skating • Searching • Very Sick • A Kiss • A Painful Goodbye • A Swan • End Credits

| | | | | | |
|-------|------|-----|-------------|---|----------------|
| 5/4/85 | 202 | 3 | 2 Key Notes ......[I] $10 | | Capitol 12405 |

Living Inside Your Love • Whiplash • Back In Central Park • Crazy For You • Magic In Your Eyes • I Don't Want To Leave You Alone Anymore • Where I Wander • Tropical Legs • I'll See You Again

### KNIGHT, Gladys, & The Pips

Born on 5/28/44 in Atlanta. R&B singer. The Pips consisted of Gladys's brother Merald "Bubba" Knight and cousins William Guest and Edward Patten. Group inducted into the Rock and Roll Hall of Fame in 1996. *Top Pop Albums*: 27.

| | | | | | |
|-------|------|-----|-------------|---|----------------|
| 1/25/75 | 207 | 1 | 1 In The Beginning ......[E] $12 | | Bell 1323 |

Letter Full Of Tears • Either Way I Lose • If Ever I Should Fall In Love • Daybreak • Maybe, Maybe Baby • Every Beat Of My Heart • Giving Up • Stop And Get A Hold Of Myself • Lovers Always Forgive • Tell Her You're Mine • Operator

| | | | | | |
|-------|------|-----|-------------|---|----------------|
| 4/7/79 | 201 | 3 | 2 Gladys Knight ...... $10 | | Columbia 35704 |

Am I Too Late • You Bring Out The Best In Me • I Just Want To Be With You • If You Ever Need Somebody • My World • I (Who Have Nothing) • You Don't Have To Say I Love You • The Best Thing We Can Do Is Say Goodbye • It's The Same Old Song • You Loved Away The Pain

### KNITTERS, The ☉

Rock group from Los Angeles: Christine "Exene" Cervenka (vocals), "John Doe" Nommensen (vocals, guitar), Dave Alvin (guitar), Jonny Ray Bartel (bass) and Done "D.J." Bonebrake (drums). Cervenka and Doe were married for a time. Cervenka, Doe, Alvin and Bonebrake were also members of X. Alvin was also with The Blasters.

| | | | | | |
|-------|------|-----|-------------|---|----------------|
| 6/15/85 | 204 | 4 | Poor Little Critter On The Road ...... $10 | | Slash 25310 |

Poor Little Critter On The Road • Someone Like You • Walkin' Cane • Silver Wings • Poor Old Heartsick Me • The New World • Cryin' But My Tears Are Far Away • Love Shack • The Call Of The Wreckin' Ball • Trail Of Time • Baby Out Of Jail • Rock Island Line

### KNOPFLER, Mark

Born on 8/12/49 in Glasgow, Scotland; raised in Newcastle, England. Singer/songwriter/guitarist. Leader of Dire Straits.

| | | | | | |
|-------|------|-----|-------------|---|----------------|
| 5/21/83 | 201 | 4 | Local Hero ...... [I-S] $10 | | Warner 23827 |

The Rocks And The Water • Wild Theme • Freeway Flyer • Boomtown • The Way It Always Starts • The Rocks And The Thunder • The Ceilidh And The Northern Lights • The Mist Covered Mountains • The Ceilidh (Louis' Favourite Billy's Tune) • Whistle Theme • Smooching • Stargazer • The Rocks And The Thunder • Going Home (Theme Of The Local Hero)

### KOLOC, Bonnie ☉

Female singer/songwriter from Chicago.

| | | | | | |
|-------|------|-----|-------------|---|----------------|
| 8/26/72 | 204 | 7 | 1 Hold On To Me ...... $15 | | Ovation 1426 |

Sailing Ship • Burgundy Wine • The Lover In Winter Plaineth For The Spring • Hold On To Me • Sweet Mama • We Are Ships • Angel From Montgomery • Jamaica • Diamond Lil • Every Day II

| | | | | | |
|-------|------|-----|-------------|---|----------------|
| 8/24/74 | 209 | 2 | 2 You're Gonna Love Yourself In The Morning ...... $15 | | Ovation 1438 |

You're Gonna Love Yourself In The Morning • Colors Of The Sun • Crazy Mary • Children's Blues • Guilty Of Rock And Roll • Roll Me On The Water • I'll Have To Say I Love You In A Song • 25th Of December • The Lion Tamer • Mother Country

### KONGOS, John ☉

Born in Johannesburg, South Africa. Pop-rock singer/songwriter.

| | | | | | |
|-------|------|-----|-------------|---|----------------|
| 2/26/72 | 204 | 2 | Kongos ...... $12 | | Elektra 75019 |

Tokoloshe Man • Jubilee Cloud • Gold • Lift Me From The Ground • Come On Down Jesus • I Would Have Had A Good Time • Try To Touch Just One • Tomorrow I'll Go • He's Gonna Step On You Again

### KOOL & THE GANG

R&B-funk group from Jersey City, New Jersey. Nucleus of group: Robert "Kool" Bell (bass) and his brother Ronald Bell (sax), Claydes Smith (guitar), Rick Westfield (keyboards), Dennis Thomas (sax), Robert Mickens (trumpet) and George Brown (drums). *Top Pop Albums*: 20.

| | | | | | |
|-------|------|-----|-------------|---|----------------|
| 4/15/78 | 208 | 2 | 1 Kool & The Gang Spin Their Top Hits ...... [G] $10 | | De-Lite 9507 |

Open Sesame • Spirit Of The Boogie • Kool & The Gang • Hollywood Swinging • Funky Stuff • More Funky Stuff • Jungle Boogie • Caribbean Festival • Love And Understanding • Summer Madness

| | | | | | |
|-------|------|-----|-------------|---|----------------|
| 11/11/78 | 207 | 2 | 2 Everybody's Dancin' ...... $10 | | De-Lite 9509 |

Everybody's Dancin' • Dancin' Shoes • Big Chief Funkum • I Like Music • You Deserve A Break Today • At The Party • Stay Awhile • It's All You Need • Peace To The Universe

### KROKUS

Heavy-metal group from Zurich, Switzerland: Marc Storace (vocals), Fernando Von Arb and Tommy Kiefer (guitars), Chris Von Rohr (bass) and Freddy Steady (drums).

| | | | | | |
|-------|------|-----|-------------|---|----------------|
| 7/5/80 | 201 | 7 | Metal Rendez-Vous ...... $10 | | Ariola America 1502 |

Heatstrokes • Bedside Radio • Come On • Streamer • Shy Kid • Tokyo Nights • Lady Double Dealer • Fire • No Way • Back-Seat Rock 'N' Roll

# L

### LAINE, Cleo
Born Clementina Dinah Campbell on 10/28/27 in Southall, England. Jazz singer. Married bandleader Johnny Dankworth in 1958.

| | | | | | |
|---|---|---|---|---|---|
| 2/9/74 | 219 | 3 | **1 I Am A Song** .................................................................................. | $12 | RCA Victor 5000 |

I'm Gonna Sit Right Down And Write Myself A Letter • Early Autumn • Friendly Persuasion • There Is A Time (Le Temps) • Day When The World Comes Alive • I Am A Song • It Might As Well Be Spring • Music • But Not For Me • Two-Part Invention • Talk To Me Baby • Thieving Boy • Hi-Heel Sneakers

| | | | | | |
|---|---|---|---|---|---|
| 9/30/78 | 201 | 3 | **2 Gonna Get Through** ....................................................................... | $10 | RCA Victor 2926 |

One More Night • When I Need You • I'll Have To Say I Love You In A Song • On And On • I Believe You • Gonna Get Through • Just The Way You Are • The Wish • Let's Have A Quiet Night In • The Merchant Song

### L.A. JETS ○
Rock group from Los Angeles: Karen Lawrence (vocals), Harlin McNees and Silver Hanson (guitars), James Lindsay (percussion), Wayne Cook (keyboards), Ron Cindrich (bass) and John DeSautels (drums).

| | | | | | |
|---|---|---|---|---|---|
| 6/19/76 | 210 | 1 | **L.A. Jets** ...................................................................................... | $10 | RCA Victor 1547 |

Dancin' Thru The Night • Bailin' Out • An Elemental Song • It Takes A Lot To Laugh, It Takes A Train To Cry • At The Dardanelle • Music Is My Life • Never Satisfied • Money Money • Carmel Dodge • Then The Rains Came • Bandido • Hi-Heel Sneakers

### LAKE
Progressive-rock group from Germany: James Hopkins-Harrison (vocals), Alex Conti (guitar), Geoffrey Peacey and Detlef Petersen (keyboards), Martin Tiefensee (bass) and Dieter Ahrendt (drums).

| | | | | | |
|---|---|---|---|---|---|
| 7/22/78 | 201 | 3 | **Lake II** ......................................................................................... | $10 | Columbia 35289 |

Welcome To The West • See Them Glow • Letters Of Love • Red Lake • Love's The Jailor • Lost By The Wayside • Highway 216 • Angel In Disguise • Scoobie Doobies

### LAKE, Greg
Born on 11/10/48 in Bournemouth, England. Singer/guitarist/bassist. Former member of King Crimson and Emerson, Lake & Palmer.

| | | | | | |
|---|---|---|---|---|---|
| 10/1/83 | 209 | 1 | **Manoeuvres** ................................................................................. | $10 | Chrysalis 41392 |

Manoeuvres • Too Young To Love • Paralysed • A Woman Like You • I Don't Wanna Lose Your Love Tonight • It's You, You've Gotta Believe • Famous Last Words • Slave To Love • Haunted • I Don't Know Why I Still Love You

### LAMONT CRANSTON BAND ○
Rock group from Minneapolis: Pat Hayes (vocals, harmonica), Larry Hayes and Charlie Bingham (guitars), Rick O'Dell and Jim Greenwell (horns), Bruce McCabe (keyboards), Terry Grant (bass) and Jim Novack (drums).

| | | | | | |
|---|---|---|---|---|---|
| 4/24/82 | 201 | 4 | **Shakedown** .................................................................................. | $10 | RCA Victor 4313 |

Two Trains Runnin' • Upper Mississippi Shakedown • Seven • Moonlight On The Broken Glass • Streets Around Here • I'm So Shy • So Much • Party Train • Cold, Broke & Hungry • What Love Will Do

### LANE, Robin, & The Chartbusters
Rock group formed in Boston by female singer Lane, with Asa Brebner and Leroy Radcliffe (guitars), Scott Baerenwald (bass) and Tim Jackson (drums).

| | | | | | |
|---|---|---|---|---|---|
| 5/24/80 | 207 | 1 | **Robin Lane & The Chartbusters** .................................................... | $10 | Warner 3424 |

When Things Go Wrong • It'll Only Hurt A Little While • Don't Cry • Without You • Why Do You Tell Lies • I Don't Want To Know • Many Years Ago • Waitin' In Line • Be Mine Tonite • Kathy Lee • Don't Wait Till Tomorrow

### LARSEN, Neil
Born on 8/7/48 in Cleveland; raised in Siesta Key, Florida. Jazz-rock keyboardist. Also see **Full Moon**.

| | | | | | |
|---|---|---|---|---|---|
| 1/20/79 | 206 | 4 | **Jungle Fever** ............................................................................... | [I] $10 | Horizon 733 |

Sudden Samba • Promenade • Windsong • Emerald City • Jungle Fever • Red Desert • Last Tango In Paris • From A Dream

### LaSALLE, Denise
Born Denise Craig on 7/16/39 in LeFlore County, Mississippi. R&B singer/songwriter.

| | | | | | |
|---|---|---|---|---|---|
| 8/4/79 | 205 | 3 | **1 Unwrapped** ................................................................................. | $10 | MCA 3098 |

Think About It • Keep On Dancin', Rock • A Miracle, You And Me • Too Little In Common To Be Lovers • Da Ya Think I'm Sexy? • Medley: Make Me Yours/Precious Memories/Trapped By A Thing Called Love

| | | | | | |
|---|---|---|---|---|---|
| 4/14/84 | 204 | 5 | **2 Right Place, Right Time** ............................................................... | $10 | Malaco 7417 |

Right Place, Right Time • He's Not Available • Treat Your Man Like A Baby • Good Man Gone Bad • Boogie Man • Your Husband Is Cheating On Us • Why Does It Feel So Right • Keep Your Pants On • Bump And Grind • Love School

### LaVETTE, Bettye ○
Born Betty Haskin in 1946 in Muskegon, Michigan. R&B singer/actress.

| | | | | | |
|---|---|---|---|---|---|
| 2/13/82 | 207 | 5 | **Tell Me A Lie** ............................................................................... | $10 | Motown 6000 |

Right In The Middle (Of Falling In Love) • Either Way We Lose • Suspicions • You Seen One You Seen 'Em All • I Heard It Through The Grapevine • Tell Me A Lie • I Like It Like That • Before I Even Knew Your Name (I Needed You) • I Can't Stop • If I Were Your Woman

### LAWRENCE, Steve — see GORME, Eydie

### LAWS, Hubert
Born in 1939 in Houston. R&B-jazz flutist. Brother of **Ronnie Laws**.

| | | | | | |
|---|---|---|---|---|---|
| 7/13/74 | 207 | 1 | **In The Beginning** ......................................................................... | [I] $15 | CTI 3 [2] |

In The Beginning • Restoration • Gymnopedie #1 • Come Ye Disconsolate • Airegin • Moment's Notice • Reconciliation • Mean Lene

### LAWS, Ronnie
Born on 10/3/50 in Houston. R&B-jazz saxophonist. Brother of **Hubert Laws**.

| | | | | | |
|---|---|---|---|---|---|
| 1/26/85 | 201 | 7 | Classic Masters ... [K] | $10 | Capitol 12375 |

City Girl • Always There • Love Is Here • Every Generation • (You Are) Paradise • Friends And Strangers • In The Groove • Stay Awake • Saturday Evening

### LEE, Brenda
Born Brenda Mae Tarpley on 12/11/44 in Lithonia, Georgia. Country-pop singer.

| | | | | | |
|---|---|---|---|---|---|
| 4/21/73 | 206 | 3 | Brenda ... | $15 | MCA 305 |

Nobody Wins • I Can See Clearly Now • Sweet Memories • Everybody's Reaching Out For Someone • Here I Am Again • Run To Me • Something's Wrong With Me • I'm A Memory • My Sweet Baby • We Had A Good Thing Going • Always On My Mind

### LEE, Johnny
Born John Lee Ham on 7/3/46 in Texas City; raised in Alta Loma, Texas. Country singer/songwriter/guitarist. Married to actress Charlene Tilton from 1982-84.

| | | | | | |
|---|---|---|---|---|---|
| 8/20/83 | 201 | 3 | 1 Hey Bartender | $10 | Warner 23889 |

Hey Bartender • Blue Monday • You Really Got A Hold On Me • My Baby Don't Slow Dance • I'll Have To Say I Love You In A Song • Women In Boots • I'm In Love Again • In My Dreams • I Just Want To Love You Forever • Gimme Little Night Time

| | | | | | |
|---|---|---|---|---|---|
| 11/12/83 | 210 | 4 | 2 Greatest Hits ... [G] | $10 | Warner 23967 |

Lookin' For Love • Cherokee Fiddle • Prisoner Of Hope • When You Fall In Love • Bet Your Heart On Me • Sounds Like Love • Pickin' Up Strangers • One In A Million • Be There For Me Baby • Hey Bartender

### LEE, Laura
Born Laura Lee Rundless on 3/9/45 in Chicago. R&B singer/songwriter.

| | | | | | |
|---|---|---|---|---|---|
| 7/15/72 | 201 | 5 | Two Sides Of Laura Lee | $15 | Hot Wax 714 |

At Last (My Love Has Come Along) • Every Little Bit Hurts • Guess Who I Saw Today • Crumbs Off The Table • If You Can Beat Me Rockin' (You Can Have My Chair) • Workin' And Lovin' Together • Rip Off • When A Man Loves A Woman • You've Got To Save Me

### LEE, Peggy
Born Norma Deloris Egstrom on 5/26/20 in Jamestown, North Dakota. Jazz-pop singer. Won Grammy's Lifetime Achievement Award in 1995.

| | | | | | |
|---|---|---|---|---|---|
| 8/19/72 | 203 | 5 | 1 Norma Deloris Egstrom From Jamestown, North Dakota ... | $12 | Capitol 11077 |

Love Song • Razor (Love Me As I Am) • When I Found You • A Song For You • It Takes Too Long To Learn To Live Alone • Superstar • Just For A Thrill • Someone Who Cares • The More I See You • I'll Be Seeing You

| | | | | | |
|---|---|---|---|---|---|
| 11/23/74 | 209 | 1 | 2 Let's Love ... | $12 | Atlantic 18103 |

Let's Love • He Is The One • Easy Evil • Don't Let Me Be Lonely Tonight • Always • You Make Me Feel Brand New • Sweet Lov'liness • The Heart Is A Lonely Hunter • Sweet Talk • Sometimes • Let's Love (Reprise)

### LENNY & SQUIGGY ✪
Duo of actors Michael McKean ("Lenny") and David L. Lander ("Squiggy") of TV's *Laverne & Shirley*. The Squigtones included Christopher Guest (as "Nigel Tufnel"). McKean and Guest went on to form Spinal Tap.

| | | | | | |
|---|---|---|---|---|---|
| 5/19/79 | 205 | 5 | Lenny And The Squigtones ... [L] | $10 | Casablanca 7149 |

recorded at The Roxy in Hollywood

Vamp On • Night After Night • Creature Without A Head • King Of The Cars • Squiggy's Wedding Day • Love Is A Terrible Thing • Babyland (For Eva Squigman) • (If Only I Had Listened To) Mama • So's Your Old Testament • Sister-In-Law • Honor Farm • Starcrossed • Only Women Cry • Foreign Legion Of Love • Vamp Off

### LE PAMPLEMOUSSE
Disco studio group led by producers Laurin Rinder and W. Michael Lewis. Band name is French for The Grapefruit.

| | | | | | |
|---|---|---|---|---|---|
| 2/3/79 | 207 | 2 | Sweet Magic ... | $10 | AVI 6053 |

Sweet Magic • Slowdown • Do You Have Any? (Ya Know Where I Can Get Some) • I Wanna Make Music With You • Deeper • No Sweat • Can't Hide It (I Came Here To Dance)

### LE ROUX
Rock group from Baton Rouge, Louisiana: Dennis Frederiksen (vocals), Tony Haseldon and Jim Odom (guitars), Rod Roddy (keyboards), Leon Medica (bass) and David Peters (drums).

| | | | | | |
|---|---|---|---|---|---|
| 4/16/83 | 203 | 4 | So Fired Up ... | $10 | RCA Victor 4510 |

So Fired Up • Lifeline • Let Me In • Yours Tonight • Line On Love • Carrie's Gone • Wait One Minute • Turning Point • Don't Take It Away • Look Out

### LE JARDIN ✪
Disco studio group produced by Jacques Simon. Group name is French for The Garden.

| | | | | | |
|---|---|---|---|---|---|
| 9/9/78 | 210 | 1 | Mirage ... | $10 | Muscle 401 |

Livin' For The Night • Le Jardin De Amour • You Are A Star • Discothèque Cherie • Rio Fever • Les Beignets • I'm In Love • Voilà!

### LEWIS, Huey, & The News
Born Hugh Cregg III on 7/5/50 in New York City. Former member of **Clover**. Formed the News in San Francisco: Lewis (vocals, harmonica), Chris Hayes (guitar), Johnny Colla (sax), Sean Hopper (keyboards), Mario Cipollina (bass) and Bill Gibson (drums). Lewis acted in the movie *Short Cuts* and had a cameo appearance in *Back To The Future*.

| | | | | | |
|---|---|---|---|---|---|
| 8/16/80 | 203 | 3 | Huey Lewis & The News ... | $10 | Chrysalis 1292 |

Some Of My Lies Are True (Sooner Or Later) • Don't Make Me Do It • Stop Trying • Now Here's You • I Want You • Don't Ever Tell Me That You Love Me • Hearts • Trouble In Paradise • Who Cares? • If You Really Love Me You'll Let Me

| DEBUT | PEAK | WKS | Album Title | $ | Label & Number |
|-------|------|-----|-------------|---|----------------|

### LEWIS, Jerry Lee
Born on 9/29/35 in Ferriday, Louisiana. Rock and roll singer/piano player. Turned to country music in 1968. Nicknamed "The Killer." Cousin of **Mickey Gilley** and **Jimmy Swaggart**. Inducted into the Rock and Roll Hall of Fame in 1986. *Top Pop Albums*: 21.

| 1/30/71 | 213 | 1 | 1 In Loving Memories: The Jerry Lee Lewis Gospel Album | $20 | Mercury 61318 |

In Loving Memories • The Lily Of The Valley • Gather 'Round Children • My God's Not Dead • He Looked Beyond My Fault • The Old Rugged Cross • I'll Fly Away • I'm Longing For Home • I Know That Jesus Will Be There • Too Much To Gain To Lose • Medley: If We Never Meet Again/I'll Meet You In The Morning

| 3/3/73 | 201 | 2 | 2 Who's Gonna Play This Old Piano...(Think About It Darlin') | $15 | Mercury 61366 |

Who's Gonna Play This Old Piano • She's Reachin' For My Mind • Too Many Rivers • We Both Know Which One Of Us Was Wrong • Wall Around Heaven • No More Hanging On • Think About It Darlin' • Bottom Dollar • No Traffic Out Of Abilene • Parting Is Such Sweet Sorrow • The Mercy Of A Letter

| 5/22/82 | 205 | 3 | 3 The Survivors ......[L] | $10 | Columbia 37961 |

**JOHNNY CASH/JERRY LEE LEWIS/CARL PERKINS**
recorded on 4/23/81 at the Sporthalle Boeblingen in Stuttgart, West Germany

Get Rhythm • I Forgot To Remember To Forget • Goin' Down The Road Feelin' Bad • That Silver Haired Daddy Of Mine • Matchbox • I'll Fly Away • Whole Lot-ta Shakin' Goin' On • Rockin' My Life Away • Blue Suede Shoes • There Will Be Peace In The Valley For Me • Can The Circle Be Unbroken • I Saw The Light

### LEWIS, Linda ☉
R&B singer/actress from London. Appeared in the movies *A Taste Of Honey* and *A Hard Day's Night*.

| 9/20/75 | 204 | 5 | Not A Little Girl Anymore | $10 | Arista 4047 |

(Remember The Days Of) The Old Schoolyard • It's In His Kiss • This Time I'll Be Sweeter • Rock And Roller Coaster • Not A Little Girl Anymore • Love Where Are You Now • My Granddaddy Could Reggae • I Do My Best To Impress • May You Never • Love, Love, Love

### LEWIS, Ramsey
Born on 5/27/35 in Chicago. Jazz-R&B keyboardist. *Top Pop Albums*: 30.

| 6/9/79 | 203 | 8 | 1 Ramsey ......[I] | $10 | Columbia 35815 |

Medley: Aquarius/Let The Sun Shine In • Wearin' It Out • I Just Can't Give You Up • Every Chance I Get (I'm Gonna Love You) • Dancin' • I'll Always Dream About You • Intermezzo • Medley: Spañoletta/Don't Cry For Me Argentina • Intermezzo

| 3/20/82 | 202 | 10 | 2 Live At The Savoy ......[I-L] | $10 | Columbia 37687 |

recorded at The Savoy Theater in New York City

Close Your Eyes And Remember • Sassy Stew • Callin' Fallin' • Baby What You Want Me To Do • You Never Know • Lynn • It's Just Called Love • Hits Medley: Wade In The Water/Hang On Sloopy/The In Crowd

| 7/9/83 | 206 | 5 | 3 Les Fleurs ......[I] | $10 | Columbia 38787 |

title is French for "The Flowers"

Super Woman (Where Were You When I Needed You) • A House Is Not A Home • Essence Of Love • Les Fleurs • Physical • With A Gentle Touch • Reasons

### LIGHT, Enoch, & The Light Brigade
Born on 8/18/07 in Canton, Ohio. Died on 7/31/78. Orchestra leader. *Top Pop Albums*: 25.

| 2/13/71 | 211 | 6 | The Big Band Hits Of The Thirties ......[I] | $12 | Project 3 5049 |

Begin The Beguine • A String Of Pearls • I'm Getting Sentimental Over You • Well, Git It • Woodchoppers Ball • One O'Clock Jump • Moonlight Serenade • Let's Dance • In The Mood • Ciribiribin • Snowfall • South Rampart Street Parade • Take The A Train

### LIGHTHOUSE
Rock group from Toronto: Skip Prokop (vocals, drums), Ralph Cole (guitar), Larry Smith (keyboards), Dale Hillary, John Naslen and Rick Stepton (horns), Dick Armin (cello), Don DiNovo (viola) and Alan Wilmont (bass).

| 10/6/73 | 220 | 1 | Can You Feel It | $12 | Polydor 5056 |

Set The Stage • Same Train • Magic's In The Dancing • Pretty Lady • Disagreeable Man • Can You Feel It • Is Love The Answer • Lonely Hours • No More Searching • Bright Side

### LINDLEY, David
Born in 1944 in San Marino, California. Session guitarist. El-Rayo X consisted of Bernie Larsen (guitar), Jorge Calderón (bass) and Ian Wallace (drums).

| 11/13/82 | 202 | 4 | Win This Record | $10 | Elektra 60178 |

**DAVID LINDLEY and El Rayo-X**

Something's Got A Hold On Me • Turning Point • Spodie • Brother John • Premature • Talk To The Lawyer • Make It On Time • Rock It With I • Ram-A-Lamb-A Man • Look So Good

### LINHART, Buzzy ☉
Male singer/songwriter.

| 10/23/71 | 210 | 1 | The Time To Live Is Now | $12 | Kama Sutra 2037 |

The Time To Live Is Now • There's No Need • Comin' Home • Heaven • Crazy • Let's Get Together • Leila • I Don't Ever Want To Say Goodbye • The Love's Still Growing • Friends • Medley: Cheat-Cheat-Lied/Hit The Road Jack • Good Face

### LIPSTIQUE ☉
Disco studio group from Germany assembled by producer Jurgen Korduletsch.

| 6/3/78 | 201 | 12 | At The Discotheque | $10 | Tom N' Jerry 4701 |

At The Discotheque Medley: At The Discotheque/Discotique/Our Song Of Love/I'm Still Dancing • Medley: I Wanna Play With You/Funny Games • Medley: Venus/Light My Fire • Mah-Nah-Mah-Nah

### LITTLE FEAT
Rock group from Los Angeles: Lowell George (vocals, guitar), **Paul Barrère** (guitar), Bill Payne (keyboards), Kenny Gradney (bass), Sam Clayton (percussion) and Richard Hayward (drums). George died of heart failure on 6/29/79 (age 34).

| 5/27/72 | 203 | 3 | 1 Sailin' Shoes | $15 | Warner 2600 |

Easy To Slip • Cold, Cold, Cold • Trible Face Boogie • Willin' • A Apolitical Blues • Sailin' Shoes • Teenage Nervous Breakdown • Got No Shadow • Cat Fever • Texas Rose Cafe

| 3/10/73 | 205 | 4 | ● 2 Dixie Chicken | $15 | Warner 2686 |

Dixie Chicken • Two Trains • Roll Um Easy • On Your Way Down • Kiss It Off • Fool Yourself • Walkin All Night • Fat Man In The Bathtub • Juliette • Lafayette Railroad

### LIVGREN, Kerry ☉
Born on 9/18/49 in Kansas. Guitarist/keyboardist of Kansas.

| 9/20/80 | 209 | 2 | **Seeds Of Change** ......................................................................... | $10 | Kirshner 36567 |

guest vocalists include Ronnie James Dio, David Pack and Steve Walsh

Just One Way • Mask Of The Great Deceiver • How Can You Live • Whiskey Seed • To Live For The King • Down To The Core • Ground Zero

### LLOYD, Charles
Born on 3/15/38 in Memphis. Jazz tenor saxophonist.

| 1/20/73 | 208 | 3 | **Waves** ...................................................................................... [I] | $12 | A&M 3044 |

TM • Pyramid • Majorca • Harvest • Waves • Rishikesha Medley: Hummingbird/Rishikesh/Seagull

### LLOYD, Ian — see STORIES

### LOBO
Born Roland Kent Lavoie on 7/31/43 in Tallahassee, Florida. Pop singer/songwriter/guitarist.

| 12/15/79 | 207 | 2 | **Lobo** ........................................................................................ | $10 | MCA 3194 |

Where Were You When I Was Falling In Love • Spendin' Time, Makin' Love And Goin' Crazy • A Day In The Life Of A Love • Heart To Heart (Person To Person) • It's Time To Face The Music And Dance • Holdin' On For Dear Love • Lay Me Down • I Don't Wanna Make Love Anymore • The Way I Came In • Gus, The Dancing Dog

### LOCOMOTIV GT ☉
Rock group: Thomas Barta (vocals, guitar), Gabor Presser (keyboards), Thomas Somlo (bass) and Joseph Laux (drums).

| 8/17/74 | 207 | 1 | **Locomotiv GT** ............................................................................ | $12 | ABC 811 |

Rock Yourself • Gimme Your Love • Free Me • Confession • She's Just 14 • Won't You Dance With Me • Hey, Get The Feelin' • Waiting For You • Serenade (To My Love If I Had One) • Back Home • Jenny's Got A New Thing

### LOFGREN, Nils
Born on 6/21/51 in Chicago; raised in Maryland. Pop-rock singer/guitarist/pianist.

| 9/17/83 | 206 | 1 | **Wonderland** .............................................................................. | $10 | Backstreet 5421 |

guest vocalists include Louise Goffin, Carly Simon and Edgar Winter

Across The Tracks • Into The Night • It's All Over Now • I Wait For You • Daddy Dream • Wonderland • Room Without Love • Confident Girl • Lonesome Ranger • Everybody Wants • Deadline

### LOMAX, Jackie
Born on 5/10/44 in Liverpool, England. Male singer/songwriter.

| 7/3/71 | 211 | 3 | 1 **Home Is In My Head** ................................................................. | $15 | Warner 1914 |

Give All You've Got • A Hundred Mountains • When I Miss You The Most • Or So It Seems • Home Is In My Head • Nothin' Ever Seems To Go My Way • She Took You Higher • Don't Do Me No Harm • Higher Ground • Helluva Woman • Turning Around • You Within Me

| 3/25/72 | 208 | 2 | 2 **Three** ..................................................................................... | $15 | Warner 2591 |

No Reason • Time Will Tell You • Hellfire, Night-Crier • Lost • Roll On • Lavender Dream • Let The Play Begin • Fever's Got Me Burnin' • Last Time Home • Rock Salt • (You've Got To) Do It All Yourself

### LOOKING GLASS
Pop-rock group from Brunswick, New Jersey: Elliot Lurie (vocals, guitar), Larry Gonsky (keyboards), Piet Sweval (bass) and Jeff Grob (drums).

| 7/21/73 | 209 | 9 | **Subway Serenade** ...................................................................... | $15 | Epic 32167 |

Jimmy Loves Mary-Anne • City Lady • For Skipper • Sweet Somethin' • Who's Gonna Sing My Rock 'N' Roll Song • Are You Dreamin' (Money In My Pockets) • Rainbow Man • Wait • Sweet Jeremiah • Wooly Eyes

### LORDS OF THE NEW CHURCH, The
British rock group: Cleveland native Stiv Bators (vocals; **Dead Boys**), Brian James (guitar), Dave Tregunna (bass) and Nicky Turner (drums). Bators died on 6/4/90 (age 40) after being hit by a car.

| 7/23/83 | 203 | 3 | 1 **Live For Today** .......................................................................... [M] | $10 | I.R.S. 70409 |

Live For Today • Opening Nightmares • Dreams And Desires

| 10/29/83 | 202 | 2 | 2 **Is Nothing Sacred?** ................................................................... | $10 | I.R.S. 70039 |

Dance With Me • Bad Timing • Johnny Too Bad • Don't Worry Children • The Night Is Calling • Black Girl White Girl • Goin' Downtown • Tale Of Two Cities • World Without End • Partners In Crime • Live For Today

### LOVE AFFAIR ☉
Rock group from Cleveland: Rich Spina (vocals, keyboards), Wes Coolbaugh and John Zdravecky (guitars), Wayne Cukras (bass) and Michal Hudak (drums).

| 9/6/80 | 209 | 3 | **Love Affair** .............................................................................. | $10 | Radio 2004 |

Seventeen (You're A Star) • Mama Sez • Touch Me • Magic Man • Can't Get Enough • I Can't Let Go • Going Down • Crazy • Does She • Cleveland Boys

### LOVE UNLIMITED ORCHESTRA
Forty-piece studio orchestra conducted and arranged by **Barry White**.

| 2/18/78 | 201 | 6 | **My Musical Bouquet** ................................................................... [I] | $10 | 20th Century 554 |

Don't You Know How Much I Love You • Stay Please And Make Love To Me • Hey Look At Me, I'm In Love • Love You, Ooh It's True I Do • Whisper Softly • Enter Love's Interlude • Can't You See

### LUCIEN, Jon ☉
Born in 1942 in St. Thomas, Virgin Islands. R&B singer/songwriter.

| 12/27/75 | 203 | 2 | **Song For My Lady** ...................................................................... | $12 | Columbia 33544 |

Soul Mate • Dindi • Motherland • You Are My Love • Maiden Voyage • Creole Lady • Song For My Lady • Follow Your Heart

| DEBUT | PEAK | WKS | Album Title | $ | Label & Number |
|---|---|---|---|---|---|

### LUCIFER'S FRIEND ☉
Rock group from Germany: John Lawton (vocal), Peter Hesslein (guitar), Peter Hecht (keyboards), Dieter Horns (bass) and Joachim Rietenbach (drums).

| | | | | | |
|---|---|---|---|---|---|
| 11/10/73 | 221 | 2 | 1 Lucifer's Friend ................................................................................ | $15 | Billingsgate 1002 |

Ride The Sky • Everybody's Clown • Keep Goin' • Toxic Shadows • Free Baby • Baby You're A Liar • In The Time Of Job When Mammon Was A Yippie • Lucifer's Friend

| | | | | | |
|---|---|---|---|---|---|
| 4/19/75 | 205 | 1 | 2 ...Where The Groupies Killed The Blues ............................................... | $12 | Passport 98008 |

Burning Ships • Prince Of Darkness • Hobo • Mother • Where The Groupies Killed The Blues • Rose On The Vine • Summerdream Medley: Delirium/No Reason Or Rhyme

### LUV YOU MADLY ORCHESTRA ☉
Disco studio group assembled by producer Steve James.

| | | | | | |
|---|---|---|---|---|---|
| 9/2/78 | 207 | 1 | Luv You Madly Orchestra ...................................................................... | $10 | Salsoul 8507 |

In The Beginning Medley: In The Beginning God/Take The "A" Train/Satin Doll/I Let A Song Go Out Of My Heart/Caravan/Mood Indigo/Melancholia • Moon Maiden • Love You Madly • Hippo Hop • Rocket Rock • Fleurette Africaine • Soda Fountain Rag • Fountain Bleu Forest • Lotus Blossom

### LYNN, Cheryl
Born on 3/11/57 in Los Angeles. R&B-disco singer.

| | | | | | |
|---|---|---|---|---|---|
| 7/27/85 | 202 | 5 | It's Gonna Be Right ............................................................................ | $10 | Columbia 40024 |

Fidelity • Fade To Black • Love's Been Here Before • It's Gonna Be Right • Let Me Love You • Find Somebody New • Loafin' • Slipped Me A Mickey • Tug 'O' War

# M

### MacGREGOR, Byron ☉
Born Gary Mack in 1948 in Calgary, Alberta, Canada. Died of pneumonia on 1/3/95 (age 46). News director at CKLW-Detroit when he did the narration for "Americans."

| | | | | | |
|---|---|---|---|---|---|
| 2/23/74 | 208 | 2 | Americans ............................................................................ | [T] $15 | Westbound 1000 |

Americans • Gettysburg Address • Star Spangled Banner • Amazing Grace (America The Beautiful) • How Good You Have It In America • America The Beautiful • The Strongest Americans • Dixie • Lincoln Lives On • Eyes Of Texas • Oh Canada • God Save The Queen • Stars & Stripes

### MACK, Jimmie, And The Jumpers ☉
Rock group: Jimmie Mack (vocals), Flasher (guitar), Gene Leppik (bass) and Steve Merola (drums).

| | | | | | |
|---|---|---|---|---|---|
| 1/17/81 | 208 | 2 | Jimmie Mack And The Jumpers ............................................................... | $10 | RCA Victor 3698 |

It's Gonna Hurt • I Need You • Hold Me Tight • Little Bit Of Lovin • Just To Be In Love Again • Main Street • When I Kiss You • I Want It All • Justelle • The Very Last Time

### MAHAL, Taj
Born Henry Fredericks on 5/17/40 in New York City. Blues singer/guitarist.

| | | | | | |
|---|---|---|---|---|---|
| 6/12/76 | 201 | 2 | Satisfied 'N Tickled Too | $12 | Columbia 34103 |

Satisfied 'N Tickled Too • New E-Z Rider Blues • Black Man, Brown Man • Baby Love • Ain't Nobody's Business • Misty Morning Ride • Easy To Love • Old Time Song-Old Time Love • We Tune

### MAIN INGREDIENT, The
R&B vocal trio from New York City: Cuba Gooding, Luther Simmons and Tony Sylvester. Gooding's son, Cuba Jr., acted in several movies.

| | | | | | |
|---|---|---|---|---|---|
| 10/20/73 | 205 | 13 | 1 Greatest Hits ............................................................ | [G] $12 | RCA Victor 0314 |

You've Been My Inspiration • Spinning Around (I Must Be Falling In Love) • I'm So Proud (Mayfield) • Black Seeds Keep On Growing • I'm Better Off Without You • Everybody Plays The Fool • You've Got To Take It (If You Want It) • No Tears (In The End) • Make It With You • Who Can I Turn To (When Nobody Needs Me)

| | | | | | |
|---|---|---|---|---|---|
| 9/4/76 | 201 | 7 | 2 Super Hits | [G] $12 | RCA Victor 1858 |

Instant Love • Rolling Down A Mountainside • I Want To Make You Glad • Happiness Is Just Around The Bend • Just Don't Want To Be Lonely • The Good Old Days • Girl Blue • Shame On The World

| | | | | | |
|---|---|---|---|---|---|
| 9/20/80 | 207 | 3 | 3 Ready For Love ............................................................... | $10 | RCA Victor 3641 |

**THE MAIN INGREDIENT Featuring Cuba Gooding**
Think Positive • Ready For Love • Evil Ways • What Can A Miracle Do • Catchin' The Fever • With You • Spoiled • Makes No Difference To Me

### MALO
Latin-rock band. Core members: Arcelio Garcia (vocals), Carlos Rivera (guitar), Sergio Brandas (bass) and Steve Arnold (drums). Malo is Spanish for "Bad."

| | | | | | |
|---|---|---|---|---|---|
| 6/12/82 | 210 | 1 | Malo V ................................................................................ | $10 | Traq 107 |

Lady I Love • I Found You Out • Good Tasting Stuff • It's A Lovely Day • Cantina • Young Man

### MAMAS & THE PAPAS, The
Folk-rock group from Los Angeles: husband-and-wife John (vocals, guitar) and Michelle (vocals) Phillips, with vocalists Dennis Doherty and "Mama" Cass Elliot. Group inducted into the Rock and Roll Hall of Fame in 1998.

| | | | | | |
|---|---|---|---|---|---|
| 4/10/71 | 226 | 2 | Monterey International Pop Festival ....................................... | [L] $20 | Dunhill 50100 |

recorded from 6/16 - 6/18/67 in Monterey, California
Straight Shooter • Got A Feelin' • California Dreamin' • Spanish Harlem • Somebody Groovy • I Call Your Name • Monday, Monday • Dancing In The Street

### MAN ☉
Pub-rock group from Wales: Micky Jones (vocals, guitar), Deke Leonard (guitar), Martin Ace (bass) and Terry Williams (drums).

| | | | | | |
|---|---|---|---|---|---|
| 3/1/75 | 205 | 3 | Slow Motion ....................................................................... | $12 | United Artists 345 |

Hard Way To Die • Grasshopper • Rock And Roll You Out • You Don't Like Us • Bedtime Bone • One More Chance • Rainbow Eyes • Day And Night

### MANCINI, Henry
Born on 4/16/24 in Cleveland; raised in Aliquippa, Pennsylvania. Died of cancer on 6/14/94. Leading movie and TV composer/arranger/conductor. *Top Pop Albums:* 39.

| | | | | | |
|---|---|---|---|---|---|
| 8/11/73 | 215 | 3 | Oklahoma Crude ................................................................................[I-S] $12 | | RCA Victor 0271 |

Oklahoma Crude • Lightfinger • Cleon And Lena • Lena's Tune • Over The Top • Send A Little Love My Way • The Big Climb • The Dude Of My Dreams • On Your Hill • In Your Hill • Send A Little Love My Way

### MANDEL, Harvey
Born on 3/11/45 in Detroit. Blues-rock guitarist. Former member of **Canned Heat**.

| | | | | | |
|---|---|---|---|---|---|
| 2/27/71 | 213 | 3 | Baby Batter ........................................................................................ [I] $15 | | Janus 3017 |

Baby Batter • Midnight Sun • One Way Street • Morton Grove Mama • Freedom Ball • El Stinger • Hank The Ripper

### MANDRÉ
Disco-funk singer/songwriter/keyboardist/bassist André Lewis. Former member of **Maxayn**.

| | | | | | |
|---|---|---|---|---|---|
| 4/22/78 | 201 | 13 | 1 Mandré Two ............................................................................................ $10 | | Motown 900 |

Love Comes Rushin' In • I Like Your Freaky Ways • Fair Game • Code Name: MM3 • Maxymus Lyte (Opus III) • Iles Dans L'Espace • Doing Nothing, Nothing Doing

| | | | | | |
|---|---|---|---|---|---|
| 4/7/79 | 209 | 1 | 2 M3000 ................................................................................................. $10 | | Motown 917 |

M3000 (Opus VI) • L'Oasis • Final Funk • Spirit Groove • Freakin's Fine • Do Whatcha Gotta Do • Swang

### MANDRELL, Barbara
Born on 12/25/48 in Houston; raised in Oceanside, California. Country singer/multi-instrumentalist. Host of own TV variety series from 1980-82.

| | | | | | |
|---|---|---|---|---|---|
| 6/16/84 | 204 | 3 | 1 Clean Cut ............................................................................................. $10 | | MCA 5474 |

Happy Birthday Dear Heartache • If It's Not One Thing It's Another • I Can Depend On You • I Wonder What The Rich Folk Are Doin' Tonight • Crossword Puzzle • Only A Lonely Heart Knows • Just Like Old Times • Look What Love Has Done • Take Care Of You • Sincerely I'm Yours

| | | | | | |
|---|---|---|---|---|---|
| 5/4/85 | 210 | 1 | 2 Greatest Hits ................................................................................... [G] $10 | | MCA 5566 |

I Was Country When Country Wasn't Cool • Years • Wish You Were Here • The Best Of Strangers • Happy Birthday Dear Heartache • (If Loving You Is Wrong) I Don't Want To Be Right • Crackers • One Of A Kind Pair Of Fools • In Times Like These • There's No Love In Tennessee

### MANGIONE, Chuck
Born on 11/29/40 in Rochester, New York. Flugelhorn player/bandleader/composer.

| | | | | | |
|---|---|---|---|---|---|
| 1/22/83 | 202 | 3 | 70 Miles Young ...................................................................................... [I] $10 | | A&M 4911 |

70 Miles Young • Feels So Good • Cannonball Run Theme • Recuerdo • Lullaby For Nancy Carol

### MANHATTAN TRANSFER, The
Vocal harmony group from New York City: Gene Pistilli, Tim Hauser, Erin Dickins, Pat Rosalia and Marty Nelson. Pistilli went on to become a prolific songwriter/producer. Hauser went on to lead a different, more successful Manhattan Transfer group.

| | | | | | |
|---|---|---|---|---|---|
| 7/12/75 | 202 | 2 | Jukin' ....................................................................................................[E] $12 | | Capitol 11405 |

THE MANHATTAN TRANSFER and GENE PISTILLI
recorded in 1971
Chicken Bone Bone • I Need A Man • Vipers Drag • Fair And Tender Ladies • Rosianna • Sunny Disposish • Java Jive • One More Time Around Rosie • Guided Missiles • Roll Daddy, Roll

### MANILOW, Barry
Born Barry Alan Pincus on 6/17/46 in Brooklyn. Singer/songwriter/pianist. *Top Pop Albums:* 24.

| | | | | | |
|---|---|---|---|---|---|
| 12/29/73+ | 206 | 5 | Barry Manilow...................................................................................... $25 | | Bell 1129 |

reissued in 1975 on Arista 4007 (#28)
Sing It • Sweetwater Jones • Cloudburst • One Of These Days • Oh My Lady • I Am Your Child • Could It Be Magic • Seven More Years • Flashy Lady • Friends • Sweet Life

### MANN, Barry ☉
Born Barry Iberman on 2/9/39 in Brooklyn. One of pop music's most prolific songwriters in a partnership with wife Cynthia Weil.

| | | | | | |
|---|---|---|---|---|---|
| 2/12/72 | 213 | 1 | Lay It All Out ...................................................................................... $15 | | New Design 30876 |

Too Many Mondays • When You Get Right Down To It • Lay It All Out • I Heard You Singing Your Song • Holy Rolling • You've Lost That Lovin' Feelin' • On Broadway • Something Better • Sweet Ophelia • Don't Give Up On Me • Ain't No Way To Go Home • Wild-Eyed Indian

### MANTOVANI And His Orchestra
Born Annunzio Paolo Mantovani on 11/15/05 in Venice, Italy. Died on 3/29/80. Orchestra leader. *Top Pop Albums:* 49.

| | | | | | |
|---|---|---|---|---|---|
| 4/7/73 | 214 | 2 | Gypsy Soul .......................................................................................... [I] $12 | | London 900 |

The Heart Of Budapest • Czardas • Golden Earrings • Theme From "Villa Rides" • Carmen: Gypsy Dance • Gypsy Carnival • The Singer Not The Song • Hejre Kati • Gypsy Flower Girl • Hora Staccato • Zapateado • Hungarian Rhapsody No. 2

### MANZANERA, Phil
Born on 1/31/51 in London. Rock singer/guitarist. Member of **Roxy Music** from 1972-83.

| | | | | | |
|---|---|---|---|---|---|
| 8/2/75 | 202 | 3 | Diamond Head ...................................................................................... $12 | | Atco 113 |

Frontera • Diamond Head • Big Day • The Flex • Same Time Next Week • Miss Shapiro • East Of Echo • Lagrima • Alma

### MARILLION
Rock group from Aylesbury, England: Derek "Fish" Dick (vocals), Steve Rotheray (guitar), Mark Kelly (keyboards), Pete Trewavas (bass) and Ian Mosely (drums).

| | | | | | |
|---|---|---|---|---|---|
| 7/21/84 | 209 | 1 | Fugazi .................................................................................................. $10 | | Capitol 12331 |

Assassing • Punch And Judy • Jigsaw • Emerald Lies • She Chameleon • Incubus • Fugazi

### MARINO, Frank
Born on 8/22/54 in Montreal. Rock singer/guitarist. Leader of Mahogany Rush.

| | | | | | |
|---|---|---|---|---|---|
| 8/22/81 | 202 | 4 | The Power Of Rock And Roll ................................................................ $10 | | Columbia 37099 |

The Power Of Rock And Roll • Play My Music • Stay With Me • Runnin' Wild • Crazy Miss Daisy • Go Strange • Young Man • Ain't Dead Yet

### MARJOE ✪
Born Marjoe Gortner on 1/14/44 in Long Beach, California. Actor/singer. Cast member of TV's *Falcon Crest*.

| 11/18/72 | 207 | 2 | **Marjoe** ...................................................................................................... [S] $15 | Warner 2667 |

Medley: Wedding Ceremony/Onward Christian Soldiers/Hell With The Lid Off • Marjoe's Testimony • Medley: My Name Is Marjoe Gortner/Glory Hallelujah (Since I Lay My Burden Down) • Medley: God's Now Given Me A Cadillac/Glory Hallelujah • Big-Time Religion Gimmicks • Medley: An Addict's Testimony/Can God Deliver A Dog • I've Got Confidence *[Holland Sisters]* • God I Love You *[Countrymen]* • Do You Know Who Jesus Really Is? • We've Come Too Far To Turn Around *[June Samuels]* • Yes He Can! • Going To Heaven To Meet The King *[June Samuels]* • Glory Gee • Save All My Brothers *[Jerry Keller]*

### MARRIOTT, Steve ✪
Born on 1/30/47 in London. Died in a fire on 4/20/91. Rock singer/guitarist. Former leader of Small Faces and Humble Pie.

| 5/15/76 | 206 | 5 | **Marriott** ...................................................................................................... $12 | A&M 4572 |

East Side Struttin' • Lookin' For A Love • Help Me Make It Through The Day • Midnight Rollin' • Wam Bam Thank You Ma'am • Star In My Life • Are You Lonely For Me Baby • You Don't Know Me • Late Night Lady • Early Evening Light

### MARSHALL TUCKER BAND, The
Southern-rock band from Spartanburg, South Carolina: Doug Gray (vocals), Toy Caldwell and George McCorkle (guitars), Jerry Eubanks (sax), Ronnie Godfrey (keyboards), Franklin Wilkie (bass) and Paul T. Riddle (drums). Caldwell died of respiratory failure on 2/25/93 (age 45). Marshall Tucker was the owner of the band's rehearsal hall.

| 3/26/83 | 204 | 3 | 1 **Just Us** ...................................................................................................... $10 | Warner 23803 |

8:05 • Stay A Step Ahead • Time Don't Pass By Here • Testify • Long Island Lady • A Place I've Never Been • Wait For You • When Love Begins To Fade • Paradise

| 2/11/84 | 202 | 4 | 2 **Greetings From South Carolina** ...................................................................................................... $10 | Warner 23997 |

Carolina Sunset • Good 'Ole Hurtin' Song • If I Could Only Have My Way • I May Be Easy But You Make It Hard • Closer To Jesus • Blood Red Eagle • Shot Down Where You Stand • Feel A Drunk Comin' On • Bags Half Packed • Rollin' River

### MARTIN, Moon
Born John Martin in Oklahoma. Pop-rock singer/songwriter/guitarist.

| 4/24/82 | 205 | 6 | **Mystery Ticket** ...................................................................................................... $10 | Capitol 12200 |

X-Ray Vision • Witness • She's In Love With My Car • Paid The Price • Firing Line • Dangerous Game • Don't You Double (Cross Me Baby) • Aces With You • Deeper (Into Love) • Chain Reaction

### MARTINO, Al
Born Alfred Cini on 10/7/27 in Philadelphia. Pop singer/actor. Portrayed singer "Johnny Fontane" in *The Godfather*.

| 3/4/72 | 204 | 2 | **Summer Of '42** ...................................................................................................... $12 | Capitol 793 |

The Summer Knows • It's Impossible • More Than Ever Now • Where Do I Begin • Come Run With Me • Losing My Mind • Look Around (You'll Find Me There) • Loving Her Was Easier • A Time For Us • Gift Of Love

### MAS, Carolyne
Rock singer/guitarist from the Bronx, New York.

| 7/19/80 | 203 | 5 | **Hold On** ...................................................................................................... $10 | Mercury 3841 |

Hold On • Stay True • You Cannot Win If You Do Not Play • Running From The High Life • Go Ahead And Cry Now • All For You • He's So Cool • Remember The Night • Thomas Dunson's Revenge • Amsterdam

### MASON PROFFIT
Country-rock group from Chicago: brothers Terry (vocals, guitar) and John (guitar, vocals) Talbot, Bruce "Creeper" Kurnow (piano), Tim Ayres (bass) and Art Nash (drums).

| 12/9/72 | 211 | 3 | 1 **Rockfish Crossing** ...................................................................................................... $12 | Warner 2657 |

Jesse • You Win Again • Better Find Jesus • Summer Side Of Love • Breakin' Down • Were You There? • Hobo • A Thousand And Two • Medley: Cripple Creek/Quit Kickin' My Dog Around • Wetback • Medley: George's Jam/Call Me The Breeze

| 1/19/74 | 203 | 2 | 2 **Come & Gone** ...................................................................................................... [R] $15 | Warner 2746 [2] |

reissue of the group's early albums *Wanted* (did not chart) and *Movin' Toward Happiness* (#177)

Voice Of Change • A Rectangle Picture • You Finally Found Your Love • Sweet Lady Love • Stewball • Two Hangmen • Buffalo • Walk On Down The Road • It's All Right • Till The Sun's Gone • Johnny's Tune • Michael Dodge • Hard Luck Woman • Children • Hokey Joe Pony • Flying Arrow • Old Joe Clark • Good Friend Of Mary's • He Loves Them • Melinda • Let Me Know Where You're Going • Everbody Was Wrong

### MASS PRODUCTION
Disco-funk group from Richmond, Virginia: Agnes "Tiny" Kelly (female vocals), Larry Marshall (male vocals), LeCoy Bryant (guitar), James "Otiste" Drumgole (trumpet), Gregory McCoy (sax), Tyrone Williams (keyboards), Emanual Redding (percussion), Kevin Douglas (bass) and Ricardo Williams (drums).

| 8/12/78 | 207 | 1 | 1 **Three Miles High** ...................................................................................................... $10 | Cotillion 5205 |

Watch Me Do It • Sky High • I Don't Want To Know • Groove Me • Our Thought (Let The Music Take You Away) • Just Wanna Make A Dream Come True (Mass In F Minor) • Scarey Love • Slow Bump • Music And Love

| 4/24/82 | 203 | 3 | 2 **In A City Groove** ...................................................................................................... $10 | Cotillion 5233 |

Maybe Maybe • Never Ever • One More Chance • Should Have Known Better • Rock • Inner City • Solid Love • Weird

### MASTERMIND ✪
Disco group: Wendell Derrick (vocals), Joe Frye (guitar), Anselm Scrubb, Mario Ford, Guy Fuertes and Lenny White (horns), Juan Clouden (percussion), Geoffrey Williams (keyboards), Carl Bain (bass) and Brian Wilson (drums).

| 11/26/77 | 207 | 1 | **Mastermind** ...................................................................................................... $10 | Prelude 12147 |

I Am Music • Hustle Bus Stop • Free And Wild • Disco Party In The Street • Mother Nature • Runnin' Away From Love • Mastermind

### MATERIAL ✪
Experimental disco group spearheaded by producer/guitarist/percussionist Bill Laswell.

| 1/15/83 | 203 | 7 | **One Down** ...................................................................................................... $10 | Elektra 60206 |

guests vocalists include Nona Hendryx and Whitney Houston

Take A Chance • I'm The One • Time Out • Let Me Have It All • Come Down • Holding On • Memories • Don't Lose Control

| DEBUT | PEAK | WKS | Album Title | $ | Label & Number |
|-------|------|-----|-------------|---|----------------|

### MATHIS, Johnny
Born on 9/30/35 in San Francisco. Popular ballad singer of the 1950s and '60s. *Top Pop Albums*: 69.

| 9/17/77 | 201 | 1 | **Hold Me, Thrill Me, Kiss Me** | $10 | Columbia 34872 |

Hold Me, Thrill Me, Kiss Me • We're All Alone • All The Things You Are • One • When I Need You • The Most Beautiful Girl • Tomorrow • Evergreen (Love Theme From "A Star Is Born") • I Always Knew I Had It In Me • Don't Give Up On Us

### MATTHEWS, Ian
Born Ian Matthew MacDonald on 6/16/46 in Lincolnshire, England. Singer/songwriter/guitarist. Founder of **Fairport Convention** and **Matthews' Southern Comfort**.

| 1/9/71 | 209 | 1 | 1 **Second Spring** | $15 | Decca 75242 |

**MATTHEWS' SOUTHERN COMFORT**
Ballad Of Obray Ramsey • Moses In The Sunshine • Jinkson Johnson • Tale Of The Trial • Blood Red Roses • Medley: Even As/D'Arcy Farrow • Something In The Way She Moves • Southern Comfort

| 7/10/71 | 208 | 6 | 2 **If You Saw Thro' My Eyes** | $15 | Vertigo 1002 |

Desert Inn • Hearts • Never Ending • Reno Nevada • Little Known • Hinge • Hinge • Southern Wind • It Came Without Warning • You Couldn't Lose • Morgan The Pirate • If You Saw Thro' My Eyes

| 12/6/80 | 206 | 3 | 3 **Spot Of Interference** | $10 | RSO 3092 |

I Survived The Seventies • She May Call You Up Tonight • I Can't Fade Away • Driftwood From Disaster • Why Am I? • No Time At All (See How They Run) • For The Lonely Hunter • See Me • Civilisation • What Do I Do?

### MAURIAT, Paul
Born in France in 1925. Orchestra leader.

| 10/21/72 | 206 | 2 | **Theme From A Summer Place** | [I] $12 | MGM/Verve 5087 |

Theme From "A Summer Place" • Adieu L'Été Adieu La Plage • Quand Vient L'Été • Rendez Vous Au Lavandou • Holidays • Aprés Toi • Ebb Tide • Summer Of 42 • Sur La Plage • Qui Saura • Summer Memories • Day By Day

### MAXAYN ✪
R&B group: Maxayn Lewis (female vocals), Marlo Henderson (guitar), Andre Lewis (keyboards, bass) and Emilio Thomas (drums). Andre Lewis later recorded as Mandré.

| 4/7/73 | 206 | 3 | **Mindful** | $12 | Capricorn 0110 |

Moan To The Music • Love Is Near • Good Things • Stone Crazy • Tellin' You • Feelin' • The Answer • Check Out Your Mind • I Want To Rest My Mind • Travelin'

### MAX WEBSTER ✪
Male rock trio from Canada: Kim Mitchell (vocals, guitar), Dave Myles (bass) and Gary McCracken (drums). McCracken later joined **Wrabit**.

| 1/10/81 | 202 | 1 | **Universal Juveniles** | $10 | Mercury 3855 |

In The World Of Giants • Check • April In Toledo • Juveniles Don't Stop • Battle Scar • Chalkers • Drive And Desire • Blue River Liquor Shine • What Do You Do With The Urge • Cry Out For Life

### MAYALL, John
Born on 11/29/33 in Macclesfield, Cheshire, England. Bluesman John Mayall and his Bluesbreakers band spawned many of Britain's leading rock musicians.

| 2/23/74 | 201 | 3 | 1 **The Best Of John Mayall** | [K] $15 | Polydor 3006 [2] |

Play The Harp • Moving On • Mess Around • Full Speed Ahead • Red Sky • The Laws Must Change • Change Your Ways • Good Looking Stranger • Room To Move • Do It • California Campground • Keep Our Country Green • Things Go Wrong • Deep Blue Sea • Prisons On The Road • Boogie Albert

| 8/28/76 | 205 | 3 | 2 **A Banquet In Blues** | $12 | ABC 958 |

Sunshine • You Can't Put Me Down • I Got Somebody • Turn Me Loose • Seven Days Too Long • Table Top Girl • Lady • Fantasyland

### MAYDAY ✪
Rock group: Steve Johnstad (vocals), Randy Fredrix (guitar), David Beck (keyboards) and Charles Mas (bass).

| 11/7/81 | 210 | 1 | **Mayday** | $10 | A&M 4873 |

Chicago Nights • So Young So Bad • New York City • Loco Love • Life In Space • Love Affair • Innocent Bystander • Getaway • Familiar Faces • Once Upon A Time

### MC5
Hard-rock group from Detroit: Rob Tyner (vocals), Fred "Sonic" Smith and Wayne Kramer (guitars), Michael Davis (bass), and Dennis Thompson (drums). Smith married Patti Smith in 1980. Tyner died of a heart attack on 9/17/91 (age 46). Smith died of a heart attack on 11/4/94 (age 45). MC5 is short for Motor City Five.

| 7/31/71 | 204 | 5 | **High Time** | $50 | Atlantic 8285 |

Sister Anne • Baby Won't Ya • Miss X • Gotta Keep Movin' • Future/Now • Poison • Over And Over • Skunk (Sonically Speaking)

### McCLINTON, Delbert
Born on 11/4/40 in Lubbock, Texas. Country-blues-rock singer/songwriter/guitarist/harmonica player. Recorded with Glen Clark as **Delbert & Glen**.

| 12/15/73 | 212 | 5 | 1 **Subject To Change** | $20 | Clean 602 |

**DELBERT & GLEN**
Oh My • If You Don't Leave Me Alone (I'm Gonna Find Somebody That Will) • Lucky Boy (Your Ramblin' Days Are Through) • Too Much • Sidewalk Diploma • Cold November • I Don't Want To Hear It Anymore • Let Me Be Your Lover • Bless 'Em • California Livin' • You Gonna Miss Me • To Be With You

| 6/6/81 | 204 | 4 | 2 **The Best Of Delbert McClinton** | [G] $10 | MCA 5197 |

Let Love Come Between Us • It's Love Baby (24 Hours A Day) • Victim Of Life's Circumstances • Love Rustler • Pledging My Love • Turn On Your Love Light • Ruby Louise • Two More Bottles Of Wine • Hold On To Your Hiney • Before You Accuse Me

### McCOY, Charlie
Born on 3/28/41 in Oak Hill, West Virginia. Top Nashville harmonica player and session musician.

| 3/23/74 | 213 | 4 | **The Fastest Harp In The South** | [I] $12 | Monument 32749 |

Silver Wings • Why Me • Paper Roses • You Are The Sunshine Of My Life • Almost Persuaded • The Fastest Harp In The South • Release Me • Rollin' In My Sweet Baby's Arms • Behind Closed Doors • A Tribute To Bob Wills: Faded Love/Maiden's Prayer • Ruby (Are You Mad At Your Man?)

| DEBUT | PEAK | WKS | Album Title | $ | Label & Number |
|-------|------|-----|-------------|---|----------------|

**McCOY, Van**
Born on 1/6/44 in Washington, D.C. Died of a heart attack on 7/6/79. Disco pianist/producer.

| 10/30/76 | 202 | 3 | Rhythms Of The World ........................................................ | $12 | H&L 69014 |

Rhythms Of The World • That's The Joint • Soul Cha Cha • The Shuffle • Oriental Boogie • Indian Warpath • Swahili Boogie

**McCREARY, Mary ✪**
R&B singer/songwriter/pianist. Married **Leon Russell** in 1976.

| 10/26/74 | 203 | 8 | Jezebel ........................................................................ | $12 | Shelter 2110 |

Singing The Blues (Reggae) • Everybody's Having Problems • Please Don't Go • High Flyin' Me • Seasons • Mighty Clouds Of Joy • Brother • Jezebel • Levon • Soothe Me • Singing The Blues

**McCULLOUGH, Ullanda ✪**
Female R&B singer from Detroit.

| 4/11/81 | 204 | 6 | Ullanda McCullough ........................................................ | $10 | Atlantic 19296 |

Bad Company • I'll Just Die • Warm And Gentle Explosion • Love Had Changed My Life • It's You • Rumors • You're Gonna Wanna Come Back • Rock Me

**McDONALD, Country Joe**
Born on 1/1/42 in Washington, D.C. Country-rock singer/songwriter/guitarist. Leader of Country Joe & The Fish.

| 6/12/71 | 205 | 5 | 1 Hold On It's Coming ........................................................ | $15 | Vanguard 79314 |

Hold On It's Coming No. 1 • Air Algiers • Only Love Is Worth This Pain • Playing With Fire • Travelling • Joe's Blues • Mr. Big Pig • Balancing On The Edge Of Time • Jamila • Hold On It's Coming No. 2

| 9/11/76 | 202 | 3 | 2 Love Is A Fire ........................................................ | $12 | Fantasy 9511 |

It Won't Burn • You're The Song • In Love Naturally • Oh, No • Baby, Baby • True Love At Last • Who's Gonna Fry Your Eggs • Colortone • I Need You (This And That) • Love Is A Fire

**McDONALD AND GILES**
Keyboardist Ian McDonald was born on 6/25/46 in London. Drummer Michael Giles was born in 1942 in Bournemouth, England. Both were members of King Crimson.

| 2/20/71 | 201 | 11 | McDonald And Giles ........................................................ | $15 | Cotillion 9042 |

Suite In C • Flight Of The Ibis. • Is She Waiting? • Tomorrow's People-The Children Of Today. • Birdman

**McGILPIN, Bob ✪**
Born in Fort Dix, New Jersey. Disco singer/songwriter.

| 9/16/78 | 204 | 4 | Superstar ........................................................ | $10 | Butterfly 010 |

I'll Always Come A Runnin' • Part Time Baby • When You Feel Love • Love Is Gonna Bring Me Back • I'm Not Alone Without You • Rainy Day • Superstar • Move In Closer • Moon Dancin' • Go For The Money

**McGOVERN, Maureen**
Born on 7/27/49 in Youngstown, Ohio. Pop singer/actress.

| 7/12/75 | 201 | 3 | Academy Award Performance | $12 | 20th Century 474 |

Thanks For The Memory • The Continental • For All We Know • Medley: When You Wish Upon A Star/Over The Rainbow • Lullaby Of Broadway • The Morning After • The Windmills Of Your Mind • Swingin' On A Star • All The Way • We May Never Love Like This Again • You'll Never Know • Thanks For The Memory

**McGRIFF, Jimmy**
Born on 4/3/36 in Philadelphia. Jazz-R&B organist/multi-instrumentalist.

| 8/7/76 | 208 | 1 | The Mean Machine .................................................... [I] | $12 | Groove Merchant 3311 |

featuring Joe Thomas (sax)
It Feels So Nice (Do It Again) • The Mean Machine • Please Don't Take Me Out • Get Back • Overweight Shark Bait • Pogo's Stick

**McGUFFEY LANE**
Country-rock group from Columbus, Ohio: Bob McNelley (vocals), Terry Efaw and John Schwab (guitars), Stephen Douglass (keyboards), Stephen Reis (bass) and John Campigotto (drums). Group name taken from a street in Athens, Ohio. Douglass died in a car accident on 1/12/84 (age 33). McNelley died from a self-inflicted gunshot wound on 1/7/87 (age 36).

| 1/31/81 | 205 | 3 | McGuffey Lane ........................................................ | $10 | Atco 133 |

People Like You • Long Time Lovin' You • Ain't No One (To Love You Like I Do) • Let Me Take You To The Rodeo • Green Country Mountains • Stagecoach • Music Man • Breakaway • Lady Autumn • Stay In Love With You

**McGUINN, Roger**
Born James McGuinn on 7/13/42 in Chicago. Founder/lead singer/guitarist of The Byrds. Changed name to Roger in 1968.

| 6/19/76 | 204 | 5 | 1 Cardiff Rose ........................................................ | $12 | Columbia 34154 |

Take Me Away • Jolly Roger • Rock And Roll Time • Friend • Partners In Crime • Up To Me • Round Table • Pretty Polly • Dreamland

| 5/14/77 | 206 | 1 | 2 Thunderbyrd........................................................ | $12 | Columbia 34656 |

All Night Long • It's Gone • Dixie Highway • American Girl • We Can Do It All Over Again • Why Baby Why • I'm Not Lonely Anymore • Golden Loom • Russian Hill

**McKUEN, Rod**
Born on 4/29/33 in Oakland, California. Poet/singer/songwriter/actor.

| 7/31/71 | 201 | 2 | Scandalous John | [I-S] | $15 | Buena Vista 5004 |

Pastures Green • Iris & Fido • Pastures Green (vocal) • Desert Lullaby • Train To Quivira • Touch & Go • Scandalous John Suite • Warbag • McCanless Country • Paco The Brave • Amanda • Mariposas D'Amora • The Tribes • Conquistador • Quivira, The City Of Gold • Paco, The Great Engineer • Pastures Green (vocal reprise)

**McLAGAN, Ian**
Born on 5/12/45 in London. Keyboardist of Small Faces and **Faces**.

| 3/14/81 | 203 | 1 | Bump In The Night........................................................ | $10 | Mercury 4007 |

Little Girl • Alligator • If It's Lovin You Want • Casualty • Told A Tale On You • Judy Judy Judy • So Lucky • Rebel Walk • Not Runnin Away • Boy's Gonna Get It

353

| DEBUT | PEAK | WKS | Album Title | $ | Label & Number |
|-------|------|-----|-------------|---|----------------|

### McLAUGHLIN, John
Born on 1/4/42 in Yorkshire, England. Jazz-fusion guitarist.

| | | | | | |
|---|---|---|---|---|---|
| 11/11/72 | 206 | 2 | **1 Devotion** .................................................................................... [I] | $15 | Douglas 31568 |

Devotion • Dragon Song • Marbles • Siren • Don't Let The Dragon Eat Your Mother • Purpose Of When

| | | | | | |
|---|---|---|---|---|---|
| 2/5/83 | 202 | 2 | **2 Music Spoken Here** ...................................................................... [I] | $10 | Warner 23723 |

Aspan • Blues For L.W. • The Translators • Honky-Tonk Haven • Viene Clareando • David • Negative Ions • Brise De Coeur • Loro

### McNEELY, Larry ☉
Born on 1/3/48 in Lafayette, Indiana. Singer/songwriter/guitarist/banjo player. Regular on **Glen Campbell**'s TV show.

| | | | | | |
|---|---|---|---|---|---|
| 3/6/71 | 215 | 1 | **Glen Campbell Presents Larry McNeely** ........................................ | $12 | Capitol 674 |

Mac Arthur Park • If You Got To Go, Go Now • Banjo Raga Number Two • Stick With Me Baby • Bethe • Alexander Freedom • Shuckin' The Corn • Payday • Haley's Comet's Comin' • Who Am I Medley: Who Am I/Refractions/Get Together/Save The Country

### MECO
Born Meco Monardo on 11/29/39 in Johnsonburg, Pennsylvania. Disco producer/arranger.

| | | | | | |
|---|---|---|---|---|---|
| 8/27/83 | 202 | 3 | **Ewok Celebration** ........................................................................ [I] | $10 | Arista 8098 |

Ewok Celebration • Lapti Nek • Themes From "Star Wars" • Nights Are Forever • Theme From Simon & Simon • Maniac • Love Theme From "Superman III" • Themes From "Wargames"

### MEISNER, Randy
Born on 3/8/46 in Scottsbluff, Nebraska. Bassist/vocalist of Poco (1968-69) and the Eagles (1971-77). Also see **Rick Nelson**.

| | | | | | |
|---|---|---|---|---|---|
| 7/22/78 | 204 | 3 | **Randy Meisner** ............................................................................ | $10 | Asylum 140 |

Bad Man • Daughter Of The Sky • It Hurts To Be In Love • Save The Last Dance For Me • Please Be With Me • Take It To The Limit • Lonesome Cowgirl • Too Many Lovers • If You Wanna Be Happy • I Really Want You Here Tonight • Every Other Day • Heartsong

### MELANIE
Born Melanie Safka on 2/3/47 in Queens, New York. Folk-pop singer/songwriter.

| | | | | | |
|---|---|---|---|---|---|
| 2/1/75 | 208 | 3 | **1 As I See It Now** | $15 | Neighborhood 3000 |

Yankee Man • You're Not A Bad Ghost, Just An Old Song • Record Machine • Eyes Of Man • Stars Up There • Don't Think Twice, It's All Right • Sweet Misery • Monongahela River • Yes Sir, That's My Baby • Autumn Lady • Chart Song • As I See It Now

| | | | | | |
|---|---|---|---|---|---|
| 2/17/79 | 207 | 2 | **2 Ballroom Streets** ...................................................................... | $12 | Tomato 9003 [2] |

Running After Love • Holdin' Out • Cyclone (Candles In The Rain) • Beautiful Sadness • Do You Believe • Nickel Song • Any Guy • Look What They Done To My Song • I Believe (Secret Of The Darkness) • Poet • Save Me • Together Alone • Ruby Tuesday • Buckle Down • Miranda • Brand New Key • Groundhog Day • Friends & Company

### MEMBERS, The ☉
Pop-rock group from Surrey, England: Nicky Tesco (vocals), J.C. and Nigel Bennett (guitars), Simon Lloyd and Steve Thompson (horns), Chris Payne (bass) and Adrian Lillywhite (drums).

| | | | | | |
|---|---|---|---|---|---|
| 4/2/83 | 202 | 5 | **Uprhythm, Downbeat** .................................................................. | $10 | Arista 6605 |

Working Girl • The Family • The Model • Chairman Of The Board • Boys Like Us • Going West • Radiodub • Fire (In My Heart) • You And Me Against The World • We, The People

### MEMPHIS HORNS, The
Studio group from Memphis: Wayne Jackson (trumpet), Andrew Love (tenor sax), James Mitchell (baritone sax), Lewis Collins (soprano sax) and Jack Hale (trombone). Jackson was a member of The Mar-Keys.

| | | | | | |
|---|---|---|---|---|---|
| 9/17/77 | 201 | 17 | **Get Up & Dance** | $10 | RCA Victor 2198 |

vocalists include James Gilstrap, John Valenti and Deniece Williams

Get Up And Dance • Just For Your Love • Waitin' For The Flood • Love Is Happiness • Memphis Nights • What The Funk • Country Soul • No Go Betweens • Don't Abuse It • Keep On Smilin'

### MENTAL AS ANYTHING ☉
Rock group from Sydney, Australia: brothers Chris "Reg Mombassa" (guitar) and Pete (bass) O'Doherty, Martin Plaza (vocals, guitar), Andrew "Greedy" Smith (keyboards) and Wayne Delisle (drums).

| | | | | | |
|---|---|---|---|---|---|
| 10/1/83 | 203 | 1 | **Creatures Of Leisure** .................................................................. | $10 | A&M 4946 |

Spirit Got Lost • Float Away • Brain Brain • Bitter To Swallow • Close Again • Nothing's Going Right Today • Working For The Man • Fiona • Seems Alright To Me • Drinking Of Her Lips • Red To Green • Let's Not Get Sentimental • Business & Pleasure

### MERCYFUL FATE ☉
Heavy-metal group from Denmark: King Diamond (vocals), Hank Sherman and Michael Denner (guitars), Timi Hansen (bass) and Kim Ruzz (drums).

| | | | | | |
|---|---|---|---|---|---|
| 1/5/85 | 210 | 1 | **Don't Break The Oath** ................................................................ | $10 | Combat 8011 |

A Dangerous Meeting • Nightmare • Desecration Of Souls • Night Of The Unborn • The Oath • Gypsy • Welcome Princess Of Hell • To One Far Away • Come To The Sabbath

### METERS, The
R&B group from New Orleans: brothers Cyril (vocals) and Art (keyboards) Neville, Leo Nocentelli (guitar), George Porter (bass) and Joseph "Zig" Modeliste (drums). Cyril and Art are brothers of Aaron Neville.

| | | | | | |
|---|---|---|---|---|---|
| 7/23/77 | 209 | 1 | **New Directions** .......................................................................... | $12 | Warner 3051 |

No More Okey Doke • I'm Gone • Be My Lady • My Name Up In Lights • Funkify Your Life • Stop That Train • We Got The Kind Of A Love • Give It What You Can

### MICHAELS, Lee
Born on 11/24/45 in Los Angeles. Rock singer/organist.

| | | | | | |
|---|---|---|---|---|---|
| 3/23/74 | 210 | 4 | **Tailface** .................................................................................... | $12 | Columbia 32846 |

Met A Toucan • Politican • Slow Dancin' Rotunda • Roochie Toochie Loochie • Drink The Water • Lovely Lisa • Garbage Gourmet

### MIDNIGHT STAR
R&B-funk group from Kentucky: Belinda Lipscomb (female vocals), Melvin Gentry (male vocals, drums), Jeffrey Cooper (guitar), brothers Reggie (trumpet) and Vincent (trombone) Calloway, William Simmons (sax), Bo Watson (keyboards) and Kenneth Gant (bass). Reggie and Vincent later formed Calloway.

| | | | | | |
| --- | --- | --- | --- | --- | --- |
| 9/11/82 | 205 | 3 | **Victory** ..................................................................................................... $10 | | Solar 60145 |

Victory • Strike A Match • Move Me • Make Time (To Fall In Love) • Hot Spot • You Can't Stop Me • Be With You • Love Is Alive

### MILES, John
Born on 4/23/49 in Jarrow, England. Rock singer/guitarist/keyboardist.

| | | | | | |
| --- | --- | --- | --- | --- | --- |
| 8/5/78 | 210 | 1 | 1 **Zaragon** ................................................................................................... $10 | | Arista 4176 |

Overture • Borderline • I Have Never Been In Love Before • No Hard Feelings • Plain Jane • Nice Man Jack: Kensington Gardens/Mitre Square/Harley Street • Zaragon

| | | | | | |
| --- | --- | --- | --- | --- | --- |
| 4/5/80 | 202 | 2 | 2 **Sympathy** ................................................................................................ $10 | | Arista 4261 |

Where Would I Be Without You • It's Not Called Angel • Sympathy • We All Fall Down • C'est La Vie • Do It All Again • Can't Keep A Good Man Down • Fella In The Cellar

### MILLER, Frankie
Born in 1950 in Glasgow, Scotland. Rock singer/guitarist.

| | | | | | |
| --- | --- | --- | --- | --- | --- |
| 6/9/79 | 209 | 1 | **A Perfect Fit** ............................................................................................ $10 | | Chrysalis 1220 |

A Woman To Love • Is This Love • Pappa Don't Know • Something About You • When I'm Away From You • Darlin' • Every Time A Tear Drop Falls • Falling In Love With You • And It's Your Love • Good To See You

### MILLER, Marcus ✪
Born on 6/14/59 in New York City. R&B-jazz singer/bassist.

| | | | | | |
| --- | --- | --- | --- | --- | --- |
| 7/14/84 | 204 | 4 | **Marcus Miller** ......................................................................................... $10 | | Warner 25074 |

Unforgettable • Is There Anything I Can Do • Superspy • Juice • I Could Give You More • Perfect Guy • My Best Friend's Girlfriend • Nadine

### MILLS BROTHERS, The
Legendary family vocal group from Piqua, Ohio: brothers Herbert (b: 4/2/12; d: 4/12/89), Harry (b: 8/19/13; d: 6/28/82) and Donald (b: 4/29/15) Mills.

| | | | | | |
| --- | --- | --- | --- | --- | --- |
| 8/18/73 | 208 | 2 | **The Best Of The Mills Brothers** ...............................................[G] $15 | | Paramount 1010 [2] |

Glow Worm • Yellow Bird • Strollin' • You're Nobody Till Somebody Loves You • Canadian Sunset • Chanson d'Amour • Hey There • Lazy River • I'll Be Around • Standing On The Corner • I'm Sorry I Answered The Phone • Cab Driver • I Love You So Much It Hurts • Paper Doll • A Million Marys • Opus One • The Jones Boy • Moon River • A Donut And A Dream • Till Then • My Shy Violet • Sally Sunshine

### MINK DeVILLE
R&B-styled punk band formed by vocalist Willy DeVille (b: William Boray on 8/27/53 in New York City).

| | | | | | |
| --- | --- | --- | --- | --- | --- |
| 2/18/84 | 208 | 3 | **Where Angels Fear To Tread** ............................................................ $10 | | Atlantic 80115 |

Each Word's A Beat Of My Heart • River Of Tears • Demasiado Corazon (Too Much Heart) • Lilly's Daddy's Cadillac • Around The Corner • Pick Up The Pieces • Love's Got A Hold On Me • Keep Your Monkey Away From My Door • Are You Lonely Tonight • The Moonlight Let Me Down

### MINNELLI, Liza
Born on 3/12/46 in Los Angeles. Singer/actress. Daughter of Judy Garland and movie director Vincente Minnelli. Starred in many movies and in Broadway shows. Married to Peter Allen from 1967-73.

| | | | | | |
| --- | --- | --- | --- | --- | --- |
| 12/8/73 | 207 | 6 | **The Liza Minnelli Foursider** .....................................................[K] $15 | | A&M 3524 [2] |

Medley: Everybody's Talkin'/Good Morning Starshine • Liza (With A "Z") • I Will Wait For You • Cabaret • The Man I Love • Love Story • Married • You'd Better Sit Down, Kids • Leavin' On A Jet Plane • Come Saturday Morning • Nevertheless (I'm In Love With You) • Lazy Bones • Come Rain Or Come Shine • My Mammy • Waiting For My Friend • Medley: Mac Arthur Park/Didn't We • Maybe This Time • God Bless The Child

### MIRACLES, The
R&B vocal group from Detroit: Billy Griffin, Ronnie White (d: 8/26/95, age 57), Bobby Rogers and Warren "Pete" Moore. Original leader Smokey Robinson left in 1972. Top Pop Albums: 25.

| | | | | | |
| --- | --- | --- | --- | --- | --- |
| 9/3/77 | 209 | 2 | **Greatest Hits** ...................................................................................[G] $12 | | Tamla 6357 |

The Power Of Music • Overture • Love Machine • Do It Baby • Take It All • Don't Cha Love It • What Is A Heart Good For • Night Life • Gemini • Don't Let It End ('Til You Let It Begin)

### MISSETT, Judi Sheppard — see AEROBIC ALBUMS

### MISS PIGGY — see AEROBIC ALBUMS

### MOB, The ✪
Pop group from Chicago: Artie Herrera (vocals), Al Herrera, Jimmy "Ford" Franz, Mike "Paris" Sistak, Tony "Roman" Nedza, Gary "Stevens" Biesbier, Bobby Raffino and Jimmy "Soul" Holvay.

| | | | | | |
| --- | --- | --- | --- | --- | --- |
| 2/6/71 | 204 | 1 | **The Mob** ................................................................................................... $15 | | Colossus 1006 |

Give It To Me • Maybe I'll Find A Way • Once A Man • Goodtime Baby • Lost • I Dig Everything About You • Love's Got A Hold On Me • More Of You • For A Little While • Back On The Road Again

### MOM'S APPLE PIE ✪
Rock group: Bob Fiorino and Tony Gigliotti (vocals), Bob Miller and Joe Ahladis (guitars), Roger Force, Bob Pinti and Fred Marzulla (horns), Dave Mazzochi (keyboards), Greg Yochman (bass) and Pat Aulizia (drums).

| | | | | | |
| --- | --- | --- | --- | --- | --- |
| 12/2/72 | 203 | 5 | **Mom's Apple Pie** ................................................................................... $25 | | Brown Bag 14200 |

label quickly replaced the original cover art with a less offensive version ($15)

I Just Wanna Make Love To You • Lay Your Money Down • Good Days • People • Dawn Of A New Day • Happy Just To Be • Secret Of Life • Mr. Skin

### MONKEES, The
Pop band formed in Los Angeles. Members chosen from over 400 applicants for new Columbia TV series. Consisted of Davy Jones (vocals), **Michael Nesmith** (guitar, vocals), Peter Tork (bass, vocals) and Micky Dolenz (drums, vocals). Group starred in the movie *Head* (1968) and 58 episodes of *The Monkees* TV show (1966-68).

**2/6/71 · 207 · 2** — Barrel Full Of Monkees .............................................. [G] $75   Colgems 1001
I'm A Believer • Cuddly Toy • Star Collector • What Am I Doing Hangin' 'Round? • Pleasant Valley Sunday • Last Train To Clarksville • Valleri • Randy Scouse Git • I Wanna Be Free • Listen To The Band • (Theme From) The Monkees • She Hangs Out • Gonna Buy Me A Dog • She • (I'm Not Your) Steppin' Stone • Daydream Believer • Your Auntie Grizelda • A Little Bit Me, A Little Bit You • Mary, Mary • Shades Of Gray

### MONTY PYTHON
British comedy troupe: Eric Idle, John Cleese, Terry Jones, Graham Chapman, Michael Palin and Terry Gilliam. Chapman died of cancer on 10/4/89 (age 48).

**5/12/73 · 217 · 3** — **1** Money Python's Previous Record ............................................. [C] $15   Charisma 1063
also see #2 below
Medley: Embarrassment/A Bed Time Book • England 1747 - Dennis Moore • Money Programme • Dennis Moore Continues • Australlan Table Wines • Argument Clinic • Putting Down Budgies And So Forth • Eric The Half A Bee • Travel Agency • Radio Quiz Game • Medley: A Massage/City Noises Quiz • Miss Anne Elk • We Love The Yangtse • How-To-Do-It Lessons • A Minute Passed • Medley: Eclipse Of The Sun/Alastair Cooke • Wonderful World Of Sounds • A Fairy Tale

**3/13/76 · 202 · 6** — **2** The Worst Best...Monty Python .............................................. [C-K] $20   Buddah 5626 [2]
record 2 is a reissue of #1 above
Apologies • Spanish Inquisition • World Forum • Gumby Theatre • The Architect • The Piranha Brothers • Death Of Mary Queen Of Scots • Penguin On The T.V. • Medley: Comfy Chair/Sound Quiz • Medley: Be A Great Actor/Theatre Critic • Royal Festival Hall Concert • Spam • Medley: The Judges/Stake Your Claim • Medley: Still No Sign Of Land/The Undertaker • Medley: Embarrassment/A Bed Time Book • England 1747 - Dennis Moore • Money Programme • Dennis Moore Continues • Australlan Table Wines • Argument Clinic • Putting Down Budgies And So Forth • Eric The Half A Bee • Travel Agency • Radio Quiz Game • Medley: A Massage/City Noises Quiz • Miss Anne Elk • We Love The Yangtse • How-To-Do-It Lessons • A Minute Passed • Medley: Eclipse Of The Sun/Alastair Cooke • Wonderful World Of Sounds • A Fairy Tale

**2/27/82 · 204 · 5** — **3** Instant Record Collection .............................................. [C-K] $12   Arista 9580
The Executive Intro • Pet Shop • Nudge Nudge • Premier Of Film Live Broadcast From London • Bring Out Your Dead • How Do You Tell A Witch • Camelot • Argument Clinic • Crunchy Frog • The Cheese Shop • The Phone-In • Sit On My Face • Another Executive Announcement • Bishop On The Landing • Elephantoplasty • The Lumberjack Song • Bookshop • Blackmail • Farewell To John Denver • World Forum • String • Wide World Of Novel Writing • Death Of Mary Queen Of Scots • Never Be Rude To An Arab

### MOORE, Melba
Born Melba Hill on 10/29/45 in New York City. R&B singer/actress.

**11/21/81 · 201 · 6** — What A Woman Needs .............................................. $10   EMI America 17060
Let's Stand Together • Your Sweet Lovin' • What A Woman Needs • Take My Love • Overnight Sensation • Each Second • Piece Of The Rock • Let's Go Back To Lovin'

### MORODER, Giorgio — see OAKEY, Philip

### MOTHER'S FINEST
R&B group from Atlanta: husband-and-wife Glenn Murdoch and Joyce Kennedy (Vocals), Gary "Mo" Moore (guitar), Michael Keck (keyboards), Jerry "Wizard" Seay (bass) and Barry "B.B." Borden (drums).

**11/17/79 · 203 · 4** — Mother's Finest Live .............................................. [L] $10   Epic 35976
recorded on the group's 1979 tour
Somebody To Love • Fire • Mickey's Monkey • Give You All The Love • Baby Love • Magic Carpet Ride • Love Changes • Watch My Stylin' • Don't Wanna Come Back

### MOTHERS OF INVENTION, The
Satirical rock group led by Frank Zappa.

**7/24/71 · 201 · 2** — The Worst Of The Mothers .............................................. [K] $40   MGM 4754
Help I'm A Rock • Anyway The Wind Blows • Flower Punk • You Didn't Try To Call Me • Take Your Clothes Off When You Dance • Motherly Love • Mom And Dad • Mother People • Wowie Zowie • Status Back Baby

### MOTÖRHEAD
Heavy-metal trio from London: Ian "Lemmy" Kilminster (vocals, bass), Eddie Clarke (guitar) and Phil Taylor (drums).

**12/27/80+ · 201 · 10** — **1** Ace Of Spades .............................................. $10   Mercury 4011
The Chase Is Better Than The Catch • Love Me Like A Reptile • Shoot You In The Back • Live To Win • Fast And Loose • (We Are) The Road Crew • Ace Of Spades • Fire, Fire • Jailbait • Dance • Bite The Bullet • The Hammer

**9/19/81 · 204 · 3** — **2** No Sleep 'Til Hammersmith .............................................. [L] $10   Mercury 4023
Ace Of Spades • Stay Clean • Metropolis • The Hammer • Iron Horse • No Class • Overkill • (We Are) The Road Crew • Capricorn • Bomber • Motorhead

**12/8/84 · 205 · 5** — **3** No Remorse .............................................. [K] $12   Bronze 90233 [2]
Ace Of Spades • Motorhead • Jailbait • Stay Clean • Too Late Too Late • Killed By Death • Bomber • Iron Fist • Shine • Dancing On Your Grave • Metropolis • Snaggletooth • Overkill • Please Don't Touch • Stone Dead Forever • Like A Nightmare • Emergency • Steal Your Face • Louie Louie • No Class • Iron Horse • We Are The Road Crew • Leaving Here • Locomotive

### MOTTOLA, Tony
Born on 4/18/18 in Kearney, New Jersey. Latin-style guitarist.

**1/30/71 · 212 · 1** — **1** Close To You .............................................. [I] $12   Project 3 5050
Close To You • Always • Medley: Moon River/What Are You Doing The Rest Of Your Life? • Autumn Leaves • Here's That Rainy Day • A Time For Love • We've Only Just Begun • Sophisticated Lady • Yesterday When I Was Young • Wave • The Christmas Song • Didn't We • Jennifer Ann

**4/8/72 · 214 · 2** — **2** Superstar Guitar .............................................. [I] $12   Project 3 5062
Superstar • I Don't Know How To Love Him • Windy • Volare • Medley: Yesterdays/Yesterday • By The Time I Get To Phoenix • Love • Something • Spanish Harlem • Spinning Wheel • Wichita Lineman • Fly Me To The Moon

### MOTT THE HOOPLE
Glitter-rock group from Hereford, England: Ian Hunter (vocals), Mick Ralphs (guitar), Verden Allen (keyboards), Pete "Overend" Watts (bass) and Dale "Buffin" Griffin (drums). Also see Ian Hunter.

| 4/17/71 | 207 | 6 | 1 **Wildlife** ........................................................................... $20  Atlantic 8284 |
Whisky Women • Angel Of Eighth Avenue • Wrong Side Of The River • Waterlow • Lay Down • It Must Be Love • Original Mixed-Up Kid • Home Is Where I Want To Be • Keep A'Knockin'

| 2/19/72 | 208 | 3 | 2 **Brain Capers** ...................................................................... $20  Atlantic 8304 |
Death May Be Your Santa Claus • Your Own Backyard • Darkness Darkness • The Journey • Sweet Angeline • Second Love • The Moon Upstairs • The Wheel Of The Quivering Meat Conception

| 11/27/76 | 206 | 1 | 3 **Greatest Hits** ............................................................ [G] $15  Columbia 34368 |
All The Way From Memphis • Honaloochie Boogie • Hymn For The Dudes • Born Late '58 • All The Young Dudes • Roll Away The Stone • Ballad Of Mott The Hoople (March 26, 1972, Zurich) • The Golden Age Of Rock 'N' Roll • Foxy Foxy • Saturday Gigs

### MOULIN ROUGE ⊙
Female disco vocal trio: Stephanie Spruill, Julia Tillman and Lorna M. Willard.

| 2/24/79 | 209 | 3 | **Moulin Rouge** ..................................................................... $10  ABC 1120 |
Holiday • Run To Me • Lonely Days • To Love Somebody • My World • Massachusetts

### MOUZON, Alphonse — see CORYELL, Larry

### MOVE, The
Progressive-rock group from Birmingham, England: Carl Wayne (vocals), Roy Wood (guitar), Trevor Burton (bass) and Bev Bevan (drums). Burton was replaced by Rick Price. Wayne was replaced by Jeff Lynne. Group evolved into the Electric Light Orchestra.

| 7/20/74 | 205 | 2 | **The Best Of The Move** ................................................... [K] $25  A&M 3625 [2] |
Yellow Rainbow • Kilroy Was Here • (Here We Go Round) The Lemon Tree • Weekend • Walk Upon The Water • Flowers In The Rain • Hey Grandma • Useless Information • Zing Went The Strings Of My Heart • The Girl Outside • Fire Brigade • Mist On A Monday Morning • Cherry Blossom Clinic • Night Of Fear • Disturbance • I Can Hear The Grass Grow • Wave Your Flag And Stop The Train • Something • Omnibus • Wild Tiger Woman • Blackberry Way • Curly • This Time Tomorrow • Lightning Never Strikes Twice • Brontosaurus

### MUHAMMAD, Idris
Born Leo Morris in 1939 in New Orleans. Prolific session drummer.

| 1/20/79 | 208 | 1 | **You Ain't No Friend Of Mine!** ............................................ [I] $10  Fantasy 9566 |
Disco Man • See Saw • The Doc • You Ain't No Friend Of Mine! • Tell Me, Where Did We Go Wrong? • Big Foot

### MULL, Martin
Born on 8/18/43 in Chicago. Comedian/actor. Appeared in several movies and TV shows.

| 7/14/73 | 203 | 5 | 1 **Martin Mull And His Fabulous Furniture In Your Living Room** ............... [C] $12  Capricorn 0117 |
Introduction And Theme To Margie The Midget • Dueling Tubas • A Simple Carpenter • Licks Off Of Records • Return Of The Big Bands • 2001 Polka • Straight Talk About The Blues • Ukulele Blues • A Tribute To Bert Parks • Billy One-Eye • Intermission • A Girl Your Size (How Could I Not Miss) • Martin, Leon, Elton And John • My Wife • Puis-Je Emprunter Votre Cuillére? • Ah, France • Something • The Nothing • (212) 349-8735 • In The Eyes Of My Dog

| 1/21/78 | 209 | 1 | 2 **No Hits, Four Errors - The Best Of Martin Mull** ........................ [C-K] $12  Capricorn 0195 |
Licks Off Of Records • Eggs • The Blacks Are Giving Me The Blues • Margie The Midget • Ukelele Blues • Flexible • Jesus Is Easy • Normal • Miami • Dueling Tubas • Hors D'Oeuvre • Santafly

| 7/7/79 | 208 | 2 | 3 **Near Perfect/Perfect** ................................................. [C] $10  Elektra 200 |
Bun And Run (No. 1) ("Daddy's Back") • Don't Put Off 'Til Tomorrow • Pig In A Blanket • This Takes The Cake • The Fruit Song • Bun And Run (No. 3) ("Happy Cows") • Bernie Don't Disco • It's All Behind Me Now • I Found It • Life Is Better Than Death

### MUPPETS, The — see DENVER, John / SOUNDTRACKS

### MURPHEY, Michael
Born on 5/5/38 in Dallas. Country-pop singer/songwriter/guitarist.

| 4/28/79 | 206 | 2 | **Peaks Valleys Honky-Tonks & Alleys** ................................... $10  Epic 35742 |
Medley: Cosmic Cowboy/Cosmic Breakdown • Medley: Another Cheap Western/Western Movies • Years Behind Bars • Backslider's Wine • Geronimo's Cadillac • South Coast • Chain Gang • Once A Drifter • Texas Morning • Lightning

### MYRICK, Gary, And The Figures
Rock group from Texas: Gary Myrick (vocals, guitar), Ed Beyer (keyboards), David Dennard (bass) and Jack White (drums).

| 9/27/80 | 203 | 1 | **Gary Myrick And The Figures** .......................................... $10  Epic 36524 |
Living Disaster • Ever Since The World Began • She Talks In Stereo • Model • She's So Teenage • You • The Party • Meaningless • Who'll Be The Next In Line • Deep In The Heartland

### MYSTERIOUS FLYING ORCHESTRA, The ⊙
Studio group assembled by producer Bob Thiele.

| 6/11/77 | 210 | 1 | **The Mysterious Flying Orchestra** ..................................... [I] $12  RCA Victor 2137 |
Improvisational Rondo for Soprano Saxophone and Guitar • Shadows • A Dream Deferred • Summer Days • There Once Was A Man Named John (Dedicated to John Coltrane) • Nice 'n Spicy

### MYSTIC MOODS, The
Hollywood studio group produced by Brad Miller.

| 6/26/71 | 222 | 3 | 1 **Country Lovin' Folk** .................................................. [I] $12  Philips 351 |
Elusive Butterfly • Everybody's Talkin' • I Guess The Lord Must Be In New York City • Catch The Wind • Simple Song Of Freedom • Where Have All The Flowers Gone • Turn, Turn, Turn • Cycles • She Belongs To Me • Don't It Make You Want To Go Home

| 7/5/75 | 201 | 24 | 2 **Erogenous** ........................................................... [I] $12  Warner 2786 |
Your Place Or Mine • Keep Me Warm • The Sound Of Love • Down Easy • The Other Side Of Midnight • Any Way You Want It • Honey Trippin' • The Magician • Fallen Angel • Get It While The Gettin' Is Good • Midnight Snack

# N

### NAILS, The
Rock group from New York City: Marc Campbell (vocals), Steve O'Rourke (guitar), David Kaufman (keyboards), Douglas Guthrie (sax) and George Kaufman (bass).

| 2/23/85 | 203 | 6 | **Mood Swing** ............................................................................... | $10 | RCA Victor 8037 |

Every Time I Touch You • Dark Brown • 88 Lines About 44 Women • Home Of The Brave • Let It All Hang Out • Mood Swing • Phantom Heart • Juanita, Juanita • She Is Everything To Me • White Wall

### NANTUCKET ✪
Southern-rock group from Jacksonville, North Carolina: Larry Uzzell (vocals), Mark Downing and Tommy Redd (guitars), Eddie Blair (keyboards), PeeWee Watson (bass) and Kenny Soule (drums).

| 8/30/80 | 206 | 1 | **Long Way To The Top** ........................................................... | $10 | Epic 36523 |

It's A Long Way To The Top • Living With You • Time Bomb • 50 More • Media Darlin' • Rugburn • Too Much Wrong In The Past (For A Future) • Over And Over Again • Turn The Radio On • Tell Me (Doctor Rhythm Method) • Rescue • Rock Of The 80's

### NASHVILLE STRING BAND, The ✪
All-star guitar trio: Chet Atkins, Homer Haynes and Jethro Burns (Homer & Jethro).

| 3/13/71 | 218 | 3 | **Identified!** ........................................................ [I] | $12 | RCA Victor 4472 |

Colonel Bogey • White Silver Sands • Red Wing • The Three Bells • Oklahoma Hills • Strollin' • Sweet Dreams • Rocky Top • Release Me (And Let Me Love Again) • Green, Green Grass Of Home

### NATIONAL LAMPOON
Comedy troupe spawned from the magazine of the same name. Members included Richard Belzer, John Belushi, **Chevy Chase**, Christopher Guest, Bill Murray, Gilda Radner and Harold Ramis.

| 5/17/75 | 206 | 2 | **Gold Turkey** .................................................... [C-K] | $12 | Epic 33410 |

Front Row Center • Medley: Public Disservice/Alternative Child • Medley: We'll Be Back/Mother Goose's Wine • My Husband • Megaphone Newsreel • Medley: The Trial/Terminal Football/Flash Bazbo • Jimmy Dugan Story • Well-Intentioned Blues • A Laugh From The Past • Medley: Stand Up/Flash Bazbo • Hockey • Prison Farm • Medley: Mr. Veal Chop/Rosenburgs • The Immigrants

### NATURAL FOUR
R&B vocal quartet from San Francisco: Delmos Whitley, Ollan Christopher James, Darryl Cannady and Steve Striplin.

| 4/27/74 | 207 | 5 | **Natural Four** .................................................................... | $20 | Curtom 8600 |

Can This Be Real • You Bring Out The Best In Me • Try Love Again • You Can't Keep Running Away • This Is What's Happening Now • Love That Really Counts • Try To Smile • Love's Society • Things Will Be Better Tomorrow

### NEELY, Sam
Born on 8/22/48 in Cuero, Texas. Singer/songwriter/guitarist.

| 10/12/74 | 202 | 3 | **Down Home** ...................................................................... | $12 | A&M 3626 |

You Can Have Her • Count Your Blessings • Sadie Take A Lover • A Woman Is The Better Part Of Home • Lord I'm Amazed • It's A Fine Morning • Rock And Roll (I Gave You The Best Years Of My Life) • Keep Me Company • Here I Go Again • Everybody Learns To Sing The Blues

### NELSON, Rick
Born Eric Hilliard Nelson on 5/8/40 in Teaneck, New Jersey. Died on 12/31/85 in a plane crash in DeKalb, Texas. Pop-rock singer/songwriter/guitarist. Son of bandleader Ozzie Nelson and vocalist Harriet Hilliard. Rick and brother David appeared on Nelson's radio show from March 1949, later on TV, 1952-66. The country-rock Stone Canyon Band consisted of Allen Kemp (guitar), Tom Brumley (steel guitar), **Randy Meisner** (bass) and Patrick Shanahan (drums). Nelson inducted into the Rock and Roll Hall of Fame in 1987.

| 11/20/71 | 204 | 3 | **Rudy The Fifth** .................................................................. | $25 | Decca 75297 |

**RICK NELSON & THE STONE CANYON BAND**
This Train • Just Like A Woman • Sing Me A Song • The Last Time Around • Song For Kristin • Honky Tonk Woman • Feel So Good • Life • Thank You Lord • Song For Kristin • Love Minus Zero/No Limit • Gypsy Pilot

### NELSON, Tracy
Born on 12/27/44 in French Camp, California. Lead singer of Mother Earth. Not to be confused with Rick Nelson's actress daughter.

| 2/26/72 | 205 | 1 | 1 **Tracy Nelson/Mother Earth** ........................................ | $15 | Reprise 2054 |

The Same Old Thing • I'm That Way • Mother Earth (Provides For Me) • Tennessee Blues • I Want To Lay Down Beside You • Someday My Love May Grow • (Staying Home And Singing) Homemade Songs • Thinking Of You • The Memory Of Your Smile • I Don't Do That Kind Of Thing Anymore

| 4/14/73 | 210 | 5 | 2 **Poor Man's Paradise** ..................................................... | $12 | Columbia 3175 |

**TRACY NELSON/MOTHER EARTH** (above 2)
Whatever I Am, You Made Me • Cruel Wind • When I Need You Most Of All • I Hate To Say Goodbye • You And Me • Jack's Waltz • I Just Can't Seem To Care • Going Back To Tennessee • Poor Man's Paradise

### NELSON, Willie
Born on 4/30/33 in Ft. Worth, Texas; raised in Abbott, Texas. Country singer/songwriter/actor. Appeared in several movies. Won Grammy's Living Legends Award in 1989. Elected to the Country Music Hall of Fame in 1993. *Top Pop Albums*: 44.

| 7/14/73 | 205 | 6 | 1 **Shotgun Willie** ............................................................... | $20 | Atlantic 7262 |

Shotgun Willie • Whiskey River • Sad Songs And Waltzes • Local Memory • Slow Down Old World • Stay All Night (Stay A Little Longer) • Devil In A Sleepin' Bag • She's Not For You • Bubbles In My Beer • You Look Like The Devil • So Much To Do • A Song For You

| 9/25/82 | 201 | 5 | 2 **The Best Of Willie** ................................................ [G] | $10 | RCA Victor 4420 |

Everybody's Talkin' • Mountain Dew • Sweet Memories • Minstrel Man • Good Times • Little Things • Bloody Mary Morning • Night Life • Me And Paul • Yesterday's Wine

| DEBUT | PEAK | WKS | Album Title | $ | Label & Number |
|-------|------|-----|-------------|---|----------------|

### NESMITH, Michael
Born on 12/30/42 in Houston. Country-rock singer/songwriter/guitarist. Member of **The Monkees**. Formed own production company, Pacific Arts, in 1977; produced several movies.

| | | | | | |
|--|--|--|--|--|--|
| 5/22/71 | 218 | 2 | 1 Nevada Fighter ............................................................................................... $30 | | RCA Victor 4497 |

**MICHAEL NESMITH & THE FIRST NATIONAL BAND**
Grand Ennui • Propinquity (I've Just Begun To Care) • Here I Am • Only Bound • Nevada Fighter • Texas Morning • Tumbling Tumbleweeds • I Looked Away • Rainmaker • René

| | | | | | |
|--|--|--|--|--|--|
| 2/12/72 | 211 | 1 | 2 Tantamount To Treason Volume One .............................................................. $30 | | RCA Victor 4563 |

**MICHAEL NESMITH AND THE SECOND NATIONAL BAND**
Mama Rocker • Lazy Lady • You Are My One • In The Afternoon • Highway 99 With Melange • Wax Minute • Bonaparte's Retreat • Talking To The Wall • She Thinks I Still Care

| | | | | | |
|--|--|--|--|--|--|
| 8/19/72 | 208 | 2 | 3 And The Hits Just Keep On Comin' ................................................................. $30 | | RCA Victor 4695 |

Tomorrow & Me • The Upside Of Good-Bye • Lady Love • Listening • Two Different Roads • The Candidate • Different Drum • Harmony Constant • Keep On • Roll With The Flow

| | | | | | |
|--|--|--|--|--|--|
| 4/9/77 | 209 | 1 | 4 From A Radio Engine To The Photon Wing ....................................................... $20 | | Pacific Arts 107 |

Rio • Casablanca Moonlight • More Than We Imagine • Navajo Trail • We Are Awake • Wisdom Has Its Way • Love's First Kiss • The Other Room

### NEVINS, Nancy ☉
Folk-rock singer. Member of **Sweetwater**.

| | | | | | |
|--|--|--|--|--|--|
| 8/16/75 | 208 | 1 | Nancy Nevins ................................................................................................ $12 | | Tom Cat 1063 |

Sunny Face • We Could Always Say It Was Rainin' • Lately • Feel So Good • Don't Hold Back • Baroquen Heart • Let Me • Joie • Just Like A Little Boy • Ten Cents A Dance

### NEWBURY, Mickey
Born Milton Newbury on 5/19/40 in Houston. Country-rock singer/songwriter.

| | | | | | |
|--|--|--|--|--|--|
| 8/10/74 | 209 | 2 | I Came To Hear The Music .............................................................................. $12 | | Elektra 1007 |

I Came To Hear The Music • Breeze Lullaby • You Only Live Once (In A While) • Yesterday's Gone • If You See Her • Dizzy Lizzy • If I Could Be • Organized Noise • Love Look (At Us Now) • Baby's Not Home • 1 X 1 Ain't 2

### NEW ENGLAND
Rock group from New York City: John Fannon (vocals, guitar), Jimmy Waldo (keyboards), Gary Shea (bass) and Hirsh Gardner (drums).

| | | | | | |
|--|--|--|--|--|--|
| 11/22/80 | 202 | 6 | Explorer Suite .............................................................................................. $10 | | Elektra 307 |

Honey Money • Livin' In The Eighties • Conversation • It's Never Too Late • Explorer Suite • Seal It With A Kiss • Hey You're On The Run • No Place To Go • Searchin' • Hope • You'll Be Born Again

### NEW HORIZONS ☉
Family funk group from Dayton, Ohio: brothers Art (vocals), Varges (keyboards), Bart (bass) and Mark (drums) Thomas, with cousin Timothy Abrams (guitar).

| | | | | | |
|--|--|--|--|--|--|
| 8/20/83 | 210 | 2 | Something New .............................................................................................. $10 | | Columbia 38709 |

Your Thing Is Your Thing • I Can't Tell You • Something New • County Line • Reaching For New Horizons • Your Thing (Rap)

### NEWMAN, Randy
Born on 11/28/43 in New Orleans. Singer/songwriter/pianist.

| | | | | | |
|--|--|--|--|--|--|
| 7/7/84 | 202 | 5 | The Natural ......................................................................................... [I-S] $10 | | Warner 25116 |

Prologue 1915-1923 • The Whammer Strikes Out • The Old Farm 1939 • The Majors: The Mind Is A Strange Thing • "Knock The Cover Off The Ball" • Memo • The Natural • Wrigley Field • Iris And Roy • Winning • A Father Makes A Difference • Penthouse Party • Medley: The Final Game/Take Me Out To The Ballgame • The End Title

### NEW RIDERS OF THE PURPLE SAGE
Country-rock group from San Francisco: guitarists/singers John Dawson, Allen Kemp, David Nelson and Buddy Cage, with drummer Patrick Shanahan.

| | | | | | |
|--|--|--|--|--|--|
| 3/7/81 | 202 | 2 | Feelin' All Right ............................................................................................. $10 | | A&M 4818 |

Night For Making Love • No Other Love • The Way She Dances • Tell Me • Fly Right • Crazy Little Girl • Full Moon At Midnite • Pakalolo Man • Day Dreamin' Girl • Saralyn

### NEW SEEKERS, The
British-Australian pop vocal group: Eve Graham, Lyn Paul, Peter Doyle, Marty Kristian and Paul Layton.

| | | | | | |
|--|--|--|--|--|--|
| 1/27/73 | 211 | 3 | Come Softly To Me ........................................................................................ $12 | | MGM/Verve 5090 |

For You We Sing • Blowin' In The Wind • Come Softly To Me • Goin' Back • Morning Has Broken • Down By The River • How I Love Them Old Songs • Captain Stormy • Day By Day • Rain • Why Can't We All Get Together • Unwithered Rose

### NEW YORK ENSEMBLE ☉
Classical-baroque rock group from New York City: Michael Kamen (vocals, keyboards), Cliff Nivison (guitar), Dorian Rudnytsky (bass) and Marty Fulterman (drums).

| | | | | | |
|--|--|--|--|--|--|
| 5/27/72 | 215 | 2 | Freedomburger ............................................................................................. $12 | | Columbia 31317 |

More Like The Master • Magic Lady • I'm Sending A Friend To You • Kiss Your Future • A Whiter Shade Of Pale • Willow Tree • Shuffle • Barrel Full Of Wine • Carry Me Up • Roll Over • Raise Your Barriers • Goodnight Irene

### NICE, The
British classical-rock trio: Keith Emerson (organ; Emerson, Lake & Palmer), Lee Jackson (bass) and Brian Davison (drums).

| | | | | | |
|--|--|--|--|--|--|
| 4/24/71 | 209 | 7 | Elegy ................................................................................................... [I-L] $12 | | Mercury 61324 |

recorded at the Fillmore East in New York City
Hang On To A Dream • My Back Pages • 3rd Movement, Pathetique Symphony • America

### NIELSEN/PEARSON ☉
Pop duo from Sacramento: singers/guitarists Reed Nielsen and Mark Pearson.

| | | | | | |
|--|--|--|--|--|--|
| 10/4/80 | 205 | 1 | Nielsen/Pearson ........................................................................................... $10 | | Capitol 12101 |

Two Lonely Nights • Don't Let Me Go • Love Me Tonight • Annie • If You Should Sail • It Could Be Trouble • Givin' Your Love To Me • Don't Forget • Hurt No More

| DEBUT | PEAK | WKS | Album Title | $ | Label & Number |
|-------|------|-----|-------------|---|----------------|

## NIGHT
Pop-rock group: Stevie Lange (female vocals), Chris Thompson (male vocals, guitar), Robbie McIntosh (guitar), Bobby Wright (keyboards), Billy Kristian (bass) and Bobby Guidotti (drums).

| 1/24/81 | 204 | 2 | Long Distance ............................................................................................ | $10 | Planet 10 |

Dr. Rock • Don't Break My Heart • Love On The Airways • The Letter • Callin' Me Back • You Cried Wolf • Stealin' • Miss You (Like I Do) • Day After Day • Good To Be Back In Your Arms

## NIGHTINGALE, Maxine
Born on 11/2/52 in Wembley, England. Singer/actress.

| 8/20/77 | 209 | 1 | Night Life............................................................................................... | $12 | United Artists 731 |

Will You Be My Lover • You Are Everything • Love Hit Me • You • Get It Up For Love • Didn't I (Blow Your Mind This Time) • Love Or Let Me Be Lonely • I Wonder Who's Waiting Up For You • How Much Love • Right Now

## NILSSON
Born Harry Edward Nelson III on 6/15/41 in Brooklyn. Died of a heart attack on 1/15/94. Pop singer/songwriter.

| 6/2/73 | 201 | 6 | Nilsson Sings Newman | $12 | RCA Victor 0203 |

all songs written by **Randy Newman**; first released on RCA Victor 4289 in 1970 ($15)
Vine St. • Love Story • Yellow Man • Caroline • Cowboy • The Beehive State • I'll Be Home • Living Without You • Dayton, Ohio 1903 • So Long Dad

## NITE CITY ✪
Rock group: Noah James (vocals), Paul Warren (guitar), Ray Manzarek (keyboards; The Doors), Nigel Harrison (bass) and Jimmy Hunter (drums).

| 4/2/77 | 204 | 5 | Nite City ................................................................................................. | $12 | 20th Century 528 |

Summer Eyes • Nite City • Love Will Make You Mellow • Angel W/No Freedom • Midnight Queen • Bitter Sky Blue • Caught In A Panic • In The Pyramid • Game Of Skill

## NIX, Don
Born on 9/27/41 in Memphis. Singer/guitarist/saxophonist. Member of **The Alabama State Troupers** and the Mar-Keys.

| 1/9/71 | 204 | 1 | In God We Trust ...................................................................................... | $12 | Shelter 8902 |

In God We Trust • Golden Mansions • I'll Fly Away • He Never Lived A Day Without Jesus • Nero My God To Thee • Amos Burke • Long Way To Nowhere • Iuka • Will The Circle Be Unbroken • I've Tried (Trucker's Lament)

## NOVO COMBO
Rock group from New York City: Pete Hewlett (vocals), Carlos Rios (guitar), Stephen Dees (bass) and Michael Shrieve (drums; Santana).

| 9/25/82 | 207 | 2 | The Animation Generation ...................................................................... | $10 | Polydor 6356 |

Animation Generation • Too Long Gone • Slow Fade • Keep Your Love Alive • Anyone Can See • Welcome Innervision • Chained Man • Follow The Love • She Runs • No Wonder

## NRBQ
Blues-rock group from Miami: Terry Adams (vocals, keyboards), Al Anderson (guitar, vocals), Joey Spampinato (bass) and Tom Ardolino (drums). Group name is short for New Rhythm & Blues Quartet.

| 5/28/83 | 202 | 3 | Grooves In Orbit.................................................................................... | $10 | Bearsville 23817 |

Smackaroo • Rain At The Drive-In • How Can I Make You Love Me • When Things Was Cheap • Daddy-"O" • 12 Bar Blues • A Girl Like That • My Girlfriend's Pretty • I Like That Girl • Get Rhythm • Hit The Hay

## NUMAN, Gary
Born Gary Webb on 3/8/58 in Hammersmith, England. Techno-rock singer/synthesizer player. Tubeway Army included bassist Paul Gardiner and drummer Jess Lidyard.

| 7/25/81 | 204 | 1 | 1 First Album .......................................................................................... | $10 | Atco 106 |

**TUBEWAY ARMY FEATURING GARY NUMAN**
Listen To The Sirens • My Shadow In Vain • The Life Machine • Friends • Something's In The House • Everyday I Die • Steel And You • My Love Is A Liquid • Are You Real? • The Dream Police • Jo The Waiter • Zero Bars

| 10/23/82 | 201 | 4 | 2 I, Assassin | $10 | Atco 90014 |

White Boys And Heroes • War Songs • A Dream Of Siam • Music For Chameleons • This Is My House • I, Assassin • The 1930's Rust • We Take Mystery To Bed

## NYRO, Laura
Born Laura Nigro on 10/18/47 in New York City. Died of cancer on 4/8/97. Singer/prolific songwriter.

| 8/19/78 | 209 | 1 | Nested ................................................................................................... | $12 | Columbia 35449 |

Mr. Blue (The Song Of Communications) • Rhythm & Blues • My Innocence • Crazy Love • American Dreamer • Springblown • The Sweet Sky • Light-Pop's Principle • Child In A Universe • The Nest

# O

## OAKEY, Philip, & Giorgio Moroder ✪
Oakey was born on 10/2/55 in Sheffield, England. Leader of electro-pop group The Human League. Moroder was born on 4/26/40 in Ortisei, Italy. Prolific disco producer.

| 8/24/85 | 201 | 1 | Philip Oakey & Giorgio Moroder | $10 | A&M 5080 |

Why Must The Show Go On • In Transit • Good-Bye Bad Times • Brand New Love (Take A Chance) • Valerie • Now • Together In Electric Dreams • Be My Lover Now • Shake It Up

### OCHS, Phil
Born on 12/19/40 in El Paso, Texas. Committed suicide on 4/9/76. Folk singer/songwriter.

| 1/15/77 | 210 | 1 | Chords Of Fame ........................................................................................ [K] $20 | A&M 4599 [2] |

I Ain't Marchin' Anymore • One More Parade • Draft Dodger Rag • Here's To The State Of Richard Nixon • The Bells • Bound For Glory • Too Many Martyrs • There But For Fortune • I'm Gonna Say It Now • Santo Domingo • Changes • Is There Anybody Here? • Love Me, I'm A Liberal • When I'm Gone • Outside Of A Small Circle Of Friends • Pleasures Of The Harbor • Tape From California • Chords Of Fame • Crucifixion • The War Is Over • Jim Dean Of Indiana • Power And The Glory • Flower Lady • No More Songs

### O'CONNOR, Hazel ☉
British singer/actress. Starred in the movie *Breaking Glass*.

| 9/13/80 | 202 | 8 | Breaking Glass ........................................................................................ [S] $10 | A&M 4820 |

Writing On The Wall • Monsters In Disguise • Come Into The Air • Big Brother • Who Needs It • Will You? • Eighth Day • Top Of The Wheel • Calls The Tune • Blackman • Give Me An Inch • If Only

### OFF BROADWAY USA
Rock group from Oak Park, Illinois: Cliff Johnson (vocals), John Ivan and Rob Harding (guitars), Mike Gorman (bass) and Ken Harck (drums).

| 1/17/81 | 208 | 1 | Quick Turns ........................................................................................ $10 | Atlantic 19286 |

Automatic • Bad Girl • Showdown • Are You Alone • Eddie's Pals • Boys Must Be Strong • Quick Turns • U.S. Girls • So Long • Alright/OK

### OHIO PLAYERS
R&B-funk group from Dayton, Ohio: Leroy "Sugar" Bonner (vocals, guitar), Marvin "Merv" Pierce (trumpet), Ralph "Pee Wee" Middlebrooks (sax) and Marshall Jones (bass).

| 12/19/81 | 201 | 6 | Ouch! ........................................................................................ $10 | Boardwalk 33247 |

Do Your Thing • The Star Of The Party • Sweet Lil Lady • Everybody Dance • My Baby Gets The Best Of My Love • Just Me • Thinkin' 'Bout You • Devoted • I'd Better Take A Coffee Break

### OLDFIELD, Mike
Born on 5/15/53 in Reading, England. Classical-rock, multi-instrumentalist/composer.

| 3/15/75 | 203 | 4 | 1 The Orchestral Tubular Bells ........................................................................................ [I] $12 | Virgin 115 |

**THE ROYAL PHILHARMONIC ORCHESTRA WITH MIKE OLDFIELD**
conducted by David Bedford; no track titles listed on this album

| 6/28/80 | 210 | 1 | 2 Airborn ........................................................................................ [I-L] $12 | Virgin 13143 [2] |

record 1: new studio recordings; record 2: recorded on his 1979 European tour
Platinum Part 1: Airborn • Platinum Part 2: Platinum • Platinum Part 3: Charleston • Platinum Part 4: North Star/Platinum Finale • Guilty • Into Wonderland • Punkadiddle • I Got Rhythm • Tubular Bells (Part 1) • Incantations

### ORBISON, Roy
Born on 4/23/36 in Vernon, Texas. Died of a heart attack on 12/6/88. Pop-rock singer/songwriter/guitarist. Inducted into the Rock and Roll Hall of Fame in 1987.

| 1/15/83 | 205 | 5 | The All-Time Greatest Hits Of Roy Orbison ........................................................................................ [G] $12 | Monument 38384 [2] |

Only The Lonely • Leah • In Dreams • Uptown • It's Over • Crying • Dream Baby • Blue Angel • Working For The Man • Candy Man • Running Scared • Falling • Love Hurts • Shadaroba • I'm Hurtin' • Mean Woman Blues • Pretty Paper • The Crowd • Blue Bayou • Oh Pretty Woman

### ORIGINAL BLUES PROJECT — see BLUES PROJECT

### ORIGINAL MIRRORS ☉
British rock group: Steve Allen (vocals), Ian Broudie (guitar), Jonathan Perkins (keyboards), Phil Spalding (bass) and Pete Kircher (drums).

| 6/21/80 | 209 | 1 | Original Mirrors ........................................................................................ $10 | Arista 4269 |

Panic In The Night • Sharp Words • Could This Be Heaven • Boys Cry • Chains Of Love • Night Of The Angels • Reflections • The Boys The Boys • Flying • Feel Like A Train

### ORPHAN ☉
Folk-pop duo from Boston: Eric Lilljequist and Dean Adrien.

| 9/2/72 | 212 | 3 | Everyone Lives To Sing ........................................................................................ $12 | London 614 |

Everyone Lives To Sing • Leave Now (Let Me Go) • Lonely Day • Sad Eyes • Down To The River • It's So Hard • Easy Now • Daylight Darkness • Look At Her • Someone Better Listen • Fisherman • Take A Look Around • I'm Alone • You Know The Way

### ORR, Bobby ☉
Born on 4/20/48 in Parry Sound, Ontario. Pro hockey player with the Boston Bruins (1966-76) and the Chicago Blackhawks (1976-79).

| 2/13/71 | 214 | 1 | The Two Sides Of Bobby Orr ........................................................................................ [T] $20 | Cori 3101 |

interviewed by Don Earle

### OSIBISA
Jazz-R&B group from Ghana, West Africa: Kofi Ayivor (vocals, congas), Teddy Osei (sax), Mac Tontoh (trumpet), Jean Dikoto Mandengue (bass) and Sol Amarfio (drums).

| 12/15/73 | 202 | 12 | Happy Children ........................................................................................ $12 | Warner 2732 |

Happy Children • We Want To Know (Mo) • Kotoku • Take Your Trouble - Go • Adwoa • Bassa Bassa • Somaja • Fire

### OTIS, Johnny — see CONCERTS/FESTIVALS

### OWENS, Gary ☉
Born on 5/10/36 in Mitchell, South Dakota. Comedian/DJ. Best known as the announcer on TV's *Laugh-In*.

| 8/12/72 | 204 | 3 | Put Your Head On My Finger ........................................................................................ [C] $15 | Pride 0002 |

Horoscope - Part I • Win That Dwarf • Tip To Gardeners • The Sky Is My Partner • Norbert T. Krelk Funeral • Foonman Home For The Perturbed News • Glur Awards • Miss Oz Sings • Golden Voice Announcer's School • Church Announcement • Nurny Creed • Incredible But True • Sure Fire Unemployment • The Presidents • Ballad Of Willie Jackson • Republican Commercial • Democrat Commercial • Harold Stassen Commercial • Dates To Remember • See Your Doctor • Lunatics' Book Of World Records • Teenage Manners • Booking Agent • Saftey Tips • School For Double Talk • Telephone Help For The Desperate • Horoscope - Part 2

## OZONE
R&B group from Nashville: Benny Wallace (vocals, guitar), Greg Hargrove (guitar), Ray Woodward, Tom Bumpass, and Bill White (horns), Jim Stewart (keyboards), Charles Glenn (bass) and Paul Hines (drums). By 1983 Herman Brown (vocals), Darren Durst (guitar) and Joe Foxworth (keyboards) joined.

| 2/28/81 | 206 | 1 | 1 Jump On It ........................................................................................ | $10 | Motown 950 |

Jump On It • Come On In • Your Love Stays On My Mind • Ozonic Bee Bop • Mighty-Mighty • Rock And Roll, Pop And Soul • Love Zone • My Fantasy

| 4/23/83 | 201 | 4 | 2 Glasses | $10 | Motown 6037 |

Glasses • You Don't Want My Love • I Can't Wait • Here I Go Again • Strutt My Thang • (Our Hearts) Will Always Shine • Don't Leave Me Now • Video King

# P

## PALUMBO, John ☺
Born on 1/13/51 in Steubenville, Ohio. Lead singer of Crack The Sky.

| 5/25/85 | 209 | 2 | Blowing Up Detroit ........................................................................... | $10 | HME 39950 |

Blowing Up Detroit • Modern Romance • Drifting Back To Motown • Electric Wire • She's The Release • Girls From Mars • In The New World • Hurt Me

## PAPPALARDI, Felix, & Creation ☺
Born on 12/30/39 in New York City. Shot to death by his wife, Gail Collins, on 4/17/83. Rock singer/bassist. Former leader of Mountain. The Japanese group Creation consisted of Kazuo "Flash" Takeda and Yoshiaki "Daybreak" Iijima (guitars), Shigeru "Sugar" Matsumoto (bass) and Masayuki "Thunder" Higuchi (drums).

| 8/21/76 | 210 | 1 | Felix Pappalardi & Creation ............................................................. | $12 | A&M 4586 |

She's Got Me • Dreams I Dream Of You • Green Rocky Road • Preachers' Daughters • Listen To The Music • Secret Power • Summer Days • Dark Eyed Lady Of The Night • Ballad Of A Sad Cafe

## PARKS, Michael
Born on 4/4/38 in Corona, California. Folk-pop singer/actor. Star of TV's *Then Came Bronson*.

| 8/7/71 | 218 | 1 | The Best Of Michael Parks ............................................................... | [G] $15 | MGM 4784 |

Big "T" Water • I Was Born In Kentucky • Sally (Was A Gentle Woman) • Sneakin' In The Back Door Of Love • Statue Of A Fool • Mountain High • Long Lonesome Highway • Tie Me To Your Apron Strings Again • There's Been A Change In Me • Sing That Song Again

## PARLIAMENT
R&B group: George Clinton (vocals), Eddie Hazel (guitar), Bernie Worrell (keyboards), William "Bootsy" Collins (bass) and Raymond "Tiki" Fulwood (drums). Clinton also spearheaded several offshoot groups such as Funkadelic.

| 8/24/74 | 201 | 2 | Up For The Down Stroke | $40 | Casablanca 7002 |

Up For The Down Stroke • Testify • The Goose • I Can Move You (If You Let Me) • I Just Got Back • All Your Goodies Are Gone • Whatever Makes Baby Feel Good • Presence Of A Brain

## PASSAGE ☺
Contemporary gospel trio: husband-and-wife Louis (vocals, bass) and Valerie (vocals) Johnson, with Richard Heath (vocals). Louis is one-half of The Brothers Johnson.

| 4/11/81 | 205 | 5 | Passage ........................................................................................... | $10 | A&M 4851 |

Have You Heard The Word • You Can't Be Livin' • Faith Walking People • I See The Light • The Great Flood • Open Up Your Heart • Power • Love Eyes • The Son Will Come Again

## PASSPORT
Jazz-fusion group from Germany led by Klaus Doldinger (sax, keyboards). Numerous personnel changes with Doldinger the only constant.

| 5/15/76 | 204 | 4 | 1 Infinity Machine ............................................................................. | [I] $12 | Atco 132 |

Ju-Ju Man • Morning Sun • Blue Aura • Infinity Machine • Ostinato • Contemplation

| 5/26/79 | 201 | 6 | 2 Garden Of Eden | [I] $10 | Atlantic 19233 |

Big Bang • Garden Of Eden: Dawn/Light I/Light II • Snake • Gates Of Paradise • Dreamware • Good Earth Smile • Children's Dance

## PASTORIUS, Jaco
Born on 12/1/51 in Norristown, Pennsylvania. Died on 9/22/87 from injuries received in a beating on 9/12/87. Bassist of jazz/rock group Weather Report.

| 5/8/76 | 203 | 6 | Jaco Pastorius ............................................................................... | [I] $12 | Epic 33949 |

guests include **Herbie Hancock**, **David Sanborn** and Wayne Shorter

Donna Lee • Come On, Come Over • Continuum • Kuru/Speak Like A Child • Portrait Of Tracy • Opus Pocus • Okonkolé Y Trompa • (Used To Be A) Cha-Cha • Forgotten Love

## PATTERSON, Kellee ☺
Born in Gary, Indiana. R&B singer/actress.

| 1/21/78 | 201 | 4 | Be Happy | $10 | Shadybrook 007 |

Overture • Heaven • If It Don't Fit, Don't Force It • Yesterday Was Love • Be Happy • Turn On The Lights • Movin' In The Right Direction • Let's Hold On To Love • I'm Coming Home

## PAUL, Billy
Born Paul Williams on 12/1/34 in Philadelphia. R&B singer.

| 2/9/80 | 205 | 2 | Best Of Billy Paul .......................................................................... | [G] $12 | Philadelphia Int'l. 36314 [2] |

Billy Boy • Me & Mrs. Jones • It's Too Late • Thanks For Saving My Life • This Is Your Life • Let 'Em In • Your Song • Let's Make A Baby • Love Buddies • I Think I'll Stay Home Today • Ebony Woman • The Whole Town's Talking • You're My Sweetness • Next To Nature • What Are We Going To Do Now That He's Back • My Old Flame

### PAVAROTTI, Luciano
Born on 10/12/35 in Modena, Italy. World-renowned operatic tenor.

| 3/26/77 | 209 | 1 | The Great Pavarotti.................................................[F-K] $10 London 26510 |

Quanto É Bella • Una Furtiva Lagrima • La Rivedra Nell'Estasi • Di' Tu Se Fedele • Questa O Quella • Ella Mi Fu Rapita..Parmi Veder Le Lagrime • O Figli Miei Ah La Paterna Mano • Ingemisco • Cujus Animam • Ah! Rimiro Il Bel Sembiante • Pour Me Rapprocher De Marie • Non Piangere, Liú! • Tu Che A Dio Spiegasti L'ali

### PAXTON, Tom
Born on 10/31/37 in Chicago. Folk singer/songwriter.

| 5/15/71 | 213 | 2 | 1 The Compleat Tom Paxton.................................................[L] $20 Elektra 2003 [2] |

Clarissa Jones • The Things I Notice Now • Medley: Jennifer's Rabbit/I Give You The Morning • Intro To "The Marvelous Toy" • The Marvelous Toy • Leaving London • Angie • All Night Long • Bayonet Rap • Talking Vietnam Pot Luck Blues • Jimmy Newman • Outward Bound • Morning Again • Can't Help But Wonder Where I'm Bound • My Lady's A Wild Flying Dove • Now That I've Taken My Life • About The Children • Ballad Of Spiro Agnew • Mr. Blue • Wish I Had A Troubadour • Ev'ry Time (When We Are Gone) • Medley: Cindy's Crying/Hooker • Ramblin' Boy • The Last Thing On My Mind

| 8/4/73 | 203 | 3 | 2 New Songs For Old Friends.................................................[L] $15 Reprise 2144 |

recorded at the Marquee Club in London
Hobo In My Mind • When We Were Good • Who's Been Passing Dreams Around? • When Annie Took Me Home • Katy Fred • Wasn't That A Party? • Faces And Places • When You Shook Your Long Hairdown • Silent Night • When Princes Meet

### PAYCHECK, Johnny
Born Donald Eugene Lytle on 5/31/37 in Greenfield, Ohio. Country singer/songwriter/guitarist.

| 3/11/72 | 204 | 1 | 1 She's All I Got.................................................$12 Epic 31141 |

She's All I Got • You Touched My Life • Love Sure Is Beautiful • She's Everything To Me • My Elusive Dreams • He Will Break Your Heart • You Once Lived Here • Only Love Can Save Us Now • Let's Walk Hand In Hand • Livin' In A House Full Of Love • A Man That's Satisfied

| 1/20/79 | 203 | 2 | 2 Armed And Crazy.................................................$10 Epic 35444 |

Friend, Lover, Wife • Armed And Crazy • Mainline • Thanks To The Cathouse (I'm In The Doghouse With You) • Leave It To Me • Me And The I.R.S. • Let's Have A Hand For The Little Lady • Just Makin' Love Don't Make It Love • Look What The Dog Drug In • The Outlaw's Prayer

### PEACHES & HERB
R&B vocal duo from Washington, D.C.: Linda "Peaches" Green and Herb Fame.

| 7/2/83 | 204 | 1 | Remember.................................................$10 Columbia 38746 |

I Got A Groove On • Remember • Keep On Smiling • Love Is Love Is Love • Be My Music • I Believe • In My World • One On One Situation • Come To Me • When The Lights Go Out

### PEARLS BEFORE SWINE
Underground folk quartet from New York City: Thomas Rapp (vocals, guitar), Elizabeth (vocals), Wayne Harley (banjo) and Jim Fairs (guitar).

| 5/15/71 | 223 | 2 | City Of Gold.................................................$30 Reprise 6442 |

**THOS. RAPP/PEARLS BEFORE SWINE**
Sonnett #65 • Once Upon A Time • Raindrops • City Of Gold • Nancy • Seasons In The Sun • My Father • The Man • Casablanca • Wedding • Did You Dream Of

### PERKINS, Carl — see CASH, Johnny / LEWIS, Jerry Lee

### PERSUASIONS, The
R&B vocal group from New York City: Jerry Lawson, Joseph Russell, Willie C. Daniels, Jimmy Hayes and Herbert Rhoad.

| 7/20/74 | 207 | 2 | More Than Before.................................................$15 A&M 3635 |

Lookin' For A Love • I've Got To Use My Imagination • Gonna Keep On Tryin' Till I Win Your Love • Beauty's Only Skin Deep • Jesus Build A Fence Around Me • Occapella • Lay Back • I Really Got It Bad For You • Until They Say Mercy • We're All Goin' Home

### P.F.M.
Progressive-rock group from Italy: Franco Mussida (vocals, guitar), Flavio Premoli (keyboards), Mauro Pagani (violin), Giorgio Piazza (bass) and Franz DiCioccio (drums). P.F.M.: Premiata Forneria Marconi.

| 7/6/74 | 201 | 1 | 1 The World Became The World.................................................$15 Manticore 66673 |

**PREMIATA FORNERIA MARCONI**
The Mountain • Just Look Away • The World Became The World • Four Holes In The Ground • Is My Face On Straight • Have Your Cake And Beat It

| 8/14/76 | 206 | 2 | 2 Chocolate Kings.................................................$12 Asylum 1071 |

From Under • Harlequin • Chocolate Kings • Out Of The Roundabout • Paper Charms

### PHILLIPS, Esther
Born Esther Mae Jones on 12/23/35 in Galveston, Texas. Died on 8/7/84. One of the first female superstars of R&B.

| 2/9/74 | 205 | 6 | Black-Eyed Blues.................................................$12 Kudu 14 |

Justified • I've Only Known A Stranger • I Got It Bad And That Ain't Good • Black-Eyed Blues • Too Many Roads • You Could Have Had Me, Baby

### PHILLIPS, Shawn
Born on 2/3/43 in Fort Worth, Texas. Male singer/songwriter/guitarist.

| 7/17/71 | 208 | 3 | 1 Second Contribution.................................................$15 A&M 4282 |

She Was Waitin' For Her Mother At The Station In Torino And You Know How I Love You Baby But It's Getting Too Heavy To Laugh • Keep On • Sleepwalker • Song For Mr. C • The Ballad Of Casey Deiss • Song For Sagittarians • Lookin Up Lookin Down • Remedial Interruption • Whaz' Zat • Schmaltz Waltz • F Sharp Splendor • Steel Eyes

| 6/5/76 | 201 | 4 | 2 Rumplestiltskin's Resolve.................................................$12 A&M 4582 |

Early Morning Hours • Spitefull • Today • Wailing Wall • Hie Away • Serendipity Peace • Rumplestiltskin's Resolve

| DEBUT | PEAK | WKS | Album Title | $ | Label & Number |
|---|---|---|---|---|---|

### PICKETT, Wilson
Born on 3/18/41 in Prattville, Alabama. R&B singer/songwriter. Inducted into the Rock and Roll Hall of Fame in 1991.

| | | | | | |
|---|---|---|---|---|---|
| 9/29/73 | 212 | 2 | 1 Miz Lena's Boy ............................................................................. $12 | | RCA Victor 0312 |

Take A Closer Look At The Woman You're With • Memphis, Tennessee • Soft Soul Boogie Woogie • Help Me Make It Through The Night • Never My Love • You Lay'd It On Me • Is Your Love Life Better • Two Women And A Wife • Why Don't You Make Up Your Mind • Take That Pollution Out Your Throat

| | | | | | |
|---|---|---|---|---|---|
| 12/22/79 | 205 | 3 | 2 I Want You........................................................................................ $10 | | EMI America 17019 |

I Want You • Love Of My Life • Shamelesss • Live With Me • Groove City • Superstar • Granny

### PINK LADY ○
Female disco duo from Japan: Mie Nemoto and Kei Masuda. Hosted own summer TV variety show in U.S., 1979.

| | | | | | |
|---|---|---|---|---|---|
| 8/4/79 | 203 | 8 | Pink Lady ........................................................................................ $10 | | Elektra 209 |

Kiss In The Dark • Dancing In The Halls Of Love • Show Me The Way To Love • Walk Away Renee • Strangers When We Kiss • Love Me Tonight • I Want To Give You My Everything • Deeply • Give Me Your Love • Love Countdown

### PIPER, Wardell ○
Female disco singer from Philadelphia.

| | | | | | |
|---|---|---|---|---|---|
| 7/7/79 | 203 | 4 | Wardell Piper ................................................................................. $10 | | Midsong Int'l. 009 |

Super Sweet • Win Your Lovin' • Captain Boogie • Don't Turn Away From Me Baby • If You Want To Make Love To Me

### PLACE, Mary Kay ○
Born on 8/23/47 in Tulsa, Oklahoma. Singer/actress. Appeared in many movies and TV shows. Played "Loretta Haggers" on TV's *Mary Hartman, Mary Hartman* (1976-78).

| | | | | | |
|---|---|---|---|---|---|
| 10/30/76+ | 202 | 10 | 1 Tonite! At The Capri Lounge Loretta Haggers ............................. $12 | | Columbia 34353 |

Vitamin L • Streets Of This Town (Ode To Fernwood) • Gold In The Ground • Settin' The Woods On Fire • Good Old Country Baptizin' • Baby Boy • Get Acquainted Waltz • Coke And Chips • Have A Little Talk With Jesus • All I Can Do

| | | | | | |
|---|---|---|---|---|---|
| 1/7/78 | 203 | 6 | 2 Aimin' To Please ........................................................................... $12 | | Columbia 34908 |

Dolly's Dive • Paintin' Her Fingernails • Don't Make Love (To A Country Music Singer) • Marlboro Man • Anybody's Darlin' (Anything But Mine) • You Can't Go To Heaven (If You Don't Have A Good Time) • Cattle Kate • Even Cowgirls Get The Blues • Something To Brag About • Save The Last Dance For Me

### POCKETS
R&B group from Baltimore: Larry Jacobs (vocals), Jacob Sheffer (guitar), Albert McKinney (keyboards), Charles Williams, Irving Madison and Kevin Barnes (horns), Gary Grainger (bass) and George Gray (drums).

| | | | | | |
|---|---|---|---|---|---|
| 10/13/79 | 209 | 1 | So Delicious ................................................................................. $10 | | Columbia 36001 |

How Do You Think It Feels? • Why'd Ya Do Dat? • Charisma • La La (Means I Love You) • Catch Me • So Delicious • Your Heart's In Trouble • Baby, Are You Coming Home With Me? • Bye-Bye

### POCO
Country-rock group from Los Angeles: Rusty Young (vocals), Paul Cotton (guitar), Kim Bullard (keyboards), Charlie Harrison (bass) and Steve Chapman (drums).

| | | | | | |
|---|---|---|---|---|---|
| 12/4/82 | 209 | 1 | Backtracks ................................................................. [G] $10 | | MCA 5363 |

Heart Of The Night • Keep On Tryin' • Midnight Rain • Widowmaker • Crazy Love • Legend • Indian Summer • Under The Gun • Rose Of Cimarron

### POINTER, June ○
Born on 11/30/54 in Oakland. Youngest member of the Pointer Sisters.

| | | | | | |
|---|---|---|---|---|---|
| 7/2/83 | 202 | 3 | Baby Sister................................................................................... $10 | | Planet 4508 |

Ready For Some Action • I Will Understand • To You, My Love • New Love, True Love • I'm Ready For Love • You Can Do It • Always • My Blues Have Gone • Don't Mess With Bill

### POINTER, Noel
Born in Brooklyn. Died of a stroke on 12/19/94 (age 39). Jazz-fusion violin player.

| | | | | | |
|---|---|---|---|---|---|
| 4/25/81 | 201 | 6 | All My Reasons | $10 | Liberty 1094 |

Classy Lady • East St. Louis Melody • All The Reasons Why • Brookline (Brooklyn, A New York City) • Savin' It Up • Virgie • I Feel Your Soul • Oh What A Beautiful City • Land Of Make Believe

### POLECATS ○
New wave group from London: Boz, Tim, Phil and Neil.

| | | | | | |
|---|---|---|---|---|---|
| 6/4/83 | 202 | 8 | Make A Circuit With Me ........................................... [M] $10 | | Mercury 812358 |

Make A Circuit With Me • Red Ready Amber • Juvenile Delinquents From A Planet Near Mars • Jeepster • Rockabilly Guy • Rockabilly Dub • John, I'm Only Dancing

### POP, The ○
New wave group from Los Angeles: David Swanson (vocals), Roger Prescott (guitar), Tim Henderson (bass) and Tim McGovern (drums).

| | | | | | |
|---|---|---|---|---|---|
| 10/27/79 | 201 | 1 | Go! | $10 | Arista 4243 |

Under The Microscope • Shakeaway • Beat Temptation • She Really Means That Much To Me • I Want To Touch You • Waiting For The Night • Go! • Falling For Carmen • Maria • Legal Tender Love

### POP, Iggy
Born James Jewel Osterberg on 4/21/47 in Muskegan, Michigan. Punk-rock pioneer. Leader of The Stooges from 1969-74. Acted in the movies *Cry Baby, Hardware* and *The Crow: City Of Angels*. "Strait" James Williamson was Iggy's regular guitarist.

| | | | | | |
|---|---|---|---|---|---|
| 4/1/78 | 204 | 3 | Kill City .......................................................................................... $15 | | Bomp 1018 |

**IGGY POP & JAMES WILLIAMSON**

Kill City • Sell Your Love • Beyond The Law • I Got Nothin' • Johanna • Night Theme • Night Theme (Reprise) • Consolation Prizes • No Sense Of Crime • Lucky Monkeys • Master Charge

### POUSETTE-DART BAND
Country-pop group: Jon Pousette-Dart (vocals), John Curtis (guitar), John Troy (bass) and Michael Dawe (drums).

| | | | | | |
|---|---|---|---|---|---|
| 8/11/79 | 203 | 2 | Never Enough ............................................................................... $10 | | Capitol 11935 |

Never Enough • Silver Stars • For Love • Cold Outside • Hallelujah I'm A Bum • Long Legs • The Loving One • We Never Give Up • Cheated • Gotta Get Far Away

| DEBUT | PEAK | WKS | Album Title | $ | Label & Number |
|-------|------|-----|-------------|---|----------------|

### POWELL, Roger ✪
Rock keyboardist. Former member of Utopia.

| 3/1/80 | 203 | 3 | **Air Pocket** ...........................................................................[I] $10 | Bearsville 6994 |

Lunar Plexus • Landmark • Air Pocket • Windows • Emergency Splashdown • Morning Chorus • March Of The Dragonslayers • Prophecy • Sands Of Arrakis • Medley: Dragons 'N' Griffins/Mr. Triscuits Theme

### PRESLEY, Elvis
Born on 1/8/35 in Tupelo, Mississippi. Died of heart failure on 8/16/77. Known as "The King Of Rock And Roll." Moved to Memphis in 1948. First recorded for Sun in 1954. Signed to RCA Records on 11/22/55. Starred in 31 feature movies. In U.S. Army from 3/24/58 to 3/5/60. Married Priscilla Beaulieu on 5/1/67; divorced on 10/11/73. Won Grammy's Lifetime Achievement Award in 1971. Inducted into the Rock and Roll Hall of Fame in 1986. *Top Pop Albums:* 98.

| 1/7/84 | 202 | 2 | 1 **Elvis-A Legendary Performer, Volume 4** ..................................[K] $15 | RCA Victor 4848 |

When It Rains, It Really Pours • Interviews By Ray And Norma Pillow • One Night • I'm Beginning To Forget You • Mona Lisa • Wooden Heart • Plantation Rock • The Lady Loves Me • Swing Down Sweet Chariot • That's All Right • Are You Lonesome Tonight? • Reconsider Baby • I'll Remember You

| 4/21/84 | 207 | 2 | 2 **Elvis' Gold Records, Volume 5** ......................................[G] $15 | RCA Victor 4941 |

Suspicious Minds • Kentucky Rain • In The Ghetto • Clean Up Your Own Backyard • If I Can Dream • Burning Love • If You Talk In Your Sleep • For The Heart • Moody Blue • Way Down

| 5/4/85 | 208 | 1 | 3 **Reconsider Baby** ..............................................................[K] $15 | RCA Victor 5418 |

Reconsider Baby • Tomorrow Night • So Glad You're Mine • One Night • When It Rains, It Really Pours • My Baby Left Me • Ain't That Loving You Baby • Feel So Bad • Down In The Alley • Hi-Heel Sneakers • Stranger In My Own Home Town • Merry Christmas Baby

### PRESSURE ✪
R&B group: Melvin Robinson (vocals), Pat Kelly (guitar), **Ronnie Laws** (sax), Barnaby Finch (keyboards), Bobby Vega (bass) and Art Rodriguez (drums).

| 2/16/80 | 207 | 2 | **Pressure** ........................................................................ $10 | L.A. 3195 |

That's The Thing To Do • Hold On • Fantastic Dreams • Can You Feel It • Shove It In The Oven • Peaceful Stream • Stay Together • I Promise

### PRESTON, Billy, & Syreeta
Preston was born on 9/9/46 in Houston. R&B singer/keyboardist. Syreeta was born Rita Wright in Pittsburgh. Married to Stevie Wonder from 1972-74.

| 5/5/79 | 208 | 2 | **Fast Break** .........................................................................[S] $10 | Motown 915 |

Go For It (Theme From "Fast Break") • Welcome To Cadwallader • More Than Just A Friend • With You I'm Born Again (instrumental) • He Didn't Stay • With You I'm Born Again • Books And Basketball • Half Time • The Big Game • Go For It (Disco)

### PREVIN, Dory ✪
Female folk singer.

| 4/10/71 | 218 | 3 | 1 **Mythical Kings & Iguanas** ............................................... $15 | United Artists 4110 |

Mythical Kings And Iguanas • Yada Yada La Scala • Lady With The Braid • Her Mother's Daughter • Angels And Devils The Following Day • Mary C. Brown And The Hollywood Sign • Lemon Haired Ladies • A Stone For Bessie Smith • The Game • Going Home (Mythical Kings And Iguanas)

| 1/8/72 | 202 | 5 | 2 **Reflections In A Mud Puddle/Taps Tremors And Timestops (One Last Dance For My Father)** ...................................... $15 | United Artists 5536 |

Doppelganger • The New Enzyme Detergent Demise Of Ali MacGraw • The Talkative Woman And The Two Star General • The Altruist And The Needy Case • Play It Again, Sam • The Earthquake In Los Angeles • The Final Flight Of The Hindenburg • I Dance And Dance And Smile And Smile • The Air Crash In New Jersey • Aftershock

| 7/21/73 | 220 | 1 | 3 **Live At Carnegie Hall** .......................................................[L] $20 | United Artists 108 [2] |

recorded on 4/18/73

Mythical Kings And Iguanas • Scared To Be Alone • I Ain't His Child • I Dance And Dance And Smile And Smile • Esther's First Communion • Medley: The Veterans Big Parade/Play It Again Sam • Don't Put Him Down • Yada Yada La Scala • The Lady With The Braid • The Midget's Lament • Left Hand Lost • When A Man Wants A Woman • Angels And Devils The Following Day • Mary C. Brown And The Hollywood Sign • Be Careful, Baby, Be Careful • Twenty-Mile Zone • Michael • Moon Rock • Going Home (Mythical Kings And Iguanas)

| 10/12/74 | 202 | 2 | 4 **Dory Previn** .......................................................... $12 | Warner 2811 |

Lover Lover Be My Cover • Coldwater Canyon • Atlantis • Mama Mama Comfort Me • Brando • New Rooms • The Empress Of China • The Obscene Phone Call • The Crooked Christmas Star '73 • Did Jesus Have A Baby Sister?

### PRIDE, Charley
Born on 3/18/38 in Sledge, Mississippi. Country singer.

| 4/8/78 | 207 | 1 | 1 **Someone Loves You Honey** ......................................... $15 | RCA Victor 2478 |

Someone Loves You Honey • Georgia Keeps Pulling On My Ring • I Live You • Play, Guitar, Play • Another I Love You Kind Of Day • More To Me • Days Of Our Lives • Daydreams About Night Things • Heaven Watches Over Fools Like Me • The Days Of Sand And Shovels • I'm Never Leavin' You

| 4/19/80 | 201 | 3 | 2 **There's A Little Bit Of Hank In Me** ......................... $12 | RCA Victor 3548 |

There's A Little Bit Of Hank In Me • My Son Calls Another Man Daddy • Moanin' The Blues • A Mansion On The Hill • Mind Your Own Business • I Can't Help It (If I'm Still In Love With You) • Honky Tonk Blues • I'm So Lonesome I Could Cry • Low Down Blues • I Could Never Be Ashamed Of You • Why Don't You Love Me • You Win Again

### PRISM
Canadian rock group: Ron Tabak (vocals), Lindsay Mitchell (guitar), John Hall (keyboards), Allen Harlow (bass) and Rocket Norton (drums). Tabak left in 1980, replaced by Henry Small. Tabak died in a car crash in 1984.

| 9/22/79 | 202 | 6 | 1 **Armageddon** ........................................................... $15 | Ariola America 50063 |

Coming Home • Jealousy • Virginia • You Walked Away Again • Take It Or Leave It • Armageddon • Night To Remember • Mirror Man

| 8/6/83 | 202 | 3 | 2 **Beat Street** ........................................................... $10 | Capitol 12266 |

Nightmare • Beat Street • Dirty Mind • Modern Times • Is He Better Than Me? • Blue Collar • Wired • State Of The Heart • I Don't Want To Want You Anymore

### PROCOL HARUM
Rock group from London led by Gary Brooker (vocals, piano) and lyricist Keith Reid. Many personnel changes.

| 12/23/72+ | 203 | 5 | A Whiter Shade Of Pale ................................................................................[R] $12 | A&M 4373 |

originally released in 1967 as *Procol Harum* on Deram 18008 (#47)
A Whiter Shade Of Pale • Conquistador • She Wandered Through The Garden Fence • Something Following Me • Mabel • Cerdes (Outside The Gates Of) • A Christmas Camel • Kaleidoscope • Salad Days (Are Here Again) • Good Captain Clack • Repent Walpurgis

### PROCTOR & BERGMAN — see FIRESIGN THEATRE

### PRODUCERS, The
Pop-rock group from Atlanta: Van Temple (vocals, guitar), Wayne Famous (keyboards), Kyle Henderson (bass) and Bryan Holmes (drums).

| 8/7/82 | 201 | 7 | You Make The Heat | $10 | Portrait 38060 |

Back To Basics • She Sheila • Operation • Dear John • Breakaway • You Make The Heat • Merry-Go-Round • Chinatown • Domino

### PROFFIT, Mason — see MASON PROFFIT

### PRYOR, Richard
Born on 12/1/40 in Peoria, Illinois. Comedian/actor. Starred in several movies.

| 11/2/74 | 202 | 4 | Craps (After Hours) ................................................................................[C] $12 | Laff 146 |

Gettin' High • Fuck From Memory • Big Tits • Gettin' Some • The President • Ass Hole • Line-Up • Masturbating • Religion • Black Preachers • Being Born • Blow Our Image • Black Jack • I Spy Cops • Sugar Ray • White Folks • Indians • Ass Wupin • Got A Dollar? • Pres.'s Black Baby • Dope • Wino Panthers • After Hours • 280 lb. Ass • Crap Game • Insurance Man • Black & Proud • Gettin The Nut • Fuck The Faggot • Jackin' Off • Snappin' Pussy • Fartin'

### PUNCH ☺
Pop/rock vocal group from Los Angeles: Kathy, Dee, Charlie & Steve.

| 8/21/71 | 225 | 1 | Punch ................................................................................ $12 | A&M 4307 |

Why Don't You Write Me • Mayflower • (I Know It's) Your Life • Piece Of My Mind • Blackbird • While My Guitar Gently Weeps • Travelin' Boy • Medley: Abraham, Martin And John/I Shall Be Released • Fallin', Lady • Love Song • Open Highway

### PURIM, Flora
Born on 3/6/42 in Rio de Janeiro. Married to **Airto**.

| 11/3/79 | 203 | 2 | Carry On ................................................................................ $10 | Warner 3344 |

Sarara • From The Lonely Afternoon • Niura Is Coming Back • Once I Ran Away • Carry On • Love Lock • Corine • Island In The Sun Interlude • Beijo Partido (Broken Kiss) • Freeway Jam

# Q

### QUATEMAN, Bill
Born in Chicago. Singer/songwriter/guitarist.

| 3/31/73 | 206 | 7 | Bill Quateman ................................................................................ $12 | Columbia 31761 |

My Music • Circles • Only Love • Keep Dreaming • Only The Bears Are The Same • Get It Right On Out There • What Are You Looking For • Your Love Can Make It Real • Too Many Mornings

# R

### RAIDERS
Pop-rock group from Portland, Oregon. Led by Paul Revere (keyboards) and Mark Lindsay (vocals).

| 3/20/71+ | 209 | 2 | 1 The Raiders' Greatest Hits Volume II ................................................................[G] $20 | Columbia 30386 |

Let Me! • Don't Take It So Hard • I Had A Dream • Too Much Talk • Just Seventeen • Gone Movin' On • The Boys In The Band • Cinderella Sunshine • Mr. Sun, Mr. Moon • Do Unto Others • We Gotta All Get Together

| 4/1/72 | 209 | 2 | 2 Country Wine ................................................................................ $20 | Columbia 31106 |

Country Wine • Powder Blue Mercedes Queen • Hungry For Some Lovin' • Baby Make Up Your Mind • Take A Stand • Where Are Your Children • Ballad Of The Unloved • American Family • Golden Girls Sometimes • Farewell To A Golden Girl

### RANK AND FILE
Country-rock group from Los Angeles: brothers Chip (vocals) and Tony (bass) Kinman, Jeff Ross (guitar) and Bobby Kahr (drums).

| 6/23/84 | 201 | 3 | Long Gone Dead | $10 | Slash 25087 |

Long Gone Dead • I'm An Old Old Man • Sound Of The Rain • Hot Wind • Tell Her I Love Her • Saddest Girl In The World • Timeless Love • John Brown • Last Night I Dreamed • It Don't Matter

### RANSOME-KUTI, Fela ☺
Born Fela Anikulapo-Kuti on 10/15/38 in Abeokuta, Nigeria. Died of heart failure on 8/2/97. Male singer. The Africa '70 was his backing group.

| 9/2/72 | 205 | 4 | Live! ................................................................................[L] $15 | Signpost 8401 |

**FELA RANSOME-KUTI and THE AFRICA '70 with GINGER BAKER**
Let's Start • Black Man's Cry • Ye Ye De Smell • Egbe Mi O (Carry Me I Want To Die)

### RASPUTIN'S STASH ✪

R&B-funk group: Martin Dumas (vocals, guitar), Paul Coleman and Vincent Willis (keyboards), Norval Taylor (congas), Wardell Peel and James Whitfield (horns), Bruce Butler (bass) and Frank Donaldson (drums).

| 10/2/71 | 204 | 4 | Rasputin's Stash ........................................................................ | $15 | Cotillion 9046 |
|---|---|---|---|---|---|

Your Love Is Certified • I'd Like To Know You Better • What's On Your Mind • Take Me On Back • Mr. Cool • You Better Think • Freaks Prayer • Dookey Shoe • You Are My Flower • I Want To Say You're Welcome

### RASTUS ✪

Rock group from Milwaukee: Danny Magelen (vocals, sax), Marc Roman (vocals, trombone), Tony Corrao and George Sopuch (guitars), Art Appleton, Mike Geraci and Vic Walkuski (horns), Don Nagy (bass) and Dave Smelko (drums).

| 2/20/71 | 207 | 3 | Rastus ...........................................................................[L] | $20 | GRT 30004 [2] |
|---|---|---|---|---|---|

record 1: recorded "live" in Milwaukee; record 2: studio recordings

Black Cat • Medley: Texas/The Bells • Walking In The Park • Goodnight Nelda Greb (The Telelphone Company Has Cut Us Off) • Sailin' Easy • Black Cat • El Congo Valiente • Warm • Multicolored Taxicabs • Wizard Of Oz Medley • Sinnin' For You • Farmer Jo • 1-75 Riff • Medley

### RAVAN, Genya

Born Goldie Zelkowitz in 1942 in Lodz, Poland; raised in New York City. Lead singer of Ten Wheel Drive.

| 2/19/72 | 205 | 3 | Genya Ravan ............................................................................ | $12 | Columbia 31001 |
|---|---|---|---|---|---|

What Kind Of Man Are You • Sit Yourself Down • I Hate Myself (For Loving You) • I'm In The Mood For Love • Medley: Takuta Kalaba/Turn On Your Love Lights • Lonely, Lonely • Flying • Every Little Bit Hurts • Bird On A Wire • I Can't Stand It

### RAWLS, Lou

Born on 12/1/35 in Chicago. R&B singer. *Top Pop Albums*: 23.

| 8/7/82 | 201 | 8 | Now Is The Time | $10 | Epic 37488 |
|---|---|---|---|---|---|

(Will You) Kiss Me One More Time • Let Me Show You How • Ain't That Love, Baby • While The Rain Comes Down • Now Is The Time For Love • Watch Your Back • It's Too Late (To Say Goodbye) • Back To You • This Love

### RAYE, Susan

Born on 10/18/44 in Eugene, Oregon. Country singer. Regular on TV's *Hee-Haw*.

| 5/29/71 | 221 | 2 | Willy Jones ............................................................................ | $20 | Capitol 736 |
|---|---|---|---|---|---|

Willy Jones • In The Arms Of Love • Heartbreak Mountain • I'll Love You Forever (If You're Sure You'll Want Me Then) • Happy Times Are Here Again • L.A. International Airport • Merry-Go-Round Of Love • Baby Sittin' With Baby • Now That I Understand • Hello Happiness, Goodbye Loneliness

### RECORDS, The

British rock group: Jude Cole (vocals, guitar), John Wicks (guitar), Phil Brown (bass) and Will Birch (drums).

| 8/9/80 | 204 | 3 | Crashes............................................................................ | $10 | Virgin 13140 |
|---|---|---|---|---|---|

Man With A Girl Proof Heart • Hearts Will Be Broken • Girl In Golden Disc • I Don't Remember Your Name • Hearts In Her Eyes • Spent A Week With You Last Night • Rumour Sets The Woods Alight • The Worriers • The Same Mistakes • Guitars In The Sky

### REDDING, Gene ✪

Born in 1945 in Anderson, Indiana. R&B singer.

| 8/3/74 | 208 | 1 | Blood Brother............................................................... | $12 | Haven 9200 |
|---|---|---|---|---|---|

Blood Brothers • Once A Fool • I Can See The Lovelight • (We've Got) More Than It Takes • This Heart • I Can't Get Arrested • Gotta Find A Way (To Keep You Lovin' Me) • What Good Is A Love Song • Easy For You To Say

### RED HOT CHILI PEPPERS, The

Alternative rock group from Los Angeles: Anthony Kiedis (vocals), Jack Sherman (guitar), Michael "Flea" Balzary (bass) and Cliff Martinez (drums). Numerous personnel changes with Kiedis and Flea the only constants.

| 9/29/84 | 201 | 8 | The Red Hot Chili Peppers | $10 | EMI America 17128 |
|---|---|---|---|---|---|

True Men Don't Kill Coyotes • Baby Appeal • Buckle Down • Get Up And Jump • Why Don't You Love Me • Green Heaven • Mommy Where's Daddy • Out In L.A. • Police Helicopter • You Always Sing • Grand Pappy Du Plenty

### RED ROCKERS

Rock group from Algiers, Louisiana: John Griffith (vocals), Shawn Paddock (guitar), Darren Hill (bass) and Jim Reilly (drums).

| 10/6/84 | 203 | 4 | Schizophrenic Circus ........................................................ | $10 | Columbia 39281 |
|---|---|---|---|---|---|

Just Like You • Blood From A Stone • Shades Of '45 • Another Day • Freedom Row • Good Thing I Know Her • Eve Of Destruction • Both Hands In The Fire • Burning Bridges

### REED, Jerry

Born Jerry Reed Hubbard on 3/20/37 in Atlanta. Country singer/songwriter/guitarist/actor. Starred on TV's *Concrete Cowboys* and acted in several movies.

| 8/26/72 | 201 | 4 | 1 Jerry Reed | $15 | RCA Victor 4750 |
|---|---|---|---|---|---|

500 Miles Away From Home • Almost Crazy • You Made My Life A Song • You're Young And You'll Forget • Alabama Wild Man • Misery Loves Company • Time For Love • Sunshine Day • Huggin' And Chalkin' • Careless Love

| 9/17/77 | 203 | 11 | 2 East Bound And Down ....................................................... | $12 | RCA Victor 2516 |
|---|---|---|---|---|---|

East Bound And Down • Lightning Rod • The Bandit • Bake • The Legend • Framed • You Took All The Rambling Out Of Me • Rainbow Ride • Just To Satisfy You • Don't Think Twice It's All Right

| 10/11/80 | 208 | 4 | 3 Texas Bound And Flyin'..................................................... | $12 | RCA Victor 3771 |
|---|---|---|---|---|---|

Texas Bound And Flying • That's The Chance I'll Have To Take • East Bound And Down • If Love's Not Around The House • Sugar Foot Rag • Caffein, Nicotine, Benzedrine (And Wish Me Luck) • Concrete Sailor • Semi-Happy • Detroit City • The Friendly Family Inn

### REED, Lou — see VELVET UNDERGROUND

### REEVES, Jim

Born on 8/20/24 in Panola County, Texas. Killed in a plane crash on 7/31/64 in Nashville. Country singer. Appeared in the 1963 movie *Kimberley Jim*. Elected to the Country Music Hall of Fame in 1967.

| 2/13/71 | 206 | 8 | Jim Reeves Writes You A Record ...................................... [K] | $25 | RCA Victor 4475 |
|---|---|---|---|---|---|

Angels Don't Lie • When Two Worlds Collide • Nobody's Fool • My Blinde Hart • The Storm • Wild Rose • After Loving You • Trying To Forget • Ding Dong • Seven Days

### REID, Terry
Born in England. Male rock singer/guitarist.

| 6/26/76 | 201 | 2 | **Seed Of Memory** | $12 | ABC 935 |

Faith To Arise • Seed Of Memory • Brave Awakening • To Be Treated • Ooh Baby (Make Me Feel So Young) • The Way You Walk • The Frame • Fooling You

### RENAISSANCE
Classical-rock group from Surrey, England: Annie Haslam (vocals), Michael Dunford (guitar) and Jon Camp (bass).

| 5/14/83 | 207 | 1 | **Time-Line** | $10 | I.R.S. 70033 |

Flight • Missing Persons • Chagrin Boulevard • Richard The IX • The Entertainer • Electric Avenue • Majik • Distant Horizons • Orient Express • Auto-Tech

### REVERE, Paul — see RAIDERS

### RHINESTONES, The
Rock group from Chicago: Kal David (vocals, guitar), Arti Funaro (guitar), Bob Leinbach (keyboards), Harvey Brooks (bass) and Eric Parker (drums). Formerly known as The Fabulous Rhinestones.

| 12/27/75+ | 204 | 4 | **The Rhinestones** | $12 | 20th Century 489 |

One Time Love • Ridin' Thumb • Party Music • Get It Up For Love • Love Jam • Another Song For You • Love On My Mind • Crossroads Of My Life • This Devil In Me • All My Love

### RHYTHM HERITAGE
Studio group from Los Angeles assembled by producers Steve Barri and Michael Omartian (keyboards). Vocals by Oren and Luther Waters.

| 2/25/78 | 202 | 5 | **Sky's The Limit** | $10 | ABC 1037 |

Sail Away With Me • Had To Fall In Love • Skippin' • Language Of Love • Theme From "Starsky & Hutch" • Holdin' Out (For Your Love) • Hedge Hog • Float On By • Sky's The Limit

### RICH, Buddy
Born Bernard Rich on 6/30/17 in New York City. Died on 4/2/87. Legendary jazz drummer.

| 3/23/74 | 212 | 4 | **The Roar Of '74** | [I] $15 | Groove Merchant 528 |

Nuttville • Kilamanjaro • Big Mac • Backwoods Sideman • Time Check • Prelude To A Kiss • Waltz Of The Mushroom Hunters • Senator Sam

### RICH, Charlie
Born on 12/14/32 in Colt, Arkansas. Died of an acute blood clot on 7/25/95. Country singer/songwriter/pianist. Known as "The Silver Fox."

| 5/4/74 | 201 | 7 | 1 **Fully Realized** | [K] $20 | Mercury 7505 [2] |

Mohair Sam • I Can't Go On • Dance Of Love • A Field Of Yellow Daisies • I Washed My Hands In Muddy Water • Everything I Do Is Wrong • She's A Yum Yum • It Ain't Gonna Be That Way • Just A Little Bit Of You • Moonshine Minnie • Down And Out • Lonely Weekends • No Home • So Long • The Best Years • Party Girl • You Can Have Her • Have I Stayed Away Too Long • Hawg Jaw • Something Just Came Over Me • Double Dog Dare Me • Just A Little Bit Of Time • Blowin' Town • Tears A Go-Go

| 2/21/76 | 204 | 2 | 2 **The World Of Charlie Rich** | [E] $12 | RCA Victor 1242 |

Now Everybody Knows • Gentleman Jim • Like Someone In Love • I'm Gonna Sit Right Down And Write Myself A Letter • There Won't Be Anymore • (My Friends Are Gonna Be) Strangers • Why, Oh Why • Lady Love • I've Got You Under My Skin • Rosanna

### RICHARD, Cliff
Born Harry Rodger Webb on 10/14/40 in Lucknow, India; raised in Surrey, England. Pop singer/actor.

| 10/30/82 | 209 | 1 | **Now You See Me, Now You Don't** | $10 | EMI America 17081 |

The Only Way Out • First Date • Thief In The Night • Where Do We Go From Here • Son Of Thunder • Little Town • It Has To Be You, It Has To Be Me • The Water Is Wide • Now You See Me, Now You Don't • Be In My Heart • Discovering

### RIFKIN, Joshua
Born on 4/22/44 in New York City. Classical/jazz/ragtime pianist.

| 2/27/71 | 223 | 1 | **Piano Rags By Scott Joplin** | [I] $15 | Nonesuch 71248 |

Maple Leaf Rag • The Entertainer • The Ragtime Dance • Gladiolus Rag • Fig Leaf Rag • Scott Joplin's New Rag • Euphonic Sounds • Magnetic Rag

### RILEY, Jeannie C.
Born Jeanne Carolyn Stephenson on 10/19/45 in Anson, Texas. Country singer.

| 7/31/71 | 206 | 5 | **Jeannie C. Riley's Greatest Hits** | [G] $15 | Plantation 13 |

Harper Valley PTA • Things Go Better With Love • The Rib • Duty Not Desire • My Man • There Never Was A Time • The Back Side Of Dallas • Country Girl • The Girl Most Likely • The Generation Gap

### RIOT
Heavy-metal group from New York City: Rhett Forrester (vocals), Mark Reale and Rick Ventura (guitars), Kip Leming (bass) and Sandy Slavin (drums). Forrester was shot to death in Atlanta on 1/22/94 (age 37).

| 6/19/82 | 201 | 7 | 1 **Restless Breed** | $10 | Elektra 60134 |

Hard Lovin' Man • CIA • Restless Breed • When I Was Young • Loanshark • Loved By You • Over To You • Showdown • Dream Away • Violent Crimes

| 2/5/83 | 203 | 6 | 2 **Riot Live** | [L-M] $10 | Elektra 67969 |

Hard Lovin' Man • Showdown • Loved By You • Loanshark • Restless Breed • Swords And Tequila

### RIPERTON, Minnie
Born on 11/8/47 in Chicago. Died of cancer on 7/12/79. R&B singer.

| 12/19/81+ | 203 | 5 | **The Best Of Minnie Riperton** | [G] $10 | Capitol 12189 |

Moment With Minnie • Perfect Angel • Memory Lane • Lovin' You • Can You Feel What I'm Saying? • Here We Go • Inside My Love • Lover And Friend • Woman Of Heart And Mind • Young Willing And Able • You Take My Breath Away • Another Moment With Minnie • Adventures In Paradise

| DEBUT | PEAK | WKS | Album Title | $ | Label & Number |
|-------|------|-----|-----------|---|----------------|

### RITCHIE FAMILY
Female disco group from Philadelphia: Vera Brown, Jacqui Smith-Lee and Dodie Draher.

| 5/22/82 | 203 | 7 | **I'll Do My Best** .................................................. $10 | RCA Victor 4323 |

I'll Do My Best (For You Baby) • This Love's On Me • One And Only • You Can Always Count On Me • Walk With Me • Alright On The Night • Tonight I Need To Have Your Love • You've Got Me Dancin'

### RIVERA, Scarlet ♦
Female violin player.

| 9/3/77 | 206 | 3 | **Scarlet Rivera** ..................................................[I] $12 | Warner 3060 |

Leftback • Wicked Witch Of The East • Gypsy Caravan • Earth Queeen • Cloak And Dagger • Ring Around The Moon

### RIVERS, Johnny
Born John Ramistella on 11/7/42 in New York City; raised in Baton Rouge, Louisiana. Rock-and-roll singer/songwriter/guitarist.

| 3/17/73 | 201 | 4 | 1 **Superpak** [K] $20 | United Artists 93 [2] |

Memphis • Brown-Eyed Handsome Man • John Lee Hooker • Silver Threads & Golden Needles • Whole Lotta Shakin' Goin' On • In The Midnight Hour • Secret Agent Man • The Promised Land • Stagger Lee • Hey Joe • Baby I Need Your Lovin' • Do You Wanna Dance • If I Were A Carpenter • Whiter Shade Of Pale • Carpet Man • Summer Rain • Rainy Night In Georgia • California Dreamin' • Jesus Is A Soul Man • Rock Me On The Water

| 7/14/73 | 212 | 2 | 2 **Blue Suede Shoes** .................................................. $15 | United Artists 075 |

Blue Suede Shoes • Medley: Searchin'/So Fine • It's All Right • Hang On Sloopy • I'll Feel A Whole Lot Better • Solitary Man • Over The Line • Willie And The Hand Jive • Got My Mojo Workin' • Turn On Your Love Light

### ROAD ♦
British rock trio: Rod Richards (vocals, guitar), Noel Redding (bass) and Leslie Sampson (drums). Redding was a member of The **Jimi Hendrix** Experience.

| 9/23/72 | 206 | 4 | **Road** .................................................. $20 | Natural Resources 105 |

I'm Trying • Going Down To The Country • Mushroom Man • Man Dressed In Red • Spaceship Earth • Friends • Road

### ROBBINS, Marty
Born Martin David Robinson on 9/26/25 in Glendale, Arizona. Died of a heart attack on 12/8/82. Country singer/songwriter/guitarist.

| 9/10/83 | 209 | 2 | **A Lifetime of Song 1951-1982** [K] $15 | Columbia 38870 [2] |

Tommorrow You'll Be Gone • I'll Go On Alone • That's All Right • Knee Deep In The Blues • Singing The Blues • A White Sport Coat (And A Pink Carnation) • The Story Of My Life • Don't Worry • Ruby Ann • Devil Woman • El Paso • Big Iron • The Hanging Tree • Ribbon Of Darkness • El Paso City • I Walk Alone • My Woman, My Woman, My Wife • Among My Souvenirs • Return To Me • Some Memories Just Won't Die

### ROBBINS, Rockie
Born Edward Robbins in Minneapolis. R&B singer.

| 6/16/79 | 204 | 3 | **Rockie Robbins** .................................................. $10 | A&M 4758 |

I Can Hardly Wait • If I Ever Lose You • Funk Street • When I Think Of You • I Love You Only • Don't Deny Me • Be Ever Wonderful • Sho' Is Bad • Miss Dynamite

### ROBERTS, Austin ♦
Born on 9/19/45 in Newport News, Virginia. Singer/songwriter.

| 12/16/72+ | 203 | 6 | **Austin Roberts** .................................................. $15 | Chelsea 1004 |

Keep On Singing • Time • There's A Shadow • What Fools We Are • Take Away The Sunshine • Something's Wrong With Me • My Song • Only Child • Believe In Me • I Can Feel It

### ROBINSON, Tom
Born on 6/1/50 in Cambridge, England. New wave singer/bassist.

| 2/21/81 | 209 | 1 | **Sector 27** .................................................. $10 | I.R.S. 70013 |

Invitation • Not Ready • Mary Lynne • Looking At You • Five Two Five • Can't Keep Away • Total Recall • Where Can We Go Tonight • Take Or Leave It • Bitterly Disappointed • One Fine Day

### RODGERS, Nile ♦
Born on 9/19/52 in New York City. R&B guitarist/producer. Member of Chic and The Honeydrippers.

| 4/16/83 | 202 | 4 | 1 **Adventures In The Land Of The Good Groove** .................... $10 | Mirage 90073 |

The Land Of The Good Groove • Yum-Yum • Beet • Get Her Crazy • It's All In Your Hands • Rock Bottom • My Love Song For You • Most Down

| 6/22/85 | 206 | 3 | 2 **B-Movie Matinee** .................................................. $10 | Warner 25290 |

Plan-9 • State Your Mind • The Face In The Window • Doll Squad • Let's Go Out Tonight • Groove Master • Wavelength • Stay Out Of The Light

### ROE, Tommy
Born on 5/9/42 in Atlanta. Pop-rock singer/songwriter/guitarist.

| 11/6/71 | 202 | 3 | **Beginnings** .................................................. $15 | ABC 732 |

Beginnings • Lawdy Miss Clawdy • Why Can't It Be Me • The Way Things Are • Brown Eyed Handsome Man • Snowman • Indulge In Love • Back Streets And Alleys • Hide Daddy's Whiskey • Your Touch Is The Best Thing In Life • Beginnings • Stagger Lee

### ROLLINS, Sonny ♦
Born on 9/7/30 in New York City. Tenor jazz saxophonist.

| 10/28/78 | 209 | 1 | **Don't Stop The Carnival** ......................................[I-L] $15 | Milestone 55005 [2] |

recorded from 4/13 - 4/15/78 at the Great American Music Hall in San Francisco
Don't Stop The Carnival • Silver City • Autumn Nocturne • Camel • Nobody Else But Me • Non-Cents • A Child's Prayer • President Hayes • Sais

### ROMAN HOLLIDAY
New wave group from London: Steve Lambert (vocals), Brian Bonhomme (guitar), Adrian York (keyboards), John Eacott (trumpet), Simeon Jones (saxophone), Jon Durno (bass) and Simon Cohen (drums). Group named after the 1953 movie starring Audrey Hepburn.

| 3/2/85 | 201 | 4 | **Fire Me Up** $10 | Jive 8252 |

One Foot Back In Your Door • Fire Me Up • Hear It In The Night • Keep The Night Away • Runaway • I'll Wait • Touch Too Much • Strangest Feeling • Don't Take It All Away • Red Turns To Blonde • You Know Me Well

| DEBUT | PEAK | WKS | Album Title | $ | Label & Number |
|-------|------|-----|-------------|---|----------------|

### ROSE, Tim ☉
Singer/songwriter.

| | | | | | |
|---|---|---|---|---|---|
| 4/29/72 | 211 | 2 | **Tim Rose** ............................................................................ | $12 | Playboy 101 |

It Takes A Little Longer • You Can't Keep Me • Hide Your Love Away • Boogie Boogie • If I Were A Carpenter • Cryin' Shame • Darling You Were All That I Had • Cotton Growin' Man • Goin' Down In Hollywood

### ROSE ROYCE
R&B group from Los Angeles: Gwen Dickey (vocals), Kenji Brown (guitar), Kenny Copeland and Freddie Dunn (trumpets), Michael Moore (sax), Terral Santiel (percussion), Victor Nix (keyboards), Lequeint "Duke" Jobe (bass) and Henry Garner (drums). Dickey left in 1980, replaced by Ricci Benson.

| | | | | | |
|---|---|---|---|---|---|
| 10/4/80 | 204 | 1 | **1 Greatest Hits** ....................................................... [G] | $10 | Whitfield 3457 |

Pop Your Fingers • It Makes You Feel Like Dancin' • First Come, First Serve • Car Wash • Is It Love You're After • Do Your Dance • You're A Winner • Ooh Boy • I Wanna Get Next To You • Wishing On A Star • I'm In Love (And I Love The Feeling) • I'm Going Down • I Wonder Where You Are Tonight • Love Don't Live Here Anymore

| | | | | | |
|---|---|---|---|---|---|
| 10/3/81 | 210 | 1 | **2 Jump Street**....................................................... | $10 | Whitfield 3620 |

Jump Street • Illusions • R.R. Express • Famous Last Words • Tell Me That I'm Dreaming • Please Return Your Love To Me • Fight It

| | | | | | |
|---|---|---|---|---|---|
| 6/5/82 | 210 | 1 | **3 Stronger Than Ever** ....................................... | $10 | Epic 37939 |

Dance With Me • Sometimesy Lady • Best Love • Still In Love • You Blew It • Somehow We Made It Through The Rain • Fire In The Funk • Talk To Me

### ROSE TATTOO
Heavy-metal group from Australia: Angry Anderson (vocals), Peter Wells and Michael Cocks (guitars), Geordie Leech (bass) and Dallas Royall (drums).

| | | | | | |
|---|---|---|---|---|---|
| 1/8/83 | 208 | 1 | **Scarred For Life**................................................. | $10 | Mirage 90022 |

Scarred For Life • We Can't Be Beaten • Juice On The Loose • Who's Got The Cash • Branded • Texas • It's Gonna Work Itself Out • Sydney Girls • Dead Set • Revenge

### ROUGH CUTT ☉
Heavy-metal group from Los Angeles: Paul Shortino (vocals), Chris Hager and Amir Derakh (guitars), Matt Thorr (bass) and David Alford (drums).

| | | | | | |
|---|---|---|---|---|---|
| 3/16/85 | 210 | 1 | **Rough Cutt**........................................................ | $10 | Warner 25268 |

Take Her • Piece Of My Heart • Never Gonna Die • Dreamin' Again • Cut Your Heart Out • Black Widow • You Keep Breaking My Heart • Kids Will Rock • Dressed To Kill • She's Too Hott

### ROUGH TRADE ☉
Rock group from Toronto: Carole Pope (vocals), Kevan Staples (guitar), Dave McMorrow (keyboards), Terry Wilkins (bass) and Bucky Berger (drums).

| | | | | | |
|---|---|---|---|---|---|
| 2/5/83 | 206 | 7 | **For Those Who Think Young** ............................... | $10 | Boardwalk 33261 |

All Touch • Attitude • For Those Who Think Young • Bodies In Collision • Prisoner Of My Skin • The Sacred And The Profane • Baptism Of Fire • Fakin' It • Blood Lust

### ROUSSOS, Demis
Born on 6/15/47 in Alexandria, Egypt. Male rock singer.

| | | | | | |
|---|---|---|---|---|---|
| 8/16/75 | 206 | 1 | **Souvenirs** ......................................................... | $12 | Big Tree 89509 |

Sing An Ode To Love • Midnight Is The Time I Need You • I'll Be Your Friend • Action Lady • Winter Rains • From Souvenirs To Souvenirs • Trying To Catch The Wind • White Wings • Tell Me Now • Names • Perdoname

### ROWANS, The ☉
Pop-rock trio from Boston: brothers Peter (vocals, guitar), Lorin (guitar) and Chris (keyboards) Rowan. Peter was a member of **Seatrain**.

| | | | | | |
|---|---|---|---|---|---|
| 7/26/75 | 210 | 1 | **The Rowans** ...................................................... | $12 | Asylum 1038 |

Take It As It Comes • Midnight-Moonlight • Me Loving You • Old Silver • Thunder On The Mountain • Beggar In Blue Jeans • Do Right • Man-Woman • Pieces On The Ground • Here Today-Gone Tomorrow

### ROXY MUSIC
Art-rock band from London. Nucleus consisted of **Bryan Ferry** (vocals, keyboards), **Phil Manzanera** (guitar) and Andy MacKay (horns).

| | | | | | |
|---|---|---|---|---|---|
| 1/21/78 | 206 | 2 | **Greatest Hits** ....................................................... [G] | $12 | Atco 103 |

Virginia Plain • Do The Strand • All I Want Is You • Out Of The Blue • Pyjamarama • Editions Of You • Love Is The Drug • Mother Of Pearl • A Song For Europe • The Thrill Of It All • Street Life

### ROYAL PHILHARMONIC ORCHESTRA — see OLDFIELD, Mike

### RUBBER RODEO ☉
Pop-rock group from Rhode Island: Trish Milliken (vocals), Bob Holmes (guitar), Mark Tomeo (steel guitar), Gary Leib (keyboards), John Doelp (bass) and Barc Holmes (drums).

| | | | | | |
|---|---|---|---|---|---|
| 7/7/84 | 205 | 5 | **Scenic Views** ..................................................... | $10 | Mercury 818477 |

Need You Need Me • Slow Me Down • Anywhere With You • Walking After Midnight • City Of God • The Hardest Thing • House Of Pain • Mess O' Me • Before I Go Away

### RUBEN AND THE JETS ☉
Rock group: Ruben Guevara (vocals), Tony Duran and Robert Camarena (guitars), Robert Roberts and Jim Sherwood (horns), Johnny Martinez (keyboards), Bill Wild (bass) and Bob Zamora (drums). Group named after **Frank Zappa**'s 1968 album *Cruising With Ruben & The Jets*.

| | | | | | |
|---|---|---|---|---|---|
| 5/5/73 | 205 | 2 | **For Real** ............................................................ | $20 | Mercury 659 |

produced by **Frank Zappa**

If I Could Only Be Your Love Again • Dedicated To The One I Love • Show Me The Way To Your Heart • Sparkie • Wedding Bells • Almost Grown • Charlena • Mah Man Flash • Santa Kari • Spider Woman • All Nite Long

| DEBUT | PEAK | WKS | Album Title | $ | Label & Number |
|-------|------|-----|-------------|---|----------------|

**RUFFIN, David**
Born Davis Eli Ruffin on 1/18/41 in Meridian, Mississippi. Died of a drug overdose on 6/1/91. Co-lead singer of **The Temptations** from 1963-68.

| 1/11/75 | 201 | 2 | 1 **Me 'N Rock 'N Roll Are Here To Stay** | $12 | Motown 818 |

I Saw You When You Met Her • Take Me Clear From Here • Smiling Faces Sometimes • Me And Rock & Roll (Are Here To Stay) • Superstar (Remember How You Got Where You Are) • No Matter Where • City Stars • I Just Want To Celebrate

| 10/27/79 | 206 | 2 | 2 **So Soon We Change** | $10 | Warner 3306 |

Let Your Love Rain Down On Me • Break My Heart • I Get Excited • Chain On The Brain • Morning Sun Looks Blue • Let's Stay Together • So Soon We Change • Sexy Dancer

**RUNDGREN, Todd**
Born on 6/22/48 in Upper Darby, Pennsylvania. Virtuoso musician/songwriter/producer/engineer. Leader of groups Nazz and Utopia.

| 7/10/71 | 214 | 3 | **Runt - The Ballad Of Todd Rundgren** | $30 | Bearsville 10116 |

Long Flowing Robe • The Ballad (Denny & Jean) • Bleeding • Wailing Wall • The Range War • Chain Letter • A Long Time, A Long Way To Go • Boat On The Charles • Be Nice To Me • Hope I'm Around • Parole • Remember Me

**RUSSELL, Leon**
Born on 4/2/41 in Lawton, Oklahoma. Rock singer/songwriter/multi-instrumentalist.

| 4/8/72 | 201 | 8 | 1 **Look Inside The Asylum Choir** | [E] $20 | Smash 67107 |

LEON RUSSELL & MARC BENNO
recorded in 1968
Welcome To Hollywood • Soul Food • Icicle Star Tree • Death Of The Flowers • Indian Style • Episode Containing 3 Songs: N.Y. OP./Land Of Dog/Mr. Henri The Clown • Thieves In The Choir • Black Sheep Boogaloo

| 7/7/79 | 204 | 2 | 2 **Life And Love** | $10 | Paradise 3341 |

One More Love Song • You Girl • Struck By Lightning • Strange Love • Life And Love • On The First Day • High Horse • Sweet Mystery • On The Borderline

# S

**SALSOUL ORCHESTRA, The**
Disco studio group assembled by producer/arranger Vincent Montana.

| 1/5/80 | 201 | 2 | **How High** | $10 | Salsoul 8528 |

How High • Have A Good Time • My Number's Up • I'll Keep You Warm • Resorts International • Stop And Think

**SANBORN, David**
Born on 7/30/45 in Tampa, Florida; raised in St. Louis. Alto saxophonist.

| 5/29/76 | 208 | 2 | 1 **Taking Off** | [I] $12 | Warner 2873 |

Butterfat • 'Way 'Cross Georgia • Duck Ankles • Funky Banana • The Whisperer • It Took A Long Time • Black Light • Blue Night • Flight

| 7/23/77 | 208 | 1 | 2 **Promise Me The Moon** | [I] $12 | Warner 3051 |

DAVID SANBORN BAND
Promise Me The Moon • Benjamin • Stranger's Arms • Heart Lake • The Rev. • We Fool Ourselves • Morning Salsa • The Legend Of Cheops

**SANCIOUS, David** ✪
Popular session keyboardist.

| 11/10/79 | 210 | 2 | **Just As I Thought** | [I] $10 | Arista 4247 |

Run • Just As I Thought • Again • The Naked I • Valley Of The Shadow • Suite (For The End Of An Age) • Remember • And Then She Said • Again (Part II)

**SANTAMARIA, Mongo**
Born Ramon Santamaria on 4/7/22 in Havana, Cuba. Bandleader/percussionist.

| 4/28/79 | 207 | 1 | **Red Hot** | [I] $10 | Columbia 35696 |

guests include **Eric Gale**, Bob James and **Hubert Laws**
Watermelon Man • A Mi No Me Engañan (You Better Believe It) • Jai Alai • Jamaican Sunrise • Afro-Cuban Fantasy • Sambita

**SANTANA, Jorge** ✪
Born on 6/13/54 in Jalisco, Mexico. Former member of **Malo**. Younger brother of Carlos Santana.

| 10/14/78 | 202 | 5 | **Jorge Santana** | $12 | Tomato 7020 |

Sandy • Tonight You're Mine • Darling I Love You • We Were There • Love You, Love You • Love The Way • Seychells • Nobody's Perfect

**SAVOY BROWN**
Male blues-rock trio from London: Ian Ellis (vocals, bass), Kim Simmonds (guitar) and Tom Farnell (drums). **Chris Youlden** was the group's original lead singer.

| 5/22/76 | 206 | 5 | 1 **Skin 'N' Bone** | $12 | London 670 |

Get On Up And Do It • Part Time Lady • This Day Is Gonna Be Our Last • She's The One • Skin 'N' Bone • Walkin' And Talkin'

| 4/9/77 | 210 | 1 | 2 **The Best Of Savoy Brown** | [G] $12 | London 5000 |

Train To Nowhere • Louisiana Blues • I'm Tired • Needle And Spoon • A Hard Way To Go • Tell Mama • Hellbound Train • Wang Dang Doodle

| 9/16/78 | 208 | 1 | 3 **Savage Return** | $12 | London 718 |

The First Night • Don't Do It Baby, Do It • Spirit High • Play It Right • Walk Before You Run • My Own Man • I'm Alright Now • Rock 'N' Roll Man • Double Lover

## SAXON
Heavy-metal group from Barnsley, England: Biff Byford (vocals), Graham Oliver and Paul Quinn (guitars), Steve Dawson (bass) and Nigel Glocker (drums).

| | | | | | |
| --- | --- | --- | --- | --- | --- |
| 12/19/81 | 207 | 3 | 1 **Denim And Leather** ....................................................................................... | $10 | Carrere 37685 |

Princess Of The Night • Never Surrender • Out Of Control • Rough And Ready • Play It Loud • And The Bands Played On • Midnight Rider • Fire In The Sky • Denim And Leather

| | | | | | |
| --- | --- | --- | --- | --- | --- |
| 7/3/82 | 208 | 2 | 2 **Strong Arm Of The Law** .................................................................................. | $10 | Carrere 37679 |

Dallas 1 PM • Strong Arm Of The Law • Sixth Form Girls • Hungry Years • Heavy Metal Thunder • Taking Your Chances • To Hell And Back Again • 20,000 FT

## SAYER, Leo
Born Gerard Sayer on 5/21/48 in Shoreham, England. Pop singer/songwriter.

| | | | | | |
| --- | --- | --- | --- | --- | --- |
| 3/2/74 | 209 | 7 | **Silverbird** .................................................................................................. | $12 | Warner 2738 |

Innocent Bystander • Goodnight Old Friend • Drop Back • Silverbird • The Show Must Go On • The Dancer • Tomorrow • Don't Say It's Over • Slow Motion • Oh Wot A Life • Why Is Everybody Going Home

## SCAGGS, Boz
Born William Royce Scaggs on 6/8/44 in Ohio; raised in Texas. Pop-blues-rock singer.

| | | | | | |
| --- | --- | --- | --- | --- | --- |
| 4/8/78 | 209 | 1 | **Boz Scaggs** .........................................................................................[R] | $10 | Atlantic 19166 |

album first released in 1969 on Atlantic 8239 (charted at #171 in 1974); this is a remixed version of that original album
I'm Easy • I'll Be Long Gone • Another Day • Finding Her • Look What I Got • Waiting For A Train • Loan Me A Dime • Sweet Release

## SCHENKER, Michael
Born on 1/10/55 in Savstedt, Germany. Hard-rock guitarist. Former member of **Scorpions** and UFO.

| | | | | | |
| --- | --- | --- | --- | --- | --- |
| 3/3/84 | 201 | 5 | **Built To Destroy** | $10 | Chrysalis 41441 |

THE MICHAEL SCHENKER GROUP
I'm Gonna Make You Mine • Time Waits • Systems Failing • Rock Will Never Die • Red Sky • Rock My Nights Away • Captain Nemo • Dogs Of War • Still Love That Little Devil

## SCHIFRIN, Lalo
Born Boris Schifrin on 6/21/32 in Buenos Aires, Argentina. Pianist/conductor/composer. Scored several movies.

| | | | | | |
| --- | --- | --- | --- | --- | --- |
| 8/7/76 | 202 | 3 | **Black Widow** ..........................................................................................[I] | $12 | CTI 5000 |

Black Widow • Flamingo • Quiet Village • Medley: Moonglow/Theme From Picnic • Theme From Jaws • Baia • Turning Point • Dragonfly

## SCORPIONS
Heavy-metal group from Hanover, Germany: Klaus Meine (vocals), Ulrich Roth and Rudolf Schenker (guitars), Francis Buchholz (bass) and Herman Rarebell (drums). Schenker is the brother of **Michael Schenker**.

| | | | | | |
| --- | --- | --- | --- | --- | --- |
| 1/6/79 | 206 | 5 | **Tokyo Tapes** ..........................................................................................[L] | $12 | RCA Victor 3039 [2] |

recorded in April 1978 at Sun Plaza Hall in Tokyo, Japan
All Night Long • Pictured Life • Backstage Queen • Polar Nights • In Trance • We'll Burn The Sky • Suspender Love • In Search Of The Peace Of Mind • Fly To The Rainbow • He's A Woman, She's A Man • Speedy's Coming • Top Of The Bill • Hound Dog • Long Tall Sally • Steamrock Fever • Dark Lady • Kojo No Tsuki • Robot Man

## SCRUGGS, Earl
Born on 1/6/24 in Flintville, North Carolina. Legendary bluegrass banjo player.

| | | | | | |
| --- | --- | --- | --- | --- | --- |
| 1/13/73 | 204 | 4 | 1 **Live At Kansas State** ....................................................................................[L] | $12 | Columbia 31758 |

EARL SCRUGGS AND THE EARL SCRUGGS REVUE
T For Texas • Bound In Jail All Night Long • Rambling 'Round Your City • Sally Gooding • Most Likely You Go Your Way (And I'll Go Mine) • Carolina Boogie • Everybody Wants To Go To Heaven • You Ain't Going Nowhere • Both Sides Now • Good Woman's Love • Bugle Call Rag • Foggy Mountain Breakdown

| | | | | | |
| --- | --- | --- | --- | --- | --- |
| 6/2/73 | 202 | 8 | 2 **Dueling Banjos** .........................................................................................[I] | $12 | Columbia 32268 |

String Bender • Peking Fling • Black Mountain Blues • Just Joshin' • Dueling Banjos • Lonesome Ruben • John Hardy • Flint Hill Special • Randy Lynn Rag • Fireball Mail

## SEATRAIN
Fusion-rock band from Marin County, California: Peter Walsh (vocals, guitar), Jim Roberts (lyricist), Bill Elliott and Lloyd Baskin (keyboards), Andy Kulberg (bass) and Julio Coronado (drums).

| | | | | | |
| --- | --- | --- | --- | --- | --- |
| 4/7/73 | 201 | 4 | **Watch** | $12 | Warner 2692 |

Pack Of Fools • Freedom Is The Reason • Bloodshot Eyes • We Are Your Children Too • Abbeville Fair • North Coast • Scratch • Watching The River Flow • Flute Thing

## SEBESKY, Don ☉
Born on 12/10/37 in Perth Amboy, New Jersey. Jazz arranger/conductor.

| | | | | | |
| --- | --- | --- | --- | --- | --- |
| 1/19/74 | 206 | 13 | **Giant Box** ...............................................................................................[I] | $15 | CTI 6031 [2] |

guests include **Airto**, **George Benson**, **Ron Carter** and **Hubert Laws**
Medley: Firebird/Birds Of Fire • Song To A Seagull • Free As A Bird • Psalm 150 • Vocalise • Medley: Fly/Circles • Semi-Tough

## SEDAKA, Neil
Born on 3/13/39 in Brooklyn. Pop singer/songwriter/pianist.

| | | | | | |
| --- | --- | --- | --- | --- | --- |
| 5/8/76 | 201 | 9 | **Sedaka Live In Australia** [L] | $12 | RCA Victor 1540 |

recorded at the South Sydney Junior Leagues Club
Sugar, Sugar • Everything Is Beautiful • Medley: Bridge Over Troubled Water/Danny Boy • Medley: Oh! Carol/Happy Birthday Sweet Sixteen/Star Crossed Lovers/Little Devil/Breaking Up Is Hard To Do/Calendar Girl • The Father Of Girls • Polonaise In A Flat • Proud Mary • Medley: Bye Bye Blackbird/I Don't Know Why (I Just Do)/I Can't Give You Anything But Love • My World Keeps Getting Smaller Every Day • Scapricciatiello • The History Of Rock And Roll Medley: Those Were The Days/Cry/Shake, Rattle And Roll/Blueberry Hill/Great Balls Of Fire/All Shook Up/She Loves You/Delilah/Those Were The Days (Reprise)

| DEBUT | PEAK | WKS | Album Title | $ | Label & Number |
|---|---|---|---|---|---|

### SEEGER, Pete
Born on 5/3/19 in New York City. Legendary folk singer/songwriter. Won Grammy's Lifetime Achievement Award in 1993. Inducted into the Rock and Roll Hall of Fame in 1996 as an early influence.

| | | | | | |
|---|---|---|---|---|---|
| 8/14/71 | **205** | 5 | Rainbow Race ................................................................. | $20 | Columbia 30739 |

Last Train To Nuremberg • Sailing Down This Golden River • Uncle Ho • Snow Snow • My Rainbow Race • Our Generation • Old Devil Time • The Clearwater • Words Words Words • Hobo's Lullaby

### SEGER, Bob
Born on 5/6/45 in Dearborn, Michigan; raised in Detroit. Rock singer/songwriter/guitarist.

| | | | | | |
|---|---|---|---|---|---|
| 12/18/71 | **210** | 1 | Brand New Morning ......................................................... | $40 | Capitol 731 |

Brand New Morning • Maybe Today • Sometimes • You Know Who You Are • Railroad Days • Louise • Song For Him • Something Like

### SELECTER, The
Ska group from Coventry, England: Pauline Black and Arthur Hendrickson (vocals), Noel Davies and Compton Amanor (guitars), Desmond Brown (keyboards), Charley Anderson (bass) and Charley Bembridge (drums).

| | | | | | |
|---|---|---|---|---|---|
| 3/28/81 | **201** | 3 | Celebrate The Bullet | $10 | Chrysalis 1306 |

Celebrate The Bullet • Red Reflections • (Who Likes) Facing Situations • Tell Me What's Wrong • Bombscare • Washed Up And Left For Dead • Selling Out Your Future • Deepwater • Cool Blue Lady • Their Dream Goes On • Bristol And Miami

### SENAY, Eddy ✪
Born in Detroit. R&B guitar instrumentalist.

| | | | | | |
|---|---|---|---|---|---|
| 7/1/72 | **204** | 4 | Hot Thang ......................................................... [I] | $12 | Sussex 7013 |

Just Feeling It • Down Home • Hot Thang • Zambezi • Jubo • Rev. Lowdown • Ain't No Sunshine • Message Of Love

### SEQUENCE, The ✪
Female funk trio from Columbia, South Carolina: Gwendolyn Chisolm, Angie Brown Stone and Cheryl Cook.

| | | | | | |
|---|---|---|---|---|---|
| 9/4/82 | **207** | 3 | The Sequence ......................................................... | $10 | SugarHill 267 |

I Don't Need Your Love • Can You Feel It • Funk That (You Mothers) • Cold Sweat • Love Changes • Unaddressed Letter • Get It Together

### SHAKATAK ✪
Jazz group from London: Jill Saward (vocals), Keith Winter (guitar), Bill Sharpe (keyboards), George Anderson (bass) and Roger Odell (drums).

| | | | | | |
|---|---|---|---|---|---|
| 11/27/82 | **202** | 3 | 1 Night Birds ......................................................... | $10 | Polydor 6354 |

Night Birds • Streetwalkin' • Rio Nights • Fly The Wind • Easier Said Than Done • Bitch To The Boys • Light On My Life • Takin' Off

| | | | | | |
|---|---|---|---|---|---|
| 4/2/83 | **204** | 2 | 2 Invitations ......................................................... | $10 | Polydor 810068 |

Invitations • Lose Myself • Lonely Afternoon • Steppin' Out • Stranger • Usual Situation • Brazil • In Shadows

| | | | | | |
|---|---|---|---|---|---|
| 2/23/85 | **203** | 7 | 3 Down On The Street ......................................................... | $10 | Polydor 823304 |

Down On The Street • Holding On • Summer Sky • Hypnotised • Don't Blame It On Love • Photograph • Watching You • Fire Dance • Lady (To Billie Holiday)

### SHANKAR, Ravi, & Ali Akbar Khan
Shankar was born on 4/7/20 in India. Sitar player. Khan was born in 1922 in Bangladesh. Sarod player.

| | | | | | |
|---|---|---|---|---|---|
| 4/7/73 | **213** | 2 | In Concert 1972 ......................................................... [I-L] | $50 | Apple 3396 [2] |

recorded in New York City

Raga - Hem Bihag • Raga - Manj Khamaj (Part I) • Raga - Manj Khamaj (Part II) • Raga - Sindhi Bhairavi

### SHARP, Dee Dee
Born Dione LaRue on 9/9/45 in Philadelphia. R&B singer. Married record producer Kenny Gamble in 1967. Also recorded as **Dee Dee Sharp Gamble**.

| | | | | | |
|---|---|---|---|---|---|
| 12/27/80+ | **204** | 4 | Dee Dee ......................................................... | $10 | Philadelphia Int'l. 36370 |

**DEE DEE SHARP GAMBLE**

Breaking And Entering • Let's Get This Party Started • I Love You Anyway • Easy Money • Invitation • Everyday Affair • If We're Gonna Stay Together • See You Later

### SHEAR, Jules ✪
Born on 3/7/52 in Pittsburgh. Leader of Funky Kings, Reckless Sleepers and Jules & The Polar Bears.

| | | | | | |
|---|---|---|---|---|---|
| 5/25/85 | **209** | 2 | The Eternal Return ......................................................... | $10 | EMI America 17156 |

If She Knew What She Wants • Stand Tall • Steady • Change (Change) • The Fever's On • Here She Comes • Memories Burn Hard • You're Not Around • Empty Out The House (Throw It All Away) • Everytime I Get The Feeling

### SHEPPARD, T.G.
Born William Browder on 7/20/42 in Alamo, Tennessee. Country singer.

| | | | | | |
|---|---|---|---|---|---|
| 1/14/84 | **204** | 4 | Slow Burn ......................................................... | $10 | Warner 23911 |

Somewhere Down The Line • Don't Fight The Night • She Put The Sad In All His Songs • Baby I'm - A Want You • Slow Burn • Blank Check • Arthur And Alice • How Lucky We Are • First Things First • It's A Sad Night For Good Girls

### SHERBS, The
Pop-rock group from Australia: Daryl Braithwaite (vocals), Tony Leigh (guitar), Garth Porter (keyboards), Tony Mitchell (bass) and Alan Sandow (drums).

| | | | | | |
|---|---|---|---|---|---|
| 5/22/82 | **202** | 4 | Defying Gravity ......................................................... | $10 | Atco 146 |

We Ride Tonight • Steppin' On Ice • We Can Make It • I'm Alive • The Danger Zone • Don't Throw It All Away

### SHERIFF
Pop-rock group from Toronto: Freddy Curci (vocals), Steve DeMarchi (guitar), Arnold Lanni (keyboards), Wolf Hassel (bass) and Rob Elliott (drums).

| | | | | | |
|---|---|---|---|---|---|
| 6/25/83 | **210** | 1 | Sheriff ......................................................... | $10 | Capitol 12227 |

reissued in 1989 on Capitol 91216 (#60)

You Remind Me • California • Makin' My Way • When I'm With You • Kept Me Coming • Mama's Baby • Crazy Without You • Elisa • Living For A Dream • Give Me Rock 'N' Roll

| DEBUT | PEAK | WKS | Album Title | $ | Label & Number |
|-------|------|-----|-------------|---|----------------|

### SHERLEY, Glen ☉
Born in Oklahoma; raised in California. Died of self-inflicted gunshot wounds on 5/11/78. Country singer/songwriter. Was an inmate at the California State Prison in Vacaville at the time of his recordings.

| | | | | | |
|---|---|---|---|---|---|
| 6/5/71 | 208 | 1 | Glen Sherley ..................................................................... [L] $12 | | Mega 1006 |

recorded on 1/31/71

Dialogue • Looking Back In Anger • Greystone Chapel • F.B.I. Top Ten • Portrait Of My Woman • Mama Had Country Soul • Pick A Bouquet • If This Prison Yard Could Talk • Step Right This Way • Frisco Song • Keep Steppin' • Measure Of A Man

### SHIPLEY, Ellen ☉
Female singer from Brooklyn.

| | | | | | |
|---|---|---|---|---|---|
| 10/25/80 | 205 | 5 | Breaking Through The Ice Age ..................................................... $10 | | RCA Victor 3626 |

Heart To Heart • Fotogenic • Jamie • This Little Girl • Talk Don't Shout • Solo • Lost Without Your Love • Promise To Keep • Living For The Tenderness

### SHORROCK, Glenn ☉
Born on 6/30/44 in England; raised in Elizabeth, Australia. Lead singer of Little River Band.

| | | | | | |
|---|---|---|---|---|---|
| 10/29/83 | 207 | 1 | Villain Of The Peace .................................................................. $10 | | Capitol 12222 |

Don't Girls Get Lonely • A Cry In A Jungle Bar • Secrets • Angry Words • Villain Of The Peace • Rock 'N Roll Soldier • Til I Loved You • Onwards And Upwards • Haunting Me • Will You Stand With Me?

### SHOTGUN
Funk group from Detroit: Billy Talbert (vocals, guitar), Ernest Lattimore (guitar), William Gentry (trumpet), Greg Ingram (sax), Larry Austin (bass) and Tyrone Steels (drums).

| | | | | | |
|---|---|---|---|---|---|
| 6/11/77 | 202 | 12 | 1 Shotgun .............................................................................. $12 | | ABC 979 |

Shotgun • Trouble Shooter • Good Thing • Concrete Jungle • Get Down With The Get Down • Mutha Funk • Shady Lady • Hot Line • Dynamite (The Bomb)

| | | | | | |
|---|---|---|---|---|---|
| 2/23/80 | 206 | 2 | 2 Shotgun IV ......................................................................... $10 | | MCA 3201 |

Come On With It • I Want You • You Deserve The Best • Go Head • Come On And Dance • Standing In Need Of Love • You Just Wanna Dance • Happy Feelin'

### SHOT IN THE DARK ☉
Pop-rock group: Krysia Kristianne (vocals), Adam Yurman (guitar), Bryan Savage (sax), Peter White (keyboards) and Robin Lamble (bass). Former backing band for Al Stewart.

| | | | | | |
|---|---|---|---|---|---|
| 5/2/81 | 210 | 1 | Shot In The Dark ...................................................................... $10 | | RSO 3096 |

Playing With Lightning • I Want The Moon • All My Life • Turn Around • Just As Well • Shot In The Dark • Make Up Your Mind • Speak My Language • Angry Song • Some Towns

### SIDE EFFECT
R&B-jazz vocal group from Los Angeles: Miki Howard, Augie Johnson, Louis Patton and Greg Matta.

| | | | | | |
|---|---|---|---|---|---|
| 5/24/80 | 208 | 1 | After The Rain .......................................................................... $10 | | Elektra 261 |

Take A Chance 'N' Dance • The Thrill Is Gone • Georgy Porgy • Close To Me • I Feel It's Real • Black Beauty • Pretty Baby • Catch It 'Fore It Falls • Eleanor Rigby • Superwoman

### SIDRAN, Ben ☉
Jazz keyboardist.

| | | | | | |
|---|---|---|---|---|---|
| 8/14/76 | 203 | 1 | Free In America ................................................................... [I] $12 | | Arista 4081 |

Feel Your Groove • After Midnight • Sunday Kind Of Love • Lets Make A Deal • Beg For It • New York State Of Mind • You Talk Too Much • The Cuban Connection • Free In America

### SIEGEL, Dan ☉
Jazz pianist.

| | | | | | |
|---|---|---|---|---|---|
| 4/11/81 | 206 | 1 | The Hot Shot ..................................................................... [I] $10 | | Inner City 1111 |

features guitarist Garry Hagberg

The Hot Shot • Sweet Talk • A Gentleman's Retreat • Once Upon A Time • The Twisted • The Wild West • Wallflower • Full Moon • Oblivion

### SIEGEL-SCHWALL BAND, The ☉
Blues-rock group from Chicago: Corky Siegel (vocals, harmonica), Jim Schwall (guitar), Rollow Radford (bass) and Sheldon Plotkin (drums).

| | | | | | |
|---|---|---|---|---|---|
| 12/18/71 | 206 | 3 | 1 The Siegel-Schwall Band ..................................................... $30 | | Wooden Nickel 1002 |

(Wish I Was On A) Country Road • Devil • Leavin' • Corrina • I Won't Hold My Breath • Next To You • Hush, Hush

| | | | | | |
|---|---|---|---|---|---|
| 10/20/73 | 201 | 7 | 2 953 West ........................................................................... $30 | | Wooden Nickel 0121 |

I'd Like To Spend Some Time Alone With You Tonight My Friend • Traitor From Decatur • Good Woman • Just Another Song About The Country Sung By A City Boy • When I've Been Drinkin' • Old Time Shimmy • Off To Denver • I Think It Was The Wine • Reed Zone (Psychiatric Institution Blues) • Blow Out The Candle

### SILENCERS, The
Rock group from Pittsburgh: Frank Czuri (vocals), Warren King (guitar), Dennis Takos (keyboards), Michael Pella (bass) and Ronnie Foster (drums).

| | | | | | |
|---|---|---|---|---|---|
| 8/16/80 | 207 | 3 | Rock 'N' Roll Enforcers ............................................................. $10 | | Precision 36529 |

Modern Love • Head On Collision • Remote Control • Illegal • Johnny Too Bad • Peter Gunn Theme • Shiver And Shake • Take Out Service • Cold Sweat • I Can't Believe It

### SILICON TEENS ☉
Group is actually solo synthesizer player Daniel Miller.

| | | | | | |
|---|---|---|---|---|---|
| 8/16/80 | 205 | 1 | Music For Parties .................................................................... $10 | | Sire 6092 |

Memphis Tennessee • Yesterday Man • Do Wah Diddy Diddy • T.V. Playtime • You Really Got Me • Chip 'N Roll • Do You Love Me • Let's Dance • Oh Boy! • Sweet Little Sixteen • State Of Shock (Part Two) • Just Like Eddie • Red River Rock • Judy In Disguise

| DEBUT | PEAK | WKS | Album Title | $ | Label & Number |
|-------|------|-----|-----------|---|----------------|

**SILK** ○
Disco studio group from Philadelphia. Vocals by Debra Henry.

| | | | | | |
|---|---|---|---|---|---|
| 8/6/77 | 208 | 2 | Smooth As Silk ........................................................... | $12 | Prelude 12145 |

I Know I Didn't Do You Wrong • Giving Yourself To Me • Leaving Me • Call Me • Live While You Can • Party Pt. 1+2 • Ain't No Need Of Crying • On Fire • Let Him Go

**SILVER CONVENTION**
Disco studio group from Germany. Vocals by Penny McLean, Ramona Wolf and Linda Thompson.

| | | | | | |
|---|---|---|---|---|---|
| 8/12/78 | 208 | 1 | Love In A Sleeper ......................................................... | $10 | Midsong Int'l. 3038 |

Spend The Night With Me • Acuestate Conmigo • Love In A Sleeper • Mission To Venus • Get It Up • Take Me, Shake Me, Wake Me • Breakfast In Bed • City In The Sun

**SILVERHEAD** ○
British rock group: Michael Des Barres (vocals), Robbie Blunt and Rod Rook Davies (guitars), Nigel Harrison (bass) and Pete Thompson (drums).

| | | | | | |
|---|---|---|---|---|---|
| 3/9/74 | 215 | 4 | 16 And Savaged ............................................................ | $12 | MCA 391 |

Hello New York • More Than Your Mouth Can Hold • Only You • Bright Light • Heavy Hammer • Cartoon Princess • Rock Out Claudette Rock Out • This Ain't A Parody • 16 And Savaged

**SIMON, Joe**
Born on 9/2/43 in Simmesport, Louisiana. R&B singer.

| | | | | | |
|---|---|---|---|---|---|
| 10/27/73 | 207 | 5 | Simon Country ............................................................. | $12 | Spring 5705 |

Do You Know What It's Like To Be Lonesome? • Five Hundred Miles • Woman Without Love • You Don't Know Me • To Get To You • Before The Next Teardrop Falls • Someone To Give My Love To • Good Things • Kiss An Angel Good Mornin'

**SINATRA, Frank**
Born Francis Albert Sinatra on 12/12/15 in Hoboken, New Jersey. Died of a heart attack on 5/14/98. Regarded by many as the greatest popular singer of all time. Acted in numerous movies. Own TV show in 1957. Won Grammy's Lifetime Achievement Award in 1965. Married to actress Ava Gardner from 1951-57. Married to actress Mia Farrow from 1966-68. Father of **Nancy Sinatra**. *Top Pop Albums*: 70.

| | | | | | |
|---|---|---|---|---|---|
| 8/3/74 | 202 | 3 | One More For The Road ..................................[K] | $12 | Capitol 11309 |

Come Fly With Me • All The Way • Love Is Here To Stay • Violets For Your Furs • Just In Time • I've Got You Under My Skin • All My Tomorrows • On The Sunny Side Of The Street • One For My Baby (And One More For The Road) • All Of Me

**SINATRA, Nancy, & Lee Hazlewood**
Sinatra was born on 6/8/40 in Jersey City, New Jersey. Daughter of **Frank Sinatra**. Hazlewood was born on 7/9/29 in Mannford, Oklahoma. Male singer/songwriter/producer.

| | | | | | |
|---|---|---|---|---|---|
| 2/26/72 | 213 | 1 | Nancy & Lee Again ........................................................ | $12 | RCA Victor 4645 |

Arkansas Coal (Suite) • Big Red Balloon • Friendship Train • Paris Summer • Congratulations • Down From Dover • Did You Ever? • Tippy Toes • Back On The Road • Got It Together

**SINCEROS, The** ○
New wave group: Mark Kjeldsen (vocals, guitar), Don Snow (keyboards), Ron Francois (bass) and Bobby Irwin (drums).

| | | | | | |
|---|---|---|---|---|---|
| 9/29/79 | 207 | 1 | The Sound Of Sunbathing ................................................. | $10 | Columbia 36134 |

Take Me To Your Leader • Worlds Apart • Little White Lie • So They Know • Hanging On Too Long • I Still Miss You • Quick, Quick Slow • My Little Letter • Break Her Heart • Good Luck (To You)

**SLICK, Grace**
Born Grace Wing on 10/30/39 in Chicago. Female lead singer of The Great Society and Jefferson Airplane/Starship.

| | | | | | |
|---|---|---|---|---|---|
| 2/6/71 | 201 | 1 | 1 Grace Slick & The Great Society ........................[K] | $20 | Columbia 30459 [2] |

Sally Go 'Round The Roses • Didn't Think So • Grimly Forming • Somebody To Love • Father Bruce • Outlaw Blues • Often As I May • Arbitration • White Rabbit • That's How It Is • Darkly Smiling • Nature Boy • You Can't Cry • Daydream Nightmare • Everybody Knows • Born To Be Burned • Father

| | | | | | |
|---|---|---|---|---|---|
| 3/10/84 | 206 | 3 | 2 Software ................................................................ | $10 | RCA Victor 4791 |

Call It Right Call It Wrong • Me And Me • All The Machines • Fox Face • Through The Window • It Just Won't Stop • Habits • Rearrange My Face • Bikini Atoll

**SMITH, Lonnie Liston**
Born on 12/28/40 in Richmond, Virginia. Jazz keyboardist/trumpeter.

| | | | | | |
|---|---|---|---|---|---|
| 10/13/79 | 208 | 2 | 1 A Song For The Children ............................................. | $10 | Columbia 36141 |

A Song For The Children • A Lover's Dream • Aquarian Cycle • Street Festival • Midsummer Magic • Nightlife • A Gift Of Love • Fruit Music

| | | | | | |
|---|---|---|---|---|---|
| 5/17/80 | 202 | 2 | 2 Love Is The Answer .................................................. | $10 | Columbia 36373 |

James Robinson (vocals, above 2)

In The Park • Love Is The Answer • Speak About It • Bridge Through Time • On The Real Side • The Enchantress • Give Peace A Chance (Make Love Not War) • Free And Easy

**SMITH, Steve** ○
Born in Boston. Drummer for Journey and The Storm. Vital Information is a jazz fusion group: Eef Albers and Dean Brown (guitars), Dave Wilczewski (sax) and Tim Landers (bass).

| | | | | | |
|---|---|---|---|---|---|
| 6/16/84 | 209 | 2 | Orion ....................................................[I] | $10 | Columbia 39375 |

**STEVE SMITH/VITAL INFORMATION**

Future Primitive • Thank You Mr. Edison • The Strut • Orion • Blade • The Adventures Of Hector And Jose • Shadows Past • Blues To Bappe II

**SMITHER, Chris** ○
Born on 11/11/44 in New Orleans. Singer/songwriter/guitarist.

| | | | | | |
|---|---|---|---|---|---|
| 2/13/71 | 204 | 1 | I'm A Stranger Too! ...................................................... | $12 | Poppy 40013 |

A Short While Ago • A Song For Susan • I Am A Child • Have You Seen My Baby • Devil Got Your Man • Homunculus • Love You Like A Man • Lonely Time • Look Down The Road • Old Kentucky Home (Turpentine And Dandelion Wine) • Time To Go Home

### SMOKE RISE ⊙
Progressive-rock group: brothers Gary (guitar), Hank (keyboards) and Stan (drums) Ruffin, with Randy Bugg (bass).

| 8/14/71 | 203 | 4 | **The Survival Of St. Joan** .................................................... $20 | | Paramount 9000 [2] |

a rock opera based on speculation that Joan of Arc survived

Survival • Someone Is Dying • Run, Run • Back In The World • I'm Here • Love Me • Stonefire • Love Me • Lady Of Light • Country Life • Run, Run • Precious Mommy • Medley: Survival/Run, Run/Back In The World • Lonely Neighbors • Cornbread • This Is How It Is • Cannonfire • It's Over • Darkwoods Lullaby • You Don't Know Why • Propitius • Burning A Witch • Love Me

### SMOKEY
British pop-rock group: Chris Norman (vocals, guitar), Alan Silson (guitar), Terry Utley (bass) and Pete Spencer (drums).

| 9/13/75 | 206 | 1 | **Smokey**.................................................... $12 | | MCA 2152 |

Pass It Around • Don't Play Your Rock N' Roll To Me • If You Think You Know How To Love Me • Give It To Me • Changing All The Time • We're Flying High • Don't Turn Out Your Light • Umbrella Day • Take Me In • Going Tomorrow

### SNIFF 'n' the TEARS
British rock group: Paul Roberts (vocals), Loz Netto and Mick Dyche (guitars), Mike Taylor (keyboards), Nick South (bass) and Paul Robinson (drums).

| 7/5/80 | 205 | 2 | **The Game's Up** .................................................... $10 | | Atlantic 19272 |

The Game's Up • Moment Of Weakness • What Can Daddy Do • Nightlife • If I Knew Then • One Love • 5 & Zero • Poison Pen Mail • Rodeo Drive

### SNOW, Phoebe
Born Phoebe Laub on 7/17/52 in New York City; raised in New Jersey. Singer/songwriter/guitarist.

| 11/20/76 | 202 | 4 | **Phoebe Snow**....................................................[R] $12 | | Shelter 52017 |

originally released in 1974 on Shelter 2109 (#4)

Good Times • Harpo's Blues • Poetry Man • Either Or Both • San Francisco Bay Blues • I Don't Want The Night To End • Take Your Children Home • It Must Be Sunday • No Show Tonight

### SOFT MACHINE
Experimental-rock group from Canterbury, England: Mike Ratledge (keyboards), Karl Jenkins (sax), Hugh Hopper (bass) and John Marshall (drums).

| 6/23/73 | 210 | 4 | **Six** ....................................................[I-L] $15 | | Columbia 32260 [2] |

record 1: recorded "live" in London; record 2: studio recording

Fanfare • All White • Between • Riff • 37 • Gesolreut • E.P.V. • Lefty • Stumble • 5 From 13 (For Phil Seamen With Love And Thanks) • Riff II • The Soft Weed Factor • Stanley Stamps Gibbon Album • Chloe And The Pirates • 1983

### SOME, Belouis ⊙
Born Neville Keighley in England. Techno-rock singer/multi-instrumentalist.

| 6/1/85 | 201 | 6 | **Some People** .................................................... $10 | | Capitol 12345 |

Some People • Stand Down • Imagination • Walk Away • Aware Of You • Target Practice • Have You Ever Been In Love • Tail Lights • Jerusalem

### SONS OF CHAMPLIN, The
Rock group from San Francisco: Bill Champlin (vocals, keyboards), Terry Haggerty (guitar), Geoffrey Palmer (keyboards), Phil Wood, Mark Isham and Michael Andreas (horns), David Schallock (bass) and James Preston (drums). Champlin joined Chicago in 1982.

| 10/11/75 | 207 | 5 | **The Sons Of Champlin**.................................................... $12 | | Ariola America 50002 |

Lookout • I'd Like To Get To Know You • Marp Interlude • Planet Ripper • All And Everything • Without Love • Rainbow's End • Geoff's Vibe • Queen Of The Rain • Gold Mine

### SOPWITH CAMEL
Pop-rock group from San Francisco: Peter Kraemer (vocals, sax), Terry MacNeil (guitar), Martin Beard (bass) and Norman Mayell (drums). Named after a type of airplane used in World War I.

| 10/20/73 | 203 | 6 | **The Miraculous Hump Returns From The Moon**.................................................... $25 | | Reprise 2108 |

Fazon • Coke, Suede And Waterbeds • Dancin' Wizard • Sleazy Street • Orange Peel • Oriental Fantasy • Sneaky Smith • Monkeys On The Moon • Astronaut Food • Brief Synthophonia

### SORENSEN, Jacki — see AEROBIC ALBUMS

### SOUL CHILDREN
R&B vocal group: Anita Louis, Shelbra Bennett, John Colbert and Norman West. Colbert later recorded as J. Blackfoot.

| 3/25/72 | 203 | 1 | **Best Of Two Worlds** .................................................... $25 | | Stax 2043 |

Bring It Here • Thanks For A Precious Nothing • Put Your World In My World • Give Me One Good Reason Why • Got To Get Away From It All • The Hang Ups Of Holding On • Wrap It Up Tonight • Let's Make A Sweet Thing Sweeter • Finish Me Off • Don't Break Away

### SOUL SEARCHERS, The
R&B-funk group from Washington, D.C.: Chuck Brown (vocals, guitar), Hilton Selton (organ), Lino Druitt (congas), John Buchanan, Lloyd Pinchback and Donald Tillery (horns), John Euell (bass) and Ken Scoggins (drums).

| 3/10/73 | 210 | 3 | **We The People** .................................................... $15 | | Sussex 7020 |

We The People • Your Love Is So Doggone Good • It's All In Your Mind • Soul To The People • Think • 1993 • When Will My Eyes See • Blowout

### SOUTH, Joe
Born Joe Souter on 2/28/40 in Atlanta. Country-pop singer/songwriter.

| 12/11/71 | 207 | 2 | **Joe South** .................................................... $15 | | Capitol 845 |

High On A Hilltop • Birds Of A Feather • For The Love Of A Woman • Rose Garden • Yo Yo • Fool Me • How Can I Unlove You • You Need Me • She's Almost You • Devil May Care

## SOUTHER, J.D.
Born John David Souther in Detroit; raised in Amarillo, Texas. Country-rock singer/songwriter.

9/23/72 | **206** | 3 — 1 **John David Souther** ............................................................ $12 — Asylum 5055
The Fast One • Run Like A Thief • Jesus In 3/4 Time • Kite Woman • Some People Call It Music • White Wing • It's The Same • How Long • Out To Sea • Lullaby

9/1/84 | **203** | 6 — 2 **Home By Dawn** ................................................................ $10 — Warner 25081
guests include Don Henley
Home By Dawn • Go Ahead And Rain • Say You Will • I'll Take Care Of You • All For You • Night • Don't Know What I'm Gonna Do • Bad News Travels Fast • All I Want

## SOUTH SHORE COMMISSION ☉
R&B group from Washington, D.C. Lead vocals by Frank McCurry and Sheryl Henry.

12/27/75+ | **205** | 5 — **South Shore Commission** ...................................................... $12 — Wand 6100
Handle With Care • Before You've Gone • I'd Rather Switch Than Fight • Free Man • We're On The Right Track • Just A Matter Of Time • Train Called Freedom • Any Day Now

## SOUTHSIDE MOVEMENT ☉
R&B group from Chicago.

8/25/73 | **207** | 1 — **The South Side Movement** ..................................................... $15 — Wand 695
I' Been Watchin' You • Love Turned Me Loose • La Dee Da • Have A Little Mercy • Can You Get To That • You're Gonna Lose My Love • Come On And Love Me • Everlasting Thrill • Superstition • Mud Wind

## SPACEK, Sissy ☉
Born Mary Elizabeth Spacek on 12/25/49 in Quitman, Texas. Actress/singer. Starred in several movies.

9/24/83 | **204** | 5 — **Hangin' Up My Heart** ......................................................... $10 — Atlantic America 90100
Hangin' Up My Heart • Have I Told You Lately That I Love You • He Don't Know Me • Lonely But Only For You • This Time I'm Gonna Beat You To The Truck • Honky Tonkin' • Old Home Town • Smooth Talkin' Daddy • If You Could Only See Me Now • If I Can Just Get Though The Night

## SPANDAU BALLET
Pop-rock group from London: brothers Gary (guitar) and Martin (bass) Kemp, Tony Hadley (vocals), Steve Norman (guitar) and John Keeble (drums). The Kemps starred in the 1990 movie *The Krays*. Gary Kemp, later in *The Bodyguard*, married actress Sadie Frost (of the 1992 movie *Bram Stoker's Dracula*).

5/16/81 | **209** | 1 — **Journeys To Glory** ........................................................... $10 — Chrysalis 1331
To Cut A Long Story Short • Reformation • Mandolin • Muscle Bound • Age Of Blows • The Freeze • Confused • Toys

## SPANOS, Danny ☉
Rock singer/songwriter.

9/24/83 | **201** | 6 — 1 **Passion In The Dark** [M] $10 — Epic 38805
One Track Heart (Passion In The Dark) • Hot Cherie • Excuse Me • Slice Of Life • Anita

3/16/85 | **208** | 1 — 2 **Looks Like Trouble** .......................................................... $10 — Epic 39459
I'd Lie To You For Your Love • Change Of Heart • Wherever There's Smoke (There's Fire) • Lorraine • Excuse Me • Comin' True • Are You Ready Now? • Molly • Looks Like Trouble • Good Girl

## SPARKS
Rock duo from Los Angeles: brothers Russell (vocals) and Ron (keyboards) Mael.

6/2/79 | **204** | 8 — 1 **No. 1 In Heaven** ............................................................. $10 — Elektra 186
Tryouts For The Human Race • Academy Award Performance • La Dolce Vita • Beat The Clock • My Other Voice • The No. 1 Song In Heaven

8/4/84 | **202** | 4 — 2 **Pulling Rabbits Out Of A Hat** ............................................... $10 — Atlantic 80160
Pulling Rabbits Out Of A Hat • Love Scenes • Pretending To Be Drunk • Progress • With All My Might • Sparks In The Dark (Part One) • Everybody Move • A Song That Sings Itself • Sisters • Kiss Me Quick • Sparks In The Dark (Part Two)

## SPECIMEN ☉
Rock group from London: Ollie Wisdom (vocals), Jon Klein (guitar), Jonny Melton (keyboards), Kev Mills (bass) and Jonathan Trevenous (drums).

2/11/84 | **207** | 1 — **Batastrophe** ................................................................ [M] $10 — Sire 25054
The Beauty Of Poisin • Syria • Kiss Kiss Bang Bang • Returning From A Journey • Tell Tail • Lovers

## SPEEDY KEEN — see KEEN, Speedy

## SPENCER, Jeremy ☉
Born on 7/4/48 in Lancashire, England. Rock singer/guitarist. Member of Fleetwood Mac from 1967-70.

9/8/79 | **208** | 2 — **Flee** ........................................................................ $10 — Atlantic 19236
THE JEREMY SPENCER BAND
Deeper • Sunshine • Love Our Way Outta Here • Flee • Cool Breeze • You've Got The Right • Travellin'

## SPINNERS
R&B vocal group from Detroit: John Edwards, Bobbie Smith, Billy Henderson, Henry Fambrough and Pervis Jackson.

4/28/84 | **201** | 7 — **Cross Fire** $10 — Atlantic 80150
Two Of A Kind • Right Or Wrong • (We Have Come Into) Our Time For Love • Cross Fire • Keep On Keepin' On • Not Just Another Lover • Love Is In Season • All Your Love • Secrets

## SPINOZZA, David ☉
Singer/songwriter/guitarist from New Jersey.

4/8/78 | **202** | 13 — **Spinozza** ................................................................... $10 — A&M 4677
Superstar • On My Way To The Liquor Store • Prelude To "The Ballerina" • The Ballerina • Edge Of The Sword • Country Bumpkin • Doesn't She Know By Now • Airborne • High Button Shoes

### SPIRIT
Rock group from Los Angeles: Jay Ferguson (vocals, guitar), Randy California (guitar), John Locke (keyboards), Mark Andes (bass) and Ed Cassidy (drums). California drowned on 1/2/97 near Molokai, Hawaii (age 45).

| 9/1/84 | 206 | 1 | **Spirit Of '84** ........................................................................ | $10 | Mercury 818514 |

Black Satin Nights • Mr. Skin • Mechanical World • Pick It Up • All Over The World • 1984 • Uncle Jack • Nature's Way • Fresh Garbage • I Got A Line On You

### SPLINTER
British vocal duo: Bill Elliott and Bob Purvis.

| 11/8/75+ | 202 | 9 | **Harder To Live** ...................................................................... | $12 | Dark Horse 22006 |

guests include George Harrison, **Billy Preston** and Tom Scott
Please Help Me • Sixty Miles Too Far • Harder To Live • Half Way There • Which Way Will I Get Home • Berkley House Hotel • After Five Years • Green Line Bus • Lonely Man • What Is It (If You Never Ever Tried It Yourself)

### SPORTS, The
Pop-rock group from Melbourne, Australia: Stephen Cummings (vocals), Andrew Pendlebury and Martin Armiger (guitars), James Niven (keyboards), Robert Glover (bass) and Paul Hitchins (drums).

| 8/16/80 | 207 | 1 | **Suddenly...** .......................................................................... | $10 | Arista 4266 |

Suddenly • No Mama No • Between Us • Go • Strangers On A Train • It Hurts • Murmurs • I Tried To Love Her • Blue Hearts • Perhaps • The Lost And The Lonely • Never Catch Her

### SPRINGFIELD, Dusty
Born Mary O'Brien on 4/16/39 in London. Pop singer.

| 3/24/73 | 212 | 2 | **Cameo** ................................................................................. | $15 | Dunhill 50128 |

Who Gets Your Love • Breakin' Up A Happy Home • Easy Evil • Mama's Little Girl • The Other Side Of Love • Comin' And Goin' • I Just Wanna Be There • Who Could Be Loving You Other Than Me • Of All The Things • Tupelo Honey • Learn To Say Goodbye

### STACKRIDGE
British rock group: Andy Davis (vocals, guitar), Mutter Slater (flute), Keith Gemmell (sax), Rod Bowkett (keyboards), Paul Karas (bass) and Roy Morgan (drums).

| 11/1/75 | 209 | 1 | **Extravaganza** ........................................................................ | $12 | Sire 7509 |

The Volunteer • Rufus T. Firefly • No One's More Important Than The Earth Worm • Greasepaint Smiles • Happy In The Lord • Benjamin's Giant Onion • Pocket Billiards • The Indifferent Hedgehog • Do The Stanley • Who's That Up There With Bill Stokes?

### STAIRSTEPS
R&B vocal group from Chicago: brothers Clarence, Dennis, Kenneth and James Burke. Previously known as The Five Stairsteps.

| 4/3/76 | 203 | 4 | **2nd Ressurection** ................................................................... | $12 | Dark Horse 22004 |

From Us To You • Pasado • Theme Of Angels • Lifting 2nd Resurrection • Time • Throwin' Stones Atcha • Far East • In The Beginning • Tell Me Why • Salaam

### STAMPLEY, Joe — see BANDY, Moe

### STANLEY, Michael
Born Michael Stanley Gee on 3/25/48 in Cleveland. Rock singer/guitarist.

| 5/5/73 | 206 | 4 | 1 **Michael Stanley** ................................................................. | $15 | Tumbleweed 106 |

guests include **Todd Rundgren** and Joe Walsh
Rosewood Bitters • Denver Rain • Louisville A.D. • A Friend And Nothing More • Rock And Roll Man • Moving Right Along • Resurrection • Good Time Charlie • Song For A Friend Soon Gone • Subterranean Homesick Blues

| 2/16/74 | 207 | 4 | 2 **Friends & Legends** ............................................................. | $12 | MCA 372 |

guests include **Dan Fogelberg** and Joe Walsh
Among My Friends Again • Help • Yours For A Song • Let's Get The Show On The Road • Just Keep Playing Your Radio • Roll On • Bad Habits • Funky Is The Drummer • Poets' Day

| 4/30/77 | 207 | 2 | 3 **Stagepass** ....................................................... [L] | $12 | Epic 34661 [2] |

**THE MICHAEL STANLEY BAND**
recorded 10/22 - 10/24/76 at the Agora Ballroom in Cleveland
Midwest Midnight • One Good Reason • Real Good Time • Nothing's Gonna Change My Mind • Calcutta Auction • Movin' Right Along • Will You Love Me Tomorrow • Waste A Little Time On Me • Pierette • Rosewood Bitters • Wild Sanctuary • Let's Get The Show On The Road • Strike Up The Band

### STARGARD
Female disco vocal trio: Rochelle Runnells, Debra Anderson and Janice Williams. Appeared as "The Diamonds" in the movie *Sgt. Pepper's Lonely Hearts Club Band*.

| 12/2/78 | 206 | 1 | **What You Waitin' For** ............................................................ | $10 | MCA 3064 |

Sensuous Woman • Blue Rain • Disco People • What You Waitin' For • Never Take You Back • Starbob • Love Me Back • How Come I Can't See You • Chameleon Lady

### STARLAND VOCAL BAND
Pop vocal group from Washington, D.C.: husband-and-wife Bill and Taffy Danoff, with future husband-and-wife Jonathan Carroll and Margot Chapman. Won the 1976 Best New Artist Grammy.

| 4/15/78 | 208 | 3 | **Late Nite Radio** .................................................................... | $10 | Windsong 2598 |

Late Nite Radio • Don't Go To Oregon • The Man Who Couldn't Get Away • Akron • Fly Away • Write Your Life • Third Rate Romance • Everyman • Please Ms. Newslady • Friends With You

### STARPOINT
R&B group from Maryland: brothers George (male vocals), Ernesto (guitar), Orlando (bass) and Gregory (drums) Phillips, with Renee Diggs (female vocals) and Kayode Adeyemo (percussion).

| 9/4/82 | 208 | 1 | **All Night Long** ...................................................................... | $10 | Chocolate City 2022 |

Bring Your Sweet Lovin' Back • Get Your Body Up • All Night Long • Show Me • I Like It • I Can Give You Love • Miracle Love • It's You

### STARR, Edwin
Born Charles Hatcher on 1/21/42 in Nashville; raised in Cleveland. R&B singer.

| | | | | | |
|---|---|---|---|---|---|
| 1/24/76 | 210 | 1 | **1 Free To Be Myself** ........................................ | $12 | Granite 1005 |

Stay With Me • Abyssinia Jones • Toys • Drunk Annie • Rainbow • Another Song For You • Best Of My Past • Beginning • Pain • Party

| | | | | | |
|---|---|---|---|---|---|
| 5/17/80 | 203 | 5 | **2 Stronger Than You Think I Am** ............................ | $10 | 20th Century 615 |

Never Turn My Back On You • Tell-A-Star • Sweet • Upside Of Down • Bigger And Better • Stronger Than You Think I Am • Get Up-Whirlpool • Boop Boop Song

### STARR, Ruby, And Grey Ghost ○
Starr was born Constance Mierzwiak. Died of cancer on 1/14/95 (age 44). Grey Ghost is her backing band.

| | | | | | |
|---|---|---|---|---|---|
| 9/27/75 | 206 | 1 | **Ruby Starr And Grey Ghost** ................................ | $12 | Capitol 11427 |

Burnin' Whiskey • Sweet, Sweet, Sweet • Witchin' Hour • Did It Again • Everything Comes And Goes • Long Wait • You Need A Chain • Fork In The Road • Living Proof

### STARZ
Rock group from New York City: Michael Lee Smith (vocals), Richie Ranno and Bobby Messano (guitars), Orville Davis (bass) and Joe X. Dube (drums). Smith is the brother of singer/actor Rex Smith.

| | | | | | |
|---|---|---|---|---|---|
| 12/9/78 | 208 | 1 | **Coliseum Rock** ............................................ | $10 | Capitol 11861 |

So Young, So Bad • Take Me • No Regrets • My Sweet Child • Don't Stop Now • Outfit • Last Night I Wrote A Letter • Coliseum Rock • It's A Riot • Where Will It End

### STATLER BROTHERS, The
Country vocal group from Staunton, Virginia: brothers Harold and Don Reid, Phil Balsley and Lew DeWitt. DeWitt died of Crohn's disease on 8/15/90 (age 52).

| | | | | | |
|---|---|---|---|---|---|
| 7/17/82 | 201 | 5 | **The Legend Goes On...** | $10 | Mercury 4048 |

Whatever • I Had Too Much To Dream • I Don't Know Why • Life's Railway To Heaven • How Do You Like Your Dream So Far • A Child Of The Fifties • That's When It Comes Home To You • I Don't Dance No More • What You Are To Me • (I'll Love You) All Over Again

### STATUS QUO, The
Rock group from London: Francis Rossi (vocals), Richard Parfitt (guitar), Alan Lancaster (bass) and John Coghlan (drums).

| | | | | | |
|---|---|---|---|---|---|
| 9/14/74 | 201 | 8 | **1 Quo** | $15 | A&M 3649 |

Backwater • Just Take Me • Break The Rules • Drifting Away • Don't Think It Matters • Fine Fine Fine • Lonely Man • Slow Train

| | | | | | |
|---|---|---|---|---|---|
| 4/5/75 | 205 | 7 | **2 On The Level** ............................................ | $12 | Capitol 11381 |

Little Lady • Most Of The Time • I Saw The Light • Over And Done • Nightride • Down Down • Broken Man • What To Do • Where I Am • Bye Bye Johnny

### STEALERS WHEEL
Pop-rock duo from Scotland: Gerry Rafferty (vocals, guitar) and Joe Egan (vocals, keyboards).

| | | | | | |
|---|---|---|---|---|---|
| 5/10/75 | 201 | 6 | **Right Or Wrong** | $12 | A&M 4517 |

Benediction • Found My Way To You • This Morning • Let Yourself Go • Home From Home • Go As You Please • Wishbone • Don't Get Me Wrong • Monday Morning • Right Or Wrong

### STEELE, Maureen ○
Female dance singer.

| | | | | | |
|---|---|---|---|---|---|
| 6/8/85 | 210 | 1 | **Nature Of The Beast** ...................................... | $10 | Motown 6141 |

Nature Of The Beast • Physical Therapy • Save The Night For Me • Sneak Preview • Rock My Heart • Bad Girls Do It Better • Sidetracked • Do You Like It When I Hurt You • My Shy Lover • Boys Will Be Boys

### STEELEYE SPAN
Folk group from England: Maddy Prior (female vocals), Tim Hart (male vocals, guitar), Robert Johnson (guitar), Peter Knight (mandolin), Rick Kemp (bass) and Nigel Pegrum (drums).

| | | | | | |
|---|---|---|---|---|---|
| 5/12/73 | 201 | 6 | **1 Parcel Of Rogues** | $15 | Chrysalis 1046 |

One Misty Moisty Morning • Alison Gross • The Bold Poachers • The Ups And Downs • Robbery With Violins • The Wee Wee Man • The Weaver And The Factory Maid • Rogues In A Nation • Cam Ye O'er Frae France • Hares On The Mountain

| | | | | | |
|---|---|---|---|---|---|
| 4/27/74 | 208 | 3 | **2 Now We Are Six** ........................................ | $15 | Chrysalis 1053 |

Thomas The Rhymer • Two Magicians • Edwin • Twinkle Twinkle Little Star • Seven Hundered Elves • The Mooncoin Jig • Drink Down The Moon • Long-A-Growing • Now We Are Six • To Know Him Is To Love Him

| | | | | | |
|---|---|---|---|---|---|
| 10/30/76 | 205 | 4 | **3 Rocket Cottage** ........................................ | $15 | Chrysalis 1123 |

London • The Bosnian Hornpipes • Medley: Orfeo/Nathan's Reel • The Twelve Witches • The Brown Girl • Fighting For Strangers • Sligo Maid • Sir James The Rose • The Drunkard

### STEVENS, Shakin' ○
Born Michael Barratt on 3/4/48 in Ely, Wales. Rockabilly singer/songwriter.

| | | | | | |
|---|---|---|---|---|---|
| 6/19/82 | 210 | 1 | **You Drive Me Crazy** ...................................... | $10 | Epic 38022 |

You Drive Me Crazy • This Ole House • Marie, Marie • Let Me Show You How • Green Door • Hot Dog • Baby You're A Child • It's Raining • Hey Mae • Make It Right Tonight

### STEVENSON, B.W.
Born Louis Stevenson on 10/5/49 in Dallas. Died on 4/28/88 after heart surgery. B.W. is short for Buck Wheat.

| | | | | | |
|---|---|---|---|---|---|
| 5/27/72 | 206 | 1 | **1 B.W. Stevenson** ........................................ | $15 | RCA Victor 4685 |

Save A Little Time For Love • Lonesome Song • Wasted Too Much Time • Long Way To Go • Highway One • Two Track Road • Say What I Feel • Texas Morning • Home Again • On My Own

| | | | | | |
|---|---|---|---|---|---|
| 4/20/74 | 206 | 2 | **2 Calabasas** ............................................ | $15 | RCA Victor 0410 |

Look For The Light • Little Bit Of Understanding • We Had It All • (Livin' It) Day By Day • Dry Land • Anna-Lisa • Please Come To Boston • Roll On • Song For Katy • Here We Go Again

| | | | | | |
|---|---|---|---|---|---|
| 2/28/76 | 201 | 1 | **3 We Be Sailin'** | $12 | Warner 2901 |

Way Down By The Ocean • East India Company • Dream Baby • Wastin' Time • Temper, Temper • Hold On • Jerry's Bar And Grill • Cold, Cold Winter • Kokomo • Quits

### STEWART, Amii
Born in 1956 in Washington, D.C. Disco singer/dancer/actress. In the Broadway musical *Bubbling Brown Sugar*.

11/24/79 — 207 — 3 — **Paradise Bird** ...................................................................................... $10 — Ariola America 50072
The Letter • Paradise Bird • He's A Burglar • Jealousy • Right Place, Wrong Time • Step Into The Love Line • Paradise Found

### STEWART, John
Born on 9/5/39 in San Diego. Singer/songwriter/guitarist. Member of The Kingston Trio from 1961-67.

4/28/73 — 202 — 6 — 1 **Cannons In The Rain** ................................................................. $12 — RCA Victor 4827
Durango • Chilly Winds • Easy Money • Anna On A Memory • All Time Woman • Road Away • Armstrong • Spirit • Wind Dies Down • Cannons In The Rain • Lady And The Outlaw

1/22/83 — 210 — 1 — 2 **Blondes** ..................................................................................... $10 — Allegiance 431
Tall Blonds • The Queen Of Hollywood High • Girl Down The River • The Eyes Of Sweet Virginia • Judy In G Major • You Won't Be Going Home • Jenny Was A Dream Girl • Blonde Star • Golden Gate • Angeles (The City Of The Angels)

### STEWART, Rod
Born on 1/10/45 in London. Pop-rock singer/songwriter. Member of **Faces** from 1969-75. Won Grammy's Living Legends Award in 1989. Married to actress Alana Hamilton from 1979-84. Married supermodel Rachel Hunter on 12/15/90. Inducted into the Rock and Roll Hall of Fame in 1994. *Top Pop Albums*: 26.

12/11/76 — 202 — 9 — **The Best Of Rod Stewart Vol. 2** .............................................[K] $15 — Mercury 7508 [2]
Man Of Constant Sorrow • Blind Prayer • Lady Day • Tomorrow Is A Long Time • Country Comforts • Mandolin Wind • That's All Right • My Way Of Giving • I Don't Want To Discuss It • Find A Reason To Believe • Italian Girls • I'd Rather Go Blind • Lost Paraguayos • True Blue • Sweet Little Rock 'N Roller • Hard Road • (You Make Me Feel Like) A Natural Man • Medley: Bring It On Home To Me/You Send Me • Twistin' The Night Away

### STEWART, Sandy ❂
Background singer and session musician for Stevie Nicks.

3/31/84 — 208 — 2 — **Cat Dancer** ............................................................................... $10 — Modern 90133
guests include Stevie Nicks
Cat Dancers • Get My Way • Think Of Me • Living End • Saddest Victory • Not Like The Others • I Pretend • Mind Over Matter • Leave It All Behind

### STILLWATER ❂
Southern-rock group from Warner Robins, Georgia: Jimmy Hall (vocals; not to be confused with leader of Wet Willie), Bobby Golden, Michael Causey and Rob Walker (guitars), Bob Spearman (keyboards), Allison Scarborough (bass) and Sebie Lacey (drums).

2/10/79 — 204 — 1 — **I Reserve The Right** .................................................................. $10 — Capricorn 0210
I Reserve The Right • Women (Beautiful Women) • Keeping Myself Alive • Kalifornia Kool • Sometimes Sunshine • Fair Warning • Alone On A Saturday Night • Ain't We A Pair

### STING — see SOUNDTRACKS (BRIMSTONE & TREACLE)

### STONEBOLT ❂
Pop-rock group from Vancouver: David Wills (vocals), Ray Roper (guitar), John Webster (keyboards), Danny Atchison (bass) and Brian Lousley (drums).

8/12/78 — 210 — 1 — 1 **Stonebolt** .................................................................................. $12 — Parachute 9006
Was It You • I Will Still Love You • One Man's Heartache • Sail On • The Shadow • Do It Right (Do It Again) • Singin' In The Streets • Queen Of The Night • Stay In Line

1/17/81 — 206 — 1 — 2 **New Set Of Changes** ................................................................ $10 — RCA Victor 3825
Take The Time • You Don't Care • Crying Again Tonight • Landing In Love • Please Please Me • New Set Of Changes • Come And See Me • All By Myself • Here Comes The Rain • Midnight Angel

### STONE CITY BAND
R&B-funk group: Levi Ruffin (vocals), Tom McDermott (guitar), OBX and Erskine Williams (keyboards), Oscar Alston (bass) and Lanise Hughes (drums). Backing group for Rick James.

2/7/81 — 205 — 3 — **The Boys Are Back** ................................................................... $10 — Gordy 1001
produced by Rick James
All Day And All Of The Night • Feel Good 'Bout Yourself • Keep Love Happy • Ganja • Freaky • Funky Reggae • Lovin' You Is Easy • Tin Soldier

### STONEGROUND ❂
Folk-rock group from San Francisco: Lynne Hughes, Deirdre LaPorte, Lydia Moreno and Annie Sampson (female vocals), Brian Godula and Cory Lerios (male vocals), Tim Barnes and Sal Valentino (guitars), John Blakeley (bass) and Stephen Price (drums).

1/29/72 — 205 — 1 — **Family Album** ...........................................................................[L] $15 — Warner 1956 [2]
recorded on 8/8/71 in San Francisco
Get Rhythm • Passion Flower • Corina • Big River • Won't Be Long • Super Clown • Richland Woman • Queen Sweet Dreams • Precious Lord • It Takes A Lot To Laugh (It Takes A Train To Cry) • I Can't Help It • No Doreen • It's Not Easy • If You Gotta Go • Total Destruction To Your Mind • You Must Be One Of Us • All My Life • Where Will I Find Love • Gonna Have A Good Time • Jam It

### STOOKEY, Paul
Born on 12/30/37 in Baltimore. Member of Peter, Paul & Mary.

2/3/73 — 204 — 4 — **One Night Stand** ......................................................................[L] $12 — Warner 2674
Desert Island • House Song • Get Together • Hymn • Who Love The Girls • Wedding Song (There Is Love) • Weave Me The Sunshine • One Note Melody • Blessed • Edgar • Funky Monkey Pt. 1 • Mermaids • Holly (One Night Stand) • Jingle Bells

### STORCH, Jeremy ❂
Singer/songwriter/pianist.

2/13/71 — 209 — 1 — **From A Naked Window** ............................................................. $12 — RCA Victor 4445
Dream City • Playground • Old Man In The Sky • Message In The Wind • Lynn And Sue Are A Country • On The Right Road • Lady In The Sand • If You Are Going Home • I Feel A New Shadow • Delia

| DEBUT | PEAK | WKS | Album Title | $ | Label & Number |
|-------|------|-----|-------------|---|----------------|

### STORIES
Rock group from New York City: Ian Lloyd (vocals), Steve Love (guitars), Ken Bichel (keyboards), Kenny Aaronson (bass) and Bryan Madey (drums).

| 1/19/74 | 208 | 2 | Traveling Underground ........................................................................... | $12 | Kama Sutra 2078 |

**IAN LLOYD & STORIES**

Bridges • Soft Rain • Hard When You're So Far Away • If It Feels Good, Do It • Mammy Blue • Stories Untold • I Can't Understand It • Medley: Earthbound/Freefall • Traveling Underground

### STRANGLERS, The
Pop-rock group from Guildford, England: Hugh Cornwell (vocals, guitar), Dave Greenfield (keyboards), Jean-Jacques Burnel (bass) and Brian "Jet Black" Duffy (drums).

| 7/8/78 | 210 | 2 | Black And White ..................................................................................... | $10 | A&M 4706 |

Tank • Nice 'N' Sleazy • Outside Tokyo • Sweden (All Quiet On The Eastern Front) • Hey! (Rise Of The Robots) • Toiler Of The Sea • Curfew • Threatened • Medley: Do You Wanna/Death And Night And Blood (Yukio) • In The Shadows • Enough Time

### STRAY DOG ☉
Rock group: Snuffy Walden (vocals, guitar), Timmy Dulaine (guitar), Luis Cabaza (keyboards), Alan Roberts (bass) and Leslie Sampson (drums).

| 1/4/75 | 210 | 1 | While You're Down There ........................................................................ | $12 | Manticore 501 |

Calamity Jane • Bits & Pieces • Pieces • I Would • Words To Say Goodbye • Junkyard Angel • Very Well • Dreams & Junk • Worldwinds

### STREETS
Rock group: Steve Walsh (vocals, keyboards), Mike Slamer (guitar), Billy Greer (bass) and Tim Gehrt (drums). Walsh was co-founder of Kansas.

| 4/13/85 | 204 | 3 | Crimes In Mind ..................................................................................... | $10 | Atlantic 81246 |

Don't Look Back • The Nightmare Begins • Broken Glass • Hit 'N Run • Crimes In Mind • I Can't Wait • Gun Runner • Desiree • Rat Race • Turn My Head

### STUFF
Group of New York's top R&B session musicians: Richard Tee (keyboards), Gordon Edwards (bass), Cornell Dupree and **Eric Gale** (guitars), and Christopher Parker and Stephen Gadd (drums). Tee died of cancer on 7/21/93 (age 49). Gale died of cancer on 5/25/94 (age 55).

| 5/31/80 | 205 | 2 | Live In New York ........................................................................... [I-L] | $10 | Warner 3417 |

recorded at Mikells nightclub in New York City

Sometimes Bubba Gets Down • You Make It Easy • You're A Great Girl • Shuffle • Medley: Love The Stuff/Ain't No Mountain High Enough • Duck Soup • The Real McCoy

### STYLISTICS, The
R&B vocal group from Philadelphia: Russell Thompkins, Airrion Love, James Smith, James Dunn and Herb Murrell.

| 1/29/77 | 209 | 1 | 1 Once Upon A Jukebox ........................................................................ | $12 | H&L 69015 |

The Great Pretender • I Got It Bad And That Ain't Good • Only You (And You Alone) • Don't Get Around Much Anymore • My Funny Valentine • Don't Worry 'Bout Me • Unchained Melody • Satin Doll • After The Lights Go Down Low • Send For Me

| 9/19/81 | 210 | 1 | 2 Closer Than Close ........................................................................... | $10 | TSOP 37458 |

What's Your Name? • I've Got This Feeling • Mine All Mine • Habit • Searchin' • It's Only Love • Closer Than Close • Almost There

### STYX
Rock group from Chicago: Dennis DeYoung (vocals, keyboards), John Curulewski and James Young (guitars), and twin brothers Chuck (bass) and John (drums) Panozzo. John Panozzo died on 7/16/96 (age 47). In Greek mythology, Styx is a river in Hades.

| 10/7/72 | 207 | 4 | 1 Styx .................................................................................................. | $15 | Wooden Nickel 1008 |

Movement For The Common Man: Children Of The Land/Street Collage/Fanfare For The Common Man/Mother Nature's Matinee • Right Away • What Has Come Between Us • Best Thing • Quick Is The Beat Of My Heart • After You Leave Me

| 4/15/78 | 201 | 17 | 2 Best Of Styx .................................................................. [K] | $12 | Wooden Nickel 2250 |

You Need Love • Lady • I'm Gonna Make You Feel It • What Has Come Between Us • Southern Woman • Rock & Roll Feeling • Winner Take All • Best Thing • Witch Wolf • The Grove Of Eglantine • Man Of Miracles

| 7/5/80 | 201 | 7 | ● 3 Best Of Styx ............................................................. [K-R] | $10 | RCA Victor 3597 |

You Need Love • Lady • I'm Gonna Make You Feel It • What Has Come Between Us • Southern Woman • Rock & Roll Feeling • Winner Take All • Best Thing • Which Wolf • The Grove Of Eglantine • Man Of Miracles

### SUE ANN ☉
Born Sue Ann Carwell in Minneapolis. R&B singer.

| 8/22/81 | 208 | 4 | Sue Ann ............................................................................................... | $10 | Warner 3562 |

Let Me Let You Rock Me • I Wanna Be The One • Company • Close Dance • Really Not That Ready • My Baby, My • Don't Treat Me Like A Fool • Sweet Talk • Heartdreams • Don't Throw It All Away

### SUGAR BEARS, The ☉
Studio production by Jimmy Bowen. **Kim Carnes** wrote and performed vocals for the group. Based on General Foods' "Sugar Crisp" cereal character.

| 1/22/72 | 209 | 1 | Presenting The Sugar Bears ............................................................... | $20 | Big Tree 2009 |

Happiness Train • All Of My Life • Right On • Feather Balloon • Kinda Friendly Things • Love You've Been A Long Time Coming • You Are The One • The Two Of Us Together • It's A Good Day • Someone Like You • Anyone But You

### SUMAC, Yma ☉
Born Amy Camus in Peru. Female singer who created a sensation with her four-octave voice. Yma Sumac is Amy Camus spelled backwards.

| 4/8/72 | 205 | 3 | Miracles ............................................................................................... | $12 | London 608 |

Remember • Medicine Man • Let Me Hear You • Tree Of Life • Flame Tree • Zebra • Azure Sands • Look Around • Magenta Mountain • El Condor Pasa

### SUN
R&B-funk group from Dayton, Ohio: Byron Byrd (vocals), Sheldon Reynolds and Anthony Thompson (guitars), Dean Francis (keyboards), Ernie Knisley (percussion), Robert Arnold, Gary King and Larry Hatchet (horns), Don Taylor (bass), and Kym Yancey (drums).

| 7/5/80 | 207 | 3 | 1 Sun Over The Universe .................................................................. $10 | Capitol 12088 |
|--------|-----|---|--------------------------------------------------------------|---------------|

Space Ranger (Majic's In The Air) • Hot Spot • Stay By My Side • Quest • You Threw My Love Away • I Want Your Love • I Made A Mistake • Fancy Feet

| 5/9/81 | 205 | 4 | 2 Sun: Force Of Nature .................................................................. $10 | Capitol 12142 |

On My Radio • Jammin' En Brazil • Guiding Light • Love Baby Love • Reaction Satisfaction • Force Of Nature • It Seems So Hard • This Is What You Wanted

### SUNRIZE ☉
Soul-funk group: Ronnie Scruggs (vocals), Dave Townsend (guitar), Kevin Jones (congas), Tony Herbert (bass) and Everett Collins (drums). Former backing band for **The Isley Brothers**.

| 10/23/82 | 206 | 3 | Sunrize .................................................................. $10 | Boardwalk 33257 |

Who's Stickin' It? • I Need You More Than Words Can Say • Someone's Taken My Hand • Come And Get My Lovin' • I Just Wanna Make Sweet Love Tonight • Honey I Love You • Hello Love • You Are The One

### SWAMP DOGG ☉
Born Jerry Williams on 7/12/42 in Portsmouth, Virginia. R&B singer/producer.

| 5/8/71 | 205 | 2 | Rat On! .................................................................. $20 | Elektra 74089 |

Do You Believe • Predicament #2 • Remember, I Said Tomorrow • Creeping Away • Got To Get A Message To You • God Bless America • I Kissed Your Face • That Ain't My Wife • She Even Woke Me Up To Say Good Bye • Do Our Thing Together

### SWAN, Billy
Born on 5/12/42 in Cape Girardeau, Missouri. Singer/songwriter/keyboardist/guitarist.

| 11/1/75 | 205 | 3 | Rock'N'Roll Moon .................................................................. $12 | Monument 33805 |

Everything's The Same (Ain't Nothing Changed) • You're The Pain (In My Heart) • (You Just) Woman Handled My Mind • Stranger • Baby My Heart • Got You On My Mind • Come By • Ubangi Stomp • Home Of The Blues • Overnite Thing (Usually) • Rock And Roll Moon Blues (Part I)

### SWEATHOG ☉
Rock group: Lenny Lee Goldsmith (vocals), Robert "B.J." Morris (guitar), Dave Johnson (bass) and Barry Eugene "Frosty" Frost (drums). Frost was also the drummer for **Lee Michaels**.

| 7/10/71 | 216 | 1 | 1 Sweathog .................................................................. $15 | Columbia 30601 |

Nonbeliever • All I Ever Do • Still On The Road • Burned • Things Yet To Come • Runneth Over • You Just Took The Ride • Lock Up My Body • Layed Back By The River

| 2/19/72 | 211 | 4 | 2 Hallelujah .................................................................. $15 | Columbia 31144 |

Road To Mexico • Ride, Louise, Ride (Change In Louise) • Rock And Roll Hoochie Koo • Questions And Conclusions • Things Yet To Come • Rejoice, Rejoice, Rejoice • Hallelujah • Darker Side • Working My Way Back Home • In The Wee Wee Hours Of The Night • Rock And Roll Revival

### SWEET THURSDAY ☉
British rock group: Jon Mark (vocals, guitar), Alun Davies (guitar), Nicky Hopkins (keyboards), Brian Odgers (bass) and Harvey Burns (drums).

| 5/12/73 | 214 | 2 | Sweet Thursday .................................................................. $15 | Great Western Gramm. 32039 |

Dealer • Jenny • Laughed At Him • Cobwebs • Rescue Me • Molly • Sweet Francesca • Side Of The Road • Gilbert Street

### SWEETWATER
Folk-rock group: **Nancy Nevins** (vocals, guitar), Albert Moore (flute), Elpidio Cobain (conga), August Burns (cello), Alex Del Zoppo (keyboards), Fred Herrera (bass) and Alan Malarowitz (drums).

| 1/23/71 | 202 | 2 | Just For You .................................................................. $15 | Reprise 6417 |

Just For You • Day Song • Windlace • Compared To What • Song For Romeo • Without Me • Look Out

### SWIMMING POOL Q's, The ☉
Rock group from Atlanta: Anne Richmond Boston (vocals, keyboards), Jeff Calder and Bob Elsey (guitars), J.E. Garnett (bass) and Billy Burton (drums).

| 10/20/84 | 202 | 5 | The Swimming Pool Q's .................................................................. $10 | A&M 5015 |

The Bells Ring • Pull Back My Spring • Purple Rivers • The Knave • Some New Highway • Just Property • Silver Slippers • She's Bringing Down The Poison • Celestion • Sacrificial Altar

### SYKES, Keith
Rockabilly singer from Memphis.

| 2/6/82 | 205 | 3 | It Don't Hurt To Flirt .................................................................. $10 | Backstreet 5277 |

Hangin' Around • Don't Go Away • In Between Lies • In My Hideaway • Love Shines Bright • Secret Life • Tell Me When It's Over • It Don't Hurt To Flirt • I Couldn't Love You Better • Buying A House (No, No, No, No, No) • Let's Drink, Let's Dance, Let's Rock

### SZABO, Gabor
Born on 3/8/36 in Budapest, Hungary. Died on 2/26/82. Jazz guitarist/composer.

| 5/19/73 | 202 | 6 | Mizrab .................................................................. [l] $12 | CTI 6026 |

Mizrab • Thirteen • It's Going To Take Some Time • Concerto #2 • Summer Breeze

| DEBUT | PEAK | WKS | Album Title | $ | Label & Number |
|-------|------|-----|-------------|---|----------------|

# T

### TANTRUM
Rock group: Barb Erber, Sandy Caulfield and Pam Bradley (vocals), Ray Sapko (guitar), Phil Balsano (keyboards), Bill Syniar (bass) and Vern Wennerstrom (drums).

| | | | | | |
|---|---|---|---|---|---|
| 3/17/79 | 209 | 2 | Tantrum ........................................................................................ | $10 | Ovation 1735 |

Listen • You Came To Me • You Are My Everything • Happy Yesterdays • Kidnapped • Flash Commander • Night On Main Street • Livin' My Life Without You • Kid Brother • No More

### TAUPIN, Bernie ✪
Born on 5/22/50 in Lincolnshire, England. Known as "The Brown Dirt Cowboy." Began highly successful songwriting collaboration with Elton John in 1969.

| | | | | | |
|---|---|---|---|---|---|
| 3/4/72 | 217 | 1 | Bernie Taupin ................................................................................ | $15 | Elektra 75020 |

Child: Birth/The Greatest Discovery/Flatters (A Beginning)/Brothers Together/Rowston Manor/End Of A Day/To A Grandfather/Solitude/Conclusion • When The Heron Wakes • Like Summer Tempests • Today's Hero • Sisters Of The Cross • Brothers Together Again • Verses After Dark: La Petite Marionette/Ratcatcher/The Visitor

### TAVARES
Family R&B-disco vocal group from New Bedford, Massachusetts: brothers Ralph, Antone "Chubby," Feliciano "Butch," Arthur "Pooch" and Perry Lee "Tiny" Tavares. Butch was married to actress/singer Lola Falana.

| | | | | | |
|---|---|---|---|---|---|
| 1/10/81 | 205 | 1 | 1 Love Uprising ................................................................................ | $10 | Capitol 12117 |

Only One I Need To Love • Break Down For Love • Love Uprising • Loneliness • Knock The Wall Down • Hot Love • Don't Wanna Say Goodnight • Do You Believe In Love • She Can Wait Forever • In This Lovely World • Life Time Of Love

| | | | | | |
|---|---|---|---|---|---|
| 10/15/83 | 208 | 1 | 2 Words And Music ........................................................................... | $10 | RCA Victor 4700 |

Ten To One • Deeper In Love • Caught Short • (You're) My All In All • Words And Music • Baby I Want You Back • I Really Miss You Baby • Don't Play So Hard To Get • Us And Love (We Go Together)

### TAXXI
British rock trio: David Cumming (vocals, guitar), Colin Payne (keyboards) and Jeffrey Nead (drums).

| | | | | | |
|---|---|---|---|---|---|
| 10/15/83 | 210 | 1 | Foreign Tongue ............................................................................... | $10 | Fantasy 9628 |

Maybe Someday • Best In The West • Runaway • Lose Myself • Walking On Air • Gold And Chains • Metro Boulot Dodo • Six Men In New York • Careless Talk

### TAYLOR, Johnnie
Born on 5/5/38 in Crawfordsville, Arkansas. R&B-disco singer. Known as "The Soul Philosopher."

| | | | | | |
|---|---|---|---|---|---|
| 1/7/78 | 202 | 4 | Disco 9000 ..................................................................................... | $12 | Columbia 35004 |

I Don't Know What I'd Do Without You • Toot Your Flute • Just A Happy Song • God Is Standing By • Disco 9000 • I Love You Woman • Right Now

### TAYLOR, Livingston
Born on 11/21/50 in Boston. Younger brother of James Taylor.

| | | | | | |
|---|---|---|---|---|---|
| 12/23/78+ | 202 | 13 | 3-Way Mirror .................................................................................. | $12 | Epic 35540 |

Going Round One More Time • L. A. Serenade • Gonna Have A Good Good Time • Train Off The Track • I Will Be In Love With You • No Thank You Skycap • I'll Come Running • Living Without You • Southern Kids • How Much Your Sweet Love Means To Me

### TELEVISION ✪
Punk group from New York City: Tom Verlaine (vocals, guitar), Richard Lloyd (guitar), Fred Smith (bass) and Billy Ficca (drums).

| | | | | | |
|---|---|---|---|---|---|
| 6/10/78 | 201 | 1 | Adventure ...................................................................................... | $12 | Elektra 133 |

Glory • Days • Foxhole • Careful • Carried Away • The Fire • Ain't That Nothin' • The Dream's Dream

### TEMPTATIONS, The
R&B vocal group from Detroit: Otis Williams, Melvin Franklin, Richard Street, Glenn Leonard and Louis Price. **David Ruffin** and **Eddie Kendricks** were lead singers during the group's prime in the 1960s. Group inducted into the Rock and Roll Hall of Fame in 1989. *Top Pop Albums:* 41.

| | | | | | |
|---|---|---|---|---|---|
| 11/4/78 | 205 | 1 | Bare Back ...................................................................................... | $12 | Atlantic 19188 |

Mystic Woman (Love Me Over) • I Just Don't Know How To Let You Go • That's When You Need Love • Bare Back • Ever Ready Love • Wake Up To Me • You're So Easy To Love • I See My Child • Touch Me Again

### 10cc
Art-rock group from Manchester, England: Eric Stewart (guitar), Graham Gouldman (bass), Lol Creme (guitar, keyboards) and Kevin Godley (drums). All share vocals. Godley and Creme left in 1976.

| | | | | | |
|---|---|---|---|---|---|
| 12/1/73 | 201 | 7 | 1 10cc ............................................................................................. | $15 | UK 53105 |

Johnny, Don't Do It • Sand In My Face • Donna • The Dean And I • Headline Hustler • Speed Kills • Rubber Bullets • The Hospital Song • Ships Don't Disappear In The Night (Do They?) • Fresh Air For My Momma

| | | | | | |
|---|---|---|---|---|---|
| 6/26/82 | 209 | 1 | 2 Ten Out Of 10 ............................................................................... | $10 | Warner 3575 |

Don't Ask • The Power Of Love • Les Nouveaux Riches • Memories • We've Heard It All Before • Don't Turn Me Away • Notell Hotel • Overdraft In Overdrive • Tomorrow's World Today • Run Away

### TEX, Joe
Born Joseph Arrington on 8/8/33 in Rogers, Texas. Died of a heart attack on 8/13/82. R&B singer.

| | | | | | |
|---|---|---|---|---|---|
| 5/20/72 | 201 | 2 | From The Roots Came The Rapper | $15 | Atlantic 8292 |

Lovin' Man • The Only Way I Know How To Love You • I Can Do It Better • Chained In The Mind • I'll Never Fall In Love Again • Oh Me Oh My (I'm A Fool For You Baby) • There's No Business Like Love • The Baby Is Mine • Somethings In Life Are Worth Dying For • Hate Yourself In The Morning

### THEM
Rock band from Belfast, Northern Ireland. Everchanging lineup included Van Morrison (vocals), Billy Harrison (guitar), Alan Henderson (bass), and brothers Jackie (piano) and Patrick (drums) McAuley.

| | | | | | |
|---|---|---|---|---|---|
| 11/2/74 | 202 | 4 | **Backtrackin'** ...........................................................[K] | $15 | London 639 |

**THEM FEATURING VAN MORRISON**
Richard Cory • I Put A Spell On You • Just A Little Bit • I Gave My Love A Diamond • Half As Much • Baby, Please Don't Go • Hey Girl • Don't Start Crying Now • All For Myself • Mighty Like A Rose

### THIRD WORLD
Reggae fusion group from Jamaica: William "Bunny Rugs" Clarke (vocals), Stephen "Cat" Coore (guitar), Michael "Ibo" Cooper (keyboards), Irvin "Carrot" Jarrett (percussion), Richard Daley (bass) and Willie Stewart (drums).

| | | | | | |
|---|---|---|---|---|---|
| 2/25/78 | 203 | 3 | 1 **96° In The Shade** | $12 | Island 9443 |

Jah Glory • Tribal War • Dreamland • Feel A Little Better • Human Market Place • Third World Man • 1865 (96° In The Shade) • Rhythm Of Life

| | | | | | |
|---|---|---|---|---|---|
| 6/14/80 | 206 | 2 | 2 **Arise In Harmony** | $12 | Island 9574 |

Arise • Stand • Visit From Mozambique • Uptown Rebel • Prisoner In The Street • Stand Up On Your Own Two Feet • Stay • Saturday Evening • Dancing In The Rain • Bridge Of Life • Give A Little Something

### 38 SPECIAL
Southern-rock group from Jacksonville, Florida: Donnie Van Zant (vocals), Don Barnes and Jeff Carlisi (guitars), Larry Junstrom (bass), and Steve Brookins and Jack Grondin (drums). Van Zant is the younger brother of Lynyrd Skynyrd's Ronnie Van Zant.

| | | | | | |
|---|---|---|---|---|---|
| 4/29/78 | 207 | 5 | **Special Delivery** | $10 | A&M 4684 |

I'm A Fool For You • Turnin' To You • Travelin' Man • I Been A Mover • What Can I Do • Who's Been Messin' • Can't Keep A Good Man Down • Take Me Back

### THOMAS, B.J.
Born Billy Joe Thomas on 8/7/42 in Hugo, Oklahoma; raised in Rosenberg, Texas. Pop singer.

| | | | | | |
|---|---|---|---|---|---|
| 11/18/72 | 209 | 2 | 1 **Country** | $12 | Scepter 5108 |

Everybody's Talkin' • Little Green Apples • No Love At All • Skip A Rope • Billy And Sue • Suspicious Minds • I'm So Lonesome I Could Cry • Four Walls • Cold, Cold Heart • I Forgot To Remember To Forget You • Wisdom Of A Fool • Without Love

| | | | | | |
|---|---|---|---|---|---|
| 6/9/73 | 221 | 5 | 2 **Songs** | $12 | Paramount 6052 |

Songs • Early Morning Hush • Down On The Street • I've Been Alone Too Long • Too Many Mondays • We're Over • Sunday Sunrise • Talkin' Confidentially • Goodbye's A Long, Long Time • Honorable Peace • People Sure Act Funny

### THOMAS, Carla
Born on 12/21/42 in Memphis. R&B singer. Daughter of **Rufus Thomas**.

| | | | | | |
|---|---|---|---|---|---|
| 8/28/71 | 213 | 2 | **Love Means...** | $30 | Stax 2044 |

Didn't We • Are You Sure? • What Is Love? • Daughter, You're Still Your Daddy's Child • Love Means You Never Have To Say You're Sorry • You've Got A Cushion To Fall On • Il Est Plus Doux Que • Cherish • I Wake Up Wanting You

### THOMAS, Ian ☉
Born in Hamilton, Ontario, Canada. Pop singer/songwriter. Brother of comedian Dave Thomas.

| | | | | | |
|---|---|---|---|---|---|
| 12/8/73 | 203 | 6 | **Ian Thomas** | $12 | Janus 3058 |

Painted Ladies • Another • One Of Those Days • Will You Still Love Me • Coming For My Life • Come The Son • When You Have Love • Evil In Your Eyes • Insecurity • White Clouds

### THOMAS, Lillo
Born in Brooklyn. Male R&B singer.

| | | | | | |
|---|---|---|---|---|---|
| 9/24/83 | 201 | 4 | **Let Me Be Yours** | $10 | Capitol 12290 |

I Love It • Trust Me • Who Do You Think You Are? • Just My Imagination (Running Away With Me) • Hot Love • (You're A) Good Girl • Joy Of Your Love • Let Me Be Yours

### THOMAS, Mickey ☉
Born on 12/3/49 in Cairo, Georgia. Lead singer of Jefferson Starship/Starship from 1979-90.

| | | | | | |
|---|---|---|---|---|---|
| 10/17/81 | 203 | 3 | **Alive Alone** | $10 | Elektra 530 |

She's Got You Running • Alive Alone • Maybe Tomorrow • Following Every Finger • This Time They Told The Truth • Survivor • You're Good With Your Love • I Don't Wanna Talk About It • Too Much Drama • Badge

### THOMAS, Rufus
Born on 3/26/17 in Cayce, Mississippi; raised in Memphis. R&B singer/songwriter/choreographer. Father of **Carla Thomas**.

| | | | | | |
|---|---|---|---|---|---|
| 4/29/72 | 203 | 2 | **Did You Heard Me?** | $25 | Stax 3004 |

(Do The) Push And Pull (Part I) • (Do The) Push And Pull (Part II) • The World Is Round • (I Love You) For Sentimental Reasons • The Breakdown (Part I) • The Breakdown (Part II) • Love Trap • Do The Funky Penguin (Part I) • Do The Funky Penguin (Part II) • Ditch Digging • 6-3-8 (That's The Number To Play)

### THOMAS, Tasha ☉
Born in Jeutyn, Alaska. Died of cancer on 11/8/84 (age 34). R&B singer/actress. Played "Auntie Em" in Broadway's *The Wiz*.

| | | | | | |
|---|---|---|---|---|---|
| 4/21/79 | 204 | 1 | **Midnight Rendezvous** | $10 | Atlantic 19223 |

Midnight Rendezvous • Street Fever • Shoot Me (With Your Love) • Hot Buttered Boogie • You Put The Music In Me • Wake Up Morning Glory • You're The One I Love (From Day To Day) • Drinking Again

### THOMAS, Timmy
Born on 11/13/44 in Evansville, Indiana. R&B singer/songwriter/keyboardist.

| | | | | | |
|---|---|---|---|---|---|
| 6/9/84 | 205 | 4 | **Gotta Give A Little Love (Ten Years After)** | $10 | Gold Mountain 80006 |

Love Is Never Too Late • Gotta Give Little Love (Ten Years After) • Hard Hat • Same Ole Song • My Last Affair • Making Up With You • Tonite Tonite • Let It Flow • Freedom Is Within

### THOMPSON, Richard & Linda
Folk-rock, husband-and-wife duo. Richard was born on 4/3/49 in London. Linda was born Linda Peters in Glasgow, Scotland. Married in 1971. Richard was a member of **Fairport Convention**.

| | | | | | |
|---|---|---|---|---|---|
| 3/5/83 | 203 | 5 | 1 **Shoot Out The Lights** .................................................................................. | $10 | Hannibal 1303 |

Don't Renege On Our Love • Walking On A Wire • A Man In Need • It's Just The Motion • Shoot Out The Lights • The Backstreet Slide • Did She Jump Or Was She Pushed? • The Wall Of Death

| | | | | | |
|---|---|---|---|---|---|
| 2/23/85 | 202 | 6 | 2 **One Clear Moment** .................................................................................. | $10 | Warner 25164 |

**LINDA THOMPSON**

Can't Stop The Girl • One Clear Moment • Telling Me Lies • In Love With The Flame • Les Trois Beaux Oiseaux De Paradis • Take Me On The Subway • Best Of Friends • Hell, High Water And Heartache • Just Enough To Keep Me Hanging On • Lover Won't You Throw Me A Line • Only A Boy

### THOMSON, Ali
Born in 1959 in Glasgow, Scotland. Pop singer/songwriter. Younger brother of Supertramp's Dougie Thomson.

| | | | | | |
|---|---|---|---|---|---|
| 4/11/81 | 201 | 2 | **Deception Is An Art** | $10 | A&M 4846 |

Safe And Warm • Foolish Child • Don't Hold Back • Art Gallery • Shells Lay Scattered • The One And Only • Man Of The Earth • A Simple Song • Secrets Hide Inside • Someone In Motion

### 3-D ☉
Rock group: Rick Zivic (vocals), Keiv Ginsberg (guitar), Ted Wender (keyboards), Nick Stevens (bass) and Mike Fink (drums).

| | | | | | |
|---|---|---|---|---|---|
| 3/1/80 | 206 | 2 | **3-D** .................................................................................. | $10 | Polydor 6254 |

Telephone Number • It's No Fun • Here Today, Gone Tomorrow • Pin Up Girl • Back To You • X-Ray Eyes • All American Boy • Carnival • All Night Televison

### THREE DOG NIGHT
Pop-rock vocal trio from Los Angeles: Danny Hutton, Chuck Negron and **Cory Wells**.

| | | | | | |
|---|---|---|---|---|---|
| 9/10/83 | 210 | 1 | **It's A Jungle** ....................................................[M] | $10 | Passport 5001 |

It's A Jungle Out There • Shot In The Dark • Livin' It Up • I Can't Help It • Somebody's Gonna Get Hurt

### TOBY BEAU
Pop group from Texas: Balde Silva (vocals, harmonica), Danny McKenna (guitar), Ron Rose (banjo), Steve Zipper (bass) and Rob Young (drums).

| | | | | | |
|---|---|---|---|---|---|
| 9/1/79 | 204 | 3 | **More Than A Love Song** .................................................................................. | $10 | RCA Victor 3119 |

Dream Girl • It Must Have Been The Moonlight • Then You Can Tell Me Goodbye • You And I Should Be Forever • Look For The Light • High Roller • I Just Wanna Love You • Boogie Woogie Melody • She Used To Be Mine • Alright Now

### TOMITA
Born Isao Tomita in Tokyo in 1932. Classical-based keyboardist.

| | | | | | |
|---|---|---|---|---|---|
| 12/8/79 | 206 | 2 | **Tomita's Greatest Hits** ....................................................[I-K] | $10 | RCA 3439 |

"Star Wars" Main Title • Clair De Lune • Close Encounters Of The Third Kind • Golliwog's Cakewalk • The Planets: Mars, The Bringer Of War • Space Fantasy • Hora Staccato • Symphony No. 5: 2nd Movement • Firebird Suite: Infernal Dance Of King Kastchei • Pictures At An Exhibition: Great Gate Of Kiev

### TONI & TERRY ☉
Country-rock female duo: Toni Brown and Terry Garthwaite. Both from the group Joy Of Cooking.

| | | | | | |
|---|---|---|---|---|---|
| 3/3/73 | 205 | 3 | **Cross-Country** .................................................................................. | $12 | Capitol 11137 |

Done My Cryin' Time • Going Isn't Easier • I Want To Be The One • Come To Me Now • As I Watch The Wind • Hey Little Girl • Midnight Blues • I Don't Want To Live Here • I've Made Up My Mind • When All Is Said • I Don't Want Nobody

### TONIO K. ☉
Born Steve Krikorian on 7/4/50 in California. Singer/songwriter. Name taken from Thomas Mann's short story *Tonio Kroger*.

| | | | | | |
|---|---|---|---|---|---|
| 4/14/79 | 203 | 4 | **Life In The Foodchain** .................................................................................. | $10 | Full Moon 35545 |

Life In The Foodchain • The Funky Western Civilization • Willie And The Pigman • The Ballad Of The Night The Clocks All Quit (And The Government Failed) • American Love Affair • How Come I Can't See You In My Mirror? • Better Late Than Never • A Lover's Plea • H-A-T-R-E-D

### TOURISTS, The ☉
Rock group from London: Annie Lennox (vocals, keyboards), David A. Stewart and Peet Coombes (guitars), Eddie Chinn (bass) and Jim Toomey (drums). Lennox and Stewart later formed Eurythmics.

| | | | | | |
|---|---|---|---|---|---|
| 4/26/80 | 204 | 4 | 1 **Reality Effect** .................................................................................. | $10 | Epic 36386 |

It Doesn't Have To Be This Way • I Only Want To Be With You • Blind Among The Flowers • In The Morning (When The Madness Has Faded) • All Life's Tragedies • Everywhere You Look • Nothing To Do • The Loneliest Man In The World • So Good To Be Back Home Again • Circular Fever • In My Mind (There's Sorrow) • Fool's Paradise

| | | | | | |
|---|---|---|---|---|---|
| 2/28/81 | 204 | 3 | 2 **Luminous Basement** .................................................................................. | $10 | Epic 36757 |

Talk To Me • Walls And Foundations • Week Days • So You Want To Go Away Now • I'm Going To Change My Mind • One Step Nearer The Edge • Don't Say I Told You So • Angels And Demons • Time Drags So Slow • Let's Take A Walk • From The Middle Room • Round Round Blues

### TOUSSAINT, Allen ☉
Born on 1/14/38 in New Orleans. Singer/songwriter/pianist.

| | | | | | |
|---|---|---|---|---|---|
| 4/19/75 | 204 | 6 | **Southern Nights** .................................................................................. | $12 | Reprise 2186 |

Last Train • World Wide • Back In Baby's Arms • Country John • Basic Lady • Southern Nights • You Will Not Lose • What Do You Want The Girl To Do? • When The Party's Over • Cruel Way To Go Down

### TRANQUILITY ☉
Rock group: Terry Shaddick (vocals), Berkeley Wright and Kevin McCarthy (guitars), Tony Lukyn (keyboards), Bernard Hagley (bass) and Paul Francis (drums).

| | | | | | |
|---|---|---|---|---|---|
| 3/3/73 | 207 | 2 | **Tranquility** .................................................................................. | $12 | Epic 31084 |

Try Again • Ride Upon The Sun • Where You Are (Where I Belong) • Look At The Time It's Late • Lady Of The Lake • Walk Along The Road • Thank You • Oyster Catcher • Black Currant Betty • Saying Good-Bye

| DEBUT | PEAK | WKS | Album Title | $ | Label & Number |
|-------|------|-----|-------------|---|----------------|

**TRANSLATOR ✪**
Rock group from Los Angeles: Steve Barton (vocals), Robert Darlington (guitar), Larry Dekker (bass) and David Scheff (drums).

9/17/83 — 206 — 3 — **No Time Like Now** .................... $10 — Columbia 38927
Un-Alone • Beyond Today • I Hear You Follow • Break Down Barriers • L.A., L.A. • I Love You • No Time Like Now • Everything Is Falling • Simple Things • The End Of Their Love • About The Truth • Circumstance Laughing

**TRAPEZE**
Rock trio from Wolverhampton, England: Glenn Hughes (vocals, bass; Deep Purple), Mel Galley (guitar) and Dave Holland (drums).

1/6/73 — 209 — 3 — **You Are The Music...We're Just The Band** .................... $50 — Threshold 8
Keepin' Time • Coast To Coast • What Is A Woman's Role • Way Back To The Bone • Feelin' So Much Better Now • Will Our Love End • Loser • You Are The Music

**TRAVERS, Pat**
Born in Toronto in 1954. Blues-rock singer/guitarist.

7/23/77 — 209 — 4 — **Makin' Magic** .................... $12 — Polydor 6103
Makin' Magic • Rock 'N' Roll Susie • You Don't Love Me • Stevie • Statesboro Blues • Need Love • Hooked On Music • What You Mean To Me

**TREMBLERS, The ✪**
Pop-rock group: Peter Noone (vocals), George Conner (guitar), Gregg Inhofer (keyboards), Mark Browne (bass) and Robert Williams (drums). Noone was lead singer of **Herman's Hermits**.

8/23/80 — 209 — 1 — **Twice Nightly** .................... $10 — Johnston 36532
You Can't Do That • Steady Eddy • She Was Something Else • I'll Be Taking Her Out Tonight • Little Lover • I Screamed Anne • Wouldn't I? • Dad Said • Maybe I'll Stay • Green Shirt • Don't Say It

**T. REX**
Rock duo from London: Marc Bolan (vocals, guitar) and Micky Finn (bass, drums). Bolan died in a car crash on 9/16/77 (age 30).

9/7/74 — 205 — 8 — **Light Of Love** .................... $12 — Casablanca 9006
Light Of Love • Solid Baby • Precious Star • Token Of My Love • Space Boss • Think Zinc • Till Dawn • Teenage Dream • Girl In The Thunderbolt Suit • Explosive Mouth • Venus Loon

**TRILLION ✪**
Rock group: Dennis Frederiksen (vocals), Frank Barbalace (guitar), Patrick Leonard (keyboards), Ron Anaman (bass) and Bill Wilkins (drums).

3/3/79 — 201 — 7 — **Trillion** .................... $10 — Epic 35460
Hold Out • Big Boy • Give Me Your Money, Honey • Never Had It So Good • May As Well Go • Fancy Action • Hand It To The Wind • Bright Night Lights • Child Upon The Earth

**TRIO**
Swedish reggae/rock trio: Stephan Remmler, Kralle Krawinkel and Peter Behrens.

1/15/83 — 207 — 4 — **Trio** .................... [M] $10 — Mercury 509
Anna-Let Me In Let Me Out • Da Da Da I Don't Love You You Don't Love Me Aha Aha Aha • Broken Hearts For You And Me • Energie • Sunday You Need Love • Ja Ja Ja

**TROGGS, The**
Rock group from Andover, England: Reg Presley (vocals), Richard Moore (guitar), Tony Murray (bass) and Ronnie "Bond" Bullis (drums). Bullis died on 11/13/92 (age 51).

8/9/75 — 210 — 1 — **The Troggs** .................... $15 — Pye 12112
I Got Lovin' If You Want It • Good Vibrations • No Particular Place To Go • Summertime • Satisfaction • Full Blooded Band • Memphis Tennessee • Peggy Sue • Jenny Come Down • Wild Thing

**TROOPER**
Rock group from Vancouver: Ramon McGuire (vocals), Brian Smith (guitar), Harry Kalensky (bass) and Tommy Stewart (drums).

10/11/75 — 207 — 2 — **Trooper** .................... $12 — Legend/MCA 2149
produced by Randy Bachman
I'm In Trouble Again • General Hand Grenade • All Of The Time • Eddy Takes It Easy • Roller Rink • Baby Woncha Please Come Home • Love Of My Life • Don't Stop Now

**TUBEWAY ARMY — see NUMAN, Gary**

**TUCKER, Marshall — see MARSHALL**

**TUCKER, Tanya**
Born on 10/10/58 in Seminole, Texas; raised in Wilcox, Arizona. Country singer.

3/8/75 — 201 — 8 — ● 1 **Tanya Tucker's Greatest Hits** .................... [G] $12 — Columbia 33355
Delta Dawn • Blood Red And Goin' Down • The Jamestown Ferry • What's Your Mama's Name • I Believe The South Is Gonna Rise Again • Would You Lay With Me (In A Field Of Stone) • Love's The Answer • Rainy Girl • No Man's Land • The Man That Turned My Mama On

10/2/76 — 203 — 4 — 2 **Here's Some Love** .................... $12 — MCA 2213
Here's Some Love • Round And Round The Bottle • Comin' Home Alone • Gonna Love You Anyway • Holding On • You Just Love The Leavin' Out Of Me • The Gospel Singer • Take Me To Heaven • Short Cut • I Use The Soap

4/8/78 — 210 — 1 — 3 **Tanya Tucker's Greatest Hits** .................... [G] $10 — MCA 3032
Here's Some Love • Ridin' Rainbows • Pride of Franklin County • Dancing The Night Away • Wait 'Til Daddy Finds Out • Let's Keep It That Way • San Antonio Stroll • Don't Believe My Heart Can Stand Another You • Short Cut • You've Got Me To Hold On To • Lizzie And The Rain Man • It's A Cowboy Lovin' Night

11/8/80 — 209 — 2 — 4 **Dreamlovers** .................... $10 — MCA 5140
Can I See You Tonight • Love Knows We Tried • I've Got Somebody • Let Me Count The Ways • Dream Lover • Somebody (Trying To Tell You Something) • All The Way • Tennessee Woman • Don't You Want To Be A Lover Tonight • My Song

10/2/82 — 203 — 3 — 5 **Changes** .................... $10 — Arista 9596
Cry • Shame On The Moon • Until You're Mine • Baby I'm Yours • I Don't Want You To Go • Heartache And A Half • Changes • Feel Right • A Thing Called Love • Too Long

## TUFANO AND GIAMMARESE ☺
Pop-rock duo from Chicago: Denny Tufano and Carl Giammarese. Both were members of The Buckinghams.

| 5/12/73 | 210 | 5 | **Tufano And Giammarese** ........................................................................... | $15 | Ode 77017 |

guests include Wilton Felder and Carole King
Music Everywhere • Wednesday Down • I'm A Loser • Rise Up • Just A Dream Away • Here We Are • Communicate • Show Me If You Can • She Takes Me There • Can You Say What You Need • Take Me Back • Give Yourself A Dream

## TURNER, Ike & Tina
Husband-and-wife R&B duo: guitarist Ike Turner (b: 11/5/31 in Clarksdale, Mississippi) and vocalist Tina Turner (born Anna Mae Bullock on 11/26/38 in Brownsville, Tennessee). Married from 1958-76. In the mid-1980s, Tina emerged as a successful solo artist. Duo inducted into the Rock and Roll Hall of Fame in 1991.

| 3/27/71 | 201 | 8 | **1 Her Man...His Woman** | $15 | Capitol 571 |

Get It - Get It! • I Believe • I Can't Believe (What You Say) • My Babe • Strange • You Weren't Ready • That's Alright • Rooster • Five Long Years • The Things That I Used To Do

| 2/17/73 | 205 | 3 | **2 Let Me Touch Your Mind** ........................................................................ | $12 | United Artists 5660 |

Let Me Touch Your Mind • Annie Had A Baby • Don't Believe Her • I Had A Notion • Popcorn • Early One Morning • Help Him • Up On The Roof • Born Free • Heaven Help Us All

| 10/6/73 | 211 | 7 | **3 The World Of Ike & Tina** ....................................................................[L] | $15 | United Artists 064 [2] |

recorded on their European tour
Theme From "Shaft" • I Gotcha • Intro To Tina • She Came In Through The Bathroom Window • You're Still My Baby • Don't Fight It • Annie Had A Baby • With A Little Help From My Friends • Get Back • Games People Play • Honky Tonk Women • If You Love Me Like You Say • I Can't Turn You Loose • I Wish It Would Rain • Just One More Day • Stand By Me • Dust My Broom • River Deep, Mountain High • Let Me Touch Your Mind • Chopper • 1-2-3

## TURRENTINE, Stanley
Born on 4/5/34 in Pittsburgh. Jazz tenor saxophonist.

| 8/11/79 | 202 | 8 | **1 Betcha** ...................................................................................................[I] | $10 | Elektra 217 |

Take Me Home • Love Is The Answer • Betcha • Concentrate On You • You • Hamlet (So Peaceful) • Long Time Gone • Together Again

| 7/19/80 | 209 | 1 | **2 Inflation** ................................................................................................[I] | $10 | Elektra 269 |

Inflation • Theme From Shaft • Song For Donny • Closer • Is It You • Deja Vu • Don't Misunderstand • Ghana

## TWITTY, Conway
Born Harold Lloyd Jenkins on 9/1/33 in Friars Point, Mississippi; raised in Helena, Arkansas. Died of an abdominal aneurysm on 6/5/93. Country singer.

| 1/31/76 | 202 | 5 | **1 Twitty** .................................................................................................... | $12 | MCA 2176 |

album also known as *This Time I've Hurt Her More Than She Loves Me*
This Time I've Hurt Her More Than She Loves Me • She Thinks I Still Care • Jason's Farm • She Sure Does Make It Hard To Go • You Love The Best Out Of Me • She Did-It Did-I Didn't • The Race Is On • She Takes Care Of Me • Woman Lovin' Kind Of Man • On My Way To Losing You

| 7/23/83 | 203 | 7 | **2 Lost In The Feeling** ............................................................................... | $10 | Warner 23869 |

Lost In The Feeling • The Best Is Yet To Come • You've Got A Good Love Coming • We're So Close • Heartache Tonight • A Stranger's Point Of View • I Think I'm In Love • Three Times A Lady • First Things First • Don't It Feel Good

| 5/26/84 | 207 | 1 | **3 By Heart** ............................................................................................... | $10 | Warner 25078 |

I Don't Know A Thing About Love • I've Never Had It Bad • Without You • All My Life • Bad Boy • Somebody's Needin' Somebody • By Heart • When The Magic Works • Call It What You Want To (It's Still Love) • A Hard Act To Follow

## TWO TONS — see WEATHER GIRLS

## TYMES, The
R&B vocal group from Philadelphia: George Williams, Albert Berry, Charles Nixon, Norman Burnett and Donald Banks. Nixon left in 1975, replaced by Wade Davis and Jerry Ferguson. Berry, Davis and Ferguson left in mid-1976, replaced by female singers Terri Gonzales and Melanie Moore.

| 12/7/74 | 205 | 2 | **1 Trustmaker** ........................................................................................... | $12 | RCA Victor 0727 |

Someway, Somehow I'm Keepin' You • The Crutch • Miss Grace • Are You Lookin' • So Much In Love • The Sha-La Bandit • Innerloop! • The North Hills • You Little Trustmaker

| 2/21/76 | 202 | 4 | **2 Tymes Up** .............................................................................................. | $12 | RCA Victor 1072 |

Only Your Love • It's Cool • If I Can't Make You Smile • God's Gonna Punish You • Hypnotized • Goin' Through The Motions • To The Max (Imum) • Good Morning Dear Lord

| 11/6/76 | 205 | 1 | **3 Turning Point** ....................................................................................... | $12 | RCA Victor 1835 |

It's So Good To Be Waking Up With You • All You Ever Wanted To Know About Love • I Need You And Your Kind Of Loving • That's The Breaks Of Love • Youth Is Wasted On The Young • Traces Of You • Love's Illusion • Savannah Sunny Sunday • The Reader • Tuning Into You

## TYNER, McCoy
Born on 12/11/38 in Philadelphia. Jazz pianist.

| 7/24/82 | 207 | 4 | **Looking Out** ...........................................................................................[I] | $10 | Columbia 38053 |

Love Surrounds Us Everywhere • Hannibal • I'll Be Around • Señor Carlos • In Search Of My Heart • Island Birdie

# U

## UFO
Hard-rock group formed in England: Phil Mogg (vocals), **Michael Schenker** (guitar), Pete Way (bass) and Andy Parker (drums).

| 8/24/74 | 202 | 2 | **Phenomenon** ......................................................................................... | $12 | Chrysalis 1059 |

Too Young To Know • Crystal Light • Doctor Doctor • Space Child • Rock Bottom • Oh My • Time On My Hands • Built For Comfort • Lipstick Traces • Queen Of The Deep

### ULTRAVOX
Electronic-rock group from London: Midge Ure (vocals, guitar), Billy Currie (synthesizer, piano), Chris Cross (bass) and Warren Cann (drums). Ure and Currie were members of **Visage**.

| | | | | | |
|---|---|---|---|---|---|
| 5/4/85 | 203 | 3 | The Collection .................................................................[K] $10 | | Chrysalis 41490 |

Dancing With Tears In My Eyes • Hymn • The Thin Wall • The Voice • Vienna • Passing Strangers • Sleepwalk • Reap The Wild Wind • All Stood Still • Visions In Blue • We Came To Dance • One Small Day • Love's Great Adventure • Lament

### UNDISPUTED TRUTH, The
R&B vocal group from Detroit: Joe Harris, Tyrone Berkeley, Tyrone Douglas, Calvin Stevens and Virginia McDonald.

| | | | | | |
|---|---|---|---|---|---|
| 9/14/74 | 208 | 3 | Down To Earth ............................................................ $20 | | Gordy 968 |

Help Yourself • Big John Is My Name • Brother Louie • I'm A Fool For You • Our Day Will Come • Just You 'N' Me • Love And Happiness • Law Of The Land • The Girl's Alright With Me • Save My Love For A Rainy Day

### UNION ☼
Canadian rock group: Randy Bachman (vocals, guitar), Frank Ludwig (keyboards), Fred Turner (bass) and Chris Leighton (drums). Bachman and Turner were leaders of Bachman-Turner Overdrive.

| | | | | | |
|---|---|---|---|---|---|
| 8/1/81 | 207 | 2 | On Strike ................................................................... $10 | | Portrait 37368 |

Mainstreet U.S.A. • Next Stop London • Stay Away From The Honky Tonks • Care Of Me • Keep The Summer Alive • On Strike • Texas Cannonball • Pacific Northwest Blues • Invitation • All Night Long

# V

### VALENTIN, Dave
Born in 1954 in New York City. Latin-jazz flutist.

| | | | | | |
|---|---|---|---|---|---|
| 8/7/82 | 201 | 5 | In Love's Time [I] $10 | | GRP 5511 |

Street Beat • In Love's Time • I Don't Wanna Fall In Love (I Just Wanna Dance) • I Got It Right This Time • Clove And Cinnamon • Dansette • The Flight • Leo And The Sun

### VALLI, Frankie
Born Francis Castellucio on 5/3/37 in Newark, New Jersey. Lead singer of The 4 Seasons.

| | | | | | |
|---|---|---|---|---|---|
| 11/15/75 | 203 | 1 | Inside You ................................................................... $15 | | Motown 852 |

Just Look What You've Done • Love Isn't Here (Like It Used To Be) • Baby I Need Your Loving • Inside You • Thank You • Hickory • Life And Breath • The Night • With My Eyes Wide Open

### VAN EATON, Lon & Derek ☼
British duo: brothers Lon and Derek Van Eaton.

| | | | | | |
|---|---|---|---|---|---|
| 4/19/75 | 210 | 1 | Who Do You Out Do.......................................................... $12 | | A&M 4507 |

Who Do You Out Do • You Lose • Do You Remember • Music Lover • Let It Grow • Wildfire • Dancing In The Dark • All You're Hungry For Is Love • Baby It's You • The Harder You Pull...The Tighter It Gets

### VANGELIS
Born Evangelos Papathanassiou on 3/29/43 in Valos, Greece. Keyboardist/composer.

| | | | | | |
|---|---|---|---|---|---|
| 3/20/76 | 204 | 5 | 1 Heaven And Hell ........................................................ [I] $12 | | RCA Victor 5110 |

Heaven And Hell (Part 1) • Heaven And Hell (Part 2)

| | | | | | |
|---|---|---|---|---|---|
| 10/2/82 | 207 | 3 | 2 To The Unknown Man ................................................... [I] $10 | | RCA Victor 4397 |

To The Unknown Man • Pulstar • Spiral • Albedo • Aries • Beaubourg Excerpt • Bacchanale • So Long Ago, So Clear

### VAN LEER, Thijs ☼
Born on 3/31/48 in Amsterdam. Male flutist. Leader of Focus.

| | | | | | |
|---|---|---|---|---|---|
| 10/20/73 | 208 | 5 | Introspection ............................................................ [I] $12 | | Columbia 32346 |

Pavane, Op. 50 • Rondo • Agnuis Dei • Focus I • Erbarme Dich • Focus II • Introspection

### VANWARMER, Randy
Born Randall Van Wormer on 3/30/55 in Indian Hills, Colorado. Singer/songwriter/guitarist.

| | | | | | |
|---|---|---|---|---|---|
| 6/27/81 | 205 | 1 | Beat Of Love ................................................................ $10 | | Bearsville 3561 |

Suzi Found A Weapon • Always Night • Medley: Babel/Don't Hide • Amen • I Guess It Never Hurts To Hurt Sometimes • Frightened By The Light Of The Day • Hanging On To Heaven • The Beat Of Love • When I'm Dead And Gone • Don't Wake Me Up

### VELVET UNDERGROUND, The
Experimental-rock group from New York City: Lou Reed (vocals, guitar), **John Cale** (keyboards), Sterling Morrison (bass) and Maureen Tucker (percussion). Various personnel included female singer Christa "Nico" Paffgen (died on 7/18/88, age 48). Morrison died of non-Hodgkin's lymphona on 8/30/95 (age 53). Highly influential group. Inducted into the Rock and Roll Hall of Fame in 1996.

| | | | | | |
|---|---|---|---|---|---|
| 1/30/71 | 202 | 1 | 1 Loaded ................................................................... $20 | | Cotillion 9034 |

Who Loves The Sun • Sweet Jane • Rock & Roll • Cool It Down • New Age • Head Held High • Lonesome Cowboy Bill • I Found A Reason • Train Round The Bend • Oh! Sweet Nuthin'

| | | | | | |
|---|---|---|---|---|---|
| 5/19/73 | 205 | 4 | 2 Lou Reed And The Velvet Underground ............................[K] $20 | | Pride 0022 |

That's The Story Of My Life • Sister Ray • Lady Godiva's Operation • Heroin • Sunday Morning • All Tomorrow's Parties • There She Goes Again • White Light/White Heat • Femme Fatale

| | | | | | |
|---|---|---|---|---|---|
| 4/27/74 | 201 | 9 | 3 1969 Velvet Underground Live With Lou Reed [L] $20 | | Mercury 7504 [2] |

recorded in Texas and San Francisco in late 1969

Waiting For My Man • Lisa Says • What Goes On • Sweet Jane • We're Gonna Have A Real Good Time Together • Femme Fatale • New Age • Rock And Roll • Beginning To See The Light • Ocean • Pale Blue Eyes • Heroin • Some Kinda Love • Over You • Medley: Sweet Bonnie Brown/It's Just Too Much • White Light/White Heat • I'll Be Your Mirror

## VELVET UNDERGROUND, The — Cont'd

| 4/6/85 | 206 | 1 | 4 **White Light/White Heat** ............................................................ [R] $10 | Verve 825119 |

originally charted in 1968 on Verve 5046 (#199)

White Light/White Heat • The Gift • Lady Godiva's Operation • Here She Comes Now • I Heard Her Call My Name • Sister Ray

| 4/13/85 | 201 | 3 | 5 **The Velvet Underground & Nico** [R] $10 | Verve 823290 |

produced by Andy Warhol; originally charted in 1967 on Verve 5008 (#171)

Sunday Morning • I'm Waiting For The Man • Femme Fatale • Venus In Furs • Run Run Run • All Tomorrow's Parties • Heroin • There She Goes Again • I'll Be Your Mirror • The Black Angel's Death Song • European Son

## VERGAT, Vic ○

Rock singer/guitarist from Switzerland.

| 11/14/81 | 207 | 1 | **Down To The Bone** ............................................................ $10 | Capitol 12187 |

Down To The Bone • Breakaway • I Don't Wanna Lose You • Walk • Hot Love • You Never Tell Me You Love Me • I Believe In Love Music • Mean Mean Cat • Hey Love

## VINEGAR JOE ○

British rock group: Elkie Brooks and Robert Palmer (vocals), Jim Mullen and Pete Gage (guitars), Mike Deaon (keyboards), Steve York (bass) and John Woods and **Keef Hartley** (drums). Palmer went on to a successful solo career.

| 2/24/73 | 201 | 2 | **Rock 'N Roll Gypsies** $12 | Atco 7016 |

So Long • Charlie's Horse • Rock 'N Roll Gypsies • Falling • It's Gettin' To The Point • Whole Lotta Shakin' (Goin' On) • Buddy Can You Spare Me A Line? • Angel • No One Ever Do • Forgive Us

## VINTON, Bobby

Born Stanley Robert Vinton on 4/16/35 in Canonsburg, Pennsylvania. Pop singer. Own musical variety TV series from 1975-78. *Top Pop Albums*: 25.

| 6/26/71 | 204 | 4 | **The Love Album** ............................................................ [K] $15 | Epic 30431 [2] |

This Guy's In Love With You • Till • For Once In My Life • When I Fall In Love • No Arms Can Ever Hold You • Please Love Me Forever • Love Me With All Your Heart • To Think You've Chosen Me • If I Didn't Care • It's All In The Game • There! I've Said It Again • Sunrise, Sunset • From Russia With Love • Too Young • Unchained Melody • All • The Shadow Of Your Smile • The End Of The World • This Is My Song • My Heart Belongs To Only You

## VISAGE

British dance-rock group: Steve "Strange" Harrington (vocals), Midge Ure (guitar), Billy Currie (voilin), Dave Formula (keyboards) and Rusty Egan (drums). Ure and Currie were members of *Ultravox*.

| 4/17/82 | 204 | 1 | **The Anvil** ............................................................ $10 | Polydor 6350 |

The Damned Don't Cry • Anvil (Night Club School) • Move Up • Night Train • The Horseman • Look What They've Done • Again We Love • Wild Life • Whispers

## VITALE, Joe

Pronounced: Vee-TAH-lay. Born in Dundalk, Maryland. Rock singer/drummer.

| 3/1/75 | 204 | 2 | **Roller Coaster Weekend** ............................................................ $12 | Atlantic 18114 |

guests include **Rick Derringer** and Joe Walsh

Roller Coaster Weekend • (Do You Feel Like) Movin' • Mad Man • Take A Chance On Love • School Yard • Shoot 'Em Up • Feeling's Gone Away • Two Of Us • Falling • Interlude • Step On You

## VITAL INFORMATION — see SMITH, Steve

## VOLMAN, Mark, And Howard Kaylan ○

Volman was born on 4/19/44 in Los Angeles. Kaylan was born on 6/22/45 in New York City. Both were founding members of The Turtles.

| 10/7/72 | 211 | 2 | **The Phlorescent Leech & Eddie** ............................................................ $20 | Reprise 2099 |

Flo And Eddie Theme • Thoughts Have Turned • It Never Happened • Burn The House • Lady Blue • Strange Girl • Who But I • I Been Born Again • Goodbye Surprise • Nikki Hoi • Really Love • Feel Older Now • There You Sit Lonely

# W

## WACKERS, The ○

Pop-rock group from Montreal: Randy Bishop (vocals), Robert Segarini (guitar), J.P. Lauzon (keyboards), Bill "Kootch" Trochim (bass) and Spencer "Ernie" Earnshaw (drums).

| 1/6/73 | 211 | 3 | **Shredder** ............................................................ $12 | Elektra 75046 |

Day & Night • Hey Lawdy Lawdy • I'll Believe In You • Put Myself To Sleep • Eventually (Even You Even Me) • Coming Apart • It's My Life • Beach Song • Buck Duckdog Memorial Jam Medley: Our Ships Comin' In/My Old Lady/You Really Got Me • Last Dance

## WADSWORTH MANSION ○

Rock quartet: brothers Steve (vocals) and Mike (drums) Jablecki, Wayne Gagnon (guitar) and John Poole (bass).

| 4/10/71 | 216 | 3 | **Wadsworth Mansion** ............................................................ $20 | Sussex 7008 |

Long Haired Brown Eyed Girl • Queenie Dew • City Gardner • She Said She Would • Sweet Mary • I Like It • Michigan Harry Slaughter • Let It Shine • Goodbye • Havin' Such A Good Time

## WAGNER, Richard ○

Singer/songwriter/guitarist from New York City.

| 6/3/78 | 203 | 7 | **Richard Wagner** ............................................................ $10 | Atlantic 19172 |

Some Things Go On Forever • Don't Stop The Music • Nightwork • Heartlands • Oceans • Go Down Together • Small Town Boy • Hand Me Down Heartaches • Motor City Showdown

### WAINWRIGHT, Loudon III
Born on 9/5/46 in Chapel Hill, North Carolina. Satirical folk singer/songwriter/actor.

| 12/22/73 | 213 | 4 | Attempted Mustache .................................................................................... | $15 | Columbia 32710 |

The Swimming Song • A.M. World • Bell Bottom Pants • Liza • I Am The Way • Clockwork Chartreuse • Down Drinking At The Bar • The Man Who Couldn't Cry • Come A Long Way • Nocturnal Stumblebutt • Dilated To Meet You • Lullaby

### WAITS, Tom
Born on 12/7/49 in Pomona, California. Gravelly-voiced monologue song stylist/actor/songwriter.

| 11/23/74 | 201 | 2 | The Heart Of Saturday Night | $12 | Asylum 1015 |

New Coat Of Paint • San Diego Serenade • Semi Suite • Shiver Me Timbers • Diamonds On My Windshield • (Looking For) The Heart Of Saturday Night • Fumblin' With The Blues • Please Call Me, Baby • Depot, Depot • Drunk On The Moon • The Ghosts Of Saturday Night

### WALDMAN, Wendy ☉
Born in 1951 in Los Angeles. Folk-pop singer/songwriter/producer.

| 5/3/75 | 207 | 2 | 1 Wendy Waldman ........................................................................................ | $12 | Warner 2859 |

Western Lullaby • Racing Boat • Explain It • Wings • Mr. Boatman • Sundown • Spring Is Here • Constant Companion • Secrets • Wild Bird • Listen To Your Own Heart • Green Rocky Road

| 6/3/78 | 203 | 10 | 2 Strange Company ...................................................................................... | $12 | Warner 3178 |

Fool To Let Him Slip Away • Long Hot Summer Nights • Train Runnin' • You'll See • The Wind In New York City • Strange Company • Hard Times • Since Love Is Gone • The Man Is Mine • Love Is The Only Goal

### WALES, Howard, & Jerry Garcia ☉
Wales is a keyboardist. Garcia was born on 8/1/42 in San Francisco. Died on 8/9/95. Founder/lead guitarist of the Grateful Dead.

| 10/9/71 | 201 | 1 | Hooteroll? | $50 | Douglas 30859 |

South Side Strut • A Trip To What Next • Up From The Desert • DC-502 • One A.M. Approach • Uncle Martin's • Da Birg Song

### WALKER, Jerry Jeff
Born Ronald Clyde Crosby on 3/16/42 in Oneonta, New York. Country-rock singer/songwriter.

| 2/24/73 | 208 | 4 | 1 Jerry Jeff Walker ...................................................................................... | $12 | Decca 75384 |

Hill Country Rain • Charlie Dunn • That Old Time Feeling • Her Good Lovin' Grace • Hairy Ass Hillbillies • David And Me • L.A. Freeway • Curly And Lil • That Old Beat Up Guitar • When I Had You • Moon Child • The Continuing Saga Of The Classic Bummer or Is This My Free One-Way Bus Ticket To Cleaveland?

| 1/6/79 | 206 | 5 | 2 Jerry Jeff ................................................................................................ | $10 | Elektra 163 |

Eastern Avenue River Railway Blues • Lone Wolf • Bad News • Boogie Mama • I'm Not Strange • Her Good Lovin' Grace • Comfort And Crazy • Follow • Banks Of The Old Bandera

### WALKER, Junior
Born Oscar Nixon on 6/14/31 in Blythesville, Arkansas. Died of cancer on 11/23/95. R&B singer/saxophonist. The All Stars included Willie Woods (guitar) and Vic Thomas (organ). Woods died on 5/27/97 (age 60).

| 6/9/73 | 202 | 3 | 1 Peace & Understanding Is Hard To Find ................................................. | $15 | Soul 738 |

**JR. WALKER & THE ALL STARS**

I Ain't Going Nowhere • I Don't Need No Reason • It's Alright, Do What You Gotta Do • It's Too Late • Soul Clappin' • I Can See Clearly Now • Gimme That Beat (Part 1) • Gimme That Beat (Part 2) • Country Boy • Peace And Understanding (Is Hard To Find)

| 9/24/83 | 210 | 1 | 2 Blow The House Down ............................................................................. | $10 | Motown 6053 |

Sexpot • Rise And Shine • Closer Than Close • Ball Baby • T-OO (T Double O) • Urgent • In And Out • Blow The House Down

### WALL OF VOODOO
Electronic-rock group from Los Angeles: Stan Ridgway (vocals), Marc Moreland (guitar), Chas Gray (keyboards), Bruce Moreland (bass) and Joe Nanini (drums).

| 1/10/81 | 204 | 3 | Wall Of Voodoo ....................................................................... | [M] $10 | Index 70401 |

Longarm • The Passenger • Can't Make Love • Struggle • Ring Of Fire • Granma's House

### WALSH, James ☉
Rock singer/keyboardist. Nicknamed "Owl." Former leader of Gypsy.

| 11/18/78 | 203 | 5 | James Walsh Gypsy Band ........................................................................ | $10 | RCA Victor 2914 |

You Make Me Feel Like Livin' • Love Is For The Best In Us • Bring Yourself Around • Don't Look Back • Cuz It's You, Girl • You • Gray Tears • My Star • Whole Lotta Givin' To Do • Lookin' Up I See • Someday

### WASHINGTON, Deborah ☉
Born on 3/16/54 in Philadelphia. R&B singer/actress.

| 10/28/78 | 205 | 2 | Any Way You Want It ............................................................................... | $10 | Ariola America 50040 |

Medley: Love Shadow/Standing In The Shadows Of Love • Fire • The Letter • Ready Or Not • Baby Love • Any Way That You Want Me • Take A Chance With Me

### WATERS, Muddy
Born McKinley Morganfield on 4/4/15 in Rolling Fork, Mississippi. Died of a heart attack on 4/30/83. Legendary blues singer/guitarist/harmonica player. Inducted into the Rock and Roll Hall of Fame in 1987 as a blues pioneer. Won Grammy's Lifetime Achievement Award in 1992.

| 4/7/79 | 203 | 3 | Muddy "Mississippi" Waters Live....................................................... | [L] $10 | Blue Sky 35712 |

Mannish Boy • She's Nineteen Years Old • Nine Below Zero • Streamline Woman • Howling Wolf • Baby Please Don't Go • Deep Down In Florida

### WATSON, Johnny "Guitar"
Born on 2/3/35 in Houston. Died on 5/17/96 of a heart attack while performing at the Yokohama Blues Cafe in Japan. R&B singer/guitarist/pianist.

| 9/27/75 | 201 | 4 | 1 I Don't Want To Be Alone, Stranger | $12 | Fantasy 9484 |

I Don't Want To Be A Lone Ranger • Your New Love Is A Player • Tripping • Lonely Man's Prayer • You Make My Heart Want To Sing • It's Way Too Late • Love Is Sweet Misery • You Can Stay But The Noise Must Go • Strong Vibrations

| 8/11/79 | 204 | 1 | 2 What The Hell Is This ............................................................................. | $10 | DJM 24 |

What The Hell Is This? • In The World • Proud Of You • Cop & Blow • I Don't Want To Be President • Mother In Law • Strung Out

## WEATHER GIRLS, The ○
Disco duo from San Francisco: Martha Wash and Izora Armstead. Formerly known as **The Two Tons** and Two Tons O' Fun.

| | | | | | |
|---|---|---|---|---|---|
| 1/10/81 | 202 | 5 | 1 **Backatcha** ............................................................................................... | $10 | Fantasy 9615 |

THE TWO TONS

Never Like This • I Depend On You • Your Love Is Gonna See Me Through • It's True I Do • Can't Do It By Myself • Cloudy With A Chance Of Rain • I've Got To Make It On My Own • I Been Down

| 12/3/83 | 206 | 1 | 2 **Success** .................................................................................................. | $10 | Columbia 38997 |
|---------|-----|---|---|---|---|

Success • Hungry For Love • Dear Santa (Bring Me A Man This Christmas) • Hope • It's Raining Men • I'm Gonna Wash That Man Right Outa My Hair

## WEBB, Jimmy ○
Born on 8/15/46 in Elk City, Oklahoma. Prolific songwriter.

| 8/12/72 | 202 | 4 | **Letters** ..................................................................................................... | $12 | Reprise 2055 |
|---------|-----|---|---|---|---|

Galveston • Campo De Encino • Love Hurts • Simile • Hurt Me Well • Once In The Morning • Catharsis • Song Seller • When Can Brown Begin • Piano

## WEBSTER, Max — see MAX WEBSTER

## WEISBERG, Tim
Born in 1943 in Hollywood. Jazz-pop flutist.

| 11/4/72 | 202 | 3 | 1 **Hurtwood Edge** ..........................................................................[I] | $12 | A&M 4352 |
|---------|-----|---|---|---|---|

Tibetan Silver • Burlington Skyway • Hurtwood Edge • Another Time • Tyme Cube • Cement City • Summers Past • Molly Mundane • Maat • Our Thing • Ojai • Song For Lisa

| 10/17/81 | 205 | 3 | 2 **Travelin' Light** ...........................................................................[I] | $10 | MCA 5245 |
|----------|-----|---|---|---|---|

Travelin' Light • All Those Nights Alone • Sooner Than Later • Gettin' Away From It All • Sundance Shuffle • King Of Cool • Sleepwalk • Audrey • Why • Paula • Trinity

## WELCH, Bob
Born on 7/31/46 in Los Angeles. Rock singer/guitarist. Member of Fleetwood Mac from 1971-74.

| 11/14/81 | 201 | 4 | **Bob Welch** | $10 | RCA Victor 4107 |
|----------|-----|---|---|---|---|

Two To Do • Remember • Bend Me Shape Me • That's What We Said • If You Think You Know How To Love Me • It's What Ya Don't Say • You Can't Do That • Secrets • Imaginary Fool • To My Heart Again • Drive

## WELK, Lawrence
Born on 3/11/03 in Strasburg, North Dakota. Died of pneumonia on 5/17/92. Accordion player and polka/sweet band leader since the mid-1920s. Band's style labeled as "champagne music." Own TV show from 1955-82. *Top Pop Albums*: 42.

| 5/8/71 | 219 | 3 | 1 **No, No, Nanette** ......................................................................... | $12 | Ranwood 8087 |
|--------|-----|---|---|---|---|

vocals by The Lawrence Welk Singers

Tea For Two • Too Many Rings Around Rosie • I've Confessed To The Breeze • I Want To Be Happy • No, No, Nanette • You Can Dance With Any Girl At All • "Where Has My Hubby Gone" Blues • Call Of The Sea • Take A Little One Step

| 2/5/72 | 202 | 2 | 2 **Go Away Little Girl** ..................................................................... | $12 | Ranwood 8091 |
|--------|-----|---|---|---|---|

vocals by Guy Hovis and Ralna English

Go Away Little Girl • Never Ending Song Of Love • Theme From "Summer Of '42" • I Hear Those Church Bells Ringing • The Night They Drove Old Dixie Down • Sweet City Woman • He's So Fine • Take Me Home, Country Roads • Never My Love • Rainy Days And Mondays • What Are You Doing Sunday • Adios, Au Revoir, Auf Wiedersehn

## WELLS, Brandi ○
Female R&B singer from Philadelphia.

| 3/20/82 | 202 | 7 | **Watch Out** .................................................................................. | $10 | WMOT 37668 |
|---------|-----|---|---|---|---|

Watch Out • When You Get Right Down To It • Fantasy • I Hate To See You Go • I Love You • What Goes Around Comes Around • You Are My Life • Falling In Love

## WELLS, Cory ○
Born on 2/5/42 in Buffalo, New York. Member of **Three Dog Night**.

| 3/4/78 | 210 | 1 | **Touch Me** ................................................................................... | $12 | A&M 4673 |
|--------|-----|---|---|---|---|

Waiting For You • When You Touch Me This Way • You're My Day • Everything's Right For Love • Midnight Lady (Hiding In The Shadows) • Starlight • Throw A Little Bit Of Love My Way • I Know You're Willin' Darlin' • Change Of Heart • Lady Put The Light Out

## WERNER, David
Rock singer/guitarist from Pittsburgh.

| 4/6/74 | 207 | 5 | **Whizz Kid** ................................................................................... | $12 | RCA Victor 0350 |
|--------|-----|---|---|---|---|

One More Wild Guitar • Whizz Kid • The Lady In Waiting • The Ballad Of Trixie Silver • It's A Little Bit Sad • Love Is Tragic • Plan 9 • Counting The Ways • The Death Of Me Yet • A Sleepless Night

## WEST, Leslie
Born Leslie Weinstein on 10/22/45 in New York City. Male rock singer/guitarist. Founding member of Mountain.

| 11/29/75 | 203 | 2 | **The Leslie West Band** ................................................................. | $12 | Phantom 1258 |
|----------|-----|---|---|---|---|

Money (Whatcha Gonna Do) • Dear Prudence • Get It Up (No Bass - Whatsoever) • Singapore Sling • By The River • The Twister • The Setting Sun • Sea Of Heartache • We'll Find A Way • We Gotta Get Out Of This Place

## WESTON, Kim ○
Born Agatha Natalie Weston on 12/30/39 in Detroit. R&B singer.

| 9/11/71 | 208 | 1 | **Kim Kim Kim** .............................................................................. | $25 | Volt 6014 |
|---------|-----|---|---|---|---|

You Just Don't Know • The Love I've Been Looking For • What Could Be Better • When Something Is Wrong With My Baby • Love Vibrations • Buy Myself A Man • Got To Get You Off My Mind • Soul On Fire • Brothers & Sisters (Get Together) • Penny Blues • The Choice Is Up To You (Walk With Me Jesus)

### WHA-KOO ☉
Pop-rock group: David Palmer (vocals), Danny Douma and Nick van Maarth (guitars), Richard Kosinski (keyboards), Don Francisco (percussion), Peter Freiberger (bass) and Claude Pepper (drums).

| | | | | | |
|---|---|---|---|---|---|
| 3/4/78 | 202 | 10 | Berkshire | $10 | ABC 1043 |

Rig-A-Marole • Fat Love • Mother Of Pearl • Midnight Kitchen • (You're Such A) Fabulous Dancer • Berkshire • I'm Here • Expire On Me • Dreaming As One

### WHISPERS, The
R&B vocal group from Los Angeles: twin brothers Walter and Wallace "Scotty" Scott, Marcus Hutson, Nicholas Cardwell and Leaveil Degree.

| | | | | | |
|---|---|---|---|---|---|
| 12/8/79+ | 201 | 5 | Happy Holidays To You | [X] $10 | Solar 3489 |

Funky Christmas • This Time Of The Year • Santa Claus Is Coming To Town • Happy Holidays To You • A Very Special Holiday • This Christmas • The Christmas Song • White Christmas

### WHITE, Alan ☉
Born on 6/14/49 in England. Session drummer.

| | | | | | |
|---|---|---|---|---|---|
| 6/26/76 | 209 | 1 | Ramshackled | $12 | Atlantic 18167 |

Oooh Baby (Goin' To Pieces) • One Way Rag • Avakak • Spring-Song Of Innocence • Giddy • Silly Woman • Marching Into A Bottle • Everybody • Darkness (Parts I,II,III)

### WHITE, Barry
Born on 9/12/44 in Galveston, Texas; raised in Los Angeles. R&B singer/songwriter/keyboardist/producer/arranger. Leader of **Love Unlimited Orchestra**. Married singer Glodean James.

| | | | | | |
|---|---|---|---|---|---|
| 4/18/81 | 201 | 3 | 1 Barry & Glodean | $10 | Unlimited Gold 37054 |

**BARRY WHITE & GLODEAN WHITE**

Our Theme - Part I • I Want You • You're The Only One For Me • This Love • The Better Love Is (The Worse It Is When It's Over) • You • We Can't Let Go Of Love • You Make My Life Easy Livin' • Didn't We Make It Happen, Baby • Our Theme - Part II

| | | | | | |
|---|---|---|---|---|---|
| 10/3/81 | 207 | 2 | 2 Beware! | $10 | Unlimited Gold 37176 |

Beware • Relax To The Max • Let Me In And Let's Begin With Love • Your Love, Your Love • Tell Me Who Do You Love • Rio de Janeiro • You're My High • Oooo....Ahhh.... • I Won't Settle For Less Than The Best (For You Baby) • Louie Louie

### WHITE, Lenny
Born on 12/19/49 in New York City. Former drummer of the jazz-rock band Return To Forever. Leader of Twennynine.

| | | | | | |
|---|---|---|---|---|---|
| 3/19/77 | 203 | 6 | 1 Big City | [I] $12 | Nemperor 441 |

Big City • Sweet Dreamer • Interludes: Egypt/Nocturne • Rapid Transit • Ritmo Loco • Dreams Come And Go Away • Enchanted Pool Suite: Prelude/Part I/Part II • And We Meet Again

| | | | | | |
|---|---|---|---|---|---|
| 1/27/79 | 205 | 2 | 2 Streamline | [I] $10 | Elektra 164 |

Struttin' • Lady Madonna • 12 Bars From Mars • Earthlings • Spazmo Strikes Again • Time • Pooh Bear • Lockie's Inspiration • I'll See You Soon • Night Games • Cosmic Indigo

### WHITE LIGHTNIN' ☉
Rock trio: brothers Donald (vocals, guitar) and Woody (drums) Kinsey, with Busta Cherry Jones (bass).

| | | | | | |
|---|---|---|---|---|---|
| 8/23/75 | 205 | 6 | White Lightnin' | $12 | Island 9325 |

Jokes On You • Without You • Bloody Tears • Return To The Underground • Wild In The Streets • Shotgun Rider • "T" In Trouble • Danger • That's No Lie • Young Blood

### WHITFIELD, Robert "Goodie" ☉
Born in Dallas. R&B singer/keyboard player.

| | | | | | |
|---|---|---|---|---|---|
| 10/2/82 | 207 | 2 | Call Me Goodie | $10 | Total Experience 3002 |

Do Something • You And I • Does Anybody Know Where The Party Is? • Puddin' Pie • L.A. • Goodie • Come Into My Life • Country Rap • Goody Goody

### WHITFORD/ST. HOLMES ☉
Rock duo. Brad Whitford was born on 2/23/52 in Winchester, Massachusetts. Guitarist for Aerosmith. Derek St. Holmes was singer/guitarist for Ted Nugent's band.

| | | | | | |
|---|---|---|---|---|---|
| 9/26/81 | 208 | 2 | Whitford/St. Holmes | $10 | Columbia 37365 |

I Need Love • Whiskey Woman • Hold On • Sharpshooter • Every Morning • Action • Shy Away • Does It Really Matter? • Spanish Boy • Mystery Girl

### WHITMAN, Slim
Born Otis Whitman on 1/20/24 in Tampa, Florida. Country balladeer/yodeller.

| | | | | | |
|---|---|---|---|---|---|
| 8/29/81 | 206 | 3 | Mr. Songman | $10 | Cleveland Int'l. 37403 |

Destiny • Can't Help Falling In Love With You • Open Up Your Heart • Flowers • My Melody Of Love • Mr. Songman • I Went To Your Wedding • Tonight Is The Night (We Fell In Love) • Oh My Darlin' (I Love You) • If I Had My Life To Live Over

### WHITTAKER, Roger
Born on 3/22/36 in Nairobi, Kenya. British singer.

| | | | | | |
|---|---|---|---|---|---|
| 4/24/76 | 202 | 8 | 1 Roger Whittaker | $12 | RCA Victor 1313 |

Every Time Is Going To Be The Last Time • All Of My Life • Hold On • Pretty Bird • Image To My Mind • From The People To The People • The Seasons (Come And Go) • Oh No Not Me • Don't Let 'Em Change • And Still The Sea • So Long

| | | | | | |
|---|---|---|---|---|---|
| 10/24/81 | 210 | 2 | 2 Changes | $10 | RCA Victor 4129 |

produced by Chet Atkins

When I Dream • Changes • Honolulu City Lights • Smooth Sailing • I Can Hear Kentucky Calling Me • How Does It Feel • Moonshine • Rocky Top • River Lady • Barroom Country Singer

### WIDOW MAKER
British hard-rock group: Steve Ellis (vocals), Luther "Ariel Bender" Grosvenor (guitar), Bob Daisley (bass) and Paul Nicholls (drums). Bender was a member of **Mott The Hoople**.

| | | | | | |
|---|---|---|---|---|---|
| 8/28/76 | 205 | 1 | Widow Maker | $12 | United Artists 642 |

Such A Shame • Pin A Rose On Me • On The Road • Straight Faced Fighter • Ain't Telling You Nothing • When I Met You • Leave The Kids Alone • Shine A Light On Me • Running Free • Got A Dream

### WILD CHERRY
White funk group from Steubenville, Ohio: Robert Parissi (vocals, guitar), Donnie Iris (guitar), Mark Avsec (keyboards), Cookie Michalchick (bass) and Ron Beitle (drums). Iris went solo in 1980.

| 5/19/79 | 204 | 2 | Only The Wild Survive .................................................. | $10 | Epic 35760 |

Try A Piece Of My Love • Look At Her Dance • Don't Wait Too Long • Starlight • Hold On To Your Hiney • All Night's All Right • Raindance • Take Me Back • Keep On Playin' That Funky Music

### WILDERNESS ROAD ☉
Rock group from Chicago: brothers Andy (bass) and Tom (drums) Haban, Warren Leming (guitar) and Nate Herman (keyboards). All share vocals.

| 3/18/72 | 213 | 2 | Wilderness Road................................................................ | $12 | Columbia 31118 |

Medley: Wilderness/Queasy Rider • Peaceful Life • Medley: Yes I Am/Revival/Testify • Medley: Ten Miles/Testify (Reprise) • Lost And Lonely Navigator • Medley: Sing Your Song To The Lord/Brother Are You Troubled? • I Had The Right • Pictures In A Gallery • Bounty Man • Dr. Morpho's Revenge • Death Dream • Don't Cry Lady • Rider's Return

### WILLIAMS, Andy
Born Howard Andrew Williams on 12/3/28 in Wall Lake, Iowa. Pop singer. Hosted own NBC-TV variety series from 1962-67, 1969-71. Formerly married to singer/actress Claudine Longet. *Top Pop Albums*: 34.

| 12/21/74 | 203 | 2 | Christmas Present ............................................................ | [X] $12 | Columbia 33191 |

Christmas Present • Joy To The World • O' Little Town Of Bethlehem • Christmas Bells • It Came Upon A Midnight Clear • Ave Maria • Oh Come All Ye Faithful • Angels We Have Heard On High • Hark! The Herald Angels Sing • Ave Maria • What Child Is This • I Heard The Bells On Christmas Day • The Lord's Prayer

### WILLIAMS, Don
Born on 5/27/39 in Floydada, Texas. Country singer/songwriter/guitarist. Leader of the Pozo-Seco Singers.

| 4/21/84 | 208 | 1 | ● The Best Of Don Williams Volume III............................ | [G] $10 | MCA 5465 |

I Believe In You • Lord, I Hope This Day Is Good • Lay Down Beside Me • Mistakes • Miracles • Good Ole Boys Like Me • It Must Be Love • Listen To The Radio • If Hollywood Don't Need You • Love Me Over Again

### WILLIAMS, Hank Jr.
Born Randall Hank Williams on 5/26/49 in Shreveport, Louisiana; raised in Nashville. Country singer/songwriter/guitarist. Son of Hank Williams. Nicknamed "Bocephus" by his father. *Top Pop Albums*: 28.

| 11/24/79 | 201 | 4 | ● Family Tradition ............................................................ | $10 | Elektra/Curb 194 |

To Love Somebody • Old Flame, New Fire • Always Loving You • We Can Work It All Out • I Fought The Law • Family Tradition • Only Daddy That Will Walk The Line • Paying On Time • I've Got Rights • I Just Ain't Been Able

### WILLIAMS, Roger
Born Louis Weertz on 10/1/24 in Omaha. Pianist. *Top Pop Albums*: 38.

| 3/13/71 | 203 | 9 | Golden Hits Vol. 2 .......................................................... | [G-I] $12 | Kapp 3638 |

Gentle On My Mind • Galveston • Alfie • Theme From Zorba The Greek • Happy Heart • The Impossible Dream • A Taste Of Honey • This Guy's In Love With You • Up-Up And Away • Love Theme From "Romeo And Juliet" • Softly, As I Leave You

### WILLIAMS, Tony
Born on 12/12/45 in Chicago. Died of a heart attack on 2/23/97. Jazz-fusion drummer.

| 7/10/71 | 214 | 1 | Ego ................................................................................ | [I] $12 | Polydor 4065 |

**THE TONY WILLIAMS LIFETIME**

Clap City • There Comes A Time • Piskow's Filigree • Circa 45 • Two Worlds • Some Hip Drum Shit • Lonesome Wells • Mom And Dad • The Urchin's Of Shermese

### WILLIAMSON, James — see POP, Iggy

### WILSON, Mary ☉
Born on 3/6/44 in Greeneville, Mississippi; raised in Detroit. Founding member of The Supremes.

| 11/3/79 | 208 | 1 | Mary Wilson .................................................................... | $10 | Motown 927 |

Red Hot • I've Got What You Need • You Make Me Feel So Good • (I Love A) Warm Summer Night • Pick Up The Pieces • You're The Light That Guides My Way • Midnight Dancer

### WILSON, Nancy
Born on 2/20/37 in Chillicothe, Ohio; raised in Columbus, Ohio. Jazz singer. *Top Pop Albums*: 34.

| 3/17/73 | 201 | 7 | I Know I Love Him .......................................................... | $12 | Capitol 11131 |

We Can Make It Baby • Morning In Your Eyes • Don't Misunderstand • Are We Losin' Touch • I Was Telling Him About You • Easy Evil • The Laughter And The Tears • Can I • I Heard You Singing Your Song • I Know I Love Him

### WINCHESTER, Jesse
Born on 5/17/44 in Shreveport, Louisiana. Male folk-pop singer/songwriter/guitarist.

| 11/6/76 | 210 | 1 | Let The Rough Side Drag ................................................ | $12 | Bearsville 6964 |

Let The Rough Side Drag • Damned If You Do • Step By Step • Lay Down Your Burden • Everybody Knows But Me • Blow On, Chilly Wind • Working In The Vineyard • How About You • It Takes More Than A Hammer And Nails To Make A House A Home • As Soon As I Get On My Feet • The Only Show In Town • The Brand New Tennessee Waltz

### WINTER, Johnny
Born on 2/23/44 in Leland, Mississippi. Blues-rock singer/guitarist. Both Johnny and brother Edgar Winter are albinos.

| 9/15/73 | 209 | 3 | 1 Austin, Texas ................................................................ | $15 | United Artists 139 |

Rollin' And Tumblin' • Tribute To Muddy • I Got Love If You Want It • Bad Luck And Trouble • Help Me • Mean Town Blues • Broke Down Engine • Black Cat Bone • My Own Fault Darlin' • Forty-Four

| 9/15/73 | 215 | 2 | 2 Before The Storm ........................................................ | $20 | Janus 3056 [2] |

Parchman Farm • Livin' In The Blues • Leavin' Blues • Thirty-Eight, Thirty-Two, Twenty • Bad News • Kind Hearted Woman • Out Of Sight • Low Down Gal Of Mine • Going Down Slow • Avocado Green • Stay By My Side • I Had To Cry • Kiss Tomorrow Goodbye • Harlem Nocturne • Easy Lovin' Girl • Spiders Of The Mind • My World Turns All Around Her • Take A Chance On My Love • Please Come Home For Christmas

**WINTER, Paul**
Born on 8/31/39 in Altoona, Pennsylvania. Soprano saxophonist.

| | | | | | |
|---|---|---|---|---|---|
| 8/12/78 | 209 | 1 | Common Ground ...................... [I] | $10 | A&M 4698 |

Ancient Voices (Nhmamusasa) • Eagle • Icarus • The Promise Of A Fisherman (Iemanja) • Ocean Dream • Trio • Common Ground (Velho Sermão) • Lay Down Your Burden • Wolf Eyes • Duet • Midnight (Minuit) • Trilogy

**WISHBONE ASH**
Progressive-rock group from Devonshire, England: Andy Powell and Ted Turner (vocals, guitars), Martin Turner (bass) and Steve Upton (drums). By 1981, Laurie Wisefield had replaced Ted Turner and John Wetton had replaced Martin Turner.

| | | | | | |
|---|---|---|---|---|---|
| 3/13/71 | 208 | 10 | 1 Wishbone Ash | $15 | Decca 75249 |

Blind Eye • Lady Whiskey • Errors Of My Way • Queen Of Torture • Handy • Phoenix

| | | | | | |
|---|---|---|---|---|---|
| 5/23/81 | 202 | 4 | 2 Number The Brave | $10 | MCA 5200 |

Get Ready • Where Is The Love • That's That • Roller Coaster • Number The Brave • Loaded • Underground • Rainstorm • Kicks On The Street • Open Road

**WOBBLE, Jah ○**
Punk singer/guitarist Wobble (from Public Image Ltd.) was born John Wardle. Guitarist The Edge (from U2) was born David Evans on 8/8/61 in Barking, England. Bassist Czukay was born on 3/24/38 in Danzig, Germany.

| | | | | | |
|---|---|---|---|---|---|
| 3/31/84 | 209 | 1 | Snake Charmer ...................... [M] | $10 | Island 90151 |

**JAH WOBBLE - THE EDGE - HOLGER CZUKAY**
Snake Charmer • Hold On To Your Dreams • It Was A Camel • Sleazy • Snake Charmer (Reprise)

**WOLFMAN JACK ○**
Born Robert Weston Smith on 1/21/38 in Brooklyn. Died of a heart attack on 7/1/95. Legendary DJ with several TV and movie appearances.

| | | | | | |
|---|---|---|---|---|---|
| 10/7/72 | 210 | 3 | Wolfman Jack | $15 | Wooden Nickel 1009 |

Sweet Caroline • There's An Old Man In Our Town • Diggin' On Mrs. Jones • Spinning Ball • Hey Wolfman • I Ain't Never Seen A White Man • Gallop • Hoodooin' Of Miss Fanny De Berry • Evil Woman • Let Me Belong To You

**WOMACK, Bobby**
Born on 3/4/44 in Cleveland. R&B singer/songwriter/guitarist. Nicknamed "The Preacher."

| | | | | | |
|---|---|---|---|---|---|
| 4/1/78 | 205 | 9 | 1 Pieces | $10 | Columbia 35083 |

It's Party Time • Trust Your Heart • Stop Before We Start • When Love Begins Friendship Ends • Wind It Up • Is This The Thanks I Get • Caught Up In The Middle • Never Let Nothing Get The Best Of You

| | | | | | |
|---|---|---|---|---|---|
| 6/16/79 | 206 | 3 | 2 Roads Of Life | $10 | Arista 4222 |

The Roads Of Life • How Could You Break My Heart • Honey Dripper Boogie • The Roots In Me • What Are You Doin' • Give It Up • Mr. D.J. Don't Stop The Music • I Honestly Love You

| | | | | | |
|---|---|---|---|---|---|
| 6/1/85 | 207 | 5 | 3 Someday We'll All Be Free | $10 | Beverly Glen 10006 |

I'm So Proud • Someday We'll All Be Free • Gifted One • Falling In Love Again • Searching For My Love • In Over My Heart • I Wish I Had Someone To Go Home To

**WOOD, Lauren ○**
Born in Pittsburgh. Female pop singer/songwriter/keyboardist.

| | | | | | |
|---|---|---|---|---|---|
| 10/20/79 | 205 | 6 | Lauren Wood | $10 | Warner 3278 |

featuring Novi Novog (synthesizer) and Ernie Eremita (bass)
Please Don't Leave • Save The Man • Hollywood • Nothin' But A Heartache • Gotta Lotta • Where Did I Get These Tears • Dirty Work • Time Zone • Overload

**WOOD, Roy**
Born on 11/8/46 in Birmingham, England. Progressive-rock guitarist. Member of **The Move** and Electric Light Orchestra.

| | | | | | |
|---|---|---|---|---|---|
| 5/5/73 | 201 | 5 | 1 Wizzard's Brew | $12 | United Artists 042 |

**ROY WOOD'S WIZZARD**
You Can Dance Your Rock 'N' Roll • Meet Me At The Jailhouse • Jolly Cup Of Tea • Buffalo Station-Going Down To Memphis • Got A Crush About You • Wear A Fast Gun

| | | | | | |
|---|---|---|---|---|---|
| 2/21/76 | 205 | 1 | 2 Mustard | $12 | United Artists 575 |

Mustard • Any Old Time Will Do • The Rain Came Down On Everything • You Sure Got It Now • Why Does Such A Pretty Girl Sing Those Sad Songs • The Song • Look Thru' The Eyes Of A Fool • Interlude • Get On Down Home

**WRABIT**
Rock group from Toronto: Lou Nadeau (vocals), John Albani (guitar), Gerald O'Brien (keyboards), Chris Brockway (bass) and Gary McCracken (drums; **Max Webster**).

| | | | | | |
|---|---|---|---|---|---|
| 10/2/82 | 210 | 1 | Tracks | $10 | MCA 5359 |

Run For Cover • Soldier Of Fortune • I'll Never Run Away • See No Evil • Bare Knuckler • Don't Lose That Feeling • Unsung Hero • Don't Stop Me Now • There Was A Time • Castles In The Sky

**WRIGHT, Richard ○**
Born on 1/28/45 in London. Singer/keyboard player. Former member of Pink Floyd.

| | | | | | |
|---|---|---|---|---|---|
| 11/4/78 | 203 | 1 | Wet Dream | $10 | Columbia 35559 |

Mediterranean C • Against The Odds • Cat Cruise • Summer Elegy • Waves • Holiday • Mad Yannis Dance • Drop In From The Top • Pink's Song • Funky Deux

**WYNETTE, Tammy**
Born Virginia Wynette Pugh on 5/5/42 in Itawamba County, Mississippi. Died of a blood clot on 4/6/98. Known as "The First Lady of Country Music." Married to **George Jones** from 1969-75.

| | | | | | |
|---|---|---|---|---|---|
| 2/3/73 | 201 | 4 | My Man | $15 | Epic 31717 |

My Man • Things I Love To Do • Hold On (To The Love I Got) • Loving You Could Never Be Better • 'Til I Get It Right • Walk Softly On The Bridges • The Bridge Of Love • You Can't Hang On (Lookin' On) • The Happiest Girl In The Whole U.S.A. • Gone With Another Man • Good Lovin'

# X

### XAVION ☉
R&B group from Memphis: Dexter Haywood (vocals), Kevan Wilkins (guitar), Johnnie Woods and Derwin Adams (keyboards), Skip Johnson (bass) and Michael "Slugger" Tucker (drums).

| | | | | | |
|---|---|---|---|---|---|
| 10/13/84 | 201 | 6 | **Burnin' Hot** | $10 | Asylum 60375 |

Eat Your Heart Out • Burnin' Hot • Don't Let It Go To Your Head • Self-Built Hell • Tell Me • Love Games • Can't Get My Connection • You're My Type • Get Me Hot

# Y

### YAMASHTA, Stomu
Born on 3/15/47 in Japan. Eclectic composer/percussionist.

| | | | | | |
|---|---|---|---|---|---|
| 8/12/78 | 205 | 2 | **Go - Live From Paris** .........................[L] | $15 | Island 10 [2] |

recorded on 6/12/76 at the Palais Des Sports in Paris; features Steve Winwood, Michael Shrieve, Klaus Schulze, Al Dimeola, Jerome Rimson, Pat Thrall, Brothers James and Karen Friedman

Space Song • Carnival • Windspin • Ghost Machine • Surf Spin • Time Is Here • Winner/Loser • Solitude • Nature • Air Voice • Crossing The Line • Man Of Leo • Stellar • Space Requiem

### YARDBIRDS, The
Rock group formed in 1963 in Surrey, England. Changing lineup featured vocalist/harmonica player Keith Relf (electrocuted on 5/14/76, age 33) and at different times included guitar heroes Eric Clapton, Jeff Beck and Jimmy Page. Disbanded in July 1968. Group inducted into the Rock and Roll Hall of Fame in 1992.

| | | | | | |
|---|---|---|---|---|---|
| 4/30/77 | 204 | 3 | **The Yardbirds Great Hits** .........................[G] | $12 | Epic 34491 |

For Your Love • Heart Full Of Soul • Still I'm Sad • I'm Not Talking • Shapes Of Things • The Train Kept A-Rollin' • I Wish You Would • I Ain't Done Wrong • I Ain't Got You • I'm A Man

### YARROW, Peter
Born on 5/31/38 in New York City. Folk singer/songwriter/guitarist. Member of Peter, Paul & Mary.

| | | | | | |
|---|---|---|---|---|---|
| 10/13/73 | 203 | 6 | **That's Enough For Me** ......................... | $12 | Warner 2730 |

That's Enough For Me • Isn't That So? • Love's Way • Groundhog • Wayfaring Stranger • The Harder They Come • O, Happy Day • Just One Pass • Whispered Words • Old Father Time

### YELLOWJACKETS
Pop-jazz trio from Los Angeles: Russell Ferrante (keyboards), Jimmy Haslip (bass) and Ricky Lawson (drums).

| | | | | | |
|---|---|---|---|---|---|
| 7/25/81 | 201 | 9 | **Yellowjackets** [I] | $10 | Warner 3573 |

Matinee Idol • Imperial Strut • Sittin' In It • Rush Hour • The Hornet • Priscilla • It's Almost Gone

### YELLOWMAN ☉
Born Winston Foster in Kingston, Jamaica. Albino reggae singer.

| | | | | | |
|---|---|---|---|---|---|
| 6/2/84 | 203 | 5 | **King Yellowman** ......................... | $10 | Columbia 39301 |

Medley: Jamaica Nice/Take Home Country Roads • Strong Me Strong • Medley: Mi Believe/Summer Holiday • Wha Dat • Medley: Moving On/Keep On Moving • Disco Reggae • Medley: Still Be A Lady/Girls Can't Do What The Guys Do • Reggae Calypso • Medley: Ooh We/Sea Cruise • Medley: If You Should Lose Me/You'll Lose A Good Thing

### YOULDEN, Chris ☉
Male lead singer of **Savoy Brown**.

| | | | | | |
|---|---|---|---|---|---|
| 7/14/73 | 210 | 4 | **Nowhere Road** ......................... | $12 | London 633 |

Nowhere Road • One October Day • Chink Of Sanity • Cryin' In The Road • Mama Don't You Talk So Loud • Standing On The Corner • In The Wood • Wake Up Neighbour • Street Sounds • Time Will Tell • Pick Up My Dogs And Gone

### YOUNG, Steve ☉
Born on 7/12/42 in Newnan, Georgia. Country-rock singer/songwriter.

| | | | | | |
|---|---|---|---|---|---|
| 9/4/76 | 201 | 2 | **Renegade Picker** | $15 | RCA Victor 1759 |

Renegade Picker • I Can't Be Myself • Old Memories (Mean Nothing To Me) • It's Not Supposed To Be That Way • Tobacco Road • Light Of My Life • Lonesome, On'ry And Mean • All Her Lovers Want To Be The Hero • Broken Hearted People (Take Me To A Barroom) • Sweet Thing • Home Sweet Home (Revisited)

# Z

### ZADORA, Pia
Born Pia Schipani on 5/4/56 in New York City. Singer/actress. Appeared in several movies.

| | | | | | |
|---|---|---|---|---|---|
| 3/23/85 | 201 | 3 | **When The Rain Begins To Fall** | $10 | MCA/Curb 5557 |

When The Rain Begins To Fall *[w/Jermaine Jackson]* • Little Bit Of Heaven *[w/Mark Spiro]* • Real Love • Follow My Heartbeat • Let's Dance Tonight • Clapping Song • Substitute • You Bring Out The Lover In Me • Rock It Out

### ZAPPA, Frank — see MOTHERS OF INVENTION

### ZOMBIES, The
Rock group from Hertfordshire, England: Colin Blunstone (vocals), Paul Atkinson (guitar), Rod Argent (keyboards), Chris White (bass) and Hugh Grundy (drums). Disbanded in late 1967. Rod formed Argent in 1969.

| 5/25/74 | 204 | 6 | Time Of The Zombies......................................................................[K] $15 | | Epic 32861 [2] |

She's Not There • Tell Her No • Whenever You're Ready • Is This The Dream • Summertime • I Love You • You Make Me Feel Good • She's Coming Home • She Loves The Way They Love Her • Imagine The Swan • Smokey Day • If It Don't Work Out • I Know She Will • Don't Cry For Me • Walking In The Sun • I'll Call You Mine • Care Of Cell 44 • A Rose For Emily • Maybe After He's Gone • Beechwood Park • Brief Candles • Hung Up On A Dream • Changes • I Want Her She Wants Me • This Will Be Our Year • Butchers Tale (Western Front 1914) • Friends Of Mine • Time Of The Season

### ZZ TOP
Rock-blues trio from Houston: Billy Gibbons (vocals, guitar), Dusty Hill (vocals, bass) and Frank "Rube" Beard (drums).

| 1/30/71 | 201 | 1 | ZZ Top's First Album | $15 | London 584 |

(Somebody Else Been) Shaking Your Tree • Brown Sugar • Squank • Goin Down To Mexico • Old Man • Neighbor, Neighbor • Certified Blues • Bedroom Thang • Just Got Back From Baby's • Backdoor Love Affair

# SOUNDTRACKS
Each movie's stars are listed below the title. Also shown are the Composer (cp), Conductor (cd), Lyricist (ly), Music Writer (mu), Performer (pf) and Songwriter [music & lyrics] (sw). The following symbols are also used in this section: [I] Instrumental, [M] Musical, [O] Oldies and [V] Various Artists.

| 9/29/79 | 208 | 1 | 1 Americathon ...........................................................................[V] $12 | | Lorimar 36174 |

It's A Beautiful Day [Beach Boys] • Get A Move On [Eddie Money] • Open Up Your Heart [Eddie Money] • (I Don't Want To Go To) Chelsea [Elvis Costello] • Crawling To The U.S.A. [Elvis Costello] • Without Love [Nick Lowe] • Car Wars [Tom Scott] • Don't You Ever Say No [Zane Buzby] • Gold [Harvey Korman]

**Animalympics -- see GOULDMAN, Graham**
animated movie; voices by: Gilda Radner/Billy Crystal/Harry Shearer

| 8/25/84 | 203 | 4 | 2 Bachelor Party ........................................................................[V] $10 | | I.R.S. 70047 |

Tom Hanks/Adrian Zmed/William Tepper/Tawny Kitaen
American Beat '84 [Fleshtones] • Something Isn't Right [Oingo Boingo] • Crazy Over You [Jools Holland] • Little Demon [Adrian Zmed] • Wind Out [R.E.M] • Bachelor Party [Oingo Boingo] • What Kind Of Hell [Alarm] • Alley Oop [Darlene Love] • Why Do Good Girls Like Bad Boys? [Angel & The Reruns] • Dream Of The West [Yip Yip Coyote]

| 12/18/71 | 208 | 5 | 3 Bedknobs And Broomsticks ....................................................[M] $20 | | Buena Vista 5003 |

Angela Lansbury/David Tomlinson/Roddy McDowall/Sam Jaffe; sw: Richard & Robert Sherman; cd: Irwin Kostal
Overture-The Old Home Guard • The Age Of Not Believing • With A Flair • A Step In The Right Direction • Medley: Eglantine/Don't Let Me Down/Reprise: Eglantine • Portobello Road • Portobello Street Dance • The Beautiful Briny • Substitutiary Locomotion • Reprises: Eglantine/Portobello Road • Finale

| 10/20/84 | 207 | 1 | 4 Body Rock ................................................................................[V] $10 | | EMI America 17140 |

Lorenzo Lamas/Vicki Frederick/Cameron Dye/Ray Sharkey
Body Rock [Maria Vidal] • Teamwork [David Lasley] • Why You Wanna Break My Heart [Dwight Twilley] • One Thing Leads To Another [Roberta Flack] • Let Your Body Rock (Don't Stop) [Ralph MacDonald] • Vanishing Point [Baxter Robertson] • Sharpshooter [Laura Branigan] • The Jungle [Ashford & Simpson] • Deliver [Martin Briley] • The Closest To Love [Ashford & Simpson]

**Breaking Glass -- see O'CONNOR, Hazel**
Hazel O'Connor/Phil Daniels/Jonathan Pryce

| 12/11/82+ | 201 | 8 | 5 Brimstone & Treacle | [V] $10 | A&M 4915 |

Sting/Denholm Elliott/Joan Plowright/Suzanna Hamilton
When The Roll Is Called Up Yonder [Finchley Children's Music Group] • Brimstone & Treacle [Sting] • Narration [Sting] • How Stupid Mr. Bates [Police] • Only You [Sting] • I Burn For You [Police] • Spread A Little Happiness [Sting] • We Got The Beat [Go-Go's] • You Know I Had The Strangest Dream [Sting] • Up The Junction [Squeeze] • Bless This House [Brimstone Chorale] • A Kind Of Loving [Police] • Brimstone 2 [Sting]

| 5/19/73 | 215 | 4 | 6 Charlotte's Web ......................................................................[M] $15 | | Paramount 1008 |

animated movie, voices by Debbie Reynolds/Henry Gibson/Agnes Moorehead; sw: Richard & Robert Sherman
Main Title • There Must Be Something More • I Can Talk • Chin Up • Mother Earth And Father Time • We've Got Lots In Common • A Veritable Smorgasbord • Deep In The Dark • Chin Up March • Zuckerman's Famous Pig • Charlotte's Farewell (Mother Earth And Father Time) • End Title

| 3/22/80 | 202 | 4 | 7 Cruising .....................................................................................[V] $12 | | Lorimar 36410 |

Al Pacino/Paul Sorvino/Karen Allen/Richard Cox
Heat Of The Moment [Willy DeVille] • Loneliness [Cripples] • Spy Boy [John Hiatt] • When I Close My Eyes I See Blood [Madelynn Von Ritz] • Lump [Mutiny] • Shakedown [Rough Trade] • Pullin' My String [Willy DeVille] • Lions Share [Germs (G.I.)] • Hypnotize [Cripples] • It's So Easy [Willy DeVille]

| 3/28/81 | 202 | 4 | 8 Dance Craze .............................................................................[V] $10 | | Chrysalis 1299 |

concert movie featuring top British ska groups
Concrete Jungle [Specials] • Mirror In The Bathroom [English Beat] • Lip Up Fatty [Bad Manners] • Razor Blade Alley [Madness] • Three Minute Hero [Selecter] • Easy Life [Bodysnatchers] • Big Shot [English Beat] • One Step Beyond [Madness] • Ranking Full Stop [English Beat] • Man At C & A [Specials] • Missing Words [Selecter] • Inner London Violence [Bad Manners] • Night Boat To Cairo [Madness] • Too Much Pressure [Selecter] • Nite Klub [Specials]

| 1/29/83 | 204 | 3 | 9 Dark Crystal, The ....................................................................[I] $10 | | Warner 23749 |

puppet performers include Jim Henson/Frank Oz/Kathryn Mullen; cp: Trevor Jones; cd: Marcus Dods; pf: London Symphony Orchestra
Overture • The Power Ceremony • The Storm • The Mystic Master Dies • Medley: The Funerals/Jen's Journey • The Skeksis Duel • The Pod Dance • Love Theme • Gelfling Song • The Gelfling Ruins • The Landstrider Journey • The Great Conjunction • Finale

| 9/8/73 | 205 | 3 | 10 Dillinger ..................................................................................[I] $12 | | MCA 360 |

Warren Oates/Ben Johnson/Michelle Phillips/Cloris Leachman; cp/cd: Barry DeVorzon
We're In The Money • Just One More Chance • Honey • Square Dance Medley • Homecoming • Happy Days Are Here Again • Honey (Reprise) • Theme From Dillinger • It's Easy To Remember • Hoe Down • Honey (Reprise) • Beyond The Blue Horizon • Super Gang Blues • One Last Time • Honey (End Title)

| DEBUT | PEAK | WKS | Album Title | $ | Label & Number |
|-------|------|-----|-----------|---|----------------|

**SOUNDTRACKS — Cont'd**

| DEBUT | PEAK | WKS | Album Title | $ | Label & Number |
|-------|------|-----|-----------|---|----------------|
| 8/25/79 | 207 | 4 | 11 **Dracula** ..........................................................................[I] | $12 | MCA 3166 |

Frank Langella/Laurence Olivier/Donald Pleasence/Kate Nelligan; cp/cd: John Williams; pf: London Symphony Orchestra
Medley: Main Title/Storm Sequence • The Night Visitor • To Scarbourough • The Abduction Of Lucy • Night Journeys • The Love Scene • Meeting In The Cave • The Bat Attack • For Mina • Dracula's Death • End Titles

| 2/5/83 | 201 | 6 | 12 **E.T. The Extra-Terrestrial** | $100 | MCA 70000 |

storybook album with music by John Williams and narration by Michael Jackson; album was pulled shortly after release due to legal problems

| 1/25/75 | 204 | 3 | 13 **Earthquake** ......................................................................[I] | $15 | MCA 2081 |

Charlton Heston/Ava Gardner/George Kennedy/Genevieve Bujold; cp/cd: John Williams
Main Title, "Earthquake" • Miles On Wheels • City Theme • Something For Rosa • Love Scene • The City Sleeps • Love Theme • Cory In Jeopardy • Something For Remy • Medley: Watching & Waiting/Miles' Pool Hall/Sam's Rescue • Finale, End Title

| 10/22/83 | 207 | 1 | 14 **Easy Money** ..................................................................... [V] | $10 | Columbia 38968 |

Rodney Dangerfield/Joe Pesci/Geraldine Fitzgerald/Candy Azzara
Easy Money [Billy Joel] • Love's Got A Line On You [Scandal] • It's Raining Men [Weather Girls] • In The Beginning [Heaven] • We Want Action [Nick Lowe] • Funiculi, Funicula [Rodney Dangerfield] • Wedding Tarantella • Willpower • Big Night On The Town • Julio's Honeymoon • Ordinary Man • Monty's Triumph

**Fast Break -- see PRESTON, Billy**
Gabriel Kaplan/Harold Sylvester/Bernard King

**Fast Forward -- see DECO**
John Scott Clough/Don Franklin/Tamara Mark/Tracy Silver

**Gospel Road, The -- see CASH, Johnny**
Johnny Cash/June Carter Cash

| 7/29/78 | 206 | 3 | 15 **Jaws 2** ............................................................................[I] | $12 | MCA 3045 |

Roy Scheider/Lorraine Gary/Murray Hamilton; cp/cd: John Wiliams
Finding The "Orca" (Main Title) • The Menu • Ballet For Divers • The Water Kite Sequence • Brody Misunderstood • The Catamaran Race • Toward Cable Junction • Attack On The Helicopter • The Open Sea • Fire Aboard And Eddie's Death • Sean's Rescue • Attack On The Water Skier • The Big Jolt! • End Title, End Cast

| 5/25/85 | 203 | 2 | 16 **Ladyhawke** ......................................................................[I] | $10 | Atlantic 81248 |

Matthew Broderick/Michelle Pfeiffer/Rutger Hauer; cp/cd: Andrew Powell; pf: The Philharmonia Orchestra
Main Title • Phillipe's Escape • The Search For Phillipe • Tavern Fight (Phillipe) • Tavern Fight (Navarre) • Phillipe Describes Isabeau • Navarre's Ambush • The Chase, The Fall & The Transformation • "She Was Sad At First..." • Navarre Returns To Aquila • Navarre's And Marquet's Duel • Marquet's Death • Bishop's Death • End Title

**Little Fauss And Big Halsy -- see CASH, Johnny**
Robert Redford/Michael J. Pollard/Lauren Hutton/Noah Beery

**Local Hero -- see KNOPFLER, Mark**
Peter Riegert/Burt Lancaster/Fulton MacKay

**Long Riders, The -- see COODER, Ry**
David, Keith & Robert Carradine/Stacy & James Keach/Randy & Dennis Quaid/Nicholas & Christopher Guest

| 1/17/81 | 207 | 1 | 17 **Loving Couples** ................................................................ [V] | $10 | Motown 949 |

Shirley MacLaine/James Coburn/Susan Sarandon/Stephen Collins
Take Me Away [Temptations] • And So It Begins (instrumental) • Turn Up The Music [Syreeta] • I'll Make It With Your Love [Billy Preston] • And So It Begins [Syreeta] • I'll Make It With Your Love (instrumental) • There's More Where That Came From [Temptations] • Bass Odyssey [Jermaine Jackson]

**Marjoe -- see MARJOE**

**Marvin & Tige -- see KLUGH, Earl**
John Cassavetes/Gibran Brown/Billy Dee Williams

| 4/25/81 | 204 | 1 | 18 **Masada** ...........................................................................[I] | $10 | MCA 5168 |

Peter O'Toole/Peter Strauss/Barbara Carrera/Anthony Quayle; cp/cd: Jerry Goldsmith
Main Title • The Old City • The Planting • The Road To Masada • Night Raid • Our Land • The Encampment • No Water • The Slaves

**Melinda -- see BUTLER, Jerry**
Calvin Lockhart/Rosalind Cash

| 2/17/79 | 201 | 2 | 19 **Moment By Moment** ....................................................... [V] | $10 | RSO 3040 |

Lily Tomlin/John Travolta
Moment By Moment [Yvonne Elliman] • The Lady Wants To Know [Michael Franks] • Everybody Needs Love [Stephen Bishop] • Moment By Moment Theme (Reprise) • You Know I Love You [Charles Lloyd] • Sometimes When We Touch [Dan Hill] • Moment By Moment (Main Theme) • For You And I [10CC] • Hollywood Boulevard • Your Heart Never Lies [Charles Lloyd] • Moment By Moment ("On the Beach") • Moment By Moment (Reprise) [Yvonne Elliman]

| 8/4/84 | 204 | 2 | 20 **Muppets Take Manhattan, The** ........................................[M] | $10 | Warner 25114 |

pf: Jim Henson/Frank Oz/Jerry Nelson/Richard Hunt/Dave Goelz
Together Again • You Can't Take No For An Answer • Saying Goodbye • Rat Scat (Something Cookin') • Together Again (Carriage Ride) • I'm Gonna Always Love You • William Tell Overture • Looking For Kermit • Right Where I Belong • Somebody's Getting Married • Waiting For The Wedding • He'll Make Me Happy • The Ceremony • Closing Medley (Final Credits)

**Natural, The -- see NEWMAN, Randy**
Robert Redford/Robert Duvall/Glenn Close/Kim Basinger

| 9/4/82 | 204 | 3 | 21 **Night Shift** ...................................................................... [V] | $10 | Warner 23702 |

Henry Winkler/Michael Keaton/Shelley Long
Night Shift [Quarterflash] • Street Talk [Burt Bacharach] • Girls Know How [Al Jarreau] • The Love Too Good To Last [Pointer Sisters] • That's What Friends Are For [Rod Stewart] • Someday, Someway [Marshall Crenshaw] • Penthouse And Pavement [Heaven 17] • Talk Talk [Talk Talk] • Everlasting Love [Rufus & Chaka Khan] • That's What Friends Are For [Burt Bacharach]

**Oklahoma Crude -- see MANCINI, Henry**
George C. Scott/Faye Dunaway/Jack Palance

| 2/9/74 | 210 | 4 | 22 **Papillon** ..........................................................................[I] | $20 | Capitol 11260 |

Steve McQueen/Dustin Hoffman/Victor Jory/Don Gordon; cp/cd: Jerry Goldsmith
Theme From Papillon • The Camp • Reunion • New Friend • Freedom • Gift From The Sea • Antonio's Death • Cruel Sea • Hospital • Survival

**SOUNDTRACKS — Cont'd**

**Paris, Texas -- see COODER, Ry**
Harry Dean Stanton/Nastassja Kinski/Dean Stockwell

| DEBUT | PEAK | WKS | | | |
|-------|------|-----|---|---|---|
| 6/11/77 | 209 | 2 | **23 Raggedy Ann & Andy** ....................................... [M] $12 | | Columbia 34686 |

animated movie, voices by: Didi Conn/Mark Baker/Joe Silver; sw: Joe Raposo
Main Title - Rag Dolly • Where'd You Go? • I Look And What Do I See • I'm No Girl's Toy • Rag Dolly • Poor Babette • A Miracle • The Abduction & Ho-Yo • Candy Hearts • Blue • Camel's Mirage • I Never Get Enough • I Love You • Hail To Our Glorious King • It's Not Easy Being King • Hooray For Me • You're My Friend • The Plot Thickens • The Tickling And The Last Laugh • Home

| 6/15/85 | 204 | 2 | **24 Rappin'** ...................................... [V] $10 | | Atlantic 81252 |

Mario Van Peebles/Tasia Valenza/Kadeem Hardison
Rappin' *[Lovebug Starski]* • Snack Attack *[Cast]* • The Fight Rap *[Lovebug Starski]* • Neighbourhood Walk *[Mario Van Peebles]* • Itchin' For A Scratch *[Force M.D.'s]* • Flame In The Fire *[Warren Mills]* • Call Me *[D. Terrell]* • If You Want To (FU12) *[Lajuan Carter]* • Golly Gee *[Tuff, Inc.]* • First Love Never Dies *[Eugene Wilde/Joanna Gardner]*

| 12/26/81+ | 202 | 8 | **25 Reds** .......................................... [I] $10 | | Columbia 37690 |

Warren Beatty/Diane Keaton/Jack Nicholson/Maureen Stapleton; cp: Stephen Sondheim; cd: Paul Gemignani
Goodbye For Now *[Jean-Pierre Rampal & Claude Bolling]* • I Don't Want To Play In Your Yard • Comrades (I) • Internationale *[Moscow Radio Chorus]* • I Don't Want To Play In Your Yard *[Heaton Vorse]* • Comrades (II) • The New York Waltz • Bloody Border • Cable Montage • Comrades (III) • The Red Army Is The Most Powerful Of All *[Moscow Radio Chorus]* • E.J. Mellinger's Rag • Winter Escape • Marriage Proposal • Comrades • The Engine *[Moscow Radio Chorus]* • Goodbye For Now

**Reggae Sunsplash '81 -- see CONCERTS/FESTIVALS**

| 2/2/74 | 216 | 5 | **26 Robin Hood** .......................................... [M] $15 | | Disneyland 3810 |

animated movie, voices by Peter Ustinov/Phil Harris/Terry-Thomas; sw: Roger Miller
Whistle Stop • Oo-De-Lally • Love • The Phony King Of England • Not In Nottingham • Reprise: Whistle Stop • Finale: Oo-De-Lally

**Scandalous John -- see McKUEN, Rod**
Brian Keith/Michele Carey/Rick Lenz/Harry Morgan

| 1/28/84 | 203 | 3 | **27 Scarface** ..................................... [V] $10 | | MCA 6126 |

Al Pacino/Steven Bauer/Michelle Pfeiffer/Mary Elizabeth Mastrantonio
Scarface (Push It To The Limit) *[Paul Engemann]* • Rush Rush *[Deborah Harry]* • Turn Out The Night *[Amy Holland]* • Vamos A Bailar *[Maria Conchita]* • Tony's Theme *[Giorgio Moroder]* • She's On Fire *[Amy Holland]* • Shake It Up *[Elizabeth Daily]* • Dance Dance Dance *[Beth Andersen]* • I'm Hot Tonight *[Elizabeth Daily]* • Gina's And Elvira's Theme *[Helen St. John]*

| 9/24/77 | 202 | 10 | **28 Smokey And The Bandit** ....................................... [I] $15 | | MCA 2099 |

Burt Reynolds/Sally Field/Jackie Gleason/**Jerry Reed**; mu: Bill Justis and **Jerry Reed**
The Legend • West Bound And Down • Foxy Lady • Orange Blossom Special • The Bandit • March Of The Rednecks • If You Leave Me Tonight I'll Cry • East Bound And Down • The Bandit • And The Fight Played On! • Ma Cousin Playz Steel • Hot Pants Fuzz Parade • The Bandit (Reprise)

**Song Of Norway -- see CONCEPT ALBUMS (Grieg's Greatest Hits)**
Florence Henderson/Toralv Maurstad/Edward G. Robinson

| 4/26/75 | 206 | 3 | **29 Stardust** ...................................... [O+V] $15 | | Arista 5000 [2] |

David Essex/Adam Faith/Larry Hagman/Keith Moon
Happy Birthday Sweet 16 *[Neil Sedaka]* • Oh No Not My Baby *[Maxine Brown]* • Take Good Care Of My Baby *[Bobby Vee]* • She's Not There *[Zombies]* • Dream Lover *[Bobby Darin]* • Do You Want To Know A Secret *[Billy J. Kramer & The Dakotas]* • Da Doo Ron Ron *[Dave Edmunds & The Electricians]* • I Get Around *[Beach Boys]* • Up On The Roof *[Drifters]* • One Fine Day *[Chiffons]* • Loco-Motion *[Little Eva]* • You've Got Your Troubles *[Fortunes]* • It Might As Well Rain Until September *[Carole King]* • Don't Let The Sun Catch You Cryin' *[Gerry & The Pacemakers]* • Surf City *[Jan & Dean]* • Matthew & Son *[Cat Stevens]* • Make Me Your Baby *[Barbara Lewis]* • Will You Love Me Tomorrow *[Shirelles]* • The Letter *[Box Tops]* • Monday, Monday *[Mamas & The Papas]* • Summer In The City *[Lovin' Spoonful]* • I'm A Believer *[Monkees]* • The House Of The Rising Sun *[Animals]* • Carrie Anne *[Hollies]* • I've Gotta Get A Message To You *[Bee Gees]* • You've Lost That Lovin' Feelin' *[Righteous Brothers]* • Eve Of Destruction *[Barry McGuire]* • White Rabbit *[Jefferson Airplane]* • (You Make Me Feel Like) A Natural Woman *[Aretha Franklin]* • When Will I Be Loved *[Stray Cats]* • Need A Shot Of Rhythm & Blues *[Stray Cats]* • Make Me Good *[Stray Cats]* • You Kept Me Waiting *[David Essex]* • Let It Be Me *[Stray Cats]* • Some Other Guy *[Stray Cats]* • Take It Away *[David Essex]* • C'mon Little Dixie *[Stray Cats]* • Americana Stray Cat Blues *[David Essex]* • Dea Sancta *[David Essex]* • Stardust *[David Essex]*

| 7/11/81 | 210 | 1 | **30 Take This Job And Shove It!** ...................................... [V] $12 | | Epic 37177 |

Robert Hays/Art Carney/Barbara Hershey/Eddie Albert/**Martin Mull**
Take This Job And Shove It *[Johnny Paycheck]* • Beer Drinkin' Christian *[Lacy J. Dalton & Bobby Bare]* • Summertime Blues *[Steve Davis]* • You Can Count On Beer *[David Allan Coe]* • I Love Robbing Banks *[David Allan Coe]* • Road Song *[Steve Davis & Janie Fricke]* • You Made It Beautiful *[Charlie Rich]* • Crazy Blue Eyes *[Lacy J. Dalton]* • How Good It Used To Be *[Charlie Rich]* • Bigfoot Theme

| 7/24/76 | 203 | 4 | **31 That's Entertainment, Part 2** ...................................... [M] $12 | | MGM 5301 |

musical highlights from MGM's greatest musicals
Overture • That's Entertainment • For Me And My Gal • I've Got A Feelin' You're Foolin' • Hi-Lili, Hi-Lo • All Of You • The Lady Is A Tramp • Smoke Gets In Your Eyes • Temptation • Takin' A Chance On Love • Inka Dinka Doo • Easter Parade • Good Morning • Triplets • The Last Time I Saw Paris • I'll Build A Stairway To Paradise • A Couple Of Swells • There's No Business Like Show Business • Have Yourself A Merry Little Christmas • I Got Rhythm • I Remember It Well • That's Entertainment (Finale)

| 9/8/73 | 211 | 5 | **32 Those Glorious MGM Musicals: Seven Brides For Seven Brothers/Rose Marie** ...................................... [M] $20 | | MGM 41 [2] |

Bless Yore Beautiful Hide • Wonderful, Wonderful Day • Goin' Co'Tin' • Sobbin' Women • Spring, Spring, Spring • Lonesome Polecat • June Bride • When You're In Love • Rose Marie • Free To Be Free • The Right Place For A Girl • Love And Kisses • Mounties • I Have The Love • I'm A Mountie Who Never Got His Man • Indian Love Call

| 8/25/73 | 205 | 9 | **33 Those Glorious MGM Musicals: The Band Wagon/Kiss Me Kate** ............ [M] $20 | | MGM 44 [2] |

That's Entertainment • By Myself • Triplets • I Love Louisa • Medley: New Sun In The Sky/I Guess I'll Have To Change My Plans • Dancing In The Dark • A Shine On Your Shoes • Louisiana Hayride • The Girl Hunt Ballet • Why Can't You Behave • I Hate Men • Tom, Dick Or Harry • Wunderbar • Always True To You In My Fashion • I've Come To Wive It Wealthily In Padua • From This Moment On • Where Is The Life That Late I Led? • Brush Up Your Shakespeare • Kiss Me Kate

| DEBUT | PEAK | WKS | Album Title | $ | Label & Number |
|---|---|---|---|---|---|

**SOUNDTRACKS — Cont'd**

| 9/1/73 | 221 | 1 | **34 Those Glorious MGM Musicals: Till The Clouds Roll By/Three Little Words** ...................[M] $20 MGM 45 [2] |

Till The Clouds Roll By • Who? • Medley: Who Cares If My Boat Goes Upstream/Make Believe • Ol' Man River • Life Upon The Wicked Stage • Can't Help Lovin' Dat Man • Leave It To Jane And Cleopaterer • Look For The Silver Lining • Medley: My Sunny Tennessee/So Long! Oo-Long (How Long You Gonna Be Gone?) • All Alone Monday • Who's Sorry Now? • I Wanna Be Loved By You • Nevertheless (I'm In Love With You) • I Love You So Much • Where Did You Get That Girl • Thinking Of You • Three Little Words

| 9/22/73 | 212 | 3 | **35 Those Glorious MGM Musicals: The Pirate/Pagan Love Song/Hit The Deck** ...................[M] $20 MGM 43 [2] |

Mack The Black • Nina • Love Of My Life • Pirate Ballet • You Can Do No Wrong • Be A Clown • Pagan Love Song • Singing In The Sun • Why Is Love So Crazy • Tahiti • Sea Of The Moon • House Of Singing Bamboo • Medley: Join The Navy/Loo-Loo • Sometimes I'm Happy • Keepin' Myself For You • Why, Oh, Why? • Lucky Bird • Chiribiribee (Ciribiribin) • I Know That You Know • A Kiss Or Two • More Than You Know • Lady From The Bayou • Sometimes I'm Happy • Hallelujah!

**Three The Hard Way -- see IMPRESSIONS, The**
Jim Brown/Fred Williamson/Jim Kelly

| 2/23/80 | 207 | 4 | **36 Together?** ........................ [V] $10 RCA Victor 3541 |

Jacqueline Bisset/Maximilian Schell/Terence Stamp
I Don't Need You Anymore [Jackie De Shannon] • I Think I'm Gonna Fall In Love • In Tune [Libby Titus] • If We Ever Get Out Of Here • On The Beach • I've Got My Mind Made Up [Michael McDonald] • Reprise: I Don't Need You Anymore [Jackie De Shannon] • Find Love [Jackie De Shannon] • Luisa

| 9/8/73 | 214 | 2 | **37 Tom Sawyer** ........................[M] $15 United Artists 057 |

Johnny Whitaker/Jodie Foster/Celeste Holm/Warren Oates
Overture • Main Title And River Song (The Theme From "Tom Sawyer") • Tom Sawyer • Gratification • A Man's Gotta Be (What He's Born To Be) • How Come? • If'n I Was God • Freebootin' • Aunt Polly Soliloquy • Hannibal Mo-(Zouree)! • River Song (The Theme From "Tom Sawyer")(Reprise) • Finale

| 7/23/83 | 210 | 1 | **38 Twilight Zone-The Movie** ........................[I] $10 Warner 23887 |

Dan Aykroyd/**Albert Brooks**/Scatman Crothers/John Lithgow; cp/cd: Jerry Goldsmith
Medley: Twilight Zone Main Title/Overture • Time Out • Kick The Can • Nights Are Forever [Jennifer Warnes] • It's A Good Life • Medley: Nightmare At 20,000 Ft./Twilight Zone End Title

**WALT DISNEY -- see CHILDREN'S ALBUMS**

| 6/7/80 | 208 | 2 | **39 Where The Buffalo Roam** ........................ [V] $10 Backstreet 5126 |

Bill Murray/Peter Boyle/Bruno Kirby/Rene Auberjonois
Buffalo Stomp [Neil Young With The Wild Bill Band Of Strings] • Ode To Wild Bill #1 [Neil Young] • All Along The Watchtower [Jimmy Hendrix] • Lucy In The Sky With Diamonds [Bill Murray] • Ode To Wild Bill #2 [Neil Young] • Papa Was A Rolling Stone [Temptations] • Home, Home On The Range [Neil Young] • Straight Answers [Bill Murray] • Highway 61 [Bob Dylan] • I Can't Help Myself (Sugar Pie Honey Bunch) [Four Tops] • Ode To Wild Bill #3 With Dialogue [Neil Young] • Keep On Chooglin' [Creedence Clearwater Revival] • Ode To Wild Bill #4 [Neil Young] • Purple Haze [Jimi Hendrix] • Buffalo Stomp Refrain [Neil Young With The Wild Bill Band Of Strings]

| 10/27/84 | 201 | 2 | **40 Wild Life, The** ........................ [V] $10 MCA 5523 |

Christopher Penn/Ilan Mitchell-Smith/Eric Stoltz/Lea Thompson
Donut City [Edward Van Halen] • Metal Of The Night [Hanover Fist] • It's Not Easy [Charlie Sexton With Ron Wood] • Human Shout [Andy Summers] • Wild Life [Bananarama] • Mind My Have Still I [What Is This] • Make It Glamorous [Van Stephenson] • Who's Gonna Break The Ice [Peter Case] • I Go Wild [Three O'Clock] • No Trespassing [Louise Goffin With Charlotte Caffey]

# ORIGINAL CASTS
The original cast stars are listed below the title.

| 8/30/80 | 205 | 2 | **1 Barnum** ........................ $10 Columbia 36576 |

Jim Dale/Glenn Close/Marianne Tatum/Terri White; mu: Cy Coleman; ly: Michael Stewart
Overture Chase • There Is A Sucker Born Ev'ry Minute • Humble Beginnings Chase • Thank God I'm Old • The Colors Of My Life (Part I) • The Colors Of My Life (Part II) • One Brick At A Time • Museum Song • Female Of The Species Chase • I Like Your Style • Bigger Isn't Better • Love Makes Such Fools Of Us All • Midway Chase • Out There • Come Follow The Band • Black And White • The Colors Of My Life (Reprise) • The Prince Of Humbug • Join The Circus • Finale Chase • The Final Event - There Is A Sucker Born Ev'ry Minute (Reprise)

| 2/9/74 | 209 | 4 | **2 Gigi** ........................ $15 RCA Victor 0404 |

Karin Wolfe/Alfred Drake/Agnes Moorehead/Maria Karnilova; mu: Frederick Loewe; ly: Alan Jay Lerner
Overture • Thank Heaven For Little Girls • It's A Bore • The Earth And Other Minor Things • Paris Is Paris Again • She Is Not Thinking Of Me • I Remember It Well • The Night They Invented Champagne • Gigi • The Contract • In This Wide, Wide World • I'm Glad I'm Not Young Anymore and Reprise • Finale/Thank Heaven For Little Girls (Reprise)

| 5/19/73 | 203 | 6 | **3 Irene** ........................ $15 Columbia 32266 |

Debbie Reynolds/Monte Markham/George S. Irving/Ruth Warrick; mu: Harry Tierney; ly: Joseph McCarthy
Overture • The World Must Be Bigger Than An Avenue • What Do You Want To Make Those Eyes At Me For? • The Family Tree • Alice Blue Gown • They Go Wild, Simply Wild, Over Me • An Irish Girl • Mother, Angel, Darling • The Riviera Rage • I'm Always Chasing Rainbows • The Last Part Of Ev'ry Party • We're Getting Away With It • Irene • The Great Lover Tango • You Made Me Love You • You Made Me Love You (Reprise) • Finale

| 1/15/83 | 209 | 5 | **4 Nine** ........................ $10 CBS 38325 |

Raul Julia/Camille Saviola/Karen Akers/Anita Morris; sw: Maury Yeston
Medley: Overture Delle Donne/Spa Music/Not Since Chaplin • Guido's Song • The Germans At The Spa • My Husband Makes Movies • A Call From The Vatican • Only With You • Folies Bergeres • Nine • Be Italian (Ti Voglio Bene) • The Bells Of St. Sebastian • Unusual Way • The Grand Canal • Simple • Be On Your Own • Medley: I Can't Make This Movie/Waltz From Nine • Medley: Getting Tall/Reprises

| DEBUT | PEAK | WKS | Album Title | $ | Label & Number |
|-------|------|-----|-------------|---|----------------|

**ORIGINAL CASTS — Cont'd**

| DEBUT | PEAK | WKS | | | |
|-------|------|-----|---|---|---|
| 2/24/73 | 211 | 2 | 5 Oh Coward! .......................................................................................... $30 | | Bell 9001 [2] |

Barbara Cason/Roderick Cook/Jamie Ross; sw: Noel Coward
Overture • Introduction • Oh Coward! • England • Family Album • Music Hall • If Love Were All • Travel • Mrs. Worthington • Mad Dogs And Englishmen • A Marvelous Party • Design For Dancing • You Were There • Theatre • Love • Women • Medley: World Weary/Let's Do It • Finale

| 11/16/74 | 207 | 1 | 6 Rocky Horror Show, The .................................................................. $20 | | Ode 77026 |
|----------|-----|---|---|---|---|

Tim Curry/Meat Loaf/Jamie Donnelly/Boni Enten; sw: Richard O'Brien
Science Fiction/Double Feature • Dammit Janet • Over At The Frankenstein Place • Sweet Transvestite • Time Warp • The Sword Of Damoclese • Charles Atlas Song • What Ever Happened To Saturday Night • Charles Atlas Song (Reprise) • Toucha, Toucha, Touch Me • Once In Awhile • Eddie's Teddy • Planet Shmanet Janet • Rose Tint My World • I'm Going Home • Super Heroes

| 7/28/73 | 201 | 2 | 7 Seesaw .......................................................................................... $25 | | Buddah 95006 |
|---------|-----|---|---|---|---|

Michele Lee/Ken Howard; mu: Cy Coleman; ly: Dorothy Fields
Seesaw • My City • Nobody Does It Like Me • In Tune • Spanglish • Welcome To Holiday Inn • You're A Lovable Lunatic • He's Good For Me • Ride Out The Storm • Entire Act • We've Got It • Poor Everybody Else • Chapter 54, Number 1909 • Seesaw Ballet • It's Not Where You Start • Finale: I'm Way Ahead/Seesaw • It's Not Where You Start (Bows)

| 6/16/73 | 211 | 2 | 8 Sondheim: A Musical Tribute.............................................................. $15 | | Warner 2705 [2] |
|---------|-----|---|---|---|---|

Angela Lansbury/Jack Cassidy/Dorothy Collins/Glynis Johns; sw: Stephen Sondheim
Overture • Do I Hear A Waltz? • If Mama Was Married • A-me-ri-ca • One More Kiss • Broadway Baby • You Could Drive A Person Crazy • Take Me To The World • I Remember • Silly People • Two Fairy Tales • Love Is In The Air • Your Eyes Are Blue • Medley: Pleasant Little Kingdom/Too Many Mornings • Entr'acte • Me And My Town • The Little Things You Do Together • Getting Married Today • Buddy's Blues • So Many People • Medley: Happily Ever After/Being Alive • We're Gonna Be All Right • Beautiful Girls • I'm Still Here • A Parade In Town • Could I Leave You? • Losing My Mind • Anyone Can Whistle • Side By Side By Side

# TELEVISION ALBUM
The stars of the show are listed directly below the title.

**Brady Bunch, The -- see BRADY**

| 6/9/73 | 205 | 5 | Strauss Family, The ................................................................ [l] $15 | | Polydor 3506 [2] |
|--------|-----|---|---|---|---|

Derek Jacobi/Margaret Whiting/Eric Woofe/Stuart Wilson; cd: Cyril Ornadel; pf: London Symphony Orchestra
Radetzky March • Einzug Gallop • Ball Racketen Waltz • Lorelei Rhein Klange • Tauberl'n Waltz • Maskenlieder Waltz • Debut Quadrille • Annen Polka • Pizzicato Polka • Moulinet Polka • Bahn Frei • Thunder And Lighting Polka • Theme From "The Strauss Family" • Overture "Die Fledermaus" • Morning Papers Waltz • Vienna Blood, Waltz • The Blue Danube Waltz • Overture "Gipsy Baron" • Tales Of The Vienna Woods • Tritsch Tratsch Polka • The Emperor Waltz • Perpertuum Mobile

# LABEL COMPILATIONS

| 7/30/83 | 209 | 1 | 1 Artists And Songs That Inspired The Motown 25th Anniversary T.V. Special, The ........................................................... $10 | | Motown 5321 |
|---------|-----|---|---|---|---|

The Temptations & The Four Tops Medley: Reach Out, I'll Be There/Get Ready/It's The Same Old Song/Ain't Too Proud To Beg/Baby I Need Your Loving/My Girl/I Can't Get Next To You/I Can't Help Myself (Sugar Pie, Honey Bunch)/(I Know) I'm Losing You/I Can't Help Myself (Sugar Pie, Honey Bunch)/I Know (I'm Losing You) • Martha Reeves & The Vandellas Medley: Nowhere To Run/Dancing In The Street/Love Is Like A Heat Wave/I'm Ready For Love • Gladys Knight & The Pips Medley: I Heard It Through The Grapevine/Friendship Train/You Need Love Like I Do (Don't You?)/If I Were Your Woman/Daddy Could Swear, I Declare/Neither One Of Us (Wants To Be The First To Say Goodbye) • Four Tops Medley: I Can't Help Myself (Sugar Pie, Honey Bunch)/Shake Me, Wake Me (When It's Over)/Standing In The Shadows Of Love/Reach Out, I'll Be There/Bernadette • Diana Ross & The Supremes Medley: Stop! In The Name Of Love/Back In My Arms Again/Come See About Me/Love Is Like An Itching In My Heart/Where Did Our Love Go • The Jackson 5 Medley: I Want You Back: ABC: The Love You Save: Dancing Machine: Never Can Say Goodbye: I'll Be There:

| 2/28/81 | 201 | 3 | 2 I.R.S. Greatest Hits Vols. 2 & 3 ...................................................... $15 | | I.R.S. 70800 [2] |
|---------|-----|---|---|---|---|

Cold, Cold Shoes [Fleshtones] • Ain't That A Shame [Brian James] • Baby Sign Here With Me [Henry Badowski] • Action Time Vision [Alternative TV] • Backtrack [Squeeze] • Disgracing The Family Name [Skafish] • Wait For The Blackout [Damned] • Thrills [Klark Kent] • Straighten Out [Stranglers] • Urban Kids [Chelsea] • Uranium Rock [Cramps] • I Live In The City [Humans] • Fallout [Police] • Can't Keep Away [Sector 27] • Memphis [John Cale] • Mess Around [Jools Holland] • Jukebox [Payola$] • Rebellious Jukebox [Fall] • Computer Datin' [Patrick D. Martin] • Only A Lad [Oingo Boingo] • You Say You Don't Love Me [Buzzcocks] • Office Girls [Klark Kent] • Lips [Wazmo Nariz] • Sodium Pentathol Negative [Fashion]

| 4/29/72 | 206 | 2 | 3 Invictus' Greatest Hits ................................................................ $15 | | Invictus 9807 |
|---------|-----|---|---|---|---|

Band Of Gold [Freda Payne] • Give Me Just A Little More Time [Chairmen of the Board] • She's Not Just Another Woman [8th Day] • Crumbs Off The Table [Glass House] • Brings The Boys Home [Freda Payne] • Everything's Tuesday [Chairmen of the Board] • You've Got To Crawl (Before You Walk) [8th Day] • Patches [Chairmen of the Board] • The Music Box [Ruth Copeland] • I Had It All [Barrino Brothers] • Pay To The Piper [Chairmen of the Board]

| 7/3/71 | 220 | 1 | 4 Motown Chartbusters Volume 3 ...................................................... $15 | | Motown 732 |
|--------|-----|---|---|---|---|

Up The Ladder To The Roof [Supremes] • Gotta Hold On To This Feeling [Jr. Walker & The All Stars] • It's All In The Game [Four Tops] • For Once In My Life [Stevie Wonder] • Baby, I'm For Real [Originals] • It's A Shame [Spinners] • Love Child [Diana Ross & The Supremes] • ABC [Jackson 5] • Psychedelic Shack [Temptations] • Friendship Train [Gladys Knight & The Pips] • Honey Chile [Martha Reeves & The Vandellas] • Twenty-Five Miles [Edwin Starr]

**LABEL COMPILATIONS — Cont'd**

| DEBUG | PEAK | WKS | | | |
|-------|------|-----|---|---|---|
| 5/22/71 | 204 | 5 | 5 **Motown Story, The**............................................................................ | $30 | Motown 726 [5] |

includes interviews with artists

Introduction [Berry Gordy, Jr.] • Money (That's What I Want) [Barrett Strong] • Shop Around [Smokey Robinson & The Miracles] • Please Mr. Postman [Marvelettes] • Playboy [Marvelettes] • Stubborn Kind Of Fellow [Marvin Gaye] • You've Really Got A Hold On Me [Smokey Robinson & The Miracles] • Pride And Joy [Marvin Gaye] • Finger Tips [Stevie Wonder] • Come And Get These Memories [Martha Reeves & The Vandellas] • Love Is Like A Heat Wave [Martha Reeves & The Vandellas] • Mickey's Monkey [Smokey Robinson & The Miracles] • Can I Get A Witness [Marvin Gaye] • My Guy [Mary Wells] • Where Did Our Love Go [Diana Ross & The Supremes] • Dancing In The Street [Martha Reeves & The Vandellas] • Baby I Need Your Loving [Four Tops] • Baby Love [Diana Ross & The Supremes] • Come See About Me [Diana Ross & The Supremes] • How Sweet It Is (To Be Loved By You) [Marvin Gaye] • My Girl [Temptations] • Shotgun [Jr. Walker & The All Stars] • Stop! In The Name Of Love [Diana Ross & The Supremes] • I'll Be Doggone [Marvin Gaye] • Back In My Arms Again [Diana Ross & The Supremes] • I Can't Help Myself [Four Tops] • The Tracks Of My Tears [Smokey Robinson & The Miracles] • Nothing But Heartaches [Diana Ross & The Supremes] • I Hear A Symphony [Diana Ross & The Supremes] • Uptight (Everything's Alright) [Stevie Wonder] • My World Is Empty Without You [Diana Ross & The Supremes] • My Baby Loves Me [Martha Reeves & The Vandellas] • Ain't Too Proud To Beg [Temptations] • What Becomes Of The Brokenhearted [Jimmy Ruffin] • You Can't Hurry Love [Diana Ross & The Supremes] • Reach Out I'll Be There [Four Tops] • You Keep Me Hangin' On [Diana Ross & The Supremes] • Standing In The Shadows Of Love [Four Tops] • Bernadette [Four Tops] • Jimmy Mack [Martha Reeves & The Vandellas] • Ain't No Mountain High Enough [Marvin Gaye & Tammi Terrell] • I Was Made To Love Her [Stevie Wonder] • Reflections [Diana Ross & The Supremes] • I Heard It Through The Grapevine [Gladys Knight & The Pips] • I Second That Emotion [Smokey Robinson & The Miracles] • I Wish It Would Rain [Temptations] • Love Child [Diana Ross & The Supremes] • For Once In My Life [Stevie Wonder] • Cloud Nine [Temptations] • I'm Gonna Make You Love Me [Diana Ross & The Supremes & The Temptations] • I Heard It Through The Grapevine [Marvin Gaye] • What Does It Take (To Win Your Love) [Jr. Walker & The All Stars] • Baby, I'm For Real [Originals] • I Want You Back [Jackson 5] • Psychedelic Shack [Temptations] • Someday We'll Be Together [Diana Ross & The Supremes] • Up The Ladder To The Roof [Supremes] • Reach Out And Touch (Somebody's Hand) [Diana Ross] • Ain't No Mountain High Enough [Diana Ross]

| DEBUG | PEAK | WKS | | | |
|-------|------|-----|---|---|---|
| 11/29/80 | 204 | 1 | 6 **Solar Galaxy Of Stars Live**................................................................[L] | $12 | Solar 3780 [2] |

recorded at the Concord Pavilion in Concord, California

Lady [Whispers] • A Song For Donny [Whispers] • And The Beat Goes On [Whispers] • Right In The Socket [Shalamar] • I Owe You One [Shalamar] • Take That To The Bank [Shalamar] • The Second Time Around [Shalamar] • Given In To Love [Lakeside] • It's All The Way Live [Lakeside] • Your Piece Of The Rock [Dynasty] • I've Just Begun To Love You [Dynasty] • I Don't Want To Be A Freak (But I Can't Help Myself) [Dynasty]

| DEBUG | PEAK | WKS | | | |
|-------|------|-----|---|---|---|
| 4/8/78 | 202 | 8 | 7 **Stiffs Live**........................................................................................[L] | $12 | Stiff 0001 |

recorded at Leicester University in London

I Knew The Bride [Nick Lowe's Last Chicken In The Shop] • Let's Eat [Nick Lowe's Last Chicken In The Shop] • Semaphore Signals [Wreckless Eric & The New Rockets] • Reconnez Cherie [Wreckless Eric & The New Rockets] • Police Car [Larry Wallis' Psychedelic Rowdies] • I Just Don't Know What To Do With Myself [Elvis Costello & The Attractions] • Miracle Man [Elvis Costello & The Attractions] • Wake Up And Make Love With Me [Ian Dury & The Blockheads] • Billericay Dickie [Ian Dury & The Blockheads] • Sex & Drugs & Rock & Roll & Chaos [All Artists]

Ze -- see CONCEPT ALBUMS (*Seize The Beat*)

*P. 402*

# CONCERTS/FESTIVALS

All are live albums.

**Alabama State Troupers -- see ALABAMA**

| DEBUG | PEAK | WKS | | | |
|-------|------|-----|---|---|---|
| 5/19/73 | 213 | 3 | 1 **Ann Arbor Blues & Jazz Festival 1972** ............................................. | $15 | Atlantic 502 [2] |

recorded from 9/8 - 9/10/72 at Otis Spann Memorial Field in Ann Arbor, Michigan

Introduction To The Festival [Michael Turner] • Kitchen Sink Boogie [Hound Dog Taylor & The Houserockers] • Wang Dang Doodle [Koko Taylor] • Ain't That Loving You [Bobby "Blue" Bland] • I Walk On Guilded Splinters [Dr. John] • Medley: (I'm A) Roadrunner/These Things Will Keep Me Loving You • Tribute To Fred McDowell: Write Me A Few Of Your Lines/Kokomo/Drop Down Mama • Highway 49 [Howlin' Wolf] • Honey Bee [Muddy Waters] • Festival Dedication To Otis Spann [John Sinclair/Muddy Waters/Lucille Spann] • Dedicated To Otis [Lucille Spann w/Mighty Joe Young] • Goin' Down [Freddie King] • Please Send Me Someone To Love [Luther Allison] • My Last Meal [Boogie Brothers w/Sister Sarah Brown] • Dust My Broom [Johnny Shines] • Gambler's Blues [Otis Rush] • Women Be Wise [Sippie Wallace w/Bonnie Raitt] • Life Is Splendid [Sun Ra & His Solar-Myth Arkestra]

| DEBUG | PEAK | WKS | | | |
|-------|------|-----|---|---|---|
| 10/20/79 | 201 | 2 | 2 **Bread & Roses** | $15 | Fantasy 79009 [2] |

recorded in October 1977 at the Greek Theater in Berkeley, California; 3-day event benefitting the community service organization founded by Mimi Farina, sister of **Joan Baez**

Intro [Mimi Farina] • Sugar Babe [Jesse Colin Young] • Swinging On A Star [Dave Van Ronk] • Little Boxes [Malvina Reynolds] • Sailing Down My Golden River [Pete Seeger] • Ramblin' Jack Elliott [John Herald Band] • San Francisco Bay Blues [Ramblin' Jack Elliott] • Boney Fingers [Hoyt Axton] • Evangelina [Hoyt Axton] • Al The Goose [Arlo Guthrie] • Medley: General Guinness/Irish Reel • San Francisco Mabel Joy [Mickey Newbury] • I Got Mine [Dan Hicks] • Another Night With The Boys [Persuasions] • What About Me? [Richie Havens] • Universal Soldier [Buffy Sainte-Marie] • Save The Whales! [Country Joe McDonald] • Committee Rap • There But For Fortune [Joan Baez] • Beginning Tomorrow [Toni Brown & Terry Garthwaite] • Walkin' One And Only [Maria Muldaur] • Last Thing On My Mind [Tom Paxton] • For Everyman [Jackson Browne & David Lindley] • Just A Closer Walk With Thee [All Artists]

| DEBUG | PEAK | WKS | | | |
|-------|------|-----|---|---|---|
| 2/14/81 | 204 | 1 | 3 **Castle Donnington: Monsters Of Rock**.............................................. | $12 | Polydor 6311 |

recorded on 8/16/80 in Castle Donnington, England

Stargazer [Rainbow] • Loving You Sunday Morning [Scorpions] • Another Piece Of Meat [Scorpions] • Backs To The Wall [Saxon] • All Night Long [Rainbow] • I Like To Rock [April Wine] • Don't Ya Know What Love Is? [Touch] • Road Racin' [Riot]

| DEBUG | PEAK | WKS | | | |
|-------|------|-----|---|---|---|
| 4/24/71 | 221 | 2 | 4 **Celebration** | $20 | Ode 77008 |

recorded in 1970 at the Big Sur Folk Festival in Monterey, California; benefitting the Institute for the Study of Nonviolence, the United Farm Workers and War Resisters International

The Night They Drove Old Dixie Down [Joan Baez] • Let It Be [Joan Baez] • The Only Mama That'll Walk The Line [Linda Ronstadt] • Lovesick Blues [Linda Ronstadt] • The Times They Are A Changin' [Merry Clayton] • Bridge Over Troubled Water [Merry Clayton] • Wouldn't It Be Nice [Beach Boys] • Entertainment Is My Business [Country Joe McDonald] • Air Algiers [Country Joe McDonald] • The Law Is For The Protection Of The People [Kris Kristofferson] • To Beat The Devil [Kris Kristofferson]

| DEBUT | PEAK | WKS | Album Title | $ | Label & Number |
|-------|------|-----|-------------|---|----------------|

**CONCERTS/FESTIVALS — Cont'd**

1/25/75 **208** 1 5 **In Concert, Volume Two** ............................................................ [I] $12 CTI 6049
two concerts recorded at the Opera House in Chicago and Ford Auditorium in Detroit featuring jazz notables **Herbie Hancock**, Freddie Hubbard, **Stanley Turrentine**, **Ron Carter**, Jack DeJohnette and Eric Gale
Hornets (Chicago) • Interlude • Hornets (Detroit) • Gibraltar (Detroit)

6/5/71 **225** 1 6 **Johnny Otis Show Live At Monterey!** ............................................. $25 Epic 30473 [2]
recorded in 1970 at Monterey, California
Willie And The Hand Jive *[Johnny Otis]* • Cry Me A River Blues *[Little Esther Phillips]* • Cleanhead's Blues *[Eddie Cleanhead Vinson]* • I Got A Gal *[Joe Turner]* • Since I Met You Baby *[Ivory Joe Hunter]* • Baby You Don't Know *[Roy Milton]* • Preacher's Blues *[Gene Connors]* • Good Rockin' Tonight *[Roy Brown]* • The Time Machine *[Shuggie Otis]* • Margie's Boogie *[Margie Evans]* • Little Esther's Blues: Blowtop Blues/T Bone Blues/Jelly Jelly • Kidney Stew *[Eddie Cleanhead Vinson]* • The Things I Used To Do *[Pee Wee Crayton]* • R. M. Blues *[Roy Milton]* • Shuggie's Boogie *[Shuggie Otis]* • You Better Look Out *[Delmar Evans]* • Goin' Back To L.A. *[Johnny Otis & Delmar Evans]* • Plastic Man *[Joe Turner]* • Boogie Woogie Bye Bye *[Ensemble]*

7/10/82 **203** 7 7 **Reggae Sunsplash '81 - A Tribute To Bob Marley** .......................... [S] $12 Elektra 60035 [2]
recorded and filmed at festival honoring late reggae great Marley at Jarrett Park in Montego Bay, Jamaica
Sound System *[Steel Pulse]* • Ku Klux Klan *[Steel Pulse]* • Handsworth Revolution *[Steel Pulse]* • Smile Jamaica *[Steel Pulse]* • Belly Full A/K/A Them Bellyful (But We Hungry) *[Rita Marley & I-Threes]* • Sugar Pie *[Melody Makers & The Wailers]* • Wa-Do-Dem *[Eek-A-Mouse & The Wailers]* • If I Had The World *[Dennis Brown]* • Plastic Smile *[Black Uhuru]* • Guess Who's Coming To Dinner *[Black Uhuru]* • The Bed's Too Big Without You *[Sheila Hylton]* • Soon Forward *[Gregory Isaacs]* • The Harder They Come *[Carlene Davis]* • Right Time *[Mighty Diamonds]* • 1865 (96° In The Shade) *[Third World]* • Rock The World *[Third World]*

**Stiffs Live -- see LABEL COMPILATIONS**

10/21/78 **206** 3 8 **Volunteer Jam III and IV** ............................................................. $15 Epic 35368 [2]
recorded on 1/8/77 and 1/14/78 at the Municipal Auditorium in Nashville; hosted by the Charlie Daniels Band
Sweet Louisiana *[Charlie Daniels Band]* • Long Haired Country Boy *[Charlie Daniels Band]* • Trudy *[Charlie Daniels Band]* • Cumberland Mountain Number Nine *[Charlie Daniels Band]* • The South's Gonna Do It *[Charlie Daniels Band/Jimmy Hall]* • Statesboro Blues *[Sea Level/Charlie Daniels/Jimmy Hall]* • Street Corner Serenade *[Wet Willie]* • You And Me *[Grinderswitch]* • Good Hearted Woman *[Willie Nelson & Band]* • Blues Medley: Funny How Time Slips Away/Crazy/Night Life • Will The Circle Be Unbroken *[Willie Nelson//Toy Caldwell/Bonnie Bramlett/Charlie Daniels/Mylon LeFevre]* • Sang Her Love Songs *[Winters Brothers Band/Joel DiGregorio/Don Murray]* • Can't You See *[All Artists]* • Tennessee Waltz *[All Artists]*

# CONCEPT ALBUMS

1/31/76 **201** 7 1 **American Graffiti Vol. III** ...................................................... [O] $15 MCA 8008 [2]
Surfer Girl *[Beach Boys]* • Lucille *[Little Richard]* • (Crazy Little Mama) At My Front Door *[El Dorados]* • For Your Precious Love *[Jerry Butler]* • Endless Sleep *[Jody Reynolds]* • Wake Up Little Susie *[Everly Brothers]* • You Talk Too Much *[Joe Jones]* • Poetry In Motion *[Johnny Tillotson]* • Poetry In Motion *[Johnny Tillotson]* • Donna *[Richie Valens]* • Honeycomb *[Jimmie Rodgers]* • Since I Fell For You *[Lenny Welch]* • Kansas City *[Wilbur Harrison]* • Surfin' *[Beach Boys]* • Hey Little One *[Dorsey Burnette]* • To Know Him Is To Love Him *[Teddy Bears]* • A Thousand Stars *[Kathy Young]* • Alley-Oop *[Hollywood Argyles]* • Shimmy Shimmy Ko Ko Bop *[Little Anthony]* • Bye Bye Love *[Everly Brothers]* • Western Movies *[Olympics]* • Mule Skinner Blues *[Fendermen]* • Rave On *[Buddy Holly]* • La Bamba *[Richie Valens]* • The Birds And The Bees *[Jewel Atkins]* • Let's Dance *[Chris Montez]* • Good Golly Miss Molly *[Little Richard]* • My Special Angel *[Bobby Helms]* • Mountain Of Love *[Harold Dorman]* • Baby, What You Want Me To Do? *[Jimmy Reed]* • The Big Hurt *[Toni Fisher]*

7/30/83 **205** 3 2 **Attack Of The Killer B's, Vol. 1** ................................................ $10 Warner 23837
B-sides and non-album tracks
You're My Favorite Waste Of Time *[Marshall Crenshaw]* • In The Sticks *[Pretenders]* • What Will Lucy Do? *[Blasters]* • Babysitter *[Ramones]* • Take Time To Know Her *[John Hiatt]* • Always Unknowing *[Roxy Music]* • Shock Den Affen *[Peter Gabriel]* • Grace *[Time]* • Love Goes To A Building On Fire *[Talking Heads]* • Producer *[Gang Of Four]* • Amnesia And Jealousy (Oh Lana) *[T-Bone Burnett]* • Walk The Dog *[Laurie Anderson]*

2/6/71 **205** 1 3 **Beautiful People** ........................................................................ $15 Harmony 11383
Square Headed People *[John Kay]* • Sally Go 'Round The Roses *[Great Society w/Grace Slick]* • Sitar Todi *[Ravi Shankar]* • Lay Down Your Weary Tune • Groovin' Is Easy *[Electric Flag]* • The American Metaphysical Circus *[United States Of America]* • Candy Man *[Rising Sons]* • Hey Joe (You Shot Your Woman Down) *[Tim Rose]* • Star Children *[Don Ellis]*

12/12/81 **210** 1 4 **Christmas Country** .................................................................... [X] $10 Elektra 554
Please Come Home For Christmas *[Johnny Lee]* • Little Drummer Boy *[Hank Williams, Jr.]* • Silver Bells *[Tompall & The Glaser Brothers]* • Blue Christmas *[Eddy Raven]* • The Christmas Song *[Sonny Curtis]* • Silent Night *[Joe Sun]* • Winter Wonderland *[Dave Rowland & Sugar]* • Rudolph The Red Nosed Reindeer *[Mel Tillis & Nancy Sinatra]* • O Holy Night *[Helen Cornelius]* • White Christmas *[Mel Tillis]*

6/6/81 **203** 1 5 **Film Classics** ............................................................................ [I] $12 RCA 4020
classical pieces that appeared in movie scores
Pachelbel: Canon In D *[Paillard Chamber Orch.]* • Mendelssohn: Symphony No. 4 ("Italian") Fourth Movement *[London Symphony Orch.]* • Corigliano: Altered States: Second Hallucination *[Dicterow/Shkolnik/Aller]* • Mascagni: Cavalleria Rusticana: Intermezzo *[Boston Pops Orch.]* • Prokofiev: Concerto No. 3: First Movement *[Dallas Symphony Orch.]* • Wagner: Die Walküre: Ride Of The Valkryries *[Boston Pops Orch.]*

5/10/75 **208** 2 6 **Flash Fearless Versus The Zorg Women Parts 5 & 6** ........................ $12 Chrysalis 1072
Trapped *[Elkie Brooks]* • I'm Flash *[Alice Cooper]* • Country Cooking *[Jim Dandy]* • What's Happening *[James Dewar]* • Space Pirates *[Alice Cooper]* • Sacrifice *[Elkie Brooks]* • To The Chop *[John Entwistle]* • Supersnatch *[Frankie Miller]* • Blast Off *[Jim Dandy]* • Trapped (Reprise) *[Eddie Jobson]*

8/11/73 **208** 3 7 **Gemini Suite** ............................................................................ [I] $15 Warner 2717
all tracks but one are instrumental; classical-rock suite composed by Jon Lord (**Deep Purple**)
Guitar *[Albert Lee]* • Piano *[Jon Lord]* • Drums *[Ian Paice]* • Vocals *[Tony Ashton & Yvonne Elliman]* • Bass Guitar *[Roger Glover]* • Organ *[Jon Lord]*

| DEBUT | PEAK | WKS | Album Title | $ | Label & Number |
|-------|------|-----|-------------|-----|----------------|

**CONCEPT ALBUMS — Cont'd**

| 2/13/71 | 212 | 2 | 8 **Grieg's Greatest Hits Made Popular In Song Of Norway** ..............................[I] | $15 | RCA Victor 3198 |

Concerto In A Minor, Op. 16 *[Philadelphia Orch. w/Van Cliburn]* • Norwegian Dance No. 2 *[New Philharmonia Orch.]* • Strange Music *[Mario Lanza]* • March Of The Dwarfs *[Boston Pops Orch.]* • I Love Thee (Ich Liebe Dich) *[Mario Lanza]* • Ingrid's Lament *[Boston Pops Orch.]* • Solvejg's Song *[Boston Pops Orch. w/Eileen Farrell]* • In The Hall Of The Mountain King *[Boston Pops Orch.]*

| 1/10/81 | 209 | 1 | 9 **Guitar Heroes** ........................................................................................ | $12 | Epic 36864 |

Rock And Roll Band *[Boston]* • Keep Pushin' *[REO Speedwagon]* • Gator Country *[Molly Hatchet]* • Highway 61 Revisited *[Johnny Winter]* • Time Warp *[Rick Derringer]* • Daddy Should Have Stayed In High School *[Cheap Trick]* • Cast The Spirit *[Russ Ballard]* • Saddle Tramp *[Charlie Daniels Band]*

| 6/9/73 | 216 | 2 | 10 **Guitars That Destroyed The World, The**........................................................ | $15 | Columbia 31998 |

Marbles *[Carlos Santana & Buddy Miles]* • Rock And Roll, Hoochie Koo *[Johnny Winter]* • The Dance Of Maya *[Mahavishnu Orch. w/John McLaughlin]* • Pleasure *[West, Bruce & Laing]* • Buck's Boogie *[Blue Oyster Cult]* • Don't Look Around *[Mountain]* • Waves Within *[Santana]* • Keep Playin' That Rock 'N' Roll *[Edgar Winter's White Trash]* • Dark Eyed Woman *[Spirit]*

| 3/27/71 | 222 | 3 | 11 **Heavenly Stars** ...................................................................................... | $15 | Cotillion 052 |

Let It Be *[Aretha Franklin]* • Steal Away *[Wilson Pickett]* • I Wish I Knew (How It Would Feel To Be Free) *[Solomon Burke]* • I Told Jesus *[Roberta Flack]* • Down By The River Side *[Sweet Inspirations]* • Heaven Help Us All *[Brook Benton]* • God Gave Me A Song *[Myrna Summers & The Interdenomonational Singers]* • Milky White Way *[Marion Williams]* • Lord Pity Us All *[Wilson Pickett]* • Without A Doubt *[Sweet Inspirations]* • People Got To Be Free *[Marion Williams]*

| 8/26/78 | 208 | 2 | 12 **Hotels, Motels and Road Shows** ..............................................................[L] | $15 | Capricorn 0208 [2] |

performances by southern-rock artists

Out On A Limb *[Stillwater]* • Mind Bender *[Stillwater]* • Grand Larceny *[Sea Level]* • Refried Funky Chicken *[Dixie Dregs]* • Fire On The Mountain *[Marshall Tucker Band]* • Superstar *[Bonnie Bramlett]* • You're So Fine *[Grinder Switch]* • Travelin' Shoes *[Elvin Bishop]* • Heard It In A Love Song *[Marshall Tucker Band]* • Teaser *[Wet Willie]* • No Hard Times *[Richard Betts]* • Are You Lonely For Me, Baby? *[Gregg Allman]* • Statesboro Blues *[Allman Brothers Band]*

| 10/30/71 | 203 | 3 | 13 **Instant Replay (Two Sides Of Football)**....................................................[C] | $15 | Decca 75300 |

skits written and performed by Tom Patchett and Jay Tarses; recorded "live" at the *Here's Lucy* soundstage at Universal Studios on 6/11/71

Sunday Morning • Getting Seated • "Red" Kneckman Interview • In The Booth • Howard Hardsell • Our National Anthem • Captains And Officials • Pre-Game Presentations • Commercial • In The Huddle • In The Men's Room • The Halftime Show • Coach And The Bench • Howard Hardsell II • The Wrap-Up • In The Locker Room • Coach At Bedtime • Run For Daylight-Song

| 12/15/79 | 209 | 3 | 14 **On This Christmas Night** ......................................................................[X] | $12 | MCA 3184 |

On This Christmas Night *[B.J. Thomas]* • The Whole World Is Colored With Love *[Reba Rambo]* • Born A Child In Bethlehem *[Tennessee Ernie Ford]* • Santa's Reindeer Ride *[Amy Grant]* • A Special Wish *[B.W. Stevenson]* • God Bless The Children *[B.J. Thomas]* • Gift Of Love *[Boones]* • Almost Christmastime *[David Meece]* • The Star *[Dan Peek]* • A Christmas Song *[Mike Warnke]*

| 11/13/76 | 209 | 1 | 15 **Peter And The Wolf**..............................................................................[I] | $12 | RSO 3001 |

Viv Stanshall (Bonzo Dog Band) narrates and instruments portray characters of classic tale; musicians include Manfred Mann, Chris Spedding, Gary Moore, Stephane Grappelli, Brian Eno, Bill Bruford, Cozy Powell and Phil Collins

Introduction • Peter's Theme • Bird And Peter • Duck's Theme • Pond • Duck And Bird • Cat Dance • Cat And Duck • Grandfather • Cat • Wolf • Wolf And Duck • Threnody For A Duck • Wolf Stalks • Cat In Tree • Peter's Chase • Capture Of Wolf • Hunters • Rock And Roll Celebration • Duck Escape • Final Theme

| 4/2/77 | 208 | 1 | 16 **Phil Spector's Greatest Hits** ................................................................[O] | $40 | Warner/Spector 9104 [2] |

Be My Baby *[Ronettes]* • Da Doo Ron Ron *[Crystals]* • You've Lost That Lovin' Feelin' *[Righteous Brothers]* • Then He Kissed Me *[Crystals]* • Baby, I Love You *[Ronettes]* • Walking In The Rain *[Ronettes]* • He's A Rebel *[Crystals]* • Uptown *[Crystals]* • Zip-A-Dee Doo-Dah *[Bob B. Soxx & The Blue Jeans]* • Not Too Young To Get Married *[Bob B. Soxx & The Blue Jeans]* • Today I Met The Boy I'm Gonna Marry *[Darlene Love]* • Wait 'Til My Bobby Gets Home *[Darlene Love]* • To Know Him Is To Love Him *[Teddy Bears]* • Pretty Little Angel Eyes *[Curtis Lee]* • I Love How You Love Me *[Paris Sisters]* • Every Breath I Take *[Gene Pitney]* • Under The Moon Of Love *[Curtis Lee]* • He's Sure The Boy I Love *[Crystals]* • Spanish Harlem *[Ben E. King]* • Unchained Melody *[Righteous Brothers]* • River Deep - Mountain High *[Ike & Tina Turner]* • Just Once In My Life *[Righteous Brothers]* • Black Pearl *[Sonny Charles & Checkmates Ltd.]* • Ebb Tide *[Righteous Brothers]*

| 9/22/79 | 202 | 4 | 17 **Propaganda** .......................................................................................... | $12 | A&M 4786 |

Go Crazy *[Granati Brothers]* • Throw It Away *[Joe Jackson]* • Come On *[Joe Jackson]* • Landlord *[Police]* • Next To You *[Police]* • Joey *[Reds]* • Head Case *[Bobby Henry]* • Don't Ask Me *[Joe Jackson]* • Slap & Tickle *[Squeeze]* • Another Lone Ranger *[David Kubinec]* • Valid Or Void *[Shrink]*

| 2/3/73 | 205 | 3 | 18 **Rock-O-Rama** ...................................................................................[O] | $20 | Abkco 4222 [2] |

Cameo/Parkway hits

The Twist *[Chubby Checker]* • So Much In Love *[Tymes]* • He's A Rebel *[Orions]* • Wild One *[Bobby Rydell]* • Gravy *[Dee Dee Sharp]* • 96 Tears *[? & The Mysterians]* • Butterfly *[Charlie Gracie]* • Mashed Potato Time *[Dee Dee Sharp]* • Let's Twist Again *[Chubby Checker]* • (I) Who Have Nothing *[Terry Knight & The Pack]* • You Can't Sit Down *[Dovells]* • Volare *[Bobby Rydell]* • South Street *[Orions]* • Wonderful Wonderful *[Tymes]* • Midnight Hour *[? & The Mysterians]* • Wa-Watusi *[Orions]* • Silhouettes *[Rays]* • Bristol Stomp *[Dovells]* • Slow Twistin' *[Chubby Checker]* • Kissin' Time *[Bobby Rydell]*

| 12/6/75 | 205 | 1 | 19 **Roots Of British Rock** .........................................................................[O] | $20 | Sire 3711 [2] |

Singin' The Blues *[Tommy Steele]* • Rock Island Line *[Lonnie Donegan]* • What Do You Want To Make Those Eyes At Me For *[Emile Ford & the Checkmates]* • Freight Train *[Chas McDevitt Group feat. Nancy Whiskey]* • Does Your Chewing Gum Lose Its Flavor On The Bedpost Overnight? *[Lonnie Donegan]* • Rainbow *[Rus Hamilton]* • I Remember You *[Frank Ifield]* • He's Got The Whole World In His Hands (Laurie London) • Stranger On The Shore *[Acker Bilk]* • Sailor (Your Home Is The Sea) *[Petula Clark]* • Look For A Star *[Gary Mills]* • Midnight In Moscow *[Kenny Ball]* • Wimoweh *[Karl Denver Trio]* • Walkin' Back To Happiness *[Helen Shapiro]* • What Do You Want *[Adam Faith]* • Petite Fleur *[Chris Barber]* • Move It *[Cliff Richard & the Shadows]* • Apache *[Shadows]* • Halfway To Paradise *[Billy Fury]* • Tell Laura I Love Her *[Ricky Valance]* • Well I Ask You *[Eden Kane]* • Diamonds *[Jet Harris & Tony Meehan]* • Only Sixteen *[Craig Douglas]* • Living Doll *[Cliff Richard & the Drifters]* • Shakin' All Over *[Johnny Kidd & the Pirates]* • Picture Of You *[Joe Brown]* • Bad Boy *[Marty Wilde]* • Tribute To Buddy Holly *[Mike Berry]* • I'm A Moody Guy *[Shane Fenton & the Fentones]* • Silver Threads And Golden Needles *[Springfields]* • You Don't Have To Be A Baby To Cry *[Caravelles]* • Telstar *[Tornadoes]*

| DEBUG | PEAK | WKS | Album Title | $ | Label & Number |
|---|---|---|---|---|---|

**CONCEPT ALBUMS — Cont'd**

| 8/15/81 | 209 | 5 | **20 Seize The Beat (Dance Ze Dance)** | $10 | Island 9667 |

dance hits released on Ze Records but previously not released on any album

Busting Out [Material w/Nona Hendryx] • Wheel Me Out [Was (Not Was)] • Drive My Car [Cristina] • Cowboys & Gangsters [Gichy Dan] • Deputy Of Love [Don Armando's 2nd Ave Rumba Band] • Que Pasa/Me No Pop I [Coati Mundi]

| 9/23/78 | 201 | 2 | **21 South's Greatest Hits Volume II, The** | $12 | Capricorn 0209 |

songs by southern-rock artists

Heard It In A Love Song [Marshall Tucker Band] • So In To You [Atlanta Rhythm Section] • Long Haired Country Boy [Charlie Daniels Band] • Hurry Sundown [Outlaws] • Jessica [Allman Brothers Band] • Struttin' My Stuff [Elvin Bishop] • That's Your Secret [Sea Level] • Mind Bender [Stillwater] • Street Corner Serenade [Wet Willie]

| 8/11/84 | 201 | 1 | **22 That's The Way I Feel Now.** [I] | $12 | A&M 6600 [2] |

tribute to the late jazz innovator Thelonious Monk

Thelonious [Bruce Fowler] • Little Rootie Tootie [NRBQ & The Whole Wheat Horns] • Reflections [Donald Fagen & Steve Khan] • Blue Monk [Dr. John] • Misterioso [Carla Bley Band w/Johnny Griffin] • Pannonica [Barry Harris] • Ba-Lue-Bolivar-Ba-Lues-Are [Was (Not Was)] • Brilliant Corners [Mark Bingham] • Ask Me Now [Steve Lacy & Charlie Rouse] • Monk's Mood [Sharon Freeman] • Four In One [Todd Rundgren & Gary Windo] • Functional [Randy Weston] • Evidence [Steve Lacy & Elvin Jones] • Shuffle Boil [John Zorn] • In Walked Bud [Terry Adams & Friends] • Criss Cross [Shockabilly] • Jackie-Ing [Mark Bingham] • 'Round Midnight [Joe Jackson] • Friday The Thirteenth [Bobby McFerrin & Bob Dorough] • Work [Chris Spedding & Peter Frampton] • Gallop's Gallop [Steve Lacy] • Bye-Ya [Steve Slagle/Dr. John/Steve Swallow/Ed Blackwell] • Bemsha Swing [Steve Lacy & Gil Evans]

# DANCE/DISCO COMPILATIONS

| 1/26/85 | 206 | 1 | **1 Breakdancing** | $10 | Columbia 39903 |

includes instructions recorded and written (on the sleeve) for breakdancing

Buffalo Gals [Malcolm McLaren & The World Famous Supreme Team] • Rockit [Herbie Hancock] • I Wonder If I Take You Home [Lisa Lisa & Cult Jam w/Full Force] • Trommeltanz (Din Daa Daa) [George Kranz] • It's Like That [Run-D.M.C.] • I Want It To Be Real [John Rocca] • Drive Me Crazy [Kid Savage & The Supreme Rockers] • One More Shot [C-Bank] • White Lines (Don't Do It) [Grand Master Melle Mel & The Furious Five] • Hey You (The Rocksteady Crew) [Rocksteady Crew]

| 6/21/75 | 206 | 15 | **2 Discotech #1** | $12 | Motown 824 |

Uptight (Everything's Alright) [Stevie Wonder] • Dancing In The Streets [Martha Reeves & The Vandellas] • (I'm A) Roadrunner [Jr. Walker & The All Stars] • You Need Love Like I Do (Don't You) [Gladys Knight & The Pips] • It's A Shame [Spinners] • Ain't Too Proud To Beg [Temptations] • I Heard It Through The Grapevine [Marvin Gaye] • Girl You Need A Change Of Mind [Eddie Kendricks] • Love Is Like An Itching In My Heart [Diana Ross & The Supremes] • Function At The Junction [Shorty Long] • Going To A Go-Go [Smokey Robinson & The Miracles] • ABC [Jackson 5]

| 7/5/75 | 206 | 3 | **3 Discotech #2** | $12 | Motown 831 |

Dancing Machine [Jackson 5] • Date With The Rain [Eddie Kendricks] • I'm A Fool For You [Undisputed Truth] • Law Of The Land [Temptations] • I Feel Sanctified [Commodores] • Chained [Rare Earth] • It's All Over But The Shoutin' [Gladys Knight & The Pips] • You Sure Know How To Love Your Man [Willie Hutch] • No Matter Where [G.C. Cameron] • What Is A Heart Good For [Miracles] • Bad Weather [Supremes]

| 9/9/78 | 202 | 6 | **4 Salsoul Saturday Night Disco Party** | $12 | Salsoul 8505 |

You Should Be Dancing [Salsoul Orchestra] • The Beat Goes On And On [Ripple] • Doctor Love [First Choice] • Hit And Run [Loleatta Holloway] • Night Fever [Salsoul Orchestra] • My Love Is Free [Double Exposure] • Stayin' Alive [Salsoul Orchestra] • Dance A Little Bit Closer [Charo & The Salsoul Orchestra]

| 8/27/77 | 203 | 6 | **5 Steppin' Out** | $12 | Midland Int'l. 2423 |

Fly, Robin, Fly [Silver Convention] • Get Up And Boogie (That's Right) [Silver Convention] • Save Me [Silver Convention] • Doctor's Orders [Carol Douglas] • Midnight Love Affair [Carol Douglas] • Take A Little [Liquid Pleasure] • I'm In Heaven [Touch Of Class] • More, More, More [Andrea True Connection]

# CHILDREN'S ALBUMS

| 12/30/72+ | 201 | 7 | **1 Amazing Spider-Man: From Beyond The Grave!** | $15 | Buddah 5119 |

5 spoken episodes plus 4 songs performed by The Webspinners

Episode I: Peter's Nightmare • Song: Theme From Spider-Man • Episode II: Spider-Man Remembers • Song: Such A Groove To Be Free • Episode III: Spider-Man's Dilemma • Episode IV: A Strange Ally • Song: Stronger The Man • Episode IV: A Strange Ally (cont'd) • Song: Goin' Cross Town • Episode V: From Beyond The Grave

| 6/12/71 | 224 | 1 | **2 Howdy Doody** | $15 | PIP 6808 |

no track titles listed on this album

| 6/12/71 | 202 | 6 | **3 It's Howdy Doody Time!** | $15 | RCA Victor 4546 |

It's Howdy Doody Time • Howdy Doody's Do's And Don'ts • Howdy Doody's Magic Juke Box

| 1/13/79 | 207 | 1 | **4 Magical Music Of Walt Disney, The** | $25 | Ovation 5000 [4] |

50-year anthology of music, dialogue and sound effects from classic Disney cartoons and movies plus music from Disneyland and Disney World theme parks; includes a 52-page Disney history book with original artwork

Mickey Mouse Review Overture • Steamboat Willie • Mickey's Early Years • Maestro Mickey Conducts • The Three Little Pigs • Snow White • Fantasia/Sorcerer's Apprentice • Pinocchio • Dumbo • Bambi • Animated Classics Of The 40's • Song Of The South • Cinderella • Peter Pan • Lady And The Tramp • Sleeping Beauty • The Vanishing Prairie • The Later Animated Years • The Rescuers • Mary Poppins • Pete's Dragon • Live Music From The Magic Kingdom • Music Of The Magic Kingdom Attractions

**MISS PIGGY -- see AEROBIC ALBUMS**

**MUPPETS, The -- see DENVER, John / SOUNDTRACKS**

| 9/15/73 | 211 | 5 | **5 Sesame Street Live!** [L] | $15 | Columbia 32343 |

"live" show featuring songs by the TV show cast; includes poster

Sesame Street Theme • Welcome • The Arm • How Do I Know I'm Here? • Tu Me Gustas (I Like You) • Show Me How You Feel • Mr. Hooper's Poem • "C" Is For Cookie • My Little Game • Believe In Yourself • What Can I Do? • Still We Like Each Other • My Name Is David • Nobody • Sing

# AEROBIC ALBUMS

### FONDA, Jane

| | | | | | |
|---|---|---|---|---|---|
| 12/15/84+ | 202 | 6 | **1 Jane Fonda Prime Time Workout**............................................ | $10 | Elektra 60382 |

cp/pf: Steps Ahead

Introduction • Warm Up • Barre Work • Arms • Waist • Aerobics • Hamstrings • Floor Work • Abdominals/Legs/Buttocks • Cool Down

### GREGGAINS, Joanie

| | | | | | |
|---|---|---|---|---|---|
| 1/14/84 | 201 | 8 | **2 Joanie Greggains - Thin Thighs, Hips & Stomach (Aerobic Shape-Up III)** | $10 | Parade 112 |

music by studio musicians; includes a 16-page book

Flash Dance (Warm-up) • Beat It (Aerobics) • Let's Dance (Stomach) • 9 To 5 (Stomach) • Fame (Stomach) • She Blinded Me With Science (Hips & Thighs) • Copacabana (Hips & Thighs) • America Swings (Hips & Thighs) • Hooked On Classics (Aerobics) • Chariots Of Fire (Cool-Down)

### MISS PIGGY

| | | | | | |
|---|---|---|---|---|---|
| 10/2/82 | 206 | 3 | **3 Miss Piggy's Aerobique Exercise Workout Album** ..................... [N] | $10 | Warner 23717 |

Frank Oz narrates as Miss Piggy and Jim Henson as Kermit

Stereau Warmup • Snackcercise • Lift The One You Love • Exercise Your Rights • Dream Dancin' • La Vie Aerobique • Sit Down • Breathe Easy • A Little Chin Music • Hairobiques Made Simple • Au Revoir

### MISSETT, Judi Sheppard

| | | | | | |
|---|---|---|---|---|---|
| 1/8/83 | 209 | 1 | **4 More Jazzercise By Judi Sheppard Missett** ............................ | $10 | MCA 5375 |

music by studio musicians; includes instruction poster

Arthur's Theme (Best That You Can Do) • Magnum P.I. • Jazzercise Theme • Rhapsody In Blue • Move Your Boogie Body • Seduced • I Want To Hold Your Hand • Dedicated To The One I Love • Push • Livingston Saturday Night • As Time Goes By • Rikki Don't Lose That Number • So Nice (Summer Samba)

### MUIR, Marcy

| | | | | | |
|---|---|---|---|---|---|
| 12/5/81 | 203 | 8 | **5 Aerobic Dancing!** ................................................................ | $10 | Parade 100 |

music by studio musicians

The Third Man Theme (Standing Warm-Ups) • Your Cheating Heart (Sitting Warm-Ups) • Le Freak (Sitting Warm-Up) • Don't Go Breaking My Heart (Moderate Tempo Aerobic Dance) • Our Day Will Come (Moderate Tempo Aerobic Dance) • I'm Your Boogie Man (Fast Tempo Aerobic Dance) • Push, Push In The Bush (Fast Tempo Aerobic Dance) • I Write The Songs (Moderate Tempo Aerobic Dance) • Afternoon Delight (Moderate Tempo Aerobic Dance) • You Make Me Feel Like Dancing (Cool Down)

| | | | | | |
|---|---|---|---|---|---|
| 1/23/82 | 208 | 4 | **6 20 Aerobic Dance Hits** .......................................................... | $12 | Parade 101 [2] |

music by studio musicians

Bette David Eyes (Floor Exercise) • Too Hot (Standing Exercise) • Elvira (Slow Tempo Aerobic Dance) • Games People Play (Moderate Tempo Aerobic Dance) • This Little Girl (Fast Tempo Aerobic Dance) • Fame (Fast Tempo Aerobic Dance) • Working My Way Back To You (Fast Tempo Aerobic Dance) • Driving My Life Away (Moderate Tempo Aerobic Dance) • Morning Train (Slow Tempo Aerobic Dance) • Lady (Cool Down Aerobic Dance) • Escape (Floor Exercise) • Funkytown (Standing Exercise) • New York, New York (Slow Tempo Aerobic Dance) • Copacabana (Moderate Tempo Aerobic Dance) • Making It (Fast Tempo Aerobic Dance) • You May Be Right (Fast Tempo Aerobic Dance) • Heatwave (Fast Tempo Aerobic Dance) • It's A Miracle (Moderate Tempo Aerobic Dance) • Stand By Me (Slow Tempo Aerobic Dance) • Magic (Cool Down Aerobic Dance)

### SORENSEN, Jacki

| | | | | | |
|---|---|---|---|---|---|
| 3/26/83 | 205 | 3 | **7 Jacki Sorensen's Aerobic Dancing** ...................................... | $10 | Lakeside 30005 |

music by studio musicians

Do Your Dance • Southern Nights • Arthur's Theme (Best That You Can Do) • Ventura Highway • Yes We Can Can • Moondance • Love Is Like Oxygen • Undercover Angel • After Midnight • Main Event • Jacki's Theme • Can You Read My Mind

# #201
# ALBUMS

This section lists, in chronological order, all 178 albums that hit the #201 position on *Billboard's Bubbling Under The Top Pop Albums* chart but <u>did not</u> go on to make the 200-position *Top Pop Albums* chart.

**DATE:** Date album first peaked at the #201 position

**WKS:** Total weeks album held the #201 position

↕: Indicates album hit #201, dropped down, and then returned to the #201 spot

# #201 ALBUMS

## 1971

| | DATE | WKS | |
|---|---|---|---|
| 1. | 1/9 | 1 | **Harvest** *Karen Beth* |
| 2. | 1/30 | 1 | **ZZ Top's First Album** *ZZ Top* |
| 3. | 2/6 | 1 | **Grace Slick & The Great Society** *Grace Slick & The Great Society* |
| 4. | 2/20 | 1 | **McDonald And Giles** *McDonald & Giles* |
| 5. | 4/24 | 2 | **Her Man...His Woman** *Ike & Tina Turner* |
| 6. | 7/24 | 1 | **The Worst Of The Mothers** *The Mothers Of Invention* |
| 7. | 8/14 | 1 | **Scandalous John** *Rod McKuen/Soundtrack* |
| 8. | 9/18 | 1 | **Ian & Sylvia** *Ian & Sylvia* |
| 9. | 10/9 | 1 | **Hooteroll?** *Howard Wales & Jerry Garcia* |
| 10. | 11/20 | 1 | **Song For You** *Jack Jones* |

## 1972

| | DATE | WKS | |
|---|---|---|---|
| 1. | 2/19 | 1 | **Coven** *Coven* |
| 2. | 4/22 | 2↕ | **Look Inside The Asylum Choir** *Leon Russell & Marc Benno* |
| 3. | 5/20 | 1 | **From The Roots Came The Rapper** *Joe Tex* |
| 4. | 5/27 | 1 | **1200 Hamburgers To Go** *Imus In The Morning* |
| 5. | 8/5 | 1 | **Two Sides Of Laura Lee** *Laura Lee* |
| 6. | 9/2 | 3 | **Jerry Reed** *Jerry Reed* |
| 7. | 9/23 | 4 | **Stratavarious** *Ginger Baker's Air Force* |
| 8. | 10/28 | 2 | **Casey Kelly** *Casey Kelly* |
| 9. | 12/16 | 2 | **Those Were The Days** *Mary Hopkin* |

## 1973

| | DATE | WKS | |
|---|---|---|---|
| 1. | 1/27 | 1 | **Amazing Spider-Man: From Beyond The Grave!** *Various Artists* |
| 2. | 2/3 | 1 | **My Man** *Tammy Wynette* |
| 3. | 3/3 | 1 | **Rock 'N Roll Gypsies** *Vinegar Joe* |
| 4. | 3/10 | 1 | **Who's Gonna Play This Old Piano...(Think About It Darlin')** *Jerry Lee Lewis* |
| 5. | 3/24 | 2 | **Keep Me In Mind** *Lynn Anderson* |
| 6. | 4/7 | 1 | **Superpak** *Johnny Rivers* |
| 7. | 4/14 | 1 | **Watch** *Seatrain* |
| 8. | 4/21 | 1 | **I Know I Love Him** *Nancy Wilson* |
| 9. | 5/19 | 1 | **Wizzard's Brew** *Roy Wood's Wizzard* |
| 10. | 5/26 | 3 | **Parcel Of Rogues** *Steeleye Span* |
| 11. | 6/16 | 4 | **Nilsson Sings Newman** *Nilsson* |
| 12. | 7/28 | 1 | **Seesaw** *Original Cast* |
| 13. | 8/18 | 2 | **The Love We Have, The Love We Had** *Jerry Butler & Brenda Lee Eager* |
| 14. | 11/3 | 2 | **Sefronia** *Tim Buckley* |
| 15. | 11/17 | 1 | **953 West** *Siegel-Schwall Band* |
| 16. | 12/8 | 3 | **10cc** *10cc* |

## 1974

| | DATE | WKS | |
|---|---|---|---|
| 1. | 3/2 | 2 | **The Best Of John Mayall** *John Mayall* |
| 2. | 3/23 | 2 | **Jamalca** *Ahmad Jamal* |
| 3. | 4/27 | 1 | **No Time To Burn** *Black Heat* |
| 4. | 5/11 | 2 | **1969 Velvet Underground Live With Lou Reed** *Velvet Underground* |
| 5. | 5/25 | 2↕ | **Fully Realized** *Charlie Rich* |
| 6. | 7/6 | 1 | **The World Became The World** *Premiata Forneria Marconi* |
| 7. | 8/31 | 1 | **Up For The Down Stroke** *Parliament* |
| 8. | 9/21 | 6↕ | **Quo** *The Status Quo* |
| 9. | 10/26 | 1 | **Bad Habits** *Headstone* |
| 10. | 11/9 | 1 | **Don't You Worry 'Bout A Thing** *Hank Crawford* |
| 11. | 11/23 | 1 | **The Heart Of Saturday Night** *Tom Waits* |
| 12. | 11/30 | 1 | **First Light** *Family Of Mann* |
| 13. | 12/14 | 1 | **Do Your Thing But Don't Touch Mine** *Goose Creek Symphony* |
| 14. | 12/21 | 3 | **Red Queen To Gryphon Three** *Gryphon* |

## 1975

| | DATE | WKS | |
|---|---|---|---|
| 1. | 1/11 | 1 | **Me 'N Rock 'N Roll Are Here To Stay** *David Ruffin* |
| 2. | 3/8 | 3↕ | **Tanya Tucker's Greatest Hits** *Tanya Tucker* |
| 3. | 4/5 | 1 | **The Dynamic Superiors** *The Dynamic Superiors* |
| 4. | 5/10 | 1 | **Right Or Wrong** *Stealers Wheel* |
| 5. | 7/19 | 1 | **Academy Award Performance** *Maureen McGovern* |
| 6. | 9/20 | 2↕ | **Erogenous** *The Mystic Moods* |
| 7. | 9/27 | 1 | **I Don't Want To Be Alone, Stranger** *Johnny "Guitar" Watson* |
| 8. | 11/8 | 2↕ | **In The Next World, You're On Your Own** *Firesign Theatre* |
| 9. | 12/20 | 1 | **By Request** *Walter Carlos* |

## 1976

| | DATE | WKS | |
|---|---|---|---|
| 1. | 2/7 | 2 | **American Graffiti Vol. III** *Various Artists* |
| 2. | 2/28 | 1 | **We Be Sailin'** *B.W. Stevenson* |
| 3. | 3/6 | 5↕ | **The Köln Concert** *Keith Jarrett* |
| 4. | 5/15 | 3↕ | **Sedaka Live In Australia** *Neil Sedaka* |
| 5. | 6/12 | 2 | **Satisfied 'N Tickled Too** *Taj Mahal* |
| 6. | 6/26 | 1 | **Rumplestiltskin's Resolve** *Shawn Phillips* |
| 7. | 7/4 | 1 | **Seed Of Memory** *Terry Reid* |
| 8. | 8/7 | 1 | **Oh, Yeah?** *Jan Hammer Group* |
| 9. | 9/4 | 1 | **Renegade Picker** *Steve Young* |
| 10. | 9/11 | 1 | **Super Hits** *The Main Ingredient* |

## 1977.

| | DATE | WKS | |
|---|---|---|---|
| 1. | 6/25 | 1 | **Engelbert Sings For You** *Engelbert Humperdinck* |
| 2. | 7/2 | 3 | **Love And Life** *Morris Albert* |
| 3. | 9/17 | 1 | **Hold Me, Thrill Me, Kiss Me** *Johnny Mathis* |
| 4. | 11/19 | 5 | **Get Up & Dance** *The Memphis Horns* |

# #201 ALBUMS

## 1978

| | DATE | WKS | |
|---|---|---|---|
| 1. | 1/28 | 1 | **Be Happy** *Kellee Patterson* |
| 2. | 2/4 | 2 | **This Is The Modern World** *The Jam* |
| 3. | 2/25 | 3 | **My Musical Bouquet** |
| | | | *Love Unlimited Orchestra* |
| 4. | 4/1 | 1 | **Bill's Best Friend** *Bill Cosby* |
| 5. | 4/15 | 3↕ | **Best Of Styx** *Styx* |
| 6. | 4/22 | 4↕ | **Mandré Two** *Mandré* |
| 7. | 6/10 | 1 | **Adventure** *Television* |
| 8. | 6/17 | 1 | **At The Discotheque** *Lipstique* |
| 9. | 7/8 | 2 | **Bop-Be** *Keith Jarrett* |
| 10. | 7/29 | 2 | **Lake II** *Lake* |
| 11. | 8/19 | 1 | **Glider** *Auracle* |
| 12. | 9/9 | 1 | **Rio De Janeiro** *Gary Criss* |
| 13. | 9/30 | 2 | **Gonna Get Through** *Cleo Laine* |
| 14. | 10/14 | 1 | **South's Greatest Hits Volume II** |
| | | | *Various Artists* |
| 15. | 11/11 | 1 | **When We Rock, We Rock And When We Roll, We Roll** *Deep Purple* |
| 16. | 12/23 | 2 | **Hog Heaven** *Elvin Bishop* |

## 1979

| | DATE | WKS | |
|---|---|---|---|
| 1. | 2/24 | 1 | **Moment By Moment** *Soundtrack* |
| 2. | 3/24 | 1 | **Trillion** *Trillion* |
| 3. | 4/7 | 1 | **Gladys Knight** *Gladys Knight* |
| 4. | 5/5 | 1 | **American Standard Band** |
| | | | *American Standard Band* |
| 5. | 6/16 | 1 | **Garden Of Eden** *Passport* |
| 6. | 6/30 | 5 | **Love's So Tough** *Iron City Houserockers* |
| 7. | 8/11 | 1 | **Hi Fi** *Walter Egan* |
| 8. | 10/13 | 1 | **The A's** *The A's* |
| 9. | 10/20 | 1 | **Bread & Roses** *Various Artists* |
| 10. | 10/27 | 1 | **Go!** *The Pop* |
| 11. | 12/8 | 2 | **Family Tradition** *Hank Williams, Jr.* |
| 12. | 12/22 | 2 | **In The Skies** *Peter Green* |

## 1980

| | DATE | WKS | |
|---|---|---|---|
| 1. | 1/5 | 1 | **Happy Holidays To You** *The Whispers* |
| 2. | 1/12 | 1 | **How High** *Salsoul Orchestra* |
| 3. | 2/9 | 1 | **Sabotage/Live** *John Cale* |
| 4. | 2/23 | 1 | **Breakwater Cat** *Thelma Houston* |
| 5. | 3/29 | 1 | **Struttin'** *Dr. Strut* |
| 6. | 5/3 | 1 | **There's A Little Bit Of Hank In Me** |
| | | | *Charley Pride* |
| 7. | 7/19 | 1 | **Best Of Styx** *Styx* |
| 8. | 7/26 | 1 | **Metal Rendez-Vous** *Krokus* |
| 9. | 9/27 | 1 | **Chevy Chase** *Chevy Chase* |
| 10. | 10/4 | 1 | **In Performance** *Donny Hathaway* |
| 11. | 11/8 | 1 | **Touch Of Silk** *Eric Gale* |
| 12. | 11/29 | 1 | **Night Song** *Ahmad Jamal* |
| 13. | 12/6 | 1 | **Gang Of Four** *Gang Of Four* |
| 14. | 12/20 | 1 | **Best Of The J. Geils Band Two** |
| | | | *The J. Geils Band* |
| 15. | 12/27 | 2 | **I Am The Living** *Jimmy Cliff* |

## 1981

| | DATE | WKS | |
|---|---|---|---|
| 1. | 2/21 | 1 | **Ace Of Spades** *Motörhead* |
| 2. | 2/28 | 3 | **I.R.S. Greatest Hits Vols. 2 & 3** |
| | | | *Various Artists* |
| 3. | 3/28 | 2 | **Celebrate The Bullet** *Selecter* |
| 4. | 4/11 | 1 | **Deception Is An Art** *Ali Thomson* |
| 5. | 4/18 | 1 | **Doc Holliday** *Doc Holliday* |
| 6. | 4/25 | 1 | **Barry & Glodean** |
| | | | *Barry White & Glodean White* |
| 7. | 5/16 | 1 | **Fantasy** *Fantasy* |
| 8. | 5/23 | 1 | **All My Reasons** *Noel Pointer* |
| 9. | 7/11 | 1 | **The Baron** *Johnny Cash* |
| 10. | 8/8 | 1 | **Yellowjackets** *Yellowjackets* |
| 11. | 8/29 | 3 | **Just A Lil' Bit Country** *Millie Jackson* |
| 12. | 9/19 | 2 | **Love Songs** *Neil Diamond* |
| 13. | 10/10 | 1 | **Good Morning America** *Charlie* |
| 14. | 10/24 | 3 | **Cheech & Chong's Greatest Hit** |
| | | | *Cheech & Chong* |
| 15. | 11/21 | 2 | **Bob Welch** *Bob Welch* |
| 16. | 12/12 | 1 | **What A Woman Needs** *Melba Moore* |
| 17. | 12/19 | 3 | **Ouch!** *Ohio Players* |

## 1982

| | DATE | WKS | |
|---|---|---|---|
| 1. | 1/9 | 4 | **The Best Of Roberta Flack** *Roberta Flack* |
| 2. | 2/13 | 1 | **Heart On A Wall** *Jimmy Destri* |
| 3. | 4/24 | 1 | **Shakedown** *Lamont Cranston Band* |
| 4. | 6/26 | 2↕ | **Restless Breed** *Riot* |
| 5. | 8/7 | 1 | **Here We Go Again** *Bobby Bland* |
| 6. | 8/14 | 1 | **In Love's Time** *Dave Valentin* |
| 7. | 8/21 | 1 | **Now Is The Time** *Lou Rawls* |
| 8. | 9/4 | 1 | **Too Fast To Live Too Young To Die** |
| | | | *Robert Gordon* |
| 9. | 9/11 | 1 | **The Legend Goes On...** |
| | | | *The Statler Brothers* |
| 10. | 9/18 | 1 | **You Make The Heat** *The Producers* |
| 11. | 10/2 | 1 | **V Deep** *The Boomtown Rats* |
| 12. | 10/9 | 2 | **The Best Of Willie** *Willie Nelson* |
| 13. | 10/23 | 2 | **I, Assassin** *Gary Numan* |
| 14. | 12/4 | 1 | **Hard Times** *Millie Jackson* |

## 1983

| | DATE | WKS | |
|---|---|---|---|
| 1. | 1/8 | 2 | **Brimstone & Treacle** *Soundtrack* |
| 2. | 2/5 | 6 | **E.T. The Extra-Terrestrial** |
| | | | *storybook album* |
| 3. | 5/28 | 2 | **Local Hero** *Mark Knopfler/Soundtrack* |
| 4. | 6/11 | 1 | **Glasses** *Ozone* |
| 5. | 8/20 | 1 | **Hey Bartender** *Johnny Lee* |
| 6. | 9/24 | 1 | **Let Me Be Yours** *Lillo Thomas* |
| 7. | 10/15 | 2↕ | **Construction Time Again** *Depeche Mode* |
| 8. | 10/22 | 1 | **Passion In The Dark** *Danny Spanos* |
| 9. | 11/5 | 1 | **The Planet Earth Rock And Roll Orchestra** *Paul Kantner* |
| 10. | 12/3 | 3↕ | **Snap!** *The Jam* |

# #201 ALBUMS

| | DATE | WKS | 1984 |
|---|---|---|---|
| 1. | 3/3 | 1 | **Lionheart** *Kate Bush* |
| 2. | 3/10 | 1 | **Built To Destroy** *Michael Schenker Group* |
| 3. | 3/31 | 1 | **Joanie Greggains - Thin Thighs, Hips & Stomach (Aerobic Shape-Up III)** *Joanie Greggains* |
| 4. | 5/5 | 1 | **Keep It Comin'** *The Jones Girls* |
| 5. | 5/19 | 1 | **Cross Fire** *Spinners* |
| 6. | 6/30 | 1 | **Long Gone Dead** *Rank & File* |
| 7. | 8/11 | 1 | **That's The Way I Feel Now** *Various Artists* |
| 8. | 9/22 | 2 | **The Coyote Sisters** *The Coyote Sisters* |
| 9. | 10/20 | 1 | **The Red Hot Chili Peppers** *The Red Hot Chili Peppers* |
| 10. | 11/3 | 1 | **The Wild Life** *Soundtrack* |
| 11. | 11/10 | 1 | **Burnin' Hot** *Xavion* |

| | DATE | WKS | 1985 |
|---|---|---|---|
| 1. | 1/26 | 1 | **In The Dark** *Roy Ayers* |
| 2. | 2/2 | 1 | **Classic Masters** *Ronnie Laws* |
| 3. | 3/2 | 1 | **Two Minute Warning** *Angel City* |
| 4. | 3/16 | 1 | **Fire Me Up** *Roman Holliday* |
| 5. | 3/23 | 2 | **When The Rain Begins To Fall** *Pia Zadora* |
| 6. | 4/20 | 1 | **The Velvet Underground & Nico** *The Velvet Underground & Nico* |
| 7. | 5/4 | 1 | **Rattlesnakes** *Lloyd Cole And The Commotions* |
| 8. | 6/8 | 2↕ | **Some People** *Belouis Some* |
| 9. | 6/15 | 1 | **Nina Hagen In Ekstasy** *Nina Hagen* |
| 10. | 7/13 | 3↕ | **They Said It Couldn't Be Done** *Grandmaster Flash & The Furious Five* |
| 11. | 8/24 | 1 | **Philip Oakey & Giorgio Moroder** *Philip Oakey & Giorgio Moroder* |

# LABEL ABBREVIATIONS

Common. United ............................................ Commonwealth United
Deutsche Gramm. ...................................... Deutsche Grammophon
Entertainment Co. ....................................... Entertainment Company
Grant Royal/Cap. .............................................. Grand Royal/Capitol
Great Western Gramm. .................... Great Western Grammophone
Midland Int'l. ...................................................... Midland International
Midsong Int'l. .................................................. Midsong International
Philadelphia Int'l. ....................................... Philadelphia International

# MISSING B-SIDES

The B-side titles are missing for the *Bubbling Under* singles listed below. Please write to us if you can verify any of the B-side titles or provide a commercial copy of the record.

| Artist | A-Side Title | Label & Number |
|---|---|---|
| CARAVAN | Stuck In A Hole | BTM 800 |
| CHEMAY, Joe, Band | Love Is A Crazy Feeling | Unicorn 95003 |
| D.A. | Ready 'N' Steady | Rascal 102 |
| GOODMAN, Steve | City Of New Orleans | Buddah 270 |
| GRAND FUNK RAILROAD | Stuck In The Middle | Full Moon 49866 |
| LEO & LIBRA | Get It While The Gettin' Is Good | Sound Bird 5003 |
| POINTER SISTERS | Who Do You Love | Planet 45908 |
| SKELLERN, Peter | Hold On To Love | Private Stock 45,028 |
| XAVION | Eat Your Heart Out | Asylum 69707 |

**When the talk turns to music, more people turn to Joel Whitburn's Record Research Collection than to any other reference source.**

That's because these are the **only** books that get right to the bottom of *Billboard's* major charts, with **complete, fully accurate chart data on every record ever charted**. So they're quoted with confidence by DJ's, music show hosts, program directors, collectors and other music enthusiasts worldwide.

Each book lists every record's significant chart data, such as peak position, debut date, peak date, weeks charted, label, record number and much more, all conveniently arranged for fast, easy reference. Most books also feature artist biographies, record notes, RIAA Platinum/Gold Record certifications, top artist and record achievements, all-time artist and record rankings, a chronological listing of all #1 hits, and additional in-depth chart information.

### TOP POP SINGLES 1955-1996
Over 22,000 pop singles — every "Hot 100" hit — arranged by artist. Features thousands of artist biographies and countless titles notes. Also, for the first time, includes the B-side title of every "Hot 100" hit, doubling the number of titles listed in any previous edition. 912 pages. $79.95 Hardcover / $69.95 Softcover.

### POP ANNUAL 1955-1994
A year-by-year ranking, based on chart performance, of over 20,000 pop hits. 880 pages. $69.95 Hardcover / $59.95 Softcover.

### POP HITS 1940-1954
Compiled strictly from *Billboard* and divided into two easy-to-use sections — one lists all the hits artist-by-artist and the other year-by-year. Filled with artist bios, title notes, and many special sections. 414 pages. Hardcover. $44.95.

### POP MEMORIES 1890-1954
Unprecedented in depth and dimension. An artist-by-artist, title-by-title chronicle of the 65 formative years of recorded popular music. Fascinating facts and statistics on over 1,600 artists and 12,000 recordings, compiled directly from America's popular music charts, surveys and record listings. 660 pages. Hardcover. $59.95.

### TOP POP ALBUMS 1955-1996
An artist-by-artist history of the over 18,300 albums that ever appeared on *Billboard's* pop albums charts, with a complete A-Z listing below each artist of <u>every</u> track from <u>every</u> charted album by that artist. 1,056 pages. Hardcover. $89.95.

### TOP POP ALBUM TRACKS 1955-1992
An all-inclusive, alphabetical index of every song track from every charted music album, with the artist's name and the album's chart debut year. 544 pages. Hardcover. $34.95.

### TOP POP ALBUM TRACKS 1993-1996
A 3 1/2-year supplement to the above Tracks book — alphabetically indexes over 21,000 tracks from the more than 1,600 albums that have appeared on *The Billboard 200* pop albums charts since 1992. 88 pages. Softcover. $14.95.

### BILLBOARD HOT 100/POP SINGLES CHARTS:

**THE EIGHTIES 1980-1989**
**THE SEVENTIES 1970-1979**
**THE SIXTIES 1960-1969**
Three complete collections of the actual weekly "Hot 100" charts from each decade; black-and-white reproductions at 70% of original size. Over 550 pages each. Deluxe Hardcover. $79.95 each.

**POP CHARTS 1955-1959**
Reproductions of every weekly pop singles chart *Billboard* published from 1955 through 1959 ("Best Sellers," "Jockeys," "Juke Box," "Top 100" and "Hot 100"). 496 pages. Deluxe Hardcover. $59.95.

### BILLBOARD POP ALBUM CHARTS 1965-1969
The greatest of all album eras...straight off the pages of *Billboard*! Every weekly *Billboard* pop albums chart, shown in its entirety, from 1965 through 1969. Black-and-white reproductions at 70% of original size. 496 pages. Deluxe Hardcover. $59.95.

### TOP COUNTRY SINGLES 1944-1993
The complete history of the most genuine of American musical genres, with an artist-by-artist listing of every "Country" single ever charted. 624 pages. Hardcover. $59.95.

### TOP R&B SINGLES 1942-1995
Revised edition of our R&B bestseller — loaded with new features! Every "Soul," "Black," "Urban Contemporary" and "Rhythm & Blues" charted single, listed by artist. 704 pages. Hardcover. $64.95.

# TOP TO BOTTOM!

## Record To Ever Appear On Every Major Billboard Chart.

### TOP COUNTRY ALBUMS 1964-1997

First edition! A music industry first and a Record Research exclusive — features an artist-by-artist listing of every album to appear on *Billboard's* Top Country Albums chart from its first appearance in 1964 through September, 1997. 304 pages. Hardcover. $49.95.

### TOP ADULT CONTEMPORARY 1961-1993

America's leading listener format is covered hit by hit in this fact-packed volume. Lists, artist by artist, the complete history of *Billboard's* "Easy Listening" and "Adult Contemporary" charts. 368 pages. Hardcover. $39.95.

### ROCK TRACKS

Two artist-by-artist listings of the over 3,700 titles that appeared on *Billboard's* "Album Rock Tracks" chart from March, 1981 through August, 1995 and the over 1,200 titles that appeared on *Billboard's* "Modern Rock Tracks" chart from September, 1988 through August, 1995. 288 pages. Softcover. $34.95.

### BUBBLING UNDER SINGLES AND ALBUMS 1959-1997

All "Bubbling Under The Hot 100" (1959-1997) and "Bubbling Under The Top Pop Albums" (1970-1985) charts covered in full and organized artist-by-artist. Also features a photo section of every EP that hit *Billboard's* "Best Selling Pop EP's" chart (1957-1960). 416 pages. Softcover. $49.95.

### BILLBOARD TOP 10 CHARTS 1958-1997

A complete listing of each weekly Top 10 chart, along with each week's "Highest Debut" and "Biggest Mover" from the entire "Hot 100" chart, and more! 780 pages. Hardcover. $39.95.

### BILLBOARD TOP 1000 x 5 1996 Edition

Includes five complete <u>separate</u> rankings — from #1 through #1000 — of the all-time top charted hits of Pop & Hot 100 Singles 1955-1996, Pop Singles 1940-1954, Adult Contemporary Singles 1961-1996, R&B Singles 1942-1996, and Country Singles 1944-1996. 288 pages. Softcover. $29.95.

### BILLBOARD SINGLES REVIEWS 1958

Reproductions of every weekly 1958 record review *Billboard* published for 1958. Reviews of nearly 10,000 record sides by 3,465 artists. 280 pages. Softcover. $29.95.

### DAILY #1 HITS 1940-1992

A desktop calendar of a half-century of #1 pop records. Lists one day of the year per page of every record that held the #1 position on the pop singles charts on that day for each of the past 53+ years. 392 pages. Spiral-bound softcover. $24.95.

### BILLBOARD #1s 1950-1991

A week-by-week listing of every #1 <u>single</u> and <u>album</u> from *Billboard's* Pop, R&B, Country and Adult Contemporary charts. 336 pages. Softcover. $24.95.

### MUSIC YEARBOOKS 1997/1996/1995/1994/1993

A complete review of '97, '96, '95, '94 or '93 charted music — as well as a superb supplemental update of our Record Research Pop Singles and Albums, Country Singles, R&B Singles, Adult Contemporary Singles, and Bubbling Under Singles books. Various page lengths. Softcover. 1997, 1996 & 1995 editions: $34.95 each / 1994 & 1993 editions: $29.95 each.

### MUSIC & VIDEO YEARBOOKS 1992/1991/1990

Comprehensive, yearly updates on *Billboard's* major singles, albums and videocassettes charts. Various page lengths. Softcover. $29.95 each.

For complete book descriptions and ordering information, call, write, fax or e-mail today.

**RECORD RESEARCH INC.**
P.O. Box 200
Menomonee Falls, WI 53052-0200   U.S.A.
Phone:   414-251-5408
Fax:   414-251-9452
E-mail:   record@execpc.com

**We're On The Internet** — If you'd like to place an order electronically, simply use the convenient order form on our Web Site: **http://www.recordresearch.com**.

# The *RECORD RESEARCH* Collection

| Book Title | Quantity | Price | Total |
|---|---|---|---|
| 1. Billboard Pop Charts 1955-1959 (hardcover) | _____ | $59.95 | _____ |
| 2. Billboard Hot 100 Charts - The Sixties (hardcover) | _____ | $79.95 | _____ |
| 3. Billboard Hot 100 Charts - The Seventies (hardcover) | _____ | $79.95 | _____ |
| 4. Billboard Hot 100 Charts - The Eighties (hardcover) | _____ | $79.95 | _____ |
| 5. Billboard Pop Album Charts 1965-1969 (hardcover) | _____ | $59.95 | _____ |
| 6. Top Pop Albums 1955-1996 (hardcover) | _____ | $89.95 | _____ |
| 7. Top Pop Album Tracks 1955-1992 (hardcover) | _____ | $34.95 | _____ |
| 8. Top Pop Album Tracks 1993-1996 (softcover) | _____ | $14.95 | _____ |
| 9. Top Pop Singles 1955-1996 (hardcover) | _____ | $79.95 | _____ |
| 10. Top Pop Singles 1955-1996 (softcover) | _____ | $69.95 | _____ |
| 11. Pop Hits 1940-1954 (hardcover) | _____ | $44.95 | _____ |
| 12. Pop Annual 1955-1994 (hardcover) | _____ | $69.95 | _____ |
| 13. Pop Annual 1955-1994 (softcover) | _____ | $59.95 | _____ |
| 14. Top Country Singles 1944-1993 (hardcover) | _____ | $59.95 | _____ |
| 15. Top R&B Singles 1942-1995 (hardcover) | _____ | $64.95 | _____ |
| 16. Pop Memories 1890-1954 (hardcover) | _____ | $59.95 | _____ |
| 17. Bubbling Under Singles And Albums 1959-1997 (softcover) | _____ | $49.95 | _____ |
| 18. Top Country Albums 1964-1997 (hardcover) | _____ | $49.95 | _____ |
| 19. Top Adult Contemporary 1961-1993 (hardcover) | _____ | $39.95 | _____ |
| 20. Top 10 Charts 1958-1997 (hardcover) | _____ | $39.95 | _____ |
| 21. Rock Tracks (softcover) | _____ | $34.95 | _____ |
| 22. Billboard Top 1000 x 5 1996 Edition (softcover) | _____ | $29.95 | _____ |
| 23. Billboard Singles Reviews 1958 (softcover) | _____ | $29.95 | _____ |
| 24. Daily #1 Hits 1940-1992 (softcover) | _____ | $24.95 | _____ |
| 25. Billboard #1s 1950-1991 (softcover) | _____ | $24.95 | _____ |

26. Music Yearbooks (softcover) ............................................................. $34.95 each  _____
   ☐ 1997    ☐ 1996    ☐ 1995

27. Music Yearbooks (softcover) ............................................................. $29.95 each  _____
   ☐ 1994    ☐ 1993

28. Music & Video Yearbooks (softcover) ................................................ $29.95 each  _____
   ☐ 1992    ☐ 1991    ☐ 1990

Shipping & Handling (see below) ...... _____

Wisconsin Residents Only (add 5.1% sales tax)...... _____

## SHIPPING & HANDLING:

| If your order subtotals: | U.S. | Foreign |
|---|---|---|
| Up to $20.00 | $4.50 | $4.50 |
| $20.01 - $50.00 | $6.00 | $6.00 |
| $50.01 - $80.00 | $7.50 | $7.50 |
| $80.01 - $130.00 | $8.50 | $10.00 |
| $130.01 - $180.00 | $9.00 | $12.50 |
| $180.01 - $230.00 | $10.00 | $16.00 |
| $230.01 - $300.00 | $11.50 | $21.00 |
| Over $300.00 | $13.00 | $25.00 |

**TOTAL PAYMENT** ........$_____

### PAYMENT METHOD:

☐ MasterCard          ☐ Check

☐ VISA                ☐ Money Order

☐ American Express

Credit Card
Expiration Date: _____ / _____
                  Mo.        Yr.

U.S. orders shipped via UPS (please give complete street address). Foreign orders shipped via surface mail; allow 8-12 weeks for delivery. Must be paid in U.S. dollars and drawn on a U.S. bank. Call for special air shipping information/rates.

Credit Card # ___ ___ ___ ___    ___ ___ ___ ___    ___ ___ ___ ___    ___ ___ ___ ___

Signature _____

To charge by phone, call **414-251-5408** or fax **414-251-9452** (office hours: 8 a.m.-noon & 1-5 p.m. CST) or e-mail to: **record@execpc.com** or mail to: **Record Research Inc., P.O. Box 200, Menomonee Falls, WI  53052-0200  U.S.A.**

Name _____

Company Name _____

Address _____ Apt/Suite # _____

City _____ State/Province _____

ZIP/Postal Code _____ Country _____